Lecture Notes in Artificial Intelligence 9332

Subseries of Lecture Notes in Computer Science

Qin Lu · Helena Hong Gao (Eds.)

Chinese Lexical Semantics

16th Workshop, CLSW 2015
Beijing, China, May 9–11, 2015
Revised Selected Papers

Editors
Qin Lu
The Hong Kong Polytechnic University
Hong Kong SAR
China

Helena Hong Gao
Nanyang Technological University
Singapore
Singapore

ISSN 0302-9743 ISSN 1611-3349 (electronic)
Lecture Notes in Artificial Intelligence
ISBN 978-3-319-27193-4 ISBN 978-3-319-27194-1 (eBook)
DOI 10.1007/978-3-319-27194-1

Library of Congress Control Number: 2015958746

LNCS Sublibrary: SL7 – Artificial Intelligence

This Springer imprint is published by SpringerNature
The registered company is Springer International Publishing AG Switzerland

Preface

The Chinese Lexical Semantics Workshop (CLSW), established in 2000, has acted as an important conference in the Asia-Pacific region to prompt the research and application of Chinese lexical semantics and other related fields, including theoretical linguistics, applied linguistics, computational linguistics, information processing, computational lexicography, etc.

The 16th Chinese Lexical Semantics Workshop (CLSW 2015) was held during May 9–11, 2015 at Beijing Normal University, China. A total of 248 papers were submitted to the workshop, an unprecedented number of submissions in the CLSW series of workshops. All submissions were reviewed by at least two independent reviewers. For the workshop, 152 papers were accepted with 97 scheduled as oral presentations and 55 as poster papers. For this volume in Springer's LNAI series, only 69 papers (27.82 % of the total submissions) were selected; 64 are regular papers (25.80 % of the total submissions) and five are short papers (2.02 % of the total submissions). This book is organized in five topical sections: Lexical Semantics, Lexical Resources, Lexicology, Natural Language Processing and Applications, and Syntax.

As the editors of this volume, we would like to thank the conference chair, all Advisory Committee members, Program Committee members, invited speakers, as well as all authors and attendees for their contribution and participation. We would also like to thank the organizing committee, Beijing Normal University and our student volunteers for their excellent arrangement and services.

September 2015
Qin Lu
Helena Hong Gao

Organization

Conference Chair

Chu-Ren Huang   Hong Kong Polytechnic University, Hong Kong SAR, China

Advisory Committee

Honorary Members

Shiwen Yu	Peking University, China
Chin-Chuan Cheng	University of Illinois, USA
Benjamin Tsou	Hong Kong Institute of Education, Hong Kong SAR, China

Members

Yanbin Diao	Beijing Normal University, China
Chu-Ren Huang	Hong Kong Polytechnic University, Hong Kong SAR, China
Donghong Ji	Wuhan University, China
Jing-Schmidt Zhuo	University of Oregon, USA
Kim Teng Lua	COLIPS, Singapore
Mei-chun Liu	National Chiao Tung University, Taiwan
Qin Lu	Hong Kong Polytechnic University, Hong Kong SAR, China
Xinchun Su	Xiamen University, China
Zhifang Sui	Peking University, China
Shu-Kai Hsieh	National Taiwan University, Taiwan
Jie Xu	University of Macau, Macau, SAR China
Hongying Zan	Zhengzhou University, China

Program Committee

Chairs

Qin Lu	Hong Kong Polytechnic University, Hong Kong SAR, China
Helena Hong Gao	Nanyang Technological University, Singapore

Members

Xiaojing Bai	Tsinghua University, China
Gong Cheng	PLA University of Foreign Language, China
Bee Chin Ng	Nanyang Technological University, Singapore
Minghui Dong	Institute for Infocomm Research, Singapore
Guohong Fu	Heilongjiang University, China
Zhiguo Gong	University of Macau, Macau, SAR China
Fuliang Guo	Hebei University, China

Jia-Fei Hong	National Taiwan Normal University, Taiwan
Jing-Schmidt Zhuo	University of Oregon, USA
Minghu Jiang	Tsinghua University, China
Guangjin Jin	Ministry of Education Institute of Applied Linguistics, China
Kathleen Ahrens	Hong Kong Baptist University, Hong Kong SAR, China
Shiyong Kang	Ludong University, China
Olivia Kwong	The Chinese University of Hong Kong, Hong Kong SAR, China
Hui-ling Lai	National Chengchi University, Taiwan
Baoli Li	Henan University of Technology, China
Jingxia Lin	Nanyang Technological University, Singapore
Ting Liu	Harbin Institute of Technology, China
Yao Liu	Institute of Scientific and Technical Information of China, China
Yao Meng	Fujitsu Research Center, China
Chong Qi	Paris Diderot University, France
Xiaodong Shi	Xiamen University, China
Jihua Song	Beijing Normal University, China
Le Sun	Chinese Academy of Sciences, China
Yinxin Sun	Beijing Normal University, China
Hongyin Tao	University of California, Los Angeles, USA
Yunfang Wu	Peking University, China
Ruifeng Xu	Harbin Institute of Technology Shenzhen Graduate School, China
Nianwen Xue	Brandeis University, USA
Erhong Yang	Beijing Language and Culture University, China
Tianfang Yao	Shanghai Jiaotong University, China
Yulin Yuan	Peking University, China
Hongying Zan	Zhengzhou University, China
Zezhi Zheng	Xiamen University, China
Qiang Zhou	Tsinghua University, China
Guodong Zhou	Soochow University, China

Organizing Committee

Chairs

Yanbin Diao	Beijing Normal University, China
Zhifang Sui	Peking University, China

Vice Chair and Secretary

Yinxin Sun	Beijing Normal University, China

Members

Zuoyan Song	Beijing Normal University, China
Xiaoying Xu	Beijing Normal University, China

Yongfang Xie	Beijing Normal University, China
Jinxia Li	Beijing Normal University, China
Shuang Hong	Beijing Normal University, China
Daxin Nie	Beijing Normal University, China
Jili Liu	Beijing Normal University, China
Rui Hao	Beijing Normal University, China

Publication Committee

Chair

| Pengyuan Liu | Beijing Language and Culture University, China |

Vice Chairs

| Xuri Tang | Huazhong University of Science and Technology, China |
| Qi Su | Peking University, China |

Members

Jia-Fei Hong	National Taiwan Normal University, Taiwan
Olivia Kwong	The Chinese University of Hong Kong, Hong Kong SAR, China
Zezhi Zheng	Xiamen University, China

Contents

Lexical Semantics

Lexicology

Syntax

Lexical Semantics

A New Categorization Framework for Chinese Adverbs

Hongzhi Xu[⊠], Dingxu Shi, and Chu-Ren Huang

The Department of Chinese and Bilingual Studies, The Hong Kong Polytechnic
University, Hong Kong, China
{hongz.xu,dingxushi,churenhuang}@gmail.com

Abstract. Previous studies on the categorization of Chinese adverbs have
not come to a conclusive end, in part due to their varying criteria. While
many studies have focused on subcategories of adverbs, the boundaries of
the subcategories themselves are not clear. As a result, there is still no clear
picture where Chinese adverbs stand in the whole field of Chinese semantics. In addition, not enough features have been explored in order to derive
highly cohesive categories. In this paper, we present a new categorization
framework for Chinese adverbs. Firstly, four coarse-grained categories are
proposed according to the semantic structures of sentences, including the
proposition, modalities, aspect and other meaning components. Then, several semantic and syntactic features are used to further divide the four
categories into more than ninety finer-grained subcategories. Based on the
new framework, we find that adverbs in the same category function in similar ways, both semantically and syntactically.

1 Introduction

Categorization of Chinese adverbs is difficult due to the fact that their function-
alities cover many different semantic components of a sentence, e.g. modality,
aspect, speaker's subjective evaluation etc. By now, there is no effective standard according to which Chinese adverbs can be categorized such that their
syntactic and semantic properties can be consequently explained and predicted.
Previous studies on Chinese adverb categorization largely depend on subjective
judgments and intuition. This has led to a trend that different researchers have
proposed different categories according to their own considerations and criteria.
For example,

Chao [3] discriminated nine categories for Chinese adverbs; Zhu [21] discriminated four categories; Li and Thompson [10] discriminates three categories
according to the syntactic position of adverbs: movable (time, attitude), non-
movable (manner, non-manner), post-verbal; Li [11] divided Chinese adverbs
into seven categories; Zhang [19] discriminates ten semantic categories. In the
newest Chinese reference grammar [9], adverbs are firstly divided into two categories: descriptive and functional. Descriptive adverbs are content and open,
while functional adverbs are closed. Functional adverbs are further divided into
four categories: temporal, degree, scope and attitudinal.

© Springer International Publishing Switzerland 2015
Q. Lu and H.H. Gao (Eds.): CLSW 2015, LNAI 9332, pp. 3–14, 2015.
DOI: 10.1007/978-3-319-27194-1_1

There are also many studies on the categorization of the subcategories of Chinese adverbs. Zhang [20] used three features to categorize scope adverbs: semantic function, syntactic property, and semantic orientation. By looking at the syntactic properties, he divided scope adverbs into two different subcategories. The first one includes adverbs that are attached to the main predicate of the sentence, e.g. 都*dou1*, 全*quan2*, 统统*tong3tong3*. The other includes adverbs that modify content words, e.g. 凡*fan2*, 仅*jin3*, 只*zhi3* etc.

Cui [5] especially focused on Chinese modal adverbs and classified them into three categories, which were then further divided into ten fine-grained categories. He used several features, including question, negation, attributive modifier, sentence type (statement, interrogative, imperative, exclamation) etc. His study doesn't include adverbs that cannot be placed in sentence initial position, such as the exclamative adverbs 真*zhen1*, 好*hao3*.

Shi [17] categorized Chinese manner adverbs [19, descriptiveadverbs] into six categories: yizhi (intention), shiji (timing), tongdu (separate-companion), yizhao (accordance), zhuangtai (stative), fangshi (manner). Shi [18] categorized Chinese frequency adverbs, which he calls dongliang fuci (adverbs of quantification), into two main categories: pindu (frequency), e.g. 频频*pin2pin2*, 常常*chang2chang2* and fudu (extent), e.g. 暂时*zan3shi2*, 长期*chang2qi1*.

Zou [22] categorized frequency adverbs into two types: judgment adverbs, e.g. 总是*zong3shi4*, 常常*chang2chang2* and descriptive adverbs, e.g. 连连*lian2lian2*, 屡次*lv3ci4*, according to whether a frequency adverb can be followed by 是*shi4*. Both of the two categories can be further divided into two subcategories.

No matter how the adverbs are categorized, it should be a principle that the adverbs categorized into the same group should behave similar, based on which we can make generalizations and predictions. In this paper, we propose a new categorization framework for Chinese adverbs that considers both their semantic and syntactic properties. In this framework, the adverbs are firstly categorized into four categories according to the semantic structures of sentences. Then the four categories can be further divided into finer-grained subcategories based on 18 semantic and syntactic features. Finally, we collected more than 1,200 Chinese adverbs from Sinica corpus [4] and Gigaword corpus [13].

The categorization framework proposed has several advantages: 1) it considers the semantic structure of sentences in intensional logic, based on which the semantic contributions of adverbs can be accurately identified; 2) we use both semantic and syntactic features rather than intuition for the categorization. This can guarantee that adverbs in the same category have similar semantic and syntactic properties. Especially, we introduce semantic entailment and situation type selection features which are important but have not been explored in previous studies; 3) the systematic study we conducted on categorization of Chinese adverbs provides a clear picture where the adverbs stand in the whole field of Chinese semantics.

The remaining of the paper is organized as follows. The semantic framework will be given in Section 2. Section 3 describes the features we proposed to be effective to categorize Chinese adverbs. Section 4 gives more detailed information of categories we found from a complete list of Chinese adverbs. Section 5 is the conclusion and our future work.

2 Categorization Framework of Chinese Adverbs

Based on our observation, Chinese adverbs can be generally divided into two categories: adverbs that function as a part of the proposition of a sentence and adverbs that are higher-order predicates beyond the main proposition. This treatment is based on the theory that modalities and evaluations are not part of the main proposition of a sentence [2, 12, 15, andothers].

In event semantics [6, 16], an event instance (including states) e of type P is introduced in the proposition of a sentence. If we follow this representation, Chinese adverbs could be divided into two categories: 1) a predicate P' which involves an instance e', which is an attribute of e, providing more information of the event; 2) a higher-order predicate Q over P which involves an independent event instance e', e.g. the speaker's evaluation or modality.

The first category can be further divided into two subcategories according to the position within a proposition:

1) Quantifier adverbs indicate the set within which a corresponding proposition P holds, including universal universal quantifier '∀', such as 全部 *quan2bu4*, 统统 *tong3tong3*, and complex quantifiers, such as 大部分 da4bu4fen4 "most" etc. As an example, 他们都是学生 *ta1men0 dou1 shi4 xue2sheng1* "They are all students" can be represented as $\forall_{x \in They}[student(x)]$. Existential quantifier '∃' is usually not expressed by adverbs.

2) Attributive adverbs are a predicate P' on certain attribute of the event instance, e.g. time, degree, manner etc. Formally, it can be represented as $\lambda_P \lambda_{P'} \exists_e \exists_{e'}[P(e) \wedge P'(e') \wedge attr(e', e)]$. For example, in 张三曾经住在北京 *zhang1san1 ceng2jing1 zhu4 zai4 bei3jing1* "Zhang San once lived in Beijing", the adverb 曾经 *ceng2jing1* "once" provides the time information, which thus affect the truth condition of the proposition by introducing a time constraint.

This category contains the largest amount of adverbs. Adverbs in this category are usually associated with certain thematic roles, the values of which can be event type specific. For example, the manner adverb 全面 *quan2mian4* "comprehensively" can modify 调查 *diao4cha2* "investigate", 讲解 *jiang3jie3* "explain", but not 聊天 *liao2tian1* "chat" or 开会 *kai1hui4* "have a meeting" etc. Such compositional semantic constraints indicate that this category is potentially open and may increase with time. These adverbs can be further divided into subcategories, according to the thematic roles they take: time, duration, degree, manner, agent's intention, frequency, and scope.

The second category can be further divided into two subcategories as well:

3) Relational predicate Q that involves another predicate P' explicitly or implicitly besides the main proposition P. Formally, they can be described as $\lambda_P \lambda_{P'} \lambda_Q \exists_e \exists_{e'}[P(e) \wedge P'(e') \wedge Q(e', e)]$. For example, the adverb 再度 *zai4du4* "the second time", in 张三再度进京 *zhang1san1 zai4du4 jin4jing1* "Zhang San went to Beijing for the second time", implies that there is another event instance of the same kind existing before the event expressed in this sentence.

4) Non-relational predicate Q that doesn't involve another predicate. It includes modality, aspect, speaker's evaluation, etc. Formally, it can be described as $\lambda_P \lambda_Q \exists_e \exists_{e'}[P(e) \wedge Q(e', e)]$. For example, the adverb 果然 *guo3ran2* "as expected"

in 张三果然来了 *zhang1san1 guo3ran2 lai2 le0* "Zhang San came as expected" implies that the speaker has expected the occurrence of the event as expressed. Non-relational predicate can possibly focus on a specific attribute or participants of an event instance. Formally, it can be described as $\lambda_P \lambda_{P'} \lambda_Q \exists_e \exists_{e'} \exists_{e''} [P(e) \wedge P'(e') \wedge attr(e', e) \wedge Q(e'', e')]$.

Adverbs expressing modalities, speaker's evaluation and aspectual information are found in this category. The evaluation can be targeted on different attributes of event instances, such as agent, patient, manner, degree, time, location etc. It can also be targeted to a certain attribute of an entity. For example, in 张三好高 *zhang1san1 hao3 gao1* "Zhang San is so tall", the speaker makes an evaluation of the degree of the tallness of the subject.

The four categories can be further divided into finer-grained categories according to more semantic and syntactic features. Based on previous studies and our own observations, we propose 18 features that we found effective to differentiate different kinds of adverbs.

3   Semantic and Syntactic Features

In this section, we describe the features that are used to categorize all Chinese adverbs.

3.1   Semantic Orientation

Modalities have been shown to be possibly related to different sources [1,14]. Hsieh [8] showed that semantic orientation is a necessary feature to study the modalities of Chinese. He discriminated speaker-oriented, situation-oriented and subject-oriented modalities. For example, in the sentence 你必须接受安检 *ni3 bi4xu1 jie1shou4 an1jian3* "You must take the security check", the deontic modality expressed by 必须 *bi4xu1* "must", could arise from the speaker, or the expectation certain situations (e.g. regularities). Here, we discriminate three semantic orientations: *speaker-oriented*, *subject-oriented* and *hearer-oriented*.

Speaker-Oriented. In English, many adverbs are speaker-oriented [7]. As in the sentence "He luckily won the lottery", the adverb 'luckily' express an evaluation by the speaker. Such speaker-oriented adverbs cannot appear in interrogative sentences, e.g. "*Does he luckily won the lottery?". The discrimination of whether an adverb is speaker oriented can also be used for Chinese. There are indeed similar adverbs in Chinese.

The most typical speaker oriented predicates are epistemic modalities, which express a speaker's commitment of the truth of a certain proposition. For example, the sentence 他绝对在家里 *ta1 jue2dui4 zai4 jia1li3* "He must be at home" includes the speaker's judgment of the possibility of the subject's being at home. So, it is not appropriate to appear in interrogative, *他绝对在家里吗？ *ta1 jue2dui4 zai4 jia1li3 ma0* "*Must he be at home?".

In the sentence 他好聪明！*ta1 hao3 cong1ming0* "He is so clever!", the adverb 好*hao3* "so" carries the exclamation (evaluation) of the speaker. On the other hand, it also carries the degree information. In this case, two different kinds of information are carried by one lexical item. This result in the fact that it can only be placed between subject and predicate. In other words, the combined adverb should obey the constraints of the both category, which results in the intersection of the possible positions where it can be place.

Subject-Oriented. Compared to speaker oriented adverbs, some adverbs are subject oriented, e.g. dynamic modal adverbs such as 无法*wu2fa3*, 不肯*bu4ken3*, or intentional adverbs such as 不经意*bu4jing1yi4*, 特意*te4yi4*.

Subject-oriented adverbs, which are also speaker oriented, require that the subject be the first person 'I' or subject for which the speaker is the representative. For example, 衷心*zhong1xin1* and 真心*zhen1xin1* are similar, both meaning "sincerely/truly" roughly. However, the former is actually speak-oriented and also subject-oriented. So, 他真心喜欢你*ta1 zhen1xin1 xi3huan1 ni3* is natural while ?他衷心祝福你*ta1 zhong1xin1 zhu4fu2 ni3* can only be used when the speaker is reporting the subject's previous utterance.

Hearer-Oriented. Some adverbs are hearer-oriented. They require that the subject must be the second person "you". For example, 你别去*ni3 bie2 qu4* 。but not *他别去*ta1 bie2 qu4* or *我别去*wo3 bie2 qu4*. 你快点走*ni3 kuai4dian3 zou3* but not *他快点走*ta1 kuai4dian3 zou3* or *我快点走*wo3 kuai4dian3 zou3*. For the third person, on possible way is to let the hearer to pass the requirements to the third person, e.g. 请你让他快点走*qing3 ni3 rang4 ta1 kuai4 dian3 zou3*. By default, we can treat such adverbs as speaker-oriented, which is different from other adverbs. Some adverbs, such as 愿意*yuan4yi4* "be willing to", can be used for first person and third person, but not second person.

Some adverbs are not compatible with third person, e.g. 尽量*jin4liang4*, the sentence 我尽量帮你*wo3 jin4liang4 bang1 ni3* "I will try my best to help you" is acceptable, while *他尽量帮你*ta1 jin4liang4 bang1 ni3* "He will try his best to help you" is bad. The English translation is acceptable. However, it is not the same meaning as the Chinese sentence. The corresponding Chinese sentence of the English is 他会尽量帮你*ta1 hui4 jin4liang4 bang1 ni3*. This shows that the adverb 尽量*jin4liang4* "try one's best" is speaker oriented and thus cannot be used for a third person. When the second person is used, e.g. 你尽量帮我*ni3 jin4liang4 bang1 wo3* "You try you best to help me", there is an implicit modality of requiring. The explicit form should be 请你尽量帮我*qing3 ni3 jin4liang4 bang1 wo3* "Please help me". Such requirements can only be expressed directly by the speaker to the hearer. Such adverbs should still be treated as subject oriented.

3.2 Position

The positions that an adverb can be placed, e.g. sentence initial position or between subject and predicate is another factor, that has been discussed in

[10,19]. We adopt this feature as it can identify the semantic role information and their combination with higher-order predicates.

Compare the two sentences 他幸亏没来*ta1 xing4kui1 mei2lai2* and 幸亏他没来*xing4kui1 ta1 mei2 lai2*, where the adverb 幸亏are placed in different positions. Some adverbs, such as degree adverbs, frequency adverbs can only be placed between the subject and the predicate. For example, the sentence 他经常出差*ta1 jing1chang2 chu1chai1* cannot be written as *经常他出差*jing1chang2 ta1 chu1chai1*.

When an adverb expresses two kinds of information at the same time, such as the speaker's evaluation on a certain attribute of an event, e.g. degree, the possible positions of the adverb will obey the rules of both kinds of semantic categories. For example, 好*hao3* and 真*zhen1* expresses both the speaker's exclamation and the degree of what is being predicated. So, the sentence 他好聪明*ta1 hao3 cong1ming2* "He is so clever" cannot be written as *好他聪明*hao3 ta1 cong1ming2*, although semantically the evaluation, i.e. exclamation, of the speaker is a higher-order predicate beyond the main proposition of 他聪明*ta1 cong1ming2* "He is clever".

Some adverbs, such as scope adverbs, 仅*jin3*, 只有*zhi3you3*, can only be placed right before the subject. For example, the sentence 仅他们去出差*jin3 ta1men0 qu4 chu1chai1* cannot be written as *仅, 他们去出差*jin3 ta1men0 qu4 chu1chai1* or *他们仅去出差*ta1men0 jin3 qu4 chu1chai1*.

We use four independent features to differentiate positional information: *Sentence initial*, *before the subject*, *between the subject and the predicate*, and *after the predicate*.

3.3   Negation

Whether an adverb can be negated is also an important factor as different adverbs behave differently in their composition with negators 不*bu4* "Bu" or 没有*mei2you3* "Mei". Since they are two different kinds of negations, e.g. Bu can be a used as a modal adverb, while Mei cannot, we use two features corresponding to *Bu-Negation* and *Mei-Negation*.

Bu-*Negation*. Most adverbs cannot co-occur with the negator 不*bu4*, such as 曾经*ceng2jing1*, 恰好*qia4hao3*, 差点*cha4dian3*, as in *他不曾经去过北京*ta1 bu4 ceng2jing1 qu4 guo4 bei3jing1*, *他不恰好碰到了张三 *ta1 bu4 qia4hao3 peng4 dao4 le0 zhang1san1*, *他不差点摔了一跤 *ta1 bu4 cha4dian3 shuai1 le0 yi1 jiao1*. Frequency adverbs such as 常常*chang2chang2*, 经常*jing1chang2*, 总*zong3*, 总是*zong3shi4*, and some quantifier adverbs such as 都*dou1*, 只*zhi3* as in sentences 他不经常出去*ta1 bu4 jing1chang2 chu1qu4*, 他们不都去*ta1men0 bu4 dou1 qu4*, 不只他们会去*bu4 zhi3 ta1men0 hui4 qu4* are examples that can take *Bu*-Negation.

Mei-*Negation*. Mei is used to negate the existence of an entity either physical object or event, i.e. '¬∃'. Some adverbs are not compatible with Mei-Negation, such as *他没有至少还可以回家*ta1 mei2you3 zhi4shao3 hai2 ke3yi3 hui2jia1* and *他没有真聪明*ta1 mei2you3 zhen1 cong1ming2*.

3.4   Semantic Entailment Test

Reality. Reality entailment is also an important factor to discriminate different adverbs. Some adverbs implies realis events. For example, the sentence 他至少还有钱*ta1 zhi4shao3 hai2 you3qian2* implies that 他有钱*ta1 you3 qian2*; the sentence 他白来了*ta1 bai2 lai2 le0* implies that 他来了*ta1 lai2 le0*. In this sense, 至少*zhi4shao3* "at least", 白*bai2* "in vain" implies realis events. 我们必须开一个会*wo3men0 bi4xu1 kai1 yi1 ge4 hui4* implies that 我们还没有开会*wo3men0 hai2 mei2you3 kai1hui4*; 他将要来香港*ta1 jiang1yao4 lai2 xiang1gang3* implies that 他还没有来香港*ta1 hai2 mei2you3 lai2 xiang1gang3*. Some adverbs do not specifically implies the reality of the event. For example, 我们只好去北京*wo3men0 zhi3hao3 qu4 bei3jing1* doesn't imply the occurrence of the event while 我们只好去了北京*wo3men0 zhi3hao3 qu4 le0 bei3jing1* does.

Yes-No Question. Previously, Cui [5] uses question to test whether an adverb is modal or not. Yes-No question is used to test whether an adverb can appear in general questions. For example, *他幸亏没来吗？ta1 xing4kui1 mei2 lai2 ma0 *他好聪明吗？ta1 hao3 cong1ming2 ma0 are bad, while 他不愿来这里吗？*ta1 bu4 yuan4yi4 lai2 zhe4li3 ma0* and 他非常聪明吗？*ta1 fei1chang2 cong1ming2 ma0* are acceptable.

Yes-No question is not totally equivalent to *speaker-oriented* feature. Some adverbs that are not compatible with Yes-No question are not speaker oriented as well. Adverbs that imply realis events for example are not possible in question as well, e.g., *他偏巧碰到李四吗？ta1 pian1qiao3 peng4dao4 li3si4 ma0 *他索性睡了一觉吗？ta1 suo3xing4 shui4 le0 yi1 jiao4 ma0*.

Controllability/Agentivity. Adverbs can be discriminated by whether the corresponding predicate expresses modality or intention of the subject, i.e. whether it can be controlled by the subject.

Controllability can be tested through their compatibility with intentional adverb, e.g. 故意*gu4yi4*, 不*bu4* etc. For example, the sentence 他不立刻站起来*ta1 bu4 li4ke4 zhan4 qi3lai2* can only be interpreted as modal negation, i.e. the subject's willingness. On the other hand, it is not acceptable for adverbs, such as 来得及*lai2de0ji2* as in *他不来得及赶上火车*ta1 bu4 lai2de0ji2 gan3shang4 huo3che1*.

3.5   Situation Type Selection

Situation type in terms of state, activity, accomplishment, achievement is also a factor for higher-order predicates, as different types of predicates select different types of situations. We discriminate six situation types: state, habitual, generic, activity, achievement and accomplishment. Some adverbs only select state, e.g. degree adverbs 非常*fei1chang2*, 很*hen3* or evaluative adverbs on degree 多么*duo1me0*, 好*hao3*, 真*zhen1* etc. Some adverbs are only compatible with habitual, such as 经常*jing1chang2*, 偶尔*ou3er3*. Some adverbs are only compatible with achievements, such as 很快*hen3kuai4*, 不久*bu4jiu3*, etc.

Generally, we can use six independent features: *state, habitual, generic, activity, achievement* and *accomplishment* to indicate whether an adverb is compatible with each of them respectively.

3.6   Thematic Roles

Thematic role here encompasses a wider scope than what was defined before, namely agent, patient, time, location, instrument, source, target, manner, beneficiary etc. As have been shown in many studies that thematic roles are key information to predict the order when adverbs are used at the same sentence, e.g. [5,7,17]. Although we don't specially study on this issue, by introducing this feature we can potentially make sure that our categorization be compatible with the result of such studies.

Thematic role adverbs are event type specific. We can expect that some attributes are applicable to most types of events, while some attributes are only applicable to certain kinds of events. It is argued that some subcategories of Chinese adverbs are relatively open than the other subcategories. It seems that they are referring to thematic role adverbs due to their semantic nature. The following are the roles what we observed that Chinese adverbs can play.

Time. adverbs express time of a certain event. Adverbs include 曾经*ceng2jing1* "once", 刚刚*gang1gang1* "just now", 近来*jin4lai2* "recently", etc. These adverbs can be placed at sentence initial position or between subject and predicate, e.g., 刚刚，他看见了李四*gang1gang1 ta1 kan4jian4 le0 li3si4* "Just now, he saw Lisi" and 他刚刚看见了李四*ta1 gang1gang1 kan4jian4 le0 li3si4* "He saw Lisi just now."

Manner. adverbs provide manner information of a certain event instance, that is how the predicated event be carried out. Such adverbs include 进一步*jin4yi1bu4* "further", 自行*zi4xing2* "by oneself", 全面*quan2mian4* "comprehensively", etc.

Degree. adverbs provide degree information of a certain gradable predicate. Such adverbs include 很*hen3* "very", 非常*fei1chang2* "very", 十分*shi2fen1* "very", etc.

Scope. adverbs express a scope within which the event happens. Such scope can be physical or abstract, such as 到处*dao4chu4* "everywhere", 四处*si4chu4* "everywhere", 四下*si4xia4* "everywhere", etc. Scope is not location, which is usually expressed by prepositional phrases rather than adverbs.

Intentionality. adverbs provide information on whether the event is intentionally carried out by the agent. Adverbs such as 刻意*ke4yi4* "deliberately", 索性*suo3xing4* "simply", 特意*te4yi4* "on purpose", etc., are intentional, while adverbs such as 不知不觉*bu4zhi1bu4jue2* "unconsciously", 不经意*bu4jing1yi4* "unconsciously", 不由自主*bu4you2zi4zhu3* "unconsciously", etc., are unintentional. These two different categories of adverbs show compatibility with different kinds of events. For example, the sentence 我不经意中了五百万 *wo3 bu4jing1yi4 zhong4 le0 wu3bai3wan4* "I won a lottery without expectation" is acceptable, but *我索性中了五百万 *wo3 suo3xing4 zhong4 le0 wu3bai3wan4* "I simply won a lottery" is not acceptable; 我特意来找你 *wo3 te4yi4 lai2 zhao3 ni3* "I'm coming to see you on purpose" is acceptable, *我不知不觉来找你 *wo3 bu4zhi1bu4jue2 lai2 zhao3 ni3* "I come to see you unconsciously" is not.

4 Semantic Categories of Chinese Adverbs

The adverbs that we categorize are extracted from two annotated corpora: Sinica [4] and Gigaword [13]. The former is annotated manually based on a balanced corpus containing text mainly from Taiwan. The latter is machine annotated, but much larger. It consists of news articles from three different districts: Mainland, Taiwan and Singapore. After excluding the noise, there are about 1,278 adverbs.

There are main two different values, namely YES, NO, for the above binary features. To be comprehensive, N/A is also introduced to indicate that this feature is not applicable to a certain adverb category. Due to the space limitation, we only give the general information here.

Table 1 shows the statistical information of the categorization. In total, there are 1,278 unique adverbs. Some of them are contained in more than one subcategories. So, there are 1,357 adverb items distributed in 94 subcategories, among which there are 8 subcategories of quantifier adverbs, 12 subcategories of attributive adverbs, 20 subcategories of relational adverbs and 54 subcategories of non-relational adverbs.

Table 1. Statistical Information of Chinese Adverb Categorization

Category	No. of Subcategories	No. of Adverb Forms	No. of Adverbs
Quantifier	8	109	109
Attributive	12	468	487
Relational	20	228	229
Non-Relational	54	508	532
Total	94	1278	1357

5 Conclusion

In this paper, we take the challenge of the study on the finer-grain categorization of Chinese adverbs. We proposed a new categorization framework with two levels. The first level considers the semantic structure of a whole sentence. The second level incorporates 18 features to further divide the adverbs into finer-grained categories. We have shown that the new categorization is good to make generalization and prediction on semantic and syntactic behaviors of Chinese adverbs.

In previous studies, temporal adverbs are usually confused with frequency adverbs. For example, both 都dou1 "all", 凡fan2 "any" are put in the fanwei (scope) category. However, the former is a universal quantifier which is usually placed between the subject and the predicate, e.g., 他们都会说英语ta1men0 dou1 hui4 shuo1 ying1yu3 "All of them can speak English". The latter, on the other hand, is usually placed before the subject, e.g. 凡年满十八岁的公民都有选举权fan2 nian2 man3 shi2ba1 sui4 de0 gong1min2 dou1 you3 xuan3ju3quan2 "Those who are above eighteen all have the right to vote".

Second, the adverbs 必须bi4xu1 "must" and 明明ming2ming2 "obviously" are both in the pingzhu (evaluative) category. However, the former can appear in interrogative sentence, while the latter cannot, e.g., 他必须来吗？ta1 bi4xu1 lai2 ma0 "Must he come?" v.s. *他明明在家吗？ta1 ming2ming2 zai4jia1 ma0 "Is it obvious that he is at home?".

Third, aspectual adverbs are mixed together with pure time adverbs in shijian (time) category. Theoretically time adverbs can be place either in sentence initial position or between subject and predicate, e.g. 曾经他是一个医生ceng2jing1 ta1 shi4 yi1 ge4 yi1sheng1 "Once, he is a doctor" or 他曾经是一个医生ta1 ceng2jing1 shi4 yi1 ge4 yi1sheng1 "He is once a doctor", while aspectual adverbs can only placed between subject and predicate, e.g., *已经他是一个医生, yi3jing1 ta1 shi4 yi1 ge4 yi1sheng1 "*Already, he is a doctor".

Forth, 白bai2 "waste doing something" is treated as negation of presupposition and is put together with 不bu4 "not" in fouding (negation) category. However, we found that 白bai2 is not the same as 不bu4. For example, in the sentence 他白来了一趟ta1 bai2 lai2 le0 yi1 tang4 "He come here for nothing", the presupposition is 他来了一趟ta1 lai2 le0 yi1 tang4 "He come here", which is not negated. On the other hand, 白bai2 actually states the fact that the purpose of his coming is not satisfied.

There are many other cases in previous studies where adverbs in the same category are actually different in both semantic and syntactic perspectives. Compared to the previous studies, we have several contributions in this paper. First, we use semantic structure of sentences to differentiates four coarse-grained categories for Chinese adverbs. Such categorization is not trivial. For example, it discriminates pure attributive adverbs and evaluative adverbs that may focus on certain attributes.

Second, we proposed both semantic and syntactic features. Besides the features we carefully adopted from previous studies, we proposed semantic tests including semantic entailments, such as realis vs. irrealis, whether the whole sentence can be questioned or not etc. This is potentially important for computational linguistics, such as event processing, factuality prediction etc.

Third, with the semantic categories, we can see the overall position of Chinese adverbs with regards to their semantic functions and contributions in the whole meaning of sentences. Third, we provide a overall picture of Chinese adverbs in terms of their semantic functions. For example, we can see that the semantic role information such as location, instrument, beneficiary etc., are usually not expressed by adverbs.

On the other hand, Chinese adverbs are more complicated than what has been described here. The classification still needs refinements due to the lack of detailed investigation on the individual adverbs, which will be our goal in future.

Acknowledgments. The work is supported by a General Research Fund (GRF) sponsored by the Research Grants Council (Project no. 543512 & 543810).

References

1. Bybee, J.L.: Morphology: A study of the relation between meaning and form, vol. 9. John Benjamins Publishing (1985)
2. Bybee, J.L., Fleischman, S.: Modality in grammar and discourse, vol. 32. John Benjamins Publishing (1995)
3. Chao, Y.R.: A grammar of spoken Chinese. University of California Press (1968)
4. Chen, K.J., Huang, C.R., Chang, L.P., Hsu, H.L.: Sinica corpus: design methodology for balanced corpora. In: Proceedings of Pacific Asia Conference on Language, Information and Computing (PACLIC), pp. 167 176 (1996)
5. Cui, C.: A study on modern Chinese language modal adverbs, Doctor of philosophy. Chinese Academa of Social Science, Beijing (2002). (in Chinese)
6. Davidson, D.: The logical form of action sentences. In: Rescher, N. (ed.) The Logic of Decision and Action. University of Pittsburgh Press (1967)
7. Ernst, T.: Speaker-oriented adverbs. Natural Language & Linguistic Theory **27**(3), 497–544 (2009)
8. Hsieh, C.L.: Modal verbs and modal adverbs in chinese: An investigation into the semantic source. UST Working Papers in Linguistics, Graduate Institute of Linguistics (National Tsing Hua University) **1**, 31–58 (2005)
9. Huang, C.R., Shi, D.: A Reference Grammar of Chinese, chap. 12. Cambridge University Press, Cambridge (2016)
10. Li, C.N., Thompson, S.A.: Mandarin Chinese: A functional reference grammar. University of California Press (1989)
11. Li, Q.: fuci he fuci de zai fenlei (adverbs and the subcategorization of adverbs). In: Hu, M. (ed.) Cilei Wenti Kaocha (Surveys on Problems of Lexical Categories), pp. 364–390. Beijing Language and Culture University Press (1996)
12. Lyons, J.: Semantics. Cambridge University Press, Cambridge (1977)
13. Ma, W.Y., Huang, C.R.: Uniform and effective tagging of a heterogeneous gigaword corpus. In: Proceedings of the Fifth International Conference on Language Resources and Evaluation (LREC), pp. 24–28 (2006)
14. Palmer, F.R.: The English Verb. Longman (1974)
15. Palmer, F.R.: Mood and modality, 2nd edn. Cambridge University Press, Cambridge (2001)
16. Parsons, T.: Events in the Semantics of English, vol. 5. MIT Press, Cambridge (1990)
17. Shi, J.: On the scope, types and order of sequential use of modal adverbs. Chinese Language **1**, 17–31 (2003)
18. Shi, J.: On the categories and co-occurrence orders of manner adverbs. Studies in Language and Linguistics **23**(4), 1–9 (2004)

19. Zhang, Y.: Xiandai hanyu fuci de xingzhi, fanwei yu fenlei (the properties, scopes and categorization of modern chinese adverbs). Linguistic Studies **2**(1), 51–63 (2000)
20. Zhang, Y.: On range adverbs of mandarin chinese. Journal of Shanghai Teachers University **30**(1), 107–113 (2001)
21. Zhu, D.: Yufa jiangyi (Lecture Notes of Chinese Grammar). The Commercial Press (1982)
22. Zou, H.: The scope and the type of frequency adverbs. Chinese Teaching in the World **3**, 36–45 (2006)

Being Assiduous: Do We Have BITTERNESS or PAIN?

The Synaesthetic and Conceptual Metaphors of BITTERNESS and PAIN in Chinese and English

Jiajuan Xiong[✉] and Chu-Ren Huang

Department of Chinese and Bilingual Studies, The Hong Kong Polytechnic University,
Hong Kong, China
jiajuanx@gmail.com, churen.huang@polyu.edu.hk

Abstract. This paper examines both synaesthetic and conceptual metaphors of BITTERNESS and PAIN in Chinese and English. In terms of synaesthetic metaphor, BITTERNESS is more versatile than PAIN, as the former can be transferred to more sensory domains than the latter. Regardless of the sensory domains, the synaesthetic metaphor basically inherits the negative polarity in both Chinese and English. Regarding conceptual metaphor, both BITTERNESS and PAIN exhibit noticeable cross-linguistic differences. Specifically, EFFORT IS BITTERNESS and INTENSITY IS PAIN are attested in Chinese, while EFFORT IS PAIN and INTENSITY IS BITTERNESS are in operation in English. Whenever EFFORT is targeted, the expression at issue obliterates the negative sense of BITTER and PAIN, probably because the concept of "effort" is cross-culturally positive.

Keywords: BITTERNESS · PAIN · Synaesthesia · Metaphor · Chinese · English

1   Introduction

This paper examines the semantic networks of BITTERNESS and PAIN in Chinese and English. In Chinese, these two concepts are expressed by *ku* 'bitterness; bitter' and *tong* 'pain; painful', respectively. Moreover, these two morphemes can be juxtaposed to form compounds as *kutong* 'bitterness-pain' and *tongku* 'pain-bitterness', which are synonymous to each other.

Cross-linguistically true is the fact that both BITTERNESS and PAIN are sensory words, which are repulsive, unpleasant and thus negative in meaning. Specifically, BITTERNESS is gustatory whereas PAIN is tactile. Albeit being specific in a particular sense domain, both BITTERNESS and PAIN exhibit cross-sensory domain mappings in the sense that their original sensory meanings can be transferred to other sensory domains, such as olfactory, auditory, tactile and mental domains.

In addition to involving synesthetic metaphors, BITTERNESS and PAIN are attested to refer to degree intensification (adverbs) and effort-marking expressions (adjectives or adverbs). These two uses are subsumed under conceptual metaphor in the current study. In particular, four types of conceptual metaphors are identified, viz.,

© Springer International Publishing Switzerland 2015
Q. Lu and H.H. Gao (Eds.): CLSW 2015, LNAI 9332, pp. 15–23, 2015.
DOI: 10.1007/978-3-319-27194-1_2

EFFORT IS BITTERNESS, INTENSITITY IS PAIN, EFFORT IS PAIN, and INTENSITY IS BITTERNESS. The former two are at work in Chinese while the latter two in English.

In section 2, we will conduct the synaesthetic study of BITTERENSS and PAIN. In section 3, we will further explore how BITTERNESS and PAIN are metaphorically used out of the sensory domains. And we conclude the paper in section 4.

2   Synaesthetic Metaphor for BITTERNESS and PAIN

2.1   Synaesthetic Metaphors for BITTERNESS and PAIN in Chinese

As mentioned in section 1, *ku* 'bitterness; bitter' is gustatory and *tong* 'pain; painful' is tactile in terms of their sensory information encoded therein.

Despite their specific sensory domains, they can modify words which belong to other sensory domains, as illustrated in Table 1 below:

Table 1. *Ku* 'bitterness; bitter' and its synaesthesia

gustatory	olfactory	auditory-mental	mental
ku-cha 'bitter-tea', *ku-wei* 'bitter-taste'	*ku-wei* 'bitter-smell'	*ku-yan* 'bitter-words; unpleasant words'	*ku-men* 'bitter-stuffy; depressed', *ku-zhong-zuo-le* 'bitter-in-do-happiness; enjoy in the mist of sorrow'
negative	negative	negative	negative

Table 2. *Tong* 'pain; painful' and its synaesthesia

tactile	mental
ya-tong 'teeth-pain'	*tong-xin* 'pain-heart; distressed'
negative	negative

As shown in Table 1, *ku* 'bitterness; bitter' belonging to the gustatory domain can modify *wei* 'smell', which is olfactory. Moreover, *ku* 'bitterness; bitter' can collate with the word *yan* 'speech' and this collocation emphasizes the unpleasant feature of the speech. This is an example involving gustatory-to-auditory synaesthetic mapping, as *yan* 'speech' is of auditory by nature. Since emotional repulsiveness, i.e., unpleasant feeling, is also induced in *ku-yan* 'unpleasant words', the mental domain is also involved. In this sense, *ku-yan* 'unpleasant words' exemplifies a three-phase synaesthetic mapping, viz., gustatory-auditory-mental mapping.

In fact, without the transitional stage, the gustatory *ku* 'bitterness; bitter' can also be directly transferred to the mental domain to refer to the unpleasant feelings, such as depression, dejection, distress or sorrow. This is exemplified by the words like *ku-men* 'bitter-stuffy; depressed' or *ku-zhong-zuo-le* 'bitter-in-do-happiness; enjoy in the mist of sorrow'. Common to those synaesthetic expressions in different sensory domains is the negative or repulsive sense, which originates in the original gustatory domain.

It is worth pointing out that, in synaesthetic metaphors, the negative sense should be understood as bodily or mental experience, which is almost spontaneous and instinctive. In other words, the negativity is experiential rather than evaluative. This distinction between experiential and evaluative emotion is by no means trivial. For example, in the expression of *liang-yao-ku-kou* 'good-medicine-bitter-mouth; a good medicine tastes bitter', *ku* 'bitterness; bitter' is positive in the evaluative sense, as the medicine with bitter taste is supposed to have the healing function. It is bitter or negative only in the experiential sense. So is the word *ku-yan* 'bitter-words', which is experientially unpleasant but might be evaluatively positive when serving as good advice or admonishment to a person. This is actually attested in *Zhanguo Ce* of Classical Chinese, in which there is a saying *ku-yan, yao ye* 'bitter words, medicine; unpleasant words serve as medicine'. Furthermore, we can say that *ku-zhong-zuo-le* 'bitter-in-do-happiness; enjoy in the mist of sorrow' is a kind of positive attitude towards life. To sum up, the experiential polarity determined by physiologically-based spontaneous response differs from the evaluative polarity arrived at by resorting to a socio-cultural value system. The polarity shown in the tables refers to the experiential polarity, as synaesthesia as cross-sensory-domain mapping is closely related to one's physiological and mental responses.

The tactile word *tong* 'pain; painful' can refer to both physical pain (tactile) and psychological suffering (mental). On a par with *ku* 'bitterness; bitter', *tong* 'pain; painful' is experientially negative in both the tactile and mental domains. Unlike *ku* 'bitterness; bitter', *tong* 'pain; painful' is more restricted in its range of cross-domain mapping.

2.2   Synaesthetic Metaphors for BITTERNESS and PAIN in English

In this section, we present the synaesthetic uses of bitterness/bitter and pain/painful in English, as in Table 3 and 4, respectively.

Table 3. *Bitterness* and its synaesthesia

gustatory	auditory-mental	tactile-mental	mental
bitter lemon	*bitter words* (sarcastic or unpleasant words)	*bitter blow; bitterly cold*	*bitter memory, bitter experience*
negative	negative	negative	negative

Table 4. *Pain* and its synaesthesia

tactile	mental
back pain	*pain of defeat, pain of imprisonment, the pain of loneliness*
negative	negative

The word *bitter* describes a gustatory sense, as shown in the expression of *bitter lemon*. This gustatory meaning can be mapped to the auditory domain, as in *bitter words*. However, the meaning of *bitter words* cannot be authentically auditory but necessarily activates mental perception. In other words, *bitter* in *bitter words* does not describe the sound quality *per se*. Instead of that, the phrase *bitter words* refers to sarcastic and unpleasant words that may emotionally hurt the hearer. Moreover, it is interesting to note that the meaning of *bitter* can also be transferred to the tactile domain, as exemplified in *bitter blow*, which indicates a heavy blow. More often than not, this *bitter blow* transcends the actual tactile meaning and refers to the heavy and undesirable impact in the mental domain. Therefore, *bitter blow* instantiates the gustatory-tactile-mental mapping. However, such a mapping is not attested in Chinese *ku* 'bitterness; bitter'. Other than the auditory and tactile domains, the mental domain can also be the target domain of *bitter* in English, without any intermediate transfer, as illustrated in *bitter memory* and *bitter experience*. In all these uses, the experiential negativity is shared.

Regarding *pain*, it is originally tactile and it can be mapped to the mental domain to describe the unpleasant state of mind.

2.3   Synaesthetic Metaphors: Similarities and Differences Between Chinese and English

In terms of the synathetic metaphors of BITTERNESS and PAIN in Chinese and English, they exhibit great similarities between Chinese and English. Firstly, the gustatory BITTERNESS, compared to the tactile PAIN is more versatile in terms of the range of target domains.

Secondly, all the synaesthetic examples of BITTERNESS and PAIN basically inherit their experiential polarity, i.e., negativity, which is rooted in their respective source domains.

There are, however, differences in the synaesthetic mapping between Chinese and English, in particular regard to BITTERNESS. Specifically, *ku* 'bitterness; bitter' in Chinese can be transferred to the olfactory domain to describe a kind of smell, whereas this mapping is not attested in English. On the other hand, *bitter* in English can be mapped to the tactile domain as in *bitter blow*, which has no Chinese counterpart.

Having examined the synesthetic metaphors of BITTERNESS and PAIN, we move to the conceptual metaphors in both Chinese and English.

3   Conceptual Metaphor for BITTERNESS and PAIN

BITTERNESS and PAIN, in both Chinese and English, are not restricted to synaesthetic metaphor. Rather, they may transcend their sensory meanings to modify non-sensory actions or concepts. To distinguish this type of metaphor from synaesthetic metaphor, we adopt the term of conceptual metaphor, of which the data are presented below:

3.1   Conceptual Metaphors for BITTERNESS and PAIN in Chinese

3.1.1   Data Presentation
We firstly present the data of *ku* 'bitterness; bitter' in Chinese, as in (1) – (4). They do not involve any cross domain mapping among the six sense domains. Rather, *ku* 'bitterness; bitter' in the examples refers to efforts put forward by an Agent.

(1) chi de ku zhong ku,   fang wei ren   shang ren
     eat can bitter in   bitter then   be person up   person
     'If you are able to take the bitterest of the bitter, you would be the best among people.'

(2) chi ku   nai   lao   de   pinde
     eat bitter endure   tiredness DE   virtue
     'the virtue of being able to endure the hardships'

(3) xia   ku   gongfu
     put   bitter   effort
     'take great effort'

(4) ku   lian   wudao
     bitter practice dance
     'painstakingly practice dancing'

We now turn to the examples of *tong* 'pain; painful' in Chinese, which are presented in (5)-(9). It is interesting to note that most of examples take [*tong*-V(P)] form. More importantly, the original meaning of PAIN is bleached in the following examples and *tong* actually serves as an intensifier to strengthen the degree of the physical or mental actions.

(5) tong-chi
     pain-rebuke
     'bitterly rebuke'

(6) tong-gai-qian-fei
     pain-correct-before-mistake
     'earnestly repent and correct one's mistakes'

(7) tong-da
     pain-beat
     'bitter relentlessly'

(8) tong-hui/xi
     pain-regret/regret
     'deeply regret'

(9) tong-hen
     pain-hate
     'bitterly resent'

The above examples of both *ku* 'bitterness; bitter' and *tong* 'pain; painful' are similar in that they are not really sensory, even though they may collocate with words that belong to one of the six sense domains. For example, *chi-ku* 'eat-bitterness; assiduous' is apparently gustatory, as the verb *chi* 'eat' is a gustatory verb. However, the meaning "being assiduous, effort-making" has nothing to do with the taste. In the case of *tong* 'pain; painful', it can collocate with the verbs within the auditory domain, such as *chi* 'rebuke', the verbs within the tactile domain, such as *da* 'beat' and the verbs within the mental domain, such as *hui* 'regret' and *hen* 'hate'. However, the original sense of PAIN is not detectable in the words cited in (5)-(9). Rather, *tong* 'pain; painful' functions as an intensifier for the verbs that follow it.

To sum up, both *ku* 'bitterness; bitter' in (1)-(4) and *tong* 'pain; painful' in (5)-(9) are not synaesthetic metaphorical expressions. In what follows, we will analyze them as conceptual metaphors.

3.1.2 Data Analyses

Regarding *ku* 'bitterness; bitter' as presented in (1) to (4), they involve the meaning of "effort". This forms a sharp contrast with the sensory usages discussed in section 2, as the "effort"-encoded uses are volitional, while sensory meanings can hardly conceived to be volitional. The volitionality can be tested by the examples in (10) and (11), in which volitional verbs *yuanyi* 'be willing' and *jueding* 'decide' are applied.

(10) Ni   **yuanyi** chi-gu   ma?
      you   willing   eat-bitter Q
      'Are you willing to take effort?'
(11) Wo **jueding** xia   ku   gongfu   xuexi.
      I decide   put   bitter effort   study
      'I decide to put efforts in my studies.'

It is thus clear that the sense of "effort" is encoded in the uses of *ku* 'bitterness; bitter' in (1)-(4). We therefore conclude that BITTERNESS can be used to convey EFFORT in Chinese, as presented in (12).

(12) The conceptual metaphor of *ku* 'bitterness; bitter":
      EFFORT IS BITTERNESS.

In terms of *tong* 'pain; painful' in (5)-(9), it intensifies the degree of the actions or mental states encoded in the post-*tong* verb or verb phrase.

(13) The conceptual metaphor of *tong* 'pain; painful":
      INTENSITY IS PAIN.

Having presented the conceptual metaphors of *ku* 'bitterness; bitter' and *tong* 'pain; painful', we delve into the polarity issue in these metaphors. In particular, we will explore whether the original polarity is retained or not in the conceptual metaphors.

3.1.3   Polarity: Retained or not?

As discussed in section 2, the polarity originally encoded in *ku* 'bitterness; bitter' and *tong* 'pain; painful' is basically retained in the synaesthetic metaphors. However, this feature cannot be extended to conceptual metaphors presented in section 3.2.

We have already mentioned that both *ku* 'bitterness; bitter' and *tong* 'pain; painful' are experientially negative in polarity. However, it is obvious that the examples in (1) to (4) are positive in polarity. This makes good sense, if we consider the fact that *ku* 'bitterness; bitter' involves the conceptual metaphor of EFFORT IS BITTERNESS. Since "effort" is something recommendable and applaudable, it naturally renders the expressions which embody this metaphor positive in polarity. In other words, the positive quality of "effort" in the conceptual metaphor EFFORT IS BITTERNESS overwrites the negative polarity of "bitterness".

As regards to the conceptual metaphor INTENSITY IS PAIN, as exemplified in (5)-(9), those words are not necessarily positive or negative. For example, *kong-gai-qian-fei* 'earnestly repent and correct one's mistakes' is evaluatively positive while *tong-hen* 'bitterly resent' negative. However, close examination shows that the verb or verb phrase that follows *tong* 'pain; painful' are very unlikely to be a positive action or mental state. For example, the verb *zan* 'praise' or the mental verb *xiang* 'miss' can hardly be modified by the intensifier *tong* 'pain; painful', as shown in (14)-(15).

(14) #tong-zan
           pain-praise
           'greatly encourage'
(15) #tong-xiang
           pain-miss
           'miss intensively'

The acceptability contrast between (5)-(9) on the one hand and (14)-(15) on the other hand indicates   that *tong* 'pain; painful', as an intensifier, is the least compatible, if possible at all, with positive actions or states. Put differently, the conceptual metaphor INTENSITY IS PAIN retains the negative polarity of *tong* 'pain; painful' to a certain degree.

3.2   *Bitterness* and *Pain* for Their Conceptual Metaphors in English

On a par with Chinese, *bitterness* and *pain* in English are not confined to synaesthetic metaphor, even though they are originally sensory. Both *bitterness* and *pain* are attested to be used metaphorically out of the sensory domains. They are termed as conceptual metaphors. The data are presented and analyzed in 3.2.1 and 3.2.2.

3.2.1   Data Presentation

The English word *bitter*, including its adverb form *bitterly*, can be used to intensify an action or emotion. They are exemplified in (16) and (18).

(16) bitter campaign/argument/opposition/dispute
(17) bitter resentment
(18) bitterly fight/attack/argue

The examples in (16) illustrate that *bitter* intensifies the actions in the form of deverbal nouns, while (17) exemplifies the intensification of an emotion. As further shown in (18), when the actions take the verb form, they can be intensified by the adverb *bitterly*.

As for the English word *pain*, let us read the examples in (19) to (25).

(19) No pain, no gain!

(20) Successful are those who are willing to take pains.

(21) We must take pains to do meticulous work among the masses.

(22) They take pains over writing and send them here for us to read.

(23) I had taken great pains with my appearance.

(24) If you want to succeed in the work, you must take pains about it.

(25) They take pains to hire people whose personalities predispose them to serve customers well.

The above examples describe the efforts required in various kinds of work.

3.2.2   Data Analyses

All the examples presented in 3.2.1 show that *bitter* and *pain* in English can give rise to non-synaesthtic metaphor mappings. Specifically, "intensity" can be encoded by bitterness, leading to INTENSITY IS BITTERNESS metaphor. By contrast, "effort" can be expressed by the word *pain*, reflecting the metaphor of EFFORT IS PAIN. They are presented in (26) and (27).

(26) The conceptual metaphor of *bitter*:
INTENSITY IS BITTERNESS.
(27) The conceptual metaphor of *pain*:
EFFORT IS PAIN.

3.2.3   Polarity: Retained or not?

The question to address in this section is whether the negative polarity is retained or not in the conceptual metaphors. We find that the collocation between *bitter* and a word with positive meaning is very unlikely. This is illustrated in (28) and (29), in which *praise* and *love* are incompatible with the intensifier *bitter*.

(28) #bitter praise

(29) #bitter love

The contrast between (16)-(18) on the one hand and (28)-(29) on the other hand reveals the fact that the negative meaning of the gustatory *bitter* is somehow inherited by the intensifier *bitter*.

When it comes to the examples of *pain* in (19)-(25), it is clear that the positive meaning is conveyed. This positivity is actually made explicit by some positive words, such as *gain, successful, meticulous, succeed* etc. in those examples. Therefore, it is quite safe to conclude that in the case of EFFORT IS PAIN, the negative sense of *pain* is obliterated.

4   Conclusions

This paper examines both the synaesthetic and conceptual metaphors of BITTERNESS and PAIN in Chinese and English.

In terms of synaesthetic metaphors, BITTERNESS and PAIN show great parallelism between Chinese and English. Firstly, BITTERNESS is more versatile than PAIN with regard to the range of their cross-sensory mapping in both Chinese and English. Secondly, the negative sense is basically retained in the synaesthetic metaphor in both Chinese and English. The only noticeable difference lies in the actual domains BITTERNESS can transfer to. Specifically, BITTERNESS in Chinese can transfer to olfactory domain, while it cannot do so in English. On the other hand, BITTERNESS in English allows gustatory-to-tactile mapping, which seems to be unattested in Chinese. Regarding the synesthetic metaphor of PAIN, no significant contrast is found between Chinese and English.

Regarding conceptual metaphors of BITTERNESS and PAIN, the contrasts are shown in table 5.

Table 5. The conceptual metaphors of BITTERNESS and PAIN

	BITTERNESS	PAIN
Chinese	EFFORT	INTENSITY (negative)
English	INTENSITY (negative)	EFFORT

In Chinese, EFFORT IS BITTERNESS and INTENSITY IS PAIN are attested, whereas in English, EFFORT IS PAIN and INTENSITY IS BITTERNESS are proven. Interestingly enough, they switch the mappings in such a neat way in Chinese and English.

References

1. Ahrens, K.: Mapping principles for conceptual metaphors. In: Lynne, C., Deignan, A., Low, G., Todd, Z. (eds.) Researching and Applying Metaphor in the Real World, pp. 185–207. John Benjamins, Amsterdam (2010)
2. Bardovskaya, A.I.: Different approaches to synesthesia. In: Zalevskaya, A.A. (ed.) Psycholinguistic Researches: Word and Text, pp. 16–22. University of Tver Press, Tver (2002)
3. Bretones-Callejas, C.: Synaesthetic metaphors in English, Technical Reports, TR 01-008, International Computer Science Institute, Berkeley, USA (2001)
4. Cacciari, C.: Crossing the senses in metaphorical language. In: Gibbs, R.W. (ed.) The Cambridge Handbook of Metaphor and Thought, pp. 425–443. Cambridge University Press, New York (2008)
5. Huang, C.-R., Chung, S.-F., Ahrens, K.: An ontology-based exploration of knowledge systems for metaphor. In: Kishore, R., Ramesh, R., Sharman, R. (eds.) Ontologies: A Handbook of Principles, Concepts and Applications in Information Systems, pp. 489–517. Springer, Berlin (2006)

Semantic Profile as a Source of Polysemy: Insight from the Spatial-Configuration Verb *fàng* in Mandarin

Mei-chun Liu[✉] and Jui-ching Chang

Graduate Institute of Foreign Literatures and Linguistics,
National Chiao Tung University, Hsinchu, Taiwan
{meichunliu0107,showtheray}@gmail.com

Abstract. This study provides a linguistic insight to the issue of polysemy. It shows that semantic profile, an important cognitive mechanism, may be the source of verbal polysemy. With a close examination of corpus distribution of the high-frequency verb 放[*fàng*], we find that the diverse range of semantically and constructionally distinct uses of *fàng* can be viewed as profiling different stages of a motion-initiated event chain. We therefore propose that a multi-faceted verb such as *fàng* may involve a cognitively salient sequence of events as its conceptual basis and the various senses of the verb may highlight various portions of the lexical base as a result of semantic profile.

Keywords: Lexical semantics · Semantic profile · Polysemy · Mandarin *fàng*

1   Introduction

The issue of polysemy has been a central concern in linguistics and NLP research. The traditional sense enumeration approach has been replaced by more cognitively based accounts [1,2,3] and more generatively oriented works [4]. Recent studies on Mandarin polysemous verbs have also advanced to a corpus-based computational approach [5,6]. This study aims to propose an important mechanism in the account of polysemy that is largely neglected in previous studies. It argues that 'semantic profile' as a basic cognitive mechanism [7,8] may be the source for polysemous relations. Earlier works on polysemy have shown that metaphorical/metonymic extensions [1,2] and contextual re-interpretation [9] may give rise to different senses of a word. But little attention has been paid to polysemous words that do not fall into either of the above categories. Liu & Chou [10] and Chou [11] conducted a case study of the Mandarin multi-faceted verb 擠[*jǐ*] and argues that the different uses of *jǐ* can be viewed as profiling different portions of a base schema. The study is a pioneering work that shows how semantic base and profile can be at work in forming verbal polysemy. In the same vein, this study examined the polysemous verb 放[*fàng*] and found that *fàng* involves a wide range of uses that can be integrated as a natural sequence of motion-initiated, path-related sub-events of a base schema. Its polysemous nature pertains to the cognitive mechanism of base vs. profile, as *fàng* lexically encodes an event chain from caused motion to directed motion to spatial relocation along a path schema that serves as the conceptual base for various sense selections profiling distinct stages of the event chain [12].

© Springer International Publishing Switzerland 2015
Q. Lu and H.H. Gao (Eds.): CLSW 2015, LNAI 9332, pp. 24–32, 2015.
DOI: 10.1007/978-3-319-27194-1_3

2   The Issue of Polysemy

The definition of polysemy is 'a word that contains different but related meanings' [3], [13]. Central to the issue are two questions: how the different meanings come about and how they are related. From the perspective of cognitive semantics, sense extension is mainly motivated by the cognitive mechanisms of metaphorical and metonymic transfers' [1], [2], [14]. That is, the sense of a word may extend from a more concrete, physio-spatial domain (the source domain) to a less tangible, more abstract domain (the target domain) by metaphorical or metonymic (part-for-whole) mapping principles.

As an illustration, Lakoff [2] looks at the English preposition OVER and proposes that the central sense of OVER is 'above and across' (as in 'The plane flew over'), which forms the basic image schema for various sense extensions through metaphorical and metonymic manipulation of the base schema.

However, the above principles may not apply to many polysemous verbs that encode equally concrete and tangible senses, such as 放[*fàng*], as it may be used to denote different but equally spatial-motional senses: 放人[*fàng rén*] (*set sb. free*), 放手[*fàng shǒu*] (*loose hand*), 放風箏[*fàng fēng zhēng*] (*fly a kite*), 放起落架[*fàng qǐ luò jià*] (*release the landing gear down*), 放書[*fàng shū*] (*put book*), etc. For such verbs, semantic profile may be the key to their polysemous extensions.

3   The Senses of *fàng*

The Mandarin verb *fàng* is found to have an extremely wide range of uses according to corpus distributions. Chinese WordNet [15] distinguishes thirty-seven different senses for *fàng*. Hwang & Chen [16] proposes eight distinct senses of *fàng* based on its frequent collocations as compared to those of the verb 擺[*bǎi*]. However, no further discussion is given as to the interrelations among the senses:

As a further attempt to minimize the number of senses, Luo [17] argues that, the different uses of *fàng* can be generalized into two major senses 'to put' and 'to release', both of which are physio-motional, as exemplified in (1)

(1)   a. To put:
　　　他們把書放在桌子上[*tā men bǎ shū fàng zài zhuō zi shàng*]
　　　'*They put the book on the table.*'
　　b. To release:
　　　他把老虎從籠子裡放了出來[*tā bǎ lǎo hǔ cóng lóng zi lǐ fàng le chū lái*]
　　　'*He releases the tiger out of the cage.*'

From the two fundamental meanings, other senses of *fàng* may be derived. For example, 'to add' is extended from 'to put', as '放鹽[*fàng yán*]' implicates the action of putting salt into the pot, thus 'adding salt' to other cooking ingredients. And 'to pasture' is extended from 'to release', as '放牛[*fàng niú*]' originally means 'releasing the cows from the cattle corral'.

Luo's study helps to reduce the multiple uses of *fàng* to two sense categories. However, there are still some unsolved problems that await for an answer. First, what is the relation between the two proposed senses of *fàng*? Are they 'ambiguous' or 'polysemous'? If they are polysemous, how are the two senses related? In other words, more detailed accounts are still needed to explain how the two senses are semantically motivated and conceptually related in the single verb form *fàng*? The question is twofolded: on one hand, it is obvious that there is no metaphorical extension between 'to release' and 'to put', as both meanings are equally spatial and physical. Hence, what motivates the two equally familiar and concrete senses? On the other hand, categories show prototype effects; hence, which sense is more prototypical in defining *fàng*? These questions beg a more detailed and principled account of the verb *fàng*.

As an attempt to answer the above questions, the present study shows that the diverse uses of *fàng* may be related by eventive inferences implicative of a causal chain [12] from motion to direction to spatial configuration. It thus proposes that the polysemous nature of *fàng* may be attributed to the cognition mechanism of semantic base and profile [7,8]. The two fundamental senses of *fàng* postulated in [17] may be integrated as denoting the two ends of a motional path which provides the conceptual base for profiling the various intermediate points along it, giving rise to the various senses of *fàng*.

4   Semantic Profile

The notion of semantic profile is first proposed by Langacker [7,8]. He argues that the meaning of a lexical unit may involve designated semantic base and profile. He stated that "a predication always has a certain scope, and within that scope it selects a particular substructure for designation.... I refer to the scope of a predication and its designatum as base and profile, respectively." [7: 183]. A semantic base functions as a cognitive frame presupposed by a lemma or a set of related lemmas, and semantic profile is the highlight within the lexical base. In other words, a word may encode a concept by profiling a certain aspect of a semantic base. For example, an 'arc' is the profile of a 'circle', as shown in Figure 1. Another example is the verb 'arrive'. While denoting the event of reaching a destination, 'arrive' presupposes an "extended path of motion on the part of its trajectory" [7: 246]. That is, with the semantic base of an entity (i.e. a trajector) moving to a destination, the verb 'arrive' profiles only the final portions of this base, where the trajector enters the vicinity of its destination and then reaches it, as illustrated in Figure 2:

Fig. 1. Semantic profile of 'arc'

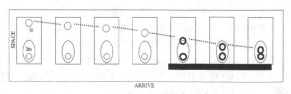

Fig. 2. Semantic profile of 'arrive'

Applying the concept of semantic base and profile, [10,11] examined the multi-faceted verb 擠[*jǐ*] and proposed that the diverse but related uses of *jǐ* may be viewed as profiling different facets of a container-containee schema. The verb denotes four major senses: 1) motion (e.g. 擠公車[*jǐ gōng chē*] (*to crowd into the bus*)), 2) spatial configuration (e.g. 擠在公車裡[*jǐ zài gōng chē lǐ*] (*crowded in the bus*)), 3) body contact (e.g. 人擠人[*rén jǐ rén*] (*people jostled against each other*)), and 4) removal (e.g. 擠牙膏[*jǐ yá gāo*] (*to squeeze the toothpaste out*)). The four senses are related as they profile various components of the designated base schema involving a confined space and its occupants, as Figure 3[1] illustrated.

In a similar vein, the notion of semantic base and profile also plays an important role in explaining the multiple senses of the spatial-configuration verb 放[*fàng*].

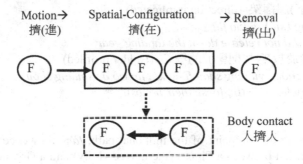

Fig. 3. Semantic base and profiles of '*j•*'arc

5   The Semantic Profile of *fàng*

5.1   Event Sequence of *fàng*

放[*fàng*] in Mandarin can be used to encode different types of motional events, such as 放書[*fàng shū*] (*to put*), 放鹽[*fàng yán*] (*to add*), 放映[*fàng yìng*] (*to play video/audio*), 放煙火[*fàng yān huǒ*] (*to set off fireworks*), 放和平鴿[*fàng hé píng gē*] (*to release*), etc. (cf. [16]). At first sight, it seems conceivable that the first two uses pertain to the meaning 'to put', and the rest 'to release', as generalized in [17].

In the following, we will show how the distinct senses of *fàng* may differ in their collo-constructional associations as observed in the corpus [19].

The 'Release' Sense

When *fàng* is used in the sense of releasing, it only takes a direct object, denoting the initial stage of a caused motion that a holdee is set free from its holding place, as exemplified in (2a-b). By implicational inference, the released entity will undertake a 'path' of motion involving a direction, as in (2c-d), where the motion may be complemented

---
[1] In the all of the Figures in this paper, 'F' stands for 'Figure' as opposed to 'Ground' [18]

with a directional phrase. In addition, the holder (source) can also be profiled as it takes on the object position and becomes the most salient argument in (2e).

(2) a. 他們六天後就放人(Source and Goal underspecified)
tā men liù tiān hòu jiù fàng rén
    'They release the ones (in custody) in 6 days.'
    b. 他們把老虎從籠子裡放了出來 (Source specified)
tā men bǎ lǎo hǔ cóng lóng zi lǐ fàng le chū lái
    'They release the tiger out of the cage.'
    c. 隨後大會放(出)和平鴿及五彩氣球 (Direction underspecified but implicated)
suí hòu dà huì fàng (chū) hé píng gē jí wǔ cǎi qì qiú
    'Later, the Assembly sent out the doves of peace and colorful balloons.'
    d. 飛機未放(下)起落架 (direction implicated)
fēi jī wèi fàng (xià) qǐ luò jià
    'The plane did not release down the landing gear.'
    e. 他們最後終於放手/放開緊握的雙手 (Holder profiled)
tā men zuì hòu zhōng yú fàng shǒu fàng kāi jǐn wò de shuāng shǒu
    'They finally let it go (lit. loose their hands).'

The 'Put' Sense
When used to refer to the endpoint of the motional path, *fàng* may encode a spatial configurational relation between a Figure (the moved entity) and a Ground (the locational endpoint), as the entity is moved toward and ends at a new location. In this sense, *fàng* behaves more like a verb of placement that requires a locative NP denoting the locational Goal (*dào* + Loc) or Ground (*zài* + Loc). The verb can then enter three different constructions expressing three salient ways of depicting the spatial relation: as a caused motion event (3a), as a Figure-oriented inchoative state (3b), or as a Ground-anchored stationary state (3c):

(3) a. 他把書包放到/在椅子上 (Caused motion)
tā bǎ shū bāo fàng dào zài yǐ zi shàng
    'He put the backpack to/on the chair.'
    b. 書包放在椅子上了 (Figure-oriented)
shū bāo fàng zài yǐ zi shàng le
    'The backpack was put on the chair.'
    c. 椅子上放著一個書包 (Ground-oriented)
yǐ zi shàng fàng zhe yí ge shū bāo
    'One the chair lay a backpack.'

The two senses of *fàng* are indeed distinct in their lexical and constructional collocations. But as stated above, a more pertinent issue is how the two senses are lexically motivated and related in the single verb *fàng*.

In view of eventive inferences along a motional path, the two senses may be taken as representing the two poles of a natural progression of motional relocation: 'to release' denotes the starting point of a motional path where an entity is moved away from a source, as schematized in Fig. 4. On the other side, 'to put' indicates the endpoint of the motional path where the entity is placed at a location, as schematized in Fig. 5.

An entity is moved away from a source   An entity is placed at a location

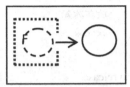   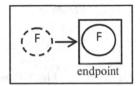

Fig. 4. Conceptual Schema of 'to release'   **Fig. 5.** Conceptual Schema of 'to put'

The two sub-schemas can be integrated into a continuous, full-scale path schema, as the motion 'to release an entity' implicates a path-directed final stage of the entity 'being put at a place'; similarly, the motion 'to put an entity at a place' presupposes its initial stage of 'being released' from a source location. Therefore, the two fundamental senses of *fang*, 'to release' and 'to put,' meet each other along a motional event chain, whereby a caused motion may start from an entity being released from its containing source and by eventive inferences, ending at a new location. The full-scale motional path schema thus provides the semantic base of *fang*, as shown in Fig. 6.

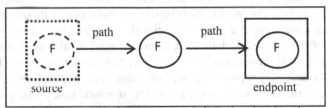

Away from a source → Toward a goal → End up in a location

Fig. 6. Integrated Conceptual Base of *fang*

With the postulation of this semantic base, the various uses of *fang* can then be plotted and anchored along the base as they lexically profile different portions of the base schema. In the corpus, we do find that *fang* may be combined with a wide array of phase markers that signal the various portions of the event schema. It ranges from an initial caused motion from a source with an underspecified direction (放出[*fang chū*]) to a directed motion (放下[*fang xià*]), to a motional path with an endpoint (放到 [*fang dào*]), and then to a positioning location (放在[*fang zài*]), as outlined in Fig. 7 and exemplified in (4) below:

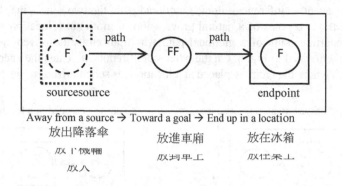

Fig. 7. Conceptual Schema of 'to release'

(4) Different stages of the event sequence of 放:

a. Release out (放出): releasing a holdee from a holder, such as 放人[*fàng rén*] (*set someone free*), 放和平鴿[*fàng hé píng gē*] (*release the peace doves*).

b. Motion with a direction (放下): the entity undergoes a direction-implicated motion, such as 放起落架[*fàng qǐ luò jià*] (*put down the landing gear*).

c. Motion to a Goal (放到): a directed path toward a goal, as in 放鹽巴(到鍋裡) [*fàng yán bā dào guō lǐ*] (*put the salt (to the pot)*).

d. Placement at an Endpoint (放在): the entity ends up at a new location, as in 放書在桌上[*fàng shū zài zhuō shàng*] (*put the book on the table*).

The proposed analysis is based on the natural inference of a caused motion event sequence that involves the motion of releasing a Figure out of its original place and then the Figure's undergoing a directed motional path to end up at a new Ground. The ending state of the motional chain is a Figure-Ground spatial configuration that is inherent in the lexical meaning of *fàng*. The proposal helps to motivate the interrelatedness of the previously separate senses 'releasing' and 'putting', by taking them as both anchored in the same conceptual frame (the semantic base). Moreover, the postulation of the semantic base itself can be evidenced from the fact that there are instances of *fàng* that are used in a way to denote the whole array of the motional path, from the initial stage of releasing to the ending result of placement, as shown in (5).

(5) a. 他們將氣球**放上**天空
     tā men jiāng qì qiú fàng shàng tiān kōng
     'They release the balloon to the sky.'
   b. 趙國忠把犯人**放出**至走道
     zhào guó zhōng bǎ fàn rén fàng chū zhì zǒu dào
     'Chao release the prisoners to the aisle.'

In the above examples, the whole path schema is referred to as the verb phrase 放上天空[*fàng shàng tiān kōng*] (*released up to the sky*) and 放出至走道[*fàng chū zhì zǒu dào*] (*released out to the hallway*) denotes both the initial stage of moving away from (an unspecified source) and the resultative stage of landing at a specified end-point-location. In sum, the different but related stages along the motional path may be profiled in the various uses of *fàng*, giving rise to the polysemous status of *fàng*. The verb *fàng*, typically categorized as a spatial-configuration verb, may actually encode a motion-related event chain with a series of progressional stages along a path schema ending at a Figure-Ground configuration. This is why *fàng* is lexically multi-faceted, with a range of equally concrete and spatially-related senses. From the basic spatial uses, other non-spatial uses, such as 放心[*fàng xīn*] (*put down worries*), 放下心頭重擔[*fàng xià xīn tóu zhòng dàn*] (*put down mental burdens*), may then be derived through commonly-recognized metaphorical extensions.

6   Conclusion

This study challenges traditional approaches to polysemy and proposes that semantic base and profile may be an important source of lexical polysemy. The case studies of the verbs 擠[*jǐ*] *and* 放[*fàng*] in Mandarin show that spatial-motional verbs may be multi-faceted in denoting various stages of a caused motion chain that involves a sequence of naturally implicated subevents. The semantically different but related senses of *fàng* can only be accounted for as deriving from a cognitively contingent frame of event chain, which serves as the base for semantic profiles. The distinct senses of *fàng* can then be related as profiling the different stages of the event chain. The study is significant as it explores the unique properties of spatial-configurational verbs that lexically involve a complicated event schema and it ultimately provides a new insight to the issue of verbal polysemy.

Acknowledgements. This study is sponsored by the Ministry of Science and Technology, Taiwan ROC. Grand no. 103-2410-H-009-022-MY3

References

1. Sweetser, E.E.: Polysemy vs. Abstraction: mutually exclusive or complementary? In: Proceedings of the Twelfth Annual Meeting of the Berkeley Linguistics Society, pp. 528–538. Berkeley Linguistics Society, Berkeley (1986)
2. Lakoff, G.: Women, fire, and dangerous things: What categories reveal about the mind. University of Chicago Press, Chicago (1990)
3. Tuggy, D.: Ambiguity, polysemy, and vagueness. Cognitive Linguistics (includes Cognitive Linguistic Bibliography) 4(3), 273–290 (1993)
4. Pustejovsky, J.: The Generative Lexicon. MIT Press (1995)
5. Liu, M.C.: Lexical information and beyond: Meaning coercion and constructional inference of the Mandarin verb gǎn. Journal of Chinese Linguistics 33(2), 310–332 (2005)
6. Hong, J.F.: Verb Sense Discovery in Mandarin Chinese—A Corpus based Knowledge-Intensive Approach. Springer, Berlin (2014)
7. Langacker, R.W.: Foundations of cognitive grammar: Theoretical prerequisites, vol. 2. Stanford University Press, Stanford (1987)

8. Langacker, R.W.: Concept, image, and symbol: The cognitive basis of grammar. Mouton de Gruyter, Berlin/New York (1990)
9. Traugott, E.C., König, E.: The semantics-pragmatics of grammaticalization revisited. In: Traugott, E.C., Bernd H. (eds.) Approaches to Grammaticalization, vol. 1, pp. 189–218. John Benjamins Publishing Co. (1991)
10. Liu, M.C., Chou, S.P.: Semantic profile in an event chain: the cross-categorial verb *jǐ* in Mandarin Chinese. Paper presented at The 22nd IACL & the 26th NACCL. University of Maryland, Maryland (2014)
11. Chou, S.P.: Semantic Profile of the Multi-faceted Verb *jǐ* in Mandarin Chinese. MA thesis. National Tsing Hua University, Hsinchu (2014)
12. Croft, W.: Syntactic categories and grammatical relations: The cognitive organization of information. University of Chicago Press, Chicago (1991)
13. Lyons, J.: Semantics, vol. 2. Cambridge University Press, Cambridge (1977)
14. Lakoff, G., Johnson, M.: Metaphors We Live By. Chicago University Press, Chicago (1980)
15. Chinese Wordnet. http://lope.linguistics.ntu.edu.tw/cwn2/
16. Hwang, Y.C., Chen, X.Y.: Relation between Lexical Collocation and Near-synonymy: A Corpus-based Study. Chinese Teaching Research 2(2), 57–71 (2005). (in Chinese)
17. Luo, Y.P.: The Study of the Polysemous Verb 'Fàng4' in Mandarin Chinese. MA thesis. National Tsing Hua University, Hsinchu (2011). (in Chinese)
18. Talmy, L.: How language structures space. In: Pick Jr., H.L., Acredolo, L.P. (eds.) Spatial Orientation, pp. 225–282. Springer, New York (1983)
19. Chinese Word Sketch Engine. http://wordsketch.ling.sinica.edu.tw/

A Contrastive Analysis of *hen* and *ting* in Chinese

Qiongpeng Luo[1] and Yuan Wang[2](✉)

[1] College of Liberal Arts, Nanjing University, Nanjing, China
qpluo@nju.edu.cn
[2] College of Liberal Arts, Nanjing Normal University, Nanjing, China
wynjnu@126.com

Abstract. Though *hen* and *ting* (both glossed as 'very'), the two widely used degree adverbs in Chinese, are interchangeable in some contexts, there arc a number of contexts in which they cannot be used in place of each other. To account for this, this study proposes that the locus of semantic difference between *hen* and *ting* lies in the ways by which they manipulate the standards of comparison: while *hen* is always associated with a norm-related standard, *ting* involves some contextually salient one. This novel semantics provides better prediction for and account of the distribution of *hen* and *ting* in a variety of constructions.

Keywords: Chinese degree words *hen* and *ting* · Degree · Norm-related standard · Saliency-related standard

1   Introduction

This study provides a contrastive analysis of the lexical semantics of *hen* and *ting*, two widely used degree words in Chinese, in a degree-based semantics framework. Traditional descriptive grammars group *hen* and *ting* in the same class of *chengdu fuci* (degree words) that refer to high degrees. In reference books of Chinese grammar and dictionaries, thcy are always defined by each other. For example, the definition for *ting* in *Xiandai Hanyu Cidian* 'the Dictionary of Modern Chinese' is done by means of *hen*:

(1) The definition of *ting*: (means) *hen*, expresses high degrees

The other reference books, such as [1], have a similar treatment. There may be some reasons for doing so. In some cases, *hen* and *ting* can be used interchangeably:[1]

(2) a. *Zhe   zuo shan   {hen/ting} gao.*
    Dem Cl mountain   very   tall
    'This mount is very tall.'

---

* Corresponding author: Yuan Wang, College of Liberal Arts, Nanjing Normal University, Nanjing, China.
[1] Abbreviations used in the glosses are as follows: BI: *bi*; Cl: classifiers; Dem: demonstrative; Neg: negation; Q: question marker. Since there is no exact counterpart of *ting* in English, *hen* and *ting* are both glossed as 'very'.

© Springer International Publishing Switzerland 2015
Q. Lu and H.H. Gao (Eds.): CLSW 2015, LNAI 9332, pp. 33–41, 2015.
DOI: 10.1007/978-3-319-27194-1_4

　　b. *Zhangsan {hen/ting} congming.*
　　Zhangsan　　very　　　　intelligent
　　'Zhang San is very intelligent.'

Another commonality between them is that both are disallowed in comparatives. The following examples are adopted from [2]:

(3) a. * *Bijiao qilai,　zhe　　ge fangzi　{hen/ting}　　ganjing.*
　　　　compare　　Dem　Cl house　　very　　　　clean
　　　　Lit.: 'Comparatively, this house is very cleaner.'
　　b. * *Zhe　ge　haizi　bi　　na　　ge　haizi　{hen/ting} ke'ai.*
　　　　Dem　Cl　child　BI　Dem　　Cl　child　　very　　lovely
　　　　Lit.: 'This child is more very lovely than that child.'
　　c. * *Zhe　gen　　zhugan　　bi　na　gen　zhugan　　{hen/ting} chang.*
　　　　Dem　Cl　bamboo-stick　BI　Dem Cl　bamboo-stick　very　　　long
　　　　Lit.: 'This bamboo stick is very longer than that one.'

Some studies thus claim that *hen* and *ting* have the same lexical semantics, and their only difference is about stylistics, that is, *hen* is used both for written and oral languages while *ting* is mainly reserved for oral uses (see [2] and references therein). In this paper, we takes issue with this descriptive generalization and argue that *hen* and *ting*, while both are degree words and have a common semantics related to degrees, have distinct lexical semantics. Their difference correlates with a systematic difference about how standards are fixed when degree adverbs apply to the scales (sets of ordered degrees) denoted by the adjectives. We propose that *hen* selects a norm-related standard in a given context or speech community, while *ting* chooses a salient standard that the speaker has in mind. The way *ting* fixes its domain of operation is reminiscent of how domain restriction is operative for quantifiers ('everyone smiled' doesn't require everyone on the planet smiled, but just the contextually salient set of persons did the smiling). This novel semantics provides better prediction for and account of the distribution of *hen* and *ting* in a variety of constructions.

　　The paper is organized as follows. Section 2 examines some differences in distribution in which *hen* and *ting* cannot be used in place of each other (due to limit of space, we focus on the modificational structure of 'Adv-Adj' in this paper). Section 3 introduces degree semantics and provides our novel and more explicit lexical semantics for *hen* and *ting* in a degree-based semantics framework. Section 4 further discusses how the facts receive a better treatment on the present account. Section 5 concludes.

2　　When Are *hen* and *ting* Different?

Despite some commonalities and interchangeable uses between them, *hen* and *ting* behave differently in a number of constructions. We focus on the adjectival domain in this paper.[2]

---

[2] Being adverbs, both *hen* and *ting* can modify VPs (*{hen/ting} xihuan X* 'very like X'). Due to the limit of space, we have to set aside the issues of their differences in verbal domains.

First, while *hen* can be used to modify almost all relative adjectives, *ting* is much more restricted: it is mainly used to modify those more casual and vernacular adjectives. The following examples and judgment are based on [2: p.10]:

(4) *{hen/*ting} hanleng*   'very chilly'
    {hen/*ting} beifen   'very indignant'
    {hen/*ting} zhuangguan   'very magnificent'
    {hen/*ting} changsheng   'very prosperous'
    {hen/*ting} shenshen   'very cautious'
    {hen/*ting} xiaotiao   'very stagnant'

The adjectives like *xiaotiao* 'stagnant', *hanleng* 'chilly', *beifen* 'indignant' are more often used in written languages. [2] thus suggests the contrast in distribution as shown in (4) is due to a stylistic difference between *hen* and *ting*: while *hen* can be used for both written and oral languages, *ting* is reserved for vernacular and oral uses. The observation itself is significant, but we don't think stylistics is the one that is responsible for the contrast as shown in (4). For two reasons. First, our informants don't think *ting* is absolutely impossible with the so-called 'formal' adjectives. For example, the adjectives such as *jijing* 'vigilant' and *anggui* 'expensive', which are formal and mostly used in written languages, are able to be modified by *ting*: *zhe haizi ting jijing* 'this child is very vigilant'; *zhe fangzi ting anggui* 'this house is very expensive', etc. Second, it is almost impossible to tell which adjective is 'for written language', and which is for 'oral language', and vice versa. The difficulty to draw a clear-cut line between 'written languages' and 'oral languages' undermines the explanatory force of the stylistic analysis.

Another difference surfaces when *hen* and *ting* are preceded by the negation word *bu* 'not' and followed by adjectives. While the sequences of *bu-hen-Adj* 'Neg very Adj' are acceptable, those of *bu-ting-Adj* 'Neg very Adj' are not:

(5) a. *bu hen ke'ai* 'not very lovely', *bu hen gaoxing* 'not very happy'
    b. **bu ting ke'ai* 'not very lovely', **bu ting gaoxing* 'not very happy'

In the literature, there has been no motivated explanation for this contrast yet.

One more difference between *hen* and *ting* concerns about their (in)compatibility with the emphatic/assertive uses of *shi* 'be'. *Hen* is possible to co-occur with *shi* to form *hen-shi-Adj* sequences. With *ting*, it is always odd to do so:

(6) a. *hen shi renao* 'very be boisterous', *hen shi congming* 'very be intelligent',
       hen shi yihan 'very be regretful'
    b. **ting shi renao* 'very be boisterous', **ting shi congming* 'very be intelligent',
       *ting shi yihan 'very be regretful'

The traditional studies that treat *hen* and *ting* the same thus miss these differences between them. We propose that the afore-mentioned differences indicate that they have different lexical semantics. To which we turn in the following section.

3   Degrees and Standards

If both *hen* and *ting* are about degrees, could it be possible to attribute their difference in lexical semantics also to degrees? So to speak, they 'select' different degrees. We demonstrate in this section that this intuition is not only possible, but also is desirable. We adopt a degree semantics framework to flesh out this idea.

A few words need to be said about the notions of 'degree' and 'scale'. Degree is the way we measure the extent of a dimension (e.g., if X is beautiful, X is beautiful to a certain extent/degree). Degrees are often represented by real numbers and their ordering by $\leq$. A scale is a set of partially ordered degrees along a certain dimension (such as *volume, weight, intelligence*, etc.). Let S be a scale, then S is a triple structure such that S = $<$D, $\leq$, DIM $>$ (DIM: dimension, such as *height, weight, intelligence*, etc.). The scheme below illustrates how a typical scale looks like:

$$S \left\{ \begin{array}{l} d_n \\ \dots \\ d_3 \\ d_2 \\ d_1 \\ d_0 \end{array} \right.$$

The part-of relation $\leq$ on S is transitive ($\forall d,d',d''[d\leq d' \wedge d'\leq d'' \rightarrow d\leq d'']$), anti-symmetric ($\forall d,d'[d\leq d' \wedge d'\leq d \rightarrow d=d']$) and reflexive ($\forall d[d\leq d']$). A scale is linear. And the degrees are dense:

(7) A set of degrees S with the ordering relation $\leq$ is a scale iff $\forall d,d' \in S$:
   (a) $\leq$ is linear: $d\leq d' \vee d'\leq d$
   (b) $\leq$ is dense: $d\leq d' \rightarrow \exists d'' \in S[d\leq d'' \wedge d'' \leq d']$

Degrees and scale provide a direct way for the representation of the lexical semantics of adjectives. An adjective always introduces some dimensions, such as height ('tall'), weight ('heavy'), intelligence ('intelligent'), prettiness ('pretty'), width ('wide'), depth ('deep'), etc. Almost for each (relative) adjective, we can think of some dimension associated with it.[3] According to one standard theory of degree semantics, adjectives denote relations from individuals to degrees. Instead of referring to properties (8a) as assumed in traditional semantics, the lexical entry of an adjective such as *piaoliang* 'beautiful' is as shown in (8b) in this degree-based semantics (cf. [3, 4, 5, 6] among many others):

(8) The lexical entry of *piaoliang* 'beautiful':
   (a) Traditional semantics: $[\![piaoliang]\!]$ = λx. **beautiful** (x)
   (b) Degree semantics: $[\![piaoliang]\!]$ = λdλx. **beautiful** (d)(x)

Adjectives are about degrees along a scale. Degrees can be operated and manipulated. One fundamental semantic contribution of the adverbs that modify adjectives is they are operators on the degrees along a certain scale. This defines the lexical seman-

---

[3] For the distinction between absolute adjectives and relative adjectives, see [3].

tics of the (degree) adverbs. Degree adverbs are functions from (gradable) predicates to individuals such that the degrees the individuals possess exceed a certain EXTENT. Different degree adverbs involve different extents of comparison. We can think of 'extent' as some standard of comparison, or in more explicit terms, the value of a degree. Lexically speaking, degree adverbs may be different from each other in the ways by which they select the standard of comparison (or the value of the standard of comparison). This is the guiding intuition that underlies our treatment of *hen* and *ting*.

A bit more formally and explicitly, we propose that the standard of comparison associated with *hen* is always a norm-related standard. A norm is a conventionalized, well-established standard that's been assumed, known to both the speaker and the hearer in a given context or a speech community. Norm-related standards are relatively fixed values. For example, language users in a speech community know, or at least take for granted, what the norm of height for 1-grade primary school students is, for 2-grade primary school students, and so on. We also know what is the norm of height for NBA players. So when people use the structure of '*hen* AP', they simply mean the degree a certain individual has exceeds some norm-related standard. Suppose the norm-related standard of height for NBA players is 2m, then *X hen gao* means X is tall to a degree which exceeds the norm-related standard, namely, 2m. It is important to note that to know a norm-related standard doesn't entail to know the exact value of the standard. It could simply be to know the (possible) range of the values.

The way *ting* selects its standard of comparison is different from that of *hen*. Unlike *hen*, *ting* is always associated with a contextually salient standard. This standard is related to a number of factors, such as the speaker's subjective evaluation, the speaker's knowledge about the object/individual in discussion, and the spatio-temporal properties of the context. Unlike the relatively fixed norm-related standard of *hen*, the salient standard of *ting* is heavily dependent on context and the factors on the part of the speakers. This salient feature of *ting* is reminiscent of the domain restriction feature of quantifiers. For example, *everyone smiled* doesn't require the total population of the earth, but the contextually salient set of people smiled. A contextually salient set can be represented by a subset of a set (cf. [7]):

(9) $[\![everyone_C \text{ smiled }]\!] = 1$ iff $\forall x \in C[\textbf{person}(x) \rightarrow \textbf{smiled }(x)]$

Taken together, the lexical entries for *hen* and *ting* are provided as (10a) and (10b) respectively (C: context variable):

(10) a. $[\![hen]\!] = \lambda G_{<d,et>}\lambda x. \exists d[G(d)(x) \wedge d \geq \textbf{Norm}_C(G)]$

    b. $[\![ting]\!] = \lambda G_{<d,et>}\lambda x. \exists C' \exists d[G(d)(x) \wedge C' \subseteq C \wedge d \geq \textbf{Standard}_{C'}(G)]$

The 'G' in (10a-b) stands for a gradable predicate. The formulas in (10a-b) mean *hen* and *ting* are functions from gradable predicates to properties. As (10) show, *hen* and *ting* have a common semantics: they both are operators on the degrees (of a certain scale), and both select degrees that exceed some standards (**Standard/Norm** are two-place predicates which operate on a set of ordered degrees and return a degree which satisfies 'standard/norm'). This common semantics explains why *hen* and *ting* are interchangeable, when no additional conditions are imposed. *Hen* and *ting* are different in the ways they fix the standards of comparison. Saliency may be about a subset of a set in a certain context. Here is an example of saliency. If there are ten faculty members in the computer science department, and their publication records for the year 2014 are as shown in (11):

(11) {<professor, number of publications>: <a, 1>, <b, 3>, <c, 4>, <d, 7>, <e, 6>, <f, 5>, <g, 10>, <h, 20>, <i, 16>, <j, 19>}

In the scenario described in (11), (12a) is false while (12b) may be true:

(12) a. *g jiaoshou   hen   duo-chan.* [false in (11)]
   g professor very productive
   'Professor g is very productive.'
   b. *g jiaoshou ting duo-chan.*
   'Professor g is very productive.'

Because *hen* is associated with a norm-related standard, and we know from (11), that Professor h published 20 papers in the year 2014. Against this standard, publishing of 10 papers a year cannot be regarded as a 'norm'. This is why (12a) is flatly false. (12b) may be true, because the speaker may utter it to talk about a salient set of the set of professors:

(13) a. Set of professor: D = {a, b, c, d, e, f, g, h, i, j}
   b. Salient set D' of D: D'⊆ D: D'={a, b, c, d, e, f, g}

In the salient set D', Professor g published the most papers in the year 2014. This satisfies the semantic requirement of *ting* (cf. (10b)). This domain-restriction semantics in terms of saliency renders (12b) acceptable in the scenario described in (11).

Furthermore, the present account correctly predicts that *X hen AP* entails *X is AP*, but *X ting AP* may not entail *X is AP*:

(14) a. *X hen AP* ⇒ *X is AP*
   (e.g., *X hen gao* 'X is very tall' ⇒ *X shi gao de* 'X is tall')
   b. *X ting AP* *⇒ *X is AP*
   (e.g., *X ting gao* 'X is very tall' *⇒ *X shi gao de* 'X is tall')

What about the syntax of *hen/ting AP*? Adopting the Degree Phrase Hypothesis (cf. [3], [8]), we argue that both *hen AP* and *ting AP* are Degree Phrases (DegPs), in which both *hen* and *ting* are heads. The structures and semantic derivations for *hen gao* and *ting gao* are provided as (15a) and (15b) respectively for illustration:

(15) a. *hen gao*

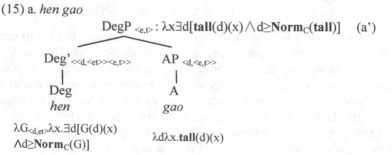

$$\text{DegP}_{<e,t>} : \lambda x \exists d[\mathbf{tall}(d)(x) \wedge d \geq \mathbf{Norm}_C(\mathbf{tall})] \quad (a')$$

$\text{Deg'}_{<<d,<et>><e,t>>}$ $\text{AP}_{<d,<e,t>>}$

Deg   A
hen   *gao*

$\lambda G_{<d,et>}\lambda x.\exists d[G(d)(x) \wedge d \geq \mathbf{Norm}_C(G)]$ $\lambda d\lambda x.\mathbf{tall}(d)(x)$

b. *ting gao*

$$DegP_{<e,t>}: \lambda x \exists C' \exists d[\textbf{tall}(d)(x) \wedge C' \subseteq C \wedge d \geq \textbf{Standard}_{C'}(\textbf{tall})] \quad (b')$$

Deg' $_{<<d,<et>><e,t>>}$ AP$_{<d,<e,t>>}$

Deg   A

ting   *gao*

$\lambda G_{<d,et>} \lambda x. \; \exists C' \exists d[G(d)(x) \wedge$ $\lambda d \lambda x. \textbf{tall}(d)(x)$
$C' \subseteq C \wedge d \geq \textbf{Standard}_{C'}(G)]$

The semantic representation (a') means some individual is tall to a certain degree d, and d exceeds the norm-related standard of 'tallness'. (b') means some individual is tall to a certain degree d, and d exceeds some salient standard of 'tallness'. These semantic representations are intuitively correct.

The syntactic treatment ('{*hen/ting*}AP' as DegPs) is also motivated by the fact that comparatives and *hen/ting* are in complementary distribution. Comparative morphemes/words are also heads of DegPs. If *hen* and *ting* are heads of DegPs, it is expected that they will not be able to support another Deg heads. The facts as shown in (3) are explained.

4   Discussion

The present account correctly predicts that, in the absence of additional restrictions, *hen* and *ting* (both are operators on degrees) are interchangeable. However, that they can be used interchangeably, i.e., they can appear in the same syntactic positions, doesn't mean they are semantically identical. The subtle semantic difference between them is captured on the present account. It has been noted that *hen* refers to a higher degree than *ting* ([1]). This is expected on the present account: because salient standard is always the standard of a subset of a set, consequently, the value for the norm-related standard is always greater than the value for the salient standard.

The contrast as shown in (4) is also explained. The fact that *ting* is always associated with a contextually salient standard means that it is interacted with language use more closely. The 'formal' adjectives that are mainly used in written languages are more difficult to incur appropriate standards of comparison, partly because their meaning are less accessible to language users, partly because their uses out of the blue make the language users bewildered.

The acceptability of the sequences of *bu-hen-Adj* versus the unacceptability of the sequences of *bu-ting-Adj* is also expected. The relevant examples are repeated below:

(5) a. *bu hen ke'ai* 'not very lovely', *bu hen gaoxing* 'not very happy'

b. **bu ting ke'ai* 'not very lovely', **bu ting gaoxing* 'not very happy'

This contrast results from the different semantic entailments of *hen* and *ting*. We have shown that 'X *hen* AP' always entails 'X is AP', while 'X *ting* AP' may not do so.

When the structure '*hen* AP' is preceded by the negation word *bu*, the semantic entailment preserves: *bu hen ke'ai* 'not very lovely' doesn't necessarily entail *bu ke'ai* 'not lovely' (that is, *X is not very lovely* only means X is not lovely to the extent of satisfying a norm related standard. X can still be lovely to some extent nonetheless). By contrast, 'X *ting* AP' doesn't entail 'X is AP', so when '*ting* AP' is preceded by the negation word *bu*, the whole sequence is uninterpretable (it is hard to distinguish *bu ting ke'ai* from *bu ke'ai* semantically). This can be salvaged in rhetoric questions. To compare (5b) with (16) below:

(16) *Bu shi ting ke'ai   de ma?*
     Neg be very   lovely de Q (rhetoric)
     'Isn't it very lovely?'

In rhetoric questions, the negative meaning is cancelled. (16) means some individual is lovely to a degree which exceeds some contextually salient standard (is it not so?). There is no problem with this semantic interpretation.

That *hen* and *ting* have different semantic entailments (resulted from their difference in lexical semantics) also explains the contrast in (6):

(6) a. *hen shi renao* 'very be boisterous', *hen shi congming* 'very be intelligent',
     hen shi yihan 'very be regretful'
   b. **ting shi renao* 'very be boisterous', **ting shi congming* 'very be intelligent',
     *ting shi yihan 'very be regretful'

Shi in (6) is used assertively/emphatically, that is, it adds some sense of assertiveness. This sense gets enhanced in the presence of *hen*, which involves a relatively fixed, norm related standard. Since *ting* doesn't involve any fixed standard, the assertive sense becomes trivial in its presence. It is this semantic triviality that is responsible for oddness of (6b).

The present account also explains the difference in distribution of *hen* and *ting* when they are preceded by *hai*. *Hai* has some concessive sense which means the degree the [Adv AP] refers to is not so bad (that it doesn't exceed the bearable limits of the speaker). Because *hen* is always associated with a norm related, fixed standard, it is semantically incompatible with *hai*. By contrast, *ting* is semantically compatible with it. This prediction is borne out: '*hai [hen AP]*'is always odd, while '*hai [ting AP]*' is acceptable:

(17) a. ^{??} *hai hen   ke'ai*
       so   very lovely
   b. *hai ting   ke'ai*
     so   very   lovely

Another elusive difference in meaning between *hen* and *ting* also gets explained. It has been reported in various descriptive studies that *hen* is more objective, and *ting* more subjective. This is expected on the present account: contextual saliency is dependent on factors on the part of speakers (speaker's knowledge, range of would-be audience, evaluation, etc.). It is the speaker who judges which (set) is more salient, and which is not. Speaker-oriented factors give rise to the effect of the subjectiveness of *ting*.

5   Conclusion

Hen and *ting*, two widely degree adverbs, used to be treated the same in traditional grammars. This blurred the subtle difference in lexical semantics between them and leaves their distributional contrast in a number of contexts unexplained. This study provides a more explicit semantic account. As degree adverbs, both *hen* and *ting* operate on a set of ordered degrees (along a certain dimension provided by the gradable adjectives) and select degrees that exceed some standards of comparison. However, *hen* and *ting* are not exactly alike: they are associated with different standards of comparison: the former is norm-related, while the latter is always about some contextually salient one that the speaker has in mind. We have shown how a cluster of facts can be better explained on the present account.

The present account has some other welcome consequence: despite the fact that all degree adverbs operate on degrees along certain scales, they may differ from each other in the values of the standards of comparison they manipulate (Kennedy 2007). We demonstrate in this study how this idea can be implemented in a formal and explicit way.

Acknowledgements. This work is financially supported by Humanities and Social Sciences Research Fund, the Ministry of Education, P. R. of China (grant 12YJC740074 to the first author and grant 14YJC740089 to the second author) and Jiangsu Provincial Social Sciences Fund (grant 14YYC002 to the second author), to which we are grateful. We'd also like to thank the anonymous reviewers for their helpful comments on an earlier draft of the paper.

References

1. Lü, S. (ed.): 800 Words in Modern Chinese (revised edition). The Commercial Press, Beijing (1999). (Xiandai Hanyu Babai Ci (in Chinese))
2. Ma, Z.: On the Degree Adverbs *hen*, *ting*, *guai* and *lao* in Mandarin Chinese. Chinese Language Learning **2**, 8–13 (1991). (Putonghua li de chengdu fuci hen, ting, guai, lao. Hanyu Xuexi (in Chinese))
3. Kennedy, C.: Vagueness and Grammar: the Semantics of Relative and Absolute Gradable Adjectives. Linguistics and Philosophy **30**, 1–45 (2007)
4. Cresswell, J.: The semantics of degree. In: Partee, B. (ed.) Montague Grammar, pp. 261–292. Academic Press, New York (1976)
5. von Stechow, A.: Comparing Semantic Theories of Comparison. Journal of Semantics **3**, 1–77 (1984)
6. Morzycki, M.: Modification. Cambridge University Press, Oxford (2015). https://www.msu.edu/~morzycki/work/papers/modification_book.pdf (to be published)
7. Westerståhl, D.: Determiners and context sets. In: van Bentham, J., ter Meulen, A. (eds.) Generalized Quantifiers in Natural Language, pp. 45–72. Foris, Dordrecht (1985)
8. Kennedy, C.: Polar Opposition and the Ontology of 'Degrees'. Linguistics and Philosophy **24**, 33–70 (2001)

Qualia Structure in Creative Metaphor

Yi Ting Tsai[✉]

National Taiwan University, No. 1, Sec. 4, Roosevelt Rd., Taipei 10617, Taiwan (R.O.C.)
r02142004@ntu.edu.tw

Abstract. In psycholinguistics, there are mixed results regarding the processes humans decode meanings to reach a metaphorical reading. However, the experimental materials have not been examined systematically using lexical-semantic approach. In this study, the experimental materials were analyzed using the qualia structure. The results verified that qualia are important in creative meaning construction, and that the Agentive quale is the one that possibly initiates the "imaginative leap" to achieve the creative meaning. Also, this phenomenon is prominent neuropsychologically in people with better image ability.

Keywords: Qualia structure · Creative metaphor · Individual difference

1   Introduction

Metaphors are one of the pervasive means we utilize to describe the world. As Lakoff and Johnson [8] stated, "our ordinary conceptual system, in terms of which we both think and act, is fundamentally metaphorical in nature." The theory has motivated abundant research over the decades on the meaning and comprehension of metaphors. In psycholinguistics, previous studies suggest at least four main models of metaphor processing: direct access model, indirect access model, parallel access model, and graded salience model. Basically, the models all suggest that for a metaphor, there is a dynamic relationship between its literal meaning and metaphorical meaning. Specifically, while the direct access model argues that metaphorical meanings are automatically accessed when people read metaphors [3,6,9], indirect access model proposes that literal meanings must be eliminated before reaching metaphorical meanings [4,11]. The parallel access model holds that literal meanings and metaphorical meanings are activated simultaneously during metaphor comprehension, [13] and the graded salience model suggests that salience, which is often modulated by familiarity, frequency, and conventionality, is the key factor influencing metaphor comprehension. [2]

However, exactly how humans decode the language to reach a metaphorical reading is still not resolved in psycholinguistics because of different tasks of the experiments, different categories of the metaphors, and individual differences on levels of various cognitive abilities. While the tasks and individual cognitive differences are sometimes difficult to be parallel in each experiment, qualities of the metaphors are actually easier to control using linguistic analysis. To our knowledge, none of the

© Springer International Publishing Switzerland 2015
Q. Lu and H.H. Gao (Eds.): CLSW 2015, LNAI 9332, pp. 42–46, 2015.
DOI: 10.1007/978-3-319-27194-1_5

experimental materials have been examined systematically using lexical-semantic approach.

In psycholinguistics, Ahrens [1] has proposed mapping principles for Chinese conceptual metaphors. The principles were verified by a series of behavioral experiment. The principles mainly suggested that for creative conceptual metaphors to be established in Chinese, they should follow the mapping principles so as to be accepted and comprehended by the readers.

In semantics, Pustejovskian semantics may give us some insights to the meaning construction of creative metaphors as he proposes that the model of the generative lexicon is open-ended in nature and accounts for the creative usages of words in various contexts.[10] In view of this, we attempt to analyze the creative metaphors in the perspectives of Pustejovskian semantics.

In parallel to Pustejovsky's theory of qualia structure, Julius M. Moravcsik [7] demonstrated his AFT analysis to explain the productive potential of words. In his analysis, humans rely on rules of language to form the underspecified concept and initiate an "imaginative leap" to achieve metaphor construction when encountering creative language. To do this, we need to master the literal use of language and recognize lexical meaning is not merely "combining parts together". Qualia structure is therefore one of the possibilities explaining our profound knowledge of the literal use of language. According to Pustejovsky, qualia structure represents the internal relations of lexical meanings and explains for a large number of senses in each word. There are four components in qualia structure: constitutive role, formal role, agentive role, and telic role. [10]

In the current study, we plan to examine the qualia structure of a set of literal words, familiar metaphors and unfamiliar metaphors that was established and verified for validity in our previous psycholinguistic research.[12] Unlike conceptual metaphors relying on structural mappings used in Ahren [1], our metaphors are ontological metaphors that do not utilize the mapping mechanisms. Therefore, we may eliminate some confounds between the quales and the conceptual rules. We aim to explore especially the qualia structure of unfamiliar metaphors and to see if they are similar with that of the familiar metaphor and/or literal words. The results may help explain for the internal meaning construction of creative metaphors and provide a perspective different from psychological paradigms.

2   Material

There were 240 Chinese sentences with the critical verb being in the sentence-final position. The critical verbs involve 80 action verbs. The sentence context is manifested to reach different readings of the same sentence-final verb in the same experimental set, leading to the three conditions: literal, familiar metaphoric, and unfamiliar metaphoric target verb. The materials were closely matched across conditions for lexical features, including familiarity, length, concreteness values, and cloze probability of the critical words; also the length, constraint and comprehensibility of the sentences. (Table 1)

Table 1. Average rating scores for lexical features of the sentence final critical words and sentential features of the materials. Standard deviations are shown in parentheses. (LIT: literal sentence; FM: familiar metaphor; UM: unfamiliar metaphor)   (Shen et al., 2015) [12]

Rating type	LIT	FM	UM
Word length	2.0 (0.6)	2.0 (0.6)	2.0 (0.6)
Word familiarity (1=very unfamiliar; 7=very familiar)	5.5 (0.7)	5.5 (0.7)	5.5 (0.7)
Word concreteness (1=very abstract; 7=very concrete)	5.7 (0.6)	5.7 (0.6)	5.7 (0.6)
Cloze probability (%)	0.0 (0.1)	0.0 (0.1)	0.0 (0.0)
Sentence length	9.3 (1.6)	9.4 (1.6)	9.4 (1.5)
Sentence constraint (%)	0.3 (0.1)	0.2 (0.1)	0.2 (0.1)
Sentence comprehensibility (1=very incomprehensible; 7=very comprehensible)	6.7 (0.4)	6.5 (0.5)	5.5 (0.8)
Sentence familiarity (1=very unfamiliar; 7=very familiar)	6.2 (0.8)	5.7 (1.0)	3.5 (0.9)
Sentence figurativeness (1=very literal; 7=very figurative)	1.5 (0.5)	4.4 (0.7)	4.8 (0.8)

3   Results

The noun combined with the critical verb in each sentence was analyzed according to its qualia role. The results show that for literal sentences, the Formal quale is the only role the noun takes. In familiar metaphor, the Telic quale is taken by most of the nouns, followed by the Formal quale, the Agentive quale, and the Constitutive quale. Finally, the Agentive quale is taken by most of the nouns in unfamiliar metaphor, followed by the Telic, the Formal, and the Constitutive quale. (Table 2)

Table 2. Results of the analysis on the qualia structure of the nouns combined with the critical verb. (LIT: literal sentence; FM: familiar metaphor; UM: unfamiliar metaphor)

	Constitutive	Formal	Telic	Agentive
LIT	0	80 (100%)	0	0
FM	2 (2%)	28 (35%)	34 (43%)	16 (20%)
UM	1 (1%)	14 (18%)	28 (35%)	37 (46%)

The Agentive quale seems to be an important role in forming creative usages. In addition, literal, familiar metaphor, and unfamiliar metaphor seem to form a continuum in which the Formal quale, the Telic quale, and the Agentive quale appear to play important roles in transforming metaphoricity of the lexical items.

4   Discussion

What do these results inspire us about the findings between our previous neuropsychological experiment and the current semantic analysis? Our previous experiment yielded that individual cognitive differences would modulate metaphor processing. Those with better imagery ability, as accessed by an established questionnaire: Visual Vividness Imagery Questionnaire (VVIQ), showed ERP imagery effect on the critical verb in LIT, FM, and UM condition compared to the abstract condition which served as a baseline. Moreover, there was a graded fashion with the imagery effect being the longest in LIT, a bit shorter in UM, and the shortest in FM. The time span actually reflected the duration in which the literal meaning was accessed and maintained. As for those with poorer imagery ability, there is no imagery effect in any of the conditions. Instead, there was an early N400 effect in UM compared to LIT and FM condition, denoting the temporary semantic difficulty in resolving unfamiliar metaphors.

The semantic analysis further verified the graded fashion seen in those with better imagery ability. The different time spans of imagery effect from LIT to FM condition could be explained by different roles the noun take from Formal to Telic roles in qualia structure. In other words, the Formal quale forms literal interpretation and causes a long imagery effect. This suggests that the Formal role in qualia structure is important for mastering the literal meaning as well as activate a mental imagery of that meaning. Next, the Agentive quale achieves creative metaphor understanding and shows a mediate imagery effect. This indicates that the Agentive quale is vital in creative language construction and mental imagery is helpful in transforming from concreteness to abstractness. Finally, the Telic quale forms familiar metaphor comprehension and arouses a short imagery effect. This represents that familiar metaphors is more abstract than literal sentences but are more concrete than the creative metaphors, and the Telic quale is the key factor in manipulating this phenomenon. Therefore, it seems that the "imaginative leap" may happen in the Agentive quale. It may be that the Agentive role is an important component for humans to access abstract as well as creative meanings. This part is what the pure results of our previous experiment cannot tell.

However, it may be wondered why such association cannot be observed in people with poorer imagery ability. One possible account is that current psychological theories of mental imagery have not recognized subjective experience such as qualia as an important element. [5] A lack of imagery effect does not necessarily equal to zero subjective qualia experience. That is to say, the qualia analysis holds true, and it is most explicit in people with better image ability while it may be more implicit in those with poorer image ability. It should not be inferred that people with low-VVIQ scores treat creative metaphor the same as literal sentence, and the best evidence is the early N400 effect seen in the low-VVIQ group.

5   Conclusion

In sum, parallel to our analysis in the experiment, different patterns of ERP effects seen in these two groups indicate two slightly different mechanisms they utilized in metaphor processing. The current study further verified that qualia are important in creative meaning construction, and that the Agentive quale is the one that possibly initiates the imaginative leap. Also, this phenomenon is prominent neuropsychologically in people with better image ability. The absence of this phenomenon in those with poorer image ability reflects both the exclusion of subjective qualia experience in current mental imagery theory and the truth that individual differences do manipulate details of creative language meaning construction online.

References

1. Ahrens, K.: Mapping Principles for Conceptual Metaphors. Researching and Applying Metaphor in the Real World **26**, 185 (2010)
2. Giora, R.: Understanding figurative and literal language: The graded salience hypothesis. Cognitive Linguistics **8**, 183–206 (1997)
3. Glucksberg, S.: The psycholinguistics of metaphor. Trends in Cognitive Sciences **7**(2), 92–96 (2003)
4. Grice, H.P.: Logic and conversation. In: Cole, P., Morgan, J.L. (eds.) Syntax and Semantics. Speech Acts, vol. 3, pp. 41–58. Seminar Press, New York (1975)
5. Hubbard, T.L.: The importance of a consideration of qualia to imagery and cognition. Consciousness and Cognition **5**(3), 327–358 (1996)
6. Hoffman, R.R., Kemper, S.: What could reaction-time studies be telling us about metaphor comprehension? Metaphor and Symbol **2**(3), 149–186 (1987)
7. Moravcsik, J.M.: Metaphor, creative understanding, and the generative lexicon. In: Bouillon, P., Busa, F. (eds.) The Language of Word Meaning. Cambridge University Press, New York (2001)
8. Lakoff, G., Johnson, M.: Metaphors we live by. University of Chicago Press (1980)
9. McElree, B., Nordlie, J.: Literal and figurative interpretations are computed in equal time. Psychonomic Bulletin & Review **6**(3), 486–494 (1999)
10. Pustejovsky, J., Boguraev, B.: A richer characterization of dictionary entries: the role of knowledge representation. In: Atkins, B.T.S., Zampolli, A. (eds.) Computational Approaches to the Lexicon, pp. 295–311. Oxford University Press, Oxford (1994)
11. Searle, J.R.: Expression and meaning: Studies in the theory of speech acts. Cambridge University Press (1979)
12. Shen, Z.Y., Tsai, Y.T., Lee, C.L.: Joint influence of metaphor familiarity and mental imagery ability on action metaphor comprehension: An ERP study. Language and Linguistics **16**(4), 615–637 (2015)
13. Glucksberg, S., Gildea, P., Bookin, H.B.: On understanding nonliteral speech: Can people ignore metaphors? Journal of Verbal Learning and Verbal Behavior **21**(1), 85–98 (1982)

The Implicit Negation and Counter-Expectation of *bai* in Mandarin Chinese

Jinghan Zeng[✉] and Yulin Yuan

Department of Chinese Language and Literature, Peking University, Beijing 100871, China
woshijinghan@126.com

Abstract. This paper studies the adverb *bai* in Mandarin Chinese, focusing on its implicit negation and counter-expectation from synchronic and diachronic perspectives. Firstly, *bai* indicates implicit negation which is able to entail an explicit negative sentence. Secondly, while studying the origin of *bai*, we are trying to trace its semantic evolution. Finally, an attempt is made to analyze counter-expectation, the pragmatic function which is caused by *bai*'s implicit negation and then triggers the deviation of speaker's expectation, and therefore to explore *bai*'s semantic construal.

Keywords: The adverb *bai* · Implicit negation · Semantic evolution · Counter-expectation

1 Introduction: The Polysemy of *bai* in Mandarin Chinese

According to *Modern Chinese Dictionary* (the 6th edition), the adverb *bai* has the following two semantic facets:

① doing something in vain or for nothing
② obtaining something for free or with no repayment

These two semantic facets are commonly used in Mandarin Chinese, take the following two sentences as examples:

(1) *Xuan chi na-lei yao-wu yao gen-ju yi-sheng-de zhun-que zhen-duan lai ding,*
　　Choose eat what kind medicine need depend-on doctor's accurate diagnose to decide,
　　fou-ze chi -le yi-xie bu-zhibing de yao deng-yu bai chi.
　　otherwise eat -INF some Neg-cure disease medicine equal *bai* eat.

This project get the foundation from *Major tender for the National Social Science Foundation: Chinese parataxis characteristic research and large knowledge base and corpus construction under the background of international Chinese language education* (12&ZD175). I would like to extend my sincere thanks.

Q. Lu and H.H. Gao (Eds.): CLSW 2015, LNAI 9332, pp. 47–61, 2015.
DOI: 10.1007/978-3-319-27194-1_6

It depends on the doctor's accurate diagnose to choose what kind of medicine to take, otherwise taking the medicine which can't cure the disease is in vain.

选吃哪类药物要根据医生的准确诊断来定,否则吃了一些不治病的药等于自吃。

(2) *Na-bang e   ren   you   shang-men-lai le,   yi-jiu shi   **bai**   chi   **bai**   he.*
Those   bad guy   again   come to door   -INF still   is   **bai**   eat   **bai**   drink.
Those bad guys came over again, eating and drinking for free as usual.
那帮恶人又来了,依旧是自吃自喝。

It is quite interesting that the adverb *bai* indicates two opposite semantic facets. Yulin Yuan(2014) used *paying out for nothing* and *getting something for free* to describe these two opposite meanings. In addition to these two semantic facets, *bai* indicates more senses in modern Mandarin Chinese, such as *unexpectedly, unreasonably, specially*, etc (Liangfu Guo 1988, Zengyi Hu 1989, 1995). However, there is few discussion in academic world that why *bai* has so variant senses in one certain period, and where they came from, let alone *bai*'s pragmatic function brought by its special semantic facet. Here, we will research the questions mentioned above one by one.

2   The Implicit Negation of *bai*

We believe that in Chinese, the adverb *bai* denotes an implicit negation. All semantic facets of *bai* share the same key cognitive foundation, that is, [+negation].

2.1   The Implicit Negative Forms in Different Languages

All languages have the function to express negation, some of them explicit and some not. The common form of negation is negative makers and its corresponding structure, or negative structures as in (3-5):

(3) a. I will go there.   b. I will <u>not</u> go there.
(4) a. Je prends du   poission.   b. Je <u>ne</u> prends <u>pas</u>   de   poission.
         I eat   INDEF-ART fish.   I   NEG$_1$ eat   NEG$_2$ INDEF-ART fish.
         I eat fish.   *I don't eat fish.*

(5) a. *wo xiang qu xue-xiao.*   b. *wo <u>**bu**</u> xiang   qu xue-xiao.*
         I   want   go school.   I   NEG want   go school.
         I want to go to school.   *I don't want to go to school.*
         我想去学校。   我<u>不</u>想去学校。

There are two types of negation in (3-5b), which are the negating of (3a-5a). In English and Chinese, negative markers such as *not* and *bu*, are usually placed in front of the verbs as in (3b) and (5b). While in French the negative structure *ne...pas* is usually added right before and after the conjugated verb as in (4b). Those negative markers and structures are explicit. However, although there are no explicit negative markers in some sentences, they are still capable of expressing negative meanings, as in (6a):

(6) a. ta ju-jue le wo-de qing-qiu. →   b. ta **bu**   jie-shou wo-de qing-qiu.
    he refuse INF my   request.   he **NEG** accept   my   request.
    He refused my request.   He didn't accept my request.
    他拒绝了我的请求。   他<u>不</u>接受我的请求。

There are not any explicit negative words or forms, but a semantic facet, [+negation], is embedded within the verb *ju-jue* as in (6a), making the VP in (6a) entails an explicit negative form, which is the ¬ V'P *bu jie-shou* in (6b), so an implication is formed between (6a) and (6b). The negation in (6a) is implicit. In this point of view, if a structure entails an explicit negative form, and along with the explicit negative form, it forms an implication, then the semantic negation in this structure is known as implicit negation.

2.2   The Implicit Negation in Adverb *bai*

Not only does verbs like *ju-jue* but also the adverb *bai* indicate implicit negation in Mandarin Chinese. In this perspective, *bai* entails a proposition which includes explicit negation, and forms an implication with the proposition. Unlike the implicit negative verbs such as *ju-jue*, *bai* negates the premise or result of VP instead of the proposition of VP, as exemplified by the ambiguous sentences in (8a-d):

(8) a. Mou-xie ke-xue-jia que-shi shi zai **bai** chi fan!
    some   scientists indeed   are ASP **bai** eat food

    某些科学家确实是在<u>白</u>吃饭。

→ b. Mou-xie ke-xue-jia que-shi shi chi-le-fan que bu chu   cheng-guo!
    some   scientists indeed are eat-INF but NEG come out   research result
    Some scientist are indeed consuming food and money in vain for research!

    某些科学家确实是吃了饭却不出成果!

→ c. Mou-xie ke-xue-jia que-shi shi bu   hua-qian jiu   chi-fan!
    some   scientists indeed   are NEG pay   CONJ   eat
    Some scientist are indeed getting things for free!

    某些科学家确实是不花钱就吃饭！

→ d. Mou-xie ke-xue-jia que-shi shi zhi   chi-fan bu   gan-huo!
    some   scientists indeed   are only eat   NEG do something
    Some scientists are indeed just getting fund but repay nothing!

    某些科学家确实是只吃饭不干活！

Bai chi fan in (8a) can be comprehended in three different ways and therefore (8a) implicates (8b), (8c) and (8d). When *bai* means *doing something in vain or for nothing*, it negates the result of VP *chi-fan*, which means *one should have results after doing something* in (8b). When *bai* means *obtaining something for free*, it negates the premise of VP, which means *one should pay before obtaining things* in (8c). When *bai* means *obtaining things with no repayment*, it negates the result of VP that *one should repay after obtaining things* in (8d). Yulin Yuan (2014) explains the two opposite semantic facets of *bai* with *the principle of the equilibrium of payment and reward* as *paying in vain for no results* and *getting profits without repayment*. We can see the implicit negation of *bai* more intuitively in Yulin Yuan's description.

Rongxiang Yang (2007) studied *bai* in Ming and Qing Dynasty, summarizing the semantic meaning of *bai* as *acting with no reasons or restrictions*, which mentioned the semantic feature [+negation] in *bai*'s meanings.[1] What we are going to amplify the explanation is that *bai's* [+negation] is an implicit implication, which is different from the [+negation] of normal negative adverbs, and thus the [+negation] of *bai* is redundant sometimes as in (9a-c):

(9) a. *Jia-ru   rang   ta-men qu   du   shu,   jiu-shi **bai** zao-ta   gong-fu.*
      if   make   them   go   read   book   then is **bai** waste   time
      If they go to school, it will be a waste of time.

      假如让他们去读书，就是白糟蹋工夫。

→ b. *Jia-ru rang ta-men qu   du   shu,   jiu-shi   zao-ta   gong-fu.*
      if   make them   go   read   book   then is   waste   time.
      If they go to school, it will be a waste of time.

      假如让他们去读书，就是糟蹋工夫。

→ c. *Ta-men   bu   ying-gai zao-ta   gong-fu qu   du   shu.*
      they   NEG   should   waste   time   go   read   book
      They shouldn't waste time to go to school.

      他们不应该糟蹋工夫去读书。

The *bai*-VP in (9a) means neither *wasting time with no results* nor *wasting time with no payment*. *Bai* can be removed and the meaning of the sentence remains the same as in (9b). As a matter of fact, the [+negation] of *bai* is carried out in a deontic category as *should not* in (9c), expressing the speaker's subjective judgement towards the behavior.

In this light, we summarize the [+negation] of *bai* into two points: one is that *bai* negates the premise or the result of VP, rather than the proposition of VP; the other is that the [+negation] of *bai* is implicated in the adverb itself, making it an implicit negative adverb.

Then what leads to this implicit negation of the adverb *bai*? In the following discussion, we would present materials in different periods in corpus and study its semantic origin.

---

[1] Yisheng Zhang (2000) also mentioned negation played an important role in *bai*' semantic meaning as *bai* can negate the presupposition of VP. Yulin Yuan(2014) did some corrections, concluding that *bai* does not negate the presupposition of VP but taking the pragmatic presupposition as the premise of its meaning in the contrary.

3 The Source and Semantic Trace of *bai*

It has been proven that the adverb *bai* in Mandarin is grammaticalized from the noun *bai* in old Chinese, and so is *bai*'s implicit negation. The implicit negation of the adverb *bai* is closely connected with the noun *bai*'s original semantic meaning.

3.1 The Original Meaning of *bai*

Researches on grammaticalization have proved that most function words originate from notional words and the adverb *bai* is one of the examples. In literatures, we can find three origins of *bai* shown as follows.

3.1.1 *bai* Represents a Kind of Color

Shuowen Jiezi (Origin of Chinese Characters) described *bai* as "白，西方色也，阴用事，物色白。从入合二。二，阴数。". (*Bai, a color of the west, is related to Yin.*) The Theory of Five Elements in Han Dynasty believes that the sun represents *tai-yang* position, and the moon represents *tai-yin* position. Besides, the five directions, which is the west, the east, the north, the south and the middle, correspond one by one with five colors which is white, cyan, black, red and yellow, so the west corresponds to white. Yucai Duan noted in *Annotation to Origin of Chinese Characters* as "出者，阳也。入者，阴也。故从入。". (*External is yang and internal is yin, so it (bai) belongs to internal.*) Thus, *bai* is a kind of color corresponding to the moon.

3.1.2 *bai* Represents the Light of the Sun

Junsheng Zhu (1833) studied the character pattern of *bai* in oracle bones and inscriptions on ancient bronze objects, and came to the conclusion that "(白)字从日，上象日未出，初生微光。按日未出地平时，先露其光恒白，今苏俗语'昧爽'日东方发白，是也，字当从日丿，指事，训太阳之明也。". (*Bai is closely connected with the sun. It represents the white light of the sun before it rises above sea level. Today the dialect in Suzhou calls it mei-shuang, which means the white light of the east. The character pattern of bai indicates the parts* 日 *and* 丿) Thus, *bai* is formed by 日 with an indicated symbol 丿, which represents sunlight.

3.1.3 *bai* Represents a Kind of Undyed Silk

Junsheng Zhu identified in *Shuo Wen Tong Xun Ding Sheng* that "白，假借为帛。". (*Bai, is the phonetically loaned character of bo*) Junsheng Zhu believed *bai* and *bo* share a similar pronunciation, so that they share the similar semantic meanings. In turn, *bo* can refer to the pronunciation of *bai,* and the actual semantic meaning of *bai* is what *bo* means. To be more precise, in *Shuowen Jiezi*, *bo* is a reference when dyeing silk or cloth; in other words, *bo* is a kind of undyed silk or cloth.

Now we must make an overall consideration about the three interpretations in literatures. *Shuowen Jiezi* is a dictionary studying the character pattern, and it interprets the motivation about how the character is made and the original meaning of a character. In this light, *bai* might be a noun and refers to a color which is similar to that of moon or sunlight. Theoretically, sunlight human can see contains light waves with different wavelengths. One certain wavelength corresponds to a certain color, so when different light waves are mixed together, sunlight appears to be colorless. In addition, *bai* can refer to undyed silks, showing the color *bai* represents is similar with something un-dyed, which is colorless. Considering the three interpretations we find a property in the semantic meaning of *bai*: there is no specific value able to refer to the color *bai* represents. Based on the property that the color of *bai* is actually colorless, we can conclude that there is a [+negation] in the semantic feature of *bai*.

By far, a brief summary could be given that in the beginning *bai* is a noun and refers to a color which has no certain color value, just like the color of the moon or sunlight.

3.2   The Extended Meaning of *bai*

The original *bai* is a noun and refers to a color. When *bai* refers to the property that the color *bai* has instead of simply referring to a color, the noun *bai* is extended to the adjective *bai*. In the following discussion, we will list the extended meanings of *bai* and show the [+negation] feature in the semantic evolution trace of *bai*.

3.2.1   The Adjective *bai* and its [+negation] Feature

There are plenty of sentences using the adjective *bai* in Old Chinese. We find three meanings of the adjective *bai* in corpus as exemplified by (10-15):

3.2.1.1   *Bai Means White*

(10) Tian-zi ju zong-zhang zuo-ge, cheng rong lu, jia **bai**-luo, zai bai qi,

    king   live all   left, take honor road ride white horse hold white flag

    yi   bai   yi,   fu   bai   yu. (Qin·LvShiChunQin·MengQiuJi)

    wear white clothes   wear white jade.

The emperor lives on the left, taking the honor road and riding a white horse, with a white flag, wearing white clothes and white jade.

天子居總章左個，乘戎路，駕白駱，載白旂，衣白衣，服白玉。（秦·呂氏春秋·孟秋紀）

(11) Mahuang cheng long er xing, Zijin gong yu **bai** he. (The Eastern Jin Dynasty·Baopuzi Neipian)

    king   ride   dragon to walk   Zijin personally master white crane

    The king rides a dragon to go and Zijin personally masters a white crane.

馬皇乘龍而行，子晉躬御白鶴。（东晋·抱朴子內篇·論仙）

3.2.1.2 Bai Means Bright

(12) Qi ru **bai**   hong,   tian ye. (The Western Han Dynasty·The book of Rites)
air as   bright fogbow   sky be
The air looks like the fogbow, and that is the sky.

氣如白虹，天也 ；（西汉·禮記·聘義）

(13) *Jun bing da jie jing guan **bai**   ri.(The Eastern Jin Dynasty·epoch of eastern han)*
king hold great morality sincerity go through bright sun
The king has great morality, and his sincerity can go up to through the bright sun.

君秉大節，精貫白日。 （东晋·後漢紀·卷三十）

3.2.1.3 Bai Means Pure

(14) *Shi gu ...   shen si   er   ming   mi   **bai**.(Warring States·Xunzi)*
is because   body die but reputation more pure.
This is the reason why... the body though die but the reputation is purer.

是故……身死而名彌白。 （战国·荀子·榮辱篇）

(15) *Ji you gong er wei zhi, ji qing-**bai** er pai zhi. (The Eastern Jin Dynasty·Baopuzi Waipian)*

scruple have feats and fear him scruple pure   and squeeze out   him
Scrupling the person who has feats and see him as a threat, being jealous of the pure persons and squeeze out them.

忌有功而危之，疾清白而排之。 （东晋·抱朴子外篇·汉过）

These three parallel examples lead us to the conclusion that the adjective *bai* also has [+negation] feature. As shown in (10-11), something white implicates the stuff has no other colors. Also, when *bai* indicates the semantic meaning of bright, it means the light consist of different waves so it has no certain color as in (12-13). Finally, as evidenced by (14-15), something pure means something with no impurities, indicating *bai* has a [+negation] feature in its semantic meaning as well.

3.2.2   The Adverb *bai* and its [+negation] Feature

The adverb *bai* emerged in Southern and Northern Dynasties. In this period of Disunity, the [+negation] feature in adjective *bai* began to be abstracted and extended to new semantic facets.[2] One of them is *additive free*, which means stuff without anything

---

[2] Jinghan Zeng, Yulin Yuan (2013) studied different semantic facets of the adverb *bai* and using semantic map to show the semantic evolution of bai.

added. As the example shown in (16) that *bai-zhou* means porridge cooked with only rice, no other ingredients being added:

(16) *Du-du yue: zuo **bai**-zhou yi tou zhi.(Southern and Northern Dynasties·A New Account of the Tales of the World)*

military governor say cook porridge to give him
The military governor said: cook some porridge to serve the guest.

都督曰：" ……作白粥以投之。（南北朝·世说新语·汰侈）

Here the adverb *bai* came into being. This is probably because under most circumstances that *bai* used as adjectives in Southern and Northern Dynasties, it refers to a method of cooking, resulting in the co-occurrence of *bai* and some cooking verbs. For this usage, *bai* always appeared in front of cooking verbs, so it could occupy the adverbial positions. As a result, in terms of part of speech, they became adverbs. However, this usage of *bai* is seldom spotted in Southern and Northern Dynasties, even till Tang Dynasty we could only find a few examples as in (17-19):

(17) Zhuo qu yi-rou,   qu   gu,   dian ru **bai** zhu zhi zhe. (Southern and Northern Dynasties·QiMinYaoShu)
cut   take breast cut off bone   put   as **bai** boil it Pron.
Cut off the bones and take the breast, and cook them as water-boiled foods.

斫取臆肉，去骨，奠如白煮之者。（南北朝·齐民要术·炙法第八十）

(18) Xiang-kan yue   wei duo, **bai** di   duan   gan chang (Tang·The female words)
look   moon NEG. fall   **bai** AUX.V broke liver intestine
Looking at each other under the moon, having deep affliction with no reason.

相看月未堕，白地断肝肠。（唐·越女词）

(19) Wu Daoxuan **bai** hua   di-yu bian. (Tang·Youyangzazu sequel)
Wu Daoxuan **bai** paint hell   change
Wu Daoxuan simply sketch Chart of Hell.

吴道玄白画地狱变。（唐·酉阳杂俎续集·寺塔记）

The *bai* in Southern and Northern Dynasties has similar semantic meaning with the adjective *bai*, meaning *additive freely*. *Bai-zhu* in (17) means boiling something in water without any ingredients. *Bai-hua* in (19) means drawing only with ink and thin lines, instead of drawing with other skills or in colors. *Bai* in (18) means doing something with no reason. In this perspective, the adverb *bai* in Southern and Northern Dynasties possesses the [+negation] feature in its semantic meaning.

The adverb *bai* became popular since Song Dynasty. The meaning of *doing something in vain or for nothing* appeared in the Northern Song Dynasty as evidenced in (20):

(20) *Gai-qi   pao   si   niu   ma,   yi   shi xia-min zhi   ku,*
   Because through dead cow   horse already is   people   AUX.V
hardship,

   *geng bu   zhi-de jia-qian, ling   ren-hu   **bai** na.(Northern Song
Dynasty·Qi fangxing niupijiaobiao)*

   even NEG   get   price   make people   ***bai*** pay

*Due to the death of the cows and the horses, the folk have already suffered a lot. They
do not have any income now, but the government still force them to pay taxes in vain.*

   盖其抛死牛马，已是下民之苦，更不支得价钱，令人户白纳。（北宋·乞

放行牛皮胶鳔）

Bai-na in (20) means the folk are obliged to pay taxes regardless of no income or
harvest, so *bai* means doing VP (paying taxes) in vain or for nothing. Here we see the
[+negation] feature in the semantic meaning of *bai*. This semantic facet remains in Contemporary Mandarin, and the very implicit negation it indicates has been preserved as well.

   As for the other semantic facet of *bai*, we have not yet found such examples in
corpus in Song and Yuan Dynasty so far. So we may as well infer that the other semantic facets emerged first in Ming Dynasty as in (21):

(21) Ta bu ceng   **bai** chi le ni   dong-xi, wen ni   qu   ta   zen-de.
   he NEG formerly **bai** eat INF you food   ask you fear him
why

   He has never eaten your food for free, why are you afraid of him?

   他不曾白吃了你东西，问你祛他怎的。（明·西游记）

Bai-chi in (21) means the subject eats for free or eats without repayment, so *bai*
means doing VP (eating) for free or with no repayment. This semantic facet also has the
[+negation] feature and even today it remains the same meaning.

   Hence, the adverb *bai* evolved through the path of *noun-adjective-adverb*. The two
opposite meanings of the adverb *bai* indicate implicit negation, which both of the two
meanings inherit from the original meaning of the noun *bai*.

4   The Subjectivity and Counter-Expectation of *bai*

4.1   Evaluation and Subjectivity of Adverbs

Now we think *bai*'s special implicit negation triggers counter-expectation, expressing
the actual situation deviate from the speaker's expectation. Expectation is a subjective
activity of human brain, and thus it must be closely connected with the subjectivity in
people's verbal communications. Yisheng Zhang (1999, 2000) and Ye Liu (2011) both
mentioned the subjectivity of *bai*. We agree with these researches, as most adverbs are
able to evaluate and so express subjectivity of the speaker, as exampled in (22-24)[3]:

---

[3] The example (22) is quoted from the Lecture notes of Professor Guo Rui, Peking University.

(22) Henan liu-ming shao-nv bei pian-zuo xi-tou-nv, huo-jiu hou **hai** wei   pian-zi shuo qing.

Henan six girl Pass. cheat massage girl save after **hai** for lier   say mercy

Six girls in Henan Province were abducted to be prostitutes, but they incredibly plead for mercy for the suspect after being saved.

河南6名少女被骗做洗头女，获救后还为骗子说情。

(23) Wo **you** bu   zhi-dao ni   shuo-de shi shui!

I   **you** NEG know   you say   is   who

I don not know who is person you talked about!

我又不知道你说的是谁！

(24) Zhe **ke** bu   neng gao-su bie-ren.

This **ke** NEG can   tell   others

We must not tell others about this.

这可不能告诉别人。

The *hai* in (22) indicates the speaker thinks VP (victims intercede for the criminal) is unreasonable, expressing the unexpected situation. The *you* in (23) indicates the speaker is impatient and unconvinced. The *ke* in (24) indicates warning and emphasis.

Now that most adverbs can express subjectivity, *bai* is no exception. This is probably because of the position of adverbs in the sentence. Rizzi (1997) divided the structure of a sentence into three layers into lexical layer, inflectional layer and complementizer layer. The lexical layer expresses the proposition meaning of the sentence and the inflectional layer includes inflections such as tense, aspect, and so on. Unlike those two layers, the complementizer layer mostly expresses the modality of the sentence, which lies on the highest layer on the syntax tree, and reflects the speaker's cognitive world. In *bai*-VP , VP lies on the lexical layer and *bai* lies on the complementizer layer. Although the adverb *bai* is an adjunct to the verb, it takes up a higher position than the entire VP. In this light, *bai* modify the entire VP so as to express the speaker's mood and mind, as in (25):

(25) Zhe-jian shi yi-dian hao-chu dou mei you, ni zhen shi **bai** chi le zhe-dun ku-tou!

This stuff a little profit at all NEG have you this is **bai** eat INF some suffering

This did not bring any profit to us at all, and you really suffered so much for nothing!

这件事一点好处都没有，你真是白吃了这顿苦头!

In (25), in terms of syntax, *bai* directly modifies the verb *chi*, and the syntactic structure of *bai*-VP is $_{VP}[_{COMP}[$ *bai* $_V[$ *chi-le*$]]$ *zhe dun ku-tou*]. However, in terms of semantics, *bai* expresses the subjective attitude and the mood of the speaker when experienced the whole event of VP. Thus, the semantic structure of this *bai*-VP should be $_{COMP}[$ *bai* $_{VP}[$ *chi-le* $_{NP}[$ *zhe dun ku-tou* $]]]$. *Bai* lies on the complementizer layer, while the aspect marker *le* on the inflectional layer and the verb phrase *chi zhe dun ku-tou* on the lexical layer.

In brief, the subjectivity and evaluation of *bai* is triggered by the syntactic structure of *bai*-VP. What's more, *bai* indicates not only subjective semantics but also counter-expectation, which depends on the semantic meaning of *bai*-VP.

4.2   The Counter-Expectation of *bai*

The implicit negation of *bai* triggers a pragmatic function of counter-expectation, which enables *bai* to present an actual situation that the proposition of VP negates the speaker's previous expectation. Construal of *bai*'s counter-expectation is based on *the principle of the equilibrium of payment and reward* in Yulin Yuan (2014). According to the principle, in verbal communication the speaker and the listener share a common sense that the payment equals to reward. Under the direction of this common sense, the process of construing counter-expectation comes in different ways: one is that when *bai* means *doing something in vain*, the result of VP (pay efforts but get no results or get no desirable results) deviates from the speaker's expectation, so it brings in counter-expectation; the other is that when *bai* means *obtaining something for free or with no repayment*, the prerequisite or premise of VP (get rewards without payment or repayment) deviates from the speaker's expectation, which brings in counter-expectation meaning of the sentence.

Our purpose is, nevertheless, more than just pointing out the counter-expectation of *bai*. The process of verbal communication includes 5 steps: encoding, sending, transmitting, receiving and decoding. The discovery on the counter-expectation of *bai* has only completed the first four steps, leaving decoding behind. The ultimate aim of verbal communication is to comprehend the speaker's intension, and this could only be realized by decoding. Then it is necessary to find out what the speaker wants to express by the usage of *bai*. Although this adverb has only two semantic facets, the speakers' expectation are more than that:

4.2.1   The Speaker Expects Results from VP

In this case, the speaker expects to benefit from the event which VP refers to. In other words, the speaker expects the result from VP. If in the actual situation the speaker did not benefit from the event or achieve what he is eager for, it will turn out to be a counter-expectation, as in (26)[4]:

(26) Ji-ran   ba-wo   bu   da,   na   hai-qu   kao   shen-me?
    since   assurance NEG   jothi then   go   exam   what

    Du   fu-xi   ban   ye   shi   **bai**   hua   qian.
    read remedial class   too   is   **bai**   pay   money

Now that you are not fully assured, what are you taking the exam for? Anyway it is a waste of money to enroll on the remedial class.

既然把握不大，那还去考什么？读复习班也是<u>白花钱</u>。

---

[4] For simplicity, we analyze only one example in each kind of the examples.

(27) Shen-me dou   mei de-dao, ni   zhe yi-tang bu shi **bai** pao le ?
     what   at all NEG get   you this time NEG is   **bai** run INF
     You did all these this time only to get nothing, aren't you?
     什么都没得到，你这一趟不是<u>白</u>跑了吗？

In (26), the speaker expects to achieve a good score after enrolling on the remedial class. But in fact the odds goes against his expectation, paying for the remedial class proven in vain for the exam.

4.2.2   The Speaker Expects that VP is Something Should not be Done

In this situation, *bai* means *doing something in vain or for nothing*. The speaker believes the event of VP is wrong, so he is never willing to let it go. Should anything unexpected took place in the actual situation, it would deviate from the speaker's expectation, as in (28):

(28) *Yi-sheng mei-you ren-zhen gei ta zhi-bing, rang ta **bai** shou-le duo nian-de   zui.*
     doctor   NEG seriously for her cure make her ***bai*** suffer   many year's   hardship
     The doctor didn't treat her illness seriously, resulting in her suffering from what she would not have had to for years.

     医生没有认真给她治病，让她白受了多年的罪。

(29) *Jia-ru rang   ta-men qu du-shu, jiu-shi   **bai**   zao-ta   gong-fu.*
     if   make   them   go read, then is   ***bai***   waste   time.
     If they go to school, then it is a waste of time.

          假如让他们去读书，就是白糟蹋工夫。

In (28) the speaker expects that the subject (*she*) shouldn't suffer so much for years. In fact, because of the barber-surgeon, the subject suffers from unnecessary pain in vain, which leads to counter-expectation of the speaker.

4.2.3   The Speaker Does not Expect any Result from VP

Bai means *doing something in vain or for nothing* in this situation. The speaker does not expect to obtain anything after doing VP. Unlike other situations, the speaker would think from the listener's point of view, so here is inter-subjectivity rather than subjectivity that works. Accordingly, the counter-expectation works from the view of the listener. In the listener's perspective, achieving VP or obtaining something should in return pay the speaker. However, the speaker seeks nothing from the listener, which ends deviating the listener's expectation, as in (30).

(30) *Zhe-xie qian shi **bai** gei ni-de, zen-me hua dou xing, bu yong huan !*
     these   money   is ***bai*** give you   how   use all   can NEG need return
     The money is given away to you. Use it whatever you wish and you don't need to pay it back.

这些钱就是<u>白</u>给你的，怎么花都行！不用还。

(31) *Zhe yin-zi lian-tong gei   nin   ban-de pu-gai,   dou shi jing-li **bai** gei ni-de.*

   this silver and   give you   purchase bedding   all   is   manager ***bai***   give you

   The money and the new beddings are all given away to you by the manager for free.

这银子连同给您办的铺盖，都是经理<u>白</u>给你的。

The speaker has no expectation of any repayment after doing VP (giving money to the listener) in (30). But in the listener's mind, the borrowed money should be paid back, so in the actual situation a counter-expectation occurs to the listener.

4.2.4   The Speaker Expects the Payment Before Achieving VP

In the situation that *bai* means *obtaining something for free*, the speaker expects that in order to achieve VP he must make efforts or pay first. If in the end the subject did not pay what he should, then it goes astray from the speaker's expectation, as in (32):

(32) *Ta-men shen-me ye   bu   gan,   **bai**   na   qian.*

   they   what   too NEG   do   ***bai*** take money

   They did nothing but can get money for free.

他们什么也不干，<u>白</u>拿钱

(33) *Lai-bin **bai** ting   yin-yue-hui zhi-wai,   hai **bai** he   yin-liao.*

   guest   ***bai*** listen concert   besides   too   *bai* drink drinks

   Apart from listening to the concert for free, the guests can drink free, too.

来宾<u>白</u>听音乐会之外，还<u>白</u>喝饮料。

In (32) the speaker expects that one can get the money only after work. To his surprise, the subject still get the money without doing anything, which deviates the speaker's expectation and brings in counter-expectation.

4.2.5   The Speaker Expects Repayment After Achieving VP

In this situation, *bai* means *obtaining something with no repayment*. The speaker has an expectation that one person should repay after getting something. Once the subject gets profits but does not repay anything, it would deviate the speaker's expectation. As presented in (34):

(34) *Ta-men bu shou   nv bu-tou,   **bai** shou   wo er-bai   liang yin-zi de bao-ming fei.*

   they NEG accept female sheriff ***bai*** charge me 2 hundred liang sliver registration fee

   They didn't accept female sheriffs, vainly charging me 22 pounds of silver for the registration fee.

他们不收女捕头，<u>白</u>收我二两银子的报名费。

(35) *Wo hen can-kui,   lao   wan-bu-cheng   ren-wu, **bai** chi ren-min-de fan.*

    I very ashamed always can't complete task ***bai*** eat people's   food

I was so ashamed that I always can't complete my task, taking the taxpayers' food for free.

我很惭愧，老完不成任务，<u>白</u>吃人民的饭。

In (34) the speaker expects that if the subject charged the registration fee, she should be given a chance to be interviewed. However, the real situation is that female sheriff is not accepted, and the subject *they* get profits (registration fee) but do not pay back (give the speaker a chance to be interviewed). So *bai* means *obtaining something with no repayment*. The actual situation deviates the speaker's expectation and brings in counter-expectation.

5   Conclusion

This paper analyzes the adverb *bai* in terms of semantics and pragmatics from both synchronic and diachronic perspectives. Based on the discussions above, we may as well come to the conclusions as follows. Firstly, *bai* indicates implicit negation with a [+negation] feature, and therefore *bai*-VP can implicate a new negative structure with an explicit negative maker. Secondly, two opposite semantic facets of the adverb *bai* (*doing something in vain or for nothing*; *obtaining something for free or with no repayment*) in Mandarin come from the noun *bai* in Old Chinese and inherit its implicit negation. Based on the evidences the semantic facets of *bai* have probably evolved through the path of *noun-adjective-adverb*. Thirdly, the implicit negation of *bai* expresses actual situation against the speaker's expectation and triggers the counter-expectation of the speaker. In real context, the construal of the speaker's expectation is closely connected with the semantic meaning of *bai*, in which certain subjectivity and inter-subjectivity are expressed.

References

1. Allwood, J., Andersson, L.-G., Dahl, O.: Logic in linguistics. Cambridge University Press, Cambridge (1977)
2. Dictionary editorial room of Institute of Linguistics, Chinese Academy of Social Sciences: Modern Chinese Dictionary. The Commercial Press, Beijing (2012). (in Chinese)
3. Sweetser, E.: From Etymology to Pragmatics: Metaphorical and Cultural Aspects of Semantic Structure. Cambridge University Press, England (1990)
4. Gui, F.: Shuowen Jiezi Yizheng (1870). QiLu Press (Photocopy), Jinan (1987). (in Chinese)
5. Zeng, J., Yuan, Y.: The Semantic evolution path of the adverb *bai* in Proto-Mandarin and Mandarin—From a perspective of semantic map (2013). (to be publish) (in Chinese)

6. Zhu, J.: Shuo Wen Tong Xun Ding Sheng (1833). Zhonghua Book Company (Photocopy), Beijing (1984). (in Chinese)

7. Guo, L.: The adverb *bai* and *baibai* in Proto-Mandarin. Journal of Chinese Linguistics **3**, 230–244 (1988). (in Chinese)

8. Rizzi, L.: The fine structure of the left periphery. In: Haegeman, L. (ed.) Elements of Grammar. Kluwer, Dordrecht (1997)

9. Xu, S.: Shuowen Jiezi (Origin of Chinese Characters). Zhonghua Book Company (Photocopy), Beijing (1963). (in Chinese)

10. Ma, S., Pan, S.: The adverb *bai* in A Dream of Red Mansions and The heroine. Studies of the Chinese Language **6**, 461–463 (1981). (in Chinese)

11. Ma, S.: A further study of the adverb *bai* in Proto-Mandarin. Studies of the Chinese Language **218**, 386–392 (1990). (in Chinese)

12. Liu, Y.: A Semantic Analysis on Subjectivity of Adverbs of Negative Presupposition "Bai" and "Xia". Journal of Zhejiang Ocean University (Humanities Sciences) **28**(2), 75–80 (2011)

13. Zhang, Y.: The semantic feature of the adverb "bai" and other similar adverbs and their potential connotations. Journal of Jiangsu Normal University (Philosophy and Social Sciences Edition) **3**, 128–132 (1994). (in Chinese)

14. Zhang, Y.: The adverb "bai" and "bai-bai" in Mandarin. Journal of Huaibei Normal University (Philosophy and Social Sciences) **1**, 113–120 (1993). (in Chinese)

15. Zhang, Y.: The study of presupposed negative adverbs in Proto-Mandarin. Research in Ancient Chinese Language **42**, 27–35 (1999). (in Chinese)

16. Zhang, Y.: The study of adverbs in Mandarin. Academia Press, Beijing (2000). (in Chinese)

17. Zhang, Y.: A Further Discussion of Modal Adverbs "bai" in Modern Chinese–A Simultaneous Study of Grammatical Pat terns and Inner Differences of Adverb "bai". Journal of Leshan Normal University **18**(1), 1–10 (2003)

18. Duan, Y.: Annotation to Origin of Chinese Characters (1815). Jiangsu Guangling engraving and printing agency for ancient books (Photocopy), Yangzhou (1997). (in Chinese)

19. Yuan, Y.: On the semantic levels and overflow conditions of the implicit negative verbs in Chinese. Studies of the Chinese Language **347**, 99–113 (2012). (in Chinese)

20. Yuan, Y.: Conception-driven and syntax-directed constructions and construal of sentences: A case study of the interpretation of sentences with the adverb *bai*. Studies of the Chinese Language **362**, 402–417 (2014). (in Chinese)

21. Hu, Z.: A semantic study of *bai* in Manchu and early vernacular works. Studies of the Chinese Language **212**, 388–396 (1989). (in Chinese)

22. Hu, Z.: The loan relationship of *bai* in Manchu and Mandarin. Journal of Chinese Linguistics **5**, 265–299 (1995). (in Chinese)

A Study of Chinese Sensation Verbs Used in Linguistic Synaesthesia

Jia-Fei Hong[1(⊠)] and Chu-Ren Huang[2]

[1] National Taiwan Normal University, Taipei, Taiwan
jiafeihong@ntnu.edu.tw
[2] The Hong Kong Polytechnic University, Hung Hom, Hong Kong
churen.huang@polyu.edu.hk

Abstract. Synaesthesia is a well-known phenomenon, both as a neural disorder (The Man Who Tasted Shapes) and a device for linguistic metaphors. The neural basis of synaesthesia is characterized by sensation stimuli or cognition that induces a different cognition spontaneously and involuntarily. Sensation verbs are rich and varied in the Chinese lexicon, but so far there has been no extensive study concerning their use in linguistic synaesthesia. To address this gap in the literature, this study will investigate linguistic synaesthesia using the visual verbs "*kan4* (look)" and "*jian4* (look)". Moreover, a discussion on semantic mappings and metaphors will be presented.

Keywords: Synaesthesia · Chinese sensation verbs · Visual verbs · Semantics · Concepts · Metaphors

1 Introduction

Synaesthesia is a cognitive state that involves multisensory integration [1] and linguistic expression. Synaesthesia in cognitive neuroscience mainly refers to a perceptual state in which a sensory stimulation or cognitive pathway leads to an involuntary and automatic sensory stimulation or cognition [1], [2], [3], [4]. Although synaesthesia has been studied in cognitive neuroscience and psychology [3], [4], [5], [6], [7], [8], [9], scant literature on the subject has been found in Chinese linguistics, despite the abundance of sensation verbs in the Chinese lexicon. In linguistics, Chinese research [10], [11] and lexical semantics [12], [13] have led to detailed discussions on Chinese sensation verbs, concepts, and knowledge representation.

Synaesthesia refers to multisensory integration that is extensively performed among the five senses— sound, sight, touch, smell, and taste—as a particular sense travels from one sensory pathway to a second sensory pathway, for example, sight elicits sound or sound elicits taste. Synaesthesia is not only the integration of reciprocal sensory modalities but also a perceptual association of language, concepts, and knowledge representation. The current study will attempt to investigate linguistic synaesthesia using "*kan4* (look)" and "*jian4* (look)" as the key words for corpus-based analyses.

Q. Lu and H.H. Gao (Eds.): CLSW 2015, LNAI 9332, pp. 62–73, 2015.
DOI: 10.1007/978-3-319-27194-1_7

2   Previous Studies: Synaesthesia and Sensation Verbs

Despite the fact that synaesthesia has not been studied extensively in Chinese linguistics, research on sensation verbs has been abundant in lexical semantics. [12] investigated the features and concepts of Chinese characters by examining Chinese semantic radicals. Through the analysis of Chinese semantic radicals and their symbolic concepts and knowledge representation, two individual words can be closely related in sensory, conceptual, and perceptual domains. Moreover, [11], [12], and [13] explored sensation words in auditory, visual, and tactile modalities by comparing "*sheng1* (sound), *ying1* (sound)", "*kan4* (look), *jian4* (look)", and "*chu4* (touch), *mo1* (touch)", respectively. Furthermore, [1], [2], and [3] indicated that synaesthesia is an involuntary and basic perception, and the types of synaesthesia expressions vary in different conditions or pathways.

This study will attempt to distinguish two semantically related words from the perspective of production and perception. Moreover, differences in agents, semantic functions, and cognitive features may lead to varied and unique collocations. As such, the current study will investigate Chinese visual verbs through the symbolic concepts and knowledge representation of Chinese radicals, the agent role of sensation verbs, semantic functions, cognitive features, and the cognitive neurological state. The degree to which synaesthesia plays a role at a linguistic level in semantic mappings and metaphors will also be discussed in this study.

3   Research Motivation and Goal

In linguistics, knowledge representation is performed through systematic contrast rather than conventional meaning. Chinese sensation verbs can be expressed in a metaphorical way. It is usually the case that the performance of a sensation verb is described by another sensation verb. For example, in the three sentences "*ta1 de5 shen1yin1 hen3 tian2* (Her voice is sweet)", "*zhe4ge5 dong1xi1 wen2qi3lui2 hen3 ci4bi2* (This thing smells pungent)", and "*zhe4ge5 nu3sheng kan4qi3lai2 hen3 la4* (The girl looks spicy)", "*shen1yin1* (voice)" is described as a "sweet" taste in the first sentence, the tactile stimulus "*ci4* (pungent)" is used to describe a smell in the second sentence, and in the third sentence a "*la4* (spicy)" taste is applied to present a visual result. These sentences are described in a metaphorical way in which certain easy or comprehensible words are applied through synaesthetic expressions.

In Chinese, visual synaesthesia is found to be more frequent than other sensory modalities. The reason for this may be that sight is the most direct sensation in an authentic description, like clear-turbid, color, long-short, brightness, and twinkle. These descriptions can be applied to sentences like "*wo3 yi3jing1 kan4tou4 zhe4ge5 ren2 le5* (I have understood this guy thoroughly)", "*ta1 hen3 hui4 kan4 zhang3guan1 de5 yan3se4* (He can understand his chief's hint)", "*ta1 shi4 hen3 you3 yuan3jian4 de5 ren2* (He is a foresighted person)", "*kan4 zhu1 cheng1 bi4* (see bright red as bluish green)", and "*bo1 yun2 jian4 ri4* (Every cloud has a silver lining)". Furthermore, sensation verbs can also be used to express an abstract outcome, like "*kan4dao4 wei4lai2* (look to the future)" and "*jian4dao4 ai4* (see the love)". This study will investigate how perceptual association is triggered in linguistics, semantic mappings, and metaphorical expressions. The most active visual verbs "*kan4* (look)" and "*jian4* (look)" will serve as the key words for corpus-based analyses.

4   Data Collection

In this study, Chinese Wordnet (CWN) (http://cwn.ling.sinica.edu.tw/) was used as the first corpus to search for visual verbs in Chinese. It was found that "*kan4*" and "*jian4*" are verbs that are most related to eye movement. Next, to find out how "*kan4*" and "*jian4*" are applied in language use, the two words were entered into Chinese Word Sketch (CWS, http://wordsketch.ling.sinica.edu.tw/) for further analysis.

4.1   Chinese Wordnet

Chinese Wordnet (CWN) is a system that characterizes words by sense division. Users can enter key words for senses or definitions [14] The interface of CWN is shown in Figure 1 below:

Fig. 1. The homepage of Chinese Wordnet (CWN)

Using CWN, it was found that "*kan4* (look)" and "*jian4* (look)" are the most common visual verbs related to eye movement. The senses and definitions of "*kan4* (look)" and "*jian4* (look)" are shown in Figures 2 and 3. Linguistic synaesthesia will be discussed based on the corpus results.

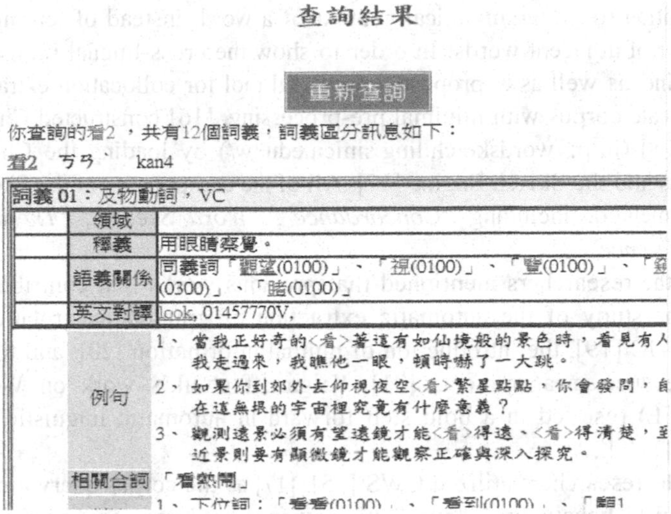

查詢結果

Fig. 2. The sense divisions of "*kan4* (look)" in CWN

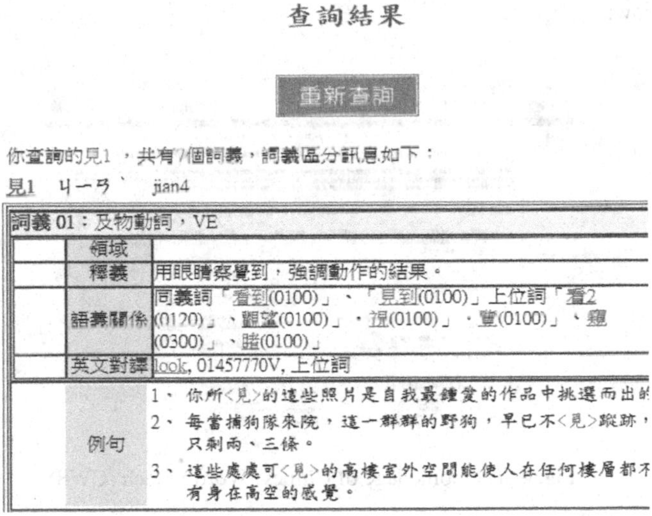

查詢結果

Fig. 3. The sense divisions of "*jian4* (look)" in CWN

4.2   Chinese Word Sketch

The Sketch Engine (SKE, also known as the Word Sketch Engine) is a novel corpus query system [15] that incorporates word sketches, grammatical relations, and a distributional thesaurus. The advantage of using the Sketch Engine as a query tool is that it pays attention to the grammatical context of a word, instead of returning an arbitrary number of adjacent words. In order to show the cross-lingual robustness of the Sketch Engine, as well as to propose a powerful tool for collocation extraction based on a large-scale corpus with minimal pre-processing, [16] constructed Chinese Word Sketch (CWS) (http://wordsketch.ling.sinica.edu.tw/) by loading the Chinese Gigaword Corpus into the Sketch Engine [17]. All of the components of the Sketch Engine were implemented, including *"Concordance"*, *"Word Sketch"*, *"Thesaurus"*, and *"Sketch Difference"*.

In [18], the researchers mentioned that previous works that contributed significantly to the study of the automatic extraction of grammatical relations include work on KWIC [19], the introduction of mutual information [20], and the introduction of relevance measurements [21]. Kilgarriff et al.'s work on Word Sketch Engine (WSE) resulted in a bold step forward in automatic linguistic knowledge acquisition [17], [22].

In [16], the researchers utilized CWS [15], [17] as the corpus query tool, by which the grammatical behaviours of two heterogeneous resources could be captured and displayed in a unified Web interface. Therefore, the best way to annotate two heterogeneous corpora to enable them to consistently compare their words' syntactic behaviours through CWS is an important concern. The homepage of CWS is shown in Figure 4 below:

Fig. 4. The homepage of Chinese Word Sketch (CWS)

Using the *"Word Sketch"* function in CWS, this study will focus on the two words *"kan4"* and *"jian4"* to observe their usages and distributions, such as related collocations and argument roles. The *"Word Sketch"* interface is shown in Figure 5 below:

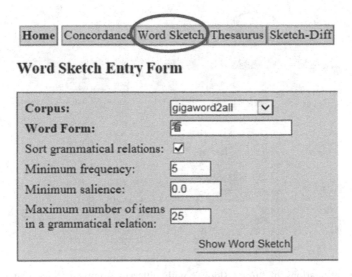

Fig. 5. The "*Word Sketch*" interface in CWS

"*Word Sketch*" is one of the four functions available in CWS. This tool's main function is to provide related syntactic information and collocations [23]. Users can observe and study linguistic distributions, usages, and results using this interface. In this study, "*kan4* (look)" and "*jian4* (look)" were compared in terms of argument roles. The collocations of the two words are shown in Figures 6 and 7, respectively.

看 gigaword2all freq = 188657

Modifier 82372 7.9		Subject 42465 5.5		PP 對 479 5.1		PP 在 1271 3.2		Object 80494 2.6	
家	43724 93.01	角度	2444 76.66	得失心	3 29.25	眼	777 91.12	臉色	328 58.79
眼睜睜	375 72.28	觀點	766 52.76	得失	11 27.13	面子	32 41.26	眼	1039 56.43
眼睜睜地	315 70.37	情況	3069 49.91	眼光	11 23.87	份	45 22.41	護工	149 55.28
回頭	443 64.3	技術線型	62 47.89	名利	6 23.52	心	11 15.12	電視	3100 55.14
還要	1301 57.51	眼光	337 47.02	利益	27 23.09	錢	9 12.18	笑話	259 52.66
要	8479 56.75	技術面	99 45.47	事情	15 22.69	比賽	5 3.52	笑話	200 47.12
一	2503 54.62	你	575 44.86	金錢	8 19.64	他	9 3.25	臺灣	533 46.79
別	688 52.56	我	1213 43.76	它	13 17.5	國家	5 0.41	今朝	86 45.54
去	2082 50.74	肉眼	67 40.7	錢	10 16.43			球	986 44.36
眼巴巴	69 48.17	明眼人	39 37.83	問題	30 14.62			遍	180 42.69
怎麼	352 43.66	眼睛	180 37.08	自己	13 13.92			誰	570 42.66
冷眼	36 39.34	大家	442 34.15	東西	5 12.98			門道	75 41.91
實在	222 38.05	總體	256 33.56	事業	5 7.43			高一線	26 40.66
幾乎	298 37.85	白天兵	11 33.21	教育	5 5.77			眼色	41 39.93
等等	26 36.77	外界	53 31.37	他	5 3.53			球賽	272 38.15

Fig. 6. The collocations of "*kan4* (look)" with different argument roles using the "*Word Sketch*" tool

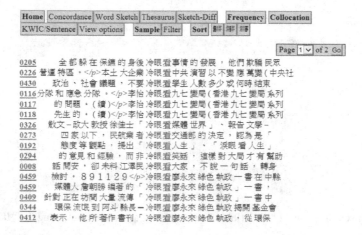

Fig. 7. The collocations of "*jian4* (look)" with different argument roles using the "*Word Sketch*" tool

5   Data Analysis

The "*Word Sketch*" tool provided the collocations and related linguistic information for "*kan4* (look)" and "*jian4* (look)". It was found that the two visual words often occurred with words that imply "temperature" and "color", for example, "*leng3yan3 kan4*", "*kan4 lian3se4*", and "*jian4 qi3se4*", which are shown in Figures 8, 9, and 10.

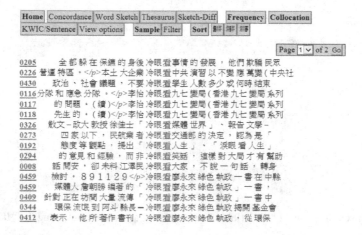

Fig. 8. Examples of "*leng3yan3 kan4*" using the "*Word Sketch*" tool

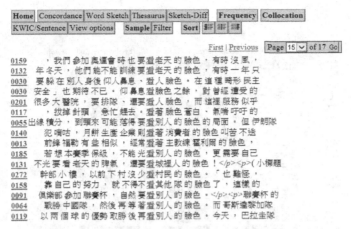

Fig. 9. Examples of "*kan4 lian3se4*" using the "*Word Sketch*" tool

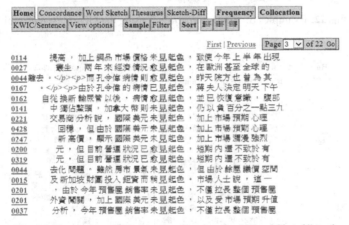

Fig. 10. Examples of "*jian4 qi3se4*" using the "*Word Sketch*" tool

In addition to the correlation of different senses, "*kan4* (look)" and "*jian4* (look)" also occurred with different consciousnesses, concepts, and experiences. These collocations conveyed inner feelings, for instance, "*ba3 de2shixin1 kan4*", "*jian4 zhen1qing2*", "*kan4 de5...zhong4*", "*kan4 de5...qing1*", and even "*kan4jian4 chun1guang1*" and "*kan4jian4 shu4guang1*", as shown in Figures 11 through 16.

Fig. 11. Examples of "*ba3 de2shi1xin1 kan4*" using the "*Word Sketch*" tool

Home
Concordance
Word Sketch
Thesaurus
Sketch-Diff
Frequency
Collocation
KWIC/Sentence
View options
Sample
Filter
Sort
First | Previous
Page 5 of 6 Go
0047 粒種子一顆心，心心相印見真情。退伍老戰士們激動
0080 副部長王光亞時說，患難之中見真情，中國是布隆迪人民
0137 大家的氣就消了。</p><p>小事見真情，真情動人心；小事不
0144 劉雲非)疾風知勁草，患難見真情。這是中非傳統友誼
0158 多日，是歡患與共，征途見真情，還是無休止的磨合
0086 表示感謝。他說：「患難見真情。我們有充分的信心
0115 的藥品。他說，患難之中見真情，此次捐助的藥品代表
0083 韓正深情地說：「困難時刻見真情。廣大外商投資企業
0094 領域的合作卓有成效。患難見真情。國際形勢的復雜變化
0067 眺望群山，他說：「患難見真情。我選擇在這個時刻
0110 尤烈。疾風知勁草，患難見真情。在抗擊非典的鬥爭
0170 而從不附加任何條件。患難見真情，多中兩國人民永遠
0129 立刻回國效力。」</p><p>患難見真情。對一批批負笈海外
0109 是兩國友誼的體現。患難見真情，津巴布韋和中國永遠
0163 馬塞爾·郎熱瓦在儀式上說，患難見真情，馬達加斯加受災後
0190 俄羅斯人民真誠的朋友。患難見真情。俄方願與中方在雙邊

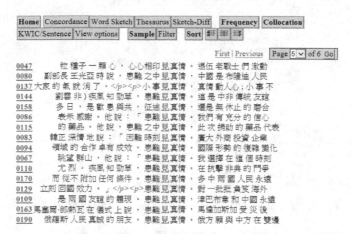

Fig. 12. Examples of "*jian4 zhen1qing2*" using the "*Word Sketch*" tool

Home
Concordance
Word Sketch
Thesaurus
Sketch-Diff
Frequency
Collocation
KWIC/Sentence
View options
Sample
Filter
Sort
0059 李長春代表把開放問題看得更重。他從遼寧調任河南
0121 說，寧可把困難和問題看得重一點，這樣可以使我們
0134 時間觀念強化了，對健康看得也越來越重。幾千年裡「
0010 參加奧運會。他對奧運會看得格外重。因此，即使是春節
0212 隊長的顏建垣，卻把教育看得很重很重。「如果把錢
0019 西班牙和中國對金牌還是看得比較重。</p><p>尚梓樹(記者
0038 說，南澳人對專業人才看得很重，已制訂了優惠的政策
0152 時，俞正聲對第三產業看得很重。他認為青島第三產業
0029 書記熊清泉代表對農業看得很重。他說，農業穩，
0252 就登台施教;</p><p>把副業看得比正業還重，搞副業他們
0232 點，才能把黨的事業看得重一分。只要大伙能多出
0044 本人也沒有把這次比賽看得很重。</p><p>她說：「這並
0072 因為他沒有把這次比賽看得很重，二是他知道自己最後
0044 身經百戰的陳子荷對這一賽事看得特別重，她說，儘管國內
0058 說，之所以把質量問題看得這麼重，主要是因為，全體
0046 地說：「知識分子把名看得比性命還重，在這個問題
0219 有的醫療單位把「錢」字看得太重，緊急危重病人因一時
0141 份量就重了。群眾把幹部看得重了，群眾與幹部的心思
0005 是咱的本分，別把官兒看得太重了。」</p><p>莽莽蒼蒼
0005 這些人哪，就是把官兒看得太重了。」他來到糧庫後

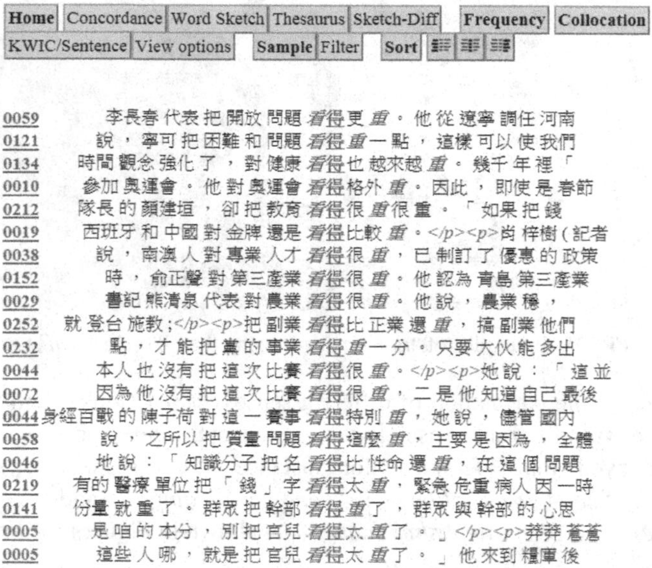

Fig. 13. Examples of "*kan4 de5...zhong4*" using the "*Word Sketch*" tool

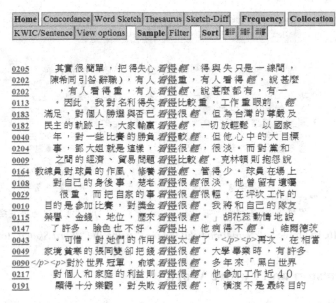

| | Home | Concordance | Word Sketch | Thesaurus | Sketch-Diff | | Frequency | Collocation |
| KWIC/Sentence | View options | | Sample | Filter | | Sort |

0205	其實很簡單，把得失心 *看得輕*，得與失只是一線間，
0202	陳希同引咎辭職），有人*看得重*，有人*看得輕*，說甚麼
0202	，有人看得重，有人*看得輕*，說甚麼都有，有一
0113	。因此，我對名利得失*看得*比較重，工作重眼前，*輕*
0183	滿足，對個人勝選與否已*看得很輕*，但為台灣的尊嚴及
0182	民主的軌跡上，大家輸贏*看得輕*，一切放輕鬆，以國家
0040	年，對一些比賽的勝負*看得較輕*，但他心中的大目標
0204	事，鄧大姐就是這樣，*看得很輕*，很淡。而對黨和
0009	之間的經濟、貿易問題*看得*比較*輕*。克林頓則抱怨說
0164	教練員對球員的作風、修養*看得輕*、管得少。球員在場上
0108	對自己的身後事，楚老*看得很輕*很淡。他曾留有遺囑
0029	很重，而把自家的事*看得輕輕*很輕。在坪坎工作的
0010	目的是參加比賽，對獎金*看得很輕*。我將和自己的隊友
0115	榮譽、金錢、地位，歷來*看得很輕*。」胡花蕊動情地說
0147	了許多，臉色也不好。*看得出*，他病得不*輕*。」維爾德茨
0043	。可惜，對她們的作用*看得太輕*了。 再次，在相當
0049	家境貧寒的張同雙卻把錢*看得很輕*。大學畢業時，有許多
0090	對於世界冠軍，俞斌*看得很輕*。多年來「黑白世界
0217	對個人和家庭的利益則*看得很輕*。他參加工作近４０
0191	顯得十分樂觀，對失敗*看得很輕*：「橫渡不是最終目的

Fig. 14. Examples of "*kan4 de5...qing1*" using the "*Word Sketch*" tool

| | Home | Concordance | Word Sketch | Thesaurus | Sketch-Diff |

看見 gigaword2all freq = 7143

PP 從 3 26.3	Modifier 2807 9.3	Subject 1243 5.5	SentObject of 182 3.4	Object 1832 2.0
出來管 2 28.09	親眼 137 61.48	內眼 22 41.17	裝作 6 32.95	身影 32 37.48
	可以 506 50.86	我 140 40.27	希望 59 31.24	影子 14 28.07
PP 被 5 13.0	沒 127 40.65	我們 82 31.24	高興 15 28.88	火光 9 27.0
蟹屍 3 34.43	能 275 36.17	你 36 29.44	裝做 4 28.6	曙光 12 23.31
	可 237 35.21	他 137 26.46	假裝 6 27.84	蟹屍 3 22.62
	仿佛 19 31.67	人們 22 22.0	怕 10 24.75	屍體 18 21.78
	遠遠地 10 31.37	你們 12 21.35	不忍 5 24.74	蹤跡 2 18.7
	沒有 185 30.05	他們 46 20.55	樂於 6 23.17	出來管 2 17.92
	突然 38 29.59	人 83 19.59	願意 11 20.49	景象 9 17.47
	隱隱約約 7 29.35	她 30 18.87	願 12 20.23	火球 4 17.34
	就 118 27.14	熟人 4 17.38	忍心 3 18.74	樣子 6 16.61
	一 59 26.4	大家 12 14.09	生怕 2 14.62	石頭房 2 16.47
	還可以 19 25.73	望遠鏡 5 13.97	喜歡 4 13.17	埃皮 2 16.37
	曾 79 25.1	別人 6 13.36	開始 6 11.31	血跡 5 16.18
	只 56 23.68	記者 69 12.82	期望 3 10.64	倩影 3 16.16
	赫然 10 23.07	顯微鏡 3 12.79	智意 2 10.6	色盲線 2 16.02
	常常 14 23.03	裁判 6 12.55	記得 2 10.57	東西 11 16.02
	不時 15 22.95	天部 3 12.23	相信 3 8.52	廖筱君 3 15.91
	隱約 7 22.9	門窗 3 11.72	擔心 2 6.73	蹤影 5 15.72
	清晰 10 22.84	王濤 3 11.64	讓 2 3.54	陽光 8 15.66
	常 22 22.77	證人 4 11.6		笑臉 4 15.29
	偶爾 8 22.31	貓咪 2 11.42		畫面 8 15.25
	清楚 15 21.87	世人 4 11.36		春光 3 14.3
	經常 23 21.69	鳥兒 2 11.22		山壁 3 14.1
	忽然 7 20.92	縫隙 2 10.95		流星雨 4 14.02

Fig. 15. Examples of "*kan4jian4 chun1guang1*" using the "*Word Sketch*" tool

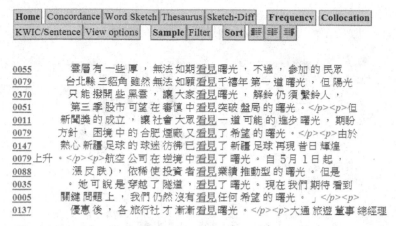

Fig. 16. Examples of "*kan4jian4 shu4guang1*" using the "*Word Sketch*" tool

6　Conclusion and Future Work

In terms of Chinese sensation verbs, linguists have focused on semantics and the knowledge representation of concepts and metaphorical expressions. However, linguistic synaesthesia in Chinese has not been studied extensively. In order to know how language is perceived in terms of psychology, cognition, and neurology, it is suggested that further research concerning linguistic synaesthesia be conducted.

In this study, we used a more scientific and empirical method to analyze linguistic synaesthesia. First, Chinese Wordnet (CWN) provided the senses and definitions of "*kan4* (look)" and "*jian4* (look)", which were most related to vision. Moreover, Chinese Word Sketch (CWS) served as another tool to show the collocations of the two visual verbs. The co-occurrence of the visual verbs and their collocations revealed linguistic synaesthesia and the perceptual associations of sensation verbs.

CWN and CWS can provide users with authentic language use, and the latter can help to explain the linguistic synaesthesia of Chinese visual verbs. Further studies regarding linguistic synaesthesia can be performed based on corpus linguistic analysis.

Acknowledgements. This research is partially supported by the "Aim for the Top University Project" and "Center of Learning Technology for Chinese" of National Taiwan Normal University (NTNU), sponsored by the Ministry of Education, Taiwan, R.O.C. and the "International Research-Intensive Center of Excellence Program" of NTNU and Ministry of Science and Technology, Taiwan, R.O.C. under Grant no. NSC 103-2911-I-003-301. In addition, this research is supported by GRF grant no. PolyU 5435/12H and GRF grant no. PolyU 5440/11H.

References

1. Cytowic, R.E.: The Man Who Tasted Shapes. MIT Press, Cambridge (1993)
2. Cytowic, R.E.: Synesthesia: A Union of the Senses, 2nd edn. MIT Press, Cambridge (2000)
3. Cytowic, R.E., Eagleman, D.M.: Wednesday Is Indigo Blue: Discovering the Brain of Synesthesia (afterword by Dmitri Nabokov), 309. MIT Press, Cambridge (2009)
4. Harrison, J.E., Baron-Cohen, S.: Synaesthesia: Classic and Contemporary Readings. Blackwell Publishing, Oxford (1996)

5. Simner, J., Mulvenna, C., Sagiv, N., et al.: Synaesthesia: The prevalence of atypical cross-modal experiences. Perception **35**(8), 1024–1033 (2006)
6. Simner, J., Ward, J., Lanz, M., et al.: Non-random associations of graphemes to colours in synaesthetic and non-synaesthetic populations. Cognitive Neuropsychology **22**(8), 1069–1085 (2005)
7. Ward, J., Huckstep, B., Tsakanikos, E.: Sound-colour synaesthesia: To what extent does it use cross-modal mechanisms common to us all? Cortex **42**(2), 264–80 (2006)
8. Rich, A.N., Bradshaw, J.L., Mattingley, J.B.: A systematic, large-scale study of synaesthesia: Implications for the role of early experience in lexical-colour associations. Cognition **98**(1), 53–84 (2005)
9. Hubbard, E.M., Ramachandran, V.S.: Neurocognitive mechanisms of synesthesia. Neuron **48**(3), 509–520 (2005)
10. Chou, Y.-M., Huang, C.-R.: Hantology: conceptual system discovery based on orthographic convention. In: Huang, C.-R., et al. (eds.) Ontology and the Lexicon. Cambridge Studies in Natural Language Processing. Cambridge University Press, Cambridge (2010)
11. Hong, J.-F., Huang, C.-R.: A hanzi radical ontology based approach towards teaching chinese characters. In: Ji, D., Xiao, G. (eds.) CLSW 2012. LNCS, vol. 7717, pp. 745–755. Springer, Heidelberg (2013)
12. Huang, C.-R., Hong, J.-F.: Deriving conceptual structures from sense: A study of near synonymous sensation verbs. Journal of Chinese Language and Computing (JCLC) **15**(3), 125–136 (2005)
13. Hong, J.-F., Huang, C.-R.: The near synonym pair Sheng and Yin: A study of the relation between sense and concept. 漢語詞彙語義研究的現狀與發展趨勢國際學術研討會。 Institute of Computational Linguistics, Peking University, November 6–8, 2004. (in Chinese)
14. Huang, C.-R., Hsieh, S.-K., Hong, J.-F., Chen, Y.-Z., Su, I.-L., Chen, Y.-X., Huang, S.-W.: Chinese Wordnet: Design, implementation, and application of an infrastructure for cross-lingual knowledge processing. Journal of Chinese Information Processing **24**(2), 14–23 (2010). (in Chinese)
15. Kilgarriff, A., Rychlý, P., Smrz, P., Tugwell, D.: The sketch engine. In: Proceedings of EURALEX, Lorient, France (2004)
16. Ma, W.-Y., Huang, C.-R.: Uniform and effective tagging of a heterogeneous Giga-word Corpus. In: Presented at the 5th International Conference on Language Resources and Evaluation (LREC 2006). Genoa, Italy, May 24–28, 2006
17. Kilgarriff, A., Huang, C.-R., Rychlý, P., Smith, S., Tugwell, D.: Chinese word sketches. In: ASIALEX 2005: Words in Asian Cultural Context, Singapore (2005)
18. Huang, C.-R., Kilgarriff, A., Wu, Y., et al.: Chinese sketch engine and the extraction of collocations. In: Proceedings of the 4th SIGHAN Workshop on Chinese Language Processing, pp. 48–55, October 14–15, 2005, Jeju, Korea (2005)
19. Sinclair, J.M. (ed.): Looking Up: An Account of the COBUILD Project in Lexical Computing. Collins (1987)
20. Church, K.W., Hanks, P.: Word association norms, mutual information and lexicography. In: Proceedings of the 27th Annual Meeting of ACL, Vancouver, pp. 76–83 (1989)
21. Lin, D.: Automatic retrieval, and clustering of similar words. In: Proceedings of COLING-ACL, Montreal, pp. 768–774 (1998)
22. Kilgarriff, A., Tugwell, D.: Sketching words. In: Corréard, M.-H. (ed.) Lexicography and Natural Language Processing. A Festschrift in Honour of B.T.S. Atkins. EURALEX (2002)
23. Hong, J.-F., Huang, C.-R.: Using Chinese gigaword corpus and chinese word sketch in linguistic research. In: The 20th Pacific Asia Conference on Language, Information and Computation (PACLIC-20). November 1–3, 2006. China Huazhong Normal University, Wu-Han (2006)

The Mirative Use of "怎么[*Zěnme*]" in Mandarin Chinese and Its Semantic Consequence

Bin Liu[✉]

Department of Chinese Language & Literature, Peking University, Beijing 100871, China
liubin198903@126.com

Abstract. Mirativity has been gradually recognized as a distinct semantic and grammatical category whose fundamental function is to illustrate information which is new or surprising to the speaker or hearer. Each language has its mirative expressions. This paper mainly discusses the mirative use of "怎么 [*zěnme*]" in Mandarin Chinese. It distinguishes between "*zěnme₁*", "*zěnme₂*" and "*zěnme₃*", and points out that "*zěnme₂*" and "*zěnme₃*" can express mirative meaning. Especially, "*zěnme₃*", which is grammaticalized from "*zěnme₂*", can be viewed as an independent marker of mirativity in Mandarin Chinese. In addition, this paper reveals that the semantic consequence of the mirative use of "*zěnme*" is promoting the rhetorical question to form negative meaning.

Keywords: "怎么[*zěnme*]" · Mirativity · Negation · Semantic consequence

1   Introduction：The Basic Meaning and Usage of "*Zěnme*"

The interrogative pronoun "怎么[*zěnme*]" has two basic usages when it is used as an adverbial in Mandarin Chinese. One is in front of verbs to ask the manner of an action. In this case, the verbs do not have negative forms and "*zěnme*" cannot be put before the subject. The other is before verbs or adjectives to ask the reason. Different from the former case, the verbs or adjectives can be negated, and this "*zěnme*" can be put before the subject (Lü, 2008/1980: 651). In this paper, we view the former "*zěnme* (how)" as "*zěnme₁*", the latter "*zěnme* (why)" as "*zěnme₂*". For instance: (quoted from Lü, 2008/1980)

(1) a. 他　怎么　学会　　广州话　　的？
　　　　he　how　master　Cantonese　DE
　　　　'How did he master Cantonese?'
　　　b. 这事　我　该　　怎么　跟　他　说？
　　　　this　I　should　how　to　he　say
　　　　'How should I tell him about this?'

This research is sponsored by the National Social Science Fund Major Project "Chinese parataxis characteristic research and large knowledge base and corpus construction under the background of international Chinese language education" (Approval No.: 12&ZD175). I would like to express my sincere gratitude to Li Qiang, WU Guoxiang, Liu Hongchao, Li Wanjun, Lin Tao and Liu Yuan for their suggestions to this paper.

Q. Lu and H.H. Gao (Eds.): CLSW 2015, LNAI 9332, pp. 74–82, 2015.
DOI: 10.1007/978-3-319-27194-1_8

（2）a. 他 怎么 这么 高兴？
      he why so happy
      'Why was he so happy?'

b. 小李 怎么 没 报名？
      XiaoLi why NEG sign up
      'Why didn't XiaoLi sign up?'

c. 怎么 他 还 不 出来？
      why he yet NEG come out
      'Why hasn't he come out yet?'

The contrast between (1) and (2) shows that "*zěnme$_1$*" is usually used before the verb (such as 1a~b), but it cannot be put in front of the subject (for example, we cannot say *"怎么他学会广州话的？"(*how did he master Cantonese*)). However, "*zěnme$_2$*" can be used both before the verb or adjective (such as 2a~b) and before the subject (such as 2c). As for why "*zěnme$_1$*" and "*zěnme$_2$*" are different in syntactic positions, Xiao (2009) indicated that the domain of "*zěnme$_2$*" has mapped to the entire sentence instead of a specific component of the sentence. In other words, "*zěnme$_2$*" was relatively semantically independent, which makes its syntactic position more flexible. In contrast, "*zěnme$_1$*" points to the action, so it could only be used before the verb.

Generally speaking, "*zěnme$_1$*" is often used in the future tense sentences (such as 1b), and also in the past tense sentences (such as 1a). However, "*zěnme$_2$*" is usually used in the past tense sentences. As we know, when we use "*zěnme*" to ask the reason for something, it must have taken place; otherwise, there is no need to ask[1]. When we use "*zěnme*" to ask the manner, there is no such restriction. That being said, things that happened before and have not happened before can both be asked.

The grammatical stresses of "*zěnme$_1$*" and "*zěnme$_2$*" are also different. Zhu (2008/1982) indicated that when asking the manner, the stress is on the interrogative pronoun "*zěnme*"; however, when asking the reason, the stress falls on the concrete words after "*zěnme*". For example, the stress of 1b is on "*zěnme*", while the one in 2b is on the verb "报名(*sign up*)".

Peng (1993) pointed out that "*zěnme$_1$*" and "*zěnme$_2$*" had their own constructions based on their different usages. For example, "*zěnme$_1$*" usually appears in "*zěnme* + VP+的(DE)" (such as 1a), but "*zěnme$_2$*" usually appears in "*zěnme*+ 这么/ 那么 (*so*)+VP" and "*zěnme* + 不/ 没有(*not*) + VP" (such as 2a~c).

After comparing the differences between "*zěnme$_1$*" and "*zěnme$_2$*" in the syntactic position, tense requirement and grammatical stress, we can generally figure out their meanings and make a distinction[2].

---

[1] Take (2b) for example, "*zěnme*" in (2b) is used to ask the reason of "没报名 (*not sign up*)", obviously, "没报名 (*not sign up*)" has happened.

[2] An interesting fact is that the meaning of "*zěnme$_1$*" and "*zěnme$_2$*" can convert in some cases. For example, "*zěnme*" in "你怎么去上班(*How do you go to work?*)" is used to ask the manner, but ask the reason in "你怎么还去上班(*Why do you still go to work?*)". We will discuss it in another research.

In addition, Lü (2008/1980) argued that "*zěnme*" can be used in front of the entire sentence, followed by a phonetic pause, and expressed the mirative meaning. At that time, "*zěnme*" was an independent component at the beginning of a sentence. For instance: (quoted from Lü, 2008/1980)

（3）a.怎么, 你 不 认识 我 了?
　　　zěnme you NEG recognize me ASP
　　≈ '*You didn't recognize me?*'
　　b.怎么 , 他 又 改变 主意 了?
　　　zěnme he again change idea ASP
　　≈ '*He changed idea again?*'

We view this "*zěnme*" as "*zěnme₃*".

This paper mainly discusses the meaning and usage of "*zěnme₂*" and "*zěnme₃*", shows the relationship of them and explains why the "*zěnme*" rhetorical question can express negative meaning.

2   The Mirative Use of "*Zěnme*"

2.1   Mirativity

Delancey (1997) firstly put forward the grammatical category of mirativtity, whose fundamental function is to convey the information which is new or surprising to the speaker or hearer. The typological studies have proved that mirativtity exists in many languages, and that there are different ways to express mirativity among languages. It seems that mirativtity is universal. However, it does not mean each language has grammatical markers of mirativtity (Aikhenvald 2004). Some researchers have proved the existence of grammatical markers or affixes of mirativtity in some languages, such as Turkish, Hare, Sunwar, Korean, etc. For example, "-miş" is a grammatical marker in Turkish. (Delancey 1997, 2001; Aikhenvald 2012)

（4）Kemal gel-miş
　　　Kemal come-MIRATIVE
　　　'*Kemal came.*'

The mirativtity is closely related to the evidentiality. There are debates about the status of mirativtity and the relationship between mirativtity and evidentiality. Some researchers view mirativtity as a sub-category of evidentiality, and others think that mirativtity should be regarded as a distinct semantic and grammatical category based on the evidence from some languages (such as Tibetan and Hare). (Delancey 1997, 2001) Furthermore, Aikhenvald (2004) has put forward three ways for the semantic evolution of mirativtity and evidentiality.

Evidentiality has been widely recognized as a distinct semantic and grammatical category, and the related studies are thorough. But there are few studies about mirativtity, especially in Chinese. We find that only Lin (2014) has discussed about mirativtity in Chinese. She discussed the relationship between evidentiality and mirativtity firstly and inspected cross-language corpora, and finally inferred that: (1) evidentiality had a tendency of becoming the strategy of mirativtity, (2) mirativtity mainly had three properties, (3) the mirative meaning of evidentiality was a result of semantic expansion, (4) 原来 (*originally*)" could be viewed as a mirative marker in Chinese.

Since the Chinese language does not have much inflectional change, unlike Turkish or Hare, there is no specific affix marker of mirativtity in Chinese. However, there are some means of mirativtity in Chinese, besides "原来 (*originally*)". Some adverbs, such as "竟然 (*unexpectedly*)", can also express mirative meanings. For example, "他竟然没去上课 (*he didn't go to class unexpectedly*)" suggests the speaker is very surprised at his absence of class. The interrogative pronoun "*zěnme*" discussed in this paper also has this mirative meaning.

In the next section, we will turn to discuss the mirative use of "*zěnme*" in Mandarin Chinese and its semantic consequence from the perspective of mirativtity.

2.2   The Mirative Use of "*Zěnme*"

As previously noted, the fundamental function of mirativtity is to convey information which is new, surprising or unprepared to the speakers, thus, the speakers feel surprised. We find the interrogative pronoun "*zěnme*" (such as "*zěnme$_2$*" and "*zěnme$_3$*") in Mandarin Chinese usually conveys this mirative meaning. In this section, we will make a specific analysis.

Lü (2008/1980) had already indicated "*zěnme$_3$*" could express mirative meaning. See the examples again.

(3) a.怎么, 你　不　　认识　我　了？
　　　　zěnme you NEG   recognize   me
　　≈ '*You didn't recognize me?*'
　　　b.怎么 ,　他　又　　改变　主意　了？
　　　　 zěnme he   again   change   idea
　　≈ '*He changed idea again?*'

Apparently, we can see that both (3a)'s information "你不认识我了 (*You didn't recognize me?*)" and (3b)'s information "他又改变主意了 (*He changed idea again?*)" are surprising and unprepared to the speakers, thus, the speakers feel so surprised that they use the sentences like (3a~b). The interrogative pronoun "*zěnme*" here obviously conveys mirative meaning, and there are phonetic pauses after "*zěnme*" (such as using the comma ","). Furthermore, "*zěnme*" here is not used to ask the specific manner or reason[3]. It functions likes a conjunction which expresses mirative meaning. Let's look at some similar examples:

(5) 他很　焦急：“怎么 ,　连　个　条子　　也　　没　　留下！”
　　he so anxious　 *zěnme*   even   a   message   also   NEG   leave
　　He was so anxious and said 'she doesn't even leave a message?'

---

[3] That is why "*zenme*" here cannot be translated into "why/how".

(6) 他 惊奇地 问："怎么，你 能 到 他卧室里 私会 议事?"
　　he surprise ask　zěnme　you can　go　his bedroom　privately meet discusss
　　He asks surprisingly 'you can go to his bedroom meeting him privately and
discussing with him?'

(7) 陶铸同志 不胜惊异，反问我："怎么，你 还 没有 收到？
　　Mr. TaoZhu　surprise　ask　me　zěnme　you　still　NEG　receive
晚上，我 再 打电话 催催。"
tonight　I　again　call　urge
　　Mr. TaoZhu was very surprised and asked 'you haven't received it? I will call
again to urge tonight.'

Actually, besides "*zěnme₃*", we find "*zěnme₂*" can also express mirative meaning, which also indicates that the information in the context is surprising or unprepared to the speakers. Let's go back to (2).

（2）a. 他 怎么 这么 高兴？
　　　　he why　so　happy
　　　　'*Why was he so happy?*'
　　　b. 小李 怎么 没 报名？
　　　　XiaoLi　why　NEG　sign up
　　　　'*Why didn't XiaoLi sign up?*'
　　　c. 怎么 他 还 不 出来？
　　　　why　he yet　NEG　come out
　　　　'*Why hasn't he come out yet?*'

We can see that (2a)'s information "他这么高兴 (*he was so happy*)", (2b)'s information "小李没报名 (*XiaoLi didn't sign up*)" and (2c)'s information "他还不出来 (*he has not come out yet*)" are all new or surprising to the speakers. The speakers use the sentences like (2a~c) to express their surprise. Therefore, we also view this usage of "*zěnme*" as its mirative use.

If the mirative meaning of "*zěnme*" in (2a~c), which asks the specific reason, is not so obvious, then the mirative meaning of "*zěnme*" in the rhetorical question is quite significant. For instance: (quoted from Liu&Yuan, 2015)

(8)你的老婆要生孩子，你他妈的 怎么 能够忍心 将她一个人丢下不管呢？
　　your wife pregnant　you　zěnme can endure　her　alone　leave
　　'*Your wife is pregnant, how can you leave her alone?*'
(9)你 哥哥 怎么 会把 我的病 放在心上？
　　your brother zěnme　can　my illness care about
　　'*How can your brother care about my illness?*'
(10)怎么一结婚，男的 就变成 这副德行了？
　　zěnme　marry man change into this appearance
　　'*How can men change into this appearance after married?*'

The contrast between (2a~c) and (8~10) indicates that "*zěnme*" in (8~10) is not asking specific reasons, but transforming the sentences into 'rhetorical question', which inquires with no doubt and expresses a negative meaning. The mirative meaning of "*zěnme*" in (8~10) is more obvious. Take (8) for example. (8)'s information "你忍心将她一个人丢下不管 (*you leave her alone*)" is so surprising and difficult to understand, thus, the speaker uses the rhetorical question "你他妈的怎么能够 忍心将她一个人丢下不管呢? (*How can you leave her alone?*)", which makes the mirative meaning prominent and expresses an emotion of blame. Similarly, (10)'s information "男的一结婚就变成这副德行了(men have changed into this appearance after married)" is surprising and confounded to the speaker, so he uses the rhetorical question "怎么一结婚，男的就变成这副德行了? (*How can men change into this appearance after married?*)" to express the information of blame and negation.

In addition, we can find that "*zěnme₃*" is actually grammaticalized from "*zěnme₂*". Its syntactic position shifted to the front of the proposition with a pause behind it. We hold that "*zěnme₃*" has become a distinct mirative marker in Mandarin Chinese and it can be regarded as a conjunction expressing mirative meaning. In contrast, "*zěnme₁*" does not convey mirative meaning. For example, (1a)'s information"学会广州话 (*master Cantonese*)" and (1b)'s information "去跟他说这事 (*to tell him about this*)" are not new or surprising to the speakers at all.

In conclusion, the evidence shows that "*zěnme₂*" and "*zěnme₃*" are the mirative use of "*zěnme*", which indicates the information is new, surprising or unprepared to the speakers. "*Zěnme₂*" in general questions can express a certain degree of mirative meaning, while in rhetorical questions its mirative meaning is much more obvious. Moreover, "*zěnme₃*" is grammaticalized from "*zěnme₂*". It can convey a strong mirative meaning, which should be viewed as a unique mirative marker in Mandarin Chinese.

3   The Semantic Consequence of "*Zěnme*"'s Mirative Use

As mentioned in Section 2, "*zěnme₂*" can express mirative meaning, especially in rhetorical questions. We know that "*zěnme*" in those questions expresses negative meaning, instead of asking for specific reasons. (8~10) are repeated below.

(8)你的老婆要生孩子，你他妈的 怎么 能够忍心 将她一个人丢下不管呢？
    your wife pregnant   you   *zěnme* can endure her alone   leave
    '*Your wife is pregnant, how can you leave her alone?*'
(9)   你   哥哥   怎么   会把 我的病   放在心上？
    your brother   *zěnme*   can my illness care about
    '*How can your brother care about my illness?*'
(10)怎么一结婚，男的   就变成   这副德行了？
    zěnme marry man   change into this appearance
    '*How can men change into this appearance after married?*'

The question is why (8~10) can express negative meaning.

After a further discussion in our last paper (Liu&Yuan, 2015) in details, the negative meaning within the "*zěnme*" rhetorical question should be generated in such a way: the context firstly implies or shows the behavior indicated by VP is unreasonable or excuseless and the purpose to give the rhetorical question of the speaker is not to ask a real question but to show suspect to the reason or excuse on purpose. The speakers "disbelieve the positive (have reasons to VP), and believe the negative (does not have reasons to VP)", instead of specifically inquiring. Both "disbelieve the positive" and "believe the negative" have a negative meaning, which make the "*zěnme*" rhetorical question emerges negative meaning: should not do something.

Take (8) for example. Why does the rhetorical question "你他妈的怎么能够忍心将她一个人丢下不管呢? (*How can you leave her alone?*)" can form negative meaning: "你不应该将她一个人丢下不管(*you shouldn't leave her alone*)"? Liu&Yuan (2015) thinks that in the context, Liu Zhaohua will leave his pregnant wife alone. Generally speaking, when someone's wife is pregnant, he should take good care of his wife, which suggests that Liu Zhaohua's behavior is unreasonable. Hence, the speaker uses the rhetorical question "你他妈的怎么能够忍心将她一个人丢下 不管呢? (*How can you leave her alone?*) " to suspect the reason on purpose. The speaker disbelieves that you have reasons to leave her alone, and believes that you do not have reasons to leave her alone. Both "disbelieve that you have reasons to leave her alone" and "believe that you do not have reasons to leave her alone" have a negative meaning, which make the rhetorical question emerges the negative meaning: "你不应该将她一个人丢下不管(*you should not leave her alone*) ".

The analysis above has explained the reason why the "*zěnme*" rhetorical question can express negative meaning, but there is still a question remains to be solved. Why does the speakers suspect about the reason of VP? Liu&Yuan (2015) has not discussed it.

After investigating the relative context, we find that the information of VP is new or surprising to the speakers, which makes the speakers feel surprised, so they suspect about the reasons of VP. While 'suspect' is an implicit negative verb (Yuan, 2012), which contains negative meaning. Under these conditions, the "*zěnme*" rhetorical question can indicate negative meaning. It is the mirative use of "*zěnme*" that makes the speakers suspect about the reason of VP, and then promotes the "*zěnme*" rhetorical question to form negative meaning. This effect can be regarded as the semantic consequence of the mirative use of "*zěnme*".

Let's go back to (8) again. The behavior "将她一个人丢下不管 (*leave her alone*)" is surprising or even incomprehensible to the speaker, so he feels very surprised and suspects about the reason of VP. "Suspect" contains negative meaning, which makes the rhetorical question "你他妈的怎么能够 忍心将她一个人丢下不管呢? (*How can you leave her alone?*) " emerge the negative meaning: "你不应该将她一个人丢下 不管 (*you shouldn't leave her alone*) ".

In conclusion, we think that the VP as a behavior in the rhetorical question is surprising or unprepared to the speakers, so they feel surprised and suspect about the reason of VP. The implicit negative verb "suspect" contains negative meaning, which makes the rhetorical question emerge negative meaning. In other words, it is the mirative use of "*zěnme*" that makes the "*zěnme*" rhetorical question form negative meaning. This explanation can make the formation mechanism of Liu&Yuan (2015) more reasonable. The revised formation mechanism is shown as follows:

The context suggests VP is unreasonable → VP is surprising to the speakers → the speakers feel surprised and suspect about the reason of VP → "suspect" (① disbelieve the positive, ② believe the negative) contains negative meaning → promoting the "zěnme" rhetorical question to form negative meaning.

4   Conclusion

This paper mainly discusses the mirative use of *"zěnme"* in Mandarin Chinese and its semantic consequence. The paper distinguishes between *"zěnme$_1$"*, *"zěnme$_2$"* and *"zěnme$_3$"*. It firstly introduces the differences between *"zěnme$_1$"* and *"zěnme$_2$"*. Secondly, it points out that *"zěnme$_2$"* and *"zěnme$_3$"* can express mirative meaning, which represents the information in the context is surprising or unexpected to the speakers. In addition, *"zěnme$_3$"* is grammaticalized from *"zěnme$_2$"*, which expresses a stronger mirative meaning and can be viewed as an independent marker of mirativity in Mandarin Chinese. Finally, the paper reveals that the semantic consequence of the mirative use of *"zěnme"* is promoting the rhetorical question to form negative meaning.

In this research, we also point out that mirativtity, as a distinct semantic and grammatical category, has been gradually recognized as an important parameter of typology, which provides a new perspective for language researching, especially for linguistic topology.

References

1. Aikhenvald, A.: Evidentiality. Oxford University Press, Oxford (2004)
2. Aikhenvald, A.: The Essence of Mirativity. Linguistic Typology **16**, 435–485 (2012)
3. DeLancey, S.: Mirativity: The Grammatical Marking of Unexpected Information. Linguistic Typology **1**, 33–52 (1997)
4. DeLancey, S.: The Mirative and Evidentiality. Journal of Pragmatics **33**, 369–382 (2001)
5. DeLancey, S.: Still Mirative after All These Years. Linguistic Typology **16**, 529–564 (2012)
6. Hu, D.: Research of Mandarin Chinese Rhetorical Question. AnHui People's Press, HeFei (2010). (现代汉语反问句研究, 合肥: 安徽人民出版社, 2010). (in Chinese)
7. Lin, Q.: Evidentiality and Mirativtity. The Third Forum of Chinese and National Language from the Perspective of Typology, Beijing Language and Culture University, BeiJing (2014). (传信和惊异, 第三届类型学视野下的汉语与民族语言研究高峰论坛, 北京语言大学, 2014). (in Chinese)
8. Liu, B., Yuan, Y.: On the Formation and Construal Mechanism of *"Zěnme"* Rhetorical Question's Negative Meaning. Special issue (2015). ("怎么"类特指反问句否定语义的形成与识解机制, 待刊, 2015). (in Chinese)
9. Lü, S.: Eight Hundred Words of Modern Chinese. The Commercial Press, BeiJing (2008/1980). (现代汉语八百词, 北京: 商务印书馆, 2008/1980). (in Chinese)
10. Peng, K.: About *"Zěnme"*. Chinese Language Learning **1**, 114–125 (1993). (说"怎么", 汉语学习, 1993:114–125). (in Chinese)

11. Xiao, Z.: On the Semantic and Syntactic Analysis of "*Zěnme*$_1$" and "*Zěnme*$_2$". Chinese Language Learning **2**, 44–49 (2009). (in Chinese)
12. Yuan, Y.: On the Semantic Level and Overflow Condition of the Implicit Negation Hidden in the Chinese verbs. Studies of the Chinese Language **2**, 99–113 (2012). (in Chinese)
13. Yuan, Y.: On the Sense Extension Mechanism and Semantic Construal Strategy of the Chinese Verb Huaiyi (怀疑). Studies in Language and Linguistics **3**, 1–12 (2014). (in Chinese)
14. Zhu, D.: Grammar- A Textbook. The Commercial Press, BeiJing (2008/1982). (语法讲义, 北京: 商务印书馆, 2008/1982). (in Chinese)

A Comparison of Chinese and English Hot Words of the Year

Weiqi Song[✉]

Guangdong University of Foreign Studies, Guangzhou, China
songweiqigd@163.com

Abstract. This paper analyzes different versions of Chinese and English "hot words of the year" in 2014 from phonology, morphology and meaning. Through contrastive analysis, it probes into both similarities and differences between Chinese and English hot words. It also tries to explore the new trends and interaction of two languages in the age of information and globalization.

Keywords: Hot words · Phonology · Morphology · Meaning · Comparison

1   Introduction

Hot words, also called "buzz words", reflect issues and things attracting the attention of people, especially people's lifestyles and thoughts in specific countries or regions in a specific period. Just as Li (2014) put it, "hot words are just hot at one time". Once a hot topic fades out of people's eyes, the corresponding words are no longer hot either. Nowadays, we can see various versions of yearly, monthly even daily hot words covering different walks of life. Even the sign and emoticon appear on the list of English hot words of the year 2014.

As part of the vocabulary, hot words have their own rationale and value which inspired the present study. Xu (2002) once pointed out that, "When making a comparison, it should be ensured that linguistic phenomena chosen from two different languages are corresponding so that the comparison is meaningful". In view of this, eight versions of hot words are used for the contrastive analysis: four in Chinese and four in English. The first version of Chinese hot words is "Chinese Inventory 2014" jointly issued by National Language Resource Monitoring and Research Center, the Commercial Press and People's Daily Online. The second is "Top Ten Hot Words in 2014" chosen by the online encyclopedia-Hudong based on online voting, expert evaluation and entry views. The third is "Historical Records of 2014" which is an annual brand activity of Baidu encyclopedia. The fourth is "Hot Words of the Year" released by a popular domestic translation software-Youdao Dictionary. Similarly, English hot words are selected from four sources: the U.S. Global Language Institute, Merriam-Webster, Inc., Oxford English Dictionary and Collins English Dictionary.

By comparing these hot words, this paper intends to find out both similarities and differences in the expression of different languages (Lü, 1942). It also tries to explore the new trends and interaction of two languages in different social and cultural contexts, aiming to provide some fresh materials for further studies.

© Springer International Publishing Switzerland 2015
Q. Lu and H.H. Gao (Eds.): CLSW 2015, LNAI 9332, pp. 83–90, 2015.
DOI: 10.1007/978-3-319-27194-1_9

2   The Analysis of Chinese Hot Words in 2014

2.1   Hot Words Collection

Chinese Inventory 2014	*Hudong Encyclopedia*	*Historical Records of 2014*	*Youdao Dictionary*
改革元年	依法治国	反腐	也是醉了
打老虎	马航	习大大	有钱任性
冰桶挑战赛	APEC蓝	中国梦	挖掘机
马航失踪事件	埃博拉病毒	新常态	撕逼大战
彭丽媛	冰桶挑战	电商	滑板鞋
壕	监狱风云	APEC蓝	冰桶挑战
埃博拉	克里米亚	依法治国	都教授
霾	《小苹果》	暖男	茶叶蛋
神曲	奶茶恋	萌萌哒	上天台
且行且珍惜	玉兔号	雾霾	国民老公

These are the four lists of Chinese hot words of the year. As far as the reference is concerned, 冰桶挑战（赛）appeared in three out of the four lists; 依法治国, 马航（失踪事件）, APEC蓝, 埃博拉（病毒）and（雾）霾 appeared in two; while other hot words appeared in only one list. The following part will focus on the six Chinese hot words which appeared more than once.

2.2   Phonetic Analysis of Six Chinese Hot Words

Generally speaking, the pronunciation of a Chinese character can be seen as a syllable. In the case of a Chinese character followed by the suffix "儿" [Er], two characters are taken as only one syllable (Huang & Liao, 2011). In terms of syllable number, we actually get ten structures for six words. For example, 冰桶挑战（赛）is the combined expression of 冰桶挑战&冰桶挑战赛. Among the ten forms of syllabic structures, 马航失踪事件 is sexisyllabic; 冰桶挑战赛&埃博拉病毒 are quinquesyllabic; 冰桶挑战, 依法治国 and APEC蓝 are quadrisyllabic; 埃博拉 is trisyllabic; 马航&雾霾 are disyllabic while only 霾 is monosyllabic. It can be seen from the syllable distribution that Chinese hot words are mainly polysyllabic. Only a few have less than three syllables.

2.3   Morphological Analysis of Six Chinese Hot Words

The six Chinese hot words fall into two types of word formation: "Chinese style" made up of Chinese characters and "Mixed style" with both Chinese and English Elements. Only APEC蓝 belongs to the mixed style ('APEC' stands for Asia-Pacific

Economic Cooperation and '蓝' for the blue sky). So, the majority of Chinese hot words are of Chinese style.

In the opinion of Zhu (1983), all words are made up of morphemes. Single-morpheme word consists of only one morpheme while compound words have two or more morphemes. Based on this, we can see that there are only two single-morpheme words, namely, 埃博拉&霾. There are five compound words with the "modifier-core" structure, they are: 马航失踪事件, 冰桶挑战赛, 埃博拉病毒, 冰桶挑战 and APEC蓝. There are also two "combined/union" structures: 依法治国&雾霾. As for 马航, it is the abbreviation of the proper noun-Malaysia Airline System (MAS). On the whole, Chinese hot words are mainly compound words.

2.4   Semantic Analysis of Six Chinese Hot Words

Firstly, let's take a look at how these hot words get hot.

冰桶挑战（赛）**[Bingtong Tiaozhan (Sai)]: [Ice Bucket Challenge]** is a new way of "playing" charity created by Americans, aiming to promote awareness of Amyotrophic Lateral Sclerosis (ALS). The participants pour a bucket of ice water on their heads, film the process and then nominate others to do the same. With the help of celebrity and social media, such an online activity gets spread very quickly.

依法治国 **[Yifa Zhiguo]: [Ruling the Country by Law]** means to rule the country by laws both representing people's will and conforming with social development. After the meeting of the 18th central committee of the Communist Party of China (CPC) on October in 2014, this expression has drawn more and more public attention.

马航（失踪事件）**[Mahang (Shizong Shijian)]: [MH 370 Tragedy]** refers to the disappearance of Flight 370 of MAS on 8 March, two hours after leaving the Kuala Lumpur International Airport. No debris from the plane has been found till 19 March.

APEC蓝 **[APEC Lan]: [APEC Blue]** refers to the blue sky in Beijing during APEC China 2014 due to control measures towards both traffic and polluting enterprises directed by Chinese government. Because of its transience, the new phrase "APEC blue" also refers to something wonderful but also fleeting.

埃博拉（病毒）**[Aibola (Bingdu)]: [Ebola (Virus)]** is a rare kind of fatal infectious disease with high mortality. Ebola got its name in 1976 when it was firstly found around the Ebola River. After the appearance of the first American Ebola patient in 2014, global concern goes to this disease.

（雾）霾 **[(Wu) Mai]: [Fog and Haze]** refers to the weather condition when the air is dirty and visibility deteriorated. On February 2014, President Xi gave some instructions to the treatment of air pollution and improvement of air quality.

It can be seen from the above explanation that these hot words are closely related to some specific phenomena and events in people's lives. For example, [Ice Bucket Challenge] involves social charity, [Ruling the Country by Law] reflects people's concern and expectation of law, [MH 370 Tragedy] shows people's care of victims and the safety issue, [Ebola (Virus)] reveals people's worry about health, while a strong desire for environmental improvement is expressed by the word change from "haze" to "blue".

Just as Saeed (1997) put it, "There is more to meaning than reference". Besides the rational meaning related to the concept itself, the word also has its color meaning attached to the rational meaning, so some special feelings in a certain context can also be expressed (Huang & Liao, 2011). [Fog and Haze] has something to do with derogatory feelings, [Ebola (Virus)] & [MH 370 Tragedy] is filled with pains and worries, while positive attitudes are attached to [Ruling the Country by Law] & [APEC Blue].

3   The Analysis of English Hot Words in 2014

3.1   Hot Words Collection

Global Language Institute	Merriam-Webster	Oxford English Dictionary	Collins English Dictionary
♥	Culture	Vape	Photobomb
#	Nostalgia	Contactless	Tinder
Vape	Insidious	Slacktivism	Bake-off
Blood moon	Legacy	Budtender	Normcore
Nano	Feminism	Normcore	Devo max
Photobomb	Je ne sais quoi	Bae	
Caliphate	Innovation	Indyref	
White privilege	Surreptitious		
Bae	Autonomy		
Bash tag	Morbidity		

[Vape] [Photobomb] [Normcore] [Bae] appeared in two out of the four lists; while other hot words appeared in only one list. For the purpose of comparison with six Chinese hot words, top words from the U. S. Global Language Institute [♥] and Merriam-Webster [Culture] are also included, so we can get six English hot words.

3.2   Phonetic Analysis of Six English Hot Words

We can see that only [♥] is a heart emoji rather than a regular word. The rest are five very common English words, no special phonetic features are found.

3.3   Morphological Analysis of Six English Hot Words

Morphology of the six selected items is relatively diversified. [♥] is a special kind of network language, [Bae] is an abbreviation, [Vape] originates from "vapor/vaporize", [Photobomb] is a compound word while [Normcore] is formed by blending.

3.4   Semantic Analysis of Six English Hot Words

According to Wang (2000), word meaning changes under the influence of the society rather than in a closed state. The English hot words can also illustrate this point.

[Vape]: a verb meaning to inhale and exhale the vapor produced by an electronic cigarette or a noun means e-cigarette. This word is strongly needed now to distinguish a new smoking fashion from the old one with tobacco. Then, marijuana vape also occurs along with voices against vape. As a highly controversial issue in close relation to health and the society, it was named as the "top word of the year".

[Photobomb]: means to drop in a photo unexpectedly or to intrude into a picture right before it is taken. It firstly became a key word in Google in 2008. In the British Commonwealth Games in 2014, Prince Harry and the Queen also "bomb" into the photos of athletes, making the word even hotter.

[Normcore]: a movement in which ordinary, unfashionable clothing is worn to add a "hardcore" to "normal" style, a new dressing fashion advocating simplicity.

[Bae]: a noun as a shortening of "baby" or "babe". Someone also take it as an acronym for "Before Anyone Else". The corresponding Chinese salutation of "baby/babe" is 宝贝 [Baobei]. When "bae" is used for anyone, this case is similar to the usage of 亲 [Qin; Dear] in Chinese.

[♥]: a symbol of love. The U. S. Global Language Institute finds that "♥" is the most frequently used sign around the world in 2014, equal to the function of a word. Because it can only be felt instead of being said, multiple meanings are possible. No wonder it beats all words, taking the first place in the hot word list.

[Culture]: Peter Sokolowski, editor at large for Merriam-Webster, explained that, "Culture is a word that we seem to be relying on more and more. It allows us to identify and isolate an idea, issue, or group with seriousness." It seems that talking about culture is also becoming a culture today.

Generally speaking, English hot words also cover different aspects of social life, which is in common with Chinese hot words. [Vape] represents a new fashion of smoking while [Normcore] is a new dressing style. Other fields such as entertainment, society and culture are reflected by hot words like [Culture], [Photobomb] and [Bae]. What's more, changes in word property and meaning can also be observed. "Bomb" is mainly used in military, but goes into the recreational life after its combination with "photo". "Hardcore" originated from music and is usually used in computer, but enters the clothing field when merged with "normal". The development of the internet has pushed the sign [♥] into the language system. [Culture] itself is being extensively used today with the diversification of culture. In some sense, it is after various changes that these words become hot words of the year.

4   A Comparison of All Chinese and English Hot Words in 2014

4.1   Phonetic Comparison

Wang (1997) once said in the book 《古代汉语》 [Gudai Hanyu; Ancient Chinese] that: "Vocabulary in ancient Chinese is mainly monosyllabic while the majority of modern Chinese are disyllabic and polysyllabic words". As regards the syllable number, disyllabic words are no longer in the absolute majority of all the four versions of Chinese hot words in 2014. Looking back on hot words of the past several years, a similar pattern can be found, which indicates a trend that Chinese hot words are becoming multi-syllables. By contrast, there is no specific orientation in syllable number of English hot words. However, an interesting breakthrough is worth mentioning, that is, the sign [♥] is also legitimate for the selection of hot words.

4.2   Morphological Comparison

On the whole, Chinese hot words are made up of Chinese characters, with a few including both Chinese and English elements. English hot words are still formed by basic methods like blending, compounding, shortening, borrowing, etc. Whatever the morphology, hot words in two languages both are trying to express the richest meanings in a simple and precise way.

4.3   Semantic Comparison

Abstract and Concrete. Lian (1993) once pointed out that, English tends to use abstract expressions as indicated by a large number of abstract nouns used to express complicated thoughts and subtle emotions. As an inflectional language, English has various means of grammaticalization like the suffix "-ity", "-ia" , "-ism", etc. The majority of the four versions of English hot words also fall into the abstract category, with only two signs excluded. In contrast, Chinese tends to use concrete words like [Ice Bucket Challenge], [MH 370 Tragedy], [Fog and Haze], 打老虎 [Da Laohu; Shoot Tigers/Punishing Corruption], 挖掘机 [Wajue Ji; Excavator], 玉兔号 [Yutu Hao; Lunar Rover], 茶叶蛋 [Chaye Dan; Tea Flavoured Eggs], 滑板鞋 [Huaban Xie; Skate Shoes], 《小苹果》 [Xiao Ping Guo; Little Apple], 上天台 [Shang Tiantai; Go to the Roof/Suicide after Losing], etc. Though most elements of Chinese hot words are concrete, word meanings are strong and profound.

Another obvious difference between Chinese and English hot words is connected with emotional colors. Most of the English hot words are neutral or professional terms while Chinese hot words always involve social and political ethics. For this reason, we can feel the public call for democracy and justice from [Ruling the Country by Law], 反腐 [Fanfu; Anti-corruption] & [Punishing Corruption]. While 中国梦 [Zhong Guo Meng; Chinese Dream] is filled with patriotism and public confidence. People's environmental claims are expressed by [Fog and Haze] & [APEC Blue]. The economic situation is implied by 壕 [Hao, Tu Hao; Mainland Chinese (people who are rich but uncultured)] & [Tea Flavoured Eggs]. Cynicism and frustration are showed by 监狱风云 [Jianyu Fengyun, Prison on Fire (celebrities were caught in prison for drug abuse)] 奶茶恋 [Naicha Lian; Milktea Girl's Love], 且行且珍惜 [Qie Xing Qie Zhenxi; Seize the Moment]. Such a contrast between Chinese and English hot words is a reflection of cognitive differences of people in different countries and cultures.

Globalization and Diversification. Chinese and English hot words in 2014 can be seen as the reflection of eastern and western features in language, society and culture against the background of globalization. From mixed style word [APEC蓝] and borrowed words like "Je ne sais quoi", "Devo max", we can find the influence of globalization on different languages. Despite that Chinese has incorporated English elements, it is impossible for Chinese characters to appear in English hot words. This is because external environment surrounding Chinese is more complex while English is mainly affected by the internal Indo-European languages. Under influences from different language families, Chinese is no longer as "pure" as before, which has raised the concern of scholars and experts (Zhu, 2011). But alphabet notations like "tuhao" & "dama" have got access to English and once even became hot words, too.

Besides, we can find something shared by Chinese and English hot words. Two languages both have worries about the threat posed by diseases, 埃博拉（病毒）in Chinese while "Insidious" & "Morbidity" in English. Care about autonomy and political rights are also showed by Chinese expression 克里米亚 [Keli Miya; Crimea] and English expressions "Autonomy" & "Indyref". As regards the political system and national policies, Chinese has 中国梦, 改革元年 [Gaige Yuan Nian], 依法治国, 习大大 [Xi Dada], 反腐, 打老虎 and English has "Caliphate", "White Privilege", "Devo max". Attention on women's rights is respectively indicated by 彭丽媛 [Peng Liyuan] in Chinese and "Feminism" in English. On one hand, Chinese women are admiring and pursuing 国民老公 [Guomin Laogong; National Husband], 都教授 [Du Jiaoshou], 暖男 [Nuan Nan], on the other hand, foreign women are affectionately called "Bae".

Apart from similarities, we do appreciate differences of the eastern and western world expressed by hot words of the year. The west is talking about "Culture" while China is talking about 新常态 [Xin Changtai; New Situation (with relatively stable economic development)]. English celebrities bomb into the public, making a hot "Photobomb" while Chinese celebrities were cast into the prison, making a hot [Prison on Fire], reminding the public to "Seize the Moment". The movie and TV circles in England and America are creating the atmosphere of "Nostalgia" while Chinese films are showing 撕逼大战 [Sibi Dazhan; War of Words]. English families are holding the "Bake-off" while Chinese are doing [Ice Bucket Challenges]. The west has developed the "Contactless" payment, however, mainland Chinese are thought as too poor to eat [Tea Flavoured Eggs]. As for technology, English has "Nano" & "Innovation" while Chinese has [Excavator] & [Lunar Rover]. Foreigners are dating with "Tinder" while a Chinese university girl is directly dating with a CEO [Milktea Girl's Love]. Foreigners use the French phrase "Je ne sais quoi" to express feelings towards good things and give a "Bash Tag" to a bad thing, but Chinese will say 也是醉了 [Yeshi Zuile; Are You Kidding] no matter good or bad cases. The sky should be the same over the earth, but the west is observing the "Blood Moon" excitedly while

Chinese are worrying about [Fog and Haze]. "Normcore" is popular in foreign dressing while [Skate Shoes] are popular in Chinese pop music. Foreign "Budtender" is profiting from marihuana while Chinese 电商 [Dianshang; Electric Business] is competing in logistics. "Vape" is running into the mouths of the foreigners while the song [Little Apple] is flooding into the ears of the Chinese. Western "Slacktivism" is "Insidious" in the internet while Chinese "tuhao" "Go to the Roof/ Suicide after Losing] in the World Cup gambling.

5   Conclusion

Pan (2002) held that contrastive linguistics should put its focus on macro-linguistics, emphasizing the combination of language with backgrounds such as culture and society. In line with this idea, the present paper made an attempt to explore both similarities and differences of people's lives and thoughts in different countries under the influence of globalization. Hot words of the year are just like a mirror which inflects various aspects of social life, embodies people's living and thinking state. It has to be admitted that this paper is just a preliminary study. More research, both synchronic and diachronic, is needed on the academic part. It's hoped that by looking at hot words, we can have a better understanding of the society.

References

1. Li, M.: Review of "Top Word of the Year" and Conceptual Analysis of Popular Words. J. Rhetoric Learning. **1**, 48–51 (2014). [李明洁. 年度词语排行榜述评与流行语的概念辨析. 当代修辞学]. (in Chinese)
2. Xu, Y.: Contrastive Linguistics. Shanghai Foreign Language Education Press, Shanghai (2002). [许余龙. 《对比语言学》. 上海: 上海外语教育出版社]. (in Chinese)
3. Lü, S.: An Outline of Chinese Grammar. The Commercial Press, Beijing (1942). [吕叔湘. 《中国文法要略》. 北京: 商务印书馆]. (in Chinese)
4. Zhu, D.: Explainations on Grammar. The Commercial Press, Beijing (1983). [朱德熙. 《语法讲义》. 北京: 商务印书馆]. (in Chinese)
5. Saeed, J.: Semantic. Blackwell, Oxford (1997)
6. Huang, B., Liao, X.: Modern Chinese, 5th edn. Higher Education Press, Beijing (2011). [黄伯荣, 廖序东. 《现代汉语(增订五版)》. 北京: 高等教育出版社]. (in Chinese)
7. Wang, R.: Studies in English Lexicology. Shanghai Foreign Language Education Press, Shanghai (2000). [汪榕培. 《英语词汇学研究》. 上海: 上海外语教育出版社]. (in Chinese)
8. Wang, L.: Ancient Chinese. The Chinese Publishing House, Beijing (1997). [王力. 《古代汉语》. 北京: 中华书局]. (in Chinese)
9. Lian, S.: Contrastive Studies of English and Chinese. Higher Education Press, Beijing (1993). [连淑能. 《英汉对比研究》. 北京: 高等教育出版社]. (in Chinese)
10. Zhu, Y.: A Contrastive Analysis of Ten Chinese and English Top Words in 2010. D. Zhejiang University (2011). [朱羽颖. 2010年汉英十大热词比较分析. 浙江大学硕士学位论文]
11. Pan, W.: An Outline of Chinese-English Contrastive Study. Beijing Language and Culture University Press, Beijing (2002). [潘文国. 《汉英语对比纲要》. 北京: 北京语言文化大学出版社]. (in Chinese)

On Detection of Synonyms Between Simplified Chinese of Mainland China and Traditional Chinese of Taiwan: A Semantic Similarity Method

Boli Wang and Xiaodong Shi[✉]

Department of Cognitive Science, Xiamen University, Xiamen 361005, China
me@bo-li.wang, mandel@xmu.edu.cn

Abstract. We present an approach for automatically detecting synonyms between simplified Chinese used in mainland China and traditional Chinese used in Taiwan from large scale corpus. After pre-processing step (including doing segmentation and POS tagging on our corpora), all words are classified into 3 categories according to their frequency: words exclusively used in mainland China, words exclusively used in Taiwan, and words commonly used in both sides. We use word vectors to represent meanings of words, calculate semantic similarities between words of both sides, and extract synonyms. The experiment shows that our approach can find synonyms that are not present in handcrafted dictionary.

Keywords: Synonyms between simplified and traditional chinese · Semantic representation · Semantic similarity · Automatic conversion between simplified and traditional chinese

1   Introduction

There is a lot of differences in language usage between simplified Chinese (SC) used in mainland China (MC) and traditional Chinese (TC) used in Taiwan (TW), including pronunciation, spelling system, punctuation marks, script, vocabulary, grammar and so on. In the aspect of vocabulary, some words have totally different meanings between MC and TW. For example, the word 土豆 [tu dou] means *potatoes* in MC but *peanuts* in TW. We call these words **homographs** between MC and TW. Meanwhile, some different words from two sides have the same meaning. For example, The English name *Obama* is translated into 奥巴马 [ao ba ma] in MC but 歐巴馬 [ou ba ma] in TW. We call these words **synonyms** between MC and TW.

Divergences in vocabulary confuse people from both MC and TW when they read articles from the other side. To handle this problem, some SC-TC automatic conversion systems integrate word conversion function using a MC-TW **synonyms table**. Typically, as reported in (Jinzhi Su, 1995) and (Xingjian Li, 2012), MC-TW synonyms table is constructed by handcrafted compiling, which is time-consuming and bounded by compilers' knowledge scope. Moreover, new words appear at all times and synonyms table thus should be renewed accordingly. In this paper, we present a

© Springer International Publishing Switzerland 2015
Q. Lu and H.H. Gao (Eds.): CLSW 2015, LNAI 9332, pp. 91–100, 2015.
DOI: 10.1007/978-3-319-27194-1_10

statistical approach to detect MC-TW synonyms from large scale corpus automatical-ly. With our method, a MC-TW synonyms table can be constructed in shorter time and include some synonyms ignored by handcrafted work.

There are two types of words that should be listed in the synonym table. (i) Some words exclusively used in one side and incomprehensible to people from the other side. E.g. 离休 [li xiu] (*honored retirement of those engaged in the revolution before 1949*) is an **exclusive word** of MC and 博爱座 [bo ai zuo] (*priority seats for the weak*) is an exclusive word of TW. (ii) Some words are commonly used in both MC and TW but have different meanings in two sides, namely homographs, such as 土豆 [tu dou] we mentioned. These words are likely to be misunderstood and need to be translated into a synonym with the same meaning in word conversion.

Therefore, our task is to find correspondences of synonyms between MC and TW. However, some correspondences are not one-to-one. For example, in conversion from TC to SC, 土豆 [tu dou] should be translated into 花生 [hua sheng] (*peanuts*). But reversely, in conversion from SC to TC, 花生 [hua sheng] does not need to be trans-lated into 土豆 [tu dou] because 花生 [hua sheng] also means *peanuts* in TW. Therefore, two different synonyms tables are needed to handle bidirectional conver-sions separately.

2   Related Work

When detecting synonyms, we need to calculate the semantic similarity between two words.

In the earlier researches, methods based on knowledge base have been commonly used on semantic similarity computing. (Richardson, 1994) measures semantic simi-larity of two words according to their relationship in WordNet, which is a knowledge base of English vocabulary. (Qun Liu, 2002) proposes a method to compute semantic similarity of Chinese words based on HowNet, which is a knowledge base of Chinese vocabulary. However, knowledge bases are handcrafted and always incomplete.

Corpus-based approaches to semantic similarity computing have received much attention lately. Since the context surrounding a given word provides important in-formation about its meaning, word meanings can be represented in distributional statistics of words' occurrence. (Chen, 2011) integrates lexical semantics consistency weight as a feature in SC-TC conversion model and semantic similarity is computed using cosine distance measure. (Shi Wang, 2013) and (Jing Shi, 2013) conduct a lot of experiments on different methods of semantic representation and similarity meas-ure. Using deep neural network, (Mikolov, 2013) proposes two novel model architec-tures for computing continuous vector representations of words and achieves large improvements in accuracy of word similarity task with much lower computational cost.

3   Our Approach

The main purpose of this research is to detect synonyms between MC and TW automatically. The flowchart of our method is shown in Fig. 1.

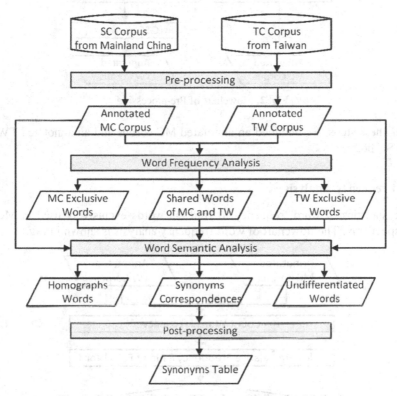

Fig. 1. General Flowchart of Synonyms Detection Method

3.1   Corpus and Pre-processing

A simplified Chinese corpus from MC and a traditional Chinese corpus from TW are needed. We choose MC and TW corpora from the same domain and at the same period, because meanings of words may differ considerably between different domains or periods. For example, in MC, 斑竹 [ban zhu] traditionally means *mottled bamboo*, but now it has a new meaning (*moderator*) in BBS.

Automatic Chinese segmentation with same granularity and POS tagging with same tag set is conducted on both two corpora[1] in pre-processing, which is shown in Fig. 2. We also convert all traditional Chinese characters in Taiwan TC corpus into SC after segmentation, because one word may have two different forms in SC and TC and TC-SC automatic conversion has a higher precision than SC-TC conversion.

---

[1]   In our experiments, we use SEGTAG toolkit (http://cloudtranslation.cc/segtag.html) on both MC and TW corpora.

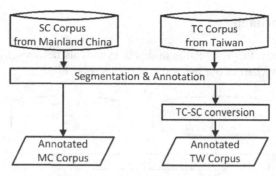

Fig. 2. Flowchart of Pre-processing

After these steps, we obtained an annotated MC corpus and an annotated TW corpus (in SC both).

3.2   Frequency Analysis

We use statistics of word frequency to find out words exclusively used in MC and TW respectively. The flowchart of word frequency analysis is shown in Fig. 3.

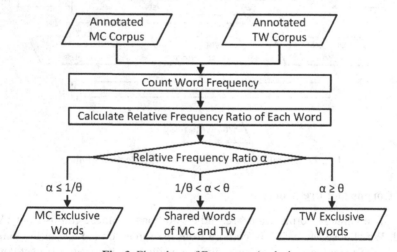

Fig. 3. Flowchart of Frequency Analysis

Let all words appear in the corpus be denoted by $W = \{w_1, w_2, \dots, w_M\}$, where M is the size of W. The relative frequency ratios α of a word w_i between MC and TW is given by:

$$\alpha(w_i) = \frac{C_s(w_i)}{\sum_\omega C_s(\omega)} \bigg/ \frac{C_t(w_i)}{\sum_\omega C_t(\omega)} \tag{1}$$

Here $C_s(w_i)$ is the number of times word w_i occurs in MC corpus and $C_t(w_i)$ is the number of times w_i occurs in TW corpus. For those words not occurring in the corpus, we assign ε (smaller than 1) as their frequency to smooth data and avoid division by zero. In our experiment, we set $\varepsilon = 0.1$.

We set a threshold θ (larger than 1) and divide all words in W into three categories: (1) If $\alpha(w_i) \geq \theta$, word w_i is supposed to be an exclusive word of MC seldom used in TW. (2) If $\alpha(w_i) \leq 1/\theta$, word w_i is supposed to be an exclusive word of TW seldom used in MC. (3) If $1/\theta < \alpha(w_i) < \theta$, word w_i is supposed to be a **shared word** that is commonly used in both MC and TW.

3.3   Semantic Analysis

In semantic analysis, we extract synonyms between MC and TW by computing semantic similarity between words. The flowchart is shown in Fig. 4.

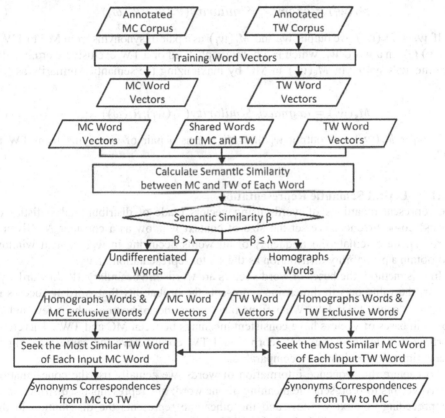

Fig. 4. Flowchart of Semantic Analysis

(i) We learn word vectors $R_s(w_i)$ and $R_t(w_i)$ as semantic representations of each word w_i from annotated MC and TW corpora respectively. Details of our learning algorithm will be described in Section 3.3.1.

(ii) Given a word w_i, which is a shared word, we calculate semantic similarity β between MC and TW as follows:

$$\beta(w_i) = Similarity(R_s(w_i), R_t(w_i)) \tag{2}$$

Details of similarity measure will be described in Session 3.3.2. We set a threshold λ and classify all shared words into two categories: (1) If $\beta(w_i) > \lambda$, word w_i is supposed to have same meaning between C and TC, namely an **undifferentiated word**. (2) If $\beta(w_i) \leq \lambda$, word w_i is supposed to have different meanings between MC and TW, namely a homograph word.

(iii) Given a word w_i, which is a homograph word or a MC exclusive word, we determine w_i's synonym $M_t(w_i)$ in TW by maximizing the semantic similarity as follows:

$$M_t(w_i) = argmax_\omega \, Similarity(R_s(w_i), R_t(\omega)) \tag{3}$$

If $w_i \neq M_t(w_i)$, we output w_i and $M_t(w_i)$ as a pair of synonyms from MC to TW.

(iv) Given a word w_i, which is a homograph word or a TW exclusive word, we determine w_i's synonym $M_s(w_i)$ in MC by maximizing the semantic similarity as follows:

$$M_s(w_i) = argmax_\omega \, Similarity(R_t(w_i), R_s(\omega)) \tag{4}$$

If $w_i \neq M_s(w_i)$, we output w_i and $M_s(w_i)$ as a pair of synonyms from TW to MC.

3.3.1 Lexical Semantic Representation

We represent meanings of words using vectors made of distributional statistics of words' co-occurrence. We set the size of context window as a constant N. Given a word w_i, we calculate the frequency of all words occurring in w_i's context window and obtain a probability distribution as the vector representation of w_i.

In this method, the bases of word vectors are words in vocabulary W. In word w_i's vector, the value on j-th dimension represents the probability that word w_j occurs in word w_i's context window. We assume that the number of homographs is few and all words in bases of vectors have consistent meanings between MC and TW[2]. Therefore, word vectors learned from MC corpus and TW corpus have the same meaning in every dimension and thus are comparable.

To capture the sequence information of words, we actually use the concatenation of two vectors to represent the meaning of one word: one represents the distribution in the preceding context window and the other one represents the distribution in the succeeding context window. Therefore, the whole word vector of w_i is given by:

$$R(w_i) = [R_l(w_i), R_r(w_i)] \tag{5}$$

---

[2] For example, when word 土豆 [tu dou] served as the basis of word vectors, we ignore the truth that it means *potatoes* in MC but *peanuts* in TW.

Here, $R_l(w_i)$ represents the distribution of word occurrence in the left window of w_i and $R_r(w_i)$ represents that in the right window of w_i. The length of $R_l(w_i)$ and $R_r(w_i)$ are all equal to M, the size of W.

3.3.2   Similarity of Lexical Semantic

Considering that word vectors are probability distributions, we use histogram intersection distance (HID) to measure the semantic similarity between words.

With the inspiration of tf-idf, we set different weights to different dimensions of word vector when computing HID. The weight of the j-th dimension is set to be the reciprocal of frequency that word w_j occurs in the whole corpora. Thus, when computing similarity, dimensions of infrequent words play a more important part than those of frequent words. The enhanced HID can be described by the following formula:

$$H(R_1, R_2) = \frac{\sum_k \frac{\min(R_1[k], R_2[k])}{C(w_k)}}{\sum_k \frac{\max(R_1[k], R_2[k])}{C(w_k)}} \tag{6}$$

Here, $H(R_1, R_2)$ is the similarity of word vectors R_1 and R_2. $R[k]$ is the value on the k-th dimension of word vector R. $C(w_k)$ is the frequency that word w_k occurs in the whole corpora.

Since representation of a word consists of two probability distribution, when computing the similarity of two words R_s and R_t, as described in (7), we firstly compute the similarity between R_{sl} and R_{tl} and similarity between R_{sr} and R_{tr} separately, and then set the average of two similarities as the similarity between R_s and R_t.

$$Similarity(R_s, R_t) = \frac{H(R_{sl}, R_{tl}) + H(R_{sr}, R_{tr})}{2} \tag{7}$$

3.4   Post-processing

After synonyms detection, we verify the result manually[3] to improve the accuracy and convert TW words into TC.

4   Experiment

4.1   Experiment Setup

To evaluate our approach, we use a MC corpus from Xinhuanet with 189 million words[4] and a TW corpus from MSN with 183 million words[5] to detect synonyms

---

[3] According to the result of manual verification, we can also update the value of thresholds in our detection algorithm to achieve better performance.

[4] The Xinhuanet corpus is available in Superfection Simplified Chinese Corpus (http://cloudtranslation.cc/corpus_sc.html).

[5] The Taiwan MSN corpus is available in Superfection Traditional Chinese Corpus (http://cloudtranslation.cc/corpus_tc.html).

from MC to TW. Contents of both two corpora are news published on Internet from 2011 to 2014. To narrow the searching space, we only focused on words with 2 or 3 Chinese characters. We also filtered out MC words with frequency lower than 2000 and TW words with frequency lower than 10. We set our program to output 5 best synonym candidates for each MC word.

4.2 Experiment Result

Our program output 421 synonyms pairs. We verified all the results manually and the precision is shown in Table 1. 148 pairs are correct synonyms and 76 results list the correct synonyms in the 2nd to 5th candidates. Some correct synonyms are shown in Table 2.

Table 1. Precision of the Experiment Result

	p@1*	**p@3***	**p@5***
Precision	35.15%	49.64%	53.21%

* p@N means precision considering N-best results.

Table 2. Synonyms Detected in the Experiment (Partial)*

Word in mainland China		**Word in Taiwan**		**Meaning**
美联储	[mei lian chu]	聯準會	[lian zhun hui]	U.S. Federal Reserve
短信	[duan xin]	簡訊	[jian xun]	SMS; short messages
硬件	[ying jian]	硬體	[ying ti]	Hardware
网点	[wang dian]	**據點**	[ju dian]	Branches; outlets
网络	[wang luo]	網路	[wang lu]	Network
群体	[qun ti]	**族群**	[zu quan]	Social groups
概率	[gai lv]	機率	[ji lv]	Probability
民警	[min jing]	**員警**	[yuan jing]	Policemen
入市	[ru shi]	**進場**	[jin chang]	Entering the stock market
芯片	[xin pian]	晶片	[jing pian]	Silicon chips
出租车	[chu zu che]	計程車	[ji cheng che]	Taxies
欺诈	[qi zha]	**詐欺**	[zha qi]	Fraud

* Pairs in bold are those not annotated as synonyms in [3].

4.3 Analysis

From Table 1 we see that our method reports a satisfactory precision. Moreover, Table 2 shows that a number of synonyms, that are hard to be found in handcrafted compilation, can be found in our method.

However, according to the experiment result, our method still has some limitations.

(i) Ambiguous words cannot be handled in our method. For example, our program output TW word 類股 [lei gu] (*sectors of stocks*) as the synonym of MC word 板块 [ban kuai] (*plates or sectors*). This correspondence is correct in text about stock market but incorrect in geology context.

(ii) Synonym phrases cannot be detected by our method. For example, TW word 殘障人士 [can zhang ren shi] (*disabled people*) is corresponding to MC word 残疾人 [can ji ren] (*disabled people*). But this correspondence cannot be found by our method because 殘障人士 [can zhang ren shi] is segmented as two words 殘障 [can zhang] and 人士 [ren shi].

5   Conclusion and Future Work

We have presented an automatic approach to detect synonyms between MC and TW, and showed that it can extract synonyms missing by traditional handcrafted compilation. Thus, our method can be also applied to computer aided dictionary compilation.

Our future work includes:

- An attempt to integrate continuous vector representations of words using deep neural network;
- An investigation into an appropriate method of synonym phrases detection;
- An attempt to apply our method to machine translation and try to extract translation rules from comparable corpora.

Acknowledgments. The work described in this paper is supported by the Special Fund Project of Ministry of Education of China (Conversion System from Simplified to Traditional Chinese Characters), National High-Tech R&D Program of China (No. 2012BAH14F03), the National Natural Science Foundation of China (Nos. 61005052 and 61303082) and the Research Fund for the Doctoral Program of Higher Education of China (No. 20130121110040).

References

1. Su, J.: Research on Homographs across the Straits. Studies of the Chinese Language **1995**(2), 107–117 (1995). (苏金智: 海峡两岸同形异义词研究. 中国语文. 1995(2), 107–117 (1995)). (in Chinese)
2. Li, X., Qiu, Z.: Determination and Treatment of Diverse Words in the Cross-Straits Dictionary. Applied Linguistics **2012**(4), 74–81 (2012). (in Chinese)
3. The Common Words Dictionary of the Cross-Straits. http://www.zhonghuayuwen.org/PageInfo.aspx?Id=375. (in Chinese)
4. Richardson, R., Smeaton, A., Murphy, J.: Using WordNet as a knowledge base for measuring semantic similarity between words. In: Proceedings of AICS Conference (1994)
5. Liu, Q., Li, S.: Word Similarity Computing Based on How-net. Computational Linguistics and Chinese Language Processing **7**(2), 59–76 (2002). (in Chinese)
6. Chen, Y., Shi, X., Zhou, C.: A simplified-traditional chinese character conversion model based on log-linear models. In: Proceedings of International Conference on Asian Language Processing (2011)
7. Wang, S., Cao, C., Pei, Y., Xia, F.: A Collocation-based Method for Semantic Similarity Measure for Chinese Words. Journal of Chinese Information Processing. **27**(1), 7–14 (2013). (in Chinese)

8. Shi, J., Wu, Y., Qiu, L., Lv, X.: Chinese Lexical Semantic Similarity Computing Based on Large-scale Corpus. Journal of Chinese Information Processing **27**(1), 1–6+80 (2013). (in Chinese)
9. Mikolov, T., Chen, K., Corrado, G., Dean, J.: Efficient estimation of word representations in vector space. In: Proceedings of Workshop at ICLR (2013)
10. Swain, M.J., Ballard, D.H.: Color Indexing. IJCV **7**(1), 11–32 (1991)
11. Salton, G., Buckley, C.: Term-weighting Approaches in Automatic Text Retrieval. Information Processing & Management **24**(5), 513–523 (1988)

Analysis on Semantic Prosody
of 'mianzi' and 'lian': A Corpus-Based Study

Yeechin Gan[(✉)]

Department of Chinese Language and Literature, Tsinghua University, Beijing 100084, China
echin_001@hotmail.com

Abstract. This paper explores the collocational behaviour and semantic prosody of the words 'miànzi' and 'liǎn' occurring in expressions pertaining to
'human relationships' or 'reputation' in modern Chinese. A statistical analysis
of a 1.2 million words of authentic texts from the CCL corpus reveals that these
two words tend to have opposite semantic prosody especially when used in the
samesentence. Through a further investigation on the semantic prototype of
'miàn' and 'liǎn' via the diachronic corpus, 'liǎn' is mainly used to refer to the
face of women or animals from the Wei-Jin Southern and Northern dynasties
until the Ming-Qing dynasties. It also often used as curse words in novels of the
Ming and Qing periods and clearly reflects the inequity between genders in the
old days. This negative connotation thus gives rise to a negative semantic prosody in 'liǎn'. This suggests that the emergence of a different semantic prosody
for 'miànzi' and 'liǎn' in modern Chinese is rather an evolution and a result of
its former use throughout history.

Keywords: Corpus-based · Semantic prosody · Mianzi · Lian · Face · Human
relations

1   Introduction

Smith (1894), an American missionary who lived in China for 54 years, emphasized
the importance of the face as a key factor in understanding Chinese behavior and
psychology. He stated that "……the word 'face' does not in China signify simply the
front part of the head, but is literally a compound of noun of multitude with more
meanings than we shall be able to describe, or perhaps to comprehend." Similarly,
Chinese linguist Lin Yutang (1939) also claimed: "[face] it is prized above all earthly
possessions. It is more powerful than face and favour, and more respectful than the
constitution." (p.200) Indeed, the notion of "face" is highly important and can be
defined in different perspectives in Chinese culture. It is rather complicated to understand especially for those visiting China or having contacts with Chinese for the first
time. The concept of "face" is related to the positive social value a person claims for
himself or herself during a line or argument to offset the feelings of embarrassment,
sometimes people also seek to save face to preserve harmony or to win honor.

According to Chinese lexicography, 面 [miàn] and 脸 [liǎn] are considered as a
pair of words pertaining to the semantic field of 'the front part of the head'. The former appeared first and has been used since the Pre-Qin dynasty. Even when the latter

© Springer International Publishing Switzerland 2015
Q. Lu and H.H. Gao (Eds.): CLSW 2015, LNAI 9332, pp. 101–111, 2015.
DOI: 10.1007/978-3-319-27194-1_11

appeared, 'miàn' was still predominant until the Song and Yuan dynasties in the relevant semantic field. After a fluctuation in use of these two words in the Chinese lexicon throughout history, 'liǎn' overtook 'miàn' and became the predominant word in this particular semantic field. (Wang 1980; Xie and Zhang 1993; Wang 2005; Yin 2009) Previous researches are mainly focus on the original semantic field. By being naturally a very distinctive part of the body, the meaning of both terms evolved to relate metaphorically to one's 'interpersonal interactions and relationships'. Expressions such as '要面子' [yàomiànzi](*to win honour*), '丢脸' [diūliǎn] (*lose face*)or '不 要脸' [búyàoliǎn] (*shameless*) are highly associated with one's self respect and dignity as well as the idea of shyness or shame. There is a need to further study on these two term in regards to their extended meaning.

Hence, this paper aims to examine the collocation behavior and semantic prosody of these two words 'miànzi' and 'liǎn', which are used to describe the moral face and social face in modern Chinese. Furthermore, the relevant semantic prosody of each word will be discussed from the perspective of ancient Chinese.

2   A Review on Collocations and Semantic Prosody

Collocational behavior refers to the systematic associative pattern with particular words of a linguistic feature. The term collocation was first proposed by Firth (1957): "I propose to bring forward as a technical term, meaning by collocation, and apply the test of collocability" (Firth 1957:194). He then defined the collocation of a given word as "statements of the habitual or customary places of that word." （Firth 1968:181） (cf. Xiao and McEnery 2006).

Semantic prosody is the affective meanings of a given mode with its typical collocates (Stubbs 2001). It refers in fact to the meaning of their interaction. Many different terms have been used in the literature on semantic prosody: positive and negative, favorable and unfavorable, desirable and undesirable, but the basic of evaluation is based on human's desire to evaluate entities in the world they inhibit as essentially as good or bad. In this study, we choose the dichotomy "positive" and "negative" for semantic prosody that has been agreed and used in most of the corpus linguistic researches. Louw stated (1993): "Semantic prosodies have been largely inaccessible to human intuition about language and they cannot be retrieved reliably through introspection." Without an extensive analysis of a large amount of occurrences, it is difficult to find typical patterns and different linguistic structures. Therefore, a corpus-based method is essential in providing an insight that will allow us to look into the nature of the prosody itself. "Semantic prosody is a constraining mechanism, like so many mechanisms in grammar. You cannot simply put any old bunch of words together." (Morley & Partington 2009). Furthermore, the use of authentic texts forming a corpus allows the examination of contextual preferences in the natural use of both words. The goal of a corpus-based investigation is not simply to report quantitative findings, but also to explore the importance of these findings for learning about the patterns of language use (Biber 2000:5).

This paper is an exploratory corpus-based study and aims to address the following questions:

1. How different are the collocation behavior and semantic prosody of 'miànzi' and 'liǎn' in modern Chinese texts?
2. How does a diachronic Chinese corpus research further explains the findings in modern Chinese?

3   Corpora and Analysis Method

3.1   Corpus of Chinese linguistics Research Center Established by Peking University (abbreviated as CCL)

CCL contains three corpora: a modern Chinese corpus, an ancient Chinese corpus and an English–Chinese parallel corpus. The entire CCL database consists approximately of 477 million words. In this study, only the first corpus was chosen and the search was limited to the modern Chinese literature. A total of 1247 texts with 'miànzi' as the node word and 37,547 texts with 'liǎn' as the node word were extracted. In sum, approximately 1.2 million words of texts were collected.

3.2   Corpus of Ancient Chinese Classic Books Established by Erudition Digital Technology Research Center

This diachronic corpus was developed by the Ai Ru Sheng Digital Technology Company. It consists of a total of 1.7 billion words. This database contains Chinese books covering the period of the Pre-Qin dynasty until the 20th century. It is divided into four major sub-corpora with 20 categories and 100 sub-categories based on genres and period of time. The system allows us to search for specific target words and also pro-vides ancient books browsing, collation, annotation, editing, downloading and printing.

3.3   Analysis Tools

Two kind of tool were used in this study, namely ICTCLAS[1] for word segmentation and annotation, and AntConc[2] for statistical analysis.

3.4   Quantitative Methods of Summarizing Concordance Data

The quantitative method used in this study is a statistical calculation of the collocations, i.e. node word and its collocation were extracted from the corpus, and statistical tools were used to measure the significant degree between them (Wei 2002). The significant degree can be identified by restricting the length of the window span between the node word and its co-occurrence (Yang 2002:111). A discontinuous

[1]   Zhang. H.P. (2014).ICTCLAS. Beijing, China: Beijing Institute of Technology. Available from http://ictclas.nlpir.org/
[2]   Anthony, L. (2014). AntConc (Version 3.4.3) [Computer Software]. Tokyo, Japan: Waseda University. Available from http://www.antlab.sci.waseda.ac.jp/

collocation analysis was also used to extract collocates that are not located right next to the node word but rather at certain distance. A number of corpus-based researches have shown that more than 95 percent of collocation information can be retrieved when the window span is set on -5/+5 words.

Mutual information (MI) is used as the statistical test to measure the collocational strength in this study. Mutual Information formula is as (1).

$$MI(w_1, w_2) = \frac{P(w_1, w_2)}{P(w_1) \, P(w_2)} \tag{1}$$

Fig. 1. w_1 is the node word and w_2 is the collocates word

Calculations for the MI compare the probability of observing the two words together with the probability of observing each word independently based on the frequencies of the words. A score around 0 shows that the words tend to co-occur at a rate greater than chance. The higher the score, the stronger the association between words (Biber 2000: 266). In this study, to be considered as a collocate of the node words 'miànzi' or 'liǎn', words extracted has to fall within a window span of -5/+5 with a minimum co-occurrence frequency of 10 and a minimum MI score of 4.0.

4 Collocation Patterns

4.1 Analysis on 'miànzi' and Its Collocates

We studied 'miànzi' and 'liǎn' in a 1.2 million words database extracted from CCL in order to carry out a broad comparison of 'miànzi' and 'liǎn', as well as to determine their semantic prosody features. First, the top ten significant collocates with the node word 'miànzi' within the window span of -5/+5 and a minimum co-occurrence frequency of 20 times and above include (rank by the MI score) as per below:

1. 找回面子 [zhǎohuímiànzi]   (to look for face) '*try to keep up appearances*'
2. 驳面子 [bómiànzi]   (to contradict face) '*not spare sb's responsibili ties; not showing due respect for sb's feelings*'
3. 碍面子[àimiànzi]   (to hinder face) '*spare sb's feeling; be afraid to hurt sb's feeling*'
4. 留面子[liúmiànzi]   (to save face) 'save sb's face (*so as not to embar rass him)*'
5. 挣面子[zhèngmiànzi]   (to earn face) '*try to win credit or honor*'
6. 赏面子[shǎngmiànzi]   (to grant face) '*have regards to sb's face*'
7. 顾面子 [gùmiànzi]   (to take into consideration face) '*save sb's face; spare ab's feelings*'
8. 争面子[zhēngmiànzi]   (to vie for face) '*try to win credit or honor*'
9. 撑面子[chēngmiànzi]   (to brace face) '*keep up appearances (as not to lose dignity)*'
10. 给面子[gěimiànzi]   (to give face) '*do sb's favor; save sb's face (so as not to embarrass)*'

Examples:

gēn wǒ zǒu   yí dìng bǎ diūdiào de miàn zi zhǎo huí
1. 跟 我 走， 一 定 把 丢 掉 的 <u>面 子 找 回</u>……

With me walk, must get the thrown face find back.
Follow me and you shall regain your face (honour)…

tā men dōu xiǎo xīn yì yì de zhù yì gěi duì fāng liú miàn zi
2. 他 们 都 小 心 翼 翼 地 注 意 给 对 方 <u>留 面 子</u>。

They all extremely careful paying attention to the other person save face.
They all carefully made sure to give face (proper consideration) to each other.

bēi fù zhe mò dà yuān qū hái qiáng chēng zhe miàn zi
3. 背 负 着 莫 大 冤 屈 还 强 撑 着 <u>面 子</u>。

Bearing with enormous injustice still keep up with the face
To defend/ preserve one's dignitiy even when facing injustice.

qiú qiúnín qǐ lái ba   gěi xiōng dì yī gè miàn zi hǎo bù hǎo
4. 求 求 您 起 来 吧， <u>给 兄 弟 一 个 面 子</u> 好 不 好 ？

Begging you stand up ba, give brother a face okay?
Please get up, do your brother the favour will you?

From examples [1] to [4], we can see that the contexts emphasize on the speakers' desire to have or keep their 'face' as in their honour or prestige. 'miànzi' shows a positive semantic prosody because it represents positive values such as honor, favour, and respect from others. It is the favourable social face that everyone desires for. As a result, it is strongly associated with collocates such as 'to keep', 'to save', 'to earn' etc, verbs that typically have a positive semantic prosody.

However, the second most significant collocate 驳[bó] seems to be an exception amongst the others. The phrase 驳面子[bómiànzi] can be directly interpreted as to 'contradict-face', which means to not spare somebody's sensibilities or to not show due respect for somebody's feelings. Thus it seems that this collocation has a rather negative semantic prosody, contrary to the rest. However a closer examination of the examples of 'bó' co-concordance with the node 'miànzi' shows otherwise.

yòng zhōng guó huà shuō   tā yào qǐng kè   bié bó tā de miàn zi
5. 用 中 国 话 说 :"他 要 请 客， <u>别 驳</u>他 的 <u>面 子</u>。"

Use Chinese words say: 'He wants treat guest, do not contradict his face.
Like they say in Chinese: 'If he insist on paying, do not deny him the honour.'

liáng yǒu zhì dà jīng   dàn bù néng bó xiǎo liú miàn zi
6. 梁 有 志 大 惊， 但 <u>不 能 驳</u> 小 刘 <u>面 子</u>……

Liang Youzhi big shock, but cannot contradict Xiaoliu's face….
Liang Youzhi was extremely shocked, yet had to spare Xiaoliusomeconsiderations…'

dà ren qí shí bú dà yuàn yì bó xiǎo hái de miàn zi
7. 大 人 其实 <u>不大</u> 愿 意 <u>驳</u> 小 孩 的 <u>面 子</u>。

Adults actually not really willing to contradict children's face.
Adults actually refuse to hurt children's feelings.

As shown in examples [5] to [7], the phrase 驳面子 [bómiànzi] is normally used in a negative sentence, i.e. with negation words such as 别 [bié] (*don't*), 不[bù] (*not*), 不能[bùnéng] (*cannot*) . Hence, the overall context of 'bómiànzi' still expresses the keenness on saving or keeping the face, in other words to give consideration to the sensibility or feelings of others. In this case, all the collocations exhibit rather a positive semantic prosody.

4.2   Analysis of 'liǎn' and Its Collocates

In comparison with 'miànzi', 'liǎn' displays a tendency towards negative semantic prosody. As shown by the result of the statistical calculation, with a span of -5/+5, minimum co-occurrence frequency of 20times, the ten most significant collocates of 'liǎn' typically include (rank by the MI score) as per below:

1. 拉长[lāchángliǎn]   (to pull long face) '*pull a long face; not to spare sb's sensibilities*'
2. 板脸 [bǎnliǎn]   (harden face) '*put on a stern expression*'
3. 不要脸[búyàoliǎn]   (not want face) '*shameless*'
4. 涎脸[xiánliǎn]   (thicken face) '*cheeky; have no sense of shame*'
5. 撕破脸[sīpòliǎn]   (to tear rip face) '*put aside all the considerations of face; come to an open break in friendship with sb*'
6. 翻脸[fānliǎn]   (to turn over face) '*turn hostile*'
7. 赏脸[shǎngliǎn]   (to grant face) '*(when requesting sb to accept one's invitation) honor me with your presence*'
8. 丢脸[diūliǎn]   (to throw face) '*lose face; be disgraced*'
9. 扯脸[chěliǎn]   (to tear face) '*fall out; turn against (an acquaintance)*'
10. 长脸[zhǎngliǎn]   (to grow face) '*to win credit or honor*'

For example:

wǒzhǔn bèi bú yào liǎn yě bú yào pí le
11. 我 准 备 <u>不 要 脸</u> 也 不 要 皮 了。

I   ready   do not want face also do not want skin le.
I am ready to be completely shameless.

liǎn pí sī pò le   zài tuán jié jiù bù xíng le a
12. <u>脸 皮 撕 破</u>了， 再 团 结 就 不 行 了啊！

Face skin tear rip le, then united would not do le a!
When your pride is all ripped apart, there is no point in uniting again!

The negative semantic prosody of 'liǎn' has been widely observed with eight out of ten collocates being semantically negative in the context of 'interpersonal relations'. Overall 'liǎn' is more likely to associate with unfavourable meaning as reflected by its significant collocates.

However, it is interesting to note that the connotation of 'liǎn' is not completely negative. It co-occurs with 赏 [shǎng] (*grant*) and 长 [zhǎng] (*grow*) which are actually associates with semantically positive, thus resulting in a collocation of positive semantic prosody.

zuò rén děijiǎng diǎn gǔ qì   děi gěi zán zhuāng lǐ rén zhǎng liǎn
13. 做 人 得 讲 点 骨气， 得 给 咱 庄 里 人 <u>长 脸</u>。

Be people have to talk a little bit moral integrity, have to our village people grow-face.
One has to show moral integrity and win face for the people of our village

huí tóu nín shǎng liǎn   gěi wǒgè jī huì qǐng nín chīdùn biàn fàn
14. 回 头 您 <u>赏 脸</u>, 给 我 个 机会 请 您 吃 顿 便 饭。

Back head you grant-face, give me a chance treat you to eat a meal.
Next time, do me the honour of inviting you for dinner.

4.3   'miàn zi' vs. 'liǎn'

In the next group of examples, we observed the co-occurrence of both 'miànzi' and 'liǎn' in the same sentence. These two synonyms displayed obvious differences on the collocational behaviour and semantic prosody.

xiǎo hái kě yǐ méi liǎn dà ren shì yí dìng yàoyǒu miàn zi
15. 小 孩 可以 <u>没 脸</u> 大 人 是 一 定 要 <u>有 面 子</u>!

Kids can no face adults must want have face!
It's ok to have no pride when you're a kid but not when you're an adult!

yì jiālǎo xiǎo dōu méi miàn zi   nǐ hái yǒu liǎn chàng gē
16. 一 家 老 小 都 <u>没 面 子</u>, 你 还 <u>有 脸</u> 唱 歌！

One family old young all with no face, you still have-face to sing!
Everyone in the family is feeling embarrassed, how can you keep singing so proudfully!

zì jǐ wú fàn kě chī ér qù chī rén jiā de fàn   shǎng miàn zi jiù yī biàn ér wéi diū liǎn
17. 自 己 无 饭 可 吃 而 去 吃 人 家 的 饭, <u>赏 面 子</u>就 一 变 而 为 <u>丢 脸</u>。

Oneself no rice to eat and eat other's rice, grant face turned to throw-face.
Being invited for a meal when one has nothing to eat is turning honour into embarrassment.

This observation echoes with the findings in section 4.1 and 4.2 where 'miànzi' and its significant collocates tend to have positive semantic prosody, while 'liǎn' and its significant collocates exhibit the opposite. This shows that even though both refer to the concept of 'face-value' in Chinese language, there is a clear distinction between the semantic tendencies. 'miànzi' is more likely to link with the positive notions of prestige, honour and dignity, whereas 'liǎn' is more related to negative notions such as shame, embarrassment and even hurting other's feeling.

5   Discussion

5.1   An Exploration on the Differences of Semantic Prosody 'miàn' and 'liǎn' from Ancient Chinese Perspective

As illustrated by the above-mentioned examples, 'miànzi' and 'liǎn' display an obvious difference on theirs semantic prosody based on their significant collocates in Modern Chinese. In this section, corpus of ancient Chinese (as mentioned in 3.2) was used to further investigate the protocol concept of 'miàn' and 'liǎn'. However, we do not intend to present a thorough analysis about their chronological development, but to explore on the original usage of these words in ancient Chinese which then influences on the semantic differences in Modern Chinese.From a character analysis perspective, the primitive form (oracle bone) of the character 'miàn' is as follow   . It is defined as "the front part of face" in the 说文解字[shuōwénjiězì] (*a dictionary of Han dynasty*). The use of 'miàn' in the semantic field of "a person physical's facet" is common until the Song dynasty.

    jing yú shuǐ   jiàn miàn zhī róng   mò zǐ fēi gōng
18. 镜 于 水 ， 见 面 之 容 。 （《墨子·非 攻 》）

    Mirror on water, see face expression.
    To see one's facial expression in the reflection of the water.

    fù xiōng lián ér wàngwǒ wǒ hé miàn mù jiàn zhī   shǐ jì xiàng yǔ běn jì
19. 父 兄 怜 而 王 我， 我 何 面 目 见 之 ？ （《史记· 项 羽 本 纪》）

    Father brother pity and king I, I how face eyes see them?
    My compatriots want me to be king, but is my face worthy?

The term 'liǎn' originated around the Wei-Jin Southern and Northern dynasty period in Northern China. According to the ancient Chinese dictionary named 集韵 [jíyùn], 'liǎn' was used to refer only to the cheeks, not the entire face. A search in the Corpus of the ancient Chinese books with 'liǎn' as the keyword revealed that 'liǎn' was mainly used in poems to describe the inner and outer beauty, expression and/or feelings of female characters from the Wei-Jin Southern and Northern dynasty to the Tang dynasty.

    cháng méi héng yù liǎn   hào wàn juǎn qīng shā   yù tái xīn yǒng
20. 长 眉 横 玉 脸 ， 皓 腕 卷 轻 纱 。 （《玉 台 新 咏 》）

    Long eyebrow straight jade face, fair wrist roll light gauze
    A face delicate like jade with long eyebrow, she gently curled up the vale as the light shone on her wrist.

yān zhī hán liǎn xiào   sū hé yì yī xiāng   bái jū yì shī quán jí
21. 胭 脂 含 <u>脸</u> 笑 , 苏合裹衣 香 。 (《白居易诗 全 集》)

Blushers contain face smiles, snow bush wine clothe smell.
A smiling face revealed by her blusher, a smell of snowdrop bush intertwined with her clothes.

qǐ zhī hóng liǎn   lèi dī rú zhū   dūn huáng qǔ zi cí guī yuàn
22. 岂知 <u>红 脸</u>, 泪滴如珠。 (《 敦 煌 曲子词·闺 怨 》)

How know red face, tear drops like pearls.
How to grasp the shyness of the face covered with pearl of tears.

In addition, 'liǎn' was also used to refer to the face of animals. Below is an example during the Song dynasty taken from the ancient Chinese corpus.

bái xián sì gē ér dà   bái sè hóng liǎn   tōng zhì běi qí
23. 白 鹇 似鸽而大, 白色 <u>红 脸</u>。 (《 通 志·北齐》)

White pheasant like dove and big, white color red face.
The white pheasant and dove are similar in size, with a white and red colored face.

Furthermore, Wang (2005) pointed out that 'miàn' was used solely to refer to the face of human beings in all four different versions of 老乞大[lǎo qi dà] whereas 'liǎn' was used twice to refer to animal's face, which are '白脸马' [báiliǎnmǎ](*white face horse*) in 老乞大原本[lǎo qi dàyuan běn] (1346)and '破脸马'[pòliǎnmǎ] (*face-scratched horse*)in老乞大谚解[lǎo qi dàyànjiě] (1670).

'liǎn' gradually replaced the physical meaning 'miàn' (*a person's face*) in usage, and then it was symbolically used to denote the relationship between individual and society. It became endowed with a symbolic significance during the Qing dynasty. (Hwang 2012)Hence, the semantic foundation of the term 'miàn' and 'liǎn' are clearly different. The term 'miàn' was mainly used to describe the face of superior such as the emperor, man's etc. However, 'liǎn' was referred as the part of cheek of female and later used as face of females or animals. This shows that the word was chosen and used due to the imbalance of the gender status in ancient Chinese society. Women were confined to the domestic sphere due to their biologically imposed roles in reproduction and child rearing which cause the declination in status. As a consequence, the term 'liǎn' is more likely to link with unfavourable affective meaning. Its semantic foundation then evolved over a long period of time towards a negative prosody. Therefore, it is often combined with words that carry the similar negative semantic prosody, such as 不要[búyào] (*not want*), 丢[diū] (*throw*), 无[wú] (*not have*) to create a negative atmosphere in the contexts. These combinations were used as curse words in many classical novels around the Ming and Qing dynasties. As illustrated by the below-mentioned examples, 'liǎn' co-occur with words which refer to a lower standard social face metaphorically.

rén jiā zhī bù zhī dào   zhè me diū liǎn   hóng lóu mèng   dì yī bǎi yī huí
24. 人 家 知 不 知 道, 这 么 <u>丢脸</u>...... (《 红 楼 梦 》第一百一回)

People know not knowing, so throw-face…
Does anyone know about it, it is so embarrassing…

25.
wú liǎn jiàn rén   suǒ yǐ zì jìn
<u>无 脸</u> 见 人 , 所 以 自 尽 。《 官 场 现 形 记 》第 三 十 回 ）
guān chǎng xiàn xíng jì   dì sān shí huí

No-face see people, so commit sucide.
It is too humiliating, therefore [he/she] has to commit suicide.

In contrast, 'miànzi' tends to co-occur with verbs that exhibit a positive semantic tendency such as 有[yǒu](*to have*), 留[liú] (*to save*), 顾全[gùquán](*to take care of*) in ancient Chinese literature. Due to its positive semantic prosody, 'miànzi' symbolises a kind of social reputation that is highly valued by the society. For example:

26.
yǒu le wáng ye de miàn zi   hái pà shàng tóu bù shōu
<u>有 了 王 爷 的 面 子</u>, 还 怕 上 头 不 收 ？ (《 官 场 现 形 记 》第
guān chǎng xiàn xíng jì   dì
sān shí wǔ huí
三 十 五 回 ）

Have le Wang Grandmaster face, still afraid the superior do not accept?
With the prestige of Wang Grandmaster, The superior would not refuse to accept [this].

27.
yǒu le yín zi   jiù yǒu miàn zi
有 了 银 子, 就 <u>有 面 子</u>。 (《 二 十 年 目 睹 怪 现 状 》第 二 十 回 ）
èr shí nián mù dǔ guài xiàn zhuàng   dì èr shí huí

Have le silvers, then have face.
Honour comes along with money.

28.
gěi nǐ men èr wèi liú miàn zi   nǐ men èr wèi shàng chē ba
给 你 们 二 位 <u>留 面 子</u>, 你 们 二 位 上 车 罢。 (《 济 公 全 传 》
jì gōng quán zhuàn
dì èr bǎi shí èr huí
第 二 百 十 二 回 ）

Give you two save-face, you two go up car ba.
As a gesture of respect, both of you are invited to get into the car.

Based on the analysis of the lexical development of 'miàn' and 'liǎn' from diachronic perspective, it shows that the initial semantic of these two words was completely different. Due to a close evolution of the language with the development of the society, the word 'liǎn' was attributed a rather negative semantic as it is mainly used in relation with women and animals since the Wei-Jin Southern-Northern dynasties. "Prosodies are undoubtedly the product of a long period of refinement through historical change and even though new prosodies may be in the process of being formed, they cannot be sued for the purpose of instantiating irony until their prosody predominates sufficiently strongly." (Louw 1993)   As a result, 'liǎn' tends to occur with negative collocates more frequent than 'miàn'. Although both words are considered synonyms in Modern Chinese, they nevertheless show a very different semantic prosody and tendency. When 'liǎn' is used in the context of interpersonal relations, it is more like to denote a negative metaphorical meaning which relates to shame, disgrace or embarrassment. In contrast, when 'miànzi' is used in the same context, it relates rather to prestige, honor or reputation.

6   Conclusion

A corpus-based study is a promising method to explore and determine collocations and semantic prosody of synonyms.This study revealed the collocational behavior and semantic prosodies of 'miànzi' and 'liǎn' in Modern Chinese through a statistical analysis on 1.2 million words of authentic texts extracted from the CCL corpus. The findings showed that 'miànzi' has a positive semantic prosody whereas 'liǎn' has a more negative one. Through a further investigation on diachronic corpus and previous studies tracing the chronological development of 'miàn' and 'liǎn', we discovered that 'liǎn' is mainly used to refer to the women's cheeks or animals' face from the Wei-Jin Southern and Northern dynasties until the Tang-Song dynasties while the term 'miàn' was mainly used to describe the face of superior such as the emperor, human's etc. This clearly reflects the inequity between genders in the old days. These initial semantic thus gives rise to different semantic prosody in'miànzi'and 'liǎn' which in turn explained their different collocation patterns and linguistic features in Modern Chinese.

References

1. Biber, D., Condrad, S., Reppen, R.: Corpus linguistics. Foreign Language Teaching and Research Publisher, Beijing (2000)
2. Hwang, K.K.: Face and morality in confucian society. In: Foundations of Chinese Psychology, pp. 265–295. Springer, New York (2012)
3. Lin, Y.T.: The Chinese. XueLin Publisher, Shanghai (1994). (in Chinese)
4. Louw, B.: Irony in the text or insincerity in the writer? The diagnostic potential of semantic prosodies. Text and technology: In honour of John Sinclair, 240–251 (1993)
5. Morley, J., Partington, A.: A few frequently asked questions about semantic— or evaluative—prosody. International Journal of Corpus Linguistics **14**(2), 139–158 (2009)
6. Smith, A.H.: Chinese Characteristic. F. H. Revell Company, New York (1894)
7. Stubbs, M.: Words and Phrases. Blackwell, Oxford (2001)
8. Xiao, R., McEnery, T.: Collocation, semantic prosody and near synonymy: A cross-linguistic perspective. Applied Linguistics **27**(1), 103–129 (2006)
9. Xie, Z.Y., Zhang, H.J.: The changes in the semantic field of face in Chinese Language and discussion about the turning in Chinese historical research methods. Ancient Chinese Research **4**, 85–93 (1993). (in Chinese)
10. Wang, L.: Articles on the historical Chinese (Re-printed 2007). Zhonghua Bookstore, Beijing (1980). (in Chinese)
11. Wang, W.H.: The changes of basic lexicons reflected in different versions of LaoQiDa. Chinese Linguistic **6**, 545–555 (2005). (in Chinese)
12. Wei, N.X.: Corpus-based and corpus-driven approaches to the study of collocation. Contemporary Linguistics **2**, 101–114 (2002). (in Chinese)
13. Yang, H.Z.: Introduction to corpus linguistic. Shanghai Foreign Language Teaching Publisher, Shanghai (2002). (in Chinese)

Study of the Place Names from the Perspective of Category Theory

Xinye Yang[✉]

School of Chinese Language and Literature, Huanggang Normal University, Huanggang, China
xinxinyeye@sina.com

Abstract. Place names constitute a cognitive category. These names are generally divided into complete names and incomplete names. From the perspective of toponym ontology, place names constitute a category hierarchy body that comprises a 'starting point' and a 'subject'. The category members of each level is connected through of 'entity' or 'relationship'. Place names gradually expanded from the center to the edge of three categories, namely, the subordinate category, superordinate category and basic level category, which are influenced by the restriction of human senses. This study proposes a place name analysis model according to the patterns of category.

Keywords: Place names · Category · Analysis

1   Introduction

Although many studies have previously investigated the place names in China and in other countries, they have mostly concentrated on record scanning, textual research, tracing, summarizing the rules, and discussing the standardization of these names. Recent studies have aimed to establish database of place names and GIS. From a linguistics perspective, this study is limited to the use of place names as auxiliary materials, and these names are seldom perceived as independent systems.

Labov and Taylor suggested a close relationship between language and category as well as posited, category as the starting point of human thought, action, and language[1][4]. Recent linguistic studies on category have mainly focused on grammar, including the interpretation of phonemes, vocabulary, and syntax, which comprise the evolution and expansion of the structure and meaning of a category. As psychological representations of namers, place name is a hierarchical category body which has a certain cognitive effect. What is the process of its categorization? How are various sub-categories connected with one another?. This paper aims to integrate category theory into the analysis of place names, to establish a category research framework for analyzing place names, and to discuss how the concept of place names is influenced by category pattern.

© Springer International Publishing Switzerland 2015
Q. Lu and H.H. Gao (Eds.): CLSW 2015, LNAI 9332, pp. 112–119, 2015.
DOI: 10.1007/978-3-319-27194-1_12

2 General Form of Place Names

Place names are typically arranged as 'proper name + general name'. However, some place names do not have a general name while others have two general names. We call the standard form of place names as 'complete place name', whereas, the non-standard form of place names is called 'incomplete place name'.

2.1 Complete Place Name

(1) 'Proper name+the only general name' type. This is the most common form of the place names. Such as哈喇巴勒图郭勒(*Karabalta-Gol*), 拔笋渠(*Basun-Qu*), 野云沟(*Yeyun-Gou*), 沙山子(*Sha-Shanzi*), etc.

(2) 'Taking general name as proper name' type. This type is usually present in regions of multi-language area.Such as达坂城(*Dawan-Cheng*), 达坂河(*Dawan-He*), 达坂水(*Dawan-Shui*), 雅尔湖(*Yar-Hu*), 布拉克渠(*Bulak-Qu*), etc.

2.2 Incomplete Place Name

This type of names may lack of general name, or may lack of proper name which are naming by general name directly.

(1) 'No general name' type. This type exists in the minority language area and Chinese place names. Such as库尔墨图(*Kurmotu*), 苏鲁图(*Suluktu*), 桦树林(*Huashulin*), 车牌子(*Chepaizi*), 石人了(*Shirenzi*), 一颗树(*Yikeshu*), etc.

(2) 'Taking general name as place name'. Although this type of information appears less, the objective facts can not be ignored. Such as雅尔(*Yar*), 塔克(*Tak*).

3 The Structure and Features of the Category Body of Place Name

Categorization is a cognitive process that based on the interaction and experience between the namer and objective world. It's the first step from psychological representation to the generation of place name. In the concrete process of cognition, the namer classifies the class genus and attribute features of reality representation which include human activity. Langacker considered that the basic cognitive structure of human beings includes time domain and spatial domain[2]. Essentially, the categorization of place name is an embodiment of the objective world in the namer's mind, is the result of the physical space internalization and then it constitutes a psychological space by means of language. According to the structural features of space, we divide the category body of place name into two subcategories. See below.

(1) Starting point category. It's a collection of semantic units of cognitive relevance in the concept of place name. This category mainly bears the concept of the semantic of the place name.

(2) Subject category. It's a collection of semantic units of gestalt cognition in the concept of place name. The members of this category mainly restrict the type of the concept of place name.

There are three main characteristics of the category body of place names. See below.

(1) Spatial ductility. Liu Yuhong believes that the reality representation is not a pure objective existence. It's based on the human's existence. The existence of human gives the objective world some basic attributes and features[3]. The namer experiences the objective reality near or distant taking his position as a reference point. And then forms a three-dimensional space relationship with its axis in which the cognitive subject interacts with the objective reality. It can be formed a psychological representation when the objective things do not appear. Although the namer's focus are diverse, people always focus on the point, line and surface. When a namer is placed in a named object, the range of his sight is limited and it is easy to focus on a certain point in geographic entities, such as some kind of plant or animal or a specific object. When the namer is outside the named object and the distance is close, it is easy to observe the characteristic of the object, and the linear feature can be observed when the distance is far away. Such as 哈喇阿萨尔(*Karasag*), 哈喇布喇郭勒(*Karabra-gol*).

(2) Complexity of category body. The category body of place name is a structure of three-dimensional structure which can be divided into the starting point category and the subject category from the horizontal point of view. Some of the starting point category of place name can further divide the feature category. This is because the cognitive categorization of namer will continue after they districted the starting point category and subject category. The namer's focus of cognition is transferred to the feature category to distinguish it from other members of the same category. Such as 库克讷克达巴 (*Kukenake-dab*). First, the namer selects 讷克(*nake*) as starting point category, then continues to choose 库克(*kuk*) as feature category to distinguish from other members of the same category. From the vertical perspective that is the level of the category, the complete place name contains the starting point category and the subject category, which is the basic-level category of the category body of place name. However, the incomplete place name or only contains the starting point category which is the superordinate category of category body of place name or only contains the subject category to form the subordinate category.

(3) Cognitive prominence. The concept of place name is a information flow generated by a series of units in a linear way. However, the cognitive economic principle thinks that the partial content of information flow only can become the focus of information. In this information flow, the subject category is always in the background that is the basement in the cognitive domain and the starting point category is always on the side position which is the most valuable part of place name. See Fig. 1.

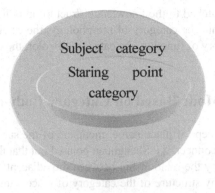

Fig. 1. Cognitive diagram of sub-category

4   Categorization Process Based on Category Body of Place Name

The categorization of place name comes from two aspects, one is the namer's perception and experience of the named object, the other is the knowledge base in the brain of namers that is the relevant cognitive experience of objects. Namers' inner knowledge, image schema and the expectation of object become the basis of category. Such as what attributes should plants have? Which attributes should animals have? All of these can be perceived by human visual, tactile, sense of taste, hearing and other sensory channels. As mentioned above, the concept of place name is a result of interaction between the namer and the natural entity. All kinds of geographical elements through the visual, auditory, taste, tactile and other sensory access to people's brain. These can be combined with the existing mental experience to promote the ultimate formation of concept.

The categorization process based on category body of place name begins with the member of the subject category. The main way of conceptual categorization based on family resemblance is comparison and summarization. Namers identify some geographic entities with the same attributes by comparison and then find the difference between the attributes and other geographical entities. After that, namers generalize distinctive features of similarity and conclude the result of recognition. This process is the basis of dividing and constructing the subject category. The statistical data of this paper includes 37 categories such as mountain category, water category, village category, lake category, platform category, dam category and so on.

The namer's process of categorization is not over after determining the members of the subject category. He shifts the focus of cognition to the distinctive feature so as to distinguish from other members of the same category, then continues to match these attributes with experience knowledge in his mind and categorizes attributes that have a distinction that is to determine the starting point category. Such as plant category, animal category, material category, mineral category, geographical features category, terrain category, event category and so on. Due to the complexity of place name, there are some non-similar characteristics in some of the starting point after the formation of the starting point category. Namers also continue to categorize these distinctive features which will be further matched to the knowledge structure in brain. These distinctive features can be classified into the category of morphology, the category of habits, the category of shape, the category of function, the category of color, the category of material and so on.

5   Connection Mode Based on Category Body of Place Name

To form a complete concept of place name, members of the sub categories also need to choose a certain way to connect. Xu Shenghuan pointed out that the class hierarchy in the category is constructed by the relationship between the adjacent and similar[5]. This can only explain the hierarchy structure of the category of place name. This study proposes two ways after the observation of the connection mode of each level of the subcategory. See below.

5.1   Entity Connection

The semantic of the concept of place name is directly presented by the words of the members of the subcategory. See below.

(1) 安济哈雅 (Ajihay. The riverside abounds in this grass, people often go to pick, so use this name.)
(2) 塔克(Tak.This place locates in Nanshan, so use this name.)

In the above two examples, the overall semantics of the concept of place name is directly presented by the lexical semantic combination of the sub categories.

5.2   Relationship Connection

Place names' semantic concept come from metaphor mapping. As a concept of the source domain, the concept of the subcategory is projected into the target domain and forms a new concept. The most frequently used in the place name is to take the category of human body and animal form as a metaphor of the shape category and the form category. The category of human body and animal category are basic category. Because human beings are quite familiar with their body and they can use the human body category as other abstract concepts' metaphor. In the long years , animals formed a close relationship with human beings. In the process of getting along with animals, human beings have a comprehensive and thorough understanding to animal's habits and physical features. See below.

(1)   博罗哈玛尔鄂拉(Borohamar-aula. Blue ridge like the human nose, so use this name.)
(2)   汗哈尔察海鄂拉(Khanhalchahy-aula. The namer used the eagle to describe the mountain.)
(3)   巴尔巴什鄂拉(Batbax-aula. The shape of the mountain like a tiger's head, so use this name.)
(4)   月牙泉(Yueya-quan. The spring's shape like the shape of crescent moon, so use this name.)

The above examples are derived from body metaphor, emotion metaphor, animal metaphor and natural object metaphor.

6   The Essence of the Categorization of Place Name

The categorization of every level of the category body is essentially forms a cognitive frame which takes the subject category of place name as the center.

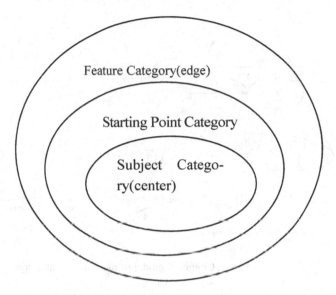

Fig. 2. Cognitive framework of the place name

As shown in Fig. 2, the subject category occupies the central position of the cognitive frame. All kinds of sub-category in the starting point category such as plants, animals, construction facilities and so on are selected and extracted by people's mental space. These categories are combined with the subject category through the entity connection or relationship connection. Some of place names also need to combine the sub-category in the feature category such as habits, colors, functions and so on to with the starting point category to distinguish the attributes. The starting point category distance center category recently. The feature category is only exist part of place names and mainly used to modify the starting point category. Thus, it is located in the edge of entire cognitive domain.

7   Conclusions

According to the category theory, the categorization of place name can be interpreted as a gradual process of expansion from center category to edge category of three categories, namely, the subordinate category, superordinate category and basic level category, which are influenced by the restriction of human senses. Each layer of the subcategory is connected by a combination of entity connection or relationship connection. So we propose a place name analysis model according to the patterns of category.

The cognitive model is shown in Fig.3.

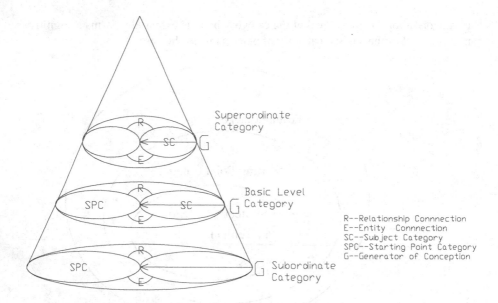

Fig. 3. Cognitive model of place name category

(1) The model is a conical structure, and the upper and the lower end of the structure are composed of the non-complete place names. The subordinate category is constituted by the starting point category. Members of this hierarchy are most dispersed and commonly native place names. With the gradual improvement of the standard of place names, members of this hierarchy are most easily covered general names become complete place names. The basic level category is composed of the complete place name, which is the combination of the starting point category and the subject category. Place names of this hierarchy are the most standard form, also are the most stable part of the category body. The subordinate category is composed of the subject category, and the number of this hierarchy is the least. However, each member of the subject catetory can constitute a category, so it can become the subordinate category. Place names of this level are also to continue to be added to general names into proper names and finally become the standard complete names.

(2) The G icon in the figure is a generator of concept. In the process of the categorization of the place name in each level, G starts from the center category that is the subject category to expand to other marginal category through entity connection and relationship connection.

References

1. Labov, W.: The boundaries of words and their meanings. In: Bailey, C., Shuy, R. (eds.) New Ways of Analysing Variation in English, pp. 340–373. Georgetown University Press, Washington (1973)
2. Langacker, R.: Foundations of Cognitive Grammar: Theoretical Prerequisites. Stanford University Press, Stanford (1987)
3. Yuhong, L.: Reality Representation, Mental representation, Linguistic Representation, Xiangtan University Jounal, 1 (2005)
4. Taylor, J.: Linguistic Categorization: Prototypes in Linguistic Theory. OUP, Oxford (1989)
5. Shenghuan, X.: Why Metaphor can Become Possible, Foreign Language Education Jounal, 3 (2003)

A Cognitive Semantic Study of Idioms from
The Book of Songs

Dong Zhang[⊠] and Jiehong Bai[⊠]

School of Foreign Languages, Hunan Normal University, Changsha, China
zhangdonne@163.com, baijh@hunnu.edu.cn

Abstract. This paper analyzes the cognitive mechanisms of meaning extension and the cognitive process of dynamic meaning construction of the idioms from *The Book of Songs* by adopting cognitive semantic theories. The findings are: conceptual metaphor and conceptual metonymy are the main conceptual motivations and cognitive mechanisms of the idioms from *The Book of Songs*; the dynamic meaning construction of the idioms is a process of blending between idiom mental space and discourse mental space, which eventually gives rise to the emergent structure.

Keywords: The Book of Songs · Idioms · Meaning construction

1   Introduction

Idioms are phrases with fixed structure, which can be independently used in terms of semantic meaning and grammatical function. The semantic meanings of idioms usually cannot be predicted from their constituent parts（Wang, 1988：174）. Linguistic structures used in *The Book of Songs* are vivid and concise, and most of them are composed of four characters. Wang（1983, 1990） and Sun (1989) investigated the semantic structures, grammatical structures and figurative functions of idioms. Zhang (2003) explored the implied regular mapping patterns and mental representation of idioms. Huang (1985) analyzed the grammatical structures of the idioms from *The Book of Songs* based on their componential meanings. Niu & Gao (2009) studied the reasons for the transformation of forms and meanings of idioms from *The Book of Songs*. He (2007, 2011) made a comprehensive study of formal structures and semantic structures of idioms from *The Book of Songs*. The previous studies mainly focus on the static analyses of the grammatical structures and semantic structures of idioms from *The Book of Songs,* ignoring their cognitive mechanisms and meaning construction of the idioms in the concrete context. On the basis of the previous studies, this paper analyzes the cognitive mechanisms underlying the meaning extension and the on-line meaning construction of the idioms from *The Book of Songs* in use.

© Springer International Publishing Switzerland 2015
Q. Lu and H.H. Gao (Eds.): CLSW 2015, LNAI 9332, pp. 120–129, 2015.
DOI: 10.1007/978-3-319-27194-1_13

2   The Cognitive Mechanisms of Meaning Extension of Idioms from *The Book of Songs*

Idioms usually contain two layers of meaning. One is called the literal meaning; the other is called the extended meaning. Literal meaning can be directly obtained from the literal meaning of constituent parts of the idioms, while extended meaning is generalized and abstracted on the basis of literal meaning. According to our observation, we have collected three hundred and two idioms from *The Book of Songs*. We argue that the extended meaning of the idioms from *The Book of Songs* is constructed through cognitive operations and mechanisms on the basis of their literal meaning, including conceptual metaphor, conceptual metonymy and the combination of conceptual metaphor and conceptual metonymy.

2.1   Conceptual Metaphor Mechanism

Conceptual metaphor theory is one of the most important theories in cognitive linguistics. It holds that metaphor is not a mere matter of words, but also an important way of categorization and conceptualization of human beings; the essence of conceptual metaphor is to understand and experience one thing or entity in terms of another; metaphor is not only a linguistic phenomenon but also a conceptual phenomenon; our thoughts, languages and action are constructed based on conceptual metaphors; metaphorical expressions are the representation of metaphorical thoughts; the essence of our thoughts is metaphorical, and the essence of metaphor is conceptual; metaphorical mapping operates between two different conceptual domains; the direction of mapping is from the source domain to the target domain, and the basis of metaphorical mapping is abstract image schema structures (Lakoff & Johnson, 1980:1-8).

Conceptual metaphor is an important cognitive mechanism, which plays a major role in the meaning extension of the idioms from *The Book of Songs*. We have observed that the number of idioms from *The Book of Songs* based on the metaphor mechanism is 139, accounting for 46% of the total idioms from *The Book of Songs*. We will take"嘤鸣求友"[*ying ming qiu you*](*People appeal to making friends with those who have common goals with them.*) as an example to explain how conceptual metaphor mechanism operates in the process of meaning extension of idioms from *The Book of Songs*. The literal meaning of "嘤鸣求友"is that the birds chirp loudly to attract their companions. People always encounter many circumstances alike. Based on metaphorical mechanism, the literal meaning is extended and thus the extended meaning of this idiom is formed, i.e., people appeal to making friends with those who have common goals with them. Therefore, we can conclude that metaphor mechanism provides the conceptual motivation and cognitive operation mechanism for the formation of the extended meaning of this idiom. In this process of metaphorical mapping, the literal meaning functions as the source domain, while the extended meaning is the target domain.

There exists the systematic resemblance between the source domain and the target domain, which provides the basis for the metaphorical mapping. The direction of the metaphorical mapping is from the literal meaning to the extended meaning, in other words, from the source domain to the target domain. The mapping between the counterpart elements in the source domain and the target domain is illustrated as follows:

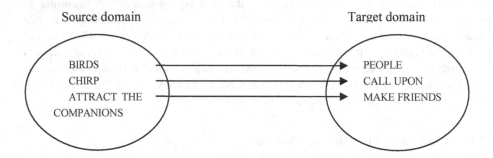

Fig. 1. The metaphorical mapping of "嘤鸣求友"

There are many other idioms from *The Book of Songs* whose extended meaning is constructed based on the metaphor mechanism, such as: "鸠占鹊巢"[*jiu zhan que chao*] (*to take possession of homes of other people*),"如圭如璋"[*ru gui ru zhang*] (*elegant temperament and good character of a person*), "深厉浅揭"[*shen li qian jie*](*to adjust measures according to the local conditions*), "龙骧麟振"[*long xiang lin zhen*](*General with both abilities and political integrity*), "高山景行"[*gao shan jing xing*](*people with noble virtue*), "琴瑟相调"[*qin se xiang tiao*](*Couples have a good and harmonious relationship with each other.*), "如花似玉"[*ru hua si yu*] (*beautiful women*).

2.2   Conceptual Metonymy Mechanism

Conceptual metonymy is also an important tool of conceptualization of human beings. The most prominent distinction between conceptual metaphor and conceptual metonymy is that conceptual metaphor maps across different conceptual domains, whereas the conceptual metonymy maps within the same conceptual domain. Langacker (1993) regards metonymy as a cognitive reference point phenomenon, in which a profiled conceptual entity as a cognitive reference point provides mental access for a relatively unprofiled conceptual entity. Cognitive semanticists hold that the nature of metonymy is conceptual; metonymy refers to the phenomenon in which one conceptual entity provides mental access to another conceptual entity within the same idealized cognitive model or conceptual domain matrix; the construal of the meaning of metonymic expressions requires cognitive processing based on the meaning of the vehicle; the basis for conceptual metaphor is similarities or resemblance between different concepts, whereas the basis for conceptual metonymy is conceptual contiguity.

Conceptual metonymy is also an important cognitive mechanism, which plays an important part in the meaning extension of idioms from *The Book of Songs*. According to our observation, the number of the idioms from *The Book of Songs* based on the conceptual metonymy mechanism is 161, accounting for 53% of the total idioms from *The Book of Songs*. This finding might provide further evidence for the findings of some scholars: conceptual metonymy is more fundamental and important than conceptual metaphor in our conceptual system (Taylor, 2003).

For example, The literal meaning of "中原板荡"[*zhong yuan ban dang*](*The whole country suffers unrest.*) is that the central plains of China suffers unrest. Here, the central plains mainly refer to the provinces located in the middle and lower reaches of the Yellow River, especially present Henan province. In the ancient time, the central plains are the main part of China. On the basis of PART FOR WHOLE metonymic pattern, here the central plains stand for China. Based on this metonymic pattern, the extended meaning is thus formed: the whole country suffers unrest. Another idiom is "自有肺肠"[*zi you fei chang*](*to do things for individual purposes*). The literal meaning of this idiom is that people have their own lungs and intestines. Human lungs, intestines and heart are adjacent, and share the physical and perceptual contiguity. Based on the contiguity, lungs and intestines can stand for the heart. In the cognitive and cultural model of ancient Chinese people, people believe that human thoughts come from human hearts. And thus human thoughts are the product and a part of the heart. Based on the WHOLE FOR PART metonymic pattern, human hearts can be used to stand for human thoughts. Therefore, the extended meaning of this idiom is that people do things for their individual purposes. Let us look at another idiom"桑中之约" [*sang zhong zhi yue*](*a date between young men and women*). In this idiom, "桑中" (*in the forest of the mulberry*) refers to the location of the date. Based on the LOCATION FOR EVENT metonymic pattern, it can stand for the dating event between young men and women. Another example is"辗转反侧"[*zhan zhuan fan ce*](*It describes that people cannot fall asleep because of anxiety or worry.*). This idiom represents an action idealized cognitive model. One action idealized cognitive model usually includes many conceptual elements in it, such as, agent, patient, action, place, time, instrument, etc. Based on the conceptual contiguity, one element can stand for another within the idealized cognitive model. This idiom represents an action idealized cognitive model of SLEEPING. Based on ACTION FOR REASON metonymic pattern, specified action can stand for the reason resulting in the action. And thus the extended meaning is constructed based on this metonymic pattern, i.e., people cannot fall asleep because of anxiety or worry.

Other idioms from *The Book of Songs* based on the conceptual metonymic mechanism are:"渭阳之情" [*wei yang zhi qing*](*the friendship between nephews and uncles*), "蒹葭之思"[*jian jia zhi si*](*to miss each other between lovers*), "主文谲谏"[*zhu wen jue jian*](*to persuade or give   advice to the emperor by writing articles*), "殷鉴不远"[*yin jian bu yuan*](*to take lessons from the previous generations*), "甘棠之爱"[*gan tang zhi ai*](*the deep affection between people and government officials*), "抱布贸丝"[*bao bu mao si*](*to make chances for approaching to beloved girls*), "元戎启行"[*yuan rong qi xing*](*Armies set out.*), "白华之怨" [*bai hua zhi yuan*](*the complaints of women for falling into disfavor*), "将伯之助" [*jiang bo zhi zhu*](*to ask for help from other people*), "桃李之馈"[*tao li zhi kui*](*to send gifts*), "采兰赠芍" [*cai lan zeng shao*](*to exchange gifts between young men and women for showing their love*), "投桃报李"[*tou tao bao li*](*to exchange valuable gifts between young men and women for showing their deep love*).

2.3   The Combination of Conceptual Metaphor and Conceptual Metonymy

The extended meanings of some idioms from *The Book of Songs* cannot be constructed by conceptual metaphor or conceptual metonymy alone, but by their combination. In this case, conceptual metaphor and conceptual metonymy function together as the conceptual motivation and cognitive mechanism of the idioms from *The Book of Songs*. Based on the literal meaning and such cognitive mechanisms as conceptual metaphor, conceptual metonymy or their combination, the extended meaning of the idioms are thus constructed with the long time conventionalized usage. According to our calculation, the number of the idioms from *The Book of Songs* based on the combination of conceptual metaphor and conceptual metonymy is 3, accounting for 1% of the total idioms from *The Book of Songs*. In the following, examples will be employed to illustrate how the conceptual metaphor and conceptual metonymy work together in the construction of the extended meaning of the idioms from *The Book of Songs*.

The extended meaning of "弄璋之喜"[*nong zhang zhi xi*] is to celebrate giving birth to a boy. The formation of this extended meaning is closely related to Chinese traditional culture of jade. Chinese people have always worshiped and deeply loved the beautiful jade. "璋"[*zhang*] is a kind of beautiful and high-quality jade. In this idiom, the pure and innocent quality of beautiful jade is metaphorically mapped to the lofty character of a virtuous man. In the ancient time, people gave a beautiful jade to the boy as a toy to expect that the boy will possess the pure and lofty character in the future. Therefore, "弄璋"[*nong zhang*] (*to play a beautiful jade*) here metonymically refers to the boy, which belongs to the ACTION FOR AGENT metonymic pattern within the same action idealized cognitive model of PLAYING JADE. Another idiom based on the combination of conceptual metaphor and conceptual metonymy is "泾渭分明" [*jing wei fen ming*] (*It refers to people with integrity.*). The literal meaning of "泾渭分明"is the distinction between Jing River and Wei River is clear. The cognitive process underlying the formation of the extended meaning of "泾渭分明"is as follows: based on the metonymy mechanism, "泾"[*jing*](*Jing River*)and "渭"[*wei*](*Wei River*) metonymically refer to water in Jing River and Wei River respectively. In the meantime, the literal meaning of "泾渭分明" as the source domain is mapped into the abstract domain of human character, which functions as the target domain of this metaphorical mapping. According to our encyclopedic knowledge relating to Jing River and Wei River, the two rivers will converge into the Yellow River, but as a result of the different color of water in the two rivers, water from the two rivers cannot be mixed harmoniously. Therefore, the extended meaning of this idiom comes into being: it refers to people who possess the character of integrity. Let us look at another idiom "蠢首蛾眉"[*qin shou e mei*](*beautiful women*). "蠢首"refers to wide forehead like the forehead of cicada, "蛾眉" here describes that the curved eyebrows of a woman are like the tentacle of the moth. Based on the partial similarities between the facial characteristics of the cicada, moth and beautiful women, the former can function as the source domain, which can be metaphorically mapped into the target domain to describe the facial characteristics of beautiful women. Meanwhile, based on the PART FOR WHOLE metonymic pattern, the literal meaning of this idiom, i.e., the wide forehead and curved eyebrows of beautiful women, stand for the beautiful women.

3   An Analysis of the On-line Meaning Construction of Idioms from *The Book of Songs*

In the previous part, the conceptual motivation and cognitive mechanisms of the idioms from *The Book of Songs* are demonstrated. In the following part, their on-line meaning construction will be analyzed.

3.1   On-line Meaning Construction

Cognitive linguistics holds that the meaning of linguistic units stems from the dynamic process of meaning construction. The nature of meaning construction is conceptual. It is equated with the conceptualization based on the encyclopedic knowledge and the contexts.

Conceptual blending theory is put forward by Gilles Fauconnier and Mark Turner on the basis of mental spaces theory and conceptual metaphor theory. It is an important theory concerning on-line meaning construction. Conceptual blending is a process of mapping between different mental spaces. Based on this interactional mapping process, the conceptual integration network is formed. The basic unit of conceptual blending is mental space, which are the small conceptual packets constructed to achieve the purpose of local understanding and action in the course of human thought and communication (Fauconnier, 1985:16-22). Basic conceptual integration network includes four mental spaces: input space I, input space II, generic space, blended space. All the mental spaces are combined through projection chains. The working process of the conceptual integration network is as follows: the shared and abstract structures of the two input spaces are projected into the generic space, which contains the schematic information and is constructed by way of analogy and schematic induction. And then, under the guidance of the generic space, the counterpart elements in the two input spaces begin to make cross-space mapping and matching. At the same time, matched elements and information in the two input spaces will be selectively projected into the blended space.   In the blended space, projected elements and structures go through three cognitive processes, which are composition, completion and elaboration (Fauconnier, 1998; Evans & Greens, 2006:405-409). Finally, the emergent structure is generated within the blended space, which does not exist before in the two input spaces. Emergent structures only exist in the blended space and contain new information and structures.

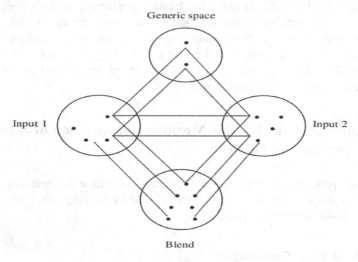

Fig. 2. The conceptual integration network

3.2   On-line Meaning Construction of Idioms from *The Book of Songs*

Based on the previous studies and analyses, we argue that the on-line meaning construction of idioms from *The Book of Songs* in the specific context is as follows: firstly, in the process of understanding an idiom in a specific context, we will construct an idiom mental space, which is generated by mapping from the literal meaning of the idiom to the extended meaning by way of conceptual metaphor, conceptual metonymy or the combination of them. And then, as the discourse develops, more information will be added and elaborated, including contextual information. The contextual information will construct a discourse mental space. Finally, the idiom mental space and discourse mental space will be integrated to achieve the on-line meaning construction of idioms. The basis of the mapping and projection is the shared structures and counterpart elements between the two spaces. In the process of blending, the idiom mental space is responsible for providing organizing frames and schematic structures, whereas the discourse mental space will provide semantic values. Based on the figure of the basic conceptual integration network, the figure of on-line meaning construction of idioms is illustrated as follows.

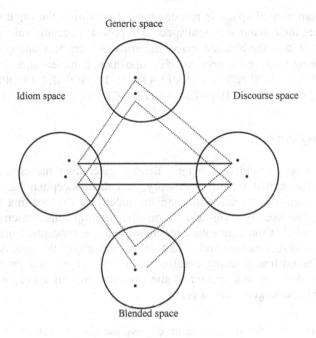

Fig. 3. The on-line meaning construction of idioms

In the following, we will take"嘤鸣求友" as an example to illustrate the on-line meaning construction of idioms from *The Book of Songs*.

"We Chinese people are in the depths of the disaster in history and in the time of needing assistance most urgently. As a saying in *The Book of Songs* "嘤鸣求友", we are at this time. "

This passage is extracted from *Stalin Was a Friend of the Chinese People*, a speech made by Mao Zedong. In the process of understanding the idiom"嘤鸣求友"in the above context, we will firstly construct the idiom mental space, which is mainly composed of its extended meaning. According to what we have analyzed before, we know that the extended meaning of this idiom is that people appeal to making friends with those who have common goals with them. This extended meaning constitute the idiom mental space, which includes many conceptual elements, such as, PEOPLE, APPEALING TO, and HOPING TO MAKE FRIENDS WITH THOSE WHO HAVE COMMON GOALS WITH THEM. The contextual information makes up the discourse mental space, which also includes many conceptual elements, such as CHINESE PEOPLE, CALLING UPON, and HOPING TO MAKE FRIENDS WITH SOVIET PEOPLE. The common structures and abstract organization constitute the generic space, which include such elements as AGENT, ACTION, and PURPOSE. Under the guidance of the generic space, counterparts in both the idiom mental space and the discourse mental space begin to map and match. Simultaneously, elements of the two spaces will be selectively projected into the blended space. In this blending process, idiom mental space is responsible for providing the organizing frame and roles, whereas the discourse mental space will provide semantic values and contextual information. Within the blended space, the emergent structure and emergent meaning come into being through the process of composition, completion, and elaboration, i.e., CHINESE PEOPLE SEND AN INVITATION TO SOVIET PEOPLE IN ORDER TO MAKE FRIENDS WITH THEM AND TO GET HELP FROM THEM.

4   Conclusion

This paper adopts cognitive semantic theories, including the conceptual metaphor theory, the conceptual metonymy theory, and the conceptual blending theory, to analyze the cognitive operation mechanism underlying the meaning extension of the idioms from *The Book of Songs* and the on-line meaning construction of the idioms. It has been found that the conceptual metaphor and the conceptual metonymy are the main conceptual motivations and cognitive mechanisms of the idioms from *The Book of Songs*. The on-line meaning construction of the idioms is a process of blending between the idiom mental space and the discourse mental space, which eventually gives rise to the emergent structures.

Acknowledgements. We would like to express our sincere gratitude to the anonymous reviewers for their valuable comments. The study is jointly supported by the Humanities and Social Science by the Ministry of Education (10YJA740003), Social Science Foundation of Hunan Province (13YBA414), and Hunan Provincial Innovation Foundation for Postgraduate (CX2015B156).

References

1. Evans, V., Greens, M.: Cognitive Linguistics: An Introduction. Edinburgh University Press, Edinburgh (2006)
2. Fauconnier, G.: Mental Spaces. MIT Press, Cambridge (1985)
3. Fauconnier, G., Turner, M.: Conceptual Integration Networks. Cognitive Science **3**, 133–187 (1998)
4. He, S.: Morphological Structure of Idioms from *The Book of Songs*. The Periodical of the Research on The Book of Songs **1**, 237–248 (2007). (in Chinese)
5. He, S.: Meanings of Idioms from *The Book of Songs*. The Periodical of the Research on The Book of Songs **3**, 114–133 (2011). (in Chinese)
6. Huang, J.: An Analysis of Grammatical Structures of Idioms in *The Book of Songs*. Journal of Xiamen University **3**, 129–136 (1985). (in Chinese)
7. Lakoff, G., Johnson, M.: Metaphors We Live By. The University of Chicago Press, Chicago (1980)
8. Langacker, R.W.: Reference-point Construction. Cognitive Linguistics **4**, 1–38 (1993)
9. Niu, Q., Gao, Y.: Research on the Evolution of Some Idioms in *The Book of Songs*. Journal of Changchun University of Science and Technology **4**, 574–575 (2009)

10. Sun, W.: A Study on Chinese Idioms. Jilin Education Press, Changchun (1989). (in Chinese)
11. Taylor, J.: Linguistic Categorization. Oxford University Press, Oxford (2003)
12. Wang, D.: A Study on Lexicology. Shandong Education Press, Jinan (1983). (in Chinese)
13. Wang, D.: General Linguistics. Jiangsu Education Press, Nanjing (1990). (in Chinese)
14. Wang, Z.: An English-Chinese Dictionary of Applied Linguistics. Hunan Education Press, Chang Sha (1988). (in Chinese)
15. Zhang, H.: Idioms: Conventionalized Mapping Patterns and Mental Representations. Modern Foreign Languages **3**, 250–258 (2003). (in Chinese)

Sum, Domain Restriction and Quantification–A Semantic Study of *Quanbu* in Mandarin

Lei Zhang[(⊠)]

School of Overseas Education, Northeast Normal University, Changchun, China
Zhangl120@nenu.edu.cn

Abstract. This paper investigates the semantics of 全部 [*quanbu*] *(all)* in Mandarin Chinese. It is argued that in the adverbial, determiner and nominal positions *quanbu* takes different meanings. To be more specific, the adverb *quanbu* serves as a quantifier which can trigger a tripartite structure. Moreover, as a quantifier, *quanbu* is compatible with a sum operator with the collective property and incompatible with a sum operator taking the distributive property. The determiner *quanbu* is a sum operator with the collective property. The noun *quanbu* implies the sum of all the parts. *Quanbu* has some similarities and differences with 全 [*quan*] *(all)* and 都 [*dou*] *(all)*. In the co-occurrence case of *quanbu* and *dou*, word order plays an important role to determine their division of labor.

Keywords: Semantics of *quanbu* · Sum operator · Domain restriction · Quantifier

1 Introduction

In Mandarin Chinese, 全部[*quanbu*] *(all)* is a frequently used word with universal meaning. Moreover, it can occur either in the determiner position, or the head position of a nominal phrase, or an adverbial position. Consider (1).

(1) a. 这　　就是　我　的　　　全部　　　　想法.[1]
　　　 this　just　I　DE　　　all　　　　　thought
　　　 'This is all my thoughts.'
　 b. 写作　　是　我　生活　的　　全部.
　　　 writing　be　I　life　DE　　all
　　　 'Writing is all my life.'
　 c. 三　　个　　月　　　后　肿块　全部　　消失.
　　　 three　CL　month　　later　lump　all　　disappear
　　　 'Three months later the lumps all are flattened out.'

In terms of form, the difference between *quanbu* and 全[*quan*] *(all)* lies in a single word. These two words have many similarities and some differences. Moreover, the adverb *quanbu* has some similarities with 都[*dou*] *(all)*.

---

[1] In this paper, the description on *quanbu* is mainly based on observing the data of some commonly used corpora such as CCL corpus and BCC corpus. Further, many examples are cited from CCL corpus, which are not pointed out here one by one.

Q. Lu and H.H. Gao (Eds.): CLSW 2015, LNAI 9332, pp. 130–140, 2015.
DOI: 10.1007/978-3-319-27194-1_14

In addition, *quanbu* can co-occur with other words with universal meanings. Consider (2).

(2) a. 所有　　　　断骨　　　全部　正常　愈合.
　　　all　　　　broken-bone　all　　normal　knit
　　　'*All the broken bones knitted normally.*'

　　b. 企业　　所有　的　　一切　全部　都　是　　　国有　　　　　　的.
　　　business　all　DE　everything　all　　all　be government-owned　DE
　　　'*Everything of the business belongs to the government.*'

Does *quanbu* have the same semantics in different syntactic positions? What are the similarities and differences between *quanbu* and *quan/dou*? Why can *quanbu* occur with other words with universal meanings? What is their division of labor in the co-occurrence case?

In this paper, I will investigate the semantics of *quanbu* and attempt to answer the above questions. Section 2 explores the semantics of the adverbial, determiner and nominal *quanbu*. Section 3 makes a comparison between *quanbu* and *quan* and between *quanbu* and *dou* respectively. Section 4 discusses the case where *quanbu* co-occurs with other words taking universal meanings. Section 5 concludes this paper.

2   The Semantics of *Quanbu*

2.1   The Adverbial *Quanbu*

This section will investigate the basic semantics of the adverb *quanbu* when used alone, including its distribution, the semantic properties of its associate element, its direction of association, its tripartite structure and so forth.

The adverbial *quanbu* generally occurs in the classic position of an adverb, i.e. a post-subject and preverbal position. In the case that 必须[*bixu*] (*must*) occurs in the sentence in question, *bixu* usually occurs to the left of *quanbu*, as shown in (3a); in a few cases it appears to the right of *quanbu*, as shown in (3b). In a similar fashion, 已/已经 [*yi/yijing*](*already*) is generally present to the left of *quanbu*, as seen in (4).

(3) a. 按　　　规定　该　签字　的　人员　必须　全部　签字.
　　　according rule　should sign　DE　staff　must　all　　sign
　　　'*According to the rule, the staff who should sign their names all must sign.*'

　　b. 这 一　笔　资金 恐怕　全部　必须　贷款　才　筹　得　出来.²
　　　this one CL　fund perhaps　all　　must　loan　only　raise　DE　out
　　　'*Only loaning all can this fund perhaps raises.*'

(4) a. 照片　　　已经　　全部　洗　出来　了.
　　　picture　already　all　　print　out　SFP
　　　'*The pictures all have already been printed.*'

　　b. 本案　　　的　　　赃款　　　　已　全部　追回.
　　　this-case DE illicit-money already　all　　recover
　　　'*The illicit money of this case all has been already recovered.*'

---

² Abbreviations used in this paper include –CL: classifiers; ASP: aspect markers; NEG: negative markers; and SFP: sentence final particles.

The adverb *quanbu* can be treated as an adverb of universal quantification, which quantifies over its interacting element and indicates that every member of the set denoted by its interacting element has the relevant property. *Quanbu* requires its associate element is semantically plural. Consider (5).

(5) a. 去年　毕业　的　学生　全部　升入　　中学。
  last-year graduate DE student   all   come-up middle-school
  'The students graduated last year all came up to middle schools.'
 b. 故障　全部　　排除　　了。
  trouble   all   remove   SFP
  'All of the troubles (s) are removed.'

In (5a), the interacting element of *quanbu* is 去年毕业的学生[*qunian biye de xuesheng*](*the students graduated last year*) which is a plural NP; in (5b) the associate element 故障[*guzhang*](*trouble(s)*) is semantically plural. Due to the unclear context here *guzhang* can denote either a set of several breakdowns or a breakdown composed of several parts.

Generally speaking, in the case of a semantically plural element to the left of *quanbu*, *quanbu* operates on this element, as shown in (6a); only in the case that there is no available semantically plural element to the left of *quanbu*, *quanbu* associates with some element to its right, which is usually the verb close to it, as shown in (6b).

(6) a. 山东　　　新疆　　　白条　全部　　兑现。
  Shandong Xinjiang   IOU   all   cash
  'In Shangdong and Xinjiang IOUs all are cashed.'
 b. 江西　　全部　兑现　白条.
  Jiangxi   all   cash   IOU
  'In Jiangxi IOUs are cashed completely.'

In (6a), *quanbu* associates with 白条[*baitiao*](*IOU*); According to the context, in (6b) 江西[*Jiangxi*](a province of China) as a province is single in semantics. Here *quanbu* interacts with the verb 兑现[*duixian*](*cash*) to its right.

In the case of leftward direction, the associate element of *quanbu* can be a normal nominal phrase, a universal phrase such as a 所有[*suoyou*](*all*)-NP, 整个[*zhengge*] (*whole, entire*)-NP or 一切[*yiqie*](*all*)-NP, or an expression with 不管/无论 [*buguan/wulun*](*no matter, whatever*). Consider (7) to (9) respectively.

(7) 本　次　　　　世锦赛　　8强　　全部　产生.
 this CL world-championship final-8   all   come-out
 'In this World Championship final 8 all came out.'
(8) a. 所有　的　私人　医院　全部　停业.
  all   DE private hospital   all   close
  'All the private hospitals were closed.'
 b. 整个　　城市　全部　被　　淹.
  entire   city   all   BEI   flood
  'The entire city was overwhelmed.'

c. 一切　　费用　全部　报销.
　　all　expense　all　reimburse
　　'*All the expenses are reimbursed.*'

(9) 被 没收 的 产品 不管 是 真 是 假，全部 公开 销毁.
BEI confiscate DE product no-matter be genuine be false   all   openly eliminate
'The confiscated products no matter whether they are genuine or false all are elim-
inated openly.'

While generally *quanbu* cannot co-occur with an interrogative expression such as a
什么[*shenme*](*what*)-NP or 谁[*shui*](*who*), and endow it with a universal interpretation,
as shown in (10). In addition, it cannot license a 连[*lian*](*even*)-NP, as shown in (11).

(10) a. *他　　什么　全部　喜欢　吃.
　　　he　what　all　like　eat
　　　'*He* likes *eating everything.*'
　　b. *谁　全部　知道　这　个　道理.
　　　who　all　know this CL reason
　　　'*Everyone knows this reason.*'
(11) *连　　傻瓜　全部　能　答　对　这　道　题.
　　even idiot　all　can answer right this　CL question
　　'*Even idiots can answer this question correctly.*'

As an adverb of universal quantification, *quanbu* can trigger its own tripartite
structure. In the leftward association case, the tripartite structure is determined by the
topic rule: the interacting element of *quanbu* is mapped to the restrictor and the rest of
the sentence considered is to the nuclear scope. For example, the possible tripartite
structure of (6a) is shown in (12). In the rightward association case, *quanbu* itself
introduces a set of all the possible parts on which it operates. For instance, the possible tripartite structure of (6b) is seen in (13).

(12) 山东新疆白条全部兑现.
　　全部$_x$ [x∈[|白条|] [山东新疆 x 兑现]
　　$\forall$ x [x∈[|白条|] → 山东新疆 x 兑现]]
　　'For every x, if x is a member of '白条', then '山东新疆 x 兑现'.'
(13) 江西全部兑现白条.
　　全部$_x$ [x∈ set of {1/3, 3/5, 80 %,……}] [江西 x 兑现白条]
　　$\forall$ x [x∈ set of {1/3,3/5, 80%,……} → 江西 x 兑现白条]
　　'For every x, if x belongs to the set of all the possible parts, then '江西 x 兑
现白条'.'

2.2   The Determiner *Quanbu*

The determiner *quanbu* can either modify a nominal phrase directly or restrict a nominal
phrase together with the particle 的[*de*](*a particle in Mandarin*). Consider (14).

(14) a. 全部（的）家当
    all   the   property
    '*all the property*'
 b.全部（的）金额
    all   the   money
    '*all the money*'

The determiner phrase (thereafter DP) composed of *quanbu* and a nominal phrase can act as either the subject or the object. See (15a) and (15b) respectively.

(15) a.最终   全部   财产   将   传给   儿子.
    final   all   property will descend   son
    '*Finally all the property will be descended to the son(s).*'
 b.他   被   没收   了   全部   财产
    he   BEI confiscate ASP   all   property
    '*He was confiscated all the property.*'

Moreover, *quanbu* can restrict a nominal expression with a numeral-classifier phrase. See (16).

(16) 全部 8 名   中国   选手 都   成功   抵达   对岸   的   终点。
    all   8 CL Chinese player all successfully reach the-other-side-of-the-river DE finishing point
    '*All of the eight Chinese players reached the finishing point on the other side of the river.*'

The literal meaning o*f quanbu* is 'the sum of every parts', in which 部[*bu*](*part*) itself already takes the flavor of classifier, and thus *quanbu* generally cannot combine with a measure word and then to restrict the nominal expression. For example, 全部 名中国选手[*quanbu ming Zhongguo xuanshou*] and 全部枚金牌[*quanbu mei jinpai*] are not acceptable.

DPs with the determiner *quanbu* show the asymmetry between the subject and the object position. The DP in the object position does not need any element to license it, whereas it in the subject position has some restriction. To be more specific, when the predicate has the distributive property, the relevant sentence usually need some element such as the quantifier *dou* to license it, otherwise it will be ungrammatical, as shown in (17).

(17) 全部 资金 ??(都)   被   冻结   了.
    all   fund   all   BEI   freeze SFP
    '*All the funds are frozen.*'

It is argued that, the determiner *quanbu* is a sum operator, which is unary and has the collective property. *Quanbu* operates on its interacting element, and sums up every part of the entity denoted by its interacting element.

In the case that the predicate has the intrinsic distributive property, the semantic property of a DP with the determiner *quanbu* is mismatched with the predicate, and thus the DP need a quantifier such as *dou* to distribute the relevant property to the entity/entities denoted by the DP.

2.3   The Nominal *Quanbu*

In the case of being a noun, *quanbu* indicates the sum of all the parts, which can be modified or restricted by other elements, as shown in (18).

(18) 生活 /生命 的　全部
     life   life DE all
     '*all of the life*'

3   A Comparative Study

3.1   A Comparison with *Quan*

In terms of lexical form, *quanbu* and *quan* have the common morpheme *quan*. These two words share many similarities, i.e. both of them can serve as sum operators in the determiner position, and adverbs of quantification in the adverbial position; as quantifiers, *quanbu* and *quan* are interchangeable in many cases.

There are many differences between these two words. First of all, in the light of part of speech, besides an adverb and determiner, *quanbu* can function as a noun, while *quan* cannot act as a noun. Second, the determiner *quan* can combine with a measure word to restrict a nominal expression, for instance 全校学生[*quan xiao xuesheng*](*all the students of the school*), 全村人[*quan cun ren*](*the whole village*), whereas as mentioned above, *quanbu* cannot combine with a measure word directly. In contrast, *quan* cannot restrict a NP with a numeral-classifier phrase, for example, expressions such as 全三项比赛[*quan san xiang bisai*](*all the three games*) are unacceptable; whereas *quanbu* does not have this restriction. Last but not least, as an adverb of quantification, *quan* is different from *quanbu* in the following five aspects.

Firstly, *quan* can occur in a post-verbal position in some cases, while the adverb *quanbu* cannot occur in that position. See the contrast in (19).

(19) a. 这 套 书　我 买　　全 了.
       this CL book　I　buy　　all SFP
       '*I have bought all of this set of books.*'
     b. *这 套 书　我 买　全部　　了.
       this CL book　I　buy　all　　SFP
       '*I have bought all of this set of books.*'

Secondly, in oral contexts *quan* can quantify over *shenme* and endow it with a universal meaning. Moreover, *quan* can license a *lian*-NP. See (20a) and (20b) respectively. However, as above-mentioned *quanbu* does not have the above uses.

(20) a. 他 什么　全 爱 吃.
       he　what　all　like eat
       '*He likes eating everything.*'
     b. 他 连　　　　山珍海味　　　　全　不 爱 吃.
       he even table-delicacies-from-land-and-sea　all　NEG like eat
       '*He does not like eating even table delicacies from land and sea.*'

Thirdly, in some cases, the preverbal *quan* can quantify over a set of degrees, while *quanbu* does not have this function. See the contrast in (21).

(21) a. 这 朵 花 全 开 了.
　　　 this CL flower all blossom ASP
　　　 '*This flower came out completely/This entire flower came out.*'

　　 b. ? 这 朵 花 全部 开 了.
　　　 this CL flower all blossom ASP
　　　 '*This entire flower came out.*'

Fourthly, although *quanbu* and *quan* both can be used in spoken and written Chinese, data in CCL corpus show that, *quanbu* usually occurs in written Chinese, especially news reports, and the aspect marker 了[*le*](*a particle in Mandarin*) rarely appears the relevant sentence, as shown in (22); while *quan* has the tendency to be used in spoken Chinese, where an aspect marker is usually present, otherwise the relevant sentence may become marginal even unacceptable, as shown in (23).

(22) 这些 产品 全部 售出.
　　 these product all sell-out
　　 '*These products all are sold out.*'

(23) 这些 产品 全 卖 出去 *(了).
　　 these product all sell out SFP
　　 '*These products all are sold out.*'

Finally, as mentioned by Lü (1980), to satisfy the requirement of rhythm, *quanbu* is inclined to co-occur with disyllabic verbs and *quan* has the tendency to precede monosyllabic verbs.

3.2   A Comparison with *Dou*

The adverb *quanbu* and *dou* have some similarities, i.e. they can function as adverbs of quantification and require that their interacting elements are semantically plural. These two adverbs also have some differences, as shown below.

First, *dou* can associate with an element to its right. More precisely, *dou* can interact with an interrogative phrase to its right, as shown in (24); *dou* and the sentence final particle *le* can form a discontinuous constituent, in which the surrounded element will introduce an alternative set. The event denoted by this element presents in the relative highest position of the scale considered. See (25). However, *quanbu* does to hold the above uses.

(24) 他 都 买 了 什么?
　　 he all buy ASP what
　　 '*What does all he bought?*'

(25) 都 八 点 了!
　　 all eight o'clock SFP
　　 '*It's already eight o'clock!*'

Second, in the case of leftward association, types of elements that *dou* can associate with are more diverse than that of *quanbu*: (a) *dou* can license a *lian*-construction, while *quanbu* cannot associate with scales; (b) *dou* can interact with interrogative expressions such as *shui* and endow them with universal readings, however, *quanbu* cannot; (c) *dou* can license a preverbal 每[*mei*](*every*)-NP, whereas *quanbu* cannot; and (d) *dou* can associate with *buguan/wulun*-constructions freely, whereas the association of *quanbu* with *buguan/wulun* needs the help of context.

Third, *dou* can quantify over 多数 [*duoshu*](*most*)/很多 [*henduo*](*many*)/许多 [*xuduo*](*many*)-NPs, whereas *quanbu* rarely operates on these expressions. See the contrast in (26).

(26) a. 很多/   许多/   多数   人   都   喜欢   唱歌.
        many   many   most   person   all   like   sing
        '*Many/most people like singing.*'
     b.*很多/   许多/   多数   人   全部   喜欢   唱歌.
        many   many   most person   all   like   sing
        '*Many/most people like singing.*'

Fourth, their relative positions with *yijing* or *bixu* are different, either. The word order of *dou-yijing* is used more frequently than the word order of *yijing-dou*. By contrast, the *yijing-quanbu* word order is used more widely than *quanbu-yijing*. *Dou* usually occurs to the left of *bixu*, whereas *quanbu* to the right of *bixu*.

Last, *dou* is neutral, which can occur in both spoken and written Chinese, whereas *quanbu* is usually used in formal contexts.

4   A Co-occurrence Study

The adverbial *quanbu* can co-occur with other universal expressions. In this section, I will first explore the cases that *quanbu* co-occurs with DPs with universal meanings and then the cases that *quanbu* and another quantifier *dou* occur in the same sentence.

4.1   The Co-occurrence with a DP with Universal Meaning

The adverb *quanbu* not only can occur with a *suoyou*-NP but also can license the sentence under consideration. Look at (27).

(27) 到 1995   年   底   为止, 所有 项目   *(全部)   实施.
     to 1995   year end till   all project   all   carry-out
     '*Until the end of 1995 all the project carried out.*'

According to Zhang, Lee and Pan (2009), *suoyou* is a sum operator, which has the inherent collective property. When the predicate has the distributive property, a preverbal *suoyou* -NP needs a quantifier to support it.

It is argued that *quanbu* is a quantifier with the collective property; therefore it is compatible with *suoyou*.

In a similar fashion, *quanbu* can license a *yiqie*-NP, as seen in (28).

(28) 一切   矜持   全部   荡然无存.
     all   reserved-manner   all   all-gone
     '*All the reserved manner is gone.*'

In addition, *quanbu* can co-occur with 满[*man*](*full*)-NPs, *zhengge*-NPs, as shown in (29).

(29) a. 他 满 嘴 牙 全部 掉 光 了.
        he full mouth tooth all drop up SFP
        '*He has no teeth left in his mouth.*'
     b. 整个   工程   全部 完工.
        entire project all complete
        '*The entire project was completed.*'

However, in general *quanbu* is incompatible with a *mei*-NP. Consider (30).

(30) *每 个 学生   全部   买 了 一 本 书.
     every CL student   all   buy ASP one CL book
     '*Every student bought a book.*'

It is assumed that, in the above cases *suoyou, yiqie, man, zhengge* and *mei* serve as sum operators, and *quanbu* functions as a quantifier. The incompatibility of *quanbu* with *mei* is due to the mismatch of their semantic properties: *quanbu* has the collective property, whereas *mei* has the distributive property. In other words, in the co-occurrence case *quanbu* requires that the sum operator co-occurring with it has the collective property.

4.2   The Co-occurrence of *Quanbu* with *Dou*

The adverb *quanbu* and another adverb of universal quantification *dou* can occur in a single sentence and there is no redundancy in meaning.   In the co-occurrence case the relative positions of these two adverbs plays an important role to determine their division of labor.

In the case that *quanbu* appears to the left of *dou*, usually *quanbu* does not serve as a quantifier any more, but act as a domain restrictor which restricts the quantificational domain of *dou*, and *dou* is still a quantifier. Consider (31).

(31) a.教师   全部 都 参加   了 培训.
       teacher all all participate ASP training
       '*The teachers all participated in training.*'

     b.我们   全部 都 长   得 很 相似.
       we   all all look   DE very similar
       '*We all look alike.*'

Suppose these two adverbs are both quantifiers, the sentence in question will get a wrong reading. For instance, (31a) will be interpreted as 'all the parts of the teachers participated in training', obviously which is a wrong interpretation.

When *dou* is stressed and a degree set is available to be quantified by *dou*, *dou* can still be a quantifier. In such a case, the quantifier *quanbu* operates on a plural element to its left. Consider (32).

(32) 这些　　花　　全部　都　　开　　了
　　　these　flower　all　　all blossom ASP
　　　'*All of these flowers came out completely.*'

In the case that *quanbu* occurs to the right of *dou*, there are still two possibilities about their division of labor: when both of them can find available plural element to quantify over, they are quantifiers, as shown in (33a); when *dou* and *quanbu* operates on the same element to their left, *dou* is used to restrict the quantificational domain of *quanbu* and *quanbu* is a quantifier, as shown in (33b).

(33) a.各　　种　　　色光　　都　全部　　被　吸收　了.
　　　　every kind chromatic-light all　all　　BEI absorb SFP
　　　　'*Every kind of chromatic light is absorbed completely.*'
　　　b. 我 的　这些　想法　都　　全部　被　否定　了.
　　　　　I DE these thought　all　　all　　BEI negate SFP
　　　　　'*These thoughts of mine all are negated.*'

5 Conclusions

In this paper I have investigated the semantics of *quanbu* in Mandarin. It is argued that, when used alone, the adverb *quanbu* functions as an adverb of universal quantification, which has the plural requirement on its interacting element. The determiner *quanbu* is a sum operator which has the collective property. The nominal *quanbu* indicates the sum of all the parts under consideration.

This paper also shows the similarities and differences between *quanbu* and *quan*, and between *quanbu* and *dou*.

As a quantifier *quanbu* can license a DP with *suoyou/yiqie/zhengge*. The co-occurrence of *quanbu* with *mei* is highly restricted due to the incompatibility of their semantic properties.

In the case that *quanbu* and *dou* co-occur in a sentence, they have different division of labor and they may change semantic functions compared with the case that they used alone.

Acknowledgements. The results reported in this paper are supported by The National Social Science Fund Project (Project No. 15BYY141), HKSAR-GRF (Project No. 9041935) and The Fundamental Research Funds for the Central Universities, The Funds for Young Team Projects of Northeast Normal University. The author thus acknowledges the generous support of the relevant parties. Sincere thanks also go to the anonymous reviewers for their invaluable comments. As usual, the author alone is responsible for all potential errors that may exist in the paper.

References

1. Hajičová, E., Partee, B.H., Sgall, P.: Topic-focus Articulation, Tripartite Structures and Semantic Content. Kluwer Academic Publishers, Dordrecht (1998)
2. Jiang, Y.: Pragmatic Reasoning and Syntactic/Semantic Characterization of *Dou*. Modern Foreign Languages. **1**, 10–24 (1998). (in Chinese)
3. Lee, P.L., Zhang, L.: Pan, H.H: The Co-occurrence Constraint and Division of Labor of Adverbial Universal Quantifiers/Distributors in Mandarin Chinese—Using Adverbials *Dou, Ge and Quan* as Examples. Chinese Linguistics. **3**, 59–70 (2009). (in Chinese)
4. Lin, J.W.: Distributivity in Chinese and Its Implications. Natural Language Semantics. **6**, 201–243 (1998)
5. Lü, S.X.: Eight Hundred Words in Modern Chinese. The Commercial Press, Beijing (1980). (in Chinese)
6. Pan, H.H., Hu, J.H., Huang, Z.H.: *Mei*-NPs' constraints on distribution and semantic interpretation. In: Formal and Functional Studies in Chinese, pp. 110–122. The Commercial Press, Beijing (2009). (in Chinese)
7. Pan, H.H.: Focus, tripartite structure and *dou* quantification. In: Grammar Study and Explore (13), pp. 163–184. The Commercial Press, Beijing (2006). (in Chinese)
8. Peng, X.C., Yan, L.M.: A Semantic Comparison of *Quanbu, Suoyou* and *Yiqie*. Chinese Teaching in the World. **4**, 33–43 (2007). (in Chinese)
9. Zhang, L., Lee, P.L., Pan, H.H.: Sum Operator *Suoyou* and Universal Quantification in Chinese. Chinese Teaching in the World. **4**, 457–464 (2009). (in Chinese)
10. Zhang, L., Lee, P.L., Pan, H.H.: A semantic study of *quan* in mandarin chinese. In: Grammar Study and Explore (15), pp. 136–151. The Commercial Press, Beijing (2010). (in Chinese)

On *ta*: The Focus Marker of Numeral Expressions

Ying Zhang[(✉)]

School of Humanities, Anqing Normal University, Anqing 246133, Anhui, China
zhangying0491@163.com

Abstract. This paper investigates the function of non-referential pronoun *ta*. Generally, a pronoun should have one possible antecedent. If there is no antecedent for the pronoun *ta* in the preceding of sentence, we will naturally look backward for its antecedent and focus on the latter. So the pronoun *ta* has evolved into the focus marker of numeral expressions, and it can make up for the limitation of the focus marker *shi*.

Keywords: *ta* · Focus marker · Double object construction · *bei*-sentence

1 Introduction

It is obvious that personal pronouns have non-referential usages in modern Chinese. In the examples below, pronouns are in bold face:

(1) 你　望着　　　我，我　望着　　　你
　　 ni　wang-zhe　　wo　wo　wang-zh e　ni
　　 you　look at-ZHE　me　I　look at-ZHE　you
　　 'Everyone looked at each other.'

As reflected through the English translation, 你[ni](*you*) and 我[wo](*I*) do not refer to any specific person. According to the Economy Principle, each word in a sentence must have its existence value. A natural question thus arises: what kind of function do the dummy pronouns play?

In the current research, we would like to have a more detailed examination of the non-referential usage of 他[ta](*HE*) and 它[ta](*IT*), and attempt to identify their function. Given the fact that there is no difference in pronunciation between them, we will not distinguish 它[ta](*IT*) from 他[ta](*HE*), which will be usually used in our account.

2 Dummy Pronouns in the Double Object Construction

At the first step in our account, consider the Chinese examples below:

(2) a. 写　　他　　一篇
　　　 xie　　ta　　yi-pian
　　　 write　HE　one-CL
　　　 'to write an essay'

Q. Lu and H.H. Gao (Eds.): CLSW 2015, LNAI 9332, pp. 141–147, 2015.
DOI: 10.1007/978-3-319-27194-1_15

b. 走　　他　　　一趟
zou　　ta　　　yi-tang
go　　HE　　　one-CL
'to go for one time'

c. 玩儿　他　个　痛快
wanr　ta　ge　tongkuai
play　HE　CL　delighted
'*to play delightedly*'

他[ta](*HE*) in the examples above are dummy pronouns that lack antecedents. Chao(1979), Zhu(1982) and Lü (1985) have pointed out that this kind of structure can be considered to double object construction. Lü (1985) notes that the structure have a very important characteristic, i.e., post-verbal numeral phrases must appear. Lü (1992) reasserts his own previous views, but states that the reason why post-verbal numeral phrases must appear in such structures is not clear. We will attempt to answer this question in the following account.

As for the function of 他[ta](*HE*) in such structure, different scholars have different opinions. For example, Hu(1995) points out that the dummy pronoun他[ta](*HE*) in such structures can only strengthen the tone. Gu(1999) claims that the dummy pronoun他[ta](*HE*), playing no semantic and syntactic functions, only strengthens the mood of the sentence, and can be omitted. The question for now is whether they are dispensable.

Yuan(2003) observes that in the light of markedness theory, the dummy pronoun他[ta](*HE*) is used to mark the verb-object construction as the focus. The following example from Yuan(2003) illustrates this.

(3)　a. A:你 要 干 什么？　～B:我 要 喝 他 一扎　啤酒。
　　　　　ni yao gan shenme?　　wo yao he ta yizha　pijiu
　　　you want do　　what　　　I　want drink HE one-CL　beer
　　　'*A: What are you going to do? B: I'm going to drink a glass of beer.*'

　　b. A:你 要 喝 什么？　～ B:我 要 喝 一扎　啤酒。
　　　　ni yao he shenme?　　wo yao he yizha　pijiu
　　　you want drink what　　　I　want drink one-CL　beer
　　　'*A:What would you like to drink? B: A glass of beer.*'

(4)　a. A: 你 打算　怎么办？～ B:我 打算 看 他　两个　通宵。
　　　　　ni dasuan zenmeban?　　wo dasuan kan ta　liangge tongxiao
　　　you want do　　what　　　I　want watch　HE two-CL whole night
　　　'*A: What are you going to do? B: I'm going to watch two whole nights.*'

　　b. A: 你 打算　看 多久？～ B: 我 打算 看 两个　通宵。
　　　　ni dasuan kan duojiu?　　　wo dasuan kan liangge tongxiao
　　　you want watch how long　　I　want　watch two-CL whole night
　　　'*A: How long are you going to watch? B: Two whole nights.*'

Yuan(2003) have pointed out that when the verb-object construction is used as the focus and the whole sentence is used to answer the question '*what are you going to do*', the dummy pronoun 他[ta](*HE*) can be used.

In fact, even if the focus of a sentence is not the verb-object construction, the dummy pronoun 他[ta](*HE*) can still be inserted, as shown below:

(5)   刘：戈玲啊，   那   红烧肉   多少钱   一份儿？
       Liu: Ge,ling-A,   na   hongshaorou   duoshaoqian   yifenr
       Name- interj., that Red-Cooked Pork   how much   one-CL
       'Hey, Ge,ling, How much that Red-Cooked Pork?'
    戈：也   就   两块   多   钱   嘛。
       Ge: ye   jiu   liangkuai duo   qian   ma
       well just two-CL   more money MA
       'Only more than two dollars'
    刘：豁 出去了，我买它两份儿。
       huo chuqu le,   wo mai   ta   liangfen
       risk it all LE,   I buy HE   two-CL
       'I am going to risk it all and buy two lots'

As it can be seen, it is the numeral expressions 两份儿[liangfen](two-CL), but not the verb-object construction 买两份儿[mai liangfen](to buy two-CL), that is used as the focus, while the dummy pronoun 他[ta](*HE*) can still be inserted. Based on the phenomena discussed above, we may speculate that the dummy pronoun 他[ta](*HE*) is used to mark the following numeral expressions as the focus, that is to say, the dummy pronoun他[ta](*HE*) is a focus marker. Xu(2001) have pointed out that numeral expressions are more likely to become a focus in a sentence.

For further the discussion, we would like to bring forth another issue: why can the dummy pronoun他[ta](*HE*) can be used as a focus maker? It is generally known that there is a direct connection between a pronoun and its antecedent. If we cannot find the antecedent, we will naturally pay attention to the elements following the pronoun, and thus the following elements are naturally emphasized.

The most typical focus marker in Chinese is the verb是[shi](*to be*). Take 是一个人也没来(No one came.) as an instance. In this example, the numeral expression 一个人(one person) in subject position is a focus, 是[shi](*to be*) is used as a focus marker. However, 是[shi](*to be*) cannot be used between a verb and its complement. Otherwise, the sentence will be ungrammatical, such as *吃了是三个苹果(*eat three apples*)，*睡了是三天三夜(*sleep for three days and nights*). Therefore, when a numeral expression used as an object or a complement needs to be focused, the dummy pronoun 他[ta](*HE*) will be the best candidate.

The account presented above can also answer Lü's question why the dummy pronoun 他[ta](*HE*) must be used before a numeral expression. The explanation goes as follows. The numeral expression immediately following a verb is the focus, no matter why it is a focus, it needs to be marked in a syntactic way, and since the typical focus marker in modern Chinese 是[shi] (to be) and other focus markers such as 连 [lian](even) cannot appear between a common verb and its object or complement, the dummy pronoun 他[ta](HE), as a focus marker, undertake the task inevitably owing to its property of being able to function as the object of a common verb.

We next turn to discuss the context in which focus marker 他[ta](*HE*) is used. Lü(1992:2) notes some very interesting examples. A few are adapted below.

(6) a. *昨天   我 买了   他 二斤   羊肉   吃   涮羊肉
        zuotian   wo mai le   ta erjin   yangrou chi shuanyangrou
        yesterday I buy-LE HE two-CL mutton   eat instant-boiled mutton
        '*Yesterday I bought two pounds of mutton to eat mutton hotpot.'
     b. 昨天   我 想 买 他 二斤   羊肉   吃   涮羊肉
        zuotian   wo xiang mai ta erjin   yangrou chi shuanyangrou
        yesterday I   want buy HE two-CL   mutton   eat instant-boiled mutton
        'Yesterday I wanted buy two pounds of mutton to eat mutton hotpot.'

(7) 每   到   春节   我   总要   买 它 二斤   羊肉
     mei   dao   chunjie   wo   zongyao   mai ta erjin   yangrou
     every at   Spring Festival I   always   buy HE two-CL   mutton
     吃   涮羊肉。
     chi   shuanyangrou
     eat   instant-boiled mutton
     'Every Spring Festival I always buy two pounds of lamb two pounds of mutton to eat mutton hotpot.'

According to Lü(1992), (6b) is more adequate than (6a), suggesting the dummy pronoun 他[ta](*HE*) is prone to be used to express unrealized things other than realized things. In addition, (7) is well-formed, suggesting the dummy pronoun他[ta](*HE*) can also express habitual things. Yuan(2003) have pointed that unrealized things and habitual things are unrealistic things. So common to all these examples above is that the focus marker 他[ta](*HE*) can only be used in non-realistic sentence. Is this the truth? The answer is no. Consider the following example as observed by Ōta Tatsuo(1958):

(8) 第一天   没 拉 他   什么   钱。 (老舍《骆驼祥子》)
     diyitian   mei la ta   shenme qian
     the first day not pull HE any   money
     'On the first day of pulling a cart , he is not making money'
                                    (Lao She, *Rickshaw Boy*)

Ōta Tatsuo(1958) argues that 他[ta](*HE*) in example (8) is an accessory word to support the verb. It is clear that 什么钱(any money) is a numeral expression, and we may approach this sentence from another point of view that 他[ta](*HE*) is also a focus maker in this sentence. In other words, the focus marker 他[ta](*HE*) can also be used in realistic sentence.

However, it is undeniable that the focus marker 他[ta](*HE*) usually be used in non-realistic sentence, because in such sentence, 他[ta](*HE*) usually has no antecedent. As a result, the pronouns' referential function weakens, and it is easier to be used as a focus maker.

3   Dummy Pronouns in *bei*-sentence

Wu(2000), Xiong(2003) and Huang et al.(2009) argue that a resumptive pronoun may be present in the long passive in which 被[bei](*BEI*) is followed by an NP. This observation is supported by the contrast in the following examples:

(9)   a. 小李ᵢ   被   小张   打了   他ᵢ   一拳。
         XiaoLi bei Xiao Zhang da le   ta   yiquan
         Name   Bei Name   beat-LE   HE   this-CL
         '*Xiao Li was punched by Xiao Zhang*'
      b. 张三ᵢ   被   李四   打了   他ᵢ   一下。
         ZhangSan bei LiSi   dale   ta   yixia
         Name   Bei Name   beat-LE   HE   one-CL
         '*ZhangSan was beaten by LiSi*'

There is controversy over how to analyze such sentences among researchers. One key point of debate has been whether a resumptive pronoun can be used in the long passive. For example, Shi and Liu(2008) claim that resumptive pronouns cannot appear in passive sentences. Putting the controversy aside for now, it is clear that sentences of this sort represented by (9a-b) can be acceptable in Modern Chinese. Later on, we will explain why resumptive pronouns can appear in passive sentences.

Many scholars have observed that a numeral expression must be present after他 [ta](*HE*) in these passive sentences, such as Li(2008), Xiong(2003), Song(2006). With the approach taken in the current account, the instances become understandable. 他 [ta](*HE*) is a focus marker, and it must precede a numeral expression needing to be focused.

However, in CCL corpus, we did not find sentences similar to (9a-b). Recall that the focus marker 他[ta](*HE*) usually be used in non-realistic sentence, but passive sentences are usually realistic sentence, the answer comes.

4   Dummy Pronouns in "*ta*+NP" Structure

As to the grammatical position in a sentence, the focus marker 他[ta](*HE*) can appear not only between a verb and its complement as shown in the examples above, but also before a noun as in (10):

(10) 有   这么   一锅   汤   垫底，   它   再多   的 萝卜，
     you   zheme   yiguo   tang   diandi, ta   zaiduo de luobo,
     there be such   a pan of soup   simmer   HE   more   DE radish
     也   能   让   群众   爱不释手。
     ye   neng   rang   quanzhong   aibushishou
     also can   make   the masses love
     '*Radish was stewed with such a soup, even if there are more radish in it, People cannot help but drink*'

For the convenience of discussion, we use "ta+N" structure to present the structure 它再多的萝卜(*more radish*). It is well known that "ta+N" structure is a very common construction in Chinese, in which the pronoun and the NP following it bear a co-referential relationship, such as 他老王(*He Laowang*). Such kind of structures is generally referred to as an appositive construction. The problem is that the pronoun and the NP following it are not always consistent in quantity, and accordingly the co-referential relationship between them cannot be guaranteed. If there is no co-referential relationship between the pronoun and the NP following it, the "*ta*+NP" structure cannot be counted as an appositive construction. The phrase 它再多的萝卜 (*more radish*) is an obvious example. Since 它[ta](*IT*) and 再多的萝卜(*more radish*) are not consistent in quantity, it can be certain that there is no co-referential relationship between them and therefore the phrase 它再多的萝卜(*more radish*) is not possible to be seen as an appositive construction. 它[ta](*IT*) in (10) can be seen as a focus marker in the view of this paper. Obviously, the typical focus marker 是[shi](*to be*) in modern Chinese cannot appear in such a position.

5   Conclusion

This paper re-examines the role of the dummy pronoun他[ta](*HE*) in Mandarin Chinese and conclude that the dummy pronoun can be used as a focus marker. It is well known that a pronoun should have one possible antecedent. If there is no antecedent for pronoun *ta* in the preceding of sentence, we will naturally look backward for its antecedent, and the latter will be emphasized. Eventually, the dummy pronoun他 [ta](*HE*) has evolved into a focus marker. It can be used between a verb and its object or complement, making up for the limitation of focus marker 是[shi](*to be*), but in such case the object complement can only be a numeral expression. It can also be used in the long passive and "*ta*+NP" structure, expressing the following numeral expressions as focus.

References

1. Huang, C.-T.J.: On Ta de laoshi dang-de hao and Related Problems. Linguistic Sciences **3**, 225–241 (2008). (黄正德: 从"他的老师当得好"谈起.语言科学3:225~241(2008)) (in Chinese)
2. Huang, C.-T.J., Li, Y.-H.A., Li, Y.: The Syntax of Chinese. Cambridge University Press, Cambridge (2009)
3. Li, X.: Comparative Analysis on resumptive pronouns. Modern Chinese **5**, 76–77 (2008). (黎小荣:英汉接应代词对比分析.现代语文5,76~77(2008)). (in Chinese)
4. Lü, S.: On Early Modern Chinese Pronoun. Academia Press, Shanghai (1985). (吕叔湘:近代汉语指代词. 上海:学林出版社(1985)) (in Chinese)
5. Lü, S.: Research on theory and usage. In: Grammar Research and Exploration (6), pp. 1–3. Commercial Press, Beijing (1992). (吕叔湘: 理论研究和用法研究.载语法研究和探索(六). 北京:商务印书馆(1992)) (in Chinese)

6. Shi, Y., Liu, C.: Pronoun Anaphora Phenomenon and Its Historical Origin in Disposal of Chinese Dialect. Linguistic Researches **3**, 52–55 (2008). (石毓智、刘春卉:汉语方言处置式的代词回指现象及其历史来源.语文研究3:52~55(2008)) (in Chinese)
7. Tatsuo, Ō.: A historical grammar of modern chinese. In: Chinese translation by Jiǎng & Xu. Peking University Press, Beijing (1958). (太田辰夫著, 蒋绍愚、徐昌华译: 中国语历史文法. 北京: 北京大学出版社(1958)) (in Chinese)
8. Wu, G.: Chinese Passives and Verb Passivization. Modern Foreign Languages **23**(3), 249–260 (2000). (吴庚堂:汉语被动式与动词被动化. 现代外语23(3): 249~260(2000)) (in Chinese)
9. Xu, J.: Grammatical principles and grammatical phenomena. In: Peking University Press, Beijing (2001). (徐杰:普遍语法原则与汉语语法现象.北京:北京大学出版社(2001)) (in Chinese)
10. Yuan, X.: Origin of non-referential Pronoun Ta in Modern Chinese. Journal of Sichuan Normal University (Social Science) **32**(6), 43–47 (2005). (袁雪梅:现代汉语虚指"他"的来源. 四川师范大学学报(社会科学版)32(6):43~47(2005)) (in Chinese)
11. Yuan, Y.: On the syntactic and semantic functions of non-referential pronoun Ta(他):from the perspective of prosodic syntax and focus theory. In: Grammar Research and Exploration (12), pp. 44–64. Commercial Press, Beijing (2003) (袁毓林: 无指代词"他"的句法语义功能——从韵律句法和焦点理论的角度看, 载语法研究与探索(十二). 北京:商务印书馆(2003)) (in Chinese)
12. Chao, Y.R.: A Grammar of Spoken Chinese, p.125. The Commercial Press, Beijing (1979)
13. Zhu, D.: Lecture Notes of Grammar. Commercial Press, Beijing (1982). (朱德熙: 语法讲义. 北京:商务印书馆(1982)) (in Chinese)

The Semantic Features of "changchang", "jingchang", "wangwang" and "tongchang"—A Corpus-Based Perspective

Yuncui Zhang and Pengyuan Liu(⊠)

Institute of Applied Linguistics,
Beijing Language and Culture University, Beijing 10083, China
zycblcu@sina.com, liupengyuan@pku.edu.cn

Abstract. In addition to indicate frequency, "changchang" (常常 [*changchang*] (*often,always;frequently,usually*)) and "jingchang" (经常[*jingchang*](*often,always; frequently,usually*)) can also be used to represent that actions or events occur, or states exist with regularity, and the sentence express people's experience summary as well as "wang wang" (往往[*wangwang*](*frequently,usually;often,always*)) and "tongchang" (通常[*tongchang*](*frequently,usually;often,always*)). This study points out: (1) The four adverbs tend to match the controllable/uncontrollable verbs when they refer to frequency/regular; (2) They are more inclined to mean regular when they match adjectives. This study applies the method of corpus linguistics, combines with the comparison methods of function words to verify with syntactic behavior. Based on the observation of a large number of data and analyze the specific facts, we get a sequence of semantic features.

Keywords: Time adverbs · Semantic features · Syntactic behavior · Corpus linguistics

1 Introduction

As the name suggests, time adverbs express time. With respect to the category about "chang chang", "jingchang", "wangwang" and "tongchang", the academic circles mainly divided into two parties. Time adverbs: scholars such as ZhaoY (1979), ZhuD (1982), Ma&Lu (1985), *Modern Chinese* compiled by Peking University (2000), *New Adaptation of Modern Chinese* by Zhang B (2002), etc. Frequency adverbs: such as Liu (1983), Zhou (1999), etc. Shi J (2002) regarded them as momentum adverbs. Zhang (2000) looked upon as frequency adverbs and then he (2004) divided them into time adverbs.Towards the study of semantic and syntactic features, many linguists concentrated mainly on "chang chang", "wangwang" and "tongchang", less for "jingchang".

Lv(1983): "changchang" represents high frequency, but "wangwang" is different from "偶尔" [Ou'er] (occasionally), which represents low frequency, nor "changchang". "wangwang" expresses more than once but not very often.

© Springer International Publishing Switzerland 2015
Q. Lu and H.H. Gao (Eds.): CLSW 2015, LNAI 9332, pp. 148–159, 2015.
DOI: 10.1007/978-3-319-27194-1_16

Ma&Lu(1985): "changchang" and "wangwang" represent often-occasional. Both of them indicate actions or events occur constantly. "wangwang" expresses something empirical, so it is always used in the past tense. No "jingchang" or "tongchang" involved in.

Zhou(1994) pointed out that "changchang" is less restricted in use than "tongchang". The semantic analysis of "tongchang" focuses on the *time, place, way, factor, frequency,* etc, which related to the predicate or attached words that modify objects.

Li(2004): "changchang" simply emphasizes that actions often appear, "wangwang" not only emphasizes that actions often appear, but also expresses the present situations happened with certain regularity.

This is the interpretations in *The dictionary of Modern Chinese* and *Eight hundred words in Modern Chinese* below:

The dictionary of Modern Chinese:

a_1.changchang: An event happens more than once at short intervals. eg:

他常常受到表扬。[*ta changchang shou dao biao yang.*] (*He has often been praised*)

b_1 jingchang: changchang, shichang. eg:

他 们 经 常 保 持 联 系 。 [*ta men jingchang bao chi lian xi*] (*They often keep in contact with each other.*)

c_1 tongchang: In general, behavior or events happen regularly. eg:

他通常六点钟起床。[*ta tongchang liu dian qi chuang.*] (*He usually gets up at six o'clock.*)

d_1 wangwang: Based on previous experience, some cases exist or happen constantly under certain conditions. eg:周日他往往去公园散步。 [*zhou ri ta wangwang qu gong yuan san bu.*]

(*He usually goes for a walk in the park on Sunday.*)

Mutual interpreting between "changchang" and "jingchang".

Eight hundred words in Modern Chinese:

a_2 changchang: Indicates that behavior or action happens more frequently. Some actions occur more than once in a not long time , which simple refers to the action of repeated but do not necessarily have regularity. eg:

他常常工作到深夜。[*ta chang chang gong zuo dao shen ye.*] (*He often worked late into the night*)

b_2 jingchang: Be used in the same way as shichang , which emphasizes the consistency; An event happens more than once at short intervals. eg:

经常打扫房间。[*jingchang da sao fang jian.*] (*(sb)often cleans the room.*)

c_2 tongchang: Refers to the actions with regularity. eg:

我们通常周四下午开会。[*wo men tongchang zhou si xia wu kai hui.*]

(*We usually meet on Thursday afternoon*)

d_2 wangwang: Some situations appear frequently, summary for events happened with a regular. The sentence indicates the situation, condition, or results related to the action. eg:

每逢节日，我们往往到厂矿去演出。[*mei feng jie ri,wo men wangwang dao chang kuang qu yan chu.*]

(*In every festival, we usually go to the factories to perform.*)

In addition, *Case of function words interpretation in Modern Chinese* compiled by Chinese literature from Beijing university (1985): "wangwang" means the shape of the situation under normal circumstances. "changchang" is usually used for representing actions occur frequently, "changchang" emphasizes that behaviors and actions without exception; "wangwang" just modifies actions often happen under some circumstances. But "changchang" is unconstrained.

To summarize the definition of dictionaries and papers, toward to the semantic, most scholars hold the view : the different between the four adverbs is "changchang" and "jingchang" presents more frequency of events or actions; "wangwang" and "tongchang" make a summing up of the experience, and emphasize that actions or events happen regularly.

Actually, based on the investigation of the large-scale corpus and analysis of a large number of language facts, we find that, in addition to indicate frequency[1], "changchang" and "jingchang" can also be used to represent that actions or events occur, or states exist with regularity, and the sentence express people's experience summary[2] as well as "wangwang" and "tongchang". At this point most of them decorate the predicate part. Furthermore, 1) The four adverbs tend to match the controllable/uncontrollable verb when they refer to frequency/regular; 2) They are more inclined to mean regular when they match adjectives. This paper applies the method of corpus linguistics, combines with the comparison methods of function words, to verify with syntactic behaviors. Based on the statistics of a large number of language facts, the result is supported by the data, and we also analyze the specific facts.

2   The Controllable/Uncontrollable Verbs Collocations

Ma Q (1988) haven given detailed descriptions of controllable/uncontrollable verb. He inspired from the Tibetan language grammar. Chinese verb can be divided into controllable verbs and uncontrollable verbs according to whether the behavior is under control. This classification is one system of Chinese verbs.

2.1   Hypothesis

The controllable verbs refer to the behavior that can be operated consciously, such as走路 [zoulu](to walk),看[kan](to look), 打[da](to hit), etc. These verbs express verbal force with flexibility. In general, controllable action can be achieved with repetition and frequency; The uncontrolled verbs are uncontrolled and unconsciously action, such as是[shi] (to be), 有 [you](have), 死[si](die), 形成[xingcheng](form),etc.They represent attributes or categories so that are not easy to achieve repetition and frequency. Hence, we come up with **hypothesis one**: when "changchang", "jingchang", "tongchang", "wangwang" refer to frequency, they tend to modify controllable verbs; when refer to regular, they are inclined to modify uncontrollable verbs. eg:

(1)a.他谢了顶，通常穿一件栗子色天鹅绒外衣。

[ta xie le ding,tongchang chuan yi jian li zi se tian'e rong wai yi]

(He has a bald head,and often wears a chestnut color velvet coat.)

---

[1]Hereinafter referred to as "frequency".
[2]Hereinafter referred to as "regular".

b..商品买卖关系中，消费者通常是弱者。

[*shang pin mai mai guan xi zhong,xiao fei zhe tong chang shi ruo zhe*]

(*In commodity business relationships, consumers generally is the weak.*)

(2)a.父亲担心他的伤，往往陪伴至深夜。[*fu qin dan xin ta de shang,wangwang pei ban zhi shen ye*]

(*He is always accompanied by his father into the middle of the nightis.*)

b.许多企业往往缺乏法制观念，造成诸多违法广告。

[*xu duo qi ye wangwang que fa fa zhi guan nian,zao cheng zhu duo wei fa guang gao*]

(*Many companies are generally lack of legal awareness, resulting in many illegal advertisements.*)

(3)a.她常常鼓励孩子要勇于实践。[*ta changchang gu li hai zi yao yong yu shi jian*]

(*She often encourages children to practice.*)

b.妇女和孩子常常成为被动吸烟受害者。

[*fu nx he hai zi changchang cheng wei bei dong xi yan shou hai zhe*]

(*Women and children are always the victims of passive smoking.*)

(4)a.每个人都应该这样经常问一问自己。(*mei ge ren dou ying gai zhe yang wen yi wen zi ji*)

(*Everyone should often asks himself like this way.*)

b.这种人像雕塑经常有一定的寓意。[*zhe zhong ren xiang diao su jingchang you yi ding de yu yi*]

(*This kind of portrait sculpture generally has implied meanings.*)

The verbs穿[*chuan*](*wear*), 陪伴[*pei ban*](*accompany*), 鼓励[*gu li*](*to encourage*) and 问[*wen*](*to ask*) in the above examples are controllable verbs indicating frequency, which are modified by "changchang", "jingchang", "tongchang", "wangwang"respectively[3]. The verbs是[*shi*](*to be*), 缺乏[*que fa*](*be lack of*), 成为[*cheng wei*](*become*) and有[*you*](*have*) are uncontrollable verbs, and they do not emphasize the frequency of a single behavior but the regular or universality under some conditions. In section2.3, we will explain in more details and describe more language facts.

2.2 Verification

We will validate from the following two perspectives: Perspective 1): It is widely believed that "changchang", "jingchang" are more inclined to mean frequency, and "tongchang", "wangwang" are more inclined to mean regular. So if the hypothesis is true, "changchang" and "jingchang" will share a high proportions of controllable verb/uncontrollable verb than "tongchang" and "wangwang". Rather than vise versa.

This article adapt 149 controllable verbs and 136 uncontrollable verbs from Ma Q (1988) *Controllable and uncontrollable verbs*. Based on BCC corpus[4], we got 19515 instances[5]. From table 1, we can see the distributed situation below correspond to perspective 1).

---

[3] The sentences including "changchang" and "wangwang" are ambiguous in different contexts. Here default modify verbs.

[4] BCC was developed by institute of big data and educational technology, Beijing Language and Culture University. It is a large-scale corpus, which contains weibo,science &technology,literature,the press,15 billion words in total.

Table 1. Collocation with controllable verbs and uncontrollable verbs

	controllable	uncontrollable	controlla-ble/uncontroll able	uncontrolla-ble/controllable
changchang	2480	2988	83.00%	120.48%
jingchang	2682	1452	184.71%	54.14%
tongchang	443	2568	17.25%	579.68%
wangwang	702	6200	11.32%	883.19%

Perspective 2): Among the frequency instances, the proportions collocate with controllable verbs should higher than the proportion collocate with uncontrollable verbs. Just contrary among the frequency instances.

We labeled the 19515 instances manually. From table 2, we can see the distribution. Through the data and proportions, we can see the results correspond well with the perspective 2). At this point, hypothesis one turns out to be correct.

We can approximately attain a semantic sequence. Frequency: "jingchang">"changchang">"wangwang">

"tongchang"; Regular: "tongchang">"wangwang">"changchang">"jingchang".

Table 2. Frequency/Regular with controllable/uncontrollable verbs

adverbs	semantic	total		controllable		uncontrollable	
		num	pct	num	pct	num	pct
changchang	frequency	2428	47.5%	2068	85%	360	15%
	regular	3040	52.5%	412	14%	2628	86%
jingchang	frequency	2756	54%	2584	94%	172	6%
	regular	1378	46%	98	7%	1280	93%
tongchang	frequency	62	5.3%	46	74%	16	26%
	regular	2949	94.7%	397	13%	2552	87%
wangwang	frequency	177	7.5%	97	55%	80	45%
	regular	6725	92.5%	605	9%	6120	91%

2.3   Description and Explanation

We have verified hypothesis one by corpus statistics and data analysis from the two perspectives above. Now adequate description, and explanation below.

(5)a.科研工作者常常有两愁：一愁没课题；二愁成果转化率低。

[*ke yan gong zuo zhe changchang you liang chou:yi chou mei ke ti;er chou chen guo zhuan hua di.*]

(*Researchers often have two kinds of troubles: the first is that they have no projects; the second is that the conversion rate of achievements is low.*)

b.他常常模仿邮票和纸币上人物的发型。

---

[5] We only searched the adverb usage of "tongchang"and "jingchang".

[*ta changchang mo fang you piao he zhi bi shang ren wu de fa xing*]

(*He often imitates the characters' hair styles on stamps and notes.*)

In the example (5) a,有[*you*](*have*) is a uncontrollable verb. The sentence means that it is an universal phenomenon among researchers, most researchers have the two troubles. It is a state of being, but not frequency of 有[*you*](*have*). (5) b模仿[*mo fang*](*to imitate*) is an controllable verb, 常常模仿[*changchang mo fang*](*often imitate*) means 模仿[*mo fang*](*to imitate*)many times。

(6)a.年轻男女在社会上经常受了磨练后会变得坚韧不拔。

[*nian qing nan nv zai she hui shang jing chang shou le mo lian hou hui bian de jian ren bu ba*]

(*The young will always become strong after they were educated in society.*)

b.太太喜欢他们姊妹们在一起经常打闹。[*tai tai xi huan ta men jie mei men zai yi qi jingchang da nao*]

(*The lady prefers the sisters often play together.*)

In the example (6) a, "jingchang" modifies the whole predicate section obviously, the sentence indicates that年轻男女会变得坚韧[*nian qing nan nv hui bian de jian ren*](*the young will be strong*) is universal. (6) b , "jingchang" modifies the single controllable verb打闹[*da nao*](*play*), and represents the frequency of打闹[*da nao*](*play*)。

(7)a.雷雨之后往往出现这样的春寒。[*chun lei zhi hou wangwang chu xian zhe yang de chun han*]

(*Cold spell in spring always appears after thunderstorms.*)

b.凡是母亲给哥哥的物件，弟弟往往想占为己有。

[*fan shi mu qin gei ge ge de wu jian,di di wang wang xiang zhan wei ji you*]

(*The little brother often wants to appropriate to himself what his mum sent for his older brother.*)

(7)a "wangwang"emphasizes the condition在雷雨之后[*zai lei yu zhi hou*](*after thunderstorms*), 出现这样的春寒[*chun xian zhe yang de chun han*](*Cold spell in spring always appears)* is the law of nature. b往往想[*wangwang xiang*](*often wants to*) conveys the times of想[*xiang*](*want*).

(8)a.被围困的萨拉热窝穆斯林通常是通过机场地下通道同外界来往的。

[*bei wei kun de sa la re wo mu si lin tongchang shi tong guo ji chang di xia tong dao tong wai jie lai wang de*]

(*Generally, the trapped Sarajevo Muslim kept in touch with the outside world through the underground passage at the airport.*)

b.她通常戴一副亮晶晶的耳环，据说是未婚夫送的。

[*ta tongchang dai yi fu liang jing jing de er huan,ju shuo shi wei hun fu song de.*]

(*She always wears a pair of sparkling earrings that his fiance proposed.*)

(8) a means that the way穆斯林[*mu si lin*](*the Muslim*)来往[*lai wang*](*kept in touch with*) is机场地下通道[*ji chang di xia tong dao*](*the underground passage at the airport*). It is the way that is emphasized. b.戴[*dai*](*wear*) is an controllable verb with strong action, modified by "tongcahng",which indicates the frequency.

Actually, another special controllable verbs can not achieve repetition and frequency. The following sentences can not established. For example:

(9)* 小 王 常 常 / 经 常 / 往 往 / 通 常 娶 小 李 。 [*xiao wang chang-chang/jingchang/wangwang/tongchang qu xiao li] (*Mr.Wang often marries Miss Li)

However, in certain contexts, similar verbs can be matched with the four adverbs. eg:

(10)现代男人多数早婚，而职业女性却常常/经常/往往/通常迟嫁。

[xian dai nan ren duo shu zao hun,er zhi ye nv xing que chang-chang/jingchang/wangwang/tongchang chi jia]

(In modern society, males get married in an early age, but professional females get married in an old age generally.)

The reasons of the above situation is complicated. Due to the length of the article, we won't explain in this paper. Based on the analysis, we can see that not only "tongchang" and "wangwang" hold the regular semantic, but also "changchang"and "jingchang" do. This is the problem ignored in the past research, and we also find the relations between the semantic features and the verbs.

3   Adjectives Collocations

3.1   Hypothesis and Verification

Inspired by the same semantic features between adjectives and uncontrollable verbs, we put forward **hypothesis two**: The four adverbs are more inclined to express regular when they modify adjectives,and they especially refer to some kinds of state.

As we all know, other adverbs is generally not modify adjectives expect for negative adverbs and degree adverbs. As a consequence, there aren't too many instances cases in the corpus. Table 3 includes the quantities and percents about collocations with adjectives. and the semantic features of frequency and regular respectively in this case.

Table 3. The distributions about collocations with adjectives

adverbs semantic	changchang		jingchang		tongchang		wangwang	
	num	pct	num	pct	num	pct	num	pct
Frequency	15	12%	18	41%	0	0%	4	0.9%
Regular	111	88%	26	59%	136	100%	427	99.1%

From table3, the frequency percents from high to low is 100%, 99.1%, 88%, 59%, higher than the regular percents, and then the data has verified **hypothesis two**.

3.2   Description and Explanation

There are two cases when the four adverbs modify adjective: 1)single adjective, 2)another adverb before, What's more, predicate-complement structures where adjective as the central word.[6] Except for "jingchang", 2) occupies the largest number and proportion, followed by the number of 1).

---

[6] No separate section as the quantity is less.

3.2.1 Single Adjective

(11)小女生姿态的哀兵政策对男人通常管用。

[*xiao nv sheng zi tai de ai bing zheng ce dui nan ren tong chang guan yong*]

(*Beautiful girls' underdog policy usually works on men.*)

饲养蛇的人，性格经常古怪。[*si yang she de ren,xing ge jing chang gu guai.*]

(*Snake people generally have an eccentric personality.*)

人生是坎坷的，好景往往短暂。[*ren sheng shi kan ke de,hao jing wang wang duan zan*]

(*The road of life is rocky, happiness is always transient.*)

诚实的人说话又常常乏味。[*cheng shi de ren shuo hua you chang chang fan wei*]

(*But an honest man's words is often boring.*)

(11)通常管用[*tongchang guan yong*](*usually works*) means that the policy works in an ordinary way, not works again and again. (12) Means that most养蛇人[*yang she ren*](*snake people*) have an eccentric personality, which is a common feature. (13)往往短暂[*wangwang duan zan*](*always transient*) refers to the experience summary of life. (14)常常乏味[*chang chang fan wei*] indicates a common phenomenon about the honest man's words.

In a word, all the examples above signify the universality or regular of certain states or attributes.

There is a part of emotion adjectives among all the adjectives, such as 激动 [*ji dong*](*excite*), 苦闷 [*ku men*](*depressed*), 头痛 [*tou tong*](*have a headache*), 难受 [*nan shou*](*uncomfortable*), 恐惧[*kong ju*](*scared*), 内疚[*nei jiu*](*guilty*),愤怒[*fen nu*](*angry*),失望[*shi wang*](*disappointed*),etc, which express feelings and affections.This type of adjective has characteristics of variability, thus they express frequency when modified by the four adverbs. eg:

(15)每每念及大哥的事，母亲经常失望，什么都不说。

[*mei mei nian ji da ge de shi,mu qi jingchang shi wang,shen me dou bu shuo*]

(*My mother was often disappointed when she thought of my brother, and said nothing.*)

(16)张信忠常常内疚，感到没有尽到做父亲的责任。

[*Zhang Xinzhong chang chang nei jiu,gandao mei you jin dao zuo fu qin de ze ren*]

(*Zhang Xinzhong often feels guilty because he failed to live up to a father's responsibility.*)

In (15) and (16) 失望[*shi wang*](*disappoint*) and 内疚 [*nei jiu*](*feel guilty*) are emotion adjectives, which can be controlled by the subjects 母亲 [*mu qin*](*the mother*)and 张信忠 *Zhang Xinzhong*.

In table3, all the 18 examples modified by "jingchang" are emotion adjectives. The quantity is higher than the other three words. This is why the percent of frequency is higher.

3.2.2 Another Adverb Before

"changchang"/"jingchang"/"wangwang"/"tongchang"+adverb+adjective, the adverbs in the middle are mainly degree adverbs and negative adverbs, such as"很"[*hen*](*very*),"特别"[*tebie*](*specially*), "比较"[*bi jiao*](*relatively*),"不"[*bu*](*not*),"过于"[*guo yu*](*too*),etc.例如：

(17)检索引擎不能对所有的信息进行分类和索引，而且检索结果常常过于庞大。

[*jian suo yin qing bu neng dui suo you de xin xi jin xing fen lei he suo yin,er qie jian suo jie guo chang chang guo yu pang da*]

(*Search engines can't categorize all of the information and indexes, and the results are often too enormous.*)

(18)孝忆国气候经常很温暖，冬天草木也不凋落。[*xiao yi guo qi hou jing chang hen wen nuan,dong tian cao mu ye bu diao luo*](*The weather in Xiao Yi is always very warm, the vegetation doesn't wither even in winter.*)

(19)领导市场经济靠命令往往不灵。

[*ling dao shi chang jing ji kao ming ling wangwang bu ling*]

(*The management of the market economy,is generally ineffective if rely on command.*)

(20)泥火山有两个特点，一是火山口通常比较浅，二是泥火山易受侵蚀。

[*ni huo shan you liang ge te dian,yi shi huo shan kou tong chang bi jiao qian, er shi ni huo shan yi shou qin shi*]

(*The mud volcanoes have two characters:one is that the crater is usually very shallow,another is that volcano is susceptible to erosion.*)

In (17),过于庞大[*guo yu pang da*](*too enormous*) is modified by "changchang", and refers to the common faults of the 检索引擎 [*jian suo yin qing*](*search engines*); (18) "jing chang" modifies 很温暖 [*hen wen nuan*](*very warm*) means the ordinary state of the natural environment in that place.

Similarly, (19), (20) "generally ineffective" and "usually very shallow" also refer to certain normal or an ordinary state. The examples above express the speakers' experience.

3.2.3 Adjective as the Central Word in Predicate-complement Structures

(21)土著地权对矿业开采和外资构成了障碍，赔偿金也常常高得令投资者望而却步。

[*tu zhu di quan dui kuang ye kai cai he wai zi gou cheng le zhang ai,pei chang jin ye chang chang gao de ling tou zi zhe wang er que bu*]

(*The aboriginal land rights have formed a barrier for mining exploitation and foreign investment,and the compensation is often too high for investors.*)

(22)女人的情绪反应往往强男人百倍；她们复原的时间也经常快些。

[*nv ren de qing xu fan ying wang wang qiang nan ren bai bei,ta men fu yuan de shi jian ye jing chang kuai xie*]

(*A woman's emotional response is often one hundred times stronger than a man's, and they restore much faster, too.*)

(23)实际下雪量比预报的往往大许多。[shi ji xia xue liang bi yu bao de wangwang da xu duo]

(*The actual amount of snow is often much larger than forecast.*)

(24)实际应用中，m与n相比，通常少得几乎可以忽略。

[*shi ji ying yong zhong,m yu n xiang bi tongchang shao de ji hu ke yi hu lue*]

(*In reality,compared with n, m is usually so less that almost can be ignored.*)

(21) "changchang" modifies the whole predicate-complement structure. "常常高得令投资者望而却步" [*changchang gao de ling tou zi zhe wang er que bu*](*often too high for investors*)refers to the speaker's summary of experiences. (22) "jingchang" modifies 快些

[*kuai xie*](*much faster*), explains that 女人复原的时间[*nv ren fu yuan de shi jian*](*the women's recovery time*) is shorter than the men's. (23), (24) "wangwang" and "tongchang" also modify the whole structure behind. 大许多[*da xu duo*] (*much larger*) means the actual amount of snow is much larger in general.

The examples above includes "tongchang" and "wangwang" can be replaced with "jingchang" and "changchang" without changing the meaning of sentence .

4 Conclusions

According to the article, apart from indicating frequency, "changchang" and "jing chang" can also be used to represent that actions or events occur, or states exist with regularity, and the sentence express people's experience summary as well as "wang wang" and "tongchang". The four adverbs tend to match the controllable when they refer to frequency, and match the uncontrollable verb when they refer to regular. They are more inclined to mean regular when they match adjectives. This paper applies the method of corpus linguistics, combines with the comparison methods of function words to verify with syntactic behaviors.

Based on the observation of a large number of data, and analysis of specific facts, try to avoid the subjectivity of the syntactic analysis and semantic analysis, we get a sequence of the two kinds of semantic features. Frequency:"jingchang">"changchang">"wangwang">"tongchang";Regular:"tongchang">"wangwang">"changchang">"jingchang".

In the process of the analysis of the corpus, we found that the reasons for the different semantic features are complex. We can find more syntactic rules and syntactic relationships, and will continue to in-depth study.

Acknowledgements. The study was supported by the Fundamental Research Funds for the Central Universities, and the Research Funds of Beijing Language and Culture University (No.15YCX101)

References

1. Shuxiang, L.: Eight hundred words in Modern Chinese (Revised and Enlarged). Commercial Press, Beijing (2013). (吕叔湘主编.现代汉语八百词(增订本).北京:商务印书馆. 2013). (in Chinese)
2. The Linguistics Institute of Chinese Academy of Social Sciences: The dictionary of Modern Chinese, 6th edn. Commercial Press, Beijing (2014). (中国社会科学院语言研究所.现代汉语词典(第6版).北京:商务印刷馆, 2014). (in Chinese)
3. Yuehua, L., et al.: Practical modern Chinese grammar. Commercial Press, Beijing (1983). (刘月华,等.实用现代汉语语法.北京:商务印书馆出版社, 1983). (in Chinese)
4. Xiaoqi, L.: Modern Chinese function words. Peking University Press, Beijing (2003). (李晓琪.现代汉语虚词手册.北京:北京大学出版社, 2003). (in Chinese)
5. Yisheng, Z.: Modern Chinese adverb research. Akademia Press, Shanghai (2004). (张谊生.现代汉语副词研究.上海:学林出版社, 2004). (in Chinese)
6. Yisheng, Zhang: Modern Chinese adverb analysis. Akademia Press, Shanghai (2000). (张谊生.现代汉语副词分析.上海:学林出版社, 2000). (in Chinese)

7. Xiaoqi, L.: Modern Chinese function words notes. Commercial Press, Beijing (2005). (李晓琪.现代汉语虚词讲义,北京:北京大学出版社, 2005). (in Chinese)

8. Haiqing, Z.: The function of the time adverbs in modern Chinese research. World Book Press, Beijing (2011). (邹海清.现代汉语时间副词的功能研究.北京:世界图书出版社, 2011). (in Chinese)

9. Haibo, R., et al.: Based on the corpus comparative study on the synonym function words in Modern Chinese. Akademia Press, Shanghai (2013). (任海波,等.基于语料库的现代汉语近义虚词对比研究.上海:学林出版, 2013). (in Chinese)

10. Dexi, Z.: Grammar notes. Commercial Press, Beijing (2011). (朱德熙,语法讲义.北京:商务印书馆, 2011). (in Chinese)

11. Jianming, L., Zhen, M.: The theory of modern Chinese function words. Language Press, Beijing (1999). (陆俭明,马真.现代汉语虚词散论.北京:语文出版社. 1999). (in Chinese)

12. Jianming, L.: Modern Chinese grammar research tutoria. Peking University Press, Beijing (2005). (陆俭明.现代汉语语法研究教程.北京:北京大学出版社, 2005.) (in Chinese)

13. Jianming, L.: Modern Chinese adverbs individual usage. Language Teaching and Linguistic Studies (1982). (陆俭明 现代汉语副词独用刍议.语言教学研究. 1982). (in Chinese)

14. Jianming, L.: The modern Chinese temporal words. Language Teaching and Linguistic Studies (1991). (陆俭明.现代汉语时间词说略.语言教学与研究. 1991). (in Chinese)

15. Xiaobing, Z.: The classification and usage rules of frequency adverbs. Journal of East China Normal University (1999). (周小兵.频度副词的划类与使用规则.华东师范大学学报, 1999). (in Chinese)

16. Zhou Xiaobing "chang" and"tongchang". Chinese Language Learning (1994). (周小兵."常常"和"通常".汉语学习, 1994). (in Chinese)

17. Jiaxuan, S.: Semantic uncertainty and Indivisible Polysemous Sentences. Studies of The Chinese Language (1991). (沈家煊.语义的不确定性和不可分化的多义句.中国语文, 1991). (in Chinese)

18. JinSheng, S.: Semantic function research of modern Chinese adverbs. Doctoral thesis, Nankai University (2002). (史金生.现代汉语副词的语义功能研究,南开大学博士论文, 2002). (in Chinese)

19. Jingshang, S., Xiaoping, H.: Category of Momentum adverb and its selectivity. Linguistic Research (2001). (史金生,胡晓萍.动量副词的类别及其选择性.语文研究, 2004). (in Chinese)

20. Mingyang, H.: Single contrast analysis-attempt to develop a kind of function words semantic analysis. Studies of The Chinese Language (2000). (胡明扬.单项对比分析法—制定一种虚词语义分析法的尝试.中国语文) 2000. (in Chinese)

21. Qingzhu, M.: Controllable verb and uncontrollable verb. Journal of Chinese Linguistics (1988). (马庆株.自主动词和非自主动词,中国语言学报, 1988). (in Chinese)

22. Chunli, Z.: The co-occurrence rules between emotion adjectives and nouns. Studies of The Chinese Language (2007). (赵春利.情感形容词与名词同现的原则.中国语文, 2007). (in Chinese)

23. Guoxian, Z.: The dynamic adjectives in modern Chinese. Studies of The Chinese Language (1995). (张国宪.现代汉语的动态形容词,中国语文, 1995). (in Chinese)

24. Guoxian, Z.: Typical characteristics of modern Chinese adjectives. Studies of The Chinese Language (2000). (张国宪.现代汉语形容词的典型特征,中国语文, 2000). (in Chinese)

25. Jun, W.: A comparative study of "changchang" and "tongchang". Master Thesis, HeNan University (2011). (王 俊."常常"和"通常"的比较研究.河南大学,硕士论文, 2011). (in Chinese)

26. Haiqing, Z.: The modern Chinese frequency adverbs. Master Thesis, Shanghai Normal University (2005). (邹海清.现代汉语频率副词研究.上海师范大学,硕士论文, 2005). (in Chinese)
27. Haiqing, Z.: The scope and categories of frequency adverbs. Chinese Teaching in the World (2006). (邹海清.频率副词的范围和类别.世界汉语教学, 2006). (in Chinese)
28. Yupei, W.: A comparative study of frequency adverbs "changchang" and "wangwang" in modern Chinese. Master Thesis, JiLin University (2007). (王宇培.现代汉语表频时间副词"常常"与"往往"的比较研究.吉林大学,硕士论文, 2007). (in Chinese)
29. Shujuan, D.: The study of frequency adverbs in modern Chinese. Master Thesis, Yanbian University. (丁淑娟.现代汉语频率副词研究.延边大学.硕士论文, 2004). (in Chinese)
30. Chunxiang, W., et al.: The modern Chinese frequency adverbs of hierarchy and semantic research. Chinese Language Learning (2005). (吴春相,等.现代汉语频率副词的层级和语义研究.汉语学习, 2005). (in Chinese)
31. Xiqiang, X., et al.: Modern Chinese adverb research summary. Journal of Yunnan Normal University (2006). (肖奚强,等.现代汉语副词研究综述.云南师范大学报, 2006). (in Chinese)
32. Yang, Z.: Highlight differences between "tongchang" and "changchang". Chinese Language Learning (2013). (杨智渤."通常"与"常常"的凸显差异.汉语学习, 2013). (in Chinese)
33. Pai, P., et al.: "meimei" and "wangwang", "changchang". Journal of Chengdu University (彭湃,等."每每"与"往往"、"常常".成都大学学报, 2004). (in Chinese)
34. Yongming, S.: The semantic and grammatical features of "changchang" and "wangwang". Journal of Zhe Jian Normal University (2002). (寿永明."常常"与"往往"的语义语法特征.浙江师范学报, 2002). (in Chinese)

A Semantic Study of Modal Words in Mandarin Chinese

Jianshe Zhou[1,2(✉)], Narentuya[1], and Jinsheng Shi[1]

[1] School of Literature, Capital Normal University, Beijing 100089, China
nrty0607@hotmail.com, shijsh@aliyun.com
[2] Jiangsu Normal University, Capital Normal University, Xuzhou 221116, China
zhoujs@mail.cnu.edu.cn

Abstract. Generating Chinese sentences require three kinds of words, including object words (lexical item), attribute words and relational words. Modal words (modal auxiliaries) are nature words which express a speaker's attitude. They help to generate modal sentences and express modal meanings. In terms of modal meanings, modal words can be divided into three categories, expressing necessity, expectation, and disjunction respectively. Different types of modal words can be discovered by data mining and their semantic strength can be calculated. In the use of modal words the relationship between speaker's identity and power should be considered.

Keywords: Sentence generation · Modal words · Semantic analysis · Modal intensity

1 Introduction

Classification of parts of speech has been a hot spot in the field of modern Chinese grammar. Due to different criteria for classification, many different word classes have been proposed. The syntactic analysis of parts of speech is usually based on the grammatical function of words, with the categories identified ranging from 11 to 15. Computational linguists focus on the criteria of grammatical function and meaning combination in their classification of Chinese parts of speech, and their differences are usually larger. According to "Dictionary of Modern Chinese Grammar" (1998), used for natural language processing, words in Chinese are divided into 25 classes. This classification is intended to facilitate the calculation and recognition of chunks as a holistic unit of grammar.[1]

The existing approaches to classification, whether based on the grammatical function or based on the identification of the language chunks, fail to consider the issue from the perspective of sentence generation. With the development of information technology, intelligent machine intelligence has gradually taken the place of people; and one of its tasks is to simulate the human brain's generation of sentences in writing. So, it is necessary to match the classification of words in Chinese to the needs of machines. This paper will explore the mechanisms of sentence generation in Chinese

---

[1] Yu, Shiwen, Zhui Zhifang, and Zhu Xuefeng. A Discussion of Comprehensive Linguistic Knowledge Databases and Their Prospects. *Journal of Chinese Information Processing,* 2011 (6).

© Springer International Publishing Switzerland 2015
Q. Lu and H.H. Gao (Eds.): CLSW 2015, LNAI 9332, pp. 160–172, 2015.
DOI: 10.1007/978-3-319-27194-1_17

grammar, using modal words as an example. We will focus on their semantic features and semantic types.

2   The Generative Nature of Modal Verbs

With regard to the semantics of sentences containing modal words, there are two levels. On one level there is an objective description of state of affairs in the world; on the other there is an expression of emotions and attitudes conveyed by modal words. Look at the example "张三去海淀图书城购买图书" (*Zhang San goes to Haidian Bookstore to buy some books*). This sentence, called the original sentence, is a statement of a situation, which can be called the original situation. It merely describes a state of affairs. However, if we embed the word "必须 [*bixu*] (*must*)" in the original sentence, we will generate "张三必须去海淀图书城购买图书" (*Zhang San must go to Haidian Bookstore to buy some books*). This is an expression that conveys a certain attitude toward the original situation. There are two levels involved in the semantic description of the sentence. On the first level, we have an objective description of the original situation, and on the sentence level, we have an expression of modality.[2] Suppose the original situation is A, then the modal statement is "A是必须的" (*A is a must*). Modal words do not describe objects, but conveys the emotions and attitudes of human beings. Therefore, they belong to the category of attribute words.

The nature of modality can be explored from three points of view. First, look at the basic meaning of modal words. This point used to be neglected in previous studies of Chinese grammar. Most grammarians have not made an in-depth study of them, often including them in the category of *volitional verbs* (能愿动词) such as "能够、会、要、肯、敢、愿意、应该、可以 (*be able, will do something, want to, want to, dare to, be willing to, should, be able*)", referred to as auxiliary verbs. This paper argues that modal words are those that express certain emotions and attitudes toward a particular situation. Modal words in Chinese include "务必、必须、必需、必要、要、须得、得、不得不、不能不、不可不、应当、应该、理当、理应、最好、是否、可否、不妨、可以 (*essential, necessary, should, must, must, have to, cannot, cannot, shall, should, must, ought to, had better, if can, can, can*)" etc...[3]

Secondly, we will look at how modal words are involved in the generation of modal sentences. The generative nature of modal verbs is reflected in two aspects. The first aspect is that a modal statement is constructed on the basis of an original sentence, and the second aspect is that additional meanings are created on a higher level. Look at the following examples.

---

[2] Lü (1979) argues that verbs like能、会、必须[*neng, hui, and bixu*]are higher-level predicates in a sentence, and they can transformed into pre-positioned predicates.

[3] There are different understandings of modality in linguistics. For instance, Lyons(1977) considers modality to be the speaker's opinions or attitudes toward a proposition expressed in a sentence or a situation described by a sentence, including truth-value modality, epistemic modality, and deontic modality. Palmer (1986/2001) argues that modality is the manifestation of a speaker's attitudes and opinions in grammar, including epistemic modality, deontic modality and dynamic modality. This paper will discuss deontic modality.

(1) 国家大剧院的房顶是椭圆形的。
Guojiadajuyuan de fangding shi yuanxing de.
The roof of the National Theatre is round in shape.
(2) 国家大剧院的房顶应当是椭圆形的。
Guojiadajuyuan de fangding yingdang shi tuoyuan xing de.
The roof of the National Theatre should be round in shape.

Example (1) is the original statement, and Example (2) is a modal statement. The former is a basic semantic description of the situation, while the latter has a modal orientation, with two different levels of understanding.

Third, modal sentences are not relevant to the truth-value of a statement. The truth-value depends on the basis meaning of an original sentence and reflects the actual situation. Hearers make their own judgment as to whether a statement is true or false. By contrast, a modal statement merely reflects the attitude of a speaker toward a situation, not whether the situation described conforms to the actual situation. Therefore, it has no direct effect on the truth-value of a statement.

(3) 国家大剧院的房顶是方形的。（假）
Guojiadajuyuan de fangding shi fangxing de. (jia)
The roof of the National Theatre is square in shape. (false)
(4) 国家大剧院的房顶是椭圆形的。（真）
Guojiadajuyuan de fangding shi tuoyuan xing de. (zhen)
The roof of the National Theatre is oval in shape. (true)

Example (3) and Example (4) are two statements that do not express the attitude of the speaker. It is concerned with objective knowledge, the truth-value is obvious. However, the following statements are different.

(3a) 国家大剧院的房顶应当是方形的。（假）
Guojiadajuyuan de fangding yingdang shi fangxing de. (jia)
The roof of the National Theatre should be square in shape. (false)
(4a) 国家大剧院的房顶应当是椭圆形的（真）
Guojiadajuyuan de fangding yingdang shi tuoyuan xing de. (zhen)
The roof of the National Theatre should be oval in shape. (true)

Modal statements mainly function to express the speaker's subjective attitude, so their truth value is not important. Example (3a) can be understood either in a deontic sense or in an epistemic sense. In the former case, it means that the National theatre should have been square in shape but is now round. In the latter case, it means that the speaker believes that the National Theatre is probably round in shape.

3   Semantic Analysis of Modal Verbs

In terms of semantic strength, modal words in Chinese are divided into three categories, expressing necessity, expectancy, and option respectively.

(I) Modality of Necessity
Verbs expressing modality of necessity include "务必、必须、必需、必要、要、须得、得 [*wubi, bixu, bixu, biyao, yao, xudei, dei*] (*must*)" and phrases like "不得不、

不能不、不可不、非……不可 [*budebu, bunengbu,bukebu, fei……buke*] (*cannot*)". "必须 [*bixu*] (*must*)", according to "Modern Chinese Dictionary", means "*reasonable and necessary; must be*" or "*to strengthen the tone of the command*". They express a variety of modality of necessity.

First, they can convey a speaker's strong commitment to his statement that certain necessary conditions must be fulfilled before a particular state of affairs comes into being. However, these conditions are governed by objective circumstances instead of the speaker's own judgment. For instance:

(5) 电脑必须有电才能用。

Diannao bixu you dian caineng yong .

Computers can only be operated with electricity.

(6) 汽车通行必须有等于或宽于汽车宽度的道路。

Qiche tongxing bixu you dengyu huo kuan yu qiche kuandu de daolu.

A vehicle can only run on a road that is as wide as or wider than itself.

(7) 春采者必须长梯高机，数人一树，还条复枝，务令净尽。

Chuncai zhe bixu changti gao ji,shu ren yi shu,huan tiao fu zhi,wu ling jing jin.

Those who pick leaves in spring must climb up a ladder, with several people working on one tree.

Example (5) indicates the condition for a particular state of affairs. When one condition becomes a necessary condition for an event to happen, the obligation indicated in "必须 [*bixu*] (*must*)" is decided by objective factors. The verb "必须 [*bixu*] (*must*)" is used for emphasis. That is to say, the subjective element of a speaker is not so strong in this case. In Example (6), "必须 [*bixu*] (*must*)" expresses an attitude toward necessary conditions. That is to say, one condition is the car's running, and the other condition is the width of the road. When the car is running, if the road width is less than the width of the car, the car cannot pass. The modal verb "必须 [*bixu*] (*must*)" is the expression of the speaker's commitment to his knowledge that the necessary condition (road width), otherwise, there would not be such a situation of a car running on the road.

Second, modal verbs of necessity can express the speaker's strong belief that certain conditions should obtain before a particular state of affairs come into being. In this case, there is a sense of obligation involved, but unlike the emphasis in normal situations. For instance:

(8) 将军所仗，必须良材。

Jiangjun suo zhang,bixu liang cai.

You, as a general, must depend on some talented people to help you.

(9) 必须大刀阔斧进行改革。

Bixu dadaokuofu jinxing gaige.

Drastic reform must be carried out.

(10)张同学必须跟李院士到科技部取资料。

Zhangtongxue bixu gen Liyuanshi dao kejibu qu ziliao.

Student Zhang must, together with Professor Li, go to the Department of Science and Technology to take back the documents.

This kind of sentence and the first class are different in terms of their strength. The first class reflects an objective link between two events, not subject to the will of the speaker. The modal verb merely serves to emphasize the link and to remind hearers to note the link. In the situation described by Example (6), a car's passage depends on the width of the road. The force implied in the sentence does not come from the modal verb, not reflecting the will of the speaker. Rather, the force comes from objective factors involved. However, in Example (10) "必须 [*bixu*] (*must*)" expresses a strong attitude on the part of the speaker, somewhat like an order that a particular state of affairs must obtain.

Analysis shows that the modal characteristics of "必须 [*bixu*] (*must*)" is nothing more than two aspects. One indicates a purely objective situation, emphasizing the connections between two things and reminding the hearer of the role of objective conditions. In this case, "必须 [*bixu*] (*must*)" has an effect on the subject of the sentence. The other aspect indicates that the speaker believes in the role of human beings in a certain situation people, making it clear that he expects the subject of the clause to take certain action. .

Like "必须 [*bixu*] (*must*)", "务必 [*wubi*] (*has to; must*)" is also strong modal level. According to Modern Chinese Dictionary, 务必 [*wubi*] (*has to; must*) means the same as "必须 [*bixu*] (*must*)" and "一定要 [*yidingyao*] (*has to; must*)". However, it is different from "必须 [*bixu*] (*must*)" in that it has a slightly stronger force.

(11) 务必在明天十点前提交。
   Wubi zai mingtian shidian qian tijiao.
   It must be submitted before ten tomorrow.

(12) 汝等诸官，各受重爵，务必赤心报国，休得怠慢。
   Rudeng zhu guan,ge shou zhong jue,wubi chixin baoguo,xiude daiman.
   You, as high-ranking officials, must be loyal to the nation and work hard.

(13) 务必继续保持谦虚、谨慎、不骄、不躁的作风，务必继续保持艰苦奋斗的作风。
   Wubi jixu baochi qianxu,jinshen,bujiao,buzao de zuofeng,wubi jixu baochi jiankufendou de zuofeng.
   We must continue to be modest, prudent while avoiding pretension and impatience.

"务必 [*wubi*] (*has to; must*)" does not emphasize the connection between two objective things, but stresses that the situation of human action should be in accordance with the wishes of the people.

"必要 [*biyao*]", according to *Modern Chinese Dictionary*, means "*indispensable; be necessary*". "必要 [*biyao*] (*be necessary*)" although containing modality, stresses that the speaker believes that an important condition should be present before a particular state of affairs comes into being. Syntactically, "必要 [*biyao*] (*be necessary*)" is often used as a predicate, indicating an affirmative judgment of a situation.

(14) 春节慰问老教授是必要的。
   Chunjie weiwen lao jiaoshou shi biyao de.
   Visiting those retired professors during the Spring Festival is necessary.

（15） 出门前断电是必要的。

　　　Chumen qian duan dian shi biyao de.

　　　Cutting off electricity before going out is necessary.

（16） 半年体检一次还是必要的。

　　　Bannian tijian yici haishi biyao de.

　　　Having a medical examination every six months is necessary.

The three sentences listed above has two layers of semantic content, one concerning a particular state of affairs and the other concerning the speaker's attitude, namely, it is necessary to do to achieve the state of affairs mentioned before.

If "必要 [biyao] (*be necessary*)" is replaced by "必须 [bixu] (*must*)" in a sentence, its modal force becomes stronger, with the necessity of a particular condition weakened. Look at the following example.

（14a） 春节慰问老教授是必须的。

　　　Chunjie weiwen lao jiaoshou shi bixu de.

　　　Visiting retired professors during the Spring Festival is a must.

（15a） 出门前断电是必须的。

　　　Chumen qian duan dian shi bixu de.

　　　Turning off electricity before going out is a must.

（16a） 半年体检一次还是必须的。

　　　Bannian tijian yici haishi bixu de.

　　　Having a medical examination every six months is a must.

Syntactically, "必要 [biyao] (*be necessary*)" and "必须 [bixu] (*must*)" is different. "必要[biyao] (*be necessary*)" can be used with "有 [you] (*have*)", such as "有必要 [you biyao]", while "必须 [bixu] (*must*)" cannot be used with "有 [you] (*have*)". Therefore, "有必须 [you bixu]" is not acceptable. Besides, "必须 [bixu] (*must*)" directly modifies a predicate verb, while "必要[biyao] (*be necessary*)" does not modify a predicate verb. For example, "张三必要去上海" (*Zhang San going to Shanghai is necessary*) is not acceptable. If the same meaning is expressed with constructions containing "必要 [biyao] (*be necessary*)", the expression should be "张三有必要去上海" (*Zhang San must go to Shanghai*).

According to Modern Chinese Dictionary, "必需 [bixu] (*must*)" is different from "必须 [bixu] (*must*)". The former is interpreted as "*something must be present*". It contains modal elements, also emphasizing a particular state of affairs.

（17） 酿酒用酵母是必需的。

　　　Niangjiu yong jiaomu shi bixu de.

　　　Brewing wine requires an enzyme.

（18） 第一手资料是必需的。

　　　Diyishou ziliao shi bixu de.

　　　First-hand material is indispensable.

（19） 煤铁等是发展工业所必需的原料。

　　　Meitan deng shi fazhan gongye suo bixu de yuanliao.

　　　Coal and iron are raw materials indispensable to the development of industry.

"必需 [*bixu*] (must)" is different from "必要 [*biyao*] (*be necessary*)" in that it focuses on need or necessity. Syntactically, like "必要 [*biyao*] (*be necessary*)", it can serve as a predicate, such as "**酿酒用酵母是必需的。**" (*Enzyme is necessary for brewing wine*). However, it does not be used with "有 [*you*] (*have*)". That is to say, "有必需 (*you bixu*)" is not acceptable.

"要 [*yao*]" is richer in meaning. It can mean the same as "必须 [*bixu*] (*must*)", such as: "养花要浇水。" (*Watering is necessary for growing flowers*). It can also mean the same as "必要[*biyao*] (*be necessary*)", such as: "上课要认真听讲。"(*Being attentive in class is necessary*). Besides, it can mean "必需 [*bixu*] (must)", such as: "开车要携带驾驶证。"(*Having one's driving license while driving is necessary*).

In addition, "不得不 [*budebu*] (*must*)" and "非……不可 [*fei……buke*] (*must*)" can express the same modality as "必须 [*bixu*] (*must*)". "不得不 [*budebu*]" emphasizes the fact that a particular choice is imposed on the party concerned, such as "门槛太低，不得不低头走进去。" (*He had to lower his head when entering the room as the doorframe is not tall*). And "非……不可[*fei……buke*]" indicates an essential condition, such as: "还有这么长的路程，我们非走夜路不可。" (*There is still such a long way to go, so we have no other choice but to continue our journey in the night*).

In summary, understanding of "*must*" modality depends on the original statement of the objective conditions. When the original statement reflects the relationship between two objective conditions of the situation, "必须 [*bixu*] (*must*)" indicates less mandatory or compulsory force on the part of the speaker, with the subjective color relatively weak. However, when the original statement describes human activities or events, people use "必须 [*bixu*] (*must*)" to express a strong subjective will, with the expectation that the agents concerned should facilitate the occurrence of a particular outcome.

(II) Modality of Expectation

Verbs that express modality of expectation, or "*should be*", include "应当、应该、理当、理应 [*yingdang, yinggai, lidang, liying*] (*should, should, must, ought to be*)". They reflect a speaker's expectation that a particular situation should occur. Inferential discourse to engage in activities.

(20) 学生应当多去图书馆、体育馆。
    Xuesheng yingdang duo qu tushuguan,tiyuguan.
    Students should often go the library and the gymnasium.
(21) 这项软件开发项目应当由工程院院士主持。
    Zhe xiang ruanjian kaifa xiangmu yingdang you gongchengyuan yuanshi zhuchi.
    The development of this software should be under the charge of the Chinese Academy of Engineering.
(22) 大年期间，若初次见到百岁老人，应当行个礼。
    Danian qijian,ruo chuci jiandao baisui laoren,yingdang xinggeli.

    During the period of the Chinese New Year, one should salute if one meets a one-hundred-year-old person.

Verbs expressing modality of expectation reflects the attitude of a speaker toward the situation described. Therefore, they have the following three characteristics. First, it is a statement of events. Secondly, the speaker expresses a particular attitude towards this statement. Thirdly, the modality of discourse situation means expectation or speculation. The speaker makes clear his expectation that an event should proceed in a particular direction. However, this expectation is not mandatory, with a much weaker force than that expressed by "必须 [*bixu*] (*must*)".

For verbs expressing modality of expectation, it is not easy to determine the truth conditions concerned. They merely indicate the attitude of a speaker. For instance, statement (21) means that it is reasonable for the Chinese Academy of Engineering to be in charge of software development. If such an event does not occur, it is not reasonable. However, we cannot say it is true or false. In other words, whether the academic is actually in charge of software development is not relevant.

An important difference between modality of expectation and modality of necessity is that the former indicates the speaker hopes that a particular situation will occur, as if bound by a particular moral obligation. An interesting verb of expectation is "理当 [*lidang*] (*should; ought to*)", similar to "应当 [*yingdang*] (*should; ought to*)". And the latter can be replaced by the former in discourse, emphasizing that someone has the duty or responsibility to do something. Statements containing "理当 [*lidang*] (*should; ought to*)" can be used either before or after a certain situation occurs, expressing retrospective inferences or prospective inferences. Look at the following examples.

(20a) 学生理当多去图书馆、体育馆。
   Xuesheng ligdang duo qu tushuguan,tiyuguan.
   Students have the duty to go to the library and the gymnasium frequently.
(21a) 这项软件开发项目理当由工程院院士主持。
   Zhe xiang ruanjian kaifa xiangmu lidang you gongchengyuan yuanshi zhuchi.
   It is reasonable for the Chinese Academy of Engineering to be in charge of the development of this software.
(22a) 大年期间，若初次见到百岁老人，理当行个礼。
   Danian qijian,ruo chuci jiandao baisui laoren,lidang xinggeli.
   During the period of the Chinese New Year, one has the duty to salute if one meets a one-hundred-year-old person.

The three sentences are not true or false. For example, in the situation described by (22a), the speaker merely expresses his attitude and expectation. So whether one actually salutes to the elderly people is not relevant to the truth-value of the statement.

"可以 [*keyi*] (*may*)" is similar to "应当 [*yingdang*] (*should; ought to*)" in meaning, but with a weaker force. It merely reflects a suggestion or advice given by the speaker. For instance:

(20b) 学生可以多去图书馆、体育馆。
   Xuesheng keyi duo qu tushuguan,tiyuguan.
   Students may go to the library or gymnasium.

(21b) 这项软件开发项目可以由工程院院士主持。

    Zhe xiang ruanjian kaifa xiangmu keyi you gongchengyuan yuanshi zhuchi.

The development of this software may be under the charge of the Chinese Academy of Engineering.

(22b) 大年期间，若初次见到百岁老人，可以行个礼。

    Danian qijian,ruo chuci jiandao baisui laoren,keyi xinggeli.

During the period of the Chinese New Year, one may salute if one meets a one-hundred-year-old person.

The speaker does not have a strong expectation that his advice is accepted by the parties concerned. Example (22b) means that one may salute to express one's respect if one meets a one-hundred-year-old person. It is a mandatory requirement.[①4]

In addition, "可以 [keyi] (may)" indicates that what the speaker suggests is only one way to solve the problem, not ruling out other choices that are open the parties concerned. The following examples are a case in point.

(23) 累了可以睡个觉。

    Lei le keyi shuigejiao.

You may go to bed if you are tied.

(24) 累了可以睡个觉。

    You shiqing keyi gei ta da dianhua.

You may call him if you have a problem.

(25) 为提高汉语水平可以读一些中文报纸。

    Wei tigao hanyu shuiping keyi du yixie zhongwen baozhi.

You may read some Chinese newspapers if you want to improve your Chinese.

In the above examples the speakers do not mean that his advice or suggestion is the only way to solve a problem, or that there are no other solutions available.

(III) Modality of Disjunction

Verbs expressing modality of disjunction include simple constructions like "最好 [zuihao] (better to; best to)", "可否 [kefou] (is it possible or not?)" and "不妨 [bufang] (might as well)" and more complex construction like "是否 [shifou] (whether; shall)" and "是不是 [shibushi] (whether or not)" etc. Statements containing these verbs normally introduce one choice open to the parties concerned, while omitting all alternatives. For instance:

(20c) 学生最好多去图书馆、体育馆。

    Xuesheng zuihao duo qu tushuguan,tiyuguan.

Students had better go to the library and the gymnasium.

---

4 In actual language use there are circumstances where a weaker expression like许可"xuke" (permission; be allowed) is used to convey the message that the hearer should or must take a certain course of action. For instance, we may say "你可以走了" (You may go), implying that the speaker orders the hearer to go. This shift in meaning is a result of the working of the Politeness Principle, the Cooperative Principle (the Quantity Maxim), and pragmatic inferencing (abduction).

(21c) 这项软件开发项目最好由工程院院士主持。

Zhe xiang ruanjian kaifa xiangmu zuihao you gongchengyuan yuanshi zhuchi.

The developement of this software had best be left under the charge of the Chinese Academy of Engineering.

(22c) 大年期间，若初次见到百岁老人，最好行个礼。

Danian qijian,ruo chuci jiandao baisui laoren,zuihao xinggeli.

During the period of the Chinese New Year, one had better salute if one meets a one-hundred-year-old person.

These examples clearly show the attitude of the speaker. For example, in (21c) the Chinese Academy of Engineering is considered the most suitable of all the possible candidates to be responsible for the software development.

The verb "最好 [*zuihao*] (*better to; best to*)", according to Modern Chinese Dictionary, means "*the most appropriate*", used by a speaker in the face of a variety of factors in the choice of discourse modality. It indicates an evaluation on the higher level of conceptual organization.

In terms of modal strength, "最好 [*zuihao*] (*better to; best to*)" is not as strong as "必须 [*bixu*] (*must*)". It is also different from "应当 [*yingdang*] (*should; ought to*)" in that the latter indicates that a particular course of action is reasonable and expected. "最好 [*zuihao*] (*better to; best to*)" indicates that the speaker does not object to many other possible courses of action, but implies that the hearer should choose what the speaker considers the best course of action. However, since the speaker merely offers an option, "最好 [*zuihao*] (*better to; best to*)" implies a respect for the hearer or the natural path of development of an event, but without imposing anything mandatory on the hearer.

"是否 [*shifou*] (*whether; shall*)" is gentler than "最好 [*zuihao*] (*better to; best to*)". The former contains two components of modality semantics: One indicating a disjunction, and the other leaving enough room for people to negotiate. Its magnitude of the euphemism was significantly greater than "最好 [*zuihao*] (*better to; best to*)".

(26) 资料是否打印出来？

Ziliao shifou dayin chulai?

Shall we have the material printed?

(27) 是否先打个电话确认一下？

Shifou xian dagedianhua queren yixia?

Shall we make a phone call to see whether it is the case or not?

(28) 会议开始前，是否让秘书列个议程？

Huiyi kaishi qian shifou rang mishu lie ge yicheng?

Shall we set the agenda before the meeting begins?

In Example (28), the speaker's intention is to make a general meeting agenda, but he does not use "最好 [*zuihao*] (*better to; best to*)", but uses "是否 [*shifou*] (*whether; shall*)" to solicit the hearer's opinion. The implied meaning is that the speaker takes a positive attitude toward the suggestion.

"可否 [*kefou*] (is it possible or not?)" is the same as "是否 [*shifou*] (*whether; shall*)" in its basic meaning, but is slightly different in style. The latter is more informal, and the former more formal and elegant.

To sum up, "最好 [*zuihao*] (*better to; best to*)" refers to the speaker's expectation of an event to occur, as he believes that a particular event is the best course of action available. The course of action may be a particular good thing or a good outcome of a bad thing, both involving the emotion and attitude of the speaker. Verbs expressing modality of disjunction all indicate an obvious expectation or negotiability. Precisely because of negotiability, "可否 [*kefou*] (is it possible or not?)", "是否 [*shifou*] (*whether; shall*)" and "是不是 [*shibushi*] (*whether or not*)" can all occur and are interchangeable in most cases.

"最好 [*zuihao*] (*better to; best to*)" and "不妨 [*bufang*] (*might as well*)" indicates a shift from evaluation to suggestion, requesting the hearer to engage in a particular course of action. By contrast, "可否 [*kefou*] (is it possible or not?)" and "是不是 [*shibushi*] (*whether or not*)" indicates a shift from choice to will, expressing the speaker's own wish that a particular state of affairs should occur. Since "最好 [*zuihao*] (*better to; best to*)" and "不妨 [*bufang*] (*might as well*)" expresses an evaluation, their modal force is stronger than that of "可否 [*kefou*] (is it possible or not?)" and "是不是 [*shibushi*] (*whether or not*)".

4   Calculation of Strength of Modal Verbs

The semantic strength of modal verbs can be calculated by data-mining of Chinese corpora, (Realistic calculation will be discussed in another paper). Here we will offer a preliminary understanding of the issue in terms of their basic strength and the emotional influence of the identity or social status of the speaker.

First, in terms of basic semantic strength, there are considerable differences among different modal verbs in Chinese. For example, roughly speaking, there is a scale ranging from "务必 [*wubi*] (*has to; must*)", "必须 [*bixu*] (must)", "应当 [*yingdang*] (*should; ought to*)", to "可以 [*keyi*] (may)" in a declining order.

The strength of modality can also be seen through levels of combination. If a clause containing a modal verb is considered a modal structure, this structure can contain smaller modal structures, and the latter can in its turn contain even smaller modal structures, as shown in the following table:

Agree with this thing──→ have to agree with this thing──→must agree with this.

The modal strength of smaller modal structures is generally weak, while the strength of larger structures is strong.[5]

Second, in terms of the identity and social status of speakers, sentences containing modal verbs also show differences in modal force. There are three cases divided according to the relations between the strength of the modal verb and the identity of the speaker, including equivalence, overstatement, and understatement.

---

[5] When several modal verbs are used together, the sequence of "subjective > objective" should be followed. If modal elements of the same type occur together, the sequence of "strong > weak" is normally followed, and the mechanism involved remains to explored.

Equivalence refers to the fact that the strength of a modal verb matches the status of the speaker. The speaker merely expresses his own evaluation of the situation and chooses the appropriate modal verb that conforms to the situation concerned. That is to say, different verbs of necessity, expectation, or disjunction are selected according to the actual situation. For example: "今天讲课最好要一个同志来帮忙做个记录" (*There ought to be someone taking notes in this lecture today*). This statement indicates equality, and leaves room for negotiation.

There are also cases of mismatch between the strength of modality and the status of the speaker. For instance, a person of relatively lower status and power, with weaker modal force, often uses stronger modal verbs. This may be called an overstatement. By contrast, a person of relatively higher status and power, with stronger modal force, often uses weaker modal verbs. This may be called an understatement. The reason why the two cases mentioned above occur is that pragmatic presuppositions are at work in communication as a result of the status and power of the parties concerned. Power itself carries an influence in communication, and this is the background information shared by communicators. And this has an important influence on the speaker and the hearer.

Take the following case for example. The president and a department manager in a company may use different modal verbs when assigning an employee to take a certain course of action. The manager, not sure whether the employee will obey his order, will probably use the sentence: "你必须在10月份底完成这项任务!" (*You must finish the job by the end of October.*) By contrast, the president may use the statement "你应当在10月份完成这项任务!" (*You should complete the task in October*). The modal force of the first statement and that of the second is different, though there may not be a difference in their effect on the hearer. It seems that a person of less power and status tend to use a modal verb of strong force, while a person of more power and status tend to use a modal verb of weak force.

The above discussion indicates that there is a close relationship between the choice of modal verbs and the identities of the communicator. And equivalence, overstatement, and understatement all point to the combination of a variety of complex factors at work in the choice of modal verbs in mandarin Chinese.

5   Summary

To conclude, from the perspective of generating sentences in mandarin Chinese, there are three kinds of words: object words (lexical item), attribute words and relational words. Modal words (modal auxiliaries) are nature words which express a speaker's attitude. They help to generate modal sentences and express modal meanings. In terms of modal meanings, modal words can be divided into three categories, expressing necessity, expectation, and disjunction respectively. Different types of modal words can be discovered by data mining and their semantic strength can be calculated. In the use of modal words, the relationship between speaker's identity and power should be considered. A profound understanding of modal verbs in Chinese may be helpful to the choice of appropriate linguistic expressions in communication, and facilitate the process of communication.

References

1. Ma, Q.Z.: Language of can wish verbs (1) (1988). (马庆株.能愿动词的连用.语言研究. 1988(1)). (in Chinese)
2. Lizhen, P.: A Study of Modern Chinese Modal. Chinese Social Science Publishing House, Beijing (2007). (彭利贞.现代汉语情态研究.北京:中国社会科学出版社, 2007). (in Chinese)
3. Shen, J.: How to Evaluate the Semantic Strength of Words. Chinese language **1989**(1). (沈家煊.判断语词的语义强度[J].中国语文.1989(1)). (in Chinese)
4. Shen, J.: The language of the "subjectivity" and "subjective". foreign language teaching and research of **2001**(4). (沈家煊.语言的"主观性"和"主观化".外语教学与研究. 2001(4)). (in Chinese)
5. Jialing, X.: The Modal Verb in Chinese. Tsinghua University, Hsinchu (2002). (谢佳玲.汉语的情态动词,台湾新竹:清华大学, 2002). (in Chinese)
6. Yu, S.: Dictionary of Modern Chinese Grammar Information. Tsinghua University Press, Beijing (1998). (俞士汶.现代汉语语法信息词典.北京:清华大学出版社,1998). (in Chinese)
7. Zhou, J.: Semantics, Logic and Philosophy of language. Academic Press, Beijing (2006). (周建设. 语义、逻辑与语言哲学.北京:学苑出版社, 2006). (in Chinese)
8. Jianshe, Z. (ed.): A Course in Modern Chinese. People's Education Press, Beijing (2014). (周建设主编.现代汉语教程.北京:人民教育出版社, 2014). (in Chinese)
9. Lyons, J.: Semantics. CUP, Cambridge (1977)
10. Palmer, F.: Mood and Modality, 2nd edn. CUP, Cambridge (2001)

Conceptual Integration and Construction Coercion —— on the Neologism *"Tangqiang"*

Minli Zhou(✉)

School of Liberal Arts, Jiangxi Normal University, Nanchang,
Jiangxi Province, People's Republic of China
minlizhou@163.com

Abstract. *"Tangqiang"* means that due to some relations with Object A, Object B gets embroiled or affected in the event in which Object A is mainly involved. This word entirely inherits the metaphorical meaning from its complete form and undergoes construction coercion, behind which metonymy mechanism plays an important role. In addition, the syntactic demands of functional diversification, the pragmatic causes of expression elaboration, and the rhetorical motivations of specific effect-pursuing have also joined hands to promote its formation together.

Keywords: Conceptual integration · Metaphor · Metonymy · Construction coercion

1 Introduction

As an abbreviation, *"tangqiang"* [1] has frequently appeared on the Internet and in the traditional media in the past few years. With *"tangqiang"* as a keyword, I conducted a full-text search in "Baidu News" [2] and found about 978,000 pieces of news containing the word *"tangqiang"*. It is worth noting that *"tangqiang"* appeared 44 times when I conducted a search in CNKI's [3] Newspaper Full-text Database (2013-2014) [4], as shown below:

（1）"躺枪"之后，红会如何重拾尊严(*"tangqiang" zhihou, Honghui ruhe chongshi zunyan*; After being criticized and affected through some relations with other persons and organizations, how can Red Cross redeem its dignity) (*People's Daily*, 08/05/2014)
（2）欧佩克瞄准美国 中国页岩油躺枪(*Oupeike miaozhun Meiguo Zhong-guo Yeyanyou tangqiang*; OPEC aims at the USA, and Chinese shale oil got affected.) (*Financial Times*, 12/10/2014)

---

[1] *"Tangqiang"* is the pinyin for the Chinese word "躺枪".
[2] A news search engine in China.
[3] CNKI is short for China National Knowledge Infrastructure.
[4] The deadline for network corpus search is Dec. 21st, 2014.

© Springer International Publishing Switzerland 2015
Q. Lu and H.H. Gao (Eds.): CLSW 2015, LNAI 9332, pp. 173–184, 2015.
DOI: 10.1007/978-3-319-27194-1_18

This shows that "*tangqiang*" has been gradually accepted by the official media. As mentioned above, it appeared 44 times and was not enclosed in double quotation marks for 12 times (about 30%). This partly indicates that in some language users' minds, "*tangqiang*" has become a word unmarked. Then, as a neologism, in what syntactic and semantic environment should "*tangqiang*" be used? From a semantic collocation perspective, the verbal morpheme "*tang*" [5] (to lie somewhere) generally follows a locative object such as "*shafa*" [6] (sofa), but the noun morpheme "*qiang*" [7] (gun) itself has no locative meaning, then why can the two morphemes be joined together and form a compound word? What have been the results of "*tangqiang*" in the competition against "*zhongqiang*" [8] (to get shot)? This paper will make an effort to answer these questions.

2   The Distribution of "*Tangqiang*" in Semantic Perspective

The relevant researches on the meaning of "*tangqiang*" are listed below: Shantao Liu (2012) argued that "*zhongqiang*", a word derived from "*tangzhe ye zhongqiang*" [9] (got shot even when lying), meant that someone was embroiled in some trouble for no reason at all; Yunfeng Huang（2013）pointed out that the phrase "*tangzhe ye zhong-qiang*" meant that someone was implicated and fell on hard times accidentally or without any cause; Wu'ai Xiang（2013）thought that "*tangzhe ye zhongqiang*" meant that somebody was incriminated wrongly. I think these explanations are basically correct, but there is still something worthy to be further discussed. For instance, is it true that a person or an object is indeed embroiled "wrongly" or affected "without any reason" in some events? Let's take a look at the following example:

（3）楼市遇冷　钢市会否"躺枪"(*Loushi yuleng Gangshi huifou"tangqiang"*; Will the steel market get affected when the real estate market is in depression?）(*Modern Logistics*, 05/11/2014)

In Example (3), the reason why the steel market is questioned is that there is an obvious dependence relationship between the steel market and the real estate market. In my view, the meaning of "*tangqiang*" can be summarized as follows: Due to some relations with Object A, Object B gets embroiled or affected in the event in which Object A is mainly involved.

2.1   Background Event and Current Event

The usage of "*tangqiang*" actually involves two events: background event and current event. The background event refers to the one in which Object A is mainly involved, while the current event refers to the one in which Object B is embroiled or affected.

---

[5] Pinyin for Chinese word "躺".

[6] Pinyin for Chinese word "沙发". In Chinese "躺沙发" means lying on the sofa.

[7] Pinyin for Chinese word "枪".

[8] Pinyin for Chinese word "中枪".

[9] Pinyin for Chinese phrase "躺着 也 中枪".

（4）12306 "斗法" 抢票软件 买票群众 "躺枪"？（*12306 "doufa" qiangpiao ruanjian Maipiao qunzhong "tangqiang"*; Will the ticket buyers be affected when 12306[10] website cracks down on ticket-snatching software?) (*Xinhua Daily Telegraph*, 01/03/2014)

In Example (4), the background event is that the ticket-snatching software is blocked by 12306 website, and the current event is that the ticket buyers encounter difficulty in buying tickets once again. There is a causal relationship between the background event and the current event in that the background event results in the current event. Syntactically, there are causative verbs such as "*rang*" [11] (cause to do; cause to happen) and "*shi*" [12] (cause to be; cause to occur) shown below:

（5）虚假广告让院士 "躺枪"（*Xūjia guanggao rang yuanshi "tangqiang"*; Fake advertisements made the academician embroiled.）(*People's Daily*, 05/20/2013)

It is Object A, not Object B, that mainly gets involved in the background event, Object B sometimes is not so obviously correlated to Object A, and the relation between them can only be activated in a specific context, so it's often surprising when Object B is embroiled or affected.   Syntactically, there are often such adverbial modifiers as "*yiwai*" [13] (unexpectedly) and "*pianpian*" [14] (unluckily) in front of "*tangqiang*", as shown in the example below:

（6）加多宝王老吉被指难去火 十花汤意外躺枪（*Jiaduobao Wanglaoji bei zhi nan quhuo Shihuatang yiwai tangqiang*; Chivaton[15] drew criticism unexpectedly when JDB and Wong Lo Kat were accused of not being able to reduce internal heat.）(*21CN Financial Network*, 09/25/2014)

2.2   Relations between Object A and Object B

Object B in the current event will not be embroiled or affected out of thin air, and it always has some relations with Object A in the background event. I can reveal the relations between them based on an analysis of the 44 examples in Newspaper Full-text Database, as shown below:

Objects A and B belong to the Same System. As Objects A and B belong to the same system, any change of Object A will inevitably affect Object B. For instance, in the example below, both online businesses and offline businesses are in sales industry, when the consumers' purchasing power remains the same, the online businesses' earning money means that the market shares of offline businesses will decrease, and that offline businesses will be impacted accordingly.

---

[10] 12306 is a name of a website where the Chinese people buy train tickets.
[11] Pinyin for Chinese word "让".
[12] Pinyin for Chinese word "使".
[13] Pinyin for Chinese word "意外".
[14] Pinyin for Chinese word "偏偏".
[15] Here Chivaton, JDB and Wong Lo Kat are brands of drinks, in their advertisements these drinks can help to reduce internal heat.

（7）电商都是赢家 线下企业躺枪（*Dianshang doushi yingjia Xianxia qiye tangqiang*; All online businesses are winners while the offline businesses are impacted.）（*Chongqing Commercial Daily*, 06/20/2013）

Object B's Dependency on Object A. Due to Object B's dependency on Object A, if a change takes place to Object A, Object B will be affected accordingly. For instance, in Example (8), traffic control means that a traffic management measure is taken for the passenger service vehicles not licensed by the local city, and Jinshazhou[16] becomes a key vehicle restricted zone. As we know, the quantity of real estate sales depends on whether transportation is convenient. So when a change takes place to the transportation, people will naturally think over whether the real estate market will be affected.

（8）广州"限外" 金沙洲楼盘"躺枪"？（*Guangzhou "xianwai" Jinshazhou loupan "tangqiang"*; Guangzhou adopts a traffic control measure, and will the real estate market in Jinshazhou be affected?）（*Private Economy News*, 04/12/2013）

Object A and Object B: System and Element. Object A is an overall system and Object B is an element in the system, so when the overall system changes, the element(s) in the system may be influenced. In Example (9), investigation tours abroad include many activities, and scientific research exchange is just one of them, but since time limits are put on all investigation tours abroad, restrictions are imposed upon scientific research exchanges as well.

（9）出国考察"一刀切"，科研交流也"躺枪"（*Chuguo kaocha yidaoqie keyan jiaoliu ye tangqiang*; Restrictions have been imposed on all investigation tours abroad, and scientific research exchange has also been restricted.）（*Xinhua Daily Telegraph*, 06/17/2014）

Object A and Object B: Part and Whole. Object B is a whole and Object A is part of it. If the part changes, the whole may also be influenced. In Example (10), collagen is a product produced by Dongbao Biology Company. When somebody says that all oral collagen products are deceptive, an adverse influence may be exerted upon Dongbao Biology Company at large.

（10）东宝生物"躺枪"：胶原蛋白"气球吹破"？（*Dongbao shengwu tangqiang: Jiaoyuandanbai qiqiu chui po*; Dongbao Biology Company has been influenced: Does collagen do have the effects just as the advertisements said?）（*21st Century Business Herald*, 05/23/2013）

A Similarity between Object A and Object B. Object A is similar to Object B in some way. Originally, Object A becomes involved in something, but Object B may be wrongly identified as Object A and thus gets affected. For instance, in Example (11), Jinjin Foods' packaging bags are similar to those of bogus products, so they may be mistakenly identified as counterfeit and shoddy products, and thus Jinjin Foods suffer a loss.

---

[16] Here Jinshazhou and Guangzhou are both place names, Guangzhou is a city and Jinshazhou belongs to it.

（11）包装袋被仿冒 津津食品"躺枪"（*Baozhuangdai bei fangmao Jinjin Shipin tangqiang*; Jinjin Foods fell victim to the counterfeited packaging bags.）（*China Food Newspaper*, 04/10/2014)

The above five categories can basically be summarized as: the background event in which Object A is involved results in the current event in which Object B is involved. In a nutshell, I hold the view that when "*tangqiang*" is used, there is always a reason behind the occurrence of the event, and nothing or nobody should be embroiled or affected for no reason whatsoever.

2.3   The Unhappy Outcome of Current Event

For the subject of the verb "*tangqiang*", he or she is unhappy with the fact that he or she is embroiled, so "*tangqiang*" is often modified by the adverb "*buxing*"[17] (unfortunately), as shown below:

（12）范玮琪怀双胞胎男孩被热议 闺蜜大小S不幸躺枪（*Fan Weiqi huai shuangbaotai nanhai bei reyi Guimi daxiao S buxing tangqiang*; Christine Fan has become a hot topic after expecting twin boys, but her best friends Barbie Hsu and Dee Hsu are made fun of having only daughters unfortunately.）（*cnhuadong.net*, 10/10/2014)

Of course, there are different degrees of unhappiness. For instance, in Example (13), the question "*Ni tangqiang le ma?*"[18] (Have you got shot even when lying?) means whether you have the features of Chinese people observable to Americans. You may be ridiculed because of these features, and this may make you unhappy slightly.

（13）美国人眼里的中国人 你躺枪了吗（*Meiguoren yanli de zhongguoren Ni tangqiang le ma*; Americans' view on Chinese people; Do you have these features or how many features of these do you have?）（*NetEase Education Forum*, 04/08/2014)

3   Conceptual Integration and the Meaning of "*Tangqiang*"

Because "*tangqiang*" is closely related to "*tangzhe ye zhongqiang*" (got shot even when lying) both formally and semantically, I will begin with "*tangzhe ye zhongqiang*" when discussing its formation hereinafter.

3.1   Haplology Integration of "*Tangzhe ye zhongqiang*"

"*Tangzhe ye zhongqiang*" is a compressed complex sentence with implied adversative or concessive meaning, and the adverb "*ye*"[19] (also, as well) means that the result is the same. There is a presupposition here: if an object sits, stands, walks or runs, it will

---

[17] Pinyin for Chinese word "不幸".

[18] Pinyin for Chinese sentence "你 躺枪 了 吗".

[19] Pinyin for Chinese word "也".

easily become a target and thus get shot; if the object lies down, it will be unlikely to become a target and thus it will not get shot. This is based on a common sense of cognition, and the common sense contains a rational relationship between a way (also known as a reason in a general sense) and a result. That is, such movements as sitting, standing, walking, and running are negative ways (or reasons in general senses) and "being shot" is a negative result; conversely, there will also be a positive way (or reason) and result. In "*tangzhe ye zhongqiang*", the positive way and the negative result are combined together, so this is a marked case. According to Jiaxuan Shen(2006), the formation of such an expression as "*tangzhe ye zhongqiang*" is a kind of "haplology integration" [20] of concepts, that is, "two interrelated events are integrated together to generate a new conceptual meaning".

"*Tangzhe*" [21] (lying somewhere), which indicates a way of an action, and "*zhongqiang*" (to get shot), which indicates a result, are integrated together through the adverb "*ye*"(also, as well), so that the first event (about the way) serves as a background to highlight the unexpectedness of the second event (about the result). This is a new meaning given to "*tangzhe ye zhongqiang*" after the haplology integration. When the speaker doesn't want to emphasize the meaning implied by the adverb "*ye*", this structure can be simplified as "*tangzhe   zhongqiang*" [22].

3.2   Blending Integration of "*Tangzhe   ye zhongqiang*"

"*Tangzhe ye zhongqiang*" was originally used to describe some events in battlefields, but actually it's used more frequently now to describe some events in cognitive domains similar to battlefields. This is why "*tangzhe ye zhongqiang*" doesn't stay at the stage of being a compressed complex sentence, whose integration degree is not so high, and the sentence has further generated a metaphorical meaning as a whole.

The Market is a Battlefield.   Conceptual integration theory holds that "none of the things, states of affairs, events, and their processes in the world can do without a certain framework, human's mental space is organized in line with conceptual framework under the induction of cognitive models, and the conceptual frameworks consist of activation relationships and relevant members" (Weishan Wu 2011:256). What are activated by "*tangzhe ye zhongqiang*" are such things, relations, and processes in battlefields: gun-bearers, target objects, third parties, and coping strategies; the gun-bearers aim at the target objects, originally there is no relations between the third parties and the gun-bearers, but there may be some relations between the third parties and the target objects, or just because they stay together with the target objects, and thus within the range of the guns, they are also likely to get shot.

---

[20] The term "haplology" is mentioned by Jiaxuan Shen in his paper *Blending and Haplology*. Actually early in 2003, Fauconnier & Turner had pointed out that both word formation by integration and sentence formation by integration are based on conceptual integration. Jiaxuan Shen in his paper further divided integration of concepts and expressions into two types---blending and haplology. The detailed definitions will be introduced below.

[21] Pinyin for Chinese phrase "躺着".

[22] Pinyin for Chinese phrase "躺着 中枪".

（14）白酒中检出塑化剂，家装塑料管企业躺着也中枪（*Baijiu zhong jianchu suhuaji, jiazhuang suliaoguan qiye tangzhe ye zhongqiang*; Family housing decoration plastic pipe manufacturers got affected after plasticizer was found in white spirits.）（*China Construction News*, 12/20/2012）

The example mentioned above contains a metaphor that the market is a battlefield. The members within the conceptual framework of market include supervisors, managers, consumers, dealers, products etc. In Example (14), the supervisors and consumers in the market correspond to the gun-bearers in the battlefield and the liquor-making companies correspond to the target objects in the battlefield. The supervisors and consumers are directed against the white spirits containing plasticizer. The family housing decoration plastic pipe manufacturers correspond to the third party in the battlefield. They were originally not directly aimed at by the supervisors and consumers, but just because their products may contain plasticizer, their sales are also impacted. This process corresponds to the one in the battlefield where the third party gets shot since it has some relations with the target objects or just stays with them within the range of the guns. According to Jiaxuan Shen(2006), the use of "*tangzhe ye zhongqiang*" in this sentence is known as a kind of "blending integration" of concepts, that is, "two similar events are integrated together to generate a new conceptual meaning".

The Media is a Battlefield. Here "media" refers to newspapers, websites etc. People make speeches in newspapers or on websites, and in this cognitive domain there are speech makers, speech acceptors, and the people or things affected by speeches as well as the impacts they receive. So the media domain is also similar or corresponding to the battlefield, as shown below:

（15）不点名报道引发猜想 海天酱油"躺着也中枪"（*Budianming baodao yinfa caixiang Haitian jiangyou "tangzhe ye zhongqiang"*; An anonymous report triggers a guess, and Haitian Soy Sauce gets affected.）（*People's Court Daily*, 08/15/2012）

In Example (15), the newspaper is a battlefield metaphorically. The news report (or its issuer) corresponds to the gun-bearer in the battlefield. The news report is directed against some large company which has produced nearly ten thousand boxes of soy sauce with carcinogenic industrial salt and the so-called large company corresponds to the target object in the battlefield. Haitian Company corresponds to the third party in the battlefield, and the news report doesn't aim at it. But because Haitian Company has something in common with the company aimed at by the news report that both of them are large companies and produce soy sauce, so the relations between them corresponds to the one between the third party and the target object in the battlefield; finally, Haitian Company became caught in the soy sauce scandal and its business reputation as well as sales declined sharply. This process corresponds to the third party's getting shot in the battlefield.

3.3   Haplology Integration and Semantic Inheritance of "*Tangqiang*"

With the increase of its metaphorical use, the metaphorical meaning has gradually been integrated into the structure "*tangzhe ye zhongqiang*", so when used in sentences, it is functionally equivalent to a word as a whole. On top of that, with the role played by the principle of economy, "*tangzhe ye zhongqiang*" has been further compressed in terms of form. Language users select the verbal morpheme "*tang*" and the noun morpheme "*qiang*" to create a neologism "*tangqiang*", which accords with the conventional structures of Chinese words, and the neologism has completely inherited the metaphorical meaning of "*tangzhe ye zhongqiang*".

（16）董秘自述工作如履薄冰太易"躺枪"（*Dongmi zishu gongzuo rulübobing taiyi "tangqiang"*; The president secretaries said that they worked as if treading on eggs and were easily embroiled in violation of securities trading rules.）(*Securities Daily*, 06/20/2014)

（17）世界杯：亚洲全覆没，中国恐"躺枪"（*Shijiebei: Yazhou quan fumo, Zhongguo kong "tangqiang"*; World Cup: Asia has been completely eliminated, China may be influenced in qualifying for the world cup.）(*Xinhua Daily Telegraph*, 06/28/2014)

Both examples mentioned above exhibit blending integration of concepts, the metaphor in the former being that the workplace is a battlefield, and the metaphor in the latter being that the arena is a battlefield.

4   Construction Coercion and the Formation of "*Tangqiang*"

4.1   The Development of *Tangqiang*'s Syntactic Functions

An analysis of the usages in Newspaper Full-text Database shows that the main syntactic functions of "*tangzhe ye zhongqiang*" are the same as those of "*tangqiang*". In Chinese, both of them serve as a predicate and occasionally as an object (Example 18 and 20) and attribute (Example 19 and 21), as shown below:

（18）如何避免"躺着中枪"（*Ruhe bimian "tangzhe zhongqiang"*; How to avoid getting embroiled.）   (*Chinese Territory Resource News*, 03/19/2013)

（19）躺着中枪的张裕在替滞后国标埋单（*Tangzhe zhongqiang de Zhangyu zaiti zhihou guobiao maidan*; Getting affected by the Pesticide Residue Scandal, Changyu[23] paid the bill for the lagging national standards.）   (*China Economic Times*, 08/17/2012)

（20）奔驰中国遭总部内部"整顿" 公关服务公司表示"躺枪"（*Benchi zhongguo zao zongbu neibu "zhengdun" Gongguan fuwu gongsi biaoshi "tangqiang"*; Mercedes-Benz China was reorganized by the headquarters, and the PR service company expressed that the rumor that it had been investigated had caused great damage to its reputation.）(*Securities Daily*, 06/28/2013)

（21）"躺枪"的社保基金无碍稳健之名（"*Tangqiang*" *de shebao jijin wu'ai wenjian zhi ming*; The affected social security funds still remain stable.）   (*Securities Daily*, 11/14/2014)

---

[23]   Changyu is a brand of wine made in China.

However, "*tangqiang*" can also serve as a predicate in subordinate predication structures and downgraded predication structures, and even be followed by an object in some sentences. For instance, in Example (22), the subject is "*honghui 'maixue huoli' 'tangqiang'* "[24] (the Red Cross was influenced by the rumor of selling blood to make profits) and in this subject, "*tangqiang*" serves as a predicate. In Example (23), the whole structure "*fangqi 'tangqiang'* "[25] (the enterprises got impacted) serves as an attribute proceeding "*zhongsheng xiang*"[26](different cases), and "*tangqiang*" is a predicate of the attributive clause. In Example (24), "*tangqiang*" is followed by a locative object "*Zhangzi Dao*"[27] (a name of an island). These examples demonstrate that after the haplology integration, the functions of "*tangqiang*" get richer and richer. Obviously, this has something to do with the fact that the verb "*tangqiang*" itself is a simpler form compared with "*tangzhe ye zhongqiang*".

(22) 红会"卖血获利""躺枪"能否促进用血公开？（*Honghui "maixue huoli" "tangqiang" nengfou cujin yongxue gongkai*; Will the event that the Red Cross was influenced by the rumor of selling blood to make profits promote the transparency of blood-using？）(*Workers Daily*, 09/24/2014)

(23) 房企"躺枪"众生相 （*Fangqi "tangqiang" zhongsheng xiang*; Many real estate enterprises got impacted by different events and suffered losses to various degrees）(*China Real Estate Business*, 01/28/2013)

(24) 7只公募基金躺枪獐子岛（*Qizhi gongmu jijin tangqiang Zhangzi Dao*; Seven Public Offering Funds got affected by the great deficit of Zhangzi Island and suffered great losses.）(*Beijing Business Today*, 11/03/2014)

4.2   A Comparison between "*Tangqiang*" and "*Zhongqiang*"

According to *Modern Chinese Dictionary* (Edition VI), "*zhong*"[28] means "*suffer*", such as "*zhongdu*" [29] (to be poisoned), "*zhongshu*" [30] (to suffer from sunstroke), "*zhongle yiqiang*" [31] (got a shot), but "*zhongqiang*" isn't included in *Modern Chinese Dictionary*. As a matter of fact, before the year 2012 when "*tangzhe ye zhongqiang*" became popular, "*zhongqiang*" had already appeared in newspapers, as shown below:

(25) 本周，连胜文中枪案仍是话题焦点。（*Benzhou, Lian Shengwen zhongqiang'an rengshi huati jiaodian*; Sean Lien's getting shot is still a hot topic this week.）(*People's Daily*, 12/06/2010)

(26) 对在环保专项行动中"中枪"的违法排污企业实施"零容忍"政策 （*Dui zai huanbao zhuanxiang xingdong zhong "zhongqiang" de weifa paiwu qiye shishi "lingrongren" zhengce*; As to enterprises that were found to have problems of illegal

---

[24] Pinyin for Chinese clause "红会 '卖血获利' '躺枪'".
[25] Pinyin for Chinese clause "房企 '躺枪'".
[26] Pinyin for Chinese phrase "众生 相".
[27] Pinyin for Chinese phrase "獐子 岛".
[28] Pinyin for Chinese word "中".
[29] Pinyin for Chinese word "中毒".
[30] Pinyin for Chinese word "中暑".
[31] Pinyin for Chinese phrase "中了 一枪".

sewage discharge during Environmental Protection Special Action, zero tolerance policy will be implemented.) (*Jiaxing Daily* 11-16-2011)

The meaning of *"zhongqiang"*(to get shot) in Example (25) is simply composed of the basic meanings of *"zhong"* (to suffer) and *"qiang"*(gun) , so the integration degree of the whole structure is relatively low. But in Example (26), the meaning of *"zhongqiang"* is derivational, which means suffering a blow or being influenced, so the integration degree is higher. Statistics shows that there are totally 112 cases of *"zhongqiang"* with this meaning in Newspaper Full-text Database from 2011 to 2014; the data are as follows: 5 in 2011, 36 in 2012, 37 in 2013, and 34 in 2014. This shows that at least judging from the present situation, the use of *"zhongqiang"* is more frequent than that of *"tangqiang"*. However, compared with *"zhongqiang"*, *"tangqiang"* has a more simplistic meaning; it only means suffering a blow or being influenced indirectly. Especially when a speaker or a writer wants to emphasize the indirectness of the blow or influence, *"tangqiang"* is undoubtedly a more appropriate choice, hence the rationality of the rise and existence of *"tangqiang"*.

4.3   Construction Coercion

In the verb *"tangqiang"* , *"qiang"* serves as an object of the verbal morpheme *"tang"*, but this kind of collocation between *"tang"* and *"qiang"* is unusual, since language users cannot get the meaning of *"tangqiang"* just from its components' meaning, so the verb *"tangqiang"* can be regarded as a rhetorical construction mentioned by Da-wei Liu (2010). In my opinion, *"tangqiang"* is generated on the basis of the construction "V+*qiang*(gun)".

The construction "V+*qiang*" mainly expresses the V's dominance over *"qiang"*, just like *"zhongqiang"*, whose literal meaning is suffering from a gun, here *"zhong"* , as a verbal morpheme, dominates the noun morpheme *"qiang"*. In the construction *"tangzhe ye zhongqiang"*, *"tangzhe"*(lying somewhere) is just a concrete way of *"zhongqiang"* (to get shot), but in the abbreviation *"tangqiang"*, *"tang"*(to lie somewhere) not only refers to the way that something gets shot, but also presupposes or implies the action *"zhong"*(to suffer), so actually here *"tang"* has dominated *"qiang"*. This is the result of construction coercion, and the cognitive mechanism behind it is metonymy, that is, a concrete way of an action is used to refer to the action itself, so that a constituent, like *"tang"*, which originally cannot be used in the construction "V+*qiang*", can now be qualified to enter into this construction. Chunhong Shi (2012) points out that "the premise for the success of construction coercion is that a coerced lexical item must have some features that fit with the construction, so when the lexical item was coerced into the construction, the features would become prominent". When the verbal morpheme *"tang"* enters into the construction, the meaning of the construction has been enriched. It not only expresses the meaning which *"zhongqiang"* expresses, but also adds up a new meaning "indirectness". There are a large number of cases in languages where a concrete way of an action is used to refer to the action itself, such as *"tuan"* [32] (group) in example (27) :

---

[32]   Pinyin for Chinese word "团".

(27) 想买什么上网团一个 (*Xiang mai shenme shangwang tuan yige*; Online group buying can help you to buy anything you want.) (*China Consumer News*, 01/15/2010)

In the original word "*tuangou*" [33] (group buying), "*tuan*"just expresses a way of "*gou*" [34] (to buy), but in example(27), "*tuan*" is used independently as a verb, meaning group buying.

4.4 Interaction between Syntax and Rhetoric

The above mainly zooms in on the internal causes behind construction coercion. From the perspective of external causes, however, the coercion is strongly motivated by a pragmatic request of expression elaboration. "*Tangqiang*" can meet a speaker or writer's expression demand if he or she wants to emphasize the loss or influence caused by indirect involvement. Besides, the subtle difference of meaning has also led to different rhetorical effects between "*tangqiang*" and "*zhongqiang*". If language users have to select a verbal morpheme from the structure "*tangzhe ye zhongqiang*" to form a new word like "V+*qiang*", then "*zhongqiang*" may have a stronger derivability, while the comprehension of "*tangqiang*" is more dependent on a particular context. As pointed out by Dawei Liu (2010), "compared with the easy realization of grammatical functions dependent on derivability, rhetoric causes will leave a deeper and more lasting impression on us owing to the process we undergo (the process of derivation and experience)". Of course, with a rise in usage frequency, especially with the popularity of "*tangzhe ye zhongqiang*", a structure closely related to it, the comprehensibility of "*tangqiang*" will increase to a great extent, and its derivability will also be strengthened, so that the new word will change gradually from a rhetorical construction to a grammatical construction.

5   A View on "*Tangqiang*" from a Social Perspective

Language is a social phenomenon, which is affected by the society to a great extent. Especially, the vocabulary is most sensitive to social development and to the needs of communication. As a social animal, a language user always stays in various kinds of relations from his or her birth, so he or she is likely to be implicated or affected at any time due to some relations with others or other things. In addition, the advent of the information era, particularly the popularity of the Internet, has led to a sudden increase in this probability. Nowadays, not only are those celebrities or famous enterprises (or institutions) liable to be embroiled in something and get affected, but also an ordinary company or citizen is very likely to be influenced due to some indirect relations with other persons or things, as shown below:

(28) 高管落马绊倒上市公司，股民"躺枪" (*Gaoguan luoma bandao shangshi gongsi, gumin "tangqiang"*; The executive of the quoted company was

---

[33] Pinyin for Chinese word "团购".
[34] Pinyin for Chinese morpheme "购".

discharged from his post and the share prices sank; as a result, the investors were hurt.) (*Xinhua Daily Telegraph*, 11/01/2013)

What's more, even a lifeless object may be embroiled in something. For instance, in Example (29), the small cucumber is a commodity, but its sales was influenced by people's suspicion of genetically modified foods.

（29）"圣女"被辱 小黄瓜"躺枪"（*"Shengnü" beiru Xiao huanggua "tang-qiang"*; When cherry tomatoes were suspected of genetically modified foods, small cucumbers' sales declined.）(*Consumer Daily*, 07/19/2013)

More pessimistically, the influence sometimes even cannot be avoided by the subjective efforts of an individual or a collective. The existence of the word "*tangqiang*" exactly reflects language users' helplessness to the social reality. They use "*tang-qiang*" to express their dissatisfaction after being slandered accidentally, to clear off their grievances and sometimes, to banter with others or just ridicule themselves.

References

1. Shi, C.: A View on the Interaction between Grammar and Rhetoric from the Perspective of Construction Coercion (in Chinese). DANGDAI XIUCIXUE, no.1 (2012)
2. Liu, D.: From Grammatical Construction to Rhetorical Construction (in Chinese). DANGDAI XIUCIXUE, no. 3 (2010)
3. Gilles, F., Turner, M.: The Way We Think: Conceptual Blending and the Mind's Hidden Complexities. Basic Books, New York (2003)
4. Shen, J.: Blending and Haplology (in Chinese). Chinese Teaching in the World, no.1 (2006)
5. Liu, S.: The Generation of the New Meaning of 'Zhongqiang' (in Chinese). Yuwen Jianshe, no. 7 (2012)
6. Weishan, W.: Cognitive Linguistics and Chinese Research. Fudan University Press, Shanghai (2011). (in Chinese)
7. Xiang, W.: 'Tangzhe ye zhongqiang' Means Groundless Embroilment (in Chinese). Yao-wenjiaozi, no. 4 (2013)
8. Yuan, Y.: Motivation, Mechanism and Condition of Interaction between Argument Structure and Sentence Construction: On the Effects of Expression Elaboration on Verbal Valence and Sentence Construction (in Chinese). Studies in Language and Linguistics, no. 4 (2004)
9. Huang, Y.: An Analysis on the Buzzword 'Tangzhe ye zhongqiang' (in Chinese). Yuwen Xuexi, no. 2 (2013)

A Linguistic Analysis of Implicit Emotions

Sophia Yat Mei Lee[✉]

The Hong Kong Polytechnic University, Hong Kong, China
ym.lee@polyu.edu.hk

Abstract. Emotions are found to be frequently expressed in implicit ways. However, most existing approaches solely deal with the emotions explicitly described using emotion-bearing words. This work aims to examine an important yet underdeveloped branch of emotion analysis, i.e. implicit emotion. By constructing and analyzing the Chinese emotion annotated corpus, we recognize the importance of implicit emotion analysis. We propose a list of linguistic cues, such as adjectives and adverbs, for implicit emotion detection in Chinese. It shows that adverbs, in particular, are of great value in detecting implicit emotions when no other cues are found in text, as some adverbs have obvious semantic orientations.

1   Introduction

In recent years, text-based emotion processing has attracted plenty of attention in natural language processing (NLP). Most research in NLP has focused on explicit emotion detection using a list of emotion-bearing words such as *angry*, *upset*, and *happy* (Mihalcea and Liu 2006; Wiebe et al. 2005; Lee et al. 2012). The expression of emotion is, however, commonly presented not by using emotion-bearing words but by describing emotion-triggered situations based on commonsense knowledge which can be interpreted in an affective manner (Balahur and Montoyo 2008, Pavlenko 2008). This has greatly limited the identification of emotions as a considerable portion of emotions are not explicitly described using emotion-bearing words. More emphasis should therefore be placed on the implicit ones for the emotion concepts to be better understood.

This paper aims to explore linguistic features of implicit information for emotion detection and classification in Chinese. In doing so, we first construct a Chinese corpus annotated with emotion-related information. We then propose various linguistic cues such as adverbs. We believe that this study will contribute to the better understanding of emotion concepts as well as enriching existing emotion frameworks with a view to enhancing the robustness of the emotion classification system currently in use.

2   Related Work

2.1   Emotion Class and Word

Researchers have proposed different lists of primary emotions, varying from two to ten basic emotions (Plutchik 1980; Ekman 1984; Turner 2000). Among these

© Springer International Publishing Switzerland 2015
Q. Lu and H.H. Gao (Eds.): CLSW 2015, LNAI 9332, pp. 185–194, 2015.
DOI: 10.1007/978-3-319-27194-1_19

proposals, *fear* and *anger* appear on every list, whereas *happiness* and *sadness* appear on most of the lists. These four emotions—*fear, anger, happiness*, and *sadness*—are the most common primary emotions. Other less common primary emotions are *surprise, disgust, shame, distress, guilt, interest, pain*, and *acceptance*. In this study, we will adopt the emotion classifications by Turner (2000), who identifies five primary emotions (namely, *happiness, sadness, fear, anger*, and *surprise*) and we will focus on the underlying expressions of these five basic emotions in text.

2.2   Implicit Emotion Processing in Text

Textual emotion processing is still in its early stages in NLP where implicit emotion analysis is a relatively new area in the field. There are only few works done in investigating implicit sentiment. Greene and Resnik (2009) identified implicit sentiment based on a set of grammatically relevant semantic features that characterizes the interface between syntax and lexical semantics. Toprak et al. (2010) explored the factual sentences that capture evaluations in consumer reviews by identifying deep level information such as opinion target, opinion holder, and anaphoric expressions.

Explicit emotions can be easily detected by most of the existing approaches due to the presence of emotion keywords (Mihalcea and Liu 2006; Wiebe et al. 2005; Lee et al. 2012). Dealing with the implicit ones, an approach to overcome this issue is proposed by Sentic computing (Cambria et al. 2009), which aims at acquiring commonsense knowledge on the emotional effect of different concepts. This system is able to identify the emotions certain kinds of things produce. Balahur et al. (2011), however, indicated that sentences with more complex contexts may not be correctly detected and classified by the system. They further explain the idea by giving an example "*I am going to a party*". "*Going to a party*" is something that produces happiness which can be accurately marked by Sentic computing. However, in the more complex sentence like "*I am going to the party, although I should study for my exam*", the emotion *guilt* cannot be correctly identified. We believe that a large amount of the detection errors are attributed to both the subjectivity of human judgments as well as the contexts in text. In light of these considerations, identifying how implicit emotions are generally expressed in text may help reveal their tangibility.

3   Explicit vs. Implicit Emotions

The term *explicit emotion* refers to the presence of emotion-related information denoted by emotion keywords. For instance, in the sentence "*She was angry that he didn't make it*", whereby the word "*angry*" directly refer to the emotion state of *anger*. This is similar to the category "emotion words" defined by Pavlenko (2008). Implicit emotion refers to the emotion-related information that requires inference or connotation instead of being conveyed by emotion keywords (including but not restricted to the category "emotion-laden words" in Pavlenko's work (2008)). An example of such a sentence is "*I don't want to hear that*" which denotes the *anger* emotion while none of the individual words in the sentence expresses such an emotion. Implicit emotions in contexts have no clues of emotion-bearing words for detection. Without presenting emotion keywords explicitly, implicit emotions are expressed by means of some linguistic cues or patterns with adjectives being the most direct ones, as shown in (1).

1. <emo>喜</emo>真的好可愛

Implicit emotions can also be expressed by means of verbs, adverbs, and conjunctions as illustrated in (2) - (4), respectively.

2. <emo>喜</emo>笑死了
3. <emo>哀</emo>又夢見了～到底要怎樣！！
4. <emo>哀</emo>別說我不在意，就算在意了又能怎樣，我只不過是把一切看得更開了

Apart from the abovementioned lexical cues, syntactic patterns also play a part in detecting implicit emotions, as seen in (5).

5. <emo>哀</emo>真再也不相信愛情了…

4   The Chinese Emotion Corpus

4.1   Corpus Data

In order to study the features of implicit emotions, a corpus containing both explicit and implicit emotions was constructed. The corpus was made up of 8,529 posts randomly extracted from the Chinese micro-blog *Sina Weibo*. The posts were contributed by 51 users. Each post contains no more than 140 characters with emoticons taken into account for annotation.

There are in total 5,819 posts (68%) with emotions. This validates our hypothesis that texts on social-mediated websites contain more emotion expressions as compared to other genres such as news. The posts expressing emotions were further classified into two groups, i.e. explicit and implicit. Posts with emotion keywords or emoticons are all considered as explicit, and the rest are implicit. The number of explicit posts and implicit posts are 3,088 (53%) and 2,731 (47%). This proves that a considerable amount of emotions are expressed implicitly in text. An in-depth analysis of implicit emotion is thus considered a necessary component of emotion analysis, which will greatly help improve the consistently unsatisfying performance of the existing work on emotion.

4.2   Annotation Scheme

Given that contexts are relatively important for implicit emotion annotation, other comments made on the same post were simultaneously shown to the annotators for reference. It is believed that the results of the annotation would be least affected by this factor. For each post, we manually identified the existence of emotions and classified them into five primary emotions if there is any, i.e. *happiness, sadness, anger, fear,* and *surprise.* More than one emotion can be presented in a post with each of them tagged as <emo> × </emo>. Some emotions were not marked even with the presence of the corresponding cues as these emotions were not the major ones in each text. An example of an unmarked emotion is given in boldface as in (6).

6. <emo>喜</emo>雖然看起來有點寒磣，但也有好好過多至了

In that case, the adjective 寒磣 would trigger the *embarrassment* emotion which belongs to the emotion of *fear.* Since *fear* was the peripheral emotion in that case, only *happiness* was annotated.

5   Corpus Analysis

5.1   Distributions of Explicit and Implicit Emotions

Table 1 shows that out of 5,819 instances of emotions, 53% are explicit and 47% are implicit. This indicates explicit and implicit emotions are of equal importance.

Table 1. Distribution of Explicit and Implicit Emotions

Emotions	Frequency	
	Explicit	Implicit
Happiness	2,041	1,332
Sadness	751	771
Anger	308	413
Fear	143	145
Surprise	159	312
No. of annotated emotions	3,402 (53.4%)	2,973 (46.6%)
Total post	3,088 (53%)	2,731 (47%)

Lack of research on implicit emotions has restricted the existing approaches to detect implicit emotions accurately. It is obviously one of the reasons why the performance of emotion detection and classification are far from satisfactory. For a promising performance of emotion detection to be achieved, more emphasis should be placed on the linguistic account of implicit emotions.

Table 2 shows that among the five primary emotions, *happiness* occurred most frequently. Unlike the other four emotions (i.e. *sadness, anger, fear,* and *surprise*), *happiness* is the only emotion that is more frequently expressed explicitly.

The statistics suggest that neutral and negative emotions are more likely to be expressed implicitly. In the following section, we will discuss how and what linguistic cues may help detect implicit emotions.

Table 2. Frequency of Each Emotion Type

Emotions	Frequency		Total no. of emotion
	Explicit	Implicit	
Happiness	**2,041 (60.5%)**	1,332 (39.5%)	3,373
Sadness	751 (49.3%)	**771 (50.7%)**	1,522
Anger	308 (42.7%)	**413 (57.3%)**	721
Fear	143 (49.7%)	**145 (50.3%)**	288
Surprise	159 (33.8%)	**312 (66.2%)**	471

5.2 Linguistic Cues for Implicit Emotion Detection

By analyzing the corpus data, we examined the existence of implicit emotions in terms of two groups of linguistic cues: adjectives and adverbs. We manually identified the linguistic cues for each of the emotion that may facilitate the detection of implicit emotions.

Adjectives
We identified some adjectives that are closely connected with particular emotions, as shown in Table 3.

Table 3. Linguistic Cues - Adjectives

	Cue words (Adjectives)
Happiness	走運, 可愛, 美, 帥, 搞笑, 逗
Sadness	孤單, 虐, 失落, 心疼, 心酸, 可憐, 無奈, 可惜
Anger	可惡, 過份, 缺德, 令人髮指
Fear	可怕, 恐怖, 迷茫, 驚險, 丟臉, 糾結, 危險, 尷尬
Surprise	厲害, 神奇, 壯觀, 矚目, 猛, 牛, 不可思議

The cue words listed in Table 3 are adjectives that often appeared in the corpus. It is observed that people sometimes do not express emotions directly by means of emotion keywords. Instead, they do so by using these cues to describe the situations (arguments/events). Since these adjectives are open-classed content words, it is believed that many more sentimental words need to be collected for the detection of implicit emotions to be well-developed.

Adverbs
In addition to the adjectives, we also identified a group of adverbs that are highly associated with implicit emotions, as shown in Table 4.

Table 4. Linguistic Cues - Adverbs

Group	Cue words
Adverbs	終於 'eventually', 卻 'but', 只是 'just', 簡直 'absolutely', 竟然 'unexpectedly', 居然 'unexpectedly', 原來 'actually'

The cues shown in Table 4 are some adverbs that can help detect the existence of implicit emotions. In order to identify which emotion each of these cues was shown to be collocated with, we calculated the emotion distribution of each cue word. Table 5 shows that the adverb 終於 occurred 29 times in implicit posts of which over 93% were annotated as *happiness* while 卻 (88.9%) and 只是 (66.7%) were highly collocated with *sadness*. 簡直 was mostly associated with *anger* (70%) whereas the other three adverbs 居然 (75%), 竟然 (73.3%) and 原來 (62.5%) often co-occurred with *surprise*. For each cue word, there are only a few of them falling into other categories. Examples of each cue, as well as its exceptions, are given for further analysis and explanations.

Table 5. No. of occurrences of each adverb

Adverbs	Emotions						
	Happiness	Sadness	Anger	Fear	Surprise	N/A	Total
終於	27	1	1	0	0	0	29
卻	1	24	0	1	0	1	27
只是	0	10	3	1	0	1	15
簡直	1	0	7	0	2	0	10
居然	1	0	3	0	12	0	16
竟然	0	0	4	0	11	0	15
原來	1	4	1	0	10	0	16

Analysis of "終於"

Over 93% of sentences containing 終於 were associated with *happiness* as shown in Table 5. A typical example is given in (7).

7. <emo>喜</emo>終於要熬到天亮了。

In (7), 熬到天亮 is not an event of *happiness*. If we delete the cue 終於, "要熬到天亮了" should be annotated as *sadness* instead of *happiness*. Therefore, 終於 is proved to be the indicator of *happiness*. There are two exceptional cases as given in (8) and (9).

8. <emo>哀</emo>傷不起 終於來了
9. <emo>怒</emo>媽的姐終於記起來要去買六級練習了他媽的沒了！！

In (8) and (9), 傷不起 and 媽的 are obviously sentimental words of *sadness* and *anger*. These affective cues have stronger emotions in determining the major emotion. The semantic orientation of 終於 is therefore overridden. Similar cases can also be found in other cue words.

Analysis of "卻"

Approximately 88.9% of 卻 were collocated with *sadness*, an example was extracted as in (10).

10. <emo>哀</emo>沒有你的未來，還是不是未來？沒有我的現在，你卻平靜安
然。難道，這就是愛？

In (10), the word 卻 implies that the speaker is not as calm as the recipient after the
break-up. *Sadness* is therefore annotated. Two exceptions of 卻 are given in (11)-
(12).

11. <emo>恐</emo> 你總有一種魅力吸引著我，但我卻不敢靠近，只敢在遠處
守護著
12. <emo>喜</emo>謝謝那些沒有義務陪我但卻一直陪我的人

The annotated emotions of (11) and (12), however, are *fear* and *happiness* instead
of *sadness*. It is observed that most of the non-*sadness* cases, if not all, co-occur with
other notable cues. For example, the word "不敢" in (11) is an emotion-post-event of
fear (Lee et al. 2014) and "謝謝" in (12) is obviously an appreciation which is highly
associated with *happiness*.

Analysis of "只是"
The semantic orientation of 只是 points to the emotion of *sadness* (66.7%) in the
corpus.

13. <emo>哀</emo>我愛你只是我的事，跟你沒關係～

只是 in (13) implies that the speaker's feelings are unreciprocated. *Sadness* is therefore the emotion expressed. Example (14), on the other hand, shows an example of a
different emotion, i.e. *anger*.

14. <emo>怒</emo>如果只是為了推銷，請不要關注我…

In (14), the action is understood to be irritating in this case, but how it can be ma-
chine-learned is still an issue to be overcome.

Analysis of "簡直"
70% of the adverb 簡直 appeared in association with the emotion *anger*. An example
is given in (15).

15. <emo>怒</emo>終於安頓好了，簡直是太熱了！

In (15), 熱 is not clear enough to be a cue of *anger*. With the help of "簡直", the
degree of *anger* is enhanced. Exceptions fell into the categories of *happiness* and
surprise as illustrated in (16) and (17).

16. <emo>驚</emo>媽媽說這比自己坐車到實體店去買都快啊，簡直就是神速啊
17. <emo>喜</emo>前兩天感冒了，絕無僅有的只花了三天就基本痊癒了……而
且是趕在跨年之前，簡直太貼心~

The two words "神速" and "貼心" are no doubt the cues of *surprise* and *happiness*. With the presence of other cues, 簡直 functions as an emotion indicator instead.

Analysis of "居然"
It is not surprising that sentences containing 居然 were mostly annotated as *surprise* (75%) as its semantic orientation is obviously pointing to that specific emotion.

18. <emo>驚</emo>回復@黑米和草:社會進步了麼，居然央視公開放映了！

Example (18) shows that even without any other cue words, *surprise* can easily be detected with the presence of the adverb 居然. The corpus data suggest that 居然 occasionally co-occur with *anger* (18.75%). Examples are given in (19) and (20).

19. <emo>怒</emo>氣死我了～ 淘寶買個東西居然給我差4角！！！
20. <emo>怒</emo>居然笑的出來

In (19), "氣死" and "居然給我差4角" correspond to the emotion *anger*. The former can be detected whereas the latter cannot since the words used may vary in different situations. In (20), the situation is even more complicated. "笑的出來" is seemingly a cue of *happiness*, but when it follows "居然" which mainly marks *surprise*, the emotion is neither *happiness* nor *surprise* but *anger*. The question is how *anger* can be detected automatically in such a circumstance. Similar situations create a big challenge for the automatic detection of implicit emotion.

Analysis of "竟然
73.3% of posts containing 竟然 were annotated as *surprise* and the rest were *anger*. A typical example is presented in (21).

21. <emo>驚</emo>我竟然可以畫出這種東西

If one says "我可以畫出這種東西！", the emotion expressed would be *happiness (pride)* instead of *surprise*. It is the presence of 竟然 that implies the emotion *surprise*. There are also instances containing 竟然 which were not considered as *surprise*, as shown are given in (22).

22. <emo>怒</emo>悶鍋。我是真的暈辣椒了。明明是微辣竟然可以把我辣到想死！

Analysis of "原來".
62.5% of 原來 were collocated with *surprise* while 25% were *sadness*.

23. <emo>驚</emo>分享圖片 原來這個也有盜版?

In (23), it is difficult to determine whether the sentence "這個也有盜版?" expresses *surprise* or neutral in emotion. However, with the presence of 原來, it helps confirm the existence of *surprise*. Posts fallen into other categories are all with other emotion cue words. Most of the cue words are simple verbs (i.e. 笑, 氣, 受傷) or adjectives (i.e. 淚流滿面). There are situations with more complex combination of words, as seen in (24).

24. <emo>哀</emo>原來我還是沒法控制自己不想。

"沒法控制自己不想" is the reason for *sadness* to be evoked. The double negation (i.e. "沒法" and "不") poses a great challenge to automatic detection of emotion.

In conclusion, the statistics suggest that these adverbs have certain semantic orientations pointing to a particular emotion. When these cues appear without any other notable lexical cues in text, they play an important role in determining the implicit emotions expressed. Sometimes, the emotion marked by these adverbs may be overridden as in (8) and (9). However, it is also possible for these adverbs to be combined with other cues that determine the emotion as in (20).

As the number of adverbs is relatively limited as compared with other open class words, gaining an insight into such kind of words would be a great help in developing a promising automatic detection system for implicit emotions.

6   Conclusion

Explicit emotion processing has been a great challenge in NLP, let alone the implicit one. We propose some linguistic cues, including adjectives and adverbs, for implicit emotion detection. In particular, adverbs are proven to be of great value in detecting implicit emotions when no other cues are found in text. Since some adverbs have certain semantic orientation pointing to a particular emotion, we believe that such a study will shed light on emotion processing as these cues can serve as clues for the identification of implicit emotions.

Acknowledgements. The work is supported by an Early Career Scheme (ECS) project sponsored by the Research Grants Council (Project no. PolyU 5593/13H) and a PolyU Faculty Grant (Project no. 1-ZVB2).

References

1. Balahur, A., Montoyo, A.: Applying a culture dependent emotion triggers database for text valence and emotion classification. In: Proceedings of the AISB 2008 Convention "Communication, Interaction and Social Intelligence" (2008)
2. Balahur, A., Hermida, J.M., Montoyo, A.: Detecting implicit expressions of sentiment in text based on commonsense knowledge. In: Proceedings of the 2nd Workshop on Computational Approaches to Subjectivity and Sentiment Analysis, pp. 53–60. Association for Computational Linguistics (2011)

3. Cambria, E., Hussain, A., Havasi, C., Eckl, C.: Affective space: blending common sense and affective knowledge to perform emotive reasoning. In: WOMSA at CAEPIA, Seville, pp. 32–41 (2009)
4. Ekman, P.: Expression and the nature of emotion. In: Scherer, K., Ekman, P. (eds.) Approaches to Emotion, pp. 319–343. Lawrence Erlbaum, Hillsdale (1984)
5. Greene, S., Resnik, P.: More than words: Syntactic Packaging and Implicit Sentiment. Proceedings of NAACL **2009**, 503–511 (2009)
6. Lee, S.Y.M., Li, S., Huang, C.-R.: Annotating events in an emotion corpus. In: Proceedings of LREC 2014 (2014)
7. Lee, S.Y.M., Chen, Y., Huang, C.-R., Li, S.: Detecting emotion causes with a linguistic rule-based approach. In: Computational Intelligence, Special Issues on Computational Approaches to Analysis of Emotion in Text. Wiley-Blackwell (2012)
8. Mihalcea, R., Liu, H.: A corpus-based approach to finding happiness. In: Proceedings of the AAAI Spring Symposium on Computational Approaches to Weblogs (2006)
9. Pavlenko, A.: Emotion and emotion-laden words in the bilingual lexicon. Bilingualism: Language and Cognition **11**, 197–201 (2008)
10. Plutchik, R.: Emotions: A Psychoevolutionary Synthesis. Harper & Row, New York (1980)
11. Toprak, C., Jakob, N., Gurevych, I.: Sentence and expression level annotation of opinions in user-generated discourse. In: Proceedings of ACL 2010, pp. 575–584 (2010)
12. Turner, J.H.: On the Origins of Human Emotions: A Sociological Inquiry into the Evolution of Human Affect. Stanford University Press, California (2000)
13. Wiebe, J., Wilson, T., Cardie, C.: Annotating Expressions of Opinions and Emotions in Language. Language Resources and Evaluation **39**(2/3) (2005)

Lexical Resources

Emotional Classification of Chinese Idioms
Based on Chinese Idiom Knowledge Base

Lei Wang[1,2(✉)], Shiwen Yu[1], Zhimin Wang[3], Weiguang Qu[4], and Houfeng Wang[1]

[1] Key Lab of Computational Linguistics of Ministry of Education,
Peking University, Beijing 100871, China
{yusw,wanghf,wangleics}@pku.edu.cn
[2] School of Foreign Languages, Peking University, Beijing 100871, China
[3] College of Chinese Studies, Beijing Language and Culture University, Beijing 100083, China
wangzm000@gmail.com
[4] School of Computer Science, Nanjing Normal University, Nanjing 210000, China
wgqu@njnu.edu.cn

Abstract. Idioms are not only interesting but also distinctive in a language for its continuity and metaphorical meaning in its context. This paper introduces the construction of a Chinese idiom knowledge base by the Institute of Computational Linguistics at Peking University and describes an experiment that aims at the automatic emotion classification of Chinese idioms. In the process, we expect to know more about how the constituents in a fossilized composition like an idiom function so as to affect its emotional properties.

Keywords: Chinese idiom knowledge base · Chinese idiom · Emotional classification

1   Introduction

An idiom is a multi-word expression that has a figurative meaning that is comprehended in regard to a common use of that expression that is separate from the literal meaning or definition of the words of which it is made(McArthur, 1992). An idiom is also used, in most cases, with some intention of the writer or to express certain emotion or attitude. Thus in nature, idioms are exaggerative and descriptive and do not belong to the plain type.

Therefore, to classify idioms according to its emotional property or descriptive property is important for many practical applications. In recent years, emotion classification has become a very popular task in the area of Natural Language Processing(NLP), which tries to predict sentiment(opinion, emotion, etc.) from texts. Most research has focused on subjectivity(subjective/objective) or polarity(positive/neutral/negative) classification. The applications with this respect include human or machine translation, automatic text classification or Teaching Chinese as a Foreign Language(TCFL). For example, when a student learning Chinese as a foreign language encounters an idiom in his or her reading or conversation, for better understanding it is important for him or her to know whether the idiom is used to indicate

© Springer International Publishing Switzerland 2015
Q. Lu and H.H. Gao (Eds.): CLSW 2015, LNAI 9332, pp. 197–203, 2015.
DOI: 10.1007/978-3-319-27194-1_20

an appreciative or derogatory sense which is very crucial to understand the attitude of the idiom user. Another example is that long articles about politics in newspapers often include a lot of idiom usage to boost their expressiveness and these idioms may carry emotional information. Obviously by knowing the emotional inclination we may easily obtain a clue about the general attitude of the particular medium. We may even be able to detect or monitor automatically the possible hostile attitude from certain electronic media which today provide so huge amount of information that seems hard for human processing on a daily basis.

2   Chinese Idioms and Chinese Idiom Knowledge Base

Generally an idiom is a metaphor, a term requiring some background knowledge, contextual information, or cultural experience, mostly to use only within a particular language, where conversational parties must possess common cultural references. Therefore, idioms are not considered part of the language, but part of a nation's history, society or culture. As culture typically is localized, idioms often can only be understood within the same cultural background; nevertheless, this is not a definite rule because some idioms can overcome cultural barriers and easily be translated across languages, and their metaphoric meanings can still be deduced. Contrary to common knowledge that language is a living thing, idioms do not readily change as time passes. Some idioms gain and lose favor in popular literature or speeches, but they rarely have any actual shift in their constructs as long as they do not become extinct. In real life, people also have a natural tendency to over exaggerate what they mean or over describe what they see or hear sometimes and this gives birth to new idioms by accident.

For the importance of idioms in Chinese language and culture, an idiom bank with about 6,790 entries were included in the most influential Chinese language knowledge base – the Grammatical Knowledge base of Contemporary Chinese(GKB) completed by the Institute of Computational Linguistics at Peking University(ICL), which has been working on language resources for over 20 years and building many knowledge bases on Chinese language. Based on that, the Chinese Idiom Knowledge Base(CIKB) had been constructed from the year 2004 to 2009 and collects more than 35, 000 idioms with more semantic and pragmatic properties added.

Upon the completion of CIKB, a few research projects have been conducted to investigate possible applications. Li(2006) investigates the frequency and formation of idiom usage in People's Daily and Wang(2010) selects 1,000 popular idioms from CIKB to compile a book for Chinese learners. On the basis of CIKB, we also made a couple of attempts on the automatic classification of idioms to identify the token-level characteristics of an idiom. This paper will focus on the emotion classification of idioms with machine learning method and the work will be elaborated in section 4. Here we define the emotion types as "Appreciative(A)", "Derogatory(D)" and "Neutral(N)".

3   Related Work on Idiom Knowledge Base and Its Applications

There has not been much work on the construction of an idiom corpus or an idiom knowledge base. With this respect, Birke and Sarkar(2006) and Fellbaum(2007) are exceptions. Birke and Sarkar(2006) constructed a corpus of English idiomatic expressions with automatic method. They selected 50 expressions and collected about 6,600 examples. They call the corpus TroFi Example Base, which is available on the Web.

As far as idiom identification is concerned, the work is classified into two kinds: one is for idiom types and the other is for idiom tokens. With the former, phrases that can be interpreted as idioms are found in text corpora, typically for lexicographers to compile idiom dictionaries. Previous studies have mostly focused on the idiom type identification(Lin, 1999; Baldwin et al., 2003; Shudo et al., 2004). However, there has been a growing interest in idiom token identification recently(Katz and Giesbrecht, 2006; Hashimoto et al., 2006; Cook et al., 2007). Our work elaborated in section 4 is also an attempt in this regard.

Despite the recent enthusiasm for multiword expressions, the idiom token identification is in an early stage of its development. Given that many language teaching and learning tasks like TCFL have been developed as a result of the availability of language resources, idiom token identification should also be developed when adequate idiom resources are provided. To this end, we have constructed the CIKB and hope to find applications of value, for example, emotion classification, event classification and text analysis based on idiom usage and its context.

According to the granularity of text, emotion analysis of texts can be divided into three levels: text(Pang et al., 2002; Cui et al., 2006), sentence(Pang et al., 2004), word(Hatzivassiloglou et al., 1997; Wiebe 2000). According to the sources of emotion prediction, classification methods can be divided into knowledge based methods and machine learning based methods. The former uses lexicons or knowledge bases to build a new lexicon that contains emotion words. WordNet is often used to compute the emotion prediction of words(Hatzivassiloglou et al., 1997; Andrea 2005). Meanwhile, incorporating knowledge into the machine learning architecture as features is a popular trend and untagged copra are often used to do emotion classification research(Turney et al., 2002; Akkaya et al., 2009).

4   An NLP Application of Emotion Classification on CIKB

In this paper, we focus on the emotion prediction of idioms conducted by machine learning method. To do this, we aim to investigate how the compositional constituents of an idiom affect its emotion orientation from the token level, especially for multiword expressions with so obvious an exaggerative and descriptive nature like idioms. From CIKB, 20,000 idioms are selected as the training corpus and 3,000 idioms as the test corpus. The detailed distribution of idioms in each emotion group is shown in Table 1.

Table 1. The distribution of idioms in each emotion group.

	Training corpus		Test corpus	
	number	percentage	number	Percentage
Appreciative(A)	6967	34.84%	1011	33.70%
Neutral(N)	8216	41.08%	1100	36.67%
Derogatory(D)	4817	24.08%	889	29.63%

We can see that neutral has the largest number of idioms, accounting for 41.08% and 36.67% in the training and test corpus respectively, but there is not a big difference between groups. Support Vector Machine(SVM)(Cortes and Vapnik, 1995) is adopted as the classification method to predict emotions in idioms. LIBLINEAR(Fan et al., 2008), a library for large SVM linear classification, is used for implementation. The solver is set be L2-loss SVM dual. Parameter C is set to be 2-5. Three classes of features and their various combinations are examined and used, including Chinese characters, words and part-of-speeches. Detailed features and related abbreviations are shown as in Table 2.

Table 2. Features selected for emotion prediction.

Features and their abbreviations		Idiom(i)	Explanation(e)
Chinese characters	character unigram(i_cu, e_cu)	√	√
	character bigram(i_cb, e_cb)	√	√
Words	word unigram(i_wu, e_wu)	√	√
	word bigram(i_wb, e_wb)	×	√
Word/part-of-speech	word/pos unigram(i_wpu, e_wpu)	√	√
	word/pos bigram(i_wpb, e_wpb)	×	×

Because Chinese sentences are written in a consecutive string of characters, we need to segment a sentence into individual words to obtain the word feature. ICTCLAS(Zhang et al., 2003), a tool developed by the Institute of Computing Technology of Chinese Academy of Sciences(ICT), is used for word segmentation and part-of-speech tagging. We adopt precision, recall and F-score($\beta=1$) as the evaluation parameters. From Table 3 we can see that i_cb has a better performance than i_cu, which indicates that a bigram model usually performs better than a unigram model. But when we segment the idioms and use i_wu, we find that the performance gets bad. This may be because the compositionality of Chinese idioms is quite fossilized and the errors caused by segmentation introduce some noise.

We want to know whether we will have a better performance if we add more features from the other fields of CIKB. Obviously the most relevant feature will be the explanation of an idiom. Therefore we add the texts in the explanation field as features in the experiment. We find that by adding more features from the explanation field, the performance does improve. But when the POS feature is introduced, the performance gets bad. This may be because as Chinese idioms keep grammatical properties of ancient Chinese language and its POS is very different from the setting of the tool designed primarily for modern Chinese, more noise is introduced by using POS here. Finally we can see that the combination "i_cu+i_cb+e_wu+e_wb" achieves the best performance in both Chinese character features and word features.

Table 3. The result of emotion classification with idioms and their explanations.

Features or features combined	Result		
	Precision	Recall	F-score
i_cu	63.23%	75.16%	68.68%
i_cb	65.78%	78.24%	71.47%
i_wu	62.51%	73.42%	68.35%
i_wpu	60.03%	71.89%	65.43%
i_cu+e_wu	66.40%	80.05%	72.59%
i_cu+e_wpu	65.68%	77.95%	71.29%
i_cu+e_wb	65.08%	76.14%	70.18%
I_cu+i_cb	67.33%	80.82%	73.46%
i_cu+i_cb+e_wu	68.55%	81.37%	74.41%
i_cu+i_cb+e_wu+e_wb	70.18%	82.71%	75.93%

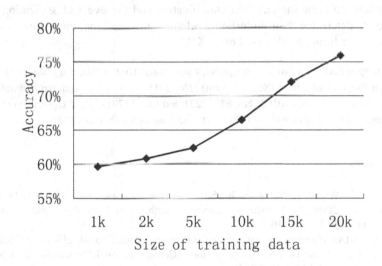

Fig. 1. Learning curve of the feature combination i_cu+i_cb+e_wu+e_wb.

Most importantly, we notice that although for idioms themselves segmentation does not affect the performance in a positive way, segmentation of the explanations does improve the performance. Thus we may conclude that the compositionality of an idiom is very different from its explanation which is written in modern Chinese while the idiom itself is still character-based and keeps its original morphemes that are inherited from ancient Chinese language. Figure 1 shows the learning curve of the best classifier with the feature combination "i_cu+i_cb+e_wu+e_wb". We can see that the accuracy keeps improving with the increase of the size of training set, and peaks at 20,000 idioms. It shows the potential to improve the performance of emotion classification by enlarging the training data set.

5   Conclusions and Future Work

This paper introduces the construction of CIKB by ICL at Peking University and its several applications so far. One application – the emotion classification of idioms – was elaborated to show our effort in exploring the token-level characteristics of Chinese idioms. Therefore we select a number of idioms from CIKB to classify them into three emotion groups. SVM is employed for automatic classification. Three classes of features are examined and experiments show that certain feature combinations achieve good performance. The learning curve indicates that performance may be further improved with the increase of training data size.

Now we also hope to classify the idioms into categories according to their usage in context, i.e., under what circumstances they are often used(event classification). Various linguistic features and real-world knowledge will be considered to incorporate into the machine learning classifier to improve classification result. The work is in progress and we hope the emotion classification and the event classification will be compared to determine their underlining relations and hope that more applications can be found in our future work based on CIKB.

Acknowledgements. Our work is supported by National High Technology Research and Development Program of China (863 Program) (No. 2015AA015402), National Natural Science Foundation (Grant No. 61170163, No. 61272221 and No.61370117) and Open Project Foundation of National Key Laboratory of Computational Linguistics (No. 201302).

References

1. Akkaya, C., Wiebe, J., Mihalcea, R.: Subjectivity word sense disambiguation. In: Proceedings of the 2009 Conference on Empirical Methods in Natural Language Processing, vol. 1, pp. 190–199 (2009)
2. Esuli, A.: Determining the semantic orientation of terms through gloss classification. In: Proceedings of the 14th ACM International Conference on Information and Knowledge Management, pp. 617–624 (2005)
3. Baldwin, T., Bannard, C., Tanaka, T., Widdows, D.: An empirical model of multiword expression decomposability. In: Proceedings of the ACL 2003 Workshop on Multiword Expressions: Analysis, Acquisition and Treatment, vol. 18, pp. 89–96 (2003)
4. Cook, P., Fazly, A., Stevenson, S.: Pulling their weight: exploiting syntactic forms for the automatic identification of idiomatic expressions in context. In: Proceedings of the Workshop on A Broader Perspective on Multiword Expressions, pp. 41–48 (2007)
5. Cortes, C., Vapnik, V.: Support-Vector Networks. Machine Learning 20(3), 273–297 (1995)

6. Cui, H., Mittal, V., Datar, M.: Comparative experiments on sentiment classification for on-line product reviews. In: Proceedings of the 21st National Conference on Artificial Intelligence, vol. 2, pp. 1265–1270 (2006)
7. Fan, R.-E., Chang, K.-W., Hsieh, C.-J., Wang, X.-R., Lin, C.-J.: LIBLINEAR: A Library for Large Linear Classification. Journal of Machine Learning Research 9(2008), 1871–1874 (2008)
8. Fellbaum, C.: Idioms and Collocations: Corpus-based Linguistic and Lexicographic Studies(Research in Corpus and Discourse). Continuum International Publishing Group Ltd., London (2007)
9. Hashimoto, C., Sato, S., Utsuro, T.: Japanese idiom recognition: drawing a line between literal and idiomatic meanings. In: Proceedings of the COLING/ACL on Main Conference Poster Sessions, pp. 353–360 (2006)
10. Hatzivassiloglou, V., McKeown, K.: Predicting the semantic orientation of adjectives. In: Proceedings of the Eighth Conference on European Chapter of the Association for Computational Linguistics, pp. 174–181 (1997)
11. Katz, G., Giesbrecht, E.: Automatic identification of non-compositional multi-word expressions using latent semantic analysis. In: Proceedings of the Workshop on Multiword Expressions: Identifying and Exploiting Underlying Properties, pp. 12–19 (2006)
12. Li, Y., Huarui, Z., Hongjun, W., Shiwen, Y.: Investigation on the frequency and formation of idioms in people's daily. In: Proceedings of the 7th Chinese Lexicon and Semantics Workshop, pp. 241–248 (2006)
13. Lin, D.: Automatic identification of noncompositional phrases. In: Proceedings of the 37th Annual Meeting of the Association for Computational Linguistics on Computational Linguistics, pp. 317–324 (1999)
14. McArthur, T.: The Oxford Companion to the English Language. Oxford University Press, Oxford (1992)
15. Pang, B., Lee, L.: A sentimental education: sentiment analysis using subjectivity summarization based on minimum cuts. In: Proceedings of the 42nd Annual Meeting on Association for Computational Linguistics, pp. 271–278 (2004)
16. Pang, B., Lee, L., Vaithyanathan, S.: Thumb up? sentiment classification using machine learning techniques. In: Proceedings of the ACL-2002 Conference on Empirical Methods in Natural Language Processing, pp. 79–86 (2002)
17. Shudo, K., Tanabe, T., Takahashi, M., Yoshimura, K.: MWEs as nonpropositional content indicators. In: Proceedings of the Workshop on Multiword Expressions: Integrating Processing, pp. 32–39 (2004)
18. Turney, P.D.: Thumps up or thumps down? semantic orientation applied to unsupervised classification of reviews. In: Proceedings of the 40th Annual Meeting on Association for Computational Linguistics, pp. 417–424 (2002)
19. Wang, L.: 1,000 Idioms for Chinese Learners. Peking University Press, Beijing (2010). Forthcoming
20. Wiebe, J.: Learning subjective adjectives from corpora. In: Proceedings of the Seventeenth National Conference on Artificial Intelligence and Twelfth Conference on Innovative Applications of Artificial Intelligence, pp. 735–740 (2000)
21. Zhang, H., Yu, H., Xiong, D., Liu, Q.: HHMM-based chinese lexical analyzer ICTCLAS. In: Proceedings of the Second SIGHAN Workshop on Chinese Language Processing, pp. 184–187 (2003)

Emotion Corpus Construction on Microblog Text

Lei Huang, Shoushan Li[✉], and Guodong Zhou

Natural Language Processing Lab, School of Computer Science and Technology,
Soochow University, Suzhou, China
lei.huang2013@gmail.com, {lishoushan,gdzhou}@suda.edu.cn

Abstract. The construction of emotion corpus is a basic task in emotion analysis, which aims to annotate the emotions, such as *joy*, *sadness*, and *angry*, expressed in the text. Previous studies generally focused on the basic emotions in their emotion taxonomies. We find that, however, many emotions expressed in microblog text are difficult to be mapped to basic emotions, which poses a great challenge to emotion annotation. To address this problem, this paper proposes a novel emotion taxonomy which contains both basic emotions and complex emotions for annotating emotions expressed in microblog text. Specially, the basic emotions include four emotion classes, i.e., *joy*, *angry*, *sadness*, and *fear* while the complex emotions include *positive* emotions, *neutral* emotions, and *negative* emotions. Experimental results demonstrate that the emotion annotation with the proposed emotion taxonomy achieves a much higher consistency, providing a good foundation for further emotion recognition task.

Keywords: Emotion corpus · Emotion analysis · Consistency

1 Introduction

With the emergence and development of Web2.0, the amount of information on the web is increasing rapidly. Microblog, or Weibo in Chinese, has become one of the most popular internet applications due to its expression features like more free and convenient among social media. Under this background, text emotion analysis provides important technical means for automatic processing and analyzing mass data in the microblogs. The text emotion analysis has become a hot research task in computational linguistics due to its wide potentials applications, e.g. public opinion monitor, intelligent advertisement, emergency warning, etc. In addition, emotion analysis can also help other researches fields, such as psychology, sociology, finance.

Emotion refers to the inner psychological reactions and feelings, such as *joy*, *angry*, *sadness*, *fear*, etc. Emotion analysis aims to automatic identify author's mood, psychological reaction and emotional state expressed by a piece of text. Generally, emotion analysis has two basic tasks: emotion recognition and emotion classification (Aman and Szpakowiczm, 2007). The existing approaches of emotion analysis are commonly based on corpus classification methods. Corpus construction is the basic technological means in natural language processing. The key of corpus construction is to build practical annotation system. In the construction of emotion analysis corpus, the emotion taxonomy is foundation and difficulty of emotion analysis research.

© Springer International Publishing Switzerland 2015
Q. Lu and H.H. Gao (Eds.): CLSW 2015, LNAI 9332, pp. 204–212, 2015.
DOI: 10.1007/978-3-319-27194-1_21

Although there are large divergences in categories and quantities of the emotion, researchers from different research fields all agree that emotions can be divided into two categories, i.e., basic emotions and complex emotions (Arnold, 1960; Ortony and Turner, 1990). In previous researches, the basic emotions classes are divided into 4, 6, 8, 10 or even more than 20, which is mainly because of the complexity and variability of emotions, and there is no complete and systematic understanding in the academic world. Such as Gray (1982) considered the basic emotions are *joy, rage, anxiety, fear*; Ekman (1982) divided the basic emotions into *joy, sadness, anger, fear, disgust, surprise*; Pultchik (1980) proposed 8 basic emotions classes, i.e., *acceptance, anger, anticipation, disgust, joy, fear, sadness, surprise*.

The complex emotions are difficult to list them all, common ones include *gratitude, pride, guilt*, etc. The existing text emotion taxonomies tend to map a variety of complex emotions to the basic emotions, such as we can map annoyance to *sadness*, satisfactory to *joy*. However, in the practical annotation process, all the complex emotions were mapped to the basic emotions is not easy task. For example, see the following two sentences:

(a) Chinese: 感谢你们这一路的陪伴。
    Pinyin: *gǎn xiè nǐ men zhè yí lù de péi bàn.*
    English: *Thank you for you company.*
(b) Chinese: 今天父亲节，祝爸爸身体健康！
    Pinyin: *jīn tiān fù qīn jié, zhù bà ba shēn tǐ jiàn kang.*
    English: *Today is father's day, I wish my father good health!*

From the above two examples, we can see that the sentence (a) expresses gratitude emotion and the sentence (b) reveals blessing emotion. These two emotions are complex emotion and are difficult to be mapped to the basic emotions. In addition, obviously, the two sentences were labeled as *emotionlessness* is unreasonable. Therefore, it is very difficult to only use some basic emotions to map all emotions for annotating corpus.

This paper aims to construct emotion corpus on microblog text. We propose a novel emotion taxonomy which contains basic emotions and complex emotions for annotating emotions expressed in microblog text. The basic emotions include four emotion classes, i.e., *joy, angry, sadness*, and *fear*. These emotions are basically all relevant researches consistent with the basic emotions (Ortony and Turner, 1990). Emotions except for the basic emotions are complex emotions. The complex emotions include *positive* emotions, *neutral* emotions, and *negative* emotions. In addition, we have set *emotionlessness* category. Empirical studies on emotion corpus demonstrate that our proposed emotion taxonomy improves the efficiency of annotating corpus and achieves a much higher consistency.

The remainder of this paper is organized as follows. Section 2 overviews the related work on emotion analysis and emotion corpus construction. Section 3 explores the description and construction methods of emotion corpus. Section 4 presents the statistics and analysis of constructed corpus. Finally, Section 5 gives the conclusion and future work.

2   Related Work

Over the last decade, emotion analysis has been a hot research topic and involve various aspects, such as emotion resource creation (Wiebe et al., 2005; Quan and Ren, 2009; Xu et al., 2010), writer's emotion vs. reader's emotion analysis (Lin et al., 2008; Liu et al., 2013), emotion cause event analysis (Chen et al., 2010), document-level emotion classification (Alm et al., 2005; Li et al., 2014) and sentence-level or short text-level emotion classification (Tokushisa et al., 2008; Bhowmick et al., 2009; Xu et al., 2012). This work focuses on construction of emotion analysis corpus.

Mishne (2005) selected 132 common moods and constructed a corpus of 815494 blog posts in Livejournal. Pak and Paroubek (2010) collected a corpus of text posts and formed a dataset of three classes: positive sentiments, negative sentiment, and a set of objective texts by using Twitter API. Quan and Ren (2009) proposed an emotional expression space model and described a relatively fine-grained annotation scheme and annotated emotion in text. In aspects of Chinese emotion corpus, Xu et al. (2008) adopted emotion classification contains 7 coarse classes, 22 fine classes for emotion annotating on sentence level in primary school textbooks, screenplays, and completed 39488 sentences of annotation. Yao et al. (2014) used seven emotion classes for annotating emotions on microblog level and sentence level on Sina microblog text, this corpus consists of 14000 microblogs, totaling 45431 sentences.

3   Emotion Corpus Construction

3.1   Datasets and Pre-processing

Up to now, the researches on emotion corpus construction on Chinese microblog are relatively small, and lack of related public corpus. The primary task of this paper is to collect relevant data. We download microblogs from the website http://t.qq.com. The data were collected by using the Tencent Microblog API, and contain 260000 users' personal information and their tweets. Specially, microblogs of each user were collected at most 210. The types of microblog are divided into seven types, i.e., original published, retweet, private message, reply, empty reply, comment, mention, according to the Type values of Tencent Microblog API. In this emotion taxonomy, we only focus on the emotion status of microblog publisher. Thus, we only choose the original published tweet to construct emotion corpus. Currently, this emotion annotated corpus consists of 150 users, totaling 15540 microblogs.

3.2   Emotion Taxonomy

The construction of annotation system of emotion analysis corpus is the mainly emotion classification problem. Because of the complexity and variability of emotion, and the number of emotion make it difficult for researchers to determine its type. The existing emotion classification systems are inconsistent. The granularity of emotion taxonomy is too detailed, not only increases the difficulty of annotation work, but also reduces the consistency of annotation. If the granularity of emotion taxonomy is too coarse, it is difficult to cover some common emotions. Therefore, this paper proposes a novel emotion taxonomy which both basic emotions and complex emotions. Specially, the basic emotions include four emotion classes, i.e., *joy, angry, sadness, fear*. While complex emotions contain three emotion classes, i.e., *positive* emotions, *neutral* emotions, and *negative* emotions. In addition, we have set *emotionlessness* category. Figure 1 illustrates the emotion taxonomy in detail as follows.

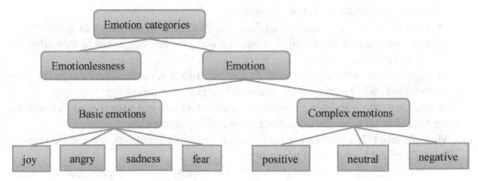

Fig. 1. Emotion taxonomy

3.3   Annotation Guidelines

The annotation guidelines can help to reduce error operation, improve the speed of annotation and increase the consistency of annotation. A microblog can have a maximum of 140 characters, colloquial and brief expression, have more network language. Moreover, Microblog platform also provides rich emoticons, such as "😢", the text elements corresponding to "\大哭"[*dà kū*](*crying*). These emoticons often represent user's emotional tendency. Therefore, the annotation guidelines were designed by combining with the characteristics of the microblog for constructing emotion corpus on microblog text is of great significance. The guidelines of this paper are as follows:

1) Annotating process: In the annotation process, we should follow the basic emotions before complex emotions, namely, for a microblog text containing emotion, we firstly judge whether the emotion belongs to the basic emotions, if it belongs to basic emotions, we choose the basic emotions for annotation. Otherwise, judge the type of complex emotions which it belongs to, we choose the appropriate complex emotions for annotating. For example,
    Chinese: *最近好烦啊*
    Pinyin: *zuì jìn hǎo fán ā*
    English: *It's been a very annoying.*
    Obviously, the text contains emotion. We firstly should judge whether the emotion belongs to the basic emotions, after finding no appropriate type of the basic emotions, therefore, choose *negative* emotion from the complex emotions category for annotating.

2) The number of Annotators: Each microblog was respectively annotated by two annotators, if the results of annotation are consistent, this results as the final results. If the results are inconsistent, so that the third annotator take part in annotation work, the consistent results as the final results.

3) Emoticon microblog: If a microblog text only contains emoticon, then directly annotate according to the meaning of emoticon. For instance, "∨大哭"[dà kū](*crying*) annotate *sadness*. If the meaning of emoticon is different from the meaning of the microblog text semantics, we should label microblog according to microblog text semantics. For example,

> Chinese: 火大，去了邮局几趟都没有把我的支付宝弄好，一群笨蛋，😊
>
> Pinyin: *huǒ dà qù le yóu jú jǐ tang dōu méi yǒu bǎ wǒ de zhī fù bǎo nòng hǎ o, yì qún bèn dàn,* 😊
>
> English: *I was very angry, went to the post office several times, the post office employees didn't make my Paypal ready, a group of idiots.* 😊

In this case, the microblog expresses *anger* emotion, but uses a smile emoticon, we should label as *anger* according to microblog semantics.

4) Multiple label: If a microblog text contains multiple emotions, we should respectively label each emotion. For example,

> Chinese: 爸爸，我们之间不仅是父子，还是师生，当你的学生真好，祝你快乐一生！
>
> Pinyin: *bà ba wǒ men zhī jiān bù jǐn shì fù zǐ, hái shì shī sheng, dāng nǐ de xué sheng zhēn hǎo, zhù nǐ kuài lè yì sheng.*
>
> English: *Dad, we are not only father and son, or teachers and students, it's good to be as your student, I wish you a happy life.*

This text contains two emotion types, happy and bless, so we label as *joy* and *neutral*.

5) Joke microblog: if the content of microblog text is a joke or the author joking, we uniformly label as *joy*. For example,

> Chinese: 我买了一只仓鼠和一个笼子，有天和朋友抱怨：你说，这笼子竟然比仓鼠还贵。朋友说：难道你认为你会比现在的房价高吗？
>
> Pinyin: *wǒ mǎi le yī zhī cāng shǔ hé yī gè long zi, yǒu tiān hé péng yǒu bào yuan: nǐ shuō zhè long zi jìng rán bǐ cāng shǔ hái guì. Péng yǒu shuō nán dào nǐ rèn wéi nǐ huì bǐ xiàn zài de fang jià gāo ma?*
>
> English: *I bought a hamster and a cage. One day with friends complained: you said, this cage is more expensive than the hamster. Friend said: do you think you will be higher than the current house price?*

6) Swearing microblog: If the content of microblog text contains dirty words, we can give priority to determine whether it contains *anger* emotion. For example,

> Chinese: 草泥马的铁路公司，尼玛的车就不能准时到站一回。
>
> Pinyin: *cǎo ní mǎ de tiě lù gong sī, ní mǎ de chē jiù bù néng zhǔn shí dào zhàn yī huí.*
>
> English: *Fuck the railroad, fuck the train can't arrive on time one time.*

7) Share microblog: If the content of a microblog text is about the shares of games, songs, shopping ads, etc., we should label as *emotionlessness*.

Chinese: 龙是桀骜的力量。我参加了《剑灵》人龙灵天种族投票，你的种族选好了吗？还有免费参加#剑灵不删档激活码抽奖#

Pinyin: *long shì jié ào de lì liang, wǒ cān jiā le jiàn líng rén long líng tiān zh ǒng zú tóu piào, nǐ de zhǒng zú xuǎn hǎo le ma? Hái yǒu miǎn fèi cān jiā jiàn líng bù shān dàng jī huó mǎ chōu jiǎng*

English: *The dragon is an unruly power. I participated in four races (Gon, Jin, Yun, Lyn) vote of BNS (Blade and Soul). Did your race choose? There are free to participate in activity for obtaining activation code.*

4   Analysis of Corpus

As discussed in Section 3.3, we annotate the emotional microblog texts. The annotated corpus consist of 150 users published 15540 microblogs. Table 1 summarizes the distribution of emotion on the corpus. Table 2 shows the distribution of emotion categories expressed in emotional microblog text.

Table 1. The distribution of emotion

	Emotional microblog		Emotionless microblog
	Single label	Multiple label	
amount	6431	117	8992
proportion/%	41.38%	0.76%	57.86%
total/%	42.14%		57.86%

Table 2. The distribution of emotional texts in each emotion category

Categories	Amount	Proportion/%
joy	1038	15.56%
angry	472	7.08%
sadness	581	8.71%
fear	94	1.41%
Positive complex emotion	1178	17.66%
Neutral complex emotion	1131	16.96%
Negative complex emotion	2175	32.61%
ALL	6669	100%

From the Table 1, we can see that the proportion of emotional and emotionless microblog is about 1:1.36. It is worth nothing that the proportion of multiple label microblog text is small compared with single microblog text. This is mainly due to our proposed emotion taxonomy in this paper can sufficient reflect the distinction between categories, and has a good degree of discrimination.

Obviously, the distribution is a bit imbalanced in Table 2. In basic emotions, the proportion of *joy* is the biggest, and the proportion of *anger* is the smallest. In complex emotions, the proportion of negative is the most.

This paper adopts kappa value to measure the consistency of annotating. From the two aspects of the consistency measurement, one is whether microblog text contains emotion, and the other is the emotion category. The consistencies of our annotation on the microblog text are given in Table 3.

Table 3. Analysis of consistency

	Kappa value
Emotion or emotionlessness	0.7186
Emotion category	0.7156

From the results of Table 3, we can see that the consistency of emotion category reach 0.7156, while the consistency of emotion or emotionlessness is about 0.7186. This results demonstrate our annotation work achieve a much higher consistency.

In order to reflect the advantages of our proposed emotion taxonomy, we randomly select 492 microblogs that 6 users published and use the basic emotions to annotate. Based on this, we carry out some statistics and analyses.

Table 4 shows the number of inconsistencies under the two emotion taxonomy. One is only containing four basic emotions, i.e., *joy*, *angry*, *sadness*, *fear* while another is our proposed emotion taxonomy which contains both basic emotions and complex emotions. The number of inconsistency is the number of inconsistent micro-blog text that different annotators label under the same samples.

Table 4. The statistic of the two emotion taxonomies

User	Only four basic emotions	Our proposed emotion taxonomy
1	31 (26.27%)	3 (2.54%)
2	67 (46.53%)	27 (18.75%)
3	9 (30.00%)	4 (13.33%)
4	22 (25.29%)	16 (18.39%)
5	34 (44.74%)	17 (22.37%)
6	20 (54.05%)	4 (10.81%)

From the statistics of Table 4, we can find that in our proposed emotion taxonomy, the proportion of inconsistency of microblog texts, the worst is 22.37%, and the best is 2.54%. While in the only four basic emotions, under the same sample, the proportion of microblog text annotation, the best is 25.29%. In contrast, this paper proposed emotion taxonomy can better distinguish different emotion categories, therefore, achieves a much higher annotation results.

5   Conclusion and Future Work

In this paper, we propose a novel emotion taxonomy which contains both basic emotions and complex emotions in order to construct emotion corpus on microblog text. Up to now, we have annotated 15540 microblogs that 150 users published. On this basis, we have carried on statistic and analysis for results of annotation. The results show that the emotion taxonomy that we proposed can well construct emotion corpus on microblog text, and the consistency of the annotation is about 0.72. In addition, we find that compared with the traditional emotion classification system, the emotion taxonomy can improve the quality and efficiency of annotating corpus.

In the future work, we would like to annotate corpus work in order to further expand the scale of corpus, and apply our annotated emotion corpus in more applications, e.g. microblog emotion classification.

Acknowledgments. This research work has been partially supported by two NSFC grants, No.61375073 and No.61273320, one the State Key Program of National Natural Science of China No.61331011.

References

1. Alm, C., Roth, D., Sproat, R., Emotions from text: machine learning for text-based emotion prediction. In: Proceedings of EMNLP, pp. 579–586 (2005)
2. Aman, S., Szpakowicz, S.: Identifying expressions of emotion in text. In: Matoušek, V., Mautner, P. (eds.) TSD 2007. LNCS (LNAI), vol. 4629, pp. 196–205. Springer, Heidelberg (2007)
3. Arnold, M.: Emotion and Personality. Columbia University Press, New York (1960)
4. Bhowmick, P.K., Basu, A., Mitra, P., Prasad, A.: Multi-label text classification approach for sentence level news emotion analysis. In: Chaudhury, S., Mitra, S., Murthy, C.A., Sastry, P.S., Pal, S.K. (eds.) PReMI 2009. LNCS, vol. 5909, pp. 261–266. Springer, Heidelberg (2009)
5. Chen, Y., Lee, S., Li, S., Huang, C.: Emotion cause detection with linguistic constructions. In: Proceedings of COLING, pp. 179–187 (2010)
6. Ekman, P., Friesen, V., Ellsworth, P.: What emotion categories or dimensions can observers judge from facial behavior? In: Ekman, P. (ed.) Emotion in Human Face, pp. 39–55. Cambridge University Press, New York
7. Gray, A.: The neuropsychology of anxiety. Oxford University Press, Oxford (1982)
8. Li, C., Wu, H., Jin, Q.: Emotion classification of chinese microblog text via fusion of bow and evector feature representations. In: Zong, C., Nie, J.-Y., Zhao, D., Feng, Y. (eds.) NLPCC 2014. CCIS, vol. 496, pp. 217–228. Springer, Heidelberg (2014)
9. Lin, K., Yang, C., Chen, H.: Emotion classification of online news articles from the reader's perspective. In: Proceedings of the International Conference on Web Intelligence and Intelligent Agent Technology, pp. 220–226 (2008)
10. Liu, H., Li, S., Zhou, G., Huang, C., Li, P.: Joint modeling of news reader's and comment writer's emotions. In: Proceedings of ACL, pp. 511–515 (2013)
11. Mishne, G.: Experiments with mood classification in blog posts. In: Proceedings of ACM SIGIR 2005 Workshop on Stylistic Analysis of Text for Information Access (2005)
12. Ortony, A., Turer, T.: What's Basic about Basic Emotions? Psychological Review, 315–331 (1990)
13. Pak, A., Paroubek, P.: Twitter as a corpus for sentiment analysis and opinion mining. In: Proceedings of Language Resource and Evalutation Conference, pp. 1320–1326 (2010)
14. Plutchik, R.: A general psychoevolutionary theory of emotion. In: Plutchik, R., Kellerman, H. (eds.) Emotions: Theory, Research, and Experience. Theories of emotion, vol. 1, pp. 3–31. Academic Press, New York
15. Quan, C, Ren, F.: Construction of a blog emotion corpus for Chinese emotional expression analysis. In: Proceedings of the 2009 Conference on Empirical Methods in Natural Language Processing, pp. 1446–1454 (2009)

16. Tokuhisa, R., Inui, K., Matsumoto, Y.: Emotion classification using massive examples extracted from the web. In: Proceedings of COLING, pp. 881–888 (2008)
17. Wiebe, J., Wilson, T., Cardie, C.: Annotating expressions of opinions and emotions in language. Language Resources and Evaluation **39**, 65–210 (2005)
18. Xu, G., Meng, X., Wang, H.: Build Chinese emotion lexicons using a graph-based algorithm and multiple resources. In: Proceedings of COLING, pp. 1209–1217 (2010)
19. Xu, J., Xu, R., Lu, Q., Wang, X.: Coarse-to-fine sentence-level emotion classification based on the intra-sentence features and sentential context. In: Proceedings of CIKM-2012, poster, pp. 2455–2458 (2012)
20. Xu, L., Lin, H., Zhao, J.: Construction and Analysis of Emotional Corpus. Journal of Chinese Information Processing **22**(1), 116–122 (2008)
21. Yao, Y., Wang, S., Xu, R., et al.: The Construction of an Emotion Annotated Corpus on Micro blog Text. Journal of Chinese Information Processing **28**(5), 83–91 (2014)

The Research on the Knowledge Base Construction of Pragmatic Information on Confusable Words in TCSL

Juan Li[1(✉)], Lijiao Yang[1], and Yongjie Lu[2]

[1] Institute of Chinese Information Processing,
Beijing Normal University, Beijing 100875, China
lijuan@mail.bnu.edu.cn
[2] College of Chinese Language and Culture, Beijing Normal University, Beijing 100875, China

Abstract. By studying the Chinese Learner's Dictionaries in recent years, this paper discovers that pragmatic information has been increased in the discrimination of confusable words. However, there is no consensus for the dimension of pragmatic information. This paper proposes to construct a knowledge base which can be applied to the field of Teaching Chinese as a Second Language (TCSL). The knowledge base focuses on the frequently-used confusable words of TCSL, and it provides referential information for words discrimination. Specifically, this research adopts fifteen dimensions to describe the dynamic pragmatic meaning of the confusable Chinese words by classifying them into several categories.

Keywords: Teaching Chinese as a Second Language (TCSL) · Confusable words · Knowledge base · Pragmatic information

1   Introduction

Vocabulary teaching is both the key point and the difficult point in TCSL. The latest studies indicate that the errors in using synonyms account for more than one third of the total errors of word use (Li, 2004). Zhang (2008) pointed out that the errors of word use occur when you should understand a word as A but you misunderstand it as B, or when you should use word A but misuse it as word B. However, words mentioned here refer to confusable words instead of synonyms. Zhang (2007) argued that confusable words and synonyms cross with each other without any inclusive or parallel relationship, for they are clusters of words put forward by researchers from different standpoints, perspectives and criteria.

For foreigners learning Chinese, it is not difficult to master the static meaning of confusable words. The difficult part lies in the flexible use of the words. In the field of TCSL, researchers and teachers attach great importance to the discrimination of confusable words. Zhang (2009) has discriminated confusable words with good results from such pragmatic information as emotive, stylistic and image color, as well as specific use. Through comparative analysis of the Chinese synonyms dictionaries for foreign learners that are published in recent years, it is found that introduction of

© Springer International Publishing Switzerland 2015
Q. Lu and H.H. Gao (Eds.): CLSW 2015, LNAI 9332, pp. 213–221, 2015.
DOI: 10.1007/978-3-319-27194-1_22

pragmatic information has become the general trend in the field of dictionary compilation. From the pragmatic perspective, Bu (2014) employs theories of pragmatics, including the context theory, the politeness principle, and the speech act theory, to study the pragmatic information in dictionaries and specify the connotation of pragmatic information in the dictionaries. However, as pragmatic information is flexible, complex and difficult to grasp, it is worthwhile to further explore the scientific and reasonable application of them to the discrimination of words.

Currently, it has become a very compelling research orientation to study linguistic problems by employing corpus and knowledge base. For instance, Comprehensive Language Knowledge Base (CLKB), which is constructed by the Institute of Computational Linguistics (ICL) of Peking University, has imposed a tremendous influence on the academic world of Chinese information processing. Yu and Zhu (2013, 2014) maintained that CLKB can also make a difference in the following fields: the research of language teaching and of teaching Chinese as a second language. However, there are few research achievements in the combination of the knowledge base with language teaching. In addition to using traditional methods like explanations by teachers and consulting the dictionaries, we should, concerning the difficulties discriminating words, take advantage of a variety of knowledge resources to facilitate this work. On the 6th Chinese Lexical Semantics Workshop, Su, et al. (2005) pointed out that traditional methods of words discrimination focus more on the static lexical meaning, at the cost of ignoring the pragmatic, stylistic and context differences presented by the lexical meaning in actual usage. Hence it is of great necessity and value to construct a knowledge base of words, which features sufficient discrimination dimensions, independent display of key information, as well as self-contained and self-verified capabilities.

Consequently, it is of great importance to build a scientific, data-oriented, explicit pragmatic information knowledge base of confusable words: (1) it can be widely applied to various aspects of TCSL and research, and can provide targeted references for TCSL. Besides, it can help researchers and learners quickly and efficiently extract confused points from confusable words. Learners can verify usage from relevant example sentences and thereby quickly master them. Meanwhile, the pragmatic information knowledge base can systematize and formalize the complicated, dynamic pragmatic information, so that compilers of dictionaries can purposefully select valid pragmatic information from it; (2) it is conducive to the development of natural language processing. Syntax, semantics and pragmatics constitute a trinity. So far, the construction of syntactic and semantic resources is relatively mature, but the pragmatic knowledge base is still in slow construction. Besides, the construction of TCSL corpus is still in its infancy, so it cannot fully meet the multi-dimensional needs in TCSL and research. As the fundamental knowledge resources, pragmatic information knowledge base can specifically provide theoretical background and design specifications for the construction of TCSL Corpus. Moreover, the pragmatic information knowledge base and other vocabulary knowledge bases can be cross-referenced, with a view to further explore language knowledge and push the construction of language knowledge base to a brand new level.

2   Design Scheme of Pragmatic Information Knowledge Base

2.1   Design Scheme of Pragmatic Information Knowledge Base

At present, there are many dictionaries published by China, which are used for discriminating synonyms or near-synonyms. The criterion of discrimination is semantic similarity, which is incomplete. With reference to 346 groups of confusable words from Xiao Pin's dissertation——the Study on Confusable words of Indonesian Learners' Inter-language (2008). It is discovered that the following three types of words may confuse foreign learners who study Chinese. First, words are similar in semantics, such as 爱护[aihu] (*care*)/爱惜[aixi] (*cherish*), 知道[zhidao] (*know*)/了解 [liaojie] (*understand*). Second, words are similar in usage, such as 对不起[duibuqi] (*sorry*)/抱歉[baoqian] (*excuse me*), 只[zhi]/支[zhi]. Third, words are entirely unrelated in semantics or usage, such as 匆匆[congcong] (*quickly*)/冲冲[congcong] (*flush*), 行[xing] (*walk*)/行[hang] (*line*). Words of the first type are compiled into a thesaurus, while the second and the third ones are almost excluded from dictionaries, leading to the predicament that they cannot be checked in those dictionaries.

By analyzing misused words in HSK dynamic Composition Corpus (The total number of words in the corpus is 2825427), it is discovered that not only the word group 诞生[dansheng] (*born*)/出生[chusheng] (*born*) is confusing, but the group 生 [sheng] (*born*)/出生[chusheng] (*born*) is. However, 生[sheng] (*born*)/出生[chusheng] (*born*) is not compiled in several extroversive dictionaries for language learners.

Therefore, we can come to this conclusion that confusable words are not completely compiled in the synonym dictionaries. To meet the demand of Chinese learners specifically, the research establishes a knowledge base of pragmatic information, which focuses on the frequently-used confusable words of TCSL, and it provides reference information for words discrimination.

But, how large it is? How to establish a knowledge base with the high quality and appropriate capacity? Based on what criteria can the research systematically and scientifically classify the confusable words?

In terms of the scale of the knowledge base, bigger is not better. It is important that the range of vocabulary in the base should be balanced, that is, coverage should be at a high level. Specifically speaking, words are taken in the base in accordance with different word categories and in an appropriate proportion. The study of confusable words is still in development, thus there is no certain word list absorbed into the base. Besides, due to the effect of Negative Transfer of Mother Tongue, learners from different countries have their own problems when encountering confusable words, leading to difficulties in making a vocabulary list.

With regard to the classification of vocabulary, Su (2005) pointed out that the trend in construction of a language knowledge base is internalization and refinement, that is, language information of words interior is increasingly concerned in the process of knowledge base construction. The method to classify words in accordance with the part of speech can only roughly segregate synonyms, or near-synonyms. For the subtle differences in meaning and usage of words in the same cluster, the research holds it is necessary to classify words by the combination of the deep semantic relevance of words. Specifically speaking, it may be feasible to classify confusable words in the frame work of content words (noun, verb, adjective, adverb, numeral and classifier) and function words.

First, the meaning of function words is context dependent, thus it is more flexible than content words. And the misuse frequency of the former is higher, so it is necessary to place them into one category in the word list of the base.

Second, the address words in nouns have high frequency of use, which can form one category. Also, the classification of other nouns can be refined.

Third, there are psychological words in verbs. And they can be classified into the following three categories: (1) Emotion: such as 喜欢[xihuan] (*like*)/爱好[aihao] (*hobby*), 讨厌 [taoyan] (*dislike*)/憎恨 [zenghen] (*hate*), 嫉妒 [jidu] (*envy*)/羡慕 [xianmu] (*admire*); (2) Perception: such as 知道 [zhidao] (*realize*)/了解 [liaojie] (*know*)/明白[mingbai] (*understand*); (3) Auxiliary: such as 能[neng] (*can*)/会[hui] (*be able to*)/愿意[yuanyi] (*be willing to*); (4) Existence: such as 显现[xianxian] (*appear*)/泄露 [xielu] (*reveal*)/暴露 [baolu] (*expose*), 出生 [chusheng] (*born*)/诞生 [dansheng] (*born*), etc.

Fourth, the category of Space-time (including adverbs and verbs): (1)Time: such as 曾经[cengjing] (*once*)/已经[yijing] (*already*), 突然[turan] (*suddenly*)/忽然[huran] (*abruptly*), 常常[changchang] (*usually*)/往往[wangwang] (*often*),etc. (2)Space ① Shift: 寻[xun] (*look for*)/ 找[zhao] (*find*), ② Movement: 改变[gaibian] (*change*)/变化[bianhua] (*alter*)/转化[zhuanhua] (*transform*), 中断[zhongduan] (*suspend*)/间断 [jianduan] (*discontinue*), etc.

Fifth, the category of Quantity: such as 二[er] (*two*)/两[liang] (*two*)/俩[liang] (*two*), 个[ge] /只[zhi]/支[zhi], etc.

Sixth, the category of Measurement: (1)big or small: such as 肥[fei] (*fat*) /粗[cu] (*wide*) /胖[pang] (*stout*); (2) height or short: such as 低[di] (*low*)/矮[ai] (*short*); (3)sparse or dense: such as 稀[xi] (*sparse*)/细[xi] (*thin*), etc.

2.2   Classify the Dimension of Pragmatic Information

The term "pragmatics" was first introduced by Charles Morris, the American philosopher. Until now, there is still no consensus on the definition of pragmatics in linguistics circles. He (1989) pointed out in his *Essentials of Pragmatics* "In most definition of pragmatics, there are two basic concepts: meaning and context. Although meaning and usage are respectively classified into different research categories, they are inseparable in language research. By drawing pragmatics into lexical study added with lexicography, the term 'pragmatic information' comes into being."

The term "pragmatic information" was first introduced by Leech and Thomas who wrote a preface named Pragmatics and the Dictionary for *Longman Dictionary of Contemporary English* (the second version). They pointed out the importance of the pragmatic information in foreign language learning and they proposed that it is practicable to place pragmatic information into dictionaries for foreign learners. From then on, compilers of dictionary for learning English pay more attention to showing pragmatic information.

What is the content of pragmatic information? Which categories and elements in particular does it include? And what is the standard of classification and the basis? All of these questions have no unified answers in an academic world. Dr. Leech and Dr. Thomas first defined pragmatic information in the preface of *Longman Dictionary of Contemporary English* (Second Edition): (1) formality in occasion; (2) familiarity between speakers and listeners; (3) intention and power of speakers; (4) social status and background, age, gender and occupation of speakers. Qian (1996) believed that there are two categories of pragmatic information shown by dictionaries. One category is the typical utterance meaning of words, which can help readers to understand the intention of speakers. Another is the general usage rule of words, which can instruct readers to choose appropriate usage based on factors like the context and relations between speakers and listener. And this part is one of the most important information in dictionaries for language learners, which directly connects very directly to the improvement of pragmatic competence of learners.

The following four dictionaries show the content of pragmatic information in compilation.

First, *Longman Dictionary of Contemporary English* (Second Edition) defines the content of pragmatic information, which includes the information defined by Leech and Thomas.

Second, *Longman Dictionary of Contemporary English* (Fourth Edition) divides pragmatic information into two parts. One is about emotion and attitude, which in particular includes the attitude of praise and dispraise, the strength of feeling, politeness and fuzziness phenomena. Another is about speech act, which includes advice, approval and disapproval, apology, permission, licenses and refusal, request, invitation, acceptance and rejection.

Third, there are six elements of pragmatic information in *Collins COBUILD Advanced Learner's English Dictionary*: (1) the attitude of praise and dispraise; (2) strong or weak tone; (3) emotion; (4) polite formula; (5) politeness; (6) fuzziness phenomena.

Fourth, the information in *Macmillan English Dictionary for Advanced Learners* includes speech act, the extent of politeness, emotive attitude, and fuzziness phenomena.

These four dictionaries reflect the content of pragmatic information, but not all. He (1987) pointed out that the discussion of meaning should be made in the range of pragmatics. Leech proposed the following four criteria: (1) speakers and listeners; (2) intention of speakers and understanding of listeners; (3) context; (4) act implemented by language.

Again, our subject to construct a knowledge base of confusable words is continued. Combing pragmatics with pragmatic information shown in dictionaries, the paper believes that pragmatic information includes context, emotive, attitude, the principle of politeness, speech act, style, deixis, space-time, and etc. Preliminarily, the paper divides pragmatic information into six categories as the first class, and then under each category set up a secondary dimensions. Here is the project:

First, pragmatic information of communicators is presented.

Include: (1) personal information: age, identity, vocation, gender, social status, literacy level; (2) relations: relatives, friends, teachers and students, hosts and guests, the older and the younger, the upper and the lower.

Second, information of emotive attitude is presented.

Include: praise, neutral and dispraise.

Third: information of social contact is presented.

Include: (1) politeness, honorific title, respect term, humble term, euphemism, polite formula; (2) occasion: formal and informal; (3) tone: statement, question, imperative, exclamatory, the extent of tone (strong or weak); (4) speech act: greetings, farewell, congratulation, apology, acknowledgement, request for help, advice ,urge, speculation and estimation, caution, discussion and suggestion, approval and agreement, disapproval and disagreement, criticism and reprimand, compliment, supplementary instruction, discourse markers, exaggeration;   (5) style: oral, written language.

Fourth, sentence information.

Include: (1) deixis: person deixis, time deixis; (2) presupposition.

Fifth, space-time.

Include: (1) era: ancient Chinese, vernacular Chinese; (2) space: dialect.

Sixth, fixed usage.

Include: front collocation, back collocation.

2.3   Engineering Method

In the engineering, we consider the following aspects.

First of all, how to determine the capacity of the base? How to classify words into different categories? At present, our research is still at the theoretical level. We selected 200 groups of confusable words and classified them into different categories based on their meanings and parts of speech. The 200 groups of tagged words mainly come from the doctoral dissertation of Dr. Xiao Pin (2008), and some of them come from HSK Dynamic Composition Corpus. In his paper, he displayed 545 groups of quasi confusable words, and 346 groups of confusable words.

Second, the pragmatic information is carefully considered. By extracting and inducing pragmatic information, we selected six categories of pragmatic information and refined them into fifteen secondary dimensions. These fifteen dimensions, which respectively include specific items, are in a relatively comprehensive coverage in the preliminary process of tagging. In future researches, deletion and modification could be made depending on the actual situation.

Last but not least, currently, the amount of the confusable words is about 200 groups, which are mainly used in similar situation. In the process of tagging, ID, phonetic, parts of speech, and example sentence are common attributes while others are optional. We classify the confusable words by choosing different pragmatic information. For instance, function words mostly use the dimension of mood modality, style, front collocations, back collocations, speech acts and so on. And salutations usually use dimensions related to communication participants, while the psychology words mostly use dimensions of emotions and attitudes.

3 Pragmatic Information Dimension Test

By classifying pragmatic information into six categories, we believe that the knowledge base can better cover confusable words and show word usage and features. It is illustrated by the following:

HSK Dynamic Composition Corpus contains some compositions written by non-native Chinese speakers who attend the high lever language examination. We queried the words "或者[huozhe] (*or*)"and"还是[haishi] (*or*)"of which the total occurrence frequency are 1146 times and 2781 times. By contrast, errors of using these two words mainly belong to the following three types.

(1) Error of sentence patterns. "或者[huozhe] (*or*) " cannot be used in interrogative sentences.

a.法律或者人情? (*Law or humanity?*)

b.他们要选择工作或者家庭? (*For them, work or family?*)

(2) Error of fixed usage. "......无论......还是...... [......wulun......haishi......]" (*Whether ...or ...*)" is a fixed usage, which indicates generalization. However, "......无论......或者...... [......wulun......huozhe......]" is not the right collocation.

a.是的, 我无论对衣服上或者房间里的色彩都很注意的。(*Yes, I am attentive to the color of the clothes or the room.*)

b.据此推测,无论在世界发达国家或者发展中国家,一律致力于严格地限制吸烟。 (*It can be presumed that smoking is strictly restricted whether in developed countries or developing countries.*)

(3) Language sense is not strong. When both words can be used in the below sentences, learners often don't know which to use.

a.我的看法是"安乐死"如果在病人说过还是写过"我要死"、"你帮我自杀"这样的话以后, 就没有什么问题。(*In my opinion, it doesn't matter to use euthanasia if a patient says or writes down "I want to die." or "Please help me die."*)

b.至今我学了三年多汉语,一听到汉语歌曲还是中国电影我就可以放下一切去欣赏它们。(*So far, I have learned Chinese for more than three years. Thus, when I hear Chinese songs or films, I can drop everything to enjoy them.*)

First, test on function words by using the dimensions of the pragmatic information.

The three dimensions in the system of our annotation are aimed at different error types as I mentioned before. Specifically speaking, "sentence pattern", "fixed usage" and "example sentence" correspond to error types of (1), (2) and (3), respectively. These pragmatic information can provide discrimination dimensions for function words, such as conjunctions (或者[huozhe] (*or*) /还是[haishi] (*or*), and auxiliary words (吧[ba] /吗[ma] /嘛[ma] /呢[ne]).

Second, test on salutations. For example, there exists no confusing points between 医生[yisheng] (*doctor*) and 先生[xiansheng] (*gentleman*), 小姐[xiaojie] (*Miss*) and 姑娘[guniang] (*girl*) for native Chinese speakers. However, these words are confusing for some learners of non-native Chinese speakers. Nevertheless, we can distinguish them from the following 8 dimensions: (1) pragmatic information of interlocutors (vocation, gender, identity); (2) relations of interlocutors; (3) style; (4) politeness; (5) occasion; (6) time; (7) space; (8) example sentence.

In addition, according to 346 groups of confusable words from the doctoral dissertation of Xiao (2008), it is discovered that psychological words easily confuse foreign learners of Chinese, such as 喜欢[xihuan] (*like*)/爱好[aihao] (*be fond of*), 爱护[aihu] (*care*)/爱惜[aixi] (*cherish*), 爱护[aihu] (*care*)/保护[baohu] (*protect*), 爱惜[aixi] (*cherish*)/珍惜[zhenxi] (*treasure*), etc. Words from this category can be discriminated by the pragmatic information like emotive attitude, front collocation, back collocation and style. Due to space limitation, we cannot show more examples. Overall, these six classifications can better generalize the pragmatic information of confusable words. Also, they can relatively cover the word categories. Hence, they can make a contribution to the discrimination of confusable words.

4   Conclusion

The paper intends to discriminate confusable words by constructing a pragmatic information knowledge base, and thus provides the solution and design scheme that extracts the classification dimensions of pragmatic information. Confusable words are described by the extracted fifteen secondary pragmatic information labeling dimensions. The knowledge base will contain frequently-used confusable words in TCSL. Through preliminary comparative examination, confusable words have been described perfectly by these pragmatic information dimensions. Thus, they will provide references for the discrimination of confusable words.

So far, the study of constructing the pragmatic information knowledge base of confusable words is still at the preliminary stage. In future researches, we should: (1) establish a more scientific classification system of confusable words; (2) modify and improve the dimensions of pragmatic information; (3) construct several pragmatic information sub-knowledge bases for learners of different mother tongues; (4) design a simple, user-friendly query system for explicit displaying of the unorganized pragmatic information of words through coding and formatting.

Acknowledgement. This work was supported by the National Hi-Tech Research and Development Program of China (No.2012AA011104), and by the "Twelfth Five" Scientific Research Project (YB125-124) of the China State Language Affairs Commission.

References

1. Bu, Y.: The Study of Pragmatic Information in Chinese Learning Dictionaries. Master Dissertation of Xiamen University (2014). (in Chinese)
2. He, Z.: Pragmatics, Meaning and Context. Journal of Foreign Languages **5**, 10–14 (1987). (in Chinese)
3. He, Z.: An Introduction to Pragmatics. Shanghai Foreign Language Education Press (1989). (in Chinese)
4. Liu, Y., Yu, S.W.: The Building of Knowledge Database of Contemporary Chinese Functional Words. Applied Linguistics **2**, 131–135 (2005). (in Chinese)

5. Li, S.L.: The Object and Principles of Discriminating Word Meanings in Teaching Chinese as a Second Language. Chinese Teaching in the World **3**, 406–414 (2010). (in Chinese)
6. Qian, H.S.: The Design and the Compilation of Dictionaries on Language and Culture. Lexicographical Studies **1**, 31–41 (1996). (in Chinese)
7. Su, X.C., et al.: The internalization and the refinement of language knowledge base-the assumption of the improvement of semantic knowledge base. In: Proceedings on the Sixth Chinese Lexical Semantics Seminar (2005). (in Chinese)
8. Xiao, P.: The Research on Confusable Words of Indonesian Students in Chinese Interlanguage. PhD Dissertation of Beijing Language and Culture University (2008). (in Chinese)
9. Yu, S.W., Zhu, X.F.: Comprehensive Language Knowledge Base and Its Preliminary Application in International Chinese Language Education. International Chinese Language Education **1**, 023 (2013). (in Chinese)
10. Yu, S.W., Zhu, X.F.: Comprehensive Language Knowledge Base and Its Applications in Language Teaching. Journal of Beihua University (Social Sciences) **15**(3), 4–9 (2014). (in Chinese)
11. Yang, W.X.: The Research on the Pragmatic Information in the English-Chinese Learner's Dictionary. Shanghai Translation Publishing House (2005). (in Chinese)
12. Zhang, B.: Synonym, Near-Synonym and Confusable Word: A Perspective Transformation from Chinese to inter-language. Chinese Teaching in the World **3**(95), 201 (2007). (in Chinese)
13. Zhang, B.: Compiling Principles and Style Designing of Export-oriented Dictionaries of Confusable Words. Chinese Language Learning **1**, 85–92 (2008). (in Chinese)
14. Zhang, L.: The Shallows: the Teaching of Confusable Words in Teaching Chinese as a Second Language. The Science Education Article Collects **11**, 104–105 (2009). (in Chinese)

Proofreading and Revision of the Semantic Classes in the Contemporary Chinese Semantic Dictionary

Lingling Mu[✉], Hao Li, Hongying Zan, Xiaobo Feng,
Yinlong Bi, and Mengshuang Li

School of Information Engineering, Zhengzhou University, Zhengzhou 450001, China
iellmu@zzu.edu.cn

Abstract. The Contemporary Chinese Semantic Dictionary(CSD) is a semantic knowledge base which is developed on the basis of GKB: Grammatical Knowledge Base of Contemporary Chinese. It can support automatic semantic analysis in various natural language processing systems, such as machine translation systems. In order to improve the CSD and prepare it for a wider range of application, the NLP laboratory of Zhengzhou University investigates the current distribution of its semantic classes and revises the unreasonable aspects of its semantic classification according to the latest development of linguistic research, particularly that in lexical semantics. This paper introduces the rules and specifications for proofreading and revising the semantic classes in CSD, the tools developed for these tasks, the statistical analysis of the current distribution of semantic classes and Part-of-Speech in CSD, the problems found in this process, and our reflections on the rules of semantic classification and semantic taxonomy. Our research provides reference and tools for the construction of semantic dictionaries in the future.

Keywords: Semantic dictionary · Semantic knowledge base · Semantic class · Lexical semantic · NLP

1   Introduction

In order to meet the requirements of automatic semantic computing, a variety of semantic dictionaries have been developed, such as Wordnet[1], Mindnet[2], Framenet[3], Thesaurus Dictionary of the Contemporary Chinese for Information Processing[4], the Machine Tractable Dictionary of Contemporary Chinese Predicate Verbs, Hownet[5], Chinese Concept Dictionary (CCD)[6], the Thesaurus of Modern Chinese[7], Wordmap[8], Tongyici Cilin[9], GKB: Grammatical Knowledge Base of Contemporary Chinese(GKB)[10] and so on.

The Contemporary Chinese Semantic Dictionary(CSD)[11,12] builds a reasonable semantic knowledge description framework on the basis of the grammatical knowledge base, which is closely related to its applications in language engineering. Currently, CSD has collected about 6.6 million Chinese content words in a database. It can support automatic semantic analysis in various natural language processing sys-

© Springer International Publishing Switzerland 2015
Q. Lu and H.H. Gao (Eds.): CLSW 2015, LNAI 9332, pp. 222–233, 2015.
DOI: 10.1007/978-3-319-27194-1_23

tems including machine translation systems. Canon, Sail-labs and more than 20 companies have bought the licenses to use it [13].

In order to improve the CSD's development and promote its application, we objectively and systematically investigated the current distribution of semantic classes in CSD and revised the unreasonable semantic classes according to the latest development of linguistic research, particularly that in lexical semantics, providing an important foundation for further improving CSD. The revised semantic taxonomy of words in CSD is more reasonable, which provides better support for research areas such as machine translation, phrase recognition and so on. The software for proofreading and revision can be used to construct semantic dictionaries in the future.

In this paper, Section 2 describes the current specifications of semantic taxonomy in CSD; Section 3 describes the specifications and standards of proofreading and revision as well as the proofreading process; Section 4 presents the statistics of the distribution of parts of speech (Part-of-Speech) and semantic classes of CSD; Section 5 summarizes the semantic classification criteria in semantic proofreading process and discusses the problems in the CSD taxonomy.

2   The Semantic Taxonomy of CSD

Mei Jiaju[9], Lin Xingguang [14,15], Chen Xiuqun [16], Chen Xiaohe [17], Dong Danian [18], Dong Zhendong [5,19], Su Xinchun [7], Zhao Jing [8] etc. have respectively used different Chinese semantic taxonomies which are independent of the syntax. In order to meet the requirements of automatic lexical semantic computing and machine translation, CSD has designed a semantic taxonomy on the basis of syntax, with reference to the various existing semantic taxonomies. It only describes the semantic taxonomies of nouns, verbs, adjectives, adverbs and numerals, among which the taxonomy of nouns is the most detailed and the taxonomies of verbs, adjectives, numerals, adverbs are simple and only reveal the different classes when they collocate with nouns and verbs. The semantic relations, which have obvious signs and can usually be expressed in syntactic forms, such as the function words, are not the focus of semantic taxonomy study [13].

The semantic taxonomy in CSD defines 151 semantic classes totally, in which there are six semantic classes that use the same names for different Part-of-Speech. They are "关系|relationship", "时间|time", "气象|weather", "外形|shape", "颜色|color" and "处所|location".

3   The Proofreading and Revision of Semantic Classes

In order to ensure the consistency of semantic proofreading standards, make it easy to do the proofreading and revising simultaneously, avoid mis-modifying the source data and make it convenient to post-process and merge data, we took some methods such as preprocessing CSD, and at the same time developed a tool for semantic proofreading and revision to enhance the proficiency. We preprocessed CSD to make it easy to do the proofreading and revision simultaneously, avoid mis-modifying the source data and make it convenient to post-process and merge data, made proofreading standards to ensure the consistency of semantic proofreading standards and developed a tool for semantic proofreading and revision to enhance the proficiency.

3.1   The Preprocessing of CSD

Before proofreading semantic classes, the CSD database was divided into three tables according to the Part-of-Speech of the entries, which contain nouns, verbs, numerals and words of other Part-of-Speech classes respectively

The purpose of proofreading CSD semantic classes is to check whether each word is classified to the correct semantic class according to the taxonomy. In order to better adapt to the development of lexical semantics, it is necessary to refer to the latest development of linguistic research, particularly that in lexical semantics, to make evidence-based proofreading. Our work mainly refers to Modern Chinese Dictionary (6th Edition) (XH) [20] and GKB [10] which are widely recognized and applied in the field of linguistics.

In order to refer to the knowledge of XH and GKB and record the revision process and the corresponding results, we supplement the original CSD structure by adding some fields as "ID", "GKB义项(GKB meanings)", "修改后的语义类(revised semantic class)", "备注(remarks)", "确信度(certainty)" and "现汉义项(XH meanings)" without changing the original contents of CSD.

3.2   Semantic Classes Proofreading

The purpose of proofreading CSD semantic classes is to check whether semantic classification in CSD is appropriate according to the CSD semantic taxonomy. It mainly includes four parts:

1. Checking the consistency of semantic classes that are annotated in CSD with those in CSD's semantic taxonomy;
2. Checking whether the annotated semantic class in CSD is classified to the appropriate standard semantic classes;
3. Classifying the words which have semantic losses in the dictionary;
4. Identifying and classifying the words annotated with multiple semantic classes as one semantic class.

3.2.1   Proofreading Specifications

1. If the words can be classified into a standard semantic class, then fill in the field of "修改后的语义类(*revised semantic class*)" with a correct standard semantic class, and make notes in the "备注(*remarks*)" field;
2. If it is considered to have no proper semantic class in the standard semantic classes, then make notes in the "备注(*remarks*)" field;

3. If the correctness of semantic class is unsure, then make notes in the "备注 (*remarks*)" field;
4. The criteria of distinction of the semantic classes: distinguishing the semantic classes according to the meanings of XH;

- If the words have no XH meanings, distinguish the semantic classes according to the explanation of "GKB义项 (*GKB meanings*)" field;
- If the words do not have XH meanings or GKB meanings, then either classify the words by referring to the word meanings in "Baidu Encyclopedia" and record the specific interpretation or examples in the "备注(*remarks*)" field, or make no changes to them.

5. The principles of semantic classification: if possible, classify the words to the semantic classes on leaf node. If there is no proper leaf node, then classify it to the classes on parent nodes. There are two cases of classifying the words to the classes on parent node:

- The semantic class of the words is right the parent class;
- The words which have no other appropriate leaf classes are classified to the parent classes. In this case, fill the "确信度(*certainty*)" field with "*";

6. When errors are found in other fields during proofreading, do not change them and only make notes in the "备注(*remarks*)" field.

3.2.2   The Requirements of Filling the Proofreading Results
According to CSD semantic taxonomy and the proofreading specifications in 3.2.1, proofread the semantic classes word by word.

1. If the semantic class is considered to be right, make no changes or records.
2. If the semantic class is considered to be wrong:

- If the words can be classified to a standard semantic class, then fill in the field of "修改后的语义类(*revised semantic class*)" with a correct standard semantic class, and make notes in the "备注(*remarks*)" field;
- Or if there is no proper standard semantic class, make notes in the "备注 (*remarks*)" field.

3. If the correctness of semantic class is unsure, make notes in the "备注(*remarks*)" field.
4. If the semantic class is missing:

- If the words can be classified to a standard semantic class, then fill in the field of "修改后的语义类(*revised semantic class*)" with a correct standard semantic class, and make notes in the "备注(*remarks*)" field;
- Or there is no proper standard semantic class, make notes in the "备注(*remarks*)" field.

3.3   The Tools for Proofreading the Semantic Classes

CSD is stored in the form of ACCESS database, the direct operations on database can result in mis-modifying the data. Therefore, we develop a tool for proofreading the semantic classes, which has such functions as displaying, searching, proofreading, revising and doing statistics, through which, we can scan the words by "Part-of-Speech" or "semantic class", count the number of all kinds of words and proofread the semantic classes directly and save the revised results. The tool greatly facilitates the proofreading and revising process and ensures we complete the work efficiently.

4   The Statistics and Analysis of Part-of-Speech and Semantic Classes in CSD

CSD is stored in the form of ACCESS database, including the following fields: "word", "Part-of-Speech", "pinyin", "meaning", "homograph", "semantic class" and other fields. Our focus is on proofreading the accuracy of the semantic class. Since the semantic specifications and Part-of-Speech are closely related, we have also examined the accuracy of Part-of-Speech, and made a simple comparison with GKB and XH.

4.1   The Statistics and Analysis of Part-of-Speech

At present, the CSD includes 65676 words, covering altogether 11 Parts-of-Speech including nouns, verbs, adjectives, adverbs, numerals, direction, pronouns, time words, status words, location words and distinguishing words. The number of entries in different Part-of-Speech classes is distributed as shown in table 1.

Table 1. The distribution statistics of the Part-of-Speech in CSD

Part-of-Speech	Nouns (n)	Verbs (v)	Adjectives (a)	Adverbs (d)	Status words(z)	Time words(t)
Quantity	37565	20952	3557	996	993	567

Part-of-Speech	Distin-guishing words(b)	Pronouns (r)	Direction (f)	Location (s)	Numerals (m)	Total (11)
Quantity	315	235	203	185	108	65676

The table shows that words having the largest number in CSD are nouns and verbs, and then adjectives and adverbs. Numerals are also a big Part-of-Speech class defined by the standard semantic classification, but the number of it is only 108, which is the least in all Part-of-Speech. Direction, pronouns, time words, status words, location and distinguishing words are not defined in standard semantic classification, the number of which is 3494 in the semantic dictionary.

Status words, time words, distinguishing words, pronouns, direction and location words are not defined in CSD, but they are related to the semantics. In CSD, status words and distinguishing words are taken as adjectives, pronouns, direction, location and time words as nouns.

4.1.1   The Comparison with XH and GKB

The semantic classification of CSD is based on the meanings of XH and the semantic information of GKB. So the compatibility of CSD with XH and GKB will affect the result of semantic classification. This paper makes a simple comparison of CSD with XH and GKB respectively.

1. The comparison with GKB

In CSD, we found that the "义项(*meanings*)" field is not from GKB and   its source is unable to determine. Since the "同形(*homographs*)" field is from GKB, we obtained

the corresponding explanation from GKB and filled in the new field "GKB同形(*GKB homographs*)". Through the comparison between CSD and GKB, it is discovered that the number of words in the intersection between CSD and GKB is 61,427 in total; those in the difference set between CSD and GKB is 166 in total. In the intersection, the number of words that are different in "同形(*homographs*)" field is 97, those that are different in Part-of-Speech is altogether 7536 and most of the words are idioms. 222 words in CSD are blank   in "同形(*homographs*)" field

2. The comparison with XH

Through the comparison between CSD and XH, it is discovered that the number of words in the intersection between CSD and XH is   39,657 in total; those in the difference set between CSD and XH is 21,936 words in total. In the intersection, the number of words in different Part-of-Speech is 6961, and that which are blank in "义项(meanings)" field is altogether 3118 in CSD.

4.1.2   The Division of Part-of-Speech in CSD

The words in CSD are limited to 11 Part-of-Speech such as nouns, verbs, adjectives, adverbs, numerals, direction, pronouns, time words, status words, location, and distinguishing words. Since the semantic of CSD is based on the Part-of-Speech, the accuracy of Part-of-Speech classification will directly affect the result of the semantic classification.

1. The Part-of-Speech of inconsistency compared with GKB and XH

From 4.1.1 we can see that there are 7536 words in CSD of which the Part-of-Speech are different from GKB, most of them are idioms. But in GKB, the Part-of-Speech of idioms is "i" and then they cannot be regarded as a reference for CSD.

At the same time, the number of the words of which the Part-of-Speech classes are different from XH is 6961 in CSD, which account for almost 10% in CSD. The different Part-of-Speech classes include three situations:

- The Part-of-Speech in XH is empty. Such as " 明日黄花 [*mingrihuanghua*] (*things that are unfashionable*)", "此起彼伏[*ciqibifu*] (*as one falls another rises*)". In this case, most of the words are four-character words and cannot find a standard Part-of-Speech in XH. But in CSD, the Part-of-Speech is annotated according to its usage. Under this situation, the Part-of-Speech in XH cannot be used as a reference.
- The Part-of-Speech is different, while the Part-of-Speech in CSD can be regarded as a subclass of XH. For example "铁青[*tieqing*]", in XH, its Part-of-Speech is adjective, but it is status words in CSD. The status words can be regarded as a subclass of the adjective. In this case, it is correct.
- The Part-of-Speech is different and totally incompatible between XH and CSD; for example "噤若寒蝉 [*jinruohanchan*] (*keep quiet out of fear*)", "限额 [*xian'e*] (*quota*)". In CSD, the Part-of-Speech are both verbs, while in XH are adjectives and nouns respectively. In this case, we should consider whether the Part-of-Speech are correct in CSD.

2. The Part-of-Speech of four-character words

During the proofreading, the division of the Part-of-Speech of the four-character words (including the idioms) in CSD are more problematic issues. There are 8786 four-character words in CSD, the distribution of their Part-of-Speech includes v, n, a, r, s, t and z, as shown in table 2.

Table 2. The distribution of the Part-of-Speech about the four-character words

Part-of-Speech	n	v	a	r	s	t	z
Quantity	2917	5170	460	3	2	4	228

In CSD, most of the four-character words are annotated as verbs and used to describe a person's or a thing's qualities or properties. For example "阴险毒辣 [*yinxiandula*] (*sinister and ruthless*)", "忠肝义胆[*zhongganyidan*] (virtue and patriotism)", "忠厚老实[*zhonghoulaoshi*](*honest*)", "忠贞不二[*zhongzhenbuer*] (*faithful*)" and so on. It is more accurate to annotate them as adjectives. The four-character words which are annotated as "其他词类(other Part-of-Speech)" are considered to be almost correct. The Part-of-Speech of the four-character words in GKB are annotated as "i" but in XH the majority of the four-character words are not annotated. Therefore, the annotations are more relied on subjective views since there are not too many the objective referential standards of the Part-of-Speech about the four-character words in CSD.

4.2   The Distribution and Revision of CSD Semantic Classes

The focus of this paper is to investigate the distribution of the semantic classes in CSD and revise the errors in semantic classification based on the CSD semantic taxonomy and the Part-of-Speech.

4.2.1   The Statistics of Semantic Class Distribution in CSD

There are 65676 entries in CSD, 164 semantic classes, and 18 of them are not in the CSD taxonomy. They are "地貌[*dimao*](*landforms*), 非身体构件 [*feishentigoujian*] (*non body component*), 集体[*jiti*](*the collective*), 建筑为[*jianzhuwei*], 节控 [*jiekong*], 其他[*qita*] (*others*), 人名 [*renming*] (*name*), 社会行为 [*shehuixingwei*](*social behavior*), 时点 [*shidian*] (*time point*), 时段 [*shiduan*] (*time period*), 事件构件 [*shijiangoujian*](*things component*), 数量[*shuliang*](*quantity*), 外观 [*waiguan*] (*appearance*), 用在动词后作补语[*yongzaidongcihouzuobuyu*](*with the complement after a verb*), 语气 [*yuqi*] (*tone*),正：人[*zheng:ren*],专名[*zhuanming*] (*proper name*), 自为 [*ziwei*]". There are 336 entries of which the original semantic classes and Part-of-Speech are different from those defined by CSD. For example the Part-of-Speech of "纺织[*fangzhi*] (*spin*)"is verb in CSD and its semantic class is "抽象事物(*abstract things*)". However, in the CSD semantic taxonomy, "抽象事物(*abstract things*)" is the semantic class of nouns instead of verbs. This case occurs in five Part-of-Speech classes.

In CSD, the words which have more than one semantic class are totally 2579, and those that are empty in the "语义(*semantic*)" field are 180.

Since the semantic class path is not marked in CSD, therefore we can't determine the parent class of the semantic classes which with the same name. According to the proofreading specifications, the words which have same name in semantic class should be marked semantic class path during proofreading. In addition to those Part-of-Speech that are defined in semantic classification taxonomy such as nouns, verbs, adjectives, adverbs and numerals, the Part-of-Speech distribution of the semantic class with same name also includes undefined Part-of-Speech such as direction, pronouns, time words, status words, location, distinguishing words and so on. For those words of which the semantic classes have the same name, their Part-of-Speech can be determined by their semantics in the proofreading.

Table 3. The revised semantic classes statistics

Part-of-Speech	Number of entries in CSD	Number of revised semantic classes		Part-of-Speech	Number of entries in CSD	Number of revised semantic classes
n	37565	3554		f	203	24
v	20953	1250		r	235	114
m	107	13		s	185	13
a	3557	283		t	567	98
b	315	46		z	993	253
d	996	191				

4.2.2   The Results of Semantic Revision in CSD

CSD altogether has 65676 entries, according to the requirements of section 3.2, we have revised a total of 5839 semantic classes (including 37 indefinite semantic classes). The statistics of proofreading results based on different Part-of-Speech is shown in Table 3.

5   Reflections on the Revision of the Semantic Classes

In the process of semantic class proofreading, we have discussed some questions, and worked out a number of semantic classification standards.

5.1   The Standards of Semantic Classification

For the words with vague class segmentation, we define the operational standards of semantic classification, such as:

1. The words indicating title and position, such as "教授[*jiaoshou*](*professor*), 秘书长[*mishu zhang*] (*secretary-general*), 主任[*zhuren*](*director*)" and so on should be classified as "身份(identity)".
2. The words indicating specific time, whether they are time point or time period, both belong to "绝对时间(absolute time)". Such as: "节气[*jieqi*](*solar terms*), 星期[*xingqi*](*week*), 节日[*jieri*](*festival*),初一[*chuyi*](*the first day in lunar calendar*), 冰川期[*bingchuanqi*](*ice age*), 三夏[*sanxia*], 明末清初[*mingmoqingchu*](*at the end of the Ming Dynasty and in the early Qing Dynasty*),中午[*zhongwu*](*noon*), 春季[*chunji*](*spring*)" and so on; the words that represent imprecise time should be classified as "相对时间(*relative time*)", like "生长期[*shengzhangqi*](*growth*), 儿童期[*ertongqi*](*childhood*), 晚唐[*wantang*](*late tang*)"and so on.
3. To determine the semantic class based on the Part-of-Speech. For example, "一下[*yixia*] (soon),一番[*yifan*],一整套[*yizhengtao*](*a whole set of*), 一路[*yilu*](*all the way*)", if considered to be adverbs, they should belong to the "程度(*degree*)" semantic class; if considered to be numerals, they should belong to the "基数(*base numbers*)" semantic class.
4. The quantifiers such as "两手[*liangshou*](*two hands*)", "一本[*yiben*] (*one*) " are not to be classified and modified temporarily.
5. The interrogative pronouns are divided as much as possible according to the meanings of XH.
6. "经心[*jingxin*](*attentive*)" as an adjective, is classified to "心理活动(*mental activity*)". "盘山 [*panshan*] (*climbing mountain*)" as a verb, is classified to "位移(displacement)".
7. The fruits and nuts such as "桃[*tao*](*peach*),梨[*li*](*pear*),苹果[*pingguo*] (*apple*),核桃[*hetao*](*walnut*),栗子[*lizi*](*chestnut*),松子[*songzi*](*pine nut*)" are classified to the "食物(*food*)".

8. The plants which are able to bear eatable fruits, such as "番木瓜 [*fanmugua*](*papaya*), 番茄[*fanqie*](*tomato*),四季豆[*sijidou*](*green beans*)" and so on are classified to "植物 (*plants*)".

9. The mathematical terms and the musical terms such as "联立方程 [*lianlifang-cheng*](*simultaneous equations*)", "合成词[*hecheng ci*](*compound words*)" and other terms are classified to "领域(*field*)".

5.2   The Discussion on the CSD Semantic Taxonomy

Some issues concerning the CSD semantic taxonomy need to be further discussed.

Inheritance of Semantic Classes

Some parent semantic classes are not unique. For example, in the standard semantics, the parent node of "食物(food)" semantic class is "人工物(artificial objects)", but "食物(food)" is not all "人工物(artificial objects)", many food are "自然物(natural objects)", such as "桃 [*tao*](*peach*), 梨[*li*](*pear*), 苹果 [*pingguo*](*apple*), 核桃 [*hetao*] (*walnut*), 栗子[*lizi*](*chestnut*),松子[*songzi*](*pine nut*)" and so on, so that some words in "食物(*food*)" are "人工物(*artificial objects*)", such as "荤菜 [*huncai*](*meat dish*), 馄饨[*huntun*](*wonton*)", while the others are "自然物(*natural objects*)", such as "茴香 [*huixiang*] (*fennel*),凤梨[*fengli*] (*pineapple*)" and so on.

Lack of Semantic Classes

The semantic classes of some words are not reflected in the current CSD semantic taxonomy. For example: in the current system taxonomy, "构件(*component*)" only includes "身体构件(*body component*)" and "非生物构件(*non-biological compo-nent*)", while the words such as "花骨朵 [*huaguduo*] (*bud*), 嫩芽 [*nenya*](*shoot*), 嫩叶[*nenye*](green leaves), 树根[*shugen*] (*root*) " are components of a tree, have no proper semantic class on leaf node, therefore they can only be classified to parent node "component".

Uncertainty of Semantic Classes

Some verb entries which have more than one semantic classes cannot be determined their semantic classes based on meanings in proofreading. This situation have two cases. One is that they are not suitable for any subclass of the standard semantic classes, for example "做好 [*zuohao*](*do well*), 尊称[*zuncheng*] (*honorific title*), 照准 [*zhaozhun*]"and so on. We believe that these words are not appropriate to be classified to any of the existing verb semantics. The other is that they belong to more than one standard verb semantic classes, such as "倒腾 [*daoteng*], 倒退 [*daotui*] (*back*)". It seems reasonable to classify them to "displacement", "physical activity", or "other behaviors".

The semantic class of the adverbial and pronominal words which indicating tones is also not clear, such as the adverbs "横竖 [*hengshu*] (*anyway*)、姑且[*guqie*] (*tenta-tively*)"and the pronouns "何如[*heru*](*how about*), 哪里 [*nali*] (*where*)". This kind of words can be regarded as function words which are not defined by CSD semantic taxonomy. We think the CSD need not cover these words.

6   Summary and Prospect

With a reference to the new findings of research on XH and GKB and a systematic investigation on the current semantic classification in CSD, the NLP research group of Zhengzhou University has revised the improper semantic classes in CSD. At present the group has completed the tasks of the statistical analyses of the semantic information of the original CSD vocabulary, the development of the semantic revision tool, the formulation of the semantic proofreading rules, the semantic class proofreading by Part-of-Speech in CSD, and the comparison of its consistency with GKB and XH5 with 5839 semantic classes in CSD revised. The focus of our research has been put on resolving the following problems in CSD: the empty semantic classes, words with more than one meaning, and words with incorrect semantic classification. The completion of semantics proofreading in CSD makes the semantic classification more reasonable and provides an important basis for the further revision of CSD. The tools we developed can also provide effective help for the construction of semantic dictionaries in the future.

However, in our work, the semantic class division is mostly decided according to the proofreaders' understanding of XH and GKB meanings, so it has subjectivity and defects in comprehensiveness. At present, we are trying to achieve automatic clustering and classification of CSD entries, which can be referred to by proofreaders in the process of proofreading.

Acknowledgments. This work was supported by the Natural Science Foundation of China(No.61402419, No.60970083, No.61272221), the National Social Science Foundation of China (No.14BYY096), 863 Projects of National High Technology Research and Development (No.2012AA011101), Science and Technology Key Project of Science and Technology Department of Henan Province (No.132102210407), Basic research project of Science and Technology Department of Henan Province(No. 142300410231,No.142300410308) Key Technology Project of the Education Department of Henan Province (No.12B520055,No.13B520381) and the Open Projects Program of Key Laboratory of Computational Linguistics(Peking University) (No. 201401), Ministry of Education of PRC.

References

1. Fellbaum, C.: WordNet: An Electronic Lexical Database. MIT Press, Mass (1998)
2. Richardson, S.D.: MindNet: acquiring and structuring semantic information from text. In: Coling 1998, pp. 1098–1102 (1998)
3. Bake, C.F., Fillmore, C.J., Lowe, J.B.: The berkeley framenet project. In: Proceedings of COLING 1998, pp. 86–90 (1998)
4. Chen, L.W., Yuan, Q.: Application Platform Project of Chinese Information Processing(中文信息处理应用平台工程). Publishing House of Electronics Industry, Beijing (1995). (in Chinese)
5. Dong, Z., Dong, Q.: Hownet Literature [OL] (1999). http://www.keenage.com (in Chinese)
6. Jiangsheng, Y., Shiwen, Y.: The Structure of Chinese Concept Dictionary(CCD 的结构与设计思想). Journal of Chinese Information Processing 16(4), 12–20 (2002). (in Chinese)

7. Su, X.C.: A Consideration about Development of A Thesaurus of Modern Chinese(现代汉语语义分类词典(TMC) 研制中若干问题的思考). Journal of Chinese Information Processing **22**(5), 12–21 (2008). (in Chinese)

8. Zhao, J.: Building A Large Scale Chinese Semantic Dictionary(大规模汉语语义词典构建). Master Thesis, Harbin Institute of Technology (2011). (in Chinese)

9. Mei, J.J.: Tongyici Cilin(《同义词词林》). Shanghai Dictionary Press, Shanghai (1983). (in Chinese)

10. Yu, S.W., Zhu, X.F., Wang, H., Zhang, H.R.: The Explanation of Contemporary Chinese Grammar Information Dictionary(《现代汉语语法信息词典详解》(第二版)), 2nd edn. Tsinghua University Press, Beijing (2002). (in Chinese)

11. Wang, H., Zhan, W.D., Liu, Q.: The design and outline of semantic knowledge-base of contemporary chinese (SKCC)(现代汉语语义词典的设计与概要). In: Proceedings of 1998 Chinese Information Processing International Conference, pp. 361–367. Tsinghua University Press, Beijing (1998). (in Chinese)

12. Wang, H., Yu, S.W., Zhan, W.D.: New progress of the semantic knowledge-base of contemporary chinese (SKCC). In: The 7th National Joint Academic Conference of Computational Linguistics (2008). (in Chinese)

13. Wu, Y.F., Wang, H., Zhan, W.D., Yu, S.W.: The Specification of the Semantic Knowledge-base of Contemporary Chinese(现代汉语语义词典规范). The Technical Report by the Institute of Computational Linguistics, Peking University (2014). (in Chinese)

14. Lin, X.G.: Concise Chinese Semantic Dictionary(《简明汉语义类词典》). The Commercial Press, Beijing (1987). (in Chinese)

15. Lin, X.G.: The Semantic Study of the Chinese Information Field(中文信息界的语义研究谭要). Language Application **3** (1998). (in Chinese)

16. Chen, Q.: The design ideas of contemporary chinese semantic taxonomy in information processing(信息处理用现代汉语语义分类体系的设计思想). In: Study on Chinese and Chinese Characters in Computer Age. Tsinghua University Press, Beijing (1996). (in Chinese)

17. Chen, X.: A Semantic Taxonomy for Engineering(一个面向工程的语义分类体系). Language Application **2** (1998). (in Chinese)

18. Dong, D.N.: A Thesaurus of Modern Chinese(《现代汉语分类词典》). Chinese Dictionary Press, Beijing (1998). (in Chinese)

19. Dong, Z.: The Expression of Semantic Relationship and the Construction of Knowledge System(语义关系的表达和知识系统的建造). Application of Language and Writing **3** (1998). (in Chinese)

20. Linguistics Institute of Chinese Academy of Social Sciences. Modern Chinese Dictionary (6th edn.). (《现代汉语词典(第六版)》). The Commercial Press, Beijing (2012). (in Chinese)

The Word Sense Annotation Based on Corpus of Teaching Chinese as a Second Language

Jing Wang[1(✉)], Mingfu Liao[2], Renfen Hu[1], and Shuanghong Wang[3]

[1] The Institute of Chinese Information Processing, Beijing Normal University, Beijing, China
wangjing1204@foxmail.com
[2] Jiangxi Agricultural University, Nanchang, China
jxaulmf@163.com
[3] Tianjin Wutong Middle School, Tianjin, China
wangshuanghong19@163.com

Abstract. This paper discusses the word sense annotation based on real corpus in the field of Teaching Chinese as a Second Language. We choose 1173 polysemous words to do the labeling in Corpus of Teaching Chinese as a Second Language based on word sense definition in Modern Chinese Dictionary. At last, 237 polysemous words are selected for quantitative analysis of the word sense distribution. By investigating the reappearance rate of polysemous words in the sense tagged corpus, we summarize their sense distribution patterns to offer important references for vocabulary teaching to non-native students.

Keywords: Polysemous words · Corpus · Sense annotation · Quantitative analysis

1 Introduction

Word sense annotation refers to annotating the appropriate meaning for a polysemous word with a certain context. Leech (1993) said that the word sense annotation was the most useful task among various semantic annotations. Word sense annotation can offer basic resources for tasks of natural language processing such as Machine Translation, Information Retrieval, as well as the tasks in language learning and lexicography. Sinclair (1991) proposed that the sense entry of the dictionary COBUILD could be arranged by the statistics of the word sense annotation corpus.

Sense tagged Corpus has been built in some languages, like Chinese and English. Currently, most English sense tagged corpus utilize semantic knowledge base like WordNet as labeling references, i.e. SemCor Corpus, SenseVal Corpus and DSO corpus.

Chinese Word Sense Tagged Corpus (STC) was built by Institute of Computational Linguistics in Peking University. Texts in the corpus come from China Daily, containing 6.42 million words, in which 966 polysemous nouns and verbs are tagged based on the Modern Chinese Semantic Dictionary (Peng Jin, 2008). In addition to STC, Hang Xiao (2009) conducted sense annotation for polysemous words in Chinese

© Springer International Publishing Switzerland 2015
Q. Lu and H.H. Gao (Eds.): CLSW 2015, LNAI 9332, pp. 234–243, 2015.
DOI: 10.1007/978-3-319-27194-1_24

Textbook Corpus based on Modern Chinese Dictionary, and thus built a sense tagged corpus containing 2 million words.

Word sense annotation is very important for the field of Teaching Chinese as a Second Language (TCSL), but the corpus in this field only focuses on the interlanguage corpus, such as, the HSK Dynamic Composition Corpus of Beijing Language and Culture University, the Chinese Error Interlanguage Corpus of Sun Yat-Sen University, the Lengthways Oral Chinese for International Students Corpus and the Lengthways Chinese Composition of American Students Corpus of Nanjing University. The interlanguage corpus usually annotates the error information of Chinese characters, words and sentences in the corpus.

To promote vocabulary study, we built a Chinese sense tagged corpus for TCSL. We used the sense definitions in the Modern Chinese Dictionary (the 6th edition) as the annotation guidelines to tag the word sense of polysemous words in Chinese textbooks for second language learners. This paper presents quantitative statistics of the annotating results. This work fills up the blank of the word sense research based on corpus in the field of TCSL.

2   Annotation of the Polysemous Words' Sense Based on the Lexicon

2.1   Annotation Materials

This paper uses Chinese textbook parts from the Corpus of Chinese International Education Dynamic developed by the Institute of Chinese Information Processing, Beijing Normal University. This part contains 58 sets, 189 volumes of textbooks, about 3.4 million words (containing English letters, numbers and Chinese characters) and 12 thousand sentences. Figure 1 shows the part of the textbooks.

序号	系列教材序号	教材名称	出版信息			学习者信息				教材信息	
			主编	作者	出版社	出版时间	适用年龄	汉语水平	适用课型	教材类型	教材性质
7	当代中文	当代中文	吴中伟		华语教学出版社	2010	成人	初级	综合	语言技能	国别化教材
8	标准中文1	《标准中文第一级第一册》	课程教材研究所		人民教育出版社	1998	中小学	初级	综合	语言技能	通用型教材
9	标准中文2	《标准中文第一级第一册》	课程教材研究所		人民教育出版社	1999	中小学	初级	综合	语言技能	通用型教材
10	标准中文3	《标准中文第一级第二册》	课程教材研究所		人民教育出版社	1998	中小学	初级	综合	语言技能	通用型教材
11	标准中文4	《标准中文第一级第二册》	课程教材研究所		人民教育出版社	1998	中小学	中级	综合	语言技能	通用型教材
12	标准中文5	《标准中文第二级第一册》	课程教材研究所		人民教育出版社	1998	中小学	中级	综合	语言技能	通用型教材
13	标准中文6	《标准中文第二级第二册》	课程教材研究所		人民教育出版社	1998	中小学	中级	综合	语言技能	通用型教材
14	标准中文7	《标准中文第二级第一册》(缺)	课程教材研究所		人民教育出版社	1999	中小学	高级	综合	语言技能	通用型教材
15	标准中文8	《标准中文第三级第一册》	课程教材研究所		人民教育出版社	1999	中小学	高级	综合	语言技能	通用型教材
16	标准中文9	《标准中文第三级第二册》	课程教材研究所		人民教育出版社	1999	中小学	高级	综合	语言技能	通用型教材
17	博雅汉语1	《博雅汉语·初级·起步篇 I 》	李晓琪	任雪梅、徐晶凝	北京大学出版社	2004	成人	初级	综合	语言技能	通用型教材
18	博雅汉语2	《博雅汉语·初级·起步篇 II 》	李晓琪	徐晶凝、任雪梅	北京大学出版社	2005	成人	初级	综合	语言技能	通用型教材
19	博雅汉语3	《博雅汉语·准中级·加速篇 I 》	李晓琪	黄立、钱旭菁	北京大学出版社	2005	成人	中级	综合	语言技能	通用型教材
20	博雅汉语4	《博雅汉语·准中级·加速篇 II 》	李晓琪	黄立、钱旭菁	北京大学出版社	2005	成人	中级	综合	语言技能	通用型教材
21	博雅汉语5	《博雅汉语·中级·冲刺篇 I 》	李晓琪	赵延风	北京大学出版社	2005	成人	中级	综合	语言技能	通用型教材
22	博雅汉语6	《博雅汉语·中级·冲刺篇 II 》	李晓琪	张明莹	北京大学出版社	2006	成人	中级	综合	语言技能	通用型教材
23	博雅汉语7	《博雅汉语·高级·飞翔篇 I 》	李晓琪	金舒年、陈莉	北京大学出版社	2004	成人	高级	综合	语言技能	通用型教材
24	博雅汉语8	《博雅汉语·高级·飞翔篇 II 》	李晓琪	金舒年、陈莉	北京大学出版社	2006	成人	高级	综合	语言技能	通用型教材
25	博雅汉语9	《博雅汉语·高级·飞翔篇 III 》	李晓琪	金舒年、陈莉	北京大学出版社	2008	成人	高级	综合	语言技能	通用型教材
26	成功之路01	《成功之路·入门篇》	邱军	张辉	北京语言大学出版社	2008	成人	初级	综合	语言技能	通用型教材
27	成功之路02	《成功之路·起步篇1》	邱军	杨楠	北京语言大学出版社	2008	成人	初级	综合	语言技能	通用型教材
28	成功之路03	《成功之路·起步篇2》	邱军	杨楠	北京语言大学出版社	2008	成人	初级	综合	语言技能	通用型教材
29	成功之路04	《成功之路·顺利篇1》	邱军	张莉	北京语言大学出版社	2008	成人	中级	综合	语言技能	通用型教材
30	成功之路05	《成功之路·顺利篇2》	邱军	张莉	北京语言大学出版社	2008	成人	中级	综合	语言技能	通用型教材
31	成功之路06	《成功之路·进步篇1》	邱军	单世荣	北京语言大学出版社	2008	成人	中级	综合	语言技能	通用型教材
32	成功之路07	《成功之路·进步篇2》	邱军	张辉	北京语言大学出版社	2008	成人	中级	综合	语言技能	通用型教材
33	成功之路08	《成功之路·进步篇3》	邱军	单世荣、张辉	北京语言大学出版社	2009	成人	初级	综合	语言技能	通用型教材
34	成功之路09	《成功之路·进步篇·听和说1》	邱军	王小澜	北京语言大学出版社	2008	成人	初级	听说	语言技能	通用型教材

Fig. 1. Information of the TCSL textbooks

The publication year, the age and the Chinese level of the learners, the nature, type and the lessons' type of all the textbooks are taken into account in our study. The textbooks above are the classical ones from 1989 to 2012. The age of the learners covers from the children, primary students, and middle school students, to the adults. The Chinese level of the learners covers from zero, primary, and middle, to high level. And the types of the lessons include oral, listening, writing and comprehensive ones. All the textbooks are mainly used for teaching language skills, and some for medicine and business Chinese.

The semantic system and lexicon resources for word sense annotation mainly contain traditional language dictionary (like Cihai and Modern Chinese Dictionary), semantic lexicon (like Tonyici Cilin) and word sense knowledge base for NLP (like WordNet and HowNet) (Hang Xiao,2010). This paper selects the Modern Chinese Dictionary (the 6th edition) as the annotation system which is widely and representatively used in the field of Chinese language research and Chinese teaching research.

The word sense annotation can be divided into part-words and all-words annotation according to the scale of annotated words in the corpus. Our study focuses on the part-words sense annotation. We choose 1173 polysemous words to form a polysemous words' sense annotation set, called WordSet.

The polysemous word in the paper is a generalized definition, namely if one word form has more than 2 senses, we call it a polysemous word. Because both the machine and the non-native students can't discern different words which have the same form.

The WordSet contains 812 disyllabic words, 517 monosyllabic words, and only 8 polysyllabic words.

2.2   Annotating Method

This paper tags the word sense on the corpus manually. Word segmentation and POS tagging had been done before annotating, and then we proofread the results manually. The sample form of the word segmentation and POS tagging are shown in Figure 2.

```
3418      皇上/n 跑/v 了/u , /w 丈夫/n 死/v 了/u , /w 鬼子/n
来/v 了/u , /w 满/a 城/n 是/vl 血光/n 火焰/n , /w 可是/d 母亲/n
不/d 怕/v , /w 她/r 要/vu 在/p 刺刀/n 下/nd , /w 饥荒/n 中/nd
, /w 保护/v 着/u 儿女/n 。/w
```

Fig. 2. Sample of the word segmentation and POS tagging

The number at the head of a sentence is its sequence number in the corpus, the words are divided by blank character, and the part of speech tags are after "/".

20 students of language master are selected to do the first tagging, and then do collation in pairs, and at last the results are checked up by the third student. We developed an auxiliary tool for word sense annotation, and the user interface of the tool is shown in Figure 3.

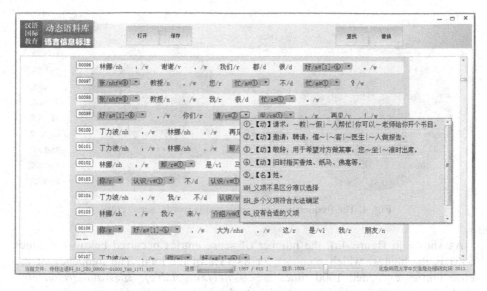

Fig. 3. The auxiliary tool for word sense annotation

The tool uploads the WordSet on the corpus, and the annotators choose the appropriate sense for every target polysemous word. The number after "#" means the number of sense entries in the WordSet.

Because the word senses in the dictionary cannot explain all the words in the corpus (Ide & Wilks, 2006), 4 flexible sense entries are added to every words: MH presents the sense that can't be distinguished, BH presents words that have several appropriate sense, QS presents words that have no suitable sense, and UN presents words need not to be annotated.

3   Statistics and Analysis of the Polysemous Words' Sense Entry

The WordSet contains 1173 polysemous and 4855 word sense entries, so every word has 4.13 sense entries averagely. We extract the annotation results of the first 237 words in the WordSet to do statistics. The 237 words account for 20% of the Word-Set, with 998 sense entries, and their average sense entry number is 4.32, which is similar to that of the whole words in the WordSet, so the sample can reflect the whole results of the WordSet to some extent.

3.1   The Frequency of the Polysemous Words' Sense Entry

The total sense entries of the 237 sample words are 767, all of them appeared 72794 times, and one sense entry appeared 94.91 times averagely. The occurrence frequency of every word sense entry is counted by every 100 times, and the results are shown as Figure 4a).

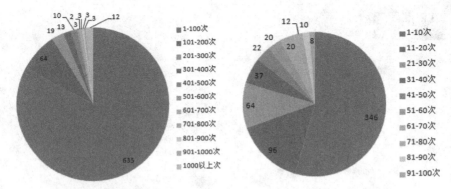

Fig. 4. The frequency of the polysemous words' sense entry

As shown in figure 4a), the number of sense entries occurred below 100 times (635) is the biggest which accounts for 83.13% of the total. The frequency of the sense entries exceeded 1000 times are 菜/n#④(vegetable), 比较/d#③(relatively), 才/d#[2]-③(newly/just/only)、发展/v#①(develop)、地方/n#[2]-①(place)、大家/r#[2](everyone)、东西/n#[2]-①(thing)、等/u#[1]-⑤(and so on)、次/q#⑤(time)、吃/v#[1]-①(eat)、得/u#[3]-③(be able to)、把/p#[1]-⑪(ba, a preposition for introduce object in Chinese)，among which the most frequent one is把/p#[1]-⑪, and its frequency is 5125.

According to the results above, the sense entries whose frequency from 1 to 100 are calculated by every 10 times, and the results are shown in Figure 4b). Figure 4b) shows that the number of the sense entries occurring from 1 to 10 times is the biggest (346), accounting for 45.11% of the total sense entries, and so is the most one, and the sense entries decline with the frequency adding up.

Then the sense entries appearing from 1 to 10 times are counted, and the results are shown as follows.

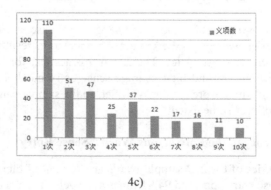

4c)

Fig. 5. The frequency of the polysemous words' sense entry

Figure 4c) shows that the number of sense entries occurring once (110) is the biggest, accounting for 14.34% of all the senses entries. 231 sense entries have not occurred in the corpus, and the reasons are shown as follows:

1. The sense entries of a word are always the local and classical Chinese senses which are commonly used in Chinese. For example, the [2]-④ sense entry of the word 扒(stew) means: a cooking method, stew the raw materials to half-cooked and fry them, and then boil them out by slow fire.
2. The sense of the polysemous word is too narrow to cover words in the corpus. For example, the second and third sense entries of the word 编辑(editor) means: ② [noun] the editor; ③ [noun] the middle professional ranks in the agency for press and publications. The third sense is so narrow that 90% words 编辑 /n(editor) in the corpus select entry 2.
3. The limitation of the corpus. The corpus comes from teaching materials of the TCSL, and a large part of the corpus are for intermediate level's students, so the sense of the polysemous occurring in the corpus always concentrated on the basic and common sense. For example, the sense entry 把/p#[1]-⑪ (ba) appears 5000 times totally, and the other senses of word 把(ba) appear rarely or do not even appear. It is concluded that the Chinese textbooks have their limitation on selecting the word and word sense, and the repetition rates of the word sense in the textbooks are uneven.

3.2   The Distribution of the Common Words' Sense and their Frequency

Because the word sense of polysemous words appears in the real corpus, and most of the sense entry frequency are uneven, so that is why some sense entries appeared frequently and others appeared rarely. The analysis of the distribution of the common word sense may reflect the selection of a word sense in the textbooks, which can offer the objective data base for the textbook editor. This paper counts the sense entries whose frequencies are over 50 only.

The Polysemous Words with 1 High-Frequency Sense Entry

That a polysemous word only has 1 sense entry with the absence of other sense entries in the corpus is an extreme case of the word sense frequency. 14 such words like this appear in the corpus accounting for 5.96% of the sample WordSet. And some words with several sense entries appear in the corpus, but they only have 1 high-frequency sense entry. 54 such words like this appear in the corpus which account for 22.98% of the whole sample WordSet when the high-frequency equals to 80%. Some polysemouse words with 1 high-frequency sense entry are listed in Table 1.

Table 1. The polysemous words with 1 high-frequency sense entry

Sense Entry	Sense entry number in corpus	Sense entry number in dictionary	Oc-cur-rence	Frequen-cy (%)	HSK level
参加/v#① (participant)	1	2	769	100.00	3
东/n#①(east)	1	4	215	100.00	3
戴/v#①(wear)	1	3	151	100.00	4
当时/n#① (at that time)	1	2	591	100.00	4
宝贵/a#① (precious)	1	2	60	100.00	5
采取/v#①(adopt)	1	2	129	100.00	5
承受/v#①(bear)	1	2	64	100.00	5
从事 /v#①(engage)	1	2	161	100.00	5
醋/n#①(vigenar)	1	2	52	100.00	5
地位/n#①(status)	1	2	259	100.00	5
大家/r#[2] (everyone)	3	3	1443	99.65	2
大概/d#③ (probably)	2	3	348	99.43	4
当然/d#② (of course)	3	2	980	99.29	3
发挥/v#① (give play to)	2	2	136	99.27	5
表现 /v#①(express)	2	2	387	98.72	5
次/q#⑤(time)	5	8	2674	98.45	2
大约/d#②(about)	2	2	181	98.37	4
超过/v#②(exceed)	2	2	221	97.79	4
饿/a#①(hungry)	2	2	166	97.65	3
承认/v#① (acknowledge)	2	2	129	96.99	5

The Polysemous Words with 2 High-Frequency Sense Entry

Some words with several sense entries appear in the corpus, but only have 2 high-frequency sense entries, and the others are not common sense. 54 such words appear in the corpus accounting for 22.78% of the whole sample WordSet when the high-frequency equals to 30%. Some polysemouse words with 2 high-frequency sense entries are listed in Table 2.

Table 2. The polysemous words with 2 high-frequency sense entries

Sense Entry	Sense entry number in corpus	Sense entry number in dictionary	Occur-rence	Frequen-cy(%)	HSK level
矮/a#①(shot)	2	3	56	69.14%	3
矮/a#②(low)	2	3	25	30.86%	3
把握/n#③ (chance)	2	3	23	30.26%	5
把握/v#②(hold)	2	3	53	69.74%	5
搭配/v#①(collate)	2	3	18	58.06%	6
搭配/v#②(match)	2	3	13	41.94%	6
挡/v#①(keep off)	2	5	33	68.75%	5
挡/v#②(cover)	2	5	15	31.25%	5
地步/n#①(status)	2	3	18	52.94%	6
地步/n#②(degree)	2	3	16	47.06%	6

The Polysemous Words with All High-Frequency Sense Entries

Some words distribute evenly and all their sense entries appear frequently in the corpus. Only 6 words appear in the corpus when their high-frequency is not below 20%. 4 words are listed in Table 3.

We can conclude from the above results in the corpus of Chinese textbooks:

1. Some common polysemous words' sense may occur rarely;
2. Some sense entries of a polysemous word have a higher frequency but skip the other senses;
3. Some uncommon senses like local and classical Chinese sense instead of the common sense would perplex the learners.

In a word, when compiling a Chinese textbook, the distribution of the polysemous words' sense and the recurrence rate of a sense entry should be taken into consideration, so that an exact Chinese textbook can be compiled by the editors.

Table 3. The polysemous words with all high-frequency sense entry

Sense Entry	Sense entry number in corpus	Sense entry number in dictionary	Occurrence	Frequency(%)	HSK level
背/n#[2]-①(back)	9	14	73	34.11	5
背/v#[1]-① (carry on the cack)	9	14	69	32.24	5
背/v#[2]-⑥(recite)	9	14	55	25.70	5
材料/n#①(material)	4	4	68	48.23	4
材料/n#② (writing material)	4	4	29	20.57	4
材料/n#③ (information)	4	4	42	29.79	4
吵/a#①(noisy)	3	3	19	23.17	4
吵/v#②(disturb)	3	3	27	32.93	4
吵/v#③(quarrel)	3	3	36	43.90	4
淡/a#②(light)	4	7	22	29.33	5
淡/a#③(tasteless)	4	7	30	40.00	5
淡/a#④(slack)	4	7	15	20.00	5
倒/d#[3]-⑤(but)	9	13	216	43.03	5
倒/v#[1]-①(fall)	9	13	102	20.32	5
倒/v#[3]- ④(reverse)	9	13	107	21.31	5
读/v#①(read aloud)	5	4	134	24.59	1
读/v#②(read)	5	4	283	51.93	1
读/v#③ (attend school)	5	4	125	22.94	1

4   Conclusion

This paper researches the distribution of the polysemous word sense in the Chinese textbook corpus annotated by word sense. The results show that the number of the sense entry declines with the recurrence rate of the sense entries rising up; the polysemous words with 1-2 high-frequency sense entries account for about 30% of the sample WordSet, while the polysemous words with all high-frequency sense entries are only 6. However, this paper only researches 237 words instead of the whole WordSet, so the data of this research can not reflect the whole distribution of polysemous words' sense in the Chinese textbook.

Acknowledgment. This work was supported by the Hi-Tech Research and Development Program of China (2012AA011104), and by China State Language Affairs Commission "Twelfth Five" Scientific Research Project (YB125-124).

References

1. Leech, G.: Corpus annotation schemes. Literary and Linguistic Computing **8**(4), 275–281 (1993)
2. Ide, N., Wilks, Y.: Making sense about sense. In: Agirre, E., Edmonds, P.G. (eds.) Word Sense Disambiguation, pp. 47–73. Springer, Dordrecht (2006)
3. Sinclair, J.: Corpus, concordance, collocation. Oxford University Press, Oxford
4. Jin, P., Wu, Y.F., Yu, S.W.: Survey of Word Sense Annotated Corpus Construction. Journal of Chinese Information Processing **3** (2008). (in Chinese)
5. Xiao, H., Yang, L.J.: Dictionary Informed Corpus Word Sense Annotation. Applied Linguistics **2** (2010). (in Chinese)
6. Xiao, H.: Dictionary Based Corpus Sense Tagging (2009). (in Chinese)
7. Dictionary editorial room of Language Institute of Chinese Academy of Social Sciences, Modern Chinese Dictionary (the 6th edn.). The Commercial Press (2012). (in Chinese)

Mining Chinese Polarity Shifters

Ge Xu[1](✉) and Churen Huang[2]

[1] Department of Computer Science, Minjiang University, Fuzhou 350108, China
xuge@pku.edu.cn
[2] Faculty of Humanities, The Hong Kong Polytechnic University, Hong Kong, China
churenhuang@gmail.com

Abstract. In sentiment analysis, polarity shifting means to shift the polarity of a sentiment clue. Compared with other natural language processing (NLP) tasks, to extract polarity shifters (polarity shifting patterns) in corpora is a challenging one, since the polarity shifters sometimes are very subtle, which often invalidates fully automatic approaches. In this paper, aiming to extract polarity shifters that invert or attenuate polarity, we use a semi-automatic approach based on pattern mining. The approach can greatly reduce the human annotating cost and cover as many polarity shifters as possible. We tested this approach on domain corpora, and encouraging experimental results are reported.

Keywords: Sentiment analysis · Polarity shifting · Sequence mining · Prior polarity

1 Introduction

Polarity shifting is a phenomenon in sentiment analysis, which denotes to invert or attenuate the polarity of a sentiment clue. A polarity shifter is a pattern to perform polarity shifting.

Previous research work has reported performance improvement when considering polarity shifting in their tasks. For example, Ikeda et al. [2008] presented a model to detect polarity shifting in sentences and improved sentiment classification. In Li et al. [2010], the authors offered 8 types of polarity shifting structures, including:

- Explicit Negation(not, no, without)
- Contrast Transition(but, however, unfortunately)
- Implicit Negation(avoid, hardly)
- False Impression(look, seem)
- Likelihood (probably, perhaps)
- Counter-factual(should, would)
- Exception (the only)
- Until (until)

Other related work is Kennedy and Inkpen [2005], Morsy and Rafea [2012] etc.

© Springer International Publishing Switzerland 2015
Q. Lu and H.H. Gao (Eds.): CLSW 2015, LNAI 9332, pp. 244–251, 2015.
DOI: 10.1007/978-3-319-27194-1_25

To find polarity shifters in a large corpus is not easy. The density of polarity shifting is low, and shifting patterns are subtle and have various expressions, making it an even harder task. Currently, human annotating is the main way to obtain polarity shifters, which is time-consuming.

Boubel et al. [2013] presents an automatic approach to extracting contextual valence shifters (polarity shifters). The system depends on two resources in French, a corpus of reviews and a lexicon of valence terms, to build a list of French contextual valence shifters. The work has the similar target with our approach which is aiming to build a list of Chinese phrase-level polarity shifters. However, our work didn't use syntactic parsers and the extracted patterns are word sequences other than a term in a syntactic tree, which makes our approach more general.

2 Our Approach

In Polanyi and Zaenen [2004], Quirk et al. [1985], Kennedy and Inkpen [2006], they classify contextual valence shifters (polarity shifters) into three classes: **inversers** invert the polarity of a polarized item, **intensifiers** intensify it and **attenuators** diminish it. Recent work on polarity shifting mainly pursues two of the three classes, that is to say, **inverser** (invert the polarity) and **attenuators** (attenuate the polarity).

In our paper, we also limit our research in those two classes of polarity shifters, and on phrase level where polarity shifters occur frequently. Basic steps of our approach are shown in section 2.1.

2.1 Basic Steps

Our approach is based on sequence mining. A sequence mining algorithm can extract frequent sequences from a corpus. PrefixSpan (Pei et al. [2001] etc.) is one of the algorithms. The "frequent" here means that the frequency of an extracted sequence should be higher than a threshold, which is called "minimum support" in the industry of data mining. In our paper, a sequence is a sequence of tokens (word or POSTAG[1]) and intervals are allowed between tokens. Given a corpus, to find the the polarity shifters in it, our approach takes the following steps:

1. Initialize PS, the set of polarity shifters;
2. Perform segmentation and POS tagging on the corpus, the result is C;
3. Choose N words from C, and manually annotate whether they are prior positive words or not, the result is POSLIST;
4. Break C into phrases, the result is PHRASE;
5. Retrieve all lines which contain at least one word in POSLIST from PHRASE, all the positive words are replaced by POSTAG, the result is POSLINE;

---

[1] In this paper, we use X to denote POSTAG, which is a symbol for all selected positive words.

6. Given a **minimum support**, run the sequence mining algorithm on POSLINE, the result is PATLIST;
7. If PATLIST is empty, END.
8. Prune PATLIST by keeping the patterns that contain at least one positive word in POSLIST;
9. Annotate PATLIST for polarity shifters, which are added to PS;compress PHRASE
10. Reduce the **minimum support**, go to step 6;

2.2 Annotating Positive Words

According to Pollyanna theory, people are inclined to use positive words. In free texts, "like" occurs much more frequent than "hate", and "good" than "bad". Furthermore, when expressing negative concepts, people are inclined to use negation on positive expression to alleviate sentiments, instead of using negative expressions directly. So, having witnessed such phenomenon (see table 1),we believe that polarity shifting has higher correlation with positive words than with negative words. In our experiments, we only consider polarity shifting on positive words.

Two issues are considered when we select positive words:

1. Contextual polarity words are not selected, such as "大"(big),"高"(high), "长"(long) etc. If these words are included, the set of phrases that is input into the sequence mining algorithm will become much larger, and the portion of phrases containing polarity shifting become smaller, thus costs more time for annotating.
2. Words about **desire** is not selected because **desire** is one type of polarity shifting, such as "希望"(hope),"建议"(recommend) etc.
3. We only consider nouns, verbs, and adjectives.
4. Some words have lost their positive semantics in language development or in specified domain. For example, in chatting about online sales, "朋友"(friend) and "美女"(beauty) can be understood as "buyer" and "female" respectively. We do not regard them as positive words.

We have three schemes to choose the positive words when deciding how many words to annotate:

1. Choosing the N most frequent words in the corpus to annotate, where N depends on how many manpower you are willing to spend. This scheme is the most time-consuming one, but also is of the highest coverage.

Table 1. Pollyanna phenomenon

Phrase	Google hits
不喜欢(not like)	16,000,000
不讨厌(not hate)	587,000
不好(not good)	30,300,000
不坏(not bad)	914,000

2. Intersecting words in the corpus with positive words in a general sentiment lexicon. By our experience, the general lexicon covers few domain-related sentiment words, and is not of high-quality from the perspective of a specific domain. Normally this scheme cannot satisfy the experimental requirement.
3. Tradeoff between the first scheme and the second one, manually annotating the intersection set of the second scheme.

In our experiments, due to limit both on time and human labor, we choose the third scheme.

2.3   Retrieving Phrases With Positive Words

After obtaining the set of positive words, we use it to find the phrases that contain at least one positive word.

Of cause, you can skip steps described by section 2.2 and this step, directly annotate polarity shifting in any given corpus using the following steps. However, according to our experience, the possibility that annotators detect polarity shifters in an arbitrary unlabeled corpus is quite low. So we will find some ways to obtain specified corpus where polarity shifters occur frequently. In our experiments, we use the bad comments with at least one positive word, assuming that polarity shifting inverts or attenuates the polarity of the positive word, see section 3.1 for more details.

2.4   Annotating Polarity Shifting

To annotate polarity shifting on patterns (output of the sequence mining algorithm), we have three options.

1. Yes. Meaning that the pattern **is** a polarity shifter, or it contains a polarity shifter.
2. No. Meaning that the pattern **has nothing to do** with polarity shifting. Any word in the pattern will not be a part of a polarity shifter.
3. Not sure. Meaning that the current pattern (or its part) maybe a part of a polarity shifting, and hope to see longer patterns containing current pattern (or its part) in next runs, then make a decision.

Two issues should be paid attention.

At first, we pay much attention on words about cognition(surprised etc.), desire(hope, wish, should),possibility(probably, maybe),limitation(only), it is much possible that these words can form a polarity shifter.

Secondly, a specially type of polarity shifting is simply to use a negative clue to negate the positive clues, such as "傻瓜喜欢" (the stupid like it), "鬼相信"(ghost believes). In our experiments, we do not regard such negative clues as polarity shifters.

After each run of annotating, we can compress the set of phrases used for next run of sequence mining.

1. If a pattern contains a polarity shifter, any phrase containing the pattern is removed from the set of phrases.
2. If a pattern has nothing to do with polarity shifting, any word of it has no contribution to detect polarity shifting, and should be removed from phrases[2].

In both cases, the set of phrases is compressed, making the task easier.

For example, the pattern "不X"(not X) is a polarity shifter, where X is the POSTAG, meaning a positive word. Patterns such as "很不X"(not X very much), "不X！"(not X!) etc. contain "不X"(not X), and also are supposed to contain polarity shifting, so we do not have to annotate them manually. The pattern "桌子的X"(table's X) has nothing to do with polarity shifting, so "table", "'s" can be deleted from phrases before they are input into the next run of sequence mining, thus compress the set of phrases.

For "Not sure" case, we will postpone decision-making to following runs. Let's assume that there is a pattern "以为X"(think X). At present, we cannot say it is a polarity shifter or not, so annotate it as "Not sure". Any phrase containing the pattern will be still input into the next run of sequence mining, and probably you will see a less frequent pattern "原本以为X"(had thought X) in the next run. At this time, we can annotate it as "Yes", meaning it contains polarity shifting.

3   Experiments

3.1   Experimental Setting

We choose PrefixSpan as the sequence mining algorithm. We set MinSupRatio=0.05 and MinSup=3. At first, we will extract frequent patterns by the support computed from multiplying MinSupRatio with the number of phrases, then gradually decrease the MinSupRatio to find less frequent patterns in following runs. When the support equals MinSup and no patterns are mined, we stop our algorithm.

Unlabeled Corpus. To obtain texts where polarity shifting may frequently occurs, we collect negative descriptions in which positive words occur. So, we at first collected bad comments on several best-selling products from 京东[3], a famous online shopping platform. Then, we broke the comments into sentences (by 。！？；：) and phrases (by ，). In our experiments, there are 440,000+ phrases, from which we selected 18936 phrases that contain at least one positive word from the existing set of positive words. We use the Jieba package[4] to perform word segmentation and POS tagging on the corpus.

---

[2] If a phrase is too short after removing such words, the phrase is removed from the set.

[3] http://www.jd.com

[4] github.com/fxsjy/jieba

Sentiment Lexicons. In section 2.2, we choose the third scheme to annotating positive words, so we need a set of positive words extracted from sentiment lexicons. Three Chinese sentiment lexicons are used:

1. Hownet sentiment lexicon[5]
2. NTUSD (NTU Sentiment Dictionary)[6]
3. Emotion Ontology published by Dalian University of Technology[7]

These three sentiment lexicons contain positive and negative terms, we merge all the positive terms as one set of positive terms to help in annotating positive words in our corpus.

3.2   Experimental Results

The main statistics of annotating process is shown in table 2.

Using our approach, from table 2, we can see that only 1065 (sum of the last column) patterns need to be annotated, of which some are automatically annotated according to nesting relationship. The whole annotating takes about one and half hour. Otherwise, we will have to annotate approximately 15000+ (18936-3695) patterns and will take much longer time.

We categorize the polarity shifters extracted from the above iterative anno-tating into 9 classes, and some of them are shown in the table 3.

Table 2. Process of Annotating

run	MinSupRatio	Num of phrases	Num of patterns
1	0.05	18936	16
2	0.05	10818	2
3	0.025	9849	9
4	0.0125	9602	29
5	0.0125	8688	7
6	0.0125	8480	2
7	0.00625	8374	48
8	0.00625	7652	8
9	0.00625	7510	1
10	0.003125	7498	92
11	0.003125	6713	14
12	0.0015625	6610	159
13	0.0015625	5135	48
14	0.0015625	4879	30
15	0.00078125	4766	392
16	0.00078125	3695	208

---

[5] http://www.keenage.com/download/sentiment.rar
[6] http://nlg18.csie.ntu.edu.tw
[7] http://ir.dlut.edu.cn/

Table 3. Some of extracted polarity shifters

Negation	真不X, 再也不能X, 不够X, 再也不会X, 不该X, 没什么X, 不敢X, 不X, 不X！, 非X, 没法X, 超不X, 不是X, 别X, 没有X, 不能X, 不要X, 没X, 不会X, 不怎么X, X不会, 再再X, 无法X, 没X, 真不知道X, 除了X, 白X, X不了, X啥, 哪X
Doubt	怎么X啊, 搞不懂X, 奇怪X, X？, 为什么X, 怀疑X, 是不是X, 怎么X！, 是否X, 难道X, 如何X, 是否是X
Desire	望X, 不想X, 希望X, 辜负X, 枉费X, 亏这么X, 但愿X, 枉X
Comparison	原先X, 原以为X, 以前X啊, 之前X才, 本来以为X, 本来应该X, 本以为X, 本来X才, 本来想X, 不如X, 随便比X, 本想X, 原本X, 原本以为X, 别的X
Transition	才X, X就是, 虽然X, X但是, X但, X可是, 就算X, X不过
Condition:	如果X, 若X, 要是X
Limitation	只有X, 勉强X, 唯一X, 才能X, 仅仅X, 要不是X, X而已
Uncertainty	也许X, 像是X
Others	失去X, 过于X, 怪我太X

After the 16th run of annotation, the minimum support is 3, and no frequent patterns are extracted, and the last 3695 phrases mainly contain low-frequent words. By our observation, most of phrases are composed of domain-dependent nouns and verbs. Furthermore, we assume that an adjective should not be a part of a polarity shifter, so we remove nouns, verbs and adjectives from phrases, and only keep the phrases longer than 2 words, thus we obtain a set of 616 phrases. In our consideration, fully manual annotating can be applied now.

Since we broke a bad comment to sentences and to phrases, not every phrase is a bad comment. Of the 616 phrases, many do not contain polarity shifting. We will not report the detailed annotation on these 616 phrases in this paper, from which the detected polarity shifters normally have low frequency and are long.

4   Conclusion and Future work

In this paper, we offer an iterative annotating approach to find frequent polarity shifters, which can greatly reduce the labor used for annotating. In the future, we would choose different corpora to perform the experiments and see if there is difference when negating a negative concept or when shifting polarity beyond phrases. Furthermore, we also would like to generalize this approach to cover more similar annotation tasks.

Acknowledgments. This research is supported by National Natural Science Foundation of China (No.61300156 and No.61300152), and Education Office Foundation of Fujian Province in China(No.JA13257).

References

Boubel, N., François, T., Naets, H.: Automatic extraction of contextual valence shifters. In: RANLP, pp. 98–104 (2013)

Ikeda, D., Takamura, H., Ratinov, L., Okumura, M.: Learning to shift the polarity of words for sentiment classification. In: IJCNLP, pp. 296–303 (2008)

Kennedy, A., Inkpen, D.: Sentiment classification of movie reviews using contextual valence shifters. In: Computational Intelligence (2006)

Kennedy, A., Inkpen, D.: Sentiment classification of movie and product reviews using contextual valence shifters. In: Proceedings of FINEXIN 2005, Workshop on the Analysis of Informal and Formal Information Exchange during Negotiations, Ottawa, CA (2005). http://www.site.uottawa.ca/~diana/publications/sentiment.pdf

Li, S., Lee, S., Chen, Y., Huang, C., Zhou, G.: Sentiment classification and polarity shifting. In: Proceedings of COLING 2010, pp. 635–643 (2010)

Morsy, S.A., Rafea, A.: Improving document-level sentiment classification using contextual valence shifters. In: Bouma, G., Ittoo, A., Métais, E., Wortmann, H. (eds.) NLDB 2012. LNCS, vol. 7337, pp. 253–258. Springer, Heidelberg (2012)

Pei, J., Han, J., Mortazavi-Asl, B., Pinto, H., Chen, Q., Dayal, U., Hsu, M.-C.: Pro fixspan: mining sequential patterns efficiently by prefix-projected pattern growth. In: Proceeding of the 2001 International Conference on Data Engineering (ICDE 2001), pp. 215–224, Heidelberg, Germany (2001)

Polanyi, L., Zaenen, A.: Contextual lexical valence shifters. In: Proceedings of the AAAI Spring Symposium on Exploring Attitude and Affect in Text: Theories and Applications (2004)

Quirk, R., Greenbaum, S., Leech, G., Svartvik, J.: A comprehensive grammar of the English language. Longman (1985)

Lexicology

Degree Modification in Mandarin: A Case Study of Creative Degree Modifier 各種 [*Gezhong*]

Minhsin Chen[✉] and Shukai Hsieh

Graduate Institute of Linguistics, National Taiwan University, Taipei, Taiwan (R.O.C.)
{r02142003,shukaihsieh}@ntu.edu.tw

Abstract. This paper aims to investigate degree modification in Mandarin through the case of creative degree modifier 各種 [*gezhong*] (all kinds of; very). We provide a theoretical analysis following the Generative Lexicon Theory and show that 各種 [*gezhong*] not only selects gradable adjectival predicates but also restricts the possible combinations as well as interpretation by means of qualia structure. The restrictions of the modification in turn reflect the pragmatic function of 各種 [*gezhong*], and mark the distinction between traditional degree modifiers and the creative one.

Keywords: Degree modification · Qualia structure · The generative lexicon

1 Introduction

Past studies addressing the issue of creative use of words have pointed out different ways to form new meanings, including introducing new lexical items from loan words, dialects, and jargon. New senses of words, on the other hand, often derive from new combinations of two old words. New senses of degree adverbials such as 爆 [*bao*] (high degree of) and 翻 [*fan*] (high degree of), as in 難爆 [*nanbao*] (very difficult) and 美翻 [*meifan*] (very beautiful) are examples that have been investigated [1]. As more and more creative use of degree adverbs emerges from the Internet, few has applied a generative system to disambiguate new senses and to see with what patterns new senses usually come into being. This paper aims to investigate a case of creative use of degree modifier which has become fairly common today:

(1) 外拍　　　　　　　　真是　　各種　　　　歡樂
Outdoors shooting　really　*gezhong*　happy
'*Outdoors shooting is seriously very happy*'

In example (1) 各種 [*gezhong*] carries an expressive function, allowing a degree reading which denotes 'very happy' for the proposition 各種歡樂 [*gezhong huanle*].

Past literature of Mandarin degree modifiers such as 有點 [*youdian*] (somewhat) and 很 [hen] (quite) has explored the distribution as well as diverse collocations of these lexical items, in which the pragmatic functions of different expressions are suggested to play the key role of their distinctions [2]. Following the previous research of degree modifiers, the present paper utilizes the Generative Lexicon Theory proposed

© Springer International Publishing Switzerland 2015
Q. Lu and H.H. Gao (Eds.): CLSW 2015, LNAI 9332, pp. 255–261, 2015.
DOI: 10.1007/978-3-319-27194-1_26

by Pustejovsky [3,4] to study the lexical semantics derived from the new combination of the creative degree modifier 各種 [*gezhong*] and adjectival predicates. To start the analysis, several research questions are proposed:

- What senses have derived from the new combination of 各種 [*gezhong*] following an adjectival predicate?
- What are the semantic properties of the predicates 各種 [*gezhong*] combine with?
- What is the pragmatic function of the new combination?
- What are the constraints for such combination and interpretation?

2   Generative Lexicon Theory

To directly address the issue of compositionality and creative use of words, Pustejovsky proposes the Generative Lexicon Theory, in which four levels of representations are organized within the generative lexicon: argument structure, event structure, qualia structure, and lexical inheritance structure. In the present paper we will focus on the qualia structure, which includes following rules:

- Constitutive role: the relation between an object and its constituents, or proper parts.
- Formal role: that which distinguishes the object within a larger domain.
- Agentive role: factors involved in the origin or "bringing about" of an object.
- Telic role: purpose and function of the object. [4]

A set of generative mechanisms is also proposed by Pustejovsky to connect the four levels. One of the mechanisms, selective binding, refers to the mechanism in which adjectives select and binds with a certain quale of a noun to realize a legitimate composition and brings out possible interpretation. With the selection of two corresponding properties in a proposition, the meaning of a given lexical item can bring out infinite senses and allow great flexibility in language. The Generative Lexicon Theory is argued in this way to accounts for polysemy and creative use in language.

Past literature investigating mental state adjectives has utilized Generative Lexicon Theory to account for various semantic and syntactic polymorphism [5]. Two representative classes of adjectives, namely stage-level predicates and individual-level predicates, were highly discussed. Through the process of selective binding, various senses of the same adjectival predicate can be distinguished by means of their qualia structure. For stage-level predicates, three senses can be found, as shown below.

Table 1. Three senses of stage-level predicates

sense	example	QUALIA
(1) stative: in a state of	I'm sad.	FORMAL
(2) causative: causes one to feel	The book is sad.	AGENTIVE
(3) resultative: a manifestation of	a sad book	TELIC

For individual-level predicates, on the other hand, two senses can be achieved, as shown below.

Table 2. Two senses of individual-level predicates

sense	example	QUALIA
(1) stative: in a state of	a clever man	FORMAL
(2) resultative: a manifestation of	a clever book	TELIC

Following the generative analysis of adjectives, senses and distribution of adjectival predicates following 各種 [*gezhong*] will be examined and discussed in section 4.

3   Method

The present paper includes 85 instances of the creative use of 各種 [*gezhong*] as degree modifier. They are collected on December 8th, 2014, from social network websites plurk.com and PTT by searching on the google search engine. These websites are chosen because they are where most creative use of 各種 [*gezhong*] is found. For our current purpose, the data being investigated is restricted to Taiwanese websites from the past year (2014).

The senses and categorical classes of the following predicates are defined and classified according to Chinese WordNet (CWN) and Academia Sinica Balanced Corpus of Modern Chinese. As for some new words from the online data that haven't been established in the two corpora, their word classes are decided according to the definition for word categories from the Sinica Corpus. To focus on the research of creative degree modifier, only instances of 各種 [*gezhong*] following an adjectival predicate are included and discussed in the present paper.

4   Analysis of Different Senses of 各種 [*gezhong*]

The new sense of 各種 [*gezhong*] has been demonstrated in example (1) above, which denotes a degree reading. In this section the derived senses of the combination of 各種 [*gezhong*] following adjectival predicates will be examined.

4.1   Distribution of 各種 [*gezhong*] and Adjectival Predicates

Out of the 85 instances, nearly half of them are stage-level predicates while the other half are individual-level predicates, as summarized below.

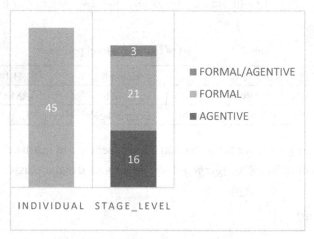

Fig. 1. Numbers of Different Types of Predicates

As demonstrated in example (1), 各種 [*gezhong*] denotes a degree reading when followed by an adjectival predicate such as 歡樂 [*huanle*] (happy). An important observation is that all of the predicates here denote a state that is gradable. That is, these predicates refer to states that can be combined with degree modifiers, as defined by the traditional view of gradable adjectives [7]. For instance, the state 'happy' in example (1) can be modified by degree modifier 'very' or 'fairly' and becomes 'very happy' or 'fairly happy'. The gradable state of adjectival predicates allow the legitimate combination of 各種 [*gezhong*] and 歡樂 [*huanle*], bringing out the interpretation of 'very happy' for this composition. The same interpretation can be achieved for other gradable adjectival predicates such as 各種累到脫力 [*gezhong leidaotuoli*] (very tired) or 各種哀傷 [*gezhong aishang*] (very sad). 'Tired' and 'sad' are both gradable adjectival predicates that can be interpreted into 'very tired' and 'very sad'.

Beside taking single-word predicates, the degree reading of 各種 [*gezhong*] also allows phrasal predicates. Consider example (2) below.

(2)   漫畫   完結   結局... 各種   意義   不明
        Comic   over   end   *gezhong* meaning unclear
        '*The comic has come to an end. The meaning of the ending is very unclear.*'

Here the phrasal predicate is an NP with a state describing the preceding head noun. The part of the phrase that can be characterized by the degree reading of 各種 [*gezhong*] is the state 'unclear'. The gradability of 'unclear' allows the interpretation 'very unclear'.

In this fashion, it comes as no surprise that there are adjectival predicates that cannot combine with 各種 [*gezhong*] to achieve the degree reading. That is, nongradable adjectival predicates such as 凍僵 [*dongjiang*] (freezing) or 死 [*si*] (dead) cannot be a legitimate predicate for 各種 [*gezhong*] in the degree reading.

Other than the gradability observation, two senses for stage-level predicates and one for individual-level predicates are found in the combination of 各種 [*gezhong*] following an adjectival predicate, as illustrated below.

Stage-level predicates

(3) 各種　　　臉紅噴血
    Gezhong　　blush
    '*I blushed.*'
    →I am in a state of blush
    (stative: FORMAL)
    →Something causes me to blush
    (causative: AGENTIVE)
    →*I/something is a manifestation of blush
    (resultative: TELIC)

Individual-level predicates

(4) 覺得　　　學弟妹 都　　　各種　　高
    I think　　juniors　are all　*gezhong* tall
    '*I think juniors are all tall.*'
    →The juniors are in a state of tall
    (stative: FORMAL)
    ›*The juniors are the manifestation of tall
    (resultative: TELIC)

For an individual-level predicate, its combination with 各種 [*gezhong*] can only extract a stative sense by means of the FORMAL role. That is, such combination cannot perform the interpretation achieved by a selection of the TELIC role. This can be seen as a distinction between traditional degree modifiers such as 很 [hen] (quite) and the creative one 各種 [*gezhong*]. While 這本書很聰明 [*zhebenshu hen congming*] (This book is very smart) can be legitimately interpreted into 'this book is the manifestation of clever', 這本書各種聰明 [*zhebenshu gezhong congming*] cannot.

For stage-level predicates, the same can be observed. The combination with 各種 [*gezhong*] can extract a stative sense by means of the FORMAL role and a causative sense by the AGENTIVE role while the resultative sense is nowhere to be found. Example (3) can be interpreted into stative, causative, or both senses. When it comes to the TELIC role, however, 這本書各種臉紅噴血 [*zhebenshu gezhong lienhongpenxie*] (This book blush a lot) sounds strange and results in an illegitimate expression.

4.2   Pragmatic Function of 各種 [*gezhong*]

Whether a stage-level or an individual-level predicate, resultative senses achieved by a selection of the TELIC role are excluded in the predication preceded by 各種 [*gezhong*]. Such phenomenon marks the distinction between 各種 [*gezhong*] and other degree modifiers. While combinations with traditional degree modifiers such as hen '很' can be used to subjectively express one's feelings as well as objectively describe a fact, the pragmatic function carried out by 各種 [*gezhong*] is to express one's own feelings toward something instead of portraying an objective fact. In cases for a fact that someone may write a book as a manifestation of his sadness, expressions such as 各種悲傷 [*gezhong beishang*] (very sad) is not ready to modify the manifestation (i.e. that book). Instead, it is more possible to be used to describe one's immediate feelings (e.g. the resultative sadness from reading the book). The user-oriented and subjective preference of using 各種 [*gezhong*] shapes the distribution of its possible combination and the derived interpretation.

4.3   Constraints of the Combination with 各種 [*gezhong*]

Above we present instances which different senses of the combination of 各種 [*gezhong*] and adjectival predicates can be achieved by utilizing different qualia roles of adjectival predicates. There, of course, exist several constraints for such combination:

- Only gradable adjectival predicates can be combined with 各種 [*gezhong*] to achieve the degree reading.
- Modification of a subjective expression can be modified by 各種 [*gezhong*] and extract stative and causitive senses by means of the FORMAL and AGENTIVE role respectively. Description of an objective fact, however, cannot be modified by 各種 [*gezhong*] and brings out the resultative sense.

5   Conclusion

In the present paper we apply the Generative Lexicon Theory and demonstrate how the different senses of 各種 [*gezhong*] combining an adjectival predicate can be disambiguated by means of its qualia structure. In sum, the degree reading of 各種 [*gezhong*] comes in combination with gradable stage-level or individual-level predicates. By using the creative degree modifier 各種 [*gezhong*], users express their subjective feelings toward the target, bringing out either stative or causative meaning of the predication. The subjectivity constrains the distribution of such combination and in turn reflects the distinction between 各種 [*gezhong*] and traditional degree modifiers, carrying an effect that cannot be achieved by old expressions.

Creative use of language may be popular for solely a short while or it may sustain and finally come into our daily lexicon. Language itself has a mechanism of selection, through which creative use that is structurally strong and carries the most effective functions survives the experimentation. While scrutinizing the pattern of a case of creative degree modification, many questions such as the limitations of the proposed method have been left unanswered. As 各種 [*gezhong*] can also be used to modify a wide variety of lexical items on the Internet (e.g. 各種勾搭 [*gezhong gouda*] all kinds of ways to know someone), further research is needed for the fuller picture regarding sense extensions and creative use of words.

References

1. Liu, H.Y., Kuo, C.C.: Excessive Extent in Cognition—A Contrastive Study on Mandarin and English. Journal of Language Teaching and Research **2**(5), 1015–1022 (2011)
2. Chang, C., Liu, M.C.: Constructional Coercions in Semantic Representation: The Evaluative 'Degree-Adverb+ X' Construction in Mandarin, Doctoral Dissertation. National Chiao Tung University (2004)
3. Pustejovsky, J.: Type Coercion and Lexical Selection. In: Semantics and the Lexicon, pp. 73–94. Springer, Netherlands (1993)
4. Pustejovsky, J.: The Generative Lexicon. MIT Press (1995)
5. Bouillon, P.: Mental state adjectives: the perspective of generative lexicon. In: Proceedings of the 16th Conference on Computational Linguistics-volume 1, pp. 143–148. Association for Computational Linguistics, August, 1996
6. Paradis, C.: Reinforcing Adjectives: A Cognitive Semantic Perspective on Grammaticalization. Topics in English Linguistics **31**, 233–260 (2000)
7. Paradis, C.: Adjectives and Boundedness 47–65 (2001)
8. Carlson, G.N.: Reference to Kinds in English, Doctoral Dissertation, University of Massachusetts (1977)

A Study on the Taxonomy of Chinese Noun Compounds

Lulu Wang[1(⊠)] and Meng Wang[2]

[1] Communication University of China, Beijing 100024, China
lulu.wang@cuc.edu.cn
[2] School of Humanity, Jiangnan University, Wuxi 214122, China
wangmengly@163.com

Abstract. This paper deals with the semantic interpretation of Chinese noun compounds. We first propose a novel taxonomy of Chinese noun compounds based on the syntagmatic possibility and semantic transparency. Further, we analyze the qualia structure of the nouns and their relations with the hidden verbs. In the end, we propose a fine-grained classification and the interpretation patterns of the noun compounds.

Keywords: Noun compound · Semantic relation · Qualia roles

1 Introduction

A Noun Compound[1] syntactically behaves as a single noun, but is semantically interpreted as a compressed proposition, which could be elaborated by the hidden verb (Yuan 1995). For example, "爱情故事" (love story) could be illustrated as "讲述爱情的故事" (a story that tells about love), in which the verb "讲述" (to tell) infers the missing relation between "爱情" (love) and "故事" (story). Many researchers (Tan 2010, Zhou 2010, Wang 2010 and Wei 2013) suggest that the hidden verbs are crucial to the interpretation of noun compounds and design various ways to reveal the hidden verbs. However, some noun compounds could not be reconstructed by the hidden verbs, such as (4a) below.

(1) a.机组 成员 （crew member）

b.机组 的 成员[2] （crew PART member）

c.构成 机组 的 成员 （constitute crew PART member）

(2) a.钻石 戒指 （diamond ring）

b.?钻石 的 戒指 （diamond PART ring）

c.镶嵌 钻石 的 戒指 （inlay diamond PART ring）

---

[1] We only analyze the noun compounds (N1-N2) that N1 behaves as the modifier of N2.

[2] "的" is an attribute particle in Chinese and here it is shorted for as PART.

© Springer International Publishing Switzerland 2015
Q. Lu and H.H. Gao (Eds.): CLSW 2015, LNAI 9332, pp. 262–269, 2015.
DOI: 10.1007/978-3-319-27194-1_27

(3)   a.试管　婴儿　（ test tube　baby ）

      b.*试管　的　婴儿　（test　tube　PART　baby ）

      c.?试管　培育　的　婴儿　（test　tube fertilize　PART　baby ）

(4)   a.夫妻　肺片　(the　spouse　pork　lungs)

      b.*夫妻　的　肺片　(the　spouse　PART　pork　lungs)

      c.*夫妻　制作　的　肺片　（the　spouse　make　PART　pork lungs)

In the above examples, only (1a) allows the attribute particle "的" inserted in between the noun compounds, while others are not grammatical as (2b-4b) show. Notably, the noun compounds in (1c-3c) could be interpreted by the hidden verbs. However, (4c) is not acceptable with the hidden verb "制作" (make), this is because "夫妻肺片" means a famous Sichuan style dish of pork lungs in chili source, which entails an idiomatical meaning which could not be reconstructed compositionally. Thus, we suggest that the semantic interpretation of noun compounds varies in the semantic transparency: some expressions are literal, some are inferable by verbs and some are idiomatic.

In this paper, we focus on the semantic interpretation on Chinese noun compounds. We will suggest a novel taxonomy of Chinese noun compounds based on the transparency of the compounds. Further, we will have a deep understanding on the qualia structure of the nouns. A fine-grained classification of the noun compounds is provided in the end.

2   Previous Studies

2.1   Noun Compound Semantics

In the theoretical field, linguists describe the semantics of the noun compounds via a set of abstract relations, as represented in the work of Levi (1978) and Warren (1978). Following this tradition, some researchers in the computational field focus on the taxonomies of noun compounds. Ó Séaghdha (2007) proposed six semantic relations: BE, HAVE, IN, ACTOR, INST, ABOUT, and each relation is subdivided into subcategories. For example, HAVE is subdivided into the subcategories of possession, condition-experiencer, property-object, part-whole and group-member. Tratz and Hovy (2010) presented a large, fine-grained taxonomy of 43 noun compound relations, which are notably tested by the Amazon's Mechanical Turk service. However, the approach of abstract rela-tions is problematic in several ways. As Nakov and Hearst (2013) pointed out that (1) it is unclear which relation inventory is best, (2) relations capture only part of the semantics, and (3) multiple relations are possible. For example, Wei (2012: 40) assumes that "中国电影" (Chinese movies) is classified into the categories of LOCATION and CONTENT.

Considering these drawbacks, other researchers use verbal paraphrases to interpret the noun compounds. Finn (1980) interpreted "salt water" with dissolved in. Butnariu and Veale (2008) summarized 8 relational possibilities. For example, "headache pill" might be paraphrased as "headache-inducing pill", "headache prevention pill", "pill for treating headaches", "pill that causes headaches", "pill that is prescribed for headache" and "pill that prevents headaches". With these verbs, the paraphrases are more specific than that of the abstract relations.

Accordingly, there are two ways to interpret the noun compounds semantics in Chinese. Wang (2010) adopts a bottom-up strategy to capture the verbs of noun compounds and provides four types of paraphrase patterns. As Wei (2012) pointed out, these four types are not specific enough to give proper interpretations. Instead, Wei classifies the noun compounds into 8 major types and 346 subcategories, which are proved to be fine-grained. However, some of these subcategories can be merged, and some noun compounds belong to more than one subcategory. Further, they all neglected the semantic transparency of the noun compounds, which should be taken serious consideration.

2.2   Semantic Transparencies

Recalling the above example of (4a), the noun compound "夫妻肺片" is not decomposable, that is, the meaning of the compound is not simply the combinations of the literal meanings of the parts. Levi (1978) argues for a transparency scale for the noun compounds as in the following table.

Table 1. Levi's transparency scale of noun compounds

	types	examples
a	transparent	orange peel
b	partly opaque	grammar school
c	exocentric	ladybird
d	partly idiomatic	flea market
e	completely idiomatic	honeymoon

In the table above, Levi summarizes five types of noun compounds based on the semantic transparency. These different types show the different interpretation patterns of the noun compounds. For example, "orange peel" is simply the combination of the parts of "orange" and "peel". But "grammar school" cannot be combined literally, that is because a hidden verb should be revealed to illustrate this compound as in "grammar teaching school". In contrast, the other types cannot be combined literally, nor be interpreted by the hidden verb. For instance, "ladybird" is not a kind of bird, but a kind of bug "Coccinellidae"[3]. And "honeymoon" has nothing to do with "honey" or "moon", but refers to the vacation that brides and grooms celebrate their marriage. The Type of "partly idiomatic" is special, because it is partly idiomatic that verbs are not easy to recover. It is not acceptable to say "flea selling market", but means market selling small commodities. Enlightened by Levi's ideas, we will present a novel taxonomy of Chinese noun compounds based on the semantic transparency.

---

[3] Here "lady" is named after "Virgin Mary", see more: http://www.hkhk.edu.ee/nature/ladybird_legends.html

3   Taxonomy of Chinese Noun Compounds

In light of Levi's transparence scale and Nun-berg, Sag and Wasow (1994)'s claim on idioms, we collected 428 noun-noun compounds (N1-N2) and classified them into the following four categories.

Table 2. Basic types of noun compounds

	transparency scale	examples
a	transparent	机组人员 (crew member)
b	partly opaque	钻石戒指 (diamond ring)
c	partly idiomatic	试管婴儿 (test tube baby)
d	completely idiomatic	夫妻肺片 (the spouse pork lung)

As the table shows, the first three types are decomposable at the syntagmatic level, but the last one is non-decomposable. We suggest that non-decomposable idioms should be analyzed as a whole unit both syntactically and semantically. The other types are decomposable, which can be divided into N1 and N2. However, the semantic relations of these types are different in semantic transparency. We will illustrate these differences with the following examples.

(5)   a.机组 人员 （crew-member *crew members*）

      b.印尼 火山 （Indonesia-volcano *an Indonesia volcano*）

The examples in (5) belong to type a, which are decomposable and the semantic relations are transparent. Syntactically, N1 is the attribute of N2. The attribute particle "的" can be inserted in between N1 and N2. Semantically, the meaning of the compound is the combination of the literal meaning of the parts. We suggest that this type is the default type of the noun-noun pairs in Chinese, where N2 is the head noun and N1 is the modifier of the noun. The semantic relations are possessive, locative and time.

(6)   a.钻石 戒指 （diamond-ring *diamond rings*）

      b.围棋 高手 （chess-master *chess masters*）

The examples in (6) are decomposable as well, but the attribute particle cannot be inserted in between. If it is inserted in between, it sounds odd to native speakers. That is because they are different from type 'a' that there are hidden verbs in between the nouns. For example, "钻石" (diamond) and"戒指" (ring) imply the verb of "镶嵌" (inlay); "围棋" (chess) and "高手" (master) imply the verb of "下". Hence, these expressions are partly opaque that we need to reveal the hidden verbs to interpret these noun compounds. In the next section, we will further explore the subcategories of this type within the qualia structure theory.

(7)   a.试管 婴儿 （test tube-baby *test tube babies*）
       b.皮包 公司 （suitcase-company *paper company*）

Similar to type b, the examples in (7) are also decomposable, but the semantic relations are more complex than the former one. In (7a), "试管" (test tube) and "婴儿" (baby) cannot be combined literally, that is because "试管" (test tube) metaphors as in vitro (glass) fertilization. Such compressed concept cannot be simply revealed by the lexical semantics, such as "装" (fill in), but can be revealed by the verbs co-occurred in the text, such as "培育" (fertilize). As for (7b), the case is the same in that we cannot analyze the compound by the literal meanings of "皮包" (suitcase), but comprehend them as an idiomatic expression. Hence, such type is the most complex in semantic relations that they are not simply the combinations of the literal meanings of the parts, but involve a process of metaphors, which enhance the difficulty in revealing the hidden verbs.

4   Revealing the Hidden Verbs

In light of Aristotle's arguments on the four causes, Pustejovsky (1995) proposed four qualia roles of nouns: formal, constitutive, agentive and telic. Wei (2012) first adopts this idea into the interpretation of Chinese noun compounds and discovers some relations between the qualia structure and the noun compounds interpretations. Further, Yuan (2014) analyzes the qualia structure of nouns in Chinese and proposes some new qualia roles based the data of Chinese, such as action and handle. To take "食品" (food) for example, the qualia roles of food are listed in the following table.

Table 3. The qualia roles of "食品" (*food*)

	食品	food
formal	商品	commodity
constitutive	快餐	fast food
unit	篮子	basket
evaluation	新鲜	fresh
agentive	制作	make
telic	吃	eat
handle	购买	buy

We believe that the above qualia roles are more fine-grained to Chinese data, and thus we analyze the qualia structure of nouns based on Yuan's qualia structure knowledge system.

We analyzed 428 noun compounds on their semantic relations and the qualia roles of the Head noun. It appears to us that there is a clear correspondent relationship between the semantic relations and the qualia roles of the head noun. To illustrate, we summarize this correspondence in the following table.

Table 4. The semantic relations of noun compounds

	semantic relations	qualia roles	interpretation patterns	examples
1	possessive	CON	"属于" (be-long)+N1+*de*+N2	机组人员 (*crew member*)
2	property	EVA/TEL	"性质是"(*the feature is*) +N1+*de*+N2	可行性报告 (*operative report*)
3	locative	CON/AGE	"位于" (*locate*) +N1+*de*+N2; "在" (*at*) +N1+V+*de*+N2	雅典奥运会 (*Athens Olympics*)
4	time	CON/AGE	"在" (*in*)+N1+*de*+N2	梅雨季节 (*plum rain season*)
5	content	CON/TEL	"关于" (*about*) +N1+*de*+N2; V+N1+*de*+N2	爱情故事 (*love story*)
6	material	AGE	"用" (*with*) +N1+V+*de*+N2	钻石戒指 (*diamond ring*)
7	patient	TEL	V+N1+*de*+N2	围棋高手 (*chess master*)
8	actor	ACT	N1+V+*de*+N2	教委文件 (*the board of education document*)
9	cause	AGE	N1+V+*de*+N2	考试焦虑 (*test anxiety*)
10	partly-idiomatic	-	metaphoric or metonymic meaning of N1+*de*+N2	试管婴儿 (*test tube baby*)
11	idiomatic	-	idiom	夫妻肺片 (*the spouse pork lungs*)

In the table above, we have summarized 10 subcategories of noun compounds based on their semantic relation. To interpret these noun compounds, we present different interpretation patterns with different conditions. The first category of "possessive" in the above table corresponds to the noun compounds of type 'a' in table 2, which could be interpreted as the literal meanings of the parts. To illustrate, the paraphrasing sentence of "机组人员" (*crew members*) is "属于机组的人员" (*the members that belonged to the crew*).

From (2) to (5), these four types correspond to both type 'a' and type 'b', since the meaning of the compound could not only be interpreted by the fixed pattern of the components, but also could be predicted by the hidden verb. For instance, the paraphrasing verb of the compound "雅典奥运会" (Athens Olympics) could be "举办" (to hold), and thus the paraphrasing sentence will be "在雅典举办的奥运会" (The Olympic Games that was held in Athens.). As for "爱情故事" (love story), it could be paraphrased as "关于爱情的故事" (the story about love), and also "讲述爱情的故事" (the story telling about love).

Moreover, categories from (6) to (8) correspond to type 'b', in which the hidden verb must be revealed. In this group, the qualia roles of the head noun are different in each type. For example, the qualia role in (6) is AGE, which is because material usually relates to the MAKE relation. And the relation of "patient" in (7) relates more with TELIC roles, which are interpreted as the functions of N1. For example, "围棋高手" (chess master) could be paraphrased as "下围棋的高手" (the masters of playing chess). Here, "下（棋）" (to play) is the TELIC role of "围棋" (chess).

The last two types correspond to type c and the non-decomposable idioms separately. Noun compounds as in (10) should be interpreted with the metaphoric meaning, and thus they cannot be interpreted with the hidden verbs. To take "试管婴儿" (test tube babies) as an example, we cannot illustrate the compound using the expressions like "在试管里孕育的婴儿" (the babies that are fertilized in test tubes). The word "试管" (test tubes) has the metonymic meaning as a "试管孕育技术" (in glass fertilization). Therefore, we need to infer the metaphoric meaning of such compounds as "用试管技术孕育的婴儿" (the babies that are fertilized by the technic using test tubes). For the idioms, they are not decomposable at all and should be treated as a whole unit. For example, "夫妻肺片" only refers to the name of a dish.

5   Concluding Remarks

This paper deals with the semantic interpretation of Chinese noun compounds. We first propose a novel taxonomy of Chinese noun compounds based on the transparency of the compounds. Further, we analyze the qualia structure of the nouns and propose a fine-grained classification of the noun compounds. In the future, we will implement this taxonomy of noun compounds in some practical NLP tasks, such as semantic similarity computation, question answering system and search query engines.

Acknowledgments. We would like to thank the anonymous reviewers of CLSW 2015 for the comments. The paper is supported by the Natural Science Foundation of China (61300152, 61375074, and 61371129) and the Social Science Foundation of China (12&ZD175 and 12&ZD227).

References

1. Butnariu, C., Veale, T.: A concept-centered approach to noun-compound interpretation. In: Proceedings of the 22nd International Conference on Computational Linguistics, pp. 81–88 (2008)
2. Finn, T.: The semantic interpretation of compound nominal. Ph.D. Dissertation, University of Illinois, Urbana (1980)
3. Levi, J.: The Syntax and Semantics of Complex Nominals. Academic Press, New York (1978)
4. Nakov, P.I., Hearst, M.A.: Semantic Interpretation of Noun Compounds using Verbal and Other Paraphrases. ACM Trans. Speech Lang. Process. **10**(3), 13 (2013)
5. Nunberg, G., Sag, I.A., Wasow, T.: Idioms. Language **70**(3), 491–538 (1994)

6. Séaghdha, D.O.: Designing and evaluating a semantic annotation scheme for compound nouns. In: Proceedings of the 4th Corpus Linguistics Conference (2007)
7. Pustejovsky, J.: The Generative Lexicon. The MIT Press (1995)
8. Tan, J.C.: Semantic Relations between nouns and noun modifiers and their roles in dictionary definition. Studies of Chinese Language **4** (2010). (in Chinese)
9. Tratz, S., Hovy, E.: A taxonomy, dataset, and classifier for automatic noun compound interpretation. In: Proceedings of the 48th Annual Meeting of the Association for Computational Linguistics, pp. 678–687 (2010)
10. Wang, M.: Linguistic Knowledge Acquisition of Noun for the Construction of Probablistic Lexical Knowledge-base. Ph.D. Dissertation, Peking University (2010). (in Chinese)
11. Warren, B.: Semantic patterns of noun-noun compounds. In: Gothenburg studies in English 41, Acta Universitatis Gothoburgensis, Goteburg (1978)
12. Wei, X.: Research on Chinese Noun Compound Interpretation for Semantic-Query. Master Thesis. Peking University (2012). (in Chinese)
13. Yuan, Y.L.: Weici Yinhan Jiqi Jufa Houguo: de zi jiegou de chengdai guize he de de yufa, yuyigongneng. Studies of Chinese Language **4** (1995). (in Chinese)
14. Yuan, Y.L.: A Study of Chinese Semantic Knowledge System Based on the Theory of Generative Lexicon and Argument Structure. Journal of Chinese Information Procession **27**(6), 23–30 (2013). (in Chinese)
15. Zhou, R.A.: Studies on the syntax and semantics of noun-noun compounds. China Social Science Press (2010). (in Chinese)

A Study on the Interactive Relationships Between the Formation of Three-Syllable Abbreviations and the Prosody

Shan Chen[1] and Jianfei Luo[2(✉)]

[1] Changde Vocational Technical College, Hunan, China
chen2shan1@163.com
[2] Beijing Language and Culture University, Beijing, China
nch1980s@163.com

Abstract. Most Chinese abbreviations consist of two syllables, but in certain cases, they are composed of three syllables in the form of super-prosody. On the basis of how to make up three-syllable abbreviations, this paper aims at exploring the interactive relationships between the forms of three-syllable abbreviations and the prosody. It is pointed out that the prosody makes a lot of contributions in terms of checking and adjusting the creation and usage of three-syllable abbreviations, during which, some components of three-syllable abbreviations will adapt themselves to the structure of prosodic morphology.

Keywords: Three-syllabic abbreviations · Prosody · Standard prosodic words · Natural foot

1 Studies on Abbreviations and Their Syllables

Some common phrases or words are shortened into another form so that they can be used in a concise, clear and convenient way, from which abbreviation comes into being. Some people call the shortened form as "shortening", while other people call it as "acronym". However, in this paper, it is believed that "shortening" is so general that it can create any words just in their shortened forms, whereas "acronym" is so narrow that it tends to leave out the shortened phrases which should belong to this range. As a result, according to its particularity, we still call it "abbreviations".

Yuan (2002) pointed out that when phrases or words are shortened into abbreviations, these abbreviations must conform to the morphological construction of the native language. Most Chinese abbreviations are just morphemes extracted from words, while in modern Chinese language, except for monosyllable, most words are composed of two or three syllables, among which disyllables take up the most, three-syllable is much lesser than disyllables, and four-syllable is the least kind. Disyllable is the most representative and the most classical phonetic form, therefore, not only are four-syllable phrases shortened as disyllable, but also some three-syllable words are contracted into disyllable. For some abbreviations, disyllable and three-syllable coexist, but disyllable is used more commonly especially in spoken language.

© Springer International Publishing Switzerland 2015
Q. Lu and H.H. Gao (Eds.): CLSW 2015, LNAI 9332, pp. 270–280, 2015.
DOI: 10.1007/978-3-319-27194-1_28

Liu (2004) analyzed the syllable numbers of abbreviations and proposed that most abbreviations are in the form of disyllable. The prosodic rules for modern Chinese words' being disyllabic decide the syllable numbers of abbreviation. Statistics show that disyllabic abbreviations take up 84.2% of the whole, while other 15.8% are forced to take the form of more than two syllables, because over-omitting of some components will lead to misunderstanding or confusion.

Niu (2004), on the basis of principles for creating an abbreviation, discussed the number of abbreviations and figured out that being brief and concise features the abbreviations of modern Chinese, namely, replacing long parts with concise parts to make the communication more convenient, which can really reflect the Economy Principle and the Least Effort Principle of words in usage. Therefore, abbreviations of modern Chinese should exist in their simplest forms without influencing their conceptual expression.

Taking these researches into consideration, it is admitted that most of the abbreviations are disyllabic, but why are there still some three-syllabic abbreviations? Which factors have affected or constrained these three-syllabic abbreviations' establishment and development?   What features do they possess in their internal constructions? This paper will focus on these three questions.

2   Relationship Between the Formation of Three-syllable Abbreviations and the Prosody

2.1   Chinese Prosodic Words and the Related Theories

Having researched how to form a word and a sentence in the prosody, Feng (1996, 1998) and other scholars pointed out that "prosodic words" are mainly decided by the "foot" in the prosodic morphology, whereas "foot" are decided by a smaller unit— "syllable", and the most basic syllable in Chinese is disyllable. In terms of the components of three-syllable, Feng insisted that [2+1] structures form a word, while [1+2] structures cannot. For example, 皮鞋厂 [*pi xie chang*](*shoes factory*) is acceptable, but *鞋工厂 [*xie gong chang*](*shoes factory*) is not like authentic Chinese. That is to say, like figure 1 and figure 2, [1+2] structures cannot form a three-syllabic prosodic word. (Thereafter, σ refers to syllable.)

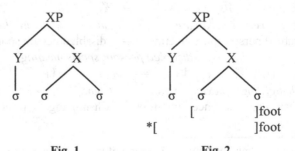

Fig. 1   **Fig. 2**

In Figure 3, only a monosyllable is under the rightmost node, while the left node covers a disyllable, which is called [2+1] structure. According to the "right to left" principle, the component under the right node X cannot form a foot; therefore, foot in this structure must involve the component under node Y. However, when it comes to the left boundary for the foot, there comes a dilemma: the two components under node Y are unified before this combination, and it is insisted that formation of new prosodic words cannot ruin the existed combinations, so the left boundary can only go to the leftmost syllable, which gives birth to a super-foot. Therefore, only super-foot in [2+1] structure can make a word, such as[[电影]院] [*dian ying yuan*](*the movie house*) and [[游击]队] [*youji dui*](*a guerrilla detachment*).

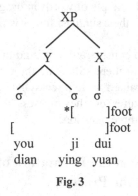

Fig. 3

2.2   Construction and Reanalysis of Abbreviations in [N+[N+N]]

Some abbreviations are not generated just at one time; instead, they may be contracted or extracted from the original structure. Therefore, besides the constraints from the basic morphology and the prosodic words, they can be affected by the original word, leading to some expressions beyond these principles. For example,

Structure for安徽师范大学[*Anhui shifan daxue*](*Anhui Normal University*) is N+(N+N) and its abbreviation is 安师大[*An shi da*](*the abbreviation of Anhui Normal University*), which is obtained by selecting a representative word from each foot. After this contracting, the final structure of its abbreviation is still N+(N+N). As is shown in figure 4 and figure 5, the structures are still nouns in [1+2], but they are not allowed in prosodic morphology, while in abbreviations, they make sense. For example,

(1) 残 疾 人 运 动 会   —— 残   运 会
     canji   ren   yundonghui   *can*   *yun hui*
     disabled person sport meeting —— disabled person sport meeting
                    disabled persons sports meeting[1]

(2) 长 江 科 学 院 —— 长   科   院
     Changjiang kexue yuan   *Chang*   *ke*   *yuan*
     Changjiang science institute   Changjiang science institute

---

[1] Since the latter is only the abbreviation form of the former structure, we only give one translation of the two parallel phrases.

Changjiang scientific research institute

(3) 德意志 新闻 社   —— 德   新   社
Deyizhi xinwen she   De   xin   she
Germany news agency   Germany news agency
Germany's Deutsche Presse-Agentur

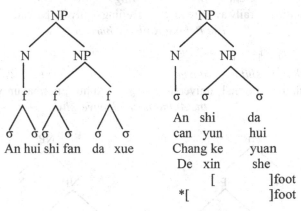

Fig. 4   **Fig. 5**

According to Feng's prediction (2004, 2006), this structure does not exist, because it violates the basis principle of morphology for natural feet. If N is replaced by NP, the same thing will also appear. For example:

(4) 表 演 艺 术 委 员 会   —— 表   委   会
biaoyan yishu weiyuahui   biao   wei   hui
perform art   committee   perform art committee
the performing arts committee

(5) 村 民 委 员 会 办 公 所 ——村   公   所
cunmin   weiyuanhui bangongsuo   cun   gong   suo
villager committee   office   villager committee office
the villagers committee office

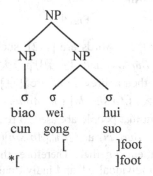

Fig. 6

In fact, do these words go beyond the principle of prosodic morphology? Do they have other constraints, or transformation rules?

A vast of researches on three-syllable abbreviations illustrate that a lot of abbreviations are in [1+2] structure, but when used, they show a tendency towards [2+1] structure, among which the first and the second syllable are bound together. For instance,

(6)   北 京 铁 路 局 ── 京 铁 局
       Beijing tielu ju   *Jing tie ju*
       Beijing   railway bureau   Beijing railway bureau
              The Beijing Railway Bureau

(7)   安 徽 师 范 大 学 ── 安 师 大
       Anhui shifan daxue   *An shi da*
       Anhui   normal university   Anhui normal university
              the Anhui normal university

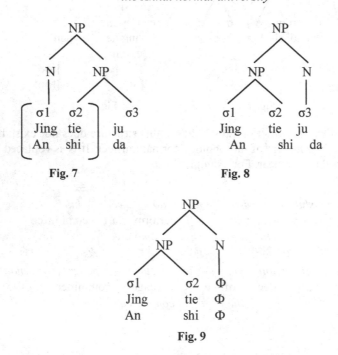

Fig. 7   Fig. 8

Fig. 9

The original structures for these words are [1+2], such as [[北京]铁路局] [*Beijing tielu ju*](*the Beijing Railway Bureau*) and [[安徽]师范大学] [*Anhui shifan daxue*](*the Anhui normal university*), and their abbreviations are [[京]铁局] [*Jing tie ju*](*the Beijing Railway Bureau*) and[[安]师大] [*An shi da*] (*the Anhui normal university*) (Figure 7), but in actual use it is found out that people are used to reading the two syllables in京铁 [*Jing tie*](*the Beijing Railway Bureau*) and安师[*An shi*](*the Anhui normal university*) together, and understanding them together. Therefore, there exists a reconstruction in the three-syllable structures. Individual σ1 and individual σ2 abandon σ3 and become unified after the reanalysis (Figure 8), during which prosodic constraint plays a key role. In morphology, [2+1] structure is valid, while [1+2] is invalid. This conflict forces the structure to adjust itself, after which a valid word can be created. After this, σ3 separates itself from the structure and becomes an "unimportant" component. Used for a long time, σ3 can also gradually fall off this structure, so that the structure in this abbreviation can be a standard disyllabic prosodic word (Figure 9).

Therefore, a hypothesis is made, namely, for three-syllabic abbreviations in [N/NP+[N+N]] structure, transformation rule is just like:

(8) **[σ1+[σ2+σ3]]→[[σ1+σ2]+σ3]→[[σ1+σ2]+Φ]**

Based on this rule, constructions of some abbreviations are testified.

(9) [上海 [电 影 制 片 厂]]→[上 [影 厂]]→[[上 影] 厂]→[[上 影]Φ]

Shanghai dianying zhipianchang   shang ying chang shangying chang shang ying

the Shanghai film studio

(10) [工 人[体 育 场]]→[工[体 场]]→[[工 体] 场]→[[工 体]Φ]

gongren tiyuchang   gong ti chang   gongti chang   gong ti

the worker sport stadium

(11) [奥 林 匹 克 [运 动 会]]→[奥[运会]]→[[奥运]会]→[[奥运]Φ]

Ao linpike   yun dong hui Ao yun hui   Aoyunhui   Aoyun

the Olympics Games

If this rule does exist, it means that prosody plays a pivotal role in forming an abbreviation, because prosody does not only adjust the structure itself in light of the natural feet, but also transform its structure. In the system of prosodic words, three-syllables are not very common and stable, so even though those words are adjusted to [2+1] structure under the rules of natural feet, they are not as stable as disyllabic standard feet. Therefore, prosody will further shorten three-syllables, mainly finished by deleting the [1] part from [2+1] structure. Thus, prosodically dependent parts become disyllabic standard feet (also standard prosodic words). That is to say, prosody adjusts the structure itself before transformation, and further adapts it in the usage. The detail is just like:

| Prosody adjusts the structure itself | | Prosody further adapts it in the usage | |

(12) [σ1+[σ2+σ3]] ⟶ [[σ1+σ2]+σ3] ⟶ [[σ1+σ2]+Φ]

2.3   The Second Change of [N+[N+N]] Abbreviations

In the three-syllable abbreviations, a certain type still cannot be adjusted by this structure, such as 党支部书记[*Dangzhibu shuji*](*Party branch secretary*) – 党支书[*Dang zhi shu*](*Party branch secretary*).

In this case, it cannot be changed to [*Dangzhi*] + [*shu*], so it cannot be transformed to [2+1] structure. Through observations, it is obvious to find out that words that can be put in the N position mainly include:

(13)   第   二   附   属   中   学   ——   二   附   中

di   er   fu   shu zhong xue   er   fu   zhong
second affiliated middle school   second affiliated middle school
the second affiliated middle school   *the second affiliated middle school*

(14) 总   通   讯   枢   纽——   总   枢   纽
zong   tong   xun   shu   niu   zong   shu   niu
total communication   hub   total   hub
the total communication hub   *the total communication hub*

(15) 中   共   总   支 部   书 记 ——   总   支   书
zhong gong   zong zhi bu   shu ji   zong   zhi   shu
Chinese communist party   general branch secretary general branch   secretary
the Chinese Communist Party general branch secretary

Fig.10

The functions of these words seem different from the common nouns. Qiu (2013) argued that in words such as 纸老虎[*zhi laohu*](*the paper tiger*), 金项链[*jin xian-glian*](*golden necklace*), the character 纸[*zhi*](*paper*), 金[*jin*](*gold*) do not have the typical characters of nouns. Instead, it has been used to differentiate the part of speech. Therefore, they can be compared:

(16) 纸   老   虎 —— *纸   工   厂
zhi   lao   hu   zhi   gong   chang
paper   tiger   paper   factory
the paper tiger   *the paper factory*

(17) 金   项   链 —— *金   商   店
jin   xiang lian   jin   shang dian
gold   necklace   gold   shop
golden necklace   *golden shop*

Therefore, it is reasonable to say that the single syllable part of abbreviations such as 党支书[*Dang zhishu*](*Party branch secretary*) has become the word to differentiate the part of speech, or as it is called quasi-affix . Thus, they are not the typical [N+N] structure, which do not fit the word formation rules of valid [2+1] structure and invalid [1+2] structure. They should fit the phrase formation rules, which is in accordance with the 纸老虎[*zhi laohu*](*the paper tiger*) and 金项链[*jin xian-glian*](*golden necklace*) type.

The rules can be concluded as follow:

(18) $[N\sigma1+[N\sigma2+N\sigma3]]\rightarrow[A\sigma1+[N\sigma2+N\sigma3]]$

The restriction of prosody is mainly displayed in this aspect: It is the prosody that forces No1 to be changed to an adjective (or distinctive) part of speech so as to make up of the new structure under the rules of prosody.

$$\text{Prosody forcing N}\sigma1\text{ to become A}\sigma1$$

(19) $[\text{N}\sigma1+[\text{N}\sigma2+\text{N}\sigma3]] \xrightarrow{\hspace{4cm}} [\text{A}\sigma1+[\text{N}\sigma2+\text{N}\sigma3]]$

2.4   The Formation of Three-syllabic Coordination Abbreviations

Another important type of three-syllable abbreviation is the coordination structure. It is made up of three parts that have been shortened to a three-syllable abbreviation. For instance:

(20)   党　组织、　政　府　部　门、军　队——党　　政　　军
　　　　dang   zu zhi,　zheng fu   bu   men, jun dui   dang　zheng　jun
　　　　party organization, government department, army Party,　government, army
　　　　　party organization ,government department and the army

(21)   采　访、　编　辑　和　播　音　——　采　　编　　播
　　　　cai   fang　bian   ji　he　bo   yīn　cai　bian　bo
　　　　interview,　edit　and　transmit　interview, edit　transmit
　　　　　interview, edit and transmit

(22)   德　　育、　　智　　育　和　休　育——德　智　体
　　　　de　yu　zhi　yu　he　ti　yu   de　zhi　ti
　　　　moral education,   intellectual education   and   physical education
　　　　　　　　　　　　　　　　　　moral intellectual physical
　　　　moral education, intellectual education and physical education

For these kinds of abbreviation, the internal structure must be [1+1+1], which has no connection with each other. Feng (1998) suggested that in the Chinese three-syllabic coordination words, there should be no pause between any two characters such as 墨西哥[*mo xi ge*](*Mexico*), 加拿大[*jia na da*](*Canada*), 数理化[*shu li hua*](*mathematics, physics, chemistry*), 福禄寿[*fu lu shou*](*happiness emolument and longevity*) etc. That is to say, these three syllables make up of an independent foot, which does not match [1+2] and [2+1] structure. According to that, all the three-syllabic coordination abbreviations were calculated through trial and error in *Modern Chinese Acronym Dictionary* edited by Yuan (2002) and BCC data were also intro-duced to search the individual usage frequency of [$\sigma1+\sigma2$] and [$\sigma2+\sigma3$].

According to the result, there is no significant difference between the combination of the first two syllables and the combination of the last two syllables, and there is no obvious tendency.

2.5   Construction of Coordination +Class-noun Abbreviations

In the three-syllable abbreviations, many structures fit the [2+1] structure naturally when they are formed at the beginning. For these kinds of structures, there is no conflict between the structure and the prosody, so it is not necessary to make any adjustment but to be formed naturally. For example:

(23)   中 学 和 小 学→ 中   小   学
     zhong xue he xiao xue zhong   xiao   xue
     middle school and primary school middle   primary school
     middle school and primary school

(24)   本 科 和 专 科→ 本   专   科
     ben ke he zhuan ke ben   zhuan   ke
     undergraduate   and   specialist undergraduate   specialist
     undergraduate and specialist

(25)   边 料 和 角 料→ 边 角 料
     bian liao he jiao liao bian jiao liao
     angle of material and material   angle of material and material

     The angle of material and material   The angle of material and material

(26)   病 害 和 虫 害→ 病 虫 害
     bing hai he chong hai bing chong hai

     disease and pest   disease and pest
     diseases and insect pests   diseases and insect pests

The structure of these words is:

(27)   [Nσ1+class-noun]+[Nσ2+class-noun]→[[Nσ1+Nσ2]+class-noun]

They fit the [2+1] foot naturally and thus can be formed smoothly.

(28)   [Nσ1+class-noun]+[Nσ2+ class-noun]→[[Nσ1+Nσ2]+ class-noun]

3   Conclusion

In the generation and usage of three-syllabic abbreviations, there are some exceptions. Thus, this paper, through analyzing the interactive relationships between the structures of three-syllabic abbreviations and the prosody, researched the internal structures of three-syllabic abbreviations and the structure adjustment. The research shows that most three-syllabic abbreviations are nominal structures, and the standard prosodic structure for these nominal compound words is [1+2]. However, in the construction of three-syllabic abbreviations, even though the internal structures of them vary, constrained by the prosody, all of these structures tend to transform into [2+1] structures (with the exception of the coordination structure). With reanalysis, all of these structures finally conform to prosodic morphology, which is shown in the figure 11:

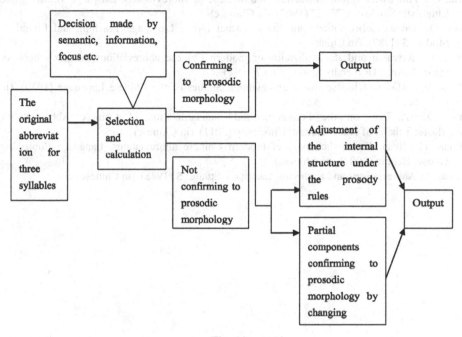

Fig. 11

Acknowledgments. The study is supported by the Beijing Language and Culture University scientific research project (Grant No. 15YJ080207), and the Youth Elite Project of Beijing Language and Culture University.

References

Chen, J.: In modern Chinese abbreviation–Discussing generally referred to as and words abbreviated. Studies of the Chinese Language (1963) (in Chinese)

Cheng, R.: Try discussing words abbreviation. Language Planning **7**, 15–18 (1992). (in Chinese)

Feng, S.: A study on prosodic words in Chinese. Social Sciences in China **1**, 161–176 (1996). (in Chinese)

Feng, S.: A study on Chinese natural foot. Studies of the Chinese Language **1**, 40–47 (1998). (in Chinese)

Feng, S.: Chinese prosodic syntax. Shanghai education Press, Shanghai (2000). (in Chinese)

Feng, S.: Research on prosodic syntax of Chinese. Peking University Press, Beijing (2005). (in Chinese)

Feng, S.: The initial compilation of Chinese written language. Beijing Language and Culture University Press, Beijing (2006). (in Chinese)

Feng, S.: Chinese prosody, morphology and syntax. Peking University Press, Beijing (2009). (in Chinese)

Liu, J.: The analysis of modern Chinese abbreviations. Master's thesis of Anhui University (2004). (in Chinese)

Ma, Q.: Tthe nature, grammatical function and use of abbreviations. Language Teaching and Linguistic Studies. **3**, 20–27 (1987). (in Chinese)

Ma, Q.: On the abbreviations and the construct forms. Language Teaching and Linguistic Studies **5** (1987). (in Chinese)

Niu, X.: Research and standardization of modern Chinese abbreviations. Master's thesis of Hebei Normal University (2004). (in Chinese)

Xiao, W.: Modern Chinese words abbreviated. Studies of the Chinese Language (1959). (in Chinese)

Yu, D.: A Talk on the Formation and Standardization of Chinese Abbreviations. Master's thesis of Hubei Normal University (2011). (in Chinese)

Yuan, H., Ruan, X.: A dictionary of modern Chinese abbreviations. Language Publishing House, Beijing (2002). (in Chinese)

Zhou, J.: Abbreviations and acronyms. Language Studies **5** (1988). (in Chinese)

Word Formation in Chinese Dialects: A Case Study of Hailu Hakka

Shengyu Teng[✉]

Department of Taiwan Language and Communication,
National United University, Miaoli 36063, Taiwan
shengyu@nuu.edu.tw

Abstract. The study of word formation consists of analyzing the processes through which and the conditions under which neologisms are formed, including the concepts and cognition of language users. To establish a complete theory of Chinese words, it is also necessary to survey and research Chinese dialect vocabularies. A wider understanding of neologisms in Chinese dialects can help clarify how new Chinese words are formed. This study, which utilized data from field surveys, was the first to investigate word formation in the Hailu Hakka dialect in both Taiwan and China. Seven types of neologisms were identified and explored. The results can serve as a reference for all studies on Chinese word formation and as a foundation for a theory of Chinese vocabulary.

Keywords: Word formation · Chinese dialect vocabulary · Hailu Hakka

1   Introduction

Xu (1999) urged the academic community to expand its research into Chinese dialect vocabulary and, to that end, developed a dialect vocabulary survey to study the dimensions of vocabulary in order to raise the standard of research into Chinese and dialect vocabularies. Su (1996) claimed that "words are best at displaying the nationality of the language and are worst at displaying the universality of human language. Establishing a theory of Chinese language that truly encompasses the characteristics of ethnic groups must start with lexicology. Neglecting studies on Chinese vocabulary negates the value of their work." Linguistic theories cannot be made light of, assumed, or applied in all cases; they must be created with reference to specific linguistic research. As such, establishing a complete theory of Chinese vocabulary requires research into the vocabularies of Chinese dialects. There have been few studies thus far, however, on word formation in Chinese dialects. In fact, this study was the first to investigate and analyze word formation in the Hailu Hakka dialect in both Taiwan and China, and could thus serve as a foundation for a theory of Chinese vocabulary.

Hailu Hakka is the second-most common dialect of Hakka in Taiwan. Taiwanese Hailu Hakka people descended mainly from immigrants from Haifeng County and Lufeng City[1] in Guangdong Province, China. The corpus used in this study was

---

[1] Due to changes in administrative districts, the range covered parts of Haifeng County, Lufeng City, and Jiexi County and all of Luhe County.

© Springer International Publishing Switzerland 2015
Q. Lu and H.H. Gao (Eds.): CLSW 2015, LNAI 9332, pp. 281–293, 2015.
DOI: 10.1007/978-3-319-27194-1_29

compiled by the author during field research. Locations representative of Hailu Hakka in Taiwan and China were selected for this study; the location selected in Taiwan was Zhudong Township[2], Hsinchu County, and the locations selected in China were Ping-dong and Huangqiang Townships in Haifeng County, Bawan and Beiyang Townships in Lufeng City, Hekou and Dongkeng Townships in Luhe County, and Wuyun and Shangsha Townships in Jiexi County.

2   Types of Word Formation in Hailu Hakka

All populations have their own methods of word formation. This section discusses the methods used in Hailu Hakka. Comparative analysis was conducted on the corpus compiled by the author and relevant literature, after which seven types of word formation were summarized.

2.1   Arbitrary Phono-semantic Combinations

Some words in Hailu Hakka are arbitrary combinations of phonetic values and meanings; this is a common strategy used to coin new words during the primary stages of language formation. This method uses a phonetic sound to represent a semantic meaning where there is no definite connection between the sound and the meaning. The new word then becomes established after repeated use. Many words in Hailu Hakka have been created as a result of arbitrary phono-semantic combinations. For example, $k^hoŋ^3$ (囥; hide), p^hat^4 (劈; reap), $laŋ^1$ (冷; cold), kau^2 (搞; rotate), ts^hen^7 (增; help), t^hiam^5 (甜; sweet), pau^2 (飽; having eaten until full), $ŋiet^8$ (月; moon), vu^1 (烏; black), leu^5 (撈; pick out of water), fo^2 (火; fire), $ŋiun^5$ (銀; silver), tai^7 (住; live), $ŋiu^5$ (牛; cow), $kiok^4$ (腳; foot), kim^1 (金; gold), sok^4 (索; rope), pen^1 (冰; ice), p^hak^8 (白; white), $ʃui^2$ (水; water), kui^1 (龜; turtle), $siet^4$ (雪; snow), sun^2 (筍; bamboo shoot), nun^3 (嫩; tender), keu^2 (狗; dog), and $ʃau^1$ (燒; hot).

The majority of words created via arbitrary phono-semantic combinations are monosyllabic. After a time, once there is a certain number of phono-semantically combined words, these morphemes are then used to create new words. Therefore, in later stages of language development, fewer new words are created using this method.

2.2   Descriptive Word Formation

Many words in Hailu Hakka include modifiers that enhance the form or nature of an object to clarify the meaning of the word. This method of making words easier to understand is called descriptive word formation. Words created using this method are

---

[2] The majority of Taiwan's Hailu Hakka population is concentrated in Hsinchu County. The ancestors of the Hailu Hakka people in Zhudong Township were from Lufeng County in what was Huizhou Prefecture during the Qing Dynasty. Hailu Hakka is predominantly spoken in the area and is representative of the political and economic center of early Hsinchu.

often more formal words, and the majority of these words are nouns. As people have different ways of describing objects, some differences are evident in Hailu Hakka.

2.2.1 Descriptions of Outward Appearance

This type of word is formed using external factors, such as an object's distinctive features, shape, actions, color, or circumstances. For example, in Chinese Hailu Hakka, the mortar used to make Hakka ground tea is called a "ŋa⁵ pat⁴" (牙𬂯; tooth bowl) because it has grooves used to grind ingredients. These grooves, referred to as teeth in Hakka, are the distinctive feature that was used to form this word. In Taiwanese Hailu Hakka, "ŋat⁴ tam³ kon¹" (齾擔竿; nicked shoulder pole) is a type of carrying pole that has notches in either end used to secure the ropes used to carry the objects. This feature was used to create this word.[3] Both Taiwanese and Chinese Hailu Hakka use the word "kʰio⁵ set⁴" (茄色; eggplant color) for the color purple because of the similarity between the colors; therefore, this color was used to form this new word. In Taiwanese Hailu Hakka, "pʰoŋ³ mui¹ tsʰu²" (膨尾鼠; inflated tail mouse) is used for squirrel because squirrels' tails are large.

2.2.2 Descriptions of Inner Traits

These Hakka words were formed using the inner characteristics of the object being described. For example, in Chinese Hailu Hakka, magnets are called "hiap⁴ ʃak⁸" (吸石; inhaling rocks) because magnets attract metal objects. Cholera is referred to as "o¹ eu² tʃin³" (屙嘔症; defecate and vomit disease) in Chinese Hailu Hakka because the symptoms include diarrhea and vomiting. In Taiwanese Hailu Hakka, clay is called "kiap⁸ nai⁵" (浹泥; sticky mud) because of its adhesive nature. In Taiwanese Hailu Hakka, elastic is called "kiu⁵dai" (勾帶; contracting band) because elastic contracts. The aster *Bidens pilosa* is known as "ŋiam⁵ ŋin⁵ tsʰo²" (黏人草; grass that sticks to people) because it often attaches itself to people's clothing.

2.2.3 Descriptions of Functionality

This type of Hakka word is formed using the function of the object being described; it is worth noting that the modifier is most often a nominalized verb. For example, a temporary bamboo chicken cage is referred to as "kai¹ kʰem⁵" (雞蓋; chicken lid) in both Taiwanese and Chinese Hailu Hakka. A type of wooden frame used to carry sugar cane on one's back is called "tʃa³ kʰia⁵" (蔗擎; sugar cane support) in Taiwanese Hailu Hakka. A type of mouse trap that kills mice is called "lo³ tʃʰu¹ tep⁸" (老鼠擲; rat thrower) in Chinese Hailu Hakka. In both Taiwanese and Chinese Hailu

---

[3] There are many classifications for carrying poles in Taiwanese Hailu Hakka. Aside from "ŋat⁴ tam³ kon¹," there are "tsʰoŋ⁵ tam³ kon¹" (長擔竿; long shoulder pole), "keu¹ tsui¹ tam³ kon¹" (鉤觜擔竿; hooked beak shoulder pole), and "ʃu³ tam³ kon¹" (樹擔竿; tree shoulder pole) (generally made of oak *Cyclobalanopsis morii*). These distinctions arose because carrying poles are an important type of farming tool for the mountain Hakka people.

Hakka, a vegetable and fruit peeler is called a "kua¹ pʰau⁵" (瓜刨; melon peeler). In both Taiwanese and Chinese Hailu Hakka, a bamboo sieve for separating rice bran is called a "mi² tsʰi¹" (米篩; rice sifter). The index finger is called "ŋiam¹ ʃit⁸ tʃi²" (拈食指; food-pinching finger) in Chinese Hailu Hakka because people often pick up food between the index finger and thumb. These Hailu Hakka words were all formed by describing the function of the object.

2.2.4   Descriptions of Possession

This type of Hakka word is formed using the manufacturing methods or the materials, place of origin, or place used or seen of the object being described. For example, ban-tiao (粄條) noodles in Chinese Hailu Hakka can be called "pʰa³ ə²pan²" (帕仔粄; cheesecloth noodles), "to¹ tsʰiet⁴pan²" (刀切粄; knife-cut noodles), or "ho⁵ fun²" (河粉; river rice noodles); they are called "pʰa³ ə²pan²" because a cheesecloth is used to wrap the noodle dough before it is steamed. After the dough is steamed, it is cut into noodles; thus, the noodles are also called "to¹ tsʰiet⁴pan²" after this production method. Chinese Hailu Hakka also calls these noodles "ho⁵ fun²" because a distributary of the Sha River in Guangzhou has sweet water that makes the bantiao noodles made there especially delicious and well-known. After the Chinese economic reform, these noodles were called "shahefen" which was later shortened to "ho⁵ fun²." This word was created using its place of origin. In Taiwanese Hailu Hakka, a gecko is called "piak⁴ ʃa⁵" (壁蛇; wall snake) and in Chinese Hailu Hakka it is called "tsʰioŋ⁵ ʃa⁵" (牆蛇; wall snake) because these animals are often seen crawling on walls. Puppet shows in both Taiwanese and Chinese Hailu Hakka are called "tsʰiau⁵ tʰeu⁵ hi³" (樵頭戲; wood play) because the puppets are made out of wood. In Chinese Hailu Hakka, a weevil is called "tsuk⁴ ʃun² ku¹" (竹筍蛄; bamboo cricket) or "ʃun² tʃuŋ⁵" (筍蟲; bamboo insect) because these insects are often seen on bamboo foraging for food.

Descriptive word formation creates new words by attaching explanations to other words. In Hailu Hakka, this is a highly productive method of word formation as there are many words that were introduced in this way.

2.3   Onomatopoeia

Phonetic sounds used to describe a sound are manipulated to conform to Hailu Hakka practice, thus creating a new word. Put another way, the sound being described is given a meaning to become a new Hailu Hakka word. There are two types of onoma-topoeias in Hailu Hakka that describe sounds that occur naturally.

2.3.1   Naming an Object After its Sound

These words refer to an object by using a modified version of the sound it makes. For example, burping in Taiwanese Hailu Hakka is called "ta¹ da et⁸ tuk⁸" (打耶嘟; produce the sound "ettuk") and in Chinese Hailu Hakka is called "ta¹ tuk⁴ et⁸" (打嘟耶; produce the sound "tuket") because "et⁸ tuk⁸" and "tuk⁴ et⁸" are both burping noises. Collared doves are called "pʰuk^8 ku^1 zai" (布咕仔; thing that goes "pukku") in both Taiwanese and Chinese Hailu Hakka because "pʰuk^8 ku^1" is the sound doves make. In Taiwanese Hailu Hakka, babies are called "o^1 ŋa^5 zai" (阿伢仔; thing that goes "onga") or "aŋ^{55} ku^3" (卬咕; [the sound] "an-goo") because "o^1 ŋa^5" is the sound of a baby's cry and "aŋ^{55} gu" is a sound often made by babies.

2.3.2   Describing a Situation After the Sound an Object Makes

This type of word often includes repeated sounds. For example, in Chinese Hailu Hakka, "ŋat^8 ŋat^8 hioŋ^1" (□□響; echoing "ngat ngat") and "ŋat^8 ŋat^8 kiau^3" (□□叫; shouting "ngat ngat") are used to describe geese honking incessantly because "ŋat^8 ŋat^8" is the sound geese make.[4] Dongkeng Hailu Hakka describes continuous thunder as "kuŋ^3 kuŋ^3 hioŋ^1" (倥倥響; echoing "kong kong") because "kuŋ^3 kuŋ^3" is the sound of thunder. In Taiwanese Hailu Hakka, "nuŋ^5 nuŋ^5 nuŋ^3 nuŋ^3" (噥噥哢哢; [the sounds] "nong nong nong nong") is used to describe incessant talking because "nuŋ^5 nuŋ^5" and "nuŋ^3 nuŋ^3" are onomatopoeias for mumbling. In Taiwanese Hailu Hakka, "tsi^3 tsi^3 tsio^3 tsio^3" (嘰嘰啾啾; [the sounds] "gee gee geo geo") is used to describe crowded and congested places because "tsi^3 tsi^3" and "tsio^3 tsio^3" are onomatopoeias for large crowds of talking people.

2.4   Conceptual Relevance

Some words in Hailu Hakka are formed based on correlations between objects; these correlations may be similar features or related characteristics that are used to then establish a systematic correlation. This method of word formation involves conceptual metaphor (Lakoff & Turner, 1989) and conceptual metonymy (Warren, 1999) in cognitive linguistics. We refer to this method as conceptual relevance and this can be divided into two categories.

2.4.1   Metaphors

Metaphorical word formation uses the mapping between a source domain and target domain to create words. In other words, a more concrete source domain is used to explain a more abstract target domain where the similarities between the source and target domains are the foundation for the metaphor. There are two types of metaphorical word formation in Hailu Hakka.

2.4.1.1   The New Word is a Complete Metaphor

Many words in Hailu Hakka use metaphors for vivid acts. For example, rain gear placed on the back during farm work is called "piet^4 hok^4" (鼈殼; soft-shelled turtle shell) or "kui^1 hok^4" (龜殼; turtle shell) because the shape of the rain gear looks like a

---

[4] A □ is used where there is no Chinese character to approximate the morpheme used in Hailu Hakka.

turtle shell. The aster *Bidens pilosa* is known as "ʒit⁴ pau¹ tʃim¹" (一包針; bundle of needles) in Chinese Hailu Hakka because the achenes of this aster are long, thin, and grouped together like a bag of needles. "ŋiau³ sai¹ teu³" (貓徙竇; cat moves to a new home) was originally used to describe feline behavior or moving to new places; in both Taiwanese and Chinese Hailu Hakka, the term is used to describe people who often move or change jobs.

2.4.1.2   Part of the New Word is a Metaphor
This type of word uses a component of a metaphor combined with a morpheme that clarifies the category of the object. Such words can further be divided into two types.

2.4.1.2.1   Metaphor Morpheme + Category Morpheme
For example, "kui² ŋien² tsuk⁴" (鬼拑竹; ghost-clutched bamboo) is used to describe Buddha's Belly Bamboo which has swollen lower internodes that give it a wavy appearance, like it is being grabbed by a ghost. "lo³ ki³ fa¹" (老妓花; dancer flower) is used to describe *Lantana camara* because the flowers are multicolored and sway in the wind like a dancing woman.

2.4.1.2.2   Category Morpheme + Metaphor Morpheme
For example, "lai⁵ tʰeu⁵ ʃi⁵" (犁頭匙; plow spoon) is used to decribe the block of wood used to secure a plow because it is shaped like a spoon. "mo³ ʃat⁸" (帽舌; hat tongue) is used to describe the bill of a hat because it is shaped like a tongue. "lai⁵ sioŋ³ pʰi⁷" (犁象鼻; plow elephant trunk) is used to describe the part that connects the plow to the yoke because it is shaped like an elephant's trunk. "iu⁵ kiaŋ³" (油鏡; oil mirror) is used to describe a layer of oil floating on water because the oil reflects light like a mirror.

2.4.2   Metonymy
Similar to metaphorical word formation, metonymical word formation also uses the mapping between a source domain and target domain to create words. However, metonymical word formation uses the experiential relationship between two concrete objects to create words. It is easy to make connections with this type of word that make an object's appearance more concrete and clear. The closeness of the source and target domains are the foundation for the metonymy; i.e., the new words uses this pre-established correlation. For example, childbirth in Chinese Hailu Hakka is called "tso³ ŋiet⁸" (做月; sitting out a month) because women rest at home for a month after giving birth to recuperate and are not allowed to leave at will or do any physical labor. Hakka uses the source domain "tso³ ŋiet⁸" to create this new word. In both Taiwanese and Chinese Hailu Hakka, "ŋa⁵ tʃʰi² pʰo⁵ pʰo⁵" (牙齒浮浮; unstable teeth) describes the Chinese medical condition of having too much fire in the body because this

presents with the symptom of tooth discomfort. Both Taiwanese and Chinese Hailu Hakka use "kuan¹ ŋa⁵ kau³" (關牙鉸; closed teeth) to describe a severe illness or shock because sometimes patients are unable to open their mouth if they are in shock or have a serious disease.

2.5   Rhetorical Word Formation

Some Hailu Hakka words are created using rhetoric. There are three types of rhetorical word formation.

2.5.1   Comparison

This type of word compares people with phenomena or animal behavior to create a vivid, lasting impression. This can be further divided into two groups.

2.5.1.1   The New Word is a Complete Comparison

For example, earthquake in Chinese Hailu Hakka is "tʰi⁵ ŋiu⁵ tʃon² kien¹" (地牛轉肩; earth ox shakes its shoulders). People get tired after a while of carrying a load on one's shoulder, so they shift it to the other shoulder; Hakka people believed that an ox was carrying the earth on its shoulder, so it, too, would periodically shift the load to its other shoulder causing an earthquake. In Taiwanese Hailu Hakka, "tʰin⁵ kiok⁴" (停腳; stop feet) means allow an object to settle; this compares a person stopping to rest with an object being set down. Contact with the milky sap of maple trees causes a rash; Chinese Hailu Hakka uses "ŋau¹ ŋin⁵" (咬人; bite person) comparing the pain and itch to being bitten by the tree.

2.5.1.2   Part of the Word is a Comparison and the Other Part is a Morpheme that Clarifies the Category of the Object

For example, to describe when rice is approaching maturation, Taiwanese Hailu Hakka uses "vo⁵ ə⁵ keu¹ tʰeu⁵" (禾仔勾頭; grain bends its head) and Chinese Hailu Hakka uses "vo⁵ tai¹ tʰeu⁵" (禾低頭; grain lowers its head) because ears of rice grain droop down. Both "keu¹ tʰeu⁵" and "tai¹ tʰeu⁵" compare this to a person lowering their head and "vo⁵ ə⁵" refers to the rice. The sensitive plant *Mimosa pudica* is called "tsa³ si² tsʰo²" (詐死草; feigning death plant) in Hailu Hakka because the leaves fold inward and droop when touched like a person feigning death. A meteor shower in Hailu Hakka is called "siaŋ¹ ə⁵ sia³ ʃi²" (星仔洩屎; defecating stars) because as meteors stream across the sky, the trail behind them is like a rain of feces. The Adam's apple in Hailu Hakka is called "tsʰioŋ¹ ʃit⁴ koi¹" (搶食胲; food-grabbing neck) because the Adam's apple moves up and down when swallowing as if it were trying to grab the food. "tsʰioŋ¹ ʃit⁴" is used as the comparison and "koi¹" is used to clarify the object.

2.5.2 Euphemism

Some words in Hailu Hakka were formed using euphemisms or implicit correlations. These words can be used to ease tension or for indirect stimulation. For example, Chinese Hailu Hakka uses "kʰoi³ kia¹ fun¹" (開佢葷;) to replace more vulgar language such as "tiau² ŋia⁵ me¹" (屌若姆; fuck your mother). Hailu Hakka uses "tʃon² tʃʰoŋ⁵ san¹" (轉長山; go back to hometown) or "tʃon² lo⁷ vuk⁴" (轉老屋; go back home) in place of "to die" because when someone passes away, it is as if they are returning home and this phrasing is not as disheartening. Taiwanese Hailu Hakka uses "se³ moi³ kien¹" (細妹間; room with many girls), "tʃʰon³ ʃit⁸ kien¹"(賺食間; room to earn money), "heu³ tʃʰa¹ lu³" (後車路; street behind the train station), or "tʃu¹ ma⁵ liau⁵" (豬嫲寮; place that auctions swine) to replace the word brothel as it may be too offensive or demeaning to some people; therefore, these situations or areas are used to imply a brothel.[5]

2.5.3 Description

This type of word often uses repeated sounds to describe an object's coloration, appearance, character, or mood in order to give the listener a vivid picture of the object. This can be further divided into two groups.

2.5.3.1 Description of Color

For example, "pʰak⁸ siet⁴ siet⁴" (白雪雪; snow white); "tsʰiaŋ¹ sim³ sim³"(青□□; emerald green), "fuŋ⁵ taŋ³ taŋ³" (紅□□; bright red), "voŋ⁵ lem⁵ lem⁵" (黃□□; extremely yellow), and "vu¹ so⁵ so⁵"(烏□□; pitch black).

2.5.3.2 Description of Mood

For example, "han⁵ tʃʰok⁴ tʃʰok⁴" (閒□□; have a lot of free time), "hap⁴ tsiet⁸ tsiet⁸" (狹□□; very narrow), "tʰen⁵ het⁸ het⁸" (跈□□; follow very close behind), "tsin¹ kuak⁸ kuak⁸" (精□□; very astute), "lo⁷ kʰiau³ kʰiau³" (老□□; aged and feeble), "tʃʰuŋ¹ kʰui⁵ kʰui⁵" (重□□; appears very heavy), and "ʃi² put⁸ put⁸" (屎□□arrogant and cocky).

2.6 Affixation

Some words in Hailu Hakka include an empty affix that give a special meaning or feeling to the new word. This is another important method of word formation in Hailu Hakka that can be divided into three types based on the placement of the affix.

---

[5] "tʃu¹ ma⁵ liau⁵" was originally a place where pigs were sold in the Zhudong area which later became a red-light district; thus, it is used as a euphemism for brothel. The area behind the train station in Hsinchu also contains many brothels which is why this term is used.

2.6.1 Prefix

Many words include the prefix "a^3" (阿), such as "a^3 kuŋ^1" (阿公; paternal grandfather), "a^3 pʰo^5" (阿婆; paternal grandmother), "a^3 pa^1" (阿爸; father), "a^3 ʃuk^4" (阿叔; uncle [father's younger brother]), and "a^3 hiuŋ^5" (阿雄; [given name]). Words with this prefix display affection and familiarity. Other words include the prefix "lo^7" (老), such as "lo^7 lai^3 e^2" (老賴仔; [surname]), "lo^7 lim^5" (老林; [surname]), "lo^7 tʰai^1" (老弟; younger brother), "lo^7 kuŋ^1" (老公; husband), and "lo^7 moi^3" (老妹; younger sister). This prefix in Hailu Hakka is used when referring to relatives of approximately the same age and also displays affection and closeness. However, using "lo^7" when referring to an animal portrays disgust or fear; for example, "lo^7 tʃu^2" (老鼠; mouse) and "lo^7 fu^2" (老虎; tiger).

2.6.2 Infix

Many words include an infix in the middle of a word. For example, "tsʰɿ^3" (姐) can be added in "lioŋ^2 tsʰɿ^3 ia^3" (兩姐爺; father and son), "lioŋ^2 tsʰɿ^3 ʃuk^4" (兩姐叔; [paternal] uncle and nephew), "lioŋ^2 tsʰɿ^3 kʰiu^1" (兩姐舅; [maternal] uncle and nephew), and "lioŋ^2 tsʰɿ^3 a^7 kuŋ^1" (兩姐阿公; grandfather and grandson). Words with this infix display affection and closeness. The infix "pu^1" (晡) can be added in Hailu Hakka to represent a certain time, such as "kin^1 pu^1 ŋit^4" (今晡日; today), "tsʰo^1 pu^1 ŋit^4" (昨晡日; yesterday), "am^3 pu^1 ʒia^3" (暗晡夜; tonight), and "tsʰo^1 pu^1 am^3" (昨晡暗; last night). The infix "a^7" (阿) can be added in Hailu Hakka to display affection and familiarity, such as "san^1 a^7 siak^4" (山阿鵲; magpie) and "voŋ^5 a^7 kok^4" (黃阿角; fish in a river). The infix "ha^3" (下) can be added in Hailu Hakka to indicate a short period of time, such as "o^1 ha^3 ŋiau^3" (屙下尿; urinate), "ʃoi^1 ha^3 muk^4" (睡下目; take a nap), and "ʃit^8 ha^3 tsʰa^5" (食下茶; have tea).

2.6.3 Suffix

Many words in Hailu Hakka include a suffix; for example, "ə^5" (仔), such as "kam^1 ə^5" (柑仔; tangerine), "sok^4 ə^5" (索仔; rope), "tsok^4 ə^5" (桌仔; table), "ʒiu^3 ə^5" (柚仔; pomelo), "tʰeu^3 ə^5" (豆仔; bean), "keu^2 ə^5" (狗仔; dog), "lai^3 ə^5" (倈仔; son), and "sun^1 ə^5" (孫仔; grandson). The suffix "ten^2" (等) can be added in Hailu Hakka to indicate an ongoing action, such as "haŋ^5 ten^2" (行等; walking), "ʃit^8 ten^2" (食等; eating), "kʰoŋ^3 ten^2" (囥等; hiding), and "kʰu^5 ten^2" (跍等; crouching). The suffix "teu^2" (斗) can be added in Hailu Hakka to indicate an ability or situation, such as "kʰiaŋ^3 teu^2" (慶斗; good), "tsam^3 teu^2" (讚斗; wonderful), "liaŋ^3 teu^2" (亮斗; pretty), "li^3 teu^2" (利斗; talented), and "ŋaŋ^3 teu^2" (硬斗; difficult [situation]). The suffix "sien^3" (線) can be added in Hailu Hakka to indicate a person's or object's mood, such as "kap^4 sien^3" (合線; peaceful and harmonious), "kuk^4 sien^3" (穀線; hurried), "liaŋ^3 sien^3" (亮線; eye-catching), "ten^5 sien^3" (矋線; pretty and imposing), "lok^8 sien^3" (樂線; optimistic), and "li^3 sien^3" (利線; firm and unwavering).

2.7   Synthetic Word Formation

Some words in Hailu Hakka are formed using more than one method; we referred to this method as sythetic word formation. For example, a wooden fish in Hailu Hakka is called "muk⁴ kʰok⁴ ə⁵" (木槌仔; wooden knocker); the middle morpheme "kʰok⁴" describes the sound the wooden fish makes (onomatopoeia), the first morpheme "muk⁴" is derived from descriptive word formation as it designates the material from which it is made, and the last morpheme "ə⁵" is a nominalization suffix. Therefore, "muk⁴ kʰok⁴ ə⁵" was created using three word formation methods. In Taiwanese Hailu Hakka, mud is called "nam³ ko¹ moi³" (濫膏糜); the last morpheme "moi³" is a metaphor whose source domain is "rice porridge" and maps the target domain "watery mud." Descriptive word formation is also used utilizing the thick, sticky nature of mud, "nam³ ko¹," combining a description of an inner trait with a metaphor. "Ve⁵ ve⁵ kun¹" (□□滾) is used in Taiwanese Hailu Hakka to describe a child crying incessantly; "ve⁵ ve⁵" is an onomatopoeia for a child's loud crying and "kun¹" is a suffix indicating a persistent action. Therefore, "ve⁵ ve⁵ kun¹" is a synthesis of an onomatopoeia and a suffix. Other Hailu Hakka words using synthetic word formation include "pot⁴ tʃʰak⁴ muk⁴" (發赤目; conjunctivitis), "piak⁸ no²" (僻腦; stroke), "pot⁴ laŋ¹ ə⁵" (發冷仔; malaria), "pot⁴ tʃʰiu⁵ tʰeu⁵" (發臭頭; skin ulcers on the scalp), "muk⁴ kim¹ kim¹ ə⁵" (目晶晶仔; bright-eyed), and "kiaŋ² pʰien¹ pʰien¹ ə⁵" (頸偏偏仔; cruel and disobedient).

3   Characteristics of Neologisms in Hailu Hakka

This section takes a macro perspective to observe the overall word formation methods used in Taiwanese and Chinese Hailu Hakka. We found several characteristics of Hailu Hakka neologisms.

3.1   Widespread use of Descriptive and Conceptual Relevance Word Formation

Both Taiwanese and Chinese Hailu Hakka make substantial use of descriptive and conceptual relevance word formation. Descriptive word formation is flexible and can be used in many situations; therefore, many words were created using this method. For example, in Taiwanese Hailu Hakka, a sugar-apple is called "fut⁸ ko²" (佛果; Buddha fruit), which is a relatively newly created word. The name is derived from the fruit's resemblance to the Buddha's head. Ping pong is called "tʰoi⁵ kʰiu⁵" (檯球; table ball) in Chinese Hailu Hakka because the game is played using a table. This is another newly coined word that arose from descriptive word formation. There are also many words that use conceptual relevance word formation, in particular metaphors. Words coined using this method often produce vivid imagery, such as "ŋiau³ sai² teu³"

(貓徙竇; using feline behavior to describe people who often move or change jobs, "mo⁵ pʰi⁷ ŋiu⁵" (無鼻牛; ox with no nose; an ox is hard to control without a nose ring, so this is used to describe disobedient children), and "ta² tʃoi³ ku²" (打嘴鼓; playing drums with the mouth; constantly making noise like a drum is used to describe idle chatter). This also shows that Hakka people are astutely observant and have a vivid imagination when forming new words.

3.2   Different Word Formation Methods used for the Same Objects

At times, Taiwanese and Chinese Hailu Hakka use different methods to coin words for the same object. For example, making funeral arrangements in Taiwanese Hailu Hakka is "tso³ vai¹ sï³" (做歪事; doing something negative) where "vai¹" is a euphemism for funerals. However, Chinese Hailu Hakka used conceptual relevance to form the word "tso³ pʰak⁸" (做白; make white) because funerals often use the color white. Taiwanese Hailu Hakka used conceptual relevance to coin a word for the index finger: "ʃa⁵ tʰeu⁵ tʃi²" (蛇頭指; snake head finger); whereas descriptive word formation was used in Chinese Hailu Hakka: "ŋiam¹ ʃit⁸ tʃi²" (拈食指; food-pinching finger). The Taiwanese Hailu Hakka word for the brim of a hat, "mo⁷ pʰin⁵" (帽屏; hat cover), used descriptive word formation because its function is to obstruct or cover from view; however, the Chinese Hailu Hakka word "mo⁷ ʃat⁸" (帽舌; hat tongue) used conceptual reference word formation because the shape of the brim is similar to the shape of a tongue. Word formation depends in part on people's cognitive thinking. These examples of Taiwanese and Chinese Hailu Hakka where different words are used to describe the same object show that the Hakka groups in these two places observe matters from slightly different perspectives.

3.3   Special and Habitual Morphemes

Some common morphemes are habitually used in both Taiwanese and Chinese Hailu Hakka.

For example, the morpheme "ai¹" (□) is often used in pulling or rotating motions. For example, in both Taiwanese and Chinese Hailu Hakka, "ai¹ luŋ⁵" (□礱) means rotary mill, "ai¹ hien⁵" (□弦) means to play the *huqin* (a Chinese two-stringed fiddle), and "ai¹ pan²" (□粄) means to grind rice into a paste. In Taiwanese Hailu Hakka, a mantis is called "ai¹ luŋ⁵ pʰi¹ pʰo¹" (□礱□□), a term which makes use of this morpheme because the rocking motion of mantises is similar to that a grinding mill. Words that pertain to earth or dirt in Hailu Hakka often use the morpheme "nai⁵" (泥; mud) rather than "tʰu²" (土; soil). For example, clay is "kiap⁸ nai⁵" (浹泥; sticky mud), "kiet⁴ ʃak⁸ nai⁵" (結石泥; mud that holds rocks together), or "ŋiam⁵ nai⁵" (黏泥; sticky mud) in Taiwanese Hailu Hakka and "ŋiam⁵ nai⁵" (黏泥; sticky mud) in Chinese Hailu Hakka. A mud brick house is called "nai⁵ tʃon¹ vuk⁴" (泥磚屋; mud brick house) in both Taiwanese and Chinese Hailu Hakka. Cement is called "fuŋ³ mo¹nai⁵" (紅毛泥; red hair mud) in both Taiwanese and Chinese Hailu Hakka. This preference for the morpheme "nai⁵" over "tʰu²" is opposite from the Minnan language from the same region.[6] Many diseases in Hailu Hakka use the morpheme "pot⁴" or "fat⁴" (發) as the first syllable. For example, "pot⁴ tʃʰak⁴ muk⁴" (發赤目; conjunctivitis), "pot⁴ tʃʰiu³ tʰeu⁵" (發臭頭; skin ulcers on the scalp), "pot⁴ laŋ¹ ə⁵" (發冷仔; malaria), "fat⁴ fuŋ⁵" (發紅; inflammation), and "fat⁴ ʃau¹" (發燒; fever) This morpheme has two pronunciations, and the pronunciation in a particular word has been established by popular usage and cannot be changed at will. Other common morphemes in Hailu Hakka include "tʃʰun¹" (春), which is used for eggs, "lan³" (爛), which is used for broken things, and "tsak⁴" (矺), which is used for pressing.

4   Conclusion

This study investigated the methods of word formation in Hailu Hakka and compiled seven different methods with specific characteristics. Determining the processes and manners through which words are created in dialects can serve as a reference in studies focusing on word formation in the Chinese language. Moreover, a population's understanding or observations of a particular subject may affect the method with which that population coins new terms. These different methods of word formation that stem from lifestyles, habits, ways of thinking, and personal values can reflect the unique traits of a dialect. These methods can then be used to create new words that conform to the word formation practices in that dialect. This highlights the importance for further studies on Chinese word formation.

References

1. Ren, X.L.: Chinese Morphology. China Social Science Press, Beijing (1981). (in Chinese)
2. Li, R.L.: A Comparison of Chinese Dialects. Commercial Press, Beijing (2003). (in Chinese)
3. Xu, B.H.: Enhancing Chinese Dialect Vocabulary. Dialect 1, 21–23 (1999). (in Chinese)
4. Ge, B.Y.: Modern Chinese Lexicology. Shandong University, Jinan (2004). (Revised Edition) (in Chinese)
5. Deng, S.Y.: Pronunciation and Vocabulary of Taiwanese Sihai Dialect. Journal of Hakka Studies. 5(2), 103–152 (2012). (in Chinese)

---

[6] The Minnan language often uses the morpheme "tu" (土), such as in "tuquecuo" (土确厝; mud brick house), "hongmaotu" (紅毛土; cement), and "niantu" (黏土; clay).

6. Lu, Y.J.: Hsinchu Hailu Hakka Vocabulary. Master Thesis. Graduate Institute of Taiwan Languages and Language Education, National Hsinchu University of Education (1999) (in Chinese)
7. Lakoff, G., Turner, M.: More than Cool Reason: a field guide to poetic metaphor. University of Chicago Press, Chicago (1989)
8. Warren, J.: Evaporites. Their Evolution and Economics. Blackwell Science, Oxford (1999)

A Research into the Multi-category Words of Verb-Noun in Modern Chinese Based on the Quantitative Analysis of the Collocating Classifiers

Di4zhen4(*Earthquake*), Feng4xian4(*Devote*), Ji4zai3(*Record*), Jiu4ji4(*Relief*), Pei2tong2(*Accompany*), Shen1qing3(*Apply for*)

Pengyuan Liu and Jia Ding[✉]

Institute of Applied Linguistics, Beijing Language and Culture University, Beijing, China
liupengyuan@blcu.edu.cn, dingjia46@sina.cn

Abstract. The paper studies the multi-category words of verb-noun. We use six words with different parts of speech in two dictionaries to discuss the multi-category words of verb-noun. Based on the collocation between the multi-category words of verb-noun and the corresponding classifiers in a large-scale corpus, we describe the verb-noun words phenomenon considering words' syntactic characteristics and semantic characteristics. The data shows that di4zhen4, jiu4ji4, pei2tong2, shen1qing3 can collocate with classifiers as nouns or verbs and the collocations are distinct. We could see these four as multi-category words of verb-noun because of their evident noun's and verb's characteristics. Feng4xian4, ji4zai3 do not have ample collocations with action measure words, neither do with static measure words, but we also consider these two as multi-category words of verb-noun.

Keywords: Criterion for multi-category words of noun and verb · Classifiers · Quantitative methods

1 Introduction

One of the most urgent problems about Chinese linguistics is the classification of the multi-category words. Words of noun-verb, verb-adjective and noun-adjective are the primary types of the multi-category words, and the noun-verb words dominate the two-category words in quantitative terms. According to Hu (1995), 12.91%——19.33% multi-category words are noun-verb words. Discrepancies and similarities between nouns and verbs are significant in respect of syntactic functions and semantic characteristics, which lead to a classification controversy of noun-verb words. No conclusion was drawn in China whether multi-category words should be measured in meaning, function, frequency or multi-criterion.

Multi-category words are by no means the marginal grammar phenomenon. In the literature we have noted there are three viewpoints which drew great attentions: (1) Zhu (1961) suggests that words like "yan2jiu1" (*research*) and "diao4cha2"

© Springer International Publishing Switzerland 2015
Q. Lu and H.H. Gao (Eds.): CLSW 2015, LNAI 9332, pp. 294–306, 2015.
DOI: 10.1007/978-3-319-27194-1_30

(*survey*) which have noun's syntactic character are supposed to be a sub-category of verbs named as "nouny verbs", he abstracts the major syntactic characteristics of this type of words in Yufa Jiangyi (Lecture Notes on Grammar). Lu(1995) and Guo(1999) hold the same view. (2)Some suggest the following criteria(Su, 2002) that if the part of speech is changed, and lexical meaning has been clearly transferred, then we should acknowledge that it is a multi-category word, which means that lexical meaning monitors the status of the words' category. (3)Other scholars such as Hu(1995) argued that the grammatical function is the efficient measure, and he pointed out three criteria to distinguish the noun-verb words. Recently, some scholars study multi-category words' mechanism by peering through the perspective of cognitive grammar and prototype categories. The theory of "nouny verbs" mitigating the category's controversy could not supply operational standard. For the second theory, it is hard to judge which category a word belongs to only by its lexical meaning without considering its syntactic function——which is complementary to the meaning. Formation and meaning should verify each other (Zhu, 1982), and some scholars believe that words with quantitative phrases (more specifically, phrases composed by numerals and classifiers used to modify other entities) modified should be considered as nouns.

We try to seek the resolution of the controversies surrounding multi-category words in Chinese by providing a detailed corpus-based investigation of six words' distribution and collocation with quantitative phrases. There are two authoritative dictionaries——Modern Chinese Dictionary(Xiandai Hanyu Cidian)(6th edition)[1] and Grammatical Knowledge-Base of Contemporary Chinese(GKB)[2], the first is dominant in linguistics field while the second in the field of NLP. But the words' parts of speech from these two dictionaries have some differences because the emphasis points of principle, purpose and application are different. Aiming at the frequently-used words which in one dictionary is tagged as noun, and in another tagged as verb, we study these words' syntactic function and with the help of corpora, we do quantitative analysis for these words collocated with static measure words or action measure words. After fulfilling this step, on the basis of the preliminary acquaintance we depict words' syntactic performance as verb and noun. Without the semantic analysis we couldn't see the whole situation, so we carry out a semantic research to find supports. We perform the estimation for verb-noun words in a relatively comprehensive way.

---

[1] Modern Chinese Dictionary (Xiandai Hanyu Cidian) is the most authoritative Chinese dictionary in Modern China, whose status is similar to Oxford English Dictionary in the English World. Its aim is to standardizing the words, popularizing Beijing pronunciation and promoting Chinese standardization. From the fifth edition, the words have added the POS tag and the sixth edition modified it. The overall words are more than 69000 items.

[2] GKB is aiming at Chinese Information Processing. It is a operational standard for NLP, mainly contains language information processing and grammar study, modern Chinese words' grammatical function categories and words' grammatical characteristics, possessing about 10000 words.

2 Quantitative Analysis for Six Words' (di4zhen4, feng4xian4 and so on) Collocation with Classifiers

2.1 Target Words

We seek to achieve our target words by undertaking the following procedures. First, we use the 183 two-syllable words both have verb-tag and noun-tag we filtrate from GKB with eliminating overlapped one, and we get 93 items which are above 3000 times in Chinese High Frequency Words List edited by Beijing Language and Culture University. Then we compare the words' POS tags in Modern Chinese Dictionary(the sixth edition) which leads to seven words——地震 [*di1zhen4*](*earthquake*), 奉献 [*feng4xian4*](*devote*), 记载 [*ji4zai3*](*record*), 救济 [*jiu4ji4*](*relief*), 陪同 [*pei2tong2*](*accompany*), 申请 [*shen1qing3*](*apply for*), 学会 [*xue2hui4*](*learn, academy*). In GKB, all six words are listed in nouns list and verbs list, and in Modern Chinese Dictionary are tagged as verbs, there tags are different in these two dictionaries. We choose the first six words as our target words.[3]

2.2 The Collocation with Classifiers

Static measure words are one of the subcategories in classifiers, and these words' main function is to modify nouns to signify the quantity of nouns. So we say that words modified by static measure words are nouns. In order to construct the collocation structure, we pick up some static measure words according to GKB's affluent grammatical information. We first pick up 个[*ge4*] modifies individual, 些 [*xie1*] modifies indefinite quantity entity, 场[*chang3*] and 起[*qi3*]express events' frequency. In contrast to those words, we select two action measure words 次[*ci4*] and 下[*xia4*] to do quantitative study, these two items could only express action's frequency and do not have other function(except some irregularities). Furthermore, we consider the collocation especially for "ji4zai3", "shen1qing3" and "pei2tong2", we add 份[*fen4*](for the first two words) 位[*wei4*](for the last one) respectively modify these two words. 次[*ci4*] as action measure words which can collocate with target words in two position(after the target words or before them), so we have来一次[*lai2yi1ci4*](*come once*) and 一次冒险[*yi1ci4mao4xian3*](*once adventure*). As we can observe, this item can collocate with target word in front of it or after it. Words like "yi1dianr3" have been abandoned to guarantee classifiers' exclusiveness, ensure our result's credibility, and avoid that some classifiers could collocate with both verbs and nouns. Table 1 gives the specific collocation structure.

---

[3] In Modern Chinese Dictionary,学会[*xue2hui4*]*(learn, academy)* is tagged as noun, the other six are tagged as verbs. From different viewpoint, we could see 学会[*xue2hui4*] as a phrase means "learn and acquire", also we could see it as a noun means "academy". So we put it out of this paper's target words.

Table 1. The collocation structure of classifiers and target words

Static measure words+target words	action measure words+target words
ge4+di4zhen4[ji4zai3, ……]	di4zhen4[ji4zai3, ……]+ci4
chang3+di4zhen4[ji4zai3, ……]	di4zhen4[ji4zai3, ……]+yi1xia4
qi3+di4zhen4[ji4zai3, ……]	ci4+di4zhen4[ji4zai3, ……]
yi1xie1+di4zhen4[ji4zai3, ……]	
fen4+ji4zai3[shen1qing3]	
wei4+pei2tong2	

2.3   Data and Discussion

We use BCC[4] as our research support, table 2 shows the total frequency[5] of the six words in this massive corpora.

Table 2. The total frequency of the six target words in BCC

	di4zhen4	feng4xian4	ji4zai3	jiu4ji4	pei2tong2	shen1qing3
Total frequency	34134	34072	53570	9977	17591	108933

According to table1 above, we search the collocation in BCC, there are 13364 concordance lines[6]. Through manual elimination, we got 4744 lines matching with our aim. The eliminated lines mainly have four types:

1)Non-word type. That is to say concordance lines we get contain no target words but only a cluster of characters which are in two words. For example:一次高兴地震颤 [yi1ci4 gao1xing4 *de zhen4*chan4]*(once happy tremble)*|大地震动了起来[da4*di4 zhen4*dong4 le qi3lai2]*(the earth shock)*, these two examples contain the same characters with di4zhen4.

2)Non-modify type. Classifiers and target words are in the same sentence but don't have modification relationship. It contains three sub-categories:

2a)Classifiers and target words modify the same word, as in this one:一次地震演习 [yi1ci4 di4zhen4 yan3xi2]*(one earthquake drill)*, 地震[di4zhen4]*(earthquake)* and 一次 [*yi1ci4*] *(once)* all modify 演习[*yan3xi2*]*(manoeuvre)*.

---

[4] In this paper, all examples are cited from BCC Chinese corpus. It contains 15 billion characters, has six parts which are literature(3 billion)、 journal(2 billion)、 micro-blog(3 billion)、 technology(3 billion)、 mingled corpus(1 billion)and ancient Chinese(3 billion),it can reveal nowadays social language life. We choose the first four parts as our researching basement, the scale is up to 10 billion characters.

[5] To insure the result shows words but characters, we use "target word/v" and "target words/n" as formulas.

[6] We searched the adjoining collocation and the non-adjoining collocation by using the query expression.

2b)Classifiers and target words belong to different layers of the sentence. 派一个少校来陪同[pai4 yi1ge4 shao4xiao4 lai2 pei2tong2]*(send a commander to accompany us)*|记载下来的一次重要访问[ji4zai4 xia4lai4 de yi1ci4 zhong4yao4 fang3wen4]*(record an important visit)*.

2c)"Verb+action measure word+target word"——this formation is hard to confirm its layers, as we could see. Zhu(1982) tries to solve this problem in the view of structure, and assumes that 一次[*yi1ci4*]*(once)* modifies the target word. On the contrary, some scholars put 一次[yi1ci4]*(once)* in the complement position related with the verb expressing the action's frequency. It is a far immense issue, this research takes no account of it.

3)Embedded type. Words like 地震波 [di4zhen4bo1]*(seismic wave)*, 申请书 [shen1qing3 shu1]*(requisition)*, 救济款[jiu4ji4 kuan3]*(aims)* seem to contain the target words, but it is the element in words-construction not in grammatical construction. We also eliminate this situation.

4)Characters' misuse or words' misuse, corpus from micro-blog has some inaccurate expression caused by that. We account none of them as up-to-standard concordance lines.

Then we get table 3 and figure 1, show the data of six target words collocating with the classifiers:

Table 3. Collocations between target words and action/static measure words

	static Modify	action Modify	ratio
di4zhen4	1343	1361	99%
feng4xian4	24	160	15%
ji4zai3	10	132	8%
jiu4ji4	3	137	22%
pei2tong2	16	41	39%
shen1qing3	459	861	53%

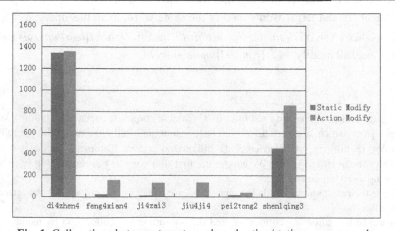

Fig. 1. Collocations between target words and action/static measure words

According to table2 and table 3, the ratio between target words and collocation is respectively 7.92%, 0.54%, 0.26%, 1.40%, 3.24%, 1.21%. Thus, the collocation strength rank is: 地震[*di4 zhen4*]>奉献[*feng4 xian4*]>记载[*ji4 zai3*]>救济[*jiu4 ji4*]>陪同[*pei2 tong2*]>申请[*shen1 qing3*]. 地震[*di4zhen4*] has the largest proportion with classifiers——7.92%, and the frequencies are 1361 and 1343 respectively corresponding to action measure words and static measure words, which the ratio is near to 1:1. The next two are 陪同[*pei2tong2*] and 救济[*jiu4ji4*], but these two words tend to collocate with action measure words. Then申请[shen1qing3], the ratio between collocating with static measure words and action measure words is about 1:2. 奉献[feng4xian4] and 记载[ji4zai3] rank at the last position, and more likely to collocate with action measure words.

We notice the other two calculating factors: the ratio of the collocation between target words and classifiers, the ratio between both action measure words and static measure words in the modifiers collocated with target words. Because some words are easily modified by classifiers, some are not, words belong to two categories have different characteristics collocating with these two types of classifiers. And the inevitable thing is the classifiers we pick may have an error. So we cannot come to an accurate conclusion. But for some words with ample collocation we might could confirm which category the words belong to. According to the data we have preliminary conclusions:1)地震[*di4zhen4*]、救济[*jiu4ji4*]、陪同[*pei2tong2*] and 申请[*shen1qing3*] collocate with classifiers more often, and the ratio of collocation with both kinds of classifiers is high, especially can be modified by static measure words. We could assure these four words are two-category words. 2)on the opposite, 奉献[*feng4xian4*] and 记载[*ji4zai3*] do not have so much chance to collocate with classifiers, for some reason such as target words' intrinsic quality, we could not come up with the conclusion to which category they belong to.

To make sure the conclusion is correct and dispel questions that data cannot resolve, we will discuss the target words in respect of syntactic and semantic layers.

3   The Analysis of Syntactic Characteristics

Zhu(1982) mentions that the dominating characters to predicate the "nouny verbs" are 1) can be the object of the preparative predicate object verb, 2)can be modified by nouns directly. Hu(1995) sums up three functional standards: 1)can be modified by measure words directly, 2)can be the subject of 有[*you3*](*have*), 3)can be modified by nouns directly. Zhong Qin(1980) points out that only in this situation that the words can be modified by static measure words, normal adjectives and nouns that fall into verb-noun category. Yang Tongyong(2008) states the criteria above has deficiencies, and disjunction or conjunction should reach the unification in syntax. Scholars' criteria and characteristics differ in both "nouny verbs" and "grammatical function", but "modified by nouns" is acknowledged by most of them. Next, we will investigate the syntactic characters of the six words when they act the function of noun and of verb.

3.1   The Syntactic Characteristics as Noun

Nouns' grammatical characteristics are summed up by three points: 1)could be the subject and object; 2)could not be modifiers or be modified by nouns; 3)could not be reduplicated normally.

1.   These words can be subject or object.

(a) 地震   造成   了   地面   青砖   的   断裂。

/di4zhen4/ zao4cheng2 le di4mian4 qing1zhuan1 de duan4lie4.

Earthquake cause ASP   earth   black brick AUX break.

'The earthquake caused the fracture of black brick.'

(b) 奉献   是   一种   最大   的   享受。

/feng4xian4/ shi4 yi1zhong3 zui4da4 de   xiang3shou4.

Devotion   is   a kind of biggest AUX enjoyment.

'Devotion is a biggest enjoyment.'

(c) 另一个   记载   是   《傅子》。

Ling4yi1ge4 ji4zai3   shi4   Fu4zi3.

Another one record   is   Fuzi.

'Another record is Fuzi.'

(d) 等 我们   走远   后,你 就   可以   给   那些   人 发 **救济** 了。

Deng3   wo3men zou3yuan3 hou4,ni3 jiu4 ke3yi3 gei3 na4xie1 ren2 fa1 jiu4ji4 le.

Wait we go away after,you can give those people give out alms ASP.

'After we go away,you can grant alms to those people.'

(e) 前 教皇   每次   下水   之前,   都   会   有   他   的   陪同。

Qian2 jiao4huang2 mei3ci4 xia4shui3 zhi1qian3,dou1 hui4 you3 ta1 de pei2tong2.

Former pope every time enter the water before,always will have his companion.

'Before the former pope went swimming,he always has his companion.'

(f) 最后,   **申请**   批   下来   了。

Zui4hou4, shen1qing3 pi1   xia4lai2   le.

Finally,   application approve come down ASP.

'Finally,the application is approved.'

记载[*ji4zai3*] normally could not be used as subject or object by itself, unless it has other modifiers. Inversely, 地震[*di4zhen4*], 奉献[*feng4xian4*], 救济[*jiu4ji4*], 陪同[*pei2tong2*], 申请[*shen1qing3*] could be subject and object. And (e) has two kind of ways to comprehend: on the one hand, 他[*ta1*]*(him)* could represent the subject "pope"; on the other hand, 他[ta1](him) represents another person, the one who accompanies the pope. In the last situation, 陪同[pei2tong2] is a verb, and 他[ta1](him) is the actor. So the accuracy of the POS is important to the comprehension of the sentence. Two target words also have the same situation which are 救济[*jiu4ji4*] and 陪同[*pei2tong2*]. In the forth section, we will discuss the semantic terms as well.

2.   These target words can be modifiers or be modified by nouns.

(g) 汶川 地震 [Wen4chuan4 di4zhen4]*(Wenchuan earthquake)*| 教师的奉献 [jiao4shi1 de feng4xian4]*(the devotion from teacher)*|类似的记载[lei4si4 de ji4zai3]*(similar record)*|人民政府的救济[ren2min2 zheng4fu3 de jiu4ji4]*(the relief from the government)*|他的陪同[ta1 de pei2tong2]*(his companion)*|入党申请[ru4dang3 shen1qing3]*(WUBC)*

(h) 地震灾区 [di4zhen4 zai1qu1]*(earthquake zone)*| 奉献 精神 [feng4xian4 jing1shen2]*(spirit of devotion)*|记载文献[ji4zai3 wen2xian4]*(recorded literature)*| 救济物资 [jiu4ji4 wu4zi1]*(relief supplies)*| 陪同人员 [pei2tong2 ren2yuan2]*(accompanying person)*|申请材料[shen1qing3 cai2liao4]*(application document)*

Attribute function are rare, and the modification thing don't need 的[de]*(AUX)* as a binder. The be modified function can use 的[de]*(AUX)* or not. In addition, 地震 [di4zhen4] can be modified by nouns directly. These words can collocate with normal adjectives formed modification relations.

3.   These words could not used as reduplicated formation.

Through the searching from BCC, these six words do not have overlapped usage. Three words have reduplicating usage but they obviously are verbs—— 奉献 *[feng4xian4]*, 记载*[jiu4ji4]*, 申请*[shen1qing3]*.

3.2   The Syntactic Characteristics as Verb

Verbs' grammatical characteristics are 1)could be predicate or the center of the predicate; 2)could be modified by 不[*bu4*]*(NEG)*, generally could be modified by adverb of degree; 3)could be the head of 了[*le*], 着[*zhe*], 过[*guo*] which present tense; 4)some action verbs could be reduplicated.

1.   These words could be predicates or centers of predicates.

(a) 汶川   地震   了！
Wen4chuan1   di4zhen4   le!
Wen4chuan1   earthquake ASP!
'Wenchuan got earthquake!'

(b) 他们   彼此   奉献   了   纯真   的 感情。
Ta1men4   bi3ci3 feng4xian4   le   chun2zhen1 de gan3qing2.
They   each other devote   ASP   pure   AUX emotion.
'They devoted their pure emotions to each other.'

(c) 正史   上   记载：......
Zheng4shi3   shang4   ji4zai3:......
The authorized history up   record:.......
'The authorized history recorded that.......'

(d) 剩下   的   一些   钱   就   先   救济   一下   你   自己。
Sheng4xia4 de   yi1xie1 qian2   jiu4 xian1 jiu4ji4 yi1xia4 ni3 zi4ji3.
Spare   AUX some money   first relieve once   yourself.

'You can use the spare money to relieve yourself first.'

(e) 我们　　这边　　由　江凌、　　林经理　　和　我　陪同。

Wo3men zhe4bian1 you2 Jiang1ling2、Lin2 jing1li3 he2　wo3 pei2tong2.

Our　　this　by　Jiang Ling、Lin manager and　me company.

'We are accompanied by Jiang Ling、Manger Lin and me.'

(f) 如果　生产　矿泉水　只要　8万，你　却　向　我　申请

Ru2guo3 sheng1chan3 kuang4quan2shui3 zhi3yao4 ba1wan4, ni3 que4 xiang4 wo3 shen1qing3

If　　produce　　mineral water　only need　　80000,you but from me apply

10万，那　多余　的　2万　就是　浪费。

shi2wan4,na4 duo1yu2 de liang3wan4 jiu4shi4 lang4fei4.

100000, that spare AUX 20000 is waste.

'If producing mineral water only needs 80000 yuan,but you apply for 100000 yuan from me,then the spare 20000 yuan is a waste.'

The main function of verbs is to be predicate or to be the center of predicate, and these six words all have this function, so we could say that they all have verbs' characteristics.

2. These words could be modified by 不[*bu4*] *(NEG, not)*.

(g) 我们的房屋别说什么经受地震了,甚至在不地震时都能莫名其妙地塌了。

Wo3men de fang2wu1 bie2shuo1 shen2me jing1shou4 di4zhen4 le,shen4zhi4 zai4 bu4 di4zhen4 shi2 dou1 neng2 mo4ming2qi2miao4 de ta1 le.

Our house don't say some suffer earthquake ASP,even here not earthquake when all can inexplicable collapse ASP.

'Our house could collapse without earthquake,never say suffering one earthquake.'

(h) 如果一味地索取爱,不奉献爱,时间长了往往会产生离异念头。

Ru2guo3 yi1wei4 de suo3qu3 ai4,bu4 feng4xian4 ai4,shi2jian1 chang2 le wang3wang3 hui4 chan3sheng1 li2yi4 nian4tou2.

If blindly ask for love,not devote love,time long ASP always could generate divorced thought.

'If one always takes love instead of giving love,he/she will have the thought of divorce after a long time.'

(i) 但松井所记下的是他的"赫赫战功",而对日本军的犯罪一点一滴也不记载。

Dan4 song1jing3 suo3 ji4 xia4 de shi4 ta1 de he4he4zhan4gong1,er2 dui4 ri4ben3jun1 de fan4zui4 yi1dian3yi1di1 ye3 bu4 ji4zai3.

But Matsui write down AUX is his contribution,but for Japanese military crime a little too not record.

'Matsui recorded his "contribution" without any trace of the Japanese military crime.'

(j) 吝啬,是指对穷困急难的人也不**救济**。

Lin4se4,shi4 zhi3 dui4 qiong2kun4 ji2nan4 de ren2 ye3 bu4 jiu4ji4.

Parsimony is point for destitute unfortunate AUX people also not relieve.

'Parsimony refers to those who do not relieve people suffering poverty.'

(k) 子秋先生,晚餐我就不陪同了。

Zi3qiu1 xian1sheng,wan3can1 wo3 jiu4 bu4 pei2tong2 le.

Ziqiu sir,dinner I would not accompany ASP.

'Mr Ziqiu,I'm afraid I could not accompany you for dinner.'

(l) 如果 你 不 **申请** 专利, 万一 让 别的 公司 捷足先得 了,咱们 可 就 被动 了。

Ru2guo3 ni3 bu4 shen1qing3 zhuan1li4,wan4yi1 rang4 bie2de gong1si1 jie2zu2xian1de2 le, zan2men ke3 jiu4 bei4dong4 le.

If you don't apply for patent, what if let other company going ahead ASP, we would passive ASP.

'If you don't apply for patent but other companies do,we would be in a dominated position.'

These words can be modified by 不[*bu4*]*(NEG,not)*, but could not be modified by degree adverb 很[*hen3*]*(very)* or 非常[*fei1chang2*]*(very)*.

    3.   These words could be the head of 了[*le*], 着[*zhe*], 过[*guo*]. For example:

(m) 地震了[*di4zhen4 le*]*(got earthquake)*|奉献着自己的生命[*feng4xian4 zhe zi4ji3 de sheng1ming4*]*(devote one's life)*|记载了一个有趣的故事[*ji4zai3 le yi1ge4 you3qu4 de gu4shi4*]*(record an interesting story)*|救济过太多寡妇[*jiu4ji4 guo4 tai4duo1 gua3fu4*]*(relieve so many widows)*|陪同着两位大将下去休息 [*pei2tong2 zhe liang3wei4 da4jiang4 xia4qu4 xiu1xi*]*(accompany two generals to rest)*|申请着最后的支援[*shen1qing3 zhe zui4hou4 de zhi1yuan2*]*(apply for the last assistance)*

We could not find any instance that 地震[*di4zhen4*] and 救济[*jiu4ji4*] collocate with 着[*zhe*]*(ASP)*, but other four target words could be followed by the aspect marker. There is a common criteria except that some nouns and adjectives with special meaning such as circulation meaning can have了[*le*], 着[*zhe*], 过[*guo*], only verbs can have aspect marker like 了[*le*], 着[*zhe*], 过[*guo*].

    4.   奉献 [*feng4xian4*], 救济 [*jiu4ji4*], 申请 [*shen1qing3*] can overlap. The examples are in 4.1.3.

    5.   These words could have objects.

(n) 奉献 爱心 [*feng4xian4 ai4xin1*]*(devote your love)*| 记载历史 [*ji4zai3 li4shi3*]*(record history)*|救济灾民[*jiu4ji4 zai1min2*]*(relieve people in the disaster-hit area)*|陪同国家领导人[*pei2tong2 guo2jia1 ling3dao3ren2*]*(accompany country leaders)*|申请入党[*shen1qing3 ru4dang3*]*(apply for joining the party)*

In addition, these words can be the objects of preparative predicate object verbs except 地震[*di4zhen4*]. For example:进行奉献[jin4xing2 feng4xian4]*(proceed devotion)*| 予 以 记 载 [yu3yi3 ji4zai3]*(grant recording)*| 进 行 救 济 [jin4xing2 jiu4ji4]*(proceed relieving)*|进行陪同[jin4xing2 pei2tong2]*(proceed company)*|进行申请[jin4xing2 shen1qing3]*(proceed application)*. We all know that 进行[*jin4xing2*], 予以[*yu3yi3*], 给予[*ji3yu3*] must be followed by verbs. Thus, these words have the characteristics of verbs.

Summing up, 地震[*di1zhen4*], 奉献[*feng4xian4*], 记载[*ji4zai3*], 救济[*jiu4ji4*], 陪同[*pei2tong2*], 申请[*shen1qing3*] all possess nouns' and verbs' syntactic characteristics. It's true that 地震[*di1zhen4*] is different from the other words in the inner structure(verb-object structure), and it could not have object when used as verb, could not used as object of the preparative predicate object verbs. Verbs all have some thing in common and these two dictionaries all consider these six target words having verbs' characteristics, but even the most similar words have its own idiosyncrasy. There must be something else influence their categories. So even words could match all the nouns' characteristics, we could not firmly predicate that these words only belong to nouns.

4   Semantic Characteristics Analysis

记载[*ji4zai3*], 陪同[*pei2tong2*], 申请[*shen1qing3*] have different meaning in various position in the sentence, the reason might be that these three words are autonomous and have strong meaning to change. 救济[jiu4ji4] as a verb means that "using money or substance help the disaster area or people suffering from life", this action is given out by a person or a social organization. When it plays the role of nouns, its meaning has been changed from an action to instrumental money or substance. 申请 [*shen1qing3*] also changed from the verb meaning——"illustrate reasons to leaders or relevant departments" to "material illustrating reasons". 陪同[*pei2tong2*] nominate the person instead of the action. These three words all transferred their meaning from action role to semantic role, a process that action categorized. In section 2.3, we point out the eliminated situation, the third one has the same meaning to the nouns' 救济 [*jiu4ji4*] and 申请[*shen1qing3*].

Hu Mingyang(1996) points out Europeanization, that many verbs and adjectives are in the situation that these words are drifting to nouns. Yu Shiwen(2005) does some calculating analysis targeted to this phenomenon, combining the qualitative and quantitative methods and inspecting some two-syllable words' drift phenomenon. In contrast, 地震[*di4zhen4*], 奉献[*feng4xian4*] and 记载[*ji4zai3*] don't have so much transfer in meaning, and they are in the transition period. That is ineluctable that the semantic role is blurred, so it's difficult to assure the category only using semantic role. Whether these words (救济[*jiu4ji4*], 申请[*shen1qing3*], 陪同[*pei2tong2*]) are action or specific things, it depends on their context. Even though the part of speech can find reliance in semantics, considering the transition period and the meaning's flexibility, we should tend to mainly rely on syntactic characteristics as formation to achieve the goal.

5   Conclusion

In conclusion, we present six target words' characteristics, as table4:

Table 4. General analysis of syntactic-semantic characteristics of the six target words (N=not)

	Collocation with classifier	static : action	noun	verb	Semantic transition
di4zhen4	7.92%	0.99	Y	Y	N-evident
feng4xian4	0.54%	0.15	Y	Y	N-evident
ji4zai3	0.26%	0.08	Y	Y	N-evident
jiu4ji4	1.40%	0.22	Y	Y	evident
pei2tong2	3.24%	0.39	Y	Y	evident
shen1qing3	1.21%	0.53	Y	Y	evident

According to the table above, we set that the main standard is the calculation of the static measure words and the action measure words, and other syntactic characteristics are the subordinate standard, the semantic characteristics the reference standard. In conclusion, 地震 [*di4zhen4*], 救济 [*jiu4ji4*], 陪同 [*pei2tong2*], 申请 [*shen1qing3*] collocate with classifiers and the ratio is considerable, and we can see apparently that they collocate with static measure words and action measure words. They have nouns' and verbs' characteristics, are multi-category words. But 奉献 [*feng4xian4*] and 记载 [*ji4zai3*] collocating with classifiers are more less, and their ratio is mostly constituted by collocating with action measure words. From other syntactic layers, their characters are obvious as a verb or as a noun. From the above, we need to combine words' syntactic characteristics and the quantitative analysis to make the final decision. We tend to regard these two words as multi-category words.

In this study, to come up with a conclusion that matches linguistic fact, we first find a calculating criteria that classifiers collocate with target words, then we explore the syntactic and semantic criteria. We could not only hang on the qualitative criteria, equinoctial line may not be the best choice, data can be more convincing at most of time. Data supports the verdict and the use of language is the basis. This is an elementary experiment, and for some uncountable noun the operation is hard to handle. And semantic analysis could not associate with formation sequentially, it's a tough mission to probe. The best expectation is that designing a proper way, putting syntactic form and data forward and taking the way combining semantic analysis and syntax. What is next for the study is expanding the target words' coverage, consummating the static measure words and collocation, penetrating into the criteria of assuring the conversion of words. Finally, we could get a reasonable and scientific solution.

Acknowledgements. This research is supported by the Fundamental Research Funds for the Central Universities, and the Research Funds of Beijing Language and Culture University (No.15YCX097).

References

1. The Chinese academy of social sciences institute of language dictionary newsroom. Modern Chinese Dictionary. The Commercial Press, Beijing (2014). (现代汉语词典) (in Chinese)

2. Yu, S., et al.: Grammatical Knowledge-Base of Contemporary Chinese. Tsinghua University Press, Beijing (1998). (现代汉语语法信息词典) (in Chinese)

3. Beijing Language and Culture University. Modern Chinese Common Words Frequency List. (现代汉语常用词词频表) (in Chinese)

4. Zhu, D.: Lecture Notes on Grammar. The Commercial Press, Beijing (1982). (语法讲义) (in Chinese)

5. Hu, M.: Study in Problems of Modern Chinese Parts of Speech. Beijing Language and Culture University Press, Beijing (1996). (现代汉语词类问题考察) (in Chinese)

6. Zhu, D.: The Study of Verbs and Adjectives' "Nominalization". Journal of Peking University (4) (1961). (关于动词形容词"名物化"的问题) (in Chinese)

7. Hu, M.: Verb-Noun Words' Quantitative Research. Language Studies (2) (1995). (动名兼类的计量考察) (in Chinese)

8. Guo, R.: The POS problem of the Chinese Dictionaries. Chinese Language (2) (1999). (语文词典的词性标注问题) (in Chinese)

9. Su, B.: Chinese Lexicographical Book's POS Work and its Influence to Paraphrasing. Lexicographical Studies (2) (2002). (汉语语文辞书的词性标注及其对释义的影响) (in Chinese)

10. Zhong, Q.: The Problem of the POS in Chinese Dictionaries. Lexicographical Studies (1) (1980). (汉语词典标注词性问题) (in Chinese)

11. Yang, T.: The Probe to the Verb-Noun Words' Complexity from the View of Grammatical Collocation. Lexicographical Studies (2) (2008). (从语法搭配看动名兼类的复杂性) (in Chinese)

12. Yu, S., Duan, H., Zhu, X.: The Quantitative Analysis on Words' conversion Phenomenon and Verbs Drifting to Nouns' Phenomenon, JSCL (2005). (词语兼类暨动词向名词漂移现象的计量分析.全国第八届计算语言学联合学术会议(JSCL-2005)论文集) (in Chinese)

13. Li, L.: The Study for Verb-Noun Words with Behavior Content Results Semantic. Heilongjiang University Master's Thesis (2012). (行为内容结果义动名兼类分歧词考察研究) (in Chinese)

A Study on the Lexicalization of Combined Idioms in Mencius

Jingxuan Guo and Erhong Yang[⊠]

Institute of Language Monitoring and Social Computation,
Beijing Language and Culture University, Beijing, China
guojingxuan0907@foxmail.com, yerhong@blcu.edu.cn

Abstract. Lexicalization is an important notion in language research. This paper discusses the lexicalization of combined idioms in Mencius in forms and meanings. Through the study, it can be concluded that most combined idioms in Mencius initially stand as two dissyllabic words alone and then transform into combined idioms after a transitional phase, accompanied with metaphorical or metonymical changes in meanings.

Keywords: Combine idioms · Lexicalization · Corpus

1 Introduction

Lexicalization is not just a means of word-formation, but a bridge between synchronic linguistics and diachronic linguistics. As Givon (1971) said: "Today's morphology is yesterday's syntax" [1]. Lexicalization is a methodology of revealing both the evolution modern Chinese and its relationship to ancient Chinese. Although there are various definitions of "lexicalization", in this paper, we use the term as defined by Dong XiuFang (2009): the lexicalization refers to an evolution from non-lexical forms into lexical. This is a broad definition which includes idiomization (an evolution from non-lexical forms to idiom) [2]. By the definition, we consider lexicalization of idioms as the integration of idioms formation and its evolution.

Most lexicalization studies have focused on the relationship between lexicalization and grammaticalization and the formation of certain disyllables or discourse markers, while neglecting the lexicalization of Chinese idioms. From a diachronic perspective, Jiang Chengsheng (2012) concluded that lexicalization is a diachronic and degenerative process which degenerates syntax to morphology [3]. From a synchronic perspective, Qian Yun (2003) has studied the lexicalization degree of the Chinese idioms on aspects of meanings and structures. She pointed out that the rhythm, analogy, and origin of idioms may affect lexicalization degree of Chinese idioms [4]. Additionally, some academics have studied the lexicalization of a single Chinese idiom. For instance, Hu Binbin(2013) studied the lexicalization of the Chinese idiom "呜呼哀哉 [wuhu'aizai]" (alas), and the factors which will lead to lexicalization such as prosody, phonetics, grammar, semantics and pragmatics [5].

Among the former studies, few touched on common lexicalization features of Chinese idioms. Therefore, this paper will study the lexicalization of combined idioms in Mencius at an evolutionary viewpoint and summarize the common features in lexicalization.

© Springer International Publishing Switzerland 2015
Q. Lu and H.H. Gao (Eds.): CLSW 2015, LNAI 9332, pp. 307–319, 2015.
DOI: 10.1007/978-3-319-27194-1_31

2   The Definition of Combined Idioms

There are two classifications of idioms in *Mencius*: one is by meanings and the other is by construction forms. For example, Hu Jiming (1999) has classified the idioms into "direct transformation", "processing and transformation" and "summarizing and combination". The "summarizing and combination" refers to summarizing two or more phrases in Mencius and extracting their essential components or adding components to form a four-syllable idiom [6]. Similarly, Xiao Yongfeng (2011) has classified idioms in Mencius into "extracting from the original", "replacing, adding or deleting words", "refining and integration" and "adjusting word order". The "refining and integration" refers to refining and integrating two phrases or clauses in one context into an idiom, such as "水深火热[shuishenhuore]" (be plunged into dire suffering), "出尔反尔[chuerfaner]" (promise and then deny in succession), "流连忘返[liulianwangfan]" (indulge in pleasures without stop), "事半功倍[shibangongbei]" (get twofold results with half the effort) etc. [7]. Similarly, Liu Jinning (2011) viewed lexicalization as the summarizing of two or more clauses by extracting the essential components into an idiom, such as "流连忘返", "事半功倍", "一毛不拔 [yimaobuba]" (as mean as a miser), "鳏寡孤独[guanguagudu]" (the widower, the widow, the orphan and the childless), "水深火热", etc.[8].

Construction forms can affect lexicalization; therefore, we adopt the second way of classification (by construction forms)to classify these idioms into five categories: "directly extracting from the original", "adding words", "truncating words", "combining" and "summarizing". To avoid controversy, we relied on the *Chinese Idiom Dictionary*[9] and selected 17 combined idioms originating from *Mencius* as a sample set:"事半功倍", "杯水车薪[beishuichexin]" (to make a useless attempt), "出类拔萃 [chuleibacui]" (outstanding), "地利人和[dilirenhe]" (hold all the aces), "自暴自弃 [zibaoziqi]" (totally give up hope and stay in desperation), "出尔反尔", "水深火热", "先知先觉[xianzhixianjue]" (having foresight), "同流合污[tongliuhewu]" (associate oneself with undesirable elements), "寸木岑楼[cunmucenlou]" (There is a vast difference between the two), "一毛不拔", "鳏寡孤独", "俯仰无愧[fuyangwukui]" (having a clear conscience), "吊民伐罪[diaominfazui]" (console the people and punish the wicked), "一曝（暴）十寒[yipushihan]" (work by fits and starts), "一傅众咻 [yifuzhongxiu]" (Cannot achieve much in a disturbing environment), "流连忘返".

3   The Lexicalization of Combined Idioms

From a diachronic perspective, the lexicalization of idioms is a long-term evolution accompanied with changes in forms and meanings. We will discuss such evolution and changes in detail.

3.1   The Changes in Forms

In terms of forms, combined idioms are mainly derived from one or more clauses. Lexicalization of such idioms can be roughly classified into two categories: The first, most combined idioms in Mencius have experienced three stages of lexicalization. At the first stage, the two disyllable components are used independently, but in the need of expression and restricted by the linguistic economic principle, the two components may be used together by chance. The second stage is a transitional stage (usually accompanied with such variations as changing order of words), with increasing occurrences, its form is gradually fixed and transforms into an idiom by the third and final stage. In the second category, a disyllable component in one idiom is used frequently. While restricted by the classical four-syllable form [10], it eventually transforms into an idiom. We will elaborate on the two categories with several examples:

A Study on the Lexicalization of "鳏寡孤独[guanguagudu]" (the Widower, the Widow, the Orphan and the Childless). In Table 1, According to the ancient Chinese corpora[1], we have summarized occurrences of the Chinese idiom "鳏寡孤独" in different historical periods.

As in Table 1, the disyllables "鳏寡[guangua]" (the widower and the widow) has already been used together in Zhou Dynasty. In the following two examples, "鳏寡" is used as the object of clauses.

a　作其即位，爰知小人之依，能保惠于庶民，不敢侮<u>鳏寡</u>。（《尚书》）

The king understood the sufferings of common people, after he came into power, he granted many benefits to the people, and never discriminated the widower and the widow (Shang Shu).

b　爰及矜人，哀此<u>鳏寡</u>。（《诗经》）

The impoverished, the widower and the widow are all people in deep sorrow (the Book of Song).

During The Spring and Autumn Period, the four monosyllabic words: "鳏[guan]" (the widower), "寡[gua]" (the widow), "孤[gu]" (the orphan), "独[du]" (the childless) had been firstly used by Mencius in one context, where their meanings were distinguished (as in example c). The word "孤独[gudu]" (the orphan and the childless) had been used independently or served as a component along with other words in a clause (as in example d).

c　老而无妻曰<u>鳏</u>，老而无夫曰<u>寡</u>，老而无子曰<u>独</u>，幼而无父曰<u>孤</u>；此四者，天下之穷民而无告者。"（《孟子·梁惠王下》）

These four, the widower, the widow, the childless and the orphan, are the poor and helpless (Mencius).

---

[1] These examples are from Ancient Chinese Corpus of Online Corpus (http://www.cncorpus.org/acindex.aspx)

d   虽然，妾闻之，勇士不以众强凌孤独，明惠之君不拂是以行其所欲。（《晏子春秋》）

I heard that the warrior would never bully the weak, and the wise monarch would never act unrestrained and reckless (Yan Zi).

Table 1. the occurrences of "鳏寡孤独" in different historical period

items \ Dynasty	Zhou(BC.1046-BC.256)	The Spring and Autumn period (BC.770-BC.476)	Han(BC.202-220)	Wei,Jin, Southern and Northern (222-589)	Sui, Tang (581-907)	Song(960-1279)	Yuan, Ming (1271-1644)	Qing (1636-1912)
鳏寡(the widower and the widow)	7	10	17	17	30	28	9	39
孤独(the orphan and the childless)	0	3	19	22	18	13	14	6
鳏寡…孤独(the widower and the widow…the orphan and the childless)	0	0	4	1	1	1	1	0
鳏寡孤独	0	0	2	21	31	6	20	25
variations	0	0	0	8	8	1	0	0

During the Han Dynasty, "鳏寡" and "孤独" had firstly been combined to describe the vulnerable, while "鳏寡孤独" had not formally formed an idiom at this phase(e.g. e). Occurrences of "鳏寡" and "孤独" are more frequent than occurrences of "鳏寡孤独". This indicates a low adhesiveness between "鳏寡" and "孤独" , the combination was just a coincidence instead of a actual inner fusion.

e   上为立后故，赐天下鳏寡孤独穷困及年八十已上孤儿九岁已下布帛米肉各有数。（《史记》）

Owing to get married, the king bestowed grants on the widower, the widow, the orphan, the childless and the poor (Shi Ji).

f   是其为人，哀鳏寡，恤孤独，振困穷，补不足。（《战国策》）

The person comforted and compensated the widower, the widow, the orphan and the childless, relieved the poverty of the helpless (Strategies of the Warring States).

During the Wei, Jin, Southern, Northern, Sui, and Tang Dynasty, occurrences of "鳏寡孤独" were more frequent, while "鳏寡" and "孤独" were rarely used separately, the speech pause between the two words had disappeared, and word fusion began to take place. In example h, "鳏寡孤独" , "癃残六疾[longcanliuji]" (the weakness and physical disability) and "不能自存者 [bunengzicunzhe]" (the person who cannot live by himself) are separated by punctuation and serves as equal syntactic components in one context, this means "鳏寡孤独" is a stand-alone syntactic component in a clause. However, "鳏寡孤独" had not then been completely lexicalized. As in example i, "各有差[geyoucha]" (differently) implies that the meaning of "鳏寡孤独" had not fused yet. In addition, this stage was accompanied with variations such as "鳏寡孤老[guanguagulao]" (the widower, the widow, the orphan and the old) (e.g. j), "孤独鳏寡[guduguangua]" (the orphan, the childless, the widower and the widow) (e.g. k), etc. The aforementioned examples indicate a transitional lexicalization period of the idiom "鳏寡孤独".

g 恤<u>鳏寡</u>, 存<u>孤独</u>。（《昭明文选》）

   The person comforted and compensated <u>the widower, the widow, the orphan and the childless</u> (Zhao Ming Selected Works).

h <u>鳏寡孤独</u>, <u>癃残六疾</u>, <u>不能自存者</u>, 郡县优量赈给。（《宋书》）

   The province and county delivered food and cloth to the <u>weak and helpless</u> (Book of Song).

i 己巳, 板授高年刺史, 守, 令, 恤<u>鳏寡孤独</u>各有差。（《北史》）

   The king authorized the office to the old governor, and compensated <u>the widower, the widow, the orphan and the childless</u> differently (History of the Northern Dynasties).

j 赐高年爵，恤<u>鳏寡孤</u>老各有差。（《北史》）

   The king authorized the office to the old governor, and compensated <u>the widower, the widow, the orphan and the old</u> differently (History of the Northern Dynasties).

k 赐<u>孤独鳏寡</u>粟帛有差, 年七十已上加衣杖。（《晋书》）

   The king granted <u>the widower, the widow, the orphan and the childless</u> food and cloth, and the person over 70 would get more (Book of Jin).

In the Song Dynasty, "鳏寡孤独" had been used as a word (e.g. l), but there are variants such as "鳏寡惸独" (the widower, the widow, the orphan and the childless) (e.g. m).

l 若分以赐<u>鳏寡孤独</u>之民, 所济实多" （《资治通鉴》）

   If give grant to <u>the helpless</u>, a great amount of people will be aided (History as a Mirror).

m 八月戊子, 免<u>鳏寡惸独</u>今岁税米。（《新唐书》）

   <u>The helpless</u> were exempted from taxation in August (New History of the Tang Dynasty).

During the Yuan Dynasty, "鳏寡孤独" started to be modified by quantifiers and had a tendency of substantivization (e.g. n). At this phase, variations of "鳏寡孤独" had not appeared in the ancient Chinese corpus, so we could deem that the form of "鳏寡孤独" had been fixed. What is more, increasing occurrences of "鳏寡孤独" indicated the completion of lexicalization.

n   有什么命夫命妇，都是些鳏寡孤独！（《牡丹亭》）

There are the helpless rather than noble (Peony Pavilion).

Table 2. the occurrences of "吊民伐罪" in different historical period

Dynasty ⟍ items	Zhou (BC. 1046–BC. 256)	The spring and Autumn period (BC. 770–BC. 476)	Han (B C. 202 –220)	Wei, Jin, Southern, Northern (222–589)	Sui, Tang (581– 907)	Song (960– 1279)	Yuan, Ming (1271– 1644)	Qing (1636– 1912)
吊民 (console the people)	0	0	0	5	4	7	2	1
伐罪 (punish the wicked)	1	1	1	13	17	19	5	6
吊民···伐罪 (console the people···punish the wicked)	0	0	0	2	0	0	1	0
吊民伐罪	0	0	0	1	1	4	22	5
伐罪吊民 (console the people and punish the wicked)	0	2	0	11	5	4	9	0
伐罪吊人 (console the people and punish the wicked)	0	0	0	2	14	1	0	0

Generally, the lexicalization of "鳏寡孤独" occurred over a long time: Initially, "鳏寡" and "孤独" were used independently as two disyllables. Almost by accident, they were used together and after a transitional stage with increasing occurrences and fixed in word order[2]. Eventually, "鳏寡孤独" had been lexicalized as an idiom. Similarly, some Chinese idioms have also experienced such kind of lexicalization, such as

---

[2] If the components coexisted as the order opposite form, the two components are phrases rather than words and these words are not allowed to change the order [11].

"水深火热[shuishenhuore]" (be plunged into dire suffering), "地利人和[dilirenhe]" (hold all the aces), "自暴自弃[zibaoziqi]" (totally give up hope and stay in desperation), "先知先觉[xianzhixianjue]" (having foresight), "寸木岑楼[cunmucenlou]" (a vast difference between two things), "一毛不拔[yimaobuba]" (as mean as a miser), "俯仰无愧[fuyangwukui]" (having a clear conscience), "流连忘返[liulianwangfan]" (indulge in pleasures without stop), "一傅众咻[yifuzhongxiu]" (so disrupted to achieve nothing), "出类拔萃[chuleibacui]" (outstanding), "出尔反尔[chuerfaner]" (promise and then deny in succession), etc.

A Study on the Lexicalization of "吊民伐罪[Diaominfazui]" (Console the People and Punish the Wicked). However, the lexicalization of "吊民伐罪" is different from "鳏寡孤独".

As in example a, "伐罪[fazui]" (punish the wicked) was always in the collocation of "奉辞伐罪[fengcifazui]" (send an expedition to punish the wicked) from Zhou Dynasty to Han Dynasty. During The Spring and Autumn Period, the original form of "吊民伐罪" had firstly appeared in *Mencius*, also, "伐罪吊民" (punish the wicked and console the people) had occurred in *"The Art of War"* (e.g. b). But this usage did not survive during the Han Dynasty. Therefore, "吊民伐罪" had not then been lexicalized.

a　民弃不保，天降之咎，肆予以尔众上，<u>奉辞伐罪</u>。（《尚书》）

> *People abandon them and the heaven give sin to them. Therefore, complying with the order of the king, I send an expedition to punish the wicked (Shang Shu).*

b　"<u>诛其罪</u>，<u>吊其民</u>，如时雨降，民大悦。"　（《孟子·滕文公下》）

> *Punish the wicked and console the people, which make people ecstatic, like a timely rain (Mencius).*

c　凡欲兴师动众，<u>伐罪吊民</u>，必任天时。（《兵法》）

> *If you want to punish the wicked and console the people, you must be according to the time (Art of War).*

Since the Wei, Jin, Southern and Northern Dynasties, occurrences of "奉辞伐罪" and "伐罪吊民" increased. Like the former dynasty, they were used between two commas to serve as a syntactic component independently (e.g. d and e). Higher occurrences of "伐罪吊民" than "吊民伐罪" implied that word order had not been fixed.

d　近者<u>奉辞伐罪</u>，旌麾南指，刘琮束手。（《三国志》）

> *Recently I send an expedition to punish the wicked to the South. Then, Liu Cong surrendered (Record of the Three Kingdoms).*

e　夫<u>伐罪吊民</u>，古之令轨（《三国志》）

> *Consoling the people and punishing the wicked is a good moral standard (Record of the Three Kingdoms).*

During the Sui and Tang Dynasties (709-960), "吊民伐罪" began to serve as a syntactic component. As in example f, it acts as an modifier of the word"义 [yi]"(righteousness). "伐罪吊人" appeared as a variant of "吊民伐罪" at this period(e.g. g). The usage was similar to "吊民伐罪", note that "伐罪吊人" had been used as an idiom and served as the object of"所谓[suowei]" (so-called) (e.g. f).

f   今魏虏贪惏,罔顾吊民伐罪之义,必欲肆其残忍,多所诛夷,俘囚士庶,并为军实。（《周书》）

> *Now, Wei Dynasty is committing all kinds of outrages, disregarding the righteousness of <u>consoling the people and punishing the wicked</u> (The Book of Zhou Dynasty).*

g   愚臣昧焉，窃恐非五帝,三王伐罪吊人之意也。（《旧唐书》）

> *I am afraid that it is not the meaning of <u>punishing the wicked and consoling the people</u> (The Old Book of Tang History).*

h   所谓伐罪吊人，威德被于遐外，为国之善者也。（《魏郑公谏录》）

> *There are the best policy to run the country, such as <u>punishing the wicked, consoling the people</u> and spreading the prestige and benevolence far away (Records of Wei Zheng).*

In records of the Song dynasty, the "伐罪吊人" only appeared once, on the contrary, the usage of"吊人伐罪" increased a little. As in example i, "吊民伐罪" had the functionality of a idiom and was used as a syntactic component.

i   太王汤武是吊民伐罪，为天下除残贼底道理。（《朱子语类》）

> *The king, Tang Wu <u>consoled the people and punished the wicked</u> to get rid of an evil for the people (Analects of Zhu Zi).*

During the Yuan and Ming Dynasties, occurrences of "吊民伐罪" had increased a lot (e.g. j) but the variant "伐罪吊人" did not occur anymore. Yet another variant, "伐罪吊民", were still in use (e.g. k).This indicates that the idiom "吊民伐罪" had been only partially lexicalized, given the unfixed word order.

j   承裔等奉诏宣扬国威，所谓' 吊民伐罪'者也。（《金史》）

> *Cheng Yi received orders to publicize national prestige, what is the so-called <u>consoling the people and punishing the wicked</u> (The History of Jin Dynasty).*

K   你今日金台拜将，要伐罪吊民，只怕你不能兵进五关，先当死于此地也！"（《封神演义》）

> *Today, you appointed a military leader to <u>punish the wicked and console the people</u>. I am afraid you will die here (The Legend of Deification).*

During the Qing Dynasty, the variant "伐罪吊民" was no longer used, the word order was fixed as "吊民伐罪", indicating the completion of lexicalization. In comparison, "吊民伐罪" is not composed of two initially separated disyllables components. Instead, its lexicalization is affected by the fixed format of four-syllable words. But they both have experienced a transitional stage during which their formats and occurrences are fixed and increasing.

A Study on the Lexicalization of "事半功倍[shibangongbei]" (get twofold results with half the effort). In addition, there are a few idioms' lexicalization is a mixture with the two categories aforementioned. These idioms have only one frequently-used disyllables component. During the transitional phase, these idioms are lexicalized under the restriction of classical four-syllable word format. We will discuss the lexicalization of "事半功倍" to illustrate this.

Table 3. Tha occurrences of "事半功倍" in different historical period

Dynasty items	The Spring and Autumn Period (BC.770 -BC.476)	Han (BC. 202 -220)	Wei,Jin, Southern, Northern (222-589)	Sui, Tang (581- 907)	Song (960 -1279)	Yuan, Ming (1271- 1644)	Qing (1636- 1912)	Contempo-rary and modern (1912- 1949)
功倍(get twofold results)	4	0	0	29	7	4	0	4
事半功倍	0	0	0	0	0	4	2	41
事半…功倍 (get twofold results…wit h half the effort)	0	1	0	2	0	0	0	13
师逸(佚)功倍 (get twofold results with less time)	0	0	4	4	0	0	0	0

The idiom "事半功倍" is originated from *Mencius*. As in Table 4, "功倍 [gongbei]" (get twofold results) had already been used in the Spring and Autumn Period, but it was a trans-layered structure[3] instead of an idiom, where "功[gong]" (results) served as a subject and "倍[bei]" (twofold) served as an object, such as example a. Also, "师逸而功倍[shiyi'ergongbei]" (get twofold results with less time) and "士（事）半而功倍[shiban'ergongbei]" (get twofold results with half the effort) appeared as variants of "事半功倍" (as the example b and c).

---

[3] Trans-layered structure refers to two components in different syntactical levels combining into a new syntactical component [12].

a 其为人君者乐思太平，得天之心，其功倍也。（《兵法》）

The king, who loves peace, will win people's hearts. Therefore, he will get twofold results (Art of war).

b 善学者，师逸而功倍，又从而庸之。（《礼记》）

The good learner always gets twofold results with less time (The Book of Rites).

c 先胜者，先见弱於敌而後战者也，故士（古通事）半而功倍焉（《兵法》）

The former winner will show weakness to the enemy then begin to fight. As a result, they will get twofold results with half the effort (Art of war).

During the Wei, Jin, Southern and Northern Dynasties, with the prosperity of parallel prose, the form of four-syllable word was fashionable. Under this background, "师逸（佚）功倍[shiyigongbei]" (get twofold results with less time) appeared in the form of four-syllable. It was always used between two commas as an independent clause. Note that in example d, "事逸而功倍" is modified by an adverb and serves as the functionality of verbs.

d 以古人之训其家者，各训乃家，不更事逸而功倍乎？（《颜氏家训》）

Using the ancient method to educate their own family, it will be easy and get twofold results (Yan's Instructions).

During the Sui and Tang Dynasties, occurrences of "功倍" increased (9 four-syllable words containing "功倍" in total), such as "力省功倍[lishenggongbei]" (get twofold results with less effort), "道尊功倍[daozungongbei]" (get twofold results with respecting teacher and knowledge), etc. However, most of these four-syllable words only appear once. Additionally, "功倍" is modified by the modal verb "可以 [keyi]" (may) and serves as the predicate, which is equivalent to the functionality of a verb (e.g. e). Also, "功倍" can be used as the object of "云[yun]" (say that…), as in the example f. Such usage lays the foundations for the lexicalization of "事半功倍".

e 如切如磋，闻《诗》闻《礼》，一年可以功倍，三多于是足用。（《陈书》）

If you learn from Shijing and Yili, you will get twofold results in one year and enjoy the benefit all one's life after three years (Book of Chen).

f 不传其习，或失於多，嗟尔寡闻，孰云功倍？（《全唐文》）

They did not inherit tradition and lost a lot. So they knew little information about it and would not get twofold results (Complete Prose Works of the Tang).

During the Yuan and Ming Dynasties, "事半功倍" had been firstly used together and occurred 4 times in the corpus, twice used as an independent clause between two commas (e.g. g, h) and twice used as an attributive (e.g. i). During Qing Dynasty, it was used twice as a predicate (e.g. j).

g 事半功倍，可为左辅永利。（《万历野获编》）

It will get twofold results with half the effort and get benefit (An unofficial history of Wan Li period).

h 丝音之最易学者，莫过于提琴，事半功倍，悦耳娱神。（《闲情偶记》）

The violin is the easiest to learn, and get twofold results with half the effort. It is sweet-sounding and joyful (Book occasional send).

i 其所造之房屋器皿，定与拙匠不同，且有事半功倍之益。（《闲情偶记》）

The buildings and vessels, who construed, must be different from the poor craftsman. And they will get twofold results with half the effort (Book occasional send).

j 倘若我找着这个姑了，托他经手，一定事半功倍。（《官场现形记》）

If I find that one to handle affairs, it must be get twofold results with half the effort (Exposure of the Official World).

After the Qing Dynasty, occurrences of "事半功倍" increased and began to act as an independent syntactic component. Apart from serving as an attributive, it can also serve as an object (e.g. k) or a predicate (e.g. l). Accordingly, we can infer that the lexicalization of "事半功倍" had been completed.

k 足下欲奋如椽之笔，提倡小家族制度以为事半功倍，不知将何说以处孝弟之道……（《新青年》）

You advocated small family system and though that will get twofold results with half the effort, but how to deal with filial piety (New Youth)?

l 是借机械的力去帮助人功自然事半功倍故此古代重农工。（《民报》）

In ancient, agriculture and industry were taken seriously, because working with machine would get twofold results with half the effort(Citizen Newspaper).

In conclusion, although "事半[shiban]" (with half the effort) had been used as early as Mencius, it never served as an independent syntactic component. However, due to the lexicalization of "功倍" and the restriction of fixed four-syllable word format, the lexicalization of "事半功倍" had been boosted. Similarly, with increasing occurrences of "同流[tongliu]" (associate) and influenced by other similar four-syllable phrases, such as "善恶同流[shanertongliu]" (mixed with kindness and evil) and "天地同流[tianditongliu]" (an integration with heaven and earth), "同流合污" have been eventually lexicalized as an idiom.

In summary, most combined idioms in Mencius are composed of two disyllable components that are initially used independently. During a transitional period, many variants will appear and disappear; with increasing occurrences and fixed in format, the idiom will be eventually lexicalized.

3.2   Changes in Meanings During the Lexicalization of Combined Idioms

From the viewpoint of methodology, most combined idioms are mainly derived from one or more clauses. There is usually a conceptual integration[4] in meanings during lexicalization. Conceptual integration is featured through metaphor and metonymy [13]. From the cognitive perspective, metaphor and metonymy are cognitive mechanisms rather than rhetorical devices. Metaphor and metonymy are respectively considered as approximation and adjacency [14].

Metaphor is based on the principle of similarity in conceptual structures, namely, the intersection of different cognitive domains and similar associations between different concepts [15]. Most combined idioms in Mencius are of metaphor. For instance, the literally meaning of "杯水车薪" is to put out a fierce fire with a cup of water. During lexicalization, it generated a metaphorical meaning of making a useless attempt. Other idioms such as "寸木岑楼", "水深火热", "一曝十寒", "同流合污", "一毛不拔", "一傅众咻" and "俯仰无愧" are the same.

Metonymy refers to a representative thing in one cognitive domain representing a thing in another cognitive domain, such as the substitutional relationship between parts and wholes [15], concrete and abstract, features and categories [16]. For instance, the idiom "鳏寡孤独" originally refers to four kinds of person: the widower, the widow, the orphan and the childless. During lexicalization, its meaning has changed to represent the helplessness or vulnerable, which is a typical substitutional relationship between parts and wholes.

4   Conclusions

Most lexicalized combined idioms in Mencius are composed with two initially independent disyllable words. Through lexicalization, the two disyllable words combine and entail metaphorical or metonymical changes in meanings. As a consequence, these idioms are more concise and expressive in meanings.

Acknowledgements. This paper was supported by the Fundamental Research Funds for the Central Universities, and the Research Funds of Beijing Language and Culture University (14YCX065).

This research project is supported by Science Foundation of Beijing Language and Culture University (supported by "the Fundamental Research Funds for the Central Universities") (13ZDY03).

---

[4] Conceptual Integration is a kind of theory framework of exploring meaning construction and information integration, which involved the merged function process of the mental space network dynamic cognitive model. Conceptual integration plays a central role on our way of learning, thinking and living [17]. In short, Conceptual Integration took the mental space as input space, communicative information as the element of input space, then manipulated and integrated them [13].

References

1. Givón, T.: Historical Syntax and Synchronic Morphology: an Archaeologist's Field Trip. Chicago Linguistic Society **7**(1), 394–415 (1971)
2. Dong, X.: Syntactic change and lexicalization in Chinese. Studies of the Chinese Language **5**, 399–409 (2009). (in Chinese)
3. Jiang, C.-S., Liang, J., Liao, D.: On Grammaticalization and Lexicalization in Idioms. Journal of South China Normal University (Social Science Edition) **2**, 128–130 (2012). (in Chinese)
4. Qian, Y., Yu, G.: A research in the lexicalization of four-character idioms in Mandarin Chinese. Linguistic Sciences **2**(6), 86–96 (2003). (in Chinese)
5. Hu, B.: The Lexicalization Course of the Idiom"Wuhu'aizai (呜呼哀哉)" and Related Issues. Language Teaching and Linguistic Studies **5**, 57–64 (2013). (in Chinese)
6. Hu, J.: The influence of *Mencius* on the culture, linguistic and vocabulary. Journal of Southwest China Normal University (Philosophy & Social Science Edition) **1**, 108–111 (1999). (胡继明.《孟子》对汉语文学语言词汇的影响.西南师范大学学报,1999第1期.) (in Chinese)
7. Xiao, Y.: Analyzing "Mencius" idioms. The Science Education Article Collects **4**, 78–79 (2011). (刘金宁.《孟子》成语初探.北方文学,2011第4期.) (in Chinese)
8. Liu, J.: The first exploration of *Mencius* idiom. Northern Literature **4**, 135–137 (2011). (in Chinese)
9. The editorial board for *Idioms Dictionary*: Idioms Dictionary. The Commercial Press, Bei Jing (2014). (《成语大词典》编委会.《成语大词典 (最新修订版)》.商务印书馆,2014). (the latest revised edition). (in Chinese)
10. Zhou, J.: The classic of idioms. Nan Kai Journal **2**, 29–35 (1997). (论成语的经典性.南开学报,1997第2期) (in Chinese)
11. Dong, X.: Lexicalization the Origin and Evolution of Chinese Disyllabic Words, revised edn. The Commercial Press, Beijing (2013). (in Chinese)
12. Dong, X.: The formation of trans-layered structure and adjustment of the language system. Journal of Hebei Normal University (Social Science) **20**(3), 83–86 (1997). (董秀芳. 跨层结构的形成与语言系统的调整.河北师范大学学报,1997第20卷第3期) (in Chinese)
13. Zhang, J.: The Lexicalization grade and derivation of Chinese antonymic compounds. Journal of International Chinese Studies **1**, 155–163 (2012). (张金竹.汉语反义复合词的衍生和词汇化等级.国际汉语学报,2012第1期) (in Chinese)
14. Shen, J.: Blending and haplology. Chinese Teaching in the World **4**, 5–12 (2006). (in Chinese)
15. Liu, X.: Lexicalization of Quantity Classifiers Phrases in Chinese. Studies in Language and Linguistics **26**(1), 103–106 (2006). (in Chinese)
16. Sun, Y., Liu, H.: The review of Idioms and Their Comprehension: A Cognitive Semantic Perspective. Foreign Languages and Their Teaching **8**, 60–63 (2004). (孙亚,刘宇红.《熟语及其理解的认知语义学研究》评介.外语与外语教学2004第8期) (in Chinese)
17. Wang, Z.: Development of Conceptual Blending and Its Frontier Issues. Journal of Sichuan International Studies University **22**(6), 65–70 (2006). (in Chinese)

A Constructional Approach to Lexical Templates in Chinese Neologisms

Xiaomei Hu[✉]

Central China Normal University, Wuhan, Hubei, China
wjshxm@126.com

Abstract. This paper first defines lexical templates in Chinese, followed by an examination of the front empty lexical templates with examples taken from Chinese neologisms within the framework of construction grammar. We hold a lexical template to be an intermediate productive construction with one variable position and a lexically specified one. The holistic meaning is not the sum of that of the constituent parts; neither does the head contribute much to the meaning.

Keywords: Lexical templates · Construction · Neologisms

1   Introduction

Neologisms are an interesting phenomenon in that their emergence demonstrates the capability of language to undergo and sustain change. In contemporary Chinese, neologisms keep entering common use, and some of them have even been accepted into mainstream language. For example, "网购" (*online shopping*), "丁克" (*DINK*), "云计算" (*cloud computing*), etc. have been included in "现代汉语词典 (第六版)" (*Contemporary Chinese Dictionary*, 6th edition), the authoritative one-volume dictionary of Chinese language.

But these neologisms are not coined in a haphazard manner. Some of them show a lot of commonalities; some even seem to follow a very obvious word-formation pattern termed "template". Look at the following three-character words taken from *Chinese New Words* (2007-2011):

A	B	C
凤凰 | 男[1]	孔雀 | 女[2]	庐舍 | 族[3]
肉食 | 男[4]	草食 | 女[5]	裸婚 | 族[6]
月亮 | 男[7]	火山 | 女[8]	咸鱼 | 族[9]

---

[1] Literally, it means "phoenix men". This refers to "young men who live and work in the city after years of study and efforts despite their humble birth." The following explanations will be shortened in the form "literal meaning: real meaning".

[2] Peacock women: silk stocking ladies brought up in the city

[3] Family house clan: the losers

[4] Carnivorous men: men with typical positive masculine features such as bravery, decisiveness, etc.

[5] Herbivorous women: not so open women

[6] Naked marriage clan: people who practice naked marriage

[7] Moon men: men who exhibit two different characters when in and out of the family, just like the two sides of the moon

[8] Volcano women: women who have a fiery temper and a straightforward character

[9] Salted fish clan: people in the workplace who idle their life all day without any planning about life and work

© Springer International Publishing Switzerland 2015
Q. Lu and H.H. Gao (Eds.): CLSW 2015, LNAI 9332, pp. 320–328, 2015.
DOI: 10.1007/978-3-319-27194-1_32

These words are names given to people sharing or having certain characteristics. They are labeled as nouns and obviously they are compounds. But average Chinese speakers may not know their exact meaning, because the meaning cannot be deduced from the parts that comprise the whole. One thing for sure is that these words refer to people or things, judging from the last character in each word which determines its categorical meaning.

A closer look at these words reveals several facts:

(1)Vertically, words in each column follow an obvious word-formation pattern, here a "P1+P2" pattern ("P" for "Part"), separated by a " | " for ease of analysis. In the pattern, P1 is variable, while P2 is lexically specified. We call this kind of word-formation pattern "lexical template". In columns A, B and C, the templates are "P1+男(*man*)", "P1+女(*woman*)" and "P1+族(*clan*)" respectively.

(2)These words are all right-headed nominal compounds, with P1 being the modifier and P2 the head under semantic analysis. This type of "modifier+head" pattern is a predominant compound-formation pattern in neologisms in Chinese language, as will be proved with statistics later. Marchand's (1969) formula of compounds "AB is B" also applies here.

(3)Meanings of the words are not totally compositionally transparent. Knowledge of the meaning of the parts does not guarantee understanding that of the whole. But basically, the meaning of the above three templates can be "people characterized by what is expressed in the variable part".

(4)Although P2 is the head in each word, it does not make a substantial contribution to its meaning; a thorough understanding of the exact meaning relies heavily on P1, which plays a pivotal part in terms of meaning contribution. So although P2 is the formal head, semantically speaking, it is only a "dummy head" which tells about a very general categorical meaning.

In the following sections, the patterns shown in (1) will be defined as "lexical templates". We will try to provide explanations for the rest three points.

Unless otherwise specified, all the Chinese examples used in this paper are taken from the closed corpus based on *Chinese New Words 2007-2011*, a total of 2681 words or phrases, of which 1526 are nouns, 233 verbs, 17 adjectives and the rest other types of words or phrases.

2   Lexical Template

2.1   The Notion of Lexical Template

In this paper, a "lexical template" in Chinese is defined as a productive schematic pattern of words or phrases, usually consisting of one open position and one lexically specified part[10]. The open position is called "slot", and the specified part "designator".

---

[10] There may be some other templates in which neither position is lexically specified. For example, XYY is a template in which X is a surname of a person, and YY is the action of the person which is usually decoded as a verb.

Formally, an "X+specified character" format is used to represent the template, hence the three templates in Section 1 are respectively "X男", "X女" and "X族". Semantically, the designator encodes the general categorical meaning, i.e. whether it is a noun or a verb; the actual slot-filling part specifies the idiosyncratic information of the word.

A template is productive because it is very easy to collect a whole bunch of words or phrases generating from a template. For example, we find altogether 212 "X族", 121 "X门(gate)", 63 "X体(genre/style)", 53 "X哥(brother)", 39 "X男", 39 "X女" and 22 "X奴(slave)" words or phrases in the corpus. It is schematic because it is an abstract generalization of a group of words which share the same specified character in the same position, and the same sense relationship between slot and designator. Fill in a word in the slot and we get an output word. The relationship between a template and the output words is one of a schema and instantiations. The output can be either words or phrases, depending on the number of the syllables. The majority of Chinese words are disyllabic, although some trisyllabic combinations are also identified as compounds. If a lexical item has more than three syllables, it is usually considered an idiom or phrase.

There are mainly three types of templates according to the position of the slot—front empty, back empty and middle empty. The table below shows the format of each type of template.

Table 1. Types &Examples of Lexical Templates

Types	Examples of Lexical Templates
Front empty	X哥(*brother*)
	X控(*complex*)
	X门(*gate*)
Middle empty	去(*de-*)X化(*-ation*)
Back empty	微(*Weibo/Microblogging*)X
	秀(*show*)X
	低碳(*low-carbon*)X

This paper focuses on the discussion of templates found in nominal compounds. From all the 1526 compound nouns in our corpus, we find 30 major front empty templates which form 670 nouns, 10 back empty templates which form 155 nouns and no middle empty template. So obviously, front empty templates account for a majority of the templates, or put differently, "modifier + head" pattern is predominant in forming new nominal compounds.

2.2   Previous Studies

Lexical template under discussion is in essence the notion of *Ciyu Mo* (*template for words and phrases*) in Chinese language, which was first put forward by Li Yuming(1999). In his article, Li introduced the notion and talked about characteristics, types and formation of *Ciyu Mo*. He defined *Ciyu Mo* as "a productive model-based device for the formation of new words or phrases, consisting of a *Mobiao(template mark)* and a *Mocao(template slot)*", redefined in this paper as designator and slot respectively.

Following Li, Su Xianghong(2010) conducted a comprehensive study of *Ciyu Mo*. She adopted Li's notion and made some extension. She was the first to point out the phenomenon of clusters of *Ciyu Mo*. For example, "X人(*man*), X民(*citizen*), X领 (*collar*), X客(*-ker*), X达人(*talent*), X族(*clan*), X友(*pal*), X盲(*ignorant person*), X虫 (*worm*), X迷(*addict*), X奴(*slave*)" are all productive people-referring templates in Mandarin Chinese. The specified Chinese characters in each template have a similar meaning—they refer to a group of people or individuals of the group. She also identified one special empty template "XYY" in which both X and Y are variable. The "XYY" form of expression is very common in children's language—the reduplication of "Y" into "YY" usually shows the speaker's affection for the thing/person being talked about or the speaker may try to be childlike. This template is seemingly an imitation of children's language, but the effect may be very different. Although the syntactic relationship between X and YY may vary, words generating from this template generally carry with them a critical, sarcastic or pejorative meaning. The table below summarizes the four subtypes of this template according to the relation between X and YY.

Table 2. Subtypes of XYY

X	YY	Example
subject	predicate	范跑跑[11]
subject	predicate	楼歪歪[12]
verb	object	躲猫猫[13]
modifier	head	鞋带带[14]

Lexical template or *Ciyu Mo* is much the same as the notion of "constructional idioms" in languages such as German, Dutch and English. Constructional idioms are

---

[11] When Wenchuan "5.12" earthquake struck in Sichuan Province in 2008, a teacher surnamed Fan was the first to dash out of his classroom, leaving his class in danger. He was nicknamed "Runner Fan" for this selfish act.

[12] This refers to the fact that two buildings tilted so much as to be very close to each other after a heavy rain in Chengdu, Sichuan Province.

[13] This term originally means a children's game of playing hide-and-seek. It refers here to the police's explanation of a convict's death in a detention center in Yunnan Province, which was finally found due to his fellow inmates' mistreatment and beating for many times.

[14] Literally it means "shoelace". This term also becomes known due to the death of a suspect, who was said by the police to have committed suicide with a shoelace.

morphological or syntactic schemas in which one or more positions are lexically fixed, whereas other positions are open slots, represented by variables (Jackendoff, 2002). Look at the syntactic structure below:

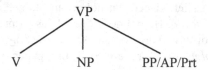

Fig. 1. A Formalization of VP (Jackendoff, 2002)

This structure can be seen as a generalization of all the possible VP structures which may differ only in the parts which are open positions. For example, *take NP to task, V one's heart out, V one's way PP, V NP[time] away* are all cases of constructional idioms of VP(Jackendoff, 2002).

Booij(2010) applied the notion "construction" in morphological analysis and theorizing and developed a theory of construction morphology. In analyzing complex words, Booij(2010) related the notion "construction" to that of "hierarchical lexicon", and argued that both complex words and the abstract schemas that they instantiate must be specified in the lexicon. Accordingly, constructional idioms intermediate between the individually listed words and the very abstract schemas can account for different patterns in morphology. Some researchers have begun to apply the theories of construction morphology in analyzing Chinese compounds, for example Arcodia(2011).

Although much has been done in analyzing the characteristics and formation mechanisms of lexical templates in Chinese, it will be a new attempt to analyze the intrastructure and the meaning of them from a constructional perspective.

3   Predominance of Right-Headed Compound Nouns

As has been noted in Section 2, most nouns in our corpus are of the front empty template, that is, they are right-headed nominal compounds. Words that can fill the slot serve to be modifiers of the designator of the template.

We can identify several explanations in the literature. As was pointed out by Lu Zhiwei(1957), the "modifier + head" type of compound nouns account for a vast majority in endocentric compounds, which in turn account for a vast majority in the commonly used words. Zhou Jian (1991) made a statistical research of the disyllabic compounds in the *Contemporary Chinese Dictionary* and found 43% of the compounds are in the pattern of "modifier + head". And from a dynamic point of view, the majority of newly emergent words are also "modifier + head" compounds. So it is very common in Chinese to form words in a "modifier+head" pattern.

The principle of combining two words arises from the natural human tendency to see a thing similar to another one already existing and at the same time different from it (Marchand, 1969). These compound nouns are mostly names for new things, phenomena and processes, so the naming will draw on the existing names to show the commonalities between the new and the already existing names while emphasizing the idiosyncrasies at the same time. Let's take the template "X男(*man*)" as an example again. The designator "男(*man*)" generally designates the category of the output words, as can be seen in examples in Section 1. We can fill in the "X" position with different words to have different output words, and the difference only consists in the difference of "X". So "凤凰男" and "月亮男"are above all a type of "男(*man*)", and the distinguishing features of the two words are specified by "凤凰"and "月亮" respectively. This is much similar to Marchand's (1969) formula "AB is B". For example, a *steamboat* is a *boat* with *steam* specifying the difference between these two words.

From the statistics in Section 2, we see 670 out of 1520 nouns are generated by front empty templates, which is due to the fact that front empty templates are very suitable for the formation of right-headed words which share the same basic category but vary in specific features.

4   Partial Semantic Compositionality and Transparency

At the beginning of this section, let's first quote Goldberg (2006:5):

> Any linguistic pattern is recognized as a construction as long as some aspect of its form or function is not strictly predictable from its component parts or from other constructions recognized to exist. In addition, patterns are stored as constructions even if they are fully predictable as long as they occur with sufficient frequency.

According to Goldberg, linguistic patterns at different levels and of different complexity can all be regarded as constructions, so it is with lexical templates, because they are also form-meaning pairings. For example, the form "X哥(*brother*)" generally refers to a man with characteristics X, but in concrete words, "哥" will convey some emotional meaning, either admirable or reproachable or neutral, which cannot be predicted from the word itself. The added meaning is achieved through non-compositionally combining "哥" which expresses a categorical meaning and "X" which expresses the marked features that distinguish the "哥" from others. "大衣哥"(*brother in cotton-padded overcoat*) is a peasant singer named Zhu Zhiwen who was wearing a cotton-padded overcoat when attending a singing talent show. "浓烟哥"(*brother in thick smoke*) is a fireman who gave his own smoke mask to a little girl when rescuing residents trapped in a flaming building. "表哥"[15](*watch brother*) refers to a corruption-committing official in Shaanxi Province, who was found to have worn several famous watches on different occasions and was finally removed from his position and convicted. Although these words may have some emotional meaning, we cannot obviously see it from the constituent parts, such as "大衣", "浓烟" and "表", which are neither positive nor negative in meaning. Only when we know the whole

---

[15] Retrieved from http://baike.baidu.com/link?url=rMS2Bf0imXOIQH1H_cSxLlUf62gTfkXN yb81p_3aRgKN04kY_rH5ZzldmyvuME8UdScCRCORWc_ezpsFdSjeJ7zgY3svkrgeD6ZA GcQbJ2ilaEUJpyItj4XWmWpMGtWUKh8tkRtmFgCyxEBLz63qTJGuKlckVsnYEBYCdS EV_qW, 2014-11-28

story related to the word can we fully know the emotional meaning. So the holistic meaning of the words is not the sum of the parts. In this sense, the meaning of the words cannot be decoded compositionally, at least partially not.

As the words that can fill in the "X" position are often used metaphorically or metonymically, the meaning is not transparent to ordinary people. Take the two words "凤凰男"and "孔雀女"as examples again. The Chinese words "凤凰"(*phoenix*)and "孔雀"(*peacock*) are names of birds, but when used to refer to people, they cannot be interpreted literally. There is a well-known Chinese saying, "A golden phoenix flies out of a small mountain valley", which metaphorically describes the case that a person of humble family background leaves his birth place and finally rises to success through his own efforts. So "凤凰" here refers to people having such experiences. Similarly, "孔雀" refers to girls born in the big city but brought up spoilt and arrogant, just as described by the English idiom "as proud as a peacock".

From the analysis above, it can be concluded that such words as listed above do not always have compositionally transparent meaning. So it is not very easy to know the meaning of the whole word simply based on the meaning of the template and the parts; a full knowledge of the meaning depends on one's understanding the origin and source of each word. Thus, it is also a support of the central idea of hierarchical lexicon: both the individual words and the template which is a schema should be simultaneously listed in the lexicon (Booij, 2010).

5   Semantic Contribution of the Head

Booij(2013) used the schema below to summarize the form-meaning correspondence that holds for English right-headed compounds:

$$[X_i Y_j]_{Yk} \quad \Longleftrightarrow \quad [SEM_{Yj} \text{ with relation R to } SEM_{Xi}]_k$$

Fig. 2. A Schema for Right-Headed Compounds

This is a very typical schema in the framework of construction morphology which schematizes a word-formation pattern as a form-meaning pairing. In this schema, on the left of the arrow is the form of a compound which is composed of two parts X and Y. On the right of the arrow is the semantic representation of the word. Booij (2013) further explained that "the schema expresses that the formal head of the compound is also its semantic head". The following is his detailed analysis:

> A *windmill*, for instance, is a type of *mill*, not a type of *wind*, and it denotes a *mill* which has some semantic relation with the left constituent wind, namely 'powered by'. This specific interpretation of the relation variable R is provided by conceptual and encyclopedic knowledge, and is conventionalized for existing, listed compounds. (p.260)

This is similar to Haspelmath's(2002) analysis of compounds. He held that "the first compound member generally serves to modify and narrow the denotation of the second compound member". For example, "a lipstick is a special kind of stick (not a special kind of lip)". So "semantically the second member is in this sense more important"; it is "the head of the compound", and the modifying element is called the "dependent".

Dong Xiufang(2004) also gave a lot of examples to illustrate her *Cifa Moshi* (morphological rules) for forming compound nouns in Chinese language. For example, the pattern "X(noun or verb)+声(*sound*)" is a rule (a front empty template in our analysis) for describing the sound of X or sound related to the action X. In compound nouns such as "风声"(*sound of wind*), "笑声"(*laughter*) and "摩擦声"(*scraping sound*), "声" is the head, while "风", "笑" and "摩擦" are either nouns or verbs.   So, whatever category X is, it is actually the head that determines the category and the basic meaning of the word. Marchand (1969) termed the relationship between modifier and head as a "determinant/determinum" relationship. The determinum is the head, the determinant being the modifier expressing the idiosyncratic information that distinguishes the word from all the other words having the same determinum.

We agree with these researchers on the dual role of the head, both formally and semantically, but we have some new findings. Examining the meaning of the compounds in our corpus, we find we cannot fully understand the words listed in Section 1, even if we know the meaning of the head words "男", "女" and "族" very well. For a complete understanding of the words, we need to know more than the meaning of the head. The modifier "X" seems to contribute a bigger part to the meaning than the head. Therefore, in terms of meaning contribution, the head is only a dummy one. The semantic focus or weight falls on the modifier rather than the head.

True that from the word *windmill* we know that it is a *mill* rather than a *wind*, but just knowing the categorical meaning doesn't help much to the full understanding of the word; it is the modifier that carries a bigger weight than the head.

6   Concluding Remarks

In this paper, we examined the lexical template identified from Chinese neologisms in recent years. Our attention is focused on the front empty templates of right-headed nominal compounds. These templates are schematic constructions which do not have a compositionally transparent meaning which can be explained in their constructional nature and the different contribution of the modifier and the head. Other types of templates will be studied in future researches.

Acknowledgements. I would like to express my grateful thanks to Prof. Weiyou Zhang, my supervisor, for his guidance and suggestions. The responsibility of the faults, if any, is entirely my own.

References

1. Arcodia, G.: A Construction Morphology Account of Derivation in Mandarin Chinese. Morphology **21**(1), 89–130 (2011)
2. Booij, G.: Morphology in Construction Grammar. In: Hoffmann, T., Trousdale, G. (eds.) The Oxford Handbook of Construction Grammar, pp. 255–273. Oxford University Press, Oxford (2013)
3. Booij, G.: Construction Morphology. Oxford University Press, Oxford (2010)
4. Chinese Academy of Social Sciences Research Institutes of Language Department of Dictionary. Xiandai Hanyu Cidian, 6th edn. The Commercial Press, Beijing (2012)
5. Dong, X.: Chinese Lexicon and Morphology. Peking University Press, Beijing (2004)
6. Goldberg, A.E.: Constructions at Work: The Nature of Generalization in Language. Oxford University Press, Oxford (2006)
7. Haspelmath, M.: Understanding morphology. Arnold (Co-published by Oxford University Press), London (2002)
8. Hou, M., Zhou, J.: Chinese New Words 2007. The Commercial Press, Beijing (2008)
9. Hou, M., Zhou, J.: Chinese New Words 2008. The Commercial Press, Beijing (2009)
10. Hou, M., Zhou, J.: Chinese New Words 2009. The Commercial Press, Beijing (2010)
11. Hou, M., Zhou, J.: Chinese New Words 2010. The Commercial Press, Beijing (2011)
12. Hou, M., Zhou, J.: Chinese New Words 2011. The Commercial Press, Beijing (2012)
13. Jackendoff, R.: Foundations of Language. Oxford University Press, Oxford (2002)
14. Li, Y.: Ciyu Mo. In: Xing, F. (ed.) Aspects of the Characteristics of Chinese grammar, pp. 146–157. Beijing Language and Culture University Press, Beijing (1999)
15. Lu, Z.: Chinese Morphology. Science Press, Beijing (1964). (revised edition)
16. Marchand, H.: The Categories and Types of Present-Day English Word-Formation: A Synchronic-Diachronic Approach, 2nd edn. C.H. Beck'sche Verlagsbuchhandlung, München (1969)
17. Su, X.: A Study of Ciyu Mo in Contemporary Chinese. Zhejiang University Press, Hangzhou (2010)
18. Zhou, J.: Meaning structure and relations between constituents of compounds. Language Studies, vol. 6. Tianjin Education Press, Tianjin (1991)

The Study on the Noun-Locative Combination from the Perspective of Nouns' Properties

Qiang Li[✉]

Department of Chinese Language and Literature, Peking University, Beijing 100871, China
leeqiang2222@163.com

Abstract. The noun-locative combination is restricted by the semantic properties of nouns, which has been discussed by some scholars. However, these discussions are not adequate and have problems. This paper points out the problems and argues that spatiality, nature, state and temporality of nouns have an important influence on the noun-locative combination. Specifically, the combination ability between spatial nouns and spatial locatives is strong; nouns with strong temporality and state can be easily combined with temporal locatives; nouns with strong nature cannot be combined with spatial and temporal locatives.

Keywords: Locative · Noun · Spatiality · Nature · State · Temporality

1 Introduction

The noun-locative combination has been discussed by some scholars. There are two research orientations about the discussion: a. study the collocation of nouns with one or more locatives or with a class of locatives, and investigate the noun-locative combination on the semantic properties; b. discuss the noun-locative combination on the whole and study whether the combination is restricted by some factors. This paper mainly discusses the latter case. On the basis of the existing results, I argue that whether nouns can be combined with locatives and which locatives nouns can be followed by are constrained by the intrinsic semantic properties of nouns.

2 A Review on Some Research Results

As to the selection of nouns on locatives, Chu (1995, 2003) pointed out that not all nouns can be located before locatives as a referent. That is to say, there is a property restriction of locatives on nouns. He argues that properties of nature and state can be found on the entities referred by nouns. State is the basis of spatiality, for example, "山 (*mountain*), 城 (*city*), 桥 (*bridge*)" are nouns with strong state, so they can be

---

This research is sponsored by the National Social Science Fund Major Project "Chinese parataxis characteristic research and large knowledge base and corpus construction under the background of international Chinese language education" (Approval No.: 12&ZD175). We hereby express our sincere thanks.

Q. Lu and H.H. Gao (Eds.): CLSW 2015, LNAI 9332, pp. 329–339, 2015.
DOI: 10.1007/978-3-319-27194-1_33

followed by locatives, while "小李 (*Xiao Li*), 司令 (*commander*), 雷 (*thunder*), 老虎 (*tiger*)" are nouns with strong nature, so they cannot be followed by locatives. Besides, he indicates that it is a continuum between nature and state of nouns. Therefore, the combination ability between nouns and locatives is different. He attempts to build the corresponding relation as follows.

- State and nature of nouns: strong nature ⟷ strong state
- Semantic feature of nouns: [+life] ⟷ [-life]
- Selection ability of nouns on locatives: weak ⟷ strong

The viewpoints in Chu (1995, 2003) can be summarized in one sentence: the stronger the state of nouns, the stronger the combination ability between them and locatives; on the contrary, the stronger the nature of nouns, the weaker the combination ability between them and locatives.

On the basis of relevant language facts, I think that several viewpoints in Chu (1995, 2003) deserve further discussion. Firstly, that article points out that "山 (*mountain*), 城 (*city*), 桥 (*bridge*)" are nouns with strong state, while "小李 (*Xiao Li*), 司令 (*commander*), 青蛙 (*frog*), 雷 (*thunder*)" are nouns of strong nature. Besides, the article argues that the reason why "小李 (*Xiao Li*), 司令 (*commander*), 青蛙 (*frog*)" cannot be combined with spatial locatives is that the nature meaning exists in these nouns. However, there are several doubts in the above statements: a. the nature meaning of "小李 (*Xiao Li*), 司令 (*commander*), 青蛙 (*frog*)" cannot be accurately grasped. Meanwhile, the state meaning of "山 (*mountain*), 城 (*city*), 桥 (*bridge*)" cannot also be explained; b. what's more, the reason why "小李 (*Xiao Li*), 司令 (*commander*), 青蛙 (*frog*)" cannot be with spatial locatives is constrained by syllable numbers. If locatives are disyllabic, then the combination ability will improve. Take "小李 (*Xiao Li*), 司令 (*commander*)" for example:

1. 小李　前面　　放着　一张　桌子。
   xiaoli front   lay   a   table
   "There is a table in front of Xiao Li."
   小李　　后面　　停着　　一辆　　车。
   xiaoli   behind   pack   a   car
   "There is a car behind Xiao Li."
   他　用　　手　　指着　　小李　　东边。
   he use hand point xiaoli east
   "He is pointing at the east of Xiao Li."
2. 司令　　前面　站着　　一排　士兵。
   commander front stand row   soldier
   "A row of soldiers stood in front of the commander."
   司令　　　后面　背着　一杆　枪。
   commander behind carry a   gun
   "The commander is carrying a gun on his back."
   军队　　部署　在　司令　　北面。
   army   deploy in commander north
   "The army is deployed to the north of the commander."

Through observing the above sentences, we can find that "小李 (*Xiao Li*), 司令 (*commander*)" cannot be combined with spatial locatives is not due to their nature meaning, but subjected to the prosodic pattern. If the prosodic requirements are satisfied, these nouns can also be combined with locatives.

Secondly, the method distinguishing the nature meaning and state meaning of nouns suggested in the article is using "全 (*all*), 满 (*full*)" as modifiers to modify nouns. If nouns can be modified by them, then the state of nouns is strong, and if not, then the nature is strong. Nevertheless, using "全 (*all*), 满 (*full*)" as a verification has problems. Take "天 (*sky*), 地 (*ground*)" and "山 (*mountain*), 城 (*city*)" as examples, these nouns can be modified by "全 (*all*), 满 (*full*)":

3. 全 (*all*)

半人马星座　是　全　天　　最　亮　　的　球状　　星团。
Centaurus　is　all　sky　most　bright　DE　ball　star-cluster
"Centaurus is the brightest ball star-cluster in the sky."

他们　上来　　遍满了　全　地，　围住　　圣徒　　的　　营。
they　come up　full　　all　ground　surround　believer　DE　camp
"They came up, full of the ground, and surrounded the believers' camp."

灵峰、　　灵岩、　大龙湫　为　全　　山　　风景　　中心。
lingfeng, lingyan, dalongqiu are all mountain scenery center.
"Lingfeng, lingyan and dalongqiu are the center of the sceneries in the entire mountain."

187米　　的　　开罗塔　　高高地　俯瞰着　全　　城。
187meter　DE　Cairo Tower　high　overlook　all　city
"Cairo Tower of 187 meters highly overlooks the entire city."

4. 满 (*full*)

满　天　繁星　构成了　一幅　　美丽　　的　　银河　图景。
full　sky　star　make　a　　beautiful　DE　galaxy　scenery
"Stars in the sky make a beautiful galaxy scenery."

风化　　下来　　的　云母　碎片　满　地　　可见。
weathering　down　DE　mica　debris　full　ground　visible
"The mica debris due to the weathering is visible on the full ground."

满　　山　　　遍野　　都　是　绿色。
full　mountain　all over the fields　all　is　　green
"Green is on the full mountain and all over the fields."

清凉　　的　　夜风　　吹过，满　城　都　是　花　香。
cool　　DE　night wind　blow　full　city　all　is　flower fragrance
"After the cool night wind blows, the city is full of the flower fragrance."

As we see, both "天(*sky*), 地(*ground*)" and "山(*mountain*), 城(*city*)" can be modified by "满"(*full*) and "全"(*all*), then there should be strong state in these nouns, and their combination ability with locatives should be the same. However, it is not the case. "天(*sky*), 地(*ground*)" can only be combined with "上(*above*), 下(*below*)", and the combination ability between them and locatives is far less than that between "山 (*mountain*), 城(*city*)" and locatives.

Moreover, the state meaning does not exist in all nouns which can be modified by "满(*full*), 全(*all*)", and the state meaning belongs to the whole structure "满(*full*)/全 (*all*)+NP". For instance:

5. 薛姑娘　　就喜欢　看着　满　桌子　好　菜　　喝　　酒。
　　Xue girl　　like　　look　full　table good　　food　drink　wine
　　"*Xue likes drinking wine looking at the good food full on the table.*"
　　全　桌子　　的　　气氛　　　都　稍稍　　轻松下来。
　　all　table　　DE　atmosphere　all　little　　relax
　　"*The atmosphere around the table is slightly relaxed.*"

6. 这　满　屋子　的　书　才是　真正　的　　财富呀，一辈子　都受用不尽的。
　　this full house DE book　is　　real　DE　wealth　　all the life　beneficial
　　"*The books full of the house are the real wealth, and beneficial for all the life.*"
　　全　　屋子　的　　人　都　转过来　望　　他。
　　full　house　DE　people　all　turn　look at　he
　　"*The people in the house all turned to look at him.*"

Even though "桌子(*table*), 屋子(*house*)" in the above sentences can be modified by "满(*full*), 全(*all*)", we cannot judge that the state meaning exists in these nouns. Shi (2001) pointed out that there are two kinds of semantic constituents in the meaning of nouns: one is aboutness semantic constituent and the other is descriptive semantic constituent. Aboutness semantic constituent exists in nouns like "桌子(*table*), 屋子(*house*)", which is the objective content illustrating and limiting the connotation of nouns, such as possession, structure, material and telic. The nature and state meaning do not exist in nouns referring to entities like "桌子(*table*), 屋子(*house*)". However, the state meaning of "满/全 (*full/all*) +NP" is obviously due to the adverbs "满/全 (*full/all*)", but not the NP. Yuan (2004) has explained the differences on meaning and usage of "满"(*full*) and "全"(*all*) through container metaphor and set metaphor. He mentioned that the reason why "满"(*full*) can modify "桌子/屋子"(*table/house*) is that an image schema about a container is activated by "满"(*full*). That is to say, in our conceptual frame, we consider the entities referring by concrete nouns and abstract nouns as entities with clear boundaries. Besides, he used the semantic expression below to describe the phrase "满桌子糖果 (*candies full of the table*)":

"table" is a container, "candies" are the entities in the container; "candies" are on the "table";
there is a table, all the "candies" are on the "table";
there are many subspaces on the "table", "candies" have many subsets;
there are some "candies" in the every subspace of the "table".

Thereinto, the "full" meaning of the word "满"(*full*) is in the last sentence of the above semantic expression. In other words, the state meaning of "满"(*full*) is presented by this scenery. Similarly, the state meaning of "全" (*all*) can be explained in the same way.

Thus it can be seen that there is a doubt to verify state and nature of nouns by "满/全"(*full/all*). The state meaning of "满/全 (*full/all*)+NP" is not expressed by NP, but through the semantic scenery of "满/全"(*full/all*). Then, is there a difference between state and nature of nouns? I argue that this difference indeed exists, but not as Chu's opinion that "山(*mountain*), 城(*city*), 桥(*bridge*)" are nouns with strong state, while "小李(*xiao Li*), 青蛙(*frog*), 司令(*commander*)" are nouns with strong nature. Besides, except for nature and state, spatiality and temporality exist in nouns. All these four properties have effects on the noun-locative combination.

3   Spatiality, Nature, State and Temporality

The basic and prototype property of nouns is spatiality. Chen (1998) referred that "as to the typical entities, they always occupy some space and own some characteristics such as big/small, high/low, thick/thin……the grammatical meaning of nouns relates to the space and location. We recognize kinds of state in spatial distribution of entities and understand the role of these nouns in specific scenery on the basis of grammatical forms." Nevertheless, in the category of nouns, there are some variations. The spatial property of nouns may not be obvious. Taylor (1989) summed up the typical characteristics of nouns: discrete, tangible, three-dimensional entity > non-spatial entity > collective entity > abstract entity. On this chain, the spatiality of nouns is stronger on left, while weaker on the right. On the level of abstract entity, because of no spatiality, a functional deviation may happen, and nouns can transform to adjectives and verbs. Zhang & Fang (1996) indicated that the function of nouns can dissociate in some cases, and nouns can develop into adjectives or verbs. They built the following path: noun > non-predicate adjective > adjective > intransitive verb > transitive verb (> means "develop into"). For instance (cited from Zhang & Fang 1996:212):

- nouns used as non-predicate adjective:
  义务劳动(*obligatory labor*), 专业水平(*expertise level*), 学院风格(*college style*), 嘉宾主持(*guest host*), 友情演出(*friendship performance*)
- nouns used as adjective:
  假装特学问(*pretend to have knowledge*), 话说得有点痞(*words are a little ruffian*), 做派那叫款(*behavior is sincere*), 怎那么事儿呀(*how is going on*)
- nouns used as intransitive verb:
  还权威着呢(*authorized*), 咱们民主民主(*democratic*), 这回可真坛子胡同了(*jar/hutong*), 褶子了(*pleat*)
- nouns used as transitive:
  结论不出我什么东西来(*make no conclusions about me*), 他爱醋谁醋谁，也醋不着我呀(*no matter who he is jealous of, I am not envied*)

From the above examples, we can find that spatiality does not exist in nouns that can transform to non-predicate adjectives and adjectives, which is the type of abstract entity that Taylor argues. Conversely, strong nature exists in these nouns, which is the semantic basis of transforming to non-predicate adjectives and adjectives.

Except for nature, the state meaning exists in nouns. Wang (2001) pointed out that people and things as entities can show different state, and then the nouns referring to them can show different state meaning. Besides, there is a close relation between nature and state meaning of nouns. Zhang (2007) also indicated that the establishment of nature (property) is the generalizing result of relevant state and it is a typical category. Nature exists in state, and there is no nature which can separate from state. The relation between nature and state is like that between language and speech. The variation of speech can derive the evolution of language or affect the property of language. Hence, it is difficult to draw a distinction between nature and state meaning of nouns. Nevertheless, there are some significant differences. Zhang (2006) argued that both nature and state are static, and the difference between them lies in the presence of timeliness. Nature represents permanence, while state represents temporary. I think there is also a difference between nature and state meaning of nouns with regard to time. That is to say, if strong nature exists in nouns, then the nature must be permanent; on the contrary, if strong state exists in nouns, then the state must be temporary. Compare the examples below:

- 典型(*prototype*) 威风(*prestige*) 热情(*enthusiasm*) 权威(*authority*) 汉奸(*traitor*) 流氓(*rogue*) 内行(*adept*) 学者(*scholar*) 模范(*model*) 傻瓜(*fool*)
- 暴雨(*rainstorm*) 阵雨(*shower*) 急病(*acute disease*) 高烧(*high fever*) 低烧(*low fever*) 狂风(*gale*) 强震(*strong shock*) 强风(*strong breeze*) 高温(*high temperature*)

The nature meaning exists in nouns in the first group. For instance, the nature of "典型" (*prototype*) is having representativeness; the nature of "威风" (*prestige*) is making people fear; the nature of "流氓" (*rogue*) is deploying dirty means, acting in a rascally manner. These natures exist in the meanings of nouns. They are stable and not easy to change over time. The state meaning exists in nouns in the second group. For instance, the state of "暴雨" (*rainstorm*) is heavy and fierce; the state of "急病" (*acute disease*) is sudden; the state of "强震" (*strong shock*) is strong power. These states are not stable and can change over time. Zhang (2006) further pointed out that the distinction of nature and state is the result of different image schemes in people's cognitive world. According to Langacker (1987), there are two different scanning ways for people to recognize things or actions. One is summary scanning and the other is sequential scanning. Objects are perceived as a whole in the summary scanning but the constituents are ignored. On the contrary, the constituents of objects are highlighted in the sequential scanning and a constituent after another is orderly processed. As to nature, Zhang thought it is the result of summary scanning and has nothing to do with time, while state is the result of sequential scanning and has temporality. The state instability of nouns can explain why nouns with state own quantative feature. For instance:

- 小雨(*light rain*)—中雨(*moderate rain*)—大雨(*heavy rain*)—暴雨(*rainstorm*)
- 阵雨(*shower*)—几个小时的雨(*rain of a few hours*)—一天的雨(*rain of a day*)
- 小病(*indisposition*)—大病(*serious illness*)—重病(*serious disease*)
- 低烧(*low fever*)—高烧(*high fever*)
- 低温(*low temperature*)—高温(*high temperature*)

State exists in these nouns, which is instable. They can change with time and constitute a quantity shaft of extension, and show the characteristic of a certain magnitude.

To sum up, I argue that the nature and state of nouns can be distinguished by [±time] and [±stability]. The strong stability exists in nouns with nature, and these nouns do not show temporality; the weak stability exists in nouns with state, and these nouns show temporality. It can be expressed as:

	time	stability
nouns of nature	-	+
nouns of state	+	-

Givón(1979,1984) argued that the main grammatical form classes reflect the temporal stability of perceived phenomenon. On this basis, he established a continuum of "noun-adjective-verb". Thereinto, nouns are stable and do not change with time; verbs are instable and change with time easily; adjectives are in the middle. This can be represented as figure 1 below.

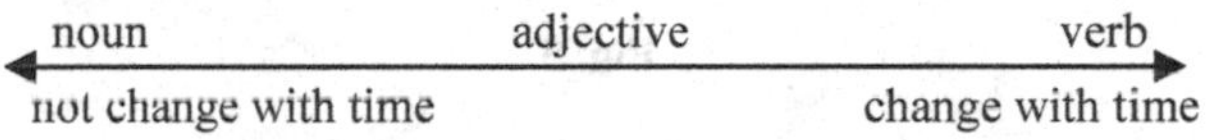

noun   adjective   verb

not change with time   change with time

Fig. 1

According to my understanding of nouns' properties, nouns in the above figure can be further refined, which is shown as figure 2.

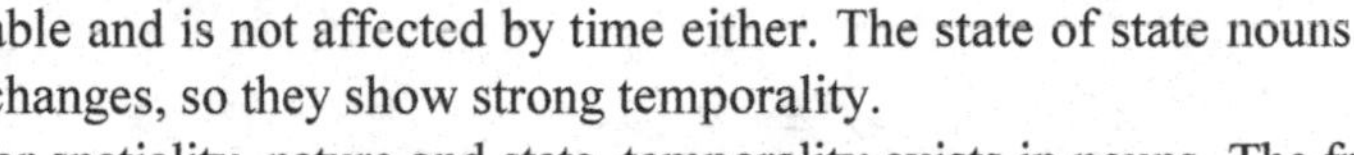

spatial noun   nature noun   state noun

no temporality   no temporality   strong temporality

Fig. 2

Entities represented by spatial nouns always occupy certain space. This class of nouns does not show temporality and is not affected by time. The nature of nature nouns is stable and is not affected by time either. The state of state nouns is temporal and easily changes, so they show strong temporality.

Except for spatiality, nature and state, temporality exists in nouns. The fruits of studying on the temporality of nouns are rich, such as Han (2004, 2006, 2007), Lu (2012), Zhong (2010). These nouns with temporality are called "event nouns" in some literatures, which always represent events. As we know, temporality exists in events. Hence, event nouns show process and tractility. In most cases, event nouns always occur with verbal measure words, time measure words and verbs containing time. For instance:

7. 梅雨　　　已经　持续　了　三　天　三　夜。
plum rains　already　last　LE　three　day　three night
"The plum rains already lasts for three days and nights."

8. 这场 旷日持久 的 战争 给 双方 造成 了 巨大 的 伤亡。
　　this prolonged DE war give both sides cause LE huge DE casualty
　　"*This prolonged war caused huge casualties for both sides.*"

9. 这顿 晚餐 吃 了 三个 小时。
　　this dinner eat LE three hour
　　"*This dinner lasted for three hours.*"

10. 两 天 小雪 之后 是 一个 晴天。
　　two day light snow after is a fine
　　"*After two days of light snow, it turned fine.*"

From the sentences above, we can see that event nouns show strong temporality. If these nouns are put in the time chain, they should be on the rightmost position, which can be represented as figure3:

spatial noun	nature noun	state noun	event noun
no temporality	no temporality	strong temporality	strongest temporality
spatiality		no spatiality	

Fig. 3

In conclusion, I argue that nouns can be divided into spatial nouns, nature nouns, state nouns and event nouns. These four kinds correspond to different temporality respectively. Meanwhile, spatial nouns have the typical feature of spatiality, because they refer to concrete entities and can be as referents to determine the spatial orientation. Nature nouns, state nouns and event nouns do not show spatiality, because they represent abstract entities and cannot be as referents to determine the spatial orientation.

4　The Effect of Nouns' Properties on the Noun-Locative Combination

First, let's make a brief analysis on the table below:

		上(面)	下(面)	前(面)	后(面)	左(边)	右(边)	里(面)	外(面)	内	中	东(边)	西(边)	南(边)	北(边)
A	山	+	+	+	+	+	+	+	+	+	+	+	+	+	+
	桥	+	+	+	+	+	+	+	+	+	+	+	+	+	+
	大楼	+	+	+	+	+	+	+	+	+	+	+	+	+	+
B	热情	-	-	-	-	-	-	+	-	-	+	-	-	-	-
	汉奸	-	-	-	-	-	-	+	-	-	+	-	-	-	-
	贵族	-	-	-	-	-	-	+	-	-	+	-	-	-	-
C	暴雨	-	-	+	+	-	-	+	-	-	+	-	-	-	-
	狂风	-	-	+	+	-	-	+	-	-	+	-	-	-	-
	高温	-	-	+	+	-	-	+	-	-	+	-	-	-	-
D	比赛	-	-	+	+	-	-	+	-	-	+	-	-	-	-
	会议	+	-	+	+	-	-	+	-	-	+	-	-	-	-
	地震	-	-	+	+	-	-	+	-	-	+	-	-	-	-

In the table, group A, B, C, D respectively represents spatial nouns, nature nouns, state nouns and event nouns. Thereinto, entities referred by nouns in group A occupy certain space, so there is a strong combination between these nouns and spatial locatives, and all the locatives in the table can collocate with them. Affected by prosody, some disyllable words cannot be combined with monosyllable words, for example, "大楼上"(*on the building*) is ungrammatical. However, it does not mean that "大楼"(*building*) cannot be followed by locatives. If the locative is disyllable word "上面"(*above*), "大楼"(*building*) can also be combined with it, for instance, "大楼上面"(*on the building*) is grammatical. Nouns in group B do not show spatiality and the temporality of them is also weak. Then, the combination ability between them and locatives is weak. Nevertheless, under the mechanism of metaphor, nouns in group B can be combined with "里"(*in*) and "中"(*in*). In this case, the nature meaning of these nouns is not highlighted. For instance, in the sentence form "汉奸中/里也有一些有良心的人"(*there are some conscientious people in traitors.*), we consider the noun "汉奸"(*traitor*) as a kind of people, but not highlight the property of their baseness, shameless and dirty. Under the mechanism of "container metaphor", people of the same feature are easily considered as a container of clear boundary. Just because of this, nature nouns can be followed by "里"(*in*) and "中"(*in*). State exists in nouns in group C, which is always connected with time. Then they can be combined with temporal locatives "(之)前"(*before*) and "(之)后"(*after*). Because spatiality does not exist in them, spatial locatives cannot be combined with them. But we can imagine that when we are under the environment of raining, blowing and high temperature, we will have a feeling that surrounded by rain and hot air. Hence, we can regard these nouns as an abstract entity with internal space. They can be combined with spatial locatives "里"(*in*) and "中"(*in*). Nouns in group D have the feature of strong temporality and contain a procedural event. So this kind of nouns can be combined with temporal locatives "(之)前"(*before*), "(之)后"(*after*) and "中"(*in*). Because they do not show spatiality, they cannot be combined with spatial locatives. However, an event has a temporal beginning and terminal, which can be regarded as a closed and bounded object. Therefore, they own the feature of space-like. Thus, nouns like "比赛"(*match*), "会议"(*meeting*) and "地震"(*earthquake*) can be combined with "里(面)"(*in*).

The basic function of locatives is spatial and temporal orientation based on the entity referred by nouns as referents. Locatives can be divided into spatial locatives and temporal locatives. Based on the table above and fig.3, the combination between nouns and locatives can be summarized as:

- When nouns refer to a concrete object of occupying space, the combination ability with spatial locatives is the strongest, because on the basis of physical entities, we can discuss the spatial location. When nouns' spatial feature is weak and temporality feature is strong, the combination ability between nouns and spatial locatives is weak, but the ability of them with temporal locatives is strong.
- Nature nouns do not show spatiality and temporality. Thus they cannot be combined with spatial and temporal locatives.

- The temporal feature of state nouns and event nouns is strong. Therefore, they can be combined with temporal locatives. Because spatiality does not exist in these nouns, they cannot be combined with spatial locatives.
- Through the cognitive mechanism of metaphor, nature nouns, state nouns and event nouns can be considered as entities with internal space, so they can be combined with some spatial locatives.

5   Conclusion

Chu (1995, 2003) put forward the noun-locative combination rule: the stronger the state feature of nouns is, the stronger the combination ability is; on the contrary, the stronger the nature feature of nouns is, the weaker the combination ability is. I think the property of nouns should be analyzed, on the basis of which the combination between nouns and locatives is investigated. The semantic features of nouns affect the noun-locative combination. Nouns with strong spatiality can be combined with spatial locatives easily. Nouns with strong temporality and state can be combined with temporal locatives easily. If there is a strong nature in nouns, namely the feature of spatiality and temporality is weak, and then the combination ability between these nouns and locatives is weak. This can be seen not only as the general rule of noun-locative combination, but also as the general trend of the bidirectional semantic choice between nouns and locatives.

References

1. Givón, T.: On Understanding Grammar. Academic Press, New York (1979)
2. Givón, T.: Syntax-A functional typological introduction. John Benjamins, Amsterdam (1984)
3. Langacker, R.W.: Foundations of Cognitive Grammar, vol. 1. Stanford University Press, Stanford (1987)
4. Taylor, J.R.: Linguistic Categorization: Prototypes in Linguistic Theory. Clarendon press, Oxford (1989)
5. Chen, P.: The Tripartite-structure of Temporal System in Modern Chinese. Studies of the Chinese Language 6, 401 – 421 (1988). (论现代汉语时间系统的三元结构, 中国语文, 1988(6): 401 – 421) (in Chinese)
6. Chu, Z.: Latent Form of Noun in Modern Chinese—about Studying Locative after Noun. Research in Ancient Chinese Language. Supplementary Issue, 48 – 53(1995). (现代汉语名词的潜形态—关于名词后添加方位词情况的考察,古汉语研究, 1995, 增刊:48 – 53) (in Chinese)
7. Chu, Z.: Study on the Location System in Modern Chinese. Central China Normal University Press, Wuhan (2003). (现代汉语方所系统研究,武汉:华中师范大学出版社, 2003) (in Chinese)
8. Chu, Z.: Study on Spatial Phrases in Chinese. Peking University Press, Beijing (2010). (汉语空间短语研究,北京:北京大学出版社, 2010) (in Chinese)
9. Han, L.: An Analysis of Event Nouns in Modern Chinese. Journal of East China Normal University (Philosophy and Social Sciences) 5, 106–113 (2004). (in Chinese)

10. Han, L.: Semantic Basis and Relevant Sentence Pattern of the Event Nouns. Studies in Language and Linguistics **3**, 26–29 (2006). (in Chinese)
11. Han, L.: The Selection of Event Nouns and Classifiers—A Case Study of "Yu" (雨). Journal of East China Normal University (Philosophy and Social Sciences) **3**, 64–68 (2007). (in Chinese)
12. Lu, B.: The semantic characteristics of event nouns in Chinese and English. Contemporary Linguistics **1**, 1–11 (2012). (in Chinese)
13. Shi, C.: The descriptive features of nouns and the probability of adverbs modifying nouns. Studies of the Chinese Language **3**, 212–224 (2001). (in Chinese)
14. Wang, J.: Study on Nouns in Modern Chinese. East China Normal University Press, Shanghai (2001). (现代汉语名词研究,上海:华东师范大学出版社, 2001) (in Chinese)
15. Yuan, Y.: On some grammatical phenomenon related to container metaphor and set metaphor: towards a cognitive explanation and a computational analysis of co-occurrence restriction of words. Studies of the Chinese Language **3**, 195–208 (2004). (in Chinese)
16. Zhang, B.: Study on the dissociation of nouns' function. In: Shao, J. (ed.) Semantic Study in Syntax Structure, pp. 30‒39. Beijing Language and Culture University Press, Beijing (1998). (名词功能游离研究,邵敬敏主编《句法结构中的语义研究》30‒39页,北京语言文化大学出版社, 1998) (in Chinese)
17. Zhang, B., Fang, M.: Functional Studies of Chinese Grammar. Jiangxi Educational Publishing House, Nanchang (1996). (in Chinese)
18. Zhang, G.: Attribute State and Change. Language Teaching and Linguistic Studies **3**, 2–11 (2006). (in Chinese)
19. Zhang, G.: On the Mirror Image of the Semantic Features of the Sub-categories of Adjectives. Chinese Linguistics **2**, 31–36 (2007). (in Chinese)
20. Zhong, M.: Study on Event Noun in Chinese and English. MA thesis of Nanchang university (2010). (in Chinese)

On the Interaction Between the Structure and the Prosody of Chinese 1 + 3 Idioms

Jianfei Luo[✉]

Beijing Language and Culture University, Beijing, China
nch1980s@163.com

Abstract. Most four-syllable Chinese idioms are in the structure of first two syllables sharing inter-relationship and the other two syllables sharing idiomatic structural interaction (thereafter, 2 + 2 structure), while some asymmetry idioms mainly refer to those with the first one syllable working independently and the other three syllables expressing idiomatic relation (thereafter 1 + 3 structure). It is interesting that the latter can also be transferred to 2 + 2 structure once affected by the prosody. In this paper, under the related principles of prosodic morphology and prosodic syntax, idiomatic structural analyses are made on 1 + 3 structure, which syntactically cover the structure of adverbial-verb, subject-predicator, verb-object, verb-complement and adjective-complement, to explore how they can be transformed to 2 + 2 structure in prosody and what will be the aftermath of this transformation.

Keywords: 1 + 3 asymmetry idioms · Prosodic morphology · Prosodic syntax · Reanalysis

1   Introduction

Chinese idioms are mainly extracted from ancient cultural classics and poems. These idioms can be summaries of the historical facts, narration of ancient wars, significant plots of legendary stories, extracts from articles and poetry implications, or just folk tales. Endowed with these cultural traits and historical connotations, Chinese idioms can be settled down in a brief and fixed way, which, together with their harmonious prosody, convey diverse language information.

In most Chinese idioms, the first two words dependently relate while the other two words work in prosody, as well as in structure, such as 铜墙铁壁[*tong qiang tie bi*](*bastion of iron: impregnable fortress*), 干柴烈火[*gan chai lie huo*](*(like) a blazing fire and dry wood*). Feng (2009) pointed out, in an analysis to the prosody of Chinese idioms, that in the prosody many Chinese idioms are in "weak-strong-weak-strong" mode, such as 守株待兔[*shou zhu dai tu*](*stand by a tree stump waiting for a hare*) (figure 1). However, it can be figured out that some idioms are not in the structure of 2+2 independently, but they are in 2+2 prosodic structure, such as 一衣带水 [*yi yi dai shui*](*be joined by a strip of water*). Therefore there are conflicts between structure and prosody. How to solve these conflicts is the focus of this thesis.

© Springer International Publishing Switzerland 2015
Q. Lu and H.H. Gao (Eds.): CLSW 2015, LNAI 9332, pp. 340–351, 2015.
DOI: 10.1007/978-3-319-27194-1_34

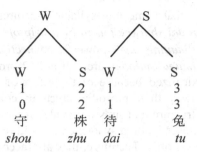

Fig. 1. the stress structure of the 守株待兔[shou zhu   dai tu](stand by a tree stump waiting for a hare)

2   Literature Review

Shi(1995) focused on asymmetry idioms. Phonological prosody of 1+3 structures and 3+1 structures were discussed in his essay. He made a further analysis and pointed out that most Chinese idioms with four syllables are in the form of 2+2 prosodic structure, even though some idioms are structurally 1+3, such as 好为人师[*hao wei ren shi*](*be fond of teaching others*), 遥相呼应[*yao xiang hu ying*](*echo each other at a distance*), 学以致用 [*xue yi zhi yong*](*learn to practise*), 掩人耳目 [*yan ren er mu*](*deceive the public*), 成人之美[*cheng ren zhi mei*](*aid sb. in doing a good deed*). Main reason for this is that the last two syllables reached a consensus in structures and prosody; and worked together in unity, so that the second syllable could do nothing but attach the first syllable to form a prosodic word (thereafter, PrWd). Namely, the last two syllables firstly form a PrWd, whereas the other two syllables are compelled to form another PrWd.

Centering on 1+3 and 3+1 phonetic segments of idioms under the structure of verb-objective and adjective-complement, Ju (1995) pointed out that the middle part among the four syllables plays a pivotal role in phonetic combination. When components of the middle part are disyllabic, which is closely related to each other in meaning, the phonetic combination for verb-objective structure will be 1+3, while that of adjective-complement will be 3+1. Whereas, when the middle part is monosyllabic, the phonetic segment for most idioms with four syllables will be 2+2.

Feng (2009) demonstrated that all standard PrWds are in two syllables, so the combination of standard PrWds would definitely create the "case" for four syllables. Therefore, the most common form would be 2+2. The "case" originated from four syllabic forms and is derived from Chinese prosodic system. Owing to this, all the compound prosodic words just show two parts independently, and these two parts form an interdependent relationship instead of individual structures. Combination of two feet leads to the fact that even though there are two different parts, they are united. Besides phonetic stresses of these four words, merging them is simply a language description of "though different but united".

Feng also found out that some four-syllable structures beyond the form of 2+2, such as 一衣带水[*yi yi dai shui*](*be joined by a strip of water*), 狐假虎威[*hu jia hu wei*](*bully people by flaunting one's powerful connections*), 井底之蛙[*jing di zhi wa*](*a person with a limited outlook*), are still in 2+2 prosodic structures, and these phrases have been lexicalized because of the effect of "prosody over syntax", in which phrases gave away their prosodic structures corresponding to syntax and adopted the prosodic structure and stressing model of the compound prosodic words. That is to say, these phrases ignored syntactic rules and respond to prosody, changing into compound prosodic words. Therefore, they also accord with the stressing model showed in Figure 1.

It can be seen that some scholars have noticed that Chinese idioms are not symmetric, and tried to explain the reasons, which is especially obvious in Feng's (2009) research. The key point for this asymmetry lies in "prosody". Prosody leads to the "reanalysis" of sentence patterns of these four-syllabic structures. However, scholars did not give detailed descriptions and explanations to these questions: how different idioms with 1+3 structures should trigger the "reanalysis" of sentence patterns under the effects of prosody; at what aspects prosody can make a "reanalysis"; and what kind of "reanalysis" prosody can trigger. Based on these literature reviews, both quantitative and qualitative ways will be introduced to give a detail analysis on the role played by prosody in asymmetric idioms, and to explain its reason. 771 idioms with 1+3 structure, coming from *Dictionary of Idioms*, are categorized into adverb-verb, subject-predicator, verb-object, verb-complement and adjective-complement.

3   Distribution and Numbers of Chinese Idioms with 1+3 Structure

3.1   General Distribution

Dictionary of Idioms issued by the Commercial Press was selected as object of the research. Firstly, syllabic numbers of these idioms were calculated and the results are followed.

Table 1. Syllabic numbers and distribution of these Chinese idioms

Syllable	3	4	5	6	7	8	9	10	11	12	13	14	Total
Number	20	**10778**	132	115	96	164	6	16	1	3	0	1	11332
Percent (%)	0.18	**95.11**	1.16	1.01	0.85	1.45	0.05	0.14	0.01	0.03	0.00	0.01	100

Among these 11,332 idioms, four-syllable idioms take up 10,778, which is overwhelmingly (more than 95%) dominant in quantity. This also accords with our language sense. Among these four-syllable idioms, 771 idioms are not symmetric, taking up 7.2%, and their structures are as follows:

(1a) adverb-complement: 饱经风霜*[bao jing feng shuang]*(have experienced years of wind and frost)

(1b) subject-predicator: 鹤立鸡群*[he li ji qun]*(stand head and shoulders above others)

(1c) verb-object: 乘人之危*[cheng ren zhi wei]*(take advantage of others' difficulties)

(1d) verb-complement: 视若草芥*[shi ruo cao jie]*(to regard as worthless)

(1e) adjective-complement: 高不可攀*[gao bu ke pan]*(too high to be reached)

(1f) coordination and others: 勇而无谋*[yong er wu mou]*(be brave but have no plans)

The table below shows the numbers and percentages of these idioms.

Table 2. Number and percentage of idioms with 1+3 structure

Type	(1a)	(1b)	(1c)	(1d)	(1e)	(1f)	Total
Number	264	298	58	27	75	49	771
Percent	34.2%	38.7%	7.5%	3.5%	9.7%	6.4%	100.0%

3.2   Analysis of Idioms with 1+3 Structure

3.2.1   Adverb-verb amid this type, the most common adverbs are: 大*[da]*(big), 别 *[bie]*(else), 独 *[du]*(unique), 各 *[ge]*(every), 一 *[yi]*(any), 久 *[jiu]*(long), 饱 *[bao]*(enough), 杳*[yao]*(remote). They have appeared more than 5 times. For example:

(2a) 大*[da](big)*: 大动干戈*[da dong gan ge]*(get into a fight)

(2b) 别*[bie](else)*: 别具匠心*[bie ju jiang xin]*(show ingenuity)

(2c) 独*[du](unique)*: 独树一帜*[du shu yi zhi]*(fly one's own colors)

(2d) 各*[ge](every)*: 各持己见*[ge chi ji jian]*(each sticks to his own view)

(2e) 一*[yi](any)*: 一无所知*[yi wu suo zhi]*(know nothing at all)

(2f) 久*[jiu](long)*: 久经沙场*[jiu jing sha chang]*(experience battlefield for a long time for a long time)

(2g) 饱*[bao](enough)*: 饱经沧桑*[bao jing cang sang]*(have seen much of the changes in human life)

(2h) 杳*[yao](remote)*: 杳无音信*[yao wu yin xin]*(not heard from ... at all)

Table 3. Type and number of adverbs in adverb-verb idioms with 1+3 structure

Type	(2a)	(2b)	(2c)	(2d)	(2e)	(2f)	(2g)	(2h)	Subtotal	Total
Number	23	16	15	12	10	7	5	5	93	264
Percent	8.7%	6.1%	5.7%	4.5%	3.8%	2.7%	1.9%	1.9%	35.2%	100.0%

3.2.2   Subject-predicator: Idioms with 1+3 structure under this category can be divided into the following six types. (Thereafter, σ is monosyllable, σσ is disyllable).

(3a) [[NP]σ+[[V]σ+[NP]σσ]: (1+(1+2)), such as 将遇良才 *[jiang yu liang cai]*(find one's match)

(3b) [[NP]σ+[[Adv]σ+[VP]σσ]: (1+(1+2)), such as 盗亦有道 [*dao yi you dao*](*there is honor among thieves*)

(3c) [[NP]σ+[[Aux]σ+[VP]σσ]: (1+(1+2)), such as 门可罗雀 [*men ke luo que*](*birds can be caught by a net at the door -- a deserted house*)

(3d) [[NP]σ+[[[Prep]σ+[NP]σ]+[VP]σ]]: (1+(2+1)), such as病从口入[*bing cong kou ru*](*diligence is the means by which one makes up for one's dullness*)

(3e) [NP]σ+[[V]σ+[PP]σ]: (1+(1+2)), such as 青出于蓝 [*qing chu yu lan*] (*green comes from blue but better than blue (surpass one's master or teacher in learning)*)

(3f) others: such as 时不我待[*shi bu wo dai*](*time and tide wait for no man*)

Table 4. Type and number of subject-predicator idioms with 1+3 structure

Type	(3a)	(3b)	(3c)	(3d)	(3e)	(3f)	Total
Number	125	132	10	13	4	14	298
Percent	41.9%	44.3%	3.4%	4.4%	1.3%	4.7%	100.0%

3.2.3   Verb-object idioms of this category with 1+3 structure can be divided into the following five types:

(4a) [V]σ+[NP1]σ+[NP2]σσ: (1+1+2), such as 傍人门户[*bang ren men hu*](*rely on sb. for a living*)

(4b) [V]σ+[NP]σσσ: (1+3), such as 乘人之危[*cheng ren zhi wei*](*take advantage of others' difficulties*)

(4c) [[V]σ+[[V]σ+[NP]σσ]]: (1+(1+2)), such as好为人师[*hao wei ren shi*](*be fond of teaching others*)

(4d) [[V]σ+[[NP]σ+[VP]σσ]]: (1+(1+2)), such as 如虎添翼[*ru hu tian yi*](*just like adding wings to a tiger*)

(4e) [[V]σ+[[NP]σσ+[VP]σ]]: (1+(2+1)), such as 如鸟兽散 [*ru niao shou san*](*scatter like birds or wild animals*)

Table 5. Type and number of verb-object idioms with 1+3 structure

Type	(4a)	(4b)	(4c)	(4d)	(4e)	Total
Number	8	8	27	14	1	58
Percent	13.8%	13.8%	46.6%	24.1%	1.7%	100.0%

3.2.4   Verb-complement idioms with 1+3 structure under this category are divided into seven different types. These are as follows:

(5a) [[V]σ[于[NP]σσ]]: 安于现状[*an yu xian zhuang*](*be satisfied with the existing state of affairs and reluctant to move forward*)

(5b) [[V]σ[若[NP]σσ]]: 奉若神明[*feng ruo shen ming*](*revere sth. as sacred*)

(5c) [[V]σ[如[NP]σσ]]: 视如草芥[*shi ru cao jie*](*to regard as worthless*)

(5d) [[V]σ[以[VP]σσ]]: 学以致用[*xue yi zhi yong*](*learn in order to practice*)

(5e) [[V]σ[不[VP]σσ]]: 爱不释手[*ai bu shi shou*](*like(love) sth. so much that one cannot bear to part with it*)

(5f) [[V]σ[无[NP]σσ]]: 查无实据*[cha wu shi ju]*(*it has been found that the report is not substantiated by facts*)

(5g) [[V]σ[为[NP]σσ]]: 奉为楷模*[feng wei kai mo]*(*hold up as a model*)

Table 6. Type and number of verb-complement idioms with 1+3 structure

Type	(5a)	(5b)	(5c)	(5d)	(5e)	(5f)	(5g)	Total
Number	4	6	4	3	6	1	3	27
Percent	14.8%	22.2%	14.8%	11.1%	22.2%	3.7%	11.1%	100.0%

3.2.5   Adjective-complement idioms with 1+3 structure under this category have been divided into the following types:

(6a) [[A]σ[不[VP]σσ]]: 安不忘危*[an bu wang wei]*(*never relax your vigilance while you live in peace*)

(6b) [[A]σ[如[NP]σσ]]: 安如磐石*[an ru pan shi]*(*be as firm (solid) as a rock*)

(6c) [[A]σ[若[NP]σσ]]: 呆若木鸡*[dai ruo mu ji]*(*dumb as a wooden chicken*)

(6d) [[A]σ[无[NP]σσ]]: 暗无天日*[an wu tian ri]*(*complete darkness*)

(6e) [[A]σ[以[VP]σσ]]: 乐以忘忧*[le yi wang you]*(*seek pleasure in order to free oneself from care*)

(6f) [[A]σ[于[NP]σσ]]: 老于世故*[lao yu shi gu]*(*have seen much of the world*)

(6g) others: 富甲一方*[fu jia yi fang]*(*one of the richest*)

Table 7. Type and number of adjective-complement idioms with 1+3 structure

Type	(6a)	(6b)	(6c)	(6d)	(6c)	(6f)	(6g)	Total
Number	34	16	10	5	3	2	5	75
Percent	45.3%	21.3%	13.3%	6.7%	4.0%	2.7%	6.7%	100.0%

4   The Reanalysis of 1+3 Idioms Under Prosodic Restriction

4.1   The Reanalysis of Adverb-Verb Idioms with 1+3 Structure

For adverb-verb idiomatic expressions, the language structure is coherent. As it shows in figure 2, a three-syllable VP, which is made up of a one-syllable Verb and two-syllable NP, is modified by Adverb. From figure 2, it is noticeable that Adverbial expressions are mostly those parts that cannot be used by themselves under the rules of prosody such as 饱*[bao]*(*enough*). They are the special parts in terms of "syntactic freedom and prosodic relation". Feng (2006) and Huang (2012), did qualitative research and quantitative research respectively, and postulated that sentence parts like the above mentioned need to be matched with one-syllable parts so as to form "even" syllables that make sense. That is what we called "Embedded Compound Monosyllabic Morpheme (thereafter, ECMM). Therefore, being driven by prosody, the 1+3 structure has changed the position of verbs and the re-analysis of 2+2 has been done under standard prosodic restriction.

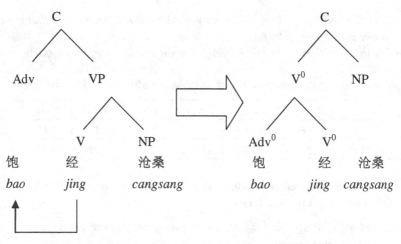

Fig. 2. the reanalysis of the adverb-verb idioms with 1+3 structure

4.2   Re-analyses of Subject Predicate Idioms with 1+3 Structure

4.2.1   Prosodic analysis of subject-predicate idioms with 1+3 structure: The inside structure of subject-predicate idioms with 1+3 structure is relatively complicated. (3a) structure above takes a large proportion and its main feature is one-syllable subject which is followed by three-syllable VP that is made up of one-syllable V and two-syllable NP, as it's being shown in the figure below.

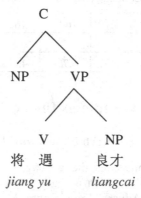

Fig. 3. structure of the idiom 将遇良才 [*jiang yu liang cai*](*find one's match*)

Let's take a look at V-O structure. Wang (2000) has studied the fundamental differences among three-character metric words. They are:

Three-syllable metric words : (雨伞厂 [*yu san chang*](*umbrella factory*)): (***)
Three-syllable bound phrases: (小雨伞 [*xiao yu san*](*small umbrella*)): (*^)(**)
Three-syllable free phrases: (买雨伞 [*mai yu san*](*to buy an umbrella*)): *(**)

She points out that three-character V-O without parentheses is free syllable, which is suggested by Duanmu (1999). This kind of syllable (e.g. 买[*mai*](*to buy*)) can not only move towards the two extremes of the foot bound, but also towards the two sidelines of stress bound, which is proper and fit to deal with the free syllables that are out of the deep rhythm.

The assumptions proposed by Wang and Duanmu appropriately explain the S+P+O [1+3] idiom metric structure. Taking 将遇良才[*jiang yu liang cai*](*find one's match*) as example, the key verb 遇[*yu*](*to meet*) as one syllable is out of the whole VP metric structure. According to Wang's (2000) predication, in regard to prosody, this is the free part that can be combined freely with the first syllable and the last syllable. However, in a four-syllable idiom, only one syllable is left to NP due to the fact that VP has taken 3 characters. On the other hand, one-syllable V, which is out of prosody structure, tends to match with the first syllable to form the two-syllable metrics rather than the last syllable, which is called super-prosodic-word. This explains how S+P+O [1+3] idiom metrics structure has been changed to 2+2 structure.

4.2.2   [S[Adverb Predicate] and [S[Auxiliary Predicate] the prosodic analysis of idioms

The structure of the idioms that have been illustrated in (3b) and (3c), as it's been shown in figure 4("I" both stands for adverb and auxiliary verb), is different from the aforementioned structure. The second syllable acts as adverb or auxiliary verb here. Therefore, they are more likely to be used as functional words than vocabulary. It demonstrates the upward movement of characters (e.g. 我往北走[*wo wang bei zou*](*I go towards the north*), the pitch model will change from 3-3-3-3 into 2-3-2-3), therefore, the second syllable in these discourse tend to move forward to 2+2 prosodic model.

4.2.3   About 青出于蓝[*qing chu yu lan*](*green comes from blue but better than blue (surpass one's master or teacher in learning)*).

A compound relationship can be found in idioms like [*qing chu yu lan*] because of the preposition and the verb (Dong, 1998; Feng, 2005). Therefore, 出 于 [*chu yu*](*come from*) firstly forms a grammatical word, so that this idiom cannot be reanalyzed into 2+2 prosodic structure, and can keep the prosodic 1+3 structure.

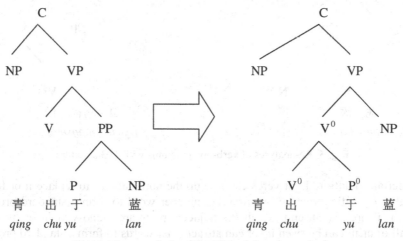

Fig. 4. The reanalysis of the idiom [qing chu yu lan]

4.3   Re-analyses of Verb-Object Idioms with 1+3 Structure

4.3.1   Light verb theory and verb-object idioms with 1+3 structure.

According to researches on light verbs in verb-object structures made by Larson(1988), Huang el(2009), the above-mentioned (4a), (4c), (4d) and (4e) can also be analyzed in the light verb theory, which can be seen in figure 5 (v refers to light verb, while V notional verb).

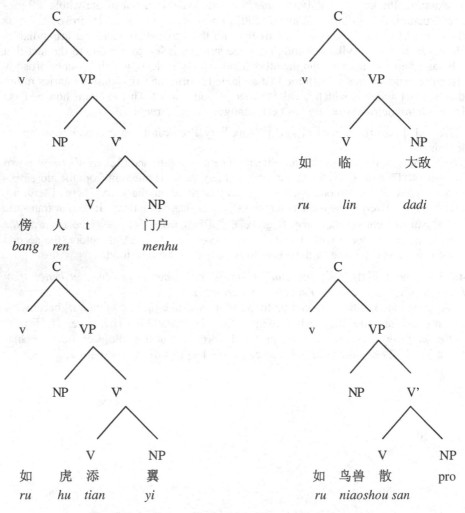

Fig. 5. Re-analyses of verb-object idioms with 1+3 structure

In certain situation, light verbs can rise up the notional part to replace it or form a disyllabic prosodic structure by attracting another word to form a standard prosodic word. In figure 5a, 5b and 5c, all the adjacent parts are monosyllabic in structure, thus, all of them can be risen up or can attract other words to form a standard prosodic word. Under this restrain, reanalysis can be made to form a 2+2 structure. However, 如鸟兽散[*ru niaoshou san*](*scatter like birds or wild animals*) at figure 5d is different, because 鸟兽[*niaoshou*](*birds and wild animals*) is disyllabic, and it cannot be embedded into 如[*ru*](like), which is beyond the restrain to standard prosodic word. Hence, it cannot be reanalyzed into 2+2 structure.

4.3.2   About 乘人之危[cheng ren zhi wei](take advantage of others' difficulties). [V+[X zhi Y]], one type under verb-object idioms, grammatically belongs to 1+3 structure, but its prosody is different from the others because of the [zhi] (Feng(2009) and Luo(2014)) have demonstrated that such kind of classical Chinese functional word will affiliate with the following part Y, after which it will form a word [zhi]-Y and then combine with the previous part to form a 2+2 prosodic structure.

4.4   Verb-Complement and Adjective-Complement Idioms with 1+3 Structure

This kind of idioms can be easily analyzed, because complement embedment exists in theory and has been proven (Feng, 2005). Thus the following does make sense in Figure 6 and 7:

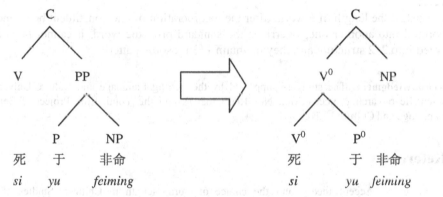

Fig. 6. Verb-complement idioms with 1+3 structure

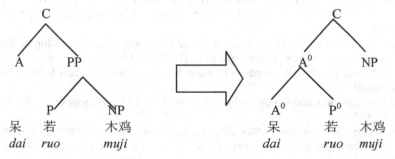

Fig. 7. Adjective-complement idioms with 1+3 structure

5   Conclusion

Taking all above analyses into consideration, re-analyses from 1+3 structure to 2+2 structure must obey these rules:

First of all, adverbs in adverb-verb structure are mostly ECMM. They are firstly combined with a monosyllabic verb to form a disyllabic grammatical word, and are later assigned to other syllables in order to create a 2+2 structure.

Second, in the structures of subject-predicator, the second syllable affiliates with the first one, thus they will be 2+2 prosodic structure.

Besides, light verb attracts other part in verb-object structure, and under the restrain of standard prosodic word, the first two words combine together to form a prosodic 2+2 structure.

In addition, some classic Chinese functional word tends to affiliate with the following part, leading to the inconsistency between its prosodic structure and grammatical structure. Finally the prosody overcomes the grammar and form a 2+2 prosodic structure.

Furthermore, verb-complement and adjective-complement idioms with 1+3 structure should be reanalyzed into 2+2 structure due to the embedment of preposition to verb.

Last, if the length of a word, after the incorporation of one constituent being incorporated into another one, overrides the standard prosodic word, it cannot be reanalyzed into 2+2 structure and they maintain 1+3 prosodic pattern.

Acknowledgment. The study is supported by the Beijing Language and Culture University scientific research project (Grant No. 15YJ080207), and the Youth Elite Project of Beijing Language and Culture University.

References

Duanmu, S.: Accent theory and the choice of words length in Chinese. Studies of the Chinese Language **4**, 246–254 (1999). (in Chinese)

Duanmu, S.: Rhythm in Chinese. Contemporary. Linguistics **4**, 203–209 (2000). (in Chinese)

Duanmu, S.: Stress, Information, and Language Typology. Linguistic Sciences **5**, 3–16 (1990). (in Chinese)

Duanmu, S.: A Formal Study of Syllable Tone, Stress and Domain in Chinese languages. Doctoral dissertation, MIT, Cambridge, Mass (1990). (in Chinese)

Feng, S.: A study on prosodic words in Chinese. Social Sciences in China **1**, 161–176 (1996). (in Chinese)

Feng, S.: A study on Chinese natural foot. Studies of the Chinese Language **1**, 40–47 (1998). (in Chinese)

Feng, S.: Chinese prosodic syntax. Shanghai education Press, Shanghai (2000). (in Chinese)

Feng, S.: Research on prosodic syntax of Chinese. Peking University Press, Beijing (2005). (in Chinese)

Feng, S.: Chinese prosody, morphology and syntax. Peking University Press, Beijing (2009). (in Chinese)

Hogg, R., McCully, C.B.: Metrical Phonology. Cambridge University Press, New York (1987)

Huang, J., Li, A., Li, Y.: The Syntax of Chinese. Cambridge University Press, UK (2009)

Ju, J.: A preliminary study on the combination of the "1 + 3" and "3 + 1" in the four word case. Chinese Language Learning 1, 37–39 (1995). (in Chinese)

Larson, R.: On the double object construction. Linguistic Inquiry 19(3), 335–391 (1988)

Liberman, M., Prince, A.: On stress and linguistic rhythm. Linguistic Inquiry, 8 (1997)

Luo, J.: Research on the Prosodic Structure of "Zhi" Structure. Journal of Shaoyang University(Social Science Edition), 69–74 (2014). (in Chinese)

Shi, Y.: On the four word lattice and its phonological rhythm. Chinese Language Learning 5, 15–21 (1995). (in Chinese)

Wang, H.: Nonlinear phonology of Chinese. Peking University Press, Beijing (2008). (in Chinese)

Wang, H.: The prosodic word and prosodic phrase of Chinese. Studies of the Chinese Language 6, 191–200. (in Chinese)

On the Licensing of Verbs in a Flip-Flop Construction from the Qualia Structure of Nouns

Changsong Wang[1(⊠)] and Wei Chin[2]

[1] School of Foreign Languages, Beijing Institute of Technology, Beijing, China
cswang@bit.edu.cn
[2] Institute of Scientific and Technical Information of China, Beijing, China
verachinbeijing@kimo.com

Abstract. This paper aims to study the licensing mechanism of the verbs in a flip-flop construction in Chinese. It is found that the selection of the verbs in a flip-flop construction is constrained by the qualia structure, to be specific, the telic role, of a noun. When the lexical semantics of a verb matches the Telic role of the noun in a preverbal or postverbal 'Num +Cl +N', it is licensed and the wellformedness of a flip-flop construction is predicted.

Keywords: Flip-flop construction · Num + Cl + N · Qualia structure · Telic role

1 Introduction

In this paper, we study a special type of sentences in Chinese, as shown in (1)-(2), which has aroused much research in the literature, for instance, Li & Fan (1960), Li (1998), Lu (1988, 2010), Shen (1995), Tsai (1996, 2001, 2015), Ren (1999), Zhang (1999), Li & Lu (2002), etc. One trait of such sentences is that the subject and the object can switch their positions, while leaving the meaning of the sentence almost unchanged. For this reason, Tsai (1996, 2001) dubs it as a flip-flop construction and Ren (1999) calls it Subject-Object convertible accommodation sentences. In this paper, we will follow Tsai (1996) and name it as a flip-flop construction.

(1) a. 三个人吃一锅饭。
     san ge ren   chi yi guo fan.
     three Cl people eat one Cl rice
     'Three people can/are to eat one pot of rice.'
   b. 一锅饭吃三个人。
     yi guo fan chi san ge ren.
     one Cl rice eat three Cl people
     'One pot of rice is enough for three people to eat.'
(2) a. 三个人睡一张床。
     san ge ren   shui yi zhang chuang.
     three Cl people sleep one Cl   bed
     'Three people can/are to sleep on a bed.'

© Springer International Publishing Switzerland 2015
Q. Lu and H.H. Gao (Eds.): CLSW 2015, LNAI 9332, pp. 352–360, 2015.
DOI: 10.1007/978-3-319-27194-1_35

b. 一张床睡三个人。

yi   zhang chuang shui san   ge ren.
one Cl   bed   sleep three Cl people
'A bed can sleep three people.'

Many aspects of this type of sentences have been investigated in the above-mentioned literature. However, there is still one question less discussed, that is, why can only some verbs appear in a flip-flop construction? For instance, if the 吃 [*chi*] (*eat*) in (1) is substituted by 做[*zuo*] (*do/make*) or 煮[*zhu*] (*cook*), as in (3), or if 睡 [*shui*] (*sleep*) in (2) is taken by 卖 [*mai*] (*sell*) or 抬 [*tai*] (*carry*), as in (4), the subject and object cannot flip-flop any longer. This could be evidenced with the ungrammaticality of (3b) and (4b). In this paper, we are going to explore the licensing mechanism of the verbs in such flip-flop sentences.

(3)   a. 三个人做/煮一锅饭。

san   ge ren   zuo/zhu yi   guo fan.
three Cl people do/cook one Cl rice
'Three people can/are to make a boil of rice.'

b. *一锅饭做/煮三个人。

**yi   guo fan zuo/zhu san   ge ren.*
one Cl rice do/cook three Cl people
*'A pot of rice can make/boil three people.'

(4)   a. 三个人卖/抬一张床。

san   ge ren   mai/tai   yi zhang chuang.
three Cl people sell/carry one Cl   bed
'Three people can/are to sell/carry a bed.'

b. *一张床卖/抬三个人

**yi zhang chuang mai/tai   san   ge ren.*
one Cl   bed   sell/carry three Cl people
*'A bed can sell/carry three people.'

2   Characteristics of a Flip-flop Construction

Besides the subject-object convertibility, there are some other syntactic and semantic properties for a flip-flop construction, which are listed as follows:

First, the subject and object should appear in the form of 'Num(eral) + Cl(assifier) + N(oun)'. What is more, this phrase must be indefinite, rather than definite. Otherwise, flip-flop sentences would be impossible to be formed, as shown in (5). Li & Lu (2002) argue to take the 'Num + Cl + N' in flip-flop sentences as Number Phrase (NumP) instead of Determiner Phrase (DP). In this paper, we adopt such a proposal and provide another piece of related evidence (Li 1998). Unlike a normal DP, the 'Num + Cl + N ' has no referentiality and couldn't be questioned with 谁[*shui*] (*who*) or 什么[*shenme*] (*what*), as in (6a, b); instead, it can be questioned with '几[*ji*] (*how many/much*) + Cl +N' , as in (7a,b).

(5) a. 张三吃了那三碗饭。

   Zhangsan chi le   na san wan fan.

   Zhangsan eat Perf. that three Cl   rice

   'Zhangsan ate those three bowls of rice.'

  b. *那三碗饭吃了张三。

   *na san wan fan chi le   Zhangsan.

   that three Cl   rice eat Perf. Zhangsan

   *'Those three bowl of rice ate Zhangsan. '

(6) a. —谁吃一锅饭？

   —*shui chi yi guo fan?*

   who eat one Cl rice

   'Who are to eat one pot of rice?'

   —*三个人。

   —**san ge ren.*

   three Cl people

   'Three people.'

  b. —三个人吃什么？

   —*san ge ren chi shenme?*

   three Cl people eat what

   'What are three people to eat?

   —*一锅饭。

   —**yi guo fan.*

   one Cl rice

   'One pot of rice.'

(7) a. —几个人吃一锅饭？

   —*ji   ge ren   chi yi guo fan?*

   how.many Cl people eat one Cl rice

   'How many people can/are to eat one pot of rice?'

   —三个人。

   —*san ge ren.*

   three Cl people

   'Three people.'

  b. —三个人吃几锅饭？

   —*san ge ren   chi ji   guo fan?*

   three Cl people eat how.many Cl rice

   'How many pots of rice can three people eat?'

   —一锅饭。

   —*yi guo fan.*

   one Cl rice

   'One pot of rice.'

Second, verbs in a flip-flop construction are different from normal action verbs. As pointed out in Ren (1999), the verbs in subject-object convertible accommodation sentences, which cover the flip-flop sentences discussed in this paper, have undergo some abstraction and tend to express the ways of accommodation rather than referring to detailed actions. Zhang (1999) agrees with such an analysis in discussing distributional sentences with double number phrases in the form of 'Num + Cl +N'. According to Zhang, the verbs in such sentences are non-dynamic and the structure tends to express a relation. Lu (2010) argues that the verbs in a flip-flop construction may bear multiple semantic relations. For example, 吃[*chi*] (*eat*) in (5a) refers to an action, which links Agent and Patient. Meanwhile, 吃[*chi*] (*eat*) can come into a 'holder - ways of holding - holdee' construction, which refers to a quantity relation, as in (1). Under such occasion, *chi* (*eat*) no longer refers to an action, but a way/manner of holding. However, Lu (1993), Tsai (2001, 2015), Li & Lu (2002) do not take the verbs in such sentences as anything different from normal verbs. According to them, what make these sentences special is that there is an unpronounced verb, i.e. 够[*gou*] (*suffice*), or a light modal verb, i.e. 能[*neng*] (*can*), and there is a covert movement from the action verb to the covert (light) verb. This analysis is also very inspiring, as it can easily explain why such sentences do not refer to an action but denote a kind of potentiality.

The above-mentioned literature is insightful. However, these analyses cannot explain one often neglected problem, that is, why some verbs can form a flip-flop construction, while others can't. In the following section, we are going to explore this problem from the perspective of qualia structure in the theory of generative lexicon.

3   Qualia Structure

The theory of generative lexicon is systematically presented by Pustejovsky (1995), in which he proposes that a generative lexicon is a computational system which consists of at least four levels of representations: argument structure, event structure, qualia structure, and lexical type structure. In this section, we will mainly review the qualia structure (Pustejovsky1995: 85-104, Song 2011, Yuan 2013, etc.), as it is related to our current research.

Pustejovsky (1995: 76) assumes that qualia structure consists of four key aspects of a word's meaning, which are Constitutive role, Formal role, Telic role, and Agentive role. According to Pustejovsky (1995: 85-86), Constitutive role describes "the relation between an object and its constituent parts or proper parts", which may include material, weight, parts and component element. Formal role "distinguishes an object within a larger domain", which may include orientation, magnitude, shape and dimensionality, color and position. Telic role refers to an object's purpose and function, which may cover two points: a "purpose that an agent has in performing an act" and a "built-in function or aim which specifies certain activities". Agentive role concerns the factors involved in the origin or "bringing about" of an object, and it may include creator, artifact, natural kind and causal chain. As noted by Pustejovsky (1995: 76), "not all lexical items carry a value for each qualia role". Take a noun *book* for example, its Formal role is *hold*, as it is mainly used to hold information; its Telic role is *read*, as it is mainly used to read; its Agentive is *write*, as books are produced through writing. The qualia structure of *book* is roughly described as below, in which *x, y* are arguments and *e/e'* refers to an event (irrelevant details not discussed).

(8)

$$
\begin{bmatrix}
\text{book} \\
\text{QULIA} = \begin{bmatrix}
\text{FORMAL} = \text{hold}(y, x) \\
\text{TELIC} = \text{read}(e,w,x.y) \\
\text{AGENTIVE} = \text{write}(e', v, x.y)
\end{bmatrix}
\end{bmatrix}
$$

(adapted from e.g. 29, Pustejovsky 1995: 116)

As for Telic role, Pustejovsky (1995: 99-101) distinguishes two types: Direct Telic and Purpose Telic. The former refers to "something which one acts on directly", *beer* is such an example. It can be taken as an object of a predicate like *drink*. The latter refers to "something which is used for facilitating a particular activity", as exemplified by *knife*, which may be used in an activity as a tool.

In the following section, we will explore the licensing mechanism of the verbs in a flip-flop construction from the Telic role of nouns.

4   Why Some Verbs Cannot Occur in a Flip-flop Construction?

As described in Section 1, if verbs in a flip-flop construction are changed, the 'Num +Cl +N' might not be able to switch and ungrammaticality arises or the accommodation/holding meaning disappears, as shown in (3-4), here repeated as (9-10).

(9)   a. 三个人做/煮一锅饭。

   san ge ren   zuo/zhu yi guo fan.
   three CL people do/cook one CL rice
   'Three people can/are to make a pot of rice.'

   b. *一锅饭做/煮三个人

   *yi guo fan zuo/zhu san ge ren.
   one Cl rice do/cook three CL people
   *'One pot of rice can make/boil three people can.'

(10)   a. 三个人卖/抬一张床。

   san ge ren   mai/tai yi zhang chuang.
   three Cl people sell/carry one Cl   bed
   'Three people can/are to sell/carry one bed.'

   b. *一张床卖/抬三个人

   *yi zhang chuang mai/tai   san   ge ren.
   one Cl   bed   sell/carry three Cl people
   *'A bed can can sell/carry three CL people.'

Many more similar examples are discussed as below. If 住 [*zhu*] (*live*) in (11) is substituted by 买 [*mai*](*buy*) /卖 [*mai*] (*sell*)/修 [*xiu*] (*repair*), as in (12a), or if 坐 [*zuo*] (*sit*) in (13) is changed as 抬[*tai*] (*carry*) /修[*xiu*] (*repair*)/ 卖 [*mai*] (*sell*), as in (14a), flip-flop is not possible, as respectively shown in (12b) and (14b). Why is there such a difference between these sentences?

The reason is quite simple if a qualia structure perspective is taken. We find that the selection of verbs in a flip-flop construction is related to the noun in either the preverbal or postverbal 'Num + CL +N'. To be specific, we find that the licensing of the verbs in a flip-construction is constrained by the Telic role of one of the nouns in the two 'Num + Cl +N'. In this line, we can explain why (9a, 10a, 12a, 14a) cannot flip-flop, as respectively shown in (9b, 10b, 12b, 14b). Take (9a) for example, the Telic role of 饭[*fan*] (rice) is 吃[*chi*] (*eat*), rather than 做 [*zuo*] (*make*) or 煮 [*zhu*] (*cook*), which is the Agentive role of *rice*. Similarly, the Telic role of 床 [*chuang*] (*bed*) in (10a) is 睡 [*shui*] (*sleep*), instead of 卖 [*mai*] (*sell*) or 抬[*tai*] (*carry*); the Telic role of 房 [*fang*] (*house*) in (12a) is 住 [*zhu*] (*live*), instead of 卖 [*mai*] (*sell*), 买 [*mai*] (*buy*) or 修 [*xiu*] (*repair*); and the Telic role of 板凳 [*bandeng*] (*bench*) is 坐 [*zuo*] (*sit*), instead of 抬 [*tai*] (*carry*), 修 [*xiu*](*repair*) or 卖 [*mai*] (*sell*).

(11) a. 三个人住一套房。
　　　 san ge ren   zhu yi   tao fang.
　　　 three Cl people live one Cl house
　　　 'Three people can/are to live in a suite.'
　　 b. 一套房住三个人。
　　　 yi tao fang zhu san ge ren.
　　　 one Cl house live three Cl people
　　　 'A suit can/are to live three people.'

(12) a. 三个人买/卖/修一套房。
　　　 san ge   ren mai/mai/xiu   yi tao fang.
　　　 three Cl people buy/sell/repair one Cl house
　　　 'Three people can/are to buy/sell/repair a suite.'
　　 b. *一套房买/卖/修三个人。
　　　 yi tao fang mai/mai/xiu   san ge ren.
　　　 one Cl house buy/sell/repair   three Cl people
　　　 *'A suit can/is to buy/sell/repair three people.'

(13) a. 二个学生坐一张板凳。
　　　 liang ge xuesheng zuo yi zhang bandeng.
　　　 two Cl student   sit one Cl   bench
　　　 'Two students can/are to sit a bench.'
　　 b. 一张板凳坐二个学生。
　　　 yi zhang bandeng zuo liang ge xuesheng.
　　　 one Cl   bench   sit two Cl studeng
　　　 'A bench can/is to sit two students.'

(14) a. 二个学生抬/修/卖一张板凳。
　　　 liang ge xuesheng tai/xiu/mai   yi zhang bandeng.
　　　 two Cl   student carry/repair/sell one Cl   bench

'Two students can/are to carry/repair/sell one bench.'

b. *一张板凳抬/修/卖三个学生。

*yi zhang bandeng tai/xiu/mai   liang ge xuesheng.

one Cl   bench carry/repair/sell two Cl student

*'A bench can/is to carry/repair/sell two students.'

This assumption is shown to be correct with many more examples, as shown in (15-17). In (15), 栽 [zai] (plant) is the Agentive role, but not the Telic role, of 树 [shu](tree); therefore, to flip-flop is not possible, as shown in (15b). Similarly 做[zuo] (make) in (16) is the Agentive role, but not Telic role, of 菜 [cai] (dishes). 写 [xie] (write) in (17) is the Agentive role, but not Telic role, of 书 [shu] (book). However, if 做 [zuo] (make) in (16a) and 写 [xie] (write) in (17a) are respectively substituted by 吃 [chi] (eat), as in (18), and 读[du] (read) or 看 [kan] (read), as in (19), to flip-flop becomes possible again. This could be predicted with our proposal. The unavailability of flip-flop in (15-17) and the availability in (18-19) show that the selection of the verbs in a flip-flop construction are constrained by the Telic role of the noun in the preverbal/postverbal [Num +Cl +N].

(15)   a. 三个人栽一颗树。

san ge ren   zai yi ke shu.

three Cl people plant one Cl tree

'Three people can/are to plant one tree.'

b. *一棵树栽三个人。

*yi ke shu zai   san ge ren.

one Cl tree plant three Cl people

*'One tree can/is to plant three people.'

(16)   a. 五个人做一桌菜。

wu ge ren   zuo yi zhuo cai.

five Cl people make one Cl dish

'Five people can/are to work together to make a table of dishes.'

b. *一桌菜做五个人。

*yi zhuo cai zuo   wu ge ren.

one Cl dish make five Cl people

*'One table of dishes can/ is to do five people.'

(17)   a. 两个人写一本书。

liang ge ren   xie yi ben shu.

two Cl people write one Cl book

'Two people can/are to write a book.'

b. *一本书写两个人。

*yi ben shu xie liang ge ren.

one Cl book write two Cl people

*'One book can write two people.'

(18) a. 五个人吃一桌菜。
　　　　wu ge ren　chi yi zhuo cai.
　　　　five Cl people eat one table dish
　　　　'Five people can/are to eat a table of dishes.'
　　　b. 一桌菜吃五个人。
　　　　yi zhuo cai chi wu ge ren.
　　　　one table dish eat five Cl people
　　　　'A table of dishes can be eaten by five people.'

(19) a. 两个人读/看一本书。
　　　　liang ge ren　du/kan yi ben shu.
　　　　two　Cl people read one Cl book
　　　　'Two people can/are to read one book.'
　　　b. 一本书读/看两个人。
　　　　yi　ben shu　du/kan　liang ge ren.
　　　　one Cl　book read　　two Cl　　people
　　　　'One book can be read by two people.'

If the above discussion is on the right track, the verbs in a flip-flop construction are different from normal action verbs in a sentence (cf. Ren 1999, Zhang 1999, Lu 2010, etc.). They are more restricted than normal action verbs. These verbs not only select two indefinite 'Num+Cl+N' as their arguments, but also are constrained by the qualia structure of a preverbal/postverbal noun in one of the two 'Num +Cl +N'. Only when the lexical meaning of the verb is in line with the Telic of one of the two nouns, a flip-flop construction may be formed.

5　Conclusion

The two NumPs in a flip-flop sentence can change their orders, while the sentence meaning stays almost unchanged. One puzzle in this construction is why some verbs can occur in such a construction while others cannot. In this paper, we explore this myth from the perspective of the qualia structure of nouns and find that one noun in a preverbal/postverbal NumP may set limits on the selection of the verbs. Only when the lexical semantics of a verb matches the Telic role of a certain noun, a flip-flop construction may be licensed.

Acknowledgment. This research is partially supported by Beijing Institute of Technology Research Fund Program for Young Scholars, Beijing Social Science Fund for Young Scholars (No. 15WYC077), China Postdoctoral Science Foundation (No. 2014M550792), and National Key Project of Scientific and Technical Supporting programs (No.2011BAH30B01). Our thanks also go to two anonymous reviewers, Dr. Song Zuoyan and other audiences in the CLSW 2015 for their valuable comments and suggestions.

References

1. Huang, C., Li, Y., Li, Y.: The Syntax of Chinese. Cambridge University Press, Cambridge (2009)
2. Li, A.: Argument determiner phrases and number phrases. Linguistic Inquiry **29**(4), 693–702 (1998)
3. Li, A., Lu, B.: On the number phrase 'number + classifier +noun". Studies of the Chinese Language **4**, 326–336 (2002). (in Chinese)
4. Li, L., Fan, F.: A tentative research on number-classifier constructions denoting *mei* 'every'. Studies of the Chinese Language (11) (1960). (in Chinese)
5. Lu, B.: zhe-guo fan chi san-ge ren' as the result of verb movement. In: Paper presented to NACCL 5. University of Dalaware. (1993)
6. Lu, J.: Function of 'number + classifier' in modern chinese. In: Grammar Research and Inquiry (4). Peking University Press, Beijing (1988). (In Chinese)
7. Lu, J.: New Inquiries into Chinese grammar and semantics (Collection of speeches from 2000–2010). The Commercial Press, Beijing (2010). (In Chinese)
8. Lu, S., Pan, H.: The semantic licensing conditions of indefinite subjects in Mandarin Chinese. Studies of the Chinese Language **6**, 528–537 (2009). (In Chinese)
9. Pustejovsky, J.: The generative lexicon. The MIT Press, Cambridge (1995)
10. Ren, Y.: Analysis on the semantic conditions on subject-object convertible accommodation sentences. Chinese Language Learning **3**, 1–6 (1999). (In Chinese)
11. Shen, Y.: On the functions and characteristics of Num-Measure compound in the transposition of noun phrase. Chinese Teaching in the world **1**, 14–20 (1995). (In Chinese)
12. Song, Z.: On the latest development of generative lexicon theory. In: Essays in Linguistics **44**, pp. 202–221. The Commercial Press, Beijing (2011)
13. Tsai, W.: Subject specificity, raising modals and extended mapping hypothesis, paper presented at the Symposium on the referential properties of noun phrases. City University of Hong Kong (1996)
14. Tsai, W.: On subject specificity and theory of syntax-semantics interface. Journal of East Asian Linguistics **10**, 129–168 (2001)
15. Tsai, W.: Bare quantity construction in Mandarin Chinese and the typology of modals, paper presented at the International Conference on Language Form & Function. Soochow University (2015)
16. Yuan, Y.: A study of Chinese semantic knowledge system based on the theory of generative lexicon and argument structure. Journal of Chinese Information Processing **27**(6), 23–31 (2013). (In Chinese)
17. Zhang, N.: Representing specificity by the internal order of indefinites. Linguistics **44**(1), 1–21 (2006)
18. Zhang, W.: A semantic study of the unique syntactic structures in Chinese. Beijing Language and Culture University Press, Beijing (1999). (In Chinese)

Polarity Sensitivity of Minimal Degree Adverbs in Modern Chinese

Zhong Wu[1,2(✉)] and Lihua Li[2]

[1] Research Center for Language and Language Education,
China Central Normal University, Wuhan 430079, Hubei, China
zhongwu2000@163.com
[2] Wuhan University of Engineering Science, Wuhan 430200, Hubei, China
lilihua0806@sina.com

Abstract. Based on the semantic and pragmatic analysis of the typical Chinese minimal degree adverbs, as well as their relative frequency in corpora, this paper examines the polarity sensitivity of these adverbs. Evidence shows that *shaowei* (a little) and *xiewei* (a little bit) are positive polarity items (PPIs) while *hao* (a little) and *sihao* (a bit) are negative polarity items (NPIs). The research findings also indicate that the semantics is not the only factor that determines the polarity of minimal degree words, the pragmatics and frequency of the examined words must also be taken into account when deciding their polarity sensitivity.

Keywords: Minimal degree adverbs · Polarity sensitivity · Frequency

1 Introduction

Many natural languages have polarity sensitive lexical elements which are called polarity items because they usually appear in the positive or negative context. They can be categorized into positive polarity items (PPIs) and negative polarity items (NPIs). Accordingly, positive polarity items often appear in affirmative declarative sentences, such as 'some' in example 1, while negative polarity items, like 'any' in example 2, are frequently used in negative contexts.

Eg. 1 He went to fetch some books.
Eg. 2 I'm not making any promises.

The negative context refers to the scope of negation which usually indicates the semantic influence of negative markers, like 'no', 'not' in English or *bu* (不'not'), *mei*(没'not') in Chinese. It is important to note that the semantic influence is heavily influenced by the order of the negative markers and their neighboring parts in a sentence. In English, the right part of the negative marker is in the scope of negation. However, linguists' opinions vary on the issue of negative scope in Chinese. Shen and Lv asserted that the negative scope in Chinese is the whole sentence while Yuan

© Springer International Publishing Switzerland 2015
Q. Lu and H.H. Gao (Eds.): CLSW 2015, LNAI 9332, pp. 361–368, 2015.
DOI: 10.1007/978-3-319-27194-1_36

argued that the scope of negation in Chinese must be restricted to the right part of the negative marker. [1][2][3] We agree with Shen and Lv when the purpose of this research is considered.

As for the semantic and pragmatic features of NPIs, Shi proposes that words indicating minimal degree, semantically, are used only in negative structures while words indicating maximal degree are used in positive structures only. [4] Israel states that the measure terms, degree adverbs, indefinite pronouns, determiners, modal verbs, temporal and aspectual adverbs are common types of polarity items. [5]

Degree adverbs in modern Chinese are closed class words with limited members. Wang divides degree adverbs into relative degree adverbs and absolute degree adverbs based on whether an explicit object of reference for comparison exists or not. [6] Ma categorizes degree adverbs in Chinese into high degree adverbs and low degree adverbs according to their scale of degree. [7]

As to the polarity sensitivity of degree adverbs, Klein examines the polarity restriction on the use of adverbs of degree in Dutch and found that a minimal or negative degree is most commonly used to express a lack of a positive quality. [8: 148] Huang explores this phenomenon in English context and has identified the relative frequency of minimal degree adverbs in large corpora as an important factor for polarity sensitivity determination. [9]

Although the phenomena of polarity sensitivity have been explored by linguists from western countries, who have made great contributions to the development of linguistic theory of English, few Chinese scholars have systematically investigated this phenomenon in Chinese. To address such need in research, this paper uses corpus data and statistics to investigate the distribution and frequency of typical modern Chinese minimal degree adverbs in positive and negative contexts, and seeks to determine their polarity sensitivity bases on their semantic and pragmatic.

2   The Design of the Research

This study examines four typical modern Chinese minimal degree adverbs, namely, *hao* (毫'a little'), *sihao* (丝毫'a bit'), *shaowei* (稍微'a little'), and *xiewei* (些微'a little bit'), to answer the following two questions:

A. Are there any differences in the distribution frequency of the four adverbs in positive or negative context?
B. What are their semantic characteristic and polarity in positive or negative context?

With regard to question A, CCL (Center for Chinese Linguistics) as the data source is selected, for it is a classic modern Chinese corpus with more than 580 million characters. The downloaded data from CCL represent the distribution of these minimal degree adverbs in the real use. Therefore, the probability of their properties in the corpus reflects their usage.

In this study, the key words are *hao*, *sihao*, *shaowei*, and *xiewei* respectively, and the span is the whole sentence. After the data having been downloaded and given serial number, the software, "RandomMaker", will be used to choose 400 sentences as the sample concordances. It is true that the same token may have several meanings which belong to different classes. For instance, *xiewei* is both an adverb and an adjective. Unfortunately, the tagging software is currently not able to accurately filter out words that are not minimal degree adverbs, and manual screening is needed to further review the sample concordances. Considering both the adequacy of sample size and the feasible workload for manual operation, this study has determined that a total number of 400 sentences is a suitable size for key word analysis in this study. After downloading, numbering, sampling, and manual screening, the selected concordances were counted and analyzed.

3   The Examination of the Polarity Characteristics of Chinese Minimal Degree Adverbs

3.1   The Four Typical Chinese Minimal-Degree Adverbs

The concordances of four Chinese adverbs, *hao, sihao, shaowei*, and *xiewei*, downloaded from CCL, are 49059, 7783, 3253 and 771 respectively. By using "RandomMaker", 400 concordances are selected for analysis. Because the token *xiewei* can also take the form of "*xie + wei*", which is not a meaningful Chinese word but the combination of two separate characters, all concordances containing such structure are deleted prior to statistical analysis. Similarly, *hao* is a component morpheme of *sihao*. Hence, the sentences containing *sihao* in these 400 *hao* concordances have also been deleted to avoid double counting.

Table 1 shows the distribution of minimum degree adverbs in sampling after manual screening. As an adverb, the percentage of *shaowei, sihao* and *hao* are 100%, 78.11%, and 69.75% respectively, while the adverb *xiewei* only accounts for 9.92% of the total sample.

Table 1. The part of speech of four Chinese minimal degree adverbs in sampling

	Adverb		Others		Total
	Frequency	Percentage	Frequency	Percentage	
hao	264	78.11%	74	21.89%	338
sihao	279	69.75%	121	30.25%	400
shaowei	400	100%	0	0%	400
xiewei	13	9.92%	118	90.08%	131

This study further investigates the positive and negative context of the chosen adverbs and the results are displayed in Table 2:

Table 2. The context-based distribution of four Chinese minimal degree adverbs

	Positive		Negative		Total
	Frequency	Percentage	Frequency	Percentage	
hao	0	0%	264	100%	264
sihao	0	0%	279	100%	279
shaowei	388	97%	12	3%	400
xiewei	12	92.31%	1	7.69%	13

From the table shown above, *shaowei* and *xiewei* are PPIs, for most of them appear in assertive sentences. Similarly, *hao* and *sihao* are NPIs because their appearances in the sample sentences are always accompanied by negative markers, such as *wu* (无'not'), *bu* (不'not'), *wei*(未'no'), *mei* (没'no') or *meiyou* (没有'no').

3.2   The Analysis of the Polarity Characteristics of Four Chinese Minimal-Degree Adverbs

3.2.1   *Shaowei* and *xiewei*

The total number of concordance containing *shaowei* is 3253 in CCL. In the selected sample, there are 400 *shaowei* and all of them are adverbs. As an adverb of degree, it modifies adjective, verbs, and sometimes adverbs.

Eg.3 *shaowei* + adjective
常昊　　决赛　　取胜率　　应该　　〈稍微〉　　大些。
Changhao　juesai　qushenglv　yinggai　<shaowei>　daxie
'ChangHao's chance to win the final should be < slightly> larger.'

Eg.4 *shaowei* + verb
我　给　大家　〈稍微〉　　解释　一下。
wo　gei　dajia　<shaowei>　jieshi　yixia
'I will explain <a little> to you.'

Eg.5 *shaowei* + adverb
这些　名字　〈稍微〉　　有点　　通俗。
zhexie mingzi <shaowei>　youdian　tongsu
'These names are <a little bit> common.'

The following example shows that *shaowei* can also be used to modify negative markers:

Eg. 6 *shaowei* + negation + adjective
〈稍微〉　　不　新鲜　的　都　不见　了。
<shaowei >　bu　xinxian　de　dou　bujian　le
'(Vegetables) staled <a little> have gone.'

Eg. 6 *shaowei* + negation + verb
如果　〈稍微〉　　不注意，　就　会　被　车　刮住　或者　　压迫　在　中间。
ruguo　<shaowei>　buzhuyi,　jiu　hui　bei　che guazhu　huozhe　yapo zai zhongjian.
'If you do not pay enough attention, it will cause a car scraping or oppression in the middle.'

Sometimes, negative markers appear before *shaowei*. This kind of situation is more likely to appear in interrogative sentences, which is in opposition to positive statements. Such finding is consistent with Klein's argument that a minimal or negative degree is mostly used to express a lack of a positive quality. [8]

Eg. 7 negation + *shaowei* + verb
你　为什么　不　〈稍微〉　松松　你　的　钱包　　呢?
ni　weishime　bu　<shao wei >　songsong ni　de　qianbao　ne ?
'Why don't you loosen your wallet < slightly >?'

In the selected sample, no sentence has the structure of "negation + *shaowei* + adjectives".

The data listed above and the figures in Table 2 show that *shaowei*, in most cases, appears in the affirmative context syntactically. Pragmatically, however, it serves to weaken the degree of positivity in those contexts. As a result, this study considers *shaowei* as a PPI and functions as a downtoner in sentences.

In the selected sample, there are 131 concordances containing the word *xiewei* and 13 of which are adverbs. Like *shaowei*, it precedes and modifies adjectives, verbs, and adverbs.

Eg.8 *xiewei* + adjective
在　暴动　有　〈些微〉　　可能　的　地方　用尽全力　　（发动）。
zai　baodong　you <xiewei>　keneng　de　difang　yongjin quanli　(fadong)
'(We) should launch an uprising with all efforts in place where revolution has <a little> possibility.'

Eg.9 *xiewei* + verb
双方　　〈些微〉　的　　交谈　了　两句。
Shuangfang <xiewei>　de　jiaotan　le　liangju
'The two sides talked <a little>.'

Eg.10 *xiewei* + negation
倩彤　　有　〈些微〉　不耐烦。
qiantong　you　<xiewei>　bunaifan
'Qiantong was < a bit> impatient.'

It is shown that only 1 of the 13 cases is used in the negative environment. Thus, *xiewei*, just like *shaowei*, is a PPI when frequency and pragmatics factors are considered. It generally has a lowering effect, scaling downwards from an assumed norm.

3.2.2   *Hao* and *sihao*

Shi and Jiang point out that *hao* has a preference for negative environment. [4][10] The statistics of this research support their statements, as all of the 264 adverbs are found in negative contexts. All *hao* modifies monosyllable negative markers like *wu*, *bu* and *mei*. A total of 161 instances of *hao* were accompanied by *wu*, and the other 102 instances of *hao* are accompanied by *bu*. Only one instance of *hao* is accompanied by *mei*. A few selected examples are listed as below:

Eg.11 *hao* + *wu* + verb
（心脏） 对   病人   的 日常   生活   〈毫〉无影响。
(xinzang) dui   bingren de   richang shenghuo   <hao >wuyingxiang
'(The heart) has no influence <at all> on patient's daily activities.'

Eg.12   *hao* + *wu* + noun
矮人 可以   〈毫〉无困难   地 挤   过去。
airen   keyi   <hao> wukunnan   de ji   guoqu
'Dwarves can squeeze without difficulty.'

Eg.13   *hao* + *bu* + verb
我   〈毫〉不在乎。
Wo   <hao> buzaihu
'I do not care <at all>.'

Eg.14 *hao* + *bu* + adjective
我 会 〈毫〉不犹豫 的 选择   13班。
wo   hui <hao>buyouyu de   xuanze   13ban
'I would not hesitate <a little> to choose class 13.'

Eg.15 *hao* + *mei* + adjective
这个 说 相声   的 〈毫〉没客气。
zhege shuo xiangsheng de   <hao>meikeqi
'The crosstalk is not polite <at all>.'

As shown in the cited examples, we can see "*hao* + *wu*" structure modifies verbs and abstract nouns while "*hao* + *bu*" has a preference for verbs and adjectives and "*hao* +*mei*" collocates with adjectives. Through the combination of the minimal degree adverbs and negative markers, they amplify the negation effects in a sentence. Therefore, *hao* is an NPI and can be used to realize negative reinforcement in all sentences.

Compared with *hao*, *sihao* is more flexible syntactically as it can precede or follow the negative marker *mei* or *meiyou*. In most cases, however, it precedes and modifies *wei* and *bu*.

Eg.16 *meiyou* + *sihao* + verb
他 都 没有 〈丝毫〉 留意。
ta   dou   meiyou   <sihao>   liuyi
'He does not pay the <slightest> attention.'

Eg.17 *sihao* + *meiyou* + verb
老人 甚至 〈丝毫〉 没有 表现 出 对 乐器 的 好奇。
laoren   shenzhi   <sihao>   meiyou biaoxian   chu   dui   yueqi   de   haoqi
'The old man does not even show <a bit> curiosity to musical instruments.'

Eg.18 *sihao* + *bu* + verb
他们 的 干劲 却 〈丝毫〉 不减。
Tamen   de   ganjin   que   <sihao>   bujian
'Their enthusiasm is unabated.'

Eg.19 *sihao* + *wei* + verb
风筝 爱好者 参加 比赛 的 热情 〈丝毫〉未减。
fengzheng   aihaozhe canjia   bisai   de   reqing   <sihao>wei jian
'The kite amateurs' enthusiasm to participate in competition is undiminished.'

There is only one example in "*wei + sihao*" collocation.

Eg.20 *wei* + *sihao* + verb
这事 并未 〈丝毫〉 增加 他 在 同行间 的 名气。
Zheshi   bingwei   <sihao>   zengjia   ta   zai   honghangjian de   mingqi.
'This incident has not increased his reputation in his peers.'

In all these collocations, *sihao*, regardless of its position to the negative marker, intensifies the negation effects in sentences. Therefore, it is an NPI like *hao*.

Shi Yuzhi points out that the semantics of degree words play a critical role when deciding their polarity characteristics. [4] However, the findings in this study do not support Shi's argument, as the four minimal adverbs discussed in this research all indicate semantics of minimal degree but not all of them are NPIs. When we inquire into the polarity characteristics of a word, both its semantic features and its relative frequencies in large corpus should also be taken into account. As shown in Table 3, *shaowei* and *xiewei* are PPIs while *hao* and *sihao* are NPIs.

Table 3. The polarity characteristic of four Chinese minimal degree adverbs

	PPI	NPI
hao	–	+
sihao	–	+
shaowei	+	–
xiewei	+	–

4   Conclusion

Semantically, a word indicating minimal degree is likely to be a negative polarity sensitive item. However, this research shows that there is not a consistent one-to-one match between minimal degree adverb and NPI. The minimum semantic degree is only one of several factors of NPI. Therefore, in addition to its semantic and pragmatic characteristics, the frequency of a minimal degree adverb should also be taken into consideration when deciding its polarity sensitivity.

References

1. Kaimu, S.: Exploration of the Negation Scope and Focus of bu. Zhongguo Yuwen **6**, 404–412 (1984)
2. Shuxiang, L.: Interrogation. Negation. Affirmation. Zhongguo Yuwen **4**, 241–250 (1985)
3. Yulin, Y.: Negative Sentence: Its FocusPresupposition and Scope Ambiguity. Zhongguo Yuwen **2**, 99–108 (2000)
4. Yuzhi, S.: Symmetry and Asymmetry Between Affirmation and Negation, 2nd edn. Beijing Language and Culture University Press, Beijing (2001)
5. Israel, M.: The pragmatics of polarity. In: Horn, L.R., Ward, G. (eds.) The Handbook of Pragmatics, pp. 701–723. Blackwell Publishing, Oxford (2005)
6. Li, W.: The Chinese Modern Grammar. The Commercial Press, Beijing (1933/1985)
7. Zhen, Ma.: An Observation on the Distribution of Degree Adverbs in Sentence Pattern of Degree. Sijie Hanyu Jiaoxue **4**, 81–86 (1988)
8. Klein, H.: Adverbs of Degree in Dutch and Related Language. John Benjamins, Amsterdam (1998)
9. Ruihong, H.: The Polarity Sensitivity of English Minimal Degree Adverbs. Foreign Language Teaching and Research (Bimonthly) **4**, 268–275 (2007)
10. Yong, J.: The Cascade Model of the Polarity Items Based on Information Theory. Foreign Language Research **1**, 65–70 (2013)

The Semantic and Pragmatic Analysis of '*wo zhidao* (*I know*)' in Fiction Style

Zhenguo Wu[1], Lijuan Li[1,2(✉)], and Zhifu Liu[2]

[1] School of Chinese Language and Literature, Central China Normal University, Wuhan, China
wu_zhenguo@126.com, lilij10@163.com
[2] School of Art and Communication, China Three Gorges University, Yi Chang, China
zhifuliu1980@163.com

Abstract. In fiction style, '*wo zhidao* (*I know*)' is used frequently, and it is often followed by a clause as object. When the verb '*zhidao* (*know*)' means 'to have information about something', '*wo zhidao* (*I know*)' is mainly used in the persuading and request speech act to indicate that the input information is accessible, or to make the potential information explicit. When the meaning of '*wo zhidao* (*I know*)' changes from 'certain information exist in my mind' to 'I believe certain information', the subjectivity of '*wo zhidao* (*I know*)' enhanced, we can consider it as a strong assertive predicate. In this case, '*wo zhidao* (*I know*)' is mainly used in the reproach or reprimanded context to express the speaker's belief and attitude.

Keywords: Fiction style · *Wo zhidao* (*I know*) · Semantic characteristics · Pragmatic function

1   Introduction

The verb '知道[*zhidao*] (*know*)', a word used to depict one's cognitive state, means 'to have information about the truth or knowledge'. There are four patterns which are composed by the first or second person pronoun and the affirmative form or negative form of the verb '知道[*zhidao*] (*know*)'. The patterns are listed as follows:

    a. the first person affirmative form: 我知道[*wo zhidao*] (*I know*);
    b. the first person negative form: 我不知道[*wo bu zhidao*] (*I don't know*);
    c. the second person affirmative form: 你知道[*ni zhidao*] (*You know*);
    d. the second person negative form: 你不知道[*ni bu zhidao*] (*You don't know*).

For convenience, the Chinese characters will be omitted in the following part.

Hongyin Tao (2003) considered that the evidence from sound patterns, syntax, and discourse pragmatics is drawn to support that constructions such as '*wo bu zhidao* (*I don't know*)' and '*ni zhidao* (*You know*)' are evolving into a pragmatic marker. Liyan Liu (2006) studied the three patterns and the function of the discourse marker '*ni zhidao* (*You know*)' in oral communication. Biji Zhou, Ying Li (2014) demonstrated

© Springer International Publishing Switzerland 2015
Q. Lu and H.H. Gao (Eds.): CLSW 2015, LNAI 9332, pp. 369–379, 2015.
DOI: 10.1007/978-3-319-27194-1_37

the evolution of the discourse marker '*ni bu zhidao* (*You don't know*)' and summarized its functions.

Regard to '*wo zhidao* (*I know*)', Hongyin Tao (2003) had pointed out that 'Although we haven't discussed this kind of pattern in this paper formally, it does not mean that the pattern has no feature. The first person affirmative form has a strong communicative meaning and shows a clear declaration of the speaker. . . The pragmatic meaning of this kind of sentence is to show the attitude of the speaker rather than the cognitive state of the speaker directly'. Mr. Tao didn't discuss '*wo zhidao* (*I know*)', because of the low frequency of '*wo zhidao* (*I know*)' in the corpus that he used. According to the instructions of Tao Hongyin (2003), his study was based on face-to-face conversational discourses corpus of about 100,000 Chinese characters. It is obvious that the size of the corpus is small and the context is single. In Tao's study, '*wo zhidao* (*I know*)' is not a pattern frequently used, which results from the single context. In order to explicitly analyze '*wo zhidao* (*I know*)', it is necessary to choose diverse context. So the further research must be based on a bigger corpus and a more diverse context. A fiction is known to have a narrative style and diverse context to shape the characters and create conflict. In this study, we employed the Contemporary Fiction Corpus developed by 'Research Center of Language and Language Education of Central China Normal University'. This corpus consists of more than 40 contemporary fictions of Chinese writers and more than 657,136 sentences.

In this paper, first, we analyze the usage of '*zhidao* (*know*)' patterns in fiction style, and compare the frequency of '*zhidao* (*know*)' patterns between fiction and conversation. Second, we discuss the semantic and pragmatic features of '*wo zhidao* (*I know*)' with an object. The pattern '*wo zhidao* (*I know*)' without an object, will not be discussed in this paper temporarily because of space limitation.

2   The Statistical Analysis of '*zhidao* (*know*)' Patterns and '*wo zhidao* (*I know*)' with an Object

2.1   The Salience of '*wo zhidao* (*I know*)' Patterns in Fiction Style

We investigated the patterns such as '*wo zhidao* (*I know*)', '*wo bu zhidao* (*I don't know*)', '*ni zhidao* (*You know*)' and '*ni bu zhidao* (*You don't know*)' in Contemporary Fiction Corpus and compared the data with the data of Tao Hongyin (2003). Specific statistics are shown in Table 1.

Table 1. The Comparison of '*zhidao* (*know*)' Patterns in Different Style

	Conversation		Fiction	
	Frequency	Proportion%	Frequency	Proportion %
wo zhidao	13	21.7	1493	47.3
wo bu zhidao	23	38.3	497	15.7
ni zhidao	18	30.0	930	29.5
ni bu zhidao	6	10.0	237	7.5

Although the sample size is different, statistic shows that, the proportion of the first person form (a total of 60% in conversation and 63% in fiction) is higher than the proportion of the second person form (a total of 40% in conversation and 37% in fiction), and the proportion of the second person affirmative form is also higher than the proportion of the second person negative form.

It can be seen that '*wo zhidao* (*I know*)' is often used in fictions (47.3%), and '*wo bu zhidao* (*I don't know*)' is often used in conversations (38.3%). So we can draw such a conclusion that '*wo zhidao* (*I know*)' is salient in the fiction. Because of the strong communication feature of '*wo zhidao* (*I know*)' and the narrative characteristic of the fiction, '*wo zhidao* (*I know*)' is often used in dialogues besides the first-person narration of the writer. Technically, in face-to-face conversations, the speaker mainly expresses his/her views, and for saving face, the speaker rarely replies with '*wo zhidao* (*I know*)', and also rarely uses '*wo zhidao* (*I know*)' to express subjective judgment. The speaker often uses '*wo bu zhidao* (*I don't know*)' to express his point of view in order to avoid being too arbitrary.

2.2   The Case of '*wo zhidao* (*I know*)' with an Object in Fiction

In conversations, the common grammatical feature of '*zhidao* (*know*)' patterns is the absence of object. In 117 cases of '*zhidao* (*know*)' patterns investigated by Mr. Tao, the number of '*zhidao* (*know*)' without object is 58 (nearly 50%). In fictions, when the subject is the first person pronoun '*wo* (*I*)', there are only 151 cases of the verb '*zhidao* (*know*)' used alone (about 10%); while the frequency of cases of the verb '*zhidao* (*know*)' with object is 1252 (about 84%); the frequency of others is 90 (about 6%). The style, frequency and proportion of the object following '*wo zhidao* (*I know*)' are shown in Table 2.

Table 2. The Statistics of Different Objects of the Verb '*zhidao*'

	Noun object	Pronoun object	Verb object	Adjective object	Clause object	Multiple clause object
Frequency	86	60	19	4	944	139
Proportion%	6.9	4.8	1.5	0.3	75.4	11.1

In the fiction, when the subject is the first person pronoun '*wo* (*I*)', the verb '*zhidao* (*know*)' can have six kinds of objects, but the most frequently used is clause object. This is different from the point of Cong Meng (2003) and Hongyin Tao (2003). It shows that the person of subject can also influence the type and frequency of the object of the verb '*zhidao* (*know*)'. Mei Fang (2005) considered that the evidential and epistemic verb can be followed by several clauses, but often by only one clause. She also considered that when a verb with predicate object followed by several objects, the characteristics of this verb as predicate will disappear and the constructions like '我觉得[*wo juede*] (*I feel*)/我想[*wo xiang*] (*I think*)/我看[*wo kan*] (*I kook*)' are grammaticalized as a pragmatic marker expressing the speaker's attitude. Based on our survey, '*wo zhidao* (*I know*)' can be subjectivized to express the speaker's belief and attitude.

In conclusion, 'wo zhidao (I know)' is salient in the fiction and often appears with a clause object. We will analyze the semantic and pragmatic features of 'wo zhidao (I know)' in the following part.

3 The Semantic and Pragmatic Analysis of 'wo zhidao (I know)'

On one hand, the basic meaning of 'zhidao (know)' is 'to have information about something or knowledge', which is similar to 'know (to have information about something)' in English. On the other hand, through the analysis, we find that 'wo zhidao (I know)' has evolved to a strong assertive predicate in modern Chinese, and that 'wo zhidao (I know)' has strong subjectivity. In this case, the meaning of 'zhidao (know)' is 'to be sure about something', which is similar to 'know (to be sure about something)' in English. 'Wo zhidao (I know)' has special pragmatic value when it means 'I have information about something or knowledge' or 'I am sure about something' in Chinese. It's necessary to note that, besides pronoun object, the objects following 'wo zhidao (I know)' are proposition. For convenience, the forms of 'wo zhidao (I know)' with objects are denoted by 'wo zhidao P (I know P)' in this paper.

3.1 'Wo zhidao (I know)' that Denotes 'P' is Accessible or Makes 'P' Explicit

In general, when the verb 'zhidao (know)' means 'to have information about something', the semantic content of the object of 'zhidao (know)' is a presupposition. The presupposition is the information that the speaker considers the hearer has already known. For example, in the sentence 'He knows John had come', 'John had come' is presupposition. In the communication, 'P' in the sentence 'wo zhidao P (I know P)', as a presupposition, is often given information or background information (such as the experience of the speaker or common sense). The pragmatic value of 'wo zhidao (I know)' can be summarized as: pointing out that the input information is accessible or making the potential information explicit. We will analyze the pragmatic value of 'wo zhidao (I know)' in detail.

Firstly, when 'wo zhidao P (I know P)' is used as a reply in the dialogue, 'P' is a given information, and 'wo zhidao P (I know P)' implies that what the speaker said is accessible and comprehensible to the hearer.

(1)楚天舒说："老乡，演习打的都是空爆弹，伤不了你的果树。"铁锁说："我知道这是演习，可硝烟一熏，挂果就要迟一年。"

Tianshu Chu says, "Hey, brother, there is only air bursting ammunition in the military exercise. It won't hurt your fruit trees." While Tiesuo says, "I know it's a military exercise. But the fruit bearing time will be delayed for one year once they are exposed to the smoke of gunpowder."

(2)宋文富也笑一笑说："只要你能想办法把王吉元买过来，花几百两银子我不心疼。""我知道你不心疼！人人说你宋大爷今年官星高照，不久就要走马上任。"

Wenfu Song smiles and says, "<u>I don't care</u> how much it will cost as long as you can buy Jiyuan Wang." "I know <u>you don't care</u>! It is known that you are bound to be an official this year and will take up an official post in the near feature."

In example (1), the clause 'it's a military exercise' is a given information. The sentence 'I know it's a military exercise' not only indicates that the hearer knows the matter of military exercise, but also the particular circumstances and influences. In example (2), the clause 'you don't care' is also a given information, the sentence 'I know you don't care' means the hearer not only has the information of 'you don't care', but also knows the reason, and the content after the sentence 'I know you don't care' directly shows the hearer's understanding. In these sentences, the literal meaning of '*wo zhidao* (*I know*)' is that the hearer knows what the speaker said. In fact, it implies that the hearer understands what the speaker said. All of these understandings show that the hearer is familiar with the background information of the communication. In other words, the information sent by the speaker is accessible to the hearer.

Secondly, sometimes, although 'P' is the shared information of the speaker and hearer, it does not appear in the preceding part of the dialogue. It can be the background information of the dialogue, for example, the experiences of the speaker, or the common sense that related to the dialogue. They are potential information of the communication. During the communication, the speaker will make the potential information explicit for a specific purpose.

(3)高庆山过去扶着犁杖说："老常哥，我给你耕一遭吧？"老常说："我知道<u>你也是庄稼人出身</u>，可是这牲口不老实，有点认生人！"

Qingshan Gao says with the plow in his hands, "Brother Chang, let me plough for you." Chang says, "I know <u>you were born as a peasant</u>. But the livestock is intractable and a little afraid of strangers."

(4)"虽然我知道<u>先亮底的人总是吃亏</u>，可谁叫我没你稳得起呢？"林凡夫先开口，"贵哥，我是来向你辞职的。"傅贵没吃惊，听他说。

"Although I know <u>those who put his cards on the table first will suffer losses</u>, I'm still less steady and calmer than you." Fanfu Lin says first, "Brother Gui, I am here to ask for resignation." Gui Fu just listens to him without any surprise.

In example (3), the clause 'you were born as a peasant' is the background information of the communication. In order to refuse the request of Qingshan Gao, Chang first delivered the background information 'you were born as a peasant' which was an admission that Qingshan Gao can plough, implying that Qingshan Gao's request is reasonable; then he indirectly refused Qingshan Gao by 'the livestock is intractable and a little afraid of strangers'. In example (4), the clause 'those who put his cards on the table first will suffer losses' is a common sense. Fanfu Lin admitted that he knew the common sense by '*wo zhidao* (*I know*)', making a concession; then he turned to show the behavior that is contrary to the common sense. The speaker highlights that he understood the common sense by '*wo zhidao* P (*I know* P)', which is beneficial to reduce his own embarrassment.

In a word, when the verb '*zhidao* (*know*)' means 'to have information about something', the pragmatic values of '*wo zhidao* (*I know*)' include: pointing out that the input information is accessible; making the potential information explicit. The syntactic and semantic characteristics relative to these two pragmatic values of '*wo zhidao* (*I know*)' include: '*wo zhidao* P (*I know* P)' is used as a concession clause in transitional complex sentence, there are 233 such examples as examples (1) (3) and (4); '*wo zhidao* P (*I know* P)' is used as a preceding clause in complex sentence of cause and effect to indicate cause, there are 143 such examples as example (5).

(5)沈伟道："我知道你和我妈不和，所以不敢瞎答应。"

Wei Shen says, "I know you don't get along well with my mother, so I couldn't answer her so casually."

From the perspective of pragmatic, whether to make a concession or to explain the reasons, all of these behaviors show the speaker pay attention to the factors affecting his speech act, and the sentence used to indicate concession and explain the reasons is often applied in the persuading and request speech act. In the persuading and request speech act, the status of the speaker is not higher than the hearer. In order to realize the purpose of the communication, it is necessary for the speaker to use a certain language strategy. As the saying goes, 'to know one's own strength and the enemy's is the sure way to victory'. To grasp the information about the speaker himself and the hearer accurately is the basis of complete communication tasks. During the communication, the speaker often uses '*wo zhidao* P (*I know* P)' to show self-knowledge or consideration for the hearer, making himself in a good position and making imperative speech act completely successful.

The success of the speech act of persuading mainly depends on the accurate analysis about the state of the hearer. In the sentence '*wo zhidao* P (*I know* P)', the content of 'P' is about the hearer, which shows the consideration of the hearer. In (6) and (7), the underlined parts indicate because of the speaker's understanding of the hearer, the speaker can win the trust of the hearer and make a good impression on the hearer, then achieves the purpose of persuading.

(6)孙若西柔声地说，"我知道，你从小失掉父母，寄人篱下，举目无亲，多孤单啊！你相信，只有我才是你唯一的亲人。咱俩结婚，我保证对你好，一心爱着你。"

Ruoxi Sun says softly, "I know you lost your parents when you were a child, and it's very lonely to live under other's roofs and have neither friends nor relations. You should believe it's I that am your sole relation. I promise I will take good care of you and love you with heart and soul after we get married."

(7)坐好之后，韩燕来劝告说："我知道你是从根据地来的老革命，经验多，道理也说的透；但这个环境可不同外边，说话要留神，咱们同姓苏的萍水相逢，可没什么深交情。"

After sitting down, Yanlai Han persuades, "I know you are a veteran from the base area and reasonable. But the situation here is different from others. You should talk with great care because Mr. Su is just a nodding acquaintance."

In the speech act of request, the speaker can express the wrongness of the speaker or the probable answer of the hearer in advance. In this way, the speaker shows the self-knowledge or consideration for the hearer, and makes the adviser in an active status to prompt success communication.

(8)她哀恳般的抬头看着奶奶："奶奶，我知道，<u>以我刚进门的身分地位，实在没有说话的资格</u>，可是，这件事和靖南息息相关，我实在无法沉默。请奶奶三思！我在这儿，给您跪下了！"说完，她就跪在奶奶面前了。

She looked up at her grandma with a pleading expression on her face, "Grandma, I know, <u>as a new member of the family, I'm not entitled a voice here</u>. But this matter is closely related to Jingnan. I can't keep silent. Please think twice, Grandma! Please." She really knelt down immediately to implore.

(9)龚跃进说："史局长，你看你看，我知道<u>你忙，到了哪儿也闲不下来</u>。我看还是先找个地方坐下来，只要坐下来……再说天也不早了，工作再忙，饭总是得吃的吧。"

"Mr. Shi, I know <u>you are busy, and can't be free for one second</u>. I think you'd better find a place to sit first…… What's more, it's a little dark outside. You need eat something no matter how busy you are." Yuejin Gong says.

In example (8), the speaker firstly said 'as a new member of the family, I'm not entitled a voice here', showing her self-identification, then she begged her grandma. If she begs her grandma immediately, her grandma maybe refuse her by 'you are not entitled a voice here'. In example (9), if Yuejin Gong requests immediately, Mr. Shi maybe refuse him by 'I'm busy now'. But Yuejin Gong uses '*wo zhidao*(*I know*)' to deliver the shared information – 'Mr. Shi is busy', which not only shows the consideration for the hearer, but also implies compliment in order to make the speaker to be in a good position.

3.2   '*Wo zhidao* (*I know*)' Indicates the Speaker's Belief and Attitude

Jiahua Zhang (2009) considered that the proposition content of the object of '*zhidao* (*know*)' is objective, it is typically shown by the syntactic characteristics of '*zhidao* (*know*)' and '认为[*renwei*] (*think*)'. For example, the sentence 'I think that he had left, but he didn't leave in fact' is accepted, but the sentence 'I know that he had left, but he didn't leave in fact' not. In the sentence 'I think that he had left', the clause 'he had left' is the speaker's judgment, the verb '认为[*renwei*] (*think*)' is often considered as a weak assertive predicate. In the sentence 'I know that he had left', the clause 'he had left' is not the speaker's judgment, but a fact, and the verb '*zhidao* (*know*)' is considered as a factive verb. Our research shows that the object of the verb '*zhidao* (*know*)' can also be the speaker's judgment.

(10)<u>连长命令我们架起大炮</u>，我知道这下是真要打仗了。

<u>The commander ordered us to set up the cannon</u>. I know the war will break out really this time.

(11)<u>天不早了，办公室的灯闭了</u>，我知道江老师要出来了。

It's a little dark. <u>The lights in the office have been turned off</u>. I know Mr Jiang will come out at once.

(12)<u>根据经验</u>，我知道现在开始好转了。

<u>According to my experience</u>, I know it has begun to change for the better now.

(13)"我知道我要出事了……<u>我有这种预感</u>。 "

<u>I have a hunch</u> that I'll meet a mishap.

In the above examples, the objects of the verb '*zhidao (know)*' are the speaker's judgments, the underlined parts are the foundations of the speaker's judgments. In example (10), it is the auditory information 'The commander ordered us to set up the cannon' that make the speaker form the judgment 'the war will break out really this time'. In example (11), the foundation of the speaker's judgment is 'the lights in the office have been turned off', it is visual information. In (12) and (13), the foundation of the speaker's judgment is the speaker's experience and hunch respectively. Because of the clause following '*zhidao (know)*' is the speaker's subjective judgment, '*zhidao (know)*' can be replaced by '认为[*renwei*](*think*)' in these sentences. For example, in (10), the sentence can be changed into 'The commander ordered us to set up the cannon. I think the war will break out really this time.' Other examples are similar to example (10). Now we can draw the following conclusion: '*wo zhidao (I know)*' can express the speaker's subjective judgment with a strong certainty. Example (14) can illustrate clearly.

(14) a."雅丽，我……我知道你不想出国。"欧正才十分肯定地说。

"Yali, I……I know you don't want to go abroad." Zhengcai Ou affirmatively said.

b.雅丽，我确信你不想出国。

Yali, I'm sure that you don't want to go abroad.

c.雅丽，我认为你不想出国。

Yali, I think you don't want to go abroad.

In example (14), if we replace '*zhidao (know)*' with '确信[*quexin*] (*be sure*)', the meaning of the sentence remains unchanged. If we replace '*zhidao (know)*' with '认为[*renwei*] (*think*)', the certainty of the sentence becomes weaker.

When the meaning of '*wo zhidao (I know)*' changes from 'certain information exist in my mind' to 'I believe certain information', the subjectivity of '*wo zhidao (I know)*' enhanced. We can consider it as a strong assertive predicate which indicates the speaker is sure of the truth of the proposition. Related syntactic and discourse characteristics are as follows.

First, the sentence stress of '*wo zhidao* P' changes. According to Jiahua Zhang (2009), '*zhidao (know)*' and '认为[*renwei*] (*think*)' focus on different information. '*wo zhidao* P (*I know* P)' focuses on '*zhidao (know)*' — 'P exist in my mind', but '*wo renwei* P (*I think* P)' focuses on 'P' — 'what exist in my mind is P'. For example, the focus of the sentence 'I know you have been rehabilitated' in example (15) is '*zhidao (know)*', and '*zhidao (know)*' is the stressed syllable, 'you have been rehabilitated' is an old information, it can't be changed into 'I think you have been rehabilitated'. But the focus of the sentence 'I know the war will break out really this time' in example (10) is 'the war will break out really this time', and '*zhidao (know)*' is not the stressed syllable.

(15)八圈……说："天成，你看看，我可是平反了呀……"呼天成点点头说："我知道。圈叔，我知道你平反了。"

Baquan says, "Tiancheng, you see, I have really been rehabilitated..."Tiancheng Hu nods and says, "I know. Uncle Quan, I know you have been rehabilitated."

Second, the proposition clause 'P' can be used with a model word, and then a modal proposition is formed.

(16)我知道<u>可能</u>我一辈子也见不到她了。

I know maybe I can't see her any longer all my life.

(17)我知道你<u>定能</u>顶住。

I'm sure that you can stand up to the pressure.

(18)我知道罗厚<u>准</u>来挑拨是非了。

I know Hou Luo must come for making mischief.

There is a model word '可能[*keneng*] (maybe)' in the object clause in example (16), indicating that the speaker's judgment 'I can't see her any longer all my life' maybe become a fact. The model word such as '定[*ding*] (*must*)' and '准[*zhun*] (*must*)' in examples (17) and (18) denotes that the speaker's judgments 'you can stand up to the pressure' and 'Hou Luo come for making mischief' will definitely become a fact. In these sentences, '*wo zhidao* (*I know*)' can be replaced by '我认为 [*wo renwei*] (*I think*)' or '我想[*wo xiang*] (*I think*)'.

Third, the speaker can use the interrogative sentence such as '对吗？[*dui ma*?] (*right*?)', and '是不是？[*shi bu shi*?] (*isn't it*?)' following '*wo zhidao* P (*I know P*)' to ask for confirmation.

(19) 我知道您找什么：九百九十九个脚印，您找到了九百九十七个，还剩下一大一小，<u>对吗</u>？

I know what you're looking for: nine hundred and ninety-nine footprints. Until now you have found nine hundred and ninety-seven ones, leaving a big one and a small one not found. <u>Am I right</u>?

(20)我知道八路军个个都是好汉，不是汉奸，你们不会替日本人收面，说不定倒是想打日本人哩，<u>是不是</u>？

I know every soldier from the Eighth Army is a brave man, not a traitor. And you'll never collect flour for Japanese army. Perhaps you want to fight against Japanese, <u>don't you</u>?

Zhaojun Guo (2004) considered that only the object clause of the weak assertive predicate can be followed with a tag question. But the above examples show that even the strong assertive predicate can also be followed with a tag question, because the proposition content of the object clause is uncertain. Sometimes, even the hearer can negate the judgment. For example, in (21), the hearer use the negative word '不[*bu*] (*no*)' to negate the speaker's judgment.

(21)"我知道，你非常讨厌我有这么一个女儿……""不！"

"I know you're disgusted to have such a daughter as me...""No!"

In a word, '*wo zhidao* (*I know*)' can be used to express the speaker's subjective judgment with a strong certainty. In this situation, '*wo zhidao* (*I know*)' has the same meaning with '我确信[*wo quexin*] (*I am sure*)', and both of them can be used to express the speaker's belief and attitude. Hongyin Tao (2003) considered that '*wo bu zhidao* (*I don't know*)' is used to express the speaker's tone of uncertainty. This point is also related to the strong assertiveness function of the verb '*zhidao* (*know*)'. That is to say, '*wo bu zhidao* (*I don't know*)' is equal to '我不确信[*wo bu quexin*] (*I am not sure*)'.

As Wittgenstein said, '*wo zhidao* (*I know*)' often indicates that I have a legitimate reason to support my statement. People say '*wo zhidao* (*I know*)' when they are ready to give a convincing reason. '*wo zhidao* (*I know*)' is often used to express the speaker's words are believable. Sometimes, in order to enhance the credibility of the speaker's judgment, the speaker often shows his own experience or status. For example, the sentence 'I killed Jackal before' in example (22) shows the speaker's experience, and the sentence 'I'm an actor in Chinese operas' in example (23) shows the speaker's status.

(22)我打死过豺狗，我知道，眼珠子不转，死了！

I killed Jackal before. I know it's dead if its eyeballs don't move.

(23)我是唱戏的，我知道，用黄缎子包的东西，那可不是一般的东西。

I'm an actor in Chinese operas. I know those wrapped with yellow satin are not ordinary things.

Because of the strong subjectivity of '*wo zhidao* (*I know*)', it is often used in the reproach or reprimanded context. In the context of reproach, the speaker can use '*wo zhidao* (*I know*)' to express anger. Example (24) can explain it well.

(24)"你就会骂我，你一天到晚，就在这儿挑我的不是！"靖南吼向了牧白："我知道，你心里只有干儿子，没有亲儿子！秋桐的事，就是被你这个干儿子办得乱七八糟，才弄到今天这个地步！"

"You're busy scolding me and finding fault with me all the day!" Jingnan roared at Mubai, "I know there is only your nominal son in your heart. No place for your own son! As for the matter of Qiutong, it's just because he screwed it up that it got into such a mess!"

In (24), '*wo zhidao* (*I know*)' is equal to 'You don't think that I don't know'. From the perspective of information transfer, the speaker makes the information that the hearer thinks he/she doesn't know and will not tell him/her explicit. In the reprimanded context, the speaker uses '*wo zhidao* P (*I know* P)' to express a judgment that is disadvantageous to the hearer. For example, the clauses 'you are getting older' and 'you are getting more ideas' in (25) are the speaker's judgments, expressing the negative evaluation about the hearer.

(25)"你看看你的零件，我想我闭着眼也能做得比你好。我知道，你年龄大了，心也野了，既然这样，我看你还是回家嫁人去吧！"

"Look at your parts. I think I can do it better than you with my eyes closed. I know that you are getting older, and you are getting more ideas. In that case, I think you'd better go home and get married!"

4   Conclusion

In conclusion, the pattern 'wo zhidao (I know)', salient in fiction style, is often followed by clause object and used in conversations. When the verb 'zhidao (know)'
means 'to have information about something', 'wo zhidao (I know)' is mainly used in
the persuading and request speech act to indicate that the input information is accessible or to make the potential information explicit. When the meaning of 'wo zhidao
(I know)' changes from 'certain information exist in my mind' to 'I believe certain
information', the subjectivity of 'wo zhidao (I know)' enhanced, we can consider it as
a strong assertive predicate. In this case, 'wo zhidao (I know)' is mainly used in the
reproach or reprimanded context to express the speaker's belief and attitude.
The interesting question is that the truth-value of the proposition clause 'P' is not
influenced by 'wo zhidao (I know)'. That is to say, the logic meaning of the object
clause is independent. This is the characteristic of a typical discourse marker. Further
study is needed.

References

1. Chu, Z.: On the thinking way of grammar study in investigating tendentiousness based on
   diversity. Journal of Huazhong Normal University (Humanities and Social Sciences). **2**,
   90–94 (2011). (in Chinese)
2. Fang, M.: On Grammartical bleaching of the evidential and epistemic verb: from comple-
   ment-taking predicates to pragmatic markers. Chinese Language. **6**, 495–507 (2005)
3. Guo, Z.: The Weak Assertive Predicate 'WO XIANG' in Mandarin Chinese Linguistics
   Study **2**, 43–47 (2004). (in Chinese)
4. Liu, L.: The discourse marker nizhidao(你知道). Chinese Language **5**, 423–432 (2006).
   (in Chinese)
5. Meng, C., et al.: Chinese verb usage dictionary. The Commercial Press, Beijing (2003).
   (in Chinese)
6. Tao, H.: Phonological, grammatical, and discourse evidence for the emergence of zhidao
   constructions. Chinese Language **4**, 291–302 (2003). (in Chinese)
7. Wang, D.: The co-variation between the semantics of the main verb and the nominalization
   of its predicative object. Chinese Language **4**, 315–328 (2003). (in Chinese)
8. Zhang, J.: A semantic and pragmatic account of the differences between syntactic Characteristics of zhidao(知道)and renwei(认为). Contemporary Linguistics **3**, 244–251 (2009).
   (in Chinese)
9. Zhou, B., Li, Y.: the evolution of discourse markers 'you don't know'. Chinese Linguistics
   1, 78–84 (2014). (in Chinese)

The Characteristics and the Whole Conversion Analysis of Quantitative Antonymous Compounds

Jinzhu Zhang[1(✉)] and Shan Xiao[2(✉)]

[1] The PLA University of Foreign Languages, Kunshan 215300, Jiangsu, China
95339041@qq.com
[2] International Education School, China University of Geosciences,
Wuhan 430074, Hubei, China
84781725@qq.com

Abstract. Based on the corpus (Center for Chinese Linguistics PKU corpus), we exhaustively analyze the semantics and syntactic function of quantitative antonymous compounds and morphemes. Through the coordination of two antonymous quantitative morphemes, antonymous compounds can refer to all the attribute values or the superior attribute category with universal quantification. The universal quantification determines the syntactic properties, which shows the bottom-up restriction mechanism. This study provides some references for the teaching Chinese as a foreign language, especially for vocabulary teaching.

Keywords: Antonymous compounds · Universal quantification · Conversion · Non self-sufficiency of semantics

1 Introduction

There is a small class in character adjectives representing space and quality, such as 大 / 小 [da/xiao](big/small), 多 / 少 [duo/shao](more/less), 长 / 短 [chang/duan] (long/short), 宽 / 窄 [kuan/zhai](wide/narrow), 高 / 低 [gao/di](high/low), 深 / 浅 [shen/qian](deep/shallow) etc, which contains [+measurement] semantic features, so we call them "Quantitative Adjectives".[1] These words are all pairs of antonyms.

In Chinese, there are a kind of coordinate compounds composed of quantitative adjectives, such as 大小 [daxiao](size), 多少 [duoshao](how much, how many), 长短 [changduan](length), 宽窄 [kuanzhai](width), 高低 [gaodi](height), 深浅 [shenqian](depth) etc, which we called "Quantitative Antonymous Compounds" (expressed in A1A2).

From the surface, we find that this kind of words are very simple in that the component morphemes are high frequency words, appearing in the outline of HSK vocabulary level A and B. Coordinate structure is centripetal structure from the perspective of structural linguistics. And compared to the synonymy and homologous coordinate structure, the semantic and syntactic function difference between component morphemes of antonymous compounds and the whole antonymous compounds is much bigger.[2] The surface grammatical structure and the deep semantic structure of

© Springer International Publishing Switzerland 2015
Q. Lu and H.H. Gao (Eds.): CLSW 2015, LNAI 9332, pp. 380–391, 2015.
DOI: 10.1007/978-3-319-27194-1_38

A1A2 is not corresponding. In other words, the semantic transparency of A1A2 is very low, because of which the second language learners tend to make errors in the acquisition of such words. For example[1]:

（1）这个高低是什么高低呢?

[*Zhe ge gaodi shi shenme gaodi ne?*]

What is the height?

（2）这都是为了农作物的大小大一些，还有长得好看一些。

[*Zhe dou shi weile nongzuowu de daxiao da yixie, hai you zhang de haokan yixie.*]

This is to make the size of corps grow larger and better.

（3）只有不管长短的假期来临之际，我才能背着大包去那儿。

[*Zhiyou buguan changduan de jiaqi lailin zhiji, wo caineng bei zhe da bao qu nar.*]

When the long and low vocations is coming, I am able to carry a big bag to go there.

Apparently, these three sentences are wrong. (1)高低[*gaodi*](*height*) should be replaced by高度[*gaodu*](*height*); (2)大小[*daxiao*](*size*) should be omitted; (3)长短[*changduan*](*length*) should be replaced by 长[*chang*](*long*).

Chinese academic circles have conducted a lot of studies on monosyllabic quantitative adjectives from the perspective of ontology and second language acquisition. At present the studies on antonymous compounds mainly focus on the description and interpretation of its diachronic evolution, describing their sources, forming process, the lexicalization mechanism and grammaticalization level etc.[3-6]But still there is a lack of comprehensive and systematic studies on the semantics, syntactic function and the differences between the components and the whole word. On the basis of previous research, we exhaustively analyze the semantics and syntactic function of the whole word and morphemes, and further manifest the characteristics of existing category, which can provide some reference and guidance for the teaching Chinese as a foreign language, especially for vocabulary teaching.

2   Semantics and Syntactic Analysis of Quantitative Antonymous Compounds

2.1   Selection of Quantitative Antonymous Compounds

In Chinese, there are numerous objectives representing quantitative category. In view of the frequency of A1A2, we mainly talk about the following five words: 大小 [*daxiao*](*size*), which represents the overall dimension; 多少 [*duoshao*](*how much, how many*), which represents the overall number; 高低[*gaodi*](*height*), which represents the height of the upward; 长短[*changduan*](*length*), which represents the

---

[1] Cases of errors are from Beijing Language and Culture University "HSK Dynamic Composition Corpus" (about 4.24 million words).

distance between two points, and深浅[*shenqian*](*depth*), which represents the length of the upward and the inside.

2.2　Semantics and Syntactic Analysis of 大小[*daxiao*](*size*)

2.2.1　大小[*daxiao/da xiao*](*size*) Representing the Quantitative

When大小[*daxiao*](*size*) represents the quantitative, it can refer to the specific amount of space, such as volume and the abstract number, time, degree or size, etc. 大小[*daxiao*](*size*) can appear in the following syntactic structures:

（一）大小[*daxiao/da xiao*](*size*)+NP(Noun Phrases)

大小[*daxiao/da xiao*](*size*)acts as an attributive in front of NP. The NP can be a single word, such as "大小湖泊"[*daxiao/da xiao hupo*](*big and small lakes*) , or be composed of more than one word, such as "大小环形山、平原和盆地"[*daxiao/da xiao huanshan, pingyuan he pendi*](*big and small craters, plains and basins*). 大小[*daxiao/da xiao*](*size*)implies a composite quantity, which determines that NP cannot be a individual , such as "*大小总统[*daxiao/da xiao zongtong*](*big and small presidents*), *大小世界[*daxiao/da xiao shijie*](*big and small worlds*), *大小校长[*daxiao/da xiao xiaozhang*](*big and small headmasters*)"etc. NP should be measurable, for example:

（4）他并没有问多少钱雇来的，而把<u>大小</u>三张钱票交给老张。

[Ta bing meiyou wen duoshao qian gu lai de, er ba daxiao/da xiao san zhang qian piao jiao gei laozhang.]

He didn't ask how much it is hired but gave LaoZhang three big and small pieces of paper currency.

NP can be either a single word or a quantitative structure, and the quantifiers must be individual quantifiers. 大小[*daxiao/da xiao*](*size*) highlights the specific properties of things--a certain value ofthe property. In example(4)大小[*daxiao/da xiao*](*size*)can refer to the physical properties of "area" of "money" or the social properties of "value", which have many kinds of intercommunity, which means when the "area" is large, the "value" is big. Clearly, the semantics of 大小[*daxiao/da xiao*](*size*) is not the addition of two component morphemes "大/小 [*da/xiao*](*big/small*) ", but covers all the values in a property category, with universal quantification, as shown in Fig. 1.

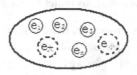

Fig. 1. Universal quantification schema of大小[*daxiao/da xiao*](*size*) in "大小[*daxiao/da xiao*](*size*)+NP"

In Fig. 1, as the typical entities in this category, the semantics of "e$_大$" and "e$_小$" is restrained(with a dotted line), highlighting all the values in the dimension category, and emphasizing the integrity of category(with a heavy line).

(二) 大小[*daxiao/da xiao*](*size*) In Unconditional Sentence

The typical structure of 大小[*daxiao/da xiao*](*size*) in unconditional sentences is "S$_1$+无论[*wulun*](*whatever*)/无论[*wulun*](*whatever*)+S$_1$+大小[*daxiao/da xiao*](*size*), S$_2$+都[*dou*](*all*) +VP". The relation between S$_1$ and大小[*daxiao/da xiao*](*size*) is a kind of statement. S$_1$ and S$_2$ can be either same or different. If the same, S$_2$ can be canceled. S$_1$ in this structure must have quantity and plural semantic features. For example:

（5）报无论大小，都有个品位的问题。

> [*Bao wulun daxiao/da xiao, dou you ge pinwei de wenti.*]
> *Whatever the size of newspaper is, the newspaper has its own taste.*

In example(5), 大小[*daxiao/da xiao*](*size*) refers to any properties value of the newspapers size category, such as "biggest, very big, quite big, bigger, small, smaller, very small, smallest". The quantity of newspapers is plural. Here,大小[*daxiao/da xiao*](*size*)refers to the specific properties of things--that is the value of properties, also with universal quantification. When it comes to the usage of 无论 [*wulun*](*whatever*), Shuxiang Lv[7] pointed out that they can be used in the kind of sentences that have interrogative pronouns expressing arbitrary reference or coordinate elements expressing selective relation, which means in any cases the result or the conclusion won't change with "都[*dou*](*all*), 也[*ye*](*also*) ". His point of view has also supported our conclusion. Although the relation between coordinate elements after无论[*wulun*](*whatever*) is selective, they can constitute a common reference category or collection together, expressing universal quantification. We call this "arbitrary universal quantification". In arbitrary universal quantification, 大小[*daxiao/da xiao*](*size*) and大/小[*da/xiao*](*big/small*) are still at the same level. This type is illustrated in Fig. 2, where solid lines represent all values or entities, the dotted lines represent the entirety.

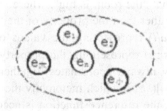

Fig. 2. Universal quantification schema of大小[*daxiao/da xiao*](*size*) in unconditional sentences

(三) VP+大小[daxiao/da xiao](size)

In this structure, 大小[*daxiao/da xiao*](*size*) is the object of VP, usually used in negative sentences. For example:

（6）中国一贯主张国家不分大小，都一律平等。

[Zhongguo yiguan zhuzhang guojia bu fen daxiao/da xiao, dou yilv pingdeng.]
China has always maintained that all nations, big or small, are equal.

In example(6), the meaning of 大小[*daxiao/da xiao*](*size*) is the addition of components, referring to the specific properties value, emphasizing the quantity, without any degree. Predicate verbs in the sentence commonly have comparison meaning, such as "分[*fen*](*distinguish*), 比较[*bijiao*](*compare*)" etc.

（四）数量名 [shu liang ming](Number + Measure word + Noun)+大小 [daxiao](size)

In this structure, 数量名[*shu liang ming*](*Number + Measure word + Noun*) is used to clarify the specific quantity of大小[*daxiao*](*size*). For example:

（7）科学家能够在1毫升血液中检查出只有25微米大小的癌细胞。

> [*Kexuejia nenggou zai 1 haosheng xueye zhong jiancha chu zhiyou 25 weimi daxiao de aixibao.*]
> *Scientists can able to check out 25 micron size of cancer cells only in 1 ml blood.*

（8）只有三张榻榻米大小的空间里，她铺上一张席子。

> [*Zhiyou san zhang tatami daxiao de kongjian li, ta pu shang yi zhang xizi.*]
> *She spreaded a mat in the space of only three tatami size.*

In example(7), as a specific property value, quantitative structure "1毫升[*yi haosheng*](*1ml*)" makes the semantic meaning of "癌细胞[*aixibao*](*cancer cell*)" embodiment and quantization. In example(8), "榻榻米[*tatami*](*tatami*)" has typical spatial characteristics, which also makes the semantic meaning of "空间[*kongjian*](*space*)" embodiment and quantization. These sentences have a kind of comparison or matching meaning.

Basic category and subordinate category are important concepts in cognitive linguistics. The basic category is the generalization expression level for the classification of things. Subordinate category is more specific than the basic category. As for quantitative adjectives, we say that "the room is big", where "big" is the specific property of the "area" of the room, rather than the property of the "room". We can understand that 大/小[*da/xiao*](*big/small*) representing the values of properties has a vertical relation with大小[*daxiao*](*size*) representing the property. 大/小[*da/xiao*](*big/small*) in the subordinate category always coordinates together and gradually becomes a compound word大小[*daxiao*](*size*), which metonymy the "area" property in the basic category. The realization of the reference function is accomplished through the conception integration of the metonymy mechanism. The semantic meaning of 大小 [*daxiao*](*size*) can cover all大/小[*da/xiao*](*big/small*) magnitudes value in the subordinate category, with the governing universal quantification. The governing universal quantification is illustrated in Fig. 3.

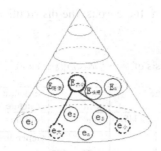

Fig. 3. Universal quantification schema of 大小 [*daxiao*](*size*) in " 数 量 名 [*shu liang ming*](*number + measure word + noun*) +大小[*daxiao*](*size*)"

（五）NP+(的[de](particle))+大小[daxiao](size)

The nominal subject NP can refer to the properties of the person or thing that exists independently, such as shape, volume and weight. However, 大小[*daxiao*](*size*), with lower self-sufficiency, can't refer to the properties independently. Instead it must be attached to the subject NP. In this structure, NP and 大小[*daxiao*](*size*) are forming a possessive construction. NP plays a limiting role, such as "宫室的大小[*gongshi de daxiao*](*the size of the palace*)". 大小[*daxiao*](*size*) is corresponding to the scale of the house property. In this structure, 大小[*daxiao*](*size*) is an attribute noun, and its utterance function is reference, not modification.[8] 大小[*daxiao*](*size*) refers to the property category covering all the property values of the subordinate category, with the governing universal quantification, which can also be illustrated by Fig. 3.

NP +大小[*daxiao*](*size*) forms a possessive relationship. NP is the attribute of possession.大小[*daxiao*](*size*) is the head. The whole structure is nominal, which can be used as the object of measurement class, comparison verb structures and individual prepositions (such as " 从 [*cong*](*from*), 根 据 [*genju*](*according to*), 通 过 [*tongguo*](*through*)", etc) and the subject of a small number of changes, iconicity and the judging class verb structures. 大小[*daxiao*](*size*) representing the property can't co-occur with 大/小[*da/xiao*](*big or small*) representing the value of property.

2.2.2 大小[*daxiao*](*size*) Representing the Social Relations and Evaluation

大小[*daxiao*](*size*) mainly refers to the level of seniority, covering all the persons within the range of a "social space", including adults and children, with universal reference, which can be illustrated by Fig. 1. 大小[*daxiao*](*size*) is mainly used in the structure of "全[*quan*](*all*)/一[*yi*](*whole*)+家[*jia*](*family*)+大小[*daxiao*](*size*)".

When大小[*daxiao*](*size*) refers to evaluation meaning, it means "either large or small" and is used as an adverb in the structure of "大小[*daxiao*](*size*)+VP". The nominal structure representing the individual generally could not co-occur with 大小 [*daxiao*](*size*).

Based on the statistics from the corpus, the distribution of大小[*daxiao*](*size*) is as follows:

Table 1. Syntactic analysis of 大小[*daxiao*](*size*) and 大/小[*da/xiao*](*big/small*)

Meanings	Syntactic structure	Percentage		Syntactic position	Semantic structure	compound	components
Quantity	(I)	1.19%	29.11%	Object	Addition	+	-
	(II)	3.17%			Generalization	+	-
	(III)	24.75%		Attributive		+	+
	(IV)	11.49%	66.34%	Head	Extension	+	+
	(V)	54.85%		Head		+	-
Social relation	VP+~	0.4%		Object	Generalization	+	-
		1.58%		Head		+	-
Evaluation	~+VP	2.57%		Adverbial	Extension	+	-

2.3   Syntactic Analysis of 多少[*duoshao*](*how much*), 高低 [*gaodi*](*height*), 长短 [*changduan*](*length*), 深浅[*shenqian*](*depth*)

Similarly, the syntactic analysis of多少[*duoshao*](*how much*), 高低[*gaodi*](*height*), 长短[*changduan*](*length*), 深浅[*shenqian*](*depth*) are also statistically analyzed. The details are as follows:

Table 2. Syntactic analysis of 多少[*duoshao*](*how much*)and 多/少[*duo/shao*](*more/less*)

Meanings	Syntactic structure	Percentage		Syntactic position	Semantic structure	compound	components
Quantity	(V)	3.08%	18.85%	Head	Extension	+	-
	(II)	1.92%				+	-
	(I)	23.45%		Object			
	~+measure word +NP	42.5%	52.11%	Attributive		+	-
	~+measure word			Attributive		+	-
Evaluation	~+VP	29.04%		Adverbial	Extension	+	-

Table 3. Syntactic analysis of 高低[*gaodi*](*height*)and 高/低[*gao/di*](*high/low*)

Meanings	Syntactic structure	Percentage		Syntactic position	Semantic structure	compound	components
Quantity	(II)	4.51%	12.35%		Generaliza-tion	+	-
	(III)	7.84%		Attribu-tive	Generaliza-tion	+	+
	(V)	65.69%	65.69%	Head	Extension	+	-
Hierarchy	VP+~	21.76%		Object	Extension	+	-
Degree		0.2%		Object		+	-

Table 4. Syntactic analysis of 长短 [*changduan*](*length*) and 长/短 [*chang/duan*](*long/short*)

Meanings	Syntactic structure	Percentage		Syntactic position	Semantic structure	compound	components
Quantity	(II)	4.0%	23.2%		Generaliza-tion	+	-
	(III)	19.2%		Attribu-tive		+	+
	(IV)	17.6%	65.6%	Head	Extension	+	-
	(V)	48.0%				+	-
Quality	VP+~/~+VP	11.0%		Object, Subject	Extension	+	-
Evalua-tion	~+VP	0.2%		Adverbial	Extension	+	-

Table 5. Syntactic Analysis of 深浅 [*shenqian*](*depth*) and 深/浅 [*shen/qian*](*deep/shallow*)

Meanings	Syntactic structure	Percentage		Syntactic position	Semantic structure	compound	components
Quantity	(II)	2.33%	9.33%		Generaliza-tion	+	-
	(III)	7.0%		Attributive		+	+
	(V)	14.33%	78.0%	Head	Extension	+	-
		63.67%				+	-
Sense of propriety	VP+~	12.67%		Object	Extension	+	-

Based on statistical data from table 1 to 5, we find that the semantic meaning of A1A2 has both the generalization and the extension of component morphemes. Through metonymy mechanism of conceptual integration, A1A2 can refer to proper-ties of basic category. The frequency of this meaning is the highest. The meaning of component morphemes of A1A2 is weakened or eliminated. Two components gradually merge into one word, which means the degree of semantic integration is higher. The semantic projection of A1A2 expands to abstract social fields based on physical space quantity, which forms a set of concepts and codes of various physical and non-physical properties expressed by different dimensions.

3   Typical Characteristics of Quantitative Antonymous Compounds

In the relationship between morphemes, lexicon and syntax, morphemes plays a decisive role. Each component is given an assignment of the same semantic features or category features by the construction of antonymous coordination and the same features or category features determines the same syntactic representation. Through the coordination of two typical quantitative antonymous adjectives, compound word A1A2 is formed and A1A2 can refer to all the properties value or the basic properties category, with universal quantification. The universal quantification determines its special syntactic representation. This is a kind of bottom-up constraint mechanism, which is from the bottom of the morphemes to the lexical semantics and then to high-level syntactic semantics. The properties reference of A1A2 is different from a typical noun referring to the person or the things. The uniqueness of A1A2 are as follows:

First, the universal quantification meaning.

Influenced by antonymous coordination morphemes, A1A2 carries the semantic characteristics of universal quantification. Restricted by the degree of lexicalization, the universal quantification represents the explicit and implicit forms at the syntactic level: that is when A1A2 expresses specific properties, the modified NP should be plural and measurable. In example(4), "三张[*san zhang*](*three pieces*)" is explicit plural quantity. while in example(5), "报[*bao*](*newspaper*)" is implicit plural quantity, referring to an arbitrary value or all values in the property category. Chinese is a language lacking of morphological changes, we can't see the marker of plural forms and can only judge from the meaning of sentences.

Secondly, non self-sufficiency of semantics.

A1A2 can't be used as the attributive in the sentence independently without attaching to the things or actions to constitute possessive construction. A few A1A2 constituting subject-predicate structure with equal verbs can be used as attributive, such as "长短不等的木棒[*changduan bu deng de mubang*](*the sticks of different length*)". In addition, A1A2 are mainly used in the structure of "NP+(的[*de*](*particle*))+A1A2)", can't be freely used as the subject and the object.

Thirdly, A1A2 tends to show a nominal tendency.

The classification of parts of speech depends on its internal descriptive function. The descriptive function of part of speech have four basic types: statement (expressed as an assertion), reference (expressed the object), modification, and auxiliary.[9] Noun mainly expresses the things and has the reference function. Clearly, nouns can refer to persons and things independently. A1A2 can refer to any one or all values of the property category and can refer to the property of its basic category. From the syntactic function, A1A2 mainly occupies the subject and the object syntactic position, which is similar to the syntactic function of nouns.

Finally, A1A2 belongs to the atypical nouns.

The typical feature of nouns is space, which can be modified by quantity structures, such as,"一支笔[yi zhi bi](one pen), 三本书[san ben shu](three books), etc" and can't be modified by adverbs.[11] Seventy-eight percent of nouns can be modified by quantitative phrases,[10] while A1A2 can't. For example:

> *三种高低[san zhong gaodi](three kinds of height)
> *一张厚薄[yi zhang houbao](one piece of thickness)
> *一个大小[yi ge daxiao](one size)
> *一根长短[yi gen changduan](one length)

Based on the above analysis, we find that A1A2 does not have the prototypical or the typical features of nouns, but is the atypical member of the noun category.

4   Whole Conversion Analysis of Quantitative Antonymous Compounds

From the specific property or the value property to metonymy the basic property category, there is a vertical relationship between the component morphemes and the compounds, which are in different semantic categories. Thus, it can be said that the semantics of A1A2 has changed, or the conversion has occurred.

The part of speech is classified by the utterance function. Since the 50's, there has been controversy about whether there is a multi-class words or conversion between word classes. A lot of studies have discussed these issues and point out that the descriptive functions can be transformed to one another.[10-12] The descriptive function of morphemes is modification, while the descriptive function of the compound A1A2 is reference. The transformation of descriptive function has been completed in the lexicon level, named as lexical transformation.[10]

The main syntactic functions of adjective in Chinese is to act as predicate or attribute, and can be modified by degree adverbs. When acted as an attribute, the opposite meanings of A1 and A2 show the asymmetry and the markedness both on the lexical level and the syntactic level, such as, "大方[dafang](generous), *小方[xiaofang]; 有多 A_1[you duo A1](how A1),*有多A_2[you duo A2] (how A2)". A1A2 can't be modified by degree adverbs and the lexical status of component morphemes is equal. The asymmetry and the markedness disappear. A1A2 can act as the head, attribute, object in modifier-head construction to generalize and metonymy the whole property category, but can't take the tense, aspect marker and directional complements. Such as:

> 大/小了[da/xiao le](getting big and small)   *大小了[daxiao le]
> 多起来/少下去[duo qi lai/shaoxiaqu](getting more/getting less)
> *多少起来/下去[duoshao qi lai/xiaqu]

Compared with the component morphemes, the whole compound A1A2 have taken place the fundamental change both at the semantic or syntactic level. The details are as follows:

Table 6. Comparison between A1A2 and component morphemes A1/A2

	Syntactic structure	Syntactic position	Utterance function		Overlapping	Negative	Markedness
			Modification	Reference			
Components	A+NP S+adv+A	Attributive, Predicate	+	-	+	不[*bu*](*negative*)+A	+
Compound	NP+ （的） +A₁A₂ VP+A₁A₂	Subject, Object	-	+	-	- 不 [*bu*](*negative*)+VP+A₁A₂	-

5   Conclusion

Through the analysis, we find that the quantitative antonymous compounds formed from antonymous quantitative adjectives, on the basis of the semantics of component morphemes, metonymy all values of property category or basic category through the generalization mechanism of the conceptual integration. The compound A1A2 loses the adjective characteristic of component morphemes A1/A2, which shows strong nominal syntactic tendency. However, the non self-sufficiency of semantics also inhibits the transformation of A1A2 to a typical noun, but to be a non-prototypical or atypical one.

There is a link between the quantitative adjectives and the quantitative antonymous compounds, but the difference is greater. In the process of lexicalization, all the A1A2 occur the whole conversion, presenting great inconsistency with the component morphemes both at the semantic and syntactic levels. The surface semantic information of A1A2 causes certain difficulties in predicting words meaning for learners of Chinese. We hope that the study can provide a reference for the acquisition of this kind of words.

Acknowledgement. This work was supported by a grant from China Educational Commission of Hubei Provice(13g048).

References

1. Lu, J.M.: Speaking of Quantitative adjective. Language Teaching and Linguistic Studies **3** (1998)
2. Dong, X.F.: Lexicalization: the Origin and Evolution of Chinese Disyllabic Words, p. 122. The Commercial Press, Beijing (2002)
3. Wei, D.C.: The Study on Antonymous Compounds in <YanShi JiaXun>. Journal of Northeast Normal University, Changchun **1** (1998)

4. Guo, Y.J.: Exploration of Antonymous Compounds, Shandong Normal University Master's Degree Thesis, Jinan (2000)
5. Yang, J.C.: The Study of Antonymous Compounds. Zhonghua Book Company, Beijing (2007)
6. Zeng, D.: A Cognitive Study of the Evolution of Antonymous Compounds, Zhejiang University PhD Thesis, Hangzhou (2007)
7. Lv, S.X.: Eight Hundred Words in Modern Chinese (An Enlarged Revision). The Commercial Press (2010)
8. Lv, J.M., Shen, Y.: Fifteen Chinese and Chinese Studies. The Peking University Press (2004)
9. Croft, W.: Syntactic Categories and Grammatical Relations. The University of Chicago Press, Chicago (1991)
10. Guo, R.: Research on the Part of Speech in Modern Chinese, pp. 84–101. The Commercial Press, Beijing (2002)
11. Zhu, D.X.: Lectures on Grammar, p. 41. The Commercial Press, Beijing (1982)
12. Shi, D.X.: Noun and noun elements. The Peking University Press, Beijing

都b[Doub(Dou2、 Dou3)] as A Counter-Expectation Discourse-Marker: On the Pragmatic Functions of Doub from the Perspective of Discourse Analysis

Hua Zhong[✉]

Overseas Education College of Fujian Normal University, Fuzhou, China
jtingshan@163.com

Abstract. The conventional implicature of Doub indicates that a speaker make a judgment on the state of affairs described by a proposition, and he/she believes that the possibility of the state of affairs is inferior-to-expectation (or normal). It is a non-truth procedural pragmatic meaning which carries interpersonal functions and textual functions in discourse. In this paper, "counter-expectation information" is divided into two main classes, "adversity-to-expectation" and "deviation-from-expectation", and four subclasses, "contradictory relation", "contrary relation", "superior-to-expectation", and "inferior-to-expectation". Based on this scheme, the semantic function and pragmatic functions of Doub as a counter-expectation discourse marker is analysed. This study has shown that the pragmatic scale of the possibility of occurrence or existence of a situation is the pragmatic scope of Doub; and the "inferior-to-expectation" is its pragmatic condition. The informative intention of Doub is to state that the possibility of occurrence or existence of a situation is lower than the expectation (or normal), and the communicative intention is to provide the proof or support for the declaration and the assertion of the speaker, namely for evidentiality or to enhance illocutionary force and mood in language. This is the meta-pragmatic awareness of Doub. In a textual structure, a Doub sentence is usually an "assistant" of a declaration or an assertion, and it is seldom used as an independent sentence/expression. The textual relevance types of Doub sentences mainly include: progressive, adversative, certificative, causation, and suppositional. And Doub is often used in spoken discourse.

Keywords: 都b[Doub] · Procedural pragmatic meaning · Interpersonal functions · Textual functions · Counter-expectation discourse markers

1   Definition of the Semantic Function of 都b[Doub]

Doub described in this article includes Dou2 (*even*), Dou3 (*already*) mentioned in the current literatures, for example:

(1) Ni   dai   wo   bi   qin   jiejie   dou hao.
    You   treat me   than   biological elder-sister   even good
    You treated me even better than my elder sister. [Dou2] *(even)*

This article uses Discourse Markers (or Pragmatic Marker) in the wide sense, i.e. those discourse ingredients that perform interpersonal functions and/or textual functions in a discourse, are Discourse Markers (see [1, 2]).

© Springer International Publishing Switzerland 2015
Q. Lu and H.H. Gao (Eds.): CLSW 2015, LNAI 9332, pp. 392–407, 2015.
DOI: 10.1007/978-3-319-27194-1_39

(2) Fan   dou   liang-le,   kuai chi ba!
Dinner already cold-Asp, hurry eat PAT
The dinner already   got cold, just have it! [Dou$_3$] *(already)*

For the ease of expression, those constructions that contain Dou$_b$ are roughly formatted as "(X) + Dou$_b$ + Y, (Z)".

Thus we can roughly say that Dou$_b$ construction contains two components, one: "(X) Y, (Z)" explicitly expresses the propositional meaning, i.e. the occurrence or existence of a state of affairs; two: Dou$_b$ implicitly makes a judgment on the state of affairs, which considers that the possibility of occurrence or existence of the state of affairs described by a proposition is inferior-to-expectation (or normal).

From the perspective of three metafunctions of functional linguistics (see [1,3]), in Dou$_b$ construction, component one "(X) Y, (Z)" has an experiential function, which describes things and their corresponding processes in the subjective and objective world, and expresses the truth-value meaning and propositional meaning; as for component two, Dou$_b$ what mainly performs is interpersonal functions and textual functions, which expresses the non-propositional meaning and procedural meaning. In other words, the meaning of Dou$_b$ is not the truth-value conditional meaning from the point of traditional semantics, but the pragmatic meaning for leading or guiding the addresee to understand the relevant discourse (see [4,5,6,7,8]), for example:

(3) a. Ta zhang-de bi ren   dou gao-le.
It grow-PAT than person even tall-Asp
It even grew taller than a man.

   b. Ta zhang-de bi ren   gao-le.
It grow   than person tall-Asp
It grew taller than a man.

(4) a. Wan shang ba wo dou ku   xing-le.
Night at   let me even cry wake-up-Asp
Cries even woke me up at night.

   b. Wan shang ba wo ku   xing-le
Night at   let me cry wake-up-Asp
Cries woke me up at night.

(5) a. Jintian dou   xingqisan   le.
Today already   Wednesday Asp
Today already is Wednesday.

   b. Jintian xingqisan   le.
Today Wednesday Asp
Today is Wednesday.

What is expressed by sentences (3-5) b is the truth-value conditional meaning, when the context is uncertain, they can be manifoldly understood. For example, sentence (4) b BA WO KU XING LE [*Cries woke me up*], which can be understood as KUSHENG DA LE [*Cries were loud*], but also can be understood as (KUSHENG HEN XIAO),WO SHUIJIAO HEN JINGXING [*(cries were lowish), I'm easy to be woken up*]. If the sentence (4) a is added with Dou$_b$, then the pragmatic reading of the proposition shall be constrained and limited, for example, sentence (4) a BA WO DOU KU XING LE [*Cries even woke me up*], normally can only be understood as KUSHENG TAI DA LE [*Cries were too loud*].

2   Pragmatic Functions of 都ᵦ[Douᵦ]

Generally speaking, Douᵦ encodes two kinds of procedural meaning: one is to introduce a kind of expectation (or normal), and another is to judge that the possibility of occurrence or existence of the situation described by a proposition is lower than the expectation (or normal). Therefore, it can be said that Douᵦ is a counter-expectation (hereafter CE) marker (see [9]).

Obviously, Douᵦ has some basic characteristics of a CE marker. For example, with the addition of Douᵦ, the original proposition changes from neutral information to CE information, and its informational value from medium to high[1]; but its truth-value condition is not affectted by Douᵦ. Although it does not added any content to the proposition, Douᵦ asserts that the propositional content has deviated from the expectation (or normal), and can undertake subjective valuation, interpersonal interaction, association in discourse context as a discourse marker. But these basic characteristics (including their contents, displaying means, extents shown in Douᵦ sentences), are also unique, and reflect the unique pragmatic functions of Douᵦ. It is illustrated as follows.

2.1   Inferiority of the Pragmatic Scale of Possibility

CE marker, in any human language, is a concept covering broadly (see [11]). Except for semantics encoded by a CE marker itself, what determines its pragmatic scope, pragmatic conditions (existing literatures haven't reviewed pragmatic features of discourse markers from this point) and other pragmatic features is also the relation between the CE information and its expectation (or normal), which is the factor that cannot be ignored (existing literatures haven't noticed this factor). For the ease of illustration of pragmatic functions of Douᵦ, according to the different relations between CE informations and expectations (or normals), CE informations can be classified as follows: *adversity-to-expectation* and *deviation-from-expectation*. If the relations between CE informations and expectations (or normals) are contradictory or contrary, then the CE information belongs to *adversity-to-expectation*; when the CE information is superior or inferior to the expectation on a certain pragmatic scale, then the CE information belongs to *deviation-from-expectation*. Accordingly, *adversity-to-expectation* can be subclassified into *contradictory relation* and *contrary relation*,

---

[1] From the point of expectation of participants of conversation, the information conveyed by linguistic elements in a discourse can be classified as "expectation information", "CE information" and "(neutral) information", and informational value: CE information > neutral information > expectation information (see [10]).

but *deviation-from-expectation* into *superior-to-expectation (over expectation)*, and *inferior-to-expectation (below expectation)* (see figure 1), such as:

A. Adversity-to-expectation: (6) Contradictory relation, (7) Contrary relation:

  (6) Tamen bujin   meiyou yinwei   tongxiao weishui   er   pibeibukan,
      They not-only haven't because   one-night sleepless and   exhausted
      <u>faner gege</u> jingshen zhenfeng
      but Cl-Cl spirits   in high
      They weren't exhausted due to the sleepless night, <u>but</u> each of them was in high spirits instead.

  (7) Shenghuo zhong <u>bushi</u> queshao mei,   <u>ershi</u> queshao faxian mei-de   yanjing
      Life   in   not   lack beauty, but   lack   find beauty-PAT eyes
      Life is <u>not</u> lacking of beauty, <u>but</u> lacking of eyes to find beauty.

B.Deviation-from-expectation:(8) superior-to-expectation, (9) inferior-to-expectation:

  (8) Juda-de   shuguan touying mianji <u>jing   da</u> 1   wan   pingfeng
      Huge-PAT canopy projection area unexpectedly to one 10-thousand square
      mi <u>zhi duo</u>, ceng rongna yizhi   jiqian   ren de jundui zai shu xia
      meter PAT many once contain one-Cl thousands people PAT army in tree under
      duobi jiaoyang
      avoid blazing sun
      Projected area of a huge canopy <u>unexpectedly</u> is <u>more than</u> 10 thousands m², which accommodated one army with thousands soldiers under the tree for sheltering from blazing sun.

  (9) Fanzheng dangshi   fan le   bantian   juben faxian <u>jingran</u>   <u>zhiyou</u>
      Anyway at-that-time flip Asp half-a-day script find unexpectedly only
      yi ju,   qishi   ye mei you yi ju,   jiushi yige ci
      one sentence, actually also not have one sentence, that-is one-Cl word
      Anyway at that time, the script was flipped over for a very long time, but <u>unexpectedly</u> <u>only</u> <u>one</u> sentence, actually it is an incomplete sentence, i.e. only one word.

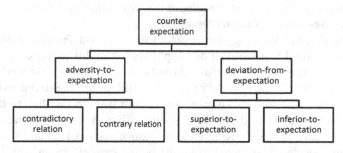

Fig. 1. The classification of CE informations

Obviously, the CE information marked by Dou₆ is inferior-to-expectation (or normal) on the pragmatic dimension of the possibility of occurrence or existence of a situation. But the pragmatic dimension of the possibility of occurrence or existence of a situation is actually the pragmatic scope of Dou_b, and inferior-to-expectation (or normal) is the pragmatic condition of Dou_b. This is different from other CE markers of deviation-from-expectation. For example, the pragmatic scope of "竟达[*Jingda*]... 之多[*Zhiduo*]" [*surprisingly is more than...*] is the quantity of things, and the pragmatic condition is superior-to-expectation (or normal), for instance, the projected area of the canopy is more than 10 thousands square meters, which is already far more than the expected.

Given the stated possibility of occurrence or existence of the situation expressed by a Dou_b sentence is lower than the expectation (or normal), it is conceivable that the occurrence or existence of situations at the lowest pragmatic scale of the possibility easily become contents of Dou_b sentences, and their pragmatic frequency is highest. For example:

(10) Pingri   Yuqing sao   shi lian   yige   haozi dou   shebu-de
     Usually Yuqing sister-in-law is   include one-Cl   dime   even reluctant-PAT
     yong de.
     use PAT
     Usually sister Yuqing was even reluctant to spend a dime.

(11) Meitian   cihou   ni,   yiju   haohua   dou   de-budao
     Everyday look-after you,   one-Cl good-word even   cannot-get
     I look after you every day, even without receiving a single good word from you.

(12) Yiwen   you de   hao-de   bi   yuanwen dou   jingcai, juanyong.
     Translations have-PAT good-PAT than original even brilliant   meaningful
     Some translations are even more brilliant and meaningful than the original itself.

(13) Wo nage   pengyou haoqi-de   dou kuai feng-le,   pinming
     My that-Cl friend surprised-PAT even almost crazy-Asp risk-his-life
     Shenzhe   bozi wang   tai   shang zhao.
     stretch-out neck toward stage on   find
     Even that friend of mine was almost crazily curious, and then he craned his neck to see what's going on the stage.

(14) Ruguo shiqu ta, wo ningyuan   sidiao! Chule ta,   wo shenmeren dou bujia!
     If   lose him, I would-rather die-Asp! Except him, I whoever even not marry!
     If I lost him, I would rather die! Even I will marry nobody but him!

Sentence (13) means "That friend of mine was curious to the extreme extent that he got almost crazy"; sentence (14) means "she doesn't want to lose him to the extreme extent that she would rather die if she lost him". Thus in existing literature, Dou_b is considered to "mark polarity" by an extreme means, such as [12] and so on, or Lian sentences are considered to "mark polarity" by the extreme means (in these literatures, Dou_b in a Lian sentence is explained as Dou_a), such as [13, 14] and so on, but all of these literatures are overgeneralized.

In turn, we can also predicate that when the possibility is higher or equivalent to that of the state of affairs expected (or normal) in a particular context, or the state of affairs is without any possibility (except the state of affairs exaggerated on purpose), because the possibility cannot be inferior-to-expectation (or normal), Douᵦ sentences are untenable. For example:

(15) *Qiche bi zixingche dou   kuai.
     Car   than bicycle   even fast
     *Cars move even faster than bicycles.

(16) * Dou   kuai   ershi-le,   zenmo hai bu tuixiu-ne?
     Already almost twenty-Asp, how   still not retire-PAT
     *You almost turn 20, why haven't retired yet?

(17) a. *Ta lian   jiejiari   dou xiuxi.
        He include holiday   even rest
        *He even rests on holidays.

    b. * Ta lian   zhoumo   dou xiuxi
        He include weekend even rest
        *He even rests at weekends.

    c. Ta lian   gongzuori dou xiuxi.
        He include weekday even rest
        He even rests on weekdays.

(18) a. *Ta lian   xiashu   dou   gan dezui
        He include subordinates even dare offend
        *He even dares to offend his subordinates.

    b. *Ta lian   pingji-tongshi dou gan dezui
        He include peers   even dare offend
        *He even dares to offend his peers.

    c. Ta lian   lingdao dou gan dezui
        He include leaders even dare offend
        He even dares to offend his leaders.

    d. Ta lian shangdi dou gan dezui
        He include god   even dare offend
        He even dares to offend God.

(19) a. *Zhewei tongxue lian   yifen   dou neng   kao dao.
        This-CL student include one-point even enable-to exam get
        *This student even can get one point in an examination.

    b. *Zhewei tongxue lian liuqishi   fen   dou neng   kao dao.
        This   student include sixty-seventy points even enable-to exam get
        *This student even can get sixty or seventy points in an examination.

    c. Zhewei tongxue lian   bashi fen   dou neng   kao dao
        This   student include eighty points even enable-to exam get
        This student even can get eighty points in an examination.

    d. Zhewei tongxue lian   yibai   fen   dou neng   kao dao
        This   student include one hundred points even enable-to exam get
        This student even can get one hundred points in an examination.

(20) a. *Xiaoming bi   jiejie   dou xiao.
        Xiaoming than   elder-sister even young
        *Xiaoming is even younger than his elder sister.

b. *Xiaoming bi   jiejie   dou da.
   Xiaoming than   elder-sister even old
   *Xiaoming is even older than his elder sister.
c. Xiaoming zhangde   bi   jiejie   dou lao (guzuo kuazhang)
   Xiaoming look-PAT   than elder-sister even old (deliberate exaggeration)
   Xiaoming looks even older than his elder sister (exaggerated on purpose).

"To rest on holidays, cars move faster than bicycles, not to retire yet at the age of 20, he dares to offend his subordinates, one can get one point in an examination" are at the high end of pragmatic scales of possibilities. "To rest at weekends, he dares to offend his peers, one can get sixty or seventy points in an examination, Xiaoming is younger than his elder sister" have the possibility almost equivalent to or close to the expectation (or normal). But the possibility of "Xiaoming is older than his elder sister" doesn't exist, so Dou$_b$ sentences are untenable. Normally the possibility of "Xiaoming looks older than his elder sister" is unlikely, but it is can be used for exaggeration on purpose. For most students who "can get sixty or seventy points" is the expected or normal possibility of exam results, but for one student who is doing very badly at school (whose exam result is expected or normally to be thirty or forty points), the possibility is inferior-to-expectation or (normal), at this point then the Dou$_b$ sentence is tenable, for example:

(21) Ta xianzai dou neng   kao   dao liuqishi   fen-le,   zhende jinbu
     He now   even enable-to exam get   sixty-seventy points-Asp, really progress
     hen da   le
     very large Asp
     He even can get sixty or seventy points, which really had made a great progress.

2.2   The Subjective Commentary function of Dou$_b$ as a Discourse Marker

Dou$_b$ as a CE marker doesn't have any objective meaning, but the subjective meaning. The presentation of this kind of subjective meaning is the definition of possibility of an expectation (or normal) firstly, which may be different due to the relevant people and situation, for example:

(22) Dou   kuai liushi-de   ren   le,   yinggai xiangshou xiangshou le,
     Already soon sixty-PAT person Asp, should   enjoy   enjoy   Asp,
     buyao zai   name   laolei le.
     don't again that   tired Asp
     You are almost 60, so you should enjoy your life, and stop working so hard.
(23) Dou   kuai liushi-de   ren   le, geng yinggai zhuajin shijian le, nenggou
     Already soon sixty-PAT person Asp, more should seize   time Asp, enable-to
     youxiao   gongzuo-de shijian bu duo   le.
     efficiently work-PAT time   not much Asp
     You are almost 60, so you should even work harder with insufficient time.

Secondly, the informative intention of a Dou$_b$ sentence is to describe the state of affairs whose possibility of occurrence or existence is inferior-to-expectation, as long as the addressee can understand the informative intention, the truth or falsehood of the proposition in a Dou_b sentence is insignificant. Therefore, a speaker even can use the things in fictions, or myths and legends for purposeful exaggeration just like extreme situations deviated from the expectation (or normal), to express attitudes and feelings of the speaker emphatically, for example:

(24) Meishi-de   youhuo   lian shangdi dou shoubuliao   le
     Delicious-food-PAT temptation include God   even cannot-stand Asp
     Even God can't stand the temptation of delicious food!

(25) Nanren   kaodezhu, muzhu dou   hui shang shu!
     Men   reliable,   sow even can climb trees
     Men only can be reliable if the sow can fly!

(26) Kanzhe   nadui   juanzi naodai dou kuai zha   le!
     Look-Asp that-pile paper   head even soon explode Asp
     Looking at piles of papers almost makes my head explode.

(27) Zhiyao   wo yidan huode-le ni, wo bi shenxian dou guangcai-ne
     As-long-as I once have-Asp you, I than god   even glorious-PAT
     As long as I got you, I would be more glorious than gods.

(28) Ningyuan yisheng dou bu shuohua, dou buxiang   shuo jiahua qipian ni.
     Prefer to whole-life all no talk   even don't-want talk lies deceive you
     I even prefer to be silent for the rest of my life, rather than lying to you.

In addition, Dou_b as a CE marker doesn't have any propositional function but a commentary function[2] to a relevant proposition, and obviously functions evaluatively (see[15]), which also can be considered as a high-level predicate (see [16]) with an "implicit assertion". As a result, Dou_b cannot to be negated, and except an echo question, a Dou_b sentence normally can't be used as an interrogative sentence [commentary: * in front of an example sentence means that it is false; ?* means that an echo question is tenable and a general question is untenable]. For example:

(29) Guangbo li napa you   yisi   xiweide   bianhua, ta dou_b
     broadcast in even-if there-be a-hint-of slight-PAT change,   he even
     neng ting chulai.
     enable hear clearly
     In the broadcasts, even if there is a slight change, he is able to distinguish it.
     →* Ta bu (mei) dou_b neng   ting chulai.
        He not   even enable-to hear clearly
     **He can't dou_b(even) distinguish it.*
     →?*Ta dou_b neng   ting chulai ?/?* Shui dou_b neng ting chulai?
        He even enable-to hear clearly?/ who even enable-to hear clearly ?
     **Can he dou_b(even) distinguish all of the changes?/ ?* who dou_b(even)
     can distinguish all of the changes?*

(30) Dou_b   kuai rudong-le,   zenme hai you   wenzi?
     Already soon winter-Asp, how   still have mosquitoes
     Winter is coming, why still have mosquitoes?
     →*Bu (mei) dou_b kuai rudong-le.
     **Winter hasn't dou_b (yet) come .*

---

[2] Some scholars call it as reflexivity, such as [3].

→?*Dou_b   kuai rudong-le?/?* Dou_b kuai   rudong-le?
already soon winter-Asp?/ already soon winter-Asp?
?*Dou_b will winter come soon?/?* Dou_b will winter come soon ?

(31) Wo kan gou youshi   bi   ren   dou hao
I   see   dog sometimes than person even good
In my point of view, sometimes dogs are even better than human beings.
→* Gou youshi   bi ren   bu (mei) dou_b hao
Dog sometimes than person not(no)   even good
*Dogs sometimes are dou_b(even) not better than human beings .
→ ? *Gou youshi   bi   ren   dou_b hao ma?
Dog sometimes   than person even good PAT
?*Do dogs dou_b(even) better than human beings sometimes?

(32) FangPei xiang dou_b mei xiang,   yimian zhuangxiang yimian shuo.
FangPei think even no   think, while packing   while talk
FangPei packed and said that even without any consideration.
→*FangPei xiang bu dou_b mei xiang→?*FangPei xiang dou_b mei xiang ma?
FangPei think not even no thinking →FangPei think even no thinking-PAT
**FangPei didn't dou_b(even) think it for a second.→ ? *Did FangPei
dou_b(even) think it for a second ?*

(33) Fan   dou   liang-le, kuai chi-ba!
Dinner already cold-Asp, hurry eat-Asp
The dinner already got cold, just eat it!
→*Fan bu (mei) dou_b liang-le →? *Fan dou_b liang-le ma?/?* Shenmo dou_b
Dinner not already cold-Asp→ Dinner already cold-PAT?/ What already
liang le?
cold Asp
**The dinner didn't dou_b(already) get cold completely.→?*Did the dinner
dou_b(already) get cold?/?*What did dou_b(already) get cold?*

(34) Ba wo rede   dou   kuai yao   tiaohai   le.
Let me hot-PAT even   soon want   jump-into-the-sea Asp
I can't stand the heat to some extent that I almost want to jump into the sea.
→*Ba wo rede   bu dou_b   kuai yao   tiaohai   le
Let me hot-PAT not even   soon want jump-into-the-sea Asp
*I can stand the heat dou_b(even) to some extent I want to jump into the sea.
→?*Ba wo rede   dou_b kuai yao   tiaohai   le ma?
let me hot-PAT even soon   want jump-into-the-sea Asp PAT ?
→? can't I stand the heat to some extent dou_b(even) I want to jump into the
sea?*

2.3   The Interpersonal Interaction of Dou_b as a CE Marker

As mentioned above, Dou_b as a CE marker roughly encodes two levels of procedural
meanings: one is to introduce some kind of expectation (or normal), another is to
judge that the possibility of a state of affairs is deviated from the expectation (or normal). And it makes a Dou_b sentence has an emphasis meaning by pragmatic interfe-

rence (length limited, interference procedure is conducted in a separate paper). As we can see, the addition of Dou_b changes the original proposition from neutral information to CE information, and its informational value from medium to high. It can give a procedural restriction or guidance on understanding the relevant discourse, which helps the addressee obtain more information contents with less pragmatic efforts. This is just the exertion of Economy Principle at discourse level.

In a Dou_b sentence, its information intention is to state that the possibility of occurrence or existence of a state of affairs is lower than the expectation (or normal). But this is not the chief purpose of a Dou_b sentence, nor its communicative intention (see[7]). Its chief purpose is to assist in expressing a variety of emotions of a speaker, such as exclamation, astonishment, blame, complain, regret and etc., through stating the state of affairs deviating from expectation(or normal), or to assist in expressing advice, reminder and so on. (see[17,18,19]). For example:

(35) Lian   Jiang Juxia dou yao ting ta-de,   zhen shi liaobuqi   de   renwu.
Include Jiang Juxia even will listen him-PAT, really is remarkable PAT figure
He is such a remarkable man, even Jiang Juxia listen to him.

(36) Ni zenme hui lian   wo shi shui dou   bu   zhidao?
You how   will include me is   who even don't know
How could you even don't know who I am?

(37) Ni   shuo lun   cai, ni shuo na koucai   na yingyu,   shuode bi
You say talk-about talent, you talk that eloquence, that English, talk-Asp than
meiguoren dou_b didao.
Americans even authentic
Speaking of talent, with such an eloquence, he even can speak English more authentic than Americans themselves.

(38) Meitian   cihou   ni,   yiju   haohua   dou   debudao.
Everyday look-after   you, one-Cl good-word even can't-get
I look after you every day, even without receiving a single good word from you.

(39) Duoshao   ren   zuomeng dou_b meng bu dao de haoshi,
How-many people dream even dream not get PAT good-thing,
ni jingran   hai tuici!
you unexpectedly still refuse
You even refuse such a wonderful thing, which tons of people can't have in their dream.

(40) Duonian   de lieren le,   lian ge   banjiu   dou dabudao,
Many-years PAT hunter Asp, include one-Cl turtledove even can't-get,
diuren ne.
shame PAT
It is such a shame for being a hunter for many years even without a turtledove caught.

(41) Ni zai gongsi   dou   kuai banian-le,   fangqi gongling dehua
You in company already almost eight-year-Asp, give-up seniority if
tai kexi-le.
too regretful-Asp

It is to be regretted that you will give up your seniority since you have worked here for almost eight years.

From the corpora of Dou_b sentences, it is not difficult to find that Dou_b sentences having communicative intention to assist in expression, which provides an evidence and support for a speaker's attitude and assertion, i.e. "evidentiality", strengthening illocutionary force, mood, and tone, such as examples (35-41). It is a kind of effort to strengthen the speaker's exclamation, astonishment, blame, complain, regret and etc., which is just the embodiment of the communicative intention or meta-pragmatic awareness of a Dou_b sentence(see [20]).Take a comparison:

(42) a. Dou   daxuesheng   le, yao   zhuyi   xingxiang!
        Already undergraduate Asp, should pay-attention-to image
     Pay attention to your image since you are already an undergraduate.
     b. Yao   zhuyi   xingxiang!
        Should pay-attention-to image
        Pay attention to your image!

(43) a. Ni dei suan chou qi   louzi le ba? Lian   nüde   dou
        You should be smelly chess basket Asp PAT, include female-PAT even
        yingbuliao.
        win-not-Asp
        You may be a bad chess player, aren't you? You even can't win a girl.
     b. Ni   dei suan chou qi   louzi le ba?
        You   should be   smelly chess basket Asp PAT
        You may be a bad chess player, aren't you?

Obviously, in comparison with sentences (42-43) b which only say "Pay attention to your image!", "You are a bad chess player, aren't you?", sentences (42-43) a are much stronger in illocutionary force, mood, and tone, which is more evidential and even make the addressee harder to refuse, and also show the communicative intention to strengthen declaring the speaker's attitude and assertion.

2.4   Relevance in Discourse Structure

From the above, it is not difficult to find that there is actually a comparison (among different pragmatic scales of possibility or between the state of affairs deviating from the expectation and the reality or result etc.) behind the procedural meaning of Dou_b as a CE marker. But the comparison itself is not the chief purpose of a Dou_b sentence, and the chief purpose of a Dou_b sentence is evidentiality for showing the speaker's attitude and assertion, and to provide relevant evidences, which can strengthen illocutionary force and obtain the best communicative effects. Therefore, in a relatively complete discourse or context, Dou_b is normally used in the sentence for assisting to declare the speaker's attitude and assertion, and is seldom used in an independent sentence, such as examples above (35-43). Thus, whether the targets of comparison are explicit or implicit, and whether sentences assisted to declare attitude and assertion are explicit or implicit, in a specific discourse, a Dou_b sentence must have very strong context dependency and textual relevance.

Moreover, the procedural meanings and pragmatic features of Douᵦ also affect the type of its textual relevance. Because when a comparison is explicitly shown in the context, the scales' differences among different members of possibility pragmatic scales are shown and the type of its textual relevance is often progressive, for example:

(44) Budan   xiaomanyao bu   bao,   jiu lian jiankang dou nan   shuo.
     not only thin-waist   not remain, but include health   even difficult speak
     Not only your thin waist can't remain, but even your health hard to be kept either.

(45) Shou doude   keneng lian   fanwan dou   duan bu zhu le,
     Hand tremble-PAT maybe include rice-bowl even   hold not can Asp,
     geng bie   shuo   xiezi   le.
     more not to   mention   writing Asp.
     The trembling hands even can't hold a rice bowl, not to mention writing.

(46) Bie shuo   bibushang   erge   le, lian women laosan   dou
     Not mention no-match-for second-brother Asp, include our   third-brother even
     bu ru.
     not compete-with
     You even can't compete with our third brother, not to mention our second brother.

(47) Chufang li   gengben lian denguang dou meiyou, geng meiyou
     Kitchen inside totally include lamplight even no, more no
     caitang de xiangqi.
     soup PAT aroma
     There is even no lamplight in this kitchen, not to mention aroma of soup.

For showing the comparison between the state of affairs deviated from the expectation and the reality or result, the type of its textual relevance is often adversative, for example:

(48) Ta yaode   zhishi shushi   er   meiyou fannaode   shenghuo, keshi lian
     He want-PAT only comfortable and   no   troubles-PAT life,   but include
     zhedian ta dou   ban bu dao.
     these   he even do not enable
     What he only wants is a comfortable life without worries or troubles, but he even can't realize it.

(49) Pingsuli neng   jiandao tamen zhizhong yiwei dou shifen bu yi, xianzai
     Usually enable-to see   they among one-Cl even very not easy, now
     jingran   you jihui tongshi   yidu sanjiemei   de   fang rong.
     unexpectedly have chance at same time see three-sisters PAT   beautiful face
     One of them can't usually be easily found, but unexpectedly there is a chance to see the three beautiful sisters in person at the same time.

(50) Zhiyou ziji erzi de   ming cai zhiqian, bieren de ming que bi gou
     Only own son PAT life is   valuable,   other PAT life but than dog
     dou bu ru.
     even no match-for
     In his eyes, only his own son is valuable, and others' are even no match for dog's.

(51) Lian   jiaren dou   duode   yuanyuan-de, Jiang jiaoshou que bu
    include families even avoid-PAT far-far -PAT, Jiang professor but not
    xianqi.

    dislike-and-avoid

*Professor Jiang hasn't ever disliked and avoided him, even his own families
have.*

When the sentence showing the speaker's attitude and assertion, which is assisted by
a Dou$_b$ sentence, explicitly occur in front or back of the Dou$_b$ sentence, the type of textual relevance is often certificative, causal, or suppositional and so on, for example:

(52) Lian   wo ziji dou peifu ziji,   jingran   hui shuochu zhemo
    include I   myself even admire myself, unexpectedly enable speak-out so
    you zheli   de   hua.

    have philosophy PAT words

I even admired myself for speaking out such philosophical words.

(53) Ni   lian   xiang dou xiang bu dao, bu keneng   zuodao.
    You include think even think not enable, not possibly achieve
    You even couldn't think of it, not to mention realization of it.

(54) Xiangyu   lian   yige   Fan Zeng dou bu   neng   yong,
    Xiangyu   include one-Cl Fan Zeng even not can   use,
    suoyi bei wo   mie   le.
    so   by me   defeat Asp
    Xiang Yu even can't employ Fan Zeng, so he was defeated by me.

(55) Dou   sidian le,   hai bu ganhuor, xiangsha   ne?
    Already 4'olock Asp, still don't work, think-what PAT
    It is already 4'olock you haven't start working yet, what are you thinking of?

(56) Ruguo lian zhe daoli   dou   bu dong,   zenme qu tansuo
    If include this reason even not understand, how go explore
    gengshen de dongxi ne?
    deeper PAT things PAT?
    If you even can't understand this, how will you explore and dig deeper?

Of course, various combinations among these types of textual relevance, such as progressive, adversative, certificative, causal, suppositional, and so on, are also possible, for example:

(57) Dan He Xiangning yinwei zaojiu bumanyu   Chiang Kai-shek de
    but He Xiangning because long-ago dissatisfied Chiang Kai-shek PAT

    daoxing nishi, yinci budan butongyi dang   zhenghunren,   shenzhi
    retroaction   so not-only disagree work-as marriage-witness even
    lian   hunli   dou buken   chuxi, Chiang Kai-shek wunai,   zhide
    include wedding even refuse-to attend, Chiang Kai-shek cannot-help, have-to
    ling   qing yiwei nüshi zhenghun.
    another invite one-Cl lady marriage-witness
    *But He Xiangning didn't agree to be the witness of wedding and also refused to
    attend the wedding for being dissatisfied with Chiang Kai-shek's retroaction
    for long, so Chiang Kai-shek was compelled to invite another madam to be his
    marriage witness.*

(58) Er yige nanren, jiaruo lian   ziji de   haizi dou bu yao,
     But one-Cl man, if include own PAT children even not keep,
     ta yejiu lian   renxing dou mei you le
     he then include humanity even not have Asp
     There's no humanity at all if a man even doesn't keep his own child.
(59) Wo shifen ganxie ta,   shenzhi juede bu haohao   xue, lian   ta   dou
     I very grateful him, even feel   not good-good learn, include him even
     duibuqi. Zhe zhong xinqing gengjia jifa-le   wo de   xuexi reqing,
     be sorry. This kind feeling still-more stimulate-Asp I PAT learn   passion,
     wo de xuexi chengji ye   you le   mingxian-de   tigao.
     I PAT learn grades also get Asp significantly-PAT   improved
     With my gratitude of him, I feel that I even would be sorry to him if I don't work
     hard. This feeling further stimulated my passion for study, and my grades were
     also improved significantly.
     Moreover, from the point of the corpora searched by me, Doub sentences are main-
ly used in spoken discourse (limited by the length, examples are omitted).

3   Conclusion

In conclusion, we have shown that: first of all, the conventional implicature of Doub is
to convey the speaker's judgment on the state of affairs described by the proposition,
which considers the possibility of occurrence or existence of the situation is inferior-
to-expectation (or normal). This is non-truth conditional procedural pragmatic meaning, which mainly performs interpersonal and textual functions in a discourse.

Secondly, in addition to its own semantics, what decides the characteristics of
pragmatic functions of each CE marker, is also the relation between CE information
marked by it and the expectation (or normal). Therefore, for a much clearer understanding of pragmatic functions of Doub as a CE marker, this article tried to make a
classification of CE information according to the relations between CE information
and expectations (or normals) as follows: *adversity-to-expectation* and *deviation-
from-expectation*, and *adversity-to-expectation* can be subclassified into *contradictory
relation* and *contrary relation*, and *deviation-from-expectation* falls into *superior-to-
expectation (over expectation),* and *inferior-to-expectation (below expectation).*

As to Doub, its non-truth conditional procedural pragmatic meaning and the CE information which is marked by it, has the inferior-to-expectation (or normal) possibility,
which makes Doub have basic characteristics of a CE marker, makes Doub and Doub
sentences show following pragmatic features in syntactic and discourse structure.

First, the pragmatic dimension of "possibilities of existence or occurrence of
things" is the pragmatic scope of Doub, and "inferior-to-expectation (or normal)" is
the pragmatic condition of Doub. Specifically, the occurrence or existence of one state
of affairs at the lowest end of pragmatic scales is mostly likely to be the content of a
Doub sentence. When its possibility is higher or equal to the expected (or normal)
situation, or even doesn't exist (except exaggerated on purpose), because the possibility cannot be lower than the expected (or normal), its Doub sentence is untenable.

Second, Dou$_b$ as a CE marker doesn't have any objective meaning, but the subjective meaning. The presentations of this kind of subjective meaning include the definition of the possibility of an expectation (or normal), which may be different due to the relevant people and situation, and in Dou$_b$ sentences a speaker even can use the things in fictions, or myths and legends for purposeful exaggeration just like extreme situations deviated from the expectation (or normal), to express his/her attitudes and feelings emphatically. In addition, Dou$_b$ as a CE marker doesn't have any propositional function but a commentary function to a relevant proposition, and obviously functions evaluatively, which also can be considered as a high-level predicate with an "implicit assertion". As a result, Dou$_b$ cannot be negated, and except an echo question, a Dou$_b$ sentence normally can't be used as an interrogative sentence. With the addition of Dou$_b$ the original proposition changes from neutral information to CE information, and its informational value from medium to high.   Dou$_b$ can give a procedural restriction or guidance on understanding the relevant discourse, which helps the addressee obtain more information contents with less pragmatic efforts. This is just the exertion of Economy Principle at discourse level. The information intention of a Dou$_b$ sentence is to describe the occurrence or existence of the state of affairs that its possibility is inferior-to-expectation, but the communicative intention is to assist in expression evidentially, which provides an evidence and support for a speaker's attitude and assertion, which enhance illocutionary force, mood and tone, which is just the embodiment of the meta-pragmatic awareness of a Dou$_b$ sentence. So Dou$_b$ is normally used in the sentence for assisting in showing the speaker's attitude and assertion, and is seldom used in an independent sentence. Thus Dou$_b$ or a Dou$_b$ sentence is characterized by very strong context dependence and textual relevance.

Finally, the procedural meanings and the pragmatic features of Dou$_b$ make Dou$_b$ sentences have main types of textual relevance which are progressive, adversative, certificative, causal, suppositional and etc., and Dou$_b$ (or a Dou$_b$ sentence) is mainly used in spoken discourse.

Acknowledgements. I would like to express my gratitude to all those who have helped me during the writing of this paper. Special thanks should go to my friends Cheng Ru Dong and Ge Xu who have managed to read my manuscripts and make suggestions for further revisions. If there are still something unacceptale, I am responsible for them.

References

1. Halliday, M.A.K.: An Introduction to Functional Grammar, pp. 79–81. Edward Arnold, London (2004)
2. Aijmer, K., Simon-Vandenbergen, A.-M.: Pragmatic markers. In: Zienkowski, J., et al. (eds.) Discursive Pragmatics, pp. 223–247 (2011)
3. Halliday, M.A.K.: An Introduction to Functional Grammar. Edward Arnold, London (1994)
4. Blakemore, D.: Semantic Constraints on Relevance. Basil Blackwell, Oxford (1987)
5. Blakemore, D.: Understanding Utterances. Basil Blackwell, Oxford (1992)

6. Blakemore, D.: Relevance and Linguistic Meaning: The Semantics and Pragmatics of Discourse Markers. Cambridge University Press (2002)
7. Sperber, D., Wilson, D.: Relevance: Communication & cognition, 2nd edn, pp. 58–61. Blackwell, Oxford (1995)
8. Roulet, E.: The description of text relation markers in the Geneva model of discourse organization. In: Fischer, K. (ed.), pp. 115–132 (2006)
9. Heine, B., Claudi, U., Hünnemeyer, F.: Grammaticalization: A Conceptual Framework, p. 192. University of Chicago Press, Chicago (1991)
10. Dahl, O.: Grammaticalization and the lift cycles of construction, p. 27. Ms. Stockholm University (2000)
11. Wu, F.: On the pragmatic function of the construction X bu-bi Y·Z. Chinese Language **3**, 222–231 (2004). (in Chinese)
12. Yan, J.: Pragmatic Reasoning and Syntactic/Semantic Characterization of Dou (都). Modern Foreign Languages **1**, 11–24 (1998). (in Chinese)
13. Cui, Y.: Sentence pattern analysis of "Lian (连)…Ye (也)/Dou (都)". Language Teaching and Linguistic Studies **4**, 30–44 (1984). (in Chinese)
14. Yuan, Y.: The Information Structure of the lian (连) construction in Mandarin. Linguistic Science **2**, 14–28 (2006). (in Chinese)
15. Fraser, B.: Towards a theory of discourse markers. In: Fischer, K. (ed.), pp. 189–204 (2006)
16. Zhang, Y.: On Adverbs in Mandarin Chinese, pp. 46–47. Xuelin Publishing House (2000). (in Chinese)
17. Guo, C.: Similarities and Differences of Temporal Adverbs of Yijing (已经) and Dou (都). Chinese Teaching in the World **2**, 35–41 (1997). (in Chinese)
18. Li, W.: On the Construction of "Dou (都) XP le (了)" and Its Formation Mechanism. Language Teaching and Linguistic Studies **5**, 57–63 (2010). (in Chinese)
19. Yuan, Y.: Focus Structure and Semantic Interpretation of Chinese Sentence, pp. 177–203. The Commercial Press (2012). (in Chinese)
20. Verschueren, J.: Understanding Pragmatics. Arnold, London and New York (1987)

Syntactic Behaviors Driven by Lexical Semantics

A Study on *geng* (更) and *hai* (還) in Chinese Comparatives

Chen-chun E[✉]

Department of Chinese and Bilingual Studies, The Hong Kong Polytechnic University,
Hong Kong, China
echenchun@gmail.com

Abstract. The two Chinese degree adverbs *geng*(更)and *hai* (還) can modify gradable predicates in comparative structures. They can be interchangeable in many cases.
However, data extracted from BCC corpus show that their distribution is structurally
constrained. This paper aims to account for their differences in syntactic behaviors. I
argue that the value of the lexical semantic feature [degree] is inherently [+] in the
adverb *geng* while the value is indefinite in *hai*. To realize the comparitive reading,
the legitimate occurrence of *hai* is constrained by a certain syntactic configuration so
that the indefinite [degree] value can be structurally licensed. Assuming X-bar
theory, I propose that the legitimate occurrence of *hai* in comparative structures is licensed in the domain of m-command.

Keywords: Chinese comparatives · Degree adverbs · Feature-licensing

1 Introduction

1.1 The Observed Phenomenon

In Chinese comparative structures, both *geng* (更) and *hai* (還) function to indicate
comparison on the scale defined by the predicate, as shown in (1):

(1) a. 他跑得比我更快。

    Ta pao-de   bi   wo   geng   kuai.

    He run-DE_2 than me GENG fast[1]

    'He runs faster than me.'

  b. 他跑得比我還快。

    Ta pao-de   bi   wo   hai kuai.

    He run -DE_2 than me HAI fast

    'He runs faster than me.'

---

[1] Abbreviations used in this paper are listed as follows:
DE_1: Pre-nominal modification marker
DE_2: Postverbal resultative marker
PART: Particle
PredP: Predicate Phrase

© Springer International Publishing Switzerland 2015
Q. Lu and H.H. Gao (Eds.): CLSW 2015, LNAI 9332, pp. 408–417, 2015.
DOI: 10.1007/978-3-319-27194-1_40

The two examples in (1) express the proposition that two individuals are compared on the scale of speed in the activity of running. The degree modifying adverb *geng* or *hai* forms a comparative constituent with the gradable adjective *kuai* 'fast'. Replacing one with the other would not affect the intended semantic meaning that the third singular person is faster in running than the first singular person.

Although both *hai* and *geng* can modify the degree denoted by the predicate in comparative structures, data extracted from Beijing Language and Culture University Chinese Corpus (hereafter BCC for short) indicate differences in their syntactic behaviors. The realization of the comparative reading of *hai* is shown to be context-dependent in syntax while its near synonym *geng* can convey the comparative reading on its own and is less restricted by the syntactic configuration where it occurs.

1.2   The Theoretical Framework

This study is grounded on Pustejovsky's (1991, 1995) contention that lexical semantics cannot be completely separated from the syntactic structure where the lexical word occurs. It is assumed that in computing the meaning of a lexical item, there is interactive relationship at the interface between lexicon and syntax. It is not reasonable to treat lexicon as a module independent from syntax in modeling natural language processing. Although *hai* can function as a degree modifier as *geng* to convey comparative reading, it in fact has multiple semantic meanings and pragmatic use (Donazzan 2008, Liu 2000). The research question in this study mainly concerns how the comparison reading is encoded when *hai* enters syntax. Given that *hai* and *geng* can be interchangeable in some comparative structures but not always, it is reasonable to surmise that *geng* and *hai* possess different lexical semantic constitutions. Only through knowledge of a word's use in the syntactic configuration can an appropriate representational structure for it be established (Verspoor 1993).

1.3   The Aim of the Study

Earlier studies contribute to our better understanding of the nuance in the two words' semantic meanings and pragmatic usage (Donazzan 2008, Liu 2000). This study aims to account for the two words' different syntactic behaviors assuming X-bar Theory. I argue that the difference in their syntactic behaviors is driven by the inherent value of the semantic feature [degree]: It is inherently [+] for *geng* but 'indefinite' (represented as [α]) for *hai* in lexicon. In language processing, when *hai* is extracted from the lexicon, its [degree] value is not determined until it enters syntax of the comparative construction. When the syntactic context is legitimate to license a [+] value to the [degree] feature carried by *hai*, the comparative reading of *hai* then can be realized.

The paper is organized as follows. Section 2 first presents cases where *geng* and *hai* can be interchangeable. Then their differences in syntactic behaviors are examined. An analysis implicating the lexical semantic feature [degree] and the m-command structural relationship is accordingly proposed to account for the differences. Data extracted from BCC showing the interaction between modals and *geng*/ *hai* will lend further support for the proposed analysis. Section 3 concludes.

2   *Geng* and *hai* in Comparative Structures

2.1   The Near Synonym Pair: *geng* and *hai*

Geng and *hai* are both adverbs that indicate degree. They can precede a gradable predicate and denote a comparative meaning. Examples are given in (2) and (3), where the two degree adverbs are marked grey:

(2) a. 照顧小孩比工作更累。
     Zhaogu   xiaohai bi gongzuo geng   lei.
     Look.after kids   han work   GENG exhausting
     'Looking after a kid is more exhausting than working.'

  b. 照顧小孩比工作還累。
     Zhaogu   xiaohai bi gongzuo hai   lei.
     Look.after kids   than work   HAI exhausting
     'Looking after a kid is more exhausting than working.'

(3) a. 名利和權勢比起地獄裡的魔鬼更可怕。
     Ming-li   han quanshi   bi(qi) diyu li de mogui geng kepa
     Fame-gain and power compared.with hell in DE$_1$ devil GENG frightening
     'Compared with the devil in hell, fame, gain, and power are more terrifying.'

  b. 名利和權勢比起地獄裡的魔鬼還可怕。
     Ming-li   han quanshi   bi(qi)   diyu li de mogui hai kepa
     Fame-gain and power compared.with hell in DE$_1$ devil HAI frightening
     'Compared with the devil in hell, fame, gain, and power are more terrifying.'

In above examples, two individuals or things are compared in a dimension--- the degree of exhaustion in (2) and the degree of fright in (3). The structure [X bi(qi) Y *geng/hai* Pred.] represents the proposition that X has a higher degree of the property denoted by the predicate than Y. The lexical item *geng* or *hai* immediately precedes the predicate *lei* 'tiresome' in (2), and *kepa* 'frightening' in (3), resulting in a comparative reading 'more exhausting' and 'more frightening'.

2.2   The Structurally Licensed [Degree] Feature in *hai*

It seem that *geng* and *hai* in above examples are synonymous and that replacing one with the other does not affect the intended semantic meaning. However it is noted that the two lexical items as degree modifiers cannot be always interchangable. Consider the following examples:

(4) a. 這些年的生活讓他變得更/*還成熟了。
     Zhexie nian de shenghuo rang ta bian-de   geng / *hai   chenshou le.
     These   year DE$_1$ life   let him become-Mod. GENG/* HAI mature Part.
     'Life in the past years has made him become more mature.'

b. 升級後的速度應該會更/ *還快。

Shengji hou de   shudu yinggai hui   geng / *hai   kuai
Upgrade after DE$_1$ speed should capable   GENG/ *HAI fast
'After upgrading, the speed should be faster.'

In (4a), the third person singular is compared with himself in old days on the scale of maturity. *Geng* in the constituent *geng chenshou* 'more mature' precedes and modifies the predicate *chengshou* 'mature' and denotes a higher degree of maturity. Unlike the comparative sentences in (1), (2), and (3), *geng* cannot be replaced with *hai*, as indicated by the asterisk symbol. The puzzle becomes more salient when we compare (4b) with (1b): It is not felicitous for *hai* to modify the degree on the scale of being fast in (4b), but it is felicitous in (1b). It is therefore reasonable to surmise that the proper occurrence of *hai* in comparative structure is constrained by the overall syntactic configuration beyond the constituent where *hai* occurs, but not by the predicate it modifies.

When the *bi*-phrase in comparative structures is present, *geng* and *hai* are both possible to precede the gradable predicate and form a comparative reading, as illustrated in (1), (2), and (3) above. However, when the *bi*-phrase is absent, the two words demonstrate different syntactic behaviors. Consider the contrast in (5) and (6), where the b-sentence is distinct from the a-sentence in the absence of the *bi*-phrase:

(5) a.   他的想法比你的更/還吸引人。

Tade xiangfa bi   nide geng/ hai   xiyingren.
His   idea   than yours GENG/ HAI attractive
'His idea is more attractive than yours.'

b.   他的想法更/*還吸引人。

Tade xiangfa   geng / *hai   xiyinren.
His   idea   GENG/ *HAI attractive
'His idea is more attractive (than yours).'

(6) a.   北部缺水的情況比南部更/還嚴重。

Beibu que-shui   de   qingkuang bi nanbu   geng/ hai   yanzhong.
North lack-water DE$_1$ situation   than south   GENG/ HAI serious
'The situation of drought in the north is more serious than it is in the south.'

b.   北部缺水的情況更/*還嚴重。

Beibu que-shui   de   qingkuang geng   /*hai   yanzhong.
North water.shortage DE$_1$ situation   GENG/ HAI   serious
'The situation of water shortage in the north is more serious (than it is in the south).'

When *bi*-phrase is absent, *geng* still can convey the meaning of comparison but *hai* cannot, as indicated by the asterisk symbol. To account for this discrepancy, it is hypothesized that the difference between *geng* and *hai* lies in how the degree feature is realized: *Geng* has inherent degree feature with the [+] value while the value of the degree feature in *hai* is underspecified and needs to be structurally licensed. This explains why *hai* cannot generate the comparison reading by itself without co-occurrence of the *bi*-phrase. Therefore in processing comparative sentences containing *hai*, a linking needs to be established between the lexical item *hai* and the syntactic constituent of the *bi*-phrase.

Such a linking can be explained via the structural relationship of m-command, which is a broader version of c-command in that the specifier is included in the commanding domain (Haegeman 1994). If α and β are two nodes in a syntactic tree, α m-commands β iff:

    a.   α does not dominate β, and
    b.   the first maximal projection that dominates α also dominates β.

The structural relationship is schematized in (7):

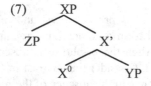

(7)

According to the definition, if ZP in the above x-bar structure is α, then it m-commands everything below the first maximal projection, i.e. XP. The m-command relationship between the internal structure of the predicate in (5a) and (6a) is shown in (8):

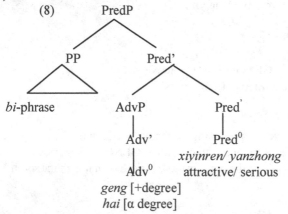

(8)

The above layout of the syntactic structure shows that the AdvP and the *bi*-phrase mutually m-command each other. The PredP is projected by the head *xiyinren* 'attractive' in (5a) and by *yanzhong* 'serious' in (6a). The lexical word *geng* or *hai* projects into an AdvP, as an adjunct adjoining to the intermediate projection Pred'. The [degree] feature in Adv^0 percolates up to the maximal projection of AdvP (cf. discussion about feature percolation in Cole et al (1993)). The *bi*-phrase is realized in the specifier position. When Adv^0 is realized as *geng*, which carries the [+degree] feature, the occurrence of the *bi*-phrase is optional. In other words, the inherent [+degree] feature allows the lexical word *geng* to occur and express degree by itself. By contrast, when it is *hai* that projects into the AdvP, its [degree] feature's value is underspecified and needs to be licensed by the *bi*-phrase. This indicates the dependency between *hai* and the *bi*-phrase is tighter than it is between *geng* and the *bi*-phrase.

The structural relationship of m-command can offer a feasible account for the dependency between *hai* and the *bi*-phrase. The evidence comes from the ungrammaticality caused by dislocation of the *bi(qi)*- phrase. Consider the ungrammaticality of the b-sentence in the following examples where the b-sentence contrasts with the a-sentence in the position of the *bi(qi)*- phrase, highlighted in grey. To avoid redundancy, the English translation for the b-sentence is omitted.

(9)   a. 他現在的態度比(起)以前更/還保守。
        Ta xianzai de   taidu   bi(qi)   yiqian geng/hai   baoshou.
        He   now   DE₁ attitude compared.with past   GENG/HAI conservative.
        'His attitude nowadays is more conservative than before.'

      b. Bi(qi)   yiqian, ta xianzai de   taidu   geng/*hai   baoshou.
        compared.with past   he now   DE₁ attitude GENG/*HAI conservative

(10) a. 的想法比起你的更/ 還吸引人。
        Tade xiangfa   bi(qi)   nide   geng/ hai   xiyingren.
        His   idea   compare.with yours   GENG/ HAI attractive
        'Compared with yours, his idea is more attractive.'

      b. Bi(qi)   nide,   tade xiangfa Geng /*hai   xiyingren.
        Compare-with. yours, his   idea   GENG/*HAI attractive

(11) a. 北部缺水的情況比(起)南部更/還嚴重。
        Beibu que-shui   de qingkuang bi(qi)   nanbu   geng /hai
        north   water.shortage DE₁ situation compare.with south   GENG/ HAI
        yanzhong.
        serious
        'The situation of water shortage in the north is more serious than the south.'

      b. Biqi   nanbu, beibu que-shui   de qingkuang geng /*hai
        Compare-Part. south, north water.shortage DE₁ situation   GENG/ HAI
        yanzhong.
        serious

The b-sentence in (9), (10) and (11) shows that ungrammaticality is caused when the *bi(qi)*-phrase is dislocated and separate from the comparative constituent formed by *geng/ hai* and the gradable predicate. As presented above, the *bi(qi)*-phrase is analyzed to be in the specifier position of the PredP and form an m-command relationship with the AdvP projected by *geng/ hai*. The degree feature of the lexical word *hai* is analyzed to be structurally licensed by the *bi(qi)*-phrase via the m-command relationship. The dislocation makes the *bi(qi)*-phrase not able to m-command the AdvP, projected by *hai*, anymore and the degree feature in *hai* thus would fail to be licensed. This accounts for the infelicity of the b-sentences.

2.3   Interaction with Modals

The constraint that the occurrence of the degree *hai* is structurally constrained can be further evidenced by the following examples, where *geng*, but not *hai*, is compatible with modals marked in grey:

(12) a. 升級後的速度應該會更/*還快。

Shengji hou   de shudu yinggai hui   geng /* hai   kuai.
Update after DE speed should able GENG/*HAI fast
'After upgrading, the speed should be faster.'

b. 如果再加个冰淇淋，應該會更/*還吸引人。

Ruguo zai   jia   ge bingqilin, yinggai hui geng/*hai   xiyinren.
If   further add CL ice.cream should   able GENG/*HAI   inviting.
'If ice cream is added (to it), it would be even more inviting.'

Data extracted from BCC further support the claim that *geng* has a much higher frequency than *hai* to co-occur with modals. Table 1 shows the number of entries in BCC with *hai* and *geng* co-occurring with a preceding modal respectively. In the search pattern, the underline ___ stands for the position of *geng/ hai*, and 'a' stands for 'adjective' according to the search convention of BCC. For example, by keying in '*keneng hui geng* a' (可能會更a) in BCC, we obtained 259 entries, but zero entry for '*keneng hui hai* a' (可能會還a).

Table 1. Interactions between modals and *geng/ hai* when the *bi*-phrase is absent

Search Pattern	*hai* (還)	*geng* (更)
kenenghui__a (可能會__a)	0	259
yinggahui__a (應該會__a)	0	83
keyi__a (可以__a)	0	2137
bixu__a (必须__a)	0	146
buxiang__a (不想__a)	0	11

The zeros shown in the column for *hai* indicate that the [degree] feature of *hai* is not licensed in the syntactic structure and therefore cannot convey the comparative meaning as *geng* can.

On the other hand, when *bi*-phrase is present, *hai* is legitimate to co-occur with a modal by following it. Two examples are given in (13) where the modal is marked grey and the *bi*-phrase underlined:

(13) a. 不久的將來, 水會比石油還貴。

   Bujiou   de jianglai, shui hui   bi shiyou   hai   gui.
   No.long DE future, water would   than petroleum HAI expensive.
   'It will not be long before water becomes more expensive than petroleum.'

b. 狗可以比狼还凶猛

   Gou keyi bi   lang   hai xungmeng.
   Dog can   than wolf HAI ferocious
   'Dogs can be more ferocious than wolves.'

The result of data extraction from BCC lends further support for the proposal that the *bi*-phrase needs to be within the m-command domain so as to license the [degree] feature carried by *hai*. Table 2 shows that results of data extraction. The underline __ between n and a in the search pattern stands for the position of *geng/ hai*, 'a' stands for 'adjective', and 'n' stands for 'noun' according to the search convention of BCC. For example, by keying in '*keyi bi* n *geng a*' (可以比n更a) in BCC, we obtained 34 entries, and 12 entries for '*keyi bi* n *hai* a' (可以比n還a). By comparing Table 1 and Table 2, we can see more clearly the *bi*-phrase has a much tighter structural relationship with *hai* than it does with *geng*.

Table 2. Interactions between modality and *geng/ hai* when the *bi*-phrase is present

Search Pattern	*hai* (還)	*geng* (更)
可以比n__a	12	34
Kenenghui bi n_ a 可能會比n___a	0	2
yinggai bi n__a 應該比n___a	4	17
hui bi n__a 會比n___a	40	78
yao bi n___a 要比n___a	30	103
bixu bi n___a 必須比n___a	1	5

As discussed in the previous section, the *bi*-phrase can license the legitimate occurrence of *hai* via the m-command relationship. The proposed structure implicating the m-command relationship (cf. the tree structure in (8)) can predict that if *bi*-phrase is out of the m-command domain, the sentence would be illegitimate. Ungrammaticality caused by the dislocation of the *bi*-phrase in the examples of (14) supports this prediction:

(14) a. *不久的將來，水比石油會還貴。
         *Bujiou   de jianglai, shui bi shiyou   hui   hai   gui.
         No.long DE future, water than petroleum would   HAI expensive.
         'It will not be long before water becomes more expensive than petroleum.'

   b.   *狗比狼可以還凶猛。
        *Gou bi   lang   keyi hai xungmeng.
        Dog than wolf can   HAI ferocious
        'Dogs can be more ferocious than wolves.'

3   Conclusions

It has been shown that *geng* and *hai* are both possible to precede the gradable predicate they modify and convey a comparative meaning on a scale denoted by the predicate. There are cases showing that *geng* and *hai* are interchangeable. However, it has been shown that the potential for *hai* to code comparison is restricted by the syntactic structure where it occurs. To account for the different syntactic behaviors between *geng* and *hai* in Chinese comparative structures, I have proposed that the inherent [+degree] feature makes *geng* able to mark comparative reading without being constrained by the occurrence of the *bi(qi)*-phrase. By contrast, the value of the [degree] feature encoded in *hai* is underspecified in the lexicon and is structurally licensed in syntax. It is further argued that when the *bi(qi)*-phrase is absent or not included in the domain of m-command, the licensing relationship would crash.

Acknowledgements. This study is supported and funded by The HK PolyU-PekingU Research Centre on Chinese Linguistics, a collaborative research center set up jointly in 2009 by the Hong Kong Polytechnic University (PolyU) and Peking University. I benefit greatly from suggestions from Prof. Chu-Ren Huang, Prof. Ding-Xu Shi (PolyU), Prof. Rui Guo (Peking University) and colleagues in the Department of Chinese and Bilingual Studies at PolyU. Special thanks go to my colleague Dr. Hongzhi Xu at PolyU, who helped me with technics of using Regular Expressions to extract data from corpora. All remaining errors are my own.

References

Cole, P., Hermon, G., Sung, L.-M.: Feature percolation. Journal of East Asian Linguistics **2**(1), 91–118 (1993)

Donazzan, M.: Presupposition on times and degrees: the semantics of mandarin *hái*. In: Chan, M.K.M., Kang, H. (eds.) Proceedings of the 20th North American Conference on Chinese Linguistics (NACCL-20), vol. 2, pp. 597–610 (2008)

Haegeman, L.: Introduction to Government and Binding Theory, pp. 132–137, Oxford, Cambridge (1994)

Liu, F.-H.: The scalar particle *hai* in Chinese. Cahiers de linguistique-Asie orientale **29**(1), 41–84 (2000)

Pustejovsky, J.: The generative lexicon. Computational Linguistics **17**(4), 409–441 (1991)

Pustejovsky, J.: The Generative Lexicon. MIT Press, Cambridge (1995)

Verspoor, C.M.: Contextually-dependent lexical semantics. Doctoral dissertation. The University of Edinburgh (1997)

Natural Language Processing and Applications

Chinese Text Analysis Based on Minimal Recursion Semantics

Chao Su[1], Heyan Huang[1,2(✉)], Shumin Shi[1,2], and Ping Jian[1]

[1] School of Computer Science and Technology, Beijing Institute of Technology, Beijing, China
{suchao,hhy63,bjssm,pjian}@bit.edu.cn
[2] Beijing Engineering Research Center of High Volume Language Information Processing and Cloud Computing Applications, 5 South Zhongguancun Street, Beijing 100081, China

Abstract. Minimal Recursion Semantics (MRS) is a framework for computational semantics that is suitable for parsing and generation. To represent Chinese texts using MRS, we built a lexicon with the rich semantic knowledge of HowNet and defined36 grammar rules and 47 types. The types, words, and rules are described by TDL (Type Description Language) and implemented in the LKB (Linguistic Knowledge Builder) system. The results show that MRS is also suitable for Chinese semantic representation.

Keywords: Semantics · Minimal recursion semantics · Verb-object semantic collocation · HowNet

1   Introduction

The semantic representation of natural language is useful for multiple applications, such as text classification, information retrieval, text entailment recognition, machine translation, et al.. Minimal recursion semantics (MRS) is a framework for computational semantics that is suitable for parsing and generation (Copestake et al., 2005).

The DELPH-IN[1](Deep Linguistic Processing with HPSG) community has adopted Head-Driven Phrase Structure Grammar (HPSG) and MRS to get the meaning of texts and utterances. In recent years, MRS in dozens of languages, such as English, Japanese, has achieved great results (Zeng et al., 2012).Compared with that of English, the research of Chinese on this topic is still insufficient. (Wang et al., 2007) proposed an analysis of Chinese NPs in the framework of HPSG, especially focusing on the noun-classifier matching. (Zeng et al., 2012) represented quantitative noun phrase using MRS. However, it is quite limited: the scale of its grammar is too small and it only analysis quantitative noun phrase. Therefore, this paper tries to explore the applicability of the MRS framework for Chinese semantic representation.

For Chinese, in most cases, the verb is the core element of the sentence. And the verb-object semantic collocation is one of the most important in many kinds of relationships between the verb and the noun. (Q. Li & Z. Li, 2010) described three

---

[1]   DELPH-IN: http://www.delph-in.net/

© Springer International Publishing Switzerland 2015
Q. Lu and H.H. Gao (Eds.): CLSW 2015, LNAI 9332, pp. 421–429, 2015.
DOI: 10.1007/978-3-319-27194-1_41

elements for verb-object semantic collocation: semantic role, semantic category and semantic features. Semantic role is the semantic type of the object which collocates with the verb. Semantic category reflects the relation among the objects of the world. And Semantic feature is a supplement to semantic role and category. Due to the complexity of the linguistic phenomena in Chinese, we begin with only the verb-object phrases.

2   Background

2.1   Minimal Recursion Semantics

MRS is a framework for computational semantics which can be used for both parsing and generation. MRS is a syntactically 'flat' representation and includes a treatment of scope which is straightforwardly related to conventional logical representations. MRS representations are expressive, have a clear interface with syntax, and are suitable for processing (Lien, 2014).

MRS takes the elementary predications (EP) as the primary unites of semantics. An EP usually corresponds to a single word. An EP contains three components: a handle, a relation, and a list of arguments. An MRS structure is a tuple <GT, R, C> where GT is the top handle, R is a set of EPs, and C is a bag of handle constraints.

For example, the sentence "Every dog chases some white cat" is semantically ambiguous. Here are two representations of the sentence in (1) and (2):

(1) a. some (y, white (y) ∧ cat (y), every (x, dog (x), chase (x, y)))

   b.

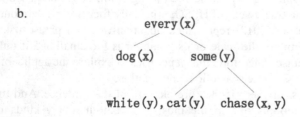

(2) a. every (x, dog (x), some (y, white (y) ∧ cat (y), chase (x, y)))

   b.

         every (x)
        /   \
    dog (x)   some (y)
               /   \
    white (y), cat (y)   chase (x, y)

To represent them as one single MRS structure, Copestake represented the pieces of the tree that are constant between two readings, and stipulated some constraints on how they may be joined together. Then the two structures could be generalized as shown in (3):

(3) <h0, {h1: every (x, h3, h8), h3: dog (x), h7: white (y), h7: cat (y), h5: some (y, h7, h9), h4: chase (x, y)}, {}>

2.2 HowNet

HowNet, which is first released in 1999, has been applied in various areas of NLP (Z. Dong & Q. Dong, 2000). It is a computer-oriented common-sense knowledge base. The representation of "水饺 (*dumpling*)" in HowNet is as follows:

```
NO=078963
W_C=水饺
G_C=N
E_C=
W_E=dumpling
G_E=N
E_E=
DEF=food|食品
```

In the above, "food |食品" is one of the sememe in HowNet. Thus the definition of the concept of "水饺 (*dumpling*)" means that: a dumpling is (a) a kind of food.

2.3 TFS (Typed Feature Structure) and Unification

TFS is used to express the multi-level language information. It always appears as an attribute-value matrix (AVM). A TFS described by AVM is shown in fig. 1.

$$\begin{bmatrix} \text{type1} \\ \text{FEATURE1} & \text{type2} \\ \text{FEATURE2} & \text{type3} \end{bmatrix}$$

Fig. 1. A TFS described by AVM

In the above, type1 is the type of this AVM. FEATURE1 and FEATURE2 are features of type1. The types of them are typ2 and type3, respectively.

Unification operation is the basis of text analyzing based on TFS. Two TFSs are combined if they are compatible, which is like combining words into a sentence. For example, in fig. 2, two TFSs, (a) and (b), can be combined into (c), because they have a greatest lower bounds (GLB).

$$\begin{bmatrix} \text{word} \\ \text{ORTH} & 读 \end{bmatrix} \quad \begin{bmatrix} \text{word} \\ \text{POS} & v \end{bmatrix} \quad \begin{bmatrix} \text{word} \\ \text{ORTH} & 读 \\ \text{POS} & v \end{bmatrix}$$

(a)   (b)   (c)

Fig. 2. Examples of Typed Feature Structure

If we transform a text into some TFSs and combine them according to some grammar rules (both syntactic and semantic), we will get a correct sentence.

Both the TFSs and rules are defined by TDL (Type Description Language). Restricted to the length of the article, please refer to *The (new) LKB system* (Copestake et al., 1999).

3   Representing Chinese Text using MRS

To represent Chinese text using MRS, we built the type file, the lexicon file, and the grammar rule files. In this section, we introduce our system and the files.

3.1   System Design

We implement our analysis in the LKB (Linguistic Knowledge Building) system (Copestake et al., 1999). It is a grammar and lexicon development environment for use with constraint-based linguistic formalisms. It is suitable for unification-based linguistic formalisms for parsing and/or generation and has been widely used in developing grammars based on HPSG.

The structure of our system is shown in fig. 3.

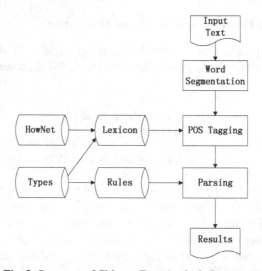

Fig. 3. Structure of Chinese Text Analysis System

First, we need to construct the files of types and rules, and build lexicon using HowNet. Then we load them into the LKB system. We segment each sentence in the input Chinese text and put them in to the LKB system. The system uses lexicon files for part-of-speech tagging, and then makes use of grammar rules to parse and outputs the results.

3.2   Type Definition

The type system defines the framework for the rest of the grammar. For instance, the categories, n, v, np and so on, are represented as types. Some basic types of TFS (Typed Feature Structure), such as *top*, *list*, are built in the LKB system (Copestake et al., 2002).

We built 47 types, which were shown in fig. 4, in our system. In fig. 4& table 1, "DNP" and "DZNP" represent "NP with 的[de](*of*)", "Ding Zhong NP (NP with attribute-head structure)", respectively; "DAP", "ZZAP" and "LHAP" represent "AP with的[de](*of*)", "Zhuang Zhong AP (AP with adverbial-head structure)", "Lian He AP (AP which is the union of two adjectives)"; "SBVP", "SBinVP", "ZZVP" and "LHVP" represent "Shu Bu VP (VP with Predicate-complement structure)", "Shu Bin VP (VP with predicative-object structure)", "Zhuang Zhong VP (VP with verb-adverbial structure)", "Lian He VP (VP with predicative- predicative structure)", respectively.

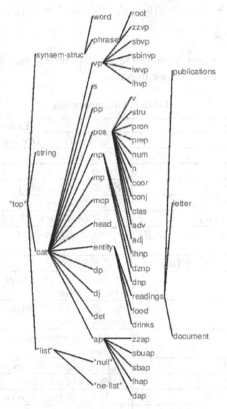

Fig. 4. The Type Hierarchy

3.3   Lexicon

The lexicon mainly consists of type, morphology, and semantic relations of each word. We built it using TDL with the knowledge in HowNet. For example, the words "书 (*book*)", "喝 (*drink*)", and "读 (*read*)" described by TFS are shown in fig. 5.

In fig. 5, "ORTH" is short for "orthography". "POS" stands for "part of speech" of the word. "ENTITY" for noun is the sememe, which can be got from HowNet. "ENTITY" for verb is the sememe of its object. Both "POS" and "ENTITY", which make up a new feature "HEAD", participate in the unification.

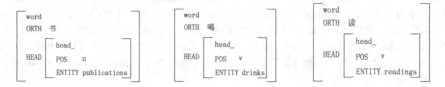

Fig. 5. TFS of "书(*book*)", "喝(*drink*)", and "读(*read*)"

3.4   Grammar Rules

Grammar rules describe how to combine lexical entries and phrases to make further phrases. Table 1 shows the rules we used.

Table 1. Grammar rules

Rule	Example
S→NP + VP	他是善良的人。(*He is a kind person.*)
NP→n	专家(*expert*)
NP→pron	他(*he*)
DNP→n (head) + stru<的[*de*]>	老师的(*the teacher's*)
DNP→adj (head) + stru<的[*de*]>	时毛的(*fashionable*)
DNP→v (head)　+ n + stru<的[*de*]>	打人的(*torturer*)，卖菜的(*vegetable vendor*)
DNP→mp + vp (head)　+ stru<的 [*de*]>	一个开车的(*a driver*)
DNP→n + v (head)　+ stru<的[*de*]>	工人做的(*made by workers*)
DZNP→n + n(head)	计算机专家(*computer expert*)，木头房子 (*wooden house*)
DZNP→v + n(head)	起飞时间(*departure time*)，庆祝会 (*celebration*)
DZNP→AP + n(head)	大规模(*large-scale*)，干净的衣服(*clean clothes*)
DZNP→num + n(head)	八百壮士(*eight hundred heroes*)
DZNP→mp + n(head)	一块石头(*a stone*)，一杯水(*a cup of water*)
DZNP→mp + ap + n(head)	一个非常善良的人(*a very kind person*)
DZNP→pron (head)　+ num	他们俩(*they two*)
DZNP→pron (head)　+ num + clas	他们两位(*both of them*)
AP→adj	干净(*clean*)
DAP→adj(head) + stru<的>	干净的(*clean*)

Table1. Grammar rules (continued)

ZZAP→adj + adj(head)	空前紧张(*an unprecedented tension*)
ZZAP→adj + adj(head) + stru<的>	空前紧张的(*an unprecedented tension*)
ZZAP→ adv + adj(head)	非常复杂(*very complex*)
LHAP→adj(head) + conj + adj	轻松而愉快(*relaxed and happy*)
VP→v	踢(*kick*)
SBVP→v(head) + v	转换成(*convert into*)
SBVP→v(head) + adj	洗干净(*wash clean*)，收拾整齐(*tidy out*)
SBinVP→v(head) + np	交换礼物(*exchange gifts*)，打人(*hit somebody*)
ZZVP→adv + v(head)	马上集合(*get together quickly*)，立即报告 (*report at once*)
ZZVP→pp + v(head)	被他看见(*be seen by him*)
ZZVP→pp + v(head) + stru	从船上跳下去(*jump down from the ship*)
ZZVP→adv + v(head) + np	都是计算机专家(*are all computer expert*)
ZZVP→adv + lhvp(head) + np	都研究并开发计算机(*all research and develop computer*)
LHVP→v (head) + v	唱歌跳舞(*sing and dance*)
LHVP→v (head) + conj + v	研究与开发(*research and develop*)
LHVP→v (head) + np + conj + v + np	烧毁证物并袭击警察(*destroy the evidence and assaulting a police officer*)
MP→num(head) + clas	一个(*one*)
MCP→num (head) + num	一百(*one hundred*)

Take the rule "SBinVP→v(head) + np" for example. It is defined using TDL as follows:

```
sbinvp_rule1 := phrase &
[ CATEGORY sbinvp,
   ARGS [ FIRST [ HEAD.POS v, HEAD.ENTITY #en ],
          REST [ FIRST [ HEAD.POS n, HEAD.ENTITY #en],
                 REST *null* ]]] .
```

A verb and a noun form a verb phrase. We should note that the value of the feature "ENTITY" must be the same, which assures the compatibility of the two sub-TFSs.

4   Experiments

We built a small test set, which consists of twenty sentences. Then we loaded the sentences into the LKB system. The output was a text file in which the LKB showed whether each sentence could be analyzed correctly.

The result is shown in fig. 6. The figure after each sentence shows whether the analysis is successful or not. It fails only if the figure is zero. In all of the twenty sentences, eighteen are analyzed successfully, while two unsuccessfully. We can see that the grammar can analyze the basic noun phrase, verb phrase, and the SVO (Subject-Verb-Object) structure. It should be noted that the first 8 sentences prove that the semantic information of verb-object collocation is useful for sentence analysis and generation.

1 我 吃 水饺. (*I eat dumplings.*) 2 25

2 我 喝 水饺. (*I drink dumplings.*) 0 22

3 我 喝 矿泉水. (*I drink mineral water.*) 2 25

4 我 吃 矿泉水. (*I eat mineral water.*) 0 22

5 宝宝 喝 矿泉水. (*The baby drinks mineral water.*) 2 25

6 爷爷 看 报纸. (*Grandpa reads newspapers.*) 2 25

7 学生 读 书. (*The students read the books.*) 2 25

8 我 写 信. (*I write a letter.*) 2 25

9 他 是 善良 的 人. (*He is a kind person.*) 4 53

10 他 是 一 个 人. (*He is a man.*) 2 34

11 这 是 老师 的. (*This is the teacher's.*) 3 33

12 他 是 开 车 的. (*He is a driver.*) 9 73

13 这 是 工人 做 的. (*This is made by the worker.*) 4 55

14 他 是 计算机 专家. (*He is a computer expert.*) 3 33

15 他们 两 位 都 是 计算机 专家. (*Both of them are computer experts.*) 3 66

16 他们 都 研究 并 开发 计算机. (*Both of them research and develop computers.*) 6 76

17 双方 交换 礼物. (*They two exchange gifts.*) 2 25

18 他们 立即 集合. (*They immediately get together.*) 2 19

19 APEC 景观 吸引 了 众多 市民. (*The APEC attracts many people.*) 9 84

20 罪犯 烧毁 证物 并 袭击 警察. (*The criminals burned the evidence and attacked the policeman.*) 6 107

```
;;; Total CPU time: 100 msecs

;;; Mean edges: 42.60

;;; Mean parses: 3.25
```

Fig. 6. Result for MRS Analysis

5   Conclusion and Future Work

We built some resources to analyze Chinese text using MRS, including some types, a lexicon, and some grammar rules. Besides, we represented the verb-object semantic collocation in Chinese with MRS. The experiment showed that MRS is applicable to represent Chinese text semantics.

In the future, we should continue our work in two directions. First, we will build more Chinese syntax and semantics into the MRS. Second, we will try to generate Chinese text using MRS. Furthermore, we will use MRS to translate between Chinese and other languages for which MRS grammars have been built.

Acknowledgments. This work is supported by the National Basic Research Program of China (973 Program, Grant No. 2013CB329303, 2013CB329606) and the National Natural Science Foundation of China (Grant No.61132009, 61201352).

References

1. Copestake, A., Flickinger, D., Pollard, C., Sag, I.A.: Minimal recursion semantics: An introduction. Research on Language and Computation 3(2–3), 281–332 (2005)
2. Wang, L., Liu, H., Stefan, M.: A description of Chinese NPs using head-driven phrase structure grammar. In: 14th International Conference on Head-Driven Phrase Structure Grammar, CSLI, Stanford (2007)
3. Zeng, S., Wang, H., Zhangm, Y.: Mandarin Text Representation Based on Minimal Recursion Semantics-Illustrate by Quantitative Noun Phrases. New Technology of Library and Information Service 10 (2012). (in Chinese)
4. Li, Q., Li, Z.: Elements of Framework Describing for Verb-Object Semantic Collocation. Journal of Yangtze University (Social Sciences Edition) 1, 016 (2010). (in Chinese)
5. Qin, Y., Wang, X., Zhong, Y.: Identification of noun phrase with various granularities. In: Natural Language Processing and Knowledge Engineering, NLP-KE 2007 (2007)
6. Lien, E.: Using minimal recursion semantics for entailment recognition. In: EACL 2014, p. 76 (2014)
7. Dong, Z., Dong, Q.: HowNet (2000). http://www.keenage.com (in Chinese)
8. Dong, Z., Dong, Q.: HowNet-a hybrid language and knowledge resource. In: Natural Language Processing and Knowledge Engineering. IEEE (2003)
9. Copestake, A., Carroll, J., Malouf, R., Oepen, S.: The (new) LKB system. Center for the Study of Language and Information. Stanford University (1999)
10. Copestake, A.: Implementing typed feature structure grammars, vol. 110. CSLI Publications Stanford (2002)
11. Zhan, W.: A Study of Constructing Rules of Phrases in Contemporary Chinese for Chinese Information Processing. Peking University (1999). (in Chinese)
12. Li, Q.: Combination of Mandarin Chinese verb "xie" and nouns from the perspective of generative lexicon theory. In: Su, X., He, T. (eds.) CLSW 2014. LNCS, vol. 8922, pp. 55–65. Springer, Heidelberg (2014)
13. Qiu, X.: Semantic derivation of the "吃 [chi] (eat) + object" idiom in Mandarin, Taiwanese and Hakka. In: Su, X., He, T. (eds.) CLSW 2014. LNCS, vol. 8922, pp. 31–42. Springer, Heidelberg (2014)

Canonicity of Chinese Opposite Pairings

A Corpus-Based Measurement

Jing Ding[✉] and Chu-Ren Huang

Department of Chinese and Bilingual Studies,
The Hong Kong Polytechnic University, Hong Kong, China
amanda.ding@connect.polyu.hk, churen.huang@polyu.edu.hk

Abstract. Being a canonical opposite pairing means it has a higher frequency in collocation and a wider distribution in syntactic frames. Based on Chinese GigaWord Corpus, this study questions the previous findings from English and other languages that "canonicity is a gradable property" (Jones *et al.* 2012), and explores, in Chinese, whether for each opposite conceptual pair there is a canonical pairing, and, the characteristics of opposite parings.

Keywords: Chinese opposites · Canonictiy · Gigaword

1 Introduction

For an opposite conceptual pair, such as COLD: HOT, it is possible to have more than one lexicalized pairing, for example, cold: tropical, icy: hot, or, chilly: heated. So, does the conceptual pair of COLD: HOT has a "canonical pairing"? Or, how we define a "canonical pairing"?

Previous studies on similar questions on English (Cf., Jones 2002, 2006; Murphy and Jones 2008; Murphy *et al.* 2009; Jones *et al.* 2012) assumed that the canonical opposite pairs should be the ones having the highest hit frequency in co-occurrence and the widest distribution in various syntactic frames.

Our study follows the way of previous studies and distinguishes three sub-types of opposites. They are antonyms (gradable opposites), complementary (ungradable opposites) and converse (oppositional relations). This paper is going to explore the features of being canonical opposite pairings in Chinese.

2 Literature Review

Justeson and Katz (1991) pointed out that the distinction between being antonymous (gradable opposites) and not, might not be dichotomous, but "may be more or less antonymous" (1991: 147), Jones *et al.* (2007) continued to question whether lexico-grammatical constructions can be used to measure the canonicity of antonym pairings. By using the World Wide Web as a corpus to better reflect language use, their experiment was based on constructions in which antonym pairings were expected to co-occur much more frequently than the average rate. Fourteen contrastive constructions, such as X and Y alike, between X and Y, both X and Y, either X or Y, from X

© Springer International Publishing Switzerland 2015
Q. Lu and H.H. Gao (Eds.): CLSW 2015, LNAI 9332, pp. 430–437, 2015.
DOI: 10.1007/978-3-319-27194-1_42

to Y, X versus Y and whether X or Y, were built to tackle antonym co-occurrence in discourse. These constructions were applied to a range of contrasting items across a list of adjectives as seed words, which were borrowed from the result of the eliciting experiment by Paradis *et al.* (2006). The World Wide Web was chosen as the research data source since they aimed to have "a more accurate and detailed antonym profile for many more adjectives" (Jones *et al.*, 2007: 137).

Jones et al. concluded "repeated co-occurrence across a wide range of antonyms frames is a better indicator of canonicity than either raw frequency counting or meta-linguistic experimentation" (2007: 150-1).

Paradis *et al.* (2009) used a psycholinguistic experiment and its final result indicated that: first, non-canonical antonym reaction times are found to be affected by "the semantic divergence between the members of the pair" (Charles *et al.* 1994, Cf. Paradis *et al.* 2009: 384), which means the farther one antonym candidate lies from the given word, the longer time subjects would need to react to it; second, "canonical antonyms have been found to prime each other more strongly than non-canonical opposites (Becker, 1980)" (2009: 384).

The results of Paradis *et al.*'s (2009) elicitation experiment suggests – and as also confirmed by similar results in Jones *et al.*'s (2007) web study – that there is a scale of canonicity from the perfect antonym candidate to the "no preferred partners" or "not-so-good ones". For some words, their antonym members are very easily defined and elicited in test as the same ones by different language users, while for some other words, the answers vary to different persons or in different contexts.

Jones *et al.* (2012) summarized the above series of work on antonym canonicity into the following points:

1. "there is a dichpotomy between good and bad antonyms";
2. for the group of non-canonical antonyms, there is a continuum of the canonicity curve;
3. "canonicity is a gradable property" and antonyms are a conceptual relation. (2012: 70).

3   Methodology

Our Chinese experiment is separated into four steps:

Step 1: using the candidate pairings in a sample corpus for collocation;
Step 2: generalizing syntactic frames from these collocated sentences;
Step 3: with the syntactic frames (from Step 2) and candidate pairings (from Step 1), extracting sentences from a main corpus;
Step 4: counting the hit number and frame number of each paring, and measuring the canonicity of the pairing.

Chinese GigaWord Simplified Corpus (here forth GigaWord or GigaWord Corpus) is chosen because of its large size (250,124,239 tokens) and high quality segmentation and POS labeling (the accuracy reaches around 95%, according to Hong & Huang 2006). The segmentation and POS information are important for Chinese corpus-based experiment and that is why we cannot use raw data from open resources like Google.

In Step 1 of our experiment, we choose Sinica Corpus as the sample corpus. Sinica Corpus is one part of the GigaWord Corpus so the segmentation and POS information generalized from sample test may be inherited by GigaWord, in Step 3.

We select 22 opposite conceptual pairs, including 5 complementary, 12 antonym and 5 converse pairs. *Tongyici Cilin* (2005), the biggest synonym dictionary of Chinese, is used to complete the synonym group of each concept. The final candidate list includes 2662 candidate pairings.

For the syntactic frames, we firstly translated the ones used in Jones (2002) and then modified them with the sentences from our sample test (in Step 2).

4   Discussion

We define a Dominance_Score to measure the canonicity of a pairing and its formula is:

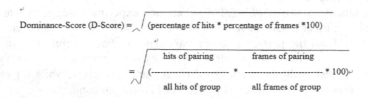

Fig. 1. Formula of Dominance

The Dominance-Score (D-Score) is decided by two factors: the hit number and the distribution of syntactic frames. If the D-Score were 5 or more, the matched pairing is defined as a canonical one.

Basically, within the same conceptual pair, the percentage of frames goes down with the reduction of hits. In other words, the more frequent one pairing members co-occur, the more frames they tend to occupy. For example, strong Vs. week

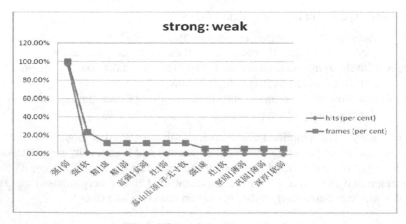

Fig. 2. Hit trends in *Strong: Weak*

Table 1. Ranks of D-Score in *Strong: Weak*

rank	pairing	D-Score	hits	frames
1	强|弱	9.84	959(96.77%)	17(100.00%)
2	强|软	0.51	11(1.11%)	4(23.53%)
3	精|虚	0.24	5(0.50%)	2(11.76%)
4	精|弱	0.22	4(0.40%)	2(11.76%)
5	富强|贫弱	0.19	3(0.30%)	2(11.76%)
6	壮|弱	0.15	2(0.20%)	2(11.76%)
7	泰山压顶|手无寸铁	0.15	2(0.20%)	2(11.76%)
8	强|虚	0.08	1(0.10%)	1(5.88%)
9	壮|软	0.08	1(0.10%)	1(5.88%)
10	坚固|薄弱	0.08	1(0.10%)	1(5.88%)
11	巩固|薄弱	0.08	1(0.10%)	1(5.88%)
12	深厚|软弱	0.08	1(0.10%)	1(5.88%)
		total	991	17

As we can see, the trends of hit numbers agree with the trends of frame distributions in the case of *strong: weak*.

In cases like *Receive: Give*, the two ranks of hits and frame distributions conflict with each other.

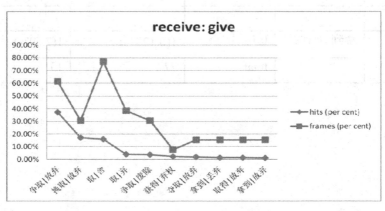

Fig. 3. Hit trends in *Receive: Give*

In this case, the trends of hits percentage and frames percentage do not parallel with each other. *Zheng1qu3: fang4qi4* is the pairing co-occurring in the largest percentage of extracted sentences but it is not the one which has the widest distribution in frames. The one with widest distribution of frames is that of *qu3: she3*, in the third position of hits number. *Huang4qu3: fang3qi4* is the most but one frequent pairing in sentences number but forth in frames number. Hence, in the table X, *qu3: she3* replaces *huang4qu3: fang4qi4* in the second position of D-Score rank. We also notice that, the sixth most frequent co-occurring pairing, *huo4de2: qi4quan2*, significantly takes less frames than its followers, *duo2qu3: fang4qi4*, *na2dao4: diu1qi4* and so on. So it is unsurprising to see its rank drops to tenth for D-Score.

Table 2. Ranks of D-Score in *Receive: Give*

rank	pairing	D-Score	hits (per cent)	frames (per cent)
1	争取|放弃	4.80	290(37.32%)	8(61.54%)
2	取|舍	3.52	125(16.09%)	10(76.92%)
3	换取|放弃	2.29	133(17.12%)	4(30.77%)
4	取|弃	1.24	31(3.99%)	5(38.46%)
5	争取|废除	1.07	29(3.73%)	4(30.77%)
6	夺取|放弃	0.53	14(1.80%)	2(15.38%)
7	拿到|丢弃	0.47	11(1.42%)	2(15.38%)
8	取得|放弃	0.44	10(1.29%)	2(15.38%)
9	拿到|放弃	0.42	9(1.16%)	2(15.38%)
10	获得|弃权	0.40	16(2.06%)	1(7.69%)
…	…	…	…	…
60	拿到|废弃	0.10	1(0.129%)	1(7.69%)
		total	777	13

The result of 22 conceptual groups is as follow:

Table 3. Top 5 D-Score Pairings in 22 Opposite Groups

		D-Score rank 1	2	3	4	5
complementary	生:死	活:死 (7.07)	生:死 (2.72)	生存:死亡 (1.13)	生还:死亡 (0.84)	生还:丧生 (0.51)
	男:女	男:女 (5.31)	男子:女子 (2.94)	男性:女性 (2.31)	子:女 (1.01)	男人:女人 (0.99)
	真:假	真:假 (7.28)	实:虚 (3.27)	真实:虚假 (1.19)	真:幻 (0.49)	真实:虚伪 (0.42)
	开:合	开:关 (6.67)	打开:关闭 (2.37)	开:闭 (1.84)	开启:关闭 (1.51)	票:关 (0.80)
	奇:偶	双:单 (9.60)	双数:单数 (1.22)	偶数:奇数 (0.53)	双:独 (0.43)	偶:独 (0.31)
Antonym	快:慢	快:慢 (6.31)	急:缓 (2.59)	急性:慢性 (2.01)	迅:慢 (1.13)	急:缓 (0.84)
	明:暗	光明:黑暗 (4.95)	明:暗 (4.50)	亮:暗 (2.01)	亮:黑 (1.78)	明:黑 (1.03)
	强:弱	强:弱 (9.84)	强:软 (0.51)	硬:虚 (0.24)	强:弱 (0.22)	坚强:软弱 (0.19)
	大:小	大:小 (9.78)	大型:小型 (0.91)	大:粗 (0.34)	大:纤 (0.19)	大型:微型 (0.14)
	宽:窄	宽:窄 (7.79)	广:窄 (0.79)	宽敞:狭小 (0.79)	宽广:狭窄 (0.68)	宽大:狭窄 (0.68)
	好:坏	好:坏 (5.27)	好:差 (2.93)	优:劣 (2.05)	佳:差 (0.73)	好:糟 (0.63)
	厚:薄	厚:薄 (7.78)	浓:淡 (2.68)	浓:稀 (1.81)	腻:淡 (0.57)	稠:稀 (0.47)
	冷:热	寒冷:酷热 (3.97)	寒冷:炎热 (2.56)	严寒:酷 (2.15)	冰冷:火热 (1.62)	冰冷:炎热 (1.15)
	高:低	高:低 (9.05)	高:贱 (0.88)	高昂:低廉 (0.59)	贵:低 (0.53)	昂贵:便宜 (0.32)
	肥:瘦	肥:瘦 (6.29)	粗:细 (5.05)	丰满:苗条 (0.98)	肥胖:苗条 (0.57)	肥胖:纤细 (0.44)
	美:丑	美:丑 (6.12)	美丽:丑陋 (4.68)	漂亮:丑陋 (2.65)	好看:难看 (1.25)	华丽:难看 (1.25)
	智:愚	明白:糊涂 (4.08)	聪明:愚蠢 (1.77)	敏锐:笨拙 (1.77)	聪明:愚蠢 (1.67)	敏慧:迟钝 (1.44)
Converse	买:卖	买进:卖出 (3.02)	购买:出售 (1.63)	购:销 (1.44)	买入:卖出 (1.39)	买购:销售 (1.22)
	来:去	来:去 (8.35)	过来:过去 (0.60)	前来:前往 (0.57)	光顾:前往 (0.54)	来到:前往 (0.41)
	教:学	教育:学习 (4.97)	辅导:学习 (1.98)	指导:学习 (1.93)	辅导:被学 (1.45)	授导:学习 (1.42)
	取:舍	争取:放弃 (4.80)	取:舍 (3.52)	换取:放弃 (2.39)	取:弃 (1.24)	争取:缴除 (1.07)
	施:受	捐赠:接受 (7.22)	赠送:接受 (2.74)	赠与:接受 (2.01)	给:受 (1.45)	捐赠:收受 (1.45)

In the 22 opposite concepts, 16 out of them have one canonical pairing, and only 6 pairs do not have canonical pairings. Within these 16 pairs, some of the so-called canonical pairings, however, are not accepted in certain contexts. For example, for the opposite group of "fat: slim", the pairs of *pang4: shou4* and *cu1: xi4* are close in D-Score, but *pang4: shoud4* usually used to describe the body shape. Besides, compared with complementary and antonym pairs, converse pairs are less likely to have canonical pairings, since 3 out of 6 non-canonical pairs are in converse group.

We also notice that Chinese opposite pairings prefer to have syllabic matched members.

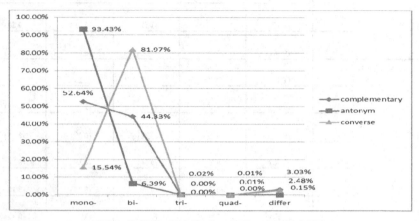

Fig. 4. Syllable Distribution in Opposite Pairings

As we can see in this figure for both complementary and antonym pairs, the most common pairings are mono-syllabic ones; but for converse pairs, the most common ones are bi-syllabic. Our data also supports the fact that an opposite pairing can be built with words having different numbers of syllables, but the ones with the same syllable number are dominant in usage.

5   Conclusion

In our study, frequency and distribution of syntactic frames are used to determine the canonicity of being opposites. As we can see in the data, the two factors clash in some cases. It suggests that canonical pairing does exist in some conceptual opposite groups. Converse pairs are less likely to have canonical pairings in the three sub-types of opposites. Moreover, our data suggests, in Chinese, there is a relation between the syllable number and of being opposite pairing. Opposite pairings prefer to have syllabic matched members.

This study uncovers the features of being canonical opposite pairings in Chinese but leaves us a new question: why converse pairs show differences with the other two sub-types in both canonicity and syllabic matching? We need a further study to answer it.

References

1. Jones, S.: Antonymy: A Corpus-based Perspective. Routledge, London (2002)
2. Johns, S.: A Lexico-syntactic analysis of antonym co-occurrence in spoken English. Text & Talk 26(2), 191–216 (2006)
3. Jones, S., Paradis, C., Murphy, M.L., Willners, C.: Googling for 'Opposites': a web-based study of antonym canonicity. Corpora 2(2), 129–154 (2007)
4. Jones, S., Murphy, M.L., Paradis, C., Willners, C.: Antonyms in English: Construals, Constructions and Canonicity. Cambridge University Press (2012)
5. Justeson, J.S., Katz, S.M.: Co-occurrences of antonymous adjectives and their contexts. Computational Linguistics Archive 17(1), 1–19 (1991)
6. Murphy, M.L., Jones, S.: Antonyms in Children's and Child-Directed speech. First Language 28, 403–430 (2008)
7. Murphy, M.L., Paradis, C., Willners, C.: Discourse functions of antonymy: a cross-linguistic investigation of Swedish and English. Journal of Pragmatics 41, 2159–2184 (2009)
8. Paradis, C., Willners, C.: What a corpus-based dictionary tells us about antonyms. In: Corino, E., Marello, C., Ornesti, C. (eds.) Proceedings XII Euralex International Congress, vol. I, pp. 213–220 (2006)
9. Paradis, C., Willners, C., Murphy, M.L., Jones, S.: Good and bad opposites: using textual and experimental techniques to measure canonicity. The Mental Lexicon 4(3), 380–429 (2009)
10. Hong, J.-F., Huang, C.-R.: Using Chinese gigaword corpus and chinese word sketch in linguistic research. In: Proceedings of the 20th Pacific Asian Conference on Language, Information and Computation (PACLIC'20), Wuhan, China, November (2006)

Politicize and Depoliticize: A Study of Semantic Shifts on People's Daily Fifty Years' Corpus via Distributed Word Representation Space

Wenlong Mou[1], Ni Sun[2], Junhao Zhang[2], Zhixuan Yang[1],
and Junfeng Hu[1,2(✉)]

[1] School of Electronics Engineering and Computer Science,
Peking University, Beijing, China
huif@pku.edu.cn
[2] Key Laboratory of Computational Linguistics, Ministry of Education,
Peking University, Beijing, China

Abstract. The semantic meanings of words are always changing with time. In this paper, we focus on semantic shifts, a certain type of semantic change, which indicates the meaning changes of a bunch of words that are influenced by social trends in specific time period. By training distributed word representation spaces for segmented time periods in diachronic corpus and mapping them into a universal semantic space, the semantic shifts of a certain cluster of words can be reflected as an offset vector in the universal space.

Further study shows that this semantic shift vector can be used as standard pattern to trace the words which have the similar semantic shift between other time periods.

Keywords: Semantics · Diachronic semantic change · Word embedding space

1 Introduction

Language is always changing over time, and the change in semantic meanings of words is a common phenomenon which deserves to be investigated. Studies on semantic change of words combine corpus linguistics and sociolinguistics. Related work such as Baker[1] and Gabrielatos et al.,[4] analyzed frequencies and contexts of words in diachronic corpus and discussed the trends in semantic meaning of words which is affected by social events, cultural evolution and political environments. For example, Baker[1] found that the meaning of money is stable and words such as family and children increasingly draws more attention in diachronic British English corpus. On the other hand, meanings of some words may also be radically altered, added or removed. Rohrdantz et al.,[12] uses topic model to identify the new meaning of words in diachronic corpus. In this paper, we focus on the previous aspect, which is a subset of semantic change, referred as semantic shift, which describes the phenomenon that meanings of a cluster

© Springer International Publishing Switzerland 2015
Q. Lu and H.H. Gao (Eds.): CLSW 2015, LNAI 9332, pp. 438–447, 2015.
DOI: 10.1007/978-3-319-27194-1_43

of words are influenced by a certain social, cultural or political trend. A set of computational methods is developed to systematically analyze semantic shifts.

Distributed word embedding such as Bengio et al.,[2] and Mikolov et al.,[9] represent each word with a real-valued low-dimensional vector. Since such models are trained based on the contexts of a word, they can capture both semantic and syntactic features of this word. Semantic shift, exposed as changes in the contexts of a word, can be captured by word embedding models. Mikolov et al.,[11] showed that a relationship between words can be characterized by a relation-specified offset vector. So we can study the semantic shifts of words by studying the geometry of the word embedding space trained on the diachronic corpus. There are related works on modeling semantic changes using word embedding models. Kulkami et al.,[7] discussed detection of statistical significant changes in this space. Kruszewski et al.,[6] analyzed effects of adjectives on nouns in phrases, which is comparable to our model.

Sun et al.,[13] introduced the diachronic deviation feature in a diachronic corpus. And they showed that a cluster of words with similar deviation features may imply certain trends of semantic shifts. However, they did not give a quantitative description of the semantic shifts. In this paper, we propose a method to obtain an offset vector to express the semantic shift in a word embedding space. As compared with traditional linguistic methods, our model can figure out semantic shifts systematically and gives out a quantitative measurement in the semantic vector space. On this basis, this model is potentially applicable in two aspects: it not only helps to build a more accurate word embedding model with concerns about semantic shift, but also serves as a systematic method to trace the effect of social trends on language.

Our approach is based on the previous work in Sun et al.,[13]. We select clusters with the most eminent semantic shifts, and segment the corpus into different partitions that the semantic meanings in each segment are relatively consistent. By training word embedding space for each segmented corpus, linear transformations can be made to mapping the different word semantic representations

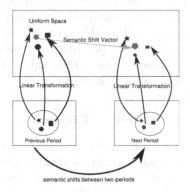

Fig. 1. Graphic Illustration of semantic shift vector

into a universal semantic space. Then we can find out the offset vector between items come from different space, which can reflect a certain trend of semantic shift in different time periods.

The semantic shift vector obtained in two typical time periods can be used as a standard pattern to trace similar semantic shifts between other time periods.

The rest of this paper is organized as follows. Section 2 introduces how we split the corpus into several adjacent periods, between which a typical semantic shift occurs. In section 3, we propose a method to estimate the semantic shift vector and illustrate the politicizing and depoliticizing vector obtained by this method. Politicization and depoliticization between adjacent years are traced and verified in Section 4. Section 5 concludes our model and describes future work.

2   Corpus Segmentation for the Study of Semantic Shift

In this section, we proposed how we extend previous work in Sun et al.,[13] to segment the diachronic corpus into relevant time periods to discover the typical semantic shift between time periods.

2.1   Diachronic Deviation Feature

In Sun et al.,[13], the whole diachronic corpus is divided into contiguous overlapping segments by a fixed size sliding window in temporal order. In this paper, the window size is set as 5 years, so the 50-year (1947 to 1996) People's Daily diachronic corpus is divided into 46 segments. Each segment contains approximately 30 million words.

For each segment, a distributed word representation space is trained individually, by the method proposed in Mikolov et al.,[9]. All of which are then transformed into a universal space trained on the whole corpus by a linear transformation learned from these spaces. Following Sun et al., we search for words with the smallest covariance vector norm in order to find a reference points set with relatively small size (usually not more than 500) but stable semantic meaning. Compared with the linear transformation in Mikolov et al.,[10] which is typically learned with 5000 reference points, this approach will not overfit on the semantic changed words, which enables analysis on semantic shifts.

Now there are many points corresponding to a specific word in the uniform space, and the variance of these points in each axis is extracted to characterize the diachronic deviation feature of this word.

2.2   Selection of Semantic Shifted Clusters

Since we are interested in the word cluster whose semantic meaning shifted similarly due to the influence of social or historical trends, the hierarchical clustering algorithm proposed in He et al.,[5] is applied to the diachronic deviation features of all words. Compared with traditional clustering methods, the algorithm proposed by He et al. does not need to specify the number of clusters in advance and since it is a hierarchical clustering method, we can choose clusters in different levels, enabling us to tradeoff between within-cluster similarity and cluster size.

In our experiment, words occurred less than 50 times are dropped out before clustering. And we choose the cluster with largest size (around 100 words) in the second level to study in the succeeding steps. Clusters with deviation feature close to zero are also discarded, because they correspond to words with stable meanings.

Words in the same cluster may not have the same meaning, but the meanings of them shift due to the same trends, which we will investigate further.

2.3   Corpus Partition Based on Clusters

Though semantic meanings shift unceasingly and continuously, certain historical and social trends can dramatically affect the flavor and attitude of a word, resulting in semantic shifts. Thus, given a selected cluster, we seek to split the corpus into several disjoint slices, during each of which the meaning of words inside the cluster can be seen as stable, and between which semantic meaning of the cluster shifted. On this basis, we can observe semantic shifts associated with the cluster in a clear and unbiased view, by comparing the semantic meaning between two adjacent periods.

Michel et al.,[8] proved that change in diachronic frequency of a cluster of words can serve as a clue for the social trend which results in semantic shifts. Thus we can partition the corpus based on the word frequency curve for the cluster.

Let $C = \{w_1, w_2, ..., w_l\}$ be a word cluster and $f_j^{(t)}$ be the frequency of word w_j at year t. We seek to partition the corpus into several contiguous and disjoint slices $\Delta : t_0 < t_1 < ... < t_K$, such that overall frequency of the cluster should be relatively stable during each period and change sharply between periods.

In order to get the best partitioning of total frequency curve, we minimize sum of intra-group variances explicitly:

$$\underset{t_0 < t_1 < ... < t_K}{\arg \min} \left\{ \sum_{i=1}^{K} \sum_{t \in [t_{i-1}, t_i)} \left(\sum_{j=1}^{l} f_j^t - \sum_{j=1}^{l} \overline{f_j^{(i)}} \right)^2 \right\}$$

The number of partitioned periods K is set fixed manually (usually 2 or 3). This can be solved by the dynamic programming method by Fisher[3].

3   Estimation of Semantic Shift Vectors

In this section, we describe how to estimate the semantic shift vector based on partitioned periods. By applying our methods to Peoples Daily fifty years corpus, we mine out a trend of semantic shift related to politics. A vector representing politicizing and depoliticizing of words is obtained.

3.1   Offset Vector Between Periods

Now we are ready to introduce the semantic shift vector which can describe the influence that certain trends imposed on word sense. For each period partitioned in section 2.3, we train a distributed word embedding space. A linear transformation from each periods space to the uniform one is also learned, using semantic stable words discovered in Section 2.1 as reference points. For word w_j in the ith period, let the projected vector be $y_j^{(i)}$ in the target space. We define the semantic shift vector of a word as the difference between its corresponding vectors, projected from the adjacent period, namely $y_j^{(i)} - y_j^{(i-1)}$. For a cluster of words C, we define its shift vector as the weighted average of individual shift vectors. If $\lambda_j^{(c)}$ is the weight of word in the cluster calculated by the hierarchical clustering algorithm, then we can calculate the semantic shift vector as follows:

$$v_i\left(C\right) = \frac{\sum\limits_{w_j \in C} \lambda_j^{(c)} \left(y_j^{(i)} - y_j^{(i-1)}\right)}{\sum\limits_{w_j \in C} \lambda_j^{(c)}}$$

Despite its simplicity, the semantic shift vector has certain meaning related to the trend which induces the semantic shifts of the given cluster. It turns out that the semantic shift vector is not only applicable to words within the selected cluster or related to the periods when this kind of semantic shift occurs, but can also be applied to any words in any periods. In other words, the shift vector can serve as a standard pattern for semantic shifts.

3.2   Politicizing and Depoliticizing Vector

In the hierarchical clustering tree acquired in Section 2.2, the largest subtrees at the second level in the clustering tree are identified as the words associated with semantic shifts. The obtained clusters are illustrated in Table 1.

As the table shows, the first cluster is closely related to politics and ideology, and their semantic shifts are assumed to be induced by politics. Thus, we conduct a case study on this cluster and seek to find the politicizing and depoliticizing vector.

Table 1. Some of selected clusters in Peoples Daily fifty years corpus

"本性"(natural instincts), "贵族"(aristocrat), "灭亡"(perish), "没落"(wane), "列强"(western political power), "堕落"(depravity), "意识形态"(ideology), "帝国主义"(imperialism), "阶级"(social class), "封建"(feudalism), "官僚"(bureaucrat), "统治"(rule), "专制"(autocracy), "势力"(force), "剥削阶级"(exploiting class), etc.
"演奏"(play music), "演唱"(sing), "歌曲"(song), "舞蹈"(dance), "表演"(perform), "歌舞"(sing and dance), "合唱"(chorus), "乐器"(musical instruments), "朗诵"(reading aloud), etc.
"镍" (nickel), "硫酸" (sulphuric acid), "合金" (alloy), "合成" (synthesis), "氧气"(oxygen), "人工" (man-made), "高速" (high-speed), "轧钢" (steel rolling), "炼钢" (steel making), "炼油" (petroleum refining), "高炉" (blast furnace), etc.

We partitioned the diachronic corpus based on the total frequency of this cluster, the curve of which is shown in Figure 2.

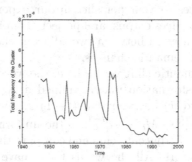

Fig. 2. Graphic Illustration of semantic shift vector

Using the algorithm described in Section 2.3, the whole corpus is segmented into two parts: one starts from 1947 and ends at 1976, another starts from 1977 and ends at 1996. In a historical view, the semantic meanings of these words shifted between before and after 1977. In the former period, those words are influenced by strong political and ideological flavor, while in the latter the influence get much weaker. We calculated the offset vector as described in Section 3.1. In our model, the vector is supposed to represent semantic shift induced by this change on political influences. We name the vector as depoliticizing vector, and its opposite vector as politicizing vector. We will then prove that the politicizing and depoliticizing vectors really represent the acquisition and removal of political flavor.

4   Tracing Semantic Shifts and Verification

In this section, we applied the politicizing and depoliticizing vector obtained in Section 3.2 to diachronic corpus. We will first trace this kind of semantic shift across years, and then prove that semantic shifts do occur on the words that are mined out to be politicized or depoliticized.

4.1   Experiment Settings and Preliminaries

Experiments are conducted on Peoples Daily fifty years corpus (from 1947 to 1996). CBOW model by Mikolov et al.,[9] is used for constructing distributed word representation space. The dimension of the vectors is set to be 50.

4.2   Tracing Semantic Shifts

With a semantic shift vector described above, we can use it as a tool to trace semantic shifts between adjacent years. We split the corpus uniformly into several non-overlapping slices (a year per slice in our experiments), train a word embedding space on each slices corpus, and project them into the uniform space. The difference vector of a word between two adjacent slices is expected to represent the corresponding semantic changes.

Let the estimated semantic shift vector be v, the word vector for w_i. at year t be $\alpha_i^{(t)}$, and the transformation matrix trained at year t be M_t. Then the semantic change for word w_i between year $(t-1)$ and year t can be described as a vector $\delta_i^{(t)} = M_t \cdot \alpha_i^{(t)} - M_{t-1} \cdot \alpha_i^{(t-1)}$ in the uniform space.

We consider all pairs of adjacent years and compare the semantic shift vector v with all difference vectors. All the words those have $\delta_i^{(t)}$ similar to v are expected to shift in the same way at year t. In our experiments similarity between vectors is measured by cosine similarity, while a threshold for the vector norm of $\delta_i^{(t)}$ is imposed.

We trace diachronic semantic shifts using politicizing and depoliticizing vector respectively. This approach is supposed to mine out words whose semantic shifts happened at the end of previous year or the beginning of next year. Some of the results are illustrated in the tables below:

Table 2. Words traced by politicizing vector

Time	Retrieved words
1951-1952	"北面" (the north side), "侦察" (reconnoitre) "南飞" (fly to the south), "咸兴"(a city in Korea), "东面" (the east side), "重炮" (heavy artillery), "长白" (a mountain in north-eastern China), "开赴" (march to), "伊川" (a county in Korea), "海上" (In the sea), "南面" (the north side), "榴弹炮" (howitzer)
1961-1962	"曲轴"(crank shaft), "溜" (slide), "管线" (pipe), "齿轮" (gear), "活塞环" (piston ring), "隔热" (heat insulation), "运转" (operate), "流水作业" (pipeline), "连杆" (link rod), "标定" (calibration), "绞盘" (winch), "轴" (axle bearing), "行驶" (running of a car), "故障" (breakdown)

With a historical view, semantic shifts retrieved by our methods can be explained by certain social events which may impose influence on the semantic meaning of words: For the first group of words in Table 2, a batch of words are found to be politicized from 1951 to 1952, just at the time when China participated in the Korean War and presumably enhanced the official propaganda. From 1961 to 1962, terms about machinery are found politicized, indicating the upsurge of industrial production related to war in 1962.

Similarly, explanations can be found for Table 3. The batch of words that were found to be depoliticized from 1958 to 1959 reflects the end of military conflicts between Taiwan and mainland China in 1958. Many economic terms were found to get rid of political flavor in 1978, which indicates the economic reform and opening up in China.

Table 3. Words traced by depoliticizing vector

Time	Retrieved words
1958-1959	"侵犯" (offend), "可欺" (gullible), "无耻" (shameless), "狂妄" (arrogant), "义愤" (indignation), "容许" (permit), "落花" (falling flowers, usually metaphor for complete failure), "不容" (no tolerance), "低估" (underestimate), "外人" (aliens), "软弱" (feeble), "绝" (absolutely), "内政" (civil affairs)
1977-1978	"趋于" (tend to), "英镑" (UK pound), "超额利润" (super profit), "实惠" (real benefits), "顺差" (favorable trade balance), "预期" (expectation), "停滞" (stagnation), "增长" (economic growth), "悬殊" (wide gap), "耐用" (durable goods), "库存" (repertory), "市场" (market), "货币" (currency)

4.3 Comparison and Verification

We have mined out the politicizing and depoliticizing vector. Semantic shifted words are traced in for adjacent years. Though some historical explanation can be given, we need more evidence to verify that they are truly politicized or depoliticized. In this subsection, we will show with experimental results that these semantic shifts really happened.

For a word w_i, we examined its semantic meaning at year $(t - 1)$ and year t, which can be characterized by its k nearest neighbors in the word embedding space for two years. If more political words appear in its neighborhood, the politicization is considered to happen. We compare the 20 nearest neighbors of some retrieved words between adjacent years. Some of the results are shown below (the words with political flavor are underlined):

As Table 2 shows, the word "超额利润" (super-profit) is retrieved to be depoliticized from 1977 to 1978. We compare its nearest neighbors between two years.

As shown in Table 4, there are really more political words appearing in 1977. Therefore, the word "超额利润" (super-profit) is really depoliticized. For the politicizing vector, we can also verify that semantic shifts really occurred on the retrieved words, using the methods described above. Word "东面" (east side) in 1951 and 1952, results are shown in Table 5:

As shown in Table 5, more political words appear in the neighbor of "东面" (east side), which indicates that this word is really politicized in 1952.

Therefore, we proved that the semantic shift vector obtained by this method can really express the concept of politicization and depoliticization. Thus it serve as a standard pattern for the corresponding kind of semantic shifts.

Table 4. Twenty Nearest Neighbors for word "超额利润" (super-profit)

k-N-N in 1977	k-N-N in 1978
"弹头" (warhead), "班机" (flight), "后起" (rising country), "销售额" (volume of sales), "交战" (in war), "股票" (stock), "剩余价值" (surplus value), "萧条" (depression), "买进" (buy), "征兵" (conscription), "多国公司" (multinational company), "牟取暴利" (profiteer), "数十亿" (billions of), "获取" (acquire), "疆界" (border), "食物" (food), "借贷" (debt), "追逐" (seek), "粮价" (price of grain), "掠取" (robbery)	"提留" (withdraw and retain), "博利瓦" (currency of Venezuela), "能力" (capability), "涨价" (increase price), "支配权" (administration), "数额" (quantity), "竞争力" (competitiveness), "必需" (necessity), "抵消" (counteract), "物化" (materialize), "牟取" (profiteer), "固定" (fix), "百分之二点七" (2.7%), "流转" (circulate), "数量" (quantity), "留成" (preserve), "资产" (capital), "生产率" (productivity), "倒流" (reverse flow), "比率" (ratio)

Table 5. Twenty Nearest Neighbors for word "东面" (east side)

k-N-N in 1951	k-N-N in 1952
"岩洞" (cave), "附近" (neighbourhood), "西面" (west side), "山前" (front of a mountain), "乌江" (a river in China), "正西" (west side), "偷渡" (illegal immigration), "横" (across), "低空" (low in the sky), "东南角" (south-eastern corner), "狭长" (narrow and long), "浪头" (wave), "朴达峰" (a mountain in Korea), "踞" (be based on), "洪川", "天德山", "金川"(all of three are places in Korea), "小山" (little mountain), "南面" (south side), "北面" (north side)	"社稷" (nation), "山前" (front of a mountain), "一线" (forefront), "北麓" (north side of mountain), "纷飞" (fly), "陡峭" (steep), "清川江" (river in Korea), "南边" (south side), "大同江"(river in Korea) , "公路" (highway), "交叉点" (crossroads), "海岛" (island), "河川", "莱州" (place in Korea), "绝壁" (cliff), "附近" (neighbourhood), "南面" (south side), "制高点" (high ground), "北面" (north side), "西面" (west side)

5 Conclusion and Future Work

In this study, we introduced semantic shift vector as a quantitative description for semantic shift induced by social trends.

A study in Peoples Daily fifty years corpus mined out semantic shift vector induced by politic trend. Experiments show that this vector is applicable to find other words that are politicized or depoliticized between any time periods.

Politicize and depoliticize, as an example, is one of the many semantic aspects that can be remarkably influenced by social trends. The quantitative study of these language phenomena may leads to more accurate description of the word semantic mean in the future. Researches in this field may also benefit studies on figurative or metaphorical meaning of words.

Acknowledgments. This work is supported by the National Natural Science Foundation of China (grant No. M1321005, 61472017).

References

1. Baker, P.: Times may change, but we will always have money: Diachronic variation in recent british english. Journal of English Linguistics **39**(1), 65–88 (2011)
2. Bengio, Y., Ducharme, R., Vincent, P., Janvin, C.: A neural probabilistic language model. The Journal of Machine Learning Research **3**, 1137–1155 (2003)
3. Fisher, W.D.: On grouping for maximum homogeneity. Journal of the American Statistical Association **53**(284), 789–798 (1958)
4. Gabrielatos, C., McEnery, T., Diggle, P.J., Baker, P.: The peaks and troughs of corpus-based contextual analysis. International Journal of Corpus Linguistics **17**(2), 151–175 (2012)
5. He, S., Zou, X., Xiao, L., Hu, J.: Construction of diachronic ontologies from people's daily of fifty years. In: Language Resources and Evaluation Conference, pp. 3258–3263 (2014)
6. Kruszewski, G., Baroni, M.: Dead parrots make bad pets: exploring modifier effects in noun phrases. In: Lexical and Computational Semantics (* SEM 2014), p. 171 (2014)
7. Kulkarni, V., Al-Rfou, R., Perozzi, B., Skiena, S.: Statistically significant detection of linguistic change. arXiv preprint arXiv:1411.3315 (2014)
8. Michel, J.B., Shen, Y.K., Aiden, A.P., Veres, A., Gray, M.K., Pickett, J.P., Hoiberg, D., Clancy, D., Norvig, P., Orwant, J., et al.: Quantitative analysis of culture using millions of digitized books. Science **331**(6014), 176–182 (2011)
9. Mikolov, T., Chen, K., Corrado, G., Dean, J.: Efficient estimation of word representations in vector space. arXiv preprint arXiv:1301.3781 (2013)
10. Mikolov, T., Le, Q.V., Sutskever, I.: Exploiting similarities among languages for machine translation. arXiv preprint arXiv:1309.4168 (2013)
11. Mikolov, T., Yih, W.T., Zweig, G.: Linguistic regularities in continuous space word representations. In: HLT-NAACL, pp. 746–751 (2013)
12. Rohrdantz, C., Hautli, A., Mayer, T., Butt, M., Keim, D.A., Plank, F.: Towards tracking semantic change by visual analytics. In: Proceedings of the 49th Annual Meeting of the Association for Computational Linguistics: Human Language Technologies: Short Papers. Association for Computational Linguistics, vol. 2, pp. 305–310 (2011)
13. Sun, N., Chen, T., Xiao, L., Hu, J.: Diachronic deviation features in continuous space word representations. In: Sun, M., Liu, Y., Zhao, J. (eds.) NLP-NABD 2014 and CCL 2014. LNCS, vol. 8801, pp. 23–33. Springer, Heidelberg (2014)

PoS Tagging for Classical Chinese Text

Tin-shing Chiu[1(⊠)], Qin Lu[1], Jian Xu[1], Dan Xiong[1], and Fengju Lo[2]

[1] Department of Computing, The Hong Kong Polytechnic University, Hung Hom, Hong Kong
{cstschiu,csluqin}@comp.polyu.edu.hk, wyatt198258@126.com,
csdxiong@comp.polyu.edu.hk
[2] Department of Chinese Linguistics & Literature, Yuan Ze University, Taoyuan City, Taiwan
gefjulo@saturn.yzu.edu.tw

Abstract. The Chinese language is evolving over the centuries. In order to study the changes of Chinese language using computational methods, segmentation and PoS tagging of Chinese are essential. However, segmentation and PoS tagging methods developed for Modern Standard Chinese do not perform well for Classical Chinese. The cost of segmenting and annotation is high if they are done manually. In this work, we present a CRF based method for PoS tagging for Classical Chinese text in the Ming and Qing dynasties. One of the key issues is the preparation of the training data for CRF. Our initial experiment shows that PoS tagging based on Modern Standard Chinese text can achieve a precision of 83%; and by adding as little as 12,000-word annotated Classical Chinese texts, we were able to improve the precision to over 90%.

Keywords: Part-of-speech tagging · Novels in the ming and qing dynasties · Chinese classics · Ancient chinese

1 Introduction

Segmentation and part-of-speech (PoS) tagging are essential for analysing Classical Chinese texts. Because of the great difference in syntax and semantics between modern Chinese and ancient Chinese, the performance of the tools or resources built for or trained from modern Chinese is not satisfactory when applied to Classical Chinese. This makes the research on computational study of Classical Chinese more difficult. In this paper, we present a Conditional Random Field (CRF) based PoS tagging algorithm for Classical Chinese. The key issue, however, is not so much on the computational method, but on the proper use of available language resources and how to prepare the necessary training data for the machine learning algorithm. Our preliminary study shows that with a little over 10,000 words of annotated Classical Chinese text, we can improve the performance by about 9%.

The paper is organized as follows. Section 2 provides some information on related work. Section 3 briefly describes the PoS tagging model. Section 4 presents our annotation process in details. Section 5 shows the setup and presents the results of our experiment.

© Springer International Publishing Switzerland 2015
Q. Lu and H.H. Gao (Eds.): CLSW 2015, LNAI 9332, pp. 448–456, 2015.
DOI: 10.1007/978-3-319-27194-1_44

2   Related Works

Because of the nature of Chinese language, segmentation and PoS tagging play a very important role in Chinese linguistics and related natural language processing (NLP) applications, such as text-to-speech [9,10]. However, NLP tools, such as segmentation, developed for Modern Standard Chinese would have very poor performance when directly applied to Classical Chinese text because of the evolution of Chinese, such as the change of lexical form from single-character to multi-character. Results show that a segmentor which can reach 97% precision for Modern Standard Chinese [7] can only obtain about 90.14% precision [4] for Classical Chinese.

Due to the lack of computational tools, most digitization work for Classical Chinese text has to rely mainly on manual annotation. In 1995, Academia Sinica started annotating an old Chinese corpus. In 2001, the Academia Sinica Tagged Corpus of Early Mandarin Chinese was made online for public access. At present, there are 19 literatures available in total, including *Water Margin* (《水滸傳》), *The Golden Lotus* (《金瓶梅》) and *A Dream of Red Mansions* (《紅樓夢》)[1]. Another annotation work on segmentation was conducted based on Specification for Corpus Processing at Peking University [8] which was meant for Modern Chinese text. To make segmentation suitable for Classical Chinese text, our team has developed a specification for both word segmentation and named entity annotation for Classical Chinese text applicable to Ming and Qing literature and also ancient script in the pre-Ming/Qing period [3]. Four Chinese classical novels, *Romance of the Three Kingdoms* (《三國演義》), *Water Margin* (《水滸傳》), *The Golden Lotus* (《金瓶梅》) and *A Dream of Red Mansions* (《紅樓夢》) are segmented by using a semi-automatic method with a strict quality assurance process. After a quality assurance process through manual checking, the precision from an automatic method which can reach 90.14% in precision can be improved to reach 99.44% as the end result [4].

In computational linguistics, many algorithms are derived to label sequential data, such as hidden Markov models (HMMs), maximum entropy Markov models (MEMMs) and conditional random fields (CRFs). They are all probabilistic models and obey Markov property. Simply put, the Markov property states that the transition to the next state is controlled by the current state. From Lafferty (2001) experiment, in terms of accuracy, the error rate of CRF is 5.55% which is better than HMM (5.69%) and MEMM (6.37%) [6]. While in Modern Standard Chinese PoS tagging, the accuracy of PoS tagging can reach 91.9% [5] and 96.2% [2].

3   PoS Tagging

In this work, we choose to use the CRF model for PoS tagging. Generally speaking, CRFs are built based on a discriminative undirected graphical model which models the conditional probability $p(Y|X)$ with a set of pre-defined features extracted from the

---

[1] Academia Sinica Tagged Corpus of Early Mandarin Chinese (http://app.sinica.edu.tw/cgi-bin/kiwi/pkiwi/kiwi.sh)

training data set. In PoS tagging task, X is a random variable sequence that ranges over natural language sentences while Y is a hidden random variable sequence that ranges over the corresponding PoS labels of those sentences. Fig. 1 shows the graphical representation between hidden and observable nodes in a linear-chain structure.

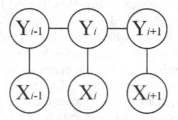

Fig. 1. Graphical structure of CRFs for sequences

If a linear-chain CRF is defined by a graph G with a feature set, F, and each feature $f_k \in F$, is weighted by λ_k, then, the conditional probability is defined by

$$p(Y|X) = \frac{\exp\left(\sum_k \sum_i \lambda_k f_k(y_{i-1}, y_i, X)\right)}{\sum_y \exp\left(\sum_k \sum_i \lambda_k f_k(y_{i-1}, y_i, X)\right)}$$

Features f_k defines the set of functions that encode the relationship of graph G. The features are extracted from a window of size 5, with two words before and two words after the current word including their tags. Since the prediction is evaluated by Boolean values, the model can be solved by optimizing λ_k as f_k is considered a given value in G. In our PoS tagger, the previous/next one word and the previous/next two words with PoS are used as features. No other feature is considered.

4   Preparation of Annotation Process

In order for the CRF model to work, training data must be annotated with PoS tags. The annotation process for Chinese classics, if started from scratch, can be done manually. However, this task is time consuming and error prone. On the other hand, PoS tagged language resources for Modern Standard Chinese have already been developed and made available for many years [7,8]. Thus, we make use of the Modern Standard Chinese corpus as the initial training data and set up an iterative annotation process to speed up the annotation process of Chinese classics as shown in Fig. 2. Each iteration contains four steps as follows.

Step 1: Take a section of Classical Chinese text as input. This section will be annotated by the PoS tagger.

Step 2: Use the Modern Standard Chinese corpus with PoS tags as the training data to train the CRF model, and then, label the input Classical Chinese text to produce automated PoS tags.

Step 3: The output in Step 2 is manually reviewed and confirmed. To ensure quality, the manual revision can be cross-checked by more than one person.

Step 4: The manually verified Classical Chinese text with PoS is merged into the training data set for the next iteration of annotation.

When the iteration continues, the portion of Classical Chinese text in the training data set is increased, and thus, PoS tagger's performance is expected to improve until it reaches the saturation point. The next section will illustrate the performance in our experiment.

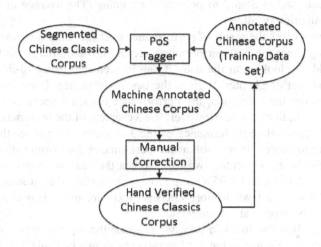

Fig. 2. The process of PoS annotation

5   Experiment

The objective of the project is to have the 4 Chinese classics all tagged with PoS. To train the CRF initially, we used 2 months of People's Daily corpus with PoS as the training set and the initial training data contains 2,270,249 words. So, the PoS labelling set used is based on Specification for Corpus Processing at Peking University version 2001. The PoS tagger uses CRF model for prediction. Since the training time is proportional to the size of training data, we set the number of iteration of each execution to 20 for CRF.

In the evaluation, we use three randomly selected chapters from the novel, *A Dream of Red Mansions*, for training and testing (Chapter 9, Chapter 52, and Chapter 91). Based on the training/testing process shown in Fig. 2, we put one chapter into the system at a time. Thus, in the second and the third iteration, we would already be using manually verified Classical Chinese text as part of the training data. In the first iteration, we select a chapter randomly from the novel, and the outcome is then reviewed manually. After the review is completed, the annotated text is merged into the training data to have 2,274,651 words, an increase of 4,402 words which translates to

0.1934% increase in training data only. After the third iteration, the training data set reaches 2,281,192 words.

To evaluate the performance, we conduct 4 sets of experiments. The first experiment is our baseline where only People's Daily data is used and applied to all the 3 chapters separately. The second experiment, labelled 0-fold, is to use the People's Daily data as the initial training, and take the result of the previous iteration using Classical Chinese text to annotate the next chapter. For the 3-fold and 10-fold and 3-fold cross validation, the text in the current iteration is divided into 3 parts (or 10 parts). One part is used as the testing data, and the remaining parts are merged into the training data set used in Step 2 to be used for training. The average of the N-fold is used as the evaluation result.

Table 1 summarizes the result of performance over the three iterations. Obviously 10-fold training gives the best performance because more training data is used compared to 3-fold. By looking at the data, it can be seen that using 10-fold after using Chapter 1 (and part of Chapter 2) gives the best performance. Even if more training data is used in the third iteration, the performance does not seem to achieve better result as it has a slight decrease. However, the 3 chapters of the texts may be different. By looking at the baseline performance of the 3 chapters, we can see that Chapter 2 has the best performance. If we look at the performance improvement of the 10-fold compared to the baseline method, we can see that the improvements for the 3 iterations are 7.02%, 8.63%, and 8.95%, respectively, indicating that greater performance improvement is obtained when more classical texts are used. However, the performance seems to be capped at around 90%.

To further analyse the errors in PoS, we examine the top five types of PoS tag errors in the chapter we select in the third iteration as shown in Table 2. It is Chapter 91 of *A Dream of Red Mansions*. Out of the 4,158 words, 596 words are incorrectly labelled. So, the error rate is 14.33%. However, 226 of them are errors of named entities, accounting for around 38% of all errors. The number of named entities in this chapter is 300. In other words, more than 75% of named entities cannot be predicted.

Table 1. Accuracy of 10-fold and 3-fold cross validation

	First Iteration	Second Iteration	Third Iteration
10-fold	86.41%	90.13%	89.95%
3-fold	84.80%	88.96%	89.59%
0-fold	80.74%	86.04%	85.67%
2 months People's Daily	80.74%	82.97%	82.56%
Best improvement	7.02%	8.63%	8.95%

To further analyse the errors related to named entities, Table 3 shows the statistics of named entities in all the three chapters of *A Dream of Red Mansions* used in this work.

Table 2. Top five categories of error in the third iteration

Category	Count	Ratio
Named Entities	226	37.92%
Noun	80	13.42%
Verb	72	12.08%
Adverb	35	5.87%
Adjective	28	4.7%
Top 5 Total	441	73.99%

Table 3. Error rate of named entities

	First Iteration	Second Iteration	Third Iteration
Number of Named Entities	298	377	300
Number of Errors	298	251	226
Error Rate	100%	66.58%	75.33%
Total Number of Words	4402	6541	4158

It is not surprising to see that the error rate of predicting named entities in the first chapter is 100%. This is because the training data set does not have any sample that follows our specification on named entities and named entities in classical Chinese are very different from that of the modern time. When named entity samples are added to the training data set after the first iteration, the error rate is dropped to 66.58%. However, as more samples of named entities are added, the error rate is increased to 75.33%. Further analysis is needed to identify the problems.

Table 4. Examples of word incorrectly labelled

Word	Possible Labels in Training Data Set
奶奶 (*madam*)	n
婆婆 (*mother-in-law*)	n
大爺 (*mister/sir*)	n
孩子 (*child/kid*)	n
媳婦 (*daughter-in-law*)	n

In chapter 91, there are a total of 300 named entities identified manually. Only 149 of them are correctly predicted by the PoS tagger. The remaining 151 are incorrectly labelled. They are not presented in the training set or labelled as named entities. So the decrease of the accuracy is reasonable. Table 4 lists some of the words that we have marked as named entities manually but not listed as named entities in the training data set.

In our specification for word segmentation and name entity tagging, if a word is actually used to refer to a person, we will label it as a named entity. For example, one of sentences in Chapter 91 is "寶蟾/也/笑/道/：/「/他/辜負/奶奶/的/心√/，/" ("*He has not repaid your kindness with gratitude, Madam," Baochan sniggered*). The word "奶奶 (*Madam*)", in general, is a common noun. But in this sentence, it is the conversation between "寶蟾 (*Baochan*)" and her mistress "金桂 (*Jingui*)". "奶奶" in this sentence actually refers to "金桂 (*Jingui*)" so that, according to our specification, "奶奶 (*Madam*)" is labelled with "na2". Since we have already manually annotated named entities, they should be labelled as named entities. The PoS tagger need not predict those words which has been labelled as named entities. If name entities are not predicted by PoS tagger, the performance would reach 91.1% as shown in Table 5. Fig. 3 shows a pairwise comparison to show the performance differences between when named entities are predicted by PoS tagger and when they are not predicted by PoS tagger. From the figure, it is easy to see that in the first iteration where named entities cannot be learned from People's daily data, the difference in performance for 0-fold has the largest contrast. As the training iteration proceeds, the learning of named entity has taken much better shape.

Table 5. Accuracy of 10-fold and 3-fold cross validation if named entities are not predicted by PoS tagger

	First Iteration	Second Iteration	Third Iteration
10-fold	88.89%	91.76%	91.46%
3-fold	88.59%	91.00%	91.49%
0-fold	87.51%	89.88%	91.10%

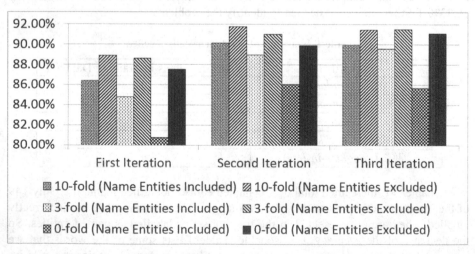

Fig. 3. Comparison of named entities predicted by PoS tagger and not predicted by PoS tagger

In the next experiment, we remove the People's Daily data as training data. Instead, we use only the first two chapters of *A Dream of Red Mansions* to train the PoS tagger to annotate the third chapter (Chapter 91). Table 6 shows the result with CRF using different iterations. In Table 6, the accuracy of using two chapters of *A Dream of Red Mansions* is around 87% (if named entities are not predicted) or 83% (if named entities are predicted). Compared to the result of including Modern Standard Chinese corpus in the training data set, we can see that the Modern Standard Chinese corpus is still essential as it distributes 3-4% gain to accuracy. Of course, one of the reasons is that the Modern Standard Chinese corpus is much larger than the Classical Chinese text we have now. If we have enough annotated Classical Chinese text, we can further improve performance without the use of Modern Standard Chinese text.

In the last experiment, we evaluate the use of three chapters of training data from the result of the three chapters in *A Dream of Red Mansions* to annotate one chapter from *Romance of the Three Kingdoms*. The accuracy of using two months' People's Daily and the three chapters of *A Dream of Red Mansions* is 72.17% (84.29% if named entities are not predicted), while the accuracy of using only the three chapters is 61.12% (73.24% if named entities are not predicted). It is not surprising that the accuracy of annotating *Romance of the Three Kingdoms* is low since the style of *A Dream of Red Mansions* is much closer to Modern Standard Chinese. But, the style of *Romance of the Three Kingdoms* is closer to Classical Chinese. The grammar and meaning of Chinese between Modern Standard Chinese and Classical Chinese are highly different. From the experiment, we can see that Modern Standard Chinese corpus is still a very important resource for annotating Classical Chinese.

Table 6. Accuracy of annotating Chapter 91 using two chapters of *A Dream of Red Mansions*

Iteration of CRF PoS Tagger	Accuracy Excluding Named Entities	Accuracy Including Named Entities
1	78.74%	73.21%
2	83.55%	78.48%
5	85.55%	80.78%
10	86.70%	82.23%
20	86.89%	82.56%
50	87.13%	82.71%
100	86.89%	82.54%
500	87.01%	82.56%

6   Conclusion and Future Work

The use of segmentation and PoS tagging tools developed for Modern Standard Chinese cannot yield good result for Classical Chinese. Thus, manually annotated texts for Classical Chinese are still very much needed if we want to use them to process ancient Chinese. In this work, we make use of the CRF model to conduct PoS tagging for Classical Chinese text. Experiments show that the Modern Standard Chinese corpus is still a very essential resource for annotating Classical Chinese text. The accuracy can be increased to around 86% if the style of Chinese is similar to Modern Standard Chinese or to around 72% if the style of Chinese is more ancient. Because

Chinese classics contain a lot of named entities which are different from the Modern Standard Chinese, we anticipate that more work is needed to develop special methods to handle named entities in Chinese classics.

Acknowledgment. This work is partially supported by the Chiang Ching-kuo Foundation for International Scholarly Exchange under the project "Building a Diachronic Language Knowledge-base" (RG013-D-09).

References

1. Academia Sinica Tagged Corpus of Early Mandarin Chinese. http://app.sinica.edu.tw/cgi-bin/kiwi/pkiwi/kiwi.sh
2. Chang, C.-H., Chen, C.-D.: HMM-based part-or-speech tagging for Chinese corpora. In: Proceedings of the Workshop on Very Large Corpora, Columbus, OH, pp. 40–47, June 1993
3. Xiong, D., Lu, Q., Lo, F., Shi, D., Chiu, T.-S., Li, W.: Specification for segmentation and named entity annotation of chinese classics in the ming and qing dynasties. In: Ji, D., Xiao, G. (eds.) CLSW 2012. LNCS, vol. 7717, pp. 280–293. Springer, Heidelberg (2013)
4. Xiong, D., Lu, Q., Lo, F., Shi, D., Chiu, T.-S.: Quality assurance for segmentation and annotation of Chinese novels in the ming and qing dynasties. In: Proceedings of 2012 International Conference on Asian Language Processing (IALP 2012), November 13–15, 2012, Hanoi, Vietnam, pp. 77–80 (2012)
5. Ng, H.T., Low, J.K.: Chinese part-of-speech tagging: one-at-a-time or all-at-once? Word-based or character-based? In: EMNLP 2004, pp. 277–284 (2004)
6. Lafferty, J., McCallum, A., Pereira, F.: Conditional random fields: probabilistic models for segmenting and labeling sequence data. In: Proceedings of the Eighteenth International Conference on Machine Learning, pp. 282–289. Morgan Kaufmann, San Francisco (2001)
7. Zhou, Q., Yu, S.: Blending segmentation with tagging in Chinese language corpus processing. In: COLING 1994, pp. 1274–1278 (1994)
8. Shiwen, Y., Duan, H., Zhu, X., Swen, B., Chang, B.: Specification for Corpus Processing at Peking University: Word Segmentation, POS Tagging and Phonetic Notation. Journal of Chinese Language and Computing **13**(2), 121–158 (2003). (in Chinese)
9. Chou, F.-C., Tseng, C.-Y., Chen, K.-J., Fen, Q.: A Chinese text-to-speech system based on part-of-speech analysis, prosodic modeling and non-uniform units. In: Proceedings of Acoustics, Speech, and Signal Processing, (ICASSP 1997), April 21–24 1997, vol. 2, Munich, pp. 923–926 (1997)
10. Schlunz, G.I., Barnard, E., van Huyssteen, G.B.: Part-of-speech effects on text-to-speech synthesis. In: 21st Annual Symposium of the Pattern Recognition Association of South Africa (PRASA), November 22–23 2010, pp. 257–262, Stellenbosch, South Africa (2010)

Narrative Idioms for Elementary-Level Chinese as a Second Language Learners

Yaqi An and Shan Wang[✉]

Department of Chinese Language Studies, The Hong Kong Institute of Education,
Tai Po, Hong Kong
s1114431@s.ied.edu.hk, swang@ied.edu.hk

Abstract. There is relatively little research on the teaching of idioms to elementary-level learners in the field of teaching Chinese as a second language (CSL). Due to the absence of an idiom syllabus based on different Chinese proficiency levels, teachers hardly know what to teach. In order to solve the problem of what and how to teach at the elementary level, this paper suggests teaching narrative idioms to beginners. It analyzed the definition of narrative idioms and their pedagogical values, discussed the difficulties of teaching idioms at the elementary level, and suggests some effective teaching methods. This study demonstrated that it is necessary and possible to start idiom teaching for elementary-level CSL learners.

Keywords: Narrative idiom · Elementary level · CSL (Chinese as a second language) · Teaching strategy

1   Introduction

The idiom is a very important part of Chinese vocabulary, but it is also a weak part in Chinese teaching and learning. So far, compared to the study of other types of vocabulary, the research on idiom teaching and learning is inadequate. Meanwhile, there is no specialized syllabus or reference book for idiom teaching, which makes it a tricky problem. When referring to vocabulary books, such as the *Chinese Proficiency Syllabus of Words and Characters* (National Office for Teaching Chinese as a Foreigner Language, Chinese Proficiency Test, 1997), we find that idioms are mostly concentrated in the intermediate and advanced stages, few in the elementary stage. But vocabulary selected in the syllabus needs to be revised constantly. Based on this point, whether teaching beginners idioms, what to teach, and how to teach are still worth discussing. Idioms are the crystallization of Chinese culture. Learning idioms can help Chinese learners understand Chinese culture, cultivate their Chinese thinking, enhance their language sense, and facilitate daily communication. Moreover, most idioms have allusions and interesting plots which increase students' interests in learning Chinese. Therefore, it is significant to examine how to teach narrative idioms to the elementary-level students. Based on previous studies, this paper discussed what a narrative idiom is and its pedagogical value, analyzed the difficulties of teaching

© Springer International Publishing Switzerland 2015
Q. Lu and H.H. Gao (Eds.): CLSW 2015, LNAI 9332, pp. 457–464, 2015.
DOI: 10.1007/978-3-319-27194-1_45

idioms in the elementary level, and suggested some effective teaching strategies, which are helpful to Chinese learners and teachers.

2   Literature Review

Previous studies are mainly concentrated on the study of idioms themselves, including their structure, pragmatics, origin, and categories, etc. Ma (1968) first established the original type system of idioms. He categorized the origin of idioms into newly-created, ones and inherited ones. The "inherited" ones are divided into "fables, mythologies and legends, historical stories, and logia." Chen (2012) mentioned that there are four types of origins: from fables such as 愚公移山 *yú gōng yí shān* "(lit. the foolish man who removes the mountains) the determination to win victory and the courage to surmount every difficulty"; from historic stories, such as 破釜沉舟 *pò fǔ chén zhōu* "(lit. break the caldrons and sink the boats) after crossing) cut off all means of retreat"; from poems, for example, 勾心斗角 *gōu xīn dòu jiǎo* "intrigue against each other"; and from slangs, like 众志成城 *zhòng zhì chéng chéng* "(lit. Our wills unite like a fortress) unity is strength". Liu and Xing (2000) held that symmetrical idioms with four characters account for a large proportion. These symmetrical idioms are easy to learn; therefore, teachers can utilize this feature to teach. However, the above research has not categorized narrative idioms into an independent category.

Tan (2010) pointed that the cultural function of idioms is mainly expressed through three aspects: the cognitive function, the educational function, and the creative function. Actually, idioms are the essence of Chinese. They contain plentiful historical and cultural information, and carry Chinese values, ways of thinking and attitude to life. At the same time, the idiom is an important media of Chinese teaching; the idiom itself contains certain travel application value in tourism. Therefore, idiom teaching should get the position it deserves in teaching Chinese as a second language (TCSL). Learning idioms can help students understand Chinese culture, cultivate Chinese thinking, and stimulate learners' interests.

With the development of Chinese teaching and learning, more and more scholars are concern about idiom teaching in TCSL. Zhang (1999) summarized 3 types of errors of international students in idiom learning: errors caused by the grammatical meanings of idioms; errors caused by not understanding the meanings of idioms; errors caused by disassembling idioms arbitrarily. She pointed out that learning idioms in isolation and statically is also one of the important reasons that cause errors. As long as teachers know those error types, they can adjust their old teaching strategies, and design some more targeted teaching strategies for those error-prone types.

From the perspective of teaching strategies, Zhang (2013), based on international students' common error types when they learn idioms, proposed "characters-based" theory to guide teaching, which is "taking the individual characters in an idiom as the starting point". The steps are: first introduce the form pronunciation and meaning of each character, its level in the *Chinese Proficiency Syllabus of Words and Characters* (National Office for Teaching Chinese as a Foreigner Language, Chinese Proficiency Test. 1997), and its relation with other characters; then introduce the cultural background of the idiom; finally use the idiom in sentences. However, character-based theory is not fully mature, which is still controversial.

Xie (2013) proposed to adopt the approach of new media style to teach idioms. Cheng (2012) suggested four teaching methods to conduct the teaching: student-level based teaching, theme-based teaching, character meaning based teaching, origin teaching, and deduction teaching and induction teaching. Xia (2010) suggested to combine many famous methods together "the direct method, the dictation method, the translation method, and the active comparative method" in the teaching of idiom. Through a questionnaire survey, Xu (2013) explored the problems in idiom teaching. He examined the potential disadvantages that international students may have in their Chinese learning process. Based on these findings, Xu suggested that teachers can actively include the cultural elements in their teaching and extensively exploit the potentials of using stories in teaching idioms.

The teaching methods that these researchers suggested are not specific to the new beginners who learn idioms, and thus there is still room to develop in this specific field.

Some of the researchers have also noticed that the current teaching of Chinese idiom lacks a basic direction. For example, Wan (2013) mentioned three problems: "(i) because of the absence of a syllabus, there is no focus on teaching; (ii) the content is dismissive because the teaching is not systematical but rather improvisational; (iii) students don't know how to conduct the proper use of idioms" Thus, Wan (2013) constructed a Chinese idiom syllabus for learners who study Chinese as a second language. However, there is still a need to improve Wan's work because this general syllabus has the following three drawbacks: (i) it fails to get enough scholarly attention; (ii) this syllabus is only a proposed one, lacking many important contents, such as the POS; (iii) this syllabus does not make clear the level each idiom belongs to. Thus to formulate a more practical teaching syllabus of idioms, especially what kind of idioms to teach for new beginners is of urgent need.

3   Introduction to Narrative Idioms

This section first discussed the definition and characteristics of idioms, then introduced narrative idioms.

3.1   The Definition and the Characteristics of Idioms

From the reference books to the research monographs and textbooks, there are dozens of definitions of what is an idiom. Just as Li (2001) says: "What is an idiom? This is a simple problem, but simultaneously it is also a problem that is not yet completely solved." It is generally agreed that idioms are fixed phrases with long-term use and many of them are made up of four characters. This paper summarizes the following several characteristics of idioms: (i) stable structure; (ii) historicity, the majority of idioms originated from historical events, fables and so on; (iii) short but with rich meanings; (iv) the quantity is huge; (v) the utilization scope is broad.

3.2   Narrative Idioms

There are many kinds of classifications of idioms. A narrative idiom, as the name suggests, is an idiom that has a story with far-reaching implications behind, which after the historical precipitation, has been passed down orally, spread until now, and is inseparable with the idiom. People may misunderstand the meaning of the idiom without the stories of those idioms. For example, 塞翁失马 *sài wēng shī mǎ* "(*lit.* the old man's loss of horse may be a fortune in disguise) a blessing in disguise". The historical story of the idiom is: in the Warring States time, an old person has lost a horse, but obtained two horses back. The idiom is used to mean that afflictions are sometimes blessings in disguise. If a people only know the idiom, but don't know the story, he/she may misunderstand the meaning that somebody lost a horse. That is not the implicated meaning of the idiom; in the meantime, if people only know the historical story, but don't know the idiom, he/she can also lose the essence of the Chinese culture, and the communications in daily life will be insufficiently simplified and unexpressive. A nonnarrative idiom is in contrast to the narrative one. The former kind of idioms either comes from people's oral language, such as 一干二净 *yī gān èr jìng* "(*lit.* one and all") completely", 三长两短 *sān cháng liǎng duǎn* "(*lit.* three longs and two shorts) unexpected misfortune *esp.* death" or from literary quotations, but without a story. For example, 五颜六色 *wǔ yán liù sè* "of various colors" comes from 镜花缘 Jìng huā yuán "Flowers in the Mirror", a novel written by Li Ruzhen in Qing dynasty: "惟各人所登之云，五颜六色，其形不一。" *Wéi gè rén suǒ dēng zhī yún, wǔyánliùsè, qí xíng bù yī.* "Every one boards a cloud with different colors and shapes."

Compared with the non-narrative idioms, this paper classifies narrative idioms into two groups:

(i) myths and legends, which come from Chinese ancient tales but are not recorded accurately in the history, they are not real stories, such as 愚公移山 *yú gōng yí shān* "(*lit.* the foolish man who removes the mountains) the determination to win victory and the courage to surmount every difficulty", 夸父逐日 *kuā fù zhú rì* "(*lit.* Kuafu runs after the sun)" means "doing something beyond one's ability", 女娲补天 *nǚ wā bǔ tiān* "Goddess Nǚwa patches up the sky", 画龙点睛 *huà lóng diǎn jīng* "(*lit.* bring the painted dragon to life by putting in the pupils of its eyes) add the finishing touch", etc.

(ii) historical allusions, which are from Chinese historical events. The characters and the events in them were accurately occurred in the past. These idioms were recorded in history books and spread until now. For example, 破釜沉舟 *pò fǔ chén zhōu* "[*lit.* break the caldrons and sink the boats (after crossing)] cut off all means of retreat", 一鼓作气 *yī gǔ zuò qì* "(*lit.* At the first drum courage is aroused) at one fling", 一言既出，驷马难追 *Yī yán jìchū sìmǎ nán zhuī* "(*lit.* a word once spoken cannot be overtaken even by a team of four horses) A real man never goes back on his words", etc.

4   Idiom Teaching for the Elementary-level Chinese Learners

This section investigated the present situation of the idiom teaching and the difficulties in idiom teaching, especially at the elementary level.

4.1   The Present Situation of the Idiom Teaching

As an important part of vocabulary teaching, the idiom teaching is different from common vocabulary teaching. Most of the idioms have rich meanings and contain stories, which become a burden in the teaching process.

For intermediate and advanced level students, if they want to break the bottleneck of Chinese study, the difficulty in learning idioms should be necessarily overcome. The overall situation of idiom learning and teaching shows that they are in a dilemma of "important +unimportant". For students, on the one hand, idioms are interesting because they are short, meaningful and concise; on the other hand, idioms are difficult to understand, have large quantities, and are prone to be wrongly used. At the same time, there are still rare authoritative idiom reference books for CSL learners, which raised the study difficulties. For teachers, idiom teaching is a challenging problem. On the one hand, teachers agree that the idiom occupies an important position in the vocabulary teaching; on the other hand, due to the characteristics of idioms, such as pragmatic complexity, it is hard for students to grasp them immediately after teachers teach them.

4.2   The Difficulties in the Idiom Teaching

There are 6 levels of *Chinese proficiency in International Curriculum for Chinese Language Education* (The Confucius institute headquarters / Hanban, 2014). The first and second levels belong to the elementary level. Learners at this level have two difficulties when learning idioms.

(i)   Students at the elementary level know very limited Chinese. *International Curriculum for Chinese Language Education* indicates that students at this level should learn 300 characters. Though they can distinguish simple characters, there are many characters beyond those required characters and some new characters could be very complicated. For example, in 画蛇添足 *huà shé tiān zú* "(*lit.* paint a snake with feet) ruin the effect by adding sth. superfluous", the four characters are not contained in the elementary-level glossary, which increases the difficulty.

(ii)   Narrative idioms contain Chinese culture and represent Chinese minds and values. Some students have difficulty in understanding them because of different growth, education and life background. For example, 愚公移山 *yú gōng yí shān* "(*lit.* the foolish man who removes the mountains) the determination to win victory and the courage to surmount every difficulty", from the Chinese respect, it is a commendatory term which praises the spirits of working with perseverance; while from the western respect, it is not a wise solution, because moving house can reach the goal much faster than "move the mountain". Meanwhile, descendants do not have to live for the desire of the older generation. Therefore there may be some problems in cross-cultural communication.

5   Pedagogical Strategies of Chinese Idioms Teaching at the Elementary Level

This section suggested the Pedagogical Arrangements for teaching narrative idioms at the elementary level in the respect of short and long term courses. Then it suggested some effective instructional strategies.

5.1   Pedagogical Arrangements

At the elementary level, the narrative idioms should be selected in accordance with the proficiency level as well as the arrangement of the lessons. It is important to realize that those idioms simply serve as assistive tools instead of the main teaching contents. For example, in the short-term Chinese classes of Jinan University in winter vacation for Chinese starters, there are 5 weeks' duration of study for the whole winter, totally 100 class hours. That is, 4 class hours for each day, five days for each week. The teaching contents include integrated Chinese, Chinese reading, Chinese listening and speaking, and Chinese cultural. Therefore, due to the time limitation, the teaching of narrative idioms could be arranged in the cultural class, or, in a more loose and relaxed way. Teachers can select one idiom for each week.

For the long-term course, most colleges who offer Chinese learning classes have their own designated course books. For example, *Boya Chinese* (Li, 2004-2008) was adapted as the books by School of Literature, Beijing Normal University, Zhuhai. At the elementary level, teachers could select some of the easy narrative idioms in their integrated Chinese class. For example, teach the idiom 一诺千金 *yī nuò qiān jīn* "A promise is weightier than one thousand bars of gold" A promise is a promise, which has a short and simple story and is relatively easy to understand. It can also forster students' interest in the integrated Chinese class. For the long-term Chinese course, it is suggested that the teaching of narrative idioms could be arranged only once in three to four weeks. Such a strategy has brought the benefits of narrative idioms teaching to its maximum, and also has guaranteed a proper pace of the course teaching. Generally, the number of selected idioms needs to be limited within a reasonable range, because the teaching of the narrative idioms is mainly aimed at fostering the students' interests and improving their Chinese thinking ability.

5.2   Teaching Strategies

By combining personal teaching experience and previous research results, this paper suggests three effective approaches which are considered as suitable for teaching narrative idioms.

(i) The Audio-visual approach: there is a variety of animated videos about idioms which can be used as course resources for realistic teaching practice. Though the targeted audience is mostly teenagers whose mother language is Chinese, the content is easy to understand. However, for the students of CSL at the elementary level, some explanations and translations from teachers would be helpful.

(ii) The Total Physical Response Approach: it encourages students to perform the stories contained by idioms they have learned in class, which can deepen their understandings to those idioms. The content of the performance should not be limited to the mimic of the original story. For instance, when students designing the performance of the idiom 拔苗助长 *bá miáo zhù zhǎng* "(*lit.* try to help the shoots grow by pulling them upward) spoil things by excessive enthusiasm", it does not necessarily need to be restricted to the short-tempered farmer, who was one of the characters in original story. Instead students are encouraged to interpret its meaning through a different story expressing the same connotation contained by this idiom. They can take another example, for instance, a teacher imposes the cramming method of teaching onto his students, which finally results in a declined performance instead of progress. Therefore, through the connection to students' own life experience in reality, this strategy guides them to draw inferences about other cases from one instance.

(iii) The Conscious-comparative Approach: it was proposed by Xia (2010). She argues that there are some sorts of analogous mentalities and similar fables existing in all nationalities in the world. For example, the story of Xiang Yu contained in the idiom 破釜沉舟 *pò fǔ chén zhōu* "(*lit.* break the caldrons and sink the boats) cut off all means of retreat" is similar to the story that Julius Caesar ordered his troops to burn ships when crossing a river. Other common idioms, such as 爱屋及乌 *ài wū jí wū* "*lit.* The love for the house extends even to the crows perching on its roof" love me love my dog, 一朝被蛇咬，十年怕井绳 *Yī zhāo bèi shé yǎo, shí nián pà jǐng shéng* "(*lit.* Once bitten by a snake, ten years in fear of a well rope.) once burnt, twice cautious", can also find their counterparts in English. Referring to those idioms that have similar foundations in other cultures can stimulate students' resonance and create a deeper impression of idioms in their minds. However, this method can be a challenge as well, because the cultural backgrounds of each student are various, which requires Chinese teachers to be knowledgeable enough to learn about students' cultures.

6   Conclusion

Research is rare on teaching idioms to the elementary-level CSL learners. Due to the lack of a Chinese proficiency level based idiom syllabus, teachers hardly know what to teach and how to teach. Targeting at these problems, this paper proposed teaching narrative idioms at the elementary level. The paper first discussed the definition of narrative idioms and their pedagogical values, then analyzed the difficulties of teaching narrative idioms at the elementary level, and finally suggested some effective teaching strategies. This study has demonstrated that it is necessary and possible to start idiom teaching for elementary-level CSL learners.

Acknowledgement. This research is supported by the start-up research grant of The Hong Kong Institute of Education. The reference number is RG 71/2014-2015R.

References

1. National Office for Teaching Chinese as a Foreign Language: The Outline of Chinese Vocabulary and Chinese Character Level, 1st edn. (汉语考试,.汉语水平词汇与汉字等级大纲). Beijing Language and Culture University Press, Beijing (1997)
2. Chen, H.: Analysis for Strategies of Teaching Idioms—Taking Idioms Course as the example (对外汉语成语教学策略浅探—以《成语教程》为例. Modern Chinese: Language Study (5) (2012)
3. Chen, X.: Summarize of the Source of Chinese Idioms Type (汉语成语来源类型问题综述). The Silk Road **231**(14) (2012)
4. College Chinese Study (大学语文研究) (2009). http://www.eyjx.com/eyjx/1/ReadNews.asp?NewsID=4574 (accessed September 30, 2009)

5. National Office for Teaching Chinese as a Foreign Language: The Outline of HSK Level Standards and Grammatical level (汉语水平等级标准与语法等级大纲). Higher Educational Press, Beijing, 180 (1996)

6. Huang, B., Liao, X.: Modern Chinese (现代汉语), p. 137. Higher Educational Press, Beijing (2002)

7. School of Literature, Jinan University (2014). http://hwy.jnu.edu.cn/zhaosheng/contents.aspx?id=5679 (accessed October 28, 2014)

8. The Confucius Institute Hdeadquarters/ Hanban: International Curriculum for Chinese Language Education (国际汉语教学通用课程大纲). Beijing Language and Culture University Press, Beijing (2014)

9. Liu, Y., Li, M.: The Compilation and Location of Grammar Level Outline (《语法等级大纲》的编制与定位). Language Teaching and Study **4**, 81–93 (1997)

10. Liu, Z., Xing, M.: Symmetry of Semantic Structure of Four-characters Idiom and Cognition of Global Chinese Language Teaching (四字格成语语义结构的对称性与认知). Chinese Teaching in the World (世界汉语教学) (1) (2000)

11. Li, X., et al.: Boya Chinese (博雅汉语). Peking University Press, Beijing (2004–2008)

12. Li, X.: The Problem of Idioms Specification (成语规范问题). Lexicographical Studies (2) (2001)

13. Ma, Q.: HSK Lexical Classification Book (汉语水平考试HSK词汇分类手册). The Commercial Press, Beijing (2010)

14. Ma, G.: A Brief Introduction to Idioms (成语简论). Liaoning People's Publishing House of Shenyang, Shenyang (1968)

15. Tan, K.: The Theory of the Culture Function of Idioms (论成语的文化功能). Journal of Changzhou Institute of Technology (3) (2010)

16. Wan, B.: Study on Syllabus of Chinese Idioms for Second Language Learners (面向二语学习者的汉语成语教学大纲研究). Shandong University (2013)

17. Wang, L., et al.: Modern Chinese Dictionary (现代汉语词典), p. 191. Zhonghua Book Company, Beijing (2009)

18. Xia, L.: Using Multiple Teaching Methods to Teach Chinese Idioms (运用多种教学法进行汉语成语教学). Shanxi Radio & TV University **76**(3) 2010

19. Xie, G.: Theory of Film and Television Teaching Application in Idioms Teaching Chinese as a Foreign Language (论影视教学法在对外汉语成语教学中的实际运用). Guangxi University (2013)

20. Yang, J.: The Teaching Program of Chinese as a Foreign Language at the Elementary Stage (对外汉语初级阶段教学大纲), p. 144. Beijing Language and Culture University Press, Beijing (1999)

21. Yang, Q.: Commentary of the Dictionary of the Idioms (成语词典述评). Lexicographical Studies (6) (1994)

22. Zhang, X.: A Corpus-based Study of Using Frequencies of Chinese and English Idioms (基于语料库的汉英成语使用频率研究). Ocean University of China (2009)

23. Zhang, Y.: Error Analysis About the Foreign Students Using Chinese (外国留学生使用汉语成语的偏误分析). Language Application **31**(3) (1999)

24. Zhang, C.: Review on the research of Chinese as a foreign language teaching and Acquisition (对外汉语成语教学与习得研究综述). Journal of Chongqing University of Education **26**(1) (2013)

25. Xu, Z.: A Study on the Culture Lead-in in TCFL Chinese Idiom Teaching (对外汉语成语教学的文化导入研究). Zhejiang University (2013)

Lexicalized Token Subcategory and Complex Context Based Shallow Parsing

Shui Liu[1(✉)], Zheng Zhang[1], and Pengyuan Liu[2]

[1] School of Foreign Languags and Literature, Beijing Normal University, Beijing, China
water1981@gmail.com
[2] Institute of Information Science and Technology, Beijing Language and Culture University,
Beijing, China

Abstract. Based on second order hidden markov model (HMM), this paper proposed a Viterbi-decoding chunking algorithm and a novel chunking post-processing algorithm. The method for estimating the parameter in HMM makes use of token subcategory and lexicalization information, which balances the disambiguation ability and data sparseness problem in maximum likelihood estimate (MLE) caused by the token subcategory and lexicalization. To compensate for the absence of complex context during HMM based chunking, this paper proposed a post-processing algorithm which makes a stable improvement to chunking algorithm and avolds the illegal token path in chunking. The experiment indicates that the performance of this chunking system achieves 93% f-measure on the CoNLL 2000 standard testing corpus.

Keywords: Shallow parsing · HMM · Post-processing algorithm

1   Introduction

Parsing is an important NLP technology.   However, parsing cannot perfectly meet the requirement of research and application because of its weak robustness and inefficiency. In order to overcome these problems, chunking is proposed by Abney [1]. Different from parsing, chunking merely analyses the boundary of non-overlapping phrases rather than the complete relationship among phrases [2,3]. Compared to parsing, chunking is a simple NLP technique, which is mature enough with the development of sequence labeling methods to be widely applied in the statistical machine translation (SMT) and Information Extraction (IE) fields.

According to the definition of chunking, the output of chunk is a sequence of non-overlapping phrases. Thus, each word in a chunk could be tagged with a unique label, which makes chunking as sequence labelling problem [4-6].

Applying discriminant machine learning methods are widely used in chunking, and achieve state-of-the-art experimental result [7]. Meanwhile, these approaches always cost very expensive effort in training, feature selection and on-line prediction, which limited the application of chunking in some way. On the other hand, the maximum likelihood will not afford the same burden, with simpler parameter estimation and

© Springer International Publishing Switzerland 2015
Q. Lu and H.H. Gao (Eds.): CLSW 2015, LNAI 9332, pp. 465–470, 2015.
DOI: 10.1007/978-3-319-27194-1_46

higher efficiency. However, the sparseness brought by lexicalization is the key challenge of this type of chunking methods. In this paper, we would like to find an approach which can solve chunking problem in efficiency and acceptable performance.

Ambiguity is the key problem in chunking. Lexicalization technology and phrase subcategory are the important approaches to solve this problem in chunking. In this paper, these two methods are comprehensively used in order to enhance the ability of disambiguation in chunking by employ smooth technology, which relieve the conflict between data sparseness and disambiguation.

The following sections are organized as: the second session will have a brief introduction of HMM using Viterbi decoding methods; the third session will propose the baseline method; the fourth session will propose a post-process method; the fifth session will give the experimental result and sixth session will have come to the conclusion of this paper.

2   HMM Based Chunking Algorithm

As previously discussion, sequence labeling method is employed in chunking. The sequence labeling problem is always considered as to maximized problem: give input sentence $I(n)=\{i_0,i_1,...,i_{n-1}: \forall j,i_j \in I\}$, the algorithm is to find a output sequence $O^{(n)}= \{o_0,o_1,...,o_{n-1}: \forall j,i_j \in I\}$, which has the highest probability:

$$O=argmax(P(O^{(n)})P(I^{(n)}|O^{(n)})P(I^{(n)})) \tag{1}$$

The observe sequence is fixed, thus above equation is equal to:

$$O=argmax\, P(O^{(n)})\, P(I^{(n)}|O^{(n)}) \tag{2}$$

HMM model is the most common algorithm to solve above problem, which further decompose above equation to below:

$$\hat{O} = argmax \prod P(o_j|o_{j-1},o_{j-2})P(I^{(n)}|O^{(n)})=argmax\ \pi_0 i_0 \prod a^2_{j-1} o_j b_{o_j i_j} \tag{3}$$

where $\pi_0 i_0$ is the initially parameter of sequence, $a^2_{j-1} o_j = P(o_j|o_{j-1},o_{j-2})$ is the transition probability and $b_{o_j i_j} = P(o_j|i_j)$ is emit probability.

Viterbi algorithm is further applied to efficiently find the best labelling sequence, which guarantee that the algorithm be finished in acceptable time.

3   The Parameter Estimation in HMM

Lexicalization and subcategory are 2 key approaches in enhancing the performance of chunking in many successful parsing models [8,9], thus these 2 approaches are further applied to enhance to disambiguation ability in chunking.

The most likelihood estimation is adopted in this paper. However the data sparse problem is the key problem, which cause 0 probability problem and enlarge statistical error.

In order to encounter data sparse problem, 2 smooth method are employed: additive and Interpolation smooth algorithm [10,11].

3.1   Lexicalization Free Parameter Estimation

In this chapter, only the original chunking tags are applied in parameter estimation, which is considered as baseline of this paper. As proposed below, the estimation of transition probability $a_{j-1}^2 o_j$ is related the original chunking tags only with simply smooth method to avoid 0 probability problem:

$$a_{j-1}^2 o_j = P(o_j|o_{j-1}, o_{j-2})$$
$$= \frac{count(o_j, o_{j-1}, o_{j-2}) + \alpha}{count(o_{j-1}, o_{j-2}) + |S| \times \alpha} \tag{4}$$

where a is a constant, |S| is the number of tags.

In lexical free emit probability estimation, only part-of-speech (POS) tags are employed:

$$b_{o_j l_j} = P(p_j|o_j) = \frac{count(o_j, p_j)}{count(o_j)} \tag{5}$$

Where p_j is the POS of j_{th} word in the sentence.

3.2   Lexicalized Emit Probability Estimation

The lexicalized parameter estimation is carried out in 2 ways: employ lexical information in tags and attach lexical information to POS.

Firstly, interpolation method is applied to simply combine the lexical free emit probability and lexical emit probability.

$$b_{o_j l_j} = P(p_j|o_j) = \lambda \times \frac{count(o_j, p_j)}{count(o_j)} + (1 - \lambda) \times \frac{count(w_j, o_j, p_j)}{count(w_j, o_j)} \tag{6}$$

Then lexicalized information is further employed to POS, that we attached considerable lexical information to POS.

$$b_{o_j l_j} = P(p_j|o_j) = \frac{count(o_j, \widetilde{p_j})}{count(o_j) + \alpha \times |\tilde{P}|} \tag{7}$$

where $\widetilde{p_j}$ is the lexicalized POS tags.

3.3   Subcategory Tags Based Transition Probability Estimation

Some researches [12,13] indicated that even simple subcategories can significantly improve the performance of language analysis. Thus, the POS is attached to chunking tags to improve the performance of chunking. The additive smooth is employed to solve the data sparse problem.

$$a_{j-1}^2 o_j = P(\tilde{o}_j|\tilde{o}_{j-1}, \tilde{o}_{j-2}) = \frac{count(\tilde{o}_j, \tilde{o}_{j-1}, \tilde{o}_{j-2}) + \alpha}{count(\tilde{o}_{j-1}, \tilde{o}_{j-2}) + |\tilde{S}| \times \alpha} \tag{8}$$

Where $\tilde{o}_j, \tilde{o}_{j-1}, \tilde{o}_{j-2} \in \tilde{S}, \in S \times P$, P is the POS (part of speech) tag set, $|\tilde{S}|$ is the number of subcategory tags.

Then interpolation is applied to make a tradeoff between specialized parameter estimation and data sparse problem:

$$a_{j-1}^2 o_j = P_\lambda(\tilde{o}_j|\tilde{o}_{j-1}, \tilde{o}_{j-2}) = \lambda \times P(\tilde{o}_j|\tilde{o}_{j-1}, \tilde{o}_{j-2}) + (1-\lambda) \times P(o_j|o_{j-1}, o_{j-2}) \quad (9)$$

To further enhance the performance of the system, lexical information is attached to chunking tags:

$$a_{j-1}^2 o_j = P_{\lambda-lex}(\tilde{o}_j|\tilde{o}_{j-1}, \tilde{o}_{j-2}) = \lambda \times \frac{count(\ddot{o}_j, \ddot{o}_{j-1}, \ddot{o}_{j-2})+\alpha}{count(\ddot{o}_{j-1}, \ddot{o}_{j-2})+|\tilde{S}|\times\alpha} + (1-\lambda) \times P_\lambda(\tilde{o}_j|\tilde{o}_{j-1}, \tilde{o}_{j-2})$$

$$(10)$$

Where $\ddot{o}_j, \ddot{o}_{j-1}, \ddot{o}_{j-2} \in \tilde{S}, \tilde{S} \subset \{W \times P \times T \cup P \times T\}$

4   Experimental Results

To study the detailed effect of lexicalized method, subcategory method and lexical free method in chunking, ten experimental settings are applied, which are:

- System1: lexical free transition probability estimation (equation 4) and lexical free emit probability estimation (equation 5).
- System2: interpolation based subcategory transition probability estimation (equation 9) and lexical free emit probability estimation (equation 5).
- System3: subcategory transition probability estimation (equation 8) and lexical free emit probability estimation (equation 5).
- System4: lexical free transition probability estimation (equation 4) and interpolation based lexical emit probability estimation (equation 6).
- System5: lexical free transition probability estimation (equation 4) and lexical emit probability estimation (equation 7).
- System6: interpolation based subcategory transition probability estimation (equation 9) and interpolation based lexical emit probability estimation (equation 6).
- System7: interpolation based subcategory transition probability estimation (equation 9) and lexical emit probability estimation (equation 7).
- System8: subcategory transition probability estimation (equation 8) and interpolation based lexical emit probability estimation (equation 6).
- System9: subcategory transition probability estimation (equation 8) and lexical emit probability estimation (equation 10).
- System10: interpolation based lexical subcategory transition probability estimation (equation 10) and lexical emit probability estimation (equation 7).

Table 1. Experimental Results

	P	R	F
System1	86▷44%	86▷74%	86▷59
System2	88▷91%	89▷76%	89▷33%
System3	88▷14%	90▷26%	89▷19%
System4	88▷83%	88▷80%	88▷81%
System5	88▷82%	89▷10%	88▷96%
System6	90▷99%	91▷49%	91▷24%
System7	91▷40%	91▷95%	91▷67%
System8	89▷93%	91▷65%	90▷78%
System9	90▷74%	92▷32%	91▷52%
System10	92▷38%	93▷20%	92▷79%

5 Conclusions and Future Work

From the table, we can conclude that the lexical information can benefit the performance of chunking. The subcategory can also significantly improve the performance of chunking as a compensation of lexical technology. Simple parameter estimation can achieve satisfactory performance level. In the future, we will explore clustering methods to further enrich the types of subcategory.

References

1. Abney, S.: Parsring by chunks. In: Principle-Based Parsing: Computation and Psycholinguistics, pp. 257–278. Kluwer Academic Publishers (1991)
2. Honglin, S., Shiwen, Y.: Survey of shallow paring. Contemporary Linguistics **2**, 74–83 (2000)
3. Qiang, G., Maosun, S., Changning, H.: Chunk system of Chines sentence. JOS **11**, 1158–1165 (1999)
4. Ramshaw, L.A., Marcus, M.P.: Text chunking using transformaiton-based learning. In: Proceedings of the Third ACL Workshop on Very Large Corpora, Cambridge, MA, USA, pp. 82–94 (1995)
5. Sang, E.F., Veenstra, J.: Representing text chunks. In: Proceedings of EACL 1999, Bergen, Norway, pp. 173–179 (1999)
6. Sujian, L., Qun, L., Zhifeng, Y.: Chunk system in Chinese sentence. JOS **26**, 1722–1727 (2003)
7. Kudoh, T., Matsumoto, Y.: Use of support vector learning for chunking identification. In: Proceedings of the 2nd Workshop on Learning Language in Logic and the 4th Conference on Computational Natural Language Learning, pp. 142–144 (2000)
8. Collins, M.: Head Driven Statistical Models for Natural Language Parsing. Ph.D. thesis. The University of Pennsylvania (1999)

9. Klein, D., Manning, C.D.: Accurate unlexicalized parsing. In: Proceedings of the 41st Annual Meeting on Association for Computational Linguistics, pp. 423–430 (2003)
10. Gale, W.A., Church, K.: What's wrong with adding one? In: Oostdijk, N., de Haan, P. (eds.) Corpus-Based Research into Language, Rodolpi, Amsterdam
11. Chen, S.F., Goodman, J.: An empirical study of smoothing techniques for language modeling. In: Proceedings of the 34th Annual Meeting on Association for Computational Linguistics, pp. 310–318 (1996)
12. Johnson, M.: PCFG models of linguistic tree representations. Computational Linguistics **24**, 613–632 (1998)
13. Molina, A., Pla, F.: Shallow Parsing using Specialized HMMs. Journal of Machine learning Research **2**, 595–613 (2002)

The Multi-language Knowledge Representation Based on Hierarchical Network of Concepts

Zhiying Liu[✉], Renfen Hu, Yaohong Jin, and Wei Li

Institute of Chinese Information Processing, Beijing Normal University, Beijing, China
{liuzhy,jinyaohong}@bnu.edu.cn, irishere@mail.bnu.edu.cn,
litsyj@163.com

Abstract. Ontology deals with knowledge sharing and reusing with standardized description of concepts, entities and their relations. This paper presents a multidimensional and unified semantic knowledge representation method covering words, sentences and discourses based on the Theory of Hierarchical Network of Concepts (HNC). With this method, we built a multi-language ontology based knowledge base (KB), which can provide theoretical reference for the semantic processing study of large-scale Chinese texts, and supports for the construction of knowledge resources in specific domains.

Keywords: Multi-language ontology · Knowledge representation · Knowledge base

1 Introduction

Ontology, a term which comes from philosophical study, has been widely used in artificial intelligence as the structural framework for organizing information and knowledge.[1,6] In general, ontology is considered an explicit formal specification of a shared conceptual model for capturing the knowledge of relevant domains, providing a common understanding of the domain knowledge, and giving an explicit definition of the relations between different entities.[3] Briefly, ontology deals with knowledge sharing and reusing with standardized description of concepts, entities and their relations.

The theory of Hierarchical Network of Concepts (HNC) presented a semantic network with comprehensive description of concepts in natural language. [4,5] According to HNC Theory, semantic network is the basis of the concept association network, which has salient characteristics of conceptuality, primitivity, hierarchy and networking. Each node in the semantic network is a concept rather than a word with specific meaning, and the concept primitives can be combined to generate numerous complex concepts. This semantic network also has hierarchical structures in which concept nodes locate in different levels. Besides, there are different relations between these concept nodes. Thus HNC semantic network is a type of language ontology.

This paper discusses how to build multi-language knowledge representation based on HNC Theory. Specifically, each concept node in HNC semantic network is explained and the corresponding multi-language words are given, currently in Chinese and English.

Q. Lu and H.H. Gao (Eds.): CLSW 2015, LNAI 9332, pp. 471–477, 2015.
DOI: 10.1007/978-3-319-27194-1_47

2   Related Work

Semantic ontology knowledge base plays an important role in lots of text processing tasks, e.g. cross-language information retrieval, information extraction and machine translation. [6, 7, 8] Previously, there are some works done on semantic ontology for natural language processing. WordNet and SUMO (The Suggested Upper Merged Ontology)   are prominent examples.

WordNet is a Semantic Knowledge base covering a wide range of words, which has a great influence in computer science field and has become one of the most important semantic resources for the research of natural language processing. [9] As an English lexical database, it groups English words into synonyms sets called synsets, and each synset has short definitions and usage examples. WordNet can be considered as a dictionary representing ontology. However, semantic relations are built for only a few notional words, and the relation types are also limited, which makes it difficult to meet the needs of users.

SUMO and its domain ontologies form the largest existing formal public ontology. [10] They have been used for research and applications in search, linguistics and reasoning. The developers designe SUMO as an upper ontology for the knowledge otology in specific domains, as well as various information processing systems. SUMO has been mapped to all of the lexicons in WorNet. However, description to the general ontology in SUMO is still not enough.

3   Multi-language Ontology

The paper introduces a multi-language ontology and a knowledge base based on the HNC semantic network. Specifically, for each concept, we will give a literal interpretation, the corresponding lexicons and semantic knowledge at sentence and discourse level. In the labeling process, the relevance between concepts is very important. HNC concept association network reveals a reasonable correlation between the concepts, and reflects the essential features of human cognition. [11] The relevance of the concept association network includes vertical and horizontal relevance. The vertical relevance is mainly shown by the top level concepts in the hierarchical concept tree, and the horizontal relevance is mainly shown by the middle level concepts, two types of extension of the bottom level concepts, cross-correlation, chain correlation, affiliated correlation and parallel correlation. Thus, when describing a concept, we must list all the concepts associated with it.

3.1   Concept Description of Multi-language Ontology

HNC theory divides concepts into abstract and concrete types. Only the concrete concepts have the physical attributes. This division is very important for the knowledge representation.

The abstract concepts are represented in the quintuple features in HNC theory. Each concept can be described in different aspects. The words with the same root and different parts of speech are derived from the same concept in English. While in Chinese an abstract word always has several parts of speech such as verb, noun or adjective. Both the parts of speech ambiguity in Chinese and the morphological change in English reflect the diversity of abstract concepts.

The diversity performance of the concrete concept is too complex to be expressed normatively since there is a lot of world knowledge in the concrete concepts. In HNC theory, the concrete concepts are represented as the affiliated concepts of the abstract concepts as a solution.

3.2   Concept Correlation of Multi-language Ontology

Compared with SUMO and WordNet, HNC performs better in the description of concept relations.

The concept description system in HNC theory is characterized by hierarchy and networking. The top level of the symbolic expression describes the hierarchy, the middle and bottom level of the concept extension structure describe the networking. The extension structures are divided into two categories: First Extension Structure includes the dual extension structure, contrastive extension structure and the inclusive extension structure; Second Extension Structure includes the interweaving extension structure (t extension), the parallel extension structure (k extension) and the directional extension structure (i extension).

Among these extension categories, the interleaving extension structure is the most important extension structure in which there are cross-correlations between the extensive items. The parallel extension structure is simpler than the others since the extensive items are the same type. The directional extension structure is tied to one side, with a particular character. The specific categories and examples are as follows in Table 1:

Table 1. Concept Extension Structure Categories and Examples

Categories		Symbols	Examples
1	dual	cnk/dnk	j02c22(far) ; j02c21(near)
	contrastive	ekm//ekn	j11e51(past); j11e52(future); j11e53(present)
	inclusive	-,-0,-00,…	pj2(country); pj2-0(province); pj2-00(city); pj2-000(village)
2	interleaving	t	24at=b (substitute) 24a9 (thing substitute) 24aa (information substitute) 24ab (human substitute)
	parallel	\k	24bb\k (energy conversion) 24bb\1 (mechanical energy conversion) 24bb\2 (thermal energy conversion) 24bb\3 (electromagnetic energy conversion)
	directional	i	a21i (agriculture) a21ii (processing of agricultural products)

The correlations above are mainly disclosed by the hierarchical symbols. In addition, several special symbols are also designed to correlate the concepts in HNC theory which are called the concept correlation expressions shown as table 2.

Table 2. Concept Correlation Expressions

Correlation Types	Correlation Symbols	Examples
definition	::=	351a::=209bu20be90("Recovery 351a " is defined as "Back to the original state 209bu20be90".)
equation	=:	710=:6502("Mood 710" is equivalent to "human perceptual response 6502".)
correspondence	:=	a629c35:=53a20\1 ("Technological invention a629c35" corresponds to the "trend commodity53a20\1".)
cross	=	a02eb37e15=a02eb1e21=a02eb2^e21 (The three parts correlated crossly.)
strong	≡	a25a≡a10t ("Social security system a25a" is correlated strongly with "Times a10t".)
flow	=>	a01be2m =>a01b3e5n ("Profit, Deficit, Balance a01b3e5n" is the effect of "Financial revenue a01be2m".)
source	<=	a5<=d ("Legal activities a5" is from "Idea activities d".)
reciprocal causation	<=>	
possessive	=%	a01b7t=%a01be22("Pay and wages a01b7t" are the daily basic expenses of any institution)
inclusive	%=	a103%=a143("Policy a103" includes "foreign policy a143")
virtual or real	==	

3.3   Multi-language Ontology Representation

The HNC symbol system is used to represent multilingual ontology which can be used to build a semantic mapping to any words in natural languages for its comprehensive semantic description. In HNC symbol system, each symbol with digital form has its special meaning and can serve as the correlative activators. The relationship between the word meanings can be expressed formally by this system. For example,

u1009c22 (Rapid)	v10a8 (Develop)
va34; pa34 (Edit; Editor)	pea34 (Newspaper office)
v901 (Assum)	rc010 (Responsibility)

Fig. 1. The Expression of Word Meaning

The strong correlations between the word "Rapid" and "Develop" are reflected in the near node distance of "u1009c22" and "v10a8" since both the nodes start with the number "10".

There is concise and rich knowledge for the concept correlation in the HNC symbol system, which can be used by the computer for digging the correlation between concepts.

4   Ontology Knowledge Representation

As a prerequisite and basis for knowledge organization, knowledge representation associates knowledge units and knowledge to facilitate the identification and understanding of knowledge.

HNC multi-language ontology base describes the following four features in XML forms [12].

4.1   HNC Concept Nodes

HNC concept nodes are built based on HNC concept primitive system. Currently, the knowledge base contains 5000 nodes, including the entire top-level nodes and some bottom-level nodes. Fig. 2 shows an example describing the concept node "01" (bearing of action) with Chinese and English definitions.

```
<hncnode>01</hncnode>
<definition>
      <chinesename>作用的承受( ZuoYong De ChengShou)</chinesename>
      <englishname>bearing of action</englishname>
      <explain/>
</definition>
```

Fig. 2. Concept Node Definition

4.2   Correlations Between Concept Nodes

The hierarchy of the concept nodes is the most important feature among concept relations, indicating the hyponymy of the concept nodes.

```
<upper>
      <hncnode>01</hncnode>
</upper>
<lower>
     <hncnode estype="m">01m</hncnode>
     <hncnode estype="t">01t</hncnode>
     <hncnode estype="\k">01\k</hncnode>
</lower>
```

Fig. 3. Correlations between Concept Nodes

Fig 3 shows an example which uses the elements "upper" and "lower" to describe the hypernym and the hyponym of a concept node to reveal the hierarchical relationship between two concept nodes. The hypemym "01" indicates the role of the bearing of action, and the hyponym indicates the basic characteristics of bearing. "01t" indicates the interleaving performance of bearing and reaction. "01\k" indicates the basic form of bearing (material and spiritual). Three hyponyms correspond to different types of extension.

Other important relations such as dual, contrastive and inclusive are also used in ontology knowledge representation. For example, "strong" and "weak" form a contrastive relation, "positive" and "negative" form a dual relation, and "year", "month" and "day" form an inclusive relation.

4.3   Words Mapping for Concept Nodes

There are two types of concepts: concrete concept and abstract concept. For the concrete concept, only one semantic type corresponds to it, while abstract concept has several corresponding in different semantic types, such as verb, static, attribute, value and effect. That is to say, a concept in HNC ontology knowledge base can be mapped to words in different parts of speech.

```
<category>
    <v>         <chineseword>承担(ChengDan);承受(ChengShou) </chineseword>
                <englishword>bear;handle;tolerate</englishword>
    </v>
    <u>
                <chineseword>重大(ZhongDa);繁重(FanZhong)</chineseword>
                <englishword>bearable;tolerable </englishword>
    </u>
    <r>
                <chineseword>责任(ZeRen);重担(ZhongDan)</chineseword>
                <englishword>responsibility</englishword>
    </r>
</category>
```

Fig. 4. Words Mapping for Concept Nodes

In Fig. 4, the concept node "01" can be represented with dynamic concept "bear", attributive concept "bearable" and effect concept "responsibility".

5   Conclusion

To deal with the language understanding issue, this paper presents a multidimensional and unified semantic knowledge representation method covering words, sentences and discourses based on the Theory of Hierarchical Network of Concepts (HNC).

With this method, we built a multi-language ontology based knowledge base (KB), with 5,000 concept nodes described based on HNC concept primitive system. In the future, we will improve the otology knowledge base and explore its application in practical fields.

Acknowledgments. This work is supported by the Hi-Tech Research and Development Program of China(2012AA011104), and China State Language Affairs Commission "Twelfth Five" Scientific Research Project(YB125-124).

References

1. William, S., Austin, T.: Ontologies. IEEE Intelligent Systems, 18–19 (1999)
2. Li, S., Yin, Q., Hu, Y.: Overview of Researches on Ontology. Journal of Computer Research and Development (7), 1041–1052 (2004). (in Chinese)
3. Gruber, T.: Towards Principles for the Design of Ontologies Used for Knowledge Sharing. International Journal of Human-Computer Studies **43**(5/6), 907–928 (1995)
4. Huang, Z.: HNC (Hierarchical Network of Concepts) Theory. Tsinghua University Press (1998). (in Chinese)
5. Miao, C.: HNC (Hierarchical Network of Concepts) Theory Introduction. Tsinghua University Press (2005). (in Chinese)
6. Hu, T.: Ontology-based semantic study. Journal of Modern Information **2**, 153–156 (2006). (in Chinese)
7. Liu, W.: Multilingual Ontology Building and Application in Cross Language Information Retrieval. Journal of Wuhan University of Science and Technology(Social Science Edition) (1), 73–76 (2008). (in Chinese)
8. Yao, W., Wang, L., Wang, C.: Design and Implementation of knowledge Retrieval System Based on Ontology. China Information Technology and Applications Academic Forum Proceedings, 40–42 (2008). (in Chinese)
9. Li, X.: Mapping of Ontology Based on WordNet. Central South University (2008). (in Chinese)
10. Wang, H., Ding, Y., Zhang J.: SUMO- Introduction and Enlightenment of Upper Ontology. Library Theory and Practice (3), 96–98 (2007). (in Chinese)
11. Chen, X.: Study on the Ontology Knowledge Base based on HNC Theory. Public Communication of Science & Technology 7, 217–218 (2011). (in Chinese)
12. Wang, J.: Web Information Resources Integration of Digital Library Based on the XML Ontology Description Language. Modern Information (11), 84–86 (2007). (in Chinese)

Using Keyword Features to Automatically Classify Genre of Song Ci Poem

Yong Mu[✉]

Department of Chinese Language and Literature, School of Humanities,
Tsinghua University, Beijing 100084, China
muyong2004@126.com

Abstract. The category of subjective aesthetic was distinguished into automatic text categorization of natural language processing problem. The Song dynasty poems were collected and randomly divided into training set and testing set based on keyword features. Three classification methods, which are K-nearest neighbor, naive Bayes classifier and support vector machine, were used to classify the poems' genres. Results showed that support vector machine can classify best and achieved above 95% accuracy.

Keywords: Text classification · Keyness · Genre of song-Ci poem · Natural language processing

1 Introduction

The Song-Ci (宋词) poem classification was first introduced by Zhang Yan (张綖) in the Ming Dynasty. He classified Song-Ci poems in one of his writings named "Shiyu Tupu • Fanli (诗余图谱·凡例). " There are two different styles of Song-Ci poetry: the Wan-Yue (婉约, delicate restraint), and the Hao-Fang (豪放, heroic abandon). Wan-Yue has a graceful and restrained characteristic, similar to Qin Shao-you (秦少游) 's works, whereas Hao-Fang is more like the works of Su Zi-zhan (苏子瞻) that makes readers feel bold and unconstrained. This classification was made based on personal knowledge, experience and perception, which effectively grasped the connotation and artistic conception. However, the process of classification necessitates a lot of time and energy, and the result could be biased by subjective judgment of personal preference.

Since the 1980's, Chinese scholars began to combine features of ancient poetry and natural language processing (NLP) technology to conduct computer-aided research on poetry understanding, such as "Computer supportive in Ancient poems research" laboratory, which was a cooperation between the Institute of Computational Linguistics of Peking University and Institute of Ancient Literature in Yuanze University. However, there is still not much research in this field. Zhou [10][6] introduced the concept of "Computational Poetics" and carried out a series of related research work. Li [2] proposed natural language processing technology based on word connection and applied it to understand the meaning of poetry.

© Springer International Publishing Switzerland 2015
Q. Lu and H.H. Gao (Eds.): CLSW 2015, LNAI 9332, pp. 478–485, 2015.
DOI: 10.1007/978-3-319-27194-1_48

Training computers to learn to "understand" and "categorize" the human language is still a challenge. Word, phrase and grammatical level have already been widely studied in NLP, but the semantic and emotional aspects are still narrow, particularly in style and genre, which is classified as the embodiment of personality in literary language.

Generally, the original document must be converted into a data structure that a computer can understand through the process called "pretreatment" before the computer is trained. This pretreatment process consists of many steps, such as word segmentation, tagging, stop word filtering, and so on. Because there is no space as the boundary between one word to another in Chinese language, one of the most important steps in the pretreatment process of Chinese language is text representation.

At present, there are two studies that researched how to classify the Song Ci genre in different text representation policies. The first was done by Yi in 2005 [8]. The researcher used the word segmentation policy in the text representation step, and applied a genetic algorithm with the three classification methods, which are Naïve Bayes, decision tree, and support vector machine, to categorize Song-Ci genre. The result found that the support vector machine gave the best solution set with 85% of average accuracy. In 2008, Wu introduced the frequent words co-occurrence policy to improve the result [9]. In the experiment, a vector space model with three classification methods, which are K-nearest neighbor, naive Bayes classifier, and support vector machine, was applied. The best result achieved 91.45% of average accuracy. Recently, Li [1] published an interesting piece that compared the effect of classifying the artistic conception of Tang Poetry based on single-word segmentation policy and word segmentation policy. The result found that the solution of word segmentation policy is slightly lower in accuracy.

Based on the characteristics of the language used in Chinese classical poems, Song-Ci is very concise and exquisite, normally using single characters to express complicated mood and emotion. Therefore, using the word segmentation system of modern Chinese to classify Song-Ci, as done in Yi [8] and Wu [9], proved to be a less efficient system. The significance of this research shows that text representation based on single-word segmentation policy and building keyness based on big data of Song-Ci [7] is more effective. Three classification methods, which are K-nearest neighbor, naive Bayes classifier and support vector machine, were trained to classify the poems' genre of 151 poems in Song Dynasty, in order to building the Song-Ci classification machine and classifying the big data of Song-Ci. The results were compared with the works of Yi and Wu [8][9].

2   Methodology

2.1   Experimental Design

The two categories of Wan-Yue and Hao-Fang from the Song-Ci genres were translated as text representation in this research. Evaluating which poem belonged to which genre can be classified as a text categorization problem. In the study, the preprocessed corpus was divided into two categories: Wan-Yue and Hao-Fang. Automatic text classifying was composed of three steps, which are the representation step, algorithm classifying step and result evaluation step.

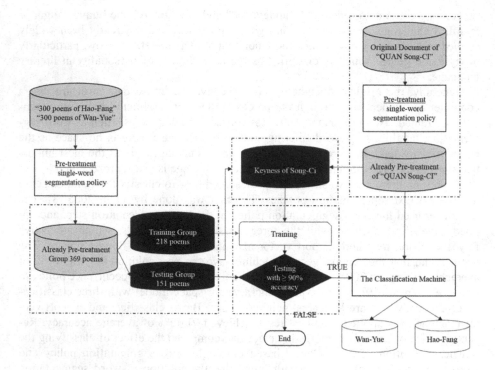

Fig. 1. Experimental flow chart

The representation step extracts features from documents by feature-selection strategy, and then transforms the document into a vector-space model for features. The algorithm classifying step chooses the most suitable algorithm for this type of document. Lastly, the result evaluation step chooses some classic evaluation indexes in the field of information retrieval, such as accuracy, recall rate, equilibrium value. The experiment procedure can be described as shown in figure 1 and figure 2.

Step 1.	Selecting artificial classified works from Quan Song Ci (全宋词, The Whole Collection of Song Poetry) as the training set and testing set.
Step 2.	Feature extraction from the training set and test set.
Step 3.	Numeralization of the training set and test set by the features; each work is transformed into a vector.
Step 4.	Modeling by using classification algorithm to train the data of training set, creating a classifier.
Step 5.	Classifying the test set using the trained classifier and evaluating the results, selecting the highest score of the test model as the Song Ci genre classifier.
Step 6.	Distinguishing the genre of Song Ci automatically by this classifier

Fig. 2. Experimental Step

2.2   Data Generating

The details of experimental data were shown in table 1 and table 2. Table 1 shows the number of samples in the training group and testing group. Testing groups are divided according to author's names and shown in table 2. This found that there is an author named Lu You who wrote both types of Song-Ci genre poetry.

Table 1. The number of sample in training group and testing group

Group	Song-Ci genre		Total
	Hao-Fang	Wan-Yue	
Training group	110	108	218
Testing group	66	85	151
Total	176	193	369

Table 2. Testing group divided by authors

Song-Ci genre			
Hao-Fang		Wan-Yue	
Author	Quantity	Author	Quantity
Ouyang Xiu	4	Zhang Xian	5
Huang Tingjian	4	Yan Shu	5
He Zhu	5	Liu Yong	13
Shu Shi	14	Yan Jidao	5
Ye Mengde	4	Zhou Bangyan	8
Zhang Yuangan	4	Qin Guan	6
Lu You	9	Fan Chengda	4
Zhang Xiaoxiang	6	**Lu You**	8
Liu Guo	4	Jiang Kui	10
Liu Kezhuang	8	Shi Dazhu	7
Wen Tianxiang	4	Wu Wenying	14

To generate the experimental data, two books of "Three Hundred poems of Hao-Fang" [4] and "Three Hundred poems of Wan-Yue" [5] were used as the reference for experimental data. According to these books that consist of poems from the Tang, Song, Ming and Qing Dynasty, it is necessary to classify poetry according to the time period before starting the experiment. After the classifying, 231 poems in Tang, Ming and Qing Dynasty were filtered out. The example group had 369 poetry from the Song dynasty, which can be divided into 176 poems of Hao-Fang and 193 poems of Wan-Yue. After that 369 poetry in example group were randomly divided into two groups, which were the training group and testing group by 3:2 ratio. The details are shown in table 1.

2.3   Solution Procedures

2.3.1   K-Nearest Neighbor

K-Nearest Neighbor (KNN) is a widely used method of classification that is based on learning the training data examples to classify new data and make predictions. Given a test document, the system finds the nearest K "neighbors" in it, and gives grades to the candidates according to the classification of these neighbors. Taking the similarity of neighbor texts and test texts as the weight of neighbor classification, if part of the texts of the K "neighbors" belong to the same category, sum the weight of each neighbors in this category for the similarity of the document which will be classified and test. By sorting the scores of the candidate classification then giving a threshold, we can determine the classification of test documents. The decision rules can written as follows:

$$y(x, c_i) = \sum_{d_i \epsilon kNN} sim(x, d_i) y(d_i, c_j) - b_j$$

The value of $y(d_i, c_j)$ is 0 or 1, 1 said that the document d_i belongs to the classification C_j, 0 said that the document d_i does not belong to the classification C_j; $sim(x, d_i)$ is the similarity of test text x and training text d_i; b_j is the binary decision threshold , which is generally taken by including the angle cosine of two vectors.

2.3.2   Naive Bayes Classifier

Naive Bayes Classifier (NBC) is a method of classification that analyzes the probability of class variables and data features set. The hypothesis of Naive Bayes is that the data features and specific categories are independent of each other. When the text vector component is a Boolean value, 0 indicates that the corresponding keyword does not appear in the document while 1 indicates it appears. The probability of the document Doc belongs to the class C is:

$$P(Doc(F_j)|C) = \frac{1 + N(Doc(F_j)|C)}{2 + |D_c|}$$

$P(Doc(F_j)|C)$ is the Plath estimate of the conditional probability of feature F_j which appears in the class C, $N(Doc(F_j)|C)$ is the number of documents that features F_j which appears in the class C, $|D_c|$ is the number of documents in class C.

2.3.3   Support Vector Machine

The original Support Vector Machine (SVM) algorithm was invented by Vladimir N. Vapnik and Alexey Ya. Chervonenkis in 1963, but the current standard incarnation was proposed by Corinna Cortes and Vapnik in 1993 and published in 1995 [1]. The SVM showed good effect to solve nonlinear, small sample problems. The idea of SVM, in simple terms, is to find a decision surface in an vector space, and the plane can segment two class data points best [11].

2.4   Keyness

Keyness is a term used in linguistics to describe the likelihood a word or phrase has of being "key" in its context. Compare this with collocation, the quality linking two words or phrases usually assumed to be within a given span of each other. Keyness is a textual feature, not a language feature (a word has keyness in a certain textual context but may well not have keyness in other contexts), so it is very suitable for feature genre classification.

Table 3. The 45 keywords of Hao-Fang

Keyword	江	山	百	万	兴	雄	旗	北
Pinyin	jiang1	shan1	bai3	wan4	xing1	xiong2	qi2	bei3
Meaning	river	mountain	hundred	ten hundred	prosper	hero	flag	north
Keyword	经	事	关	战	剑	朝	英	军
Pinyin	jing1	shi4	guan1	zhan4	jian4	chao2	ying1	jun1
Meaning	pass through	affair	barrier	war	sword	court	hero	army
Keyword	吾	涛	可	问	胡	冲	帆	南
Pinyin	wu1	tao1	ke3	wen4	hu2	chong1	fan1	nan2
Meaning	I	billow	can	ask	barbarian	rush	sail	south
Keyword	壮	血	投	矣	要	之	白	神
Pinyin	zhuang4	xue3	tou2	yi1	yao4	zhi1	bai2	shen2
Meaning	strong	blood	cast	interjection	need	this	white	deity
Keyword	物	古	封	汉	潇	安	虎	诸
Pinyin	wu4	gu3	feng1	han4	xiao1	an1	hu3	zhu1
Meaning	thing	ancient	envelop	Chinese	sound	safe	tiger	Every
Keyword	磨	铁	发	名	闻			
Pinyin	mo2	tie3	fa1	ming2	wen2			
Meaning	grind	iron	send out	name	hear			

Table 4. The 49 keywords of Wan-Yue

Keyword	华	春	情	帘	莺	愁	娇	暖
Pinyin	hua2	chun1	qing2	lian2	ying1	chou2	jiao1	nuan3
Meaning	flower	spring	feeling	curtain	warbler	anxious	tender	warm
Keyword	转	香	怕	寄	宝	阑	小	薄
Pinyin	zhuan3	xiang1	pa4	ji4	bao3	lan2	xiao2	bo2
Meaning	turn	fragrant	fear	send	treasure	separate	small	thin
Keyword	思	甚	院	琴	禁	留	水	肠
Pinyin	si1	shen4	yuan4	qin2	jin1	liu2	shui3	chang2
Meaning	miss	very	yard	lyre	bear	stay	water	bowel
Keyword	芳	窗	梅	寒	碎	棠	团	拈
Pinyin	fang4	chuang1	mei2	han2	sui4	tang2	tuan2	nian1
Meaning	fragrant	window	winter sweet	cold	fragmentary	begonia	group	pick up
Keyword	红	半	又	燕	新	悄	眉	绿
Pinyin	hong2	ban4	you4	yan4	xin1	qiao1	mei2	lv4
Meaning	red	half	again	swallow	new	quiet	eyebrow	green
Keyword	魂	涯	晴	雁	还	夜	梳	腮
Pinyin	hun2	ya2	qing2	yan4	huan2	ye4	shu1	sai1
Meaning	spirit	margin	fine	wild goose	back	night	comb	cheek
Keyword	玉							
Pinyin	yu4							
Meaning	jade							

In this research, the concept of "keyness" was used to extract keywords from the training sets of Wan-Yue and Hao-Fang. The feature sets according to a certain threshold number were established. This study used Antconc to extract keywords from sample groups of Wan-Yue and Hao-Fang with the keyness ≥ 3. The results after extracting found that there were 49 and 45 keywords in Wan-Yue and Hao-fang, as shown in table 3 and table 4 respectively. These 94 keywords were used as the feature items (each keyword is a feature) to calculate the frequency of each feature in different texts in both the training set and testing set.

3   Results

To compare the performance of the classification methods, Precision (P) and Recall (R) were used——the most common evaluation standard index in the field of information retrieval. The precision indicates what proportion is correct among the selected document; the recall rate indicates how much was selected by the classifier in all the correct results. Table 4 shows the experimental results of the three classification methods compared with the work of Wu in 2008.

Table 5. The Comparison Performance of classification method (Unit :%)

	P%		R%	
	Hao-Fang	Wan-Yue	Hao-Fang	Wan-Yue
KNN w-fwc (Wu, 2008)	83.3	77.3	75.0	85.0
KKK w/o-fwc (Wu, 2008)	84.6	98.3	93.1	88.5
KNN	**90.9**	72.7	76.9	88.9
NBC	63.6	**100.0**	**100.0**	73.3
SVM	**90.9**	**100.0**	**100.0**	**91.7**

From table 5 we can see, KNN classification algorithm is more accurate on the Hao-Fang set than on the Wan-Yue set. NBC algorithm is very accurate on the Wan-Yue set, but undesirable on Wan-Yue set. For SVM algorithm, it shows 100% precision and a high recall rate on Wan-Yue set, 90.9% precision and perfect recall rate on Hao-Fang set. SVM with single-word segmentation had the best performance out of the three classification methods. When comparing with previous research, the performance of SVM with single-word segmentation is better than Wu 2008 [9].

4   Conclusion

In view of the human errors and limitations, this research considers using modern computer technology to support the classification of the large number of Ci poems. This does not only significantly reduce manpower and time, but also improve the efficiency. Moreover, by the quantitative method, the machine learning can deal with poems that are considered as "only to be sensed, not explained," and also provide some new information and reference, which the traditional research method in the literature cannot easily find. In this paper, we extract keywords where the keyness is more than 3. If the threshold is relaxed, with Keyness$\geq$2 as selection criteria, the feature vector space will be constructed by more dimensions. This may further improve the classification accuracy, but of course this remains to be tested.

References

1. Qi, L.: Research and Implement of Classical Poetry Artistic Conception Classification. The master degree thesis of Donghua University (2014). (in Chinese)
2. Ly, L.: A study on term connection oriented NLP technique and its applications [Ph.D. Thesis]. Chongqing: Chongqing University (2004). (in Chinese)
3. Ying, L.: Statistical Linguistics. Tsinghua University Press, Beijing (2014)
4. Zhuqin, L.: 300 Hao Fang Ci. San Qin Press, Xi'an (2003). (in Chinese)
5. Yin, L.: 300 Wan Yue Ci. San Qin Press, Xi'an (2003). (in Chinese)
6. Jingsong, S., Changle, Z., Yihong, L.: The Establishment of the Annotated Corpus of Song Dynasty PoetryBased on the Statistical Word Extraction and Rules and Forms. Journal of Chinese Information Processing 3 (2007). (in Chinese)
7. Guizhang, T.: Quan Song Ci. Zhonghua Book Company, Beijing (1965). (in Chinese)
8. Yong, Y.: A Study on Style Identification and Chinese Couplet Responses Oriented Computer Aided Poetry Composing. Ph.D. Dissertation of Chongqing University (2005). (in Chinese)
9. Chunlong, W.: The Research of Computer Assistant Analysis on Chinese Song Poems' Style. The master degree thesis of Xiamen University (2008). (in Chinese)
10. Zhou, C.L.: An Introduction to Computation of Mind and Brain. Tsinghua University Press, Beijing (2003). (in Chinese)
11. Cortes, C., Vapnik, V.: Support-vector networks. Machine Learning 20(3), 273 (1995)

A Corpus-Based Analysis of Lexical Bundles in English Introductions of Chinese and International Students' Theses

Guiling Niu[✉]

Zhengzhou University, Zhengzhou, Henan, China
mayerniu@163.com

Abstract. Phraseology is attracting an increasing number of linguistics researchers' attention. Based on the data from our self-made corpus, this paper aimed to make a comparative analysis of the lexical bundles in the English introductions of Chinese graduate students' theses and those written by the graduate students in the international prestigious universities. The most frequently used four-word lexical bundles in the corpus were identified and classified structurally and functionally and corresponding analysis was made. Results indicated that lexical bundles in the English introductions of Chinese students' theses were structurally incomplete in comparison with those in the international students' papers, and that lexical bundles were less varied in form, meaning and function in Chinese students' English thesis introductions despite the larger number both in type and token. It is necessary to strengthen the richness, diversity and fluency of lexical bundles in them.

Keywords: Thesis · Introduction · Lexical bundle

1   Introduction

Lexical bundle is defined as "sequences of word forms that commonly go together in natural discourse" [2].

'Lexical bundle' is also identified as cluster [18], phraseology [20], lexical chunk [19], formulaic sequence [7], lexical phrase [13], prefab or prefabricated patterns [1], multi-word expressions/unit (MWE) [16], recurrent word combination [1], etc. In computational linguistics, it is termed as 'N-gram', in which N stands for the number of words in a lexical bundle.

Recent research in computer-based analysis of language has revealed a widespread occurrence of lexical patterns in discourse. Pawley and Syder [15] asserted, "lexicalized sentence stems and other memorized strings form the main building blocks of fluent connected speech." Nattinger and DeCarrico [13] concluded, "Formulaic sequences, as called the recurrent sequence of words, are ubiquitous in language use and they make up a large proportion of any discourse." Erman and Warren (2000) affirmed that formulaic sequences of various types constituted 58.6% of the spoken English discourse and 52.3% of the written discourse. Using different criteria and procedures, Foster's raters judged that 32.3% of the unplanned native speech they analyzed was made up of formulaic language. Alternberg [1] found that 96% of native language discourses conformed

© Springer International Publishing Switzerland 2015
Q. Lu and H.H. Gao (Eds.): CLSW 2015, LNAI 9332, pp. 486–493, 2015.
DOI: 10.1007/978-3-319-27194-1_49

to certain prefabricated patterns. All these prior studies suggest that lexical bundles are ubiquitous in discourse, and the co-occurrence of one word with another or others is not by accident. Lexical bundles deserve researchers' attention.

2   Literature Review

Research indicates that the generic difference of texts is not only revealed in the use of words, including word frequency, semantic prosody, semantic preference and word functions, but also in the use of lexical bundles.

Numerous linguists have explored either the structural or functional features of lexical bundles. Biber and other researchers [3, 4, 5, 6, 7] have conducted successive studies on lexical bundles for years and contributed much to the research of this field, including the taxonomy of lexical bundles and some other related studies in both spoken and written registers [4, 5].

Wray [23] pointed out that lexical bundles serve two main functions: 1) the reduction of processing effort; 2) achievement of socio-interactional functions.

Biber et. al.'s [5] empirical research findings indicate that lexical bundles are more frequently used in academic oral register than in academic written register; In general, referential functions are the dominant use of lexical bundles in the written university registers.

In China, Pu [17] first explored the patterns of lexical bundles in students' written English based on corpus CLEC; Wei [21] analyzed the use of lexical bundles systematically and suggested a taxonomy of lexical bundles applicable to Chinese English learners by using the data in corpus COLSEC; Wang & Qian (2009) investigated the lexical bundle features of Chinese students' English contest language; Besides, Wei [21] found that a sentence or discourse always begins with lexical bundles with certain functions. Niu [14] made a detailed comparative analysis on the features of Lexical Bundles in the English abstracts of Chinese and international journal papers. Cortes [8] investigated the lexical bundle features in the part of Introduction of English research articles.

Despite the many studies abroad and at home on lexical bundles from varied perspectives, there is much less systematic research regarding the structural and functional difference of lexical bundles between second language research article introductions and native language research article introductions based on a large-scale corpus so far.

This study aims to make a comprehensive comparison between the English lexical bundles in the introductions of Chinese students' theses and those in international students' theses by using our self-made corpus - Chinese-English Comparable Introduction Corpus (CECIC), and the number of Introduction files we chose were both 30. We intended to make a comparative analysis between the lexical bundles in the introductions of Chinese graduate students' English theses and those written by the graduate students in the international prestigious universities. We also categorized and summarized the shortcomings of these introductions, with the purpose to improve Chinese students' English thesis writing, which might be pedagogically meaningful.

3   Methodology and Results

Four-word lexical bundles are most common [4]. We extracted the four-word recurrent words by employing the perspective of frequency and the cluster function in Wordsmith Tools, in the two sub-corpora, CE (English Introduction Corpus of Chinese

English-major Students' Theses) and EE (English Introduction Corpus of International English-major Students' Theses). We referred to prior research concerning structural and functional taxonomy of lexical bundles [3][4][6][8][14] to classify the bundles, processed the data, and made corresponding statistical and comparative analysis.

Besides, we set a relatively low minimum frequency, 3, in the process of cluster retrieval to remove those clusters which appeared accidentally in only one or two files. For instance, the frequency for "big breasts and wide" is 40, but this bundle was present in only one file and was left out of the bundle list. Introductions are written texts, and there are often fewer lexical bundles found in written texts than in spoken discourse. We also manually removed those non-discourse attributes or obviously influent word sequences in spite of their high frequency, for instance, "out the similarities and", "of the study and", and thus we got the final data for analysis from the two sub-corpora.

3.1   Structural and Functional Classification of Lexical Bundles

Although lexical bundles look like random word clusters and takes no position in linguistics, they can be reasonably interpreted structurally and functionally [4]. Lexical chunks are stored as a whole and are the main constituents of texts, serving the function to frame the texts.

3.1.1   Structural Features of Lexical Bundles

With respect to taxonomy of the structural features of lexical bundles in introductions, we adopted Biber et al.'s [3] and Cortes' [6] [8] classification and in combination with the bundle features in our self-made CECIC corpus, we classified lexical bundles into 10 main types structurally (See Table 1).

Table 1. Structural Distribution of 4-word Lexical Bundles in Corpus CE and EE

Structure	Bundle Types		Bundle Tokens	
	CE Corpus	EE Corpus	CE Corpus	EE Corpus
1.Noun phrase + of	20	7	115	42
2.Noun phrase + post nominal clause fragment	0	1	0	9
3.Other noun phrases	7	1	43	5
4.Prepositional phrase + of	6	10	66	52
5.Other prepositional phrases	15	7	96	61
6.Anticipatory it + Vbe + adj./pp. + (clause fragment)	3	0	15	0
7.Passive + prep. phrase fragment/infinite	2	0	9	0
8.(Modal)Verb/Be + (complement noun /adj. phrase)	7	1	44	10
9.(noun phrase/pronoun)+ V + (Complement)	9	3	44	14
10.Others	1	0	4	0
Total	70	30	436	193

According to Biber et al. [5], lexical bundles are the main building blocks in discourse and they provide a kind of pragmatic 'head' for larger phrases and clauses, where they serve as discourse frames for the expression of new information. Therefore, lexical bundles supply interpretive frames for the developing discourse. For example,

(1) Since a different reality such as, *for the purpose of* this paper, the one associated with Québec identity, cannot continue to exist in this new context of 'nation' where every culture is equal, it must exist at a distance, as an image from the past.

(2) It can be deduced that the common understanding of reality *in the sense of* being material, practical and pragmatic is a rather late invent ion.

As is shown in Table 1, the lexical bundle features in Corpus CE vary greatly from those in Corpus EE. The most salient features are: First, there are no **'Noun phrase + post nominal clause fragment'** 4-word lexical bundles in Corpus CE while there are 'the ways in which' in 4 texts and with a frequency of 9 in Corpus EE, which indicates that this kind of structure is apparently underused in CE. Besides, either in the types or tokens of lexical bundles in the two sub-corpora, there is larger number in CE than in EE, but there are much more 4-word clusters which fail to be categorized into the 10 main types, and many of them are incomplete, for example, 'out the similarities and', and therefore they are removed from the list. In addition, While there are more 4-word lexical bundles in CE, and manifests a higher frequency, but the bundles bear a relatively single model, in which there are 10 types expressing the main content of the papers, for instance, 'this thesis consists of, the structure of the'. In contrast, despite the fewer types and lower frequency of lexical bundles in CE, the wider diversity feature is prominent in these bundles and they bear more complete meanings and serve a better function in framing the structure of the other parts of whole sentence, for example, 'the ways in which' serves the function to connect the whole sentence structure and meaning, and this kind of bundles fail to appear in CE.

(3) Lastly, and perhaps most importantly, no author, to my knowledge, has compared and contrasted *the ways in which* Silko uses descriptive language and landscape illustrations to reflect culture in all three novels collectively.

3.1.2   Functional Features of Lexical Bundles

In terms of the functional taxonomy of lexical bundles, we mainly referred to Cortes [5][6][8] and Biber et al. [3, 4] and three primary discourse functions could be distinguished for lexical bundles in CECIC: (1) stance bundles, (2) discourse/text organizers, and (3) referential bundles, and the rest bundles are termed as 'others'. As is interpreted by Cortes, stance bundles indicate the speakers' attitude or appraisal to another idea, "I don't know if", "I think it was", for instance; Discourse /text organizers help to organize such discourse or texts as "if you look at", "on the other hand"; Referential bundles refer to the objective or abstract targets or the text itself or its features, eg. "there's a lot of", "a little bit more". Referential bundles are mainly used to indicate time, place or the quantity used to introduce a person or an item, "at home and abroad", "at the same time", for example.

Both Cortes' and Biber et al.'s structural taxonomies of lexical bundles are mainly based on Halliday's (1994) three metafunctions, interpersonal and organizational functions. In fact, the three core functions can also be subclassified. Based on our research needs and by referring to Corts' [6][8] and Biber et al.'s [3, 4] taxonomy of lexical bundles, we employed the structural taxonomy of lexical bundles as follows:

That a lexical bundle is categorized into one type doesn't mean that this bundle is only applicable to this use. The functional type of a lexical bundle is mainly determined by its function this bundle serves on most occasions.

Table 2. Functional Distribution of 4-word Lexical Bundles in Corpus CE and EE

CLASSIFICATION			CE Corpus		EE Corpus	
			Tokens	Types	Tokens	Types
STANCE BUNDLES	Epistemic stance		8	2	12	3
	Attitudinal/Modality stance	Desire	0	0	0	0
		Obligation/Directive	0	0	0	0
		Intention/Prediction	0	0	0	0
		Ability	10	2	13	2
DISCOURSE ORGANIZERS	Topic introduction/focus		50	14	30	12
	Topic elaboration / clarification		44	2	8	5
	Research findings/ focus		62	18	20	5
REFERENTIAL EXPRESSIONS	Identification/focus		30	2	32	2
	Specification of attributes	Quantity specification	30	33	27	4
		Framing attributes	42	38	28	5
	Time/place/text reference	Place reference	6	1	20	3
		Time reference	52	3	6	2
		Multi-functional reference (both time and place)	13	2	5	1
OTHER BUNDLES			35	5	0	0
Total			436	70	193	30

As is shown in Table 2, there is a significant difference between the functional lexical bundles in CE and those in EE in several aspects. First, bundles belonging to Epistemic stance, Topic introduction/focus and Time reference are underused in Corpus CE. Because of the objectiveness of introductions in students' theses, there is a very small percentage of Attitudinal/Modality stance which helps to express personal subjective attitude and evaluation in Corpus CECIC, indicating an obvious academic register characteristics. There are much fewer types and tokens of Attitudinal lexical bundles in both the two sub-corpora, CE and EE, compared with Biber et al.'s findings [4, 5], which investigated the use of lexical bundles in both spoken and written registers (college classroom teaching and textbooks). In Corpus EE, the Attitudinal lexical bundles that authors used to express the authors' definite attitude and stance, for example, "I would like to", "I will argue that" to introduce the authors' new idea, new information, and it is more acceptable for readers. For instance,

(4) Here, *I would like to* use a more neutral term, overlapping talk, used by Bargiela-Chiappini and Harris (1997).

(5) In this essay, *I will argue that* noir is not just a specific genre, locked into certain prose styles and literary formulations, but rather an ethos and logic that integrates itself into a wide variety of novels dealing with questions of intrigue and the individual in the mid-20th century.

The main function of 'Topic introduction/focus' bundles is to introduce the author(s) and lead the readers to the aim and topic of the research, and most of them are supposed to belong to "Move 3: Presenting the Present Work" of an introduction. This kind of bundles are prominent in Corpus EE where there is a larger percentage in types and tokens, while in CE, there are much fewer types and tokens in the use of this category of lexical bundles.

Besides, as is shown in Table 2, those bundle types of 'Framing Attributes' 'Quantity specification' are significantly overused, esp. 'Framing Attributes' bundles, the tokens of which in CE is much more than those in EE. The usage feature of this kind of bundles is closely related to another kind of overused lexical bundles in CE, Research findings/ focus, for both of them are used to describe the important findings and data features. The tokens of these two kinds of bundles take up nearly one third of all lexical bundles (tokens) in CE. Whether in bundle tokens or types, there is a larger number in CE than in EE, but there is a shortage of diversity of bundles in CE. As for 'Quantity specification', despite the absolute high frequency of bundle types in CE, most of the bundles belong to comparison type such as"The thesis consists of", "the structure of the", which means a relatively few bundle types, indicating that Chinese stuedents are active in introducing the frame or structure of a thesis, but they favor some simple lexical types, and thus the lexical bundles in their introductions lack a kind of diversity in form and meaning.

In Modality stance, Identification/focus and Topic elaboration / clarification, the type and token distributions in both CE and EE are similar, indicating Chinese students' thesis introductions and the international ones have much in common in these features.

Moreover, there are many bundles which fail to fall into none of the three core functions of lexical bundles. These bundles are not coherent enough, incomplete in form and meaning, and thus lacks a clear function, and we will not discuss them in this research.

4   Conclusion

Structurally, there is a shortage of 'Noun phrase + post nominal clause fragment' lexical bundles (eg, the ways in which) in Corpus CE, which are very useful and functional to frame other parts of the whole sentence [10].

Functionally, compared with Corpus EE, the lexical bundles used to introduce the author(s) and then the topics, classified as Topic introduction/focus, are underused in CE, while those bundle types of 'Framing attributes' and 'Quantity specification' are overused, which are manifested in the bundle features of single form, meaning and function in spite of the larger bundle types and tokens.

This research on lexical bundles in Chinese and international students' thesis introductions may facilitate the understanding of the structural and functional distribution of lexical bundles in them and the distinguishing of the different traits in respective introductions. This study may also be beneficial to develop the second language learners' genre consciousness, to promote the fluency of English introduction language and to enhance the richness and diversity of lexical bundles in theses introductions.

Acknowledgement. This work was supported by Henan Project of Philosophy and Social Science (2014BYY003), the Creative Team Foundation of Zhengzhou University, the Humanities and Social Sciences Research Project of the Education Department of China (10YJA740074), the Natural Science Fund of China (No.60970083, No.61272221), the National Social Science Fund (No.14BYY096), 863 Projects of National High Technology Research and Development (No.2012AA011101), Science and Technology Key Project of Science and Technology Department of Henan Province (No.132102210407), Basic research project of Science and Technology Department of Henan Province (No. 142300410231; No.142300410308) and Key Technology Project of the Education Department of Henan Province (No.12B520055; No. 13B520381).

References

1. Altenberg, B., Tapper, M.: The use of adverbial connectors in advanced swedish learners' written english. In: Learner English on Computer. Addition Wesley Publishing Company, London (1998)
2. Biber, D., et al.: Longman Grammar of Spoken and Written English. Foreign Language Teaching and Research Press, Beijing (1999)
3. Biber, D., Conrad, S., Cortes, V.: Lexical bundles in speech and writing: an initial taxonomy. In: Wilson, A., Rayson, P., McEnery, T. (eds.) Corpus Linguistics by the Lune: A Festschrift for Geoffrey Leech, pp. 71–92. Peter Lang, Frankfurt (2003)
4. Biber, D., Conrad, S., Cortes, V.: If you look at … Lexical Bundles in University Teaching and Textbooks. Applied Linguistics **25**(3), 371–405 (2004)
5. Biber, D., et al.: Lexical bundles in university spoken and written registers. English for Specific Purposes **26**, 263–286 (2007)
6. Cortes, V.: Lexical bundles in published and student disciplinary writing: Examples from history and biology. English for Specific Purposes **23**(3), 397–423 (2004)
7. Cortes, V.: Teaching lexical bundles in the disciplinary class: An example from history. Manuscript submitted for publication (2006)
8. Cortes, V.: The purpose of this study is to: Connecting lexical bundles and moves in research article introductions. Journal of English for Academic Purposes (2013)
9. De Cock, D.: A recurrent word combination approach to the study of formulae in the speech of native and non-native speakers of English. International Journal of Corpus Linguistics **3**(1), 59–80 (1998)
10. Niu, G.: Structurally and functionally comparative analysis of lexlical bundles in the english abstracts of chinese and international journals. In: Su, X., He, T. (eds.) CLSW 2014. LNCS, vol. 8922, pp. 349–357. Springer, Heidelberg (2014)

11. Li, X., Wei, N.: Exploring lexical connotation and semantic prosody from the bilingual perspective. Modern Foreign Languages **35**(1), 30–38 (2012). (in Chinese)
12. Liang, M., Li, W., Xu, J.: Using Corpora: A Practical Coursebook. Foreign Language Teaching and Research Press, Beijing (2010). (in Chinese)
13. Nattinger, J., DeCarrico, J.: Lexical Phrases and Language Teaching. CUP, Oxford (1992)
14. Niu, G.: A Corpus-based Study on Explicitation in English Translation of Chinese Research Paper Abstract. Journal of Xi'an International Studies University **21**(2), 112–116 (2013). (in Chinese)
15. Parley, A., Syder, F.: Two puzzles for linguistic theory: native-like selection and native-like influence. In: Richards, J., Sehmit, R. (eds.) Language and Communication, pp. 191–225. Longman, London (1983)
16. Rayson, P.: From key words to key semantic domains. International Journal of Corpus Linguistics **13**(4), 519–549 (2008)
17. Pu, J.: Colligation, Collocation and Lexical Bundles in English Word Teaching. Foreign Teaching and Research **35**(6), 438–445+481 (2003). (in Chinese)
18. Scott, M.: Oxford Wordsmith Tools 4.0 Manual. CUP, Oxford (2004)
19. Sinclair, J.: Corpus, Concordance, Collocation. CUP, Oxford (1991)
20. Stubbs, M.: Two quantitative methods of studying phraseology in English. International Journal of Corpus Linguistics **7**(2), 215–244 (2002)
21. Wei, N.: A Preliminary Study of the Characteristics of Chinese Learners' Spoken English. Modern Foreign Languages **27**(2), 140–149 (2004). (in Chinese)
22. Wei, N.: Phraseological characteristics of Chinese learners' spoken English: Evidence of lexical chunks from COLSEC. Modern Foreign Languages **30**(3), 280–291 (2007). (in Chinese)
23. Wray, A.: Formulaic sequences in second language teaching: Principle and practice. Applied Linguistics **21**(4), 463–489 (2000)
24. Wray, A.: Formulaic Language and the Lexicon. CUP, Cambridge (2002)
25. Zhang, X.A.: Corpus-based Study on the Characteristics of Lexical Chunks Used by Chinese Advanced EFL learners. Foreign Language World **140**(5), 48–57 (2010). (in Chinese)

Chinese Event Co-reference Resolution Based on Trigger Semantics and Combined Features

Jiayue Teng[1,2(✉)], Peifeng Li[1,2], and Qiaoming Zhu[1,2]

[1] Natural Language Processing Lab, Soochow University, Suzhou 215006, Jiangsu, China
tjyemail@sina.com, {pfli,qmzhu}@suda.edu.cn
[2] School of Computer Science and Technology, Soochow University,
Suzhou 215006, Jiangsu, China

Abstract. Co-reference events occur frequently in texts and recognizing the co-reference events correctly is helpful for many NLP applications, including information extraction and text summarization. This paper presents an approach to Chinese event co-reference resolution. Due to the arbitrariness and polysemy of Chinese language, more effective features are introduced, such as word similarity, word distance and word matching for special words, to improve co-reference resolution performance. Furthermore, features transformation and combination are better used by classifiers for resolution by consideration of their characteristics, and then further improve resolution performance.

Keywords: Events Co-reference recognition · Words matching · Feature transformation and combination

1   Introduction

Event co-reference resolution is an important subtask for many NLP applications such as discourse understanding, text summarization and information extraction. Commonly, an article may contain many events, which have various kinds of relationships between each other. From a linguistics view, an event is a particular occurrence with participants, which is often described as a state of change. When two events refer to the same event ontology, they are considered to have a co-reference relationship[1]. For example:

Fund Projects: National Natural Science Foundation of China (61472265), National Natural Science Fund Project (61331011), Joint Research Project of Jiangsu Province (BY2014059-08), New Technology of Software and The Collaborative Innovation Center of Industrialization funded in part.

Author Profile: Jiayue Teng (1990--), male, Master graduate student, the majority is Chinese Information Processing. Peifeng Li (1971--), male, Associate Professor, the majority is Chinese Computing and Information Extraction. Qiaoming Zhu (1963--), male, Professor, the majority is Chinese Computing and Information Extraction.

[1] ACE Guidelines 5.5.1, http://www.ldc.upenn.edu/Projects/ACE/

© Springer International Publishing Switzerland 2015
Q. Lu and H.H. Gao (Eds.): CLSW 2015, LNAI 9332, pp. 494–503, 2015.
DOI: 10.1007/978-3-319-27194-1_50

a) 两国首脑今天在巴黎举行**会谈**。双方在**会谈**中讨论了中东和平问题。
(The leaders of two states held a **talk** in Paris today. The two sides discussed the peace of the Middle East in this **talk**.)

b) 恐怖分子于2001年9月11日对美国本土发动了恐怖**袭击**。**这一事件**对美国乃至全世界产生了深远的影响。(The terrorists launched a terrorist **attack** in the United States on September 11, 2011. **This incident** has a profound impact on the United States and the world.)

In example a), the two tokens of *"会谈" (talk)* refer to the same event ontology in the sentences. Therefore, they have a co-reference relationship. In the same way, *"这一事件" (this incident)* and *"袭击" (attack)* point to the same event of attack in example b). In this paper, we call a subsequent event mention (e.g., *"袭击" (attack))* a candidate, and the preceding mention (e.g., *"这一事件" (this incident))* an anaphor. Consequently, event co-reference recognition is converted to the problem of computing semantic similarity between a candidate and an anaphor, which are combined as an event pair [1].

However, there are some differences between event co-references and entity anaphora which regularly occur in adjacent sentences. Co-reference events often cross sentences and paragraphs, and even discourses, which makes event co-reference resolution. There are also a number of differences between Chinese and English co-reference events. As is well-known, English grammar is more rigorous and less polysemy than Chinese. Unfortunately, Chinese often omits the subject and has no obvious tenses and plural forms, bringing about a complex and free Chinese grammar. Moreover, there is a large amount of Chinese vocabularies and frequent polysemy, resulting in Chinese event co-reference resolution being difficult and recognition rates low.

In this paper, we transform the event co-reference resolution problem into the semantic similarity problem of event. That means we select any two events which come from the same article and combine them as an event pair. While considering an event's basic properties, triggers, arguments, head words and so on, as the basic attributes, we append novel features for Chinese words similarity and word matching rules. In addition, some distance features are also considered. Finally, we build an event co-reference resolution classifier for Chinese text. Specifically, after full consideration of the characteristics of the Maxent classifier[2], we combine parts of the features and convert them to an easy use form, making substantial improvements in event co-reference resolution.

2   Related Works

With little early co-reference event research, more people focus on entity anaphora and event anaphora in the field of information extraction. Ahn [1] referred to the problem of co-reference event resolution when researching event extraction. According Florian's idea [2] computing entity co-reference, Ahn converted event co-reference into the

---

[2] Maximum Entropy classifier, http://homepages.inf.ed.ac.uk/lzhang10/maxent_toolkit.html

similarity calculation of event pairs, validating it on the MegaM corpus. Afterward Adrian [3] specified the features of event pairs, considering that event structure contains a certain relation or state between events. The technique made use of structural features for event co-reference, providing tag rules and corpus. Chen [4] built a pairwise event co-reference model based on feature impact using the ACE corpus, presenting an agglomerative clustering algorithm. The work compared three evaluation metrics that were previously adopted in entity co-reference resolution: MUC, B-Cubed and ECM. In addition, Chen [5] modelled event co-reference resolution as a spectral graph clustering problem and evaluated the clustering algorithm on ground truth event mentions, which provides a new method of event co-reference resolution. Apart from the above, event co-reference resolution based on large-scale data across documents is more difficult than within a single document. Fatemeh [6] broke the task of event co-reference resolution across documents into two steps: semantic class detection and similarity-based matching. The work annotated manually co-reference links on the AQUAINT TimeML corpus, revealing how semantic conventions and information available in the context of event mentions affect decisions in co-reference analysis.

However, Chinese event co-reference research is less studied. Aiming at anaphora resolution on Chinese corpus, Hu [7] built a Chinese anaphora resolution system based on the Maximum Entropy Model and validated it on the ACE05 BNews corpus with some improvements. Zhang [8] proposed a new method for exploiting head information in co-reference resolution. Based on simple instance matching, he introduced the head string of an antecedent and anaphora as a new feature and proposed a competition mode to integrate the head-string feature into instance-matching. Pang [9-10] present an approach to co-reference event resolution in emergency news based on multiple semantic features. With context features extracted from Wikipedia, the co-reference resolution model had some improvement. However, due to differences between Chinese and English linguistics, there are huge numbers of vocabularies and more widespread polysemy phenomena. Furthermore, unlike strict English grammar, Chinese grammar is loose and free, which has no obvious tenses, plural forms, etc. Even from the syntax parse tree it is difficult to grasp the major event information in the sentence. As a result, Chinese event co-reference resolution performance is so difficult that the performance is lower than when using English.

With previous research, this paper chooses the ACE Chinese corpus for the experimental samples. Based on the idea of pairwise comparisons, we convert event co-reference resolution into the semantic similarity of event pairs. Integrating related work on co-reference resolution research, we add word similarity and word matching as new features, and supplement distance features. In addition, based on characteristics of the Maxent classifier, we transform and combine some features to be better used by the classifier, resulting further improvement to the system's performance.

3   The Basic Framework

In this paper, we model Chinese event co-reference resolution using the Maximum Entropy classifier (Maxent) on the current ACE Chinese corpus, including feature selection, semantic similarity calculation, word matching, transformation and combinations of features, Maximum Entropy classification, statistical experiment results and several other steps. The basic framework is shown in Figure 1, while MUC-6 is used as the evaluation metric.

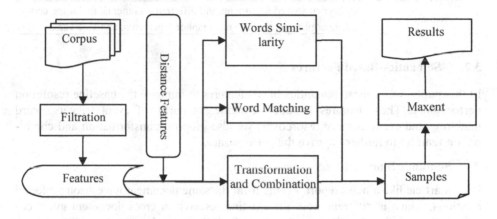

Fig. 1. The Basic Framework

According to Ahn's idea [1], we put ACE corpus into grouped documents, and make pairs with any two events in the same document. Then we use the Maxent classifier to judge whether this event pair has a co-reference relationship. Because the ACE corpus is not specifically for event co-reference resolution, sample filtration is necessary. First, we remove the documents which have no co-reference events to avoid event pairs from those documents erroneously increasing the proportion of negative samples, leading to misleading experiment results. Secondly, we also reject the event pairs where the two events have different event types, because they are easy to recognize, bring an increase in negative samples, and result in the accuracy of event pairs being very high but the MUC F-Measure very low.

3.1   Baseline

We employ a baseline for event co-reference resolution that collects features from previous studies. As shown in Table 1, those features include basic attributes [11], lexical features, distance features, and argument features. Consistent with the ACE 2005 corpus, the co-reference events are considered as having the same basic attributes. We introduce these features to train a model using a Maxent classifier and then apply it to identify the co-reference events.

Table 1. Event Co-reference Resolution Baseline

Category	Details
Attributes	Event Type, Subtype, Modality, Polarity, Genericity, Tense, and the coherence of attributes between event pairs
Lexical features	Event trigger, head words of argument, and the number of same head words, different head words.
Distances	Trigger distances, LDC-scope distances, extent distances, Depth of trigger in parse tree and their difference.
Arguments	Number of shared arguments and different arguments, including candidate arguments that are not anaphor arguments, and vice versa.

3.2 Semantics-Based Features

In this paper, we propose semantics-based features to improve the baseline resolution performance. These features include Semantic Similarity of event triggers, word matching and event distance. Moreover, we also propose transformation and combination features to further improve the performance.

● **Semantic Similarity**

For an article like a news report, events from the same document have strong internal relations, which is different from the existing research in cross-document event co-reference resolution. In other words, events from the same document usually have the same part of the basic attributes, such as an article about a traffic accident, which may contain event subtypes of Injure or Die. Semantic features can make up for the shortage of basic attributes. Although event triggers are the best performance of event characteristics, there are many Chinese vocabularies so that it is difficult to compare directly. For example:

c) 中国国务院总理朱镕基昨天致电加拿大总理克雷蒂安，对加拿大前总理特鲁多**去世(EV1)**，表示深切哀悼。(Chinese Premier ZHU Rongji called the Canadian Premier Christian, and expressed deep condolences for **the death (EV1)** of former Canadian Premier Trudeau.)

d) 朱镕基在唁电中说："惊悉，加拿大前总理皮埃尔·艾里奥特·特鲁多先生不幸**逝世(EV2)**深为悲痛。" (ZHU Rongji said in the condolence: "I am shocked to know that, the former Canadian Premier, Mr. Pierre Elliot Trudeau **died (EV2)**, with deep sorrow.")

Although the two event triggers above are different, "*去世*" *(the death)* and "*逝世*" *(died)*, their semantics are similar and the two events have a co-reference relationship. Therefore, in this paper, we employ the Word Similarity Calculation tool [12] developed by Chinese Academy of Sciences as the basis of trigger word similarity. When the similarity value θ reaches a threshold, we consider the two trigger words to be coherent. The head words of argument are also taken into account.

● **Word Matching**

Nevertheless, semantic similarity pays more attention to the differences between words. Furthermore, the recognition result is poor when calculating the unregistered words, such as the word pair: *"逼死 (force to die) + 死 (die)"*, *"募捐 (collect donations) + 捐款 (contribute money)"*. According to Word Similarity Calculation, the similarities of the word pairs above are all less than 0.3. However, from the view of event triggers in ACE corpus, the words *"逼死" (force to die)* and *"死" (die)* are coherent. Also the words *"募捐" (collect donations)* and *"捐款" (contribute money)* are coherent. Based on this, we propose the word matching rules below:

1) If two words are equal from the string point of view, then they are coherent directly;
2) Otherwise, if the word similarity $\geq$ 0.8, then they are coherent;
3) Otherwise, if two words have the same prefix or suffix, then they are coherent (such as *"举行 (hold)+ 举办 (hold)"*, *"大选 (general election)+ 民选 (elected by people)"*);
4) Otherwise, if the word's length $\leq$ 3 and two words have the same character, then they are coherent (such as *"募捐" (collect donations)* and *"捐款" (contribute money))*;
5) Otherwise, they are not consistent.

Apart from dealing with triggers and head words above, we employ the Stanford Parser[3] to generate parse trees for the sentence events occurred (LDC-Scope), and count the leaves (words) of each. That means we calculate the shared words of every two event sentences and normalize it, avoiding skew from long sentences that have more shared words or short sentences have less shared words. In other words, we measure two sentences' similarity from the words point of view, leading to an improvement in the resolution model.

● **Event Distance**

When focusing on the ACE corpus, it's easy to find that co-reference events often occur continuously. For example, if an event A was mentioned in the context above, then the consequence caused by the event A may be introduced in succession. Using the absolute distance measures lacks an   ideal effect. From the ACE corpus we make a conclusion that articles that come from news report have relatively normal expressions and more complex, long sentences. Nevertheless, web blogs usually contain more short and simple sentences. Besides the basic distance features included in the baseline, we add relative distance measures including event LDC-Scope at the same sentence, adjacent sentences and others.

Apart from above, we also make statistics for the event count which appear between candidate and anaphor, denoted as pairwise bias. Obviously, if the pairwise bias is 1 even 0 (*0 means this event pair is adjacent*), then this event pair has high coupling degree hence the two events have a high probability of having a co-reference relationship.

---

[3] http://nlp.stanford.edu/software/lex-parser.shtml

- **Transformation and Combination**

The Maxent classifier can flexibly apply context features thus researchers only pay attention to seeking features. It has no requirement for the independence of features which is an advantage. Occasionally, some features have no obvious performance for the resolution results. However, we make those features combined based on a rule, resulting in a great improvement. Take the *argument count* as an example, the number of arguments shared (called AS), the number of arguments in candidate but not in anaphor (called AAN) and the number of arguments in anaphor but not in candidate (called CAN) cannot be exploited by the classifier well. Some event sentences are so long that they contain many arguments, leading to many shared arguments and many different arguments. Considering this, we propose the transformation and combination rules below (take the *argument* count as an example):

1) If AS > 0 then set this flag as 1 else 0;
2) If AAN > 0 AND CAN > 0 then set this flag as 0 else 1;
3) If AS ≥ AAN OR AS ≥ CAN then set this flag as 1 else 0.

After following the rules above, the effects of shared arguments are amplified. An example is when the event pair has no co-reference relationship. In fact, there are two rules including 2) and 3) that strengthen the negative probability of event pairs. Experiments show that it is helpful for increasing the recall rate. In addition, we also consider the shared and different numbers of argument roles and head words using rules similar to the above.

Apart from the rules, some features such as the basic attributes of an event [11] are not directly employed, instead using the digital value: 0, 1 and etc. We also combine this digital value into a pairwise candidate-anaphor form as the new features, bringing about ample advantages for event features.

4   Experiments

4.1   Experiment Design

In our experiments, we get rid of the documents that contain no co-reference events from the ACE2005 Chinese corpus, leaving 294 documents with experimental values. Taking the document as the unit, we consider any two events as pairwise. We also remove event pairs that have the same event type, resulting in 12302 event pairs including 2692 positive event pairs and 9610 negative event pairs, with a ratio of about 1:4.

When filtering the ACE corpus, we note that the documents can be grouped by their sources into 13 categories. Each category's documents have slight linguistic differences, such as articles coming from the category CBS which are the majority of the broadcast news articles. Nevertheless, the majority of articles coming from NJWSL are web. There are slight differences between diverse categories' articles in the strictness and style of expressions. When generating the training and test sets, we try to cover all categories of documents in order from a variety of sources. While maintaining the training and test sets' ratio is about 4:1, we perform 5 fold cross validation to reduce bias of results.

However, we only obtain the results in pairwise format due to the sample data being event pairs after classification. To be more persuasive, we convert the pairwise results into chain form. Afterward, we calculate MUC-Precision, MUC-Recall and MUC-F1 under the MUC-6 evaluation metrics using the Conll2012-scorer-8.0 tool[4]. All the results above are shown in the micro average.

4.2   Experiment Results and Analysis

In this paper, we consider the results of the basic features as the baseline. Thus we add several categories of features of section 3.3 in turn. Table 2 shown the results of the 5 fold cross validation, from which we can make a conclusion that every category of features contributes to the overall resolution performance.

Table 2. Experiment Results

	Recall (%)	Precision (%)	F1 (%)
Baseline	62.447	67.142	64.710
+Semantic Similarity	62.677	70.311	66.275 (+**1.565**)
+Words Matching	64.599	69.186	66.813 (+**2.103**)
+Supplement of Distance	63.412	69.013	66.094 (+**1.384**)
+Transform and Combine	72.634	69.608	71.089 (+**6.379**)
All the features	74.673	71.577	73.092 (+**8.382**)

After joining the features for semantic similarity, the precision of the system increases by 3.169%, which is the highest improvement for the precision in all categories of features, although it has no substantial improvement in recall. There is no doubt that semantic comprehension especially comprehension of triggers and head words has substantial increases, such as the word pair: *"死亡 (death) +丧生 (lose one's life)"*, which have the largest probability of semantic similarity according to the Word Similarity tool. In fact, those two events have co-reference relationship usually.

Unlike the features of the semantic similarity, words matching rules have both increases in precision and recall, resulting in great improvement for the F1 measure by 2.103%. On the one hand, words matching rules consider words which have the same prefix or suffix to be similar, such as word pairs: *"购买 (buy)+ 购物 (shopping)"* and *"形成 (form)+合成 (compose)"*. Although these word pairs have certain differences from a linguistic point of view, they usually occur in the co-reference event sentences in real corpus. On the other hand, these words matching rules have the same effect as weakening strict semantic similarity, making certain word pairs that have a low probability of semantic similarity considered coherent. In other words, these rules enhance the recall measure with little sacrifice to the precision.

From the ACE corpus, adjacent events often have the greatest probability of co-reference relationship. According to the normal expression habits, we ordinarily introduce the event brief when first when describing an event. Furthermore we expound

---

[4] http://conll.cemantix.org/2012/software.html/

on this event in detail including the time, place, person, etc. With regard to the traffic accident, the damage may appear with follows, such as an event sentence *"一辆汽车追尾，撞坏前面正常行驶的货车。(A car **bumped into rear end**, **crashed** the front truck which were running normally)"*. The supplement distances implicate certain relations from relative distance measures, leading to some increase of both precision and recall.

The transformation and combination rules have the great contributions to the resolution system. Compared with the baseline, these features enhance recall by more than approximately 10 percentage points with a little increase in precision. In light of the rules in Section 3.3, some unobvious features can be transformed into more available features. There is no doubt that the influence factor of the same arguments number is enlarged invisibly and the number of head words shared is as well. In other words, this has the same effect as assigning weights to the features. However, there are important differences because assigning weights may lead to excessive tuning parameters. Finally, we transform and combine several features under the rules above, bringing about substantial performance increase. For example:

e)   为苏建何案奔走将近10年的苏建何的父亲<苏春常><今天下午>因为肺癌病逝。 (SU Jianhe's father <SU Chunchang> who has worked for the case of SU Jianhe for nearly 10 years **died** of lung cancer <this afternoon>.)

f)   <时隔半个月>苏建何的父亲<苏春常>因为肺癌在<台大医院>过世。 (<Half a month later>, SU Jianhe's father <SU Chunchang> **died** of lung cancer in <NTU hospital>.)

From the trigger word point of view, word pair: *"病逝 (die of sickness) +过世 (pass away)"* can't be considered as coherent according to the semantic similarity and word matching. Nevertheless, these two events share the same argument: *"苏春常" (SU Chunchang)*, which may cause a co-reference relationship. On the basis of the statistical method above, this event pair has AS: 1, AAN: 1, CAN: 2, which looks like they have less probability of co-reference relationship than general logic. However, according to the transformation and combination rules, once the shared arguments count is not equal to zero, its factor will be expanded, leading it to be considered as a co-reference event. Although, it may have a side effect on the precision measure, the recall measure has a substantial improvement by 10 percentage points, resulting in good increases of the F1 measure.

Integrating several categories of features above, we also obtain great improvement in co-reference resolution, but not the sum of these features' contributions, on account of that semantic similarity and words matching have partial overlaps. Additionally, transformation and combination synthesize several features above in fact, enhancing the recall measure greatly.

5   Summary

In this paper, we study the problem of co-reference event resolution. Firstly, we choose four angles including the basic attributes of an event, lexical features, distance measures and arguments based on current research to model the baseline of Chinese event co-reference resolution. Secondly, considering the characteristics of Chinese linguistics, we append semantic similarity, propose simple words matching rules and supplement several relative distance features. For the several unobvious features, we transform and combine them in order to enhance the resolution performance.

From the ACE corpus, we discover that the time and place an event occurred appear little in the plaintext form. It is helpful for the co-reference resolution to extract and infer the temporal and spatial relations automatically. Furthermore, in order to reduce the differences in linguistic expression styles, we will convert and cut the syntax parse tree of the event sentence, supplementing the few contributions of the distance features.

References

1. Ahn, D.: The stages of event extraction. In: Proceedings of the Workshop of the ACL on Annotating and Reasoning About Time and Events, pp. 1–8 (2006)
2. Florian, R., Hassan, H., Ittycheriah, A., Jing, H., Kambhatla, N., Luo, X., Nicolov, N., Roukos, S.: A statistical model for multilingual entity detection and tracking. In: Proceedings of HLT/NAACL-2004 (2004)
3. Bejan, C.A., Harabagiu, S.: A linguistic resource for discovering event structures and resolving event coreference. In: Proceedings of ACL 2008, Hawaii, USA, pp. 2881–2887 (2008)
4. Chen, Z., Ji, H., Haralick, R.: A pairwise event coreference model, feature impact and evaluation for event coreference resolution. In: Proceedings of Events in Emerging Text Types (eETTs), RANLP 2009, pp. 17–22 (2009)
5. Chen, Z., Ji, H.: Graph-based event coreference resolution. In: Proceedings of the 2009 Workshop, ACL-IJCNLP 2009, pp. 54–57 (2009)
6. Asr, F.T., Sonntag, J., Grishina, Y., Stede, M.: Conceptual and practical steps in event co-reference analysis of large-scale data. In: Proceedings of the 2nd Workshop on EVENTS, ACL 2014, pp. 35–44 (2014)
7. Hu, N., Kong, F., Wang, H., Zhou, G., Zhu, Q.: Realization on Chinese Coreference Resolution System Based on Maximum Entropy Model. Application Research of Computers 8 (2009). (in Chinese)
8. Zhang, M., Li, Y., Qin, B., Liu, T.: Coreference Resolution Based on Head Match. Journal of Chinese Information Processing, May 2011. (in Chinese)
9. Pang, N., Yang, E.: The Research on Coreference Resolution Based on Maximum Entropy Model. Journal of Chinese Information Processing, 24–27 (2008). (in Chinese)
10. Pang, N., Yang, E.: Multiple Semantic Features Based on Coreference Resolution in Emergency News. Journal of Chinese Information Processing, 26–32, January 2014. (in Chinese)
11. Mani, I., Verhagen, M., Wellner, B., Lee, C.M., Pustejovsky, J.: Machine learning of temporal relations. In: Proceedings of the 21st International Conference on Computational Linguistics and the 44th Annual Meeting of the Association for Computational Linguistics, pp. 753–760 (2006)
12. Liu, Q., Li, S.: Word Similarity Computing Method Based on HowNet. Journal of Chinese Information Processing 7(2), 59–76 (2002). (in Chinese)

Morpheme Inversion in Disyllabic Compounds—Cases in Chinese Diachronic Corpora

Dan Xiong[1], Qin Lu[1(⊠)], Fengju Lo[2], Dingxu Shi[3], and Tin-shing Chiu[1]

[1] Department of Computing, The Hong Kong Polytechnic University, Hong Kong, China
{Csdxiong,Csluqin,Cstschiu}@comp.polyu.edu.hk
[2] Department of Chinese Linguistics & Literature, Yuan Ze University, Taoyuan, Taiwan
gefjulo@saturn.yzu.edu.tw
[3] Department of Chinese & Bilingual Studies, The Hong Kong Polytechnic University,
Hong Kong, China
dingxu.shi@polyu.edu.hk

Abstract. Morpheme inversion is a significant lexical phenomenon in the evolution of Chinese words, and it poses additional difficulties in Chinese word segmentation, especially in computer processing of Chinese classics. This paper reports a study on the disyllabic morpheme-inverted compounds in the Chinese diachronic corpora from the perspective of natural language processing. The corpora include two pre-Qin classics and four notable novels created in the Ming and Qing dynasties, in which words are segmented and proper nouns are tagged. Based on the full statistics and analysis, a comparative study is carried out on the use of disyllabic morpheme-inverted compounds in the two types of Chinese text, that is, historical works and fictions. Results show that there are many more morpheme-inverted compounds in the Ming-Qing novels than in the pre-Qin classics in terms of both lexical item and frequency. The morpheme-inverted compounds in the Ming-Qing novels are also closer to their modern counterparts.

Keywords: Disyllabic morpheme-inverted compounds · Chinese diachronic corpora · Chinese segmentation

1   Introduction

In both ancient and modern Chinese, compounds with the same constituent morphemes which appear in reversed order are not uncommon. Since morpheme inversion is a rather significant phenomenon, it plays an important role in the fields of linguistics and Chinese language teaching. When computers are used to automatically segment words, these morpheme-inverted compounds may cause troubles. This paper reports a study of the disyllabic morpheme-inverted compounds in the corpora built under the project "Building a Diachronic Language Knowledge-base" (hereinafter referred to as the Diachronic Corpora) [1] from the perspective of natural language processing. The Diachronic Corpora include two historical classics from the pre-Qin

© Springer International Publishing Switzerland 2015
Q. Lu and H.H. Gao (Eds.): CLSW 2015, LNAI 9332, pp. 504–515, 2015.
DOI: 10.1007/978-3-319-27194-1_51

period, that is, *The Commentary of Zuo* (《左傳》) and *Discourses of the States* (《國語》), as well as four notable novels from the Ming and Qing dynasties, namely, *Romance of the Three Kingdoms* (《三國演義》), *Water Margin* (《水滸傳》), *The Golden Lotus* (《金瓶梅》), and *A Dream of Red Mansions* (《紅樓夢》). In the Diachronic Corpora, words are segmented and proper nouns are tagged. Through statistics and analysis, this paper looks at the distribution of disyllabic morpheme-inverted compounds in these two types of text and presents the findings. The results will be useful for investigating the preference of word in these two genres as well as the evolution of such compounds from the pre-Qin period to the Ming and Qing dynasties.

The paper is organized as follows. Section 2 gives a brief review of related works. Section 3 describes the research scope. Section 4 presents the distribution of the disyllabic morpheme-inverted compounds in the Diachronic Corpora. Section 5 conducts a comparative study of the disyllabic morpheme-inverted compounds in the two different styles of text with data and examples. The examples given in this paper are all cited from the Diachronic Corpora.

2   Related Works

The phenomenon of morpheme inversion in Chinese has attracted much attention in the field of Chinese studies. However, existing researches mainly focus on synchronic studies, such as analysis on a pair of or a certain type of morpheme-inverted words, or those in a single book or a series of works of a certain author. Generally speaking, past researches are mainly on synchronic data, such as lexical meaning analysis, etymology, rhetoric, dialectology, cross-language and cross-cultural studies, Chinese language teaching, and lexicography. These studies are described in details in references [2-3] and pages 6-9 of [4], and they will not be repeated here. On the other hand, there are few diachronic studies on the topic. Although there are some works dedicated to the morpheme-inverted words in novels of the Ming and Qing dynasties, they are mostly focused on individual books. Based on a full statistical analysis, this paper carries out a comparative study on the disyllabic morpheme-inverted compounds in the Diachronic Corpora containing six Chinese books in two different genres from the perspective of natural language processing. This paper thus presents a study quite different from the existing researches.

3   Research Scope

3.1   Definition of Disyllabic Morpheme-Inverted Compounds

Disyllabic morpheme-inverted compounds in this paper refer to pairs of disyllabic compounds with the same constituent morphemes which are combined in reversed order. There have been different opinions about the exact nature and range of morpheme-inverted compounds. With reference to the mainstream views [4-5], we have established our principles based on our research objectives and the features of such compounds in the Diachronic Corpora. The following sections specify our research scope from two aspects: (1) compound and (2) morpheme inversion. The analysis of character glyph, pronunciation, morpheme meaning, and lexical meaning is based on relevant dictionaries [6-8] as well as previous studies on the two pre-Qin classics and four Ming-Qing novels [9-14].

3.2   Compounds

Disyllabic Morphemes. Although these morphemes contain two syllables and are written with two characters, these characters are used as syllables only and do not represent meaning. They do not need further segmenting and are therefore excluded from this study. For instance:

唧咕 [*jīgu*] —— 咕唧 [*gūji*] (*whisper*)   蹊蹺 [*qīqiao*] —— 蹺蹊 [*qiāoqi*] (*queer*)

Multi-word Expressions. When building the Diachronic Corpora, we adhere to the fundamental principle of segmenting text strings into the smallest linguistic units with independent semantic or grammatical functions so that there will be no risk of meaning loss, distortion, misinterpretation, or ambiguity [1]. Word segmentation and annotation specification is established specifically for classical Chinese based on (1) the specification developed by Peking University [15] which has been widely accepted for modern Chinese segmentation in Mainland China and (2) the standard of Chinese segmentation used in Taiwan [16]. Accordingly, idiomatic phrases and multi-word expressions such as fixed expressions, idioms, and phrases with meaning not derived directly from the sense of constituent characters are not segmented. This kind of phrases is considered a single segmentation unit, that is, "the smallest linguistic unit that has specific semantic or grammatical function" [17]. Therefore, the basic units coming out of segmentation in the Diachronic Corpora include not only words in the traditional sense, but also some idiomatic phrases and multi-word expressions. For example, "心多 [*xīnduō*] (*sensitive*)" is a subject-predicate construction that will lose some semantic information if it is segmented. Because of this, it is treated as a single unit in the Diachronic Corpora. Therefore, the pair "心多 [*xīnduō*] — 多心 [*duōxīn*] (*sensitive*)" is included in this work. For the convenience of description, this kind of phrases is also called morpheme-inverted compound in this paper.

3.3   Morpheme Inversion

A pair of disyllabic morpheme-inverted compounds should have the same constituent morphemes. This requires that a constituent morpheme and its counterpart have the same glyph and pronunciation as well as the same or similar meaning. This section gives several types of examples to illustrate this point in details.

Identical Glyph, Pronunciation, and Meaning. There is no doubt that they will be treated as disyllabic morpheme-inverted compounds if the two corresponding constituent morphemes have the same glyph, pronunciation, and meaning. For example:

驛館 [yìguǎn] —— 館驛 [guǎnyì] (courier hostel)
較計 [jiàojì] —— 計較 [jìjiào] (mind; think over; plan...)

Identical Pronunciation and Meaning but Different Glyph. Some constituent morphemes have the same pronunciation and meaning but different glyphs, due to character variants, interchangeable characters, and ancient/modern character variations. For example:

熟嫻 [shúxián] —— 嫻熟 [xiánshú] (skilled)
報荅 [bàodá] —— 答報 [dábào] (repay)

In principle, this kind of words should be treated as disyllabic morpheme-inverted compounds. However, in order to recognize them correctly, a separate knowledge base is needed. To avoid getting into arguments on variants in general, they are excluded from this paper but will be included in our future study.

Identical Glyph and Pronunciation but Different Meaning. According to our principle, these pseudo-morpheme-inverted compounds are excluded since the meaning of at least one morpheme has no clear relation to the other. For example:

道人 [dàorén] (Taoist priest; monk) — 人道 [réndào] (humanity)
　　↓　　　　　　　　　　　　　　　　↓
　Taoism　　　　　　　　　　　　　morality

男子 [nánzǐ] (man) — 子男 [zǐnán] (viscount and baron)
　↓　↓　　　　　　　　　↓　　↓
male person　　　　　viscount baron

Identical Glyph but Different Pronunciation. Morphemes with different pronunciations usually have different meanings, and compounds with these morphemes are thus not included in this paper. For example:

家當 [jiādàng] (family belongings) —— 當家 [dāngjiā] (manage household affairs)
好學 [hàoxué] (eager to learn) —— 學好 [xuéhǎo] (learn from good examples)

The neutral tone in Mandarin (or Putonghua) is a reduced form of the four basic tones, in terms of duration, loudness, and contour. Some morphemes are always pronounced with a neutral tone, such as the particles "了 [le]", "地 [de]", "得 [de]", and "的 [de]". However, some morphemes are pronounced with a neutral tone only in certain compounds. Whether such compounds are included in this paper depends on the meaning of the morphemes. If the morpheme with a neutral tone has the same meaning as the one with a normal tone, the compound containing it will be qualified for a morpheme-inverted compound. In the following example, "酬₁" is pronounced with a neutral tone in Mandarin[1], but it has the same meaning as its counterpart "酬₂" which is pronounced with a second tone. The two compounds are therefore treated as morpheme-inverted compounds.

應酬₁ [*yìngchou*] — 酬₂應 [*chóuyìng*]

social intercourse

If the morpheme bearing a neutral tone has a different meaning, the related compound will not be considered a morpheme-inverted one, as shown in the following example.

人家₁ [*rénjia*] (*personal pronoun*) — 家₂人 [*jiārén*] (*family member*)

particle   *family*

> A personal pronoun referring to oneself or other people, such as the following examples in *A Dream of Red Mansions*:
> (1) 人家/睡覺/，/你/進來/作/什麼 [*rénjia shuìjiào，nǐ jìnlái zuò shénme*] (*What do you mean by coming in when I am asleep?*)
> (2) 議論/人家/的/好歹 [*yìlùn rénjia de hǎodǎi*] (*criticize other people's suggestions*)

Since the semantic content is context-sensitive, morpheme meaning and word meaning in this paper refer to their senses in the context of the Diachronic Corpora. A morpheme or word may have several senses. In the above example, the meaning of the constituent morpheme "家₁" is different from that of "家₂", and these two words do not form a morpheme-inverted compound pair. While in the following example, "人家₃ — 家₂人" are morpheme-inverted compounds since their constituent morphemes have identical/similar meaning.

人家₃ [*rénjiā*] (*household; family…*) — 家₂人 [*jiārén*] (*family member*)

family; residence…   *family*

> Some examples in the novels:
> (1) *Water Margin*: 五七百/人家 [*wǔqībǎi rénjiā*] (*hundreds of households*)
> (2) *The Golden Lotus*: 詩禮/人家 [*shīlǐ rénjiā*] (*a family of scholars*)
> (3) *A Dream of Red Mansions*: 已/有/了/人家 [*yǐ yǒu le rénjiā*] (*was betrothed*)

3.4   Others

Novels from the Ming and Qing dynasties contain a large number of traditional verses, such as poems, couplets, prose poems, and lyrics, in which morphemes can be

---

[1] Regional differences may exist sometimes. It is pronounced with a neutral tone in Mainland China but with a second tone in Taiwan (http://dict.revised.moe.edu.tw/).

inverted for the sake of rhyming or for certain rhetorical purpose. These special cases should be analyzed separately and are excluded from this work.

There are also some other special cases that are excluded:

- Numerals: Since Chinese numerals are represented by combinations of basic digitals and counting units, the order of their constituents will determine the value of the numerals. The two numerals "一十 [yīshí] (ten) — 十一 [shíyī] (eleven)" thus have predetermined different values. Numerals are thus not included in this paper.
- Proper nouns: When building the Diachronic Corpora, we tagged proper nouns such as personal names, terms of address, names of official position, titles of nobility or honour, place names, building names, and organization names. Since it is not appropriate to study these proper nouns together with common words, they are not included in this paper. Proper nouns with several senses are treated separately. For example, "巡按 [xúnàn]" can be a name of official position or a common word with the meaning of making an inspection tour. This paper only includes the latter case.
- Nonce words: Some words are occasionally invented in literature to make the description more vivid or produce certain rhetorical effect. Since these nonce words are created for particular occasions, they are excluded from this paper. For example, in the sentence "不/偷/漢子/，/只/偷/子漢 [bù/tōu/hànzi/,/zhǐ/tōu/zǐhàn] (implying that the female role in the novel had an adulterous affair with others in an ironic manner)", "子漢" is a nonce word created for this occasion only, and this pair of words is not considered morpheme-inverted compounds.

4   Distribution of Disyllabic Morpheme-Inverted Compounds in the Diachronic Corpora

The data in this paper only consist of cases within the research scope specified in Section 3. For words with multiple senses in the Diachronic Corpora, only the cases within the scope are included.

Table 1 lists the number of disyllabic morpheme-inverted compounds in each type of text. The data in this table focus on lexical item, which means that the same compound is counted only once. "C/A (%)" is the ratio of the disyllabic morpheme-inverted compounds (pair) to all the segmentation units in the Diachronic Corpora, and "C/B (%)" is the ratio of the compound pairs to the disyllabic segmentation units. The ratios reflect the diversity of the disyllabic morpheme-inverted compounds. In general, there are more such compounds in the Ming-Qing novels than in the pre-Qin classics. Possible reasons for this contrast include:

- Genre differences: The pre-Qin classics are serious historical records and belong to a formal written genre. While the Ming-Qing novels depict the life of ordinary townspeople who frequently use casual speech, local dialects, and even slangs. These novels thus belong to an informal narrative genre and contain a lot of colloquial expressions not found in formal genres.

- Language diversity: The geographical areas described in the pre-Qin classics are relatively small and the relevant population is also small. Because of the lack of appropriate means of transportation, population mobility is also limited. The lack of language diversity in the pre-Qin classics is thus expected.

Table 1. Distribution of disyllabic morpheme-inverted compounds (lexical item)

		Pre-Qin classics		Ming-Qing novels			
		1	2	3	4	5	6
A: All segmentation units in the Diachronic Corpora		6,396	4,392	12,933	18,984	21,164	20,290
B: Disyllabic units in the Diachronic Corpora		3,761	2,407	8,943	13,171	13,762	13,399
C: Disyllabic morpheme-inverted compounds (pair)		37	19	150	288	208	228
C/A (%)		0.58%	0.43%	1.16%	1.52%	0.98%	1.12%
C/B (%)		0.98%	0.79%	1.68%	2.19%	1.51%	1.70%
C (pair)	Consolidation of the text in the same style	71					819
	Intersection of the text in the same style	6					17
	Consolidation of all						956
	Intersection of the two styles						9
Pre-Qin classics: 1: The Commentary of Zuo 2: Discourses of the States Ming-Qing novels: 3: Romance of the Three Kingdoms 4: Water Margin 5: The Golden Lotus 6: A Dream of Red Mansions							

The "C/A (%)" and "C/B (%)" indicate that among the four Ming-Qing novels, the book *Water Margin* has the largest number of disyllabic morpheme-inverted compounds. A most likely reason is that this novel was based on scripts of talk shows which were very popular and widely spread before the novel was written. Therefore, the language being used in *Water Margin* has the characteristics of folklore, in which dialects and slangs are common. When the data from the four Ming-Qing novels are consolidated, there are 819 pairs of the disyllabic morpheme-inverted compounds. This number reflects the importance of such compounds in the novels.

The "intersection" shows the overlap of the disyllabic morpheme-inverted compounds in different datasets. The two pre-Qin classics have 6 pairs of disyllabic morpheme-inverted compounds in common, and the four Ming-Qing novels have 17. When all the six books are consolidated, 956 pairs of such compounds are found. The results are useful for comparing the distribution of words in different times and different styles of text. For example, the pre-Qin classics prefer the word "氏姓 [*shìxìng*] (*surname*)", while the Ming-Qing novels prefer to use "姓氏 [*xìngshì*] (*surname*)". The two sets of text have 9 pairs of disyllabic morpheme-inverted compounds in common, such as "甲兵 [*jiǎbīng*] (*weapon; soldier; war*) — 兵甲 [*bīngjiǎ*] (*weapon; soldier*)". The findings are helpful for investigating the evolution of these words.

For example, the word "甲兵 [*jiǎbīng*]" has several senses, but the sense of "war" is found only in *The Commentary of Zuo* but not in the Ming-Qing novels or the two dictionaries published in modern times [7-8]. This phenomenon reflects the semantic narrowing of the word.

甲兵 [*jiǎbīng*]

Examples in the pre-Qin classics:
(1) *The Commentary of Zuo*: 繕/甲兵 [*shàn/jiǎbīng*]
(*repair the armor and weaponry*)
(2) *Discourses of the States*: 簡服/吳國/之/士/于/甲兵
[*jiǎnfú/wúguó/zhī/shì/yú/jiǎbīng*] (*train the young people of the State of Wu to become soldiers*)
(3) *The Commentary of Zuo*: 甲兵/之/事, /未/之/聞/也
[*jiǎbīng/zhī/shì, /wèi/zhī/wén/yě*] (*never heard about war*)

Examples in the Ming-Qing novel *Romance of the Three Kingdoms*:
(1) 甲兵/不/完 [*jiǎbīng/bù/wán*] (*poor weapons*)
(2) 領/五十/甲兵 [*lǐng/wǔshi/jiǎbīng*] (*take fifty soldiers*)

Table 2 shows the number of all disyllabic morpheme-inverted compound occurrences in the Diachronic Corpora, which means that the compound as a lexical unit is counted every time when it appears. The method of consolidation and intersection in this table is the same as that in Table 1. The data of "C/A (%)" and C/B (%) indicate that compared to the pre-Qin classics, the frequency of disyllabic morpheme-inverted compounds in the Ming-Qing novels is much higher. A main reason is that monosyllabic words are dominant in the pre-Qin classics, accounting for more than 85% of the segmentation units in the Diachronic Corpora in terms of frequency.

Table 2. Distribution of disyllabic morpheme-inverted compounds (frequency)

		Pre-Qin classics		Ming-Qing novels			
		1	2	3	4	5	6
A: Segmentation units in the Diachronic Corpora		130,678	54,025	318,780	486,204	411,174	494,194
B: Disyllabic units in the Diachronic Corpora		11,729	5,725	52,223	111,043	90,553	112,611
C: Disyllabic morpheme-inverted compounds		200	109	2,570	8,212	4,337	5,432
C/A (%)		0.15%	0.20%	0.81%	1.69%	1.05%	1.10%
C/B (%)		1.71%	1.90%	4.92%	7.40%	4.79%	4.82%
C	Consolidation of the text in the same style	459					28,461
	Intersection of the text in the same style	128					6,094
	Consolidation of all						31,414
	Intersection of the two styles						2,632
Pre-Qin classics: 1: The Commentary of Zuo 2: Discourses of the States							
Ming-Qing novels: 3: Romance of the Three Kingdoms 4: Water Margin							
5: The Golden Lotus 6: A Dream of Red Mansions							

Within a pair of disyllabic morpheme-inverted compounds, even when the two are synonyms, the occurrence frequency for each member is usually different. The ratio of frequency indicates the preference of word. When the pre-Qin classics are consolidated, the three morpheme-inverted compound pairs with the highest frequency ratio are "子弟 [zǐdì] (*son and younger brother; young generations...*)/20² — 弟子 [dìzǐ] (*disciple; pupil*)/1", "民人 [mínrén] (*people*)/21 —人民 [rénmín] (*people*)/2", and "甥舅 [shēngjiù] (*nephew and uncle*)/10 — 舅甥 [jiùshēng] (*uncle and nephew*)/1". The 2nd and 3rd pairs are synonyms, and the data of occurrence frequency indicate that the pre-Qin classics prefer "民人" and "甥舅". When the four Ming-Qing novels are consolidated in the same way, the top three pairs are "吩咐 [fēnfù] (*order, instruct...*)/765 — 咐吩 [fùfēn] (*order, instruct...*)/1", "背後 [bèihòu] (*behind*)/468 — 後背 [hòubèi] (*back*)/1", and "方纔 [fāngcái] (*just now*)/227 — 纔方 [cáifāng] (*just now*)/1". The 1st and 3rd pairs are synonyms, and the data indicate that the novels obviously prefer "吩咐" and "方纔", indicating that the language is evolving towards modern Chinese.

5   Comparative Study of the Disyllabic Morpheme-Inverted Compounds in the Two Genres

In this section, data from the two pre-Qin classics and the four Ming-Qing novels are consolidated for a comparative study of the disyllabic morpheme-inverted compounds from the perspective of semantics based on statistics and typical examples. The findings are expected to help investigations on the evolution of the words. Based on the use of such compounds in the two genres, they are classified into the following categories.

5.1   Used in Both Pre-Qin Classics and Ming-Qing Novels

Due to the great difference of the two genres, the pre-Qin classics and Ming-Qing novels have only 9 pairs of disyllabic morpheme-inverted compounds in common. The word frequency of the pair of morpheme-inverted synonyms listed in Table 3 reflects their development and the tendency towards stability. That is, "長短" is more frequently used in the Ming-Qing novels which are closer to modern Chinese.

Table 3. Examples of words used in both the pre-Qin classics and Ming-Qing novels

Word pair	Word frequency	
	Classics	Novels
短長 [duǎncháng] (*short and long; weak and strong points...*)	1	1
長短 [chángduǎn] (*long and short; strong and weak points...*)	1	26

---

² It occurs 20 times in the Diachronic Corpora.

5.2 Used in Pre-Qin Classics Only

There are 29 pairs of disyllabic morpheme-inverted compounds which are used in the pre-Qin classics but not used in the Ming-Qing novels. It should be noted that some words are used in modern Chinese even though they do not appear in the four Ming-Qing novels. The frequency of the following pairs of morpheme-inverted synonyms reflects the preference of word in the pre-Qin classics.

惠慈 [*huìcí*]/1 —— 慈惠 [*cíhuì*]/3 (*benevolent*)

侈驕 [*chǐjiāo*]/1 —— 驕侈 [*jiāochǐ*]/2 (*arrogant and willful*)

5.3 Used in Ming-Qing Novels Only

There are 735 pairs of disyllabic morpheme-inverted compounds which are only used in the Ming-Qing novels. The frequency of the following pairs of morpheme-inverted synonyms indicates that the language of the Ming-Qing novels is evolving towards modern Chinese.

據占 [*jùzhàn*]/1 —— 占據 [*zhànjù*]/18 (*occupy*)

鬧熱 [*nàorè*]/4 —— 熱鬧 [*rènao*]/124 (*lively, boisterous, jolly...*)

5.4 A in Pre-Qin Classics and B in Ming-Qing Novels

There are 76 pairs of such disyllabic morpheme-inverted compounds, and they can be further classified into the following categories based on meaning.

- Lexical meanings of A and B are identical or similar. The analysis on this category of word pairs is helpful for investigating the evolution tendency of the words. Many words in the Ming-Qing novels are the same as modern Chinese. In the pairs of morpheme-inverted synonyms listed in Table 4, the latter ones used in the Ming-Qing novels are commonly used in modern Chinese.

Table 4. Examples of A and B with the same lexical meaning

Word in Pre-Qin classics (A)	Word in Ming-Qing novels (B)	Lexical meaning
禍災 [*huòzāi*]	災禍 [*zāihuò*]	disaster
寶財 [*bǎocái*]	財寶 [*cáibǎo*]	treasure

- The meaning of A is different from that of B, as the following example shows.

弄戲 [*nòngxì*] — 戲弄 [*xìnòng*]

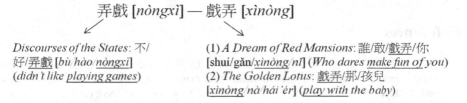

Discourses of the States: 不/好/弄戲 [*bù hào nòngxì*] (*didn't like playing games*)

(1) *A Dream of Red Mansions*: 誰/敢/戲弄/你 [*shuí/gǎn/xìnòng/nǐ*] (*Who dares make fun of you*)
(2) *The Golden Lotus*: 戲弄/那/孩兒 [*xìnòng/nà/hái 'ér*] (*play with the baby*)

- The meaning of A comes directly from that of the constituent morphemes according to the internal structure of A, while the meaning of B is derived indirectly from that of the morphemes. For example:

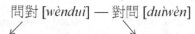

The Commentary of Zuo: 雪霜/風雨/之/不時
[*xuěshuāng/fēngyǔ/zhī/bùshí*] (*the unseasonable occurrence of snow, frost, wind, or rain*)

Romance of the Three Kingdoms: 志/懷/霜雪
[*zhì/huái/shuāngxuě*] (*his ambition is unsullied*)

- The lexical meaning of A is close to that of B, but the two compounds have different pragmatic implications. For example:

問對 [*wènduì*] — 對問 [*duìwèn*]

The Commentary of Zuo: 齊侯/問對/於/晏桓
子 [*qíhóu/wènduì/yú/yànhuánzi*] (*the Marquis of Qi asked Yan Huanzi*)

Water Margin: 拿/宋江/來/對問
[*ná/sòngjiāng/lái/duìwèn*] (*bring Song Jiang here for interrogation*)

6   Conclusion

This is a study on disyllabic morpheme-inverted compounds in the Chinese diachronic corpora from the perspective of natural language processing, based on statistics and a wide range of observations. The diachronic corpora contain two pre-Qin classics and four Ming-Qing novels, in which words are segmented, proper nouns are tagged, but POS tags are not added. The results show that there are many more morpheme-inverted compounds in the Ming-Qing novels than in the pre-Qin classics, in terms of lexical item (same compound counted only once) and frequency. Possible explanations for the contrast include the difference in genres, the diversity in language/dialect background, and the high frequency of monosyllabic words in the pre-Qin classics. This paper further compares the use of the disyllabic morpheme-inverted compounds in the two genres, which is helpful for investigating the preference of word as well as the evolution of the words throughout the history. In the future, it is planned to add POS tags to the corpora so that the study can be carried out from the perspective of word class and grammatical function. It is also planned to build the knowledge base of Chinese character variants, interchangeable characters, and ancient/modern character variations to make the data more complete.

Acknowledgments. This work is partially supported by the Chiang Ching-kuo Foundation for International Scholarly Exchange under the project "Building a Diachronic Language Knowledge-base" (RG013-D-09).

References

1. Xiong, D., Lu, Q., Lo, F., Shi, D., Chiu, T.-s., Li, W.: Specification for segmentation and named entity annotation of chinese classics in the ming and qing dynasties. In: Ji, D., Xiao, G. (eds.) CLSW 2012. LNCS, vol. 7717, pp. 280–293. Springer, Heidelberg (2013)

2. Jiang, L.L.: General Review on Flip-flop Disyllable Words in Ancient Chinese. Journal of Jiangnan University (Human & Social Sciences) **8**(3), 108–112 (2009). (in Chinese)

3. Yang, F.: Literature Review of Researches on Morpheme-Inverted Words. Science and Technology Innovation Herald (6), 10－11 (2010). (楊芬:同素異序詞研究現狀綜述.科技創新導報) (in Chinese)

4. Zhang, W.: Research on the Evolution of Inverse Morphemes Words in Mid-Classical Chinese. Doctoral dissertation of Fudan University (2005). (張巍:中古漢語同素逆序詞演變研究.復旦大學博士學位論文) (in Chinese)

5. Ai, F.M.: Defining Morpheme-Inverted Words. Journal of Language and Literature Studies (24), 118－126 (2008). (艾鳳美:關於同素異序詞的界定.語文學刊) (in Chinese)

6. Editorial Board of the Great Dictionary of Chinese Characters: The Great Dictionary of Chinese Characters. Hubei Lexicographical Publishing House, Wuhan, Sichuan Lexicographical Publishing House, Chengdu (1986－1990). (漢語大字典編輯委員會:漢語大字典.湖北辭書出版社,武漢,四川辭書出版社,成都) (in Chinese)

7. Guangdong, Guangxi, Hunan, Henan Etymological Dictionary Revision Group: Etymological Dictionary (Revised Edition). The Commercial Press, Beijing (1998). (廣東、廣西、湖南、河南辭源修訂組:辭源修訂本.商務印書館,北京) (in Chinese)

8. Department of Dictionary, Research Institutes of Language, Chinese Academy of Social Sciences: Contemporary Chinese Dictionary, 6th edn. The Commercial Press, Beijing (2012). (中國社會科學院語言研究所詞典編輯室:現代漢語詞典第6版.商務印書館,北京) (in Chinese)

9. Yang, B.J., Xu, T.: Dictionary of the Commentary of Zuo. Zhonghua Book Company, Beijing (1985). (楊伯峻,徐提·春秋左傳詞典 中華書局, 北京) (in Chinese)

10. Chen, C.S.: A Study of the Vocabulary in Discourses of the States. Doctoral dissertation of Shandong University (2005). (陳長書:《國語》詞彙研究.山東大學博士學位論文) (in Chinese)

11. Shen, B.J., Tan, L.X.: Dictionary of Romance of the Three Kingdoms. Zhonghua Book Company, Beijing (2007). (沈伯俊,譚良嘯:三國演義大辭典.中華書局, 北京) (in Chinese)

12. Li, F.B., Liu, J.F.: Dictionary of Water Margin. Shanghai Lexicographical Publishing House, Shanghai (1989). (李法白,劉鏡芙:水滸語詞詞典.上海辭書出版社, 上海) (in Chinese)

13. Bai, W.G.: Dictionary of the Golden Lotus. Zhonghua Book Company, Beijing (1991). (白維國:金瓶梅詞典.中華書局, 北京) (in Chinese)

14. Zhou, R.C.: Dictionary of A Dream of Red Mansions. Guangdong People's Press, Guangzhou (1987). (周汝昌:紅樓夢辭典.廣東人民出版社, 廣州) (in Chinese)

15. Yu, S.W., Duan, H.M., Zhu, X.F., Swen, B., Chang, B.B.: Specification for Corpus Processing at Peking University: Word Segmentation, POS Tagging and Phonetic Notation. Journal of Chinese Language and Computing **13**(2), 121–158 (2003). (in Chinese)

16. Segmentation Principle for Chinese Language Processing (CNS14366). National Bureau of Standard, Taiwan (1999). (中文資訊處理分詞規範.臺灣經濟部中央標準局印行) (in Chinese)

17. Liu, Y., Tan, Q., Shen, X.K.: Segmentation standard for modern chinese information processing (GB13715). In: Segmentation Standard for Modern Chinese Information Processing and Automatic Segmentation Methodology. Qinghua University Press, Beijing (1994). (劉源,譚強,沈旭昆:中國國家標準GB13715 信息處理用現代漢語分詞規範.信息處理用現代漢語分詞規範及自動分詞方法,清華大學出版社,北京) (in Chinese)

A Preliminary Contrastive Study on the Part-of-Speech Classifications of Two Lexicons

Likun Qiu[1]([✉]), Hongying Zan[2], Xuefeng Zhu[3], and Shiwen Yu[3,4]

[1] School of Chinese Language and Literature, Ludong University, Yantai, China
qiulikun@pku.edu.cn
[2] School of Information Engineering, Zhengzhou University, Zhengzhou, China
iehyzan@zzu.edu.cn
[3] Key Laboratory of Computational Linguistics(Peking University),
Ministry of Education, Beijing, China
yusw@pku.edu.cn
[4] Collaborative Innovation Center for Language Ability, Xuzhou, China

Abstract. Having been debated and studied for more than one century, the part-of-speech classifications of contemporary Chinese words is still attracting considerable attention from many linguists today. In this study, we aim to compare the classification systems of two lexicons C *Dictionary of Contemporary Chinese (Fifth Edition)* and *Grammatical Knowledge-Base of Contemporary Chinese*, and to observe the similarities and differences between their part-of-speech classifications of words in a comprehensive way. This paper discusses our preliminary observations, especially on the comparison of prepositions in the two lexicons. We expect that this type of contrastive studies will contribute to a deeper understanding of the parts-of-speech in Chinese, especially to the part-of-speech classification of certain Chinese words, which has long been debated.

Keywords: Part-of-speech classification · Dictionary of Contemporary Chinese · Grammatical Knowledge-Base of Contemporary Chinese · Contrastive study

1 Introduction

With the advent of the Big Data Age, Chinese information processing has been developed into the semantic level. From the perspective of computer processing, there are no essential differences between semantical analysis and grammatical analysis, both of which represent lexical knowledge of syntagmatic and paradigmatic relations. Semantical knowledge can be taken as the refinement of the grammatical knowledge used for grammatical analysis. For instance, the part-of-speech "noun", which is a syntagmatic category at the grammatical level, can be classified into a set of semantic categories, including human, animal, plant,

© Springer International Publishing Switzerland 2015
Q. Lu and H.H. Gao (Eds.): CLSW 2015, LNAI 9332, pp. 516–523, 2015.
DOI: 10.1007/978-3-319-27194-1_52

mineral, appliance, information and regulation; the syntactic constituents "subject" and "object" can be grouped into a set of semantic roles such as agent, patient, experiencer and result.

Lexical knowledge is the most fundamental and most widely used language knowledge. Research and debates on Chinese parts-of-speech have continued for more than 100 years, and remain as one of the focuses in linguistics[1, 2]. This paper compares two large-scale Chinese lexicons, *Grammatical Knowledge-Base for Contemporary Chinese* (GKB) and *Dictionary of Contemporary Chinese (Fifth Edition)* (DCC), and summarizes the achievements of studies on Chinese parts-of-speech.

GKB is an electronic dictionary designed for Chinese information processing. We have introduced the content and design principles in the two versions of *An Introduction to The Grammatical Knowledge-Base of Contemporary Chinese*[3] (*Introduction*) published in 1998 and 2003, respectively, with 10,000 words as examples. One of the major contributions of GKB is to classify each word in it into proper parts-of-speech. As for classification principles and classification results, we refer to the second edition of this book (*Introduction*) and the latest version of GKB, respectively.

DCC is the most influential contemporary Chinese lexicon. The fifth edition of DCC[4] was published in 2005. As pointed out in *Introduction to The Part-of-speech Annotation of the Fifth Edition of DCC*, one of the most important aspects of this edition is to attach parts-of-speech to each word, which has been expected by readers for many years and is also a new demand of the information age on Chinese lexicons. The sixth edition of DCC was published in 2012 and only a small number of words were modified in terms of part-of-speech annotation. Thus, we use the classification results of the fifth edition of DCC, and also refer to the paper of Xu and Tan (2006)[5] for classification principles of DCC. We haven't compared the fifth and sixth editions systematically, although we will mention the differences between the two editions in passing.

In this paper, *part-of-speech classification* denotes the work of classifying each word in a dictionary into one or several parts-of-speech based on the grammatical functions of the word. It is quite different from the work of *part-of-speech tagging*, which is popular in Chinese information processing and denotes the work of tagging each word in a sentence with one part-of-speech according to the context. We compare the classification results of tens of thousands of words in GKB and DCC. Since their design objectives, structures and sense granularities are remarkably different, it is difficult to compare them adequately, and thus we only introduce our overall scheme and take the contrastive study on prepositions as a case study.

2   Classification Principles and Results of GKB

We summarize the major principles and contributions of GKB on part-of-speech classification as follows.

First, the grammatical functions of a word indicate whether a word can form valid syntactic structures with other words. In the phrase-standard grammatical

Table 1. The part-of-speech system of GKB.

basic category	content word	nominal	1	noun	n
			2	temporal word	t
			3	location word	s
			4	directional word	f
			5	numeral	m
			6	measure word	q
			7	pronoun (nominal)	r
		predicate		pronoun (predicate)	r
			8	verb	v
			9	adjective	a
			10	descriptive word	z
		others	11	attributive word	b
			12	adverb	d
	function word		13	preposition	p
			14	conjunction	c
			15	auxiliary word	u
			16	modal particle	y
	others		17	onomatopoetic word	o
			18	interjection	e
additional category	below words		19	left additional element	h
			20	right additional element	k
			21	morpheme	g
			22	noe-morpheme character	x
	above words		23	idiom	i
			24	idiomatic phrase	l
			25	abbreviation	j
			26	punctuation	w

system, Mr. Dexi Zhu claimed that there are no one-to-one corresponding relations between Chinese parts-of-speech (e.g., verbs, adjectives and nouns) and syntactic constituents (e.g., subject, object, attribute). Following this principle, words are grouped into grammatical categories (parts-of-speech) according to their dominant grammatical functions.

Second, to meet the need of processing large-scale real Chinese text, a part-of-speech system for contemporary Chinese is designed, as shown in Table 1. The judgment standards of most categories in this system are based on their dominant grammatical functions, except for several parts-of-speech including numeral, the meaning of which is simple and definite. The basic categories in this system mainly follow the system of Mr. Dexi Zhu [6] with minor adjustment. The additional categories in this system are not parts-of-speech and used to annotate the categories of other types of linguistic units such as morpheme, abbreviation and idiom. The judgment of these additional categories is not according to grammatical functions. Further, each additional category is classified into

Table 2. The part-of-speech system of DCC.

word	content word	nominal	1	noun (subcategories: temporal word, directional word)
			4	numeral
			5	measure word
			6	pronoun (nominal)
		predicate	2	verb (subcategories: auxiliary verb, directional verb)
			3	adjective (subcategories: attributive word, descriptive word)
		others	12	onomatopoetic word
	function word		7	adverb
			8	preposition
			9	conjunction
			10	auxiliary word
			11	interjection
			12	onomatopoetic word
non-word				single-character entry (morpheme and non-morpheme character) multi-character entry (phrase, idiom and idiomatic phrase)

several subcategories based on their grammatical functions. The construction of this system is one of the milestones of GKB.

Third, more than 80,000 Chinese words are classified into proper parts-of-speech. Each word is classified into one or more parts-of-speech. This work is the basis of the overall GKB project. Yu et al. (2003)[3] describe the judgment standards for each part-of-speech, taking 10,000 words for example. In the classification process, the issues of homographic words and multi-category words are also discussed.

Finally, grammatical functions of each word are described in detail. For instance, each noun and each verb are described with more than twenty attributes and one hundred attributes, respectively. This type of descriptions form the main body of GKB.

3   Classification Principles and Results of DCC

There is a short introduction at the beginning of DCC, which describes the major principles used in the compiling process. A subsection of this introduction discusses the issue of part-of-speech classification and thus is very simple. In addition, DCC includes some linguistic terms such as "词(word)", "词类(part-of-speech)", "实词(content word)", "体词(nominal)", "谓词(predicate)", "名词(noun)" and "动词(verb)". The paraphrases of these terms supplement the descriptions of DCC on the issues of part-of-speech classification. Moreover, Xu and Tan (2006)[5] introduce the part-of-speech classification system, principles, difficulties and corresponding solutions for annotating parts-of-speech for DCC. From these discussions, we may summarize the part-of-speech classification principles and judgment standards in DCC as follows.

First, "词类(part-of-speech)" and "名词(noun)" are interpreted as "classification of word at the grammatical level" and "words that denote human beings or objects", respectively. It seems that words are classified according to their grammatical meanings. However, Xu and Tan (2006)[5] give more definite descriptions, saying that grammatical meanings are the internal basis for part-of-speech classification while grammatical functions are external representations of grammatical meanings. Thus, both grammatical meanings and functions are involved in the classification process of DCC, and in most cases grammatical functions are used as the major standards.

Second, the part-of-speech system of DCC is shown in Table 2. Since DCC has not illustrated its classification system explicitly, this system is summarized from [4] and [5].

Third, both words and morphemes are included in DCC, while only words are classified at the grammatical level. Homographic words are takens as different entries and then classified into different parts-of-speech, respectively. In addition, the different meanings of a word are also classified, respectively.

4   Overall Comparison Between GKB and DCC

From Table 1 and 2, we may find that the systems of GKB and DCC are very similar. Both of them contain four levels of categories. First, "词(word)" and "语(morpheme and phrase)" are distinguished from each other. In GKB, *basic category* and *additional category* are used to indicate them, respectively, while in DCC, *word* and *non-word* are used.

Second, in GKB and DCC, words are classified into content word and function word. They differ in that onomatopoetic word and interjection are considered as categories besides content word and function word in GKB, while onomatopoetic word is classified into content word and function word simultaneously, and interjection is taken as function word in DCC.

Third, content word contains nominal, predicate, attributive word and adverb in GKB, while contains nominal, predicate and onomatopoetic word in DCC. They differ in that adverb is classified into content word in GKB and function word in DCC. In the system of Mr. Dexi Zhu, adverb is also a type of function words, because he believe that content word should have the function of acting as subject, object or predicate. In the system of GKB, if a word can act as one of the basic grammatical constituents such as subject, object, predicate, attributive, adverbial and complement, it would be taken as a content word. Thus, attributive word and adverb are classified into content word, because they can act as attributive and adverbial, respectively.

Finally, the core parts of the two systems are the fourth levels. At this level, GKB contains 18 parts-of-speech, while DCC contains only 12 categories.

The system of GKB contains more categories, because it is used for computer processing while DCC is mainly used by humans. However, some categories have been annotated explicitly as subcategories in DCC. Specifically, noun contains two subcategories *temporal word* and *directional word*, and adjective contains two subcategories *attributive word* and *descriptive word*. Each subcategory can be mapped into a corresponding category in GKB. In addition, some auxiliary words in DCC (e.g. "啊(a)", "吧(ba)", "呢(ne)") are modal particles, and the definitions of these words contain the word "语气(mood)". So, we can pick out all modal particles from DCC easily. Thus, 17 of the 18 parts-of-speech in GKB have a corresponding part-of-speech in DCC. The only exception is the location word. In addition, verb also contains two subcategories *auxiliary verb* and *directional verb* in DCC. However, there are no corresponding parts-of-speech in GKB. Instead, GKB contains two properties "auxiliary verb" and "directional verb" in the verb bank to indicate whether a verb belongs to these subcategories.

To sum up, there are no essential differences between GKB and DCC on the classification principles and systems. The two classification systems, part-of-speech tags at all levels and their connotations are basically the same. They mainly differ in that GKB uses the dominant grammatical functions of words as judgment standards for part-of-speech classification, while DCC considers grammatical meaning and functions simultaneously.

5   Contrastive Study on Prepositions – A Case Study

The comparison between the part-of-speech classifications of GKB and DCC is a big project. Due to space limitation, we only take the comparison on prepositions as a case study.

5.1   Overall Comparison Based on Statistics

For overall comparison, we should solve the problem of word identification[6]. In other words, we need to judge whether an entry in DCC corresponds to the same entry in GKB when the two entries share the same characters.

For prepositions, DCC and GKB contains 105 and 114 words, respectively. 79 of these prepositions are shared by the two lexicons. In particular, "把(ba)", "除了(except)", "冲(towards)" and "为(for)" contain 8, 3, 2 and 2 meanings in DCC, respectively. In contrast, both "把(ba)" and "除了(except)" only contain one meaning, and "冲(towards)" and "为(for)" contain two meanings in GKB. Thus, both "把(ba)" and "除了(except)" are regarded as only one prepositional entry, and both "冲(towards)" and "为(for)" are regarded as two prepositional entries in DCC and GKB.

26 prepositions in DCC are not included in GKB. 21 of them are not included in GKB because they are only used in written or spoken Chinese. The remaining 5 words have been included in GKB, yet not considered as prepositions.

35 prepositions in GKB are not included in DCC. 16 of them are regarded as phrases yet DCC mainly includes words. The remaining 19 words are already in DCC, but their parts-of-speech are not prepositions.

5.2   Specific Difference Analysis

The rest 5 prepositions in DCC are "除开(except)", "除去(except)", "除却(except)", "讲(as for)" and "连(even)". The first four words are annotated as verbs, and the last word is taken as an auxiliary word in GKB. The differentiation between prepositions and verbs is an open issue in Chinese linguistics, because the boundary between the two parts-of-speech is not very clear. We will not discuss this problem in detail. The last preposition "连(even)" is usually used as a focus marker. For instance, in the sentence "连(even) 爷爷(grandfather) 都(also) 笑(smiled) 了(le) (The grandfather smiled too)", "连(even)" is a focus marker. If the marker is removed from the sentence, it is still a grammatical sentence and its meaning remains unchanged. This is just one of the main characteristics of Chinese auxiliary words. In most cases, prepositions can not be omitted. That's why GKB takes "连(even)" as an auxiliary word rather than a preposition.

Similarly, 18 of the rest 19 prepositions in GKB are taken as verbs in DCC. Only the preposition "连同(with)" in GKB are taken as a conjunction in DCC. An example sentence given by DCC is "货物(goods) 连同(with) 清单(inventory) 一并(together) 送去(deliver) (Goods should be delivered together with inventories)". Generally, the left and right words of a conjunction usually can swap positions while the two constituents besides a preposition cannot. In addition, an additional modifier can be placed before a preposition. In this sentence, the two constituents on each side of the word "连同(with)" cannot swap positions, and we can place an adverb "必须(necessarily)" before "连同(with)". Thus, it is taken as a preposition in GKB.

6   Conclusions

We compared the part-of-speech classifications of two large-scale Chinese lexicons. This work might contribute to in-depth studies on some controversial issues in Chinese part-of-speech classification. Obviously, an overall comparison is a big project. The two lexicons share many identical classification results, which cover most words in the two lexicons. Based on this discovery, researchers can pay more attention to other controversial issues. This goal can be achieved by analyzing the words annotated with different parts-of-speech in the two lexicons one by one, and then classifying them into several groups. Thus, we may make a breakthrough on the issues of Chinese parts-of-speech.

Acknowledgments. We thank the anonymous reviewers for their constructive comments, and gratefully acknowledge the support of the National Basic Research Program of China (No. 2014CB340504), National Science Foundation of China (No. 61272221, No. 61170163), National Social Science Foundation of China (No.14BYY096) and Scientific Research Foundation of Shandong Province Outstanding Young Scientist Award (No. BS2013DX020).

References

1. Lu, J.: More discussions on issues of chinese parts-of-speech. In: Proceedings of Senior Forum of Language Science and Technology, pp. 13–32. World Publishing Corporation, Beijing (2014). (in Chinese)
2. Shen, J.: I Only Have Taken a Half Step Forward — More Discussions on Chinese Nouns and Verbs. Essays on Linguistics **40**, 3–22 (2009). (in Chinese)
3. Yu, S., et al.: An Introduction to The Grammatical Knowledgse-Base of Contemporary Chinese, 2nd edn. Tsinghua University Press, Beijing (2003). (in Chinese)
4. Dictionary Editorial Office, Institute of Linguistics, Chineses Academy of Social Science: Dictionary of Contemporary Chinese, 5th edn. Commercial Press, Beijing (2005). (in Chinese)
5. Xu, S., Tan, J.: Introduction to The Part-of-speech Annotation of the Fifth Edition of Dictionary of Contemporary Chinese. Chinese Language **1**, 74–86 (2006). (in Chinese)
6. Zhu, D.: Grammar finder and questions and answers on grammar. In: the First Volume of Selected Works of Dexi Zhu (1999). (in Chinese)

Analysis of Typical Annotation Problems in Bilingual Case Grammar Treebank Construction

Hongying Zan[✉], Wanli Chen[✉], Kunli Zhang[✉], and Yuxiang Jia[✉]

School of Information Engineering, Zhengzhou University, Zhengzhou 450001, China
{iehyzan,ieklzhang,ieyxjia}@zzu.edu.cn, wanli2013nlp@foxmail.com

Abstract. In recent years, the study of machine translation has made great progress. However there are still many things to do for machine translation to reach the semantic level. In this paper, case grammar's features that could well describe the semantic relationships in sentences were concluded. 23 thousand annotation errors that occurred in treebank construction were analyzed. 13 typical problems were summarized and the corresponding revolutions were proposed. The application of case grammar may contribute a new way of thinking for machine translation.

Keywords: Machine translation · Case grammar · Bilingual treebank · Semantic relation · Annotation analysis

1   Introduction

Although machine translation has been moving upward constantly along the machine translation pyramid and made significant progress in the past 20 years, it hasn't approached the level of semantics yet. It is the target of machine translation that the source language and the target language should have the same semantic meaning. How to implement the statistical modeling for semantic analysis, transformation, and generation, and how to obtain the semantic knowledge of translation from large-scale data have been the key for machine translation to approach its target [1].

Case grammar is a kind of syntactic theory and semantic theory which was put forward by American linguist Fillmore in the mid-1960s to discuss the relations between syntactic structures and semantics [2,3]. Case grammar focuses on the relations between structures and semantics and emphasizes the particularity of different languages' surface structures and the universality of deep structures. Case, which is the deep semantic case of sentences, is a universal phenomenon in all languages and can support machine translation in the semantic level very well. Detailed case relation description can greatly improve the performance of machine translation systems [4].

Although case grammar can well support machine translation, one available bilingual case grammar treebank is needed. Therefore we together with Harbin institute of technology developed bilingual case grammar treebank for machine translation and attempted to provide a new thinking for the machine translation research. This paper

© Springer International Publishing Switzerland 2015
Q. Lu and H.H. Gao (Eds.): CLSW 2015, LNAI 9332, pp. 524–534, 2015.
DOI: 10.1007/978-3-319-27194-1_53

mainly introduced the basic theory of case grammar, summarized typical annotation problems while constructing the treebank, and proposed corresponding solutions.

2   Related Works

The development of machine translation has experienced a tortuous process. In 1954 Georgetown University carried out a machine translation experiment on an IBM computer for the first time by adopting the method of dictionary and word frequency statistics. From 1970s to 1980s, translation methods based on rules developed and prospered step by step. ARIANE translation system in France and TAU-METEO translation system in Canada, which was in view of weather forecast information service, were the typical representatives [5]. Since 1980 corpus techniques and statistical learning methods have promoted the development of translation methods based on corpus and statistics. In 1984 a famous Japanese scholar Makoto Nagao proposed an example-based machine translation method [6]. In 1990 IBM researchers proposed translation method based on noise channel model and developed 5 word-based translation methods in succession [7]. Around the year of 2000, a large number of scholars, including Wang, Zens, Koehn et al., proposed and improved phrase-based statistical translation models [8,9,10]. This method matured gradually and became the mainstream of statistical machine translation, widely used by Google, Microsoft, Baidu and other companies. In 2007 Jiang Wei(2005) proposed a hierarchical phrase-based translation model [11]. The method used rules to describe the nesting relationship between phrases on the base of the phrase-based method and improved the characterization ability of translation model greatly. Liu Yang(2006) proposed a translation model based on tree-to-string alignment templates [12]. The method analyzed syntactic structures of the source language, generated the target language word sequence based on syntactic structures, and achieved good practical effects. Between 2009 and 2011, some scholars from Carnegie Mellon University, Rochester University and the Hong Kong University of Science and Technology attempted to introduce semantics into statistical machine translation [13,14,15]. But the semantic role labeling and latent semantic analysis they used were still in shallow semantic levels, and couldn't take advantage of deep semantic knowledge to guide the translation process [1].

Bilingual corpora are important resources of statistical machine translation [16]. American Language Resource Alliance has collected a lot of large-scale bilingual corpora. News of Xinhua News Agency, proceedings of Hong Kong Legislative Council and laws of Hong Kong are Chinese-English bilingual corpora that is widely used internationally. Institute of Computational Linguistics of Peking University developed a Chinese-English bilingual corpus called Babel, which served for machine translation in the news field [17]. Institute of Computing Technology and Institute of Automation of Chinese Academy of Science together developed a bilingual corpus with the amount of 200,000 aligned sentences. Harbin Institute of Technology developed a bilingual corpus with the amount of 100,000 aligned sentences. HIT-Microsoft Machine Translation Joint Lab developed a bilingual corpus with the amount of 60,000 word-aligned sentences [18].

3   Case Grammar Theory

The case of case grammar represents the deep semantic relationship. Exactly it is the semantic relationship between the nominal(noun or pronoun) and predicate(verb or adjective). And it is a common phenomenon in all languages. The category of case depends on the semantic relation between the noun and verb in the underlying structure. What's more, semantic relations are changeless, which can't be affected by surface irritation such as conversion operations they have experienced, locations in the surface structure, grammatical relations with verbs and so on.

In case grammar theory, a sentence S consists of a modal M and a proposition P, which can be formed as following.

$$S \rightarrow M + P \tag{1}$$

The verb is the central word of a sentence. A proposition P consists of a verb V and other correlative cases C_i (i=1,2,3…).

$$P \rightarrow V + C1 + C2 + C3 + …+Cn \tag{2}$$

A case C consists of a case tag K and a noun phrase NP.

$$C \rightarrow K + NP \tag{3}$$

Case tag, which can be omitted, is a preposition that leads the noun phrase and defines the relation with the verb.

Case tags and semantic relations are closely linked. Fillmore suggested that 10 kinds of case tags be needed in propositions, including agentive, instrumental, dative, factitive, locative, objective, benefactive, accompaniment, destinative and source. Harbin Institute of Technology defined 54 kinds of case tags according to the need of describing semantic relations (Table 1).

4   Annotation Problems Analysis of Case Grammar

Proofreading work of annotation took the 54 kinds of case tags defined by HIT as the standard, and tried the best to maintain the consistency of the annotation in both English and Chinese on the basis of referencing text semantic relations. In the process of proofreading, about 230 thousand errors were discovered , 13 kinds of typical problems were summarized, which were analyzed as following one by one according to the type of problems.

Table 1. Table of HIT Case Grammar Treebank Tags

Category	Tag	Name	Category	Tag	Name
Headword	VACTN	Action Verb	Secondary Semantic Case	HSCOP	Scope of Head
	VCLAS	Classification Verb		DET	Determiner
	HEAD	Headword		POS	Possessive
Main Semantic Case	AG	Agent		UNT	Unit
	CA	Causer		QNT	Quantifier
	TH	Theme		APO	Apposition
	GO	Goal		REL	Relative Clause
	RA	Range		MOD	Modifier
	OBJT	Object	Modal Semantic Case	CMPR	Comparative
	BNFY	Beneficiary		MANR	Manner
	T_TIM	Time		DEGR	Degree
	S_LOC	Location		NEG	Negation
	T_SRC	Time Source		SCOP	Scope
	T_DST	Time Destination		XIMP	Imperative
	S_SRC	Location Source		QUES	Question
	S_DST	Location Destination	Semantic Structure Relation Case	PROP	Proposition
	INST	Instrument		QPROP	Question Proposition
	MEAN	Means		IMPROP	Imperative Proposition
	STND	Standard		RESN	Reason
	ACOM	Accompany		REST	Result
	S_DIR	Direction		COND	Condition
	S_PAS	Passage		INFR	Inferential
	S_AWAY	Away		PURP	Purpose
	T_DUR	Duration		CONC	Concession
	T_FRQ	Frequency		EXCP	Exception
	T_SEQ	Sequence		EXMP	Example
	LIST	Listing		CJHD	Conjunction Head

4.1   Headword

4.1.1   Nouns-Joint Headword

Combination that consists of more than one nouns should be annotated as two cases. They are nouns-joint headwords (HEAD + HEAD) and headword with modifier as the prefix(MOD + HEAD). In the original corpus, the second condition was often annotated as the first case mistakenly.

In order to describe the internal semantic relations in noun phrases in detail, the corpus should be annotated according to the word-aligned result. If the corresponding phrase of the noun phrase to be annotated in the other language consists of only one word, nouns of the phrase should be annotated as nouns-joint headword (HEAD + HEAD); if not, nouns of the phrase should be annotated as headword with modifier as the prefix (MOD + HEAD). For example, the phrase " 共 和 国 "[*gong he guo*](*republic*), whose corresponding translation is "republic", should be annotated as following: "((HEAD 共和)(HEAD 国))". The phrase "中国 公民[*zhong guo gong min*](*Chinese citizen*)", whose corresponding translation is "*Chinese citizen* ", should be annotated as "((MOD 中国) (HEAD 公民))".

4.1.2   Verbs-Joint Headword

Combination that consists of two verbs may lead to the result that two action verbs exists in the same layer of the syntax tree, which is not tolerated in case grammar. To solve this problem, the phrase should be annotated as two following forms: (VACTN (HEAD verb1)(HEAD verb2)) and ((VACTN verb1) (MANR verb2)). In the first case, the two verbs are the same in the view of semantics and none is dispensable. For example, the phrase "退耕 还林"[*tui geng huan lin*](*Returning farmland to forest*) should be annotated as "(VACTN (HEAD 退耕)(HEAD 还林))". In the second case, one verb is the implement of the other verb. For example, the phrase "增加 到"[*zeng jia dao*](*Increase to*) should be annotated as "((VACTN 增加) (MANR 到))".

Sometimes the word segment's size of verb phrases is too small. For example, the phrase "有 没 有" [*you mei you*] (*whether there exist or not*) should be annotated as following: (VACTN (HEAD 有) (HEAD 没) (HEAD 有)). Some other similar examples are "是 不 是" [*shi bu shi*] (*whether it is or not*) and "会 不 会" [*hui bu hui*] (*whether it could or not*).

According to above principles, we were able to annotate internal semantic relations in the verb phrases in detail on the premise of case grammar theory framework.

4.2   Main Semantic Case

In the main semantic case, the passive sentence pattern, pivotal construction, causer, goal, and beneficiary were easy to be annotated by mistake. The discussion and analysis would be showed as follows in detail.

4.2.1   Passive Sentence Pattern

The annotation of passive sentence pattern is easy to be interfered with by the surface structure and lead to the result that the agent and object are inversed. In this situation, the sentence should be annotated according to the semantic relations to point out the actual agent and object of the action verb. For example, "书 被 小马 借出 了"[*shu bei xiao ma jie chu le*](*the book was borrowed out by Xiaoma*) should be annotated as "(PROP (TH 书) (AG 小马) (VACTN 借出))". Similar with this is "分子 由 原子 组成"[*fen zi you yuan zi zu cheng*](*Molecules consists of atoms*).

4.2.2   Pivotal Construction

Sometimes there exists two verb phrases in one sentence, subject of which is not only the agent of the first verb phrase but also the object of the second verb phrase. The annotation in original corpus is always one-sided and could only reflect one of the semantic relations, or can't reflect any of the semantic relations. In order to take both of the semantic relations into account, the subject should be annotated unknown (UNK), and the detailed semantic relation should be judged by context,such as: whether the verb phrase has its agent/object or not.

Eg. 自愿 基金 由 人权 事务 中心 经管 , 并且 听取 董事会 的 建议 。
[*Zi yuan ji jin you ren quan shi wu zhong xin jing guan , bing ting qu dong shi hui de jian yi.*]
The voluntary fund is managed by the human rights center, and listen to the advice of the board of directors.

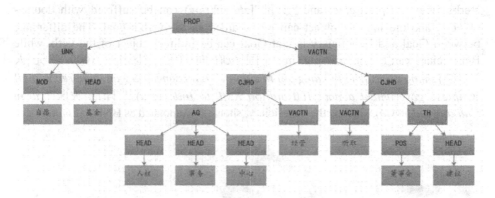

Fig. 1. Pivotal Construction

4.2.3   Discriminate of Causer and Goal

As the name implies, causer is the cause of one event and is always a subject clause or a description of one event. Predicate usually exists in a causer. Causer(CA) and goal(GO) are often difficult to distinguish in form. But CA focuses on natural cause and effect, and GO focuses on the subjective purpose. For example, in "违规 操作 设备 会 引发 火灾"[*wei gui cao zuo she bei hui yin fa huo zhai*] (*operating equipments irregularly may cause a fire*), "违规 操作 设备"[*wei gui cao zuo she bei*](*operating equipments irregularly*) should be annotated as CA.

It is important to note that CA and GO can exist in one sentence at the same time that expresses the meaning of "make sb to do sth" like "使"[*shi*],"令"[*ling*],"让"[*rang*].
Eg. 资产 价值 下跌 使 消费者 和 投资者 都 受到 影响。
[*zi chan jia zhi xia tie shi xiao fei zhe he tou zi zhe dou shou dao ying xiang*]
That the asset values fell made consumers and investors to be affected.

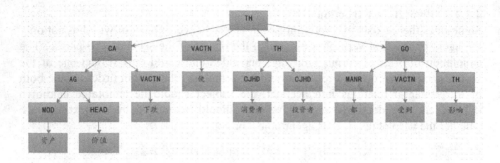

Fig. 2. Discriminate of Causer and Goal

4.2.4   Discriminate of Goal and Beneficiary

Verbs like "给"[*gei*](*give*) and "支付"[*zhi fu*](*pay*) can be suffixed with double-objects, and the indirect object can be regarded as the verb's goal. The difference between Goal and Beneficiary is that Goal can be indirect object of the verb, while Beneficiary can't. For example, in "中国 政府 向 印尼 灾区 捐赠1000 万 元 人民币" [*zhong guo zheng fu xiang yin ni zhai qu   juan zeng 100 wan yuan ren min bi*] (*Chinese government donate 100 million RMB to Indonesia*) ," 印尼 灾区"[*yin ni zhai qu*](*Indonesia*),which is the beneficiary, should be annotated as BNFY (Figure 4).

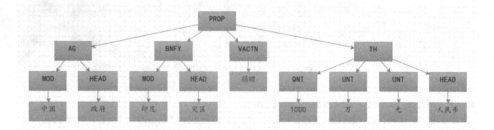

Fig. 3. Discriminate of Goal and Beneficiary

4.2.5   Combination of Range and Verb

Rang is the rang of classification and is usually combined with a classificatory verb(VCLAS). However, sometimes rang can be also combined with an action verb(VACTN) to represent the degree or amount. In original corpus, rang was often annotated as object by mistake.

Eg. 向 64000 名 索赔者 赔偿 的 总额 超出 去年 3.2亿 美元 。
[*xiang 64000 ming suo pei zhe pei chang de zong e chao chu qu nian 3.2 yi mei yuan*]
The amount payed to 64,000 claimants exceeds that of last year 320 million dollar.

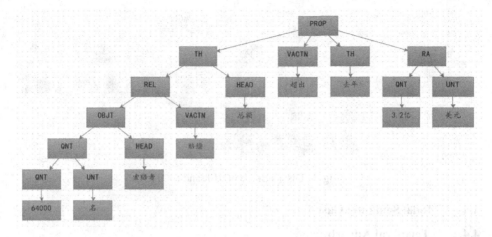

Fig. 4. Combination of Range and Verb

4.3   Secondary Semantic Case

4.3.1   Discriminate of POS and MOD

Two nouns combined by "的"[de](of) can be represented in two forms: ((POS nouns1)(HEAD nouns2)) and ((MOD nouns1)(HEAD nouns2)). If the nouns have obvious ownership relation, the phrase should be annotated as the first form; if not, the second form. For example, 〞荷兰 的 汉斯 先生〞[he lan de han si xian sheng] (*Mr. Hans of Holland*) should be annotated as the second form.

4.3.2   Discriminate of REL and MOD

In the view of semantics, the roles of MOD and REL are similar. They can both modify nouns. But MOD is usually used to annotate the phrase that consists of several simple words and REL is usually used to annotate a complex clause, which usually contains a verb.

Eg. 海平面 上升 对 经济 依赖 旅游业 的 岛屿 也 有 影响。

[*hai ping mian shang sheng dui jing ji yi lai lv you ye de dao yu ye you ying xiang*]

The rise of sea level also has effect on the island economy of which depends on tourism.

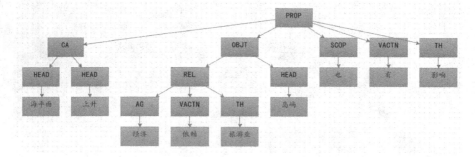

Fig. 5. Discriminate of REL and MOD

4.4   Modal Semantic Case

4.4.1   Temporal Adverb

The temporal adverbs like "已"[*yi*](*done*), "在"[*zai*](*doing*), "将"[*jiang*](*will*), "曾"[*zeng*](*did*) are reserved in Chinese case grammar, and the annotations are usually wrong in the original corpus. Since temporal adverbs are the implement of verb, they should be annotated as "MANR". For example, in "雷蒙·巴雷 曾 任 法国 总理"[*lei meng ba lei ceng ren fa guo zong li*](*Raymond Barre had been French prime minister*), "曾"[*ceng*](*had*) should be annotated as MANR.

4.4.2   Modal Verb Representing Possibility

Modal verbs like "可能"[*ke neng*](*may*),"也许"[*ye xu*](*may*),"应该"[*ying gai*](*should*) and "必须"[*bi xu*](*must*) are also reserved in Chinese case grammar. Since they described the degree of verbs, they should be annotated as "DEGR". For example, in "该 国 陷入 混乱 的 局面 也许 可以 避免"[*gai guo xian ru hun luan de ju mian ye xu ke yi bi mian*](*it might have been avoided that the nation fell into chaos*), "也许"[*ye xu*](*might*) should be annotated as DEGR.

4.5   Semantic Structure Relation Case

4.5.1   Usage of Example Case

The verb phrases prefixed with "比如"[*bi ru*](*for example*) or "包含"[*bao han*](*including*) are used to give examples for the front noun. In this situation the verb phrases should be annotated as "EXMP". For example, in "顾客 来自 各 海湾 国家 ， 包括 迪拜 科威特 沙特阿拉伯"[*gu ke lai zi ge hai wan guo jia, bao kuo di bai ke wei te sha te a la bo*](*Customers come from gulf states, including dubai, Kuwait, Saudi Arabia*), "包括 ... 沙特阿拉伯"[*bao kuo... sha te a la bo*] (*including ... Saudi Arabia*) should be annotated as EXMP.

4.5.2   Parallel Component Division Errors' Handling

Layer of parallel components sometimes may be divided by mistake. At this time, we regard it as ambiguity, and try to keep this kind of ambiguity leaving the work of disambiguation to the successor task. Accordingly every word of the components should be annotated as headword(HEAD). For example, in "此外, 雷达 图象 提供 有关 表面 结构 和 湿度 的 信息"[*ci wai, lei da tu xiang ti gong you guan biao mian jie gou he shi du de xin xi*](*In addition, the radar image provides information about surface structure and humidity*), "表面 结构 和 湿度"[*biao mian jie gou he shi du*](*surface structure and humidity*) should be annotated as "(MOD (HEAD 表面)(HEAD 结构)(HEAD 湿度))".

5   Conclusion

This paper introduced the basic theory of case grammar briefly, illustrated the good support of case grammar for machine translation in semantic layer by its detailed description of semantic relations, combed the annotation work of Chinese-English bilingual case grammar treebank construction, analyzed the typical annotation problems we had encountered and proposed corresponding solutions.

Next, we are going to research the automatic annotation of case grammar to enhance the annotation accuracy on basis of the case grammar treebank, and explore the statistical modeling of semantic analysis, transform, conversion and generation to develop a broad space for the application of bilingual case grammar treebank.

Acknowledgments. This work was supported by the Natural Science Foundation of China(No.61402419, No.60970083, No.61272221), the National Social Science Foundation of China (No.14BYY096), 863 Projects of National High Technology Research and Development (No.2012AA011101), Science and Technology Key Project of Science and Technology Department of Henan Province (No.132102210407), Basic research project of Science and Technology Department of Henan Province (No. 142300410231,No.142300410308) Key Technology Project of the Education Department of Henan Province (No.12B520055,No. 13B520381) and the Open Projects Program of Key Laboratory of Computational Linguistics(Peking University)(No. 201401), Ministry of Education of PRC.

References

1. Maosong, S., Ting, L., Donghong, J.: Frontiers of Language Computing. Journal of Chinese Information Processing **28**(1), 1–8 (2014). (in Chinese)
2. Fillmore, C.J.: The case for case. Universals in Linguistic Theory,1–88 (1967)
3. Fillmore, C.J.: The case for case reopened. Syntax and semantics **8**, 59–82 (1977)
4. Lingling, W.: Case Grammar and its Application in Chinese Research (格语法及其在汉语研究中的应用). Applied Linguistics **4**, 97–101 (1994). (in Chinese)
5. Chengqing, Z.: Statistical Natural Language Processing(统计自然语言处理). Tsinghua University Press, Beijing (2013). (in Chinese)
6. Nagao, M: A framework of a mechanical translation between Japanese and English by analogy principle. Artificial and Human Intelligence 351–354 (1984)
7. Brown, P.F., Pietra, V.J.D., Pietra, S.A.D., Mercer, R.L.: The mathematics of statistical machine translation: Parameter estimation. Computational linguistics **19**(2), 263–311 (1993)

8. Zens, R., Och, F.J., Ney, H.: Phrase-based statistical machine translation. In: KI 2002: Advances in Artificial Intelligence, pp. 18–32. Springer, Heidelberg (2002)

9. Koehn, P., Och, F.J., Marcu, D.: Statistical phrase-based translation. In: Proceedings of the 2003 Conference of the North American Chapter of the Association for Computational Linguistics on Human Language Technology-Volume 1, pp. 48–54. Association for Computational Linguistics (2003)

10. Wang, Y.Y., Waibel, A.: Modeling with structures in statistical machine translation. In: Proceedings of the 17th international conference on Computational linguistics-Volume 2, pp. 1357–1363. Association for Computational Linguistics (1998)

11. Chiang, D.: A hierarchical phrase-based model for statistical machine translation. In: Proceedings of the 43rd Annual Meeting on Association for Computational Linguistics, pp. 263–270. Association for Computational Linguistics (2005)

12. Liu, Y., Liu, Q., Lin, S.: Tree-to-string alignment template for statistical machine translation. In: Proceedings of the 21st International Conference on Computational Linguistics and the 44th annual meeting of the Association for Computational Linguistics, pp. 609–616. Association for Computational Linguistics (2006)

13. Wu, D., Fung, P.: Semantic roles for SMT: a hybrid two-pass model. In: Proceedings of Human Language Technologies: The 2009 Annual Conference of the North American Chapter of the Association for Computational Linguistics, Companion Volume: Short Papers, pp. 13–16. Association for Computational Linguistics (2009)

14. Gao, Q., Vogel, S.: Corpus expansion for statistical machine translation with semantic role label substitution rules. In: Proceedings of the 49th Annual Meeting of the Association for Computational Linguistics: Human Language Technologies: short papers-Volume 2, pp. 294–298. Association for Computational Linguistics (2011)

15. Liu, D., Gildea, D.: Semantic role features for machine translation. In: Proceedings of the 23rd International Conference on Computational Linguistics, pp. 716-724. Association for Computational Linguistics (2010)

16. Zhang, K., Zan, H., Han, Y., Mu, L.: Preliminary study on the construction of bilingual phrase structure treebank. In: Su, X., He, T. (eds.) CLSW 2014. LNCS, vol. 8922, pp. 403–413. Springer, Heidelberg (2014)

17. Baobao, C., Weidong, Z., Huarui, Z.: Bilingual Corpus Construction and its Management for Chinese-English Machine Translation. Terminology Standardization & Information Technology 1, 28–31 (2003). (in Chinese)

18. Tse ring rgyal: Research on Large-scale Sino-Tibetan Bilingual Corpus Construction for Natural Language Processing. Journal of Chinese Information Processing 25(6), 157–161 (2011). (in Chinese)

A Corpus-Based Study on Synaesthetic Adjectives in Modern Chinese

Qingqing Zhao[✉] and Chu-Ren Huang

The Department of Chinese and Bilingual Studies, The Hong Kong Polytechnic University,
Hong Kong, China
zhaoqingqing0611@163.com, churen.huang@polyu.edu.hk

Abstract. This paper focuses on 15 sensory adjectives from the gustatory sense, the tactile sense and the olfactory sense in Modern Chinese, and summarizes their synaesthetic distributions. Based on the corpus, we find some tendency among synaesthetic transfers of these 15 adjectives. The first important finding is related to the directionality of synaesthetic transfers, that is, the transfer direction is mostly from the gustatory sense to both tactile and olfactory senses, and from the tactile sense to the olfactory sense, while the reverse direction is rare. Another interesting tendency is the priority of synaesthesia over the embodied metaphor. Our data shows that sensory adjectives that have synaesthetic distributions tend to also have distributions in embodied metaphors, but not vice versa.

Keywords: Synaesthesia · Sensory · Adjectives · Chinese

1 Introduction

Synaesthesia is a phenomenon involving the connection of one sensation to another, which has been characterized as a neural disorder (Cytowic [1, 2]) and frequently studied in the fields of psychology and neuroscience (Hubbard and Ramachandran [3]).

In terms of linguistics, synaesthesia, as a kind of metaphor (Williams [4]; Day [5]), has been noticed and mentioned by scholars in the early 19th century (Geeraerts [6]), and it occurs both commonly and naturally in languages (Huang [7]), such as *sweet sound* in English and 冷色 'cold color' in Chinese, in which *sweet* and 冷 'cold' belong to the domains of gustatory sense and tactile sense respectively but *sweet* can be used to describe the auditory sense and 冷 is mapped into the visual domain, for perceiving sound is normally the sense of hearing and color is the vision.

Unlike inquiries on synaesthesia in psychological and neuroscientific areas, linguistically synaesthetic phenomena have not received the attention they deserve, which can be manifested in two aspects.

The first aspect is reflected in the data which is selected for research. Most previous scholars concentrate on the synaesthetic examples in poetic languages. For instance, Ullmann [8] collects 2000 synaesthetic examples from poems in the 19th century and points that there is a tendency of hierarchical distribution in the synaesthesia.

© Springer International Publishing Switzerland 2015
Q. Lu and H.H. Gao (Eds.): CLSW 2015, LNAI 9332, pp. 535–542, 2015.
DOI: 10.1007/978-3-319-27194-1_54

Similarly, Day [5], Callejas [9] and Yu [10] also focus on creative usages of synaesthesia and claim that there are some orientations in synaesthetic transfers, namely usually from more accessible domains (such as touch and taste) to less accessible domains (such as hearing and vision). One exception regarding research data is Williams [4], who collects synaesthetic adjectives from dictionaries. He proposes that synaesthesia is the most common type of metaphorical transfers in all languages, and the diachronic meaning change of synaesthetic adjectives obeys a strict rule which can be universal for all human languages, as shown as Fig. 1.

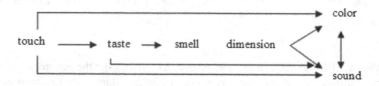

Fig. 1. The meaning change of synaesthetic adjectives (Source: Williams [4], P. 463)

The other aspect is concerned with the relationship between synaesthesia and typical metaphors that linguists have widely recognized. As Lakoff and Johnson [11] claims that metaphor is a cognitive way in our daily life enabling humans to perceive and understand more abstract and complex things in the world, the theory of embodiment has been widely regarded as providing the epistemological foundation for metaphors (cf. Lakoff and Johnson [11]; Johnson [12]; and Gibbs [13]). In other words, perceptual interactions between bodies and the world as well as motor programs of humans' bodies make the metaphor possible. However, compared with typical embodied metaphors, synaesthesia is the transfer from one sensory domain to another sensory domain, so both the source domain and the target domain of synaesthetic transfers are bodily perceptions of humans, and more importantly there is little evidence to support whether one sensory domain is more abstract and complex than another. Therefore, Taylor [14] thinks that synaesthesia is not a typical metaphor. Unfortunately, the detailed comparison between synaesthesia and embodied metaphors has been ignored.

Given the previous research gap on synaesthesia in linguistics, we plan to carry out a case study from the corpus-based approach to examine the two issues mentioned above. In this paper, we attempt to check whether there is the directionality on synaesthesia in daily Chinese, and at the same time we try to figure out the relationship between synaesthesia and the embodied metaphor. This paper will be organized as follows: in Section 2, we will introduce our method for collecting and annotating the data and Section 3 will focus on the synaesthetic distributions of our data. Then, we will compare the synaesthesia with the embodied metaphor in Section 4. Finally we will summarize our findings in Section 5, in which section we will also point out the limitation of this paper and thus propose our future work.

2   Methodology and Data

Our study will focus on synaesthetic adjectives in Modern Chinese based on the corpus from a synchronic perspective, thus attempting to explore synaesthesia in the ordinary language. We select 15 commonly-used sensory adjectives from the gustatory domain, the tactile domain and the olfactory domain, that is, 苦 'bitter', 甜 'sweet', 酸 'sour', 辣 'spicy', 咸 'salty' in taste; 冷 'cold', 热 'hot', 寒 'icy cold', 暖 'warm', 温 'moderate warm' in touch; and 臭 'smelly', 香 'fragrant', 腥 'smell usually related to fish', 骚 'foul smell usually related to urine', 膻 'smell usually related to mutton' in smell.[1]

The reason why we focus on adjectives from these three sensory domains is that basically previous studies have gained the consensus that the transfer order of synaesthesia is relatively fixed in these three domains, namely from touch to taste and then to smell (cf. Fig. 1). Therefore, we plan to examine whether the transfer hierarchy can also be applicable to synaesthesia in Modern Chinese.

Another issue is concerned with the selected words. In Chinese culture, 苦, 甜, 酸, 辣, 咸 are normally called 'five flavors' and nearly exhausted for the gustatory sensation. In order to make our work more comparable, we thus select five words from tactile and olfactory domains respectively.

As our research is based on the corpus, we use these 15 adjectives as keywords to extract all the examples from Sinica Corpus[2] (Chen et al. [15]). Some examples that are from our intuition but do not appear in Sinica Corpus are also considered if they can be found in CCL[3] corpus or BCC[4] corpus.[5]

We distinguish 6 sub-types of bodily perceptions, namely touch, taste, smell, hearing, vision and emotion. There are two reasons why we consider emotion: 1) Based on cognitive research, some researchers think emotions of humans are both physical and conceptual (cf. Johnson [12]).Typically speaking, synaesthesia is more physical and embodied metaphor is more conceptual. Therefore, we think that the emotional domain can provide more clues for the relationship between synaesthesia and the embodied metaphor; 2) In Chinese culture, 心 'heart' is in close relation to emotions as if it would be a kind of organ to perceive emotions, which can be parallel with hands as well as skins for touch, tongues for taste, noses for smelling, ears for hearing and eyes for vision. Thus, emotion is worthy to being taken into the comparison study with other purely physical sensations to some degree in Chinese.

In terms of the annotation, we first distinguish the original meaning and derived meaning for each keyword in their usages. And for the derived meaning, we further

---

[1] We cannot always find the word-to-word translation for Chinese sensory adjectives into English, so sometimes we have to utilize phrases to paraphrase the Chinese adjectives.

[2] Accessed at: http://app.sinica.edu.tw/kiwi/mkiwi/

[3] Accessed at: http://ccl.pku.edu.cn:8080/ccl_corpus/

[4] Accessed at: http://bcc.blcu.edu.cn/

[5] Please note that we do not consider compounds consisting of these 15 words, except that the compound is formed by reduplicating the keywords. For example, we take 温温 'moderate warm' into consideration, but exclude 温暖 'warm'.

differentiate synaesthesia and the embodied metaphor. If the adjective and its collocations belong to different sensory domains, we think that this adjective has synaesthetic distributions; otherwise we consider that it involves embodied metaphorical transfers.

3   Synaesthetic Distributions

Eventually, the synaesthetic distributions of the 15 selected sensory adjectives are summarized in Table 1, Table 2 and Table 3.

According to the tables, we can see that these sensory adjectives are quite frequently used to describe other senses beyond their own original sensory domains. However, there are some asymmetries among synaesthetic distributions of these 15 adjectives. The first asymmetry is that gustatory and tactile adjectives transfer more frequently than olfactory adjectives, and the second asymmetry is that for adjectives in the same domain, distinctive adjectives have different transferability, for example, 咸 in taste cannot transfer to other sensations, and 温 has the least transfers in touch, while in taste only 臭 and 香 have synaesthetic transfers.

Table 1. The synaesthetic distribution of gustatory adjectives

Source Domain (TASTE)	Target Domain				
	TOUCH	**SMELL**	**HEARING**	**VISION**	**EMOTION**
苦 'bitter'	冬日苦寒 'winter is freezing'	淡淡的苦香 'light bitter fragrance'	苦调调 'sad tune'	一脸苦相 'sorrow appearance'	心里很苦 'deep sad'
甜 'sweet'	一个甜吻 'a sweet kiss'	一股甜香 'a piece of sweet fragrance'	声音很甜 'the voice is quite sweet'	长相甜 'the appearance is sweet'	心里很甜 'deep happy'
酸 'sour'	腰酸背痛 'backache'	一股酸香 'a piece of sour fragrance'	声音酸的可以 'the voice is acid'	一副酸相 'pedantic appearance'	心头一酸 'distressed'
辣 'spicy'	洋葱辣眼 'onions making eyes painful'	辣香扑鼻 'tangy spicy fragrance'		身材辣 'figure is sexy (only for females)'	
咸 'salty'					

Table 2. The synaesthetic distribution of tactile adjectives

Source Domain (TOUCH)	Target Domain				
	TASTE	SMELL	HEARING	VISION	EMOTION
冷 'cold'		一股<u>冷</u>香 'a piece of cold fragrance'	<u>冷</u>言<u>冷</u>语 'cold words'	<u>冷</u>色 'cold color'	心<u>冷</u>了半截 'disappointed'
热 'hot'		阵阵<u>热</u>香 'flocks of hot fragrance'	声声<u>热</u>语 'words making audience warm'	劲歌<u>热</u>舞 'pop song and hot dance'	心头一<u>热</u> 'deep moved'
寒 'icy cold'		<u>寒</u>香 'cold fragrance'	<u>寒</u>声 'freezing voice'	两道<u>寒</u>光 'two lines of cold light'	心中一<u>寒</u> 'deep disappointed'
暖 'warm'		咖啡的<u>暖</u>香 'warm fragrance of coffee'	<u>暖</u>声细语 'soft voice'	<u>暖</u>色 'warm color'	心中一<u>暖</u> 'moved'
温 'moderate warm'		<u>温</u>香扑鼻 'tangy warm fragrance'	<u>温</u>声细语 'soft voice'		<u>温心</u> 'moved'

Table 3. The synaesthetic distribution of olfactory adjectives

Source Domain (SMELL)	Target Domain				
	TOUCH	TASTE	HEARING	VISION	EMOTION
臭 'smelly'			<u>臭</u>话 'bad words'	<u>臭</u>脸 'disgusting appearance'	心情很<u>臭</u> 'unhappy'
香 'fragrant'		<u>香</u>吻 'kiss'	<u>香</u>话 'good words'	<u>香</u>脸 'beautiful appearance'	
腥 'smell usually related to fish'					
骚 'foul smell usually related to urine'					
膻 'smell usually related to mutton'					

Although we only take adjectives in the gustatory sense, tactile sense and olfactory sense into consideration, we can still see some transfer directions among these three sensory domains. Olfactory adjectives are unlikely to be mapped to the gustatory sense and the tactile sense, and the only exceptional example is 香吻 ''kiss', while the transfers from taste and touch to smell are quite common. On the other hand, there are synaesthetic examples for the olfactory sense to hearing, vision and emotion, so the transfer pattern proposed by Williams [4] cannot apply to synaesthesia in Chinese, in which smell cannot transfer to other sensory domains.

In terms of the transfer orientation between the gustatory sense and the tactile sense for our selected adjectives, we can see that it is more likely for the gustatory sense to map into the tactile sense, rather than vice versa, which conflicts with previous studies, in which the gustatory sense cannot transfer back to the tactile domain. Therefore, according to our data, the hierarchy of synaesthetic transfers among taste, touch and smell is more likely to be as follows:

taste ⟶ touch ⟶ smell

Fig. 2. The hierarchy of synaesthetic transfers among taste, touch and smell in Chinese

In conclusion, the synaesthetic transfer in Modern Chinese also exhibits a direction to some degree, but it is quite different from the hierarchy proposed by previous scholars. Therefore, the previous hierarchy that is claimed to be universal is problematic, and at least it needs to be modified and refined.

4   Synaesthesia and Embodied Metaphor

As we mentioned above, synaesthesia is not a typical embodied metaphor, for both the source domain and the target domain are bodily perceptions of human beings. However there is some interesting tendency of synaesthesia that could shed light on the embodiment theory of metaphor.

As Table 4 shows, these 15 sensory adjectives can also frequently transfer into embodied metaphors, in which these adjectives are not bodily specific perceptions of humans. Rather, they are used to describe and express things that are not in real perceptual interactions with humans' sensory systems. For example, we can hardly perceive other people's personalities through any specific sensory neuro, but we still can use bodily perceptions generated by bodily neuros to describe them, such as 热心'warm-hearted', 心狠手辣 'vicious', 臭男人 'disgusting man' in the Table 4.

Comparing Table 4 with Table 1, 2 and 3 above, we can find an interesting priority of synaesthesia over the embodied metaphor, that is, if the sensory adjectives have synaesthetic distributions, all of them can be transferred into embodied metaphorical domains, but not the vice versa.

Table 4. The polarity of tactile, gustatory and olfactory adjectives in embodied metaphor

Tactile adjectives		Gustatory adjectives		Olfactory adjectives	
polarity	examples	polarity	examples	polarity	examples
冷 Negative	冷箭 'arrow shot from hiding'	苦 Negative	苦头 'suffering'	臭 Negative	臭男人 'disgusting man'
热 Positive	热心 'warm-hearted'	甜 Positive	甜梦 'sweet dream'	香 Positive	睡得香 'sleep well'
寒 Negative	寒门 'poor family'	酸 Negative	酸文人 'pedantic literati'	腥 Negative	偷腥 'extra-marital mating'
暖 Positive	暖场 'warm-up'	辣 Negative	心狠手辣 'vicious'	骚 Negative	骚女人 'sultry woman'
温 Positive	温情 'warm-atmosphere'	咸 Negative	Not found	膻 Negative	Not found

Another issue is concerned with the polarity of the sentiment. As illustrated in Table 4, embodied metaphors of these 15 adjectives normally imply the polarity of evaluation. As we re-examine the data in Table 1, 2 and 3, it is important to note that their polarities are not always obvious. For instance, it is not easy to judge whether 苦香 'bitter fragrance' and 冷色 'cold color' are negative or positive. However, in terms of the polarity of emotion expressions, it is usually clearly identifiable. 热, 暖, 温, 甜 are always positive and 冷, 寒, 酸, 苦, 臭 are always negative when expressing sentiments. This is in line with the prediction of their polarities in terms of embodiment theory of metaphors. Therefore, we infer that emotion should be a crucial domain to connect physical synaesthesia with conceptual embodied metaphors, which we will further examine in future study.

In summary, there seem to be some correlations between synaesthesia and embodied metaphors for these 15 sensory adjectives. However, further examination of the data is needed to explicate the nature of their correlations.

5   Summary

This study is a preliminary inquiry on synaesthesia in Chinese. We show that synaesthetic linguistic expressions are common in Modern Chinese.

In terms of the 15 selected sensory adjectives in this paper, we can see some tendency in synaesthetic transfers. There are some asymmetries among synaesthetic transfers of these 15 adjectives: olfactory adjectives have less synaesthetic distributions than gustatory adjectives and tactile adjectives, and for different adjectives in the same sensory domains, the transferability in synaesthesia is also distinctive.

In terms of the transfer order among different sensory domains, olfactory adjectives are unlikely to transfer into the gustatory sense and the tactile sense, but they have distributions in the hearing, vision and emotion. As for the transfer between gustatory and tactile domains, it is possible for the gustatory sense to be mapped into the tactile domain. These findings imply that the hierarchical order of synaesthesia proposed by previous scholars for English (e.g. Williams [4]) does not apply to Chinese.

There are also some correlations between synaesthetic transfers and embodied metaphors of the selected sensory adjectives. For example, all adjectives that have synaesthetic distributions can also have embodied metaphors, but not vice versa. The polarity of adjectives in embodied metaphors tends to be in line with them in emotional transfers.

Although some interesting findings and tendency have been observed in this paper, we still need to expand our data scope, to check the existence of synaesthetic hierarchy and to figure out the transfer pattern for Chinese, which may contribute to the theory of Chinese lexical semantics eventually. More importantly, we should further detect the processing details of synesthetic linguistic expressions in human brains, which can bridge the synaesthesia in linguistics and the synaesthesia in neuroscience.

References

1. Cytowic, R.: The Man Who Tasted Shapes. MIT Press, Massachusetts (1993)
2. Cytowic, R.: Synesthesia: A Union of the Senses, 2nd edn. MIT Press, Massachusetts (2002)
3. Hubbard, M.E., Ramachandran, V.S.: Neurocognitive Mechanisms of Synesthesia. J. Neuron **48**, 509–520 (2005)
4. Williams, J.: Synesthetic adjectives: A possible law of sematic change. J. Language **52**(2), 461–478 (1976)
5. Day, S.: Synaesthesia and Synaesthetic Metaphors. J. Psyche. **2**(32), 1–16 (1996)
6. Geeraerts, D.: Theories of Lexical Semantics. Oxford University Press, New York (2010)
7. Huang, C.-R.: Towards a lexical semantic theory of synaesthesia in chinese. In: Keynote Speech in the 16th Chinese Lexical Semantics Workshop, Beijing (2015)
8. Ullmann, S.: Language and Style. Basil Blackwell, Oxford (1964)
9. Callejas, B.: Synaesthetic Metaphors in English (2001). http://www.icsi.berkeley.edu/ftp/pub/techreports/20
10. Yu, N.: Synesthetic metaphor: A cognitive perspective. J. Journal of Literary Semantics **32**(1), 19–34 (2003)
11. Lakoff, G., Johnson, M.: Metaphors we live by. The University of Chicago Press, Chicago (1980)
12. Johnson, M.: The Body in the Mind: The Bodily Basis of Meaning, Imagination, and Reason. The University of Chicago Press, Chicago (1987)
13. Gibbs, R.: Embodiment and Cognitive Science. Cambridge University Press, New York (2006)
14. Taylor, J.: Cognitive Grammar. Oxford University Press, Oxford (2002)
15. Chen, K.-J., Chu-Ren, H., Li-ping, C., Hui-Li, H.: Sinica corpus: design methodology for balanced corpora. In: Proceeding of the 11th Pacific Asia Conference on Language, Information and Computation, pp.167–176. Kyung Hee University, Seoul (1996)

An Approach to Recognize Temporal Relations Between Chinese Events

Xin Zheng[1,2(✉)], Peifeng Li[1,2], Yilong Huang[1,2], and Qiaoming Zhu[1,2]

[1] Natural Language Processing Lab, Soochow University, Suzhou 215006, Jiangsu, China
358581959@qq.com, {pfli,qmzhu}@suda.edu.cn,
20144227007@stu.suda.edu.cn
[2] School of Computer Science and Technology, Soochow University,
Suzhou 215006, Jiangsu, China

Abstract. The research on temporal relations between events plays an important role in natural language processing tasks, such as information extraction, question answering and text summarization. In this paper, we first annotate a document-level corpus to be used for the recognition of temporal relations between Chinese events. We then introduce several effective features according to the characteristics of Chinese, such as trigger semantics, special words, event arguments, event co-reference relation, etc. to improve system performance over the baseline. The experimental results on our annotated corpus show that our system outperforms the baseline by 3.55% of relative improvement in F1.

Keywords: Corpus · Event · Temporal relation · Machine learning

1 Introduction

In recent years, temporal information encoded in textual descriptions of events has been of interest in the field of natural language processing, and has become a new hotspot. Temporal relation recognition is an important task of temporal information extraction, which addresses the temporal relations between events or events and time expressions. The semantic evaluations (SemEval) workshop organized by Association for Computational Linguistics (ACL) has also referred to the temporal evaluation (TempEval) task several times. TempEval consists of three main subtasks: (i) determine the temporal relation between an event and a time expression in the same sentence; (ii) determine the temporal relation between an event and the document creation time; (iii) determine the temporal relation between two events in the same sentence or consecutive sentences. This paper focuses on recognition of temporal relations between Chinese events.

Given a pair of event mentions, we predict one of the four following relations between them: *before*, *after*, *overlap* and *unknown*. Consider the following discourse as an example:

© Springer International Publishing Switzerland 2015
Q. Lu and H.H. Gao (Eds.): CLSW 2015, LNAI 9332, pp. 543–553, 2015.
DOI: 10.1007/978-3-319-27194-1_55

(a) Chinese: 墨西哥航空公司一架客机6日在墨西哥北部边境城市雷诺萨机场
降落时*滑出(E1)*跑道，至少造成5人*死亡(E2)*，6人*受伤(E3)*）。
Pinyin: *mò xī gē háng kōng gōng sī yī jià kè jī 6 rì zài mò xī gē běi bù biān jìng
chéng shì léi nuò sà jī chǎng jiàng luò shí huá chū pǎo dào, zhì shǎo zào chéng
5 rén sǐ wáng , 6 rén shòu shāng.*
English: *A Mexican airlines passenger plane **overshot (E1)** the runway when
landing at Mexico's northern city of Reynosa airport on 6th, at least 5 people
were **killed (E2)** and 6 people were **injured (E3)**.*

In the above discourse, there are three event mentions, *overshoot* (E1), *kill* (E2)
and *injure* (E3). It is not difficult to see that *overshoot* occurred before *kill* and *injure*
(*overshoot before kill, overshoot before injure*), and *kill* and *injure* occurred at the
same time (*kill overlap injure*). Similar to the example above, for a series of news
reports, by understanding the temporal relation between events, we can better summarize the contents of the article so that people can quickly get valid information.
Likewise, in "text-to-scene" systems, we need to know the sequence of events in the
article in order to arrange the animation scene, and ensure the continuity of the whole
narration.

In this paper, we first annotate a document-level corpus to be used for the recognition
of temporal relations between Chinese events. We then introduce several effective features according to the characteristics of Chinese, such as trigger semantics, special
words, event arguments, event co-reference relation, etc. to improve system performance over the baseline. The experimental results on our annotated corpus show that
our system outperforms the baseline by 3.55% of relative improvement in F1.

The rest of this paper is organized as follows. Section 2 overviews the related
work. Section 3 describes the annotation of our corpus. Section 4 introduces an approach to recognize temporal relation between Chinese events. Section 5 reports
experimental results and gives detailed analysis. Finally, we conclude our work in
Section 6.

2   Related Work

At present, most researchers study recognition of temporal relations between events
on English corpus. With the development of TimeML (Time Markup Language) and
the appearance of the Timebank corpus, statistical machine learning methods have
been widely applied to this task, which replace the early rules-based methods. Timebank corpus has become an important corpus for many scholars studying temporal
relations between English events. For example, Mani et al. (2006) proposed event
attribute features (called "perfect features"): event-class, aspect, modality, tense and
negation. Chambers et al. (2007, 2008) further expand Mani et al.'s feature space,
adding lexical features, discourse features and syntactic features, etc. Tatu et al.
(2008) used temporal relation reasoning rules (such as: *A before B and B before C →
A before C*) to improve the performance of recognition of temporal relations between
events. Yoshikawa et al. (2009) employ a Markov Logic Network model for recognition of temporal relations between events. D'Souza et al. (2013) summarize a lot of

the features used in the task of recognizing temporal relations between events, and propose several discourse-level features which can improve the system performance.

In recent years, there have been several works that have used the ACE corpus for this task (e.g., Do et al. 2012 and Ng et al. 2013). Do et al. present an event timeline which lays out sequentially event mentions in the order they take place in a given text, and then uses a joint inference model to optimize the temporal structure by coupling local classifiers. Ng et al. use several discourse analysis frameworks, which provide more useful semantic information, to further improve the performance of Do's model. An annotated event in the ACE corpus is a specific occurrence involving participants which is often a phrase or a sentence, and it consists of an event trigger and arguments. But an event in the Timebank corpus is represented by a word (trigger), therefore, the definitions of their events are very different. In addition, the density of annotated events in the Timebank corpus is greater than that in the ACE corpus, so the experimental performances on the two kinds of corpuses are not directly comparable.

The research targeting recognition of temporal relations between Chinese events is very few due primarily to the lack of temporal relation corpuses of Chinese. Cheng et al. (2008) construct a temporal relation corpus of Chinese events based on the Timebank corpus, and identify temporal relations between Chinese events by event types. Lin et al. (2009) introduce the approach of extracting and computing temporal relations between time and time, event and time as well as event and event in Chinese on the basis of information extraction and temporal annotation. Zhong et al. (2009) propose a model of event relation representation, and carry out an experiment investigating event reasoning. Zou et al. (2010) present a strategy for annotation of relations between events and annotation of the functional attributes which provide a simple way to represent event schema. Wang et al. (2012) study the recognition of temporal relations between two events where one event syntactically dominates the other event in one sentence, and propose a method based on a maximum entropy model.

3   Corpus

3.1   Definition of Temporal Relations between Events

A temporal relation is the relation of time sequences of events. There are different kinds of temporal relation type classifications between events. The TimeML uses 13 relations based on James Allen's interval logic (Allen, 1983). However,owever, the TempEval-1 uses a smaller set of 6 relations. We use the simplified relation types of TempEval-1 including the three core relations of TempEval-1 (*before*, *after* and *overlap*), and the relation *unknown* instead of others in TempEval-1 (*before-or-overlap*, *overlap-or-after* and *vague*) for ambiguous cases or no particular relation between events.

BEFORE: The first event fully precedes the second, denoted by *e1 before e2*

AFTER: The second event fully precedes the first, denoted by *e1 after e2*

OVERLAP: Two events happen at the same time or the periods they occur are overlapping, denoted by *e1 overlap e2*

UNKNOWN: There is no particular relation between two events, or it is unable to determine which kind of relation they belong to, denoted by *e1 unknown e2*

3.2 Corpus Annotation

To create an experimental data set for our work, we selected 331 news articles from the ACE 2005 Chinese corpus, Chinese Treebank and Chinese Gigaword corpus (163 articles from ACE 2005 Chinese corpus, 168 articles from Chinese Treebank and Chinese Gigaword). According to the annotation rules of the ACE 2005 corpus, the articles selected from Chinese Treebank and Chinese Gigaword are annotated in a format similar to the ACE 2005 format. Our experimental data set contains 2485 event instances and 21,132 event pairs. Table 1 shows the data statistics of each temporal relation. *Before* and *after* relations are in the majority, and *unknown* relations makes up just 7.07% of the data set.

Table 1. Statistics of our experimental data set

Relation	Before	After	Overlap	Unknown
Number	7402	7402	4834	1494
Proportion	35.03%	35.03%	22.87%	7.07%

In addition, we compute the annotator agreement in order to verify the reliability of our experimental data set. The overall value of kappa is greater than 0.7, therefore, our experimental data set is considered to be reliable.

4   Temporal Relation Recognition

In this paper, we regard temporal recognition as a classification problem, and employ a supervised learning method to solve it. Given a pair of event mentions, we can build a classifier that predicts one of the four temporal relations between them: *before, after, overlap and unknown*. The key to building the classifier is features selection, and the set of features we defined includes some basic features used in temporal relation recognition between English events, as well as new more effective features which are designed according to characteristics of the Chinese language, such as trigger semantics, special words, event arguments, and event co-reference relation.

4.1 Baseline

Table 2 summarizes many features from temporal relation research between English events, including lexical features, syntactic features, discourse features, and attribute features. In this paper, the features are called "basic features". The lexical, syntactic and discourse features, which can be applied to the study on Chinese documents, are selected from the feature set that Do et al. and D'Souza used for English in the related work. Lastly, the event attribute features are the "perfect" features proposed by Mani et al. (2006).

Some lexical and syntactic features are limited to a single sentence, but this paper studies the temporal relations between any two events within the same article, so those features might not play a major role when two events appear in different sentences or far apart. Therefore, we present some semantic and discourse-level features to improve the performance of temporal relation recognition between Chinese events.

Table 2. Basic features

Feature	Description
Lexical Features	(1) The word and part-of-speech of events and the context surrounding them, where the context is defined as a window of 3 words before and after the event; (2) the word and part-of-speech of the trigger's parent node in dependency parse tree.
Syntactic Features	(1) The dependency relation between a trigger and its parent node in the dependency parse tree; (2) the dependency relation of two triggers in dependency parse tree if they are in the same sentence; (3) the syntactic relation of the two triggers in syntactic parse tree if they are in the same sentence.
Discourse Features	(1) Which event appears first in the text; (2) whether the two events appear in the same sentence; (3) the quantized number of sentences between the two events.
Attribute Features	(1) The class, modality, polarity, genericity and tense of the events; (2) the agreement of the two events' attributes.

4.2 New Features

(1) Trigger semantics

An event's trigger is the word that most clearly expresses its occurrence. If the trigger words of two events in the same article are very similar in semantics, the events are likely to be identical or related events.

Semantic similarity: The semantic similarity of two event trigger words is calculated by HowNet. Its value ranges from 0 to 1.

Synonyms: Determining whether the two event trigger words are synonymous by TongYiCi CiLin.

(2) Special words

Negative words and imprecise words: There are not many commonly used negative words and imprecise words in modern Chinese, so we summarize the negative words and imprecise words that often appear in news corpus, and construct a negative word list and an imprecise word list. The negative word list contains a total of 29 negative words (such as "不"[bù] (no) and "没有"[méi yǒu] (none)), the imprecise word list contains a total of 18 negative words (such as "也许"[yě xǔ] (maybe) and "可能"[kě néng] (possible)).

The negative or imprecise word is searched for in the context surrounding a trigger whether it appears in the above definition of word lists, or in a window of 3 words before or after the trigger. We regard the word as a feature if the word exists, if there are multiple negative or imprecise words at the same time we adopt the principle of proximity and take the word closest to the trigger word.

Conjunctive: The word between two event triggers that is part of speech is a conjunctive (CC CS), andis regarded as a connective feature, such as "并且"[bìng qiě] (and) and "但是"[dàn shì] (but). If there are multiple conjunctives between the two event triggers, we also take the word closest to the trigger word.

Signal words: A signal word is the word that can make the temporal relation between two events clearer. We construct a signal word dictionary for news corpus through manually annotating 200 news articles (from the ACE 2005 Chinese corpus, also avoiding any overlap with the articles mentioned in Section 3). These words are mostly nouns of locality, conjunctives of causality, progressive conjunctives and a small number of verbs such as "之后"[zhī hòu] (after), "同时"[tóng shí] (simultaneous), "因此"[yīn cǐ] (therefore), and "造成"[zào chéng] (cause).

We consider the word between two events in the same sentence or adjacent sentences, and whether it appears in the signal word dictionary. We also take the word closest to the trigger word if there are multiple signal words between the two events.

(3) Event arguments

Event arguments are entities or values that play additional roles different from above, which we will refer collectively to as event participants and event attributes as event arguments.

The ACE 2005 Chinese corpus defines 35 kinds of argument roles, and different types of events corresponding to different roles. Most types of events include the initiator of the event (agent), the bearer of event (patient), when and where the event is taking place (time, place). In this paper, we consider four basic event arguments: agent, patient, time and place. The event argument features used in our experiments include the agents (or patients, time and places) of the event-pair, whether the agents (or patients, time and places) of the event-pair are the same, and whether the agent of one event is the patient of the other event.

4.3   Co-reference

Definition: When two event mentions refer to the same event, then they co-refer. For example:

Chinese: 两国首脑今天在巴黎举行会谈。双方在会谈中讨论了中东和平问题。

Pinyin: *liǎng guò shǒu nǎo jīn tiān zài bā lí jǔ xíng huì tán. shuāng fāng zài huì tán zhōng tǎo lùn le zhōng dōng hé píng wèn tǐ.*

English: *The leaders of two countries held talks in Paris today. The two sides discussed the issue of the Middle East peace in the talks.*

"会谈"*[huì tán] (talk)* in both sentences are referring to the same event and should be identified as co-reference events.

Table 3. Features for co-reference event recognition

Feature	Description	Feature	Description
(1)	Event triggers and their POS	(5)	Whether attributes are the same (five)
(2)	Semantic similarity of two triggers	(6)	Event arguments (four)
(3)	Whether two triggers are synonymous	(7)	Whether the roles of two events are the same
(4)	Event attributes (five)		

There are several studies on co-reference identification between English events, but there is no related system to identify co-reference between Chinese events. In this paper, we implement a simple co-reference identification system for Chinese events. Table 3 shows the feature set used in our co-reference identification of Chinese events, including event trigger semantics, event attribute features defined by the ACE 2005 Chinese corpus (class, modality, polarity, genericity, and tense), and the features related to the event arguments.

5   Evaluation

5.1   Experimental Setup

All sentences in the corpus are divided into words using a Chinese word segmentation tool (*ICTCLAS*) with all of the entities annotated in the corpus kept. We use the well-known Stanford Parser to create the constituent and dependency parse trees. Taking an article as a unit, the 331 articles mentioned in Section 3 are divided into five parts equally, the ME tool (*Maxent*) is employed to build our model and 5-fold cross validation is performed. The experimental evaluation indicators are: accuracy, precision, recall and F1-score. We take the results of the 5-fold cross validation in microaverage as the final experimental performance.

5.2   Results and Discussion

Firstly, we implement a simple co-reference identification system for Chinese events that can be compared with the manually annotated event co-reference results. The training set contains 300 articles which are selected from the ACE 2005 Chinese corpus (and don't repeat with the 163 articles mentioned in Section 3), including 1768 events and 15200 event pairs. There are 1610 event pairs that co-refer in the training data, which accounts for about 10.59%. The test set is the data mentioned in Section 3, including 331 articles, 2485 events, and 21132 event pairs. There are 1940 event pairs that co-refer in the test data, which accounts for about 9.18%.

The ME tool is employed to train the event co-reference classifier. Table 4 shows the experimental results. The F1-score of system is 83.71%. If two events are co-reference events, their triggers are often synonyms or near synonyms and their arguments in the same role are the same. Therefore, trigger semantic features and event arguments features are an asset to the identification of event co-reference.

Table 4. Experimental results for co-reference events recognition

Accuracy (%)	Precision (%)	Recall (%)	F1 (%)
97.12	84.87	82.58	83.71

We take the results that used the "basic features" as the baseline for of our system, and then separately add the new features mentioned in Section 4.2 and event co-reference, including the learned event co-reference and the gold event co-reference, to make direct comparisons to the baseline. The results of 5-fold cross validation in mi-cro-average, includingthe overall performance of the three relations *before*, *after*, *overlap*, are shown in Table 5. The results indicate that each of our new features con-tributes to the performance improvement of our system.

Overall, the results show that our system outperformed the baseline by 3.55% in F1-score. After adding trigger semantic features, the F1-score of the system is 0.48% higher than the F1-score of the baseline. The semantic features of this paper are the semantic similarity between two event triggers, and the two event mentions in the same article are very likely to be the same event or related events if the semantic simi-larity if their triggers is very high. For example, a "death" event is described by words with the same meaning such as *"死亡"[sǐ wáng](die)* and *"去世"[qù shì] (pass away)*, and the event mentions may happen at the same time.

Table 5. Experimental results of our system

	Accuracy(%)	Precision (%)	Recall (%)	F1 (%)
Baseline	65.79	66.91	68.37	67.63
Baseline + Semantics	66.23	67.18	69.07	68.11(+0.48)
Baseline + Special Words	66.53	67.37	69.20	68.28(+0.65)
Baseline + Arguments	67.49	68.19	70.01	69.09(+1.46)
Baseline + Co-reference1	67.52	68.51	70.36	69.42(+1.79)
Baseline + Co-reference2	67.62	68.89	70.50	69.69(+2.06)
All	69.61	70.18	72.20	71.18(+3.55)

(Note: "Co-reference1" is learned event co-reference, "Co-reference2" is gold event co-reference.)

With the addition of special words, the F1-score of the system increases by 0.65%, because special words can make the before relation of two events near in distance clearer. For example:

Chinese: 冲突之后，警方封锁了现场。

Pinyin: *chōng tū zhī hòu, jǐng fāng fēng suǒ le xiàn chǎng.*

English: *Police **cordoned off** the area after the **conflict.***

The word "之后"[zhī hòu] (after) makes the before relation between event "冲突"[chōng tū] (conflict) and event "封锁"[fēng suǒ] (cordon off) more obvious.

The F1-score of the system is 1.46% higher than the baseline after adding event argument features. If two events have common arguments (e.g., agent or patient), they often have a close connection. For example:

Chinese: 歹徒用木棍打了保安的头部，保安随即昏倒在地。

Pinyin: *dǎi túu yòng mù gùn dǎ le bǎo ān de tòu bù, bǎo ān suí jì hūn dǎo zài dì.*

English: *The gangster **hit** the security guard's head, the security guard immediately **collapsed** to the ground.*

The agents of event "打"*[dǎ] (hit)* and event "昏倒"*[hūn dǎo] (collapse)* are all "歹徒"*[dǎi tú] (gangster)*, the patients of the two events are all "保安"*[bǎo ān] (security guard)*, and the two events happened one after another. For another example:

Chinese: 张三因抢劫被警察逮捕。

Pinyin: *zhāng sān yīn qiǎng jié bèi jǐng chá dǎi bǔ.*

English: *Zhang San was **arrested** by the police for **robbery**.*

The agents of event "抢劫"*[qiǎng jié] (robbery)* and event "逮捕"*[dǎi bǔ] (arrest)* are common ("张三"*[zhāng sān] (Zhang San)*), and the two events also occurred successively.

Compared with other features, the improved performance of system is highest when adding event co-reference features. The reason is simple, if two events are co-reference events, they must happen at the same time, and the temporal relation between them must be *overlap*. Because the F1-score of the event co-reference identification system is only 83.71%, part of the event co-references could not be correctly identified, and some event pairs which are not co-reference are mistakenly identified as co-reference events. Therefore, the performance of our system when the learned event co-references is added is worse than that adding the gold event co-references.

We can find that the overall improvement of our system's performance is not the sum of the improvement of our system's performance after adding each feature successively from Table 5. For example, considering trigger semantics and the event co-references, two events in the same article are likely to be co-reference events if their triggers have the same semantics.

Our experimental method is consistent with Do's classification method [7] in that the temporal relation classifications are the same and the evaluations are conducted using the ACE 2005 Chinese corpus. Further, the performance of our method is demonstrably higher than that of Do's for several reasons reasons: 1) the difference between temporal relation annotation guidelines causes the proportions of each temporal relation to be different. Also, Do's *unknown* (*no relation*) relation accounts for 30%, but the proportion of our *unknown* relation is less than 10%. 2) Do's experimental data is sparse in that it only contains 20 articles (for 324 events), and the minimum number of event pairs in one article is 2 and the maximum number is several thousand.

In order to verify the effect of different classifiers on the performance of our system, we use the CRF (Conditional Random Field) tool to train another classifier. We also use the multiplication rule to fuse the prediction probabilities of the two classifiers ME and CRF. The results are shown in Table 6.

Table 6. Results usingmultiple classifiers and their fusion

	Accuracy (%)	Precision (%)	Recall (%)	F1 (%)
ME	69.61	70.18	72.20	71.18
CRF	67.83	68.79	71.12	69.93
ME+CRF	70.95	71.36	73.96	72.64

The results in Table 6 show that the performance of CRF classifier is slightly worse than that of ME classifier, however, the F1-score of the system after fusing the two classifiers is 1.46% higher than the F1-score of ME classifier. The fusion of different classifiers can play a complementary role, and can improve the accuracy of classification results.

6   Conclusions

In this paper we employ a supervised learning method to recognize temporal relations between Chinese events. Several effective features, such as trigger semantics, special words, event arguments, and event co-reference relations are used in our model. The experimental results illustrate that the features are effective in identifying temporal relations between Chinese event mentions. In addition, we also compare the performance of different classifiers, and use classifier fusion methods to improve the performance of our system.

In future work, we will focus on mining more effective features according to the characteristics of the Chinese language. We will also consider how temporal reasoning might assist in temporal relation recognition.

Acknowledgement. This research was supported by the National Natural Science Foundation of China (Grant No. 61472265), the State Key Program of National Natural Science Foundation of China (Grant No. 61331011), and partially supported by Collaborative Innovation Center of Novel Software Technology and Industrialization.

References

1. Mani, I., Verhagen, M., Wellner, B., Lee, C.M., Pustejovsky, J.: Machine learning of temporal relations. In: Proceeding of ACL 2006, pp. 753–760 (2006)
2. Chambers, N., Wang, S., Jurafsky, D.: Classifying temporal relations between events. In: Proceeding of ACL 2007, pp. 173–176 (2007)
3. Chambers, N., Jurafsky, D.: Jointly combining implicit constraints improves temporal ordering. In: Proceeding of EMNLP 2008, pp. 698–706 (2008)
4. Tatu, M., Srikanth, M.: Experiments with reasoning for temporal relations between events. In: Proceeding of COLING 2008, pp. 857–864 (2008)
5. Yoshikawa, K., Riedel, S.: Jointly identifying temporal relations with markov logic. In: Proceeding of ACL 2009, pp. 405–413 (2009)
6. D'Souza, J., Ng, V.: Classifying temporal relations with rich linguistic knowledge. In: Proceeding of NAACL-HLT 2013, pp. 918–927 (2013)
7. Do, Q.X., Lu, W., Roth, D.: Joint inference for event timeline construction. In: Proceeding of EMNLP 2012, pp. 677–687 (2012)
8. Ng, J.-P., Kan, M.-Y., Lin, Z., Feng, W., Chen, B., Su, J., Tan, C.-L.: Exploiting discourse analysis for article-wide temporal classification. In: Proceeding of EMNLP 2013, pp. 12–23 (2013)
9. Cheng, Y.C., Asahara, M., Matsumoto, Y.: Use of event types for temporal relation identification in chinese text. In: Proceeding of IJCNLP 2008, pp. 31–38 (2008)
10. Lin, J., Yuan, C.: Extraction and Computation of Chinese Temporal Relation. Journal of Chinese Information Processing 23(5), 62–67 (2009). (in Chinese)
11. Zhong, Z., Liu, Z., Zhou, W., Fu, J.: The Model of Event Relation Representation. Journal of Chinese Information Processing, 2009 23(6), 56–60 (2008). (in Chinese)
12. Zou, H., Yang, E., Gao, Y., Zeng, Q.: The annotation of event schema in chinese. In: 23rd International Conference on Computational Linguistics 2010, pp. 72–79 (2010)
13. Wang, F.-E., Tan, H., Qian, Y.-L.: Recognition of Temporal Relation in One Sentence Based on Maximum Entropy. Computer Engineering 38(4), 37–39 (2012). (in Chinese)

A Study of Manner Adverbs' Sememe Collocation in Modern Chinese

Lu Zhou[✉] and Rui Liu

Department of Chinese Literature and Language, Xiamen University, Xiamen, China
{zhou1829,liuruioscar}@hotmail.com

Abstract. The characteristics of manner adverbs' collocation are unique in modern Chinese, but they are rarely given much attention. After designing and proposing a descriptive and analytical methodological framework for these adverbs' sememe collocation, this research takes typical manner adverbs as examples and achieves automatic semantic clustering for their collocations by using the semantic resource (*A Thesaurus of Modern Chinese*); then it presents an analysis of the sememe collocation features of the example words under the current framework. This study proposes that the descriptive and analytical methodological framework of sememe collocation is feasible for the semantic analysis of collocations of other word categories. Additionally, the result of the sememe collocation's descriptive analysis can also contribute to deciding typical collocations.

Keywords: Manner adverbs · Sememe · Collocation · Semantic category

1 Introduction

Manner adverbs in modern Chinese include "亲手[*qinshou*](*with one's own hand, personally*)", "故意 [*guyi*](*deliberately*)", "有意 [*youyi*](*intentionally*)", "特意 [*teyi*](*with the special intention of*)", "存心[*cunxin*](*purposely*)", etc. Unlike other types of adverbs in contemporary Chinese, they possess substantial meanings and distinctive characteristics in collocation at grammatical and semantic levels, which results in their semi-fixed collocations.

Lexical collocation involves a series of selections in grammar, semantics and pragmatics. Instead of taking collocation merely as the superficial combination of words, we can start from collocation and analyze the paradigmatic relations of the collocation in terms of grammar, semantics, and pragmatics so as to summarize the features and rules about the collocation. Typical collocations are generally considered to be decided by high frequency collocates, but we reckon that on the basis of collocation frequency, factors like grammar, semantics and pragmatics should also be considered when we investigate collocation. At present scholars in this field study collocations on the basis of corpora, and most of them count, describe and analyze collocations from such grammatical and pragmatic angles as colligation and semantic prosody, rather than come up with a semantics analysis framework for collocations.

Q. Lu and H.H. Gao (Eds.): CLSW 2015, LNAI 9332, pp. 554–565, 2015.
DOI: 10.1007/978-3-319-27194-1_56

Zhang [8] offered an explicit account for sememe combination: "sememe combination includes two categories: one is the morphemic meaning combination within a sememe, and the other is the combination among sememes, which is also known as sememe collocation." Sememe collocation can be seen as a kind of sememe combination, and can also be termed as semantic combination or semantic collocation. Therefore collocations can be deeply studied from the perspective of sememe collocation. It is not enough to know which are the frequent collocates of the node words; we need to study the rules of their sememe collocation.

This paper proposes a descriptive and analytical methodological framework for sememe collocation. It takes the manner adverbs "故意[guyi](*deliberately*)", "有意 [*youyi*](*intentionally*)" and "存心[*cunxin*](*purposely*)" as node words to study their sememe collocation characteristics (the use frequency of the three node words are high, medium and low respectively). Taking "semantic category" as the point of entry, we observe the semantic clustering degree of the three node words' collocates in the semantic category system. If the clustering degree is not high, then this collocation is a common sememe collocation, with "distinctive sememe collocation features"; otherwise, it is indicated that the corresponding node words tend to choose collocates of one or more specific semantic categories. In this case, semantic category collocation is highly typical with "distinctive semantic category collocation features". This can be used to analyze the characteristics of sememe collocation.

2   Collocation Extraction and Data Arrangement

As collocation is highly field-dependent, the balance of the corpus structure should be taken into consideration when we are about to study the general rules of collocation. Thus, a balanced corpus of contemporary Chinese consisting of 300 million words is used to extract collocations automatically.

Firstly based on the segmented and POS tagged corpus, all co-occurring words that fall into the left/right span of [-2, +4] of the node words are extracted automatically and the frequency of the co-occurring words are counted; as collocates only refer to those co-occurring words syntactically connecting and semantically compatible with node words, we need to determine the threshold value, semantic and grammatical features for filtering. The concordance is conducted online based on the corpus and a manual proofreading is assisted with the "collocation filtering software" to preserve valid collocates; finally the word type number and the frequencies of each node words' valid collocates are calculated. According to the statistics, the collocates of " 故 意 [*guyi*](*deliberately*)", " 有 意 [*youyi*](*intentionally*)" and " 存 心 [*cunxin*](*purposely*)" are almost in the right position, and 95.84% of them are verbs, while 2.87% are adjectives and 1.29% are nouns. This paper will present a targeted analysis of the semantic characteristics of right collocates of the three node words respectively.

3   The Descriptive and Analytical Methodological Framework of Sememe Collocation

3.1   An Introduction to the Methodological Framework

Sememe collocation can be described and analyzed from the frequency, types and semantic categories of collocates. Word frequency reflects the co-occurrence degree of collocates with the node words while word types reflect node words' collocability with different words. Both word frequency and type represent sememe collocation features at the lexical level. If we cluster collocates according to the semantic category system, the sememe collocation can then be analyzed from the perspective of semantic category.

This paper proposes an approach to describe and analyze sememe collocation from the perspectives of semantic category, word type number and word frequency.

(i)   With a reference to the semantic category system of TMC[1] (we mainly refer to the third-level semantic category)[2], we can achieve automatic semantic clustering for the collocates of the node words "故意[guyi](deliberately)", "有意[youyi](intentionally)" and "存心[cunxin](purposely)" respectively by use of ACCESS software. When collocates are polysemy, their meaning and frequency can be determined according to their surrounding context in the corpus. For example, when "设计[sheji](design, set a trap for)" is in collocation with "有意[youyi](intentionally)" it denotes two different meanings and belongs to different semantic categories. Thus "设计[sheji] (design, set a trap for)" with different meanings are marked with lower digitals on the words for distinction. Hence the two meanings are respectively represented as "设计$_1$[sheji](design)" and "设计$_2$[sheji](set a trap for)".

(ii)   Obtain the number of word types of collocates (hereinafter W) and total frequency of collocates (hereinafter F) under each semantic category that collocates clustered into in step (i).

---

[1]   "TMC" is short for "A Thesaurus of Modern Chinese", which embodies more than 80,000 modern Chinese words with high frequency and constructs a five-level lexical semantic classification system in which there are 9 classes in the first level, 62 in the second level, 518 in the third level, 2,076 in the forth level and 72,613 in the fifth level [4].

[2]   There should be a special note about the selection of thesaurus system. "The type names of the third level are mainly the topic concepts of the type. Their features are: broad meanings, which represent the basic common usage of the type; high universality; the pragmatic features that tend to be neutral."[4] Collocates in this study are mainly the common words, which are covered by the word system TMC. The meaning coverage of the third-level semantic category in TMC is moderate, thanks to its representativeness, universality and pragmatic neutrality. If choose the first/second-level semantic categories, the coverage range of each level is too broad and the classification is vague; if choose the four/five level semantic categories, the coverage range of meanings and the classification is too narrow. Thus the third level in TMC is the most appropriate clustering level for this research.

(iii) Classify W and F in different semantic categories and draw out the grades of the semantic categories.
(iv) Evaluate the typicality of a certain semantic category by standard deviation (s) of collocates' frequency in the same semantic category.
(v) Conclude the overall features of the sememe collocation of node words and mainly evaluates the clustering degree of the sememe collocation: high clustering degree means this semantic category possesses high typicality that the node word is more likely to select, while low clustering degree or abnormal standard deviation in step (iv) means low typicality.

3.2   Analytical Demonstration of the Methodological Framework

The following takes "故意[*guyi*] (*deliberately*)" as an example to describe its sememe collocation with the above method.

(i)   If we take "故意[*guyi*] (*deliberately*)" as the node word, the total frequency of its collocates is 4877 and the total number of word types is 447. After clustering collocates according to the semantic category system in TMC, their first-level and second-level semantic category distribution is showed in Figure 1.

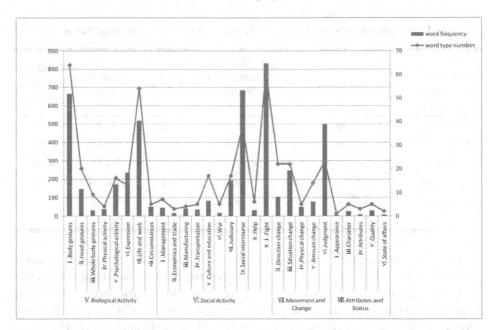

Fig. 1. The first-level and second-level semantic category distribution of the collocates of "故意 [*guyi*] (*deliberately*)"

There are 4 types of first-level semantic categories, including "biological activity", "social activity", "movement and change" and "attributes and status"; and 28 types of second-level semantic categories including "body gesture", etc. It is evident that for the collocates of "故意[*guyi*] (*deliberately*)"collocates, their word frequency and word type number are distributed in disproportion under different semantic categories. Generally speaking, word frequency is positively correlated to word type number.

Semantic categories in the first and second levels primarily display the semantic distribution of the collocations, but if we hope to describe the sememe collocation conditions to a deeper level, it is necessary to conduct further observation into the third-level semantic category.

(ii) There are up to 128 types of collocates at the third level for "故意[*guyi*] (*deliberately*)". W, F and its relative cumulative frequency and standard deviation in each semantic category are calculated.

(iii) According to our statistics, W is classified into three levels (high, medium and low) with 10 and 2 as the cut-off values respectively; F is also categorized into three grades (high, medium and low) by use of 66th and 90th percentile as the cut-off values. Table 1 shows the calculation and classification results of the six semantic categories of "VI-xi".

Table 1. The calculation and classification results of the six semantic categories of "VI-xi"

Semantic category	W	W grade[3]	F	Relative cumulative frequency of F	F grade	Grading type	Standard deviation (25.39)
VI-xi-A	5	*m*	133	54.23%	*h*	W*m* F*h*	54.45
VI-xi-B	6	*m*	27	82.86%	*m*	W*m* F*m*	1.87
VI-xi-C	27	*h*	297	15.11%	*h*	W*h* F*h*	13.63
VI-xi-D	5	*m*	66	69.65%	*m*	W*m* F*m*	21.74
VI-xi-F	2	*l*	23	85.48%	*m*	W*l* F*m*	7.78
VI-xi-G	2	*l*	7	96.39%	*l*	W*l* F*l*	0.71

The "semantic category" column represents the abbreviated type name of semantic category in TMC. For instance, " VI-xi-A" represents "A argue" (third level) under " xi, fight" (second level) under " VI, social activity" (first level). "W" is the number of word types in the corresponding semantic category. For example, there are five collocates in "Six eleven A", namely " 诡辩 [*guibian*](*quibble*)(2), 抬杠 [*taigang*](*bicker*) (2), 打闹 [*danao*](*roughhouse*) (2), 骂 [*ma*](*curse*) (3) and 作对 [*zuodui*](*oppose*) (124)". The numbers in the brackets are the frequencies of these

---

[3]   Hereinafter, we refer to "high" as "*h*", "medium" as "*m*" and "low" as "*l*".

words. "W grade" is classified according to the standards: " Ⅵ- x i -A" has five word types, thus it is counted as "medium" in word type grade. "F" refers to the total frequency of the collocates in the corresponding semantic category. For example, the word frequency of " Ⅵ- x i -A" is 133, which is the total amount of the frequency of five collocates previously mentioned. "Relative cumulative frequency of F" means the relative cumulative frequency calculated after ranking F from high to low to evaluate the significance of the collocates in the current semantic category on frequency. The relative cumulative frequency of F of "Ⅵ- x i -A" is 54.23%. According to the standard, its "F grade" is "high". "W grade" and "F grade" constitute the "grading type" of a certain semantic category. For instance, the "grading type" of "Ⅵ- x i -A" is "W*m* F*h*".

(iv) Evaluate the typicality of a certain semantic category through calculating the word frequency standard deviation (s) of collocates in the same semantic category. From the frequency distribution of "诡辩 [*guibian*](*quibble*)(2), 抬杠 [*taigang*](*bicker*) (2), 打闹 [*danao*](*roughhouse*) (2), 骂 [*ma*](*curse*) (3) and作对[*zuodui*](*oppose*) (124)" in "Ⅵ-xi-A" we can find that the frequency of collocates in one semantic category is not in equilibrium. The "Ⅵ-xi-D" which has the same W value of 5, with an F value of 66. Hence we must also comprehensively consider the dispersion degree of word frequency distribution in a semantic category, which is the "standard deviation". Let's take "Ⅵ-xi-A" as an example of the calculation method. Its standard deviation equals the standard deviation of the frequencies (namely 2, 2, 2, 3, 124) of the five collocates, which is "54.45". We also calculated the standard deviation for all the collocates' frequencies of "故意[*guyi*] (*deliberately*)", which is 25.39. When the standard deviation value of a semantic category is greater than that of the whole, it indicates that the collocations' frequency distribution is of high dispersion degree and thus requires further analysis of its semantic clustering degree to determine its typicality. This will be elaborated in the following sections.

(v) After the previous four steps, we can obtain the information of a node word about its sememe collocation, including the semantic category's "grading type", "word type number (W)", "word frequency (F)" and "standard deviation (s)". By integrating the information, we can conduct valid analysis of the clustering degree of sememe collocation.

4   The Sememe Collocation Features of "故意[*guyi*] (*deliberately*)", "有意 [*youyi*](*intentionally*)" and "存心 [*cunxin*](*purposely*)"

4.1   The Sememe Collocation of "故意[*guyi*] (*deliberately*)"

The semantic category grading hierarchy of collocates of "故意 [*guyi*] (*deliberately*)" is shown in Table 2:

Table 2. The semantic category grading hierarchy of the collocates of "故意[*guyi*] (*deliberately*)"

Semantic category grading type	Total semantic category number	No. of semantic categories with high word frequency dispersion degree	No. of semantic categories with word frequency under 10	Word type number	Total frequency
W*h* F*h*	10	3	0	141	2027
W*m* F*h*	7	7	0	41	1155
W*m* F*m*	29	1	8	133	1037
W*m* F*l*	11	0	10	37	108
W*l* F*m*	6	0	0	10	155
W*l* F*l*	65	0	18	85	395
Total	128	11	36	447	4877

According to the grade of W, there are three scenarios:

When the grade of W is low, there are two types. The difference between the two types lies in the frequency of individual words. Due to the low W value of each semantic category, the semantic clustering feature is not evident, but the sememe collocation is distinct.

When the grade of W is medium, there are three types. These three types resemble each other in W but vary in F. The reason lies in that "W*m* F*m*" type and "W*m* F*h*" type contain collocates of high frequency. Although the F value in "W*m* F*h*" is high, the dispersion degree of the collocation frequency of all the semantic categories in this type is high. Coupled with the fact that the word type number is few, its semantic clustering degree is actually not high and the semantic category collocation is not significant.

When the grade of W is high, there is only "W*h* F*h*" type. Three semantic categories' word frequencies are of high dispersion degree. The semantic clustering degree of these three is relatively weaker than the others in this type. Generally speaking, however, this collocation type is quite large in number and high in frequency, thus its semantic clustering degree is high and its semantic category collocation is distinctive.

In summary, in the hierarchies of "Wl Fl", "Wl Fm", "Wm Fl", "Wm Fm", "Wm Fh" and "Wh Fh", the semantic clustering degree goes higher and the semantic category collocation feature becomes more and more distinctive, but the sememe collocation feature becomes weaker; the semantic categories in the "Wh Fh" type is typical that "故意 [guyi](deliberately)" prefers and they are "social activity-social intercourse-speaking, social activity-social intercourse-express, social activity-judiciary- law-breaking", "social activity- fight- bully, deceive", "social activity-fight-encroach", "biological activity-life and work- provoke", "biological activity- life and work- walk", "biological activity- body gesture- touch and press", "biological activity- body gesture- pull and drag", "biological activity- body gesture- put and place". The high frequency collocates are distributed mainly in "Wh Fh" and "Wm Fh" types. We consider the high-frequency collocates in the former type are more typical.

4.2   The Sememe Collocation of "有意[youyi](intentionally)"

The semantic category grading hierarchy of the collocates of "有意[youyi](intentionally)" is shown in Table 3:

Table 3. The semantic category grading hierarchy of the collocates of "有意[youyi] (intentionally)"

Semantic category grading type	Total semantic category number	No. of semantic categories with high word frequency dispersion degree	No. of semantic categories with word frequency under 10	Word type number	Total frequency
Wh Fh	2	0	1	29	154
Wm Fh	5	3	0	30	299
Wm Fm	14	0	13	61	229
Wl Fh	2	0	0	2	119
Wl Fm	18	1	6	28	210
Wl Fl	34	0	6	40	112
Total	75	4	26	190	1123

According to the grade of W, it can be analyzed under three conditions:

When the grade of W is low, there are three types. The difference between the three lies in individual words' frequency. Due to the low W value of each semantic category, the clustering degree of the collocates in these semantic categories is quite low.

When the grade of W is medium, there are two types. The W values of all semantic categories in "Wm Fm" type are not high, nor are the total frequency of collocates and the frequency of each collocate. Thus semantic category collocation is not distinctive. Although the F value in "Wm Fh" is high, the dispersion degree of the collocation frequency inside the semantic categories is high. Coupled with the fact that the word type number is few, the semantic category collocation is not counted as significant.

When the grade of W is high, there is only "Wh Fh" type, which contains only two semantic categories. Their collocation frequencies are distributed evenly, with one semantic category having all of its collocation frequencies under 10. As the word type number and word frequency of the collocates in these two semantic categories are both of "high" grade, its semantic clustering degree is still high.

Generally, in the hierarchies of "Wl Fl", "Wl Fm", "Wl Fh", "Wm Fm", "Wm Fh" and "Wh Fh", the semantic clustering degree goes higher and the semantic category collocation feature becomes more and more distinctive, but the sememe collocation feature becomes weaker. "有意[*youyi*](*intentionally*)" tends to choose words from the semantic category of "Wh Fh" type. Thus this type can be considered as the typical semantic category that "有意[*youyi*](*intentionally*)" collocates with, which is "social activity- fight- bully and deceive, biological activity- life and work- provoke". There are only a few high frequency collocates and they are distributed mainly in the "Wm Fh" and "Wl Fm" types.

4.3   The Sememe Collocation of "存心[*cunxin*](*purposely*)"

The semantic category grading hierarchy of the collocates of "存心 [*cunxin*](*purposely*)" is shown in Table 4:

Table 4. The semantic category grading hierarchy of the collocates of "存心[*cunxin*] (*purposely*)"

Semantic category grading type	Total semantic category number	No. of semantic categories with high word frequency dispersion degree	No. of semantic categories with word frequency under 10	Word type number	Total frequency
Wh Fh	2	1	0	12	72
Wl Fh	1	0	0	1	27
Wl Fm	8	0	1	9	57
Wl Fl	6	0	0	6	13
Total	17	1	1	28	169

There are four grade types of semantic category in collocates of " 存 心 [*cunxin*](*purposely*)". It shows that both the total word type number and word frequency of the collocates of "存心[*cunxin*](*purposely*)" are not high. Even with the "W high" type, the word type number is still low. The high frequency words are distributed mainly in the two types of "W*h* F*h*" and "W*l* F*h*". Therefore, the semantic category collocation feature of "存心[*cunxin*](*purposely*)" is not distinctive, but the sememe collocation feature is.

4.4   Comparison Analysis

The semantic category number, word type number and word frequency of "W*h* F*h*" type indicate the semantic clustering degree of collocates. Through comparing the semantic category numbers, word type numbers and word frequencies in the "W*h* F*h*" type of the three node words' collocates, we can find that they differ greatly. From Table 2, we can see that "故意 [*guyi*] (*deliberately*)" has distinctive feature for semantic category collocation. The word type number and word frequency covered by the "W*h*F*h*" type are higher than other types. Compared with " 有 意 [*youyi*](*intentionally*)" and "存心[*cunxin*](*purposely*)", from Table 2, 3 and 4, the semantic category number, word type number and word frequency of "W*h*F*h*" type of "故意[*guyi*](*deliberately*)" are much higher. "有意 [*youyi*] (*intentionally*)" ranks the second in distinctiveness of semantic category collocation feature while "存心 [*cunxin*](*purposely*)" possesses distinctive sememe collocation features.

Among the semantic categories of the collocates of "故意[*guyi*](*deliberately*)", "有意[*youyi*](*intentionally*)" and "存心[*cunxin*](*purposely*)", "social activity- fight- bully and deceive" all belong to the "W*h*F*h*" type. The semantic category of the "W*h*F*h*" type, which both "故意[*guyi*](*deliberately*)" and "存心[*cunxin*](*purposely*)" choose, is "social activity-fight- encroach", while the semantic category of the same type, which both "故意[*guyi*](*deliberately*)" and "有意[*youyi*](*intentionally*)" prefer, is "biological activity- life and work- provoke". The "W*h*F*h*" type that only the semantic categories of the collocates of "故意[*guyi*](*deliberately*)" fall into include "biological activity- body gesture- pull and drag", "biological activity- body gesture- touch and press", "biological activity- life and work- walk", "biological activity- body gesture- put and place", "social activity-judiciary- law-breaking", "social activity- social intercourse- express", "social activity- social intercourse- speaking" ranking from low to high according to the standard deviations (namely the distribution dispersion degree of collocation frequency inside each semantic category).

"故意[*guyi*](*deliberately*)" has distinctive semantic category collocation features and its typical collocation should be the semantic categories of "W*h*F*h*" type. The typical collocates should be the words of high frequency in these semantic categories, while the high frequency collocates in semantic categories of "W*m*F*h*" type rank the second in typicality. " 存 心 [*cunxin*](*purposely*)" possesses distinctive sememe collocation features and its typical collocation should be determined in the high frequency collocates. Neither the semantic category collocation feature nor sememe collocation feature of "有意[*youyi*](*intentionally*)" are distinctive. There are semantic categories that possess large word type number and high word frequency, but the individual collocate frequency is not high enough. The high frequency collocates are mainly distributed in the semantic categories that have small word type number and high word frequency, which means the clustering degree of collocates of "有意 [*youyi*](*intentionally*)" inside these semantic categories is low. Besides, there also exist individual high frequency collocates without any semantic clustering features. Hence the typical semantic categories for collocation of "有意[*youyi*](*intentionally*)" are the ones that have large word type number and high word frequency, while the high frequency ones are the typical collocates.

5   Discussion and Conclusion

The three node words that are under the same semantic category with different frequencies from high to low tend to have different collocation characteristics. "故意 [*guyi*] (*deliberately*)", of which the frequency is high, displays high semantic clustering degree and distinctive semantic category collocation features. Therefore we may infer that words with high frequency of use tend to collocate with a certain type of words. Examples are the collocations of some high frequency verbs, adjectives and nouns. This requires further research.

The semantic category that the three node words' collocates fall in with both large word type number and high word frequency is "social activity- fight- bully and deceive". There might exist situations where words in a certain semantic category tend to collocate with words of another one or more semantic categories. Similar methods can be employed to further investigate the collocations of node words that belong to the same semantic category.

The core parts of the sememe collocation analysis framework are word type number of collocates, word frequency of collocates and the semantic category resource. Thereupon the framework can also be applied to the sememe collocation research of any other node words. Moreover, the research findings about sememe collocation can be applied to developing collocation lists and compiling dictionaries for language learning, especially for second language learning.

Typical collocations are not just determined by high frequency. The clustering features of collocates should also be taken into consideration. For node words, of which collocates have obvious features in grammar and semantic clustering (e.g. "故 意[*guyi*] (*deliberately*)"), they prefer to combine with typical categories of grammar and semantics with large word type number and high frequency of collocates, rather than merely high frequency words. The framework proposed in this research is helpful to find out the semantic categories.

Acknowledgements. We would like to express our appreciation to Pro. Hua Liu who developed collocation filtering software and provided the corpora in our research.

References

1. Sinclair, J.: Corpus, Concordance Collocation. Shanghai Foreign Language Education Press, Shanghai (1999)
2. Kang, S.: The Restrictions of Word Combination in Selection of Semantics. Journal of Yan' an University (Social Science Edition) **14**(3), 94–97 (1992). (亢世勇. 词语组合在语义选择上所受的限制. 延安大学学报 14(3), 94-97 (1992)). (in Chinese)
3. Su, X.: A Thesaurus of Modern Chinese. The Commercial Press, Beijing (2013). (in Chinese)
4. Su, X.: A Consideration about Development of A Thesaurus of Modern Chinese. Journal of Chinese information processing **22**(5), 12–21 (2008). (in Chinese)
5. Wang, H.: A Grammatical Study on Restricted Meaning of Chinese Nouns. Studies in Language and Linguistics **26**(1), 1–8 (2006). (in Chinese)
6. Xing, H.: Collocation Knowledge and Second Language Lexical Acquisition. Applied Linguistics **4**, 117–126 (2013). (in Chinese)
7. Ye, N.: The Motivation of Selection between the Components in Sememe Combination. Journal of Southwest University for Nationalities (Humanities and Social Science) **11**, 213–216 (2010). (叶南.义位组合中的选择理据. 西南民族大学学报(人文社科版) (11), 213-216 (2010)) (in Chinese)
8. Zhang, Q.: The Meaning of Sememe Combination. Lexicographical Studies **1**, 68–74 (1995). (张庆云.义位的组合意义. 辞书研究(1), 68-74(1995)) (in Chinese)
9. Zhang, Z., Zhang, Q.: Lexical Semantics. The Commercial Press, Beijing (2001). (in Chinese)
10. Zhou, L.: A Study of Descriptive Adverbs' Collocations Based on Corpus. Jinan University, Guangzhou (2012). (in Chinese)

Incorporating Prepositional Phrase Classification Knowledge in Prepositional Phrase Identification

Qiaoli Zhou[✉], Ling Zhang, Na Ye, and Dongfeng Cai

Knowledge Engineering Research Center, Shenyang Aerospace University,
Shenyang 110136, China
zhou_qiao_li@hotmail.com, 710138892@QQ.com, yena_1@126.com,
caidf@vip.163.com

Abstract. This paper proposes a method of prepositional phrase (PP) identification by incorporating PP classification knowledge. When PPs act as different syntactic constituents, they have different characteristics in terms of location and context. In this paper, PPs are classified based on the context in which they appear. We select features based on the category of PPs to train multiple machine learning models for PP identification, and recombine these identification results. In this way, we can make full use of the complementary advantage of multiple models.

Keywords: Chinese information processing · Prepositional phrase identification · Multi-model · Prepositional phrase classification

1   Introduction

Preposition belongs to function word and is a closed set. There is a preposition list in *the Contemporary Chinese Grammatical Knowledge Base* [1] which has 85 prepositions. PP consists of two parts: the front part is the preposition, and the latter part is a word or phrase that is the attachment of preposition. In the process of PP identification, the first word of PP is preposition, so the first word can be identified based on the part of speech, and the identification of tail word of PP is our main task. In a sentence, PP always plays the role of attributive, adverbial and complement component. Therefore the PP identification result can help sentence framework (subject, predicate and object) identification, and make the parsing easier in the next step. There are significant differences in the words adjacent to the tail word of PP, due to the different components of PP in a sentence (Detailed analysis see section 3). In this paper PP was classified, and then we select features based on the category of PPs to train models of machine learning for PP identification, and recombine these results. In this way, we can make full use of the complementary advantage of multi-model.

This work is supported by Humanities and Social Sciences Foundation for the Youth Scholars of Ministry of Education of China (№-14YJC740126) and National Natural Science Foundation of China (№-61402299).
Q. Lu and H.H. Gao (Eds.): CLSW 2015, LNAI 9332, pp. 566–576, 2015.
DOI: 10.1007/978-3-319-27194-1_57

2   Related Work

State-of-the-art PP identification methods can be classified into two types. One is based on statistical method, the other is a combination of statistical and rule method. The statistical method is based on machine learning. For instance, Support Vector Machine (SVM) [2], Conditional Random Fields (CRFs) [3] model and Maximum Entropy (ME) [4] model were applied to identify PP. Zhang Kunli et al. [5] use the "People's Daily" as corpus to identify PP based on SVM, ME and CRFs models respectively and the result shows that CRFs model obtain the best result. In the paper of Dongfeng Cai et al. [6] PP identification is transformed into the collocation identification of preposition itself and the tail word of PP. The Cascaded Conditional Random Fields (CCRFs) is used in this approach. This approach obtains breakthrough in this specific field as the current F1 is about 8.6% higher than any publicly published paper at that time.

For the combination of rule and statistical methods, the rules were used as a post-processing method to correct errors of the statistical recognition results. Xi Jianqing [7] proposed a model based on Hidden Markov Model (HMM) for identifying the boundaries of PP. They correct the mistakes of HMM recognition by using dependence grammar. Lu Zhaohua et al. [8,9] proposed a model based on ME for identifying the boundaries of PP. They also correct the mistakes in the identification results of ME model by using dependence grammar knowledge. Hu Silei and Huang Degen [10] proposed a two-layer PP identification approach based on CRFs. Their experiment involved many features for statistical decision and 22 rules to correct the result. However, the 22 rules are extracted from the experiment result and the error-prone PPs in test set, therefore these rules are perhaps not applicable to other corpora. Besides, this method can only work for the sentences that have less than two nested PPs. Song Guizhe et al. [11] use dual-layer CRFs to identify PP, and the PP rules are used for post-processing.

When the method of machine learning (ML) was used to identify PP, feature selection is very important. Experimental results show the same ML model combining different features will get different recognition results. In these papers [6,12] experimental results show that the same ML method combined different features will create nearly 9% precision gap. We do deep analysis on the PP, and discover the classification knowledge of PP. Therefore this paper proposes the strategy of multi-model advantage complementation to identify PP based on the classification knowledge of PP.

3   Classification of PP

Preposition is a closed set, and the absolute number is limited, but in Chinese grammar system the preposition played an important role. Preposition definition is different from other parts of speech. PP was formed by preposition combinations with other word, and act as modifiers in Chinese sentences, which can be used as adverbial, attributive, complement, or other components [13]. PPs serve as different sentence constituents, so the locations in the sentences will be different, and have different features of context. The main syntactic constituent PP serves as is the adverbial. When PP serves as the adverbial, PP appears in different positions in the sentence. Some may be around the subject, some only appear between subject and predicate, and some only appear before the subject [14]. The Category Description of PP is as follows:

- When PP serves as the adverbial before the subject, a pause usually appears between the adverbial and main sentence. Examples are shown in Table 1.

Table 1. PP Serves as Adverbial before the Subject

Adverbial of time	PP【在国家队效力的时候】 ，他打进了５４个球。 *(When he worked for the national team, he scored 54 goals.)*
Adverbial of place	PP【在国际关系中】 ，两国确立发展友好合作关系。 *(In international relations, the two countries have established friendly relations and cooperation.)*
Adverbial of action	PP【对于公司的决定】 ，与会领导给予了高度评价。 *(For the decision of the company, the leaders gave a high degree of evaluation.)*
Adverbial of scope	PP【除了节省时间外】 ，它还可降低费用。 *(In addition to saving time, it also reduces the cost.)*
Adverbial of reason	PP【由于历史的原因】 ，铁路的国际联运曾两度中断。 *(Due to historical reasons, the international intermodal rail was twice interrupted.)*

- PP serves as the adverbial and appears between subject and predicate. As we all know agent, patient and beneficiaries have a close relationship with predicate. When a preposition is combined with agent, patient or beneficiaries to form PP, this kind of PP has a significant characteristic that the tail word of PP is most close to predicate. Examples are shown in Table 2.

Table 2. PP Serves as Adverbial between the Subject and Predicate

Adverbial of patient	他 PP【把/p 桌子】擦干净了 *(He cleaned the table.)*
Adverbial of agent	杯子 PP【被/p 我】打破了 *(The cup was broken by me)*
Adverbial of beneficiary	他 PP【替/p 妈妈】干活 *(He works for his mother.)*
Adverbial of recipient	我们 PP【同/p 他】讨论合作的事 *(We discuss cooperation with him.)*
Adverbial of action direction and source	我 PP【从/p 图书馆】回来 *(I come back from the library.)*
Adverbial of tool	他 PP【用/p 那把刀】切菜 *(He used the knife for cutting.)*

- There are some prepositional phrases that can act as attributive. Such as "关于", "对于", "随着", "在" and "为了". Examples are shown as following.

"PP【关于/P 事件/NN 全貌/NN 问题/NN】 的/DEG 诉讼/NN"
(Litigation concerning the outline of the problem)
"PP【对于/P 民间/NN 投资/NN 】 的/DEG 拉动/NN 作用/NN"
(Stimulating role for private investment)
"PP【 在/P 中国/NR 高速/JJ 公路网/NN 中/LC】 的/DEG 枢纽/NN 地位/NN"。
(The position of the hub in the Chinese highway network)

Based on the above analysis and examples PP usually combining with "的" (*de*) act as attributive. That is to say, when PP acts as attributive, the adjacent word of tail word is "的" (*de*).

- When PP acts as complement, the sentence structure is "V + preposition + noun phrase". Such as "来/v 自/p 北京/n" (*came from Beijing*), "写/v 于/p 上海/n" (*written in Shanghai*).

From the above 4 classification of PP, we could conclude that adjacent words of PP tail word are associated with the sentence constituent PP acted as and the position PP appeared. Adjacent sign of PP tail word are shown in table 3.

Table 3. Adjacent Sign of PP Tail Word

Sentence Constituent of PP	Adjacent sign of PP tail word
Adverbial (before the subject)	comma
Adverbial (between subject and predicate)	predicate
Attributive	"的" (*de*)

4   Identification of PP Based on Multi-model

This paper uses CRFs model to identify PP, so we need to choose the feature of Model according to the training corpus. Identification Model was classified according to the characteristics of PP, so features are needed to correspond to Model. This paper therefore trains multi-model as the same time and use the advantage of multi-model to identify PP.

4.1   Identification Model Category

According to section 3 of this paper PP was summarized and analyzed, and identification Model of PP was divided into three categories.

- There is a collocation between preposition and the tail word of PP. For example, "在……上" (*on*), "除了……外" (*except*), "对于……而言" (*for*).
- The adjacent words of the tail word of PP belong to some kind of word or sign due to the syntactic constituent PP served as in sentence as shown in table 3.
- The internal structure of the PP is simple and the tail word of PP is easy to be identified by CRFs Model. For example, "在/p 上海/n" (*at Shanghai*), "自/p 去年/n" (*last year*).

4.2   Feature Selection Based on the Category

This paper uses CRFs model to identify PP, so we need to select feature sets respectively for every category from section 4.1. Through the experiments on the development set this paper selects feature sets as table 4.

Table 4. Features of Different Models

	Model	Feature
1	Model1	O|W, W, P, O
2	Model2	O|W, W, P, O, F|B|W, |B|P
3	Model3	W, P, O

'W' represents the current word, 'P' represents the part-of-speech of the current word, 'O' represents the preposition, 'F' represents the left adjacent word of preposition that appears first in the left position of current word, and 'B' represents the right adjacent word of current word. Because the first word and the tail word is a collocation in some PP, we treat the first word and tail word of PP as a collocation. Therefore the combination of features is used. "o|w" represents the combination of the first word and the candidate tail word of PP.

4.3 Tagging Sets

This paper transforms the PP identification into collocation identification of PP as Dongfeng Cai [6]. In this paper the tagging sets were composed of "OIEN", wherein 'O' represents the collocation before the PP; 'I' represents the inner collocation of PP; 'E' represents the collocation that was formed by the first word with tail word of PP, and 'N' represents behind collocation of PP. Detailed introduction is given in the following sentence. 李鹏/NR PP[对/P 韦奇立/NR 再次/AD 来访/VV] 表示/VV 欢迎/NN 。/PU (*Li Peng expressed welcome at the periodic visit of Viera.*) For this sentence, the tagging set of "OIEN" in Table 5.

Table 5. Tagging Sets

Tagging set of CRF		
O|W	P	Tag
|李鹏(|*Li Peng*)	NR	O
|对(|*at*)	P	O
对|韦奇立(*at*| *Viera*)	NR	I
对|再次(*at*| *the periodic*)	AD	I
对|来访(*at*| *visit*)	VV	E
对|表示(*at*| *expressed*)	VV	N
对|欢迎(*at*| *welcome*)	NN	N
对|。(*at*|.)	PU	N

In table 5 'w' represents the current word, which is the candidate tail word of PP. 'P' represents the part-of-speech of the current word. The 'tag' shows the tagging sets. "*\|李鹏" (*\|*Li Peng*) shows that there is no preposition before the current word "李鹏" (*Li Peng*), the preposition is represented by "*"; "对\|韦奇力" (*at*\| *Viera*) represents that the first word of PP is "对" (*at*), "韦奇力" (*Viera*) is the candidate tail word that may form collocation, at the same time "对" (*at*) appears before "韦奇力" (*Viera*); "*|对" (*|at*)means that when the preposition "对" (*at*) itself appears as a candidate tail word, the first word of PP is replaced by "*".

4.4   Experiments on Three Models

We perform the experiments on the Penn Chinese Treebank 4. The corpus contains 1064 files and 15165 sentences. We test on sentences 14126-15162, train on sentences 0-13074 and develop on sentences 13075-14125. The experiment result is tested by recall rate, precision rate and F1. The one with highest F1 has the best performance.

The method that identifies PP of nested structure uses the bottom-up strategy. The identification process is as follows:

1) Scan the sentence from right to left to check for the first preposition. If there is preposition in the sentence, go to step 2, otherwise output the result and finish the algorithm.
2) Use CRFs model to identify the PP.
3) Delete the PP that has been identified in original sentence and generate a new sentence.
4) Repeat step 1 for the new sentence.

Table 6 shows the results of different models on the identification of PP.

Table 6. Comparison of Models

	Model1	Model2	Model3
Development Set	83.59%	84.40%	80.95%
Test Set	85.53%	87.22%	85.53%

As shown in table 6 Model2 is the best Model among the three Models.

4.5   Multi-model Complementary Advantage

Multi-model complementary advantage (MCA) this paper proposed is the fusion results of multiple models based on the multi-model complementary advantage table (MCAT). Based on a combination of the features mentioned in table 4 we trained three models, and used the three models to identify PP on development sets. After analyzing the different identification results of three models, we obtained MCAT as shown in Table 7.

Parts of prepositions in the MCAT are shown in table 7. The first word of PP always is a preposition, so in this test PPs are divided into categories according to the preposition. Table 7 shows the comparative experiments of three models on the same kind of PP. As shown from Table 7, the same preposition has different experimental results based on different models. For instance, PP that was conducted by the preposition of "向"(*xiang*) gained the best identification results on the Model3, so the final Model of "向"(*xiang*) is Model3; PP that was conducted by the preposition "透过 "(*touguo*) gained the best identification results on the three models.

Table 7. Comparison of Models on the Same Kind of PP

P	Count	Model1	Model2	Model3	Best Model	Final Model
以(*yi*)	78	92.31%	93.59%	88.46%	2	2
因(*yin*)	26	65.38%	69.23%	61.54%	2	2
向(*xiang*)	17	82.35%	82.35%	88.24%	3	3
由(*you*)	41	90.24%	90.24%	87.80%	1,2	2
在(*zai*)	284	90.49%	91.20%	89.44%	2	2
透过(*touguo*)	8	87.50%	87.50%	87.50%	1,2,3	2
当(*dang*)	10	100%	90%	90%	1	1
与(*yu*)	39	94.87%	94.87%	92.31%	1,2	2
从(*cong*)	35	82.86%	82.86%	85.71%	3	3

When some kind of PP did not appear in the complementary table because it was not included in the development sets, the priority of models was set according to the table 6. Based on the overall recognition performance of the three models shown in table 6, Model1 is the highest-priority, Model2 is the second and Model3 is the lowest-priority. For instance, PP that was conducted by the preposition of "与"(*yu*) gained the best identification results on Model1 and Model2, so the final Model corresponding to "与"(*yu*) is Model2 on the priority of models. For preposition that did not appear in development set, the default choice is Model2, which is the optimal model corresponding to the priority of Model.

Each kind of PP has an optimal model corresponding to MCAT, so each kind of PP can obtain the best identification results from the three models based on MCAT. According to the above mentioned MCAT was shown in table 8.

Table 8. Part of MCAT

P	Final Model	P	Final Model	P	Final Model
以(*yi*)	2	透过(*touguo*)	2	在(*zai*)	2
因(*yin*)	2	当(*dang*)	1	由(*you*)	2
向(*xiang*)	3	与(*yu*)	2	从(*cong*)	3

5   Experiments

5.1   Methods

Our PP identification system design is shown in Figure 1. Every Model represents applying the CRFs sequence-labeling method to the extracted feature vectors to train the identification PP model. First, we identify PP on development set by use three Models respectively and obtain three results of each PP. Every kind of PP is fed to the

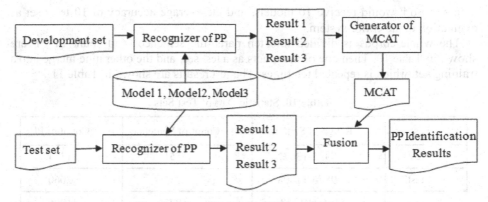

Fig. 1. System Design for PP Identification.

selection process of optimal model, which is generator of MCAT, to build MCAT. Finally, we apply MCAT to choose the PP that was identified by using three Models on the test set and obtained the final results.

5.2   Dataset

We perform the experiments on the Penn Chinese Treebank 4. The corpus contains 1064 files and 15165 sentences. We test on sentences 14126-15162, train on sentences 0-13074 and develop on sentences 13075-14125. We make statistic on corpus of CTB4, and got the average length and count in term of PPs and sentences we show in table 9. Al represents the average of length in table 9.

Table 9. Statistic Data of Corpus

	Training set	Development set	Test set
Count of Sentences	13077	1051	1037
Count of Words	343457	30847	30455
Count of PP	12578	987	1009
AL of Sentence	26.3	29.4	29.4
AL of PP	5.3	5.0	4.7

5.3   PP Identification

In order to enhance the accuracy and authenticity of the experiment and to avoid over fitting phenomenon, Models were tested using ten-fold cross validation method. Ten-fold cross-validation is to collect all the samples and the samples were divided into 10 parts, each subset of the data makes a test set, the remaining 9 parts make the training data set. So it would receive 10 models, and the average accuracy of 10 tests set as evaluation of the entire-system.

The whole corpus is divided into ten parts, the sentences and count of PP are shown in Table 10. Then one of them acts as a test set, and the other nine merge into a training set, which is repeated ten times. The test results are shown in Table 11.

Table 10. Statistic Data of Test Sets

Test set	Range of Sentence	Count of Sentence	Count of PP
test1	8325-13077	1551	1374
test2	9876-11608	1733	2060
test3	11609-13483	1875	1906
test4	13484-15162	1679	1628
test5	1-1370	1371	1338
test6	1371-2755	1385	1260
test7	2756-4135	1380	1245
test8	4136-5514	1379	1318
test9	5515-6927	1413	1245
test10	6928-8324	1396	1200

Table 11. Ten-fold Cross Validation

Test set	Model1	Model2	Model3	MCA
test1	90.9025%	92.2125%	90.393%	91.6303%
test2	86.9417%	87.3301%	86.1650%	87.2333%
test3	84.5226%	85.5194%	84.1028%	85.0472%
test4	85.5037%	86.6708%	83.7224%	87.2236%
test5	90.8072%	91.3303%	89.4619%	91.4798%
test6	91.3492%	91.9048%	88.8095%	92.4603%
test7	91.8876%	91.9679%	89.6386%	92.5301%
test8	89.2261%	90.2124%	88.6191%	90.0607%
test9	90.2811%	90.8434%	88.9960%	90.6024%
test10	90.2500%	91.6667%	88.1667%	91.0833%
Average	89.1671%	**89.9658%**	87.8075%	**90.1351%**

After a ten-fold cross-validation, as can be seen from Table 11, the recognition results of PP based on MCA increased by about 0.2 percentage points over the best single model that is Model2 , 1 percentage point higher than Model1 and 2.3 percentage points higher than Model3. It can be concluded that the MCA is efficient.

As can be seen from Table 11, not every test set of MCA results are the best, which is caused by the following reasons: First, There are great differences in the type and quantity of PP in the ten test sets. Second, types of preposition in development set are unevenly distributed, so development set cannot cover all types of preposition. Third, there are certain limitations on MCAT that was generated only based on the development set. These above issues will also be the focus of further work.

6   Conclusions

Based on the classification knowledge of PP, MCA was proposed for the recognition of PP. Ten-fold cross-validation and comparative experiments also demonstrate the effectiveness and applicability of MCA we proposed. For Chinese sentences, what makes PP different from other kind of phrase is that preposition is closed set and is the first word of PP, so we classify PP precisely according to preposition. Multi Models can be trained according to the type of PP, and we take advantage of multi Models to improve the recognition accuracy of PP.

References

1. Yu, S.: Grammatical Knowledge-base of Contemporary. Tsinghua University Press, Chinese Beijing (1998). (in Chinese)
2. Wen, M., Wu, Y.: Feature-rich Prepositional Phrase Boundary Identification based on SVM. Journal Of Chinese Information Processing 23(5), 19–24 (2008). (in Chinese)
3. Zhu, D., Wang, D., Xie, J.: Automatic Identification of Propositional Phrase Based on Conditional Random Field. New Technology of Library and Information Service 26(7/8), 79–83 (2010). (in Chinese)
4. Yu, J., Huang, D.: Automatic Identification of Chinese Prepositional Phrase Based on Maximum Entropy (Master's degree thesis) Dalian University of technology (2011). (in Chinese)
5. Zhang, K., Han, Y., Zan, H.: Prepositional Phrase Boundary Identification Based on Statistical Models. Journal of Henan University (Natural Science) 41(6), 636–640 (2011). (in Chinese)
6. Cai, D., Zhang, L., Zhou, Q., Zhao, Y.: A collocation based approach for preposition phrase identification. In: Processing of the 7th International Conference on Natural Language Processing and Knowledge Engineering (NLP-KE 2011), Tokushima, Japan, November 27–29, 2011 (in Chinese)
7. Xi, J., Luo, Q.: Research on Automatic Identification for Chinese Prepositional Phrase Based on HMM. Computer Engineering 33(3), 172–182 (2007). (in Chinese)
8. Lu, Z., Huang, G., Guo, Z.: Identification of Chinese Prepositional Phrase. Communications Technology 43(5), 181–183 (2010). 186 (in Chinese)

9. Lu, Z., Xu, H., Wang, Y.: Re-search on Identification Method of Chinese Prepositional Phrase Based on Semantic Analysis. Computer and Telecommunication **3**, 46–50 (2012). (in Chinese)
10. Hu, S.: Automatic Identification of Chinese Prepositional Phrase Based on CRF (Master's de-gree thesis) Dalian University of technology (2008). (in Chinese)
11. Song, G., Huang, D.: Recognition of Chinese Propositional Phrase (Master's degree thesis). Dalian University of technology (2011). (in Chinese)
12. Zhang, L.: Research on Chinese Preposition Phrase Identification Based on Cascaded Conditional Random Fields (Master's degree thesis). Shenyang Aerospace University (2013). (in Chinese)
13. Zhang, B.: Function Words In Modern Chinese. East China Normal University Press, Shanghai (2000). (in Chinese)
14. Shi, Y.: Chinese Grammatical. The Commercial Press, Beijing (2010). (in Chinese)

A Chinese Event Argument Inference Approach Based on Entity Semantics and Event Relevance

Shaohua Zhu[1,2], Peifeng Li[1,2(✉)], and Qiaoming Zhu[1,2]

[1] Natural Language Processing Lab, Soochow University, Suzhou 215006, Jiangsu, China
20134227017@stu.suda.edu.cn, {pfli,qmzhu}@suda.edu.cn
[2] School of Computer Science and Technology, Soochow University,
Suzhou 215006, Jiangsu, China

Abstract. Currently, Chinese argument extraction mainly focuses on feature engineering, which cannot exploit inner relationships between event mentions in the same document. To address this issue, this paper learns the probabilities of entities fulfilling a specific role from the training set and the relationship among events to infer more arguments using Markov Logic Networks. Experimental results on the ACE 2005 Chinese corpus show that our approach outperforms the baseline significantly, with an improvement of 8.6% and 8.2% in argument identification and role determination respectively.

Keywords: Argument extraction · Markov Logic Network · Argument inference

1 Introduction

The task of event extraction is to recognize event mentions of a predefined event type and their arguments (participants and attributes). Generally, it can be divided into two subtasks: trigger extraction, which aims to identify event mentions and determine their event types, and argument extraction, which aims to extract various arguments of a specific event and assign roles to them. In this paper, we focus on argument extraction in Chinese language event extraction. Take the following sentence as an example:

(E1) Chinese:米洛舍维奇被迫**逃离**贝尔格勒。
    English:*Milosevic was forced to **flee** Belgrade.*

In the above example, E1 is an event mention, whose event type is *Transport*, involving trigger mention 逃离(flee) and corresponding arguments 米洛舍维奇 (Milosevic) and 贝尔格勒(Belgrade).The two arguments of 米洛舍维奇(Milosevic) and 贝尔格勒(Belgrade) act as *Artifact* and *Origin* roles in E1, respectively. All of the examples in this paper are taken from the ACE2005 Chinese corpus.

Currently, Chinese argument extraction approaches mainly focus on feature engineering, which cannot exploit inner relationships among event mentions in the same document. Additionally, semantic information in the existing Chinese event argument extraction methods is less used. These deficiencies result in poor performance in Chi-

© Springer International Publishing Switzerland 2015
Q. Lu and H.H. Gao (Eds.): CLSW 2015, LNAI 9332, pp. 577–586, 2015.
DOI: 10.1007/978-3-319-27194-1_58

nese event argument extraction. To address this issue, this paper exploits Bei-sentences, entity semantics information, relative position of entity and trigger, entity type information and event relevance inference rules, and learns the probabilities of entities fulfilling a specific role from the training set and the relationship among events to infer more arguments in the event type of *Justice*, which is based on Markov Logic Networks.

2   Related Work

Compared with English, research on Chinese event extraction is relatively recent, with some focus on event trigger extraction. Using the ACE2005 Chinese corpus [1], Zhao et al. [2] proposed a method combining event trigger expansion and a binary classifier for event identification and solved the unbalanced data problem in training models and the data sparseness problem brought by the small set of training data effectively. Tan et al. [3] modeled event extraction as a pipeline of classification tasks. Specially, they used a local feature selection approach and combined positive features with negative features to ensure the performance of trigger identification and trigger type classification. Li et al. [4] employed compositional semantics inside Chinese triggers to expand triggers for Chinese event extraction.

Studies on Chinese event argument extraction are relatively less than Chinese event trigger extraction. Tan et al. [3] put forward an approach based on multi-level patterns in order to improve the coverage of patterns and to use various language information. Hou et al. [5] proposed a trigger word detection method based on character and used a CRF-based model in view of the inconsistency between Chinese word segmentation and trigger word boundaries to identify event mentions. Chen and Ji [6] referenced the pipeline framework of Ahn [7], applied various kinds of lexical, syntactic and semantic features to address the specific issues in Chinese. They also constructed a global errata table to record inconsistency in the training set and used it to correct inconsistency in the testing set. Fu et al. [8] used a feature weighing scheme to re-weight various features for Chinese argument extraction. Li et al. [9] proposed a global argument inference model to extract those inter-sentence arguments due to the nature of Chinese being a discourse-driven pro-drop language with the wide spread use of ellipsis and an open flexible sentence structure.

As an important hypothesis in natural languages, discourse consistency has been widely applied to many natural language processing applications, such as named entity recognition and coreference resolution. In particular, several studies have successfully incorporated trigger or entity consistency constraints into English event extraction. Liao and Grishman [10] mainly focused on employing cross-event consistency information to improve sentence-level trigger extraction and proposed an inference method to infer the arguments following role consistency in a document. Hong et al. [11] employed the background information to divide an entity type into more cohesive subtypes to create the bridge between two entities, and then inferred arguments and their roles using cross-entity inference on the subtypes of the entities. In Chinese event extraction, the discourse information has not been fully used. Li et al. [9] proposed a global argument inference model to recover inter-sentence arguments in the sentence, discourse and document layers.

3   Chinese Argument Inference

As a statistical relational learning language, Markov Logic Networks are based on the First Order Logic and Markov Networks. Basically, it can be seen as an expressive template language that uses First Order Logic formulas to instantiate Markov Networks of repetitive structure. Recently, MLNs have been used successfully in many NLP applications, such as entity resolution, link prediction, information extraction and coreference resolution.

3.1   Predicates Definition

MLN inference mainly includes predicate descriptions and inference formulas. Table 1 includes all of the predicates used in this paper. In addition, only one query predicate $Role(ent_1, role_1, evType_1)$ appears in this paper, which means entity ent_1 acts as the $role_1$ role in the $evType_1$ event type.

Table 1. Predicates and their description in our MLN

Predicate	Description
$Entity(ent_1, evType_1)$	Entity ent_1 appears in the $evType_1$ event type;
$EntAndTriRel(ent_1, evType_1, rel_1)$	Entity ent_1 is next to the trigger and ent_1 appears in the $evType_1$ event type, relative position of the entity and trigger is rel_1;
$SameEnt(ent_1, ent_2)$	Entity ent_1 is same to ent_2;
$InSameDoc(tri_1, fn_1, tri_2, fn_2)$	Trigger tri_1 and tri_2 appear in document fn_1 and fn_2 respectively. Document fn_1 is same to fn_2;
$SameEv(tri_1, fn_1, tri_2, fn_2)$	Triggers tri_1 and tri_2 trigger the same event and appear in documents fn_1 and fn_2 respectively. Document fn_1 is identical to fn_2;
$Role(ent_1, role_1, evType_1)$	Entity ent_1 acts as the $role_1$ role in the $evType_1$ event type;
$EntType(ent_1, entType_1)$	Entity type of entity ent_1 is $entType_1$ (e.g., PER or TIME);
$EvType(ent_1, tri_1, evType_1)$	Trigger tri_1 has entity ent_1 and triggers event of type $evType_1$;
$InSameSen(ent_1, tri_1, evType_1, tri_2, evType_2)$	Triggers tri_1 and tri_2 appear in same sentence and they have the same entity ent_1;

3.2   Inference Theory Basis and Rules

In this paper, we exploit Bei-sentence, entity information, relative positions of entity and trigger, entity type information and event relevance inference rules for argument inference. Because information extraction is domain specific, we only proceed to argument inference in the event type of *Justice* in the ACE 2005 Chinese corpus.

There are many Bei-sentences in the event type of *Justice*. These Bei-sentences provide evidence for argument inference. For instance, in a Bei-sentence, if the event type is *Charge-Indict*, the entity before character "被" will act as *Defendant* role with high probability. E2 is an event mention of event type *Charge-Indict* and trigger is指控 (accused), entity 他 (He) is before character "被" and it acts as *Defendant* role.

(E2) Chinese: *他被指控以学术研究为名为美国政府收集军事情报。*

    English: *He was **accused** of collecting military intelligence in the name of the academic research.*

Bei-sentence Inference: When event type $evType_1$ is the subtype of the *Justice* event type, if entity ent_1 is before character "被", the entity role $role_1$ will act as recipient (**Rule1**).

$$\text{Entity } (ent_1, +evType_1) => \text{Role } (ent_1, role_1, +evType_1) \qquad (1)$$

Some entities always act as specific roles in specific event types. For instance, courts, judges and courtrooms entities always act as *Adjudicator* role as well as policemen, police and public security bureau entities always act *Agent* role in the event type of *Justice*. According to entity semantics, all the entities in the event type of *Justice* are divided into three types, judicial organ, law enforcement agency and others. In the two types of entities judicial organ and law enforcement agency, we will respectively employ the following two entity semantics information inference rules, named judicial organ semantics information inference and law enforcement agency semantics information inference.

In the *Justice* event type, the proportion of the top three entities act as *Adjudicator* role are courts, courtrooms, and judges, with 54.7%, 16.5% and 9.4%, respectively. In addition, 83.5% of the entities in the three types act as the *Adjudicator* role. In training, the entity of the court, the courtroom and the judge will be added to the reasoning training set. In testing, if an entity is included in the training set, then it will be added to the reasoning testing set, otherwise, we judge whether the entity is synonymous with any entity in the reasoning training set. If it is, the entity is added to reasoning testing set, otherwise we judge whether the entity is synonymous to any entity in reasoning training set by TongYiCiCiLin[1]. If it is, the entity is added to the reasoning testing set, otherwise, we drop the entity. Take the following sentence for example, E3 is an event mention of event type *Appeal* and the trigger is上诉(appeal), and entity 美国最高法院(U.S. Supreme Court) of semantic type judicial organ acts as the *Adjudicator* role.

---

[1] http://www.ltp-cloud.com/download/

(E3) Chinese: 同一天，美国最高法院驳回了布什竞选阵营的另一项上诉。

English: *On the same day, the U.S. Supreme Court dismissed another **appeal** from the Bush campaign.*

Judicial Organ Semantics Information Inference: When the event type $evType_1$ is a subtype of the *Justice* event type, and if the semantics type of entity ent_1 is judicial organ, the entity role $role_1$ will act as *Adjudicator* (**Rule 2**).

$$Entity\ (ent_1, +evType_1) => Role\ (ent_1, role_1, +evType_1) \qquad (2)$$

For the *Justice* event type, the proportion of the top four entities acting as *Agent* role are police, organ, public security and policemen, with 29.3%, 9.8%, 8.5%, and 7.3%, respectively. In addition, 80.0% of the entities in the four types act as *Agent* role. The method to select the reasoning training set and testing set is similar to that of judicial organ semantics information inference. For instance, E4 is an event mention of event type *Arrest-Jail* and the trigger is 逮捕 (arrested), entity 警方(police) of semantics type of law enforcement agency acts as the *Agent* role.

(E4) Chinese: 日本警方昨天说，警方在东京逮捕了一名用棒球攻击行人的17岁男学生。

English: *Japanese police said yesterday the police **arrested** a 17-year-old male student who attacked pedestrians with baseball in Tokyo.*

Law Enforcement Agency Semantics Information Inference: When event type $evType_1$ is a subtype of the *Justice* Event type, and if semantics type of entity ent_1 is law enforcement agency, the entity role $role_1$ will act as *Agent* (**Rule 3**).

$$Entity\ (ent_1, +evType_1) => Role\ (ent_1, role_1, +evType_1) \qquad (3)$$

When the types of triggers are the subtypes of the *Justice* event type, they are typically fixed. For instance, triggers for the event type of *Arrest-Jail* and *Sue* are always"逮捕"and"诉讼"or"上诉"respectively. Therefore, in a non-Bei-sentence, the role of the entity can be deduced by the position relationship between the entity and the trigger. For instance, E5 is an event mention of event type *Sentence*, entity 法院 (court) is before trigger 判处 (sentence) and it acts as *Adjudicator* role, entity 王国清 (Guoqing Wang) is after trigger and it acts as the *Defendant* role.

(E5) Chinese: 法院当庭作出了以抢劫罪、故意伤害罪、盗窃罪，判处王国清死刑，剥夺政治权利终身，并处没收个人全部财产的一审判决。

English: *The court found for robbery, intentional injury, theft, and **sentenced** Guoqing Wang to death and deprivation of political rights for life and confiscation of all personal property in the first instance judgement.*

Relative Position of Entity and Trigger Inference: When event type $evType_1$ is the subtype of the *Justice* event type and the entity type is PER, and if the relative position rel_1 is that of entity ent_1 before the corresponding trigger, the entity role $role_1$ will act as the agent, otherwise, the entity role $role_1$ will act as recipient (**Rule 4**).

$$EntAndTriRel(ent_1,+evType_1,rel_1) => Role(ent_1,role_1,+evType_1) \qquad (4)$$

In the *Justice* event type, the type of entities which act as the *Sentence* role can only be SEN. 61.3% of entities of type SEN act as the *Sentence* role. For example, E6 is an event mention of event type *Sentence* and the trigger is判处 (sentenced), types of entity 有期徒刑1年 (1 year imprisonment) and 罚金5万元 (fined 50,000 yuan) are both SEN. Therefore, the two entities both act as the *Sentence* role.

(E6) Chinese: *女"蛇头"申明哲被判处有期徒刑1年，并处罚金5万元。*
    English: *The female felon Mingzhe Shen was **sentenced** to 1 year imprisonment, and fined 50000 yuan.*

Entity Type Information Inference: When the event type $evType_1$ is a subtype of the *Justice* event type, and if type of entity ent_1 is SEN, the entity role $role_1$ will act as *Sentence* (**Rule 5**).

$$\text{Entity } (ent_1, +evType_1) => \text{Role } (ent_1, role_1, +evType_1) \tag{5}$$

Roles of relevant events are consistent. For instance, the *Sentence* event may occur when the *Trial-Hearing* event occurs, and the *Appeal* event may occur when the *Sentence* event occurs. Take the following sentence for example:

(E7) Chinese:*在今天的"现身说法"警示教育会上，原陕西省人民银行营业部柜台负责人淡东晖等7名因贪污、受贿、挪用公款等罪被判刑的服刑人员，……*
    English: *In today's "appearing" warning education conference, the former business department of the people's bank of shaanxi province Donghui Tan, head of the counter Bribes, and other six because of corruption embezzlement and other crimes **sentenced** prisoners,……*

There are two event mentions in example E7, including one *Sentence* event mention (EM1) and one *Arrest-Jail* (EM2) event mention. If the entity 原陕西省人民银行营业部柜台负责人淡东晖等 7 名因贪污、受贿、挪用公款等罪被判刑的服刑人员(the former business department of the people's bank of Shanxi province Donghui Tan, head of the counter Bribes, and other six because of corruption embezzlement and other crimes sentenced prisoners) acts as *Defendant* role in the EM1 is given, it is easy to infer that the entity acts as *Person* role in the EM2.

Event Relevance Inference: Inference according to roles consistency between relevant events (**Rule 6**).

$$Role(e_1,+role_1,+evType_1)^\wedge EntType(e_1,+entType_1)^\wedge EvType(e_1,+tri_1,+type_1)$$
$$^\wedge SameEnt\ (e_1, e2)\ ^\wedge InSameSen\ (e_1, +tri_1, +evType_1, +tri_2, +evType_2)$$
$$^\wedge EvType(e_2,tri_2,+evType_2)=>Role(e_2,+role_2,+evType_2) \tag{6}$$

Roles of relevant event are consistent. In *Justice* event, the entity as *Defendant* role in certain event subtypes as *Person* or *Plaintiff* role in certain event subtypes, and *Agent* role in certain event subtypes as *Agent* or *Adjudicator* role in certain event subtypes. In many event subtypes, *Place* and *Time* roles are consistent.

3.3   Implementation Method

In this paper, we employ the argument extraction system of Li [9] as the inference basis. In our implementation, the following two methods are applied:

1) In Bei-sentence, entity semantics information, relative position of entity and trigger, entity type information inference rules, firstly, we extract the reasoning training set from the training set of the baseline complying with above-mentioned three rules, and learn the probabilities of the entities fulfilling a specific role. Secondly, we extract the reasoning testing set from the testing set of the baseline system complying with rules and using the learned model to infer arguments.

2) In event relevance inference rule, firstly, we extract the reasoning training set from the training set of the baseline complying with above-mentioned rule. Secondly, we set a threshold T in the testing set of the baseline. A classification probability that is higher than or equal to T is considered credible, while lower than T is considered incredible. The threshold is learned from the development set and set to be 0.73.The credible part of the testing set will serve as evidences of the incredible part and incredible part will serve as queries, namely the reasoning testing set. Meanwhile, it is also necessary to establish the link between credible entities and incredible entities. Lastly, we exploit reasoning training set and various evidences to learn a model for reasoning.

4   Experiments

4.1   Experimental Settings

This paper adopts the ACE 2005 Chinese Corpus as our experiment corpus which contains 633 Chinese documents, with most of them related to news. We chose 629 documents of the corpus for our experiments. We experiment on the event type of *Justice*, in which there are 1386 argument roles. 5-fold cross validation is used to report the results of the experiment.

This experiment takes the usual Precision (P), Recall(R) and F1-measure as our evaluation standard. For the baseline, the Maximum Entropy Classifier[2] in the mallet toolkit with the default parameters used. In the learning and inference step, the open-source Alchemy[3] package from the university of Washington is employed. We introduce MC-SAT, a slice sampling Markov Chain Monte Carlo algorithm, to make inference.

This paper is based on Li's auto triggers extraction system, in which F1 is 70.5% and adopts Li's arguments extraction system as a baseline. The following is a list of the features adopted in our baseline.

1) Basic features: trigger, POS (Part Of Speech) of the trigger, event type, head word of the entity, and entity type;

---

[2]   http://mallet.cs.umass.edu/download.php
[3]   http://alchemy.cs.washington.edu

2) Neighboring features: left neighboring word of the entity + its POS, left neighboring word of the trigger + its POS, left neighboring word of the trigger + its POS;

3) Dependency features: the path from the trigger and the entity (or head word of the entity), makes differences on the depths of the trigger and entity;

4) Syntactic features: shortest path from the entity to the trigger, relative position of the entity and the trigger;

Maximum Entropy Classifier employs the above-mentioned features for argument identification and argument role classification. Due to negative cases being too much to infer, two filtering methods must be adopted. Firstly, the paper supposes the extent of entity is given. If the entity has no extent, the clause of corresponding trigger of the entity acts as the extent. After that, we filter entities that are not contained in the extent. Secondly, if two entities are next to each other and the former one decorates the latter one, we filtered the former one.

4.2   Experimental Results Analysis

The performance of the baseline and all of the inference rules is shown in Table 2. Compared to the baseline, our inference mechanism gains 8.6% and 8.2% improvements for argument identification and argument role determination, respectively. From Table 2, it can be seen that the overall performance of the experiment is not the synthesis of the performance of several reasoning methods, because of the overlap of several reasoning methods, such as Bei-sentence and event relevance inference rules. In addition, the experimental results show that these reasoning methods are very effective, especially the entity semantics information, Bei-sentence and relative position of the entity and the trigger inference rules, which is mainly due to the number of entities that correspond to these three kinds of inference rules, accounting for 10.06% of the total number of test sets, respectively, 11.14% and 28.62%.

Table 2. Performance comparison of argument identification and argument role classification

	Argument identification (%)			Argument role classification (%)		
	P	R	F1	P	R	F1
baseline	65.75	27.56	38.84	62.48	26.19	36.91
our system	55.00	41.63	47.39	52.34	39.61	45.09
+Bei-sentence	-3.47	+3.18	+2.32	-2.98	+3.18	+2.42
+entity semantics information	-0.35	+3.54	+3.31	+0.65	+3.82	+3.77
+relative position of entity and trigger	-8.16	+5.85	+3.42	-8.87	+4.91	+2.45
+entity type information	-1.07	+1.37	+1.14	-0.87	+1.37	+1.17
+event relevance	-2.48	+2.89	+2.27	-4.31	+1.80	+0.88

In event relevance inference, because of the assumption that each of the inferred entities must be a true argument, this causes pseudo arguments inferred as true arguments, but it also avoids the missing of arguments. Moreover, the inference rule may be based on the wrong evidences, and this will lower the effectiveness of inference. As is shown in the E8, 中级人民法院 (intermediate people's court) is incorrectly recognized as an argument of Trial-Hearing event mention, thus the entity is incorrectly inferred as Defendant role of Sentence event mention.

(E8) Chinese: 曾先后１４次组织偷渡活动的"蛇头"翁金顺今天被江苏省连云港
市中级人民法院一审 *(Trial-Hearing)* 判处*(Sentence)* 无期徒刑。

English: *With 14 times the organized smuggling activities, "felon" Weng Jinshun today was **sentenced (Sentence)** to life imprisonment, Lianyungang City, Jiangsu Province Intermediate People's Court of **first instance (Trial-Hearing)**.)*

In the relative position of entity and trigger inference, the precision of argument identification and argument role determination declines badly. The reason is that a large part of entities that correspond with the rule are pseudo arguments, but they will be inferred as true arguments with MLNs. For instance, pseudo argument 军人 (soldier) is incorrectly inferred as the *Plaintiff* role of *Sue* event mention in the E9.

(E9) Chinese: 美国《华盛顿邮报》：美国共和党总统候选人小布什放弃海外军人
选票**诉讼**（*Sue*）案。

English: *U.S. "Washington Post": Republican presidential candidate George W.Bush abandoned overseas military ballots **lawsuit (Sue)**.*

5   Conclusion

In this paper, we used Bei-sentences, entity semantics information, relative positions of entity and trigger, entity type information and event relevance inference rules for argument inference with Markov Logic Networks. Experimental results show that the system performance is improved by 8.6% for argument identification and 8.2% for argument role determination from the baseline.

For future work, we will focus on argument inference in the *Justice* type of event, and will also consider how to utilize the theory of consistency across events for argument filling in Chinese event.

Acknowledgement. This research was supported by the National Natural Science Foundation of China (Grant No. 61472265), the State Key Program of National Natural Science Foundation of China (Grant No. 61331011), and partially supported by Collaborative Innovation Center of Novel Software Technology and Industrialization.

References

1. Linguistic Data Consortium. ACE (Automatic Content Extraction) Chinese Annotation Guidelines for Events. 2009–09–08. Version5.5.1. http://www.ldc.upenn.edu/Projects/
2. Zhao, Y.Y., Qin, B., Che, W., et al.: Research on Chinese event extraction. Journal of Chinese Information Processing **22**(1), 3–8 (2008). (in Chinese)
3. Tan, H.Y.: Research on Chinese event extraction. Harbin Institute of Technology (2008). (in Chinese)
4. Li, P., Zhou, G., Zhu, Q., Hou, L.: Employing compositional semantics and discourse consistency in chinese event extraction. In: Proc. EMNLP 2012, pp. 1006–1016, Jeju, Korea (2012a)
5. Hou, L.B., Li, P.F., Zhu, Q.M.: Study of Event Recognition Based on CRFs and Cross-event. Jisuanji Gongcheng/ Computer Engineering **38**(24) (2012). (in Chinese)
6. Chen, Z., Ji, H.: Language specific issue and feature exploration in Chinese event extraction. In: Proceeding of the 2009 Annual Conference of the North American Chapter of the Association for Computational Linguistics Boulder, Colorado, USA, pp. 209–212 (2009)
7. Ahn, D.: The stages of event extraction. In: Proceedings of the Workshop on Annotations and Reasoning about Time and Events, pp. 1–8 (2006)
8. Fu, J., Liu, Z., Zhong, Z., Shan, J.: Chinese Event Extraction Based on Feature Weighting. Information Technology Journal **9**, 184–187 (2010)
9. Li, P., Zhou, G., Zhu, Q.: Argument inference from relevant event mentions in chinese argument extraction. In: Proceedings of ACL, pp. 1477–1487 (2013)
10. Liao, S., Grishman, R.: Using document level cross-event inference to improve event extraction. In: Porc. ACL–2010, Uppsala, Sweden, July, pp. 789–797 (2010)
11. Yu, H., Zhang, J., Ma, B., at el.: Using cross-entity inference to improve event extraction. In: Proceedings of the 49th Annual Meeting of the Association for Computational Linguistics, Stroudsburg, PA, USA, pp. 1127–1136 (2011)
12. Li, P., Zhou, G.: Employing morphological structures and sememes for chinese event extraction. In: COLING, pp. 1619–1634 (2012)

Syntax

Verbal Predicates in Chinese Fictive Motion Expressions

Sai Ma[⊠]

University of Auckland, Room 436, Building 206, 14a Symonds Street,
Auckland Central, Auckland 1142, New Zealand
sma330@aucklanduni.ac.nz

Abstract. This article explores the verbal predicates employed in one type of
Chinese fictive motion expressions, namely, coextension paths. Eight patterns
were identified, encompassing compound verbs, verb-complement constructions, polysyllabic words, monosyllabic verbs, *monosyllabic adverbial modifier*
+ monosyllabic verb constructions, *nouns of locality + monosyllabic verb* constructions, Chinese idioms, and *AAérB* constructions. The results show that the
verbal predicates adopted in fictive motion expressions in Modern Standard
Chinese are similar to those in expressions encoding translational motion events
in ancient Chinese.

Keywords: Fictive motion · Coextension paths · Verbs · Chinese

1   Introduction

This study aims to explore the verbal predicate patterns employed in coextension path
expressions in Modern Standard Chinese[1] with usage-based data gathered from published written texts.

A coextension path is one type of fictive motion within the categorization[2] made
by Talmy [1]. Fictive motion expressions depict a physical entity or scene involving
no actual motion with dynamic linguistic forms (motion verbs, directional prepositions, etc.), as illustrated in (1) from Talmy [1].

(1) This fence **goes from** the plateau **to** the valley.

A coextension path sentence pertains to the "depiction of the form, orientation, or
location of a spatially extended object in terms of a path over the object's extent" [1].
The above coextension path sentence in (1) conceptualizes the fence with a long linear configuration as an entity moving along a path formed by the fence from the
plateau to the valley.

---

[1]   The term "Modern Standard Chinese" is adopted here to contrast both languages other than
Chinese and classical Chinese. A simplified version "Chinese" is sometimes used in this
sense.

[2]   Six types of fictive motion were proposed in Talmy [1], including emanation paths, pattern
paths, frame-relative motion, advent paths, access paths, and coextension paths. For detailed
information, see [1].

© Springer International Publishing Switzerland 2015
Q. Lu and H.H. Gao (Eds.): CLSW 2015, LNAI 9332, pp. 589–598, 2015.
DOI: 10.1007/978-3-319-27194-1_59

2   Theoretical Framework

A coextension path sentence can be seen as a semantically locative motion event being encoded linguistically as a translational motion event. A Motion event involves either a translational motion event or a stationary locational event[3]. There are four basic semantic elements involved in a Motion event, namely, the Figure, the Ground, the activating process, and the association function. The Figure is the object whose path of motion (for translational motion events) or location (for stationary location events) is being characterized, and the Ground is the object with respect to which the figural object is characterized. The Figure and the Ground are involved in both translational motion events and locative motion events. The two types of motion events differ from each other in terms of the activating process and the association function. The activating process is motion in translational motion events whereas it is stationariness in locative motion events. The association function is represented as the path of the movement performed by the Figure with respect to the Ground in a translational motion event but as the location occupied by the Figure with respect to the Ground in a locative motion event [2]. The sentences in (2) and (3) from [1] can be used to describe the same locative event, in which a Figure is located statically with respect to two Ground entities. The sentence in (3) encodes this locative event faithfully as being static, while the sentence in (2) describes the figural entity as a dynamic one moving from one Ground entity to the other. In sentence (2), the semantic locative event is linguistically conceptualized as a translational motion event.

(2) That mountain range **goes from** Canada **to** Mexico.
(3) That mountain range **lies** (longitudinally) **between** Canada and Mexico.

Path serves as the core schema in a motion event. The linguistic slot encoding Path in a language decides the type of that language. It is a verb-framed language if the verb is the slot encoding the path information; whereas it is a satellite-framed language if the satellite[4] is the slot conflating the path information. The Spanish sentence in (4) [2] is an example where Path is encoded in the verb, and the sentence in (5) [2] illustrates the case where Path is encoded in the satellite.

(4) La   botella **entró**   a   la   cueva (flotando).
    *The bottle **entered*** (Path conflated in the verb) *to   the   cave   (floating)*
(5) The bottle floated **into** (Path conflated in the satellite) the cave.

Whether Modern Standard Chinese is a satellite-framed language or a verb-framed language is still contentious [3-6]. Ancient Chinese, which was abundant with monosyllabic words, tended to encode Path in the verb slot, and thus was more like a verb-framed language. As language develops, the pattern *manner verb+path complement* (i.e., the directional-verb construction) becomes the dominant pattern to encode a

---

[3]   An example of the translational motion event is "t(T)he pencil rolled off the table" [2]. An example of the locative motion event is "t(T)he pencil lay on the table" [2].

[4]   Satellite "is a grammatical category of any constituent other than a nominal or prepositional-phrase complement that is in a sister relation to the verb root" [2]. Verb particles in English and verb complements in Chinese are considered as satellites.

translational motion event and Path tends to be encoded in the path complement. There is no consensus as to whether the manner verb or the path complement should be called "the main verb", but this disagreement will not be discussed here.

In addition to the different linguistic forms expressing the path information, satellite-framed languages and verb-framed languages also exhibit other differences. One of them is that manner information can be more readily encoded in satellite-framed languages than in verb-framed languages. Satellite-framed languages can encode the manner information in the main verb by default, whereas the verb slot in verb-framed languages is occupied by the path information and thus the manner information have to be encoded in other linguistic slots (which will add additional encoding effort) or left unexpressed [5]. Since the usual verbal pattern for Modern Standard Chinese to encode a motion event is *manner verb+path complement* and the manner information can be encoded in the manner verb effortlessly, it is assumed that manner information should have a high salience degree in modern Chinese motion event expressions.

The expressiveness of path information and manner information is also studied for fictive motion expressions, or more specifically, coextension path expressions. Through comparing English and Japanese coextension path expressions, Matsumoto [7] came up with two conditions concerning the encoding of path and manner information [7]:

a.   The path condition: Some property of the path of motion must be expressed.
b.   The manner condition: No property of the manner of motion can be expressed unless it is used to represent some correlated property of the path.

The path information must be encoded because it is what a coextension path expression is motivated by and concerned with. Pure manner information cannot be encoded because it would highlight the moving entity in coextension path expressions, which is normally suppressed at the linguistic level and is supposed to be backgrounded. The path condition and manner condition are met by both English and Japanese, which are two very different languages genetically and areally. It indicates that these two conditions may be motivated by cognitive mechanisms underlying coextension paths and may be applicable to other languages as well [7].

What types of verbal predicates are employed in Chinese coextension path expressions are interesting since, on the one hand, coextension path expressions borrow the linguistic terms from translational motion event expressions, for which manner information is supposed to be relatively salient and the usual verbal predicate pattern is *manner verb+path complement*, and on the other hand, studies on coextension paths indicate that manner information in coextension paths should be suppressed. If Chinese coextension path expressions are similar to English and Japanese ones in that they seldom contain manner information, then it would be interesting to look at what kinds of verbal predicates are used in coextension path expressions, since the verb is the most important linguistic strategy to convey the motion sense and it is canonical for Modern Standard Chinese to encode the manner information in motion verbs.

3   Data

The data are collected from a specialized self-built corpus which is assumed to be rich in coextension path expressions. This corpus is composed of a set of published written texts.

It is motivated by the assumption that authentic language data should be taken as the study object in the investigation of languages. According to mother tongue intuition as well as examples from existing literature on coextension path expressions, books and magazines focusing on geography, travel, and scenic spots tend to use coextension path expressions more, and thus they are adopted as the data sources. Detailed information of the data sources can be found in the Appendix.

All the written books and magazines are read sentence by sentence and all the coextension path expressions are collected manually. Altogether there are 1290[5] coextension path sentences collected. Since sometimes more than one coextension path expressions are contained in one sentence, the number of coextension path expressions in those sentences is more than 1290.

4   Results

Eight patterns of verbal predicates were identified, as shown in the following table with the corresponding token and percentage.

Table 1. Eight verbal predicate patterns

verbal predicate patterns	examples	token & percentage
compound verbs	伸展 [shēnzhǎn] (extend)	523 (30.58%)
verb-complement constructions	刺穿 [cìchuān] (pierce-through)	332 (19.42%)
polysyllabic verbs	绵延 [miányán] (stretch)	230 (13.45%)
monosyllabic verbs	入 [rù] (enter)	195 (11.40%)
monosyllabic adverbial modifier+monosyllabic verb constructions	斜射 [xiéshè] (obliquely-radiate)	180 (10.53%)
noun of locality+monosyllabic verb constructions	南达 [nándá] (south-arrive)	126 (7.37%)
Chinese idioms	拔地而起 [bádìérqǐ] (rise-abruptly-from-the-ground)	70 (4.09%)
AAérB constructions	奔涌而出 [bēnyǒngérchū] (surging-exit)	54 (3.16%)

---

[5] Ambiguous sentences with regard to whether they encode a coextension path or an advent path are not included in this study.

These eight cases will be illustrated briefly with one example for each case in this section.

4.1   Compound Verbs

Compound verbs are verbs containing more than one syllables as well as morphemes. Most of them are collected into Modern Chinese Dictionary [8] as a verb, but some of them are not. However, they are judged to be a compound verb based on the linguistic context. Compound verbs can be considered as a linguistic strategy in modern Chinese since the closer it is to modern society, the fewer monosyllabic words are in use, and the more disyllabic words appear [9-10]. Both manner information and path information can be encoded in compound verbs. The sentence in (6) contains a compound verb 伸展 [*shēnzhǎn*] (*extend*).

(6) 从大陆伸展过来的道路在这里走到了尽头。

    cóng   dàlù **shēnzhǎn** guòlái   de   dàolù zàizhèlǐ zǒu dào le   jìntóu
    from mainland **extend** towards-here NOM road at-here walk-to CRS end
    The road extending from the mainland walks to its end here.

4.2   Verb-Complement Constructions

In verb-complement constructions, it is possible for the verb to encode either the manner or path information apart from the movement, and the complement specifies the path of the movement. The verb-complement construction is a feature of modern Chinese [11]. Sentence (7) contains two verb-complement constructions, i.e. 冲下来 [*chōngxiàlái*] (*rush-down-come*) and 扎进 [*zhājìn*] (*jump-into*).

(7) 这万里长城，从燕山支脉的角山上直冲下来，一头扎进了渤海岸边。

    zhè wànlǐchángchéng cóng   yānshān   zhīmài   de   jiǎoshānshàng
    this   Great-Wall   from Yan-Mountain- branch-ASSOC Cape-Mount-on
    zhí   **chōngxiàlái**   yìtóu   **zhājìn** le   bóhǎi   ànbiān
    all-the-way **rush-down-come** head **jump-into** CRS   Bohai-Sea bank
    The Great Wall rushes down all the way from the Cape Mount of Yan Mountain,
    and jumps into the bank of the Bohai Sea.

4.3   Polysyllabic Verbs

Polysyllabic words are composed of two characters which bind together to form one morpheme [12]. The two characters in a polysyllabic word are inseparable. This set of words can usually be traced back to ancient Chinese [13]. The verb 蔓延 [*mànyán*] (*spread*) in (8) is a polysyllabic word.

(8) 六月，青草在秦岭的高山上蔓延开来。

    liùyuè   qīngcǎo   zàiqínlǐng de   gāoshānshàng   **mànyán**

June green-grass on-Qinling-Mountains-ASSOC-high-mountains **spread-**
kāilái
open-come
In June, green grass is spreading around on Qinling Mountains.

4.4   Monosyllabic Verbs

Monosyllabic verbs are identified when there is no other grammatical element obviously attaching to the verb. In most cases, monosyllabic verbs encode path information while manner information is occasionally encoded. Monosyllabic verbs create a
formal sense, since Modern Chinese is abundant with disyllabic words and monosyllabic words are relatively less employed in spoken language [14]. The verbs including
经 [*jīng*] (*pass*), 转 [*zhuǎn*] (*turn*), and 到 [*dào*] (*arrive*) in (9) are instantiations of
monosyllabic verbs.

(9) 欧亚大草原西自欧洲多瑙河下游，呈带状往东延伸，经匈牙利、罗马尼亚
、乌克兰、俄罗斯、哈萨克斯坦、蒙古，直至中国的东北平原，然后转向
西南，经内蒙古高原、黄土高原到青藏高原的南缘。

ōuyàdàcǎoyuán   xī   zì   ōuzhōu   duō nǎohé   xiàyóu，chéngdàizhuàng
Eurasian-Steppe west-from Europe   the- Danube downstream   in-belt-shape
wǎng dōng yánshēn，**jīng** xiōngyálì… měnggǔ， zhízhì   zhōngguó
towards east extend   **pass** Hungary   Mongolia all-the-way-to China
de   dōngběipíngyuán，   ránhòu **zhuǎn**xiàng xīnán，   **jīng**
-ASSOC the-Northeast-Plain   then   **turn**-to   southwest   **pass**
nèiménggǔgāoyuán、   huángtǔgāoyuán **dào**   qīngzànggāoyuán de
Inner-Mongolian-Plateau Loess-Plateau **arrive** Tibetan-Plateau-ASSOC
nányuán
south-part
The west of the Eurasian Steppe starts from the downstream of the Danube in
Europe, extends eastwards like a belt, and all the way goes to the Northeast
Plain in China through Hungary, Mongolia, and then it turns towards southwest
and goes through Inner-Mongolian Plateau, Loess Plateau, and arrives at the
southern part of Tibetan Plateau. It extends from the east to the west for more
than 8000 kilometres.

4.5   *Monosyllabic Adverbial Modifier+Monosyllabic Verb* Constructions

For this construction, the monosyllabic verb usually depicts the path rather than the
manner of the movement and the adverbial modifier is normally monosyllabic expressing further information about the path. The monosyllabic adverbial word preceding the verb usually has a root in ancient Chinese [15]. The verbal predicate 纵贯
[*zòngguàn*] (*from-north-to-south-pass-through*) is a *monosyllabic adverbial modifi-*
er+monosyllabic verb construction.

(10) 洋中脊纵贯四大洋，绵延80000多公里。

yángzhōngjǐ   **zòng guàn**   sìdàyáng   miányán
ocean-ridge   **from-north-to-south-pass-through**   four-ocean   stretch
80,000 duō   gōnglǐ
80,000-plus   kilometre
The ocean ridge runs through the four oceans from the north to the south, stretching more than 80,000 kilometres.

4.6   Noun of Locality+Monosyllabic Verb Constructions

For the construction *noun of locality+monosyllabic verb*, the noun of locality helps to specify the direction of the movement expressed by the verb following it. It is found that this construction is inherited from ancient Chinese [16]. Four such constructions are involved in (11), including 东起 [*dōngqǐ*] (*east-start*), 西抵 [*xīdǐ*] (*west-reach*), 南到 [*nándào*] (*south-arrive*), and 北达 [*běidá*] (*north-reach*).

(11) 鄂尔多斯盆地的地质结构，东起吕梁，西抵贺兰，南到秦岭，北达阴山。
ěěrduōsīpéndì de   dìzhìjiégòu   **dōngqǐ**   lǔliáng   **xīdǐ**
Ordos-Basin-ASSOC   geological-structure **east-start** Lvliang   **west-reach**
hèlán **nán   dào**   qínlǐng   **běi dá**   yīnshān
Helan **south-arrive** Qinling-Mountains   **north- reach** Yin-Mountains
The geological structure of Ordos Basin starts from Lvliang on its east border, reaches Helan on its west border. It arrives at Qinling Mountains on its south border and reaches Yin Mountains on its north border.

4.7   Chinese Idioms

In some cases, fictive motion paths are involved in conventionalized Chinese idioms, as illustrated in 古木参天 [*gǔmùcāntiān*] (*ancient-tree-rise-up-into-sky*) in sentence (12). It is self-evident that fictive motion expressions in this case have a flavor of ancient Chinese.

(12) 凭窗远眺，但见近处古木参天。
píng   chuāng   yuǎntiào   dànjiàn   jìnchù   **gǔmùcāntiān**
stand-by   window faraway-look   see   nearby   **ancient-tree rise-up-into-sky**
(I) stood by the window and looked into the distance, and saw ancient trees rising upwards into the sky nearby.

4.8   *AAérB* Constructions

For the construction *AAérB*, *AA* is a disyllabic adverbial word, *B* is a monosyllabic verb, and *ér* is a function word indicting that the motion encoded by *B* is modified by the word *AA*. The semantic elements encoded in *AA* can either be manner or path information, whereas what is encoded in *B* is usually the path information. This construction can also be traced back to ancient Chinese [14], [17]. The coextension path sentence in (13) employs an *AAérB* construction, namely, 贴地而行 [*tiēdìérxíng*] (*walk-in-the-manner-of-being-close-to-the-ground*).

(13) 一条绵延的石壁……黑森森地贴地而行，看不到尽头。
yītiáo miányánde shíbì   hēisēnsēndì   **tiēdìérxíng**   kànbùdào jìntóu
a-CL rolling   cliff   gloomily   **close-to-the-ground-walk**   see-no   end
A rolling cliff walks gloomily in the manner of being close to the ground, and there is no end.

5   Discussion and Conclusion

This paper explores the verbal predicate patterns in Chinese coextension path expressions. Eight patterns are identified, among which polysyllabic verbs, monosyllabic verbs, *monosyllabic adverbial modifier+monosyllabic verb* constructions, *noun of locality+monosyllabic verb* constructions, Chinese idioms, and *AAérB* constructions are related to ancient Chinese, while verb-complement constructions and compound verbs are patterns in modern Chinese. The former six types and the latter two types split the whole verbal predicate patterns evenly, with each accounting for 50%.

The results show that Matsumoto's manner condition can generally be satisfied but not in the strict sense. It is possible for manner information to be encoded in coextension path sentences, such as in compound verbs, the manner verb in verb-complement constructions, the *AA* section of *AAérB* constructions, and monosyllabic verbs encoding manner information. Nevertheless, manner information is not a frequent semantic element expressed in coextension path expressions, which is different from the case in translational motion event expressions. As the core semantic element in translational motion events, Path is retained in coextension path expressions.

The lexicalization patterns of coextension path expressions differ from that of translational motion event expressions in which the pattern *manner verb+path complement* dominates. A lot of verbs in coextension path sentences encode path information, which is consistent with the lexicalization pattern of verb-framed languages. This indicates that coextension path expressions in modern Chinese may have some relationship with ancient Chinese, which was more like a verb-framed language. This point is also evidenced by specific verbal predicate patterns discussed in the analysis part, such as Chinese idioms, polysyllabic words, and *X+verb*, in which *X* can be either nouns of locality or adverbial modifiers [18]. The employment of verbal predicate patterns from ancient Chinese, which is a verb-framed language, supports the hypothesis that fictive motion expressions occur more in verb-framed languages and less in manner-salient satellite-framed languages [19]. Another possible factor may be that the data were collected from written texts[6]. Further studies are needed to explore the relationship between coextension path expressions and ancient Chinese.

---

[6]   This was kindly pointed out by the anonymous reviewers.

Appendix Data Source

《彩图科技百科全书》编辑部 (Ed.): 地球. 上海科学技术出版社, 上海 (2005)
余秋雨: 山居笔记. 尔雅出版社, 台北 (1995)
余秋雨: 文化苦旅. 东方出版中心, 上海 (2001)
余秋雨: 行者无疆. 华艺出版社, 北京 (2001)
余秋雨: 千年一叹. 作家出版社, 北京 (2002)
余秋雨: 出走十五年. 南海出版公司, 海口 (2004)
余秋雨: 余秋雨散文: 插图珍藏版. 人民文学出版社, 北京 (2005)
博文 (Ed.): 东西南北人: 中国人的性格与文化. 当代世界出版社, 北京 (2001)
林非 (Ed.): 中华游记百年精选. 人民文学出版社, 北京 (2004)
《现当代名家游记散文摄影珍藏版丛书》系列:
史铁生: 我与地坛. 山东画报出版社, 济南 (2002)
汪曾祺: 昆明的雨. 山东画报出版社, 济南 (2004)
萧红: 呼兰河传. 山东画报出版社, 济南 (2003)
朱自清: 桨声灯影里的秦淮河. 山东画报出版社, 济南 (2002)
朱自清: 欧游杂记. 山东画报出版社, 济南 (2002)
徐志摩: 我所知道的康桥. 山东画报出版社, 济南 (2002)
郁达夫: 钓台的春昼. 山东画报出版社, 济南 (2002)
钟敬文: 西湖的雪景. 山东画报出版社, 济南 (2004)
曹聚仁: 湖上杂忆. 山东画报出版社, 济南 (2002)
朱湘: 北海纪游. 山东画报出版社, 济南 (2003)
季羡林: 火焰山下. 山东画报出版社, 济南 (2004)
《中国国家地理》, 月刊, 主编: 单之蔷, 北京: 《中国国家地理》杂志社,
    2012年1月-2012年12月, 12期
《中国国家旅游》, 月刊, 主编: 刘天北, 北京: 《中国国家旅游》杂志社,
    2012年1月-2012年12月, 12期
《世界》, 月刊, 主编: 王建梅, 北京: 《世界》杂志社, 2012年1月-2012年
    12月, 12期
《物理》, 《地理》, 《化学》, 《生物》, 共十一册, 人民教育出版社, 北京

References

1. Talmy, L.: Toward a Cognitive Semantics, vol. 1. MIT Press, Cambridge (2000)
2. Talmy, L.: Toward a Cognitive Semantics, vol. 2. MIT Press, Cambridge (2000)
3. Chen, L.: The Acquisition and Use of Motion Event Expressions in Chinese. Lincom, Europa, Munich (2007)
4. Shen, J.: A Typological Study of Verb-complement Structure in Modern Chinese. Chinese Teaching in the World **3**, 17–23 (2003). (in Chinese)
5. Slobin, D.I.: The many ways to search for a frog: linguistic typology and the expression of motion events. In: Strömqvist, S., Verhoeven, L. (eds.) Relating Events in Narrative: Typological and Contextual Perspectives, pp. 219–257. Lawrence Erlbaum Associates, Mahwah (2004)

6. Tai, J.H.-Y.: Cognitive Relativism: Resultative Construction in Chinese. Language and Linguistics **4**(2), 301–316 (2003)

7. Matsumoto, Y.: Subjective Motion and English and Japanese Verbs. Cognitive Linguistics **7**(2), 183–226 (1996)

8. Modern Chinese Dictionary, 6th edn. The Commercial Press, Beijing (2012) (现代汉语词典 (第六版). 商务出版社, 北京 (2012)) (in Chinese)

9. Li, C.N., Thompson, S.A.: Mandarin Chinese: A Functional Reference Grammar. University of California Press, Berkeley (1981)

10. Lv, S.: A Preliminary Study of the Problem of Monosyllabism and Disyllabism in Modern Chinese. Chinese Language **1**, 11‒23 (1963). (吕叔湘: 现代汉语单双音节问题初探. 中国语文. 第一期, 11‒23 (1963)) (in Chinese)

11. Shi, Y.: The Motivation of the Disyllabification for the Emergence of the Resultative Construction. Linguistics Study **1**, 1–14 (2002). (in Chinese)

12. Xu, Z.: Introduction to Polysyllabic Words. Popular Culture and Arts Publishing House, Beijing (1998). (徐振邦: 连绵词概论. 大众文艺出版社, 北京 (1998)) (in Chinese)

13. Shao, J.: General Theories in Modern Chinese. Shanghai Educational Publishing House, Shanghai (2007). (邵敬敏: 现代汉语通论. 上海教育出版社, 上海 (2007)) (in Chinese)

14. Wang, L.: History of Chinese. Science Press, Beijing (1958). (王力: 汉语史稿. 科学出版社, 北京 (1958)) (in Chinese)

15. Li, T.: A Study of Modal Words in Modern Chinese (MA Thesis). Shanghai Normal University (2005) (in Chinese)

16. Zhang, J.: A Study on Modification Construction "Monosyllabic Location Words+Monosyllabic Verbs" (PhD Thesis). Huazhong Normal University (2011) (in Chinese)

17. Wang, L.: Ancient Chinese (revised edition), vol. 2. Zhonghua Book Company, Beijing (1981). (王力: 古代汉语 (修订版) (第二册). 中华书局, 北京 (1981)) (in Chinese)

18. Ma, S.: Coextension Paths in Modern Standard Chinese. International Journal of Cognitive Linguistics **5**(1), 119–151 (2014)

19. Stosic, D., Sarda, L.: The many ways to be located: the expression of fictive motion in French and Serbian. In: Vukanović, M.B., Grmuša, L.G. (eds.) Space and Time in Language and Literature, pp. 39–60. Cambridge Scholars Publishing, Newcastle (2009)

A Brief Analysis of [V *ge* N] in Chinese: A Construction Grammar Account

Ziming Lu[✉]

School of Philosophy, Psychology and Language Sciences, University of Edinburgh,
Dugald Stewart Building, 3 Charles Street, Edinburgh EH8 9AD, UK
z.lu-6@sms.ed.ac.uk

Abstract. The General classifier 个 [*ge*] is normally located between a numeral and a noun. In a post-verbal position, *ge* is found to be used in some unusual positions, e.g. in compound verbs or between the verb and an adjective. *Ge* in this |V *ge* X] pattern has attracted much attention in Chinese linguistic research (Zhang, 2003; Lü, 1984; Biq, 2004). Most of the research focuses on the properties of *ge*, but the discussion about the [V *ge* X] pattern as a whole is limited. The main task of this research is to argue that the post-verbal *ge* and its context form a construction with a telic and bounded aspectual meaning within the framework of Construction Grammar. In addition, the omission of numeral - [*yi*] (*one*) in post-verbal NPs triggers the emergence of this construction.

Keywords: *Ge* · Aspect marker · Construction grammar

1   Introduction

个 [*ge*] is widely considered as a general classifier in Mandarin Chinese (Li and Thompson 1981, Lü 1984) which is normally located between a numeral and a noun. In a post-verbal position, when the numeral before *ge* is 一 [*yi*] (*one*), the numeral tends to be omitted. The 'bare *ge*' is found to be used in some unusual positions, as illustrated in (1.1) and (1.2).

(1.1) 刷个牙 [*shua ge ya*] (*brush teeth*)
(1.2) 吃个饱 [*chi ge bao*] (*eat till feeling full*)

In (1.1), 牙(*tooth*) is nonreferential and refers to no specific entity. It is a collocational object of the verb 刷(*brush*) and they altogether denote an activity of brushing teeth. 刷牙（*to brush teeth*) is widely considered as a splitable verb-object compound (Li and Thompson 1981) and even in the dictionary it is listed as one lexical item. In other words, 刷(*to brush*) and 牙(*teeth*) are used together to mean 'to brush teeth' and no other elements are needed to legislate it. In (1.2), *ge* is followed by an element which is even not a typical noun. 饱 (*full*) is generally used as an adjective and when used together with 吃 (*to eat*) it helps to provide more information about the activity denoted by the head verb. For both examples, the existence of *ge* does not affect the

© Springer International Publishing Switzerland 2015
Q. Lu and H.H. Gao (Eds.): CLSW 2015, LNAI 9332, pp. 599–607, 2015.
DOI: 10.1007/978-3-319-27194-1_60

grammaticality of the expressions and even without *ge*, they are still well-formed. Similarly, there are other examples where *ge* in this post verbal position is followed by adverbs and Chinese four character idioms[1].

These patterns altogether can be generalized as [V *ge* X], and the function of *ge* in these unusual positions has attracted much attention in Chinese linguistic research (Li and Thompson 1981, Zhu 1982, Lü 1984, He 2001, Zhang 2003, Biq 2004, Shi and Lei 2004). Zhu (1982) considers *ge* is still a classifier. Zhang (2003) argues that *ge* here especially in the expression like (1.2) has the similar function to the complement marker 得[*de*](1.3)

(1.3) 吃得饱 [*chi de bao*] (*eat and feel full*)

Shi and Lei (2004) mention *ge* is an 'object marker' or 'nominalizer' which nominalizes the following element. Although all these arguments seem to be demonstrated with sufficient evidence and analysis, they focus on the properties of *ge* alone. The discussion about *ge* altogether with the context it appears is limited.

This research applies Construction Grammar and aims to discuss the function of *ge* in post-verbal position and argue that *ge* and its context form a construction with a particular meaning. Due to the limitation of space, this paper will mainly discuss the [V *ge* N] construction, a micro-construction of [V *ge* X]. To be more specific, two main issues about the [V *ge* N] construction will be addressed in this paper: its syntactic and semantic properties and its construction identity. In addition, the paper will briefly discuss the constructionalization of [V *ge* N] in relation to the omission of numeral 一[*yi*] (*one*) in section 4.

2   Properties of [V *ge* N] Construction

The [V *ge* N] construction is a partially schematic construction which consists of three signs, a verb, *ge* and a noun. *Ge* in between is normally not replaceable but in some instances in modern Chinese, 一[*yi*] (*one*) could be added back before *ge* in this construction. There is no obvious semantic difference between these two forms and the [V *yige* N] is not used as frequently as [V *ge* N] (Lü, 1984), so in this research they are treated as one construction. As mentioned above, the N represents the collocational object of a verb in a splitable verb-object compound. In this construction, nouns fill in the N slot are normally nonreferential and do not denote any existing entities. As in (1.1), 牙 (*tooth*) does not refer to any tooth or teeth but it conveys a concept of a type of entities. This nonreferential property of N sets certain constraint to the V slot as well. Verbs in this construction, therefore especially excludes the existential/ possessive verb 有[*you*] (*there be/ have*) and copular 是[*shi*](*be*) or other verbs indicating existence because their semantic features conflict with the nonreferential constraint to the N slot in this construction.

---

[1] V *ge* Adverb: 哭个不停 [*ku ge buting*] (*to cry without stop*)

   V *ge* Idiom: 查个水落石出 [*cha ge shuiluoshichu*] (*to investigate till clear*).

As to the semantic features of the construction, the most significant one is that the construction has a telic and bounded reading. The presence of *ge* in [V *ge* N] arises this semantic significance. Compare (2.1) below:

(2.1) a. 洗个澡 [*xi ge zao*] (*have a bath/shower*)

b. 洗澡 [*xi zao*] (*bathe/shower*)

(2.1a) is a construct, an instance of [V *ge* N] construction and (2.1b) is its [V N] counterpart. Similar to their English translation, both events denoted by (2.1a) and (2.1b) occupy some time, but (2.1a) also indicates an end comprised in the process (Kearns 2000), while for (2.1b), there is no obvious endpoint or outcome. That is to say, (2.1a) describes an event which has an endpoint and is expected to be completed but the scenario denoted by (2.1b) does not have this kind of outcome and it is possible to be on forever. In other words, (2.1a) is telic and (2.1b) is atelic. We can further test the intuition about this difference of these two patterns with the methods Kearns (2000: 204) suggests as follows:

Two kinds of syntactic tests:

a.   The effect of adverbials which target aspectual properties of events, such as their duration or temporal bounds.
b.   The effect of tense and aspect verb forms on predicates of different classes.

In Chinese we can adopt the adverbial clause initiated with 就[*jiu*] (*as soon as*) for telicity. When we test (2.1a) and (2.1b) by this method, we get the sentences below.

(2.2) a 他洗个澡就走
      [*ta xi ge zao jiu zou*]
      (*He will leave immediately after having a   bath*)

b * 他洗澡就走
      [*ta xi zao jiu zou*]
      (*He wash bath as.soon.as leave*)

(2.2b) is not acceptable for most native Chinese speakers and if we want to make (2.2b) grammatical, we need to put an end point to the event, like (2.3):

(2.3) 他洗完澡就走
      [*ta xi wan zao jiu zou*]
      (*He will leave as soon as he finishes bathing*)

Given to the second test method mentioned by Kearns (2000), Chinese progressive marker 在[*zai*], which is usually used with a predicate, will come to serve.

(2.4) a. *他在洗个澡
      [*ta zai xi ge zao*]
      (*he progressive.marker wash ge bath*)

b. 他在洗澡
      [*ta zai xi zao*]
      (*He is bathing*)

Now it is evident that [V *ge* N] is telic and bounded while [V N], to the contrary, is atelic and unbounded. The only difference with these two patterns is the presence of *ge*. When *ge* is used as a general classifier, its basic function is to individualize entities denoted by the following nouns and helps Chinese nouns to be countable (Chierchia, 1998). Inherited from this basic semantic property, *ge* in [V *ge* N] construction can be interpreted as individualizing events from unbounded activities.

Similarly, in (1.2), the presence of *ge* between the verb and adjective denotes a resultative degree of the action and the eating event ends with the status that the eating action agent is full. (1.2) can be interpreted as that the eating activity denoted by the verb 吃[*chi*] (*eat*) is accomplished until the subject who undergoes this activity acquires the quality described by the adjective 饱[*bao*] (*full*).

Based on the discussion above, *ge* in this construction is not a classifier which is normally used to modify its following noun; instead, it functions over the whole construction. Therefore, the syntactic relationship between these three signs should be reanalyzed. When *ge* functions as a general classifier in a post-verbal position, by using the bracketed expression, the syntactic structure is [V [[Num *ge*] N]]. In [V *ge* N] pattern, the noun following *ge* is normally the collocational object of the verb and nonreferential, so it does not need to be quantified or individualized by any classifiers. Furthermore, in (1.1), 牙[*ya*] (*tooth*) can be classified by classifier *ge* when being counted. But if *ge* functions as a classifier, the meaning of the expression would be 'to brush one tooth', which is not the most natural interpretation. In other words, *ge* in [V *ge* N] pattern is not a classifier and is less attached to the noun. Based on the analysis above, due to the presence of *ge*, the event denoted by the construction is telic and bounded, so *ge* functions over the whole predicate verb phrase. Accordingly, the internal structure of the [V *ge* N] pattern can be re-analyzed as [[V [*ge*]] N]. The [V *ge* N] construction can be formalized as following:

FORM: [[V [*ge*]] N]*e* ←→ **MEANING**:[telic, bounded]*e*

In order to further illustrate that [V *ge* N] is a construction which is different from normal predicate-object construction, the next section will discuss the aspectual meaning of the construction along with its syntactic structure.

3   [V *ge* N] as an Aspectual Construction

As analyzed in previous sections, [V *ge* N] construction expresses a 'telic and aspectually bounded' meaning (Bisang 2010). According to Lin (2003), a quantified NP as an object directly affects the event's telicity as well since it provides a natural endpoint to the activity. However, telicity is important for situation aspect, but it does not determine aspect alone. Boundedness, which determines the viewpoint aspect, should be taken into consideration as well (Depraetere, 1995).

(3.1) a. 我吃了个苹果
         [*wo chi le ge pingguo*]
         (*I ate an apple*)
      b. 我吃了个饭
         [*wo chi le ge fan*].
         (*I had a meal*).

(3.1a) is a normal SVO structure with a classifier *ge* in the quantified object NP. Although there is no overt numeral preceding the classifier, the only possible quantity of apples denoted in (3.1a) is one. In other words, the omitted numeral in (3.1a) is 一[*yi*] (*one*). This qualified NP provides a natural endpoint to this 'apple-eating' activity. When this apple is finished, the eating activity ends. (3.1b) is a [V *ge* N] construct while *ge* is used to individualize the event. (3.1a) and (3.1b) both denote telic and perfective situation, but they are different in deeper level. These differences can be tested by adding adverbial 差点[*chadian*] (*almost*) and by canceling the completion of the event.

(3.2) a. 我差点吃了个苹果
    [*wo chadian chi le ge pingguo*]
    (*I almost ate an apple*)

b.我差点吃了个饭
    [*wo chadian chi le ge fan*]
    (*I almost had a meal*)

(3.2a) is ambiguous and can be interpreted in two ways: interruption of completion and interruption of intention. It could mean 'I started eating the apple but I did not finish all' or mean 'I did not start eating the apple at all'. Both interpretations can be naturally accessed. (3.2b) has only the interruption of intention meaning which means 'I did not even start having the meal'. That is to say, in (3.2a) the adverbial's semantic scope can cover either the whole activity or part of the activity; in (3.2b), the adverbial can only be interpreted as functioning over the whole [V *ge* N] event.

Another test as (3.3) can also illustrate the difference.

(3.3) a. 我吃了个苹果，但是没吃完。
    [*wo chi le ge pingguo, danshi mei chi wan*]
    (*I ate an apple, but I did not finish it*)

b.* 我吃了个饭，但是没吃完。
    [*wo chi le ge fan, danshi meichi wan*].
    (*I had a meal, but I did not finish it*)

By adding the second clause to (3.3), the completion of the event is canceled. (3.3a) is still acceptable after the cancelation although the English translation may sound strange to native speakers. (3.3b) is not grammatical, which indicates the event in the first clause is already bounded and is not able to break or intervene. This suggests that (3.3a) is telic but not necessarily bounded, so the inherent endpoint denoted by the object can be canceled by interrupting.

In (3.1),(3.2),(3.3), all the examples contain the Chinese traditional aspect marker 了 [le], but its presence does not seem to have any influence on the tests applied above. This may suggest that 了 [le]'s aspectual function is similar to that of classifiers which only provide an inherent endpoint and this endpoint can be canceled or intervened. Furthermore, 吃了饭[*chilefan*] (*eat le dinner*), as Li and Thompson (1981) mentioned, sounds like something missing. If an overt endpoint is provided, this expression will be more natural.

To sum up, although classifiers in Chinese appear in telic phrases, they are not aspect markers. On the contrary, [V *ge* N] construction is telic and bounded which guarantees its perfective aspect. As analyzed above, these aspectual features are directly affected by *ge*, so it can be assumed that *ge*, different from other classifiers, is an aspect marker to establish an unbreakable entirety view of the event. From another perspective, *ge* can be interpreted as an aspect marker when it appears in this [V *ge* X] construction, so *ge's* aspectual function is not independent from its context. Its aspectual meaning is denoted by the whole construction not by *ge* itself. Therefore, *ge*, like other aspect markers in Chinese, is more attached to the verb rather than the following noun. These semantic and syntactic features enable [V *ge* N] as a distinctive construction from normal predicate-object constructions.

4   The Emergence of [V *ge* N] Construction

The [V *ge* N] construction does not appear abruptly but it is a gradual process of constructionalization. Based on the data collected from CCL corpus (Centre for Chinese Linguistics PKU), *ge* as a classifier is first found in 4th B.C. and since then *ge* is used together with numerals in NPs. Around 8th century, more and more instances of pattern [Zero+*ge*+Noun] are found in literatures where there is no numeral before *ge*. Lü (1984) explores the drop of numeral 一[*yi*] (*one*) before *ge* and other classifiers in details and according to him, this pattern mainly occurs in post verbal position. Furthermore, when the numeral一[*yi*](*one*) is omitted, *ge* acquires more freedom to collocate with nouns especially with those which have specialized classifiers. Compare (4.1).

(4.1) a. 下有一条路
       [*xia you yitiao lu*].
       (*There is a road below*).

   b. 乞和尚指示个入路
       [*qi heshang zhishi ge rulu*]
       (*Master, please show me a way to enter*)

   c. ...做得一领布衫
       [...*zuode yiling bushan*]
       (...*(I ask someone) to make an upper garment*)

   d. 着个绯衫倚势行
       [*zhou ge feishan yishi   xing*]
       (*(someone) walks along the road wearing a red upper garment*)

路[*lu*] (*road*) is normally modified by classifier 条[*tiao*] which is used to count long entities as in (4.1a) but in (b), the word路[*lu*] (*road*) collocates with classifier *ge*. Similarly, classifier 领[*ling*] in (c) is specialized for counting the garment but in (d) *ge* is used with 衫[*shan*] (*upper garment*). In (b), 路[*lu*] (*road*) does not refer to the concrete path that people can walk on but refers to an abstract method to acquire certain knowledge. In (d), although衫[*shan*] (*upper garment*) here refers to a concrete piece of cloth like (c), but wearing the garment in (d) serves as a background information for the walking activity and the garment may never be mentioned again. Unlike (d), in (c) making a piece of garment is new information and the following story will start to describe the newly made clothes. In other word, 衫[*shan*] (*upper garment*) in (d) means a type of clothes and not specific individual. Thus, the comparison between these two pairs of examples in (4.1) indicates that the concepts denoted by the nouns following *ge* without numeral are less referential and more abstract. At this time, although there is some semantic change with the [V *ge* N] pattern, the internal structure remains the same, and *ge* is still attached to the noun. So this change is simply a constructional change, or pre-constructionalization.

In later 9th century and 10th century, the category of elements following 'bare *ge*' is further enlarged, including either nominal (4.2) or less nominal (4.3).

(4.2) ...充个耳还聋...
    [*Chong ge er huanlong*]
    (*Turn a deaf ear to...*)

(4.3) ...尽学个驰求走做...
    [...*jinxue ge chiqiuzouzuo*]
    (*You only know to go to different places to learn the knowledge (about Buddha)*)

In (4.2), the noun following *ge* is a normal single syllable noun, however *ge* is not necessary to be used between the verb and the noun. 充耳还聋[*chongerhuanlong*] (*to turn a deaf ear to*) is a well formed expression. The verb 充[*chong*] (*to fill*) and its object 耳[*er*] (*ear*) together form an expression like the modern verb-object splitable compound because they together have a fixed meaning 'to listen' and not simply the combination of two words. In addition, if the numeral 一[*yi*] (*one*) is added back to (4.2), the meaning of the expression will change. It means the sound fills in one of the ears and it is like deaf. This suggests that *ge* here is not simply a classifier and the presence of numeral restricts this new function of *ge*. This usage of *ge* is quite similar to the example (1.1) from modern Chinese. In (4.3), *ge* is followed by a clause which means 'running around to look for the knowledge'. Thus, in (4.2), *ge* is still followed by a nominal structure but in (4.3) the structure after *ge* is not nominal. These instances indicate that the host class of *ge* in post verbal position is not only restricted to nouns and the types of elements following *ge* are expanding. The function of *ge* is not simply a classifier and the productivity of the [V *ge* N] pattern increases. Accordingly, since *ge* in the post verbal position has acquired new function, it is less attached to the elements following it and the internal structure of the pattern changes. By now, both new meaning and new form are established for [V *ge* N] and it starts to be constructionalized.

According to the brief analysis above, it is highly possible that the omission of numeral一[*yi*] (*one*) before *ge* in a post verbal NP triggers the emergence of [V *ge* N] construction. The omission of一[*yi*] (*one*) enables semantic bleaching on *ge* and as a result, the collocates with *ge* expand to non-referential nouns and then even to non-nominal elements. Thus, neoanalysis is required and a new form-meaning pair appears.

5   Conclusion

When the general classifier *ge* is in a post-verbal position, its relationship with its context is complex. When *ge* is inserted between a splitable verb-object compound, they tend to form a construction [V *ge* N] with telic and bounded aspectual meaning. Similarly, this construction can be further generalized as [V *ge* X] because when *ge* in post verbal position is followed by adjectives, adverbs or idioms, they have similar syntactic and semantic features.

The [V *ge* N] construction is distinctive from normal predicate-object construction, not only in syntactic structures but also in meanings. The differences can be formalized as follows:

FORM: [V [[Num+ge_{cl}]+Noun$_i$]] => [[V [*ge*]] N]$_e$

MEANING: [Individualizing, Quantificaltion]$_i$ => [Telic, Bounded]$_e$

But this construction is also linked with normal predicate-object construction, since the emergence of [V *ge* N] construction is triggered by the omission of numeral 一[yi] (one) in post-verbal NPs.

In the [V *ge* N] construction, *ge* is not a classifier but functions as an aspectual marker, and accordingly, it is less attached to the following noun but moves closer to the verb precedes it. *Ge* individualizes an event from the activity denoted by the construction and therefore enables a telic and bounded aspectual meaning in the whole construction.

References

1. Biq, Y.-O.: Construction, reanalysis, and stance: 'V yi ge N' and variations in Mandarin Chinese. Journal of Pragmatics **36**(9), 1655–1672 (2004)
2. Bisang, W.: Grammaticalization in Chinese: a construction-based account. In: Traugott, E.C., Trousdale, G. (eds.) Gradience, Gradualness and Grammaticalization. John Benjamins Publishing Company (2010)
3. Chen, Z.: Ge Yongfa Fanhua de Jufa Fenxi 'The Syntax Results of the Overuse of ge'. Language and Translation (Chinese) (3), 29–31 (2007). (in Chinese)
4. Chierchia, G.: Reference to Kinds across Language. Natural Language Semantics **6**(4), 339–405 (1998)
5. Depraetere, I.: On the Necessity of Distinguishing between (Un)Boundedness and (A)Telicity. Linguistics and Philosophy **18**(1), 1–19 (1995)
6. He, J.: Xiandai Hanyu Liangci Yanjiu. Modern Chinese Classifier. Minzu, Beijing (2001). (in Chinese)
7. Kearns, K.: Semantics. St. Martin's Press (2000)

8. Li, C.N., Thompson, S.A.: Mandarin Chinese: a functional reference grammar. University of California Press, Berkeley (1981)
9. Lin, J.-W.: Temporal Reference in Mandarin Chinese. Journal of East Asian Linguistics **12**(3), 259–311 (2003)
10. Lin, X.: Hanyu Liangci de Renzhi Tantao. Department of Chinese Studies, National University of Singapore. Degree of Master of Art (2006). (in Chinese)
11. Lü, S.: Ge Zi de Yingyong Fanwei, Fulun Danweici qian Yizi de Tuoluo 'The Uses of Ge as a Classifier, with Pemarks Concerning the Dropping of Yi before Ge and Other Classifiers'. Chinese Grammar, pp. 139–168. Shangwu Press, Beijing (1984). (in Chinese)
12. Mi, J.: Jindai Hanyu Tongyong Geti Liangci de Lishi Yanjiu 'A Diachronic Study on the Modern Chinese General Quantifier ge'. Chinese Linguistics. Language and Culture University, Beijing (2009). Master Degree (in Chinese)
13. Okochi, A.: Liangci de Getihua Gongneng, 'Individualizing Function of Chinese Classifiers'. Chinese Study **6**, 8–12 (1988). (in Chinese)
14. Shi, Y., Lei, Y.: The Object Marking Function of ge. Chinese Linguistics Research (4), 14–19 (2004). (in Chinese)
15. Smith, C.S.: The Parameter of Aspect. Springer, Netherlands (1997)
16. Tang Chih-Chen, J.: A note on the DP analysis of the Chinese noun phrase. Linguistics **28**, 337 (1990)
17. Traugott, E.C., Trousdale, G.: Constructionalization and Constructional Changes. OUP Oxford (2013)
18. Xue, J.: Liangci Gehua Wenti Guanjian 'Problems Concerning the Overuse of Ge'. Nanjing Radio and Television University (5), pp. 22–27 (2006). (in Chinese)
19. Yang, S.: The parameter of temporal endpoint and the basic function of -le. Journal of East Asian Linguistics **20**(4), 383–415 (2011)
20. Zhang, Y.: From a Measure Word to an Auxiliary Word– a Case Study of the Grammaticalization of the Chinese Measure Word ge. Modern Linguistics **5**(3), 193–205 (2003). (in Chinese)
21. Zhao, R.: Shuo Ge 'About Ge'. Language Teaching and Research (2), 36–52 (1999). (in Chinese)
22. Zhou, L.: Cong Liangci Ge de Yuyi Fazhan he Xingzhi Chufa Qianxi V ge N jiegou 'Study on VgeN Structure Based on the Development of Ge's Semantic Features'. Exploration of Chinese (3), 208–209 (2013). (in Chinese)
23. Zhu, D.: YuFa JiangYi. Shangwu, Beijing (1982). (in Chinese)

Linguistic Features of "歇后语" (The Two-Part Allegorical Sayings): A Perspective from the Usage of Punctuations

Changshu Chen[✉]

School of Literature, Shandong Normal University, Jinan, Shandong, China
jnchangshu@163.com

Abstract. In this paper, it is been found that both the quantity of punctuations and a variety ways on the usage of punctuations in two-part allegorical sayings are not restricted to the only one common view, namely "using dash between the introduction and the interpretation (I-I)". It exists some complex phenomenon such as "different punctuations, same saying" and "same punctuation, different sayings". On the basis of static analysis, this paper focuses on the rules of punctuations between the I-I and combines with illustrating the dynamic changes of the I-I structure. As a result, we found that punctuations between the I-I are limited by the dynamic change rules of two-part allegorical sayings, which contain the rule of structure, function and semantics.

Keywords: Two-part allegorical sayings · Punctuation · I-I structure

1 Introduction

For a long time, there is a fixed usage on the usage of punctuations in Chinese two-part allegorical sayings. To some extent, it obeys the Chinese national usage of punctuation, that is, "a pattern which is integrated in principle but not in detail"(Guo P., 2009:258). However, as to some micro and specific questions like "which punctuation mark should be used in Chinese two-part allegorical sayings"[1] are not involved. In reaction to this problem, after interpreting the standard of punctuation in two-part allegorical sayings and analyzing the punctuations of two-part allegorical sayings, many scholars such as Wang H. (2000), Shao J.(2000), Lin H.(2001), Lan B. (2006) only reached one consensus, which is "using dash between I-I", and a small group of academics also noticed that "comma may be used between the I-I except dash", "it is more acceptable to use dash when there is a long pause between two parts". (Lei W. 1980: 120-121)

Therefore, it has been admitted in the dictionaries of Chinese Two-part Allegorical Sayings and some other research works published after 1949. In dictionaries of Chinese

---

[1] According ours investigation, national standard of the punctuations – *the Usages of Punctuations,* which was promulgated by government (there were 4 times to promulgate the national standard before 2015. They were 1951, 1995, 2006 and 2012) had not made any provision about the punctuations of the Chinese Two-part Allegorical Sayings.

© Springer International Publishing Switzerland 2015
Q. Lu and H.H. Gao (Eds.): CLSW 2015, LNAI 9332, pp. 608–624, 2015.
DOI: 10.1007/978-3-319-27194-1_61

two-part allegorical sayings, most entries are connected by dash between introduction and interpretation. So far, there is only one exception: in *Standard Dictionary of Modern Chinese Idioms, Proverbs and Two-part Allegorical Sayings*, edited by Li X.(2011), comma is used to connect introduction to interpretation; in the other research of Chinese two-part allegorical sayings, this problem has been generically mentioned or omitted. Apparently, most scholars agree on this rule, but sometimes we do not follow this rule when it comes to practical application, that is because punctuations are in multiforms and complicated, and in turn it brings controversial issues. Until now, lots of questions are not settled and Chinese two-part allegorical sayings cannot be simply generalized as "using dash between I-I". We will discuss it in detail below.

2 Analysis on the Usage of the Punctuation in Chinese Two-part Allegorical Sayings

Towards the journey of discussing the usages of punctuations in Chinese two-part allegorical sayings, example collecting is step one. However, Chinese two-part allegorical sayings with a high degree of colloquialism are rarely used in written language, as we all know that punctuation is a kind of written symbol. So it is difficult to collect enough examples especially on specific saying. After investigating and selecting, two example sources will mainly be used:

The first one called "Corpus of Chinese Idiomatic Phrases", created by the Institute of Linguistics, Shanxi Academy of Social Sciences. The corpus embodies 9353 pieces of Chinese two-part allegorical sayings as retrieving objects, and when retrieved these sayings in CCL Modern Chinese Corpus of Beijing University, 975 pieces could be found. (The other pieces could not be found).

The second source comes from the *Great Dictionary of Chinese two-part allegorical sayings,* edited by Wen D.(2012). It contains 7000 pieces of Chinese two-part allegorical sayings (include variants). "The example sentences refer to the original text and without modification"(Wen D. 2012:2) and the original contents of punctuations are remained.

To begin with, we make detailed statistical analysis of the data above and in turn receive following results: first, there are 3 types of the positions of punctuations, which are between the I-I, in the front/back of the I-I, inside the I-I; second, there are four kinds of punctuations, which include dash, comma, quotation mark and parentheses. It is shown in the table below as to the positions and types of the punctuations.

Table 1. The correspondence between the positions and punctuations in the two-part allegorical saying

Position	Punctuation
Between the I-I	Dash or comma, sometimes no punctuation [2]
In front/back of the I-I structure	In most cases, no punctuation, sometimes quotation marks
Inside the introduction or interpretation	Quotation marks, brackets, comma etc.

---

[2] Sometimes, colons and ellipsis are used between the I-I rarely.

According to the two points above, dynamic usages of punctuations in Chinese two-part allegorical sayings are as follows.

2.1   Same Punctuation, Different Sayings

This refers to the consistency of different Chinese two-part allegorical sayings. It includes general and individual features.

2.1.1   General "Same Punctuation, Different Sayings"

At this time, the punctuations are used in the front and back of I-I structure, or be used inside of introduction or interpretation. It is the general rules of punctuations used in not only two-part allegorical sayings, but also in every other language forms. For example, generally quotation marks should be used in the front/back of the I-I structure for emphasizing (in this paper, all the instructions of sayings are marked by double underlines and all the interpretations are marked by single underline. The other punctuations as well as the contents refer to the original text and without any modification）：

(1) 比如他争强好胜，为了比别人"强"和"胜"，在工作和学习中，就常常是急于求成，总免不了"百年松树，五月芭蕉——粗枝大叶"的，"孙猴子坐天下——毛手毛脚"的。（张作为《原林深处》六章）

Bǐrú tā zhēngqiánghàoshèng, wèile bǐ biérén "qiáng"hé"shèng", zài gōngzuò hé xuéxí zhōng, jiù chángcháng shì jíyú qiúchéng, zǒng miǎnbùliǎo "báinián sōngshù, wǔyuè bājiāo ——cūzhīdàyè"de , "sūnhóuzi zuò tiānxià——máoshǒumáojiǎo"de。 (Zhāng Zuòwéi 《Yuánlín shēnchù》 liù zhāng)

Eg1. He is so competitive that in order to compete with others, he is always in a hurry to succeed in work and study, which leads him to be "like <u>pine of hundreds years old and Chinese banana in May</u>—— with stout branches and big leafs/being crude and careless" and "<u>the Monkey King rules the world</u>—— the hands and feet with much fur/do things recklessly". (Zhang Zuowei, In the Deep Forest, Chapter6）

It is obvious that sometimes quotation marks do not appear in the sayings. It is more common than the case when they appear.

2.1.2   Only with Chinese Two-part Allegorical Sayings

This kind of usage is only found in Chinese two-part allegorical sayings and it is not exist in the other language forms. It is mainly reflected in the usage of punctuation between I-I. There are 3 conditions in the dynamic usage: first, using dash such as eg2; second, using comma such as eg3; third, without using any punctuation such as eg4. Besides, colon and ellipsis may be used in a handful of conditions, such as eg5 and eg6.

（2）一上了山，<u>可就成了没脚蟹——寸步难行了</u>。（吴越《括苍山恩仇记》）

Yī shàng le shān , kě jiù chéngle méijiǎoxiè——cùnbùnánxíng le 。
（*Wú Yuè 《Kuòcāng shān Ēnchóu jì 》*）

Eg2. Go up the mountain, and you will be like <u>the crab with no feet</u>—— <u>difficult to move even one step</u>.　(Wu Yue, the Revenge of Kuocangshan)

（3）咱们做的是<u>没本钱的买卖</u>，<u>赚起赔不起</u>，大家伙出个主意，想个计策才好！
　　（马烽等《吕梁英雄传》）

Zánmen zuò de shì méi běnqián de mǎimài,zhuàn qǐ péi bù qǐ, dàjiāhuǒ chū gè zhúyi, xiǎng gè jìcè cái hǎo !（Má Fēng 《Lǔliáng Yīngxióng zhuàn》）

...Eg3. We should devote ourselves to this matter, because it is as <u>business without capital,only make a prfit but lose the money</u>. (Ma Feng etc, A Tale of Heros of Lvliang)

（4）要是<u>铁锚碰礁石硬对硬</u>，碰崩了还不好办呢！（唐亢双等《闹海记》）

Yàoshì tiěmáo pèng jiāoshí yìngduìyìng, pèng bēng le hái bù hǎo bàn ne !
（*TángKàng shuāng děng 《Nàohǎi jì》*）

Eg4. <u>Anchor against rock hard things meet with each other</u>.It is no good for us.
（*Tang Kangshuang etc,Fight Against the Sea*）

（5）让她嫁给大梁，就如同<u>老鼠掉到面缸里</u>：<u>巴望着这一步哩</u>。（张景秀《联姻风波》）

Ràng tā jià gěi dàliáng, jiù rútóng láoshǔ diào dào miàngāng lǐ : bāwàng zhe zhè yī bù li.(Zhāng Jǐngxiù 《Liányīn fēngbō》

Eg5. She married Daliang just as <u>a mouse fell into flour bag:be wild with joy</u>".
（*Zhang Jingxiu, Tempest of Intermarriage*）

（6）你呀！<u>瘸了屁眼儿</u>……<u>斜门儿</u>，爱好什么不行，就爱听姑奶奶骂你，不挨骂长不大……"（韩冬《原欲》二章）

Nǐ ya ! Quézi pìyǎnr …….xiéménr, àihào shēnme bù xíng, jiù ài tīng gūnǎinai mà nǐ, bù āimà zhǎng bù dà …….."（Hán Dōng《Yuányù》èr zhāng）

Eg6. You are just like <u>a cripple's asshole— an oblique hole(abnormal)</u>.You just loves to be chided, or you will not be intelligent.　(Han Dong, Original Lust, chapter 2)

According to the statistics in *the Great Dictionary of Chinese Two-part Allegorical Sayings （Wen D.2012）*, 4964 pieces of Chinese two-part allegorical sayings are main entries, 4724 of which show only one example sentence. Among these examples, 4684 pieces of Chinese two-part allegorical sayings use no words between I-I; 40 pieces of them use words to insert between I-I. Details are shown in Table 2.

Table 2. The statistics of punctuations between the I-I of the two-part allegorical sayings that only have one example sentence in the *Great Dictionary*.

No other words between the I-I					There are words between the I-I	Total
Comma	Dash	No punctuation	Colon	Ellipsis		
2595	1807	269	9	4	40	4724

From table 2, we can see that the ways of using the same punctuation in different sayings mainly focuses on using comma, dash and no punctuation between I-I.

Among them, comma and dash are most commonly used, and comma using is more frequent than dash using. There are conditions that there are no punctuation between introduction and interpretation. It shows that the range of the three kinds of "same punctuation, different sayings" is different.

The above analysis is about "same punctuation,different sayings" at the same position. Many times, "same punctuation, different sayings" may also appear in two positions of one Chinese two-part allegorical saying all at once; the most common condition is that "same punctuation,different sayings" shows between I-I or in the front/back of I-I structure at the same time, that is to say the universality and specificity of punctuations are interrelated, and in turn there are some complex conditions.

First, dash is used between I-I, and quotation mark is used at both sides of the whole Chinese two-part allegorical saying. For example:

（7）还有，年终评比，有"大闹铃"拖后腿，咱们班准是"瘸子赛跑——笃定老末"。（张任《漩涡》三章）

Háiyǒu, niánzhōng píngbǐ, yǒu "dà nàolíng"tuōhòutuǐ, zánmen bān zhǔn shì "quézi sàipǎo——dǔdìng lǎomò". (ZhāngRèn《Xuànwō》sān zhāng)

Eg7. In addition, in the year-end appraisal of work, squealing girl is dragging it down. Our class is just like a lame person takes part in a race— the last one. (Zhang Ren, Whirlpool, Chapter 3)

Second, comma is used between I-I, and quotation mark is used at both sides of the whole Chinese two-part allegorical saying. For example:

（8）那小伙子不服："这是好家什。""什么好家什！你没听俗话说：'三眼铳打兔子，没准'。"（曲波《桥隆飙》二五）

Nà xiǎohuǒzi bù fú : "Zhè shì hǎo jiāshi。""Shénme hǎo jiāshi！Nǐ méi tīng súhuà shuō : 'sānyǎnchòng dǎ tùzi, méi zhǔn'. " (QúBō《Qiáolóngbiāo》èr wǔ)

Eg8. The guy doesn't summit: "It is a good tool." "I don't think so.Haven't you ever heard that 'shooting the rabbit with a three-loophole gun,cannot shoot it exactly'." (Qu Bo, Qiaolongbiao,25)

In addition, there are some unusual conditions such as dash are used between I-I, and quotation mark is used at both sides of introduction. For example:

（9）分农金会经营的窘况，却使基层人民银行无法举起尚方宝剑，犹如"豆腐掉进灰堆里"——吹不得，打不得。（1994年报刊精选）

Fēnnóngjīnhuì jīngyíng de jiǒngkuàng, què shǐ jīcéng rénmín yínháng wúfǎ jǔ qǐ shàngfāngbǎojiàn, yōurú"dòufu diào jìn huīduī li "——chuī bù de, dá bù de。 （1994nián bàokān jīngxuǎn)

Eg9. The difficulties of rural cooperative foundation made Basic people's Bank can not perform obligations just like "the beancurd dropps into the ambers"—there is no way to clean it up. （selection of newspaper,1994)

2.2   Different Punctuations, Same Saying

It refers to the phenomenon that the same Chinese two-part allegorical saying shows inconsistency when punctuations are used, which is mainly caused by the change of the structure of dynamic state. When a Chinese two-part allegorical sayings is used, the relations of the structure between I-I, the structure of the introduction or interpretation and the structure between the whole I-I structures and the proximity, may all be changed and use different punctuations. For example: "哑巴吃黄连——有苦说不出 *Yǎba chī huánglián——yǒu kǔ shuō bù chū*" ("A dumb person eats the bitter herb——suffering in silence" or "A dumb person eats the bitter herb——unable to express his discomfort/suffering in mind"). There are 60 examples of the saying in CCL Modern Chinese Corpus of Beijing University. We will take 10 of them as examples:

（10）比起明"宰"来，暗"宰"更具隐蔽性，让你哑巴吃黄连———有苦说不出。（1993年人民日报）

Bǐqǐ míng "zǎi" lái, àn "zǎi" gèng jù yǐnbìxìng, ràng nǐ yǎba chī huánglián——yǒu kǔ shuō bù chū。 (1993nián rénmín rìbào)

Eg10. Ripping off in the dark is more covert than ripping off aboveboard. You will be as a dumb person eats the bitter herb—— suffering in silence and unable to express his discomfort.（People's Daily 1993）

（11）她常常在文电上挑一些毛病，弄得那些人颇为头疼，但仔细看看，文字上确有不妥之处，真是哑巴吃黄连——有苦说不出。（《宋氏家族全传》）

Tā chángchang zài wéndiàn shàng tiāo yì xiē máobìng, nòng de nàxiē rén pōwéi tóuténg, dàn zǐxì kànkan, wénzì shàng què yǒu bù tuǒ zhī chù, zhēn shì yǎba chī huánglián ——yǒu kǔ shuō bù chū。（《Sòngshì Jiāzú Quánzhuàn》）

Eg11. She often found fault with the telegram messages and made those men vexed. But when they looked carefully, there were some wrongs with the messages. They are just as a dumb person eats the bitter herb suffering in silence and unable to express his discomfort.（The Life Story of Song family）

（12）以酒瓶盖为例，一个防伪酒瓶盖的成本是普通瓶盖的几倍甚至几十倍，企业根本不想做，但不做又不行，真是哑巴吃黄连———有苦难言。（2000年人民日报）

Yǐ jiǔpínggài wéi lì, yí gè fángwěi jiǔpínggài de chéngběn shì pǔtōng pínggài de jǐbèi shènzhì jǐshí bèi, qǐyè gēnběn bù xiǎng zuò, dàn bú zuò yòu bù xíng, zhēn shì yǎba chī huánglián ——yǒu kǔ nán yán。 (2000nián rénmín rìbào)

Eg12. Take the top as an example; the cost of an anti-fake top is several times or dozens of times. Enterprises do not want to do is, but had to do it, just as a dumb person eats the bitter herb——suffering in silence and unable to express his discomfort. (People's Daily, 2000)

（13）稽察长叫反动派给炸了酱，哑巴吃黄连，有苦说不出！（老舍短篇）

Jīcházhǎng jiào fǎndòngpài gěi zhà le jiàng, yǎba chī huánglián, yǒu kǔ shuō bù chū！(Lǎoshě Duǎnpiān)

Eg13. Inspector was defeated by reactionaries, just as a dumb person eats the bitter herb, suffering in silence and unable to express his discomfort. (Lao She, Short Stories)

（14）在9年前的那桩军售中，法商是见利忘义，助桀为虐，台湾当局则是哑巴吃黄连，至今有苦难言。

Zài 9 nián qián de nà zhuāng jūnshòu zhōng, fǎshāng shì jiànlìwàngyì, zhùjiéwéinuè, táiwān dāngjú zé shì yǎba chī huánglián, zhìjīn yǒu kǔ nányán。

Eg14.*In the arms sales before 9 years, French businessmen are cynical and are as much as holding a light to the devil. Taiwan authorities are as <u>a dumb person eats the bitter herb suffering in silence and unable to express his discomfort</u>.*

（15）这位技师，<u>哑巴吃黄连</u>,<u>有苦说不出</u>。

Zhè wèi jìshī, yǎba chī huánglián, yǒu kǔ shuō bù chū。

Eg15. *This artificer is like <u>a dumb person eats the bitter herb, suffering in silence and unable to express his discomfort</u>.*

（16）无论是"退团"还是"硬撑"，旅行社都是"<u>哑巴吃黄连——有苦说不出</u>"。

Wúlùn shì "tuìtuán" háishì "yìngchēng", lǚxíngshè dōu shì "yǎba chī huánglián ——yǒu kǔ shuō bù chū"。

Eg16. *Travel agency is like "<u>a dumb person eats the bitter herb—— suffering in silence and unable to express his discomfort</u>", being cancelled or strained.*

（17）这样一来，被"服务"的单位"<u>哑巴吃黄连——有苦说不出</u>"。（1993年人民日报）

Zhèyàng yīlái, bèi "fúwù" de dānwèi "yǎba chī huánglián ——yǒu kǔ shuō bù chū"。（1993nián rénmín rìbào）

Eg17. *Thus, "be served" company is like "<u>a dumb person eats the bitter herb——suffering in silence and unable to express his discomfort</u>". （People's Daily,1993）*

（18）一家国营书店的店员告诉记者,他们是"<u>哑巴吃黄连</u>,<u>有苦说不出</u>"。

Yījiā guóyíng shūdiàn de diànyuán gàosù jìzhě, tāmen shì "yǎba chī huánglián, yǒu kǔ shuō bù chū"。

Eg18. *One shop assistant of state-owned bookstore told reporter that they are like "<u>a dumb person eats the bitter her, suffering in silence and unable to express his discomfort</u>."*

（19）再说，他和我三七分账，我受了累，他白拿钱，我是<u>哑巴吃黄连有苦说不出</u>！（老舍《四世同堂》）

Zàishuō, tā hé wǒ sānqī fēnzhàng, wǒ shòu le lèi, tā bái ná qián, wǒ shì yába chī huánglián yǒu kǔ shuō bù chū！（Lǎoshě《Sìshìtóngtāng》）

Eg19. *Furthermore, he and me took a seventy-thirty ratio. I suffered and he took money in vain. I am as <u>a dumb person eats the bitter herb</u> suffering in silence and unable to express his discomfort. （Lao She, Four Generations Live under One Roof）*

（20）我真想拉那位厂长去法庭上说理，谁让自己是'穴头'呢？真是<u>哑巴吃黄连有苦说不出</u>。（《作家文摘》1993年）

Wǒ zhēn xiǎng lā nà wèi chángzhǎng qù fǎtíng shàng shuōlǐ, shuí ràng zìjǐ shì 'xuètou'ne？Zhēn shì yába chī huánglián yǒu kǔ shuō bù chū。（《Zuòjiāwénzhāi》1993nián）

Eg20. I want to rope the factory manager in courtroom to reason things out with him. As a broker, I am as <u>a dumb person eats the bitter herb</u>——<u>suffering in silence and unable to express his discomfort</u>. （Writer Digest,1993）

Dashes are used between I-I in Eg10-Eg12. Commas are used between the I-I in Eg13-Eg15. In Eg16-Eg17 dashes are used between the I-I. Quotation marks are used at both sides of the whole I-I structures. Eg18 puts comma between the I-I and quotation marks are used at both sides of the whole I-I structures. There are no punctuations in the whole I-I structures in Eg19 and Eg20.

Under investigation, we noticed that most Chinese two-part allegorical sayings show the character that "different punctuations,same saying". Only in parts of homophonic two-part allegorical sayings, dash is more frequently used than both comma and no punctuation between I-I, such as "a nephew lights a lantern——to give light to his uncle(remain unchanged)" （Note : in Chinese "旧" (unchanged) has homophony with "舅" (uncle)）. There are 9 examples in *CCL Modern Chinese Corpus of Beijing University* that only put dashes between the I-I without any comma. The only difference is the way of using quotation marks parentheses. For example:

（21）喊过一阵响亮口号，做过一阵表面文章，一切还是"<u>外甥打灯笼——照旧（照舅）</u>"。（新华社2004年5月份新闻）

Hăn guò yī zhèn xiǎngliàng kǒuhào, zuò guò yī zhèn biǎomiàn wénzhāng, yī qiè hái shì "wàishēng dǎ dēnglóng ——zhàojiù (zhàojiù)". （Xīnhuáshè 2004nián 5 yuè fèn xīnwén）

Eg21. After resounding slogan and show, all the things are like "<u>a nephew lights a lantern</u>—— <u>to give light to his uncle(remain unchanged)</u>". （Xinhua News Agency, May, 2004）

（22）所谓"翻牌"，即企业只换个名，而产品、工艺等方面依然是"<u>外甥打灯笼——照舅（旧）</u>"。（《人民日报》1993年2月文章）

Suǒwèi "fānpái ", jí qǐyè zhǐ huàn gè míng, ér chǎnpǐn、gōngyì děng fāngmiàn yīrán shì "wàishēng dǎ dēnglóng ——zhàojiù (jiù) "。 （《Rénmín Rìbào》 1993nián 2yuè wénzhāng）

Eg22. So called government-body-turned mean that the enterprise only change a name, but the products and technology are like "<u>a nephew lights a lantern</u>——<u>to give light to his uncle(remain unchanged)</u>". （People's Daily , Feb ,1993）

（23）而老钟来了个"<u>外甥打灯笼——照旧（舅）</u>"，医院仍旧受到严肃处理。（《人民日报》1995年3月文章）

Ér lǎozhōng lái le gè "wàishēng dǎ dēnglóng ——zhàojiù (jiù) ", yīyuàn rēngjiù shòudào yánsù chùlǐ 。 （《Rénmín Rìbào》 1995nián 3 yuè wénzhāng）

Eg23. Lao Zhong took a attitude just as "<u>a nephew lights a lantern</u>—— <u>to give light to his uncle(remain unchanged)</u>",So the hospital was severely dealt with. （People's Daily, Mar ,1995）

（24）对外国人，对洋人那份爱称还是"<u>外甥打灯笼——照舅（照旧）</u>！"
（《市场报》1994年文章）

Duì wàiguó rén, duì yángrén nà fèn àichēng hái shì "wàishēng dǎ dēnglóng——zhàojiù (zhàojiù)！" (《Shìchǎngbào》1994 nián wénzhāng)

Eg24. The pet name for the foreigner is as "<u>a nephew lights a lantern— to give light to his uncle(remain unchanged)</u>". (Market News,1994)

（25）前面两次都一样效果，再试还不是<u>外甥打灯笼——照旧（舅）</u>。（《故事会》2005年文章）

Qiánmiàn liǎng cì dōu yīyàng xiàoguǒ, zàishì hái bú shì wàishēng dǎ dēnglóng——zhàojiù (jiù)。(《Gùshìhuì》2005 nián wénzhāng)

Eg25. The same effect was gotten twice before.If try again, it will be as <u>a nephew lights a lantern—— to give light to his uncle(remain unchanged)</u>. (Stories Magazine, 2005)

（26）谈起来，"心有戚戚焉"，做起来，"<u>外甥打灯笼——照旧</u>"。
（《读书》191期）

Tán qǐlái, "xīn yǒu qīqī yān", zuò qǐlái, "wàishēng dǎ dēnglóng——zhàojiù"。(《Dúshū》191 qī)

Eg26. If a conversation does start, it strikes a sympathetic chord. However, once take up, it will be as "<u>a nephew lights a lantern—— to give light to his uncle(remain unchanged)</u>". (Reading,191)

（27）爷们对老百姓是<u>外甥打灯笼——照舅（旧）</u>！（冯志《敌后武工队》）

Yémen duì lǎobǎixìng shì wàishēng dǎ dēnglóng——zhàojiù (jiù)！(FéngZhì 《Díhòu Wǔgōngduì》)

Eg27. I will took a attitude to civilian as <u>a nephew lights a lantern——to give light to his uncle(remain unchanged)</u>. (Feng Zhi, The Military Team Behind the Enemy)

（28）没有多久，<u>外甥打灯笼——照旧</u>，不是过期，就是又发本票。（周而复《上海的早晨》）

Méiyǒu duō jiǔ, wàishēng dǎ dēnglóng——zhàojiù, bú shì guòqī, jiù shì yòu fā běnpiào。(Zhōu ěrfù 《Shànghǎi de Zǎochén》)

Eg28. Before long, all are as <u>a nephew lights a lantern—— to give light to his uncle(remain unchanged)</u>, out of date or making out a promissory note (Zhou Erfu, The Morning of Shanghai)

（29）再试纺，顶多忙一阵子，过了几天，还不是<u>外甥打灯笼——找舅（照旧）</u>。（同上）

Zài shìfǎng, dǐngduō máng yī zhènzi, guò le jǐ tiān, hái bú shì wàishēng dǎ dēnglóng——zhǎo jiù (zhàojiù)。(Tóng shàng)

Eg29. Try again, at the most, it will be busy for some time. And after a few days, it will be as <u>a nephew lights a lantern— to give light to his uncle(remain unchanged)</u>. (Zhou Erfu, the Morning of Shanghai)

Sometimes, even in the same article, the usages of the punctuations maybe same, maybe different. For example:

（30）可是，叫天子却是个榆木疙瘩死心眼子，偏要<u>小葱拌豆腐</u>，<u>一清二白</u>，辜负了水芹的一片苦心。（刘绍堂《绿杨堤》）

Kěshì, jiàotiānzǐ què shì gè yúmù gēda sǐ xīnyǎnzi, piān yào xiǎocōng bàn dòufu, yīqīng èrbái, gūfù le shuǐqín de yī piàn kǔxīn。（Liúshàotáng《Lùyángdī》）

Eg30. However, Jiaotianzi is <u>an elm knot</u> <u>a person with a one-track mind;insists on</u> that <u>bean curd mixed with chopped green onion,perfectly clear</u>. Let ShuiQin's heart down.（Liu Shaotang,The Embankment of Lvyang）

Eg30 shows three two-part allegorical sayings in all: in the first example, there are no punctuations between the I-I; in the second and third examples, a comma is used between the I-I.

From the examples mentioned above, we can conclude that, practically, it is not limits in "using dash between the (I-I)", actually the punctuations could be used in many positions. According to the distribution of punctuations in Chinese two-part allegorical sayings, there are "different punctuations,same saying" and "same punctuation,different sayings".

3　Study on Dynamic Rules of Punctuations in Modern Chinese Two-part Allegorical Sayings

By the time punctuations come into dynamic using, the usage of punctuations stays the same as the static condition or shows something different。 This kind of "unsteadiness" and "steadiness" sheds light on the "unsteadiness" and "steadiness" of the linguistic units in structure and semantics.

To be clear, from the analysis above we have already knew that it is not constant when it comes to dynamic using, punctuations could be put between I-I, at each side of the I-I structure, inside of the introductions or inside of the interpretations, and sometimes even no punctuations are used. The usage of punctuations between I-I is the most complicated situation, which also will be the key point of analysis in the following context.

3.1　The Constant Usage of Punctuations in Both Dynamic and Static Conditions of the Chinese Two-part Allegorical Sayings

It has been mentioned above that, the only agreement about usage of punctuations in Chinese two–part allegorical sayings is "using dash between I-I". When it comes to the dynamic using, dash is still the common use. It is the result of correspondence on the static features of the I-I structure and the long-standing rules of using dashes. This correspondence in turn extends and remains from the dynamic using.

In order to clarify this correspondence, it is necessary to discuss some related static features of Chinese two–part allegorical sayings. In the static system, the structure of the sayings is "introduction + pause + interpretation", and it contains 3 points:

First, from the perspective of phonetic form, it is pause between I-I and generally this pause stays quit long.

Second, from the perspective of semantics, there are two kinds of relationships of I-I. One is metaphorical relationship in terms of the metaphorical sayings. It takes the introduction as the metaphorical object and the interpretation as the metaphorical explain (otology). Its relationship shows in Fig.1.

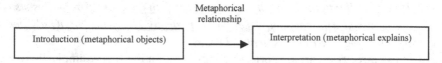

Fig. 1. The semantic relationship of the metaphorical Chinese two-part allegorical sayings

For example: 断　了　线　的　风筝　——永远　　收　不　回来　了

　　　　　Duàn le xiàn de fēngzhēng——Yǒngyuǎn shōu bù húilái le

（The sting of kite breaks——it can never be taken back）

The introduction "the sting of kite breaks" is the metaphorical object, and the interpretation "it can never be taken back" is the metaphorical explain. The two parts are linked by the metaphorical relationship and then become a whole Chinese two-part allegorical saying.

The other relationship is the relationship of extension in terms of the punning Chinese two-part allegorical sayings. In this situation, in virtue of the homophonic (or transferred meaning), the introduction could go trough the exterior meanings and connect with the interior meanings; as a result, the introduction may get an extra meaning. Then, the semantic relationship between I-I is actually the extended relationship, and it is shown in Fig.2.

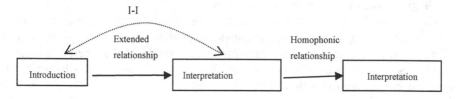

Fig. 2. The semantic relationship of the homophonic Chinese two-part allegorical sayings

For example: 大　爆仗　　掉　进　河　里——没　响　（想）

　　　　Dà bàozhàng diào jìn hé lǐ——méi xiǎng(xiǎng)

（The big firecracker falls into the river ——it's not possible to make noise by explosion, note: there is homophony in "响"（noise）and "想"（look forward to））.

Both the introduction "the big firecracker falls into the river" and the exterior meaning of "it's not possible to make noise by explosion" show the extended relationship. "响"（noise）and "想"（look forward to）are phonetic pun in Chinese and are related to the interior of the meaning "there is nothing to look forward to".

Third, from the perspective of the grammatical relationship, when the introduction and interpretation of the Chinese two-part allegorical sayings are both sentences, the relationship between I-I is the relationship of complex sentences.[3]

Dash is generically used to "show the explanation of the content, the changes or leaps of the meaning, stops or extension of the languages"(Wu B., 1990:141). These usages are corresponding to the three characters of I-I relationships above:

First, both metaphorical relationship of "metaphorical object" and "metaphorical explain" in metaphorical sayings and extended relationship of the phonetic pun in homophonic sayings are illustrative relationships. And explanation is one of the common usages of dash, so we could take it for granted.

Second, there should be meaning consistency between I-I; meanwhile, due to the jocosity and ambiguity of Chinese two-part allegorical sayings (Wen D., 2006: 295-315), distance may exist from the semantics, and then semantic zigs appear. The structure "consistency + zig" fits the usage of the dash well, just as what Lv S. and Zhu D. have mentioned:" If comma is used then the inconsistency could not be shown; if period is used then the consistency could not be shown. Here, dash is the most appropriate punctuation, but if it lacks this condition then dash could not be used either." (2013:260)

Third, from the phonetic perspective, the pause or dash between I-I means stop or the extension of the languages.

Moreover, there is an additional function about the dash between I-I: it could tell the two-part allegorical sayings from idiom, phrase, proverb and some other static linguistic unit. It is because that in written language, these units do not use dash, to be specific, they either use no punctuations or use comma. In a word, showing the I-I relationship and features are the main function of the dash between I-I.

In dynamic using, the structure of static condition "introduction + pause + interpretation" is completely be used, especially when this structure is an independent sentence or it acts as a syntactic constituent. At that time, the whole saying still shows as a complete fixed structure and the constancy of structure becomes much more obvious. Furthermore, usually the long pause remains, too. Under all those restriction, language users use dashes much more frequently than commas or no punctuations. For example:

（31）山燕政治热情高，但她还不懂啥叫条件，她是<u>黄连豆用嘴嚼——自找苦吃</u>。（杨大群《山燕》）

Shānyàn zhèngzhì rèqíng gāo, dàn tā hái bù dǒng shá jiào tiáojiàn, tā shì huángliándòu yòng zuǐ jiáo ——zìzhǎokǔchī。 (Yángdàqún 《Shānyàn》)

Eg31. Shan Yan has passionate enthusiasm for politics, but she didn't know what the condition was. She was just like <u>chewing the bitter herb</u>—— <u>asking for trouble</u>. （Yanng Daqu, Hill Swallow）

---

[3] Fan Xiao（2001）regarded it as a kind of special supplementary complex – sentence. But we regarded it as a kind of explanation complex – sentence. Chen Changshu （2014：84-85）

Certainly, the Chinese two-part allegorical sayings also add some new dynamic contents. For example, dash also distinguishes from the similar dynamic phenomenon such as general phrases and sentences on grammar, general metaphors and puns etc. But these new contents are less important contents, which derive from the fixities of the structures. It can be argued that whether static forms or dynamic forms, fixities of the structure are the main causes, which decide that dash is used between I-I.

3.2   The Inconstant Usage of Punctuations in both Dynamic and Static Conditions of the Chinese Two-part Allegorical Sayings

Certainly, the punctuations used between I-I are not only dash, but also comma, and even no punctuation. These usages are not summarized as the standards of the usages of punctuations, but often are used in dynamic condition. The forms of the dynamic usages also benefit from the relationship of correspondence: the features of the I-I structure in dynamic conditions and changes are fit for the usages rules of other punctuations specifically. What kind of dynamic changes has happened in the I-I structure?

Through the observation, we think that analyzability of the structure of I-I structure is strengthened and the fixity of the structure is weakened. Firstly, we will discuss the analyzability, which is also the character of the I-I structure in static condition. The static characters as follows.

Firstly, on grammar, both the introduction and interpretation possess the sense of analyzability. There are no differences between their forms and general phrases, sentences (in rare cases, they are words). Secondly, on semantics, there are metaphors and funs. On rhetorical structures, Chinese two-part allegorical sayings also have the features of the metaphor and pun, and there is nothing special about them. The features of the structures in dynamic condition are similar to those in static condition.

It is different from the static condition that the introduction and interpretation are not only interrelated but also connected with other units separately. The syntactic structure gets into the I-I structure by many means. Because of the differences of the language users and the individual situations, lack of special marks of the I-I structure may cause difficult understanding for people to distinguish the Chinese two-part allegorical sayings from the general phrases and sentences, as well as metaphors and puns. For example:

（32）你们可真好，一个急性子，一个好脾气，芥麦地里种萝卜，搭配得当呀！

　　（孟千等《决战》）

Nǐmen kě zhēn hǎo, yī gè jí xìngzi, yī gè hǎo píqì, qiáomàidì lǐ zhòng luóbo, dāpèi dédàng ya !　(Mèng Qiān děng 《Juézhàn》)

Eg32. You are so nice. One is impetuous, the other is good-tempered. You are just like planting radish in the field of the buckwheat—a good match!(Mengqian etc, Decisive Battle)

In Eg32, the introduction and interpretation are not dissimilar to the general sentence form. The introduction and interpretation are all explained through the context. And this process of transition from introduction to interpretation is very natural.

It is coherent in semantics and there is no need for pause to keep long time, so comma is often used in Chinese two-part allegorical sayings.

Sometimes, words are added into the Chinese two-part allegorical sayings because of contexts. One of the introduction and interpretation must be placed into the different construction. I-I structure becomes the intra-sentence structure hidden in the structure of complex sentences. The semantic zig in semantics becomes weak. And at the same time it becomes more coherent. For example:

（33）小孬说："管他娘嫁给谁——咱只管跟着喝喜酒。半夜里尿床，他想流到哪儿就流到哪儿。"

（李準《黄河东流去》）

Xiǎonāo shuō : "Guǎn tā niáng jià gěi shuí ——zán zhǐ guǎn gēn zhe hē xǐjiǔ. Bànyè lǐ niàochuáng, tā xiǎng liú dào nǎr jiù liú dào nǎr." (Lǐ zhǔn 《Huánghé Dōng Liú Qù》)

Eg33. Xiaonao said that whom she will marry doesn't matter. We only drink at the wedding feast. He is just like <u>wetting the bed in the midnight</u> , <u>having no good idea to stop him</u>. (Li Zhun, The Huanghe River Flows To The EAST)

In Eg33, the interpretation "想流到哪儿就流到哪儿" (having no good idea to stop him) and "他" （him） become one sentence , then the sentence combines with the introduction "wet the bed at midnight". The introduction and interpretation are placed into different clauses. The whole Chinese two-part allegorical saying is placed into a complex sentence.

In this way, language users usually consider the relation of the structure of the clauses before choosing the punctuations. And instead of using comma, they will choose dash. On this point, it is more obvious in metaphorical two-part allegorical sayings. "Introduction (the metaphorical objects) +interpretation (the metaphorical explains)" will be easier to go back to the regular metaphorical structure as they come into the dynamic contexts. Parts of language users know metaphorical structure much more than the fixed structure. So the frequencies of commas, which are used between I-I of metaphorical Chinese two-part allegorical sayings in dynamic context, are no less than dashes.

It is very easy for people to regard the homophonic Chinese two-part allegorical saying as a whole unit and regard it as a whole stereotyped structure. Sometimes, the introduction and interpretation are separately in different sentences, so the exterior relationship of puns is weakened. However, the introduction remains a distant relationship with the interior meaning of the interpretation, so the sudden turn of meaning between I-I is preserved. Dash can indicate this point, and so becomes the top choice of the punctuations between I-I.

According to the previous investigation result, it is different from the metaphorical two-part allegorical saying that dash is often used in homophonic two-part allegorical saying. Especially in the same homophonic two-part allegorical saying of different contexts, dash is used more than comma. The same punctuation of the same content is more obvious. We think that it is related to the special structure of "extending+ homophony". For example:

（34）你看她还是哇哩哇啦的，我敢保险她连瑶话也是<u>井里丢石头——不咚（懂）</u>啊。

Nǐ kàn tā hái shì wāliwāla de, wǒ gǎn bǎoxiǎn tā lián yáohuà yě shì jǐng lǐ diū shítou ——búdǒng （dǒng） a 。

Eg34. Look, she still gabbled. I'm sure she doesn't know the language of Yao at all just as <u>a stone is dropped into a well—flop (don't know).</u>

In Eg34, the meaning is changed dramatically from the introduction "drop a stone into a well" to the homophonic "flop", then to the interpretation "don't know". So, dash can explain the change of the meaning.

Overall, in dynamic state of the homophonic two-part allegorical sayings, the fixity of structure exceeds the analyzability of the structure. Accordingly in this kind of two-part allegorical sayings, dash is more frequently used than commas between I-I.

Of course, comma is also used between I-I in homophonic two-part allegorical saying. It indicates that people put introduction and interpretation into different individual structures and analyze them. People analyze the extended relationship of the I-I structure, and regard the introduction and interpretation as the two clauses of a complex sentence. However, people regard "extending+ homophony" as a fixed structure more often.

In dynamic conditions, the change of the punctuations between I-I is related to the pause. Sometimes, the pause between I-I can become very short, then the comma will be used. For example:

（35）刘春两道浓眉一竖，嚷道："<u>老虎头上抓虱子，好大的胆</u>！走！"（武剑青《云飞嶂》）

Liúchūn liǎng dào nóngméi yī shù, rǎngdào : "Lǎohǔ tóu shàng zhuā shīzi, hǎo dà de dǎn ! zǒu ! " （Wǔ Jiànqīng 《Yúnfēi zhàng》 ）

Eg35. <u>Search tiger's hair for lice</u>, <u>how dare you are</u>! Go! "Liuchun yelled with his strong dark eyebrows standing on end. （Wu Jianqing, Yunfeizhang）

Sometimes, there is no obvious pause between I-I. In this example, no punctuation is used .For example:

（36）王院长欲去周华处，被宋凯拦住，"算了，院长，甭管了，这时候了，只有<u>闭眼跳河听天由命</u>了。"（王海等《爱你没商量》）

Wáng yuànzhǎng yù qù zhōuhuá chù, bèi sòngkǎi lán zhù, "Suàn le, yuànzhǎng, béng guǎn le, zhè shíhòu le, zhǐyǒu bìyǎn tiàohé tīngtiānyóumìng le。 " （Wáng Hǎi děng 《Ài Nǐ Méi Shāngliang》 ）

Eg36. Dean Wang wanted to have a meet with Zhou Hua, but Song Kai held him back and said: "Forget it, dean, leave it alone, by this time, just like <u>jumping into the river when the eyes are closed</u> our lives are in the lap of the gods. （WangHai etc, No way to love you）

It is very easy to judge whether there are stops. But it is difficult to judge the length of a stop in the speech flow. Some subjective differences such as the habit of talking and familiarity with the two-part allegorical sayings contribute to the different length of stop in different people in the same condition. As a result, in the dynamic conditions, different punctuations may be used between I-I in the same two-part allegorical sayings.

Except the punctuations between I-I, the punctuations of the two flanks of the two-part allegorical saying are added temporarily in the dynamic states and do not appear in the static conditions. And the use and the disuse about the punctuations of the two flanks of the Chinese two-part allegorical sayings depend on the key point: quotation marks aim to emphasize the characters of the two-part allegorical sayings with an eye to the fixity of the I-I structure. If quotation marks are not used, the introduction and interpretation will be regarded as one general word group or one component with an eye to the analyticity of I-I structure. The use of the quotation marks is optional and confused. For example:

（37）他当保管是 "玉茭地里种豆角——捎办"。（张旺模《马大爷和电扇的故事》）

Tā dāng bǎoguǎn shì "yùjiāo dì lǐ zhòng dòujiǎo ——shāobàn ".
(Zhāng Wàngmó 《Mǎ Dàyé hé Diànshàn de Gùshì 》)

Eg37. <u>It is for him to be a storekeeper just like "growing green beans in Corn— it is easy".</u> *(Zhang Mowang, the Story about Uncle Ma and Electric Fan)*

In few examples, quotation marks are only used for introduction but not for interpretation. It may because sometimes the meanings and the contents of introductions are not true, and quotation marks are needed for emphasizing this quality. It is regarded as an individual temporary usage without regularity. For example:

（38）你倒成了 "太平洋的警察"，才管得宽咧！（应泽民《a·p案件》）

Nǐ dào chéng le "tàipíngyáng de jǐngchá", cái guǎn de kuān lie ! (Yìng zémín 《a·p ànjiàn》)

Eg38. You became "<u>the police of the the Pacific</u>", <u>who control too much</u>. (Ying Zemin, A·P law Case)

In addition, the homophonic two-part allegorical sayings often indicate the homophonic parts by the brackets. For example: 孔夫子搬家——尽是书（输）*when Confucius moves—there is nothing but books(To lose all the time)*. This is a static and solidified usage. But under investigation, there are some temporary usages of punctuations in homophonic Chinese two-part allegorical sayings, just as some homophonic parts are in quotes.

（39）她半开玩笑地说："再刻苦有啥用？小庙里的菩萨——不会有多少 '香' 的！"

（德咏等《幕边春秋》）

Tā bàn kāi wánxiào de shuō : "Zài kèkǔ yǒu shá yòng ？Xiǎomiào lǐ de púsà —— bù huì yǒu duōshǎo 'xiāng' de ！" (Dé Yǒng děng 《Mùbiān Chūnqiū》)

Eg39. "What is the point of working hard? You are just like <u>Bodhisattva of small temple— can't bear big consecration</u> ! " She jibed, tongue in cheek. (Deyong etc, Mubian Chunqiu)

4   Conclusions

In this paper,according to the structure of the two-part allegorical sayings and the basic usage of punctuations, we have discussed their features and rules above. From the sayings themselves, during the dynamic period, sayings have changed in inner structure, semantic content and syntactic function. And as a result, on the basis of the regular use, the usage of punctuations must adapt to the dynamic changes.

References

1. Chen, C.: Dynamic Studies on the Structure of Two-part Allegorical Sayings in Modern Chinese. Academic Journal of LIYUN **2**, 84–85 (2014). (in Chinese)
2. Fan, X.: About Three-Plane Theory of Chinese Grammar. Beijing Language and Culture University Press, Beijing (2001). (in Chinese)
3. Guo, P.: Research on the Chines Punctuation Since the 20th Century. Central China Normal University Press, Wuhan (2009). (in Chinese)
4. Lan, B.: Artistic usage of Punctuation. Zhonghua Book Company, Beijing (2006). (in Chinese)
5. Lei, W.: Discussion on the Usage of the Punctuation by Example. Tianjin People's Press, Tianjin (1980). (in Chinese)
6. Li, X.: Standard Dictionary of Modern Chinese Idioms, Proverbs Two-part Allegorical Sayings. Sinolingua, Beijing (2011). (in Chinese)
7. Lin, H.: Study and Application of the Punctuation. People's Press, Beijing (2001). (in Chinese)
8. Lv, S., Zhu, D.: Grammar and Rhetoric in Speech. The Commercial Press, Beijing (2013). (in Chinese)
9. Shao, J.: Knack of the Punctuation. Truth & Wisdom Press, Shanghai (2000). (in Chinese)
10. Wang, H.: Usage of the Punctuation. Jindun Publishing House, Beijing (2000). (in Chinese)
11. Wang, Q.: Introduction to Proverb and Chinese Two-part Allegorical Sayings. Hunan People's Publishing House, Changsha (1981). (in Chinese)
12. Wen, D.: Chinese Lexicology Course. The Commercial Press, Beijing (2006). (in Chinese)
13. Wen, D.: Great Dictionary of Chinese Two-part Allegorical Sayings. Shanghai Lexicographic Publishing House, Shanghai (2012). (in Chinese)
14. Wu, B.: Usage of the Punctuation Marks. Academy Press, Beijing (1990). (in Chinese)

A Constructional Approach to a Personal Pronoun Marked Construction in Mandarin Chinese

Sisi Huang and Weidong Zhan[✉]

Department of Chinese Language and Literature, Center for Chinese Linguistics,
Key Laboratory of Computational Linguistics, Ministry of Education,
Peking University, Beijing, China
huanglingyu_hi@126.com, zwd@pku.edu.cn

Abstract. This paper discusses the syntactic features as well as the semantics and typical contexts of use of a personal pronoun marked construction in Mandarin Chinese, which is formalized as Pronoun + Verb + Pronoun + de + Noun, or the simplified form "r+v+r+de+n". It also explains how different contexts determine the meaning expressed by this construction.

Keywords: R+v+r+de+n · Construction · Context · Meaning difference

1 Introduction

In this paper we discuss the interpretation of a personal pronoun marked construction in Mandarin Chinese and the various contexts in which the construction can be used. The examples below illustrate the construction (form and meaning) we are interested in.[1]

(1) 葡 萄, 你睡你的 去, 啥 事 不 愁。
    Pu Tao ni shui ni de qu sha shi bu chou
    Pu Tao, you sleep yours go, what thing NEG worry
    Pu Tao, sleep easy, don't worry about anything.

(2) 白花蛇： 师姐！你好哇？ 也 学会 扭秧歌 了 吧？
    Bai Huashe shi jie ni hao wa ye xue hui niu yang ge le ba
    Bai Huashe: sister how are you also learn dance ASP
    Bai Huashe: Sister, how are you, have you also learned how to dance?
    方太太： 滚！ 吃你的饭 去, 别 招 我 生气！
    Fang Taitai gun chi ni de fan qu bie zhao wo sheng qi
    Mrs. Fang: get out eat your supper go, NEG make me annoyed
    Mrs. Fang: Get out! Just eat your supper, don't annoy me!

(3) 他 丝毫 没有 注意 那 门房 说的话，他 睡 他的……
    Ta si hao mei you zhu yi na men fang shuo de hua ta shui ta de
    He a bit NEG pay attention to that porter words, he sleep his
    He did not pay any attention to what the doorman said and just kept sleeping.

---

[1] In this paper, examples quoted from Lv Shuxiang(1988) are marked with "Lv" and followed by the pages in which they can be found; the ones self generated are marked "self-made"; and the rest come from the Center for Chinese Linguistics PKU Corpus (CCL).

© Springer International Publishing Switzerland 2015
Q. Lu and H.H. Gao (Eds.): CLSW 2015, LNAI 9332, pp. 625–637, 2015.
DOI: 10.1007/978-3-319-27194-1_62

(4) 宋霭龄　　　说：　唐绍仪　　　是　袁世凯的　　　代表。
Song Ailing　shuo　Tang Shaoyi　shi　Yuan Shikai de　dai biao
Song Ailing　say　Tang Shaoyi　is　Yuan Shikai's　representative.

<u>他　　撤　　　他的</u>,　　您　又何必　惊慌
ta　　che　　ta de　　nin you he bi jing huang
he　　dismiss　his　　you why　　alarmed

Song Ailing said: Tang Shaoyi is the representative of Yuan Shikai. Why should you alarm yourself about the dismissal of Mr. Tang?

(5) 三　车　印度　一齐　吹打　起来, 可是 <u>你　吹　你的, 我 打　我的</u>……
San　che yin du　yi qi　chui da qi lai ke shi　ni chui　ni de　wo da wo de
Three cars Indians together play ASP,　but　you play yours, I　play mine……

The Indians in the three cars begun to play music together. But they played at will and even at random as if they are not a team at all.

Lv Shuxiang (1988) considers the structures underlined as a special usage of the "personal possessive pronouns". He states that the structure means "the subject of the structure does not care about other people or other matters". He also points out that this structure means "other people do not care about something or someone" in relatively rare situations.[1]

The grammatical form of this construction is as follows:

Pronoun + Verb + Pronoun + de + Noun. The most obvious feature is that the two pronouns in the construction are identical. The first one functions syntactically as the subject and the second one forms a possessive pronoun functioning as the modifier in an object phrase. In this paper we use the following symbols to represent each part of the construction: 'r' for personal pronoun, 'v' for predicate, 'n' for noun. Hence the construction mentioned above can be formalized as "r+v+r+de+n".

Both meaning, i.e. "the subject does not care" and "others do not care", cannot be derived directly from the structure of the construction. As defined by Goldberg(1995):"C is a CONSTRUCTION iff$_{def}$ C is a form-meaning pair <F$_i$, S$_i$> such that some aspect of F$_i$ or some aspect of S$_i$ is not strictly predictable from C's component parts or from some other previously established constructions". Therefore "r+v+r+de+n" can be regarded as a construction.[2]

Lv (1988) defines the use of this construction accurately yet some questions remain. In example (1), "你睡你的去[*ni shui ni de qu*]" can be interpreted as "Go sleep, don't worry about other matters". It expresses consolation, which is positive. However, in example (2), "吃你的饭去[*chi ni de fan qu*]" means "You should go eat your supper rather than disturb me". It expresses the discontent of the speaker, which is negative. One question naturally arises: Why do these two sentences using the same construction exhibit different meanings? If we attribute this difference to the contexts, then another question arises: What is the difference between these two contexts? In example (3), "他睡他的[*ta shui ta de*]" can be interpreted as "He sleeps, and doesn't care about what the porter says"; while in example (4), "他撤他的[*ta che ta de*]" can NOT be interpreted as "He dismisses Tang and doesn't care about other things", but as "You do not need to worry about his dismissing". In this case why do these examples exhibit a different meaning? Finally in example (5), the phrase "你吹你的, 我打我的[*ni chui ni de ,wo da wo de*]" which means "*you play by yourselves and I play by myself, none of them interferes with each other*", contains two "r+v+r+de+n" structures (namely called a double-chunk construction). In contrast, examples (1-4) contain only one "r+v+r+de+n" structure (namely a single-chunk construction). What are then the differences and relations between these two kinds of constructions?

In an attempt to answer these questions, we organized the rest of the paper as follows: Section 2 describes the syntactic features of this construction in details; Section 3 analyzes the semantics of this construction; Section 4 and Section 5 discuss the construction with the meanings "not to care about" and "not to interfere with each other" respectively, focusing on the contexts in which they can occur. These two sections also analyze how different contexts determine the meaning expressed by this construction.

2   Constraints on the Components of the Construction "r+v+r+de+n"

2.1   Constraints on the "r" and "n"

In the construction "r+v+r+de+n", "n" can be omitted (as seen in example 1,3,4) and the first "r" (subject) can also be omitted in imperative sentences. However, the two "r" must be the same. If not, the whole construction may be incorrect (example 6) or become a different construction (example 7).

(6) *你睡 他的   觉   (7) 你   帮   他的   忙
    Ni shui ta de jiao   Ni   bang ta de mang
    You sleep his sleep (*You sleep him.*)   You help his   help (*You help him.*)

2.2   Constraints on the "v"

The predicate "v" in this construction is always a bare verb and mostly single-syllable. It can be a transitive verb (for example 吃[*chi*](*eat*)), the verbal part of a of separable verb (for example 挂号[*gua hao*](*register*)) or an intransitive verb (for example 跑 [*pao*](*run*)). Most verbs in this construction are autonomous. In few situations, some non-autonomous verbs (example 8), adjectives (example 9,10) and some double-syllable verbs (example 10) may also occur.

(8) 你 死 你的, 关 我   什么 事?   (9) 我 胖   我的, 与你 何   干?
    Ni si ni de guan wo shen me shi   Wo pang wo de   yu ni he   gan
    You die yours, to me what thing   I   fat   mine to you what relation
(It's none of my business if you want to kill yourself) (That I am fat has nothing to do
with you)
(10) 我颓丧   我的, 他 积极 他的.
    Wo tui sang wo de ta ji ji   ta de
    I dispirited mine he active his (*While I am quite dispirited, he just keeps active.*)

2.3   The Relation Between the "v" and the "r+de+n"

The structure "v+r+de+n" can be regarded as a predicate-object structure, in which "v" is a transitive verb and functions as the predicate, while "r+de+n" functions as the object. This kind of structure is shown in example (11). However, compared with a regular predicate-object structure, some semantic constraints should be noticed in this particular structure. Wu Huaicheng (2008) points out that the head of "quasi-attributive" has the feature [+non-referential]. [4] In this construction, the "n" is also non-referential. If "n" is modified by a this/that + quantitative phrase, this construction becomes a regular structure (example 12). In addition, "v" and "n" can also be two components of a separable verb (example 13), such as 挂号[*gua hao*](*to register*). "v" can also be an intransitive verb or adjective (example 14), such as " 胖[*pao*] (*be fat*)". In these two situations, "v+r+de+n" is an irregular structure, in which the syntactic function of "v" and "r+de+n" is hard to determine.

(11) 你 吃 你的 饭
     Ni chi ni de fan
     You eat your meal
(You eat your meal and do not care about other matters.)

(12) 你   吃   你的   这碗   饭
     Ni   chi ni de zhe wan fan
     You eat your   this bowl rice
(You eat this bowl of rice which belongs to you.)

(13) 你 挂   你的   号
     Ni gua ni de   hao
     You register your register
(You register and do not care about other matters.)

(14) 我 胖 我的，与 你 何   干？
     Wo pang wo de yu ni he   gan
     I   fat mine to you what   relation.
(That I am fat has nothing to do with you.)

2.4   The Relation Between the "r" and the "n"

In the construction "r+v+r+de+n", the relation between "r" and "n" is of four types. In the first type, "n" must belong to "r"(example 15). In general, people brush their own teeth. Therefore in the sentence "你刷你的牙"[*ni shua ni de ya*] (*you brush your teeth*), the teeth must belong to the subject. In the second type, "n" may belong to "r" or not (example 16). In the sentence "你念你的书[*ni nian ni de shu*](*you read your book*)", the book may belong to the subject or be borrowed. In the third type, "r" and "n" have no specific relation (example 17). In the structure "你做你的杀猪匠[*ni zuo ni de sha zhu jiang*](*you act as a butcher*)", it is hard to determine the relation between "you" and "butcher". In the fourth type, the relation between "r" and "n" is not a regular syntactic relation as found in separable verbs.

(15) 你 刷 你 的 牙
     Ni shua ni de ya
     You brush your teeth
(You brush your teeth and don't care about other matters.)

(16) 你 看   你的   书
     Ni kan   ni de   shu
     You read your   book
(You read your book and don't care about other matters.)

(17) 你 做 你的   杀猪匠
     Ni zuo ni de   sha zhu jiang
     You act as your   butcher
(You be a butcher and don't care about other matters).

(18) 你   睡   你的   觉
     Ni   shui ni de jiao
     You sleep your   sleep.
(Go sleep and don't care about other matters.)

In general, "r" has no direct relation with "n", but has a direct relation with "v+n". What should be noted is that in the construction "r+v+r+de+n", "v+n" is accomplished by "r". This action can only involve "r" and no other subject.

2.5   Elements that usually Co-occur with the Structure "v+r+de+n"

In real speech, many elements usually co-occur with the structure "v+r+de+n". This sentence pattern can be modified by adverbs (example 19), which are mainly"尽管 [jin guan](merely) 安心[an xin](relived) 继续[ji xu](go on)" and so on. The structure "v+r+de+n" can also be the latter component of a serial predicate structure (example 20). It can also be the former component of a serial predicate structure (example 1,2), of which the latter component must be去[qu](go).

(19) 你 只管   打   你的 县城   (20) 回去   放   你的   哨.
　　Ni zhi guan da   ni de xian cheng   Hui qu fang   ni de   shao
　　You only care about attack your county   Go back stand   your sentry
(You should just care about attacking the country.)(Go back on sentry duty, don't care about other matters.)

3   The Two Meanings of the Construction "r+v+r+de+n"

Lv (1988) states that the single-chunk construction can be paraphrased in two ways:
(M1) do not care about other people and other matters;
(M2) other people do not care about something or someone

(21) 你们 把 这些 零碎东西 索性 都   交给 我, 你们 去逛 你们的(Lv 173)
　　Ni men ba zhe xie ling sui dong xi , suo xing dou jiao gei wo ni men qu guang ni men de
　　You BA these small things merely all entrust me   you   go sightseeing yours
Trust me with all the small things and just go sightseeing.
(22) 我 作践 了   我的 身子, 我 死 我的, 与 你   何   干 (Lv 174)
　　Wo zuo jian le   wo de shen zi wo si wo de   yu ni   he gan
　　I   harm ASP   my   body I die mine to you what relation
I harmed myself and even if I die,   it is none of your business.

In example (21), "你们去逛你们的[ni men qu guang ni men de]"can be interpreted as " Go sightseeing, and do not care about the small things". The person "who should not care" is the same acting as the subject of the sentence. In example (22), " 我死我的[wo si wo de]" can not be interpreted as "I die and I do not care about other people and other matters" but rather "I die and you should not care about my dying". The person who should not care is different from the subject. Hence Lv interprets such context as "other people do not care about".

He also states that the double-chunk construction can also be paraphrased in two ways:
(M3) do not interfere with each other
(M4) do not interfere with each other, but the latter chunk is emphasized

(23) 你　作　你的　官，　我们　上　我们的　山
　　　Ni　zuo　ni de　guan　wo men shang wo men de shan
　　　You　be　your officer,　we　climb our　mountain
You go be an officer, we go be bandits
(24) 他　闹　　　他的，人家　　　过　人家的
　　　Ta　nao　　　ta de　ren jia　　　guo　ren jia de
　　　He　make trouble his　other people　live　other people's
He makes a lot of trouble, but other people live well and do not care about him.

Example (23) means that "You go be an officer and we go be bandits, we do not interfere with each other". In this type of construction, the two chunks are closely intertwined yet the meaning is not affected by the sequence. Example (24) means that "He makes a lot of trouble, but other people live their lives and do not care about him". Here, the relation between the two chunks is sequential, i.e. sequence affects the meaning. Besides, the double-chunk construction with the meaning of M3 cannot be transformed into a single-chunk construction without changing the meaning, whereas the double-chunk construction with the meaning of M4 can be. Therefore M4 can also be interpreted as "not to care about" (example 25).

(25) 他　不管　怎么　闹，　人家　过　人家的。　　　(self-made)
　　　Ta bu guan　zen me nao　ren jia　guo　ren jia de
　　　He no matter　how　make trouble　other people live others people's
No matter how much trouble he makes, other people live their lives and do not care about him.

Regardless of the relation between the subject and the person "who should not care" in both M1 and M2, the single-chunk and the double-chunk constructions only have two meanings, which are "not to care about someone or something" and "not to interfere with each other". In the following sections, we can see that the context determines the intention expressed by the sentence, i.e. the meaning of the construction.

4 Contexts in which the Construction with the Meaning "Not To Care About" Occurs

4.1 Context of Consolation and Encouragement

Both the single-chunk construction (examples (26-27)) and the double-chunk construction (example (28)) can occur in this context. This context is defined as follows:

The listener (the person who hears this construction) is doing or going to do something, but is negatively influenced by something or someone else. In this situation, the speaker (the person who says this construction) will use this construction to encourage the listener to do what he or she wants to do or just to make him or her feel at ease. The construction in this context can be paraphrased as "Go vn, do not need to care about X".

(26)方英达   正在   唱戏   (看到陈皓若之后停唱)
   Fang Yingda zheng zai   chang xi
   Fang Yingda   PRES   sing   (stop singing after seeing Chen Haoruo)
   Fang Yingda is singing (and stops after seeing Chen Haoruo),
   陈皓若   拿着   一份   电报   走   了   过来[X]
   Chen Haoruo   na zhe   yi fen   dian bao   zou   le   guo lai
   Chen Haoruo   take   a piece of   telegram   come   ASP
   说: "你   唱,   你   唱   你的……"
   shuo ni chang   ni chang ni de
   say   you sing   you sing   yours
   Chen Haoruo goes to Fang Yingda with a telegram in his hand and says to him,
   "Go on singing and don't care about me".

(27) 伍廷芳   说:"刚刚   得到   报告…… 袁世凯   撤销   了
   Wu Tingfang shuo gang gang de dao bao gao Yuan Shikai che xiao le
   Wu Tingfang say   just now receive report,   Yuan Shikai dismiss ASP
   唐的   和谈   总代表职务[X]...."
   Tang de   he tan   zong dai biao zhi wu
   Tang's   negotiation   chief delegate.
   Wu Tingfang says that just now we have received a report saying that Yuan Shikai
   has dismissed Tang Shaoyi of his chief delegate.
   宋霭龄   说:唐绍仪   是   袁世凯的   代表。   他 撤 他的
   Song Ailing shuo Tang Shaoy shi Yuan Shikai de dai biao   ta che ta de
   Song Ailing   say   Tang Shaoyi is Yuan Shikai 's delegate ,   he dismiss his
   您   又何必 惊慌。
   nin you he bi jing huang
   you   why   alarmed
   Song Ailing says: "The dismissing of delegate Tang Shaoyi is Yuan Shikai's busi-
   ness,,why are you so shocked?.

(28) 彭德怀   听后   很   不高兴,   把   部队   撵走   了[X]。
   Peng Dehuai ting hou hen bu gao xing ba bu dui nian zou   le
   Peng Dehuai hear very unhappy   BA army   order away   ASP
   Peng Dehuai is very unhappy after hearing this and orders the army away.
   洪学智   说: 他   说   他的, 你们   挖   你们的, 继续   施工。
   Hong Xuezhi shuo ta   shuo ta de ni men wa   ni men de ji xu shi gong
   Hong Xuezhi say   he   say his   you excavate yours   go on construct
   Hong Xuezhi says: "We keep excavating, who cares what he's saying?"

In example (26), Fang Yingda is singing while Chen Haoruo comes in. Fang
Yingda is worried that Chen Haoruo may have some important matters to talk with
him. Therefore he stops singing. Knowing that this might affect Fang's activity, Chen
Haoruo says "你唱你的[*ni chang ni de*]" to give him some peace of mind, i.e. that he
should sing without worrying about anything or caring about him.

In example (27), Wu Tingfang knows that Yuan Shikai has dismissed Tang Shaoyi
of his chief delegate and is worried about this. In order to ease his mind, Song Ailing
says "他撤他的[*ta che ta de*]", telling him not to worry too much about it.

In example (28), the army is excavating a dugout but is interrupted by Peng Dehuai. Hong Xuezhi says "你们挖你们的[*ni men wa ni men de*]" to not distract the army, expressing that they should continue digging without caring about him.

In this context, the modal meaning of "not to care about someone or something" is "not to need to care about someone or something". When the listener is forced to give up what he is doing or what he wants to do, the speaker, who agrees with the listener's wish, will use this construction to encourage the listener to follow his own heart and not to care about the negative influence. As a result, the listener's wish can be achieved. This construction is therefore used to relieve someone or show consolation or encouragement.

4.2   Context of Reprimand

Only the single-chunk construction (examples (29-30)) can occur in this context, and this context is defined as follows:

The listener is doing something or has done something (X), which has a negative impact on someone else. In this situation, the speaker will use this construction to stop what the speaker is doing or express the discontent for what the speaker has done. The construction in this context can be paraphrased as "You should vn rather than care about others".

(29) 瞎瞎   被   铐   了[X],   看热闹的人   就起了吼声,   说
    Xia xia   bei   kao   le   kan re nao de ren jiu qi le hou sheng shuo
    Xia xia   BEI   arrest ASP   the crowd   make noise,   say
    The people were unhappy about the arrest of Xia xia and said:
"你   收   你的   税费,   你   铐人   干啥"
Ni   shou   ni de   shui fei ni   kao ren gan sha
you   collect your   taxes   you   arrest   why
"Why arrest him, you should just collect your taxes!"

(30) 周炳   举起 斗大的拳头, 在   罗吉脸上晃了两晃[X],
Zhou Bing   ju qi dou da de quan tou zai   luo ji lian shang huang le liang huang
Zhou Bing   lift up   big fists   in front of Luo Ji's face
Zhou Bing lifts up his big fists in front of Luo Ji's face to alarm him
问道: 你   想   怎样?
wen dao   ni   xiang zen yang
and ask: you   want how
and asks what does he want to do.
罗吉   脸色苍白,   说:炳哥,   我 走   我的 路,   与 你 什么 相干?
Luo ji lian se cang bai shuo bing ge   wo zou   wo de lu yu ni shen me xiang gan
Luo Ji white-faced   say brother Bing   I walk   my way to you what relation
Luo Ji's face turned white and said: "Brother Bing, I walk my own way, why should you care?"

In example (29), the officers have arrested Xia xia, which has a negative impact on him. The crowd is unhappy about this, so they use this construction "你收你的税费 [*ni shou ni de shui fei*]" to stop them, to tell them that they should collect taxes rather than arrest Xia xia.

In example (30), Zhou Bing shows his fists to Luo Ji, which has a negative impact on Luo ji who then uses this sentence structure "我走我的路，与你什么相干[*wo zou wo de lu, yu ni shen me xiang gan*]" to express that he is walking his own way and that it is none of Zhou's business.

In such context, the listener has a negative impact on the others and his or her action causes discontent to the speaker. The speaker therefore uses this construction to stop the listener and tell him or her not to care about the others. The construction in this context indicates the speaker's disapproval to the listener, which implies a negative meaning.

4.3   Context of Impatience

Only the single-chunk construction (examples (31-32)) can occur in this context, and this context is defined as follows:

When the speaker is impatient with regards to what the listener does, he or she will use this construction to express the idea: "I do not care about whatever you do". The speaker expresses a discontent through the idea of "Not to care about what the lisntener is doing".

(31) 赵敏　　　脸红 了，　　道：你　　死 你的, 关 我 什么 事？
　　　Zhao Min　lian hong le　dao　ni　si　ni de　guan wo shen me shi
　　　Zhao Min　shy ASP　　say　you die yours　to me what thing
Zhao Min felt embarrassed and said: I do not care about your dying, it is none of my business.

(32) 他 说：你　有　不来　　的 自由，　我 有　　等你　　的 自由。
　　　Ta shuo ni you　bu lai　de zi you　wo you deng ni　de zi you
　　　He say　you have　not to come de　freedom　I have wait for you de freedom
He says that you have the freedom not to come but I have the freedom to wait for you.

她　　说：你　等　你的 吧！我　反正　不　　来。
Ta　shuo ni　deng ni de ba　wo　fan zheng bu　lai
She say　you wait yours　　I　anyway　NEG come
She says that she doesn't care about his waiting; it is none of her business.

In example (31), "你死你的[*ni si ni de*]" means that I don't care about whether you die or not, and it is none of my business.

In example (32), "你等你的[*ni deng ni de*]" means that I don't care about whether you wait or not, and it is none of my business.

4.4   Context of Narrative

Both the single-chunk (examples (33-34)) and the double-chunk (example 35) constructions can occur in this context. The context is defined as follows:

A person wants to do something, but is negatively impacted by something or someone (X). This person does as he or she pleases without caring about the obstacles. The construction in this context can be paraphrased as "someone does something according to their own desires without caring about other things".

(33) 他   丝毫   没有   注意 <u>那   门房   说的话</u>[X], <u>他   睡   他的</u>……

     Ta   si hao mei you zhu yi na men fang shuo de hua   ta   shui ta de
     He   a bit   NEG   notice that porter words   he   sleep his……

He did not pay any attention to what the doorman said and just kept sleeping.

(34) 在 城市   街道   和   公路   上,   <u>你的   警灯   闪   你的</u>[X],

     Zai cheng shi jie dao he   gong lu shang   ni de jing deng shan   ni de
     In   city   street and   road,   your   police light glitter yours

<u>我   自岿然不动</u>   的 情景   太多了。

     wo zi kui ran bu dong   de qing jing   tai duo le
     I   do not react   situation   too much

There are just too many cases in the city where the reaction to a police intervention is "You flash your lights, I don't care".

(35) 罚   多   了   反而   使   一些   单位、财务 人员 形成

     Fa   duo   le   fan er   shi yi xie   dan wei cai wu ren yuan xing cheng
     Fine too much ASP instead   lead   some   units   financial staff   form

一种   逆反   心理,   <u>你   罚   你的</u>[X], <u>我   做   我的</u>……

     yi   zhong ni fan   xin li   ni   fa   ni de   wo zuo wo de
     a kind of   rebellious emotions   you   fine   yours   I   do mine

Too much fines creates a feeling of rebellion within some units and the staff of the finance department, leading them to keep doing what they are doing regardless of the fines.

In example (33), the porter's words have a negative impact on his sleep, yet the sentence "他睡他的[*ta shui ta de*]" means that he went to sleep without caring about giving it much consideration.

In example (34), the cops flashing their lights has a negative influence on the subject. The sentence "你的警灯闪你的[*ni de jing deng shan ni de*]" means that he does not care about them.

In example (35), the fines have a negative impact on "me". The sentence "你罚你的, 我做我的[*ni fa ni de, wo zuo wo de*]" means that "I" do as "I" please and do not care about the fining.

4.5   How to Determine the Person who "Does not Care About Someone or Something"

For the double-chunk construction, the person who "does not care about someone or something" must be identical to the subject of the latter chunk. For the single-chunk construction, as shown in examples above, the person may be identical or different to the subject.

The contexts of encouraging/consoling, reprimand and impatience all occur in a dialogue situation. For the first two types of context, the person who is being encouraged/consoled or reprimanded must clearly be the listener. Hence the person who "does not need to care about someone or something" or "should not care about someone or something" is normally represented by the pronoun "You". In the context of patience, the construction expresses that "I am reluctant to care about whether you do or not". Hence the person "to be reluctant to care about " is often represented by the pronoun "I".

In the narrative context, we can determine the person who "does not care about someone or something" on the basis of the relation between two events. In all the examples mentioned above, there are two events (or two participants) and one of them has a negative impact on the other. This relation can only be determined in context. Besides, the relation is unidirectional, i.e. only one of the event has a negative impact on the other one but not vice versa. Moreover, the one negatively affected is the person who as "has no will to care about". For instance, in example (34), the porter's words have a negative impact on the person's sleep; therefore "he" is the one who doesn't care about. In example (35), the cops flashing their lights has a negative impact on "me", so the person who "does not care about someone or something" is "I".

5   Contexts in Which the Construction with the Meaning of "Not to Interfere with Each Other" Occurs

5.1   Context of Refutation

The construction with the meaning "Not to interfere with each other" can occur in dialogue and narrative contexts. It expresses reprimand in a dialogue and has a negative or neutral connotation in a narrative context. The context of reprimand is defined as follows:

When someone is interrupted by or impatient to other people (X), he or she can use this construction to express his or her discontent. The construction in this context can be paraphrased as "we do not interfere with each other and you should not interfere with me".

(36) 我　　俩　　如今　　井水不犯河水，　　　　　你　干 你的，我 干 我的，

　　Wo　lia　ru jin　jing shui bu fan he shui　　　ni　gan ni de　wo gan wo de
　　We　two　now　do not interfere with each other,　you do　yours,　I　do　mine
你　　无故　　　来　　找啥茬？[X]
ni　　wu gu　　　lai　　zhao sha cha
you　with no reason come disturb me
We now mind our own businesses, you do your things, I do mine, why do you disturb me with no reason?

(37) 他 宁可　　　　独力　　　支持　　一家人的　生活，也 不　愿　再
　　Ta ning ke　　du li　　zhi chi　yi jia ren de sheng huo ye bu yuan zai
　　He would rather by himself　support　a family's　life , also NEG want again
和　老二　　啰嗦[X]。'对啦！我 干 我的，你 干 你的 好啦！"他说。
he　lao er　　luo suo　　dui la　wo gan wo de ni gan ni de hao la　ta shuo
with his brother argue　　Right　I　do　mine　you do yours OK　He say
He would rather support his family by himself than argue with his brother again. "Right! You do your things, I do my own!" He says.

Both"你无故来找啥茬[*ni wu gu lai zhao sha cha*](*Why do you disturb me with no reason*) " in example 36 and "老二啰嗦[*lao er luo suo*] (*argue with his second brother*)" in example 38 indicate that the speakers are disturbed. Hence speakers use this construction to express their discontent.

5.2   Context of Narrative

The construction with the meaning "not to interfere with each other" tends to be mostly negative (example 38) or neutral (example 39). Very few instances show a positive connotation.

(38) 我   国   目前的 电缆 敷设 方式 就   落后   了,   交通   与

Wo guo   mu qian de dian lan fu she fang shi jiu luo hou le   jiao tong   yu
My country present cable lay way then out-dated ASP, traffic   and
通信   互不相干,   你 干 你的, 我 干 我的......
tong xin   hu bu xiang gan   ni gan ni de wo gan wo de
communication do not interfere with each other you do yours, I   do mine
The present cabling way in our country is out-dated,, transportation and communica-tion don't interfere with each other's affairs, each one does its own work..

(39) 三 车 印度   一齐   吹打 起来, 可是 你 吹   你的, 我打   我的......
San che yin du   yi qi   chui da qi lai ke shi ni chui ni de wo da wo de
Three cars Indians together play ASP,   but   you play yours, I   play mine......
The Indians in the three cars begun to play music together. But they played at will and even at random as if they are not a team at all.

In example 38, "交通与通信互不相干[*jiao tong yu tong xin hu bu xiang gan*](*Transportation and communication do not interfere with each other*)" means that they are out-dated for not being interconnected, expressing thus a negative connotation through the construction. In example 39, "你吹你的, 我打我的[*ni chui ni de, wo da wo de*](*You play by yourself and I play by myself, we do not interfere with each other*)" expresses a neutral meaning.

The construction with the meaning "not to interfere with each other" tend to be negative in both contexts mentioned above, which conforms with the cognitive law of human beings. "Not to interfere with each other" means "I do not interfere with you and you do not interfere with me". The relation between two events taking place at the same time can be: (a) two events that benefit each other; (b) two events that do not interfere with each other; (c) two events that interferes with each other. If we se-quence them from positive to negative, the order would be (a) (b) (c). In this se-quence, "two events do not interfere with each other" (b) is considered neither good nor bad yet appears to be passive in the context. Hence it tends to be considered slightly negative as well.

6   Conclusion

In this paper, we have analyse the syntactic and semantic features of the construction "r+v+r+de+n", as well as the contexts in which it occurs. We have also explained how the meaning differs depending on the context. This construction has two meanings, i.e. "Not to care about something or someone" and "Not to interfere with each other". The former has four kinds of variations of moods, which are "not to need to care about someone or something", "should not care about someone or something", "to be reluctant to care about someone or something" and "to have no will to care about someone or something". These four variations occur in consoling/encouraging, reprimanding, impatient and narrative context respectively. The construction with the meaning of "not to interfere with each other" occurs in contexts of reprimand and narrative, and in both contexts the construction tends to be negative.

Acknowledgement. This paper is supported by The Ministry of Education Humanities and Social Sciences base major project13JJD740001, National Social Science Fund major project 12&ZD175, National Social Science Fund Project12BYY061, and be grateful to all these support.

References

1. Lv, Sh.X: Chinese Miscellany. SDX Joint Publishing Company, Shang Hai (1988). (吕叔湘.语义杂记.上海:生活.读书.新知三联书店(1988)) (in Chinese)
2. Goldberg, A.E.: Construction Grammar Approach to Argument Structure. The University of Chicago Press, Chicago (1995)
3. Shao, J.M.: The Principles of Structure Reconstruction from the Perspective of Quai-attributes. Jounrnal of Shan xi University (Philosophy & Social Science) **32**(1), 62–66 (2009). (in Chinese)
4. Wu, H.Ch.: On the Creation Mechanism of the Sentence Pattern "Para-attribute+N+Vde(得) R". Linguistic Sciences **17**(2), 127–134 (2008). (in Chinese)
5. Wu, W.Sh: Constructional Analysis, Discourse Functions and Formation of "Adj+budaonaliqu(A不到哪里去)". Zhongguo Yuwen **4**, 326–383 (2011). (in Chinese)
6. Yuan, Y.L.: A Study on Modern Chinese Imperative Sentences. Peking University Press, Beijing (1993). (袁毓林.现代汉语祈使句研究.北京:北京大学出版社(1993)) (in Chinese)
7. Zeng, Ch.L: An Analysis of the Imperative Sentence "V Ni de N". Journal of Yun Nan Normal University **6**(1), 82–88 (2008). (in Chinese)

Lexical Semantic Constraints on the Syntactic Realization of Semantic Role Theme

Shiyong Kang$^{(\boxtimes)}$, Minghai Zhou, and Xiaorui Zhao

School of Chinese Language and Literature, Key Laboratory of Language Resource Development and Application of Shandong Province, Ludong University, Yantai 264025, China
kangsy64@163.com

Abstract. When mapped to syntactic elements, semantic roles are constrained by lexical semantic categories of words that assume the semantic roles. Based on a large-scale tagged corpus, this paper takes the semantic role "Theme" as an example and analyzes its syntactic-semantic pattern, the influence of lexical semantic category upon its mapping to syntactic elements, the collocations of the semantic categories of noun-core structures and verb-core structures. The research initially reveals the constraints of lexical semantic categories upon the mapping of the semantic role "Theme" to syntactic elements.

Keywords: Semantic role · Syntactic element · Lexical semantic category

1 Introduction

When mapped to the corresponding syntactic elements, semantic role of a word is constrained by its lexical semantics. Supported by China National Social Science Fund Program "Research on the Lexical Semantic Constraints on the Syntactic Realization of Semantic Roles Based on a Large-scale Tagged Corpus", we tagged the corpus and generalized the rules that govern the syntactic realization of semantic roles.

Based on the related researches in the field, we defined the syntactic elements, semantic roles and the labels as follows:

Table 1. Syntactic Elements and Labels

Labels	Meaning	Labels	Meaning
S	Subject chunk	D	Adverbial Chunk
P	Predicate Chunk	C	Complement Chunk
O	Object chunk	J	Concurrent Chunk
A	Attributive chunk	T	Independent Chunk

As to the lexical semantic category, we adopted the classification system and labels used in *Chinese Dictionary of Synonyms* (or *Tongyici Cilin*).

This research is supported by China National Social Science Fund Program (No.12BYY123) and China National Natural Science Fund Program (No.61272215).

Q. Lu and H.H. Gao (Eds.): CLSW 2015, LNAI 9332, pp. 638–648, 2015.
DOI: 10.1007/978-3-319-27194-1_63

Table 2. Semantic Roles and Labels

Labels	Meaning	Labels	Meaning	Labels	Meaning	Labels	Meaning
S	Agent	Z	Causer	V	Verb	P	Location
D	Theme	R	Result	I	Instrument	A	Direction
L	Genitive	T	Dative	M	Material	E	Range
Y	Comitative	X	Relative	Q	Manner	C	Reason
O	Patient	F	Partitive	W	Basis	G	Aim
K	Objective	B	Source	H	Time	N	Quantity
J	Standard	U	Miscellany				

Based on the tagged corpus, this paper generalized the lexical semantic constraints that semantic role "Theme" confronts when mapped to the syntactic elements. In this research, "Theme" is defined as the subject with non-spontaneous action or state in the event. For example, [到处的野草荒藤] (dao chu de ye cao huang teng. Literally it means "everywhere wild grass and vines") D也都茂盛得自在坦荡 (ye dou mao sheng de zi zai tan dang, literally it means "ran wild in a carefree way"). With the above labels, we tagged the Chinese texts of primary and secondary school Chinese textbooks published by People's Education Press.

2   Theme's Syntactic Semantic Patterns

According to the statistics of the tagged corpus, Theme has 9 types of syntactic semantic patterns, they are: SDPV>JDPV> SDCV> DDPV > CVOD>ODPV > JDCV > PVSD > PVOD, please see the table below.

Table 3. Distribution of syntactic-semantic patterns

Label Number	Syntactic Semantic Pattern	Number	Total	Percent
1	SDPV	10031	10831	92.61%
2	JDPV	528	10831	4.87%
3	SDCV	182	10831	1.68%
4	DDPV	22	10831	0.20%
5	CVOD	19	10831	0.18%
6	ODPV	17	10831	0.16%
7	JDCV	16	10831	0.15%
8	PVSD	15	10831	0.14%
9	PVOD	1	10831	0.01%
	Total	10831	10831	100.00%

In the table above,"SDPV"means Theme D plays the role of "subject S", "P"refers to the predicate, "V" stands for the verbs that correspond with the semantic roles. Other syntactic semantic patterns can be interpreted in the same way. The statistics reveal that Theme can also be mapped to concurrent, object and adverbial in addition to subject.

First of all, Theme is mapped to subject. There are 10034 such uses, accounting for 94.43% of the total. Some sentences are inverted. The following is a detailed classification.

(1) SDPV Most of the Theme follows this pattern when mapped to subject. There are 10031 such uses, accounting for 92.61% of the total. For example:

(1)[S 她 /r]D1D2S3D4D5[P 老 /a]V1 了 /y, [PD[SX 身 体 /n]D[D 不 /d[P 好 /a]V]V2……

　　Literal translation: [S she/r]D1D2S3D4D5[P old/a]V1 marker of present tense/y, [PD[SX her body/n]D[D not/d[P good /a]V]V2……

(2) SDCV This pattern mostly occurs when the meaning of the complement in predicate-complement structure is orientated to Theme. There are 182 such uses, accounting for 1.68% of the total number of the subject. For example:

(2)……[P等/v]V1[O[S我/r]S1D2[P长/v]V[C大/a]V2]U1[D还/d[P要/v]V2[O很 /d多/a很/d多/a天/q]O2……

　　Literal translation:……[P when/v]V1[O[S I/r]S1D2[P grow/v]V[C big/a]V2]U1[D still/d[P needs/v]V2[O too/d many/a too/d many/a days/q]O2……

In the example,"大"(Da) semantically is orientated to"我"(Wo) which is labeled as Theme.

(3) PVSD In this pattern the predicate is fronted, therefore forming a predicate-subject pattern. There are 15 such uses, accounting for 0.14% of the total number of subject. For example:

(3)[P迫于/v]V1[O生计/n]K1, [S这些/r宫廷/n侍女/n]D1S2S3[D只好/d[D向/p 战场/n附近/s的/u渔民/n]T2[P卖/v]V2[O鲜花/n]O2或/c[P提供/v]V3[O其他/r 服务/vn]O3。

　　Literal translation: [P forced by/v]V1[O sustenance/n]K1, [S these/r palace/n maids/n]D1S2S3[D had to/d[D to/p battlefield/n nearby/s attributive marker/u fishmen/n]T2[P sell/v]V2[O fresh flowers/n]O2 or/c[P provide/v]V3[O other /r services /vn]O3.

Second, Theme is mapped to concurrent. There are 544 such uses, accounting for 5.02% of the total. It is further divided into two sub-patterns.

(1) JDPV According to Fillmore's One-Instance-Per-Clause Principle, Fan Xiao's Jiange or Pluralistic Case (2003) as well as the characteristics of verbs,

we labeled concurrent into different semantic roles. There are 528 Themes used as concurrent, accounting for 4.87% of the total. For example:

(4)[S[S石原/nr先生/n]S1S2[D如此/r[P不顾/v]V1[O历史/n事实/n]O1而/c[P信口雌黄/i]V2]U1，[D实在/a[P令/v]V1[J人/n]O1+D2[P吃惊/a]V2。

Literal translation: [S[S Shiyuan/n sir/n]S1S2[D so/r[P neglect/v]V1[O history/n facts/n]O1 that/c[P make irresponsible remarks/i]V2]U1，[D really/a[P make/v]V1[J people/n]O1+D2[P startled/a]V2.

(2) JDCV This pattern is formed when a concurrent is followed by a predicate-complement structure with the complementary meaning orientated to the concurrent. There are 16 such uses, accounting for 0.15%. For example:

(5)[S这/r腰鼓/n]S1S4S7，[P使/v]V1[J冰冷/z的/u空气/n]O1+D2D3[D立即/d[P变/v得/u]V2[C燥热/a]V3了/y，[P使/v]V4[J恬静/a的/u阳光/n]O4+D5D6[D立即/d[P变/v得/u]V5[C飞溅/v]V6了/y……

Literal translation: [S this/r waist drum/n]S1S4S7, [P made/v]V1[J ice-cold/z attributive marker/u air/n]O1+D2D3[D immediately/d[P changed/v auxiliary word of degree/u]V2[C dry and hot/a]V3 modal particle/y, [P made/v]V4[J tranquil/a attributive marker/u sunlight/n]O4+D5D6[D immediately/d[P change/v auxiliary word of degree /u]V5[C to splash/v]V6 marker of past tense/y……

Third, Theme is also mapped to object. There are 37 such uses, accounting for 0.34% of the total. Themes as object include the following two sub-patterns.

(1) CVOD This pattern can be changed to DV when the semantics of Theme is orientated to the complement as object of the predicate-complement structure. For example:

(6)[S煮/v饭/n老妈子/n]O1D4[D从此/d[D就/d[P骇/v]V1[C破/v了/u]V2[O胆/n]D2……

Literal translation: [S cooking/v meal/n older male servant/n]O1D4[D since then/d[D auxiliary word/d[shocked/v]V1[C broken/v marker of past tense/u]V2[O gallbladder/n]D2……

In this example, "破了胆"(po le dan) can be changed to "胆破"(dan po).

(2) ODPV In this pattern, Theme is semantically related to verb-core structure cross sentences. Object here means that noun-core structure plays the role of object in the preceding clause. For example:

(7)……[S这/r只/q鹰/n]D1[P患/v了/u]V1[O烟雾/n诱发/v的/u肺尘病/n]K1D2，[P导致/v]V2[O血液/n{中毒/v}@和/c血管/n{破裂/v}@]K2。

Literal translation:......[S this/r measure word/q eagle/n]D1[P suffers from/v marker of past tense/u]V1[O smog/n induced/v attributive marker/u pneumokoniosis/n]K1D2, [P causing/v]V2[O blood/n{ poisoning/v}@ and/c blood vessel/n{ burst/v}@]K2.

Last but not least, Theme is also mapped to adverbial in the pattern of DDPV. There are 22 such uses, accounting for 0.20% of the total. In such sentences Theme is in the prepositional phrase indicated by such case markers as "为(wei), 被(bei), 把(ba), 以 (yi), 由(you), 给(gei)", etc. For example:

(8)......[D不/d[D能/v[D为/p大家/r]DB5所/u[P知道/v]V5罢了/y。

Literal translation:......[D not /d[D can be/v[D by/p everyone /r]DB5 auxiliary word /u[P known/v]V5 modal particle/y.

3   The Influence of Lexical Semantic Categories on the Mapping of Theme to the Syntactic Elements

Theme can be mapped to a variety of syntactic elements, but the mapping capacity is constrained by lexical semantic categories. See the table below.

Table 4. Distribution of lexical semantic categories

Elements / Semantic Category	Theme as Subject SDPV, SDCV, PVSD	Theme as Concurrent JDPV, JDCV	Theme as Object CVOD, ODPV, PVOD	Theme as Adverbial DDPV
A human being	3922	318	9	11
B object	2113	84	13	5
C time and space	462	7	1	2
D abstract things	2309	95	13	3
E features	1026	33	0	1
F movement	20	0	0	0
G psychological activity	65	4	0	0
H activity	158	2	1	0
I phenomenon & state	100	1	0	0
J relevance	22	0	0	0
K expletive	31	0	0	0
L honorific	0	0	0	0
TOTAL	10228	544	37	22

From the table above, we can see the mapping capacity of each semantic category which is shown by inequation as follows:

Semantic categories for Theme as subject: A>D>B>E>C>H>I>G>J>K>F
Semantic categories for Theme as concurrent: A>D>B>E>C>G>H>I
Semantic categories for Theme as object: D=B>A>C=H
Semantic categories for Theme as adverbial: A>B>D>C>E

For Theme as subject, concurrent and adverbial, their semantic categories share a sequence: A>D>B>E>C. But for Theme as object, the sequence is D=B>A>C=H, which can be explained by the fact that most of the semantic categories for Theme are object. Though semantic categories that play the role of Theme are scattered, they, relatively speaking, are focused on A (human being), D (abstract things), B (object), E (features) and C (time and space), accounting for 96.27% of the total.

When Theme is realized by semantic category E, C, G, H, I, J and K, on the syntactic level they appear to take more of the function of nouns which is explained by the predicate and plays the role of topic.

The 93 semantic categories from *Chinese Dictionary of Synonyms* (or *Tongyici Cilin*) are mapped to subject, concurrent, object and adverbial respectively.

Horizontally, there are three types.

(1) Full projection. Semantic categories in this type can be projected to any syntactic element served by Theme. It consists of three semantic categories: Aa (general reference), Da (general term), Dk (culture and education).

(2) Zero projection. Semantic categories that belong to this type can not be projected to any syntactic element served by Theme. This type includes 11 categories, they are: Bj (microorganism), Fd (whole body movement), Gc (ability and willingness), Hk (religious activities), Hl(superstitious activities), Jc (coordination), Kb(preposition), Kd (modal particle), Ke (interjection), Kf (onomatopoeia), L(honorific).

(3) Restricted projection. Semantic categories that belong to this type can be selectively projected to the syntactic elements served by Theme. There are 75 semantic categories such as Ab, Ac, etc.

Vertically, semantic categories can form the following inequations when Theme is mapped to different syntactic elements.

When mapped as subject, the semantic categories follow the sequence: Aa>Ed> Dk>Da>Ba>Bg>Bk>Bh>Dd>Di>Cb>Df>Ca>Ah>Dn>Bi>Ab=Bn> Db>Dc>Eb>Bp>Bd>Ae>Bm>Al>Be>Bf>Bo>De>Aj>Dj>Hi=Br> Gb>Hj=Af>Ee>Ka>Bq>Dm>Hg>Ga>Ih>Ib>Ag=Ad>Bc>Ai=Ef>Ak >Am=Id>Ie>Ec=Jd=Fa=An=Dh=Dl>Hd=Bl=Ic>Hc>Ha>Hf=If>Bb=Fb=He >Ea=Hm=Ia=Ig>Jb=Je>Ac=Dg=Fc>Hb=Hh=Ja>Hn=Kc

When mapped as concurrent, the semantic categories follow the sequence: Aa> Dk=Ed>Ba>Df>Dn>Da=Bn>Di=Ab=Ah>Bg=Bi>Bh=Bp>Ae=Bd=Cb=Dd > Aj=Eb > Bk > Bm=Dc=Al > Bo=Ga=Dj > Be=De=Ad=An=Dh=Hg > Ai=Ak= Bq=Ca=Ih=Br=Db=Gb

When mapped as object, the semantic categories follow the sequence: Aa>Bk= Dj > Ag=Bi=De=Dk=Ah=Bn>Ba=Bc= Bg=Dc=Hj=Bh=Bp =Cb=Dd=Df=Dl=Dn

When mapped as adverbial, the semantic categories follow the sequence: Aa>
Ba=Dk>Ca>Bg=Al=Bp=Ed

84 semantic categories can be mapped as subject, 42 categories be mapped as concurrent, 21 object, 8 as adverbial. Of all the semantic categories, Aa precedes the
others.

4   Collocation of Theme's Noun-core Structure (NS) Semantic Category and Verb-core Structure (VS) Semantic Category

The syntactic realization of semantic roles is a process in which noun-core structure
semantic category and verb-core structure semantic category constrain each other
reciprocally. When we study the characteristics of the syntactic realization of semantic
roles, we have to take into consideration the semantic categories of the verbs that
collocate with Theme. The following statistic table shows the verb-core structure
collocating with Theme.

Table 5. Distribution of semantci cateogories of verbs

Major Semantic Categories	Number	Total	Percent	Cumulative Percent
J relevance	3982	10831	36.76%	36.76%
E features	2337	10831	21.58%	58.34%
G psychological activity	2048	10831	18.91%	77.25%
I phenomenon and state	1336	10831	12.33%	89.59%
H activity	482	10831	4.45%	94.04%
F movement	441	10831	4.07%	98.11%
K expletive	169	10831	1.56%	99.67%
D abstract things	18	10831	0.17%	99.83%
B object	9	10831	0.08%	99.92%
A human being	7	10831	0.06%	99.98%
C time and space	1	10831	0.01%	99.99%
L honorific	1	10831	0.01%	100.00%
Total	10831	10831	100.00%	

According to the number of verb-core structure semantic categories that collocate
with Theme, we can see such a sequence: J (relevance)> E (feature)> G (psychological
state) > I (phenomenon and state)> H (activity)> F (movement)> K (expletive)>D
(abstract things)>B (object)>A (human being)>C (time and space) >L (honorific).

The collocation of Theme's syntactic elements and verb-core structure semantic
categories is shown in the table below.

Table 6. Collocation of syntactic elements and verb-core semantic categories

syntactic elements / VS semantic categories	Theme as Subject SDPV, SDCV, PVSD	Theme as Concurrent JDPV, JDCV	Theme as Object CVOD, ODPV, PVOD	Theme as Adverbial DDPV
A human being	7	/	/	/
B object	9	/	/	/
C time and space	1	/	/	/
D abstract things	17	1	/	/
E features	2236	86	15	/
F movement	416	21	/	4
G psychological activity	1874	167	1	6
H activity	460	21	/	1
I phenomenon and state	1241	85	7	3
J relevance	3803	158	/	/
K expletive	163	5	13	8
L honorific	1	/	1	/
Total	10228	544	37	22

Vertically, predicates that collocate with Theme as Subject can be any semantic category listed in *Cilin*. More semantic categories collocate with concurrent. Fewer semantic categories go with Theme as object and Theme as adverbial. Horizontally, semantic categories like G (psychological activity), I (phenomenon and state) and K(expletive) can collocate with any syntactic element of Theme.

Thus, we may divide verb-core structures that collocate with Theme into the following types:

(1) Relevance This type of verb-core structure links subjects that are relevant to each other. It has the largest number. For example:

(9)[S金/b表/n]D1[P匹配/v]V1[O这/r条/q链子/n]K1……(匹配:Jc01)

Literal translation:[S gold/b watch/n]D1[P matches/v]V1[O this/r piece /q chain /n]K1……(matched:Jc01)

(2) Feature description This type links the subjects of nature and state. For example:

(10)[D在/p一个/m孩子/n的/u眼睛/n里/f]E，[S他/r的/u老师/n]D1D2D3[D是/d[D多么/d[P慈爱/a]V1，[D多么/d[P公平/a]V2，[D多么/d[P伟大/a]V3啊/y。(慈爱:Ee01；公平:Ee40；伟大:Ed20)

Literal translation: [D in /p a /m child/n attributive marker/u eyes/n inside/f]E, [S he /r of/u teacher/n]D1D2D3[D is /d[D how/d[P kind/a]V1, [D how/d[P fair/a]V2, [D how/d[P great/a]V3 exclamatory word /y.(kind:Ee01；fair:Ee40；great:Ed20)

(3) Psychological activity   This type includes psychological verbs and some adjectives related to psychology, such as "gaoxing (happy), fennu (angry) and dongshi (thoughtful). For example:

(11)......[S心里/s]D2[P难过/a]V2[C极/d了/y。(难过:Ga01)

Literal translation:......[S heart/s]D2[feels sad/a]V2[C to the extreme/d adverb of degree /y.(feel sad:Ga01)

(4) Change of phenomenon and state   This type links the subjects that change their state and activity.

(12)[S这些/r{斗争/vn}@和/c{探索/vn}@]S1D2, ...[D又/d[D一/m次/q一/m次/q地/u[P失败/v]V2了/y。(失败:If21)

Literal translation: [S these/r{ struggles /vn}@ and/c{ exploration/vn}@]S1D2, ...[D again/d[D one /m time/q one /m time/q auxiliary marker of time/u[P failed/v]V2 past tense marker/y.(failed:If21)

(5) Social intercourse and life   This type links the subjects that engage in social intercourse and daily activities.

(13) [S他们/r]D[D向/p皇帝/n]T[P建议/v]V, [O[D用/p这/r新/a的/u、美丽/a的/u布料/n]I1[P做/v]V1[C成/v[O衣服/n]R1, ...(建议:Hc14)

Literal translation: [S they/r]D[D to /p emperor/n]T[P proposed/v]V, [O[D to use /p this/r new/a auxiliary word/u, beautiful/a auxiliary word /u cloth /n]I1[P to make /v]V1[C into /v[O clothes/n]R1,......(proposed:Hc14)

(14)[S幸福/an]D[D也/d[VT需要/v]P提醒/v]V吗/y？(提醒:Hg02)

Literal translation: [S happiness/an]D[D also/d[VT needs/v][P reminding/v]V modal particle/y？(reminding:Hg02)

(6) Head movements like looking and listening   It is used to link the subjects whose heads move.

(15)[D这时/r]H[P我/r]D1[P看见/v]V1[O他/r的/u背影/n]K1, ...(看见:Fc04)

Literal translation: [D then /r]H[P I/r]D1[P saw/v]V1[O he/r possessive marker/u back/n]K1,......(saw:Fc04)

Lexical semantic constrains on the syntactic realization of semantic roles are not only reflected in their respective semantic features of noun-core structure and verb-core structure but also in their mutual collocation constrains. They are shown in the two-dimensional collocation rule table. The following two-dimensional table shows the collocation rules of semantic categories of Theme.

Table 7. Collocation of NS and VS semantic categories

NS semantic category / VS semantic category	A	B	C	D	E	F	G	H	I	J	K	L	Total
A	2	/	1	2	/	/	/	/	1	1	1	/	8
B	1	1	/	/	/	/	/	/	1	/	1	/	4
C	/	1	/	/	/	/	/	/	/	/	/	/	1
D	10	2	/	3	4	/	/	/	/	/	/	/	19
E	512	731	154	731	127	3	8	36	19	1	15	/	2337
F	366	56	3	13	1		1	1	/	/	/	/	441
G	1807	88	7	105	31	1	/	3	3	2	1	/	2048
H	257	76	11	95	24	2	5	8	3	/	1	/	482
I	478	403	62	302	45	1	10	23	9	2	1	/	1336
J	787	823	226	1121	798	13	42	86	62	13	11	/	3982
K	39	34	8	48	27	/	3	4	3	3	/	/	169
L	1	/	/	/	/	/	/	/	/	/	/	/	1
Total	4260	2215	472	2420	1060	20	69	161	101	22	31	0	10831

The meanings of verbs and nouns are intertwined in a sentence. The precondition for the combination of two lexical semantic units is that they have common sememe, that is to say, the well-formedness of a sentence is the result of the synergy of the lexical meanings of both verbs and nouns. Here we would like to show the constrain characteristics of the syntactic realization of Theme through collocation rules of semantic categories. Category L is very special for it seldom combines with other categories, so we exclude it in our discussion. From the table above, horizontally we can see Category E, I and J can collocate with any semantic category of noun-core structure. Vertically, no semantic category of noun-core structure can freely collocate with those of verb-core structure. Only Category A, B, D, C have more collocations than others, accounting for 86.48% of the total. This means Theme is mainly realized by Category A, B, D and C. The top ten rules are: A+G (1807)>D+J (1121) >B+J (823)>E+J (798)>A+J (787)>B+E (731)>D+E (731)> A+E (502)>A+ I (478)>B+ I (403). Meanwhile, in the closed domain the above table can also be seen as a two-dimensional truth table. It can provide useful knowledge for automatic tagging of semantic roles together with probability statistics.

5   Conclusions

In this paper, we analyzed the lexical-semantic constraints on the syntactic realization of the semantic role Theme. We conclude that Theme can be realized as subject, object, concurrent and adverbial syntactically, and subject is the most typical one. In addition, the words that belong to the A category are the main type of words that act as Theme.

References

1. WordNet: http://wordnet.princeton.edu/
2. Chen, C.: Research on the Semantic Issues of Modern Chinese. Xuelin Press, Shanghai (2003)
3. Fillmore, C.J.: Case for Case. Commercial Press, Beijing (2002). Mingyang Hu (Trans.)
4. Fan, X., Zhang, Y.: A Compendium of Grammar Theory. Shanghai Translation Publishing House, Shanghai (2003)
5. Kang, S., Xu, X., Ma, Y.: Semantic Constrains on the Syntactic Realization of Agent and Patient. Linguistics Research **4**, 36–40 (2011)
6. Lin, X., Lu, C.: Subjective and Objective Information of Chinese Sentences on the Semantic Dimension. Chinese Language Learning **5**, 8–11 (1997)
7. Lu, C.: Parataxis Network of Chinese Grammar. Commercial Press, Beijing (2001)
8. Lu, J.: On Interface between Syntax and Semantics. Journal of Foreign Languages **3**, 30–35 (2006)
9. Mei, J., et al.: Tongyici Cilin. Shanghai Lexicographical Publishing House, Shanghai (1983)
10. Shao, Y., Sui, Z., Wu, Y.: On the Tagging of Chinese Semantic Roles based on the Lexic-semantic Characteristics. Journal of Chinese Information Processing **6**, 3–10 (2009)
11. Shao, J.: On Bi-directional Semantic Selection Principle of Chinese Grammar. Journal of Chinese Language (8) (1997)
12. Sun, D., Li, B.: A Study on the "Lexical-semantic and Syntactic-semantic" Cohesion in Verb-core Structures. Applied Linguistics **1**, 134–141 (2009)
13. Wang, B.: On the Relationship Between the Lexical Meaning of Verbs and Their Argument Realization. Chinese Linguistics **1**, 76–82 (2006)
14. Wu, Y., Yu, S.: The Principles and Methods of Sense Discrimination for Information Processing. Applied Linguistics **2**, 126–133 (2006)
15. Yuan, Y.: The Fineness Hierarchy of Semantic Roles and its Application in NLP. Journal of Chinese Information Processing **4**, 10–20 (2007)

Research on Chinese Parsing Based on the Improved Compositional Vector Grammar

Jingyi Li[✉], Lingling Mu[✉], Hongying Zan[✉], and Kunli Zhang[✉]

College of Information Engineering, Zhengzhou University, Zhengzhou, China
zzunlp_jy@foxmail.com, {iellmu,iehyzan,ieklzhang}@zzu.edu.cn

Abstract. The basic task of syntactic parsing is to determine the syntactic structure of the sentence. Because the natural language is very complex, syntactic structure has a lot of ambiguities. Resolving ambiguity need to introduce a lot of information, and Compositional Vector Grammar (CVG) can well capture fine-grained syntactic and compositional-semantic information on phrases and words. In this paper, we first use a standard CVG model for Chinese parsing, and then we have made improvements on the CVG model. In order to introduce more information, for the word vector, we add the part of speech information; for the type of newborn node after binarization, add temporary node basic type; when computing node score, add the node type information. We also propose a solution for unknown word, replaced with structural vector. Our CVG parser improves the standard CVG parser by nearly 1% F1 on the development set of CTB8.0.

Keywords: Parsing · Ambiguity · CVG · Word vector · Unknown word

1 Introduction

Syntactic parsing is a bridge between linguistic expression and language understanding, and it is one of most fundamental tasks in Natural Language Processing (NLP). Many studies of NLP have shown the importance of syntactic parsing. For example, semantic role labeling, machine translation, text information extraction. Ambiguity is ubiquitous in natural language, and it is one of inevitable problem and difficult to solve in parsing. Human beings can rely on a lot of prior knowledge to effectively disambiguate, while parser is difficult to eliminate these ambiguity like human, due to lack of such knowledge. So a lot of knowledge should be introduced to disambiguate, such as semantic information.

Socher (2013) proposes a Compositional Vector Grammar (CVG), which merges ideas from both generative models that assume discrete syntactic categories and discriminative models that are trained using continuous vectors. The model uses PCFG model for generating candidate trees, a syntactically untied recursive neural network (SU-RNN) for learning syntactico-semantic, compositional vector representations. SU-RNN rerank candidate trees use these vector to recalculate scores of tree. Socher does the experiment on the WSJ. Experiments show CVG improves the PCFG of Stanford Parser by 3.8% to obtain an F1 score of 90.4%.

© Springer International Publishing Switzerland 2015
Q. Lu and H.H. Gao (Eds.): CLSW 2015, LNAI 9332, pp. 649–658, 2015.
DOI: 10.1007/978-3-319-27194-1_64

This paper firstly attempts to use CVG model for Chinese syntactic analysis, then for the some problems existing in the application, we introduce some measures to further improve the performance of the model. In this paper, the experiment was based on the Chinese Treebank (CTB) 8.0. Experiments show that the F1 value in the improved model increases by nearly 1% compared with the original.

2   CVG

CVG combines PCFG with a syntactically untied recursive neural network (SU-RNN) that learns syntactico-semantic, compositional vector representations. For a sentence to be analyzed, the process is shown in Figure1. PCFG model create candidate trees which as one of the inputs of SU-RNN. The embedding matrix L is the word representations. By L, words are mapped into a vector representation which is input into the SU-RNN. SU-RNN uses the information to recalculate the score of candidate tree. The highest scoring tree is chosen based on both PCFG and SU-RNN score.

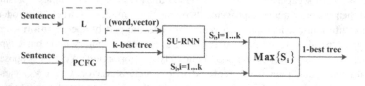

Fig. 1. This is the schematic diagram of the CVG model. The embedding matrix L and candidate tree generated by PCFG model are SU-RNN inputs. SU-RNN recalculates the score of candidate tree, and combines with the PCFG score to select the one-best tree.

2.1   Word Vector Representations

In the system that use a n-dimensional vector representation for Word. These representations should capture syntactic and semantic information. The input vectors $(x_1,...,x_n)$ come from a look-up table of dimensionality $L \in R^{n \times |V|}$, where $|V|$ is the size of the vocabulary. Each word w has an index $[w] = i$ into this table. This index is used to retrieve the word's vector representation a_w using a simple multiplication with a binary vector e, which is zero everywhere, except at the ith index. So $a_w = Le_i \in R^n$.

There are two ways to generate the table of L. The first is the word vector tools directly generate these vectors. The second is the word vector as SU-RNN model parameters for training. The second method takes into account tree structure information, which may make the performance of the model slightly better, but the model will be relatively complex. So we use the first method to generate the table L.

2.2   SU-RNN

SU-RNN compute parent vectors with syntactically untied weights. It has a set of weights. The size of this set depends on the number of sibling category combinations in the PCFG. Then use these vectors to compute the score of each node except the POS nodes and leaf nodes.

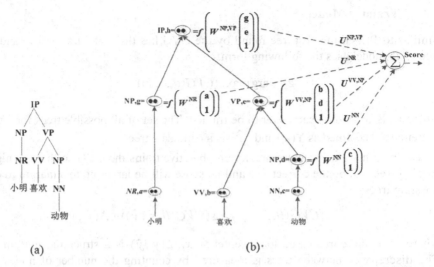

(a)   (b)·

Fig. 2. (a) is an example of a binary tree, (b) is the example of the binary   tree (a) processed by SU-RNN.

Given this tree structure such as figure 2(a), we can now compute activations for each node from the bottom up. First, we can get the word representations as (vector,POS) pairs: ((a,NR), (b,VV), (c,NN)) by the embedding matrix L. We begin by computing the activation for parent node using the children's word vectors according to Eq.1. Concatenate the children's representations into a vector c_con. Then the composition function multiplies this vector by the parameter weights of W^{c_type} and applies an element-wise nonlinearity function to the output vector. The c_type shows the weight matrix W depending on the categories of the children.   The weight matrix W includes the bias in the last column.

$$p = f\left(W^{c\_type}\begin{bmatrix} c\_con \\ 1 \end{bmatrix}\right) \tag{1}$$

The SU-RNN score of a complete tree is the sum of the scores at each node. The score of node is computed via:

$$s(p^{(i)}) = \left(U^{c\_type}\right)^T p^{(i)} \tag{2}$$

where U^{c_type} is a vector of parameters that need to be trained. The c_type shows the weight matrix U depends on the categories of the children.

While the final sore of the tree referred to the scores of PCFG and SU-RNN, which could be the summation based on a certain rule among nodes, or the summation for a certain rate of the tree. This paper uses the latter:

$$S = S_{SU-RNN} + t \cdot S_{PCFG} \tag{3}$$

where S_{SU-RNN} is the score of SU-RNN, S_{PCFG} is the score of PCFG, t is an adjustable parameter.

2.3   Training Model

Similar to PCFG, the best tree found by the CVG has the highest score of candidate tree. The model uses the following form:

$$g_\theta = \arg\max_{\hat{y} \in Y(x_i)} s(CVG(\theta, x_i, \hat{y})) \tag{4}$$

where θ is the model parameter to be trained. The set of all possible trees for a given sentence x_i is defined as $Y(x_i)$ and $\hat{y}$ is a candidate tree.

The max-margin, structure-prediction objective trains the CVG so that the highest scoring tree will be the correct tree and its score will be larger up to a margin to other possible trees:

$$s(CVG(\theta, x_i, y_i)) \geq s(CVG(\theta, x_i, \hat{y})) + \Delta(y_i, \hat{y}) \tag{5}$$

where y_i is the correct tree for a sentence x_i, $\Delta(y_i, \hat{y})$ is a structured margin loss. The discrepancy between trees is measured by counting the number of nodes N(y) with an incorrect span (or label) in the proposed tree:

$$\Delta(y_i, \hat{y}) = \kappa \left(\sum_{d \in N(\hat{y})} 1\{d \notin N(y_i)\} + \sum_{d \in N(y_i)} 1\{d \notin N(\hat{y})\} \right) \tag{6}$$

This leads to the regularized risk function for m training examples:

$$J(\theta) = \frac{1}{m} \sum_{i=1}^{m} r_i(\theta) + \frac{\lambda}{2} \|\theta\|_2^2, \text{ where}$$

$$r_i(\theta) = \max\left(\max_{\hat{y} \in Y(x_i)} (s(CVG(x_i, \hat{y})) + \Delta(y_i, \hat{y})) - s(CVG(x_i, y_i)), 0 \right) \tag{7}$$

The loss function of the model is not differentiable due to the hinge loss. Therefore, it can adjust parameter via subgradient method.

3   Improvement of CVG Model

3.1   Word Vector Fusing POS Information

Chinese semantics is very complicated. A word may have several parts of speech, and each part of speech may correspond to several meanings. For example, the word "活动" [huodong] (activity), there are at least 6 meanings, 3 parts of speech. If we use only one word vector to represent the word "活动" [huodong] (activity), the semantic expression is very limited. If each item is given a vector, firstly, there is no readily available corpus can be trained. In addition it is very difficult to achieve. This paper uses a compromise approach. Apart from the use of the existing features--part of speech, use (word, part of speech) as a whole to train, and get its vector representation. One word is not mapped to the n-dimensional space. Instead (word, part of speech) is mapped to the n-dimensional space. The word w's corresponding word vector is V(w,POS). When SU-RNN calculates the parent node vector representation, it will be able to capture more accurate information of the child node.

3.2   Unknown Word Processing

In the syntactic analysis, the unknown word is the inevitable problem. In the CVG model, unknown word refers to the word whose corresponding word vector is. For the unknown word, this paper makes a simple processing for CVG model, unified as zero vector, which indicates that unknown word does not introduce any information.

In the improved model, unknown word is not a single word, but (word, POS). For the unknown word, the structure information can be used instead of it. When the corresponding vector is not found in the vector table, the corresponding vector is found by its structure. For example, you can use POS node and its parent node and grandfather node type to form a whole. Using a similar structure corresponding to know word to weighted average, or randomly added the date in the corpus to train the vector and add to the vector table. Hypothesis "精致化" [*jingzhihua*] (*refinement*) in "(VP (VV 走向) (NP (NN 精致化)))" is the unknown word, you can use "NN^#NP_VP" instead, from the vector table to find the corresponding vector. Considering that such an alternative is imprecise, adding a parameter here to weigh the amount of information it brings, its range of [0,1].

3.3   Newborn Node Category Refinement

To reduce the complexity of model, and improve efficiency, firstly use SU-RNN to binarize input tree. This paper uses head binarization. Figure 3(a) show an example of binarization. In the process of binary to generate new node, circle is a new node. The new node needs to label it. The labeling rule uses the rules of Standford Parser, and uses the parent node and its sibling node to label its type as follows: NP: ...NP. Eq. 1 and Eq. 2 use simplified categories, so the category of newborn node becomes VP. It and the other candidate tree Figure 3(b) show are the same. Obviously these two sub tree scores will be the same, and this result is clearly not what we want.

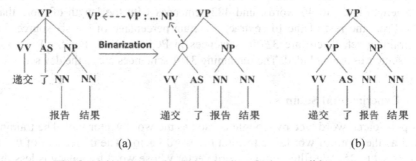

(a)   (b)

Fig. 3. (a) is an example of binarization ,(b) is a candidate tree

In order to solve the above problems, in this paper, a tag bit is added in the category of the newborn node, to distinguish the newborn node and original node. When computing the parent node vector, the captured semantic information is also more exact.

3.4   Improved Scoring Function

By the Eq.4, the values of parameters W depend on the categories of children when calculating the parent vectors. The parent vectors can not only capture the information captured by the children, but also introduce the information of the children categories. When the score of the parent node is calculated by Eq.2, the values of parameters U are still dependent on the categories of the children.

This paper considers that this is the introduction of redundant information. Parent vector representation already contains the information of the children categories. So calculating the parent node score can no longer consider the children categories. In this paper, parameters U depends on the current node category instead of the children categories. Eq.2 can be written in form:

$$s(p^{(i)}) = \left(U^{self\_type}\right)^T p^{(i)} \tag{8}$$

where self_type represents current node category, $U^{self\_type} \in \Re^{n \times 1}$ is a weight matrix corresponding to the self_type. Such a modification not only retains the information of the children categories, but also introduces the parent node category information. Then the node score will be more accurate.

4   Experiments

4.1   Experimental Data

We perform experiments using the Penn Chinese Treebank 8.0(CTB8.0).There are 114 gold standard treebank file as a test set. According to sentence length it is divided into three parts, 920 sentences whose length is less than or equal to 20 words, 885 sentences whose length is 21 to 40 words, and 482 sentences with the length of more than 40 words. From the rest of the file extract a certain percentage of the six source files to form training set. There are 32758 sentences in PCFG model. For SU-RNN model, 33223 sentences are included. The remaining 3101 sentences are as the dev set.

4.2   Experimental Setup

The open source word2vec by Google is used as the word vector tool. The training set is used as the input of word2vec to train the word vector. The dimension of the word vector is set to 25. We filter out the word vector whose word frequency is less than 2. The original word vector has 35478 vectors. The improved CVG model is with 43070 vectors of which there are 1742 structural vectors.

Use Stanford Parser to train a Chinese PCFG model as the base model, and use it to train CVG model. In order to achieve a better performance of CVG model, through experiments on the dev set, we fix the scoring function weights t=1, the regularization of $\lambda = 10^{-5}$, the learning rate $\alpha = 0.1$, structured margin loss of. The minibatch size was set to 200. The number of candidate trees is 200. The maximum number of iterations was 30. For the improved model, we set the unknown word weights r=0.2, other settings as above.

The Labeled Precision (LP), Labeled Recall (LR) and F1 of the PARSEVAL are used as the evaluation criteria in the experiment. While these results give a useful measure of overall performance, they provide no information about the nature, or relative importance, of the remaining errors. Therefore, this paper also uses Berkeley Parser Analyser to analyze error types of parsing results.

4.3   Results

Table 1 compares our results between the Chinese PCFG model (Levy R and Manning C, 2003) and CVG model (Socher R, 2013). In additin to LP, LR and F1, the table also shows the average sentence running time (Time column), the average number of unknown word per sentence (Un_word column) and result in the dev set. In the model evaluation, sentence punctuation is reserved.

Table 1. Comparison of Model on the CTB8.0. Chinese PCFG model is the base model. CVG_m is an improved model.

Model	Words	LP/%	LR/%	F1/%	Time/sec	Un_Word	F1/%,dev
Chinese PCFG	1-20	77.74	74.62	76.15	0.07	—	
	21-40	74.48	69.84	72.09	0.60	—	69.08
	>40	70.23	65.39	67.72	4.06	—	
CVG	1-20	81.16	80.36	80.76	0.12	0.47	
	21-40	77.83	75.74	76.77	0.77	1.16	73.54
	>40	73.02	69.51	71.22	4.43	2.60	
CVG_m	1-20	82.69	80.56	81.61	0.13	0.55	
	21-40	79.12	76.23	77.65	0.77	1.36	74.36
	>40	73.80	69.99	71.84	4.70	3.07	

Table 1 shows that the CVG model has a better improvement than the PCFG model. For dev set, it achieves an increase of nearly 4.5% in F1. For the test set, both the short sentence and the long sentence have an increase of about 4% in F1. As to the running time, the CVG model is slightly slower then PCFG model, but it is acceptable. The model also preserves certain unknown words for the test set, which is close to the actual application.

The CVG_m model has some improvement compared with CVG model. On the dev set, the F1 has nearly 1% increase. For the test set, the sentences whose lengths are length is less than or equal to 40 words have increased by 0.8% in F1. Long sentences also have 0.6% increase. As to the running time, it has basically no change. For the unknown word, because POS information is introduced, unknown words in CVG_m are more than CVG.

4.4   Analysis of Error Types

The results of error types in test set are shown in Table 2. Top ten error types are listed in the table. Others are represented by "other". Value indicates the average number of bracket errors per sentence attributed to that error type. The data shown in bold compared to the former are not ideal.

Table 2 shows that error numbers of CVG syntax analysis are greatly decreased compared to the PCFG model. The error number of CVG_m relative to CVG also decreased. However, some errors have increased. We analyzed these error types. Diff Label represents the span is correct but the label is wrong. This error type at least reflects the span is correct. Wrong Sense applies when the head word of a phrase receives the wrong POS, leading to an attachment error. The input vector of CVG_m model is introduced into POS information, so the error increases. In Noun Edge error, a span is moved to a position where the POS tags of its new siblings all belong to the list of NP-internal structure tags, reflecting the inclusion of additional material into an NP. The CVG model and CVG_m model have fluctuations in this error type, possibly because of the addition of semantic information, which makes certain combination of the adhesion enhancement, and makes some of the unusual combination separate. Mod. Attach is incorrect modifier scope caused by modifier phrase attachment level. Coord is the cases in which a conjunction is an immediate sibling of the nodes being

Table 2. Detailed comparison of different parsers. Values are the number of bracket errors per sentence attributed to that error type.

Error Type	PCFG			CVG			CVG_m		
	1-20	21-40	>40	1-20	21-40	>40	1-20	21-40	>40
NP Internal	1.314	3.588	6.946	1.147	3.404	6.481	1.075	3.293	6.394
Verb Args	0.504	2.206	5.147	0.451	1.819	4.411	0.412	1.754	4.317
1-Word Span	0.432	1.108	2.597	0.354	1.000	2.361	0.352	0.934	2.327
Unary	0.412	1.424	3.240	0.337	1.221	3.007	0.326	1.195	2.977
Diff Label	0.354	0.915	2.199	0.217	0.784	2.017	**0.257**	**0.806**	**2.091**
Mod. Attach	0.329	1.447	3.272	0.328	1.267	2.971	**0.345**	1.207	**3.017**
Wrong Sense	0.314	0.896	1.897	0.234	0.659	1.614	0.225	**0.669**	**1.616**
Coord	0.240	1.500	4.176	0.176	1.329	4.056	**0.177**	**1.352**	3.921
Noun Edge	0.171	0.547	0.927	0.159	0.495	**0.934**	0.122	**0.505**	0.883
PP Attach	0.138	0.522	1.164	0.103	0.384	1.127	**0.106**	**0.394**	1.120
other	0.846	3.709	8.248	0.633	2.778	6.904	0.582	2.398	6.350

moved, or is the leftmost or rightmost node being moved. PP Attach represents the transformation involved moving a Prepositional Phrase or the incorrect bracket is over a PP. These three error types may require more accurate semantic information.

5   Conclusion

In this paper, CVG is used in Chinese syntax analysis, and the results are improved compared with the base model. CVG model is improved to solve the existing problems。We also analyzed the error types of syntax analysis, thus found out on which error types the improved model performed badly and why. Next we will further improve the model and do some post-processing for specific error types. For example, combine semantic modification of the components in the dependency tree to add more semantic information, and introduce function word usage information and so on.

Acknowledgments. This work was supported by the Natural Science Foundation of China(No.61402419, No.60970083, No.61272221), the National Social Science Foundation of China (No.14BYY096), 863 Projects of National High Technology Research and Development (No.2012AA011101), Science and Technology Key Project of Science and Technology Department of Henan Province(No.132102210407), Basic research project of Science and Technology Department of Henan Province(No. 142300410231,No.142300410308) Key Technology Project of the Education Department of Henan Province (No.12B520055,No. 13B520381), 973 Projects of National Key Basic Research and Development (2014CB340504), Key Project of Science Research in Colleges and Universities in Henan Province (15A520098) and the Open Projects Program of Key Laboratory of Computational Linguistics(Peking University)(No. 201401), Ministry of Education of PRC.

References

1. Wu, W.C., Zhou, J.S., Qu, W.G.: A Survey of Syntactic Parsing Based on Statistical Learning. Journal of Chinese Information Processing **27**(3), 9–19 (2013). (in Chinese)
2. Socher, R., Bauer, J., Manning, C.D., et al.: Parsing with compositional vector grammars. In: Proceedings of the ACL Conference (2013)
3. Socher, R., Manning, C.D., Ng, A.Y.: Learning continuous phrase representations and syntactic parsing with recursive neural networks. In: Proceedings of the NIPS-2010 Deep Learning and Unsupervised Feature Learning Workshop, pp.1–9 (2010)
4. Socher, R., Lin, C.C., Manning, C., et al.: Parsing natural scenes and natural language with recursive neural networks. In: Proceedings of the 28th International Conference on Machine Learning (ICML 2011), pp. 129–136 (2011)
5. Charniak, E., Johnson, M., Elsner, M., et al.: Multilevel coarse-to-fine PCFG parsing. In: Proceedings of the Main Conference on Human Language Technology Conference of the North American Chapter of the Association of Computational Linguistics, pp. 168–175. Association for Computational Linguistics (2006)
6. Xue, N., Xia, F., Chiou, F.-D., Palmer, M.: The Penn Chinese TreeBank: Phrase Structure Annotation of a Large Corpus. Natural Language Engineering **11**(2), 207–238 (2005)

7. Mikolov, T., Chen, K., Corrado, G., Dean, J.: Efficient estimation of word representations in vector space. In: Proceedings of Workshop at ICLR (2013)
8. Levy, R., Manning, C.: Is it harder to parse Chinese, or the Chinese treebank?. In: Proceedings of the 41st Annual Meeting on Association for Computational Linguistics-Volume 1, pp. 439–446. ACL (2003)
9. Abney, S., Flickenger, S., Gdaniec, C., et al.: Procedure for quantitatively comparing the syntactic coverage of English grammars. In: Proceedings of the workshop on Speech and Natural Language, pp. 306–311. Association for Computational Linguistics (1991)
10. Kummerfeld, J.K., Tse, D., Curran, J.R., et al.: An empirical examination of challenges in Chinese parsing. In: ACL (2), pp. 98–103 (2013)

Constructional Meaning Selection for "A+Yi (*One*) +X, B+Yi (*One*) +Y" in Mandarin Chinese

Hongchao Liu[1(✉)], Weidong Zhan[2], and Chu-Ren Huang[1]

[1] CBS of Hong Kong Polytechnic University, Hung Hom, Hong Kong
jiye12yuran@126.com, churen.huang@polyu.edu.hk
[2] Center for Chinese Linguistics, Key Laboratory of Computational Linguistics, Ministry of Education, Peking University, Beijing, China
zwd@pku.edu.cn

Abstract. Mandarin "A+Yi(*one*)+X, B+Yi(*one*)+Y" construction has multiple constructional meanings encoded by the same syntactic form. We study the conditions for selection and/or preference of constructional meanings of this construction in this paper. Study of corpus data showed that POS and semantic roles of A/B X/Y cannot reliably predict different constructional meanings. We further show that conditions that can predict the differences in constructional meaning are the event structures of A and B's, as well as referential relationship between "Yi(*one*)+X"and "Yi(*one*)+Y". The context and logic relationship between A and B can also influence the constructional meaning.

Keywords: Mandarin chinese construction · "A+yi(*one*)+X, B+yi(*one*)+Y" · Constructional meaning selection · Event structure

1   Introduction

We have drawn the constructional meaning hierarchy of "A+Yi(*one*)+X, B+Yi(*one*)+Y" in Liu et. (2014) and here we copy it below with some minor adjustments:

Previous studies on "A+Yi(*one*)+X, B+Yi(*one*)+Y" has made the same mistake on describing the form's constrains as they regard it as one construction although when they analyze its meaning, they differentiate multiple senses within the same form which otherwise imply that it is not a single construction but a series of constructions share the same form . The result of taking this methodology help nothing with predicting the different constructional meanings of "A+Yi (*one*) +X, B+Yi(*one*)+Y" and thus we try to clarify the factors which can influence the meaning selection for "A+Yi(*one*)+X, B+Yi(*one*)+Y" aiming to differentiate meanings according to the concrete values of these factors.

This study has been supported by Word Chinese and Their Grammatical Variations: Empirical Studies based on Comparable Corpora (GRF project 543512), major project of humanities & social science fund of Ministry of Education of China (project no. 13JJD740001), national social science fund major project (project no. 12&ZD175) and national social science fund major project (project no. 12BYY061).

Q. Lu and H.H. Gao (Eds.): CLSW 2015, LNAI 9332, pp. 659–670, 2015.
DOI: 10.1007/978-3-319-27194-1_65

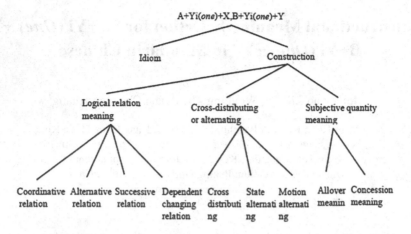

Fig. 1. "A+Yi(one)+X, B+Yi(*one*)+Y" constructional meaning hierarchy

Table 1. The constructional meanings and examples of "A+Yi(*one*)+X, B+Yi(*one*)+Y"

	Construction	Meaning	Example
a	Dependent changing	The more it As, the more it Bs.	用一吨，少一吨 'Each time you use one ton, it reduce one ton.' 'The more you use, the less it is.'
		The time for A become less and less.	看一眼，少一眼 'Each time you have a look at her, the chances for another looking at become less.' 'The time for you to look at her has become less and less.'
b	Cross-distributing	The things that Yi (*one*) +X+A and Yi (*one*) +X+B represent are cross-distributed.	深一道，浅一道 'Here a streak of deep color and there a streak of light color.' 'Many streaks of deep color and light color are cross-distributed on one flat.'
c	State alternating	The state that Yi (*one*) +X+A and Yi (*one*) +X+B represent appear alternatively.	热一阵，冷一阵 'Hot for a while and cold for a while.' 'Hot and cold are alternating.'
d	Motion alternating	The motion that Yi (*one*) +X+A and Yi (*one*) +X+B represent appear alternatively.	走一阵，歇一阵 'walk for a while and rest for a while' 'Walk and rest are alternating.'
e	Allover meaning	All of the X that has been A-ed, they has also been B-ed.	有一个，杀一个 'As long as there is one, he will kill that one.' 'No matter how many there are, he will kill them all.'

Within this paper, we focus on the "A+Yi(*one*)+X, B+Yi(*one*)+Y" whose variable A and B are predicates. As the form and meaning[1] for "coordination relation, Alternative relation and successive relation" are very simple, considering most of the previous studies have made a deep analysis on them, we will omit these meanings in our study. The examples of concession meaning show clear distinction with the rest of the meanings on its meaning and form and thus we will leave it to another study.

Here follows the subjects we will analyze with some examples for each meaning respectively:

At first, we try to find some tendencies of the variables for the examples of each constructional meaning by annotating the POS of 454 instances. It seems that only b and c show a tendency that both of their A and B are adjectives while b and c can be further differentiated through X and Y[2]. However, this factor alone cannot predict the rest of the meanings. How about expanding the scope to the variables' semantic features such as their semantic type? We choose *the Semantic Knowledge-base of Contemporary Chinese* (SKCC) as a reference and annotate all the variables' semantic type showing all the counting numbers in the following table:

Table 2. Semantic type distribution of variable A and B for motion alternating meaning "A+Yi(*one*)+X, B+Yi(*one*)+Y"

| Semantic type | Verb | | | | | | | | | | | | Total |
| | Motion behavior | | | | | | | | | | | Morpheme and phrase | |
	Body movement	Information exchange	Five senses	Social activity	displacement	Other motions	Touch	Create	Change	Possession transfer	Mental activity		
A	44	5	4	2	0	1	0	4	0	0	0	0	60
B	34	5	0	3	3	4	3	2	1	2	1	2	60

Table 3. Semantic type distribution of variable A and B for allover meaning "A+Yi(*one*)+X, B+Yi(*one*)+Y"

| Semantic type | Verb | | | | | | | | | | | | | | Total |
| | Motion behavior | | | | | | | | | | | | | | |
	Information exchange	Social activity	Five senses	displacement	Body movement	Other motions	Possession transfer	Create	Change	Touch	Static relation	Mental activity	Adjective	Phrase and abbreviation	
A	3	1	14	14	24	12	1	30	1	0	25	27	0	5	157
B	4	3	0	4	33	11	6	4	12	5	36	14	20	5	157

[1] Their variable A and B are limited to several pairs of antonyms and their meaning only contain logical relation while the other meanings are more opaque.

[2] This information has been analyzed in Liu et. (2014) and we will not repeat them within this paper and mainly focus on the differentiation between a, d and e.

Table 4. Semantic type distribution of variable A and B for concession meaning "A+Yi(*one*)+X, B+Yi(*one*)+Y"

| Semantic type | Verb | | | | | | | | Adjective | Resultative construction | Total |
| | Motion behavior | | | | | | | Mental activity | | | |
	Consume	Five senses	displacement	Body move-ment	Other motions	Possession transfer	Touch	Change			
A	1	1	2	8	1	5	4	4	1	2	4	33
B	1	1	2	8	1	5	4	4	1	2	4	33

For a, d and e, firstly, their variables' semantic types are almost randomly distributed in a wide range of scope showing a weak tendency; secondly, a, d and e share several semantic types such as 'five senses', which make it hard to differentiate them through semantic type. In total, both the POS and semantic type of the variables are not enough for predicting the different constructional meanings of "A+Yi(*one*)+X, B+Yi(*one*)+Y". We need to find more factors that can help the meaning selection of it.

2   The Influence of A and B's Event Structure

"A+Yi(*one*)+X, B+Yi(*one*)+Y" can be divided into two parts and the whole meaning is always about the relationship between the two parts. Either they are cross-distributed within one space or they are alternating on a scale of time. A and B are more like a pair of contrastive tags which are assigned by "Yi(*one*)+X" and "Yi(*one*)+Y".

It is easy to infer that when A and B are adjectives, the constructional meaning of "A+Yi(*one*)+X, B+Yi(*one*)+Y" should be about state or nature and if X and Y are nominal quantifier, the meaning should be about some things "Yi(*one*)+X" and "Yi(*one*)+Y" refer to while if X and Y are verbal or time quantifier, the meaning should be about event. However, it is not easy to differentiate the meaning in this way as When A and B are verbs, the situation would be more complex. There is a more solid construction "You (*exist*) +Yi (*one*) +X, Mei (*not exist*) +Yi (*one*) +Y":

Ex.1 *狗在有一声无一声寂寞地吠。* [3]
'*The dog is barking lonely now and then.*'

There are 34 types in the corpus instantiated by replacing X and Y with different quantifiers with a constructional meaning of 'happens sporadically with some boring, desolate or some other similar atmospheres.' "You (*exist*)" and "Mei (not *exist*)" is more like a state rather than a motion and thus when we analyze the influence of A and B on the constructional meaning, it is more useful to have a look at what semantic

---

[3]   All of the examples are extracted from CCL (Center for Chinese Linguistics PKU)'s corpus.

category[4] they belong to. For an applicable reason[5], we choose Guo(1993)'s predicate event structure system to be a reference as there is a clear mapping between the predicate's event structure type and their semantic category as well as clear standards to judge their types. Below we give Guo(1993)'s mapping scale and the event structure of a, d and e:

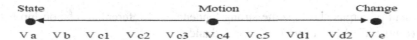

Fig. 2. Guo(1993)'s mapping scale between semantic category and event structure for verb

Table 5. Variable A and B's event structure distribution for motion alternating meaning "A+Yi(*one*)+X, B+Yi(*one*)+Y"

A	Vc5	Vc5	Vc5	Vc5	Vc5	Vc4	Vc4	Vc4	Vc4	Vc3	Vc3	Total
B	Vc5	Vc4	Vc3	Vd2	Ex.	Vc5	Vc4	Vc3	Ex.	Vc4	Vc3	
Number	8	4	1	1	1	4	30	8	2	1	1	60

Table 6. Variable A and B's event structure distribution for for allover meaning "A+Yi(*one*)+X, B+Yi(*one*)+Y"

A	Vc1	Z	Ve	Z	Z	Vc(4-5)	Vc(4-5)	Total
B	Z	Va	Z	Ve	a	Vc(1-3)	Vc(4-5)	
Number	25	14	53	26	20	10	9	157

We didn't give the distribution of A and B for concession meaning "A+Yi (*one*) +X, B+Yi(*one*)+Y" as the distributing tendency is very similar to table 6 and thus cannot be used to differentiate between a and e.

From table 5 and 6, we can observe the following tendencies:

(1) The variable "A+B" for motion alternating "A+Yi (*one*) +X, B+Yi(*one*)+Y" represent "motion+ motion". For variable A and B in table 5, their event structures almost all belong to Vc3-5 (we have three exceptions to be analyzed in the next section). According to figure 2, Vc3-5 represents typical "motion" and thus we can use "motion+motion" to represent "A+B";

(2) No less than one of the variables of allover meaning "A+Yi (*one*) +X, B+Yi(*one*)+Y" represents "state" or "change". In table 6, Va, Vc1 and Vc2 tend to represent "state"; Ve represents "change"; Vc3 is a dilemma for us as illustrated in Guo(1993) that "Vc1, Vc2 and Vc3 used to belong to stative verb, but compared with Va and Vb, even from the perspective of subjective intention, they are different......especially for Vc3, it has very strong verbal tendency." If we regard Vc3 as a

---

[4]   Here refers to motion, state and change.

[5]   This study finally aims to construct a construction knowledge database for NLP and thus all of the features should be able to judge and annotate by clear standards.

trans-class one, the problem will be solved. However, we still have 9 exceptions with no variables represent "state" or "change", we will explain them in the next section.

3   The Influence of Referential Relationship Between "Yi(*one*)+X" and "Yi(*one*)+Y"

The data of corpus shows some strong tendencies of referential relationship between "Yi (*one*) +X" and "Yi (*one*) +Y" for a, d and e:

(1)   "Yi (*one*) +X" and "Yi (*one*) +Y" usually refer to different things for motion alternating "A+Yi (*one*) +X, B+Yi(*one*)+Y".

Ex. 1. 电脑棋师的"棋艺"是人教给它的, 它只能按照现成步骤来走棋, 走一步运算一步。

'*The skill of computer chess master is taught by human and it can only take a move according to the ready-made procedures. **Each time it takes a move, it will operate the next move**.*'

'*The computer is alternating between taking a move and operating a move.*'[6]

Apparently, the move a computer takes doesn't refer to the same move it operates.

(2) "Yi (*one*) +X" and "Yi (*one*) +Y" usually refer to the same thing for allover meaning "A+Yi (*one*) +X, B+Yi(*one*)+Y".

Ex.2. 他们千方百计克服困难, 做一单成一单……

'*They try their best to overcome the difficulties and **each piece of business they did have succeeded**……*'

The piece of business that they have dong is the same piece of business that is successful.

Some more powerful evidences are the 9 exceptions we mentioned above:

Ex.3. 走一亭, 吃一亭; 走一地, 问一地; 走一处, 说一处; 走一处, 洗一处; 走一段, 问一段; 干一处, 响一处.

'*Every pavilion he passes, he will eat there; every place he passes, he will ask questions there; every place he passes, he will give a speech there; every place he passes, he will do a foot massage there; every stretch of road he passes, he will ask the direction there; every place he get a position, he will succeed there.*'

'*Walking and eating are alternating for the subject; walking and asking questions are alternating for the subject……t*'

---

6   We give another explanation for some absurd direct translation of the literal meanings which is also essential for understanding the constructional meaning.

We just give several examples here and actually, these examples have the same semantic structure with a location argument after the predicate instead of a patient. Interestingly, we call them exceptions in the second section as their variable A and B such as "走 (*walk*), 吃 (*eat*) and 问 (*ask*)" have an event structure similar to the motion alternating meaning "A+Yi (*one*) +X, B+Yi(*one*)+Y"'s variables because they share the same "motion+motion" category mapping from figure 2. However, the reference to the same thing makes them select the meaning of allover instead of motion alternating.

(3) The constructional meaning doesn't emphasize whether they refer to the same thing or not for the "Yi (*one*) +X" and "Yi (*one*) +Y" of concession meaning "A+Yi (*one*) +X, B+Yi(*one*)+Y". They usually belong to the same total.

Ex. 4.石油作为矿物质能源,不可再生,用一吨少一吨。

*'Petrol, as a fossil fuel, cannot be regenerated. **Every time we use one ton, it will become one ton less.**'*

'For the petrol, the more we use, the less it is.'

Ex. 5. 这样看上去虽然进展缓慢，却很有效果，敌人消灭一个少一个……

*'Although it seems too slowly, but the result is effective. **For the enemy, each time we eliminate one, it will become one less.**'*

'For the enemies, the more you eliminate, the less they are.'

For 4, it is hard to say the "one ton" that has been used refer to the same "one tone" that is decreased as the constructional meaning doesn't emphasize it which is the same case for example 5. But we can confirm that the "one ton" that has been used and the "one ton" that has been decreased belong to the same total.

4   The Influence of Context

4.1   The Context 's Selection of Motion Alternating Meaning

The basic features for motion alternating meaning "A+Yi (*one*) +X, B+Yi(*one*)+Y" are: (1) Both of A and B's semantic type are "motion"; (2) "Yi (*one*) +X" and "Yi (*one*) +Y" refer to different thing. There are 7 examples not following these two tendencies including 1 violation of (1), 4 violations of (2) and 2 violations of both.

The 1 violation of (1) is "哭一阵，气一阵" (*cry for a while and then angry for a while*) as "气" (angry)'s event structure cannot be decided according to Guo(1993). The selection of motion alternating meaning should owe to "一阵" (*a while*) which has a strong indication for alternating meaning. The rest of the exceptions select alternating meaning because of context.

Ex. 1. 全部完工再使用，难以尽快收回投资，就建一层用一层，滚动地把资金收回。

'It is hard to recoup the investment if waiting for its whole accomplishment and thus **every time they finished one floor and they will come into use that floor** *which can help them to recoup the investment in a rolling way.'*
　　'Building a floor and using that floor are alternating'

Ex. 2. 做一期，售一期；用上期款，供下期施工。

*'***Every time they finish one phase, they will sell that phase of building****; with the money from the last phase to build the next phase.'*
　　'Building and selling are alternating'

The "rolling way" in 1 has indicated the alternating of "建" (*build*) and "用" (*use*); "用上期款，供下期施工" (*with the money from the last phase to build the next phase*) has the similar function to select the meaning of motion alternating for example 2.

4.2　Context's Selection of Dependent Changing Meaning

Here we give an example first.

Ex. 1. 这种清茶泡一次，淡一次。

'For this kind of green tea, **you make it for one more time and it will become lighter***.'*
'The more you soak that tea leaves, the lighter the taste is.'

There is a causal relationship between the "泡" (*soak*) and "淡" (*become lighter*) in example 1 as the more you soak the tea leaves, the taste will become lighter and lighter. For most of the time, we can transfer these kinds of examples into another construction with a form of "Yue (*the more*)…Yue (*the more*)", but some cannot be transformed as there is no logical causal relationship between their A and B.

Ex. 2. 乔家这座老宅，说不定就要顶给别人了，睡一天少一天。

'Qiao's courtyard maybe taken by others to pay bills and thus **the time to sleeping here has become day and day less***.'*

Ex. 3. 回趟老家看看去，这辈子活到这年头了，回一次少一次呢。

'To go back to hometown to have a look as we have lived up so much time of this life and thus **the time for going back home has become less and less***.'*

The common property of examples like example 2 and example 3 is the time to do A is becoming less and less. It is hard to infer a direct causal relationship between "A+Yi (*one*) +X" and "B+Yi(*one*)+Y" as it will be weird to say "sleeping" leads to "being less" or "going back hometown" leads to "being less" and thus we cannot transfer them to a "Yue (*the more*)…Yue (*the more*)" construction. But when we have the context, the causal relationship has been built. In example 2, because of the "courtyard maybe taken by others", the time "for sleeping will become less and less" has become natural; in example 3, because of their age has become bigger and bigger, it is reasonable to infer that the time for going back home has become less and less.

5   The Influence of Logical Relationship Between A and B

5.1   Logical Relationship's Selection of Allover Meaning

We have explained most of the examples about their selection of allover meaning with only 2 exceptions:

Ex. 1. *我现在还存着平反时送回来的那些声泪俱下的交代书，看一回笑一回。*

'*I still keep the revealing materials in which I cried out my 'crimes', sent back when I was rehabilitated, **each time I read it, I always laugh**.*'

Ex. 2. *高晓声的《陈奂生》，我看一遍哭一遍，我觉得那写的就是我，实实在在的就是我……*

'*For Gao Xiaosheng's novel, Chen Huansheng, **each time I read it, I always cry** as I feel the role the novel is writing about is me, absolute me.*'

For example 1 and example 2: (1) variable A and B for them represent motion mapping from event structure according to figure 2; (2) "Yi (*one*) +X" and "Yi (*one*) +Y" refer to different thing. Both of these features match motion alternating meaning, however, they do select the meaning of allover. Actually, it is a very common phenomenon that causal relationship exists between "看" (*read*) and "哭" (*cry*) or other motions. To "read" is to acquire some information which can cause some natural responses such as "cry, laugh, think, touched or angry……" "听" (*listen*) is similar to "看" (*read*). The logical relationship between A and B for dependent changing meaning is also causal relation and thus the question is why example 1 and 2 don't select dependent changing meaning? For dependent changing construction, B is limited to "少" (less), "好" (good), "and 淡" (light) and "强" (strong) which is more like adjectives instead of verbs in Chinese. But for "笑" (*laugh*) and "哭" (*cry*), they are typical verb representing motion and thus it is hard to select the dependent changing meaning for them just as "少" (less), "好" (good), "and 淡" (light) and "强" (strong) do although we cannot explain the mechanism behind them.

Not all of the examples of allover meaning has a relationship of cause-result one as example 1 and 2.

Ex. 3. *对查出的制假、售假黑窝点、伪劣商品集散地，要做到发现一个端掉一个，决不手软。*

'*For the dens that make or sell forged and fake commodity, **no matter how many we find, we will crack them all**.*'

Ex. 4. 公安都是神仙？什么疑难复杂案子见一个破一个. 那是电影里演的！

'*Are all the policemen gods? It only exists in movies that **they will solve any cases in any complex degree that they encounter**!*'

The logical relationship between A and B for example 3 and 4 is conditional relation which is most of the cases for allover meaning "A+Yi (*one*) +X, B+Yi(*one*)+Y".

5.2   Logical Relationship's Selection of Dependent Changing Meaning

There is an overlapping between dependent changing meaning and allover meaning for the causal relation between A and B can select them both but the causal relationship is more powerful for dependent changing meaning as we can say A leads to B in dependent meaning examples while it is not applicable for allover meaning ones. However, the leading-to relationship is not always prominent in the surface structure of the constructional examples and sometimes they need context to make them clear. Thus, we can divide the examples of dependent changing meaning into two groups according to whether the leading-to relationship is prominent or not.

(1) 用一吨, 少一吨; 消灭一个少一个; 杀一个少一个; 泡一次淡一次;

'Each time you use one ton, it becomes one ton less; Each time you eliminate one enemy, it becomes one enemy less; each time you kill one enemy, it becomes one enemy less; each time you soak the tea leaves, it becomes lighter.'

'The more you use, the less it is; the more you eliminate, the less the enemy is; the more you kill, the less the enemy is; the more you soak the tea leaves, the lighter the taste is.'

(2) 买一件少一件; 发现一个少一个; 睡一天少一天; 回一次少一次.

'Each time you buy one piece, the storage will becomes one piece less; each time you discover one, it become one less; each time you sleep one day, it becomes one day less; each time you go back home, it becomes one time less.'

'The more you buy, the less the storage is; the more you discover, the less it is; the more you sleep, the less the time for being here is; the more you go back home, the less the time for going back is.'

For the first group, the leading-to relationship is prominent as it is natural to say "用" (*use*) leads to "少" (*less*) and "泡" (*soak*) leads to "淡" (*light*) but for the second group, the leading-to relation is implicit in the context as it is weird to say "发现" (*discover*) leads to "少" (*less*) except we have the following context.

Ex. 1. 人类的基因数目是有限的, 发现一个少一个。

'*The gene number of human being is limited and thus **the more we discover, the less the gene that need to be discovered is**.*'

As the total number of human genes is limited, every time we find a new one means the chance for finding another new one has become less.

5.3   The Logical Relationship's Selection of Cross-Distributing, State Alternating and Motion Alternating Meaning

The logical relationship between A and B is the same for cross-distributing, state alternating and motion alternating meaning "A+Yi (*one*) +X, B+Yi(*one*)+Y" as the A and B are typical antonyms for most of the time.

Cross-distributing meaning: 青一块紫一块; 粗一道细一道; 长一行短一行;
'Black and blue; thick and thin streaks are cross-distributed; long and short line of things are cross-distributed.'

State alternating meaning: 长一声短一声; 深一脚浅一脚; 冷一顿热一顿;
'Sigh long and short; walking unevenly; eat cold and hot food irregularly.'

Motion alternating meaning: 走一阵歇一阵; 哭一阵笑一阵; 走一步停一下.
'Walk for a while and rest for a while; cry for a while and laugh for a while; walk and stop alternate.'

Sometimes, the antonym relation between A and B are assigned by context.

Ex. 1. *做一期, 售一期; 用上期款, 供下期施工。*
'Every time they finish building one phase, they will sell that phase of building; with the money from the last phase to build the next phase.'

"做" (*build*) and "售" (*sell*) are not antonyms; however, they form a pair of antonyms in the context because the money for the next phase can only be collected though selling the last phase and thus "做" (*build*) and "售" (*sell*) become complementary motions within this context.

6   Conclusion

With analyzing in details, we found the factors that influence the meaning selection of "A+Yi (*one*) +X, B+Yi(*one*)+Y" which can be demonstrated in the following table.

Table 7. Factors influnce the meaning selection of "A+Yi (*one*) +X, B+Yi(*one*)+Y"

	POS	Semantic type of A+B	Referential relationship between "Yi(*one*)+X" and "Yi(*one*)+Y"	Whether influenced by context or not	Logical relationship between A and B
Cross-distributing meaning	a+a	State+state	Refer to same thing	N/A	Antonym relation
State alternating meaning	a+a	State+state	Refer to different thing	N/A	Antonym relation
Motion alternating meaning	v+v	Motion+motion	Mostly refer to different thing	Yes	Antonym relation
Allover meaning	Mostly v+v	state/change; X+state/change	Mostly refer to different thing	Yes	Conditional or causal relation
Dependent changing meaning	Mostly v+a	X+state/change	Belong to the same total	Yes	Leading-to relation

References

Guo, R.: Verb's event structure of mandarin Chinese. Studies of the Chinese Language **6**, 410–419 (1993). (in Chinese)

Liu, H., Zhan, W.: Classification and Template for Interpretation of Construction "A+一+X, B+一+Y". Journal of Chinese Information Processing **28**, 125–131 (2014). (in Chinese)

First Explorations on the Syntactic Distributions of Verb-Object Constructions in Mandarin–V+A Constructions as Examples

Pengyuan Liu[⊠] and Lin Li

Institute of Applied Linguistics, Beijing Language and Culture University, Beijing, China
liupengyuan@blcu.edu.cn, lilin7365@yeah.net

Abstract. This study aims to use a large-scale corpus to explore the syntactic distributions of V+A bound verb-object constructions which consist of single verbs and single adjectival objects. We find that the distributions of V+A constructions in the corpus come in three varieties: 1.without followed by constituents; 2. followed by nominal constituents; 3.followed by non-nominal constituents. We arrive at the following conclusions that impact on the distributions: 1.the combination degree of V and A; 2.the properties of nominal constituents and the effect of V+A collocate with nominal elements. Then we discuss a special syntactical type such as "*da-hei*""*zhao-xin*". At last, we find and analyze some verb-object constructions which usually cannot exist independently.

Keywords: V+A · Bound types · Verb-object constructions · Non-nominal objects

1 Introduction

The verb-object construction is a basic syntactical type in Mandarin. Many linguists focus on it. Zhu Dexi gave detailed descriptions of this type, in particular, of non-nominal objects (such as verbal objects and adjectival objects) in the grammatical perspective. Zhu's approaches were widely held among Chinese linguists working on Mandarin. According to his approaches, there are two kinds of verb-object constructions come in two-fold varieties. One is verb-object constructions in which the main verbs are followed by nominal objects. Examples are: 洗衣服[*xi-yifu*](*to wash clothes*),吃饭[*chi-fan*](*to eat*). We refer to these as "verb-nominal object constructions". The other is verb-object constructions in which the main verbs are followed by non-nominal objects. Examples are:感到幸福[*gandao-xingfu*](*feel happiness*),发胖 [*fa-pang*](*become fat*). We refer to these as "verb—non-nominal object constructions".

There is a lot of literature on verb-nominal object constructions both in syntax and semantics. The theoretical achievements are fruitful. Syntactically, there are many detailed formulations of the properties of verbs and objects. Ma Qingzhu(1985) explored autonomous verbs, non-autonomous verbs and nominal objects. Fan Xiao and Yuan Yulin(1993) discussed verbs in valence theory. Semantically, the increasing

© Springer International Publishing Switzerland 2015
Q. Lu and H.H. Gao (Eds.): CLSW 2015, LNAI 9332, pp. 671–683, 2015.
DOI: 10.1007/978-3-319-27194-1_66

explorations of the varieties relations between verbs and objects by linguists, such as Li Linding(1983),Meng Cong(1999).Recently, a growing popular type of "verb-object+object" (verb-object constructions followed by objects) gained some researchers' attention, such as Rao Changrong(1984),Xing Gongwan(1997),Zhang Bo(1999).They discussed the constituents' properties, origins, collocation and the pragmatic values. Moreover, some linguists such as Feng Shengli(1997) researched in prosodic.

Few researchers have already tried to described verb-non-nominal objects from verbal objects and adjectival objects. For example, in an attempt to formulated adjectival objects, they started out by formulating properties of the objects. Then they argued verbs and adjectives in grammatical meanings and rhetoric. All of these works provide a good perspective for the next working. However, compared with all researches of the verb-nominal object constructions, the research about non-nominal objects is not thoroughly enough, and need more systematical explanations.

In this study, we will manage to explore the verb—non-nominal objects constructions' syntactic distributions based on a large-scale corpus which as a database and a case foundation, with the attempt to find some regulations and reasons about the syntactic distributions. For convenience we use V+A to represents a single verb followed by a single adjectival object. We focus on V+A verb-object constructions with reasons as follows: (1)the high rate of utilization and the stability of single words, (2)and in order to focus on our objects as far as possible. Examples are: 发白[*fa-bai*](*turn white*),转好[*zhuan-hao*] (*get better*),嫌贵[*xian-gui*](*complain something is too expensive*).

2   Examples and Distributions

2.1   Examples

In an attempt to formulate the V+A bound verb-object constructions comprehensively, we use two different corpora: a web fiction corpus and a news corpus. The former one has flexible words using style which much more like spoken language, the latter one is more formal which much more like written language.

We download the web fiction texts from the website which consist of 157 million words, and the news corpus comes from Sina news which range from June to December in 2012 and consists of 288 million words. Then we use ICTCLAS[1] (Institute of Computing Technology, Chinese Lexical Analysis System) to word segmentation and PoS tagging. After this, we establish the web fiction and news corpus (we refer to it as "the fiction-news corpus") which consists of 445 million words. All statistical data and examples are from this corpus.

---

[1] Although it is the best Chinese lexical analysis auto-system， there are still some mistakes in word segmentation and PoS tagging. In this study, we directly count and extract examples without review and analyze the results manually. The examples and statistical bias from this method may have some impacts on the distributions, but in this study we pay no attention at all.

Based on the former work, we extract all the V+A constructions as many as 28487 from the fiction-news corpus. Then we analyze all these constructions manually to exclude verb-complement constructions, subject-predicate constructions, free constructions and ungrammatical constructions. As a result we acquire 1423 V+A constructions.

2.2   Syntactic Distributions

We deal with all the examples by learning from the verb-nominal object constructions, and find that there are three different syntactic distributions: V+A+None, V+A+nominal constituents, V+A+non-nominal constituents. Examples are:

①　墙壁渗水，地板发黑。
　　Qiangbi　shen-shui, diban　fa-hei.
　　Water seeped from the wall, and the floor turned black.
②　他们愿意挨穷，　不接受冷暴力。
　　Tamen　yuanyi　ai-qiong, bu　jieshou　leng　baoli.
　　They prefer suffering poor to accepting the cold violence.
③　沈冰作为央视的女主播惊艳了不少人。
　　Shen Bing　zuowei yangshi de nv zhubo　jing-yan　le　bushao　ren.
　　Shen Bing as an CCTV anchorwoman amazed many people.
④　保湿喷雾与化妆水、柔肤水有很大区别。
　　Bao-shi　penwu　yu　huazhuangshui, roufu shui you　hen da　qubie.
　　Moisture Surge Face Spray have big differences between lotion、smoothing toner.
⑤　红姑娘忍疼点了点头。
　　Hong　guniang　ren-teng　dian le　dian　tou.
　　The girl named Hong nodded her head with bearing the pain.

As we can see from the examples, many constructions have all these distributions. Table 1 is the statistics of three distributions in the corpus[2]. It shows that in these three

Table 1. The statistics of three distributions in the corpus

Distributions	Amount	Proportion
V+A+None	991	70%
V+A+Nominal Constituents	395	28%
V+A+non-nominal Constituents	37	2%

---

[2] The statistics based on the main distributions of examples in the corpus. For example, *fa-an* 'go-black' often be used as a predicate without followed by other constituents, but there are also few examples that it can modifies nominal constituents. According to the quantity advantage of distributions, we refer to *fa-an* as V+A+None.

distributions, the highest proportion is V+A+None which as high as 70%, the lowest proportion is V+A+non-nominal constituents which as low as 2%, and the middle one is V+A+nominal constituents as 28%.

3   Analysis of the Syntactic Distributions

Are there any accidental factors that result in these distributions of V+A bound verb-object constructions in the corpus? Why the members in the same type have different syntactic distributions? Following all these questions, we explicitly observe and formulate all examples in the corpus. The results are the following:

3.1   V+A+None

This kind of constructions without followed by any constituents. Its main function is as a predicate which can modified by some adjuncts. Some of them can follow mode auxiliary verbs to be as objects. Examples are:

① 全球股市似乎正在转暖。

Quanqiu gushi sihu zhengzai zhuan-nuan.

The global stock market seems becoming warm.

② 手摸上去会发黏。

Shou   mo   shangqu   hui fa-nian.

As hands touch these, you will feel sticky.

③ 他们喜欢搞怪。

Tamen   xihuan   gao-guai.

They like to make things funny.

3.2   V+A+Nominal Constituents

According to the relationships between V+A and the nominal constituents, this kind of constructions separate into verb-object constructions and head-modifier constructions:

(1) Verb-Object Constructions

V+A as verbs, the nominal constituents as objects, and the verbs dominant the nominal constituents. Some nominal constituents (such as pronouns, nouns) can be objects. Examples are:

① 不是我有意为难你。

Bu   shi   wo   youyi   wei-nan   ni.

I do not want to intimidate you on purpose.

② 庄家有意在<u>造热</u>西班牙，分流客胜热度。

Zhuangjia youyi zai zao-re Xibanya, fenliu kesheng redu.

The bookies making Spanish hot on purpose, and diverting the temperature of the away teams.

These constructions can also co-occur with prepositions such as *ba, bei, ling*. They form the "*ba/bei/ling*+ nominal constituents+[V+A]"constructions respectively with disposal meanings. Examples are:

③ A) 实际上我还是奉劝大家不要<u>拉黑</u>我。

Shiji shang wo haishi fengquan dajia buyao la-hei wo.

Actually I still advise all of you not to block me.

B) 他们会<u>把</u>你<u>拉黑</u>。

Tamen hui ba ni la-hei.

They will block you.

④ A) 他以一记360度胯下扣篮<u>惊艳</u>全场。

Ta yi yiji 360du kuaxia koulan jing-yan quanchang.

He amazed the whole audience by using a 360-degree between-the-legs duck.

B) 事实就是这样<u>令人</u><u>惊艳</u>。

Shishi jiushi zheyang ling ren jing-yan.

The truth amazed people.

(2)Head-Modifier Constructions

The modifiers are V+A which modifying the nominal heads. According to the presence or absence of *de*, we have three types:

The first type: cannot modify the head with *de*

① 宝宝发烧不要注射<u>退热针</u>。

Baobao fashao bu yao zhushe tui-re zhen.

Babies who have fevers should not inject fever-reducing injections.

② 他连在这里面找片<u>止疼</u>片也找不出来。

Ta lian zai zhe limian zhao (yi)pian zhi-teng pian ye zhao bu chulai.

He even could not find out a pill of pain medicines inside.

The second type: have to modify the head with *de*

① 没人给她洗那些白色<u>不耐脏</u>的衣服了。

Mei ren gei ta xi naxie baise bu nai-zang de yifu le.

Nobody washes those white and not dirty-resistant cloths for her any more.

② 一直躺在地上<u>装死</u>的人突然爬了起来。

Yizhi tang zai dishang zhuang-si de ren turan pa le qilai.

The person who was playing-dead on the ground all the time suddenly got up.

The third type: modify the head either with *de* or without *de*

① A) 医生给他用过各种滴耳液、抗生素和<u>止疼</u>药。

Yisheng gei ta yongguo gezhong di-er-ye, kang-sheng-su he zhi-teng yao.

The doctor used many kinds of ear drops、antibiotics and pain medi-cines for him.

B) 莫老说那<u>些止疼</u>的药吃多了不好。

Molao shuo naxie zhi-teng de yao chi duo le bu hao.

The old Mr.Mo said it was bad to your health if you take too many of those pain medicines.

② A) 抢通部队已经组织专家商定<u>排险</u>方案。

Qiangtong budui yijing zuzhi zhuanjia shangding pai-xian fang'an.

Emergency teams have already organized experts to discuss the re-move-danger plans.

B) 消防官兵立即制定搜救<u>排险</u>的方案。

Xiaofang guanbing liji zhiding soujiu pai-xian de fang'an.

Fire fighters make a search-and-rescue and remove-danger plan immediately.

3.3   V+A+non-nominal Constituents

V+A can be followed by non-nominal constituents, such as adjectives, verbs, verb-object constructions. Examples are:

① 这些恶性的药品食品安全事件让人们陷入了一种无奈的"<u>审丑</u>疲劳"。

Zhexie e'xing de yaopin shipin anquan shijian rang renmen xianru le yi zhong wunai de shen-chou pilao.

All those pernicious cases of medicines and food security make people fell into a resigned exhausted of 'appreciate the ugly'.

② 大家只懂得水会<u>遇热</u>蒸腾，<u>遇冷</u>结冰。

Dajia zhi dongde shui hui yu-re zhengteng, yu-leng jiebing.

People only know that water transpires when it is heated, while freezes in the cold.

Some of these constructions usually have badly independence and occur in four-word types. For examples:

① 海面上的鲨鱼闻腥而至。

Haimian shang   de   shayu   wen-xing-er-zhi.

The shakes smelled the fishy then came to the surface.

② 一家三口团团围着子竹嘘寒问暖。

Yijia   sankou   tuantuan   weizhe   Zi Zhu   xu-han-wen-nuan.

Zi Zhu was surrounded by the whole three-people family and was given their thoughtful attention.

3.4   Opinions about the Three Distributions

(1)Some constructions usually without followed by objects, such as转暖 [*zhuan-nuan*], 发黏[*fa-nian*],嫌贵[*xian-gui*],趋稳[*qu-wen*](*tend to steady*),发胖[*pa-pang*].While some are similar with the verb-nominal object constructions which can be followed by nominal objects. Examples are: 为难 [*wei-nan*], 造热 [*zao-re*],惊艳 [*jing-yan*], 卖空 [*mai-kong*](*sell short of stocks*),拉黑[*la-hei*].We reach the conclusion that the combination degree of V and A is an important factor to affect the distributions.

Constructions as 嫌贵[*xian-gui*],趋稳[*qu-wen*] have low combination degree, we refer to these as phrases. Constructions as 造热[*zao-re*],惊艳[*jing-yan*] have high combination degree, we refer to these as words. The latter constructions are more like single words that result in the two elements' meanings fix together. Zhang(1999) argued that the majority verbs' essential property is followed by objects, the verb-object constructions followed by objects accelerate the process which equate with the monosyllable verbs, and gradually produce some syntactical properties which they do not have before. The trend of words made constructions like 造热[*zao-re*],惊艳[*jing-yan*] can be followed by objects, and can take 着[*zhe*],了[*le*] as tenses. Examples are: 拉黑了你 [*la-hei le ni*](*blocked you*), 裹杂着树叶[*guo-za zhe shuye*](*compounding leaves*).

(2)The formulations show that the majority of V+A can be modifiers. As modifiers, some modify without *de*, some have to with *de*, others both will do. Many factors work together result in these. Reasons we considered as followed:

① The properties of nominal constituents

The properties of nominal constituents have certain effect on the syntactic distributions of V+A constructions. Some nominal constituents need to adhere with other constituents, we refer to these as compounds. As a result they are modified without *de*. For examples: 止疼片 [*zhi-teng-pian*](*pain medicines*)/ 止疼的片 [*zhi-teng-de-pian*] (*pain-de-medicines*)*, 防碎层 [*fang-sui-ceng*](*shatter-proof layer*)/ 防碎的层 [*fang-sui-de-ceng*](*shatter-proof-de layer*)*,制热价[*zhi-re-jia*](*the heating price*)/制热的价[*zhi-re-de-jia*](*the heating-de-price*)*(*represents the examples are ungrammatical).

② The effect of V+A collocate with nominal constituents

V+A is limited to collocate with nominal constituents without *de*. When 装死 [*zhuang-si*](*play dead*),发红[*fa-hong*](*turn red*),发黄[*fa-huang*](*colored yellow*),耐脏 [*nai-zang*](*easy-to-clean*) with nominal constituents form head-modifier constituents 装死人[*zhuang-si ren*](*the person who plays dead*),发红手[*fa-hong shou*](*hands which turned red*),发黄报纸[*fa-huang baozhi*](*newspapers which colored yellow*),耐脏衣服[*nai-zang yifu*](*cloths which easy-to-clean*), *de* needs to insert into these constituents to make them grammatically and smoothly. These constituents also can transform to subject-predicate constituents. Examples are: 装死的人 [*zhuang-si de ren*]→这个人装死[*zhe ge ren zhuang-si*](*The person played dead*),耐脏的衣服 [*nai-zang de yifu*]→这件衣服耐脏[*zhe jian yifu nai-zang*](*These cloths are easy-to-clean*).Some constituents without *de* can also transform to subject-predicate constituents. Examples are: 止疼（的）药[*zhi-teng(de)yao*](*pain medicines*)→这种药止疼[*zhe zhong yao zhi-teng*](*This kind of medicines can release your pain*),耐旱（的）物种[*nai-han(de)wuzhong*](*drought-tolerant species*)→这种物种耐旱[*zhe zhong wuzhong nai-han*](*This kind of species can tolerant drought*).While some constituents without *de* cannot transform to subject-predicate constituents. Examples are: 排险（的）方案 [*pai-xian(de)fang'an*](*the plan of remove danger*)→这个方案排险 [*zhe ge fang'an pai-xian*](*The plan can remove danger*)*,吸湿（的）能力 [*xi-shi(de)nengli*](*the ability of absorb humidity*)→这种能力吸湿[*zhe zhong nengli xi-shi*](*This ability can absorb humidity*)*.

In subject-predicate constructions, predicates are statements for subjects. While in head-modifier constructions, modifiers modify heads. When subject-predicate constructions transform to head-modifier constructions, *de* as an symbol of syntactic relations aims to transform the declarative predicates into modifible modifiers. Examples are: 这个人装死[*zhe ge ren zhuang-si*].装死[*zhuang-si*] declares a situation of a person and it does not modify anything, so it needs *de* when transforms the predicate into a modifier. As a result it gains modification to modify the head. It has difference with 耐旱[*nai-han*],吸湿[*xi-shi*] in 耐旱物种[*nai-han wuzhong*],吸湿能力[*xi-shi nengli*].耐旱[*Nai-han*] is an essential property of species, so it can be a predicate and a modifier, its descriptive ability becomes stronger with *de*. Other examples like 防臭鞋垫[*fang-chou xiedian*](*anti-smelly insoles*),保暖内衣[*bao-nuan neiyi*] (*warm underwear*).While 吸湿[*xi-shi*] is not an essential property of ability. It is a limited modifier to the ability which aims to distinguish from other abilities. It emphasizes it is an ability of absorb humidity, not other abilities. So it cannot used as a predicate to declare the subject. Other examples are 制热功率[*zhi-re gonglv*](*the heating power*), 遇旱面积[*yu-han mianji*](*drought areas*).

(3)We have few examples of V+A followed by non-nominal constituents. There are varieties relationships between them: verbal in series relations, modification relations, coordination relations. It needs deeper explorations to this kind of constructions.

3.5   Distributions of a Special Kind of V+A Constructions

From the corpus we find a special kind of V+A constructions. Examples are: 打假 [*da-jia*](*anti-counterfeiting*),打黑[*da-hei*](*anti-crime*).The main difference with the above we have already discussed is A represent 'A+Nominal Constituents'. We refer to these as "the omitted V+A". There are 228 examples in the corpus. Examples are:

① 重庆打黑运动进行正酣。

Chong Qing da-hei yundong   jinxing zhenghan.

Anti-crime activities in Chong Qing are in full swing.

② 贵州茅台此次公布真酒投放量的目的是为了打假。

Gui Zhou Mao Tai cici gongbu zhen jiu toufangliang de mudi shi weile da-jia.

In an attempt to anti-counterfeiting, GuiZhou Mao Tai announced the amount of delivery of the real wines this time.

We consider two reasons about these:

(1)The omission of syllables

We can refer to double syllable coordinate constructions omitted as monosyllable constructions. Such as 尊老[*zun-lao*]——尊敬老人[*zunjing laoren*](*respect the elders*), 登高[*deng-gao*]——攀登高处[*pandeng gaochu*](*climb up higher places*),招新 [*zhao-xin*]——招收新人[*zhaoshou xinren*](*recruit freshmen*).

(2)The fixed meanings

The meanings of A+nominal constituents such as 老人[*lao-ren*](*the elders*), 高处 [*gao-chu*](*the higher places*), 新人[*xin-ren*](*freshmen*) are fixed, and A have a strong ability to modify things. As a result, A can represent things or phenomena whom have these properties. Besides all these constructions have high rate of utilization, they can express clear meanings without nominal constituents.

They have similar distributions with the normal constructions, for examples:

① 生源争夺战升级：高校掐尖，中学纷纷被"加冕"。

Shengyuan zhengduo zhan shengji: gaoxiao qia-jian, zhongxue fenfen bei "jiamian".

The fight for students upgrades: Universities fighting for good students, middle schools were 'crowned'.

② 他们什么药都可以作假。

Tamen shenme yao dou keyi zuo-jia.

They can fake every kind of medicines.

③ 他可能是个啃老族。

Ta keneng shi ge ken-lao zu.

Maybe he is a boomerang kid.

④ 这正是踏野的情趣所在。

Zhe zheng shi taye de qingqu suozai.

This exactly is the interesting of go wild.

⑤ A) 一旦商家出现售假的行为，就会受到严厉制裁。

Yidan shangjia chuxian shou-jia de xingwei, jiu hui shoudao yanli zhicai.

Once businesses sell fake things, then they will be punished strictly.

B) 坚决打击任何售假行为。

Jianjue daji renhe shou-jia xingwei.

Hitting any fake-selling activities firmly.

There are some special dependent constructions usually occur in four-word types when they are followed by non-nominal constituents. Examples are: 英雄救美 [*yingxiong-jiu-mei*](*the hero saved the beauty*),截长补短[*jie-chang-bu-duan*](*cut off from the long to support the deficiency of the short*).

Furthermore, there are many constructions as 吃脆皮[*chi-cuipi*](*eat crisp food*),建新厂 *[jian-xinchang]*(*build new factories*) .They are V+[A+nominal constituents],the nominal constituents cannot omit. This kind of constructions are left out in this study, so we consider these as ungrammatical constructions during the statistic progress and pay no attention to them.

4   A Special Type: Dependent V+A Constructions

There are some dependent V+A constructions in the corpus, they almost only occur in four-word types. Four-word type is a linguistic pattern which consists of four syllables. It have strong independence, so we can consider it as an independence language unit. Examples are: 英雄救美 [*yixiong jiu-mei*], 返璞归真 [*fanpu gui-zhen*](*recover one's original simplicity*). In this study, the V+A constructions which occur in four-word types have some syntactical properties as follows:

(1)Types: they belong to verb-object constructions.

(2)Functions: they can be predicates, and be modifiers with *de*.

(3)Forms of expression: many V and A in four-word types are synonyms and antonyms.

There are 176 V+A constructions in the web fiction corpus and 98 in the news corpus, the common constructions are 16. According to their internal structures, they can be divided into four types as in Table 2: subordination type, coordination type, verbs in series type, head-modifier type.

Table 2. The distributions of Non-independent V+A constructions in the corpus

Types	Numbers	Examples
Coordination	109	避实击虚[*bi-shi ji-xu*]*evade the enemy's main force and strike his week points* 惩贪罚恶[*cheng-tan fa-e*]*punish the greedy and the evil* 偕老带幼[*xie-lao dai-you*]*bring along the old and the young* 知冷知热[*zhi-leng zhi-re*]*give every care to someone*
Subordination	82	暗影浮香[*anying fu-xiang*]*faint fragrance and dappled shadows* 师直为壮[*shi-zhi wei zhuang*]*an army fighting for a just cause has high morale* 财不露白[*cai bu lou-bai*]*hide all one's money and valuables and do not show to others* 欣喜若狂[*xinxi ruo-kuang*]*be wild with joy*
Head-modifier	37	以旧换新[*Yi-jiu huan-xin*]*trade in the old for the new* 以小称大[*yi-xiao chen-da*]*substitue the small one for the big one* 以静制静[*yi-jing zhi-dong*]*replace still by still* 以善报恶[*yi-shan bao-e*]*return good for evil*
Verbs in Series	14	闻腥而至[*Wen-xing er zhi*]*come without delay upon smelling the fishy* 蓄水备旱[*xu shui bei-han*]*store water to prepare against drought* 静而生阴[*jing er sheng-yin*]*keep stilling then Yin exists* 拍手称快[*pai shou cheng-kuai*]*clap in high spirits*

Some V+A constructions can modify nominal constituents in four-word types which have to with *de*. Examples are:

① 我最讨厌那种嫌贫爱富的人。

Wo zui taoyan na zhong xian-pin ai-fu de ren.

The kind of people who despise the poor and curry favor with the rich are whom I hate the most.

② 卢展工来到了树木成荫的长水村。

Lu Zhangong lai dao le shumu cheng-yin de Chang Shui cun.

Lu Zhangong came to Chang Shui village where have many trees.

Some V+A constructions which occur in four-word types can use A represent things that have the same properties. For examples:

③ 这种舍易取难的做法令人费解。

Zhe zhong she-yi qu-nan de zuofa ling ren feijie.

The action of abandon easy to get hard is hard to be understood.

④   两支<u>披坚执锐</u>的军队缓缓逼近。

Liangzhi pi-jian zhi-rui de jundui huanhuan bijin.

Two well armed armies approached slowly.

V+A constructions in four-word types are hardly independent, many of them are inherited from ancient Chinese. The ancient Chinese have very explicitly expressions, so we can consider these four-word types as the inheritances from the ancient Chinese. These four-word types are usually used in the literature and formal occasions.

5   Conclusions

In this study, we use a large-scale corpus to discuss the syntactic distributions and reasons of V+A bound verb-object constructions. We find that many factors have important impacts on these, such as the combination degree of V and A, the properties of nominal constituents and the effect of V+A collocate with nominal elements. Then we discuss a special constructions as 打黑[*da-hei*] and some dependent constructions in four-word types.

Because of the limitation of the corpus and other reasons, there are still many questions which we pay no attention, such as the formulations of V+A followed by non-nominal constituents, the difference between V+A followed by nominal constituents and these followed by non-nominal constituents.

Furthermore, we need to make deeper discussions about the V+A constructions. For example, what are the limited factors that form V+A constructions? Are there some differences between V and A in the same types? What are the limited factors? All these questions need us to explore deeply.

Acknowledgements. This research was supported by the Fundamental Research Funds for the Central Universities, and the Research Funds of Beijing Language and Culture University (No.13YCX001).

References

1. Shuxiang, L.: First Exploration of single and double words in Mandarin. Studies of The Chinese Language, 1963(1). 吕叔湘.现代汉语单双音节问题初探.中国语文,1963(1) (in Chinese)
2. Shuxiang, L.: An Exploration of the Usage of Adjectives. Studies of The Chinese Language, 1965(6). 吕叔湘.形容词使用情况的一个考察.中国语文,1965(6) (in Chinese)
3. Shuxiang, L.: Formulate Grammar Questions in Mandarin, pp. 23–26, 40–53, 77–80. The Commercial Press (1979). 吕叔湘.汉语语法分析问题.商务印书馆,23-26,40-53,77-80(1979) (in Chinese)
4. Shuxiang, L.: Research on Monosyllabic Adjectives in Mandarin. Studies of The Chinese Language, 1982(1). 吕叔湘.单音形容词用法研究.中国语文,1982(1) (in Chinese)
5. Dexi, Z.: Research on Adjectives in Mandarin. Linguistic Research, 1956(1). 朱德熙.现代汉语形容词研究,1956(1) (in Chinese)

6. Dexi, Z.: Grammar Notes, pp. 110–124. The Commercial Press (1982). 朱德熙.语法讲义.商务印书馆,110-124(1982) (in Chinese)
7. Shenli, F.: Interactions Between Morphology, Syntax and Prosody in Chinese (Revised Edition). Perking University Press (2009). (in Chinese)
8. Shiwen, Y.: A Dictionary of Modern Chinese Grammar, 2nd edn. Tsinghua University Press (2003). 俞士汶等.现代汉语语法信息词典详解(第二版).清华大学出版社,2003 (in Chinese)
9. Huaide, Z.: Dictionary of Chinese Adjectives Usage. The Commercial Press (2010). 郑怀德等,汉语形容词用法词典,商务印书馆,2010 (in Chinese)
10. Cong, M.: Dictionary of Chinese Verbs Usage. The Commercial Press (2012). 孟琮等.汉语动词用法词典.商务印书馆,2012 (in Chinese)
11. Guoxian, Z.: The Selective Differences of Monosyllabic and Disyllabic Adjectives. Chinese Language Learning. 1996(3). 张国宪.单双音节形容词的选择性差异.汉语学习.1996(3) (in Chinese)
12. Qingzhu, M.: The Chinese Verb and Verbal Constructions, pp. 12–85. Peking University Press (2004). (in Chinese)
13. Linding, L.: The Chinese Verbs, pp. 151–170. Chinese Social Science Press (1990). 李临定.现代汉语动词.中国社会科学出版社,151-170(1990) (in Chinese)
14. Changrong, R.: Verb-Object Constructions Followed by Objects. Studies of The Chinese Language, 1984(6). 饶长溶动宾组合带宾语中国语文,1984(6) (in Chinese)
15. Gongwan, X.: A doubtful of sentence seems to be popularity -Verb-Object compounds +Objects. Language Planning, 1997(4). 邢公畹.一种似乎要流行开来的可疑句式—动宾式动词+宾语.语文建设,1997(4) (in Chinese)
16. Bo, Z.: Conditions and Development Tendencies of Verb-Object Constructions+ Objects. Research In Ancient Chinese, 1999(3). 张博.“动宾结构+宾语”的条件及发展趋势.古汉语研究,1999(3) (in Chinese)
17. Bingfu, L.: The Basic Function and Derived Function of "de" as are viewed from its distribution. Chinese Teaching in the World, 2003(1). (in Chinese)
18. Rui, G.: The Conversion of Expressional Functions and An Analysis of the Particle *de* in Mandarin Chinese. Contemporary Linguistics, 2000(2). (in Chinese)
19. Yangchun, X., Shuxin, Q.: On the Identity of the Pragmatic Function of the Particle *de*. Chinese Teaching in the World, 2005(3). (in Chinese)

Semantic Analysis of "V+死+人" Structure

Yong Lu and Pengyuan Liu[✉]

Institute of Applied Linguistics, Beijing Language and Culture University,
Beijing 100083, China
ly_yonglu@163.com, liupengyuan@pku.edu.cn

Abstract. In this paper, we found that some Examples of language which represent the structure (This paper explores the structure "V+死+人" while "死" and Monosyllable verbs collocate, and combined into verb-complement structure to collocate with "人" phrase structure.) of "V+死+人" (The"V"in this paper just refer to monosyllable verb.) can express the meaning of "the loss of life or death", which is meaning (a); some can express the meaning of "to reach the pole", which is meaning (b); some can both express (a) and (b). Based on the large-scale corpus for obtaining language examples, this paper obtained the total of 112 monosyllable verbs which can enter the structure of "V+死+人". In this paper, we believe that the structure will express (a) if the semantic orientation point to "人", and will express (b) if the semantic orientation point to "V"; but characteristics of "V" is the fundamental reason causing the structure of different semantics. Specifically, in the structure of "V+死+人" which expresses (a), the semantic features of "V" is [+damage, +strong action, +death]; in the structure of "V+死+人" which expresses (b), the semantic features of "V" is [+psychology, +quantity, +feelings, -death] or [-psychology, +quantity, +feelings, -death]; in the structure of "V+死+人"which can both express (a) and (b), the semantic features of "V" is [+physiological, feelings, +quantity, ±death].

Keywords: The structure of "V+死+人" · Semantic orientation · Semantic feature · Semantic analysis · Monosyllable verbs

1   Introduction

The following examples apply to the structure of "V+死+人".

(1) 踩死人 [cǎi sǐ rén]   (death of treading)
(2) 愁死人 [chóu sǐ rén]   (death of worrying)
(3) 饿死人 [è sǐ rén]   (death of starving)

Those three examples are of the same architecture, in which the word-sequence are "V+死+人" (V+death+people).

© Springer International Publishing Switzerland 2015
Q. Lu and H.H. Gao (Eds.): CLSW 2015, LNAI 9332, pp. 684–700, 2015.
DOI: 10.1007/978-3-319-27194-1_67

Making an Immediate Constituent Analysis, and the segmentation and qualitative are the same. Please see the following examples:

(1) 踩　　　死　　　人　　[cǎi sǐ rén]

(2) 愁　　　死　　　人　　[chóu sǐ rén]

(3) 冻　　　死　　　人[1]　[è sǐ rén]

　　1　　　　　　2　　1—2动宾(verb-object construction)

　　　3　　4　　3—4动补(verb-complement construction)

However, we found "死" are of different meaning as the sentence constituent in the structure. In example (1), "死" is a verb functioned as result complement; in example (2), "死" is a degree adverb as degree complement; in example (3), the"死" not only acts as result complement but also degree complement. In other words,the parts of speech are uncertain.when "死" acts as a result complement, it is a verb. when as a degree complement, it is a degree adverb. In addition, the semantics which they express are not the same. Example (1) expresses the meaning of "the loss of life or death" (a). Example (2) expresses the meaning of "to reach the pole"(b).And example (3) sometimes express (a). For instance[2]:

(4) 沿途都是原始森林，来往的群众只好住岩洞、宿草丛，常常发生冻死人的事故。

[yán tú dōu shì yuán shǐ sēn lín, lái wǎng de qún zhòng zhī hǎo zhù yán dòng、xiǔ cǎo cóng, cháng cháng fā shēng dòng sǐ rén de shì gù。]

somctimes express (b). For instance:

(5) 丽鹃现在关心的是晚上怎么睡的问题，四月的天还正冷着，没个被子要冻死人的。

[lì juān xiàn zài guān xīn de shì wǎn shàng zěn me shuì de wèn tí, sì yuè de tiān hái zhèng lěng zhe, méi gè bèi zǐ yào dòng sǐ rén de。]

---

[1] In modern Chinese part of the Monosyllable verbs can be part of "V+死+人"Constructions, such as "扮 (make up), 抬 (carry) ,埋 (buried) , 有 (there) "and so on, when they exist in the Constructions, the first layer structure is verb object structure, but when "死" and "人" combined into "死人", and after that combined with Monosyllable verbs to have a verb object structure. In this paper we are discussing "V+死+人" Constructions when "V" and"人" combined as verb-complement pattern and after that combined with "人" to have a verb object structure. Therefore, the former researchers did not write about this before.

[2] The corpus of this paper coming from the Beijing university modern Chinese corpus (CCL) and Beijing language and culture university modern Chinese corpus (BCC), in this paper we calculate data from Beijing university modern Chinese corpus (CCL) (about 580 million words) and Beijing language and culture university modern Chinese corpus (BCC) (about 5.5 billion words from literature, newspaper part), putting in the consideration the two corpora features ,respective characteristics and effect etc, on the data statistics, we first used Beijing university modern Chinese corpus (CCL) and in case of CCL corpus retrieval is less than Beijing language and culture university modern Chinese corpus (BCC), we turned to calculate BCC corpus data. For corpus sources using, we are first using CCL corpus examples, and secondly using BCC corpus examples, the above method, the author consider that, no matter in quantity, or in terms of quality, has quite a degree of credibility. In addition, in order to save space and style description, this paper does not indicate the source.

The format of example(1) to (3) are the same, which is the same as inner hierarchical structure.But why some express (a), some express (b), and some both express (a) and (b)？ What is the determinant factor that causes those different situation？ That is what exactly this essay has to study. Based on the linguistic data, we obtain information of linguistic cases for the start.

We adopt Zhang Xiaojing(2009)'s research results[3], checking individually with 1691 monosyllable verbs which she put forward, of which the number of "V" according with the format of "V+死+人"this essay studies is 112, accounting for about 6%. Extracting the Chinese Corpus BLCU and Center for Chinese Linguistics PKU, which contain the 112 "V" legal illustrative sentences, we found 1661 cases. Make a distinction of all the 1661 cases to express (a), (b) and both (a) and (b) in brain work, and see the appendix for details. In this issue, all the research based on analysis of these cases.

2   The Semantic Orientation[4] of "死"

Semantic orientation refers to the particular parts of the sentence, which has a semantic relationship between components. In other words, it means a certain part of the sentence is most directly related with some components in semantic meaning.

We consider the semantic orientation of "死" in the format of "V+死+人" determines when express (a),when express (b) and when express both.

There are three situations in the semantic orientation of "死"in the structure of "V+死+人":

(1)   The semantic meaning of "死" aims at "人", which express the meaning of "the loss of life or death"(a), showing as the follows:

"V" is limited to "踩、撞₁、淹₁、捅₁、砸、戳₁₁、打¹₃、轧¹₁、拍₁、掐₁、摔₃、踢、烧₁、劈₁、刺₁、蛰₁₍zhē₎、杀₁、炸₁、捏₁、砍¹₁、医₃、治₄、咬₁、喝¹₂、射₁、勒、捶、敲₁".For instance:

踩死人(*death of treading*)   撞死人(*death of bumping*)   淹死人(*death of flooding*)
捅死人(*death of poking*)   砸死人(*death of smashing*)   戳死人(*death of prickling*)
打死人(*death of hitting*)   轧死人(*death of rolling*)   砍死人(*death of chopping*)

---

[3] Zhang Xiaojing in her master's thesis (the studies of modern Chinese monosyllabic verbs) calculate the mono verbs inside the version (5) of "modern Chinese dictionary",and the result she get was 1691 monosyllabic verb, 3244 meanings, according to the meaning she divided the modern Chinese Monosyllable verbs into the eight following categories: action verbs, psychological verb, force-border verb, existential verbs, judgment verbs, the form of a verb, modal verb, directional verb. so this paper considering that even if Zhang Xiaojing master's thesis results have high credibility but still having widely, excellence problems, so when this paper calculate Monosyllable verb which Zhang Xiaojing already classified them by meaning, the author get 112 Monosyllable verb and 120 meanings.

[4] For the "semantic" in this thesis, please see Lu Jianming(2005).

(2) The semantic meaning of "死" points to "V" itself, which expresses the meaning of "to reach the pole" (b). "V" consists of two kinds of verbs, One is "烦[3]、急[2]、愁[1]、恼[3]、恨[1]、爱[1]、迷[4]、笑[2]、羞[1][1]、疼[2]、怨[2]、想[4]、醉[2]", and the other kind is "写[1(xiě)]、坑[4]、丢·逗[1][3]、腻[2]、吵[2]、赶[2]、哄[1]、唬[1<吓>]、唱[1]、吐[1]、噎[3]《方》、绕[4]、催[1]、粘（黏）、馋[3]、磨[4]、数[1 (shǔ)]、赚[1]、卡[2]、颠[2][1]、缠[2]、抄[1][2]、哭、拖[4]、等[2][1]、逛"etc. For instance:

烦死人(*death of bothering*)   愁死人(*death of worrying*)   恨死人(*death of hating*)

迷死人(*death of fascinating*) 笑死人(*death of smiling*)   羞死人(*death of shyness*)

吵死人(*death of quarrel*)   写死人(*death of writing*)   催死人(*death of urging*)

(3) The semantic meaning of "死" both aims at "人" and points to "V" itself, which also expresses the meaning of "the loss of life or death"(a) and the meaning of "to reach the pole" (b)."V"is limited to "饿、冻[3]、挤[1]、憋[1]、扎[1]、电[3]、撑、气[9]、熏[1]、压[1]、骂[1]、晒[1][1]、烫[1]、烤[1]、辣[2]、磨[3]、逼[1]、累[2]、骗[1][1]、呛、玩、走[1]、跑[1]、整[6<方>]、搞[1]、冰[2]、淋[1]、噎[1]"etc.For instance:

饿死人(*death of starving*)   冻死人(*death of freezing*)   挤死人(*death of crushing*)

气死人(*death of getting angry*)   扎死人(*death of pricking*)   吓死人(*death of frightening*)

气死人(*death of getting angry*)   憋死人(*death of smothering*)   压死人(*death of suppressing*)

Thus it can be seen that the structure of "V+死+人" express (a)、(b), or both (a) and (b), related with the semantic orientation of result complement "死". To be specific, when "死" points to "人", "V+死+人" expresses (a); when "死" points to "V" itself, it expresses (b); when "死" both points to the two, it has two ambiguous meanings—(a) and (b).

Therefore, the reason which explains the ambiguity of the "V+死+人" structure lies in the understanding which is directly concerned with the semantic orientation of "死". Whereas the new question that arises why the examples are of the structure "V+死+人", but sometimes "死" in semantic meaning points to "V", sometimes to "人", while sometimes to the both. This issue spurs us to continue further analysis.

3   Semantic Features of "V"

What we found the different meanings of semantic orientation of "死" are much concerned with the structure of "V", specifically different meanings in the semantic orientation of "死" is radically determined by the semantic feature of structure "V" in the key position.

（一）Analysis of the verb in "V+死+人"structure which expresses (a)

After an investigation, we found an interesting phenomenon in the format of "V+死+人" which expresses (a), and it must be understood according to the context.Here are some examples:

① 李园喝斥起来："你们这些狗奴才，本相要你们不要做伤害百姓的事，你们倒好，居然在大街上**踩死人**，不杀你们不足以平民愤。"

[*lǐ yuán hē chì qǐ lái : "nǐ men zhè xiē gǒu nú cái, běn xiàng yào nǐ men bú yào zuò shāng hài bǎi xìng de shì, nǐ men dǎo hǎo, jū rán zài dà jiē shàng cǎi sǐ rén, bú shā nǐ men bú zú yǐ píng mín fèn。"*]

②再挤下去可要**踩死人**了，萧峰当下喊道："众位莫要挤，听我一言！"

[*zài jǐ xià qù kě yào cǎi sǐ rén le, xiāo fēng dāng xià hǎn dào : "zhòng wèi mò yào jǐ, tīng wǒ yī yán ! "*]

Though the same as "踩死人", in example①, which means we got the final result, expressing the meaning of "loss the life or death"; in example②, which means the result hasn't been shown, but if continues it may happen, which express a speculation. It is thus clear though to express the fact of "死(the loss of life or death)" , still due to the different context, the focus on expressing has certain discrepancy, which depend on the specific linguistic context. However, no matter to express the Present Perfect Tense or the Future Perfect Tense, both belongs to "have done". And most importantly, the two are to express the fact of "the lose of life or death", both acting as the result complement, and can be attributed to the same category. So we gather them into the meaning(a) and set another examples:

③当桑塔纳第二次撞向孙亚东时，孙亚东夫人才如梦初醒，疯狂地扑向行人稀少的大街，嘶声呼喊："救命啊！**撞死人**了……"

[*dāng sāng tǎ nà dì èr cì zhuàng xiàng sūn yà dōng shí, sūn yà dōng fū rén cái rú mèng chū xǐng, fēng kuáng dì pū xiàng háng rén xī shǎo de dà jiē, sī shēng hū hǎn : "jiù mìng ā ! zhuàng sǐ rén le ……"*]

④看到事故发生经过的群众说：大货车肇事后，司机将车停了下来，发现**撞死人**后赶紧逃逸。

[*kàn dào shì gù fā shēng jīng guò de qún zhòng shuō : dà huò chē zhào shì hòu, sī jī jiāng chē tíng le xià lái, fā xiàn zhuàng sǐ rén hòu gǎn jǐn táo yì。*]

⑤夏日游泳好，但要注意安全。以往在江河和游泳池中曾出现过**淹死人**事故。

[*xià rì yóu yǒng hǎo, dàn yào zhù yì ān quán。yǐ wǎng zài jiāng hé hé yóu yǒng chí zhōng céng chū xiàn guò yān sǐ rén shì gù。*]

⑥"姑娘呵！不要怕我，不要跳，—海水是会**淹死人**的。"

[*"gū niáng hē ! bú yào pà wǒ, bú yào tiào, —hǎi shuǐ shì huì yān sǐ rén de。*]

⑦在江干区用刀**捅死人**的重大案犯吴建明被干警抓获。

[*zài jiāng gàn qū yòng dāo tǒng sǐ rén de zhòng dà àn fàn wú jiàn míng bèi gàn jǐng zhuā huò。*]

⑧李勒手里木棍高高举起，笑道："信不信，木头棒子也能**捅死人**！"

[*lǐ lè shǒu lǐ mù gùn gāo gāo jǔ qǐ, xiào dào : "xìn bú xìn, mù tóu bàng zǐ yě néng tǒng sǐ rén !*]

⑨这时楼下有人向案犯吆喝："别砸了，要**砸死人**的！"

[*zhè shí lóu xià yǒu rén xiàng àn fàn yāo hē : "bié zá le , yào zá sǐ rén de ! "*]

⑩去年湖南有一个地区已出现危房倒塌**砸死人**的事。

⑩[*qù nián hú nán yǒu yī gè dì qū yǐ chū xiàn wēi fáng dǎo tā zá sǐ rén de shì。*]

We use 《Modern Chinese Dictionary<the sixth version>》[5] (《Dictionary》 for short in the following) to find the corresponding meanings in the situation:

踩：[动]脚底接触地面或物体；脚底在物体上向下用力

Tread:[verb]the feet hit the ground or objects;the feet have power downward the objects

撞₁：[动]运动着的物体跟别的物体猛然碰上

Bump:[verb]the moving object dashes against other objects all of a sudden

淹₁：[动]淹没；（大水）漫过；盖上　Flood:[verb]submerge;(water)submerge;rise above

捅₁：[动]戳；扎　　　　　　　　　　　Poke:[verb]prickle;prick

砸₁：[动]用沉重的东西对准物体撞击；沉重的东西落在物体上

Smash:[verb]take heavy objects to bump against other objects;heavy objects fall down the objects

Since "死" expresses "the loss of life or death" (a), V in the structure of "V+死+人" has a strong sense of causing death, in most cases expressing the meaning of "destroy、damage、disappear", and the similar verbs such as "戳₁(poke)、打¹₃(beat)、轧¹₁(roll)、拍₁(slap)、掐₁(clutch)、摔₃(throw)、踢(kick)、烧₁(burn)、噎₁(choke)、劈₁(chop)、刺₁(sting)、蜇₁(zhē)、杀₁(kill)、炸₁(bomb)、捏₁(pinch)、砍¹₁(cut)、医₃(cure)、治₄(cure)、咬₁(bite)、喝¹₂(drink)、射₁(shot)、勒(tighten)、捶(thump)、敲₁(strike)"etc.

It was found that those verbs express the results of death caused by the very actions, in which monosyllable verb in the structure of "V+死+人" which express (a) has the semantic feature of [+destroy,+strong action,+death]. Thus, we classify those verbs of such semantic features into I verbs.

The semantic feature of I verbs is described as [+破坏，+动作强，+致死]([+destroy,+strong action,+death])

（二）、Analysis of the verb in "V+死+人"structure which expresses (b)

The structure of "V+死+人" which expresses (b) is the highest degree verb-complement structure, implying "to reach the pole". Therefore we assume that verbs combined with "死" have certain semantic features.

---

[5] In version sixth of (modern Chinese dictionary) published by the commercial press in 2012 which is editing by the dictionary editing office of language institute in Chinese academy of social sciences.

Note: "撞1" has"撞" as the first verb meanings, the rest by analogy.

And the mark <口> as spoken language mark, such as "整6<方>";

The mark <方> means dialects, such as "整6<方>".

"砍11" is the first verb meanings of"砍1", number 1 on the right is to distinguish words when "砍" has the same sound and meaning, and "砍1" is the first, the rest by analogy.

Some lingual examples are as follows:

①在电话普及率不高的当时，装部电话简直烦死人，有时还会伤了邻里和气。

[*zài diàn huà pǔ jí lǜ bú gāo de dāng shí, zhuāng bù diàn huà jiǎn zhí fán sǐ rén, yǒu shí hái huì shāng le lín lǐ hé qì。*]

②他办公室响起了一阵急促的敲门声，进来的是机动处长袁桂生，张口就说："老宋，你说4号高炉移位大修这项工程搞不搞，拖了这么长的日子，急死人哩！"

[*tā bàn gōng shì xiǎng qǐ le yī zhèn jí cù de qiāo mén shēng, jìn lái de shì jī dòng chù zhǎng yuán guì shēng, zhāng kǒu jiù shuō："lǎo sòng, nǐ shuō 4hào gāo lú yí wèi dà xiū zhè xiàng gōng chéng gǎo bú gǎo, tuō le zhè me zhǎng de rì zǐ, jí sǐ rén lǐ！"*]

③她发现厂里进来一辆标有对外贸易公司的卡车，上面还有进口化肥，就问："你们还有外贸生意呀！"厂长一摆手说："别提了，从境外进口了800多吨散装化肥硬是推不出去，愁死人了！"

[*tā fā xiàn chǎng lǐ jìn lái yī liàng biāo yǒu duì wài mào yì gōng sī de kǎ chē, shàng miàn hái yǒu jìn kǒu huà féi, jiù wèn："nǐ men hái yǒu wài mào shēng yì ya！"chǎng zhǎng yī bǎi shǒu shuō："bié tí le, cóng jìng wài jìn kǒu le 800duō dūn sàn zhuāng huà féi yìng shì tuī bú chū qù, chóu sǐ rén le！"*]

④曹千里已经被狗咬过两次了，两次都破了口子，真恨死人！

[*cáo qiān lǐ yǐ jīng bèi gǒu yǎo guò liǎng cì le, liǎng cì dōu pò le kǒu zǐ, zhēn hèn sǐ rén！*]

⑤王二嫂要了来给我，我拿回家看了好一会，真爱死人咧，只那凤凰尾巴就用了四十多样线。

[*wáng èr sǎo yào le lái gěi wǒ, wǒ ná huí jiā kàn le hǎo yī huì, zhēn ài sǐ rén liě, zhī nà fèng huáng wěi bā jiù yòng le sì shí duō yàng xiàn。*]

⑥札夫拿说，"我看对我们也没有用处，就像那些基克斯人的机器之神，简直笑死人了。"

[*zhá fū ná shuō, "wǒ kàn duì wǒ men yě méi yǒu yòng chù, jiù xiàng nà xiē jī kè sī rén de jī qì zhī shén, jiǎn zhí xiào sǐ rén le。"*]

⑦"请你不要再提那件事……羞死人了！"妙子羞愧难当，将头顶在了有田的肩膀上.

[*"qǐng nǐ bú yào zài tí nà jiàn shì ……xiū sǐ rén le！"miào zǐ xiū kuì nán dāng, jiāng tóu dǐng zài le yǒu tián de jiān bǎng shàng。*]

⑧十几页路基路面设计计算，5编实训报告书，写死人了。

[*shí jǐ yè lù jī lù miàn shè jì jì suàn, 5biān shí xùn bào gào shū, xiě sǐ rén le。*]

⑨"真是的，什么妇救会青妇队的，看看吧！男女混在一起，这不出事啦？俺的闺女可不能这样啊！哼，这还是干部领头干的呢！丢死人啦……"

[*"zhēn shì de, shí me fù jiù huì qīng fù duì de, kàn kàn ba！nán nǚ hún zài yī qǐ, zhè bú chū shì lā？ǎn de guī nǚ kě bú néng zhè yàng ā！hēng, zhè hái shì gàn bù lǐng tóu gàn de ne！diū sǐ rén lā ……"*]

⑩材料组长说：“不清楚的地方标标清就行了，不一定都要重抄，都重抄，不要抄死人么！”

[*cái liào zǔ zhǎng shuō ： "bú qīng chǔ de dì fāng biāo biāo qīng jiù háng le, bú yī dìng dōu yào zhòng chāo, dōu zhòng chāo, bú yào chāo sǐ rén me！"*]

In the same way, we use 《Dictionary》 to make examples for the meanings of the above verbs:

烦₃：[动]使厌烦   Bother:[verb]make somebody feel bored
急₂：[动]使着急   Hurry:[verb]make somebody feel anxious
愁₁：[动]忧虑   Worry:[verb]make somebody feel concerned
恨₁：[动]仇视；怨恨   Hate:[verb]look upon with hatred;be hostile to
爱₂：[动]喜欢   Love:[verb]like
笑₂：[动]讥笑   Smile:[verb]ridicule
羞¹₁：[动]使难为情   Shy:[verb]make somebody feel embarrassed
写₁(xiě)：[动]用笔在纸上或其他东西上作字
Write::[verb]make words on the paper or other things by pens
丢：[动]丢脸   Shame:[verb]lose face
抄¹₂：[动]照着别人的作品、作业等写下来当作自己的
Copy: [verb]write other people's works down as one's owns

The similar verb also includes "恼₃、怨₂、醉₂、疼₂、想₄、迷₄、逗¹₃、数₁(shǔ)、哭、坑₄、腻₂、吵₂、赶₂、哄₁、唬₁<口>、唱₁、困₁、困₄、吐₁、绕₄、催₁、粘（黏）、读₁、读₃、馋₃、赚₁、卡₂、颠²₁、缠₂、拖₄、等²₁、逛" etc.

As what can be seen though those verbs may meet the structure of "V+死+人", still each of them are different, and now can be rearranged like:

Class II verbs A：烦₃、急₂、愁₁、恼₃、恨₁、爱₂、迷₄、笑₂、羞¹₁、疼₂、怨₁、想₄、醉₂

Class II verbs B：写₁(xiě)、数₁(shǔ)、丢、逗¹₃、抄¹₂、哭、骂₂、坑₄、腻₂、吵₂、赶₂、哄₁、唬₁<口>、唱₁、困₁、困₄、吐₁、噎₃《方》、绕₄、催₁、粘（黏）、读₁、读₃、馋₃、赚₁、卡₂、颠²₁、缠₂、拖₄、等²₁、逛。

Those verbs are sorted into two category, one is "Class II verb A", which are found mostly of the emotional psychological verbs to express some kinds of "dissatisfy、displeasure、disgust"(不满意、不愉快、反感), of which the reason is related to "死". "死" for its literal meaning is the end of life, which is the life movement that everything in the world must go through. While "死" means separate and disappear so to add up semantic features of positive meaning which humans are not willing to accept after all. In the process of grammaticalization, after which "死" of the degree of the part of speech has changed, but the positive meaning has not totally been erased from people psychology yet, implying derogatory sense, thus "死"in use is with negative meaning. Which is to say the semantic feature of "死" after grammaticalization is closely related with the feature of source term "死". In this sense, all those implying degree psychological verbs can be quantified, in which "死"after grammaticalization expresses degree that owns the semantic meaning of [+quantity]. Two kinds of "死" has semantic interface and are compatible in semantic meaning. Thus the semantic features of "Class II verbs A" is can be described as follows:

Class II verbs A: [+心理，＋量，＋感情，-致死] *([+psychology[6],+quantity, +feelings,-death])*

The others are marked as "Class II verb B". We found that the "II verb B"are somewhat similar to " I verb", some of which are describing actions, but they are different between each other. From the cases above, we can see that "死"in the sentences actually won't cause the result of "the loss of life or death" due to " defraud, lose, copy, write, urge", which is just a means of hyperbole to express the depth of "defraud、urge、write". It is a subjective feeling of adaptive agent's reaction to certain behaviors, which means "dissatisfy、displeasure、disgust" in most of the time. So this kind of verbs added up with semantic features of subjective feelings are being parts of the structure, and the whole structure is the verb-complement structure expressing polarity degree, of which monosyllable verbs are distinctly different with the monosyllable verbs in the expressing (a) structure. Next, "死" to express the degree has the semantic feature of [+quantity], therefore those verbs matched with "死"is absolutely has the same feature. So the semantic features of "II verb B"can be described as:

Class II verbs B: [-心理，＋量，＋感情，-致死]*([-mental,+quantity,+emotional,-death])*

It is clear that though two kinds of verbs can be put into the (b) structure of "V+死+人", still they are not the same.

In addition, according to the corpus the we searched, after becoming a part of the structure of "V+死+人", the class II verbs A and class II verbs B can both express the (b) meaning "to reach the pole". But there is a special phenomenon that in the context of "V+死+人, do not pay with life/ not a crime", like "never to die to coax someone"、"never to die to urgent someone",in which "die"truly means "the loss of life or death". Why is this phenomenon still existed? Is this kind of monosyllable verbs in "V+死+人" format really expressing (a) meaning? Actually not. The author further

---

[6] Here we used the results of Wen Yali (2007) research, in her doctoral thesis (studies of modern Chinese psychological verbs) she divided the psychological verbs into three categories: psychological activity verb (psychological activities [+]), mental state verb (psychological state) [+]) and psychological causatives (psychological causatives[+]). From 1691 Monosyllable verb retrieval can insert the Monosyllable verb of "V+死+人" Constructions, found that there are 13 psychological verbs semantic orientation, including "愁[1]、恼[3]、想[4]、爱[2]、疼[2]、恨[1]、怨[1]、醉[2]" all belongs to the mental state verb; "烦[3]、急[2]、迷[4]、羞[1][1]、想[4]、愁[1]、恨[1]" belongs to the psychological causatives, but did not belong to psychological activity verb, in order to the study t convenient, we did not add any distinctionmark, also not careful inquiry, we just only unified the 13 psychological verb semantic characteristics of the as [+psychological], and compared it with other verbs.

searched the language examples of the class I verbs, found very few sentence of the structure "V+死+人", do not pay with life/ not a crime". The reason is because class I verbs will truly cause people death, while this results is illegal in terms of law, or pay with life in the view of dated concept.It obviously to find that "I verbs+death+people" in the specific context is not matched with "do not pay with life/not a crime". Therefore we knew before class II verbs II A and the verb class B becoming parts of "V+死+人"expressing (a) meaning is not caused by the monosyllable verb in the structure, but by the context of "do not pay with life", because that just expresses (a) "the loss of life or death", so to cause the "death"in the structure expressing "the loss of life".

From the perspective of cognitive linguistics, it is believed that the class II verbs A and class II verbs B will not cause deaths, and people tend to match their feelings to those specific expressions achieve their inner intention. Therefore , we assume that such expressions like "never to die to pit"、 "never to die to bore", those "die"acting as result complement actually are not caused by the monosyllable verb in the structure, but by the element in the match of "do not pay with life/ not a crime", so this kind of linguistic examples are left out.

（三）Analysis of the monosyllable verbs expressing both (a) and (b) meanings in the format of "V+死+人".

It has been discovered that there is another kind of monosyllable verbs being part of "V+死+人" express two meanings, but when to express (a) and (b) depend on the context. For instance:

①1960年中国大陆主要是瞎指挥和贪大喜功、虚报产量，于是出现了特大饥荒，到处**饿死人**。

[*1960nián zhōng guó dà lù zhǔ yào shì xiā zhǐ huī hé tān dà xǐ gōng、xū bào chǎn liàng, yú shì chū xiàn le tè dà jī huāng, dào chù è sǐ rén。*]

②我咳嗽一声，拿筷子敲桌子："怎么还不见上菜啊！要**饿死人**。"

[*wǒ ké sòu yī shēng, ná kuài zǐ qiāo zhuō zǐ : "zěn me hái bú jiàn shàng cài ā ! yào è sǐ rén。"*]

Both are "饿死人", the "死" in example① means "the loss of life or death", that is meaning(a); the "死" in example② means "to reach the pole", that is meaning (b). For instance:

③可进场就得出示请帖，我可没弄着。不过，我幸亏没去，去了也是**挤死人**，什么也瞧不见。

[*kě jìn chǎng jiù dé chū shì qǐng tiē, wǒ kě méi nòng zhe。bú guò, wǒ xìng kuī méi qù, qù le yě shì jǐ sǐ rén, shí me yě qiáo bú jiàn*]

④为了稳定局势，政府只好颁布法令，以赋税收入为担保，发行新的货币，并回收旧的货币。但群众仍旧将信将疑，挤兑时**挤死人**的现象时有发生。如1720年7月17日就有15个人被挤死。

[*wéi le wěn dìng jú shì, zhèng fǔ zhī hǎo bān bù fǎ lìng, yǐ fù shuì shōu rù wéi dān bǎo, fā háng xīn de huò bì, bìng huí shōu jiù de huò bì。dàn qún zhòng réng jiù jiāng xìn jiāng yí, jǐ duì shí jǐ sǐ rén de xiàn xiàng shí yǒu fā shēng。rú 1720nián 7yuè 17rì jiù yǒu 15gè rén bèi jǐ sǐ。*]

⑤司机猛踩了一下刹车，希望利用惯性将歹徒摔倒，乘客乘机将其制服。谁知一车人一动不动，歹徒打开车门后仓皇而逃。这时才有乘客喊扎死人了。司机扭头发现一名乘客倒在血泊中。

[*sī jī měng cǎi le yī xià shā chē， xī wàng lì yòng guàn xìng jiāng dǎi tú shuāi dǎo, chéng kè chéng jī jiāng qí zhì fú。 shuí zhī yī chē rén yī dòng bú dòng， dǎi tú dǎ kāi chē mén hòu cāng huáng ér táo。 zhè shí cái yǒu chéng kè hǎn zhā sǐ rén le。 sī jī niǔ tóu fā xiàn yī míng chéng kè dǎo zài xuè bó zhōng。*]

⑥"你把胡子剃了，扎死人咧。""不剃！就留了来扎你！"

[*"nǐ bǎ hú zǐ tì le， zhā sǐ rén liě。""bú tì！jiù liú le lái zhā nǐ！"*]

In the same way, we use 《Dictionary》 to make examples for meanings of some verbs:

饿₂：[动]使挨饿   Starve:[verb]make somebody be angry
冻₃：[动]受冷或感到冷   Freeze:[verb]feel cold
挤₁：[动]（许多人或物）紧紧靠拢在一起；   Crush:[verb](many people or things) gather
扎₁：[动]刺   Prick:[verb]poke
电₃：[动]触电   Electric:[verb]get an electric shock
撑₅：[动]充满到容不下的程度   Overeat:[verb]can't hold any more
气₉：[动]生气，发怒   Get angry:[verb]be furious

The similar verb also includes "压₁、憋₁、晒¹₁、烫₁、烤₁、辣₂、醉₁、累₂、骗¹₁、呛、玩·走₁、跑₁、整₆<方>、搞₁、冰₂、淋₁、熏₁、噎₁"etc.

We found out that verbs expressing both (a) and (b) meanings in most cases are "physiological condition, physiological feelings" verbs, such as "饿(*starve*)、冻(*freeze*)、憋(*suffocate*)、电(*get an electric shock*)、熏₁(*smoke*)、晒¹₁(*bask*)、烫₁(*burn*)、烤₁(*bake*)、醉₁(*drunk*)、累₂(*tire*)、呛(*irritate*)、冰₂(*feel cold*)、噎(*choke*)" and so on. Those verbs reflects the abnormal situations of physical conditions caused by disturbances of certain factors, like "冻(*freeze*)" is caused by because of the low temperature that makes bodies in a low temperature environment; "熏₁(*smoke*)" that makes physiological abnormalities due to the "smoke、gas and others" hits the respiratory track; "烫₁(*burn*)" that makes physical damage caused by high temperature of the liquid that directly touch people or the surface of objects; "电(*get an electric shock*)"means charged objects come into contact with electrical conductors (people、animals or others) that caused damages; "呛(*irritate*)"refers an irritant gas into the respiratory organs and feel uncomfortable; "噎(*choke*)"means food blocked esophagus or because of the wind, the smoke choking like breathing difficulty.

In addition, some monosyllabic verbs though they themselves do not represent physiological conditions, still they represent the behavior of the actions that will cause physiological changes in the body, for example, "跑₁(*run*)"refers to two legs or four moves fast forward(feet can rise high in the air). Seeing meanings in isolation that do not seem to be able to figure out "run"may cause body injury or abnormal state, but when matched with "death"(the loss of life or death), which inevitably gets "死(*death*)"in negative sense, because the very behavior "run"causes physiological changes on human body can withstand that exceed the limit, so to result in a sudden physiological conditions or even death in the process of running.those kinds of verbs are " 走$_1$(walk)、挤(crowd)、撑(fill to the point of bursting)、压$_1$(press)、淋 1(drench)"as well. Clearly, [+physiological] is a common semantic feature of such kind of verbs.

Meanwhile, a further study has found that when treating these verbs in isolation, they themselves seem like of no degree, but the specific action always presents a certain property, and it is these different attributes presented that matters, which means these verbs implying degree meaning, so they are attached with the semantic features of [+quantity], but "死(dead)" is a polarity degree adverb which express the meaning of"to reach the pole", and conduct an operation of the verbs indicating a process of change, and performance degrees of action verbs depend on context. When there is no fact of "the loss of life or death"in the context, the degree of qualitative changes just express to the pole, but not the qualitative leap, so to express subjective feelings of "dissatisfy、displeasure、disgust"(不满意、不愉快、反感) by a means of exaggeration ; when there exists the fact of "the loss of life or death" in the context, the degree of qualitative changes pass through the pole and achieve the leap, at this time "死 (death)" means "the loss of life or death".

But there are some verbs that obviously do not express "physiological feelings", which still becoming part of the "V+死+人" and express meaning (a) and (b), like "吓 (frighten)、气(make angry)、玩(play)、整(make)、搞(do)"etc[7], So how does it transfer the meaning? Here we can see some lingual examples:

⑦他说道，"砍下的人头从义州一直铺到辽阳，几百里的路程，大道两边儿全垒满了人头，树上挂满了尸休。血淋淋的，吓死人。"

[tā shuō dào, "kǎn xià de rén tóu cóng yì zhōu yī zhí pù dào liáo yáng, jǐ bǎi lǐ de lù chéng, dà dào liǎng biān ér quán lěi mǎn le rén tóu, shù shàng guà mǎn le shī tǐ 。 xuè lín lín de, xià sǐ rén。 "]

⑧来了厂里，他下决心再也不小偷小摸，他努力克制自己进厂后再没偷东西。可是没偷，别人却污蔑他偷了，而且偷的那么大，三四万块，能吓死人。

[lái le chǎng lǐ, tā xià jué xīn zài yě bú xiǎo tōu xiǎo mō, tā nǔ lì kè zhì zì jǐ jìn chǎng hòu zài méi tōu dōng xī。 kě shì méi tōu, bié rén què wū miè tā tōu le, ér qiě tōu de nà me dà, sān sì wàn kuài, néng xià sǐ rén。]

⑨气死人要负法律责任。

[qì sǐ rén yào fù fǎ lù zé rèn。]

⑩财务说这种磁浮票票公司规定不能报。我为公司节省开支，居然还不能报销，真是气死人。

---

[7] Due to such as ""吓、气、玩、整、搞" etc. This kind of verbs will be included in the table of "physiological feelings" most single different verb in the "V+死+人" Constructions, and they are too few, sum up no universality and identity, so this article to this only analyze the reason why this kind of verbs can be included in "V+死+人" Constructions, and does not consider the semantic features reasons.

[*cái wù shuō zhè zhǒng cí fú piào piào gōng sī guī dìng bú néng bào。 wǒ wéi gōng sī jiē shěng kāi zhī, jū rán hái bú néng bào xiāo, zhēn shì qì sǐ rén。*]

⑪朱承戒苦着脸道："这个不好玩，搞不好会**玩死人**的。"

[*zhū chéng jiè kǔ zhe liǎn dào : "zhè gè bú hǎo wán, gǎo bú hǎo huì wán sǐ rén de。"*]

⑫ 这能怨球员自己吗？连点儿人情都不讲，一禁赛就两年，这不是**玩死人**了吗？

[*zhè néng yuàn qiú yuán zì jǐ ma？lián diǎn ér rén qíng dōu bú jiǎng, yī jìn sài jiù liǎng nián, zhè bú shì wán sǐ rén le ma？*]

⑬钟成亮去发动刘常贞，刚一走进他家还没开口，刘常贞即知道钟成亮的来意，就抢先说："想起去年的'互助组'，我真吃亏不少，确实**整死人**！"

[*zhōng chéng liàng qù fā dòng liú cháng zhēn, gāng yī zǒu jìn tā jiā hái méi kāi kǒu, liú cháng zhēn jí zhī dào zhōng chéng liàng de lái yì, jiù qiǎng xiān shuō : "xiǎng qǐ qù nián de 'hù zhù zǔ', wǒ zhēn chī kuī bú shǎo, què shí zhěng sǐ rén！"*]

⑭我县农村很缺乏医疗设备和卫生人员，人们生了病就只有找那些草药医生或巫师，这些草药医生或巫师很多丝毫不懂卫生常识，便给病人乱整，常常**整死人**。

[*wǒ xiàn nóng cūn hěn quē fá yī liáo shè bèi hé wèi shēng rén yuán, rén men shēng le bìng jiù zhī yǒu zhǎo nà xiē cǎo yào yī shēng huò wū shī, zhè xiē cǎo yào yī shēng huò wū shī hěn duō sī háo bú dǒng wèi shēng cháng shí, biàn gěi bìng rén luàn zhěng, cháng cháng zhěng sǐ rén。*]

⑮不少人偷偷的把手中的棍子换成了镰刀锄头这种能**搞死人**的家伙。

[*bú shǎo rén tōu tōu de bǎ shǒu zhōng de gùn zǐ huàn chéng le lián dāo chú tóu zhè zhǒng néng gǎo sǐ rén de jiā huǒ。*]

⑯咳，最近的行情，**搞死人**呐！倒是老罗一早的高抛做得真叫漂亮，马丽丽刮目相看。

[*ké, zuì jìn de háng qíng, gǎo sǐ rén nà！dǎo shì lǎo luó yī zǎo de gāo pāo zuò dé zhēn jiào piāo liàng, mǎ lì lì guā mù xiàng kàn。*]

"吓(frighten)"in cases⑦and⑧, and "气(make angry)"in cases⑨and⑩ are psychological verbs. "吓(frighten)" means "frighten or worry someone" ; "气(make angry)"is a strong feeling of being angry. Both of the two can express meaning (a) and (b) in the "V+死+人" structure. While most psychological verbs like "烦(bore)、愁(worry)、迷 (confuse)" only express (b) in the "V+死+人" structure, the reason for which the we considered was because of "吓(frighten)、气(make angry)". This kind of verbs have a greater effect on "人(human)" than other psychological verbs, and the effect is a process of degree. If the degree of "吓(frighten)、气(make angry)"exceeds the limit of psychological endurance, "the loss of life or death" tends to happen. By this time, "死 (death)" is a result complement, and the whole format is the verb-complement pattern which express the result; if the degree of "吓(frighten)、气(make angry)"just "reach the pole", the context describes the depth of "being frightened、being angry"by a means of exaggeration, which is not enough to cause the result of "the loss of life or death", so "死(*death*)"is a degree complement indicating extreme quantity, and the whole format is the verb-complement indicating degree.

Let's look at cases ⑪ ⑫, ⑬ ⑭ and ⑮ ⑯, it is clearly that "玩死人"、"整死人"、"搞死人" can be ambiguity. We assume it is because of the indeterminate meaning of "玩(*play*)、整(*make*)、搞(*do*)", which have considerable leeway in semantic space comparing with other verbs of specific behavior act. In other words, the ambiguity of semantic meaning lead to less restriction to specified context. As a result, "flirt、prank、trick"more or less always appear in sentences that is based on this character, and it is not strange to understand "玩死人"、"整死人"、"搞死人" ambiguously. In fact, there exists more or less this kind of word in different languages, such as the "do、make、turn" in English；"[遣る][yaru]、[取る][toru] in Japanese; in German there are the equivalences of the English "do"to the "tun"、"make" to the "machen"、"take"to the "nehmen、abholen"and so on.

Such monosyllabic verbs reveals semantic features that matched with according to the context. When it is to express "the loss of life or death"(a), the semantic features of this kind of monosyllable verbs are [+physiological feelings, +quantity +death]; when it is to express "to reach the pole"by a means of exaggeration, the semantic features of this kind of monosyllable verbs are [+physiological feelings, +quantity -death]. We classify those verbs of such semantic features into Ⅲ verbs.

Therefore, we describe the semantic features of classⅢverbs as [+生理感受，+量，±致死]*([+physiological,+feelings,+quantity,±death])*

The results above can be tabulated as following:

Structure	"V+死+人"(*V+ death+people*)		
Semantic meaning	Express (a)	Express (b)	Express both (a) and (b)
Semantic features of monosyllable verbs	I verbs:[+damage, +strong action, +death]	Ⅱ verbs A： [+psychology,+quantity, +feelings,-death] Ⅱ verbs B: [-psychology,+quantity, +feelings,-death]	Ⅲ verbs： [+physiological feelings, +quantity +death]

The author thinks that we could explain the different semantics of the structure of "V+死+人" as follows:

We draw a line: one end of the line means "the loss of life or death", which is meaning (a), and the other end means "to reach the pole", which is meaning (b). In between of two ends is the "free state" (also "moving state"), which indicates both meaning (a) and meaning (b). The two ends can be named as "qualitative change state". The meaning (a) end has very high extent of death ([+death]), while meaning (b) end has very low extent of death ([-death]). The extent of death of "free state" could be high or low ([±death]). The whole line indicates the quantitative change of the extent of death. If we assume the linguistic phenomena as a two-dimensional space, and the limited syntactic structures as line segments, this two-dimensional space will have limited line segments. These line segments may be paralleled (synonymous pattern), crossed (related sentences) or out of connection with each other (unrelated sentences). There are also limited verbs in this space. We assume the monosyllabic verbs that can enter into the structure of "V+死+人" are moving along the line segments of this structure while those verbs that cannot enter into this structure are excluded.

If the structure of "V+死+人" represents meaning (a), "the loss of life or death", the monosyllabic verbs that can enter into this structure will moving to the meaning (a) end. At this moment, the I verbs have very high extent of death ([+death]). If the structure of "V+死+人" represents meaning (b), "to reach the pole", the monosyllabic verbs that can enter into this structure will moving to the meaning (b) end. The II verbs A and B have very low extent of death ([-death]). If the structure of "V+死+人" represents both meaning (a) and (b), the monosyllabic verbs that can enter into this structure will moving freely between two ends. At this moment, the extent of death of III verbs could be high or low ([±death]). In other words, the III verbs are unfixed as they move freely between two ends. As the III verbs move to the end of "the loss of life or death", the structure of "V+死+人" represents meaning (a), and the III verbs will have high extent of death ([+death]). As the III verbs move to the end of "to reach the pole", the structure of "V+死+人" represents meaning (b), and the III verbs will have low extent of death ([-death]). What decides which end will the III verbs move to? In fact, the key element is the context. If there is no restriction from the context, the III verbs will aimlessly move between two ends. That is to say, if we analyze language examples such as "饿死人、冻死人" away from context, we could not identify whether they are meaning (a), "the loss of life or death" or meaning (b), "to reach the pole". The chart is as followed:

兼表（a）义和（b）义(both express (a) and (b))
（游离状态）(free state)

(a)the meaning of "the loss of life or death"   (b)the meaning of "to reach the pole"
质变状态(qualitative change state)   质变状态(qualitative change state)

In addition, this thesis summarizes the semantic features of the monosyllabic verbs in the key position of the "V+死+人" structures representing different meanings from the perspective of paradigmatic rule. As we know, compared to phonological and syntactic, semantic is less systematic and more ambiguous and has its own characters. Therefore, we should not impose uniformity in all the summaries of monosyllabic verbs of the "V+死+人" structures representing different meanings. We need to analyze them one by one, summarize those monosyllabic verbs with common feature accurately, carefully compare those exceptional ones and find out the reasons. Hence, we should have a comprehensive perspective and give consideration to the exceptions. The generalization of the semantic features of the monosyllabic verbs of the "V+死+人" structures representing different meanings in this thesis is under the guidance of this principle.

4   Conclusion

Lu Jianming (2005) mentioned that whether some notional words have certain semantic features can only be determined and summarized by combing with specific syntactic pattern. The research of semantic features of monosyllabic verbs in this thesis is also determined and summarized by combing with the syntactic pattern of the "V+死+人" structure. We have found that the "V+死+人" structure can represent meaning (a), meaning (b) and both meaning (a) and (b). The three different meaning of this structure is closely related to the semantic features of the monosyllabic verbs in the key position. The leading reason of the "V+死+人" structure's three meanings is the semantic features of the monosyllabic verbs. Generally, the semantic features of monosyllabic verbs representing meaning (a) are [+damage, +strong action, +death]; the semantic features of monosyllabic verbs representing meaning (b) are [+psychology, +quantity, +feelings, -death] or [-psychology, +quantity, +feelings, -death]; the semantic features of monosyllabic verbs representing both meaning (a) and (b) are [+physiological, +feelings, +quantity, ±death]. Besides, the semantic orientation of the complement "死" also plays an important role. From the perspective of methodology, we could use the analytical method of semantic orientation to effectively explain such phenomenon.

The classification of semantic and semantic features is fairly subjective. Which pattern the monosyllabic verbs should be categorized and which kind of meaning they can express are also based on subjective standard. The summary of semantic features in this thesis merely provides a common frame, thus inevitably having many limitations. However, based on the linguistic facts from corpus, the thesis has objectively described the linguistic phenomenon in our daily life, and provided a criterion from the perspective of semantic feature. Besides, there is many more questions in regard to this phenomenon are worth of our discussion. For instance, we can extend our research to the structure of "adj+死+人", or "adj+死+noun" or simply study the features of the semantic orientations of "死" or study the pragmatic and rhetoric aspects of "V+死+人". The author believes that because of such research, the linguistic phenomenon are truly and objectively presented in front of us.

Appendix

1.Verbs which could be the begging of "V+死+人" structure.

Class verbs I which express (a)：踩、撞₁、淹₁、捅₁、砸、戳₁、打¹₃、轧¹₁、拍₁、掐₁、摔₃、踢、烧₁、劈₁、刺₁、蜇₁(zhē)、杀₁、炸₁、捏₁、病₂、砍¹₁、医₃、治₄、咬₁、喝¹₂、噎₁、吃₁、射₁、勒、抽¹₄、缠₁、捶、敲₁、揍₁<方>、踹₁、吹₁、吹₃、卡₁、害₄

Class II verbs A which express (a)：烦₃、急₂、愁₁、恼₃、恨₁、爱₂、迷₄、笑₂、羞¹₁、疼₂、怨₂、想₄、醉₂

Class II verbs A which express (b)：坑₄、闹₃、丢、磨₃、逗¹₃、腻₂、吵₂、写₁(xiě)、赶₂、哄₁、唬₁<口>、唱₁、困₁、困₄、吹₅、吐₁、噎₃《方》、绕₄、催₁、粘

（黏）、馋$_3$、数$_{1\ (shǔ)}$、赚$_1$、卡$_2$、害$_3$、颠$^2_1$、绑、读$_1$、读$_3$、缠$_2$、捆$_1$、勾$^1_6$、搅$_2$、抄$^1_2$、哭、骂$_2$、拖$_4$、拧$_{2(níng)}$、等$^2_1$、逛

Class III verbs which express (a) and (b)：饿、吓、冻$_3$、电$_3$、憋$_1$、撑、挤$_1$、醉$_1$、压$_1$、气$_9$、熏$_1$、晒$^1_1$、扎$_1$、烫$_1$、烤$_1$、辣$_2$、磨$_3$、逼$_1$、累$_2$、呛、骗$^1_1$、玩、走$_1$、跑$_1$、整$_{6<方>}$、搞$_1$、冰$_2$、淋$_1$

References

1. Zhu, D.: Lecture Notes on Grammar. The Commercial Press (1982). (朱德熙.语法讲义 [M].北京:商务印书馆,1982) (in Chinese)
2. Lu, J.: Tutorial of Modern Chinese Grammar Research. Peking University Press (2005). (陆俭明.现代汉语语法研究教程[M].北京:北京大学出版社,2005) (in Chinese)
3. Xing, F.: Modern Chinese. Higher Education Press (1995). (刑福义.现代汉语·全1册[M]. 北京:高等教育出版社,1995) (in Chinese)
4. Xiaojing, Z.: A study on modern chinese the one-syllable verbs. SiChuan Normal University (2009). (in Chinese)
5. Linguistics Institute of Chinese Academy of Social Sciences: The Contemporary Chinese Dictionary, 6th edn. The Commercial Press (2012). (in Chinese)
6. Promrod, A.: A study on modern chinese psychological verbs. Beijing Language and Culture University (2007). (in Chinese)
7. Lu, J.: Semantic Analysis of "VA了" Structure of Verb Complement. Chinese Language Learning 1, 1–6 (1990). (陆俭明."VA了"述补结构语义分析[J]. 汉语学习,1990,01:1-6.) (in Chinese)
8. Tang, X., Chen, L.: The Diachronic Development and Cross-linguistical Investigation of "Death" as the Function of Degree Complemet. Studise in Language and Linguistics 3, 79–85 (2011). (in Chinese)
9. Zhao, J.: The Study on the Highest Degree Adverbs in Mandarin. Shanghai Normal University (2006). (in Chinese)
10. Fan, Z.: A Study on the Semantic Feature of "VP/AP+死+了". Journal of Baise University 5, 88–93 (2010). (樊中元. "VP/AP+死+了"语义特征考察[J]. 百色学院学报,2010,05:88-93). (in Chinese)
11. Hou, R.: The Sructural and Semantic Analysis of the " Verb(Adjective)+死+……". Beijing Institute of Education, 2, 16–21 (2005). (in Chinese)
12. Lan, B.: A Study on the Degree Complement and Result Complement. Journal of Shanxi Normanl University (Social Science) 3, 115–118 (1993). (兰宾汉. 也谈程度补语与结果补语[J]. 陕西师大学报(哲学社会科学版),1993,03:115-118.) (in Chinese)

Formal Schema of Diagrammatic
Chinese Syntactic Analysis

Weiming Peng[1], Jihua Song[1(✉)], Zhifang Sui[2], and Dongdong Guo[1]

[1] College of Information Science and Technology, Beijing Normal University,
Beijing 100875, China
{pengweiming,songjh}@bnu.edu.cn, 1039223908@qq.com
[2] Key Laboratory of Computational Linguistics, Ministry of Education,
Institute of Computational Linguistics, Peking University, Beijing 100871, China
szf@pku.edu.cn

Abstract. This paper reviews the research on diagrammatic Chinese syntactic analysis and its Treebank construction which use Sentence Component Analysis (SCA) as the main ideas, puts forward a new formal schema of diagrammatic Chinese syntactic analysis based on sentence pattern structure, including diagrammatic style and its XML structure. Syntactic schemes are drawn on the sentence pattern system according to the sequence of "basic sentence pattern, extend sentence pattern, complex sentence pattern and special sentence pattern", while lexical schemes are drawn on the Diagrammatic Unit which covers idioms/proper nouns, syntactic words and morphology.

Keywords: Sentence pattern structure · Sentence-based grammar · Diagrammatic syntactic analysis

1 Introduction

In the field of Chinese grammar research and teaching, there have been two prevalent sentence structure analysis methods (referred to as syntactic analysis method), one of which is Sentence Component Analysis (SCA) advocated by the traditional grammar school, and the other is Analytical Hierarchy Process (AHP) advocated by the structuralism grammar school. The latter obviously prevailed in the academic debate on Chinese syntactic analysis method in the early 1980s [1]. Chinese information processing also mainly use AHP in automatic syntactic analysis (refer to as Parsing in this field). Whether phrase structure or dependency structure, the parser analyzes the phrase-level hierarchy and syntactic relationship of the sentence essentially, since their theoretical systems are equally based on the "Immediate Component" analysis which is the core idea of AHP. The dominance of AHP in Chinese information processing owes to its concise formal structure accompanied by the pursuit of dichotomy. Under the guidance of dichotomous analysis, AHP's graphical forms (generally using frame diagram) achieve formalized implementation in computer very easily.

SCA takes "Sentence Component" as the basic element of the analysis, and concentrates on the integral pattern of the sentence structure, which is commonly called Sentence Pattern or Framework, etc. Shuxiang Lv has assessed SCA: "This method concentrates on the main points of the sentence, not only useful for language teaching,

© Springer International Publishing Switzerland 2015
Q. Lu and H.H. Gao (Eds.): CLSW 2015, LNAI 9332, pp. 701–710, 2015.
DOI: 10.1007/978-3-319-27194-1_68

but also for scientific understanding of the language [2]." However, binding with its common diagrammatic sketch, SCA is generally considered not conducive to express the hierarchy of sentence structure, and thus missed the formalization and further opportunities of Chinese information processing applications. In recent years, as the academia raise re-recognition and re-evaluation of the traditional grammar, especially Jinxi Li's grammar theory [3], Li's diagrammatic syntactic analysis method, which has exerted a significant influence in the Chinese grammar research and teaching, again looks for the new application space in Chinese Treebank building. According to our previous studies, Li's diagrammatic method can makes use of the advantages of SCA to highlight the sentence pattern, also can deal with complicated long sentences, representing the structural hierarchy. Considering being in line with the current teaching grammar system, the diagrammatic method needs a process of transformation and formalization. This paper will review on our previous research and put forward a new edition of formalization design of diagrammatic Chinese syntactic analysis.

2   Review on Previous Research

Jing He et al. designed an annotation schema for contemporary Chinese based on Li's grammar system, which proposed the syntactic formalization schema using diagram as the presentation of syntactic structure, XML as corresponding storage format, and implemented the "encode/decode" between the diagram and the XML for the first time [4]. In this schema, the grammar system inherited Li's system, only updates some terminologies.

We improved Li's diagrammatic method, and proposed a preliminary scheme of diagrammatic Chinese syntactic analysis based on the sentence pattern structure [5]. This scheme confirmed the design principle of "encode/decode" on the sentence pattern structures, introduced description forms for the double-object, multi-predicate and condensed sentence structure, and simplified the variants system. We developed the diagrammatic tagging tool, and completed a Treebank of 717,000 words (48,000 sentences). The improved diagrammatic method is easy to master for tagging stuffs, thus contributes to the efficiency of large-scale Chinese Treebank building. Although the tagging practice shows that our transformation works well, we also found the following problems:

1. Lack of clear guiding ideology, the logic of the sentence pattern system in this version is confused: the initial backbone sentence patterns consider too many factors: POS (part of speech) of the predicate, number of objects, multi-predicate, non-subject-predicate sentence, etc. Variants and condensed sentence lack clear specifications.
2. Diagrammatic styles are used to distinguish both the type of the Components and the POS of words. The excessive influence of POS to sentence pattern leads to adverse impact of sentence pattern system summarization.
3. Lack of lexical structure design. Weiming Peng et al. put forward to distinguish between syntactic and lexical factors in syntactic analysis [6], but all kinds of "provisional words" are coined by a "-" connection (such as: 朋友-们friends; 证明-信 letter of identification), and stored as a leaf node in XML. What's more, "*For All Words, the Word-class Is Based on the Component*". Although these designs ensured the regularity of the sentence pattern system, too big particle size of the XML leaf node (morphological segmentation) is not conducive to the communication with thesaurus.

To solve the above problems, this paper will propose a new formal schema of diagrammatic Chinese syntactic analysis, including two aspects: sentence pattern structure (syntax) and Diagrammatic Unit structure (morphology). For convenient writing, list firstly the tag set of the Elements and Attribute in the XML, as shown in table 1 and table 2 respectively.

Table 1. Tag Set of the Element

Tag	Component	Tag	POS
ju	Sentence	n	Noun
xj	Clause	t	Time word
sbj	Subject	f	Localizer
prd	Predicate	m	Numeral
obj	Object	q	Measure word
att	Attribute	r	Pronoun
adv	Adverbial	v	Verb
cmp	Complement	a	Adjective
ind	Independent element	d	Adverbial
pp	Position of preposition	p	Preposition
cc	Position of conjunction	c	Conjunction
uu	Position1 of auxiliary word	u	Auxiliary word
un	Position2 of auxiliary word	e	Exclamation
uv	Position3 of auxiliary word	o	Onomatopoeia
ff	Position of localizer	w	Punctuation
		x	Default

Table 2. Tag Set of the Attribute

Attribut	Value
prd/@scp (scope of Element prd)	V (single predicate word); VO (prd + obj); VC (prd + cmp); VOO (prd + obj + obj); VCO (prd + cmp + obj); VOC (prd + obj + cmp)
cc/@fun (function of Element cc)	COO (connect NPs in coordinate structure) APP (connect NPs in appositive structure) SYN (connect VPs in synthetic predicates) UNI (connect VPs in union predicates) PVT (connect VPs in pivotal sentence) SER (connect VPs in serial verb sentence)
ju/@cnt	Text of the Sentence
\<POS>/@sen	Sense code of the word, details as follow
\<POS>/@mod	Mode code of the morphology, details as follow

3   Schema of the Sentence Pattern

According to the general experience of grammar teaching, the description of the Chinese sentence pattern system follows "from simple to complex, from general to specific" rule, in accordance with the "basic sentence pattern -> extend sentence pattern -> complex sentence pattern -> special sentence pattern and complex sentence" order.

3.1   Basic Sentence Pattern

The basic pattern of Chinese sentence structure is SVO, which is defined as "basic sentence pattern", as the gestalt diagram by default: "Sbj ‖ Prd | Obj". If some of the three components omitted, the diagram pattern remains default, only leaving the corresponding position blank in the diagram. In order to maintain the pattern "NP-VP-NP" (NP and VP refer to the generalized substantive components and predicative components, the same below), analyze the so-called "noun-predicate sentence" in the mainstream Chinese grammar in accordance with Li's Grammar theory: put the noun-predicate on the position of Object and leaving the position of Predicate blank, that means the blank Predicate omitted or implied a verb "是". POS no longer influent the diagram style, but marked under the Diagrammatic Unit.

The diagram of the basic sentence pattern and corresponding XML structure are shown in figure 1. As the core structure of the sentence pattern, prd element is inevitable. "x" indicates the default placeholder element, whose role is similar to the null element in Penn Chinese Treebank [7]. Punctuation element "w" locate as the brother element of its adjacent POS, regardless of hierarchy. Set @scp attribute on the prd element to facilitate subsequent information retrieval from the XML.

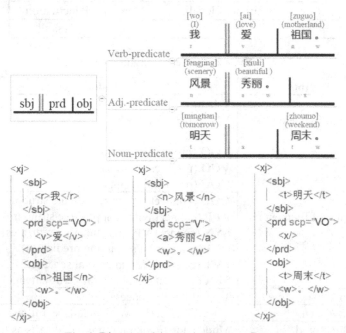

Fig. 1. Diagram of the Basic Sentence Pattern

3.2   Extended Sentence Pattern

Extended sentence pattern adds attributive, adverbial, complement, double-object, independent, coordinate, appositive structures without breaking "single-predicate" pattern of the trunk structure. Diagram formula and samples are shown in figure 2. As adjunct components, attributive, adverbial and complement all link below the horizontal line representing the trunk. Attribute, adverbial locate ahead, thus fold to the left; complement locates back, thus folds to the right. Attributive locates farther from the predicate in semantic, so triple-fold line is adopted. Further, independent component links using the dotted line.

Function words don't serve as component alone, they act in the sentence as an introducer or connector, or the marker of some affixation structure. They occupy specific "functional position" in the diagram. There are 4 main categories: prepositions, conjunctions, localizers (in location structure) and auxiliary words (including modal particles). The former 3 kinds of functional position respectively labeled "∧", "...", and "□"; while the positions of auxiliary words are divided into 3 groups as follow:

- (1) "的[de]", "地[de]", "得[de]", connecting the attribute, adverbial, and complement respectively, locate beside the connect-line;
- (2) adhere to the NP or PP structure, such as "等[deng]", "云云[yun yun]", marked "△";
- (3) adhere to the VP or clause structure, such as "者[zhe]","所[shuo]" and the modal particles etc., marked "▽".

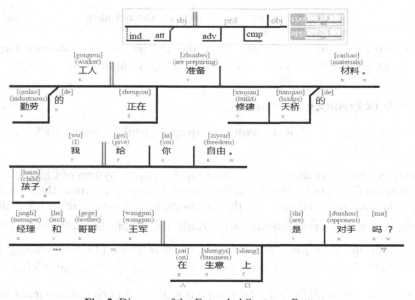

Fig. 2. Diagram of the Extended Sentence Pattern

3.3   Complex Sentence Pattern

Complex sentence pattern refers to the sentence pattern that breaks the "single-predicate" pattern of the trunk structure: multi-VP or clause serve as the predicate. 5 typical types are: synthetic predicate sentence, union predicate sentence, pivotal sentence, serial verb sentence, subject-predicate predicate sentence ("SPP sentence" for short). The diagram of the former 4 types: use " : ", "......", "//" and "/" to separate the adjacent two VPs. The diagram of SPP sentence: scaffold the predicate clause to produce a new pattern structure level.

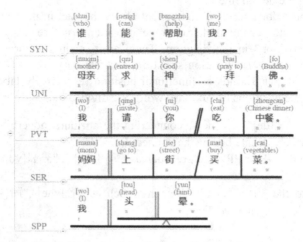

Fig. 3. Diagram of the Complex Sentence Pattern

Due to the wide difference in analysis of the complex sentence patterns among the different grammar schools, some specifications are given as follows:

(1) Synthetic Predicate Sentence

- S ∥ V₁ : V₂ | O[1], s.t.: V_1 is an auxiliary verbs or "是[shi]", semantically S ∥ V_1 and S ∥ V_2 | O both hold.

Term "synthetic predicate" comes from the Temporary System of Chinese Teaching Grammar (TSCTG for short), but the referent is slightly different. Here "auxiliary words" include the modal verb, and the directional verb using before the VP such as "来[lai](come to (do)),开始[kaishi](start to (do))" etc. "Synthetic predicate" in TSCTG mainly refers to "是[shi](be)" plus NP (such as: 他是学生。[Ta shi xuesheng] (He is a student.) [8], here only refers to the word "is" followed by a predicative VP. e.g.:

— Auxiliary verb: 谁能帮助我？[shei neng bangzhu wo] (who can help me?) 我 来 帮你。[wo lai bang ni] (Let me help you).

---

[1]   The complex sentence focuses on V, the object O is not inevitable, the same below.

— "是[shi](be)": 我是服了你！[wo shi fule ni] (I am taking you!)   他昨天是从香港回来的。[ta zuotian shi cong xianggang huilai de] (He came back yesterday from Hong Kong.)

(2) Union Predicate Sentence

- $S \parallel V_1 \mid O_1 \ldots\ldots V_2 \mid O_2$, s.t.: $S \parallel V_1 \mid O_1$和$S \parallel V_2 \mid O_2$ both hold, semantically maintain an inter-clause relation, without speech pauses.

The most typical case refers to the two coordinate structure of two VP (as distinguished from NP, renamed "Union"). Since coordinate can also be seen as a kind of inter-clause relation, classify other multi-VP structures with inter-clause relation to this type. e.g.:

— Coordinate relationship: 母亲求神拜佛。[muqin qiu shen bai fo] (Mother pray to Buddha for help).
— Other relationship: 他越想越生气。[ta yue xiang yue shengqi] (The more he think, the more he become angory).

3.4   Special Sentence Pattern and Complex Sentence

Special sentence pattern includes 3 types: holophrastic sentence, no-subject sentence and inverted sentence. The complex sentence consisting of several clauses can be diagrammatized successively according to the top-down sequence, with a dotted connective line on the left side.

The diagrams are shown in figure 4 and figure 5.

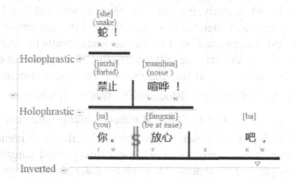

Fig. 4. Diagram of the Special Sentence Pattern

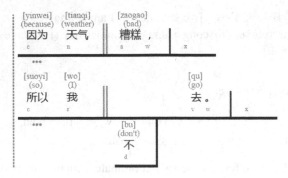

Fig. 5. Diagram of the Complex Sentence

4   Schema of Lexical Structure

The discrimination between Chinese words and phrases is a "persistent" problem in Chinese information processing. The current mainstream Treebank have admitted word-segmentation specification directly on the word granularity, which means word segmentation units would be a leaf node in the syntax tree, and there is no interme- diate state. In the viewpoint of syntactic analysis of sentence pattern, affected by the capacity of thesaurus, word segmentation units are usually too small in granularity, thus an extra lexical analysis process from the word unit to the syntactic analysis unit (Diagrammatic Unit) is needed [6]. In this process, the combination of words and morphemes is not as free as the combination at the syntactic level, but is limited more by the syllable rhythm, pragmatic habits and other aspects, and has stronger pattern. The research of Chinese message structure database of HowNet, as well as later Xiufang Dong [9] and Jinxia Li [10] suggest that it is necessary to analyze dynamic words and their structure modes while analyzing Chinese sentences and building Treebank.

Based on the above consideration, we put forward the concept of "Diagrammatic Unit" as the smallest "segmented" unit of diagrammatic syntactic analysis. The "smal- lest" here means relative to sentence pattern structure, it's equivalent to a whole word, whose interior still can carry on the analysis of the lexical structure. As shown in figure 6, "铁路工人"[tielu gongren](locoman), "铺路砖"[pu lu zhuan](paving block), "备下" [bei xia] (get ready) and "厚厚" [houhou] (thickly) are four dynamic words, one of which is equivalent to a word from the perspective of sentence pattern struc- ture. In the interior of diagrammatic units, more fine-grained constituents (words or morphemes) are separated by spaces. Through the diagrammatic tagging tool [11, 12] which can prompt candidate fine-grained senses in the lexicon in real time, the sense encoding could be tagged on each constituent expediently, thus realize the communi- cation with the lexicon.

To collect dynamic words and their structure modes, mark structure relational op- erators in the interior of diagrammatic units as shown in Figure 6. The dynamic word categories involved include: idioms / proper nouns (文字改革 [wenzi gaige] (reform of writing system), 北京师范大学[Beijing shifan daxue] (Beijing Normal University), etc.), syntactic words (resultative construction verb, quantifier, etc.) and morphology (reduplicated form, verb + "了[le], 着[zhe], 过[guo]", etc.).

Fig. 6. Diagram with Lexical Structure Information

Also, with the aid of the diagrammatic tagging tool, the relational operator is tagged after the POS and sense code of each constituent. While encoding XML, the mode code Attribute @mod is generated in the integral POS Element of a diagrammatic unit. The mode code takes the POS (or morpheme class exactly) code of each constituent; if the syllable number of the constituent is greater than 1, attached the number at the rear of the POS; at last connect them with relational operators.

5   Conclusion

Missing the advantage of summing up sentence patterns of SCA, it is a great pity for Chinese grammar teaching and Chinese information processing to realize information communication and crossover study of the two application subjects. A number of scholars from the fields of Chinese grammar and teaching Chinese as a foreign language have called for reviewing fair value of SCA. Borong Huang [13], Xudong Liao and Nairong Qian [14] have combined the two analysis methods and put forward the "Framework Core Analysis", "Centripetal Much Analysis Syntax", etc. This paper learns from the theoretical achievements of predecessors and social leaders of the time, puts forward an improved formal schema of diagrammatic Chinese syntactic analysis on the basis of the practice of Treebank tagging, and aims to lay the formalization foundation for carrying out sentence pattern analysis based on SCA.

Acknowledgement. Supported by: Open Projects Program of Key Laboratory of Computational Linguistics (Peking University), Ministry of Education of PRC; Beijing Normal University Young Teachers Fund Project (No: 2014NT39); State Key Development Program of Basic Research of China (973 Program) (No: 2014CB340504).

References

1. Ping, H.: Discussion Collected Papers of Chinese Syntactic Analysis. Shanghai Education Press, Shanghai (1984)
2. Shuxiang, L.: Problems of Chinese syntax analysis. The Commercial Press, Beijing (1979)
3. Weiming, P., Jihua, S., Ning, W.: Traditional Chinese Grammar and Its Potential Application in Chinese Information Process. Journal of Chinese Information Processing **4**, 50–60 (2012)
4. He, J., Peng, W., Song, J., Liu, H.: Annotation schema for contemporary chinese based on JinXi Li's grammar system. In: Liu, P., Su, Q. (eds.) CLSW 2013. LNCS, vol. 8229, pp. 668–681. Springer, Heidelberg (2013)
5. Weiming, P., Jihua, S., Ning, W.: Design of Diagrammatic Parsing Method of Chinese Based on Sentence Pattern Structure. Computer Engineering and Applications **50**(06), 11–18 (2014)
6. Weiming, P., Jihua, S., Shiwen, Y.: Lexical Issues in Chinese Information Processing: in the Background of Sentence-based Diagram Treebank Construction. Journal of Chinese Information Processing **28**(02), 1–7 (2014)
7. Naiwen, X., Fei, X., Fudong, C.: The Penn Chinese TreeBank: Phrase structure annotation of a large corpus. Natural language engineering **11**(2), 207–238 (2005)
8. Zhigong, Z.: Grammar and Grammar Teaching: Introduction to the Temporary Grammatical System. People's Education Press, Beijing (1956)
9. Xiufang, D.: Chinese Lexicon and Morphology. Peking University Press, Beijing (2004)
10. Jinxia, L.: The Theory and Practice of Distinguish between Words and Phrases. China Social Sciences Press, Beijing (2013)
11. Min, Z., Weiming, P., Jihua, S.: Development and Optimization of Syntax Tagging Tool on Diagrammatic Treebank. Journal of Chinese Information Processing **06**, 26–33 (2014)
12. Tianxin, Y., Weiming, P., Jihua, S.: High Efficiency Syntax Tagging System Based on the Sentence Pattern Structure. Journal of Chinese Information Processing **04**, 43–49 (2014)
13. Borong, H.: The Third Discussing on Framework Core Analysis. Journal of Yancheng Teachers University (Humanities & Social Sciences Edition) **06**, 49–52 (2010)
14. Nairong, Q.: Modern Chinese (Revised Edition). Jiangsu Education Press, Nanjing (2001)

The Derivational Analysis of the Deep and Surface Structure of Human Related Synthetic Compounds

Yan Zhang[⊠] and Chongming Ding

College of Chinese Language and Culture, Beijing Normal University, Beijing 100875, China
yyaann2005@126.com, dchm@bnu.edu.cn

Abstract. While semantics is influenced by the deep structure as well as the surface structure, the study of the deep structure should not be ignored. Focusing on some human related Chinese synthetic compounds, this paper will study the derivational relation between the deep and surface structure. First, the human related synthetic compounds in N1-V-N2 style are first classified by their surface structure. It appears differently on different kinds of such compounds when we refer to the deep cognitive structure and the surface structural structure. Next, it is pointed out that there are certain connections of these two structures, and thus we add some details and certain revision to the previous study (Gu and Shen 2001) on these compounds. In addition, we discuss the other two approaches that analyze the formation of such nominal compounds.

Keywords: N1-V-N2 · Human related chinese synthetic compounds · The deep cognitive structure · The surface structural structure

1 Introduction

Presently human related synthetic compounds lacks an explicit definition. Gu and Shen (2001) hold the idea that the OVS style, for example, 节目主持人 *[jiemu zhuchiren] (the person who hosts a program)*, is a synthetic compound. Yet, He (2004) takes a wider consideration, and he maintains that synthetic compounds include the above mentioned OVS style, as well as VOS (开创事业者 *[kaichuang shiyezhe] (the person who start a career)* style.

The synthetic compounds in this paper focus on N1-V-N2, which is an abstract describing structure. For N2, it has a semantic feature of being human related. However, since such words always refer to human beings, we call them human related synthetic compounds (henceforth HSCs). In addition, N1, V and N2 correspond to the semantic roles of agent, action and patient (theme), respectively.

We adopt the acknowledged viewpoint that the semantics is influenced by the deep structure as well as the surface structure. Nevertheless, the study of the deep structure should not be ignored when we examine this view. As is well known, some problems, which cannot be settled by surface structure, require support obtained from the analysis of the deep structure. This is an important approach in this paper.

© Springer International Publishing Switzerland 2015
Q. Lu and H.H. Gao (Eds.): CLSW 2015, LNAI 9332, pp. 711–721, 2015.
DOI: 10.1007/978-3-319-27194-1_69

2   Literature Review

The synthetic compounds are studied by different scholars in diverse ways. Wu (1982) pays attention to such words firstly. Although he does not name them as synthetic compounds, he finds out a substantive characteristic of all such compounds, i.e., they share the same syntactic structure. Take the structure of N1-N2 for example. The verb inside has a different relation with nouns. For instance, 青年服务社 [qingnian fuwushe] (the agency which serves the youth), 服务 (to serve) has a relationship with both 青年 (the youth) and 社 (agency); however, when we refer to 青年突击队 [qingnian tujidui] (the commando which is made up by the youth), 突击 (to make a sudden and violent attack) just correlates with 青年 (the youth).

Gu and Shen (2001) analyze synthetic compounds by argument structure adjustment, which receives some disagreements. He (2004) argues against Gu and Shen's (2001) proposal that OVS style synthetic compounds derive from syntactic structure, alleging that their approach is a misunderstanding of the Uniformity of Theta Assignment Hypothesis (UTAH) as well as a mix-up of syntax and morphology. Continuing his inquiry, he then analyzes VO phrases such as 播音 [boyin](to broadcast), utilizing loop theory and structure associate memory, He states that such VO style has been lexicalized as a root and thus can participate in lexical formation. However, he only mentions that the external argument will move to the right of V, without further explaining how words like 新闻播音员 [xinwen boyinyuan] (the broadcaster who broadcast news) can be derived from 播音员 [boyinyuan] (broadcaster).

Later, He (2005) puts the argument that OVS structure synthetic compounds is genuine lexical structure, while VOS structure has a mixed morphological and syntactic structure. He (2009) proposes two basic principles in the formation of synthetic compounds: the right-headedness rule and the UTAH. In addition, he indicates that we can describe such structure by Zero ternary operator. Later, (2013) abandons description, but continues to study these compounds by economy principle in turn. As for 论文指导老师 [luwenzhidaolaoshi] (the teacher who supervises students' papers), he thinks that both [Npaper [Nsupervise teacher]] and [N [VPpaper supervise] teacher] are in line with the economy principle.

Wang (2001) explains the ungrammaticality of 粉碎纸张机 [fensuizhizhang ji] (the machine that can smash paper; shredder) by using prosodic stress theory. Shi (2003) considers that verb-noun compounds, for example, 汽车修理工 [qiche xiuligong] (the repairman who repairs cars), can be explained by the structure of modification in formal syntax. Feng (2004) studies the restrictions of Chinese prosodic organization on Verb-Object inverse structures.

Besides, Cheng (2005) analyzes 者 [zhe] (a pronoun represents the person; -er) synthetic compounds in modern Chinese. Zhou (2006) debates the [[N1+V] + N2] structure by typology analysis. Zhou (2007) argues that the structural analysis of 纸张粉碎机 [zhizhang fensui ji] (shredder) should be [[zhizhang fensui] ji]. We disagree with this analysis in that 纸张粉碎 [fensui zhizhang] (to smash paper) is meaningless and unestablished in the corpus.

Feng (1998, 2004) analyzes synthetic compounds with prosody, which will be referred to in the following study.

3   The Analysis of the Surface Lexical Structure

There exists a large number of N1-V-N2 HSCs in mandarin Chinese; however, whether they share the same generating structure requires research in detail. All 81 HSCs cited from previous studies will be discussed, except 3 compounds that cannot be retrieved in BLCU Center for Chinese (BCC) or Center for Chinese Linguistics Corpus of Peking University (CCL), we have 78 HSCs in total.

We searched the 78 N1-V-N2 HSCs in the aforementioned corpora with the structures of N1-V and V-N2 respectively, and then classify them into 3 categories by surface structure. We use agent, action and theme to label N1, V and N2, for the sake of demonstrating the thematic relations between them.

3.1   The First Category: HSCs of [Theme-Action]-Agent

It represents the [N1-V]-N2 structure synthetic compounds. There are 4 lists in 76 words (5.1%): 现场搜索警员 *[xianchangsousuo jingyuan] (the policeman who searches the site)*, 花木管理临时工 *[huamuguanli linshigong] (the temporary worker who manages the flowers and trees)*, 数据分析组 *[shujufenxi zu] (the group who analyzes the data)*, 物价调控委员会 *[wujiatiaokong weiyuanhui] (the committee who controls the prices) (See appendix 1)*.

One main feature of this type is that V-N2 cannot exist or exist independently. Taking 现场搜索警员 for instance, 现场搜索 *(searching the site)* can exist separately, but 搜索警员 *(searching a policeman)* cannot exit as a nominal phrase. For example:

- （1）王祖勉训导的两条警犬奉命参加了现场搜索，不到 1 小时，两条警犬在一片杂草丛中发现了犯罪嫌疑人并将其制服。*[Wang Zumian xundao de liang tiao jingquan fengming canjia le xianchang sousuo, budao yi xiaoshi, liang tiao jingquan zai yi pian za caocong zhong faxian le fanzui xianyiren bing jiang qi zhifu.](These two police dogs who are trained by Wang Zumian took part in the searching, and they found the suspect in no more than one hour.)*

Another one, 分析组 *[fenxi zu] (the analysis group)* is not commonly acceptable, while we find many sentences in corpus with 数据分析 *[shuju fenxi] (data analysis)*.

3.2   The Second Category: HSCs of Theme-[Action-Agent]

It refers to N1-[V-N2] structure HSCs, with a total number of 22, accounting for 28.2%. Here are some examples: 坦克狙击手 *[tanke jujishou] (the sniper who snipes tanks)*, 眼膜捐献者 *[yanmo juanxianzhe] (the donor who donates cornea)*, 文物诈骗犯 *[wenwu zhapianfan] (the swindler who swindles cultural relics)*, 遗嘱执行人 *[yizhu zhixingren] (the executor who executes testaments)*, 电影出品人 *[dianying chupinren] (the person who produces movies)*.

Similarly, a characteristic of N1-V is that it cannot exist or exist independently. For example, we find examples with 狙击手 *[juji shou] (sniper)*, but no 坦克狙击 *[tanke juji] (tank snipe)* exists. *(See appendix 2)*.

3.3   The Third Category: HSCs of [Theme-Action]-agent /Theme-[Action-Agent]

It shows the feature of both [N1-V]-N2 and N1-[V-N2], and has a large amount, with 66.67% (the number is 52). Here are some examples: 论文指导老师, 汽车修理工, 节目主持人, 资料分析员 *[ziliao fenxiyuan] (the person who analyzes data)*, 文学爱好者 *[wenxue aihaozhe] (the person who is fond of literature)*, 文物走私团伙 *[wenwuzousi tuanhuo] (the gang who smuggles cultural relics)*.

From the result of corpus searching, those words share an obvious feature in that they can be segmented by two ways. Still, distinctions exist among them. For example, we might hesitate when analyzing the structure of 论文指导老师, but easily judge the word like 节目主持人. Although 节目主持 can be used as a single word, as illustrated in the example below, when deciding its internal structure, we prefer to take [主持人] as a segment.

- （2）他虚心向北京市劳模、原4702号车售票员杨本莉请教，并自学了心理学、节目主持、播音、人际交往、英语、哑语等。*[Ta xuxin xiang Beijing shi laomo, yuan si qi ling er hao che shoupiaoyuan Yang Benli qingjiao, bing zixue le xinlixue, jiemuzhuchi, boyin, renjijiaowang, yingyu, yayu deng.](He consulted Yang Benli, who is a model worker of bus 4702 in Beijing. Besides, he himself learned psychology, program host, broadcasting, interpersonal communication, English and sign language and so on.)*

3.4   Further Discussion of Structure [Theme-Action]-Agent /Theme-[Action-Agent]

After a closer analysis of the examples in 3.3, we find it more reasonable to segment 节目主持人 *(appendix 3·I)* into N1-[V-N2] structure. In comparison, 论文指导老师 *(appendix 3·II)* can be analyzed as either [N1-V]-N2 or N1-[V-N2].

According to Feng's study (1998) on the Chinese natural prosodic foot, 5-Chinese-character string can only form the [2#3] rhythm, for that [3#2] rhythm is not orally acceptable. 6-character string can be read in any rhythm, except [2#2/2]. 7-character string can only be read in [2/2#3] rhythm. His research sheds light on the current issue; however, there still remains some questions, as prosodic foot theory has its limitations in explaining lexical structure. On the other hand, we can get some inspirations from Li's study (2004) on the understanding preference of disyllabic V + disyllabic N structure (i.e., whether the structure is treated as a verb phrase or as a whole or a nominal phrase). It is shown that when the disyllabic N cannot refer to a specific entity, the whole word will be easily regarded as nominal with a [modifier + head noun] structure. From this perspective, we take a closer look at head morphemes such as 员 *[yuan] (-er)*, 人 *[ren] (-er)*, 人员 *[renyuan] (-er)*, 工 *[gong] (-er)*, 家 *[jia] (-er)*, 商 *[shang] (-er)*, 师 *[shi] (-er)*, 者 *[zhe] (-er)*. We find that they all, with a high productivity, cannot clearly refer to a specific entity. At the same time, they are highly grammaticalized, and some of them – like 者, 家, 员 – are treated as nominal affixes, while others – like 人, 商, 师 – are regarded as quasi-affixes. This is the reason why certain V-N2 are considered as a nominal structure. It is so prominent in our cognition when we analyze those words such as 播音员 *(broadcaster)*, 主持人 *(host)*, 修理工 *(repairman)*, 演奏家 *(concert performer)*, 批发商 *(wholesaler)*, 设计师 *(designer)*, 志愿者 *(volunteer)*, that we will easily consider N1 as an attribute. That is to say, we are inclined to think these words as N1-[V-N2] structure. However, both 论文指导 and 指导老师 can be distinctly understood, so we categorize such words separately.

4   The Analysis of the Deep Cognitive and the Surface Structural Structure

As we all known, language has a tight relationship with cognition. Furthermore, the process of thinking forms the structure of cognition, and is presented by different language structures. For instance, the sentence 我吃饭 *[wo chi fan] (I have a meal)* can be abstracted as a cognition structure of agent-action-theme, which is a combination of a series of concepts. And the structure can be used to express infinite and massive sentences. Of course, speakers or listeners will complete the structure if some linguistic components of this cognition structure disappears. Take the following dialogue as an example:

- （3）——你吃饭吗？ *(Have you had meals?)*
- ——我吃了。 *(I had.)*

Though it lacks an object (theme) in the response, we will intuitively complete the answer.

'Agent-Action-Theme' is a general cognitive structure in human thinking despite of the language differences. In actually expression, however, 'Theme-Action-Agent' structure also exists, and it can be seen as a surface structure of the previous structure.

He and Wang (2005) refers to UTAH in analyzing HSCs, which requires that identical thematic relationships between predicates and their arguments are represented syntactically by identical structural relationships. As to N1-V-N2 HSCs, they are coherent with their syntax description—N2-V-N1, the cognitive structure. Therefore, our task to describe and explain the generation types and causes of the formation of N1-V-N2 is converted to analyze the derivation relationship from N2-V-N1 to N1-V-N2, Which can be shown respectively in Fig. 1, Fig. 2.

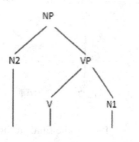   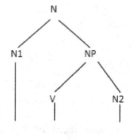

Fig. 1.   **Fig. 2.**

5   The Derivation from Deep Cognitive Structure to Surface Structural Structure

5.1   The Derivation Analysis Under Argument Theory

Taking 论文指导老师 as an instance, utilizing Gu and Shen (2001), 老师 *(teacher)* is an external argument. Acting as the head in the structure, it is unable to be excluded, which is the head in the structure, and cannot be left out. 论文 *(papers)* is an internal argument, Which is able to be hid within synthetic compounds. And, 指导 *(to guide)* is the core component.

Moreover, the agent is the external argument and the theme is the internal one. The structure property of synthetic compounds is decided by the former argument, acting as the core of a structure. The latter one, however, can be remained under cover.

There is an interaction of the structural principles between morphology and syntax. Based on the standpoint, we explore the derivation process of the deep cognitive structure to the surface structural structure. The formation principle of the surface structure is head-final, meaning that the head will be at the right side of the structure. As a result, the internal argument, which becomes optional in the surface structure, will move to the left side. For 论文指导老师, the following figures demonstrate its derivation process.

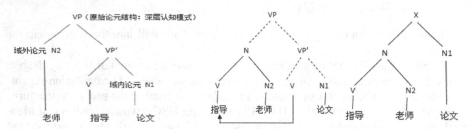

Fig. 3. The deep cognitive structure N2-V-N1

Fig. 4. The leftward movement of core component V

Fig. 5. The non-structural structure X after the second step

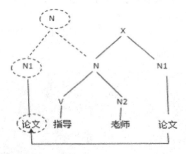

Fig. 6. The leftward movement of internal argument N1

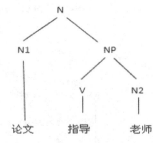

Fig. 7. The final surface structure

Based on the viewpoint of Gu and Shen, the formation of 论文指导老师 can be described with Fig. 3, Fig. 4, and Fig. 6. This, however, leaves much to be desired. Attempting to refine the process, we add a part named "the non-structural structure X "(Fig. 3) between the leftward movement of core component V and the leftward movement of internal argument N1. Such description combines the dynamic process with the static representation, aiming to better present the movement process of arguments. Additionally, it combines the derivation of the deep structure to the surface structure, utilizing the interaction of morphology and syntax. It is worth noting that the description only conveys how the deep surface forms. Hence the motivation for the formation needs to be discussed next.

5.2   The Motivation Analysis

This section focuses on relations of two structures instead of the hierarchical structure. Through restoring the surface structure of HSCs, we can deduce their deep cognitive structures.

The surface structure and deep cognitive structure of 论文指导老师 are respectively shown in Fig. 8 and Fig. 9.

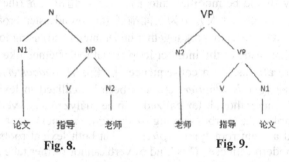

Fig. 8.   Fig. 9.

The motivation analysis will be based on the two structures.

Movement from N2-V-N1 to N1-V-N2

There exists an obvious movement between N1 and N2 when comparing Fig. 8 and Fig. 9, which results in a loop structure like Fig. 10. Actually, almost every HSCs of any type can be analyzed in this structure.

N1 and N2 can randomly shift around V, in the train of the movement between nominal compounds and verbal compounds. But there is no basic change on the semantics.

To make an assumption: N1-V-N2 derives from the loop movement of N2-V-N1. The reason for the formation of the loop movement is that both N1 and N2 have relationships with V, allowing V to act as a bridge. Furthermore, the features of N2 must not be ignored during analysis. All of them can be testified by some counter examples.

Fig. 10.

Both 影片制作人 *[yingpian zhizuoren] (the person who produces a movie)* and 电影制作人 *[dianying zhizuoren] (the person who makes a film)* are HSCs. The former follows the loop structure; however, the latter cannot shift to 人制片影片 *[ren zhipian yingpian]*. According to CSCSL (the modern Chinese language corpus of center for studying Chinese as a second language, Beijing Language and Culture University), the verb 制作 *[zhizuo] (to produce)* has a word frequency of 28.521, while, 制片 *[zhipian] (produced by)* is no more than 1. That is to say, if a verb has little to no intensity of action, it cannot derive or can just derive in a soft way between the deep structure and the surface one. This is may be considered an example of the relative concept. For example, the verb frequency of 摄影 *[sheying] (to shoot)* in 电影摄影师 *[dianying sheyingshi] (the photographer who photographs a film)* is 10.5935, but comparing with 拍摄 *[paishe] (to photograph)* with 26.0764, 10.5935 is still low.

Another counter example is that certain N1-V-N2 HSCs that cannot shift to N2-V-N1 directly need the assistance of some prepositions or other constructions. These include 超市供货商 [chaoshi gonghuoshang] (the supplier who supplies goods for supermarkets), 新闻播音员, 电视剧编剧人 [dianshiju bianjuren] (the scriptwriter who writes a TV play), 电影摄影师, 劳动互助组 [laodong huzhuzu] (the mutual aid team during work), etc. They should be modified into 商（人）给超市供货 (the supplier provides goods for supermarkets), （人）员为新闻播音 (the broadcaster broadcasts news), 组以互助的方式劳动 (the team work together under mutual aid) using loop structure.

One reason that leads to the indirect loop is that morphemes like 员, 师, 商 have already turned to affixes. As a consequence, 播音员 *(broadcaster)*, 摄影师 *(photographer)*, 供货商 *(goods supplier)* etc. has been lexicalized in lexicon. In addition, most of the verbs here, though lexicalized, can be analyzed as a 'verb + object' structure. For example, the verb 'sheying' *(photograph)* includes a verb root 'she' *(shoot/take)* and a noun root 'ying' *(picture)*, but both lexical roots cannot be separately used in modern Chinese. This kind of verb cannot further take a noun as object.

Therefore, it is obvious that some factors affect the movement may be obtained. One is the degree of action of V, another is the affixation of N2, and finally is the structural structure of V. With regard to various classifications of N1-V-N2, only the third one loops without preconditions. An example may be seen in 论文指导老师, which illustrates why there exist two different surface structural analyses of these HSCs.

Superposition of N1-V and V-N2

The superposed structure can be described by Fig. 11.

V is the core component in both N1-V, the left structure, and in V-N2, the right structure. Hence, it can combine the left side and the right side.

When we analyze the HSCs in this way, there are three situations: either of the two half-structures may exist in corpus separately or a

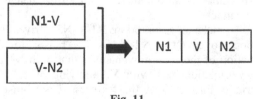

Fig. 11.

new structure exists after connecting them. It is reflected mainly by the third classification of words like 论文指导老师, 资格审查小组 *[zigeshencha xiaozu] (the examination group who exam qualification)*, 节目主持人, etc.

The left structure exists independently, while the right one does not exist or cannot exist by itself. However, a new structure exists after the two half-structures are joined together. This situation mainly appears in the first classification like 现场搜索警员, 花木管理临时工, 数据分析组, 物价调控委员会.

The left structure does not exist or cannot exist by itself, while, the right one can. Similar to that situation, another one does after the two half-structures are superposed. Mainly in the second and the third classifications, words like 坦克狙击手, 眼膜捐献者, 遗嘱执行人, 学生辅导员 *[xuesheng fudaoyuan] (the instructor who assists students)*, 超市供货商 have the feature.

6   Conclusions

The interaction between the deep cognitive structure and the surface structural structure of HSCs can be proved by the movement of arguments, loop structure, and superposed structure. Based on the derivational analysis, we have explored how different N1, V, and N2 can affect the formation of the HSCs, detailed the transformation from deep cognitive structure to surface structure, and then discussed the motivation of this structural derivation.

Still, there are some questions that require further study, such as the analysis of V, which can be made up by corpora study in some degree. This should analyzed through differing and exhaustive methods.

Appendixes

Appendix 1: 现场搜索警员 *[xianchangsousuo jingyuan](the policeman who searches the site)* 花木管理临时工 *[huamuguanli linshigong](the temporary worker who manages the flowers and trees)* 数据分析组 *[shujufenxi zu](the group who analyzes the date)* 物价调控委员会 *[wujiatiaokong weiyuanhui](the committee who controls the prices).*

Appendix 2: 坦克狙击手 *[tanke jujishou](the sniper who snipes tanks)* 眼膜捐献者 *[yanmo juanxianzhe](the donor who donates cornea)* 案件辩护律师 *[anjian bianhulvshi](the attorney who defends others)* 研究生指导教师 *[yanjiusheng zhidaojiaoshi](the teacher who guides postgraduates)* 进修生指导教师 *[jinxiusheng zhidaojiaoshi](the teacher who guides visiting students)* 仪表装配工人 *[yibiao zhuangpeigongren](the worker who assembles instruments)* 文物诈骗犯 *[wenwu zhapianfan](the swindler who swindles cultural relics)* 儿童拐骗犯 *[ertong guaipianfan](the kidnapper who kidnaps children)* 国宝盗窃犯 *[guobao daoqiefan](the larcener who steals national treasures)* 遗嘱执行人 *[yizhu zhixingren](the executor who executes testaments)* 电影出品人 *[dianying chupinren](the producer who produces movies)* 电影制片人 *[dianying zhipianren](the person who produces movies)* 产品经销人 *[chanpin jingxiaoren](the dealer who deals in products)* 超市供货商 *[chaoshi gonghuoshang](the supplier who supplies goods for supermarket)* 谣言制造者 *[yaoyan zhizaozhe](the fabricator who fabricates rumors)* 事业开创者 *[shiye kaichuangzhe](the pioneer who starts a career)* 奥运志愿者 *[aoyun zhiyuanzhe](the* volunteer who works for the Olympic Games) 病毒制造者 *[bingdu zhizaozhe](the maker who makes virus)* 学生辅导员 *[xuesheng fudaoyuan](the tutor who assists students)* 水文勘测队 *[shuiwen kancedui](the survey team who survey hydrology)* 机要保卫人员 *[jiyao baoweirenyuan](the guard who guards confidential files)* 古迹介绍专家组 *[gujijieshao zhuanjiazu](the panel who introduce historic sites).*

Appendix 3·I: 新闻播音员 *[xinwen boyinyuan](the broadcaster who broadcasts news)* 车辆检测员 *[cheliang jianceyuan](the inspector who tests vehicles)* 汽车驾驶员 *[qiche jiashiyuan](the driver who drives a car)* 仓库保管员 *[cangku baoguanyuan](the keeper who keeps a warehouse)* 比赛裁判员 *[bisai caipanyuan](the referee who referees a contest)* 动物饲养员 *[dongwu siyangyuan](the raiser who raises animals)* 宿舍管理员 *[sushe guanliyuan](the manager who manages the dormitory)* 资料分析员 *[ziliao fenxiyuan](the person who analyzes data)* 政治宣传员 *[zhengzhi xuanchuanyuan](the propagandist who propagandizes politics)* 节目主持人 *[jiemu zhuchiren](the person who hosts a program)* 财产继承人 *[caichan jichengren](the successor who succeeds property)* 影片制作人 *[yingpian zhizuoren](the person who produces a movie)* 专利代理人 *[zhuanli dailiren](the agent who agents patents)* 电视剧编剧人 *[dianshiju bianjuren](the scriptwriter who writes a TV play)* 钢琴演奏家 *[gangqin yanzoujia](the player who plays the piano)* 古董收藏家 *[gudong shoucangjia](the collector who collects antiques)* 古玩收藏家 *[guwan shoucangjia](the collector who collects antiques)* 汽车修理工 *[qiche xiuligong](the repairman who repairs cars)* 飞机修理工 *[feiji xiuligong](the repairman who repairs planes)* 水暖维修工 *[shuinuan weixiugong](the maintenance worker who maintains the plumbing)* 服装设计师 *[fuzhuang shejishi](the designer who designs costumes)* 时装设计师 *[shizhuang shejishi](the designer who designs fashion)* 飞机设计师 *[feiji shejishi](the designer who designs planes)* 商务策划师 *[shangwu cehuashi](the planner who plans commercial affairs)* 电影摄影师 *[dianying sheyingshi] (the photographer who photographs a film)* 图书出版商 *[tushu chubanshang](the publisher who publishes books)* 汽车经销商 *[qiche jingxiaoshang](the dealer who deals in cars)* 蔬菜批发商 *[shucai pifashang](the wholesaler who wholesales vegetables)* 五金批发商 *[wujin pifashang](the wholesaler who wholesales hardwares)* 汽车经销者 *[qiche jingxiaozhe](the seller who sells cars)* 歌曲演唱者 *[gequ yanchangzhe](the singer who sing a song)* 宗教信仰者 *[zongjiao xinyangzhe](the believer who believes in religion)* 课件制作者 *[kejian zhizuozhe](the maker who makes the courseware)* 文学爱好者 *[wenxue aihaozhe](the person who is fond of literature)* 技术管理者 *[jishu guanlizhe](the controller who controls the technology)* 金钱崇拜者 *[jinqian chongbaizhe](the adorer who adores money)* 计算机操作者 *[jisuanji caozuozhe](the operator who operates computers)* 通缩政策推行者 *[tongsuozhengce tuixingzhe](the executor who executes the deflation policy)* 武器核查团 *[wuqi hechatuan](the inspectors who inspect weapons)* 劳动互助组 *[laodong huzhuzu](the mutual aid team during work)* 文物走私贩 *[wenwu zousifan](the smuggler who smuggles cultural relics).*

Appendix 3·II: 论文指导老师 *[luwenzhidaolaoshi](the teacher who supervises students' papers)* 论文指导教师 *[luwenzhidaojiaoshi](the teacher who guides students' papers)* 汽车制造工人 *[qichezhizaogongren](the worker who makes cars)* 文物走私团伙 *[wenwuzousituanhuo](the gang who smuggles cultural relics)* 成果鉴定委员会 *[chengguojiandingweiyuanhui](the committee who appraise achievements)* 野生动物保护委员会 *[yeshengdongwubaohuweiyuanhui](the committee who protect wild animals)* 资格审查小组 *[zigeshenchaxiaozu](the examination group who exam qualification)* 文艺研究团体 *[wenyiyanjiutuanti](the organization who study the literature and art)* 地面攻击部队 *[dimiangongjibudui](the troops who attack ground)* 滚筒雕刻技师 *[guntongdiaokejishi](the artificer who sculptures expansion cylinders)* 首长保卫人员 *[shouzhangbaoweirenyuan](the guard who guards the leader).*

References

1. Cheng, G.: Zhe (er) synthetic compounds in Chinese and their implications for UG. Modern Foreign Languages (Quarterly), August 2005. (in Chinese)
2. Feng, S.L.: Verb-Object Inversion and Prosodic Morphology. Linguistic Sciences, May 2004. (in Chinese)
3. Feng, S.L.: The Natural Foot in Mandarin Chinese. Studies of the Chinese Language 1, 42 (1998). (冯胜利.《论汉语的"自然音步"》.中国语文,1998年第1期,42)(in Chinese)
4. Gu, Y., Shen, Y.: The derivation of synthetic compounds in Chinese. Studies of the Chinese Language **2**, 124 (2001). (in Chinese)
5. He, Y.J.: The loop theory in Chinese morphology. Contemporary Linguistics **3**, 227–231 (2004). (in Chinese)
6. He, Y.J., Wang, L.L.: Real and Pseudo Synthetic Compounds in Chinese Language. Teaching and Linguistic Studies **5**, 17–18 (2005). (in Chinese)
7. He, Y.J.: On the Logical Form of Chinese Synthetic Compounds. Linguistic Sciences, September 2009. (in Chinese)
8. He, Y.J.: A further study on Chinese synthetic compounds: Structure, typology and cues to language acquisition. Foreign Language Teaching and Research (bimonthly), July 2013. (in Chinese)
9. Li, J.X.: Factors Restraining Preference to ways to Understand V Double + N Double. Academic Journal Graduate School Chinese Academy of Social Sciences **1** (2004). (in Chinese)
10. Shi, D.X.: Chinese attributive V-N compounds. Studies of the Chinese Language **6** (2003). (in Chinese)
11. Wang, H.J.: The relations between the number of syllable, the tonal range of pitch and the grammatical structure in Chinese. Contemporary Linguistics **4** (2001). (in Chinese)
12. Wu, J.C.: Modern Chinese Syntactic Analysis, pp. 286–287. Peking University Press, Beijing, June 1982. (吴竞存.《现代汉语句法分析》.北京:北京大学出版社,1982年6月, 286-287) (in Chinese)
13. Xu, T.Q.: Foundation of Linguistics: A Course Book, p. 170. Peking University Press, Beijing, February 2001. (in Chinese)
14. Zhou, R.: A study on Chinese VON/OVN compounds under typological evidence: Universality vs. individuality. Studies of the Chinese Language **4** (2006). (in Chinese)
15. Zhou, R.: The IC Analysis On "zhizhang fensui ji". EASTLING, December 2007. (in Chinese)

Author Index

Printed in the United States
By Bookmasters